ROGET'S THESAURUS

Existence

Ens, entity, being, exist^ce   Nonentity, nullity, nihility
Essence, quintess^e quid^ty   nonexist^ce noth^g nought
Nature thing substance   void zero, cypher blank
course world frame   empty
position constitution
Reality, (v. truth) actual   unsubstantial
exist^ce — fact,   Unreal, ideal, imaginary
course of things, under; sun   visionary, fabulous
extant, present   fictitious, supposititious
                                absent, shadow: dream
                                phantom, phantasm
Positive, affirmative absolute Negative, virtual, extrinsic
intrinsic, substantive   potential. adjective
inherent
To be; exist, obtain, stand
pass, subsist, prevail, lie
— on foot, on; tapis
to constitute, form, compose   to consist of
                                scope, habitude, temperament
State, mode of exist^ce condition, nature, constitut^n habit
Affection, predicament, situat^n posit^n posture, place contingency
Circumstances, case, plight, trim, tune, — point, degree
juncture, conjuncture, pass, emergency, exigency.

— Mode, manner, style, cast, fashion, form, shape
strain, way, degree. — tenure, terms, tenor
footing, character, capacity
Relation, —ship, affinity, alliance, analogy, filiat^n (v. connect^n)
Reference about respect? regard? concerning, touching
in point of, as to — pertaining to, belong^g applicable to
relatively, according to
Comparable commensurate   incomp^ble incomm^te —ble,
correspondent —able   irreconcilable, discordant
accordant

Facsimile of the first page of the MS. classified catalogue of words completed
by Dr. P. M. Roget in 1805, which was the germ of the Thesaurus.

THESAURUS
OF ENGLISH WORDS AND PHRASES

CLASSIFIED AND ARRANGED

SO AS TO FACILITATE THE EXPRESSION OF IDEAS
AND TO ASSIST IN LITERARY COMPOSITION

BY

PETER MARK ROGET, M.D., F.R.S.

ENLARGED BY

JOHN LEWIS ROGET, M.A.

THIS CLASSIC AMERICAN EDITION WAS ORIGINALLY
REVISED AND ENLARGED BY

SAMUEL ROMILLY ROGET, M.A.

AVENEL BOOKS
New York

Library of Congress Catalog Card Number: 76-48411
This edition is published by Avenel Books
a division of Barre Publishing Inc.

        g h
Manufactured in the United States of America

Library of Congress Cataloging in Publication Data

Roget, Peter Mark, 1779-1869.
   Thesaurus of English words and phrases, classified
and arranged so as to facilitate the expression of ideas
and to assist in literary composition.

   "This classic American edition was originally revised
and enlarged by Samuel Romilly Roget."
   Reprint of the 1933 ed.
   Includes index.
   1. English language—Synonyms and antonyms.
I. Roget, John Lewis, 1828-1908.   II. Roget, Samuel
Romilly, 1875-   III. Title.
PE1591.R7 1978   423'.1   76-48411
ISBN 0-517-20985-3 lib. bdg.
ISBN 0-517-26934-1

FOREWORD
TO THE
1979 EDITION

FOR over three generations, *Roget's Thesaurus* has served the needs of writers, speakers, students, and translators. Peter Mark Roget first compiled and organized his guide to English words and phrases in 1805; the work was published in 1852 and was immediately recognized as a valuable tool for anyone concerned with the proper and creative use of the English language. Three generations of Rogets have worked to keep the thesaurus up to date, preserving Peter Mark Roget's original concept, organization, and format, while adapting the work to contemporary needs.

Roget recognized that writing and speaking difficulties are not necessarily the result of a poor vocabulary or ill-formed ideas. He grasped what many writers, orators, and translators had long had to contend with: the necessity of finding the exactly appropriate word or phrase from a group of synonyms. In every language, words are subject to a variety of shadings and implications. A living, growing language contains words that have specific meanings—meanings either embedded in the root of a word or that have developed in the course of history and usage. Words that at first seem synonymous and therefore completely interchangeable, prove otherwise in certain contexts. The word first chosen on impulse may interrupt the mood of a piece of writing or a speech and may jar the reader or the listener by its lack of specificity, or, more seriously, may imply a completely different intent than that which the author had in mind.

The translator is especially concerned with the problems of mood and intent, for even the most formal scholarly works depend on the idiomatic expressions of a language. The richness of poetry and fiction sometimes depends totally on an exact and idiomatic turn of phrase. These expressions are inaccessible to literal translation; a translator must find a matching idiom to retain the author's original sense.

A standard dictionary provides little assistance in these situations. Dictionaries serve only to define words, giving little indication of their use within a language. More importantly, dictionaries are not designed to allow the playing with words that is so important to creating individual nuance.

With the thesaurus, a whole new approach to creative expression is possible, because the thesaurus stresses the importance of the *idea* first. It functions almost as a reverse dictionary: as a dictionary goes from word to idea, a thesaurus starts with a concept and leads to specific words. In this way, the thesaurus becomes both thought-expressing and thought-provoking. A writer or speaker who has a general idea in mind must find the word or phrase that will convey his meaning most clearly and succinctly. The thesaurus, with its exhaustive compilation of synonyms, permits on-the-spot, rapid comparisons of similar words. In addition, while glancing over the list of words, one may decide to modify or strengthen his initial concept. The thesaurus user may come upon an expression or word that had not occurred to him before. And, finally, the selection of a word may start off new trains of thoughts and ideas.

THE DESIGN OF THE THESAURUS

The format of *Roget's Thesaurus* is well adapted to the needs of the user. It is organized by general categories that reflect the most common patterns of words and their usage in the English language. The six general categories are:

1) Abstract relations
2) Space
3) Matter
4) Intellect
5) Volition
6) Affections

Of course, many words fit under more than one of these categories, and they will be found in each relevant one. For example, *work*, because of its multiple meanings, has a place in "abstract relations," "space," "intellect," "volition" and "affections." An introductory synopsis of the general categories describes in detail the subcategories within each general category, making it easy for the thesaurus user to pinpoint and clarify in his own mind the precise meaning he is looking for.

The format of the thesaurus embodies the principle that form must follow function. And the function of the thesaurus is to facilitate the precise expression of ideas; it encourages the exploration of shades of meaning, of comparing directly one word with another that is almost synonymous. In addition, each subcategory is printed beside the subcategory that most nearly reflects its antithesis. For example, *superiority* and *inferiority* appear in parallel columns, as do *safety* and *danger*, *vanity* and *modesty*, and so on.

The thesaurus functions in another way also. The index at the back of the book is arranged by individual words. Within the entry, each word is further broken down into its various meanings, with references to the subcategory in the text proper. When the thought is clear, but the word is missing, the index functions as a quick, easy guide. The index is so specific that a word may have as many as twenty different references. *Rude,* for example, is broken down into ten possible contexts, reflecting the variety of meanings it may assume—"violent," "shapeless," "inelegant," "uncivil," and so on.

The arrangement of words and phrases within each subcategory remains constant throughout the book, and is again designed for easy use. The keyword of each subcategory is printed in bold-faced type. It is followed by a list of synonymous nouns, then verbs, adjectives, adverbs, etc. Under each part of speech, the most closely related synonyms are grouped together in paragraphs. Finally, there is a list of phrases and idiomatic expressions, for often a phrase is the only way to get at the true thought. Slang expressions (indicated as such) that have become a part of the language are also given. Foreign words that have been naturalized are included, as are those foreign words that have no literal translation in English and serve a distinctive role in the English language.

Because further refinements may be necessary, all entries are internally cross-referenced. For example, under *disobedience,* one finds references to *disorder, resistance, defy.*

The Thesaurus as an Indispensable Tool

The aim of *Roget's Thesaurus* is twofold. It is a quick reference of synonyms for someone looking for a fresh word or a word with a slightly different meaning than the word in the writer's mind. These thesaurus users will depend heavily on the index, where they will find references to the literal, figurative, and derivative senses of any word. Others might depend more on the general categories. These are the users who immerse themselves in the rich lists of words and phrases, thereby getting a total feeling of the concept under consideration and all its ramifications.

The purpose of the thesaurus is not to regulate word usage in the English language. Rather, it expands anyone's appreciation of English, supplying a rich vocabulary and suggesting new forms of expression, possibly even new ideas.

ELLEN LEVENTHAL

PREFACE

TO

THE FIRST EDITION

(1852)

I<small>T</small> is now nearly fifty years since I first projected a system of verbal classification similar to that on which the present Work is founded. Conceiving that such a compilation might help to supply my own deficiencies, I had, in the year 1805, completed a classed catalogue of words on a small scale, but on the same principle, and nearly in the same form, as the Thesaurus now published.* I had often during that long interval found this little collection, scanty and imperfect as it was, of much use to me in literary composition, and often contemplated its extension and improvement; but a sense of the magnitude of the task, amidst a multitude of other avocations, deterred me from the attempt. Since my retirement from the duties of Secretary of the Royal Society, however, finding myself possessed of more leisure, and believing that a repertory of which I had myself experienced the advantage might, when amplified, prove useful to others, I resolved to embark in an undertaking which, for the last three or four years, has given me incessant occupation, and has, indeed, imposed upon me an amount of labour very much greater than I had anticipated. Notwithstanding all the pains I have bestowed on its execution, I am fully aware of its numerous deficiencies and imperfections, and of its falling far short of the degree of excellence that might be attained. But, in a Work of this nature, where perfection is placed at so great a distance, I have thought it best to limit my ambition to that moderate share of merit which it may claim in its present form; trusting to the indulgence of those for whose benefit it is intended, and to the candour of critics who, while they find it easy to detect faults, can at the same time duly appreciate difficulties.

P. M. R<small>OGET</small>

April 29th, 1852

* A facsimile of the first page of this little manuscript book which is the original form of the Thesaurus is given in the frontispiece.

EDITOR'S PREFACE

(1879)

(*Slightly Abridged*)

THE FIRST EDITION of Dr. Roget's Thesaurus was published in the year 1852, and a second in the ensuing spring. On the issue of the third, in 1855, the volume was stereotyped. Since that time until now, the work has been reprinted in the same form and with little alteration, in rapidly succeeding editions, the printing of which has worn out the original plates.

During the last years of the author's life, which closed, at a very advanced age, in the month of September, 1869, he was engaged in the task of collecting additional words and phrases, for an enlarged edition which he had long projected. This he did not live to complete, and it became my duty, as his son, to attempt to carry the design into execution.

The result of the author's labours was embodied in a copy of the Thesaurus, in which the margins and spaces about the letterpress were closely covered with written words and phrases, without any very precise indication of the places in the text where additions or alterations were intended to be made. On a careful examination of these *addenda,* I came to the conclusion that, in order to introduce them with advantage, it would be necessary to make some slight changes; without, however, interfering at all with the framework of the book, and but little with the details of its system. In this proceeding my course has been mainly determined by the following considerations.

Any attempt at a philosophical arrangement under categories of the words of our language must reveal the fact that it is impossible to separate and circumscribe the several groups by absolutely distinct boundary lines. Many words, originally employed to express simple conceptions, are found to be capable, with perhaps a very slight modification of meaning, of being applied in many varied associations. Connecting links, thus formed, induce an approach between the categories; and a danger arises that the outlines of our classification may, by their means, become confused and eventually merged. Were we to disengage these interwoven ramifications, and seek to confine every word to its main or original import, we should find some secondary meaning has become so firmly associated with many words and phrases, that to sever the alliance would be to deprive our language of the richness due to an infinity of natural adaptations.

Were we, on the other hand, to attempt to include, in each category of the Thesaurus, every word and phrase which could by any possibility be appropriately used in relation to the leading idea for which that category was designed, we should impair, if not destroy, the whole use and value of the book. For, in the endeavour to enrich our treasury of expression, we might easily allow ourselves to be led imperceptibly onward by the natural association of one word with another, and to add word after word, until group after group would successively be absorbed under some single heading, and the fundamental divisions of the system be effaced. The small cluster of nearly synonymous words, which had formed the nucleus of a category, would be lost in a sea of phrases, and it would become difficult to recognize those which were peculiarly adapted to express the leading ideas.

These considerations were material in dealing with the new and multitudinous store of words and phrases which the author had accumulated. Many of these were altogether new to the Thesaurus. Many were merely repetitions in new places of words already included in its pages. With reference to cases similar to the latter, the author had declared it to have been a general rule with him 'to place words and phrases which appertain more especially to one head, also under other heads to which they have a relation,' whenever it appeared to him 'that this repetition would suit the convenience of the inquirer and spare him the trouble of turning to other parts of the work.' But, with the now increased mass of words, it became a question, in many cases, whether such repetition would still prove convenient. Where categories might by that course be unduly swollen, or where they might, by reason of their being separated from each other by subtile distinctions or faint lines of demarcation, be thereby too nearly assimilated, I thought it would often be better to confine words of the kind referred to to their primary headings. The necessity of keeping the book within reasonable dimensions had also to be borne in mind.

Under these circumstances, the best method of ensuring the ready accessibility of the multitude of words now to be dealt with, and at the same time preserving unimpaired the unity of the several categories, appeared to me to lie in the copious use of references from one place in the book to another. Relying on this contrivance as a means of opening more widely the resources of the collection, by making the groups of words mutually suggestive, and thereby leading not only to more varied forms of expression, but to kindred ideas, I have added largely to the references already inserted by the author. I have also ventured occasionally to substitute a reference for a group of words, when the identical group existed in another place, and could thus be made immediately available.

In order, at the same time, to make the value of the references more appreciable, I have (whenever it has appeared to me to be necessary) inserted, in a parenthesis, a word indicating the nature of the group or category referred to. Any one using the book will thereby be enabled to judge whether it will be worth his while to turn to the place in question.

The cross references may also be looked upon as indicating in some degree the natural points of connection between the categories, and the ramification of the ideas which they embody. As would be the case under any classification of language, a large proportion of the expressions, to find which recourse is had to the Thesaurus, lie on an ill-defined border land between one category and another; and it is not always easy, even with the aid of a carefully compiled index, to determine under which of several allied headings they should be sought. In the present edition, when the inquirer has once started on his voyage of discovery, the references enable him to pass freely from one division to another without recurring to the Index.

Many new words have also been inserted which were not contained in the author's manuscript.

Except in a very few cases, where distinct ideas were obviously united under one head, I have not had the presumption to meddle with the author's division into categories; but, within each category, I have endeavoured to carry somewhat further the sorting of words according to the ideas which they convey.

With these objects in view, I have supplied the work with a new and elaborate Index, much more complete than that which was appended to the previous editions. Although, in the original design of his work, the author appears to have conceived the process of search for a required expression as one in which the system of classification would be first consulted, and the Index afterwards called in aid if necessary, I believe that almost everyone who uses the book finds it more convenient to have recourse to the Index first.

From the peculiar nature and use of the Thesaurus, its Index will be found to differ, in some of its essential functions, from an alphabetical table of contents. The present Index does not merely afford an indication of the place where every given word or topic occurs or is dealt with in the text; but it is intended as a guide to other expressions which may be found there. The word we look out in this Index is not that which we require, but that which we wish to avoid. It is, therefore, not necessary that every word there given should be a repetition of one in the text. It may even happen that the word selected as a guide, though suggestive of the group wanted, is wholly unfit to be comprised within it.

The new Index contains not only all the *words* in the book (without needless repetition of conjugate forms), but likewise the *phrases,* all of which had been excluded from the Index to the previous editions. It is hoped that these additions, although they increase the bulk of the book, will have the effect of extending its usefulness in at least a corresponding degree.

Some changes of detail have also been made, where the form of the work seemed susceptible of improvement, and there was no reason to suppose that the author would have disapproved of the alteration. In the previous editions, the *phrases* were in general placed in separate paragraphs, under the heading **Phr.**, in each of the subdivisions assigned to the different grammatical parts of speech. In the present edition, *words* and *phrases* are placed together, and the heading **Phr.** is only employed in the case of phrases which have no convenient place in such an arrangement. Much space has been saved, and many repetitions have been avoided, by the use of lines and hyphens, where words or phrases in the same group have syllables or parts in common, and by references from one part of speech to another. These abbreviations may be best explained by examples, of which the following are a few:—

'with -relation, – reference, – respect, – regard- to'; is meant to include the phrases 'with relation to,' 'with reference to,' 'with respect to,' 'with regard to.'

'root –, weed –, grub –, rake- -up, – out;' includes 'root up,' 'root out,' 'weed up,' 'weed out,' 'grub up,' 'grub out,' 'rake up,' 'rake out.'

'away from –, foreign to –, beside- the -purpose, – question, – transaction, – point;' includes 'away from the purpose,' 'foreign to the purpose,' 'beside the purpose,' 'away from the question,' 'foreign to the question,' 'foreign to the transaction,' 'beside the question,' 'away from the point,' 'beside the transaction,' 'foreign to the point,' 'away from the transaction,' 'beside the point.'

'raze – to the ground'; includes 'raze,' and 'raze to the ground.'

'campan-iform, -ulate, -iliform;' includes 'campaniform,' 'campanulate,' and 'campaniliform.'

'goodness &c. *adj.*'; 'badly &c. *adj.*'; 'hindred &c. *v.*'; include all words similarly formed from synonyms of 'good,' 'bad,' and 'hinder,' respectively, given under the headings **Adj.** and **V.** in the same categories where the abbreviations occur.

The participle 'to' before a verb has in all cases been rejected, the heading **V.** being thought sufficiently distinctive; the use of capitals for the initial letters of the first words of paragraphs has been abandoned, as giving those words undue importance; and the title of each category has been kept distinct from the collection of words under its heading.

I should be ungrateful were I not to acknowledge the assistance derived, both by my father and myself, from various suggestions made by well-wishers to the work, some of whom have been personally unknown to either of us; and also to record my thanks to several kind friends, and to Messrs. Spottiswoode and Co.'s careful reader, for valuable aid during the passage of the sheets through the press.

JOHN L. ROGET

March 17th, 1879.

INTRODUCTION

[*Notes within brackets are by the editors.*]

THE present Work is intended to supply, with respect to the English language, a desideratum hitherto unsupplied in any language; namely, a collection of the words it contains and of the idiomatic combinations peculiar to it, arranged, not in alphabetical order as they are in a Dictionary, but according to the *ideas* which they express.* The purpose of an ordinary dictionary is simply to explain the meaning of the words; and the problem of which it professes to furnish the solution may be stated thus:—The word being given, to find its signification, or the idea it is intended to convey. The object aimed at in the present undertaking is exactly the converse of this: namely,—The idea being given, to find the word, or words, by which that idea may be most fitly and aptly expressed. For this purpose, the words and phrases of the language are here classed, not according to their sound or their orthography, but strictly according to their *signification*.

The communication of our thoughts by means of language, whether spoken or written, like every other object of mental exertion, constitutes a peculiar art, which, like other arts, cannot be acquired in any perfection but by long and continued practice. Some, indeed, there are more highly gifted than others with a facility of expression, and naturally endowed with the power of eloquence; but to none is it at all times an easy process to embody, in exact and appropriate language, the various trains of ideas that are passing through the mind, or to depict in their true colours and proportions, the diversified and nicer shades of feeling which accompany them. To those who are unpractised in the art of composition, or unused to extempore speaking, these difficulties present themselves in their most formidable aspect. However distinct may be our views, however vivid our conceptions, or however fervent our emotions, we cannot but be often conscious that the phraseology we have at our command is inadequate to do them justice. We seek in vain the words we need, and strive ineffectually to devise forms of expression which shall faithfully portray our thoughts and sentiments. The appropriate terms, notwithstanding our utmost efforts, cannot be conjured up at will. Like 'spirits from the vasty deep,' they come not when we call; and we are driven to the employment of a set of words and phrases either too general or too

* See note in p. xxi.

limited, too strong or too feeble, which suit not the occasion, which hit not the mark we aim at; and the result of our prolonged exertion is a style at once laboured and obscure, vapid and redundant, or vitiated by the still graver faults of affectation or ambiguity.

It is to those who are thus painfully groping their way and struggling with the difficulties of composition, that this Work professes to hold out a helping hand. The assistance it gives is that of furnishing on every topic a copious store of words and phrases, adapted to express all the recognizable shades and modifications of the general idea under which those words and phrases are arranged. The inquirer can readily select, out of the ample collection spread out before his eyes in the following pages, those expressions which are best suited to his purpose, and which might not have occurred to him without such assistance. In order to make this selection, he scarcely ever need engage in any critical or elaborate study of the subtle distinction existing between synonymous terms; for if the materials set before him be sufficiently abundant, an instinctive tact will rarely fail to lead him to the proper choice. Even while glancing over the columns of this Work, his eye may chance to light upon a particular term, which may save the cost of a clumsy paraphrase, or spare the labour of a tortuous circumlocution. Some felicitous turn of expression thus introduced will frequently open to the mind of the reader a whole vista of collateral ideas, which could not, without an extended and obtrusive episode, have been unfolded to his view; and often will the judicious insertion of a happy epithet, like a beam of sunshine in a landscape, illumine and adorn the subject which it touches, imparting new grace and giving life and spirit to the picture.

Every workman in the exercise of his art should be provided with proper implements. For the fabrication of complicated and curious pieces of mechanism, the artisan requires a corresponding assortment of various tools and instruments. For giving proper effect to the fictions of the drama, the actor should have at his disposal a well-furnished wardrobe, supplying the costumes best suited to the personages he is to represent. For the perfect delineation of the beauties of nature, the painter should have within reach of his pencil every variety and combination of hues and tints. Now, the writer, as well as the orator, employs for the accomplishment of his purposes the instrumentality of words; it is in words that he clothes his thoughts; it is by means of words that he depicts his feelings. It is therefore essential to his success that he be provided with a copious vocabulary, and that he possess an entire command of all the resources and appliances of his language. To the acquisition of this power no procedure appears more directly conducive than the study of a methodized system such as that now offered to his use.

The utility of the present Work will be appreciated more especially by those who are engaged in the arduous process of translating into English a work written in another language. Simple as the operation may appear, on a superficial view, of rendering into English each of its sentences, the task of transfusing, with perfect exactness, the sense of the original, preserving at the same time the style and character of its composition, and reflecting with fidelity the mind and the spirit of the author, is a task of extreme difficulty. The cultivation of this useful department of literature was in ancient times strongly recommended both by Cicero and by Quintilian, as essential to the formation of a good writer and accomplished orator. Regarded simply as a mental exercise, the practice of translation is the best training for the attainment of that mastery of language and felicity of diction, which are the sources of the highest oratory, and are requisite for the possession of a graceful and persuasive eloquence. By rendering ourselves the faithful interpreters of the thoughts and feelings of others, we are rewarded with the acquisition of greater readiness and facility in correctly expressing our own; as he who has best learned to execute the orders of a commander, becomes himself best qualified to command.

In the earliest periods of civilization, translators have been the agents for propagating knowledge from nation to nation, and the value of their labours has been inestimable; but, in the present age, when so many different languages have become the depositories of the vast treasures of literature and of science which have been accumulating for centuries, the utility of accurate translations has greatly increased, and it has become a more important object to attain perfection in the art.

The use of language is not confined to its being the medium through which we communicate our ideas to one another; it fulfils a no less important function as an *instrument of thought*; not being merely its vehicle, but giving it wings for flight. Metaphysicians are agreed that scarcely any of our intellectual operations could be carried on to any considerable extent, without the agency of words. None but those who are conversant with the philosophy of mental phenomena, can be aware of the immense influence that is exercised by language in promoting the development of our ideas, in fixing them in the mind, and in detaining them for steady contemplation. Into every process of reasoning, language enters as an essential element. Words are the instruments by which we form all our abstractions, by which we fashion and embody our ideas, and by which we are enabled to glide along a series of premises and conclusions with a rapidity so great as to leave in the memory no trace of the successive steps of the process; and we remain unconscious how much we owe to this potent auxiliary of the reasoning faculty. It is on this ground, also, that the present Work founds a claim to utility. The review of a catalogue of words of analogous signification, will often suggest by association other trains of thought, which, presenting the subject under new and varied aspects, will vastly expand the sphere of our mental vision. Amidst the many objects thus brought within the range of our contemplation, some striking similitude or appropriate image, some excursive flight or brilliant conception, may flash on the mind, giving point and force to our arguments, awakening a responsive chord in the imagination or sensibility of the reader, and procuring for our reasonings a more ready access both to his understanding and to his heart.

It is of the utmost consequence that strict accuracy should regulate our use of language, and that every one should acquire the power and the habit of expressing his thoughts with perspicuity and correctness. Few, indeed, can appreciate the real extent and importance of that influence which language has always exercised on human affairs, or can be aware how often these are determined by causes much slighter than are apparent to a superficial observer. False logic, disguised under specious phraseology, too often gains the assent of the unthinking multitude, disseminating far and wide the seeds of prejudice and error. Truisms pass current, and wear the semblance of profound wisdom, when dressed up in the tinsel garb of antithetical phrases, or set off by an imposing pomp of paradox. By a confused jargon of involved and mystical sentences, the imagination is easily inveigled into a transcendental region of clouds, and the understanding beguiled into the belief that it is acquiring knowledge and approaching truth. A misapplied or misapprehended term is sufficient to give rise to fierce and interminable disputes; a misnomer has turned the tide of popular opinion; a verbal sophism has decided a party question; an artful watchword, thrown among combustible materials, has kindled the flame of deadly warfare, and changed the destiny of an empire.

In constructing the following system of classification of the ideas which are expressible by language, my chief aim has been to obtain the greatest amount of practical utility. I have accordingly adopted such principles of arrangement as appeared to me to be the simplest and most natural, and which would not require, either for their comprehension or application, any disciplined acumen, or depth of metaphysical or antiquarian lore. Eschewing all needless refinements and subtleties, I have taken as my guide the more obvious characters of the ideas for which expressions were to be tabulated, arranging them under such classes and categories as reflection and experience had taught me would conduct the inquirer most readily and quickly to the object of his search. Commencing with the ideas expressing abstract relations, I proceeded to those which relate to space and to the phenomena of the material world, and lastly to those in which the mind is concerned, and which comprehend intellect, volition, and feeling; thus establishing six primary Classes of Categories.

1. The first of these classes comprehends ideas derived from the more general and ABSTRACT RELATIONS among things, such as *Existence, Resemblance, Quantity, Order, Number, Time, Power.*

2. The second class refers to SPACE and its various relations, including *Motion,* or change of place.

3. The third class includes all ideas that relate to the MATERIAL WORLD; namely, the *Properties of Matter,* such as *Solidity, Fluidity, Heat, Sound, Light,* and the *Phenomena* they present, as well as the simple *Perceptions* to which they give rise.

4. The fourth class embraces all ideas of phenomena relating to the INTELLECT and its operations; comprising the *Acquisition,* the *Retention,* and the *Communication of Ideas.*

5. The fifth class includes the ideas derived from the exercise of VOLITION; embracing the phenomena and results of our *Voluntary and Active Powers*; such as *Choice, Intention, Utility, Action, Antagonism, Authority, Compact, Property,* &c.

6. The sixth and last class comprehends all ideas derived from the operation of our SENTIENT AND MORAL POWERS; including our *Feelings, Emotions, Passions,* and *Moral and Religious Sentiments.**

The further subdivisions and minuter details will be best understood from an inspection of the Tabular Synopsis of Categories prefixed to the Work, in which are specified the several *topics* or *heads of signification,* under which the words have been arranged. By the aid of this table the reader will, with a little practice, readily discover the place which the particular topic he is in search of occupies in the series; and on turning to the page in the body of the Work which contains it, he will find the group of expressions he requires, out of which he may cull those that are most appropriate to his purpose. For the convenience of reference, I have designated each separate group or heading by a particular number; so that if, during the search, any doubt or difficulty should occur, recourse may be had to the copious alphabetical Index of words at the end of the volume, which will at once indicate the number of the required group.†

* It must necessarily happen in every system of classification framed with this view, that ideas and expressions arranged under one class must include also ideas relating to another class; for the operations of the *Intellect* generally involve also those of the *Will,* and *vice versâ;* and our *Affections* and *Emotions,* in like manner, generally imply the agency both of the *Intellect* and of the *Will.* All that can be effected, therefore, is to arrange the words according to the principal or dominant idea they convey. *Teaching,* for example, although a Voluntary act, relates primarily to the Communication of Ideas, and is accordingly placed at No. 537, under Class IV Division (II). On the other hand, *Choice, Conduct, Skill,* &c., although implying the co-operation of Voluntary with Intellectual acts, relate principally to the former, and are therefore arranged under Class V.

† It often happens that the same word admits of various applications, or may be used in different senses. In consulting the Index the reader will be guided to the number of the heading under which that word, in each particular acceptation, will be found, by means of *supplementary words* printed in Italics; which words, however, are not to be understood as explaining the meaning of the word to which they are annexed, but only as assisting in the required reference. I have also, for shortness' sake, generally omitted words immediately derived from the primary one inserted, which sufficiently represents the whole group of correlative words referable to the same heading. Thus the number affixed to *Beauty* applies to all its derivatives, such as *Beautiful, Beauteous, Beautifulness, Beautifully,* &c., the insertion of which was therefore needless. [In compiling the new Index the editor has adopted this principle as a general rule, from which, however, he has not scrupled to depart where he has deemed it expedient to do so.]

The object I have proposed to myself in this Work would have been put imperfectly attained if I had confined myself to a mere catalogue of words, and had omitted the numerous phrases and forms of expression composed of several words, which are of such frequent use as to entitle them to rank among the constituent parts of the language.* Very few of these verbal combinations, so essential to the knowledge of our native tongue, and so profusely abounding in its daily use, are to be met with in ordinary dictionaries. These phrases and forms of expression I have endeavoured diligently to collect and to insert in their proper places, under the general ideas that they are designed to convey. Some of these conventional forms, indeed, partake of the nature of proverbial expressions; but actual proverbs, as such, being wholly of a didactic character, do not come within the scope of the present Work; and the reader must therefore not expect to find them here inserted.†

For the purpose of exhibiting with greater distinctness the relations between words expressing opposite and correlative ideas, I have, whenever the subject admitted of such an arrangement, placed them in two parallel columns in the same page, so that each group of expressions may be readily contrasted with those which occupy the adjacent column, and constitute their antithesis. By carrying the eye from the one to the other, the inquirer may often discover forms of expression, of which he may avail himself advantageously, to diversify and infuse vigour into his phraseology. Rhetoricians, indeed, are well aware of the power derived from the skilful introduction of antitheses in giving point to an argument, and imparting force and brilliancy to the diction. A too frequent and indiscreet employment of this figure of rhetoric may, it is true, give rise to a vicious and affected style; but it is unreasonable to condemn indiscriminately the occasional and moderate use of a practice on account of its possible abuse.

The study of correlative terms existing in a particular language, may often throw valuable light on the manners and customs of the nations using it. Thus, Hume has drawn important inferences with regard to the state of society among the ancient Romans, from certain deficiencies which he remarked in the Latin language.‡

---

* For example:—To take time by the forelock;—to turn over a new leaf;—to show the white feather;—to have a finger in the pie;—to let the cat out of the bag;—to take care of number one;—to kill two birds with one stone, &c., &c.

† See Trench, *On the Lessons in Proverbs.*

‡ 'It is an universal observation,' he remarks, 'which we may form upon language, that where two related parts of a whole bear any proportion to each other, in numbers, rank, or consideration, there are always correlative terms invented which answer to both the parts, and express their mutual relation. If they bear no proportion to each other, the term is only invented for the less, and marks its distinction from the whole. Thus, *man* and *woman*, *master* and *servant*, *father* and *son*, *prince* and *subject*, *stranger* and *citizen*, are correlative terms. But the words *seaman*, *carpenter*, *smith*, *tailor*, &c., have no correspondent terms, which express those who are no seamen, no carpenters, &c. Languages differ very much with regard to the particular words where this distinction obtains; and may thence afford very strong inferences concerning the manners and customs of different nations. The military government of the

In many cases, two ideas which are completely opposed to each other, admit of an intermediate or neutral idea, equidistant from both; all these being expressible by corresponding definite terms. Thus, in the following examples, the words in the first and third columns, which express opposite ideas, admit of the intermediate terms contained in the middle column, having a neutral sense with reference to the former.

Identity	*Difference*	*Contrariety*
Beginning	*Middle*	*End*
Past	*Present*	*Future*

In other cases, the intermediate word is simply the negative to each of two opposite positions; as, for example—

Convexity	*Flatness*	*Concavity*
Desire	*Indifference*	*Aversion*

Sometimes the intermediate word is properly the standard with which each of the extremes is compared; as in the case of

Insufficiency	*Sufficiency*	*Redundance*

for here the middle term, *Sufficiency*, is equally opposed, on the one hand to *Insufficiency*, and on the other to *Redundance*.*

These forms of correlative expressions would suggest the use of triple, instead of double, columns, for tabulating this threefold order of words; but the practical inconvenience attending such an arrangement would probably overbalance its advantages.

It often happens that the same word has several correlative terms, according to the different relations in which it is considered. Thus, to the word *Giving* are opposed both *Receiving* and *Taking*; the former

Roman emperors had exalted the soldiery so high that they balanced all the other orders of the state: hence *miles* and *paganus* became relative terms; a thing, till then, unknown to ancient, and still so to modern languages.'—'The term for a slave, born and bred in the family, was *verna*. As *servus* was the name of the genius, and *verna* of the species without any correlative, this forms a strong presumption that the latter were by far the least numerous: and from the same principles I infer that if the number of slaves brought by the Romans from foreign countries had not extremely exceeded those which were bred at home, *verna* would have had a correlative, which would have expressed the former species of slaves. But these, it would seem, composed the main body of the ancient slaves, and the latter were but a few exceptions'.—HUME, *Essay on the Populousness of Ancient Nations.*

The warlike propensity of the same nation may, in like manner, be inferred from the use of the word *hostis* to denote both *a foreigner* and *an enemy.*

* [In the following cases, the intermediate word signifies an imperfect degree of each of the qualities set in opposition—

Light	*Dimness*	*Darkness*
Transparency	*Semitransparency*	*Opacity*
Vision	*Dimsightedness*	*Blindness*]

correlation having reference to the *persons* concerned in the transfer, while the latter relates to the *mode* of transfer. *Old* has for opposite both *New* and *Young,* according as it is applied to *things* or to *living things.* *Attack* and *Defence* are correlative terms; as are also *Attack* and *Resistance.* *Resistance,* again, has for its other correlative *Submission.* *Truth in the abstract* is opposed to *Error;* but the opposite of *Truth communicated* is *Falsehood.* *Acquisition* is contrasted both with *Deprivation* and with *Loss.* *Refusal* is the counterpart both of *Offer* and of *Consent.* *Disuse* and *Misuse* may either of them be considered as the correlative of *Use.* *Teaching* with reference to what is taught, is opposed to *Misteaching;* but with reference to the act itself, its proper reciprocal is *Learning.*

Words contrasted in form do not always bear the same contrast in their meaning. The word *Malefactor,* for example, would, from its derivation, appear to be exactly the opposite of *Benefactor:* but the ideas attached to these two words are far from being directly opposed; for while the latter expresses one who confers a benefit, the former denotes one who has violated the laws.

Independently of the immediate practical uses derivable from the arrangement of words in double columns, many considerations, interesting in a philosophical point of view, are presented by the study of correlative expressions. It will be found, on strict examination, that there seldom exists an exact opposition between two words which may at first sight appear to be the counterparts of one another; for in general, the one will be found to possess in reality more force or extent of meaning than the other with which it is contrasted. The correlative term sometimes assumes the form of a mere negative, although it is really endowed with a considerable positive force. Thus *Disrespect* is not merely the absence of *Respect;* its signification trenches on the opposite idea, namely, *Contempt.* In like manner, *Untruth* is not merely the negative of *Truth;* it involves a degree of *Falsehood.* *Irreligion,* which is properly *the want of Religion,* is understood as being nearly synonymous with *Impiety.* For these reasons, the reader must not expect that all the words which stand side by side in the two columns shall be the precise correlatives of each other; for the nature of the subject, as well as the imperfections of language, renders it impossible always to preserve such an exactness of correlation.

There exist comparatively few words of a general character to which no correlative term, either of negation or of opposition, can be assigned, and which therefore require no corresponding second column. The correlative idea, especially that which constitutes a sense negative to the primary one, may, indeed, be formed or conceived; but, from its occurring rarely, no word has been framed to represent it; for, in language, as in other matters, the supply fails when there is no probability of a demand. Occasionally we find this deficiency provided for by the contrivance of prefixing the syllable *non*; as, for instance, the negatives of *existence, performance, payment,* &c., are expressed by the compound words, *non-existence, non-performance, non-payment,* &c. Functions of a similar kind are performed by the prefixes *dis-*, anti-, contra-, mis-, in-,* and *un-.†* With respect to all these, and especially the last, great latitude is allowed according to the necessities of the case; a latitude which is limited only by the taste and discretion of the writer.

On the other hand, it is hardly possible to find two words having in all respects the same meaning, and being therefore interchangeable; that is, admitting of being employed indiscriminately, the one or the other, in all their applications. The investigation of the distinctions to be drawn between words apparently synonymous, forms a separate branch of inquiry, which I have not presumed here to enter upon; for the subject has already occupied the attention of much abler critics than myself, and its complete exhaustion would require the devotion of a whole life. The purpose of this Work, it must be borne in mind, is, not to explain the signification of words, but simply to classify and arrange them according to the sense in which they are now used, and which I presume to be already known to the reader. I enter into no inquiry into the changes of meaning they may have undergone in the course of time.‡ I am content to accept them at the value of their present currency, and have no concern with their etymologies, or with the history of their transformations; far less do I venture to thrid the mazes of the vast labyrinth into which I should be led by any attempt at a general discrimination of synonyms. The difficulties I have had to contend with have already been sufficiently great, without this addition to my labours.

The most cursory glance over the pages of a Dictionary will show that a great number of words are used in various senses, sometimes distinguished by slight shades of difference, but often diverging widely from their primary signification, and even, in some cases, bearing to it no perceptible relation. It may even happen that the very same word has two significations quite opposite to one another. This is the case with the verb *to cleave*, which means *to adhere tenaciously*, and also *to separate by a blow. To propugn* sometimes expressed *to attack*; at other times *to defend. To let* is *to hinder*, as well as *to permit. To*

---

* The words *disannul* and *dissever*, however, have the same meaning as *annul* and *sever; to unloose* is the same as *to loose,* and *inebriety* is synonymous with *ebriety.*

† In the case of adjectives, the addition to a substantive of the terminal syllable *less*, gives it a negative meaning: as *taste, tasteless; care, careless; hope, hopeless; friend, friendless; fault, faultless;* &c.

‡ Such changes are innumerable: for instance, the words *tyrant, parasite, sophist, churl, knave, villain,* anciently conveyed no opprobrious meaning. *Impertinent* merely expressed *irrelative,* and implied neither *rudeness* nor *intrusion,* as it does at present. *Indifferent* originally meant *impartial; extravagant* was simply *digressive;* and *to prevent* was properly *to precede* and *assist.* The old translations of the Scriptures furnish many striking examples of the alterations which time has brought in the signification of words. Much curious information on this subject is contained in Trench's *Lectures on the Study of Words.*

ravel means both *to entangle* and *to disentangle*. *Shameful* and *shameless* are nearly synonymous. *Priceless* may either mean *invaluable* or *of no value*. *Nervous* is used sometimes for *strong*, at other times for *weak*. The alphabetical Index at the end of this Work sufficiently shows the multiplicity of uses to which, by the elasticity of language, the meaning of words has been stretched, so as to adapt them to a great variety of modified significations in subservience to the nicer shades of thought, which, under peculiarity of circumstances, require corresponding expression. Words thus admitting of different meanings have therefore to be arranged under each of the respective heads corresponding to these various acceptations. There are many words, again, which express ideas compounded of two elementary ideas belonging to different classes. It is therefore necessary to place these words respectively under each of the generic heads to which they relate. The necessity of these repetitions is increased by the circumstance, that ideas included under one class are often connected by relations of the same kind as the ideas which belong to another class. Thus we find the same relations of *order* and of *quantity* existing among the ideas of *Time* as well as those of *Space*. Sequence in the one is denoted by the same terms as sequence in the other; and the measures of time also express the measures of space. The cause and the effect are often designated by the same word. The word *Sound*, for instance, denotes both the impression made upon the ear by sonorous vibrations, and also the vibrations themselves, which are the cause or source of that impression. *Mixture* is used for the act of mixing, as well as for the product of that operation. *Taste* and *Smell* express both the sensations and the qualities of material bodies giving rise to them. *Thought* is the act of thinking; but the same word denotes also the idea resulting from that act. *Judgment* is the act of deciding, and also the decision come to. *Purchase* is the acquisition of a thing by payment, as well as the thing itself so acquired. *Speech* is both the act of speaking and the words spoken; and so on with regard to an endless multiplicity of words. Mind is essentially distinct from Matter; and yet, in all languages, the attributes of the one are metaphorically transferred to those of the other. Matter, in all its forms, is endowed by the figurative genius of every language with the functions which pertain to intellect; and we perpetually talk of its phenomena and of its powers, as if they resulted from the voluntary influence of one body on another, acting and reacting, impelling and being impelled, controlling and being controlled, as if animated by spontaneous energies and guided by specific intentions. On the other hand, expressions, of which the primary signification refers exclusively to the properties and actions of matter, are metaphorically applied to the phenomena of thought and volition, and even to the feelings and passions of the soul; and in speaking of a *ray of hope*, a *shade of doubt*, a *flight of fancy*, a *flash of wit*, the *warmth of emotion*, or the *ebullitions of anger*, we are scarcely conscious that we are employing metaphors which have this material origin.

As a general rule, I have deemed it incumbent on me to place words and phrases which appertain more especially to one head, also under the other heads to which they have a relation, whenever it appeared to me that this repetition would suit the convenience of the inquirer, and spare him the trouble of turning to other parts of the work; for I have always preferred to subject myself to the imputation of redundance, rather than incur the reproach of insufficiency.* When, however, the divergence of the associated from the primary idea is sufficiently marked, I have contented myself with making a reference to the place where the modified signification will be found.† But in order to prevent needless extension, I have, in general, omitted *conjugate words,* ‡ which are so obviously derivable from those that are given in the same place, that the reader may safely be left to form them for himself. This is the case with adverbs derived from adjectives by the simple addition of the terminal syllable *-ly*; such as *closely, carefully, safely,* &c., from *close, careful, safe,* &c., and also with adjectives or participles immediately derived from the verbs which are already given. In all such cases, an '&c.' indicates that reference is understood to be made to these roots.§ I have observed the same rule in compiling the Index; retaining only the primary or more simple word, and omitting the conjugate words obviously derived from them. Thus I assume the word *short* as the representative of its immediate derivatives *shortness, shorten, shortening, shortened, shorter, shortly,* which would have had the same references, and which the reader can readily supply. ||

The same verb is frequently used indiscriminately either in the active or transitive, or in the neuter or intransitive sense. In these cases, I have generally not thought it worth while to increase the bulk of the Work by the needless repetition of that word; for the reader, whom I suppose

* Frequent repetitions of the same series of expressions, accordingly, will be met with under various headings. For example, the word *Relinquishment* with its synonyms, occurs as a heading at No. 624, where it applies to *intention,* and also at No. 782, where it refers to *property.* The word *Chance* has two significations, distinct from one another: the one implying the *absence of an assignable cause;* in which case it comes under the category of the relation of Causation, and occupies the No. 156: the other, the *absence of design,* in which latter sense it ranks under the operations of the Will, and has assigned to it the place No. 621. I have, in like manner, distinguished *Sensibility, Pleasure, Pain, Taste,* &c., according as they relate to *Physical,* or to *Moral Affections;* the fomer being found at Nos. 375, 377, 378, 390, &c., and the latter at Nos. 822, 827, 828, 850, &c.

† [See Editor's Preface, p. x.]

‡ By '*conjugate* or *paronymous* words is meant, correctly speaking, different parts of speech from the same root, which exactly corresponds in point of meaning.'— *A Selection of English Synonyms,* edited by Archbishop Whately.

§ [The author's practice, in this respect, has beeǹ followed in the present edition, and a reference to the group of adjectives, verbs, or other roots, has been added, where such suggestion has been thought expedient.]

|| [See note in p. xvii.]

to understand the use of the words, must also be presumed to be competent to apply them correctly.

There are a multitude of words of a specific character which, although they properly occupy places in the columns of a dictionary, yet, having no relation to general ideas, do not come within the scope of this compilation, and are consequently omitted.* The names of objects in Natural History, and technical terms belonging exclusively to Science or to Art, or relating to particular operations, and of which the signification is restricted to those specific objects, come under this category. Exceptions must, however, be made in favor of such words as admit of metaphorical application to general subjects, with which custom has associated them, and of which they may be cited as being typical or illustrative. Thus, the word *Lion* will find a place under the head of *Courage*, of which it is regarded as the type. *Anchor*, being emblematic of *Hope*, is introduced among the words expressing that emotion; and in like manner, *butterfly* and *weathercock*, which are suggestive of fickleness, are included in the category of *Irresolution*.

With regard to the admission of many words and expressions, which the classical reader might be disposed to condemn as vulgarisms, or which he, perhaps, might stigmatize as pertaining rather to the slang than to the legitimate language of the day, I would beg to observe, that, having due regard to the uses to which this Work was to be adapted, I did not feel myself justified in excluding them solely on that ground, if they possessed an acknowledged currency in general intercourse. It is obvious that, with respect to degrees of conventionality, I could not have attempted to draw any strict lines of demarcation; and far less could I have presumed to erect any absolute standard of purity. My object, be it remembered, is not to regulate the use of words, but simply to supply and to suggest such as may be wanted on occasion, leaving the proper selection entirely to the discretion and taste of the employer.† If a novelist or a dramatist, for example, proposed to delineate some vulgar personage, he would wish to have the power of putting into the mouth of the speaker expressions that would accord with his character; just as the actor, to revert to a former comparison, who had to personate a peasant, would choose for his attire the most homely garb, and would have just reason to complain if the theatrical wardrobe furnished him with no suitable costume.

Words which have, in process of time, become obsolete, are of course

---

* [The author did not in all cases rigidly adhere to this rule; and the editors have thought themselves justified both in retaining and in adding some words of the specific character here mentioned, which may be occasionally in request by general writers, although in categories of this nature no attempt at completeness has been made.]

† [It may be added that the Thesaurus is an aid not only in the choice of appropriate forms of expression, but in the rejection of those which are unfit; and that a vulgar phrase may often furnish a convenient clue to the group of classic synonyms among which it is placed. Moreover, the slang expressions admitted into the work bear but a small proportion to those in constant use by English writers and speakers.]

rejected from this collection.* On the other hand, I have admitted a considerable number of words and phrases borrowed from other languages, chiefly the French and Latin, some of which may be considered as already naturalized; while others, though avowedly foreign, are frequently employed in English composition, particularly in familiar style, on account of their being peculiarly expressive, and because we have no corresponding words of equal force in our own language.† The rapid advances which are being made in scientific knowledge, and consequent improvement in all the arts of life, and the extension of those arts and sciences to so many new purposes and objects, create a continual demand for the formation of new terms to express new agencies, new wants, and new combinations. Such terms, from being at first merely technical, are rendered, by more general use, familiar to the multitude, and having a well-defined acceptation, are eventually incorporated into the language, which they contribute to enlarge and to enrich. *Neologies* of this kind are perfectly legitimate, and highly advantageous; and they necessarily introduce those gradual and progressive changes which every language is destined to undergo.‡ Some modern writers, however, have indulged in a habit of arbitrarily fabricating new words and a new-fangled phraseology, without any necessity, and with manifest injury to the purity of the language. This vicious practice, the offspring of indolence or conceit, implies an ignorance or neglect of the riches in which the English language already abounds, and which would have supplied them with words of recognized legitimacy, conveying precisely the same meaning as those they so recklessly coin in the illegal mint of their own fancy.

A work constructed on the plan of classification I have proposed might, if ably executed, be of great value, in tending to limit the fluctuations to which language has always been subject, by establishing an authoritative standard for its regulation. Future historians, philologists, and lexicographers, when investigating the period when new words were introduced, or discussing the import given at the present time to the old, might find their labours lightened by being enabled to appeal to such a standard, instead of having to search for data among the scattered writings of the

---

* [A few apparently obsolete words have nevertheless found their way into the Thesaurus. In justification of their admission, it may be contended that well-known words, though no longer current, give occasional point by an archaic form of expression, and are of value to the novelist or dramatist who has to depict a bygone age.]

† All these words and phrases are printed in Italics. [A few of these expressions, although widely used by writers of English, are of a form which is really incorrect or unusual in their own language, in some more extreme cases of this kind, the more widely used or incorrect form has been given.]

‡ Thus, in framing the present classification, I have frequently felt the want of substantive terms corresponding to abstract qualities or ideas denoted by certain adjectives, and have been often tempted to invent words that might express these abstractions; but I have yielded to this temptation only in the four following instances, having framed from the adjectives *irrelative, amorphous, sinistral,* and *gaseous,* the abstract nouns *irrelation, amorphism, sinistrality,* and *gaseity.* I have ventured also to introduce the adjective *intersocial* to express the active voluntary relations between man and man.

age. Nor would its utility be confined to a single language; for the principles of its construction are universally applicable to all languages, whether living or dead. On the same plan of classification there might be formed a French, a German, a Latin, or a Greek Thesaurus, possessing, in their respective spheres, the same advantages as those of the English model.* Still more useful would be a conjunction of these methodized compilations in two languages, the French and English, for instance; the columns of each being placed in parallel juxtaposition. No means yet devised would so greatly facilitate the acquisition of the one language, by those who are acquainted with the other: none would afford such ample assistance to the translator in either language; and none would supply such ready and effectual means of instituting an accurate comparison between them, and of fairly appreciating their respective merits and defects. In a still higher degree would all those advantages be combined and multiplied in a *Polyglot Lexicon* constructed on this system.

Metaphysicians engaged in the more profound investigation of the Philosophy of Language will be materially assisted by having the ground thus prepared for them, in a previous analysis and classification of our ideas; for such classification of ideas is the true basis on which words, which are their symbols, should be classified.† It is by such analysis alone that we can arrive at a clear perception of the relation which these

* [This suggestion has been followed, in French, in a *'Dictionnaire Idéologique'* by T. Robertson (Paris, 1859); and, in German, in a *'Deutscher Sprachschatz'* by D. Sanders (Hamburg, 1878), and *'Deutscher Wortschatz oder Der passende Ausdruck'* by A. Schelling (Stuttgart, 1829).]

† The principle by which I have been guided in framing my verbal classification is the same as that which is employed in the various departments of Natural History. Thus the sectional divisions I have formed, correspond to Natural Families in Botany and Zoology, and the filiation of words presents a network analogous to the natural filiation of plants or animals.

The following are the only publications that have come to my knowledge in which any attempt has been made to construct a systematic arrangement of ideas with a view to their expression. The earliest of these, supposed to be at least nine hundred years old, is the AMERA CÓSHA, or *Vocabulary of the Sanscrit Language*, by Amera Sinha, of which an English translation, by the late Henry T. Colebrooke, was printed at Serampoor, in the year 1808. The classification of words is there, as might be expected, exceedingly imperfect and confused, especially in all that relates to abstract ideas or mental operations. This will be apparent from the very title of the first section, which comprehends 'Heaven, Gods, Demons, Fire, Air, Velocity, Eternity, Much:' while Sin, Virtue, Happiness, Destiny, Cause, Nature, Intellect, Reasoning, Knowledge, Senses, Tastes, Odours, Colours, are all included and jumbled together in the fourth section. A more logical order, however, pervades the sections relating to natural objects, such as Seas, Earth, Towns, Plants, and Animals, which form separate classes; exhibiting a remarkable effort at analysis at so remote a period of Indian literature.

The well-known work of Bishop Wilkins entitled 'An Essay towards a Real Character and a Philosophical Language,' published in 1668, had for its object the formation of a system of symbols which might serve as a universal language. It professed to be founded on a 'scheme of analysis of the things or notions to which names were to be assigned'; but notwithstanding the immense labour and ingenuity expended in the construction of this system, it was soon found to be far too abstruse and recondite for practical application.

In the year 1797, there appeared in Paris an anonymous work, entitled 'PASI-GRAPHIE, ou Premiers Eléments du nouvel Art-Science d'écrire et d'imprimer une langue

symbols bear to their corresponding ideas, or can obtain a correct knowledge of the elements which enter into the formation of compound ideas, and of the exclusions by which we arrive at the abstractions so perpetually resorted to in the process of reasoning, and in the communication of our thoughts.

Lastly, such analysis alone can determine the principles on which a strictly *Philosophical Language* might be constructed. The probable result of the construction of such a language would be its eventual adoption by every civilized nation; thus realizing that splendid aspiration of philanthropists—the establishment of a Universal Language. However utopian such a project may appear to the present generation, and however abortive may have been the former endeavours of Bishop Wilkins and others to realize it,* its accomplishment is surely not beset with greater difficulties than have impeded the progress to many other beneficial objects, which in former times appeared to be no less visionary, and which yet were successfully achieved, in later ages, by the continued and persevering exertions of the human intellect. Is there at the present day, then, any ground for despair, that at some future stage of that higher civilization to which we trust the world is gradually tending, some new and bolder effort of genius towards the solution of this great problem may be crowned with success, and compass an object of such vast and paramount utility? Nothing, indeed, would conduce more directly to bring about a golden age of union and harmony among the several nations and races of mankind than the removal of that barrier to the interchange of thought and mutual good understanding between man and man, which is now interposed by the diversity of their respective languages.

de maniere a etre lu et entendu dans toute autre langue sans traduction,' of which an edition in German was also published. It contains a great number of tabular schemes of categories; all of which appear to be excessively arbitrary and artificial, and extremely difficult of application, as well as of apprehension. [Systems of grouping with relation to ideas are also adopted in an *'Analytical Dictionary of the English Language'* by David Booth (London, 1835), a *'Dictionnaire Analogique de la Langue Française'* by P. Boissière (Paris), and a *'Dictionnaire Logique de la Langue Française'* by L'Abbé Elie Blanc (Paris, 1882).]

* 'The Languages,' observes Horne Tooke, 'which are commonly used throughout the world, are much more simple and easy, convenient and philosophical, than Wilkins' scheme for a *real character;* or than any other scheme that has been at any other time imagined or proposed for the purpose.'—'Επεα Πτερόεντα, p. 125.

PLAN OF CLASSIFICATION

TABULAR SYNOPSIS OF CATEGORIES

CLASS I. ABSTRACT RELATIONS

I. EXISTENCE

1°. ABSTRACT...........	1. Existence.	2. Inexistence.
2°. CONCRETE..........	3. Substantiality.	4. Unsubstantiality.
3°. FORMAL........... {	*Internal.*	*External.*
	5. Intrinsicality.	6. Extrinsicality.
4°. MODAL........... {	*Absolute.*	*Relative.*
	7. State.	8. Circumstance.

II. RELATION

	9. Relation.	10. Irrelation.
	11. Consanguinity.	
1°. ABSOLUTE......... {	12. Correlation.	
	13. Identity.	14. Contrariety.
	15. Difference.	
2°. CONTINUOUS........	16. Uniformity.	16*a*. Non-uniformity.
	17. Similarity.	18. Dissimilarity.
3°. PARTIAL........... {	19. Imitation.	20. Non-imitation.
	20*a*. Variation.	
	21. Copy.	22. Prototype.
4°. GENERAL..........	23. Agreement.	24. Disagreement.

III. QUANTITY

	Absolute.	*Relative.*
1°. SIMPLE.............	25. Quantity.	26. Degree.
	27. Equality.	28. Inequality.

	29. Mean.	
	30. Compensation.	
	By Comparison with a Standard.	
2°. COMPARATIVE....... {	31. Greatness.	32. Smallness.
	By Comparison with a similar Object.	
	33. Superiority.	34. Inferiority.
	Changes in Quantity.	
	35. Increase.	36. Decrease.
	37. Addition.	38. { Non-addition. Subduction.
	39. Adjunct.	40. Remainder.
		40*a*. Decrement.
3°. CONJUNCTIVE....... {	41. Mixture.	42. Simpleness.
	43. Junction.	44. Disjunction.
	45. Vinculum.	
	46. Coherence.	47. Incoherence.
	48. Combination.	49. Decomposition.

[xxix]

4°. CONCRETE	50. Whole.	51. Part.
	52. Completeness.	53. Incompleteness.
	54. Composition.	55. Exclusion.
	56. Component.	57. Extraneous.

IV. ORDER

1°. GENERAL	58. Order.	59. Disorder.
	60. Arrangement.	61. Derangement.
	62. Precedence.	63. Sequence.
	64. Precursor.	65. Sequel.
2°. CONSECUTIVE	66. Beginning.	67. End.
	68. Middle.	
	69. Continuity.	70. Discontinuity.
	71. Term.	
	72. Assemblage.	73. Non-assemblage. Dispersion.
3°. COLLECTIVE	74. Focus.	
	75. Class.	
4°. DISTRIBUTIVE	76. Inclusion.	77. Exclusion.
	78. Generality.	79. Speciality.
5°. CATEGORICAL	80. Rule.	81. Multiformity.
	82. Conformity.	83. Unconformity.

V. NUMBER

1°. ABSTRACT	84. Number.	
	85. Numeration.	
	86. List.	
	87. Unity.	88. Accompaniment.
	89. Duality.	
	90. Duplication.	91. Bisection.
	92. Triality.	
2°. DETERMINATE	93. Triplication.	96. Trisection.
	94. Quadruplication.	
	95. Quaternity.	97. Quadrisection.
	98. Five, &c.	99. Quinquesection, &c.
	100. Plurality.	100a. Fraction.
		101. Zero.
3°. INDETERMINATE	102. Multitude.	103. Fewness.
	104. Repetition.	
	105. Infinity.	

VI. TIME

	106. Time.	107. Neverness.
	Definite.	*Indefinite.*
	108. Period.	109. Course.
1°. ABSOLUTE	108a. Contingent Duration.	
	110. Diuturnity.	111. Transientness.
	112. Perpetuity.	113. Instantaneity.
	114. Chronometry.	115. Anachronism.

	1. *to Succession*	116. Priority.	117. Posteriority.
		118. Present time.	119. Different time.
		120. Synchronism.	
		121. Futurity.	122. Preterition.
		123. Newness.	124. Oldness.
2°. REL- ATIVE	2. *to a Period*	125. Morning.	126. Evening.
		127. Youth.	128. Age.
		129. Infant.	130. Veteran.
		131. Adolescence.	
	3. *to an Effect or purpose*	132. Earliness.	133. Lateness.
		134. Occasion.	135. Intempestivity.

3°. RECURRENT	136. Frequency.	137. Infrequency.
	138. Periodicity.	139. Irregularity.

VII. CHANGE

1°. SIMPLE.............
- 140. Change.
- 141. Permanence.
- 142. Cessation.
- 143. Continuance.
- 144. Conversion.
- 145. Reversion.

2°. COMPLEX..........
- 146. Revolution.
- 147. Substitution.
- 148. Interchange.
- 149. Changeableness.
- 150. Stability.
- *Present.*
- *Future.*
- 151. Eventuality.
- 152. Destiny.

VIII. CAUSATION

1°. CONSTANCY OF SE-QUENCE..........
- 153. { *Constant Antecedent.* Cause.
- 154. { *Constant Sequent.* Effect.
- 155. { *Assignment of Cause.* Attribution.
- 156. { *Absence of Assignment.* Chance.

2°. CONNECTION BE-TWEEN CAUSE AND EFFECT.......
- 157. Power.
- 158. Impotence.
- *Degrees of Power.*
- 159. Strength.
- 160. Weakness.

3°. POWER IN OPERA-TION.............
- 161. Production.
- 162. Destruction.
- 163. Reproduction.
- 164. Producer.
- 165. Destroyer.
- 166. Paternity.
- 167. Posterity.
- 168. Productiveness.
- 169. Unproductiveness.
- 170. Agency.
- 171. Energy.
- 172. Inertness.
- 173. Violence.
- 174. Moderation.

4°. INDIRECT POWER....
- 175. Influence.
- 175a. Absence of Influence.
- 176. Tendency.
- 177. Liability.

5°. COMBINATIONS OF CAUSES..........
- 178. Concurrence.
- 179. Counteraction.

CLASS II. SPACE

I. SPACE IN GENERAL

1°. ABSTRACT SPACE.....
- 180. { *Indefinite.* Space.
- 180a. Inextension.
- 181. { *Definite.* Region.
- 182. { *Limited.* Place.

2°. RELATIVE SPACE.....
- 183. Situation.
- 184. Location.
- 185. Displacement.

3°. EXISTENCE IN SPACE
- 186. Presence.
- 187. Absence.
- 188. Inhabitant.
- 189. Abode.
- 190. Contents.
- 191. Receptacle.

II. DIMENSIONS

1°. GENERAL..........
- 192. Size.
- 193. Littleness.
- 194. Expansion.
- 195. Contraction.
- 196. Distance.
- 197. Nearness.
- 198. Interval.
- 199. Contiguity.

2°. LINEAR.............
- 200. Length.
- 201. Shortness.
- 202. { Breadth. Thickness.
- 203. { Narrowness. Thinness.
- 204. Layer.
- 205. Filament.
- 206. Height.
- 207. Lowness.
- 208. Depth.
- 209. Shallowness.

2°. SENSATION

(1) *General* ....
- 375. Sensibility.
- 376. Insensibility.
- 377. Pleasure.
- 378. Pain.

(2) *Special*

1. *Touch* ..
- 379. Touch.
- 380. { Sensations of Touch.
- 381. Numbness.

2. *Heat* ...
- 382. Heat.
- 383. Cold.
- 384. Calefaction.
- 385. Refrigeration.
- 386. Furnace.
- 387. Refrigeratory.
- 388. Fuel.
- 389. Thermometer.

3. *Taste* ...
- 390. Taste.
- 391. Insipidity.
- 392. Pungency.
- 393. Condiment.
- 394. Savouriness.
- 395. Unsavouriness.
- 396. Sweetness.
- 397. Sourness.

4. *Odour* ..
- 398. Odour.
- 399. Inodorousness.
- 400. Fragrance.
- 401. Fœtor.

5. *Sound* ..

(i.) *Sound in General.*
- 402. Sound.
- 403. Silence.
- 404. Loudness.
- 405. Faintness.

(ii.) *Specific Sounds.*
- 406. Snap.
- 407. Roll.
- 408. Resonance.
- 408a. Non-resonance.
- 409. Sibilation.
- 410. Stridor.
- 411. Cry.
- 412. Ululation.

(iii.) *Musical Sounds.*
- 413. { Melody. Concord.
- 414. Discord.
- 415. Music.
- 416. Musician.
- 417. Musical Instruments.

(iv.) *Perception of Sound.*
- 418. Hearing.
- 419. Deafness.

6. *Light* ...

(i.) *Light in General.*
- 420. Light.
- 421. Darkness.
- 422. Dimness.
- 423. Luminary.
- 424. Shade.
- 425. Transparency.
- 426. Opacity.
- 427. Semitransparency.

(ii.) *Specific Light.*
- 428. Colour.
- 429. Achromatism.
- 430. Whiteness.
- 431. Blackness.
- 432. Gray.
- 433. Brown.
- 434. Redness.
- 435. Greenness.
- 436. Yellowness.
- 437. Purple.
- 438. Blueness.
- 439. Orange.
- 440. Variegation.

(iii.) *Perceptions of Light.*
- 441. Vision.
- 442. Blindness.
- 443. Dimsightedness.
- 444. Spectator.
- 445. Optical Instruments.
- 446. Visibility.
- 447. Invisibility.
- 448. Appearance.
- 449. Disappearance.

Class IV. INTELLECT

Division (I.). FORMATION OF IDEAS

I. OPERATIONS OF INTELLECT IN GENERAL.....	450. Intellect.	450a. Absence of Intellect.
	451. Thought.	452. Incogitancy.
	453. Idea.	454. Topic.
	455. Curiosity.	456. Incuriosity.
	457. Attention.	458. Inattention.
	459. Care.	460. Neglect.
II. PRECURSORY CONDITIONS AND OPERATIONS......	461. Inquiry.	462. Answer.
	463. Experiment.	
	464. Comparison.	
	465. Discrimination.	465a. Indiscrimination.
	466. Measurement.	
	467. Evidence.	468. Counter-evidence.

469. Qualification.

III. MATERIALS FOR REASONING..........

Degrees of Evidence.

470. Possibility.	471. Impossibility.
472. Probability.	473. Improbability.
474. Certainty.	475. Uncertainty.

IV. REASONING PROCESSES .	476. Reasoning.	477. { Intuition. Sophistry.
	478. Demonstration.	479. Confutation.
	480. Judgement.	481. Misjudgement.
	480a. Discovery.	
	482. Over-estimation.	483. Under-estimation.
	484. Belief.	485. { Unbelief. Doubt.
	486. Credulity.	487. Incredulity.
	488. Assent.	489. Dissent.
	490. Knowledge.	491. Ignorance.
V. RESULTS OF REASONING .	492. Scholar.	493. Ignoramus.
	494. Truth.	495. Error.
	496. Maxim.	497. Absurdity.

Faculties.

498. { Intelligence. Wisdom.	499. { Imbecility. Folly.
500. Sage.	501. Fool.
502. Sanity.	503. Insanity.
	504. Madman.

VI. EXTENSION OF THOUGHT	1°. *To the Past...*	505. Memory.	506. Oblivion.
		507. Expectation.	508. Inexpectation.
			509. Disappointment.
	2°. *To the Future.*	510. Foresight.	
		511. Prediction.	
		512. Omen.	
		513. Oracle.	
VII. CREATIVE THOUGHT...		514. Supposition.	
		515. Imagination.	

Division (II.). COMMUNICATION OF IDEAS

I. NATURE OF IDEAS COMMUNICATED......

516. Meaning.   517. Unmeaningness.
518. Intelligibility.   519. Unintelligibility.
520. Equivocalness.
521. Metaphor.
522. Interpretation.   523. Misinterpretation.
524. Interpreter.
525. Manifestation.   526. Latency.
527. Information.   528. Concealment.
529. Disclosure.   530. Ambush.
531. Publication.
532. News.   533. Secret.
534. Messenger.

II. MODES OF COMMUNICATION.............

535. Affirmation.   536. Negation.
537. Teaching.   538. Misteaching.
                             539. Learning.
540. Teacher.   541. Learner.
542. School.
543. Veracity.   544. Falsehood.
                             545. Deception.
                             546. Untruth.
547. Dupe.   548. Deceiver.
                             549. Exaggeration.

III. MEANS OF COMMUNICATION

1°. *Natural Means*......

550. Indication.
551. Record.   552. Obliteration.
553. Recorder.
554. Representation.   555. Misrepresentation.
556. Painting.
557. Sculpture.
558. Engraving.
559. Artist.

2°. *Conventional Means*

1. *Language generally*

560. Language.
561. Letter.
562. Word.   563. Neology.
564. Nomenclature.   565. Misnomer.
566. Phrase.
567. Grammar.   568. Solecism.
569. Style.

Qualities of Style.
570. Perspicuity.   571. Obscurity.
572. Conciseness.   573. Diffuseness.
574. Vigour.   575. Feebleness.
576. Plainness.   577. Ornament.
578. Elegance.   579. Inelegance.

2. *Spoken Language*

580. Voice.   581. Aphony.
582. Speech.   583. Stammering.
584. Loquacity.   585. Taciturnity.
586. Allocution.   587. Response.
588. Interlocution.   589. Soliloquy.

3. *Written Language*

590. Writing.   591. Printing.
592. Correspondence.   593. Book.
594. Description.
595. Dissertation.
596. Compendium.
597. Poetry.   598. Prose.
599. The Drama.

Class V. VOLITION

Division (I.). Individual Volition

I. Volition in General

1°. Acts....

600. Will.	601. Necessity.
602. Willingness.	603. Unwillingness.
604. Resolution.	605. Irresolution.
604a. Perseverance. } 606. Obstinacy. }	607. Tergiversation.
	608. Caprice.
609. Choice.	609a. Absence of Choice. 610. Rejection.

2°. Causes..

611. Predetermination.	612. Impulse.
613. Habit.	614. Desuetude.
615. Motive.	615a. Absence of Motive. 616. Dissuasion.
617. Plea.	

3°. Objects..

618. Good.	619. Evil.
620. Intention.	621. Chance.
622. Pursuit.	623. Avoidance.
	624. Relinquishment.

II. Prospective Volition........

1°. Conceptional..

625. Business.
626. Plan.
627. Method.
628. Mid-Course.   629. Circuit.
630. Requirement.

2°. Subservience to Ends...

1. Actual Subservience.

631. Instrumentality.
632. Means.
633. Instrument.
634. Substitute.
635. Materials.
636. Store.
637. Provision.   638. Waste.
639. Sufficiency.
641. Redundance.   640. Insufficiency.

2. Degree of Subservience.

642. Importance.	643. Unimportance.
644. Utility.	645. Inutility.
646. Expedience.	647. Inexpedience.
648. Goodness.	649. Badness.
650. Perfection.	651. Imperfection.
652. Cleanness.	653. Uncleanness.
654. Health.	655. Disease.
656. Salubrity.	657. Insalubrity.
658. Improvement.	659. Deterioration.
660. Restoration.	661. Relapse.
662. Remedy.	663. Bane.

3. Contingent Subservience.

664. Safety.	665. Danger.
666. Refuge.	667. Pitfall.
668. Warning.	
669. Alarm.	
670. Preservation.	
671. Escape.	
672. Deliverance.	

II. PROSPEC-TIVE VOLI-TION—*cont.*	3°. *Precursory Measures*	673. Preparation. 675. Essay. 676. Undertaking. 677. Use.	674. Non-preparation. 678. Disuse. 679. Misuse.	

III. ACTION	1°. *Simple*...	680. Action. 682. Activity. 684. Haste. 686. Exertion. 688. Fatigue.	681. Inaction. 683. Inactivity. 685. Leisure. 687. Repose. 689. Refreshment.
	2°. *Complex* .	690. Agent. 691. Workshop. 692. Conduct. 693. Direction. 694. Director. 695. Advice. 696. Council. 697. Precept. 698. Skill. 700. Proficient. 702. Cunning.	 699. Unskilfulness. 701. Bungler. 703. Artlessness.

IV. ANTAGONISM	1°. *Conditional*....	704. Difficulty.	705. Facility.
	2°. *Active*....	706. Hindrance. 708. Opposition. 710. Opponent. 712. Party. 713. Discord. 715. Defiance. 716. Attack. 718. Retaliation. 720. Contention. 722. Warfare. 724. Meditation. 725. Submission. 726. Combatant. 727. Arms. 728. Arena.	707. Aid. 709. Co-operation. 711. Auxiliary. 714. Concord. 717. Defence. 719. Resistance. 721. Peace. 723. Pacification.

V. RESULTS OF ACTION.....	729. Completion. 731. Success. 733. Trophy. 734. Prosperity. 736. Mediocrity.	730. Non-completion. 732. Failure. 735. Adversity.

Division (II.). INTERSOCIAL VOLITION

I. GENERAL..............	737. Authority. 739. Severity. 741. Command. 742. Disobedience. 744. Compulsion. 745. Master. 747. Sceptre. 748. Freedom. 750. Liberation. 753. Keeper. 755. Commission. 758. Consignee. 759. Deputy.	738. Laxity. 740. Lenity. 743. Obedience. 746. Servant. 749. Subjection. 751. Restraint. 752. Prison. 754. Prisoner. 756. Abrogation. 757. Resignation.

CLASS VI. AFFECTIONS

II. PERSONAL

III. SYMPATHETIC

2°. DIFFUSIVE	906. Benevolence.	907. Malevolence.
		908. Malediction.
		909. Threat.
	910. Philanthropy.	911. Misanthropy.
	912. Benefactor.	913. Evil doer.
3°. SPECIAL	914. Pity.	914a. Pitilessness.
	915. Condolence.	
	916. Gratitude.	917. Ingratitude.
4°. RETROSPECTIVE	918. Forgiveness.	919. Revenge.
		920. Jealousy.
		921. Envy.

IV. MORAL

1°. OBLIGATIONS	922. Right.	923. Wrong.
	924. Dueness.	925. Undueness.
	926. Duty.	927. Dereliction.
		927a. Exemption.
	928. Respect.	929. Disrespect.
		930. Contempt.
2°. SENTIMENTS	931. Approbation.	932. Disapprobation.
	933. Flattery.	934. Detraction.
	935. Flatterer.	936. Detractor.
	937. Vindication.	938. Accusation.
	939. Probity.	940. Improbity.
		941. Knave.
	942. Disinterestedness.	943. Selfishness.
3°. CONDITIONS	944. Virtue.	945. Vice.
	946. Innocence.	947. Guilt.
	948. Good Man.	949. Bad Man.
	950. Penitence.	951. Impenitence.
	952. Atonement.	
	953. Temperance.	954. Intemperance.
		954a. Sensualist.
	955. Asceticism.	
4°. PRACTICE	956. Fasting.	957. Gluttony.
	958. Sobriety.	959. Drunkenness.
	960. Purity.	961. Impurity.
		962. Libertine.
	963. Legality.	964. Illegality.
	965. Jurisprudence.	
	966. Tribunal.	
	967. Judge.	
5°. INSTITUTIONS	968. Lawyer.	
	969. Lawsuit.	
	970. Acquittal.	971. Condemnation.
	973. Reward.	972. Punishment.
		974. Penalty.
		975. Scourge.

V. RELIGIOUS

1°. SUPERHUMAN BE-INGS AND REGIONS	976. Deity.	
	977. Angel.	978. Satan.
	979. Jupiter.	980. Demon.
	981. Heaven.	982. Hell.
2°. DOCTRINES	983. Theology.	
	983a. Orthodoxy.	984. Heterodoxy.
	985. Revelation.	986. Pseudo-revelation.
3°. SENTIMENTS	987. Piety.	988. Impiety.
		989. Irreligion.

4°. Acts ....
- 990. Worship.
- 991. Idolatry
- 992. Sorcery.
- 993. Spell.
- 994. Sorcerer.

5°. Institutions ......
- 995. Churchdom.
- 996. Clergy.
- 997. Laity.
- 998. Rite.
- 999. Canonicals.
- 1000. Temple.

ABBREVIATIONS, &c.

Adj.	*adj.*	Adjectives, Participles, and Words having the power of Adjectives.
Adv.	*adv.*	Adverbs and Adverbial Expressions.
Int.	*int.*	Interjections.
Phr.	*phr.*	Phrases.
V.	*v.*	Verbs.

The numbers are those of the headings, or Categories.

Words in italics within parentheses are not intended to explain the meanings of the words which precede them, but to indicate the nature of allied group of words under the numbers which follow them.

See also the Editor's Preface, p. xi.

CLASS I
Words expressing ABSTRACT RELATIONS

THESAURUS

OF

ENGLISH WORDS AND PHRASES

CLASS I

WORDS EXPRESSING ABSTRACT RELATIONS

SECTION I. EXISTENCE

1°. BEING, IN THE ABSTRACT

1. Existence.—N. existence, being, entity, *ens, esse*, subsistence, quiddity.

reality, realness, actuality; positiveness &c. *adj.*; fact, matter of fact, sober reality; truth &c. 494; actual existence.

presence &c. (*existence in space*) 186; coexistence &c. 120.

stubborn fact; not a -dream &c. 515; no joke.

substance, essence, prime constituent, hypostatis.

[Science of existence], ontology.

V. exist, be; have -being &c. *n.*; subsist, live, breathe, stand, obtain, be the case; occur &c. (*event*) 151; have place, rank, prevail; find oneself, pass the time, vegetate.

consist in, lie in, reside in, inhere in.

come into -existence &c. *n.*; arise &c. (*begin*) 66; come forth &c. (*appear*) 446.

become &c. (*be converted*) 144; bring into existence &c. 161; coexist, preexist, endure &c. 141.

Adj. existing &c. *v.*; existent, subsistent, under the sun; in -existence &c. *n.*; extant; afloat, on foot, current, prevalent, rife, in force, -vogue; undestroyed.

real, actual, positive, absolute; true &c. 494; substan-tial, -tive; self-existing, -ent.

2. Inexistence.—N. inexistence; non-existence, -subsistence; nonentity, *nil*; negativeness &c. *adj.*; nullity; nihil-ity, -ism; *tabula rasa*, blank; abeyance; absence &c. 187; no such thing &c. 4; nothingness, oblivion, *non esse*.

annihilation; extinction &c. (*destruction*) 162.

V. not -exist &c. 1; have no -existence &c. 1; be null and void; cease to -exist &c. 1; pass away, perish; be –, become-extinct &c. *adj.*; die out; disappear &c. 449; melt away, dissolve, leave not a rack behind, leave no trace; go, be no more; die &c. 360.

annihilate, render null, nullify; abrogate &c. 756; destroy &c. 162; take away; remove &c. (*displace*) 185.

Adj. inexistent, non-existent &c. 1; negative, blank, null and void; missing, omitted; absent &c. 187; visionary &c. 515.

unreal, potential, virtual; baseless, *in nubibus*; unsubstantial &c. 4; vain.

un-born, -created, -begotten, -conceived, -produced, -made.

perished, annihilated &c. *v.*; extinct, exhausted, gone, lost, departed; defunct &c. (*dead*) 360; *spurlos versenkt*.

fabulous, ideal &c. (*imaginary*) 515; supposititious &c. 514.

Adv. negatively, virtually, &c. *adj.*

[1]

well-founded, -grounded; un-ideal, -imagined; not -potential &c. 2.

Adv. actually &c. *adj.*; in -fact, – point of fact, – reality; indeed; *de –, ipso-facto.*

2°. Being, in the Concrete

3. Substantiality.—N. substantiality, *hypostasis*; person, thing, object, article; something, a being, an existence; creature, body, substance, flesh and blood, stuff, *substratum*; matter &c. 316; physical nature.

[Totality of existences], world &c. 318; *plenum.*

Adj. substan-tive, -tial, concrete; hypostatic; personal, bodily; tangible &c. (*material*) 316; real, corporeal, evident.

Adv. substantially &c. *adj.*; bodily, essentially.

---

4. Unsubstantiality.—N. un-, in-substantiality; nothingness, nihility.

nothing, naught, *nil*, nullity, zero, cipher, no one, nobody; never –, ne'er -a one; no such thing, none in the world; nothing -whatever, – at all, – on earth; not a -particle &c. (*smallness*) 32; all -talk, – moonshine, – stuff and nonsense, matter of no import.

thing of naught, man of straw, John Doe and Richard Roe; *nominis umbra,* nonentity, figurehead, lay figure; flash in the pan, *vox et præterea nihil.*

shadow; phantasm, phantom &c. (*fallacy of vision*) 443; dream &c. (*imagination*) 515; *ignis fatuus* &c.

(*luminary*) 423; 'such stuff as dreams are made of'; air, thin air; bubble &c. 353; 'baseless fabric of a vision'; mockery.

hollowness, blank; vacuity, void &c. (*absence*) 187.

inanity, fool's paradise, fatuity, stupidity, emptiness of mind.

V. vanish, evaporate, fade, sink, fly –, die –, melt- away, dissolve, disappear &c. 449, become extinct, become invisible.

Adj. unsubstantial; fleeting; base-, ground-less; ungrounded; without –, having no- foundation.

visionary &c. (*imaginary*) 515; immaterial &c. 317; spectral &c. 980; dreamy; shadowy; ethereal, airy, imponderable, tenuous, vague.

vacant, vacuous; empty &c. 187; eviscerated; blank, hollow; nominal; null; inane.

Phr. there's nothing in it.

3°. Formal Existence

Internal conditions

5. Intrinsicality.—N. intrinsicality, inbeing, inherence, inhesion, immanence; subjectiveness; *ego*; essence; essentialness &c. *adj.*; essential part, essential stuff, substance, quintessence, incarnation, quiddity, gist, pith, core, kernel, marrow, sap, life-blood, backbone, heart, soul, life, flower; important part &c. (*importance*) 642.

principle, nature, constitution, character, ethos, type, quality, crasis, *diathesis.*

habit; temper, -ament; spirit, humour, grain, disposition, streak, tendency &c. 176.

External conditions

6. Extrinsicality.—N. extrinsicality, objectiveness, *non ego*; extraneousness &c. 57; accident; letter of the law.

Adj. derived from without; objective; extrin-sic, -sical; extraneous &c. (*foreign*) 57; modal, adventitious, additional, supervenient, fortuitous; a-, ad-scititious; incidental, casual, accidental, unessential, non-essential, accessory.

implanted, ingrafted, instilled, inculcated.

outward &c. (*external*) 220.

Adv. extrinsically &c. *adj.*

[2]

endowment, capacity; capability &c. (*power*) 157; moods, declensions, features, aspects; peculiarities &c. (*specialty*) 79; idiosyncrasy; idiocrasy; diagnostics.

V. be –, run- in the blood; be born so; be -intrinsic &c. *adj.*

Adj. derived from within, subjective; idiocratic, idiosyncratic, intrin-sic, -sical; fundamental, cardinal, normal; inherent, essential, natural; in-nate, -born, -bred, -dwelling, -grained, -wrought; radical, incarnate, thoroughbred, hereditary, inherited, immanent; congen-ital, -ite; connate, running in the blood; coeval with birth, genetic, ingenerate, -genite; indigenous; in the -grain &c. *n.*; bred in the bone, instinctive; inward, internal &c. 221; to the manner born; virtual.

characteristic &c. (*special*) 79, (*indicative*) 550; invariable, incurable, ineradicable, fixed, settled, constant, unchanging.

Adv. intrinsically &c. *adj.*; at bottom, in the main, in effect, essentially, practically, virtually, substantially, *au fond*; fairly.

4°. Modal Existence

Absolute	*Relative*
7. State.—**N.** state, condition, category, estate, lot, case, trim, mood, pickle, plight &c. 704; temper; aspect &c. (*appearance*) 448.	**8. Circumstance.**—**N.** circumstance, situation, phase, position, posture, attitude, place, point; terms; *régime*; footing, standing, status.
constitution, habitude, *diathesis*; frame, fabric &c. 329; stamp, set, fit, mould.	occasion, juncture, conjuncture; contingency &c. (*event*) 151.
mode, modality, schesis; fettle; form &c. (*shape*) 240.	predicament; emergen-ce, -cy; exigency, crisis, pinch, pass, push; turning point; crossroads.
tone, tenor, turn; trim, guise, fashion, light, complexion, style, character.	bearings, how the land lies.
V. be in –, possess –, enjoy –, labour under- a -state &c. *n.*; be on a footing, do, fare; come to pass.	**Adj.** circumstantial; given, conditional, provisional; critical; modal; contingent, incidental; adventitious &c. (*extrinsic*) 6.
Adj. conditional, modal, formal; structural, organic.	**Adv.** in the circumstances &c. *n.*, under the conditions &c. 7; thus, in such wise.
Adv. conditionally &c. *adj.*; as -the matter stands, – things are; such being the case &c. 8.	accordingly; that –, such- being the case; that being so, since, seeing that.
	as matters stand; as -things, – times-go.

conditionally, provided, if, in case; if -so, – so be, – it be so; if it so -happen, – turn out; in the event of; in such a -contingency, – case, – event; provisionally, unless, without.

according to -circumstances, – the occasion; as it may -happen, – turn out, – be; as the -case may be, – wind blows; *pro re natâ*.

Section II. RELATION

1°. Absolute Relation

9. Relation.—**N.** relation, bearing, reference, connection, apposition, interconnection, concern, cognation; applicability, appositeness; correlation	**10.** [Want, or absence of relation.] **Irrelation.**—**N.** irrelation, dissociation; inapplicability; inconnection; multifariousness; disconnection &c. (*dis-*

&c. 12; analogy; similarity &c. 17; affinity, intimacy, friendship; homology, alliance, homogeneity, association, rapport; approximation &c. (*nearness*) 197; filiation &c. (*consanguinity*) 11; interest; relevancy &c. 23; relationship, relative position; relativity; interrelation &c. 12.

comparison &c. 464; ratio, proportion.

link, tie, bond, bond of union.

V. be-related &c. *adj.*; have a relation &c. *n.*; relate –, refer- to; bear upon, regard, concern, touch, affect, have to do with; pertain –, belong –, appertain- to; have respect to; answer to; interest.

bring -into relation with, – to bear upon; connect, associate, draw a parallel; link &c. 43.

Adj. relative; correlative &c. 12; cognate; relating to &c. *v.*; relative to, in relation with, referable *or* referrible to; belonging to &c. *v.*; appurtenant to, in common with.

related, connected; implicated, associated, affiliated, akin, allied to; collateral, cognate, congenial, kindred, affinitive, *en rapport*, in touch with.

approxima-tive, -ting; approaching; proportion-al, -ate, -able; allusive, comparable.

in the same -category &c. 75; like &c. 17; relevant &c. (*apt*) 23.

Adv. relatively &c. *adj.*; pertinently &c. 23.

thereof; as -to, – for, – respects, – regards; about; concerning &c. *v.*; anent; relating –, as relates- to; with -relation, – reference, – respect, – regard- to; in respect of; while speaking –, *à propos-* of; in connection with; by the -way, – by; whereas; for –, in -as much as; in point of, as far as; on the -part, – score- of; *quoad hoc*; *pro re natâ*; under the -head &c. (*class*) 75- of; in the matter of, *in re*.

Phr. 'thereby hangs a tale.'

junction) 44; inconsequence, independence; incommensurability; irreconcilableness &c. (*disagreement*) 24; heterogeneity; unconformity &c. 83; irrelevancy, impertinence, *nihil ad rem*; intrusion &c. 24.

V. have no -relation &c. 9 to, – bearing upon, – concern &c. 9 with, – business with; not -concern &c. 9; have -nothing to do with, – no business there; intrude, &c. 24.

bring –, drag –, haul –, lug- in head and shoulders.

Adj. irrelative, irrespective, unrelated, irrelated; arbitrary; independent, unallied; un-, dis-connected; adrift, isolated, insular; extraneous, strange, alien, foreign, outlandish, exotic.

not comparable, incommensurable, heterogeneous; unconformable &c. 83.

irrelevant; rambling &c. 279; inapplicable; not -pertinent, – to the purpose; impertinent, inapposite, beside the mark, *à propos de bottes*; away from –, foreign to –, beside- the -purpose, – question, – transaction, – point; misplaced &c. (*intrusive*) 24.

remote, far fetched, out of the way, forced, neither here nor there, quite another thing; detached, segregated, segregate.

multifarious; discordant &c. 24.

incidental, parenthetical, *obiter dictum*, episodic.

Adv. parenthetically &c. *adj.*; by the -way, – by; *en passant*, incidentally; irrespectively &c. *adj.*; without reference, – regard- to; in the abstract &c. 87; *a se*.

---

11. [Relations of kindred.] **Consanguinity.—N.** consanguinity, relationship, kindred, blood; parentage &c. (*paternity*) 166; filiation, affiliation; lineage, agnation, connection, cognation, alliance, family -connection, – tie; ties of blood; blood relationship; nepotism.

kins-man, -folk; people; kith and kin; rela-tion, -tive; connection; sib; next of kin; uncle, aunt, nephew, niece; cousin, -german; first –, second- cousin; cousin -once, – twice &c.- removed; near –, distant-relation; brother, sister, one's own flesh and blood.

family, patriarch, matriarch; fraternity; brother-, sister-, cousin-hood. race, stock, generation; sept &c. 166; stirps, side; strain; breed, clan, tribe.

V. be -related &c. *adj.* – to; claim -relationship &c. *n.*- with.

Adj. related, akin, consanguineous, matrilinear, patrilineal, of the blood, family, allied, collateral; cog-, ag-, con-nate; kindred; affiliated, affine; fraternal, avuncular.

intimately –, nearly –, closely –, remotely –, distantly- related, – allied; german.

12. [Double or reciprocal relation.] **Correlation.—N.** reciprocalness &c. *adj.*; recipro-city, -cality, -cation; mutuality, correlation, correspondence, interdependence; interchange &c. 148; exchange, barter; interrelation, interconnection; alternation, see-saw.

V. reciprocate, alternate; interchange &c. 148; exchange; counterchange; interact, correspond, mutualize, give and take.

Adj. reciprocal, mutual, commutual, correlative; alternate; interchangeable; international; correspondent, complementary, analogous.

Adv. *mutatis mutandis*; *vice versâ*; each other; by turns &c. 148; reciprocally &c. *adj.*; to and fro &c. 314.

13. Identity.—N. identity, sameness, oneness, ditto, homogeneity; unity, coincidence, coalescence; convertibility; equality &c. 27; selfness, self, oneself; identification.

monotony, tautology &c. (*repetition*) 104.

synonym.

fac-simile &c. (*copy*) 21; *alter ego* &c. (*similar*) 17; *ipsissima verba* &c. (*exactness*) 494; same; self –, very –, one and the- same; very –, actual-thing; no other.

V. be -identical &c. *adj.*; match, coincide, coalesce.

treat as –, render- -the same, –identical; identify; recognize the identity of.

Adj. identical; self, ilk; the -same &c. *n.*; self same; synonymous; one and the same.

coincid-, coalesc-ent, -ing; indistinguishable; one; equivalent &c. (*equal*) 27; much -the same, – of a muchness; unaltered.

Adv. identically &c. *adj.*; on all fours; *ibid-*, *-em*.

14. [Non-coincidence.] **Contrariety. —N.** contrariety, contrast, foil, antithesis, oppositeness; counterpole; contradiction; antagonism &c. (*opposition*) 708; counteraction &c. 179.

inversion &c. 218; the -opposite, – reverse, – inverse, – converse, – antipodes, – other extreme &c. 237.

antonym.

V. be -contrary &c. *adj.*; contrast with, oppose; differ *toto cœlo*.

invert, reverse, turn the tables &c. 218.

contra-dict, -vene; antagonize &c. 708.

Adj. contrar-y, -ious, -iant; opposite, counter, dead against; ad-, con-, reverse; opposed, antithetical, contrasted, antipodean, antagonistic, opposing; conflicting, inconsistent, contradictory, at cross purposes; negative; hostile &c. 708.

differing *toto cœlo*; diametrically opposite; as opposite as -black and white, – light and darkness, – fire and water, – the poles, as different as chalk from cheese; 'Hyperion to a satyr'; quite the -contrary, – reverse; no such thing, just the other way, *tout au contraire*.

Adv. contrarily &c. *adj.*; *contra*, contrariwise, *per contra*, on the contrary, nay rather; topsy-turvy; *vice versâ*; on the other hand &c. (*in compensation*) 30.

15. Difference.—N. difference, unlikeness; heterogeneity; vari-ance, -ation, -ety; diversity, dissimilarity &c. 18; disagreement &c. 24; disparity &c. (*inequality*) 28; distinction, contradistinction; distinctness; discrepancy, divergence, contrast &c. 18; nonconformity, incompatibility, antithesis.

discord &c. 713.

modification, moods and tenses.

nice –, fine –, delicate –, subtle- distinction; shade of difference, *nuance;* discrimination &c. 465; *differentia.*

different thing, something else, variant, apple off another tree, horse of another colour, another pair of shoes; this that or the other.

V. be -different &c. *adj.*; differ, vary, ablude, mismatch, contrast; diverge –, depart –, deviate- -from; divaricate; differ -*toto cœlo*, – *longo intervallo.*

disagree &c. 713.

vary, modify &c. (*change*) 140.

discriminate &c. 465.

Adj. differing &c. *v.*; different, diverse, divided, heterogeneous; distinguishable; varied, modified; divergent, incongruous, diversified, various; discrepant, dissentient, differential; divers, all manner of; variform &c. 81; discordant &c. 713.

other, another, not the same; unequal &c. 28; unmatched; widely apart.

distinctive, characteristic; discriminative; distinguishing.

Adv. differently &c. *adj.*

Phr. *il y a fagots et fagots; tot nomines tot sententiæ;* one man's meat is another man's poison.

2°. Continuous Relation

16. Uniformity. — N. uniformity; homogene-ity, -ousness; continuity, stability, consistency; connatural-ity, -ness; homology; accordance; conformity &c. 82; agreement &c. 23.

regularity, constancy, even tenor, routine; monotony, evenness, sameness, dead level; steadiness, equability, unity.

V. be -uniform &c. *adj.*; accord with &c. 23; run through.

become -uniform &c. *adj.*; conform to &c. 82.

render uniform &c. *adj.*; assimilate, level, smooth, dress.

16a. [Absence or want of uniformity.] **Non-uniformity.—N.** diversity irregularity, unevenness; multiformity &c. 81; unconformity &c. 83; roughness &c. 256; heterogeneity, heteromorphism.

Adj. diversified, varied, irregular, uneven, rough &c. 256; multifarious; multiform &c. 81; of various kinds; all -manner, – sorts, – kinds- of.

Adv. in all manner of ways, here there and everywhere.

Adj. uniform; homo-geneous, -logous; of a piece, consistent, steady; connatural; monotonous, changeless, dreary, even, invariable, equable, level, regular, stereotyped, unchanged, unvarying; methodical &c. 60; habitual &c. 613.

Adv. uniformly &c. *adj.*; uniformly with &c. (*conformably*) 82; in harmony with &c. (*agreeing*) 23; in a -rut, – groove.

always, ever &c. 112; invariably, without exception, never otherwise; by clock-work; endlessly &c. 112.

Phr. *ab uno disce omnes.*

3°. Partial Relation

17. Similarity.—N. similarity, resemblance, likeness, similitude, sem-

18. Dissimilarity.—N. dissimil-arity, -itude; unlikeness, diversity, disparity,

blance; affinity, approximation, parallelism; parity; agreement &c. 23; ana-logy, -logicalness; correspondence, equality &c.

connatural-ness, -ity; brotherhood, family likeness.

alliteration, rhyme, pun.

repetition &c. 104; sameness &c. (*identity*) 13; uniformity &c. 16.

analogue; the like; match, *pendant*, fellow, companion, pair, mate, twin, double, counterpart, brother, sister; one's second self, *alter ego*, chip of the old block, *par nobile fratrum*, *Arcades ambo*, birds of a feather, *et hoc genus omne*.

parallel; simile; type &c. (*metaphor*) 521; image &c. (*representation*) 554; photograph; close -, striking -, speaking -, faithful &c. *adj.* - likeness, - resemblance.

V. be -similar &c. *adj.*; look like, resemble, bear resemblance, favour; savour -, smack- of; approximate; parallel, match, rhyme with; take after; imitate &c. 19; run in pairs.

render -similar &c. *adj.*; assimilate, approximate, bring near; connaturalize, make alike; rhyme, pun.

Adj. similar; resembling &c. *v.*; like, alike; twin.

analog-ous, -ical; parallel, of a piece; such as, so.

connatural, congeneric, allied to; corresponding, cognate; akin to &c. (*consanguineous*) 11.

approximate, much the same, near, close, something like, such like; a show of; mock, *pseudo*, simulating, representing.

exact &c. (*true*) 494; lifelike, faithful, realistic; true to -nature, - the life; the -very image - picture- of; for all the world like, *comme deux gouttes d'eau*; as like as -two peas, - it can stare; *instar omnium*, cast in the same mould, ridiculously like.

Adv. as if, so to speak; as -, as if- it were; *quasi*, just as, *veluti in speculum*.

dissemblance; divergence, inequality, difference &c. 15; novelty; variation, variety, originality, disguise.

V. be -unlike &c. *adj.*; vary &c. (*differ*) 15; bear no resemblance to, differ *toto cælo*.

render -unlike &c. *adj.*; vary &c. (*diversify*) 140.

Adj. dissimilar, unlike, disparate; of a different kind &c. (*class*) 75; unmatched, unique; new, novel; unprecedented &c. 83; original.

nothing of the kind; no such -, quite another- thing; far from it, other than, cast in a different mould, *tertium quid*, as like a dock as a daisy, 'very like a whale'; as different as -chalk from cheese, - Macedon and Monmouth; *lucus a non lucendo*.

diversified &c. 16a.

Adv. otherwise, *alias*.

---

19. Imitation.—N. imitation; copying &c. *v.*; transcription; repetition, mimeograph, mimeotype, duplication, reduplication; quotation; reproduction.

mockery, mimicry, mime, simulation, personation; representation &c. 554; semblance, simulacrum; pretence; copy &c. 21; assimilation.

paraphrase, parody &c. 21.

plagiarism; forgery &c. (*falsehood*) 544.

imitator, echo, cuckoo, parrot, ape, monkey, mocking-bird, mimic, impersonator; copyist.

V. imitate, copy, mirror, reflect, reproduce, repeat, borrow; do like, echo, re-echo, catch; transcribe; match, parallel.

20. Non-Imitation.—N. no imitation, genuineness, originality; creativeness.

Adj. unimitated, uncopied; unmatched, unparalleled; inimitable &c. 33; *unique*, original, primordial, primary, pristine, underived, first-hand, archetypal, prototypal.

---

[7]

mock, take off, mimic, ape, simulate, personate, impersonate; forge; act &c. (*drama*) 599; represent &c. 554; counterfeit, duplicate; portray, parody, travesty, caricature, burlesque.

follow –, tread- in the- -steps, – footsteps, – wake- of; pattern after, take pattern by; follow -suit, – the example of; walk in the shoes of, take a leaf out of another's book, strike in with; take –, model -after; emulate.

Adj. imitated &c. *v.*; mock, mimic; counterfeit, false, pseudo; modelled after, moulded on, paraphrastic; literal; imitative, apish; second-hand; imitable; sham &c. 545.

Adv. literally, to the letter, strictly, precisely, *verbatim, literatim, sic, totidem verbis,* word for word, *mot à mot.*

Phr. like master like man.

20a. Variation.—N. variation; alteration &c. (*change*) 140.

modification, moods and tenses; modulation.

divergency &c. 291; deviation &c. 279; aberration; innovation.

V. vary &c. (*change*) 140; deviate &c. 279; diverge &c. 291.

Adj. varied &c. *v.*; modified; dissimilar &c. 18; diversified &c. 16*a*.

21. [Result of imitation.] **Copy.—N.** copy, fac-simile, counterpart, *effigies,* effigy, symbol, image, form, likeness, similitude, semblance, resemblance, cast, electrotype, stereotype, tracing, ectype; imitation &c. 19; model, representation, adumbration, study; counterfeit presentment, portrait &c. (*representment*) 554.

duplicate; transcript, -ion; reflex, -ion; shadow, echo; chip of the old block; reprint, reproduction, casting, engraving, replica; transfer; second edition &c. (*repetition*) 104; *réchauffé;* apograph, fair copy, revise.

22. [Thing copied.] **Prototype.—N.** prototype, original, model, pattern, founding, precedent, standard, scantling, type, arche-, anti-type; protoplast, copy-book, module, exemplar, example, ensample, specimen; paradigm; guide; templet; lay-figure.

text, copy, manuscript, MS., design; fugleman, keynote.

die, mould; matrix, engraving, last, plasm; pro-, proto-plasm; mint; seal, punch, *intaglio,* negative, stamp.

V. be –, set- an example; set a copy; standardize.

parody, caricature, cartoon, burlesque, travesty, paraphrase.

servile -copy, – imitation; counterfeit &c. (*deception*) 545; *pasticcio.*

Adj. faithful; lifelike &c. (*similar*) 17.

4°. GENERAL RELATION

23. Agreement. — N. agreement; ac-cord, -cordance; unison, harmony, syntony; concord &c. 714; concordance, concert, understanding, convention, *entente -cordiale, consortium,* consensus of opinion, pact, mutual understanding, unanimity.

conformity &c. 82; conformance; uniformity &c. 16; consonance, consentaneousness, consistency; congruity, -ence; keeping; congeniality; correspondence, concinnity, parallelism, apposition, union.

fitness, aptness &c. *adj.*; relevancy;

24. Disagreement. — N. disagreement; dis-cord, -cordance; disunion, dissonance, dissidence, discrepancy; unconformity &c. 83; incongru-ity, -ence; discongruity, *mésalliance,* oxy-*moron;* jarring &c. *v.*; clash, collision, dissension &c. 713; conflict &c. (*opposition*) 708; controversy &c. 720; falling out, wrangle, argument.

disparity, mismatch, misfit, disproportion; disproportionateness &c. *adj.*; variance, divergence, repugnance.

unfitness &c. *adj.*; inaptitude, impropriety; inapplicability &c. *adj.*; in-

pertinen-ce, -cy; sortance; case in point; aptitude, coaptation, propriety, applicability, admissibility, commensurability, compatibility, suitability; cognation &c. (*relation*) 9.

adaptation, adjustment, arrangement, graduation, accommodation; reconcil-iation -ement; assimilation; attunement.

consent &c. (*assent*) 448; concurrence &c. 178; co-operation &c. 709.

right man in the right place, very thing; quite –, just- the thing.

V. be -accordant &c. *adj.*; agree, accord, harmonize; correspond, tally, respond; meet, suit, fit, befit, do, adapt itself to; fall in –, chime in –, square –, quadrate –, consort –, comport- with; dovetail, assimilate; fit like a glove; fit to a -tittle, – T; match &c. 17; become one.

consent &c. (*assent*) 488.

render -accordant &c. *adj.*; fit, suit, adapt, accommodate; graduate; adjust &c. (*render equal*) 27; dress, regulate, readjust; accord, harmonize, reconcile; fadge, dovetail, square.

Adj. agreeing, suiting &c. *v.*; in accord, accordant, concordant, consonant, congruous, consentaneous, correspondent, corresponding, homologous, congenial; becoming; harmonious, reconcilable, conformable; in -accordance, – harmony, – keeping, – unison, &c. *n.*- with; at one with, of one mind, of a piece; consistent, compatible, proportionate, answerable; commensurate; on all fours.

apt, apposite, pertinent, pat; to the -point, – purpose; happy, felicitous, germane, *ad rem*, in point, bearing upon, applicable, relevant, admissible.

fit, adapted, *in loco, à propos*, appropriate, seasonable, sortable, suitable, idoneous, deft; meet &c. (*expedient*) 646.

at home, in one's proper element.

Adv. *à propos of*; pertinently &c. *adj.*; *pro rata*.

Phr. *rem acu tetigisti*, the cap fits.

consistency, inconcinnity; irrelevancy &c. (*irrelation*) 10.

misjoin-ing, -der; syncretism, intrusion, interference; *concordia discors*.

fish out of water.

V. disagree; clash, quarrel, jar &c. (*discord*) 713; interfere, intrude, come amiss; not concern &c. 10; mismatch; *hymano capiti cervicem jungere equinam*.

Adj. disagreeing &c. *v.*; discordant, discrepant; at -variance, – war; hostile, antagonistic, repugnant, factious, contradictory, dissentious, incompatible, irreconcilable, inconsistent with; unconformable, exceptional &c. 83; intrusive, incongruous; disproportionate, -ed; unharmonious; unconsonant; divergent, repugnant to.

inapt, unapt, inappropriate, inept, infelicitous, improper; unsuit-ed, -able; inapplicable; un-fit, -fitting, -befitting; unbecoming; ill-timed, ill-adapted, unseasonable, *mal à propos*, inadmissible; inapposite &c. (*irrelevant*) 10.

uncongenial; ill-assorted, -sorted, -matched; mis-matched, -mated, -joined, -placed; unaccommodating, irreducible, uncommensurable, unsympathetic.

out of -character, – keeping, – proportion, – joint, – tune, – place, – season, – its element; at -odds, – variance with.

Adv. in -defiance, – contempt, – spite-of; discordantly &c. *adj.*; *à tort et à travers*.

Section III. QUANTITY

1°. Simple Quantity

25. [Absolute quantity.] **Quantity.—** **N.** quantity, magnitude; size &c. (*dimensions*) 192; amplitude, mass,

26. [Relative quantity.] **Degree.—** **N.** degree, grade, extent, measure, proportion, amount, ratio, stint, standard,

amount, *quantum*, measure, measurement, substance, strength.

[Science of quantity.] Mathematics, Mathesis.

[Definite or finite quantity] arm-, hand-, mouth-, spoon-, thimble-, capful; stock, batch, lot, dose, ration, quotum, quota, pittance, driblet, part, portion &c. 51.

Adj. quantitative, some, any, more or less.

Adv. to the tune of.

height, pitch; reach, amplitude, range, scope, size, calibre; gradation, shade; tenor, compass; sphere, station, rank, standing; rate, way, sort.

point, mark, step, stage &c. (*term*) 71; intensity, strength &c. (*greatness*) 31.

V. compare, graduate, calibrate, measure.

Adj. comparative; gradual, shading off, gradational; within the bounds &c. (*limit*), 233.

Adv. by degrees, gradually, inasmuch, *pro tanto*; how-ever, -soever; step by step, bit by bit, little by little, inch by inch, drop by drop, gradatim; by -inches, – slow degrees, – little and little; in some -degree, – measure; to some extent; just a bit.

2°. COMPARATIVE QUANTITY

27. [Sameness of quantity or degree.] **Equality.—N.** equality, parity, co-extension, symmetry, balance, poise; evenness, monotony, level.

equivalence; equi-pollence, -poise, -librium, -ponderance; par, quits; not a pin to choose; distinction without a difference, six of one and half a dozen of the other; identity &c. 13; similarity &c. 17; isotropism; coequality.

equalization, equation; equilibration, co-ordination, adjustment, readjustment.

drawn -game, -battle, draw, stalemate; neck and neck race; tie, dead heat.

match, peer, compeer, equal, mate, fellow, brother; equivalent.

28. [Difference of quantity or degree.] **Inequality.—N.** inequality; dis-, im-parity; odds; difference &c. 15; ill-balanced; unevenness; inclination of the balance, partiality; shortcoming; casting – make- weight; superiority &c. 33; inferiority &c. 34.

V. be -unequal &c. *adj.*; countervail; have –, give- the advantage; turn the scale; kick the beam; topple, -over; over-match &c. 33; not come up to &c. 34.

Adj. unequal, uneven, disparate, partial; un-, over-balanced; top-heavy, lop-sided.

Adv. *haud passibus æquis.*

V. be -equal &c. *adj.*; equal, match, reach, keep pace with, run abreast; come –, amount –, come up-to; be –, lie- on a level with; balance; cope with; come to the same thing; level off.

render -equal &c. *adj.*; equalize, level, dress, balance, equate, handicap, give points, trim, adjust, poise; fit, accommodate; adapt &c. (*render accordant*) 23; strike a balance; establish –, restore-equality, – equilibrium; readjust; stretch on the bed of Procrustes.

Adj. equal, even, level, monotonous, coequal, symmetrical, co-ordinate; on a -par, – level, – footing- with; up to the mark; equiparent.

equivalent, tantamount; quits; homologous; synonymous &c. 522; resolvable into, convertible, much at one, as broad as long, neither more nor less; much the same –, the same thing –, as good-as; all -one, – the same; equi-pollent, -ponderant, -ponderous, -balanced; equalized &c. *v.*; drawn; half and half; isochronous; isoperimetrical.

Adv. equally &c. *adj.*; *pari passu, ad eundem, cæteris paribus*; *in equilibrio*; to all intents and purposes.

Phr. it -comes, -adds up, – amounts- to the same thing.

29. Mean.—N. mean, medium, intermedium, average, run of the mill, normal, balance; mediocrity, generality, rule, ordinary -run, -ruck; golden mean &c. (*mid-course*) 628; middle &c. 68; compromise &c. 774; neutrality; middle point, middle course.

V. split the difference; take the -average &c. *n.*; reduce to a -mean &c. *n.*; strike a balance, pair off.

Adj. mean, intermediate; medial; middle &c. 68; average, normal, standard; neutral; middling, moderate.

médiocre, middle-class; *bourgeois*, commonplace &c. (*unimportant*) 643.

Adv. on an average, in the long run; taking -one with another, – all things together, – it for all in all; *communibus annis*, in round numbers.

30. Compensation.—N. compensation, equation; commutation; indemnification; compromise &c. 774; neutralization, nullification; counteraction &c. 179; reaction; measure for measure; retaliation &c. 718; equalization &c. 27; redemption, recoupment, recompense.

set-off, offset; make- casting-weight; counterpoise, equipoise, ballast; indemnity, reparation &c. 790; equivalent, *quid pro quo*; bribe, hush-money, tribute &c. 784; amends &c. (*atonement*) 952; counterclaim, counterbalance, equiponderance, countervail, cross demand.

V. make -amends, – compensation; com-pensate, -pense; indemnify; counter-act, -vail, -poise; equiponderate; balance; out-, over-, counter-balance; set off, offset, cancel; hedge, square, give and take; make up -for, – lee way; cover, fill up, neutralize, nullify; equalize &c. 27; make good; redeem &c. (*atone*) 952; recoup, pay &c. 973.

Adj. compensat-ing, -ory; amendatory, reparative, countervailing &c. *v.*; in the opposite scale; equivalent &c. (*equal*) 27.

Adv. in -return, – consideration; but, however, yet, still, notwithstanding; neverthe-, nath-less; although, though; al-, how-beit; in spite of, despite; maugre; at -all events, – any rate; be that as it may, for all that, even so, on the other hand, at the same time, *quoad minus*, *quand même*, however that may be; after all, – is said and done; taking one thing with another &c. (*average*) 29.

QUANTITY BY COMPARISON WITH A STANDARD

31. Greatness.—N. greatness &c. *adj.*; magnitude; size &c. (*dimensions*) 192; multitude &c. (*number*) 102; immensity, enormity; infinity &c. 105; might, strength, intensity, fulness; importance &c. 642; fame &c. 873.

great quantity, quantity, deal, power, sight, pot, volume, world; mass, heap &c. (*assemblage*) 72; stock &c. (*store*) 636; peck, bushel, load, cargo; cart -, wagon -, car -, truck -, ship- load; flood, spring tide; abundance &c. (*sufficiency*) 639.

principal -, chief -, main -, greater -,

32. Smallness.—N. smallness &c. *adj.*; littleness &c. (*small size*) 193; tenuity; paucity; fewness &c. (*small number*) 103; meanness, insignificance &c. (*unimportance*) 643; mediocrity, moderation.

small quantity, *modicum, minimum*; vanishing point; material point, electron, atom, particle, molecule, corpuscle, point, dab, fleck, speck, dot, mote, jot, iota, ace; *minutiæ*, details; look, thought, idea, *soupçon*, whit, tittle, shade, shadow; spark, *scintilla*, gleam; touch, cast; grain, scruple,

major –, best –, essential- part; bulk, mass &c. (*whole*) 50.

V. be -great &c. *adj.*; run high, soar, loom up, tower, bulk large, transcend; rise –, carry- to a great height; know no bounds; scale, overtop, ascend.

enlarge &c. (*increase*) 35, (*expand*) 194.

Adj. great; greater &c. 33; large, considerable, fair, above par; big, massive, huge &c. (*large in size*) 192; ample; abundant &c. (*enough*) 639; Herculean &c. 159; full, intense, strong, sound, passing, heavy, plenary, deep, high; signal, at its height, in the zenith.

world-wide, wide-spread, extensive; wholesale; many &c. 102.

goodly, noble, precious, mighty; sad, grave, serious; far gone, arrant, down-right; utter, -most; crass, gross, arch, profound, intense, consummate; rank, unmitigated, red-hot, desperate; glaring, flagrant, stark staring; thorough-paced, -going; roaring, thumping, thundering, strapping, whacking; extraordinary; important &c. 642; unsurpassed &c. (*supreme*) 33; complete &c. 52.

vast, immense, enormous, extreme; inordinate, excessive, extravagant, exorbitant, outrageous, preposterous, unconscionable, swinging, monstrous, over-grown; towering, stupendous, prodigious, astonishing, incredible; terrific, frightful; marvellous &c. (*wonder*) 870; grand.

unlimited &c. (*infinite*) 105; unapproachable, unutterable, indescribable, ineffable, unspeakable, inexpressible, beyond expression, fabulous.

un-diminished, -abated, -reduced, -restricted.

absolute, positive, stark, decided, unequivocal, essential, perfect, finished.

remarkable, of mark, marked, pointed, veriest; noticeable, uncommon, noteworthy, eminent &c. 873.

Adv. [in a positive degree] truly &c. (*truth*) 494; decidedly, unequivocally, purely, absolutely, seriously, essentially, fundamentally, radically, downright, in all conscience; for the most part, in the main.

[in a complete degree] entirely &c. (*completely*) 52; abundantly, &c. (*suf-*

granule, globule, minim, sup, sip, sop, spice, drop, droplet, sprinkling, dash, smack, tinge, tincture; inch, patch, scantling, dole; scrap, shred, tag, splinter, rag, tatter, cantlet, flitter, gobbet, mite, bit, morsel, crumb, seed, fritter, shive; snip, -pet; snick, snack, snatch, slip, scrag; chip, -ping; shiver, sliver, driblet, clipping, paring, shaving, hair.

nutshell; thimble-, spoon-, hand-, cap-, mouth-ful; fragment; fraction &c. (*part*) 51; drop in the ocean, drop in the bucket.

animalcule &c. 193.

trifle &c. (*unimportant thing*) 643; mere –, next to- nothing; hardly anything; just enough to swear by; the shadow of a shade.

finiteness, finite quantity.

V. be -small &c. *adj.*; lie in a nutshell.

diminish &c. (*decrease*) 36, (*contract*) 195.

Adj. small, little, tiny, weeny; diminutive &c. (*small in size*) 193; minute; minikin, fine, inconsiderable, dribbling, paltry &c. (*unimportant*) 643; faint &c. (*weak*) 160; slender, light, slight, scanty, scant, limited; meagre &c. (*insufficient*) 640; sparing; few &c. 103; low, so-so, middling, tolerable, no great shakes; below –, under--par, – the mark; at a low ebb; half-way; moderate, modest; tender, subtle; petty, shallow, skin-deep.

inappreciable, evanescent, infinitesimal, homœopathic, very small, atomic, molecular, ultra-, -microscopic.

petty, shallow &c. 499.

mere, simple, sheer, stark, bare; near run.

Adv. [in a small degree] to a small extent, on a small scale; a -little, – wee, – tiny bit; slightly &c. *adj.*; imperceptibly; miserably, wretchedly; insufficiently &c. 640; imperfectly; faintly &c. 160; passably, pretty well, well enough.

[in a certain or limited degree] partially, in part; in –, to a certain degree; to a certain extent; comparatively; some, rather; in some -degree, -measure; some-thing, -what; simply, only, purely, merely; at –, at the- -least,

ficiently) 639; widely, far and wide.

[in a great or high degree] greatly &c. *adj.*; much, muckle, well, indeed, very, very much, a deal, no end of, most not a little; pretty, – well; enough, in a great measure, passing richly; to a -large, – great, – gigantic- extent; on a large scale; so; never –, ever- so; ever so much; by wholesale; mightily, mighty, powerfully; with a witness, *ultra*, in the extreme, ex- tremely, exceedingly, intensely, ex- quisitely, acutely, indefinitely, im- measurably; beyond -compare, – comparison, – measure, – all bounds; incalculably, infinitely.

[in a supreme degree] pre-eminently, superlatively &c. (*superiority*) 33.

[in a too great degree] immoderately, unduly, monstrously, grossly, prepos- terously, inordinately, exorbitantly, excessively, enormously, out of all proportion, with a vengeance.

[in a marked degree] particularly, remarkably, singularly, curi- ously, uncommonly, unusually, peculiarly, notably, signally, strikingly, pointedly, mainly, chiefly; famously, egregiously, prom- inently, glaringly, emphatically, strangely, wonderfully, amazingly, surprisingly, astonishingly, incredibly, marvellously, awfully, stupendously.

[in an exceptional degree] peculiarly &c. (*unconformity*) 83.

[in a violent degree] furiously &c. (*violence*) 173; severely, des- perately, tremendously, extravagantly, confoundedly, deucedly, devilishly, with a vengeance; *à –, à toute- outrance*.

[in a painful degree] painfully, sadly, grossly, sorely, bitterly, piteously, grievously, miserably, cruelly, woefully, lamentably, shockingly, frightfully, dreadfully, fearfully, terribly, horribly, distressingly, balefully.

– most; ever so little, as little as may be, *tant soit peu*, in ever so small a degree; thus far, *pro tanto*, within bounds, in a manner, after a fashion.

almost, nearly, well nigh, short of, not quite, all but; near –, close- upon; *peu s'en faut*, near the mark; within an -ace, – inch- of; on the brink of; scarcely, hardly, barely, only just, no more than.

[in an uncertain degree] about, there- abouts, somewhere about, nearly, say; be the same -more, – little more- or less.

[in no degree] no- ways, – wise; not -at all, – in the least, – a bit, – a bit of it, – a whit, – a jot, – a shadow; in no -wise, – respect; by no -means, – man- ner of means; on no account, at no hand.

Quantity by Comparison with a Similar Object

33. Superiority.—N. supremacy, superiority, majority; greatness &c. 31; advantage, odds, pull; preponder- ance, -ation; predominance, vantage ground, coign of vantage, prevalence, partiality; personal superiority; sover- eignty &c. 737; nobility &c. (*rank*) 875; Triton among the minnows, *primus inter pares, nulli secundus*, superman; captain &c. 475.

supremacy, pre-eminence; primacy, lead, *maximum*; record; climax, crest, top; culmination &c. (*summit*) 210; transcendence; *ne plus ultra*; lion's share, Benjamin's mess; excess; bisque,

34. Inferiority.—N. inferiority, mi- nority, subordinancy; shortcoming, de- ficiency; handicap; *minimum*; smallness &c. 32; imperfection, shabbiness.

[personal inferiority] commonalty &c. 876; subordinate, substitute, sub.

V. be -inferior &c. *adj.*; fall –, come- short of; not -pass, – come up to; want.

become –, render- smaller &c. (*decrease*) 36, (*contract*) 195; hide its diminished head, retire into the shade, yield the palm, play second fiddle, take a back seat; bow.

Adj. inferior, smaller; small &c. 32;

surplus &c. (*remainder*) 40, (*redundance*) 641.

V. be -superior &c. *adj.*; exceed, excel, transcend; out-do, -balance, -weigh, -rival, -Herod, outrank, pass, surpass, surmount, get ahead of; over-top, -ride, -pass, -balance, -weigh, -match; top, o'er-top, cap, beat, win out, cut out; beat hollow; outstrip &c. 303; eclipse, throw into the shade, take the shine out of, put one's nose out of joint; have the -upper hand, – whip hand of, – advantage; turn the scale, play first fiddle &c. (*importance*) 642; preponderate, predominate, prevail; precede, take precedence, come first; come to a head, culminate; beat &c. all others, bear the palm; break the record, take the cake.

become –, render- -larger, &c. (*increase*) 35, (*expand*) 194.

Adj. superior, greater, major, higher; exceeding &c. *v.*; great &c. 31; distinguished, *ultra*; vaulting; more than a match for.

supreme, greatest, maximal, maximum, utmost, paramount, pre-eminent, foremost, crowning; first-rate &c. (*important*) 642, (*excellent*) 648; unrivalled; peer-, match-less; none such, second to none, *sans pareil*; un-paragoned, -paralleled, -equalled, -approached, -surpassed; superlative, inimitable, *facile princeps*, incomparable, sovereign, without parallel, *nulli secundus, ne plus ultra*; beyond -compare, – comparison; culminating &c. (*topmost*) 210; transcend-ent, -ental; *plus royaliste que le Roi.*

increased &c. (*added to*) 35; enlarged &c. (*expanded*) 194.

Adv. beyond, more, over; over –, above- the mark; above par; upwards –, in advance- of; over and above; at the top of the scale, on the crest, at its height.

[in a superior or supreme degree] eminently, egregiously, pre-eminently, surpassing, prominently, superlatively, supremely, above all, of all things, the most, to crown all, *par excellence*, principally, especially, particularly, peculiarly, *a fortiori*, even, yea, still more.

Phr. 'we shall not look upon his like again.'

minor, less, lesser, deficient, minus, lower, subordinate, secondary; second-rate &c. (*imperfect*) 651; sub, subaltern; thrown into the shade; weighed in the balance and found wanting; not fit to hold a candle to.

least, smallest &c. (*see* little, small &c. 193); lowest.

diminished &c. (*decreased*) 36; re-duced &c. (*contracted*) 195; unimpor-tant &c. 643.

Adv. less; under –, below- -the mark, – par; at -the bottom of the scale, – a low ebb, – a disadvantage; short of, under.

CHANGES IN QUANTITY

35. Increase—N. increase, augmen-tation, addition, enlargement, exten-sion; dilatation &c. (*expansion*) 194; multiplication; increment, accretion; accession &c. 37; production &c. 161; development, growth; aggrandizement, aggravation, intensification; rise; as-cent &c. 305; anabasis; ex-aggeration, -acerbation; spread &c. (*dispersion*) 73; flood-, spring-, -tide; gain, produce, profit &c. 618; booty, plunder &c. 793.

V. increase, augment, add to, en-large; dilate &c. (*expand*) 194; grow,

36. Non-Increase, Decrease.—N. decrease, diminution; lessening &c. *v.*; subtraction &c. 38; reduction, abatement, declension; shrinkage &c. (*contraction*) 195; coarctation; abridg-ment &c. (*shortening*) 201; extenuation.

subsidence, catabasis, wane, ebb-, neap-tide, decline; descent &c. 306; decrement, reflux, depreciation; ero-sion, wear and tear, deterioration &c. 659; anticlimax; mitigation &c. (*mod-eration*) 174.

V. decrease, diminish, lessen; abridge

wax, mount, swell, get ahead, gain strength; advance; run –, shoot- up; rise; ascend &c. 305; sprout &c. 194.

aggrandize; raise, exalt; deepen, heighten; lengthen; thicken; strengthen; intensify, enhance, inflate, magnify, double, redouble; multiply; aggravate, exaggerate; ex-asperate, -acerbate; add fuel to the flame, *oleum addere camino*, superadd &c. (*add*) 37; spread &c. (*disperse*) 73.

Adj. increased &c. *v.*; on the increase, undiminished; additional &c. (*added*) 37; increasing &c. *v.*; growing, crescent, intensive, cumulative.

Adv. *crescendo*, increasingly.
Phr. *vires acquirit eundo*.

&c. (*shorten*) 201; shrink &c. (*contract*) 195; drop –, fall –, tail- off; fall away, waste, wear, erode; wane, ebb, decline; descend &c. 306; subside; deliquesce, melt –, die -away; retire into the shade, hide its diminished head, fall to a low ebb, run low, languish, decay, crumble, consume away.

bate, abate, dequantitate; discount; depreciate; extenuate, lower, weaken, attenuate, fritter away; mitigate &c. (*moderate*) 174; belittle, minimize; dwarf, throw into the shade; keep down, reduce &c. 195; shorten &c. 201; subtract &c. 38.

Adj. unincreased &c. (*see* increase &c. 35); decreased &c. *v.*; decreasing &c. *v.*; on the -wane &c. *n.*; deliquescent.

Adv. *diminuendo, decrescendo*, decreasingly.

3°. Conjunctive Quantity

37. Addition.—N. addition, annexation, adjection; junction &c. 43; super-position, -addition, -junction, -fetation; accession, reinforcement; increase &c. 35; increment, supplement; accompaniment &c. 88; interposition &c. 228; insertion &c. 300; summation &c. 85; adjunct &c. 39.

V. add, annex, adject, affix, attach, superadd, subjoin, superpose; clap –, saddle- on; tack to, postfix, append, tag; ingraft; saddle with; sprinkle; introduce &c. (*interpose*) 228; insert &c. 300.

become added, accrue; ad-, supervene; add up &c. 85.

reinforce, strengthen, swell the ranks of; augment &c. 35.

Adj. added &c. *v.*; additional; supplement, -al, -ary; suppletory, subjunctive; adjec-, adsci-, asci-titious; additive, extra, spare, further, fresh, more, new, ulterior, other, auxiliary, supernumerary, accessory.

Adv. in addition, more, plus, extra; and, also, likewise, too, furthermore, further, item; and -also, – eke; else, besides, to boot, *et cætera*; &c.; and so -on, – forth; into the bargain, *cum multis aliis*, over and above, moreover.

with, withal; including, inclusive, as well as, not to mention, let

38. Non-Addition. Subduction.—N. sub-traction, -duction; deduction, retrenchment; removal; ab-, sub-lation; abstraction &c. (*taking*) 789; garbling &c. *v.*; mutilation, detruncation; amputation, severance; abs-, ex-, re-cision; curtailment &c. 201; minuend, subtrahend; decrease &c. 36; abrasion.

V. sub-tract, -duct; rebate, de-duct, -duce; bate, retrench; remove, withdraw; take -from, – away; detract.

garble, mutilate, amputate, sever, detruncate; cut -off, – away, – out; expurgate; abscind, excise; pare, thin, prune, decimate; abrade, scrape, file; geld, castrate, emasculate, unman, spay, caponize; eliminate.

diminish &c. 36; curtail &c. (*shorten*) 201; deprive of &c. (*take*) 789; weaken.

Adj. subtracted &c. *v.*; subtractive. tailless, acaudal.

Adv. in -deduction &c. *n.*; less; short of; minus, without, except, excepting, with the exception of, barring, bar, save, exclusive of, save and except, with a reservation.

alone; together -, along -, coupled -, in conjunction- with; conjointly; jointly &c. 43.

39. [Thing added.] **Adjunct.—N.** adjunct; addit-ion, -ament; *additum*, affix, appendage, annex; augment, -ation; increment, reinforcement, supernumerary, accessory, item; garnish, sauce; accompaniment &c. 88; adjective, *addendum*, accession, complement, supplement; continuation; extension, subscript, tag, appendix, postscript, interlineation, interpolation, insertion.

rider, codicil, off-shoot, episode, side issue, corollary; piece; flap, lapel, label, tab, strip, fold, lappet, apron, skirt, embroidery, trappings, *cortège*; tail, suffix &c. (*sequel*) 65; wing.

Adj. additional &c. 37.

Adv. in addition &c. 37.

40. [Thing remaining.] **Remainder·** **—N.** remainder, residue; remains, *remanet*, remnant, rest, relic, relict; leavings, heel-tap, odds and ends, cheese-parings, candle ends, orts; *residuum*; dottle, dregs &c. (*dirt*) 653; refuse &c. (*useless*) 645; stubble, result, educt; fag-end, stub; ruins, wreck, skeleton, stump; *alluvium*.

surplus, overplus, excess; balance, complement; superfluity &c. (*redundance*) 641; surviv-al, -ance; afterglow.

V. remain; be -left &c. *adj.*; exceed, survive; leave.

Adj. remaining, left; left -behind, - over; residu-al, -ary; over, odd; unconsumed, sedimentary; surviving; net; exceeding, over and above; outlying, -standing; cast off &c. 782; superfluous &c. (*redundant*) 641.

40a. [Thing deducted.] **Decrement.—N.** decrement, discount, rebate, defect, loss, deduction, eduction, tare; drawback; waste, wastage; reprise.

41. [Forming a whole without coherence.] **Mixture.—N.** mix-, admix-, commix-ture, -tion, mingling; commixion, immixture, interfusion, intermixture, alloyage, matrimony; junction &c. 43; combination &c. 48; entanglement, interlacing; miscegenation, interbreeding.

impregnation; in-, dif-, suf-, trans fusion; infiltration; seasoning, sprinkling, interlarding; interpolation &c. 228; adulteration, sophistication.

[Thing mixed] tinge, tincture, touch, dash, smack, sprinkling, spice, seasoning, infusion, *soupçon*.

[Compound resulting from mixture] alloy, brass, bronze, pewter &c.; amalgam, *magma*, blend, half-and-half, *mélange*, *tertium*, *quid*, miscellany, *ambigu*, medley, mess, hash, hotchpotch, hodgepodge, *pasticcio*, patchwork, odds and ends, all sorts; jumble &c. (*disorder*) 59; salad, sauce, mash, *omnium gatherum*, gallimaufry, ragout, *olla podrida*, *olio*, salmagundi, *potpourri*, Noah's ark; texture, mingled yarn; mosaic &c. (*variegation*) 440.

half-blood, -caste, -breed, Eurasian; mulatto; terc-, quart-, quinteron &c.; quad-, octo-roon; *griffo*, *zambo*; cross, hybrid, mongrel &c. 83.

42. [Freedom from mixture.] **Simpleness.—N.** simpleness &c. *adj.*; purity, homogeneity.

elimination; sifting &c. *v.*; purification &c. (*cleanness*) 652.

V. render -simple &c. *adj.*; simplify.

sift, winnow, bolt, eliminate; narrow down; get rid of, exclude &c. 55; clear; purify &c. (*clean*) 652; disentangle &c. (*disjoin*) 44.

Adj. simple, uniform, of a piece, homogeneous, single, pure, clear, sheer, neat; Attic.

un-mixed, -mingled, -blended, -combined, -compounded; elementary, undecomposed; un-adulterated, -sophisticated, -alloyed, -tinged, -fortified; pure and simple.

free -, exempt- from; exclusive.

Adv. simply &c. *adj.*; only.

V. mix; join &c. 43; combine &c. 48; com-, im-, inter-mix; mix up with, mingle; com-, inter-, be-mingle; shuffle &c. (*derange*) 61; pound together; hash -, stir- up; knead, brew; impregnate with; interlard &c. (*interpolate*) 228; inter-twine, -weave &c. 219; associate with, miscegenate, interbreed.

be mixed &c.; get among, be entangled with.

instil, imbue; in-, suf-, trans-fuse; infiltrate, dash, tinge, tincture, season, sprinkle, besprinkle, attemper, medicate, blend, cross; alloy, amalgamate, compound, adulterate, sophisticate, infect.

Adj. mixed &c. *v.*; implex, composite, half-and-half, linsey-wolsey, hybrid, mongrel, heterogeneous; motley &c. (*variegated*) 440; miscellaneous, promiscuous, indiscriminate; miscible.

Adv. among, amongst, amid, amidst, with; in the midst of, in the crowd.

43. Junction.—N. junction; joining &c. *v.*; joinder, union; con-nection, -junction, -jugation, compendency, annex-ion, -ation, -ment; coalition; astriction, attachment, compagination, vincture, ligation, alligation; accouplement; marriage &c. (*wedlock*) 903; infibulation, inosculation, symphysis, anastomosis, confluence, communication, concatenation; concurrence, meeting, reunion; assemblage &c. 72.

copulation, coition, intercourse.

joint, joining, juncture, chiasma, pivot, hinge, articulation, commissure, seam, suture, gusset, stitch, splice; link &c. 45; mitre, mortise.

closeness, tightness &c. *adj.*; coherence &c. 46; combination &c. 48.

V. join, unite; con-join, -nect; associate; put -, lay -, clap -, hang -, lump -, hold -, piece -, tack -, fix -, bind up- together; embody, re-embody; roll into one.

attach, fix, affix, saddle on, fasten, bind, secure, clinch, twist, make -fast &c. *adj.*; tie, pinion, string, strap, sew, lace, stitch, tack, paste, knit, button, buckle, hitch, lash, truss, bandage, braid, splice, swathe, gird, tether, moor, picket, harness, chain; fetter &c. (*restrain*) 751; lock, latch, belay, brace, hook, grapple, leash, couple, accouple, link, yoke, bracket; marry &c. (*wed*) 903; bridge over, span.

pin, nail, bolt, hasp, clasp, clamp, screw, rivet; impact, solder, braze, cement, set; weld -, fuse- together; wedge, rabbet, mortise, mitre, jam, dovetail, enchase; graft, ingraft, inosculate; en-, in-twine; inter-link, -lace,

44. Disjunction.—N. dis-junction, -connection, -unity, -union, -association, -engagement, -sociation; discontinuity &c. 70; inconnection; abstraction, -edness; isolation; insul-arity, -ation; oasis; separateness &c. *adj.*; severalty; *disjecta membra*; dispersion &c. 73; apportionment &c. 786.

separation; parting &c. *v.*; detachment, segregation; divorce, sejunction, seposition, diduction, diremption, discerption; elision; *cæsura*, division, subdivision, break, fracture, rupture; compartition; dis-memberment, -integration, -location; luxation; sever-, dis-sever-ance; scission; re-, ab-scission; circumcision; lacer-, dilacer-ation; dis-, ab-ruption; avulsion, divulsion; section, resection, cleavage; fission; separability; separatism.

fissure, breach, rent, split, rift, crack, slit, slot, incision.

dissection, anatomy; decomposition &c. 49; cutting instrument &c. (*sharpness*) 253; saw.

V. be -disjoined &c.; come -, fall- -off, - to pieces; peel off; get loose.

dis-join, -connect, -engage, -unite, -sociate, -pair; divorce, part, dispart, detach, uncouple, separate, cut off, rescind, segregate; set -, keep- apart; insulate, isolate; throw out of gear; cut adrift; loose; un-loose, -do, -bind, -tie, -hitch, -chain, -lock &c. (*fix*) 43, -pack, -ravel; disentangle; set free &c. (*liberate*) 750.

sunder, divide, subdivide, sectionalize, sever, dissever, abscind; cut; segment; in-cide, -cise; circumcise; saw, snip, nib, nip, cleave, rive, rend, slit,

-twine, -twist, -weave; entangle; twine round, belay; tighten; trice –, screw-up.

be -joined &c.; hang –, hold- together; cohere &c. 46.

Adj. joined &c. *v.*; joint; con-joint, -junct; corporate, compact; hand in hand.

firm, fast, close, tight, taut, taught, tense, secure, set, intervolved; in-separable, -dissoluble, -secable, -severable.

Adv. jointly &c. *adj.*; in conjunction with &c. (*in addition to*) 37; fast, firmly &c. *adj.*; intimately.

split, splinter, chip, crack, snap, break, tear, burst; rend &c. -asunder, – in twain; wrench, rupture, shatter, shiver, cranch, crunch, craunch, chop; rip up; hack, hew, slash; whittle; haggle, hackle, discind, lacerate, scamble, mangle, gash, hash, slice.

cut up, carve, quarter, dissect, anatomize; take –, pull –, pick –, tear- to pieces; tear to tatters, – piecemeal; divellicate; skin &c. 226; dis-integrate, -member, -branch, -band; disperse &c. 73; dis-locate, -joint; break up; mince; comminute &c. (*pulverize*) 330; distribute, apportion &c. 786.

part, – company; separate, leave; alienate, estrange.

Adj. disjoined &c. *v.*; discontinuous &c. 70; bipartite, multipartite, abstract; digitate; disjunctive; isolated &c. *v.*; insular, separate, disparate, discrete, apart, asunder, far between, loose, free; unattached, -annexed, -associated, -connected; distinct; adrift; straggling; rift, reft, cleft, split.

[capable of being divided] scissile, partible, divisible, separable, severable, detachable.

Adv. separately &c. *adj.*; one by one, severally, apart; adrift, asunder, in twain; in the abstract, abstractedly.

---

45. [Connecting medium.] **Vinculum.—N.** vinculum, link, *nexus*; connec-tive, -tion; junction &c. 43; bond of union, copula, intermedium, hyphen; bracket; bridge, stepping-stone, isthmus.

bond, tendon, tendril; fibre; cord, -age; riband, ribbon, rope, guy, cable, line, halser, hawser, painter, moorings, wire, chain; string &c. (*filament*) 205.

fastening, tie; liga-ment, -ture; strap; bowline, halliard, tackle, lanyard, rigging, shrouds; standing –, running- rigging; traces, harness; yoke; band, -age; brace, roller, fillet; inkle; with, withe, withy; thong, braid; girder, tie-beam; girt, cinch, girth, girdle, cestus, garter, braces, suspenders, halter, noose, lasso, lariat, surcingle, knot, hitch, running knot, frog.

pin, corking pin, nail, brad, tack, skewer, staple, cleat, clamp; cramp, screw, button, buckle, clasp, hasp, hinge, hank, catch, latch, bolt, ring, latchet, pawl, tag; tooth; stud; hook, – and eye; morse, lock, holdfast, padlock, rivet; anchor, grappling-iron, drawbar, coupler, drawhead, coupling, treenail, trennel, stake, pale, pile, post, bollard.

cement, glue, gum, paste, size, wafer, solder, lute, putty, bird-lime, mortar, stucco, plaster, grout.

shackle, rein &c. (*means of restraint*) 752; suspender &c. 214; prop &c. (*support*) 215.

V. bridge over, span; connect &c. 43; hang &c. 214.

46. Coherence.—N. co-, ad-herence, -hesion, -hesiveness; concretion, accretion; con-, ag-glutination, -glomeration; aggregation; consolidation, set, cementation; sticking, soldering &c. *v.*; connection.

47. [Want of adhesion, non-adhesion, immiscibility.] **Incoherence.—N.** non-adhesion; immiscibility; incoherence; looseness &c. *adj.*; laxity; relaxation; loosening &c. *v.*; freedom; disjunction &c. 44; rope of sand.

tenacity, toughness; stickiness &c. 352; insepara-bility, -bleness; bur, remora.

conglomerate, concrete &c. (*density*) 321.

V. cohere, adhere, stick, cling, cleave, hold, take hold of, hold fast, close with, embrace, clasp, hug; grow –, hang-together; twine round &c. (*join*) 43.

stick like -a leech, – wax; stick close; cling like -ivy, – a bur; adhere like -a remora, – Dejanira's shirt.

glue; ag-, con-glutinate; cement, lute, paste, gum; solder, weld; cake, coagulate, consolidate &c. (*solidify*) 321; agglomerate.

Adj. co-, ad-hesive, -hering &c. *v.*; tenacious, tough; sticky &c. 352.

united, unseparated, sessile, inseparable, inextricable, infrangible; compact &c. (*dense*) 321.

48. Combination.—N. combination; mixture &c. 41; alloy; junction &c. 43; union, unification, synthesis, incorporation, amalgamation, embodiment, coalescence, crasis, fusion, blend, blending, absorption, centralization, federation.

compound, amalgam, composition, *tertium quid*; resultant, impregnation.

V. combine, unite, incorporate, alloy, intertwine &c. 41; amalgamate, embody, absorb, re-embody, blend, merge, fuse, melt into one, consolidate, coalesce, centralize, impregnate; put –, lump- together; federate, associate; fraternize; cement a union, marry, wed, couple, pair, ally.

Adj. combined &c. *v.*; conjunctive, conjugate, conjoint, allied, confederate; impregnated with, ingrained, inoculated.

V. make -loose &c. *adj.*; loosen slacken, relax; un-glue &c. 46; detach &c. (*disjoin*) 44.

Adj. non-adhesive, immiscible; incoherent, detached, loose, slack, baggy, lax, relaxed, flapping, streaming; dishevelled; segregated, like grains of sand; un-consolidated &c. 321, -combined &c. 48; non-cohesive.

49. Decomposition.—N. decomposition, analysis, diæresis, dissection, resolution, catalysis, electrolysis, hydrolysis, photolysis, dissolution; dispersion &c. 73; disjunction &c. 44; disintegration, decay, rot, putrefaction, putrescence, caries, necrosis, corruption &c. (*uncleanness*) 653.

V. decom-pose, -pound; analyze, disembody, dissolve; resolve –, separate-into its elements; electrolyze; dissect, decentralize, break up; disintegrate; disperse &c. 73; unravel &c. (*unroll*) 313; crumble into dust; decay &c. *n.*; deteriorate &c. 659.

Adj. decomposed &c. *v.*; catalytic, analytical.

4°. Concrete Quantity

50. Whole. [Principal part.]—N. whole, totality, integrity; totalness &c. *adj.*; entirety, *ensemble*, collectiveness; unity &c. 87; completeness &c. 52; indivisibility, indiscerptibility; integration, embodiment; integer, integral.

all, the whole, total, aggregate, one and all, gross amount, sum, sum-total, *tout ensemble*, length and breadth of, Alpha and Omega, 'be all and end all,' lock, stock and barrel.

bulk, mass, lump, tissue, staple, body, torso, *compages*; trunk, bole, hull, hulk, skeleton; greater –, major

51. Part.—N. part, portion; dose; item, particular; aught, any; division, ward; subdivision, section; chapter, verse; article, clause, count, paragraph, passage; phrase; number, volume, book, fascicule; sector, segment; fraction, fragment; cantle, -t; frustum; detachment, parcel, unit, class &c. 75.

piece, lump, bit; cut, -ting; chip, chunk, collop, slice, scale, shard; lamina &c. 204; moiety; small part; morsel, scrap, crumb; particle &c. (*smallness*) 32; instalment, dividend; share &c. (*allotment*) 786.

–, best –, principal –, main- part; essential part &c. (*importance*) 642; lion's share, Benjamin's mess; the long and the short; nearly –, almost- all.

V. form –, constitute- a whole; integrate, embody, amass; aggregate &c. (*assemble*) 72; amount to, come to.

Adj. whole, total, integral, entire; complete &c. 52; one, individual.

un-broken, -cut, -divided, -severed, -clipped, -cropped, -shorn; seamless; undiminished; un-demolished, -dissolved, -destroyed, -bruised.

in-divisible, -dissoluble, -dissolvable, -discerptible.

wholesale, sweeping, comprehensive.

Adv. wholly, altogether; totally &c. (*completely*) 52; entirely, all, all in all, considering all things, in a body, collectively, all put together; in the -aggregate, – lump, – mass, – gross, – main, – long run; *en masse*, on the whole, as a whole, bodily, *en bloc*, *in extenso*, throughout, every inch; substantially.

débris, odds and ends, oddments, *detritus*; *excerpta*; member, limb, lobe, lobule, arm, wing, scion, branch, bough, joint, link, offshoot, ramification, twig, stipule, tendril, bush, spray, sprig; runner; leaf, -let; stump; constituent, ingredient, component part &c. 56.

compartment; department &c. (*class*) 75; county &c. (*region*) 181.

V. part, divide, break &c. (*disjoin*) 44; partition &c. (*apportion*) 786.

Adj. fractional, fragmentary; sectional, aliquot; divided &c. *v.*; in compartments, multifid, incomplete, partial, divided &c. 44.

Adv. partly, in part, partially; piecemeal, part by part; by -instalments, – snatches, – inches, – driblets; bit by bit, inch by inch, foot by foot, drop by drop; in -detail, – lots.

---

52. Completeness.—N. completeness &c. *adj.*; completion &c. 729; integration; integrality.

entirety; universality; totality; perfection &c. 650; solid-ity, -arity; unity; all; *ne plus ultra*, ideal, limit.

complement, supplement, make-weight; filling up &c. *v.*

impletion; satur-ation, -ity; high water; high –, flood –, spring- tide; fill, load, bumper, bellyful; brimmer; sufficiency &c. 639.

V. be -complete &c. *adj.*; come to a head.

render -complete &c. *adj.*; complete &c. (*accomplish*) 729; fill, charge, load, replenish; make-up, – good; piece –, eke- out; supply deficiencies; fill -up, – in, – to the brim, – the measure of; saturate &c. 869.

go the whole -hog, – length, go all lengths.

Adj. complete, entire; whole &c. 50; perfect &c. 650; full, good, absolute, thorough, plenary; solid, undivided; with all its parts.

exhaustive, radical, sweeping, thorough-going; dead.

regular, consummate, unmitigated, sheer, unqualified, unconditional, free; abundant &c. (*sufficient*) 639.

53. Incompleteness.—N. incompleteness &c. *adj.*; deficiency, short -measure, – weight; shortcoming &c. 304; insufficiency &c. 640; imperfection &c. 651; immaturity &c. (*non-preparation*) 674; half measures.

[part wanting] defect, deficit, shortage, ullage, defalcation, omission, *caret*; interval &c. 198; break &c. (*discontinuity*) 70; non-completion &c. 730; missing link.

V. be -incomplete &c. *adj.*; fall short of &c. 304; lack &c. (*be insufficient*) 640; neglect &c. 460.

Adj. incomplete; imperfect &c. 651; unfinished; uncompleted &c. (*see* complete &c. 729); defective, deficient, wanting; failing; in -default, – arrear; short, – of; hollow, meagre, lame, half-and-half, perfunctory, sketchy; crude &c. (*unprepared*) 674.

mutilated, garbled, mangled, docked, lopped, truncated; bobtailed, cropped, bobbed, shingled.

in -progress, – hand; going on, proceeding.

Adv. incompletely &c. *adj.*; by halves.

Phr. *cætera desunt*; *caret*.

---

brimming; brim-, top-ful; chock –, choke- full; as full as -an egg is of meat, – a vetch, – a tick; saturated, crammed; replete &c. (*redundant*) 641; fraught, laden; full-laden, -fraught, -charged; heavy laden.

completing &c. *v.*; supplement-al, -ary; ascititious.

Adv. completely &c. *adj.*; altogether, outright, wholly, totally, *in toto*, quite; over head and ears; effectually, for good and all, nicely, fully, through thick and thin, head and shoulders; neck and -heel, – crop; all out; in -all respects, – every respect; at all points, out and out, to all intents and purposes; *toto cœlo*; utterly, clean, – as a whistle; to the -full, – utmost, – backbone; hollow, stark; heart and soul, root and branch; down to the ground.

to the top of one's bent, as far as possible, *à outrance*.

throughout; from -first to last, – beginning to end, – end to end, – one end to the other, – Dan to Beersheba, – head to foot, – head to heels, – top to toe, – top to bottom; *de fond en comble*; *à fond, a capite ad calcem, ab ovo usque ad mala*, fore and aft; every -whit, – inch; *cap-à-pie*, to the end of the chapter; up to the -brim, – ears, – eyes; as . . . as can be.

on all accounts; *sous tous les rapports*; with a -vengeance, – witness.

---

54. Composition.—N. composition, constitution, crasis, synthesis; make-up; combination &c. 48; inclusion, admission, comprehension, reception; embodiment, formation, conformation, production.

compilation &c. 72; (*musical*) composition &c. 415; painting &c. 556; writing &c. 590; typography &c. 591.

V. be -composed, – made, – formed, – made up- of; consist of, be resolved into.

include &c. (*in a class*) 76; subsume; synthesize; contain, hold, comprehend, take in, admit, embrace, embody; involve; implicate, drag into.

compose, constitute, form, make; make –, fill –, build- up; weave, construct, fabricate; compile; write, draw; set up (*printing*); enter into the composition of &c. (*be a component*) 56.

Adj. containing, constituting &c. *v.*

---

56. Component.—N. component; component –, integral –, integrant-part; element, constituent, ingredient, leaven; part and parcel; contents; appurtenance; feature; member &c. (*part*) 51; personnel.

V. enter into, – the composition of; be a -component &c. *n.*; be –, form-part of; merge –, be merged- in; be

55. Exclusion.—N. exclusion, non-admission, omission, exception, rejection, repudiation; exile &c. (*seclusion*) 893; preclusion, lock out, ostracism, prohibition; disbarment, expulsion, ban.

separation, segregation, seposition, elimination, coffer-dam.

V. be excluded from &c.

exclude, bar, ban; leave –, shut –, thrust –, bar- out; reject, repudiate, spurn, blackball; ostracize, boycott; lay –, put –, set -apart, – aside; relegate, segregate; throw overboard; strike -off, – out; neglect &c. 460; banish &c. (*seclude*) 893; separate &c. (*disjoin*) 44.

pass over, omit; garble; eliminate, weed, winnow.

Adj. excluding &c. *v.*; exclusive.

excluded &c. *v.*; unrecounted, not included in; inadmissible; preventive, interdictive.

Adv. exclusive of, barring; except; with the exception of; save, bating.

57. Extraneousness.—N. extraneous-ness &c. *adj.*; extrinsicality &c. 6; exteriority &c. 220; alienism.

foreign -body, – substance, – element; alien, stranger, intruder, interloper, foreigner, tramontane, *novus homo*, new comer, immi-, emi-grant; creole, Afrikander; outsider, outlander, tenderfoot.

implicated in; share in &c. (*participate*) 778; belong –, appertain- to.

form, make, constitute, compose.

Adj. forming &c. *v.*; inclusive; inherent &c. 5.

Adj. extraneous, foreign, alien, ulterior; exterior, external, outside, outlandish; oversea; tra-, ultra-montane.

excluded &c. 55; inadmissible; exceptional.

Adv. in foreign -parts, – lands; abroad, beyond seas, overseas.

Section IV. ORDER

1°. Order in General

58. Order.—N. order, regularity &c. 80; uniformity, symmetry, *lucidus ordo*; harmony, music of the spheres.

gradation, progression; series &c. (*continuity*) 69.

subordination; course, even tenor, routine; method, disposition, arrangement, array, system, economy, discipline; orderliness &c. *adj.*

rank, place, &c. (*term*) 71.

V. be –, become- in order &c. *adj.*; form, fall in, draw up; arrange –, range –, place- itself; adjust; fall into –, take- -one's place, – rank; rally round; arrange &c. 60.

Adj. orderly, regular; in -order, – trim, – apple-pie order, according to Cocker, – its proper place, neat, neat as a pin, tidy, *en règle*, well regulated, correct, methodical, uniform, symmetrical, ship-shape, business-like, systematic; habitual; unconfused &c. (*see* confuse &c. 61) arranged &c. 60.

Adv. in order; methodically &c. *adj.*; in -turn, – its turn; step by step; by regular -steps, – gradations, – stages, – intervals; *seriatim*, systematically, by clockwork, *gradatim*; at stated periods &c. (*periodically*) 138.

59. [Absence, or want of Order, &c.] Disorder.—N. disorder; derangement &c. 61; irregularity; anomaly &c. (*unconformity*) 83; anar-chy, -chism; want of method; dishevelment, untidiness &c. *adj.*; disunion; discord &c. 24.

confusion; confusedness &c. *adj.*; disarray, jumble, mix-up, huddle, litter, lumber; *cahotage*; farrago; mess, muss, mash, muddle, hash; hotchpotch; *imbroglio*, chaos, *omnium gatherum*, medley; mere -mixture &c. 41; fortuitous concourse of atoms, *disjecta membra*, *rudis indigestaque moles*.

complexity; complexness &c. *adj.*; com-, im-plication; intri-cacy, -cation; perplexity; network, maze, labyrinth; wilderness, jungle; involution, ravelling, entanglement; coil &c. (*convolution*) 248; sleave, tangled skein, knot, Gordian knot, kink, web; wheels within wheels.

turmoil; ferment, &c. (*agitation*) 315; to do, trouble, pudder, pother, row, disturbance, convulsion, tumult, pandemonium, uproar, riot, rumpus, stour, scramble, *fracas*, embroilment, *mêlée*, spill and pelt, rough and tumble; whirlwind &c. 349; bear garden, Babel, Saturnalia, Donnybrook Fair, confusion worse confounded, most admired disorder, *concordia discors*; Bedlam –, hell- broke loose; bull in a china shop; all the fat in the fire, *diable à quatre*, Devil to pay; pretty kettle of fish; pretty piece of -work, – business.

slattern, slut, sloven, draggle-tail.

V. be -disorderly &c. *adj.*; ferment, play at cross purposes.

put out of order; derange &c. 61; ravel &c. 219; ruffle, rumple; bungle, botch.

Adj. disorderly, orderless; out of -order, – place, – gear, – whack; irregular, desultory; anomalous &c. (*unconformable*) 83; acephalous, disorganized, straggling; un-, im-methodical; unsymmetric; unsystematic; untidy, slovenly, bedraggled, messy; dislocated; out of sorts; promiscuous, indiscriminate; chaotic, anarchical, lawless; unarranged &c. 60; confused, tumultuous, turbulent, tempestuous; deranged &c. 61; topsy turvy &c. (*inverted*) 218; shapeless &c. 241; disjointed, out of joint.

com-plex, -plexed; intricate, complicated, perplexed, involved, ravelled, entangled, knotted, tangled, inextricable; irreducible.

troublous; riotous &c. (*violent*) 173.

Adv. irregularly &c. *adj.*; by fits and -snatches, – starts; pell-mell; higgledy-piggledy; helter-skelter, harum-scarum; in a ferment; at -sixes and sevens, – cross purposes; upside down &c. 218.

Phr. the cart before the horse, chaos is come again.

---

60. [Reduction to Order.] **Arrange-ment.—N.** arrangement; plan &c. 626; preparation &c. 673; dispos-al, -ition; col-, al-location; distribution; sorting &c. *v.*; assortment, allotment; group-ing; apportionment, *taxis*, taxonomy, *syn-taxis*, graduation, organization, grading; re-organization, rationaliza-tion.

analysis, classification, division, di-gestion; systematism.

[Result of arrangement] order, order-liness, form, array; digest, synopsis &c. (*compendium*) 596; *syntagma*, table, atlas; register &c. (*record*) 551; score &c. 415; cosmos, organism, architec-ture.

[Instrument for sorting] sieve &c. 260; file, card index.

V. reduce to –, bring into- order; introduce order into; rally.

arrange, dispose, place, form; put –, set –, place- in order; straighten up, tidy up; set out, collocate, allocate, pack, marshal, range, size, rank, array, group, parcel out, allot, space, dis-tribute, deal; cast –, assign- the parts; dispose of, assign places to; assort, sort; sift, riddle; put –, set- -to rights, – into shape, – in trim, – in array.

class, -ify; divide; file, string to-gether, thread; register &c. (*record*) 551; list, catalogue, tabulate, index, alphabeticize, graduate, digest, grade, codify; orchestrate, score.

methodize, regulate, systematize, standardize, co-ordinate, organ-ize, settle, fix.

unravel, disentangle, ravel, card; disembroil.

Adj. arranged &c. *v.*; embattled, in battle array; cut and dried; methodical, orderly, regular, systematic, tabular.

61. [Subversion of Order; bringing into disorder.] **Derangement.—N.** de-rangement &c. *v.*; disorder &c. 59; evection, discomposure, disturbance; dis-, de-organization; involvement; dis-location; perturbation, interruption; shuffling &c. *v.*; inversion &c. 218; corrugation &c. (*fold*) 258; insanity &c. 503.

V. derange; dis-, mis-arrange; dis-, mis-place; mislay, discompose, dis-order, de-, dis-organize; embroil, un-settle, disturb, confuse, trouble, per-turb, jumble, tumble; huddle, shuffle, muddle, toss, hustle, fumble, riot; bring –, put –, throw- into -disorder &c. 59; break the ranks, disconcert, convulse; break in upon.

unhinge, dislocate, put out of joint, throw out of gear.

turn topsy-turvy &c. (*invert*) 218; bedevil; complicate, involve, perplex, confound; im-, em-brangle; tangle, en-tangle, ravel, tousle, dishevel, ruffle, rumple &c. (*fold*) 258; dement.

litter, scatter; mix &c. 41.

Adj. deranged &c. *v.*; syncre-tic, -tistic.

2°. CONSECUTIVE ORDER

62. Precedence.—N. precedence; coming before &c. *v.*; the lead, *le pas*; superiority &c. 33; importance &c. 642; anteced-ence, -ency; anteriority &c. (*front*) 234; precursor &c. 64; priority &c. 116; precession &c. 280; anteposition, preference.

V. precede; come -before, – first; forerun, head, lead, take the lead; lead the -way, – dance; introduce, usher in; have the *pas*; set the fashion &c. (*influence*) 175; lead off, kick off, open the ball; take –, have- precedence; outrank; have the start &c. (*get before*) 280.

place before; prefix; premise, prelude, preface.

Adj. preceding &c. *v.*; pre-, antecedent; anterior; prior &c. 116; before; former, foregoing; before-, above-mentioned; aforesaid, said; precurs-ory, -ive; prevenient, preliminary, prefatory, introductory; prelus-ive, -ory; proemial, preparatory.

Adv. before; in advance &c. (*precession*) 280.

Phr. *seniores priores.*

63. Sequence.—N. sequence, coming after; going after &c. (*following*) 281; consecution, succession; posteriority &c. 117.

continuation; prolongation, order of succession; successiveness; Elijah's mantle.

secondariness; subordinancy &c. (*inferiority*) 34.

V. succeed; come -after, – on, – next; follow, ensue, step into the shoes of; alternate.

place after, suffix, append.

Adj. succeeding &c. *v.*; sequent; sub-, con-sequent; sequacious, proximate, next; consecutive &c. (*continuity*) 69; alternate, amœbæan.

latter; posterior &c. 117.

Adv. after, subsequently; behind &c. (*rear*) 235.

---

64. Precursor.—N. precursor, antecedent, precedent, predecessor; forerunner, van-courier, *avant-coureur*, pioneer, prodrome, *prodromos*, outrider; leader, bell-wether; herald, harbinger; dawn.

prelude, preamble, preface, prologue, foreword, *avant-propos*, *protasis*, prolusion, proem, *prolepsis*, *prolegomena*, prefix, introduction; lead, heading, frontispiece, groundwork; preparation &c. 673; overture, voluntary, *exordium*, symphony, *ritornello*; premises.

prefigurement &c. 511; omen &c. 512.

Adj. precursory; prelu-sive, -sory, -dious; proemial, introductory, prefatory, prodromous, inaugural, preliminary; precedent &c. (*prior*) 116.

65. Sequel.—N. sequel, suffix, successor; tail, *queue*, train, wake, trail, rear; retinue, suite; appendix, postscript, subscript; epilogue; conclusion; peroration; codicil; continuation, *sequela*; appendage &c. 39; tail –, heelpiece; tag, more last words; *colophon*.

follower, after-glow, -growth, -crop, -taste, -math.

after-part, -piece, -course, -thought, -game; *arrière pensée*, second thoughts.

---

66. Beginning.—N. beginning, commencement, opening, outset, incipience, inception, inchoation; introduction &c. (*precursor*) 64; *alpha*; initial; foundation; inauguration, *début*, *le premier pas*, embarcation, rising of the curtain; zero hour; exordium, curtain raiser; maiden speech; prelude; outbreak, onset, brunt; initiative, move, first move; gambit, narrow –, thin-

67. End.—N. end, close, termination; desinence, conclusion, *finis*, *finale*, period, term, *terminus*, last, *omega*; extreme, -tremity; gable –, butt –, fagend; tip, nib, point; tail &c. (*rear*) 235; verge &c. (*edge*) 231; tag, epilogue, peroration; *bonne bouche*; bitter end, tail end; terminal; *apodosis*; appendix.

consummation, *dénouement*; finish &c. (*completion*) 729; fate; doom, -sday;

end of the wedge; fresh start, new departure; forefront.

origin &c. (*cause*) 153; source, rise; bud, germ &c. 153; egg, rudiment; genesis, birth, nativity, cradle, infancy, incunabula; start, starting-point &c. 293; dawn &c. (*morning*) 125.

title-page; head, -ing, caption; van &c. (*front*) 234.

en-trance, -try; inlet, orifice, mouth, chops, lips, porch, portal, portico, *propylon*, door; gate, -way; postern, wicket, threshold, vestibule; skirts, border &c. (*edge*) 231; tee.

first -stage, – blush, – glance, – impression, – sight.

rudiments, elements, outlines, *principia*, grammar, *protasis*; alphabet, ABC.

V. begin, commence, inchoate, rise, arise, originate, institute, conceive, initiate, open, dawn, set in, take its rise, enter upon, start; enter; set out &c. (*depart*) 293; embark in.

usher in; lead -off, – the way; take the -lead, – initiative; inaugurate, head; stand -at the head, – first, – for; lay the foundations &c. (*prepare*) 673; found &c. (*cause*) 153; set -up, – on foot, – agoing, – abroach, – the ball in motion; apply the match to a train; launch, broach; open -up, – the door to; set -about, – to work; make a -beginning, – start; handsel; take the first step, lay the first stone, cut the first turf; break -ground, – the ice, – cover; pass –, cross- the Rubicon; open -fire, – the ball; ventilate, air; undertake &c. 676.

come into -existence, – the world; make one's *début*, take birth; burst forth, break out; spring –, crop- up.

begin -at the beginning, – *ab ovo*, – again, – *de novo*; start afresh, make a fresh start, shuffle the cards, resume, recommence.

Adj. beginning &c. *v.*; initi-al, -atory, -ative; inceptive, introductory, incipient; proemial, inaugural; incho-ate, -ative; embryonic, rudimental; primogenial; primeval &c. (*old*) 124; rudimentary, aboriginal; natal, nascent.

first, foremost, front, leading, head; maiden.

begun &c. *v.*; just -begun &c. *v.*

Adv. at –, in- the beginning &c. *n.*; first, in the first place, *imprimis*, first and foremost; *in limine*; in -the bud, – embryo, – its infancy; from -the beginning, – its birth; *ab -initio, – ovo, – incunabilis*, primarily, originally.

crack of doom, day of Judgment, fall of the curtain, wind-up; goal, destination; limit, stoppage, end all, determination; expiration, expiry; death &c. 360; end of all things; finality; eschatology.

break up, *commencement de la fin*, last stage, turning point; *coup de grâce*, death-blow; knock-out.

V. end, close, finish, terminate, conclude, be all over; expire; die &c. 360; come –, draw- to a -close &c. *n.*; have run its course; run out, pass away.

bring to an -end &c. *n.*; put an end to, make an end of; determine; get through; achieve &c. (*complete*) 729; stop &c. (*make to cease*) 142; shut up shop.

Adj. ending &c. *v.*; final, terminal, definitive, conclusive; crowning &c. (*completing*) 729; last, ultimate; hindermost; rear &c. 235; caudal.

contermin-ate, -ous, -able.

ended &c. *v.*; at an end; settled, decided, over, played out, set at rest.

penultimate; last but -one, – two, &c.

unbegun, uncommenced; fresh.

Adv. finally &c. *adj.*; in fine; at the last; once for all.

---

68. Middle.—**N.** middle, midst, mediety; mean &c. 29; medium, middle term; centre &c. 222, mid-course &c. 628; *mezzo termine*; *juste milieu* &c. 628; half-way house, nave, navel, omphalos; nucle-us, -olus.

equidistance, bisection, half-distance; equator, diaphragm, midriff; interjacence &c. 228.

Adj. middle, medial, mesial, mean, mid; middle-, mid-most; middling; mediate; intermediate &c. (*interjacent*) 228; equidistant; central &c. 222; mediterranean, equatorial.

Adv. in the middle; in the thick; mid-, half-way; midships, *in medias res.*

69. [Uninterrupted sequence.] **Continuity.—N.** continuity; consecu-tion, -tiveness &c. *adj.*; succession, round, suite, progression, series, train, chain; cat-, concat-enation; catena; scale; gradation, course, constant flow, perpetuity.

procession, column; retinue, *cortège*, cavalcade, rank and file, line of battle, array.

pedigree, genealogy, lineage, race &c. 166.

rank, file, line, row, range, tier, string, thread, team; suit; colonnade.

V. follow in -, form- a series &c. *n.*; fall in.

arrange in a -series &c. *n.*; string together, catenate, file, thread, graduate, tabulate.

Adj. continu-ous, -ed; consecutive; progressive, gradual; serial, successive; immediate, unbroken, entire; linear; in a -line, - row &c. *n.*; uninter-rupted, -mitting; unremitting; perennial, evergreen; constant.

Adv. continuously &c. *adj.*; *seriatim*; in a -line &c. *n.*; in -succession, - turn; running, gradually, step by step, *gradatim*, at a stretch; in -file, - column, - single file, - Indian file.

70. [Interrupted sequence.] **Discontinuity.—N.** discontinuity; disjunction &c. 44; anacoluthon; interruption, break, fracture, flaw, fault, split, crack, cut; gap &c. (*interval*) 198; solution of continuity, *cæsura*; broken thread; parenthesis, episode; rhapsody, patchwork; intermission; alternation &c. (*periodicity*) 138; dropping fire.

V. be -discontinuous &c. *adj.*; alternate, intermit.

discontinue, pause, interrupt; intervene; break, - in upon; interpose &c. 228; break -, snap- the thread; disconnect &c. (*disjoin*) 44.

Adj. discontinuous, unsuccessive, broken, interrupted, *décousu*; dis-, un-connected, discrete, disjunctive; fitful &c. (*irregular*) 139; spasmodic, desultory, intermit-ting &c. *v.*, -tent; alternate; recurrent &c. (*periodic*) 138; few and far between.

Adv. at intervals; by -snatches, - jerks, - skips, - catches, - fits and starts; skippingly, *per saltum*; *longo intervallo.*

71. Term.—N. term, rank, station, stage, step; degree &c. 26; scale, remove, grade, link, peg, round -, rung- of the ladder, *status*, position, place, point, mark, *pas*, period, pitch; stand, -ing; footing, range.

V. hold -, occupy -, fall into- a place &c. *n.*

3°. Collective Order

72. Assemblage.—N. assemblage; col-lection, -location, -ligation; compilation, levy, gathering, ingathering, mobilization, meet, foregathering, muster, *attroupement*; con-course, -flux, -gregation, -tesseration, -vergence &c. 290; meeting, *levée*, *réunion*, drawing room, at home; conversazione &c. (*social gathering*) 892; assembly, congress, eisteddfod; conven-tion, -ticle;

73. Non-assemblage. Dispersion.—N. dispersion; disjunction &c. 44; divergence &c. 291; scattering &c. *v.*; dissemination, broadcasting, diffusion, dissipation, distribution; apportionment &c. 786; spread, respersion, circumfusion, interspersion, spargefaction.

waifs and estrays, flotsam and jetsam, *disjecta membra.*

V. disperse, scatter, sow, dissemi-

gemote; conclave, &c. (*council*) 696; posse, *posse comitatûs*; Noah's ark.

miscellany, *collectanea*, symposium; museum, menagerie, &c. (*store*) 636.

crowd, throng, multitude; flood, rush, deluge; rout, rabble, mob, press, crush, *cohue*, jam, horde, body, tribe; crew, gang, knot, squad, band, party; swarm, shoal, school, covey, flock, herd, drove, kennel; array, bevy, galaxy; *corps*, company, troop, *troupe*; army, force, regiment, &c. (*combatants*) 726; host &c. (*multitude*) 102; populousness.

clan, brotherhood, association &c. (*party*) 712.

volley, shower, storm, cloud.

group, cluster, Pleiades, clump, pencil; set, batch, lot, pack; budget, *dossier*, assortment, bunch; parcel; pack-et, -age; bundle, *fasciculus*, fas-

nate, radiate, diffuse, shed, spread, ted, bestrew, overspread, dispense, disband, disembody, demobilize, dismember, distribute; apportion &c. 786; blow off, let out, dispel, cast forth, draught off; strew, straw, strow; spirtle, cast, sprinkle, shatter; issue, deal out, retail, utter; re-, inter-sperse; set abroach, circumfuse.

turn –, cast- adrift; scatter to the winds; sow broadcast.

spread like wildfire, disperse themselves.

Adj. unassembled &c. (*see* assemble &c. 72); dispersed &c. *v.*; sparse, dispread, broadcast, sporadic, widespread; far-flung; epidemic &c. (*general*) 78; adrift, stray; dishevelled, streaming.

Adv. *sparsim*, here and there, *passim*.

cine, bale; ser-on, -oon; faggot, wisp, truss, tuft; shock, rick, fardel, stack, sheaf, swath, gavel, haycock, stook.

accumulation &c. (*store*) 636; congeries, heap, lump, pile, *rouleau*, tissue, mass, pyramid; drift; snow-ball, -drift; acervation, cumulation; amassment, glom-, agglom-eration; conglobation; conglomeration, -ate; coacervation, coagmentation, aggregation, concentration, congestion, *omnium gatherum*, *spicilegium*, black hole of Calcutta; quantity &c. (*greatness*) 31.

collector, gatherer; whip, -per in.

V. [be or come together] assemble, collect, muster; meet, unite, join, rejoin; cluster, flock, swarm, surge, stream, herd, crowd, throng, associate; con-gregate, -glomerate, -centrate; centre round, *rendezvous*, resort; come –, flock –, get –, pig- together; forgather; huddle; reassemble.

[get or bring together] assemble, muster, mobilize; bring –, get –, put –, draw –, scrape –, lump- together; col-lect, -locate, -ligate; get –, whip- in; gather; hold a meeting; con-vene, -voke, -vocate; rake up, dredge; heap, mass, pile; pack, put up, truss, cram; acervate; ag-glomerate, -gregate; compile; group, aggroup, concentrate, unite; collect –, bring- into a focus; amass, accumulate &c. (*store*) 636; collect in a drag-net; heap Ossa upon Pelion.

Adj. assembled &c. *v.*; closely packed, dense, serried, crowded to suffocation, teeming, swarming, populous; as thick as hops; all of a heap, fasciculated; cumulative.

Phr. the plot thickens.

74. [Place of meeting.] **Focus.**—**N.** focus; point of- convergence &c. 290; corradiation; centre &c. 222; gathering-place, resort; haunt; retreat; *venue*, *rendezvous*; rallying point, head-quarters, home, club; *dépôt* &c. (*store*) 636; tryst, trysting-place; place of -meeting, – resort, – assignation; *point de –*, *lieu de- réunion*; issue.

V. bring to- a point, – a focus, – an issue; focus.

4°. Distributive Order

75. Class.—**N.** class, category, *categorema*, head, order, section; division, subdivision; department, province, domain, sphere.

kind, sort, genus, species, variety, branch, family, race, tribe, caste, sept, clan, breed; *clique, coterie*; type, kit, sect, set; assortment; feather, kidney; suit; range; gender, sex, kin.

manner, description, denomination, persuasion, connection, designation, character, stamp; predicament; conviction &c. 484.

similarity &c. 17.

76. Inclusion. [Comprehension under, or reference to a class.]—**N.** inclusion, admission, incorporation, comprehension, reception.

composition &c. (*inclusion in a compound*) 54.

V. be -included in &c.; come –, fall –, range- under; belong –, pertain- to; range with; merge in.

include, compromise, comprehend, contain, admit, embrace, receive; enclose &c. (*circumscribe*) 229; incorporate, cover, embody, encircle.

reckon –, enumerate –, number- among; refer to; place –, arrange- under, – with; take into account.

Adj. includ-ed, -ing &c. *v.*; inclusive; comprehensive, all-embracing; congen-er, -erous: of the same -class &c. 75.

Phr. *et hoc genus omne*, &c.; *et cætera*.

77. Exclusion.*—N. exclusion &c. 55.

---

78. Generality. — **N.** general-ity, -ization; universality; catholic-ity, -ism; miscel-lany, -laneousness; dragnet.

every-one, -body; all hands, all the world and his wife; any body, N or M, all sorts; *tout le monde*.

prevalence, run.

V. be -general &c. *adj.*; prevail, obtain, be going about, stalk abroad.

render -general &c. *adj.*; generalize; spread, broadcast.

Adj. general, usual, current, generic, collective; broad, comprehensive, sweeping; encyclopedical, panoramic, widespread &c. (*dispersed*) 73.

universal; catho-lic, -lical; common, world-wide; œ-, e-cumenical; transcendental; prevalent, prevailing, rife, epidemic, besetting; all over, covered with.

every, all; indeterminate, indefinite, unspecified, impersonal.

customary &c. (*habitual*) 613.

Adv. what-ever, -soever; to a man, one and all, without exception.

generally &c. *adj.*; always, for better

79. Speciality.—N. speciality, *spécialité*; individ-uality, -uity; particularity, peculiarity; idiocrasy &c. (*tendency*) 176; personality, characteristic, mannerism, idiosyncrasy, attribute specificness &c. *adj.*; singularity &c. (*unconformity*) 83; reading, version, lection; state; *trait*; distinctive feature; technicality; *differentia*.

particulars, details, minutiæ, items, counts.

I, self, I myself, *ego*; my-, him-, her-, it-self.

V. specify, particularize, individualize, realize, specialize, designate, differentiate, determine, define, denote, indicate, itemize, detail.

descend to particulars, enter into detail, come to the point.

Adj. special, particular, individual, specific, proper, personal, intimate, original, private, respective, definite, concrete, determinate, especial, certain, esoteric, endemic, partial, party, peculiar, marked, appropriate, several, characteristic, diagnostic, exact, exclusive; singular &c. (*exceptional*) 83;

---

* The same set of words is used to express *Exclusion from a class* and *Exclusion from a compound*. Reference is therefore made to the former at 55. This identity does not occur with regard to *Inclusion*, which therefore constitutes a separate category.

for worse; in general, generally speaking; speaking generally; for the most part; in the long run &c. (*on an average*) 29.

---

idiomatic; typical, representative, distinctive.

this, that; yon, -der.

Adv. specially &c. *adj.*; in particular, *in propriâ personâ*; *ad hominem*; for my part.

each, apiece, one by one; severally, respectively, each to each; *seriatim*, in detail, bit by bit; *pro hac vice, – re natâ.*

namely, that is to say, *videlicet*, viz.; to wit.

5°. ORDER AS REGARDS CATEGORIES

80. Rule.—N. regularity, uniformity &c. 16; clock-work precision; punctuality &c. (*exactness*) 494; routine &c. (*custom*) 613; formula; system; rut; canon, convention, maxim; rule &c. (*form, regulation*) 697; key-note, standard, model; precedent &c. (*prototype*) 22; conformity &c. 82.

nature, principle; law; order of things; normal –, natural –, ordinary –, model- -state, – condition; standing -dish, – order; normality; Procrustean law; law of the Medes and Persians; hard and fast rule.

Adj. regular, uniform, symmetrical, constant, steady; according to rule &c. &c. 613; orderly &c. 58.

81. Multiformity.—N. multi-, omniformity; variety, diversity; multifariousness &c. *adj.*

Adj. multi-form, -fold, -farious, -generous; multiplex, variform, manifold, many-sided, multiplicate; omni-form, -genous, -farious; polymorphic; protean; heterogeneous, motley, mosaic; epicene, indiscriminate, desultory, irregular, diversified, different, divers; all manner of; of -every description, – all sorts and kinds; *et hoc genus omne*; and what not? *de omnibus rebus et quibusdam aliis.*

(*conformable*) 82; customary

82. Conformity.—N. conform-ity, -ance; observance.

naturalization; conventionality &c. (*custom*) 613; agreement &c. 23.

example, instance, specimen, sample, quotation; exemplification, illustration, case in point; object lesson.

conventionalist, formalist, Philistine.

pattern &c. (*prototype*) 22.

V. conform to, – rule; accommodate –, adapt- oneself to; rub off corners.

be -regular &c. *adj.*; move in a groove; follow –, observe –, go by –, bend to –, obey- -rules, – precedents; comply –, tally –, chime in –, fall in-with; be -guided, – regulated- by; fall into a -custom, – usage; follow the -fashion, – multitude; pass muster, do as others do, *hurler avec les loups*; do at Rome as the Romans do; go –, swim- with the -stream, – current, – tide; tread the beaten track &c. (*habit*) 613; rubber-stamp; keep one in countenance.

exemplify, illustrate, cite, quote, put

83. Unconformity.—N. non-conformity &c. 82; un-, dis-conformity; unconventionality, informality, abnormity, anomaly; anomalousness &c. *adj.*; exception, peculiarity, &c. 79; infraction –, breach –, violation –, infringement-of -law, – custom, – usage; eccentricity, *bizarrerie*, oddity, *je ne sais quoi*, monstrosity, rarity; freak of Nature.

individuality, idiosyncrasy, singularity, originality, mannerism.

aberration; irregularity; variety; singularity; exemption; salvo &c. (*qualification*) 469.

nonconformist; nondescript, character, original, nonsuch, monster, prodigy, wonder, miracle, curiosity, missing link, flying fish, black swan, *lusus naturæ, rara avis*, queer fish; mongrel; half-caste, -blood, -breed; *métis*, cross breed, hybrid, mule, mulatto, sacatra, marabou; *tertium quid*, hermaphrodite, gynander, androgyn.

phœnix, chimera, hydra, sphinx, minotaur; griff-in, -on; centaur; hippo-

a case; produce an- instance &c. *n.*

Adj. conformable to rule, adaptable, compliant, consistent, agreeable; regular &c. 80; according to -regulation, – rule, – Cocker; *en règle, selon les règles,* well regulated, orderly; symmetric &c. 242.

conventional, commonplace &c. (*customary*) 613; of -daily, – every day-occurrence; in the natural order of things; ordinary, common, – or garden, prosaic, habitual, usual.

in the order of the day; naturalized.

typical, normal, formal; canonical, orthodox, sound, strict, rigid, positive, uncompromising, Procrustean; point device.

secundum artem, ship-shape, technical. exemplary, illustrative, in point.

Adv. conformably &c. *adj.*; by rule; agreeably to; in -conformity, – accordance, – keeping- with; according to; consistently with; as usual, *ad instar, instar omnium; more -solito,* – *majorum.*

for the sake of conformity; of –, as a matter of- course; *pro formâ,* for form's sake, by the card; according to plan.

invariably &c. (*uniformly*) 16.

for -example, – instance; *exempli gratiâ; e.g.; inter alia.*

Phr. *cela va sans dire; ex pede Herculem, noscitur a sociis.*

---

griff, -centaur; sagittary; kraken, cockatrice, wyvern, roc, liver, dragon, sea-serpent; mermaid; unicorn; Cyclops, 'men whose heads do grow beneath their shoulders'; Teratology.

fish out of water; neither -one thing nor another, – fish flesh nor fowl nor good red herring; one in a -way, – thousand; out-cast, -law; Ishmael, pariah; oasis.

V. be -unconformable &c. *adj.*; leave the beaten -track, – path; infringe –, break –, violate- a -law, – habit, – usage, – custom; drive a coach and six through; stretch a point; have no business there; baffle –, beggar- all description.

Adj. unconformable, exceptional; abnorm-al, -ous; anomal-ous, -istic; out of -order, – place, – keeping, – tune, – one's element; irregular, arbitrary; lawless, informal, aberrant, stray, wandering, wanton; peculiar, exclusive, unnatural, eccentric, crotchety, egregious; out of the -beaten track, – common, – common run, – pale of; misplaced; funny.

un-usual, -accustomed, -customary, -wonted, -common; rare, singular, *unique,* curious, odd, extraordinary, strange, monstrous; wonderful &c. 870; unexpected, unaccountable; *outré,* out of the way, remarkable, noteworthy; queer, quaint, nondescript, none such, *sui generis;* original, unconventional, Bohemian, unfashionable; un-described, -precedented, -paralleled, -exampled, -heard of, -familiar; fantastic, new-fangled, grotesque, *bizarre;* outlandish, exotic, *tombé des nues,* preternatural; denaturalized.

heterogeneous, heteroclite, amorphous, mongrel, amphibious, epicene, half-blood, hybrid; androgyn-ous, -al; unsymmetric &c. 243. qualified &c. 469.

Adv. unconformably &c. *adj.*; except, unless, save, barring, beside, without, save and except, let alone.

however, yet, but.

Int. what -on earth! – in the world!

Phr. never was -seen, – heard, – known- the like.

Section V. NUMBER

1°. Number, in the Abstract

84. Number.—N. number, symbol, numeral, figure, cipher, digit, integer; counter; round number; formula; function; series.

sum, total, aggregate, difference, complement, subtrahend; product; multipli-cand, -er, -cator; coefficient, multiple; dividend, divisor, factor, quotient, sub-multiple, fraction; mixed number; numerator, denominator; decimal, circulating decimal, repetend; common measure, aliquot part; reciprocal; prime number; totitive, totient.

permutation, combination, variation; election.

ratio, proportion; progression; arithmetical –, geometrical –, harmonical- progression; percentage.

figurate –, pyramidal –, polygonal- numbers.

power, root, exponent, index, logarithm, antilogarithm; modulus.

differential, integral, fluxion, fluent.

Adj. numeral, complementary, divisible, aliquot, reciprocal, prime, fractional, decimal, figurate, incommensurable.

proportional, exponential, logarithmic, logometric, differential, fluxional, integral.

positive, negative; rational, irrational; surd, radical, real, imaginary, impossible.

85. Numeration.—N. numeration; numbering &c. *v.*; pagination; tale, tally, recension, enumeration, summation, reckoning, computation, supputation; calcu-lation, -lus; algorithm, rhabdology, dactylonomy; measurement &c. 466; statistics.

arithmetic, analysis, algebra, fluxions; differential –, integral –, infinitesimal- calculus; calculus of differences.

[Statistics] dead reckoning, muster, poll, census, capitation, roll-call, recapitulation; account &c. (*list*) 86.

[Operations] notation, addition, subtraction, multiplication, division, proportion, rule of three, practice, equations, extraction of roots, reduction, involution, evolution, approximation, interpolation, differentiation, integration.

[Instruments] abacus, swan-pan, logometer, sliding –, slide- rule, tallies, Napier's bones, calculating –, adding- machine, difference engine; cash register.

arithmetician, calculator, abacist; mathematician, actuary, statistician, surveyor, geodesist.

V. number, count, tell; call –, run- over, take an account of, enumerate, call the roll, muster, poll, recite, recapitulate; sum; sum –, cast- up; tell off, score, cipher, compute, calculate, set a price, reckon, – up, estimate; suppute, add, subtract, multiply, divide, extract roots.

check, prove, demonstrate, balance, audit, overhaul, take stock; affix numbers to, page, foliate, paginate.

amount –, come- to.

Adj. numer-al, -ical; arithmetical, analytic, algebraic, statistical, numerable, computable, calculable; commensur-able, -ate; incommensur-able, -ate.

86. List.—N. list, catalogue, enumeration, inventory, schedule; register &c. (*record*) 551; account; bill, – of costs; syllabus; terrier, tally, file; almanac, calendar, index, table, atlas, contents, card index; rota, ticket; book, ledger; synopsis, *catalogue raisonné*; *tableau*; scroll, manifest, invoice, bill of lading; prospectus, *programme*; bill of fare, *menu, carte*; score, census, statistics, returns; Red –, Blue –, Domesday- book; *cadastre*; directory, gazetteer, dictionary, glossary, lexicon, thesaurus, gradus.

roll; check –, chequer –, bead- roll, – of honour; muster -roll, – book; roster, panel; cartulary, diptych.

V. list, enrol, schedule, register &c. *n.*; indent, post, docket; matriculate.

Adj. cadastral, listed &c. *v.*

2°. DETERMINATE NUMBER

87. Unity.—N. unity; oneness &c. *adj.*; individuality; solitude &c. (*seclusion*) 893; isolation &c. (*disjunction*) 44; unification &c. 48.

one, unit, ace; item; individual; solo, none else, no other, naught beside.

V. be -one, – alone &c. *adj.*; dine with Duke Humphrey.

isolate &c. (*disjoin*) 44.

render one; unite &c. (*join*) 43, (*combine*) 48.

Adj. one, sole, single, solitary, only-begotten; individual, apart, alone; kithless.

un-accompanied, -attended; *solus*, single-handed; singular, odd, unique, unrepeated, azygous, first and last; isolated &c. (*disjoined*) 44; insular; unitary.

lone; lone-ly, -some; desolate, dreary.

in-secable, -severable, -discerptible; compact, irresolvable.

Adv. singly &c. *adj.*; alone, by itself, *per se*, only, apart, in the singular number, in the abstract; one -by one, – at a time; simply; one and a half, *sesqui-*.

Phr. *natura il fece, e poi roppe la stampa.*

88. Accompaniment.—N. accompaniment; appurtenance, adjunct &c. 39; context.

coexistence, concomitance, company, association, companionship; part-, co-part-nership; coefficiency.

concomitant, accessory, coefficient; companion, attendant, fellow, associate, consort, spouse, colleague, *fidus Achates*; part-, co-part-ner; satellite, hanger on, shadow; escort, *entourage*, suite, *cortège*; convoy, follower &c. 65; attribute.

V. accompany, coexist, attend, convoy, chaperon; hang –, wait- on; go hand in hand with; synchronize &c. 120; bear –, keep- company; row in the same boat; bring in its train, associate –, couple- with.

Adj. accompanying &c. *v.*; concomitant, fellow, twin, joint; associated –, coupled- with; accessory, attendant, *obbligato.*

Adv. with, withal; together –, along –, in company- with; hand in hand, side by side; cheek by -jowl, – jole; arm in arm; there-, here-with; and &c. (*addition*) 37.

together, in a body, collectively.

---

89. Duality.—N. dual-ity, -ism; duplicity; bi-plicity, -formity; span, polarity.

two, deuce, couple, couplet, doublet, brace, pair, cheeks, twins, Castor and Pollux, *gemini*, Siamese twins; fellows; yoke, conjugation, dyad, distich.

V. [unite in pairs] pair, couple, bracket, yoke; conduplicate, mate.

Adj. two, twain; dual, -istic; binary, binomial; twin, biparous; dyadic; conduplicate; duplex &c. 90; *tête-à-tête*; paired; dihedral.

coupled &c. *v.*; conjugate.

both, – the one and the other.

90. Duplication.—N. duplication; doubling &c. *v.*; gemi-, ingemi-nation; reduplication; iteration &c. (*repetition*) 104; renewal.

V. double; re-double, -duplicate; geminate; repeat &c. 104; renew &c. 660; duplicate, copy &c. 21.

Adj. double; doubled &c. *v.*; bicameral, bicapital, bi-fold, -form, -lateral,

91. [Division into two parts.] **Bisection.—N.** bi-section, -partition; di-, subdi-chotomy; halving &c. *v.*; dimidiation; *hendiadis.*

bifurcation, forking, branching, furcation, ramification, divarication; fork, prong; fold.

half, moiety.

V. bisect, halve, divide, split, cut in

-farious, -facial; two-fold, -sided, -headed, -edged &c.; duplex; double-faced; twin, duplicate, ingeminate; second; dual &c. 29.

Adv. twice, once more; over again &c. (*repeatedly*) 104; as much again, twofold.

secondly, in the second place, again.

two, cleave, dimidiate, dichotomize, divaricate.

go halves, divide with.

separate, fork, bifurcate; branch -off, – out; ramify.

Adj. bisected &c. *v.*; cloven, cleft; bipartite, biconjugate, bicuspid, bifid; bifur-cous, -cate, -cated; semi-, demi-hemi-.

92. Triality.—**N.** triality, trinity,* triplicity.

three, triad, triplet, trey, trio, ternion, trinomial, leash; tierce; triennium; trefoil, triangle, trident, tripod, triumvirate, *troika*.

third power, cube.

Adj. three; tri-form, -nal, -nomial; tertiary; triune.

93. Triplication.—**N.** tripli-cation, -city; trebleness, trine, trilogy.

V. treble, triple, triplicate, cube.

Adj. treble, triple; tern, -ary; triplex, triplicate, threefold, trilogistic; third; trinal; trihedral.

Adv. three -times, – fold; thrice, in the third place, thirdly; trebly &c. *adj.*

94. [Division into three parts.] **Tri-section.** — **N.** tri-section, -partition, -chotomy; third, – part.

V. trisect, divide into three parts, trifurcate.

Adj. trifid; trisected &c. *v.*; tripartite, -chotomous, -sulcate.

---

95. Quaternity.—**N.** quaternity, four, tetrad, quartet, quaternion, square, quadrature, quarter, quadruplet; quadrilateral, quadrangle, quatrefoil; *quadriga*.

V. reduce to a square, square.

Adj. four; quat-ernary, -ernal; quadratic; quartile, quartic, tetractic, tetrad, tetrahedral; quadrennial; quadrivalent.

96. Quadruplication.—**N.** quadruplication.

V. multiply by four, quadruplicate, biquadrate.

Adj. fourfold; quad-ruple, -ruplicate, -rible; quadruplex; fourth.

Adv. four times; in the fourth place, fourthly.

97. [Division into four parts.] **Quad-risection.**—**N.** quadri-section, -parti-tion; quartering &c. *v.*; fourth; quart, -er, -ern; farthing (*i.e.* fourthing); quarto.

V. quarter, divide into four parts, quadrisect.

Adj. quartered &c. *v.*; quadri-fid, -partite.

---

98. Five, &c.—**N.** five, cinque, quint, quincunx, quintuplet, quintet, pentagon, pentameter, Pentateuch; six, half-a-dozen, sextet, hexagon, hexameter; seven, Heptarchy; eight, octet, octagon, octave; nine, three times three; ten, decade; eleven; twelve, dozen; thirteen; long –, baker's- dozen.

twenty, score; twenty-four, four and twenty, two dozen; twenty-five, five and twenty, quarter of a hundred; forty, two score; fifty, half a hundred; sixty, three score, sexagenarian; seventy, three score and ten, septuagenarian; eighty, four score, octogenarian; ninety, four score and ten, nonagenarian.

99. Quinquesection, &c.—**N.** division by -five &c. 98; quinquesection &c.; fifth &c.; decimation.

V. decimate, quinquesect.

Adj. quinque-fid, -partite; quinquarticular; octifid; decimal, tenth, tithe, teind; duodecimal, twelfth; sexagesimal, -genary; hundredth, centesimal; millesimal &c.

---

* *Trinity* is hardly ever used except in a theological sense; *see* Deity 976.

hundred, centenary, hecatomb, century; hundredweight, cwt.; one hundred and forty-four, gross; bicentenary, tercentenary &c.

thousand, chiliad; myriad, millennium, ten thousand; lac, lakh, one hundred thousand, plum; million; thousand million, *milliard*.

billion, trillion &c.

V. centuriate.

Adj. five, quinary, quintuple; fifth; senary, sextuple; sixth; seventh; octuple; eighth; ninefold, ninth; tenfold, decimal, denary, decuple, tenth; eleventh; duo-denary, -denal; twelfth; in one's 'teens, thirteenth.

vices-, viges-imal; twentieth; twenty-fourth &c. *n.*

cent-uple, -uplicate, -ennial, -enary, -urial; secular, hundredth; thousandth; millenary &c.

3°. Indeterminate Number

100. [More than one.] Plurality.—N. plurality; a -number, – certain number; one or two, two or three &c.; a few, several; multitude &c. 102.

Adj. plural, more than one, upwards of, some, certain; not -alone &c. 87.

Adv. *et cætera*, &c., etc.

Phr. *non deficit alter.*

100a. [Less than one.] Fraction.—N. fraction, fractional part, fragment; part &c. 51.

Adj. fractional, fragmentary, partial.

101. Zero.—N. zero, nothing naught, nought, duck's egg, goose egg; cipher, none, nobody; not a soul; *âme qui vive*; absence &c. 187; unsubstantiality &c. 4.

Adj. not -one, – any.

102. Multitude.—N. multitude; numerousness &c. *adj.*; numer-osity, -ality; multiplicity; profusion &c. (*plenty*) 639; legion, host; great –, large –, round –, enormous- number; a quantity, numbers, array, sight, army, sea, galaxy; scores, peck, bushel, school, shoal, swarm, draft, bevy, cloud, flock, herd, drove, flight, covey, hive, brood, litter, farrow, fry, nest; mob, crowd &c. (*assemblage*) 72; lots, loads, heaps; all the world and his wife.

[Increase of number] greater number, majority; multiplication, multiple.

V. be -numerous &c. *adj.*; swarm –, teem –, crawl –, creep -with; crowd, swarm, come thick upon; outnumber, multiply; people; swarm like -locusts, – bees.

Adj. many, several, sundry, divers, various, not a few; a -hundred, – thousand, – myriad, – million, – thousand and one; some -ten or a dozen, – forty or fifty &c.; half a -dozen, – hundred &c.; very –, full –, ever so- many; numer-ous, -ose; profuse, in profusion; manifold, multiplied, multitudinous, multiferous, multiple, multinomial, teeming, crawling, populous, peopled, crowded, thick, studded; galore.

thick coming, many more, more than one can tell, a world of; no end -of, – to; *cum multis aliis*; thick as -hops, – hail; plenty as blackberries; numerous as the -stars in the firmament, – sands on

103. Fewness.—N. fewness &c. *adj.*; paucity, small number; small quantity &c. 32; scarcity, sparsity; rarity; infrequency &c. 137; handful; maniple; minority, exiguity.

[Diminution of number] reduction; weeding &c. *v.*; elimination, sarculation, decimation.

V. be -few &c. *adj.*

render -few &c. *adj.*; reduce, diminish the number, weed, eliminate, thin decimate.

Adj. few; scarce; scant, -y; thin, rare, thinly scattered, few and far between; exiguous; infrequent &c. 137; *rari nantes*; hardly –, scarcely- any; to be counted on one's fingers; reduced &c. *v.*; unrepeated.

Adv. here and there.

the sea-shore, – hairs on the head; and -what not, – heaven knows
what; endless &c. (*infinite*) 105.

Phr. their name is 'Legion.'

104. Repetition.—N. repetition, iteration, reiteration, duplication,
ding-dong, alliteration; *epistrophe*; harping, recurrence, succession, run;
batto-, tauto-logy; monotony, tautophony; rhythm &c. 138; pleonasm,
redundancy, diffuseness.

chimes, repetend, echo, *ritornello*, burden of a song, *refrain*; rehearsal;
encore; *réchauffé*, *rifacimento*, recapitulation.

cuckoo &c. (*imitation*) 19; reverberation &c. 408; drumming &c.
(*roll*) 407; renewal &c. (*restoration*) 660.

twice-told tale; old -story, – song, chestnut; second –, new- edition;
reprint, new impression; return game, return match, reappearance,
reproduction; periodicity &c. 138.

V. repeat, iterate, reiterate, reproduce, parrot, echo, re-echo, drum,
harp upon, battologize, hammer, redouble.

recur, revert, return, reappear; renew &c. (*restore*) 660.

rehearse; do –, say- over again; ring the changes on; harp on the
same string; din –, drum- in the ear; conjugate in all its moods, tenses
and inflexions, begin again, go over the same ground, go the same round,
never hear the last of; resume, return to, recapitulate, reword.

Adj. repeated &c. *v.*; repetition-al, -ary; recur-rent, -ring; ever
recurring, thick coming; frequent, incessant, redundant, pleonastic,
tautological.

monotonous, harping, iterative; mocking, chiming; retold; aforesaid,
-named; above-mentioned, said; habitual &c. 613; another.

Adv. repeatedly, often, again, afresh, anew, over again, once more;
ditto, *encore, de novo, bis, da capo*.

again and again; over and over, – again; many times over; time-
and again, – after time; year after year; day by day &c.; many –,
several –, a number of- times; many –, full many- a time; times out of
number, year in and year out, morning, noon and night; frequently
&c. 136.

Phr. *ecce iterum Crispinus, toujours perdrix*, cut and come again;
'tomorrow and tomorrow.'

105. Infinity.—N. infini-ty, -tude, -teness &c. *adj.*; perpetuity &c. 112.

V. be -infinite &c. *adj.*; know –, have- no -limits, – bounds; go on
for ever.

Adj. infinite; immense; number-, count-, sum-, measure-less; in-
numer-, immeasur-, incalcul-, illimit-, intermin-, unfathom-, unap-
proach-able; exhaustless, inexhaustible, indefinite; without -number,
– measure, – limit, – end; incomprehensible; limit-, end-, bound-, termless; un-told, -numbered, -measured, -bounded, -limited; illimited;
perpetual &c. 112.

Adv. infinitely &c. *adj.*; *ad infinitum*.

Section VI. TIME

1°. Absolute Time

106. Time.—N. time, duration;
period, term, stage, space, span, spell,
season; the whole -time, – period;
course &c. 109.

107. Neverness.*—N. 'neverness';
absence of time, no time; *dies non*;
Tib's eve; Greek Kalends.

Adv. never; at no -time, – period;

* A term introduced by Bishop Wilkins.

intermediate time, while, *interim,* interval, bit, pendency; inter-vention, -mission, -mittence, -regnum, -lude; respite.

era, epoch, æon, cycle; time of life, age, year, date; decade &c. (*period*) 108; moment, &c. (*instant*) 113; reign &c. 737.

glass –, ravages –, whirligig –, noiseless foot- of time; scythe.

V. continue, last, endure, go on, hold out, remain, stay, persist, abide, run; intervene; elapse &c. 109.

take –, take up –, fill –, occupy- time.

pass –, pass away –, spend –, while away –, consume –, talk against –, kill- time; tide over; use –, employ- time; tarry &c. 110; seize an opportunity &c. 134; waste time &c. (*be inactive*) 683.

Adj. continuing &c. *v.*; on foot; permanent &c. (*durable*) 110.

Adv. while, whilst, during, pending; during the -time, – interval; in the course of; for the time being, day by day; in the time of, when; mean-time, -while; in the -meantime, – *interim; ad interim, pendente lite; de die in diem;* from -day to day, – hour to hour &c.; hourly, always; for a -time, – season; till, until, up to, yet; the whole –, all the- time; all along; throughout &c. (*completely*) 52; for good &c. (*diuturnity*) 110.

here-, there-, where-upon; then; *anno,* – *Domini;* A.D.; *ante Christum;* A.C.; before Christ; B.C.; *anno urbis conditæ;* A.U.C.; *anno regni;* A.R.; once upon a time, one fine morning.

Phr. time -runs, – runs against; *tempus fugit.*

on no occasion, never in all one's born days, neverm ore, *sine die.*

_____

108. [Definite duration, or portion of time.] **Period.—N.** period; second, minute, hour, day, week, sennight, octave, month, moon, quarter, semester, year, *lustrum, quinquennium,* decade, *decennium,* indiction, lifetime, generation, epoch, era, cycle.

century, age, *millennium; annus magnus.*

Adj. horary; hourly, annual &c. (*periodical*) 138.

108a. Contingent Duration.—Adv. during -pleasure, – good behaviour; *quamdiu se bene gesserit.*

_____

109. [Indefinite duration.] **Course.** **—N.** course –, progress –, process –, succession –, lapse –, flow –, flux –, effluxion, stream –, tract –, current –, sweep –, tide –, march –, step –, flight- of time; duration &c. 106.

[Indefinite time] aorist.

V. elapse, lapse, flow, run, proceed, advance, pass; roll –, wear –, press –, drag- on; flit, fly, slip, slide, glide, crawl; run -its course.

out; expire; go –, pass- by; be -past &c. 122.

Adj. elapsing &c. *v.*; aoristic; progressive, transient &c. 111.

Adv. in due -time, – season; in -course, – process, – the fulness- of time; in time.

Phr. *labitur et labetur; truditur dies die; fugaces labuntur anni;* 'tomorrow and tomorrow and tomorrow creeps in this petty pace from day to day.'

_____

110. [Long duration.] **Diuturnity.** **—N.** diuturnity; a -long –, length of- time; an age, a century, an eternity,

111. [Short duration.] **Transientness.** **—N.** transientness &c. *adj.*; evanescence, impermanence, fugacity, transi-

æons; slowness &c. 275; perpetuity &c. 112; blue moon.

dura-bleness, -bility; persistence, lastingness &c. *adj.*; continuance, assiduity, endurance, standing; permanence &c. (*stability*) 150; survi-val, -vance; longevity &c. (*age*) 128; distance of time.

protraction –, prolongation –, extension- of time; delay &c. (*lateness*) 133.

V. last, endure, stand, remain, abide, continue, brave a thousand years.

tarry &c. (*be late*) 133; drag -on, – its slow length along, – a lengthening chain; protract, prolong; spin –, eke –, draw –, lengthen- out; temporize; gain –, make –, talk against- time.

out-last, -live; survive; live to fight again.

Adj. durable; perdurable; lasting &c. *v.*; of long -duration, – standing; permanent, chronic, long-standing; intransi-ent, -tive; intransmutable, persistent; life-, live-long; longeval, long-lived, macrobiotic, diuturnal, sempervirent, evergreen, perennial; unin-, ter-, unre-mitting; perpetual &c. 112.

lingering, protracted, prolonged, spun out &c. *v.*; long-pending, -winded; slow &c. 275.

Adv. long; for -a long time, – an age, – ages, – ever so long, – many a long day; long ago &c. (*in a past time*) 122; *longo intervallo.*

all the -day long, – year round; the livelong day, as the day is long, morning, noon and night; hour after hour, day after day, &c.; for good; permanently &c. *adj.*

112. [Endless duration.] **Perpetuity.**
—**N.** perpetuity, eternity, timelessness; everness,* aye, sempiternity, immortality, athanasia; everlastingness &c. *adj.*; perpetuation; infinite duration.

V. last –, endure –, go on- for ever; have no end.

eternize, eternify, perpetuate, immortalize.

Adj. perpetual, eternal, eterne; everlasting, -living, -flowing; continual, constant, sempiternal; co-eternal; endless, unending; ceaseless, incessant, uninterrupted, indesinent, unceasing; interminable, having no end; unfad-

toriness, volatility, caducity, mortality, span; flash in the pan, nine days' wonder, bubble, May-fly; spurt; temporary arrangement, interregnum.

velocity &c. 274; suddenness &c. 113; changeableness &c. 149.

V. be -transient &c. *adj.*; flit, pass away, fly, gallop, vanish, fade, fleet, melt away, evaporate; pass away like a -cloud, – summer cloud, – shadow, – dream.

Adj. transi-ent, -tory, -tive; passing, evanescent, fleeting; flying &c. *v.*; fug-acious, -itive; shifting, slippery; spasmodic.

tempor-al, -ary; provis-ional, -ory; cursory, short-lived, ephemeral, deciduous; perishable, mortal, precarious; impermanent.

brief, quick, brisk; cometary, meteoric, extemporaneous, summary; pressed for time &c. (*haste*) 684; sudden, momentary &c. (*instantaneous*) 113.

Adv. temporarily &c. *adj.*; *pro tempore*; for -the moment, – a time; awhile, *en passant, in transitu*; in a short time; soon &c. (*early*) 132; briefly &c. *adj.*; at short notice; on the -point, – eve -of; *in articulo*; between cup and lip.

Phr. one's days are numbered; the time is up; here to-day and gone to-morrow; *non semper erit æstas; eheu! fugaces labuntur anni; sic transit gloria mundi.*

———

113. [Point of time.] **Instantaneity.**
—**N.** instantane-ity, -ousness; sudden-, abrupt-ness.

moment, instant, second, minute; twinkling, trice, flash, breath, crack, jiffy, *coup*, burst, flash of lightning, stroke of time.

epoch, time; time of -day, – night; hour, minute; very -minute &c., – time, – hour; present –, right –, true –, exact –, correct- time.

V. be -instantaneous &c. *adj.*; twinkle, flash.

Adj. instantaneous, momentary, extempore, sudden, instant, abrupt;

* Bishop Wilkins.

ing, evergreen, amaranthine; never-ending, -dying, -fading; deathless, immortal, undying, imperishable.

Adv. perpetually &c. *adj.*; always, ever, evermore, aye; for -ever, – aye, – evermore, – ever and a day, – ever and ever; in all ages, from age to age; without end; world –, time- without end; *in sæcula sæculorum*; to the -end of time, – crack of doom, – 'last syllable of recorded time'; till doomsday; constantly &c. (*very frequently*) 136.

Phr. *esto perpetuum*; *labitur et labetur in omne volubilis ævum*.

subitaneous, hasty; quick as -thought,* – lightning, – a flash; rapid as electricity.

Adv. instantaneously &c. *adj.*; in –, in less than- no time; *presto, subito, instanter*, suddenly, at a stroke, like-a shot, – greased lightning; in a trice, in a moment &c. *n.*; eftsoons, in the twinkling of -an eye, – a bed post; at one jump, in the same breath, *per saltum, uno saltu*; at –, all at- once; in one's tracks; plump, slap; 'at one fell swoop'; at the same -instant &c. *n.*; immediately &c. (*early*) 132; *ex tempore*, on the -spot, – spur of the moment, – dot; just then; slap- dash &c. (*haste*) 684; before you could -turn round, – say -knife, – Jack Robinson.

Phr. touch and go; no sooner said than done.

114. [Estimation, measurement, and record of time.] **Chronometry.—N.** chrono-, horo-metry, -logy; date, epoch; style, era.

almanac, calendar, ephemeris; register, -try; chronicle, annals, journal, diary, chronogram.

[Instruments for the measurement of time] clock, watch; chrono-meter, -scope, -graph; repeater, alarum; time-keeper, -piece; dial, sun-dial, *gnomon, pendule*, horologe, pendulum, hour-glass, water clock, clepsydra.

mean –, Greenwich –, solar –, sidereal –, local –, summer- time; daylight saving.

chrono-grapher, -loger, -logist; annalist.

V. fix –, mark- the time; date, register, chronicle; measure –, beat –, mark- time; bear date.

Adj. chrono-logical, -metrical, -grammatical; isochronal.

Adv. o'clock; *a.m., p.m.*

115. [False estimate of time.] **Anachronism.—N.** ana-, meta-, para-, pro-chronism; *prolepsis*, misdate; anticipation, antichronism.

disregard –, neglect –, oblivion- of time.

intempestivity &c. 135.

V. mis-, ante-, post-, over-date; anticipate; take no note of time.

Adj. misdated &c. *v.*; undated; over-due; out of date; anachronous &c. *n.*

2°. Relative Time

1. *Time with reference to Succession*

116. Priority.—N. priority, antecedence, anteriority, pre-existence, precedence &c. 62; precession &c. 280; precursor &c. 64; the past &c. 122; premises.

V. precede, come before; forerun; antecede, go before &c. (*lead*) 280; pre-exist; dawn; premise, presage &c. 511.

be -beforehand &c. (*be early*) 132;

117. Posteriority.—N. posteriority; succession, sequence; following &c. 281; subsequence, supervention; futurity &c. 121; successor; sequel &c. 65; remainder, reversion.

V. follow &c. 281 –, come –, go-after; ensue, result; succeed, supervene; step into the shoes of.

Adj. subsequent, posterior, following, after, later, succeeding, postliminious,

* See note on 264.

steal a march upon, anticipate, forestall; have –, gain- the start.

Adj. prior, previous; preced-ing, -ent; anterior, antecedent; pre-existing, -existent; foresighted; former, foregoing; afore –, before-, above-mentioned; aforesaid, said; introductory &c. (*precursory*) 64; pre-war.

Adv. before, prior to; earlier; previously &c. *adj.*; afore, ere, theretofore, erewhile; ere –, before- -then, – now; erewhile, already, yet, beforehand; aforetime, on the eve of, in anticipation.

118. The Present Time.—N. the present -time, – day, – moment, – juncture, – occasion; the times, existing time, time being; twentieth century; nonce, crisis, epoch, day, hour.

age, time of life.

Adj. present, actual, instant, current, latest, existing, that is.

Adv. at this -time, – moment &c. 113; at the -present time &c. *n.*; now, at present.

at this time of day, to-day, now-a-days; already; even –, but –, just-now; on the present occasion; for the -time being, – nonce; *pro hâc vice*; on the -nail, – spot; on the spur of the -moment, – occasion.

until now; to -this, – the present day.

postnate; successive &c. 63; postdiluvial, -an; *puisné*; posthumous; post-war, future &c. 121.

Adv. subsequently, after, afterwards, since, later; at a -subsequent, – later- period; next, in the sequel, close upon, thereafter, thereupon, upon which, eftsoons; from that -time, – moment; after a -while, – time; in process of time.

postcenal, postcibal, postprandial, after-dinner.

119. [Time different from the present.] **Different Time.—N.** different –, other- time.

[Indefinite time] aorist.

Adj. aoristic.

Adv. at that –, at which- -time, – moment, – instant; then, on that occasion, upon.

when; when-ever, -soever; upon which, on which occasion; at -another, – a different, – some other, – any- time; at various times; some –, one- -of these days, – fine morning, – day; sooner or later; some time or other; once upon a time, once.

120. Synchronism.—N. synchronism; coexistence, coincidence; simultaneousness &c. *adj.*; concurrence, concomitance, unity of time, interim.

[Having equal times] isochronism, syntony.

contemporary, coetanian.

V. coexist, concur, accompany, go hand in hand, keep pace with; synchronize, isochronize.

Adj. synchron-ous, -al, -ical, -istical; simultaneous, coexisting, coincident, concomitant, concurrent; coev-al, -ous; contempora-ry, -neous; coetaneous; coterminous, coeternal; isochronous.

Adv. at the same time; simultaneously &c. *adj.*; together, in concert, during the same time; in the same breath; *pari passu*; in the interim.

at the -very moment &c. 113; just as, as soon as; meanwhile &c. (*while*) 106.

121. [Prospective time.] **Futurity. —N.** futur-ity, -ition; future, hereafter, time to come; approaching –, coming –, after- -time, – age, – days, – hours, – years, – ages, – life; morrow, to-morrow, by and by; millennium, doomsday, day of judgment, crack of doom, remote future.

122. [Retrospective time.] **Preterition.—N.** preterition; priority &c. 116; the past, past time; days –, times- -of yore, – of old, – past, – gone by; bygone days, good old days; old –, ancient –, former -times; fore time; yesterdays; the olden –, good old-time; auld lang syne; eld.

approach of time, advent, time drawing on, womb of time; destiny &c. 152; eventuality.

heritage, heirs, posterity, descendants.

prospect &c. (*expectation*) 507; foresight &c. 510.

V. look forwards; anticipate &c. (*expect*) 507, (*foresee*) 510; forestall &c. (*be early*) 132.

come –, draw- on; draw near; approach, await, threaten; impend &c. (*be destined*) 152.

Adj. future, to come; coming &c. (*impending*) 152; next, near; near –, close- at hand; eventual, ulterior; expectant, prospective, in prospect &c. (*expectation*) 507.

Adv. prospectively, hereafter, on the knees of the gods, in future; to-morrow, the day after to-morrow; in -course, – process, – the fulness- of time; eventually, ultimately, sooner or later; *proximo*; *paulo post futurum*; in after time; one of these days; after a -time, – while.

from this time; hence-forth, -forwards; thence; thence-forth, -forward; whereupon, upon which.

soon &c. (*early*) 132; on the -eve, – point, – brink- of; about to; close upon.

---

antiquity, antiqueness, *status quo*; time immemorial; distance of time; remote -age, – time; ancient history; remote past; rust of antiquity; ancientness.

pale-ontology, -ography, -ology; palætiology,* archæology; archaism, antiquarianism, mediævalism, pre-Raphaelitism; retrospection, looking back, memory &c. 505.

laudator temporis acti; mediævalist, pre-Raphaelite; antiqu-ary, -arian; archæologist &c.; Oldbuck, Dryasdust.

ancestry &c. (*paternity*) 166.

V. be -past &c. adj.; have -expired &c. adj., – run its course, – had its day; pass; pass –, go- -by, – away, – off; lapse, blow over.

look –, trace –, cast the eyes- back; exhume.

Adj. past, gone, gone by, over, passed away, bygone, foregone; elapsed, lapsed, preterlapsed, expired, no more, run out, blown over, that has been, whilom, extinct, never to return, exploded, forgotten, irrecoverable; obsolete &c. (*old*) 124; extinct as the dodo.

former, pristine, *quondam, ci-devant*, late; ancestral.

foregoing; last, latter; recent, overnight; past, preterite, preter-perfect, -pluperfect, past perfect.

looking back &c. v.; retro-spective, -active; archæological &c. n.

Adv. formerly; of -old, – yore; erst, whilom, erewhile, time was, ago, over; in -the olden time &c. n.; anciently, long -ago, – since; a long -while, – time- ago; years –, ages- ago; some time -ago, – since, – back.

yesterday, the day before yesterday; last -year, – season, – month &c.; *ultimo*; lately &c. (*newly*) 123.

retrospectively; ere –, before –, till- now; hitherto, heretofore; no longer; once, – upon a time; from time immemorial; in the memory of man; time out of mind; already, yet, up to this time; *ex post facto*.

Phr. time was; the time -has, – hath- been.

2. *Time with reference to a particular Period*

123. Newness.—**N.** newness &c. adj.; neologism, neoterism; novelty, recency; immaturity; youth &c. 127; gloss of novelty.

124. Oldness.—**N.** oldness &c. adj.; age, antiquity; cobwebs of antiquity.

maturity, ripeness; decline, decay; senility &c. 128.

* Whewell.

innovation; renovation &c. (*restoration*) 660.

modernist, neologist, neoteric.

modernism, modernity; mushroom; latest fashion, *dernier cri.*

upstart, *parvenu, nouveau riche.*

V. renew &c. (*restore*) 660; modernize.

Adj. new, novel, recent, fresh, green; young &c. 127; evergreen; raw, immature; virgin; un-tried, -handseled, -used, -trodden, -beaten; fledgling.

late, modern, neoteric; new-born, -fashioned, -fangled, -fledged; of yesterday; just out, brand –, span-new, up to date, topical; vernal, renovated; innovatory.

fresh as -a rose, – a daisy, – paint; spick and span.

Adv. newly &c. *adj.*; afresh, anew, lately, just now, only yesterday, the other day; latterly, of late.

not long –, a short time- ago.

———

seniority, eldership, primogeniture.

archaism &c. (*the past*) 122; thing –, relic- of the past; megatherium.

tradition, prescription, custom, folklore, immemorial usage, common law.

V. be -old &c. *adj.*; have -had, – seen- its day; become -old &c. *adj.*; age, fade.

Adj. old, olden, ancient, antique; of long standing, time-honoured, venerable; eld-er, -est; first-born.

prime; prim-itive, -eval, -igenous; primordi-al, -nate; aboriginal &c. (*beginning*) 66; diluvian, antediluvian; pre-historic; patriarchal, preadamite; palæocrystic; fossil, paleozoic, pre-glacial, ante-mundane; archaic, classic, mediæval, pre-Raphaelite, ancestral, black-letter.

immemorial, traditional, prescriptive, customary, whereof the memory of man runneth not to the contrary; inveterate, rooted.

antiquated, of other times, rococo, of the old school, after-age, obsolete; fusty, moth-eaten; out of -date, – fashion; stale, old-fashioned, behind the -age, – times; exploded; gone out, – by; *passé,* outworn, run out; disused; senile &c. 128; time-worn; crumbling &c. (*deteriorated*) 659; second-hand.

old as -the hills, – Methuselah, – Adam, – history.

Adv. since the -world was made, – year one, – days of Methuselah.

125. Morning. [Noon.]—**N.** morning, morn, matins, forenoon, *a.m.*, prime, dawn, daybreak, daylight, sun-up, peep –, break- of day; aurora, Eos; first blush –, prime- of the morning; twilight, crepuscule, sunrise, cockcrow.

spring; vernal equinox.

noon; mid-, noon-day; noontide, meridian, prime.

summer, midsummer; summer solstice.

Adj. matin, matutinal; vernal, æstival.

Adv. at -sunrise &c. *n.*; with the lark, when the morning dawns.

127. Youth.—**N.** youth; juven- -ility, -escence; juniority; infancy; baby-, child-, boy-, girl-, youth-hood; *incunabula*; minority, immaturity, nonage, teens, tender age, bloom.

cradle, nursery, leading-strings, pupilage, puberty, *pucelage.*

126. Evening. [Midnight.]—**N.** evening, eve; decline –, fall –, close- of day; eventide, evensong, vespers; candlelight; nightfall, curfew, dusk, twilight, blind man's holiday; eleventh hour; sun-set, -down; going down of the sun, cock-shut, dewy eve, gloaming, bed-time.

afternoon, *post meridiem, p.m.*

autumn; fall, – of the leaf; autumnal equinox, Indian summer, harvest-time.

midnight; dead –, witching time- of night; winter, – solstice.

Adj. vesperine, autumnal, nocturnal, wintry, brumal, hiemal.

128. Age.—**N.** age; oldness &c. *adj.*; old –, advanced- age; sen-ility, -escence; years, anility, grey hairs, climacteric, grand climacteric, declining years, decrepitude, hoary age, caducity, superannuation; second childhood, -ishness; dotage; vale of years,

prime -, flower -, spring-tide -, seed-time -, golden season- of life; heyday of youth, school days; rising generation, younger generation.

Adj. young, youthful, juvenile, green, callow, budding, sappy, *puisné*, beardless, unfledged, unripe, under age, in one's teens; *in statu pupillari*; younger, junior.

decline of life, 'sear and yellow leaf'; three-score years and ten; green old age, ripe old age; longevity; time of life.

seniority, eldership; elders &c. (*veteran*) 130; firstling; *doyen*, dean, father; primogeniture; nostology.

V. be -aged &c. *adj.*; grow -, get-old &c. *adj.*; age; decline, wane.

Adj. aged; old &c. 124; elderly, senile; matronly, anile; in years; ripe, mellow, run to seed, declining, waning, past one's prime; grey, -headed; hoar, -y; venerable, time-worn, antiquated, *passé*, effete, doddering, decrepit, superannuated; advanced in -life, – years; stricken in years; wrinkled, marked with the crow's foot; having one foot in the grave; doting &c. (*imbecile*) 499.

old-, eld-er, -est; senior; first-born.

turned of, years old; of a certain age, no chicken, old as Methuselah; gerontic; ancestral; patriarchal &c. (*ancient*) 124.

---

129. Infant.—**N.** infant, babe, baby; nurse-, suck-, year-, wean-ling; *papoose, bambino.*

child, bairn, little- one, – tot, – mite, chick, brat, chit, pickaninny, kid, urchin; bant-, brat-ling; elf.

youth, boy, lad, slip, sprig, stripling, youngster, cub, unlicked cub, younker, callant, whipster, whipper-snapper, schoolboy, hobbledehoy, hopeful, cadet, minor, master.

scion; sap-, seed-ling; tendril, olive-branch, nestling, chicken, duckling; larva, caterpillar, chrysalis, cocoon; tadpole, whelp, cub, pullet, fry, callow; codlin, -g; *fœtus*, calf, colt, pup, foal, kitten; lamb, -kin.

girl; lass, -ie; wench, miss, damsel, *demoiselle*, damozel; maid, -en; virgin; nymph; colleen; minx, baggage, school-girl; tomboy, flapper, hoyden.

Adj. infant-ine, -ile; puerile; boy-, girl-, child-, baby-, kitten-ish; baby; new-born, unfledged, new-fledged, callow.

in -the cradle, – swaddling clothes, – long clothes, – arms, – leading strings; at the breast; in one's teens; young &c. 127.

130. Veteran.—**N.** veteran, old man, seer, patriarch, greybeard, dugout, grand-father, -sire; grandam, beldam; gaffer, gammer; hag, crone; pantaloon; sexage-, octoge-, nonage-, cente-narian; old stager; dotard &c. 501.

preadamite, Methuselah, Nestor, Rip van Winkle, old Parr; elders; forefathers &c. (*paternity*) 166.

---

131. Adolescence.—**N.** adolescence, pubescence, majority; adultness &c. *adj.*; manhood, virility, maturity; flower of age; prime -, meridian- of life.

man &c. 373; woman &c. 374; adult, no chicken.

V. come -of age, – to man's estate, – to years of discretion; attain majority, assume the *toga virilis*; have -cut one's eye-teeth, – sown one's wild oats, settle down.

Adj. adolescent, pubescent, of age; of -full, – ripe- age; out of one's teens, grown up, mature, full- blown, – grown, in one's prime, in full bloom, manly, virile, adult; womanly, matronly; marriageable, nubile.

3. *Time with reference to an Effect or Purpose*

132. Earliness.—**N.** earliness &c. *adj.*; morning &c. 125.

punctuality; promptitude &c. (*activity*) 682; haste &c. (*velocity*) 274; suddenness &c. (*instantaneity*) 113.

prematurity, precocity, precipitation, anticipation; prevenience, a stitch in time.

V. be -early &c. *adj.*, – beforehand &c. *adv.*; keep time, take time by the forelock, anticipate, forestall; have –, gain- the start; steal a march upon; gain time, draw on futurity; bespeak, secure, engage, pre-engage.

accelerate; expedite &c. (*quicken*) 274; make haste &c. (*hurry*) 684.

Adj. early, prime, timely, in time, punctual, forward; prompt &c. (*active*) 682; summary.

premature, precipitate, precocious; prevenient, anticipatory; rathe.

sudden &c. (*instantaneous*) 113; unexpected &c. 508; impending, imminent; near, – at hand; immediate.

Adv. early, soon, anon, betimes, rathe; eft, -soons; ere –, before- long; punctually &c. *adj.*; to the minute; in time; in -good, – military, – pudding, – due- time; time enough.

beforehand; prematurely &c. *adj.*; precipitately &c. (*hastily*) 684; too soon; before -its, – one's- time; in anticipation; unexpectedly &c. 508.

suddenly &c. (*instantaneously*) 113; before one can say 'Jack Robinson,' at short notice, extempore; on the spur of the -moment, – occasion; at once; on the -spot, – instant; at sight; off –, out of- hand; *à vue d'œil*; straight, -way, -forth; forthwith, incontinently, summarily, instanter, immediately, briefly, shortly, quickly, speedily, apace, before the ink is dry, almost immediately, presently, at the first opportunity, in no long time, by and by, in a while, directly.

Phr. touch and go, no sooner said than done.

134. Occasion.—**N.** occasion, opportunity, opening, room, scope, field; suitable –, proper- -time, – season; high time; opportuneness &c. *adj.*; tempestivity.

133. Lateness.—**N.** lateness &c. *adj.*; tardiness &c. (*slowness*) 275.

de-lay, -lation; cunctation, procrastination; detention; deferring &c. *v.*; filibuster, postponement, adjournment, prorogation, retardation, respite, reprieve, stay; protraction, prolongation, moratorium; contango; demurrage; remand; Fabian policy, *médecine expectante*, chancery suit; leeway; high time.

V. be -late &c. *adj.*; tarry, wait, stay, bide, take time; dawdle &c. (*be inactive*) 683; linger, loiter, saunter, lag behind; bide –, take- one's time; hang -about, – around, – back, – in the balance; gain time; hang fire; stand –, lie-over.

put off, defer, delay, lay over, suspend; shift –, stave- off; waive, retard, remand, postpone, adjourn; procrastinate; dally; prolong, protract; spin –, draw –, lengthen- out; prorogue; keep back; tide over; push –, drive- to the last; let the matter stand over; reserve &c. (*store*) 636; temporize; consult one's pillow, sleep upon it.

shelve, table, lay on the table.

lose an opportunity &c. 135; be kept waiting, dance attendance; kick –, cool- one's heels; *faire antichambre*; wait impatiently; await &c. (*expect*) 507; sit up, – at night.

Adj. late, tardy, slow, behindhand, belated, postliminious, posthumous, backward, unpunctual; dilatory &c. (*slow*), overdue 275; delayed &c. *v.*; in abeyance.

Adv. late; late-, back-ward; late in the day; at -sunset, – the eleventh hour, – length, – last, – long; ultimately; after –, behind- time; too late; too late for &c. 135.

slowly, leisurely, deliberately, at one's leisure; *ex post facto*; *sine die*.

Phr. *nonum prematur in annum.*

---

135. Intempestivity.—**N.** intempestivity; unseasonableness; unsuitable –, improper-time; unreasonableness &c. *adj.*; evil hour; *contretemps*; intrusion; anachronism &c. 115.

crisis, turn, juncture, emergency, conjuncture; turning point, given time.

nick of time; golden –, well-timed –, fine –, favourable- opportunity; clear stage, fair field; *mollia tempora*; *fata Morgana*; spare time &c. (*leisure*) 685.

V. seize &c. (*take*) 789 –, use &c. 677 –, give &c. 784- an -opportunity, – occasion; improve the occasion.

suit the occasion &c. (*be expedient*) 646.

strike the iron while it is hot, *battre le fer sur l'enclume*, make hay while the sun shines, take time by the forelock, *prendre la balle au bond*.

Adj. opportune, timely, well-timed, timeous, timeful, seasonable.

providential, lucky, fortunate, happy, favourable, propitious, auspicious, critical; suitable &c. 23; *obiter dicta*.

Adv. opportunely &c. *adj.*; in -proper, – due- -time, – course, – season; for the nonce; in the -nick, – fulness- of time; all in good time; just in time, at the eleventh hour, now or never.

by the -way, – by; *en passant, à propos; pro -re natâ, – hac vice; par parenthèse*, parenthetically, by way of parenthesis; while -speaking of, – on this subject; *ex tempore*; on the spur of the -moment, – occasion; on the spot &c. (*early*) 132.

Phr. *carpe diem; occasionem cognosce*; one's hour is come, the time is up; that reminds me.

V. be -ill timed &c. *adj.*; mistime, intrude, come amiss, break in upon; have other fish to fry; be -busy, – engaged, – tied up, – occupied.

lose –, throw away –, waste –, neglect &c. 460- an opportunity; allow –, suffer- the -opportunity, – occasion- to -pass, - slip, – go by, – escape, – lapse; waste time &c. (*be inactive*) 683; let slip through the fingers, lock the stable door when the steed is stolen.

Adj. ill-, mis-timed; untimely, intrusive, unseasonable; out of -date, – season; inopportune, timeless, untoward, *mal à propos*, unlucky, inauspicious, unpropitious, unfortunate, unfavourable; unsuited &c. 24; inexpedient &c. 647.

unpunctual &c. (*late*) 133; too late for; premature &c. (*early*) 132; too soon for; wise after the event.

Adv. inopportunely &c. *adj.*; as ill luck would have it, in an evil hour, the time having gone by, a day after the fair.

Phr. after meat mustard, after death the doctor.

3°. Recurrent Time

136. Frequency.—N. frequency, oftness; repetition, &c. 104.

V. recur &c. 104; do nothing but; keep, – on.

Adj. frequent, many times, not rare, thickcoming, incessant, perpetual, continual, constant, recurrent, repeated &c. 104; habitual &c. 613; hourly, &c. 138.

Adv. often, often to be met with, oft; oft-, often-times; frequently; repeatedly &c. 104; unseldom, not unfrequently; in -quick, – rapid- succession; many a time and oft; daily, hourly &c.; every -day, – hour, – moment &c.

perpetually, continually, constantly, incessantly, without ceasing, at all times, daily and hourly, night and day,

137. Infrequency.—N. infrequency, infrequence, rareness, rarity; fewness &c. 103; seldomness, uncommonness.

V. be -rare &c. *adj.*

Adj. un-, in-frequent; uncommon, sporadic, rare, – as a blue diamond; few &c. 103; scarce; almost unheard of, unprecedented, which has not occurred within the memory of the oldest inhabitant, not within one's previous experience.

Adv. seldom, rarely, scarcely, hardly; not often, unfrequently, infrequently, unoften; scarcely –, hardly- ever; once in a blue moon.

once; once -for all, – in a way; *pro hac vice*; like angels' visits, few and far between.

day and night, day after day, morning noon and night, ever and anon.

most often; commonly &c. (*habitually*) 613.

sometimes, occasionally, at times, now and then, from time to time, there being times when, *toties quoties*, often enough, again and again &c. 104.

138. Regularity of recurrence. **Periodicity.—N.** periodicity, intermittence; beat; oscillation &c. 314; pulse, pulsation; rhythm; alter-nation, -nate-ness, -nativeness, -nity.

bout, round, revolution, rotation, turn.

anniversary, birthday, jubilee, centenary, bi-, ter-centenary.

[Regularity of return] rota, cycle, period, stated time, routine; days of the week; Sunday, Monday &c.; months of the year; January &c.; feast, fast, saint's day &c.; Christmas, Easter, New Year's Day &c. 998; quarter-, Lady-, Midsummer-, Michaelmas-day; May Day, the King's Birthday; leap year; seasons.

punctuality, regularity, steadiness.

V. recur in regular -order, – succession; return, revolve, rotate; come -again, – in its turn; come round, – again; beat, pulsate; alternate; intermit.

Adj. periodic, -al; serial, recurrent, cyclic-, -al, rhythmic-, -al, even; recurring &c. *v.*; inter-, re-mittent; alternate, every other.

hourly; diurnal, daily; quotidian, tertian, weekly; hebdomad-al, -ary; bi-weekly, fortnightly; monthly, menstrual, catamenial; yearly, annual; biennial, triennial, &c.; bissextile; centennial, secular; paschal, lenten, &c.

regular, steady, punctual, constant, methodical, regular as clockwork.

Adv. periodically &c. *adj.*; at -regular intervals, – stated times; at -fixed, – established- periods; punctually &c. *adj.*; *de die in diem*; from day to day, day by day.

by turns; in -turn, – rotation; alternately, every other day, off and on, ride and tie, round and round.

139. Irregularity of recurrence.—**N.** irregularity, uncertainty, unpunctuality; fitfulness &c. *adj.*

Adj. irregular, uneven, uncertain, unpunctual, capricious, erratic, desultory, fitful, flickering; rambling, rhapsodical; spasmodic, unsystematic, unequal, variable, halting.

Adv. irregularly &c. *adj.*; by fits and starts &c. (*discontinuously*) 70.

Section VII. CHANGE

1°. Simple Change

140. [Difference at different times.] **Change.—N.** change, alteration, mutation, permutation, variation, modification, modulation, inflexion, mood, qualification, innovation, *metastasis*, deviation, shift, turn; diversion; break.

transformation, transfiguration; metamorphosis; metabolism; transmutation; transubstantiation; metagenesis, transanimation, transmigration, me-

141. [Absence of change.] **Permanence.—N.** stability &c. 150; quiescence &c. 265; obstinacy &c. 606.

permanence, -cy, persistence, fixity, fixity of purpose, endurance, durability; standing, *status quo*; maintenance, preservation, conservation; conservatism; *laissez-faire*; law of the Medes and Persians; standing dish.

V. let -alone, – be; persist, remain,

tempsychosis; version; metathesis; transmogrification; catalysis; *avatar*; alterative.

conversion &c. (*gradual change*) 144; revolution &c. (*sudden or radical change*) 146; inversion &c. (*reversal*) 218; displacement &c. 185; transference &c. 270.

changeableness &c. 149; tergiversation &c. (*change of mind*) 607.

V. change, alter, vary, wax and wane; modulate, diversify, qualify, tamper with; turn, shift, veer, jibe, tack, chop, shuffle, swerve, dodge, warp, deviate, turn aside, evert, intervert; pass to, take a turn, turn the corner, resume.

work a change, modify, vamp, revamp, superinduce; trans-form, –mute, -ume, -figure &c. *n.*; metamorphose, ring the changes; convert, resolve; revolutionize; chop and change; patch, re-shape.

innovate, introduce new blood, shuffle the cards, spin the wheel; give a -turn, – colour- to; influence, turn the scale; shift the scene, turn over a new leaf.

recast &c. 146; reverse &c. 218; disturb &c. 61; convert into &c. 144.

Adj. changed &c. *v.*; new-fangled; changeable &c. 149; transitional; modifiable; alterative.

Adv. *mutatis mutandis.*

Int. *quantum mutatus!*

Phr. 'a change came o'er the spirit of my dream'; *nous avons changé tout cela; tempora mutantur et nos mutamur in illis; non sum qualis eram.*

stay, tarry, rest; hold, – on; last, endure, bide, abide, aby, dwell, maintain, keep; stand, – still, – fast; subsist, live, outlive, survive; hold –, keep one's -ground, – footing; hold good.

Adj. stable &c. 150; persisting &c. *v.*; permanent; established, fixed; durable; unchanged &c. (change &c. 140); unrenewed; intact, inviolate; persistent; monotonous, uncheckered; unfailing.

un-destroyed, -repealed, -suppressed; conservative, *qualis ab incepto*; prescriptive &c. (*old*) 124; stationary &c. 265.

Adv. *in statu quo*; for good, finally; at a stand, -still; *uti possidetis*; without a shadow of turning.

Phr. as you were!; *j'y suis j'y reste; esto perpetua; nolumus leges Angliæ mutari*; let sleeping dogs lie.

---

142. [Change from action to rest.] **Cessation.**—**N.** cessation, discontinuance, desistance, desinence.

inter-, re-mission; sus-pense, -pension; interruption, hitch; hartal; stop; stopping &c. *v.*; closure, stoppage, halt; arrival &c. 292.

pause, rest, lull, respite, truce, armistice, drop; interregnum, abeyance.

closure &c. 261.

dead -stop, – stand, – lock; checkmate; comma, colon, semicolon, period, full stop; end &c. 67; death &c. 360; *cæsura.*

V. cease, discontinue, desist, stay; break –, leave- off; hold, stop, pull up, stall, stop short, check; stick, deadlock, hang fire; halt; pause, rest.

have done with, give over, surcease,

143. Continuance in action.—**N.** continu-ance, -ation; run; extension, prolongation; maintenance, perpetuation; persistence &c. (*perseverance*) 604*a*; repetition &c. 104.

V. continue, persist; go –, jog –, keep –, carry –, run – hold- on; abide, keep, pursue, stick to; endure; take –, maintain- its course; keep up.

sustain, uphold, hold up, keep on foot; follow up, perpetuate, prolong; maintain; preserve &c. 604*a*; harp upon &c. (*repeat*) 104.

keep -going, – alive, – at it, – the pot boiling, – the ball rolling, – up the ball; plod-, plug- along; slog on; die in harness; hold on –, pursue- the even tenor of one's way.

let be; *stare super antiquas vias*;

shut up shop; give up &c. (*relinquish*) 624.

hold –, stay- one's hand; rest on one's oars, repose on one's laurels.

come to a -stand, – standstill, – dead lock, – full stop; arrive &c. 292; go out, die away, peter out; wear -away, – off; pass away &c. (*be past*) 122; be at an end.

intromit, interrupt, suspend, interpel; inter-, re-mit; put -an end, – a stop, – a period- to; bring to a stand, -still; stop, cut out, cut short, arrest, avast; stem the -tide, – torrent; pull the check string; switch off.

Int. halt! hold! stop! enough! avast! have done! a truce to! soft! leave off! shut up! give over! chuck it!

quieta non movere; let things take their course.

Adj. continuing &c. *v.*; uninterrupted, unintermitting, unremitting, unvarying, unshifting; unreversed, unstopped, unrevoked, unvaried; sustained; undying &c. (*perpetual*) 112; inconvertible.

follow-up.

Int. carry on! right away!

Phr. *vestigia nulla retrorsum*; *labitur et labetur*.

---

144. [Gradual change to something different.] **Conversion.**—**N.** conversion, reduction, transmutation, transformation, development, resolution, assimilation; assumption; naturalization.

chemistry, alchemy; progress, growth, lapse, flux.

passage; transit, -ion; transmigration, shifting &c. *v.*; conjugation; convertibility.

crucible, alembic, caldron, retort, test tube &c.

convert, neophyte, proselyte, pervert, renegade, deserter, apostate, turncoat.

V. be converted into; become, get, wax; come –, turn- -to, – into; turn out, lapse, shift; run –, fall –, pass –, slide –, glide –, grow –, ripen –, open –, resolve itself –, settle –, merge- into; melt, grow, come round to, mature, mellow; assume the -form, – shape, – state, – nature, – character- of; illapse; assume a new phase, undergo a change.

convert –, resolve- into; make, render; mould, form &c. 240; remodel, new model, refound, reform, reorganize; assimilate –, bring –, reduce- to; transform.

Adj. converted into &c. *v.*; convertible, resolvable into; transitional; naturalized.

Adv. gradually &c. (*slowly*) 275; *in transitu* &c. (*transference*) 270.

145. Reversion.—**N.** reversion, return; revulsion; reaction.

turning point, turn of the tide; *status quo ante bellum*; calm before a storm.

alternation &c. (*periodicity*) 138; inversion &c. 219; recoil &c. 277; regression &c. 283; restoration &c. 660; relapse &c. 661; vicinism, atavism, throwback.

V. revert, turn back, return; relapse &c. 661; recoil &c. 277; retreat &c. 283; restore &c. 660; undo, unmake; turn the -tide, – scale; escheat.

Adj. reverting &c. *v.*; revulsive, reactionary.

Adv. *à rebours*, wrong side out.

146. [Sudden or violent change.] **Revolution.**—**N.** revolution, *bouleversement*, subversion, break up; destruction &c. 162; sudden –, radical –, sweeping –, organic- change; clean sweep, *coup d'état*, overthrow, *débâcle*; counter-revolution, rebellion &c. 742.

transilience, jump, leap, plunge, jerk, start; explosion; spasm, convulsion, throe, revulsion; storm, earthquake, eruption, upheaval, cataclysm.

legerdemain &c. (*trick*) 545.

V. revolutionize; new model, remodel, recast; strike out something new, break with the past; change the face of, unsex; revert &c. 742.

Adj. unrecognizable.

Revolutionary, Bolshevik &c. 742.

147. [Change of one thing for another.] **Substitution.—N.** substitution, subrogation, commutation; supplanting &c. *v.*, supersession, metonymy &c. (*figure of speech*) 521.

[Thing substituted] substitute, *succedaneum*, make-shift, temporary expedient, shift, *pis aller*, stop-gap, jury-mast, *locum tenens*, warming-pan, dummy, goat, scape-goat; double; changeling; *quid pro quo*, alternative; remount; representative &c. (*deputy*) 759; palimpsest.

price, purchase-money, consideration, equivalent.

V. substitute, put in the place of, change for; make way for, give place to; supply –, take- the place of; supplant, supersede, replace, cut out, serve as a substitute; step into –, stand in- the shoes of; make a shift –, put up- with; borrow of Peter to pay Paul; commute, redeem, compound for.

Adj. substituted &c. *v.*; vicarious, subdititious; substitutional.

Adv. instead; in -place, – lieu, – the stead, – the room- of; *faute de mieux*.

148. [Double or mutual change.] **Interchange.—N.** inter-, ex-change; com-, per-, inter-mutation; reciprocation, transposal, transposition, shuffling; reciprocity, castling [at chess]; hocus-pocus.

interchange-ableness, -ability.

barter &c. 794; tit for tat &c. (*retaliation*) 718; cross fire, battledore and shuttlecock; *quid pro quo.*

V. inter-, ex-, counter-change; bandy, transpose, shuffle, change hands, swap, trade, permute, reciprocate, commute; give and take, return the compliment; play at -puss in the corner, – battledore and shuttlecock; retaliate &c. 718; barter &c. 794.

Adj. interchanged &c. *v.*; reciprocal, mutual, commutative, interchanged &c. *v.*; interchangeable, intercurrent.

Adv. in exchange, *vice versâ, mutatis mutandis*, backwards and forwards, by turns, turn and turn about, turn about; each –, every one- in his turn.

2°. COMPLEX CHANGE

149. Changeableness.—N. changeableness &c. *adj.*; mutability, inconstancy; versatility, mobility; instability, unstable equilibrium; vacillation &c. (*irresolution*) 605; fluctuation, vicissitude; alternation &c. (*oscillation*) 314.

restlessness &c. *adj.*; fidgets, disquiet; dis-, in-quietude; unrest; agitation &c. 315.

moon, Proteus, chameleon, kaleidoscope, quicksilver, shifting sands, weathercock, harlequin, Cynthia of the minute, April showers; wheel of Fortune; transientness &c. 111.

V. fluctuate, vary, waver, flounder, flicker, flitter, flit, flutter, shift, shuffle, shake, totter, tremble, vacillate, wamble, turn and turn about, ring the changes; sway –, shift- to and fro; change and change about; oscillate

150. Stability.—N. stability; immutability &c. *adj.*; unchangeableness &c. *adj.*; constancy; stable equilibrium, immobility, soundness, vitality, stabiliment, stabilization, stiffness, ankylosis, solidity, *aplomb.*

establishment, fixture; rock, pillar, tower, foundation, leopard's spots, Ethiopian's skin, law of the Medes and Persians.

stabilimeter, stabilisator.

permanence &c. 141; obstinacy &c. 606.

V. be -firm &c. *adj.*; stick fast; stand –, keep –, remain- firm; weather the storm.

settle, establish, stablish, ascertain, fix, set, stabilitate, stabilize; retain, stet, keep hold; make -good, – sure; fasten &c. (*join*) 43; set on its legs, float; perpetuate.

[48]

&c. 314; vibrate –, oscillate- between two extremes; alternate; have as many phases as the moon.

Adj. change-able, -ful; changing &c. 140; mutable, variable, checkered, ever changing, kaleidoscopic, prote-an, -iform; versatile.

unstaid, inconstant; un-steady, -stable, -fixed, -settled; fluctuating &c. *v.*; restless; mercurial; agitated &c. 315; erratic, fickle; irresolute &c. 605; capricious &c. 608; touch-and-go; inconsonant, fitful, spasmodic; vibratory; vagrant, wayward, wavering; desultory; afloat; alternating; alterable, plastic, mobile; fleeting, transient &c. 111.

Adv. see-saw &c. (*oscillation*) 314; off and on.

---

settle down; strike –, take- root; take up one's abode &c. 184; build one's house on a rock.

Adj. unchangeable, immutable; unalter-ed, -able; not to be changed, constant; permanent &c. 141; invariable, undeviating; stable, durable; perennial &c. (*diuturnal*) 110.

fixed, steadfast, firm, fast, steady, balanced; confirmed, valid, fiducial, immovable, irremovable, riveted, rooted; settled, established &c. *v.*; vested; incontrovertible, stereotyped, indeclinable.

tethered, anchored, moored, at anchor, on a rock, firm as a rock; firmly -seated, – established &c. *v.*; deep-rooted, ineradicable; inveterate; obstinate &c. 606.

transfixed, stuck fast, aground, high and dry, stranded.

indefeasible, irretrievable, intransmutable, incommutable, irresoluble, irrevocable, irreversible, reverseless, inextinguishable, irreducible; indissol-uble, -vable; indestructible, undying, imperishable, indelible, indeciduous; insusceptible, – of change.

Int. *stet.*

Present Events

151. Eventuality.—**N.** eventuality, event, occurrence, incident, affair, transaction, proceeding, fact; matter of –, naked- fact; phenomenon; advent.

business, concern; circumstance, particular, casualty, happening, accident, adventure, passage, crisis, pass, emergency, contingency, consequence &c. 154.

the world, life, things, doings, affairs, matters; things –, affairs- in general; the times, state of affairs, order of the day; course –, tide –, stream –, current –, run –, march- of -things, – events; ups and downs of life; chapter of accidents &c. (*chance*) 156; situation &c. (*circumstances*) 8.

V. happen, occur; take -place, – effect; come, become of; come -off, – about, – round, – into existence, – forth, – to pass, – on; pass, present itself; fall; fall –, turn- out; run, be on foot, fall in; be-fall, -tide, -chance; prove, eventuate, draw on; turn –, crop –, spring –, cast- up; super-, sur-vene; issue, emanate, arrive, ensue,

Future Events

152. Destiny.—**N.** destiny &c. (*necessity*) 601; hereafter, future –, post-existence; future state, next world, world to come, after life; futurity &c. 121; everlasting -life, – death; prospect &c. (*expectation*) 507.

V. impend; hang –, lie –, hover-over; threaten, loom, await, come on, approach, stare one in the face; fore-, pre-ordain; predestine, doom, fore-doom, foreshadow, have in store for.

Adj. impending &c. *v.*; destined; about to -be, – happen; coming, in store, to come, going to happen, instant, at hand, near; near –, close- at hand; overhanging, hanging over one's head, imminent; brewing, preparing, forthcoming; in the wind, on the cards, in reserve; that -will, – is to- be; in prospect &c. (*expected*) 507; looming in the -distance, – horizon, – future; unborn, in embryo; in the womb of -time; – futurity; on the knees of the gods; pregnant &c. (*producing*) 161.

Adv. in -time, – the long run; all in good time; eventually &c. 151; what-

arise, start, hold, take its course; pass off &c. (*be past*) 122.

meet with; experience; fall to the lot of; be one's -chance, – fortune, – lot; find; encounter, undergo; pass –, go-through; endure &c. (*feel*) 821.

Adj. happening &c. *v.*; going on, doing, current; in the wind, afloat; on -foot, – the *tapis*; at issue, in question; incidental.

eventful, momentous, signal; stirring, bustling, full of incident.

Adv. eventually, ultimately, in -the event of, – case; in the course of things; in the -natural, – ordinary- course of things; as -things, – times- go; as the world -goes, – wags; as the -tree falls, – cat jumps; as it may -turn out, – happen.

Phr. the plot thickens.

ever may happen &c. (*certainly*) 474; as -chance &c. 156- would have it.

Section VIII.   CAUSATION

1°. Constancy of Sequence in Events

153. [Constant antecedent.] **Cause.** —**N.** cause, origin, source, principle, element; occasioner, prime mover, engine, turbine, motor, *primum mobile*; *vera causa*; author &c. (*producer*) 164; main-spring, agent; dynamo, generator, battery (electric); leaven; groundwork, foundation &c. (*support*) 215.

spring, fountain, well, font; fountain –, spring- head; *fons et origo*, genesis; descent &c. (*paternity*) 166; remote cause; influence.

pivot, hinge, turning-point, lever; key; kernel, core; proximate cause, *causa causans*; last straw that breaks the camel's back.

ground; reason, – why; why and wherefore, rationale, occasion, derivation; final cause &c. (*intention*) 620; *le dessous des cartes*; undercurrents.

rudiment, egg, germ, embryo, fœtus bud, root, *radix*, radical, etymon, nucleus, seed, stem, stalk, stock, *stirps*, trunk, tap-root; latent organism.

nest, cradle, nursery, womb, *nidus*, birth-, breeding-place, hot-bed.

caus-ality, -ation; origination; production &c. 161.

V. be the -cause &c. *n.*- of; originate; give -origin, – rise, – occasion- to; cause, occasion, sow the seeds of, kindle, suscitate; bring -on, – to pass, – about; produce; create &c. 161; set -up, – afloat, – on foot; found, broach,

154. [Constant sequent.] **Effect.**—**N.** effect, consequence, sequela; derivative, -tion; result; result-ant, -ance; upshot, issue, *dénouement*; outcome; termination, end &c. 67; development, outgrowth, fruit, crop, harvest, product, bud, blossom, florescence, ear.

production, produce, product, finished product, work, handiwork, fabric, performance; creature, creation; off-spring, -shoot; first-fruits, -lings; *prémices*.

V. be the -effect &c. *n.*- of; be -due, – owing- to; originate -in, – from; rise –, arise –, take its rise –, spring –, proceed –, emanate –, come –, grow –, bud –, sprout –, germinate –, issue –, flow –, result –, follow –, derive its origin –, accrue- from; come -to, – of, – out of; depend –, hang –, hinge –, turn- upon.

take the consequences, sow the wind and reap the whirlwind.

Adj. owing to; resulting from &c. *v.*; resultant; derivable from; due to; caused &c. by, 153; dependent upon; derived –, evolved- from; derivative; hereditary.

Adv. of course, it follows that, naturally, consequently; as a –, in- consequence; through all, all along of, necessarily, eventually.

Phr. *cela va sans dire*, thereby hangs a tale.

institute, lay the foundation of, inaugurate; lie at the root of.

procure, induce, draw down, open the door to, superinduce, evoke, entail, operate; elicit, provoke.

conduce to &c. (*tend to*) 176; contribute; promote; have a -hand in, – finger in- the pie; determine, decide, turn the scale, give the casting vote; have a common origin; derive its origin &c. (*effect*) 154.

Adj. caused &c. *v.*; causal, original; prim-ary, -itive, -ordial; aboriginal; radical; inceptive, embry-onic, -otic; *in -embryo, – ovo*; seminal, germinal; formative, productive &c. 168; at the bottom of; connate, having a common origin.

Adv. because &c. 155; behind the scenes.

155. [Assignment of cause.] **Attribution.—N.** attribution, theory, etiology, ascription, reference to, rationale; accounting for &c. *v.*; palætiology,* imputation, derivation from.

fil-, affil-iation; pedigree &c. (*paternity*) 166.

explanation &c. (*interpretation*) 522; reason why &c. (*cause*) 153.

V. attribute –, ascribe –, impute –, refer –, lay –, point –, trace –, bring home- to; put –, set- down- to; charge –, ground- on; invest with, assign as cause, charge with, blame, lay at the door of, father upon; saddle with; affiliate; account for, derive from, point out the -reason &c. 153; theorize; tell how it comes; put the saddle on the right horse.

Adj. attributed &c. *v.*; attributable &c. *v.*; refer-able, -rible; due to, derivable from; owing to &c. (*effect*) 154; putative.

Adv. hence, thence, therefore, for, since, on account of, because, owing to; on that account; from -this, – that- cause; thanks to, forasmuch as; whence, *propter hoc.*

why? wherefore? whence? how -comes, – is, – happens- it? how does it happen?

in -some, – some such- way; somehow, – or other.

Phr. that is why; *hinc illæ lachrymæ; cherchez la femme.*

156. [Absence of assignable cause.] **Chance.†—N.** chance, indetermination, accident, fortune, hazard, hap, haphazard, chance-medley, random, luck, *raccroc*, casualty, fortuity, contingence, coincidence, adventure, hit; fate &c. (*necessity*) 601; equal chance; lottery, raffle, tombola, sweepstake; toss up &c. 621; turn of the -table, – cards; hazard of the die, chapter of accidents; cast –, throw- of the dice; heads or tails, wheel of Fortune, whirligig of chance; *sortes, – Virgilianæ.*

probability, possibility, contingency, odds, long odds, run of luck; main-chance.

theory of -probabilities, – chances; book-making; assurance; speculation, gamble, gaming &c. 621.

V. chance, hap, turn up; fall to one's lot; be one's -fate &c. 601; stumble on, light –, blunder –, hit- upon; take one's chance &c. 621.

Adj. casual, fortuitous, accidental, haphazard, random, stray, adventitious, adventive, causeless, incidental. contingent, uncaused, undetermined, indeterminate; possible &c. 470; unintentional &c. 621.

Adv. by -chance, – accident; casually; perchance &c. (*possibly*) 470; for aught one knows; as -good, – bad, – ill-luck &c. *n.*- would have it; as it may -be, – chance, – turn up, – happen; as the case may be.

2°. CONNECTION BETWEEN CAUSE AND EFFECT

157. Power.—N. power; poten-cy, -tiality; puissance, might, force; energy &c. 171; dint; right -hand, – arm;

158. Impotence.—N. impotence; in-, dis-ability; disablement, impuissance, imbecility, caducity; incapa-city,

---

* Whewell, 'History of the Inductive Sciences,' book xviii, vol. iii., p. 397 (3rd edit.).

† The word *Chance* has two distinct meanings: the first, the absence of assignable *cause*, as above; and the second, the absence of *design*—for the latter see 621.

ascendency, sway, control; pre-potency, -pollence; almightiness, omnipotence; authority &c. 737; strength &c. 159.

ability; ableness &c. *adj.*; competency; effi-ciency, -cacy; validity, cogency; enablement; vantage ground; influence &c. 175; horse power; dynamometer.

pressure; elasticity; gravity, electricity, magnetism, galvanism, voltaic electricity, voltaism, electro-magnetism, electrostatics, electrification, electric current &c.; attraction, repulsion; *vis -inertiæ, – mortua, – viva*; potential –, dynamic –, kinetic –, electrical –, chemical –, atomic- energy; friction, suction.

capability, capacity; *quid valeant humeri quid ferre recusent*; faculty, quality, attribute, endowment, virtue, gift, property, qualification, susceptibility.

V. be -powerful &c. *adj.*; gain -power &c. *n.*

belong –, pertain- to; lie –, be- in one's power; can.

give –, confer –, exercise- power &c. *n.*; empower, enable, invest; in-, en-due; endow, arm; strengthen &c. 159; compel &c. 744.

Adj. powerful, puissant; potent, -ial; capable, able; equal –, up- to; cogent, valid; effect-ive, -ual; efficient, efficacious, adequate, competent; multi-, pleni-, omni-, armi- potent; mighty, ascendent; almighty.

electric, electrical &c.

forcible &c. *adj.* (*energetic*) 171; influential &c. 175; productive &c. 168.

Adv. powerfully &c. *adj.*; by -virtue, – dint- of.

———

-bility; inapt-, inept-itude; indocility; invalidity, inefficiency, incompetence, disqualification.

telum imbelle, brutum fulmen, blank cartridge, flash in the pan, *vox et præterea nihil,* dead letter, bit of waste paper, dummy; scrap of paper.

inefficacy &c. (*inutility*) 645; failure &c. 732.

helplessness &c. *adj.*; prostration, paralysis, palsy, ataxia, apoplexy, syncope, sideration, *deliquium,* collapse, exhaustion, softening of the brain, emasculation, inanition, senility &c. 128; castrato, eunuch.

cripple, old woman, muff, mollycoddle, milksop.

V. be -impotent &c. *adj.*; not have a leg to stand on.

vouloir -rompre l'anguille au genou, – prendre la lune avec les dents.

collapse, faint, swoon, fall into a swoon, drop; go by the board; end in smoke &c. (*fail*) 732.

render -powerless &c. *adj.*; deprive of power; decontrol; dis-able, -enable; disarm, incapacitate, disqualify, unfit, invalidate, undermine, deaden, cramp, tie the hands; double up, prostrate, paralyze, muzzle, cripple, becripple, maim, lame, hamstring, draw the teeth of; throttle, strangle, *garrotte;* ratten, silence, sprain, clip the wings of, render *hors de combat,* spike the guns; take the wind out of one's sails, scotch the snake, put a spoke in one's wheel; break the -neck, – back; un-hinge, -fit; put out of gear.

unman, unnerve, devitalize, attenuate, enervate; emasculate, spay, caponize, castrate, geld; effeminize.

shatter, exhaust; weaken &c. 160.

Adj. powerless, impotent, unable, incapable, incompetent; ineff-icient, -ective; inept; un-fit, -fitted; un-, dis-qualified; unendowed; in-, un-apt; crippled, decrepit, disabled &c. *v.*; armless.

harmless, unarmed, weaponless, defenceless, *sine ictu,* unfortified, indefensible, vincible, pregnable, untenable.

para-lytic, -lyzed; palsied, imbecile; nerve-, sinew-, marrow-, pith-, lust-less; emasculate, disjointed; out of -joint, – gear; un-nerved, -hinged; water-logged, on one's beam ends, rudderless; laid on one's back; done up, dead beat, exhausted, shattered, demoralized; gravelled &c. (*in difficulty*) 704; helpless, unfriended, fatherless; without a leg to stand on, *hors de combat,* laid on the shelf.

null and void, nugatory, inoperative, good for nothing; dud; invertebrate; ineffectual &c. (*failing*) 732; inadequate &c. 640; inefficacious &c. (*useless*) 645.

159. [Degree of power.] **Strength.** —N. strength; power &c. 157; energy &c. 171; vigour, force; main –, physical –, brute- force; spring, elasticity, tone, tension, tonicity.

stoutness &c. *adj*; lustihood, stamina, nerve, muscle, sinew, thews and sinews, *physique*; pith, -iness; virility, vitality.

athlet-ics, -icism; gymnastics, feats of strength.

adamant, steel, iron, oak, heart of oak; iron grip; grit, bone.

athlete, gymnast, tumbler, acrobat; Atlas, Hercules, Antæus, Samson, Cyclops, Goliath, Titan; tower of strength; giant refreshed.

strengthening &c. *v.*; invigoration, refreshment, refocillation.

[Science of forces] dynamics, statics.

V. be -strong &c. *adj.*, – stronger; overmatch.

render -strong &c. *adj.*; give -strength &c. *n.*; strengthen, invigorate, brace, nerve, fortify, buttress, sustain, harden, case-harden, steel; gird; screw –, wind –, set- up; gird –, brace- up one's loins; recruit, set on one's legs; vivify; refresh &c. 689; refect; reinforce &c. (*restore*) 660.

Adj. strong, mighty, vigorous, forcible, hard, adamantine, stout, robust, sturdy, hardy, powerful, potent, puissant, valid.

resistless, irresistible, invincible, proof against, impregnable, unconquerable, indomitable, inextinguishable, unquenchable; incontestable; more than a match for; over-powering, -whelming; all-powerful; sovereign.

able-bodied; athletic, gymnastic; Herculean, Cyclopean, Atlantean; muscular, husky, brawny, wiry, well-knit, broad-shouldered, sinewy, strapping, stalwart, gigantic.

man-ly, -like, -ful; masculine, male, virile, in the prime of manhood.

un-weakened, -allayed, -withered, -shaken, -worn, -exhausted; in full -force, – swing; in the plenitude of power.

160. Weakness.—N. weakness &c. *adj.*; debility, atony, relaxation, languor, enervation; impotence &c. 158; infirmity; effeminacy, feminality; fragility, flaccidity; inactivity &c. 683.

declension –, loss –, failure- of strength; delicacy, invalidation, decrepitude, asthenia, adynamy, cachexy, *cachexia*, anæmia, bloodlessness, sprain, strain.

reed, thread, rope of sand, broken reed, house -of cards, – built on sand.

soft-, weak-ling; infant &c. 129; youth &c. 127.

V. be -weak &c. *adj.*; drop, crumble, give way, totter, tremble, shake, halt, limp, fade, languish, decline, flag, fail, have one foot in the grave.

render -weak &c. *adj.*; weaken, enfeeble, debilitate, shake, deprive of strength, relax, enervate; un-brace, -nerve; cripple, unman, &c. (*render powerless*) 158; cramp, reduce, sprain, strain, blunt the edge of; dilute, impoverish; decimate; extenuate; reduce -in strength, – the strength of; invalidate; *mettre de l'eau dans son vin.*

Adj. weak, feeble, debile; impotent &c. 158; relaxed, unnerved &c. *v.*; sap-, strength-, power-less; weakly, unstrung, flaccid, adynamic, asthenic; nervous.

soft, effeminate, feminate, womanish.

frail, fragile, shattery, frangible, brittle &c. 328; flimsy, unsubstantial, gimcrack, gingerbread; rickety, cranky; creachy; drooping, tottering &c. *v.*; broken, lame, halt, game, withered, shattered, shaken, crazy, shaky, tumble-down; palsied &c. 158; decrepit; C3.

languid, poor, poorly, infirm; faint, -ish; sickly &c. (*disease*) 655; dull, slack, evanid, spent, short-winded, effete; weatherbeaten; decayed, rotten, worn, seedy, languishing, wasted, washy, wishy-washy, laid low, pulled down, the worse for wear.

un-strengthened &c. 159, -supported, -aided, -assisted; aidless, defenceless &c. 158.

stubborn, thick-ribbed, made of iron, deep-rooted; strong as -a lion, – a horse, – brandy; sound as a roach; in -fine, – high- feather; in fine fettle; like a giant refreshed.

Adv. strongly &c. *adj.*; by -force &c. *n.*; by main force &c. (*by compulsion*) 744.

Phr. 'our withers are unwrung.'

on its last legs; weak as a -child, – baby, – chicken, – cat, – rat; weak as -water, – water gruel, – gingerbread, – milk and water; colourless &c. 429.

Phr. *non sum qualis eram.*

3°. POWER IN OPERATION

161. Production.—N. production, creation, construction, formation, fabrication, manufacture; building, architecture, erection, edification; coinage; organization; *nisus formativus*; putting together &c. *v.*; establishment; workmanship, performance; achievement &c. (*completion*) 729; effect &c. 154.

flowering, fructification, fruition.

bringing forth &c. *v.*; parturition, birth, birth-throe, child-birth, delivery, confinement, *accouchement*, travail, labour, midwifery, obstetrics; geniture; gestation &c. (*maturation*) 673; evolution, development, growth; genesis, fertilization, breeding, conception, germination, generation, *epigenesis*, pro-creation, -generation, -pagation; fecundation, impregnation; spontaneous generation; *arche-genesis, -biosis*; *bio-, abio-, homo-, xeno-genesis.**

authorship, publication; works, *œuvre, opus.*

edifice, building, structure, fabric, erection, pile, tower, flower, fruit.

V. produce, perform, operate, do, make, gar, form, construct, fabricate, frame, contrive, manufacture; weave, forge, coin, carve, chisel; build, raise, edify, rear, erect, put together; set –, run- up; establish, constitute, compose, organize, institute, get up; achieve, accomplish &c. (*complete*) 729.

flower, sprout, blossom, burgeon, bear fruit, fructify, spawn, teem, ean, yean, farrow, drop, calf, pup, whelp, kitten, kindle; bear, lay, bring forth, give birth to, lie in, be brought to bed of, evolve, pullulate, usher into the world.

make productive &c. 168; create; beget, conceive, get, generate, fecun-

162. [Non-production.] Destruction.
—N. destruction; waste, dissolution, breaking up; di-, dis-ruption; consumption; disorganization.

fall, downfall, ruin, perdition, crash, smash, havoc, *délabrement, débâcle*; break -down, – up; prostration; desolation, *bouleversement*, wreck, crack-up, crash, wrack, shipwreck, cataclysm; Caudine Forks, Sedan.

extinction, annihilation; destruction of life &c. 361; knock-out, knock-down blow; doom, crack of doom.

destroying &c. *v.*; demo-lition, -lishment; biblioclasm; overthrow, subversion, suppression; abolition &c. (*abrogation*) 756; sacrifice; ravage, devastation, *sabotage, razzia*; incendiarism; revolution &c. 146; extirpation &c. (*extraction*) 301; *commencement de la fin*, road to ruin; dilapidation &c. (*deterioration*) 659.

V. be -destroyed &c.; perish; fall, – to the ground; tumble, topple; go –, fall- to pieces; break up; crumble, – to dust; go to -the dogs, – the wall, – smash, – shivers, – wreck, – pot, – wrack and ruin; go -by the board, – all to smash, – to pieces, – under; be all -over, – up- with; totter to its fall.

destroy; do –, make- away with; nullify; annul &c. 756; sacrifice, demolish; tear up; over-turn, -throw, -whelm; upset, subvert, put an end to; seal the doom of, do for, dish, undo; break -, cut- up; break –, cut –, pull –, mow –, blow –, beat- down; suppress, quash, put down; cut short, take off, blot out; dispel, dissipate, dissolve; consume.

smash, – to smithereens, quell, squash, squelch, crumple up, shatter,

* Huxley.

date, impregnate; pro-create, -generate, -pagate; engender; bring –, call- into -being, – existence; breed, hatch, develop, bring up.

induce, superinduce; suscitate; cause &c. 153; acquire &c. 775.

Adj. produc-ed, -ing &c. *v.*; productive of; prolific &c. 168; creative; formative; gen-etic, -ial, -ital; fertile, pregnant; *enceinte*, big –, fraught- with; with child, in the family way, teeming, parturient, in the straw, brought to bed of; puerper-al, -ous.

architectonic; constructive.

———

shiver; batter; tear –, crush –, cut –, shake –, pull –, pick- to pieces; nip; tear to -rags, – tatters; crush –, knock- to atoms; pulverize; ruin; strike out; throw –, knock- -down, – over; lay by the heels; fell, sink, swamp, scuttle, wreck, crash, shipwreck, engulf, submerge; lay in -ashes, – ruins; sweep away, erase, expunge, strike out, delete, efface, raze; level, – with the -ground, – dust.

deal destruction, lay waste, ravage, gut; disorganize; dismantle &c. (*render useless*) 645; devour, swallow up, desolate, devastate, sap, mine, blast, confound; exterminate, extinguish, quench, annihilate; snuff –, put –, stamp –, trample- out; lay –, trample- in the dust; prostrate; tread –, crush –, trample- under foot; lay the axe to the root of; make -short work, – a clean sweep, – mincemeat- of; cut up root and branch; fling –, scatter- to the winds; throw overboard; strike at the root of, sap the foundations of, spring a mine, blow up; ravage with fire and sword; cast to the dogs; eradicate &c. 301.

Adj. destroyed &c. *v.*; perishing &c. *v.*; trembling –, nodding –, tottering- to its fall; in course of -destruction &c. *n.*; extinct.

destructive, subversive, ruinous, incendiary, deletory; destroying &c. *v.*; suicidal; deadly &c. (*killing*) 361.

Adv. with -crushing effect, – a sledge-hammer.

Phr. *delenda est Carthago.*

163. Reproduction.—N. reproduction, renovation; restoration &c. 660; renewal; new edition, reprint &c. 21; revival, regeneration, palingenesia, revivification; apotheosis; resuscitation, reanimation, resurrection, resurgence, reappearance, atavism; Phœnix; reincarnation.

generation &c. (*production*) 161; multiplication.

V. reproduce; restore &c. 660; revive, renovate, renew, regenerate, revivify, resuscitate, reanimate, refashion, stir the embers, put into the crucible; multiply, repeat, resurge.

crop up, spring up like mushrooms.

Adj. reproduced &c. *v.*; renascent, reappearing; reproductive; resurgent; progenitive; Hydra-headed.

164. Producer.—N. producer, creator, deviser, designer, originator, inventor, author, founder, generator, mover, architect; grower, constructor, maker &c. (*agent*) 690.

165. Destroyer.—N. destroyer &c. (destroy &c. 162); cankerworm &c. (*bane*) 663; iconoclast; assassin &c. (*killer*) 361; executioner &c. (*punish*) 975; Hun, Vandal, nihilist, anarchist.

166. Paternity.—N. paternity; parentage; fatherhood; consanguinity &c. 11.

parent, father, sire, dad, daddy, papa, governor, *pater*, *paterfamilias*, *abba*; genitor, progenitor, procreator, begetter; ancestor; grand-sire, -father; great-grandfather.

167. Posterity.—N. posterity, progeny, breed, issue, offspring, brood, litter, seed, farrow, spawn, spat; family, children, grandchildren, heirs; great-grandchild.

child, son, daughter; kid; infant &c. 129; bantling, scion; shoot, sprout, olive branch, sprit, branch; off-shoot,

house, stem, trunk, tree, stock, *stirps*, pedigree, lineage, line, family, tribe, sept, race, clan; genealogy, descent, extraction, birth, ancestry; forefathers, forbears, patriarchs.

motherhood, maternity; mother, dam, mamma, *materfamilias*; grandmother; matriarch.

Adj. paternal, parental; maternal; matrilinear, patrilineal, patriarchal.

168. Productiveness.—N. productiveness &c. *adj.*; fecundity, fertility, luxuriance, uberty.

pregnancy, pullulation, fructification, multiplication, propagation, procreation; superfetation.

milch cow, rabbit, hydra, warren, seed-plot, land flowing with milk and honey; second crop, after-crop, -growth, -math; fertilization.

V. make -productive &c. *adj.*; fructify; procreate, generate, fertilize, spermatize, impregnate; fecund-ate, -ify; teem, pullulate, multiply; produce &c. 161; conceive.

Adj. productive, prolific; teem-ing, -ful; fertile, fruitful, frugiferous, fruit-bearing; fructiferous; fecund, luxuriant; pregnant, uberous.

procre-ant, -ative; generative, life-giving, spermatic; originative; multiparous; omnific; propagable.

parturient &c. (*producing*) 161; profitable &c. (*useful*) 644.

-set; ramification; descendant; heir, -ess; heir -apparent, – presumptive; chip of the old block; heredity; rising generation.

straight descent, sonship, line, lineage, filiation, primogeniture.

Adj. filial.

_____

family, ancestral, linear,

169. Unproductiveness.—N. unproductiveness &c. *adj.*; infertility, sterility, infecundity; impotence &c. 158-unprofitableness &c. (*inutility*) 645.

waste, desert, Sahara, wild, wilderness, howling wilderness.

V. be -unproductive &c. *adj.*; hang fire, flash in the pan, come to nothing.

Adj. unproductive, inoperative, barren, addle, unfertile, unprolific, arid, sterile, unfruitful, acarpous, infecund; *sine prole*; fallow; teem-, issue-, fruitless; unprofitable &c. (*useless*) 645; null and void, of no effect.

_____

170. Agency.—N. agency, operation, force, working, strain, function, office, maintenance, exercise, work, swing, play; inter-working, -action, procuration, procurement.

causation &c. 153; instrumentality &c. 631; influence &c. 175; action &c. (*voluntary*) 680; *modus operandi* &c. 627.

quickening –, maintaining- power; home stroke.

V. be -in action &c. *adj.*; operate, work; act, – upon; perform, play, support, sustain, strain, maintain, take effect, quicken, strike.

come –, bring- into -operation, – play; have -play, – free play; bring to bear upon.

Adj. operative, efficient, efficacious, practical, effectual.

at work, on foot; acting &c. (*doing*) 680; in -operation, – force, – action, – play, – exercise; acted –, wrought- upon.

Adv. by the -agency &c. *n.*- of; through &c. (*instrumentality*) 631; by means of &c. 632.

171. Physical Energy.—N. energy, physical energy, force; keenness &c. *adj.*; intensity, vigour, strength, elasticity; go; pep, live wire, high pressure; backbone, mettle, fire, vim.

acri-mony, -tude, -dity; causticity,

172. Physical Inertness.—N. inertness, dulness &c. *adj.*; inertia, *vis inertiæ*, inertion, inactivity, torpor, languor; dormancy, quiescence &c. 265; latency, inaction, passivity.

mental inertness; sloth &c. (*inac-*

virulence, poignancy; harshness &c.
adj.; severity, edge, point; pungency
&c. 392.

cantharides; Spanish fly; seasoning
&c. (*condiment*) 393, stimulant, ex-
citant.

activity, agitation, effervescence;
ferment, -ation; ebullition, splutter,
perturbation, stir, bustle; voluntary
energy &c. 682; quicksilver.

resolution &c. (*mental energy*) 604;
exertion &c. (*effort*) 686; excitation &c.
(*mental*) 824.

V. give -energy &c. *n.*; energize,
stimulate, kindle, excite, activate,
exert; sharpen, pep up, intensify;
inflame &c. (*render violent*) 173; wind up &c. (*strengthen*) 159.

strike, – into, – hard, – home; make an impression.

Adj. strong, energetic, forcible, active; strenuous, forceful,
mettlesome, enterprising, go ahead; intense, deep-dyed, severe,
keen, vivid, sharp, acute, incisive, trenchant, brisk, vigorous, live.

rousing, irritating; poignant; virulent, caustic, corrosive, mordant,
harsh, stringent; double-edged, – shotted, – distilled; drastic,
escharotic; racy &c. (*pungent*) 392; sarcastic &c. 932.

potent &c. (*powerful*) 157; radio-active.

Adv. strongly &c. *adj.*; *fortiter in re*; with telling effect.

Phr. the steam is up; *vires acquirit eundo.*

tivity) 683; inexcitability &c. 826;
irresolution &c. 605; obstinacy &c.
606; permanence &c. 141.

V. be -inert &c. *adj.*; hang fire,
smoulder.

Adj. inert, inactive, passive, pacific;
torpid &c. 683; sluggish, stagnant, dull,
heavy, flat, slack, tame, slow, blunt;
lifeless, dead, uninfluential.

latent, dormant, smouldering, unex-
erted.

Adv. inactively &c. *adj.*; in -suspense,
-abeyance.

---

173. Violence.—N. violence, inclemency, vehemence, might, impetuosity;
boisterousness &c. *adj.*; effervescence,
ebullition; turbulence, bluster; uproar,
riot, row, rumpus, *le diable à quatre,*
devil to pay, all the fat in the fire.

severity &c. 739; ferocity, rage,
berserk, fury; exacerbation, exasperation, malignity; fit, paroxysm, orgasm;
force, brute force; outrage; *coup de
main*; strain, shock, shog; spasm, convulsion, throe; hysterics, passion &c.
(*state of excitability*) 825.

out-break, -burst; burst, bounce,
dissilience, discharge, volley, explosion,
blow up, blast, detonation, rush, eruption, displosion, torrent.

turmoil &c. (*disorder*) 59; ferment
&c. (*agitation*) 315; storm, tempest,
rough weather; squall &c. (*wind*) 349;
earthquake, volcano, thunderstorm.

fury, dragon, demon, tiger, beldame,
Tisiphone, Megæra, Alecto, madcap,
wild beast; fire-eater &c. (*blusterer*) 887.

V. be -violent &c. *adj.*; run high;
ferment, effervesce; romp, rampage;
run -wild, – riot; break the peace;

174. Moderation.—N. moderation;
lenity &c. 740; temperance, temper-
ateness, gentleness &c. *adj.*; sobriety;
quiet; mental calmness &c. (*inexcitability*) 826.

moderating &c. *v.*; relaxation, remission, mitigation &c. 834; tranquillization, alleviation, assuagement, ap-
peasement, contemporation, pacification.

measure, *juste milieu*, golden mean
&c. 29.

moderator; lullaby, sedative, lenitive, demulcent, rose-water, balm,
soothing syrup, poppy, opiate, anodyne, milk, opium, laudanum, 'poppy
or mandragora'; wet blanket; palliative, calmative.

V. be -moderate &c. *adj.*; keep within -bounds, – compass; sober –, settle-
down; keep the peace, remit, relent;
take in sail.

moderate, soften, mitigate, temper,
accoy; at-, con-temper; mollify, lenify,
dull, take off the edge, blunt, obtund,
sheathe, subdue, chasten; sober –,
tone –, smooth- down; censor, blue-

rush, tear; rush head-long, -foremost; run amuck, raise a storm, make a riot; make –, kick up- a row, – a fuss; bluster, rage, roar, riot, storm; boil, – over; fume, foam, come in like a lion, wreak, bear down, ride rough-shod, out-Herod Herod; spread like wildfire.

break –, fly –, burst- out; bounce, shock, strain; break-, pry-, force-, prize- open.

render -violent &c. *adj.*; sharpen, stir up, quicken, excite, incite, urge, lash, stimulate; irritate, inflame, exacerbate, kindle, suscitate, foment; accelerate, aggravate, exasperate, convulse, infuriate, madden, lash into fury; fan –, add fuel to- the flame; *oleum addere camino.*

explode, go off, displode, fly, detonate, thunder, blow up, flash, flare, erupt, burst; let -off, – fly; discharge, detonize, fulminate.

Adj. violent, vehement, forcible; warm; acute, sharp; rough, rude, ungentle, bluff, boisterous, wild, vicious; brusque, abrupt, waspish; impetuous; rampant.

turbulent; disorderly; blustering, raging &c. *v.*; troublous, riotous; tumultu-ary, -ous; obstreperous, uproarious; extravagant, unmitigated; ravening, tameless; frenzied &c. (*insane*) 503; desperate &c. (*rash*) 863; infuriate, towering, furious, outrageous, frantic, hysteric, in hysterics.

fiery, flaming, scorching, hot, red-hot, ebullient.

savage, fierce, ferocious, fierce as a tiger.

excited &c. *v.*; un-quelled, -quenched, -extinguished, -repressed, -bridled, -ruly; headstrong; un-governable, -appeasable, -mitigable; un-, in-controllable; insup-, irre-pressible.

spasmodic, convulsive, explosive; detonating &c. *v.*; volcanic, meteoric; stormy &c. (*wind*) 349.

Adv. violently &c. *adj.*; amain; by -storm, – force, – main force; with might and main; tooth and nail, *vi et armis*, at the point of the -sword, – bayonet; at one fell swoop; with a high hand, through thick and thin; in desperation, with a vengeance; *à –, à toute-outrance*; head-long, -foremost, -first; like a bull at a gate.

pencil, weaken &c. 160; lessen &c: (*decrease*) 36; check; palliate.

tranquillize, assuage, appease, dulcify, swage, lull, soothe, compose, still, calm, cool, quiet, hush, quell, sober, pacify, tame, damp, lay, allay, rebate, slacken, smooth, alleviate, rock to sleep, deaden, smother; throw -cold water on, – a wet blanket over; slake; curb &c. (*restrain*) 751; tame &c. (*subjugate*) 749; smooth over; pour oil on the -waves, – troubled waters; pour balm into, *mettre de l'eau dans son vin.*

go out like a lamb, 'roar you as gently as any sucking dove.'

Adj. moderate; lenient &c: 740; gentle, mild; cool, sober, temperate, reasonable, measured; tempered &c. *v.*; calm, unruffled, quiet, tranquil, still; slow, smooth, untroubled; tame; peaceful, -able; pacific, halcyon.

un-exciting, -irritating; soft, bland, oily, demulcent, lenitive, anodyne; hypnotic &c. 683; sedative; assuaging.

mild as mother's milk; milk and water; gentle as a lamb.

Adv. moderately &c. *adj.*; gingerly; *piano*; under easy sail, at half speed; within -bounds, – compass; in reason.

Phr. *est modus in rebus.*

4°. INDIRECT POWER

175. Influence.—N. influence; importance &c. 642; weight, pressure, preponderance, prevalence, sway, pull; predomi-nance, -nancy; ascendency; control, dominance, reign; authority

175a. Absence of Influence.—N. impotence &c. 158; inertness &c. 172; irrelevancy &c. 10.

V. have no -influence &c. 175.

Adj. uninfluential; unconduc-ing,

&c. 737; capability &c. (*power*) 157; interest; spell, magic, magnetism.

footing; purchase &c. (*support*) 215; play, leverage, vantage ground.

tower of strength, host in himself; protection, patronage, auspices.

V. have -influence &c. *n.*; be -influential &c. *adj.*; carry weight, actuate, sway, bias, weigh, tell; have a hold upon, magnetize, bear upon, gain a footing, work upon; take -root, – hold; strike root in.

run through, pervade; prevail, dominate, predominate, subject; out-, over-weigh; over-ride, -bear, – come; gain head; rage; be -rife &c. *adj.*; spread like wildfire; have –, get –, gain- -the upper hand, – full play.

be -recognized, – listened to; make one's voice heard, gain a hearing; play a -part, – leading part- in; lead, control, rule, master; get the mastery over; make one's influence felt, cut ice with; take the lead, pull the strings; turn –, throw one's weight into- the scale; set the fashion, lead the dance.

Adj. influential; important &c. 642; weighty; prevailing &c. *v.*; prevalent, rife, rampant, dominant, regnant, predominant, in the ascendant, hegemonical; authoritative, recognized, telling, with authority.

Adv. with telling effect.

-ive, -ting to; powerless &c. 158; irrelevant &c. 10.

_____

176. Tendency.—N. tendency; apt-ness, -itude; proneness, proclivity, bent, turn, tone, bias, set, warp, leaning to, predisposition, inclination, conatus, propensity, susceptibility; liability &c. 177; quality, nature, temperament; characteristic, idio-crasy, -syncrasy; cast, vein, grain; humour, mood; drift &c. (*direction*) 278; con-duciveness, -ducement; applicability &c. (*utility*) 644; subservience &c. (*instrumentality*) 631.

V. tend, contribute, conduce, lead, dispose, incline, verge, bend to, warp, turn, trend, affect, carry, redound to, bid fair to, gravitate towards; promote &c. (*aid*) 707.

Adj. tending &c. *v.*; conducive, working towards, in a fair way to, calculated to; liable &c. 177; subservient &c. (*instrumental*) 631; useful &c. 644; subsidiary &c. (*helping*) 707.

Adv. for, whither.

177. Liability.—N. lia-bility, -bleness; possibility, contingency; suscepti-vity, -bility.

V. be -liable &c. *adj.*; incur, lay oneself open to; run the –, stand a- chance; lie under, expose oneself to, open a door to.

Adj. liable, subject; in danger &c. 665; open –, exposed –, obnoxious- to; answerable, responsible, accountable, amenable; unexempt from; apt to; dependent on; incident to.

contingent, incidental, possible, on the cards, within range of, at the mercy of.

5°. COMBINATIONS OF CAUSES

178. Concurrence.—N. concurrence, cooperation, coagency; coincidence, consilience; union; agreement &c. 23; consent &c. (*assent*) 488; alliance; concert &c. 709; partnership &c. 712; collaboration, conformity.

V. con-cur, -duce, -spire, -tribute;

179. Counteraction.—N. counteraction, opposition; contrariety &c. 14; antagonism, polarity; clashing &c. *v.*; collision, interference, resistance, renitency, friction; reaction; retroaction; repercussion &c. (*recoil*) 277; counterblast; neutralization &c. (*compensa-*

agree, unite, harmonize; hang –, pull-together &c. (*co-operate*) 709; help to &c. (*aid*) 707.

keep pace with, run parallel to; go –, go along –, go hand in hand- with.

Adj. concurring &c. *v.*; concurrent, conformable, joint, co-operative, concordant, coincident, concomitant, harmonious; in alliance with, banded together, of one mind, at one with; parallel.

Adv. with one consent.

tion) 30; *vis inertiæ*; check &c. (*hindrance*) 706.

voluntary -opposition &c. 708, – resistance &c. 719; repression &c. (*restraint*) 751.

V. counteract; run counter, clash, cross; interfere –, conflict- with; jostle; go –, run –, beat –, militate- against; stultify; antagonize, frustrate, oppose &c. 708; withstand &c. (*resist*) 719; hinder &c. 706; repress &c. (*restrain*) 751; react &c. (*recoil*) 277.

undo, neutralize, cancel; counterpoise &c. (*compensate*) 30; overpoise.

Adj. counteracting &c. *v.*; antagonistic, conflicting, retroactive, renitent, reactionary; contrary &c. 14.

Adv. although &c. 30; in spite of &c. 708; *malgré*; against.

CLASS II

Words Relating to SPACE

CLASS II

Words Relating to SPACE

Section I. SPACE IN GENERAL

1°. Abstract Space

180. [Indefinite space.] **Space.—N.** space, extension, extent, superficial extent, expanse, stretch; capacity, room, accommodation, scope, range, latitude, field, way, expansion, compass, sweep, play, swing, spread.

spare –, elbow –, house- room; stowage, roomage, margin; opening, sphere, arena; lee-, sea-, head-way.

open –, free- space; wide open spaces; void &c. (*absence*) 187; waste; wild-, wilder-ness; up-, bottom-, moor -land; *campagna, veldt,* prairie, steppe.

abyss &c. (*interval*) 198; unlimited space; infinity &c. 105; world, wide world; ubiquity &c. (*presence*) 186; length and breadth of the land.

proportions, acreage; acres, – roods and perches; square -inches, – yards &c.

Adj. spacious, roomy, extensive, expansive, capacious, ample; wide-spread, vast, world-wide, uncircumscribed; boundless &c. (*infinite*) 105; shore-, track-, path-less; large &c. 192.

Adv. extensively &c. *adj.*; wherever; everywhere; far and -near, – wide; right and left, all over, all the world over; throughout the -world, – length and breadth of the land; under the sun, in every quarter; in all -quarters, – lands; here, there and everywhere; from -pole to pole, – China to Peru, – Indus to the pole, – Dan to Beersheba, – end to end; on the face of the earth, in the wide world, from all points of the compass; to the -four winds, – uttermost parts of the earth.

180a. Inextension.—N. in-, non-extension; point; atom &c. (*smallness*) 32; pinprick; limitation &c. 229.

181. [Definite space.] **Region.—N.** region, sphere, sphere of influence, corridor, ground, soil, area, realm, hemisphere, quarter district, beat, orb, circuit, circle; pale &c. (*limit*) 233; com-, de-partment; domain, tract, territory, terrain, country, canton, county, shire, province, *arrondissement,* diocese, parish, township, borough, constituency, *commune,* ward, wapentake, hundred, riding, lathe, garth, soke, tithing, bailiwick; empire, kingdom, principality, duchy, grand –, arch- duchy, palatinate; republic, commonwealth, dominion, colony, state, island.

arena, precincts, *enceinte,* walk, march; patch, plot, enclosure, &c. 232; close, *enclave,* field, court; street &c. (*abode*) 189.

clime, climate, zone, meridian, latitude.

Adj. territorial, local, parochial, provincial, insular.

182. [Limited space.] **Place.—N.** place, lieu, spot, point, dot; niche, nook, &c. (*corner*) 244; hole; pigeon-hole &c. (*receptacle*) 191; compartment; premises, precinct, station, confine; area, court, yard, quadrangle, square, compound; abode &c. 189; locality &c. (*situation*) 183.

ins and outs; every hole and corner.

Adv. somewhere, in some place, wherever it may be, here and there, in various places, *passim.*

2°. Relative Space

183. Situation.—N. situation, position, locality, *locale*, *status*, latitude and longitude; footing, standing, standpoint, post; stage; aspect, attitude, posture, *pose*.

place, site, base, station, seat, *venue*, whereabouts, environment, neighbourhood; bearings &c. (*direction*) 278; spot &c. (*limited space*) 182.

top-, ge-, chor-ography; map &c. 554.

V. be -situated, – situate; lie; have its seat in.

Adj. situ-ate, -ated; local, topical, topographical &c. *n.*

Adv. *in -situ, – loco*; here and there, *passim*; here-, there-, whereabouts; in place, here, there.

in –, amidst- such and such- -surroundings, – *environs*, – *entourage*.

184. Location.—N. loca-tion, -liza-tion; lodgment; de-, re-position; stow-, pack-age; collocation; packing, lading; establishment, settlement, installation; fixation; insertion &c. 300.

anchorage, roadstead, mooring, mooring mast, encampment, camp, bivouac.

plantation, colony, settlement, cantonment, encampment, reservation; colonization, domestication, situation; habitation &c. (*abode*) 189; cohabitation; 'a local habitation and a name'; indenization, naturalization.

V. place, situate, locate, localize, make a place for, put, lay, set, seat, station, lodge, quarter, post, install; storehouse, stow; establish, fix, pin, root; graft; plant &c. (*insert*) 300; shelve, pitch, camp, lay down, deposit, reposit; cradle; moor, tether, picket; pack, tuck in; embed; vest, invest in.

billet on, quarter upon, saddle with; load, lade, freight; pocket, put up, bag.

inhabit &c. (*be present*) 186; domesticate, colonize, populate, people; take –, strike- root; anchor; cast –, come to an- anchor; sit –, settle-down; settle; take up one's -abode, – quarters; plant –, establish –, locate- oneself; squat, perch, hive, *se nicher*, bivouac, burrow, get a footing; encamp, pitch one's tent; put up -at, – one's horses at; keep house.

indenizen, naturalize, adopt.

put back, replace &c. (*restore*) 660.

Adj. placed &c. *v.*; situate, posited, ensconced, embedded, embosomed, rooted; domesticated; vested in, unremoved.

moored &c. *v.*; at anchor.

185. Displacement.—N. displacement, elocation, transposition.

ejectment &c. 297; exile &c. (*banishment*) 893; removal &c. (*transference*) 270; unshipment.

misplacement, dislocation &c. 61; fish out of water.

V. dis-place, -plant, -lodge, -nest, -establish; misplace, unseat, disturb; exile &c. (*seclude*) 893; ablegate, set aside, remove; take –, cart- away; take –, draft- off; lade &c. 184, unship.

unload, empty &c. (*eject*) 297; transfer &c. 270; dispel.

vacate; depart &c. 293.

Adj. displaced &c. *v.*; un-placed, -housed, -harboured, -established, -settled; house-, home-less; out of -place, – a situation.

misplaced, out of its element.

3°. Existence in Space

186. Presence.—N. presence; occupancy, -ation; attendance; whereness.

permeation, pervasion; diffusion &c. (*dispersion*) 73.

187. [Nullibiety.*] Absence. — N. absence; inexistence &c. 2; non-residence, absenteeism; non-attendance, *alibi*.

* Bishop Wilkins.

ubi-ety, -quity, -quitariness; omni-presence.

bystander &c. (*spectator*) 444.

V. exist in space, be -present &c. *adj.*; assist at; make one -of, – at; look on, attend, remain; find –, present- one-self; show one's face; fall in the way of, occur in a place; lie, stand; occupy.

people; inhabit, dwell, reside, stay, sojourn, live, room, abide, bunk, lodge, nestle, roost, perch; take up one's abode &c. (*be located*) 184; tenant, occupy.

resort to, frequent, haunt; revisit.

fill, pervade, permeate; be -diffused, – disseminated- through; over-spread, -run; run through; meet one at every turn.

Adj. present; occupying, inhabiting &c. *v.*; moored &c. 184; residential, resi-ant, -dent, -dentiary; domiciled.

ubiquit-ous, -ary; omnipresent.

peopled, populous, full of people, in-habited.

Adv. here, there, where, everywhere, aboard, on board, at home, afield; on the spot; here, there and everywhere &c. (*space*) 180; in presence of, before; under the -eyes, – nose- of; in the face of; *in propriâ personâ*.

emptiness &c. *adj.*; void, *vacuum*; vac-uity, -ancy; *tabula rasa*; exemp-tion; *hiatus* &c. (*interval*) 198; no man's land.

truant, absentee.

nobody; nobody -present, – on earth; no one; not a soul; *âme qui vive*.

V. be -absent &c. *adj.*; keep -away, – out of the way; play truant, absent oneself, stay away.

withdraw, make oneself scarce, va-cate; go away, slip out, slip away, retreat &c. 293.

Adj. absent, not present, away, non-resident, gone, from home; missing; lost; wanted, wanting; omitted; no-where to be found; inexistent &c. 2.

empty, void; blank, vac-ant, -uous; untenanted, -occupied, -inhabited; ten-antless; desert, -ed; devoid; un-, unin-habitable.

exempt from, not having.

Adv. without, *minus*, nowhere; else-where; neither here nor there; in de-fault of; *sans*; behind one's back.

Phr. the bird has flown, *non est inventus*.

---

188. Inhabitant. — N. inhabitant; habitant, resident, -iary; dweller, in-dweller; occup-ier, -ant, farmer, planter; householder, lodger, boarder, paying guest; inmate, tenant, renter, incum-bent, sojourner, *locum tenens*, com-morant; settler, squatter, backwoods-man, colonist; islander; denizen, citizen; burgher, oppidan, cockney, cit, towns-man, burgess; villager; cot-tager, -tier, -ter; compatriot.

native, indigene, aboriginal, aborig-ines, autochthones; Briton, English-man, John Bull; new comer &c. (*stranger*) 57.

garrison, crew; population; people &c. (*mankind*) 372; colony, settlement; household.

V. inhabit &c. (*be present*) 186; in-denizen &c. (*locate oneself*) 184.

Adj. indigenous; enchorial; national, nat-ive, -al; autochthonous; British, English; colonial; domestic; domicil-

189. [Place of habitation, or resort.] Abode.—N. abode, dwelling, lodging, -s; diggings, domicile, residence, ad-dress, habitation, where one's lot is cast, local habitation, berth, seat, lap, sojourn, housing, quarters, headquar-ters, resiance, tabernacle, throne, ark.

home, fatherland, mother country, country &c. 181; home-stead, -stall; fireside, chimney corner; hearth, – stone; household gods, *lares et penates*, roof, household, housing, *dulce domum*, paternal domicile; native -soil, – land, blighty.

nest, *nidus*, snuggery; arbour, bower &c. 191; lair, den, cave, hole, hiding-place, cell, *sanctum sanctorum*, aerie, eyry, rookery, hive; *habitat*, haunt, covert, resort, retreat, perch, roost; nidification.

bivouac, camp, encampment, can-tonment, castrametation; barrack, casemate, casern.

iated, -ed; naturalized, vernacular, domesticated; domiciliary.

in the occupation of; garrisoned –, occupied- by.

tent &c. (*covering*) 223; building &c. (*construction*) 161; chamber &c. (*receptacle*) 191.

tenement, messuage, farm, farm-house, grange, *hacienda*.

cot, cabin, log cabin, shack, hut, *châlet*, croft, shed, booth, stall, hovel, bothy, shanty, igloo, tepee, wigwam; pen &c. (*inclosure*) 232; barn, bawn; kennel, sty, dog-hole, cote, coop, hutch, byre; cow-house, -shed; stable, dove-cote, shippen.

house, mansion, place, villa, cottage, box, lodge, hermitage, *rus in urbe*, folly, rotunda, tower, *château*, castle, pavilion, hotel, court, manor-house, capital messuage, hall, palace, alcazar; country seat; kiosk, bungalow; temple &c. 1000; home of rest, alms-, poor-, work-house, asylum; boarding-, lodging-house; flat, maisonette, duplex, penthouse, suite of rooms, apartments, rooms, room, building &c. 161; Mansion House, town hall, Capitol.

assembly-room, auditorium, coliseum, meeting-house, pump-room, spa, health resort, watering-place; club; theatre &c. 840; drill hall, gymnasium, church &c. 1000; Houses of Parliament &c. 696; school &c. 542; inn; hostel, -ry; hotel, tavern, caravansary, khan, hospice; public-, ale-, pot-, mug-house; gin-palace, gin mill; coffee-, eating-house; canteen, *restaurant, rôtisserie*, cafeteria, grill-room, *buffet, café, estaminet, posada, bodega*; bar; saloon, speakeasy, shebeen.

hamlet, village, thorp, dorp, ham, kraal; borough, burgh, town, county-seat, – town, city, capital, metropolis; suburb, quarter, parish &c. 181; ghetto; province, country.

street, place, terrace, parade, esplanade, promenade, pier, embankment, road, villas, row, walk, lane, alley, court, quadrangle, quad, wynd, close, yard, passage, rents, mansions, buildings, mews.

square, polygon, circus, crescent, mall, *piazza*, arcade, colonnade, peristyle, cloister; gardens, grove, residences; block of buildings, market-place, *place*.

anchorage, roadstead, roads; dock, basin, wharf, quay, port, harbour; dry-, graving-, floating-dock.

garden, park, pleasure-ground, pleasance, demesne.

V. take up one's abode &c. (*locate oneself*) 184; inhabit &c. (*be present*) 186.

Adj. urban, oppidan, metropolitan; suburban; provincial, rural, rustic; countrified; regional, parochial, domestic; cosmopolitan; palatial.

190. [Things contained.] **Contents.—N.** contents; cargo, lading, freight, shipment, load, bale, burden; cart-, ship-load; cup –, basket –, &c. (*receptacle*) 191- of; inside &c. 221; stuffing, ullage.

V. load, lade, ship, charge, fill, stuff.

191. Receptacle.—N. receptacle, container; inclosure &c. 232; recipient, receiver, reservatory.

compartment; cell, -ule; follicle; hole, corner, niche, recess, nook; crypt, stall, pigeon-hole, cove, oriel; cave &c. (*concavity*) 252.

capsule, vesicle, cyst, pod, calyx, *cancelli*, utricle, bladder, udder.

stomach, paunch, *venter*, abdomen, ventricle, crop, craw, ingluvies, maw, gizzard, bread-basket, belly, little Mary; mouth.

pocket, pouch, fob, sheath, scabbard, socket, bag, vanity bag, compact, sac, sack, saccule, despatch –, attaché-, tachy- case, wallet, scrip, card-, note- case, billfold, poke, knit, knap-, haver-, ruck-sack, sachel, satchel, reticule, budget, net; ditty-, -box, -bag, kitbag; portfolio; saddlebags, holster; quiver &c. (*magazine*) 636.

chest, box, coffer, caddy, case, casket, pyx, pix, *caisson*, desk, *bureau*, reliquary, shrine; trunk, portmanteau, band-box, *valise*, suitcase, hand-, traveling-, overnight-, Gladstone-, carpet-bag, brief case; boot, imperial; *vache*; cage, manger, rack.

vessel, vase, bushel, barrel; canister, jar; pottle, basket, punnet, pannier, buck-basket, hopper, maund, creel, cran, crate, cradle, bassinet, wisket, whisket, *jardinière*, *corbeille*, hamper, wastepaper basket, dosser, dorser, tray, hod, scuttle, utensil, spittoon, cuspidor.

[For liquids] cistern &c. (*store*) 636; vat, caldron, barrel, cask, puncheon, keg, rundlet, tun, butt, firkin, hogshead, kilderkin, carboy, amphora, ampulla, bottle, jar, leather bottle, decanter, ewer, cruse, carafe, crock, kit, canteen, flagon; demijohn; flask, -et; stoup, noggin, vial, phial, ampoulé, cruet, caster; gourd; urn, *épergne*, salver, *patella*, *tazza*, *patera*; pig-, big-gin; tea-, coffee-pot, percolator, *samovar*; tyg, nipperkin, pocket-pistol; tub, bucket, pail, skeel, pot, tankard, jug, pitcher, toby, mug, pipkin; gal-, gall-ipot, pannikin; matrass, receiver, retort, alembic, bolthead, can, kettle; bowl, basin, jorum, punch-bowl, cup, goblet, chalice, tumbler, glass, wineglass, rummer, beaker, tass, horn, saucepan, skillet, posnet, tureen, terrine, *casserole*, sauce-, gravy-boat.

plate, platter, paten, dish, vegetable –, *entrée*- dish, trencher, calabash, porringer, potager, saucer, pan, crucible.

shovel, trowel, spoon; table-, dessert-, tea-, egg-, salt-spoon; spatula, ladle; dipper; baler; watch-glass, thimble.

closet, commode, cupboard, cellaret, *chiffonnière*, locker, bin, bunker, *buffet*, press, safe, sideboard, drawer, chest of drawers, till, *scrutoire*, *secrétaire*, *éscritoire*, davenport, book-case, cabinet, canterbury; corner cupboard, wardrobe.

chamber, apartment, room, cabin; office, court, hall, atrium; suite of rooms, flat, story; saloon, *salon*, parlour; presence-chamber; sitting-, drawing-, reception-, state-, living-, work-room; gallery, cabinet, closet, cubicle; pew, box; *boudoir*; *adytum*, *sanctum*; bed-room, dormitory, dressing-room; refectory, dining-room, *salle-à-manger*; nursery, school-room; library, study; *studio*; billiard-, bath-, smoking-room; den, canteen, mess, officers' mess; gun-, ward-, mess-room.

attic, loft, garret, cockloft, clerestory; cellar, vault, hold, cockpit; *entre-sol*; mezzanine floor; ground-floor, *rez-de-chaussée*; basement, kitchen, cook-house, galley, pantry, scullery, offices; store-room &c. (*depository*) 636; lumber-room; dust-hole, -bin; dairy, laundry, coach-house; *garage*; *hangar*; out-, pent-house; lean-to.

portico, porch, piazza, verandah, lobby, court, hall, vestibule, corridor, passage; ante-room, -chamber; lounge; *foyer*, *loggia*.

conservatory, green-house, glass-house, vinery, bower, arbour, summer-house, alcove, grotto, hermitage, pergola.

lodging &c. (*abode*) 189; bed &c. (*support*) 215; carriage &c. (*vehicle*) 272.

Adj. capsular; saccu-lar, -lated; recipient; ventricular, cystic, vascu-lar, vesicular, cellular, camerated, locular, multilocular, poly-gastric; marsupial; siliqu-ose, -ous.

Section II. DIMENSIONS

1°. General Dimensions

192. Size.—**N.** size, magnitude, dimension, bulk, volume; largeness &c. *adj.*; greatness &c. (*of quantity*) 31; expanse &c. (*space*) 180; amplitude, mass; proportions.

capacity; ton-, tun-nage; calibre, scantling.

turgidity &c. (*expansion*) 194; corpulence, obesity; plumpness, &c. *adj.*; *embonpoint*, corporation, flesh and blood, lustihood.

hugeness &c. *adj.*; enormity, immensity, monstrosity.

giant, Brobdingnagian, Antæus, Goliath, Gog and Magog, Gargantua, monster, mammoth, Cyclops; whale, porpoise, behemoth, leviathan, elephant, hippopotamus; colossus; tun, lump, bulk, block, loaf, mass, clod, nugget, bushel, thumper, whopper, spanker, strapper; Triton among the minnows.

mountain, mound; heap &c. (*assemblage*) 72.

largest portion &c. 50; full-, life-size.

V. ve- large &c. *adj.*; become -large &c. (*expand*) 194.

Adj. large, big; great &c. (*in quantity*) 31; considerable, bulky, voluminous, ample, massive, massy; capacious, comprehensive; spacious &c. 180; mighty, towering, fine, magnificent.

corpulent, stout, fat, plump, squab, full, lusty, strapping, bouncing; portly, burly, well-fed, full-grown; stalwart, brawny, fleshy; goodly; in good -case, – condition; in condition; chopping, jolly; chub-, chubby-faced.

lubberly, hulky, unwieldy, lumpish, gaunt, spanking, whacking, whopping, thumping, thundering, hulking; overgrown; puffy &c. (*swollen*) 194.

huge, immense, enormous, mighty; vast, -y; amplitudinous, stupendous; monst-er, -rous; gigantic, elephantine;

193. Littleness.—**N.** littleness &c. *adj.*; smallness &c. (*of quantity*) 32; exiguity, inextension; parvi-tude, -ty; duodecimo; Elzevir edition, epitome, microcosm; rudiment; vanishing point; thinness &c. 203.

dwarf, pigmy, atomy, Liliputian, midget, chit, pigwidgeon, urchin, elf; doll, puppet; Tom Thumb, Hop-o'-my thumb, Humpty-dumpty; man-. mannikin; *homunculus*, dapperling, fingerling, dandiprat, cock-sparrow, scalawag.

animalcule, monad, mite, insect, emmet, fly, midge, gnat, shrimp, minnow, worm, maggot, entozoon; *bacillus*, microbe, micro-organism, *bacteria*; *infusoria*; microbe; grub; tit, tomtit, runt, mouse, small fry; millet-, mustard-seed; barley-corn; pebble, grain of sand; mole-hill, button, bubble.

point; atom &c. (*small quantity*) 32; fragment &c. (*small part*) 51; powder &c. 330; point of a pin, mathematical point; *minutiæ* &c. (*unimportance*) 643.

micro-graphy, -meter, -scope; vernier; scale.

V. be -little &c. *adj.*; lie in a nutshell; become small &c. (*decrease*) 36, (*contract*) 195.

Adj. little; small &c. (*in quantity*) 32; minute, diminutive, microscopic; inconsiderable &c. (*unimportant*) 643; exiguous, puny, tiny, wee, petty, minikin, miniature, pigmy, elfin; under sized; dwarf, -ed, -ish; spare, stunted, limited; cramp, -ed; pollard, Liliputian, dapper, pocket; port-ative, -able; duodecimo; dumpy, squat; compact, handy; short &c. 201.

impalpable, intangible, evanescent, imperceptible, invisible, inappreciable, infinitesimal, homœopathic; atomic, corpuscular, molecular; rudiment-ary, -al; embryonic.

weazen, scant, scraggy, scrubby;

giant, -like; colossal, Cyclopean, Brobdingnagian, Gargantuan, Titanic; infinite &c. 105.

large as life; plump as a -dumpling,
– partridge; fat as -a pig, – a quail,
– butter, – brawn, – bacon.

194. Expansion.— N. expansion;
increase &c. 35 -of size; enlargement,
extension, augmentation; ampli-fica-
tion, -ation; aggrandizement, spread,
increment, growth, development, pullulation, swell, dilation, dilatation, rarefaction; turg-escence, -idness, -idity;
obesity &c. (*size*) 192; dropsy, tume-
faction, intumescence, swelling, tumour, *diastole*, distension; puff-ing,
-iness; inflation; pandiculation.

dilatability, expansibility.

germination, growth, upgrowth; accretion &c. 35.

over-growth, -distension; hyper-
trophy, tympany.

bulb &c. (*convexity*) 250; plumper;
superiority of size.

V. become -larger &c. (large &c. 192);
expand, widen, enlarge, extend, grow,
increase, incrassate, swell, gather; fill
out; deploy, take open order, dilate,
stretch, spread; mantle, wax; grow –,
spring- up; bud, bourgeon, shoot,
sprout, germinate, put forth, vegetate,
pullulate, open, burst forth, flower,
blow &c. 734; gain –, gather- flesh;
outgrow; spread like wildfire, overrun.

be larger than; surpass &c. (*be superior*) 33.

render -larger &c. (large &c. 192);
expand, spread, extend, aggrandize,
distend, develop, amplify, spread out,
widen, magnify, rarefy, inflate, puff,
puff out, blow up, stuff, pad, cram;
exaggerate; fatten.

Adj. expanded &c. *v.*; larger &c.
(large &c. 192); swollen; expansive;
wide-open, -spread; fan-shaped; 'flabelliform; overgrown, exaggerated,
bloated, fat, turgid, tumid, hyper-
trophied, dropsical; pot-, swag-bellied;
œdematous, obese, puffy, pursy,
blowzy, distended; patulous; bulbous &c. (*convex*) 250; full-blown,
-grown, -formed; big &c. 192.

196. Distance.—N. distance; space
&c. 180; remoteness, farness; far- cry

thin &c. (*narrow*) 203; granular &c.
(*powdery*) 330; shrunk &c. 195.

Adv. in a -small compass, – nutshell;
on a small scale.

---

195. Contraction.—N. contraction,
reduction, diminution; decrease &c. 36-
of size; defalcation, decrement; lessening, shrinkage; collapse, emaciation,
attenuation, tabefaction, consumption,
marasmus, atrophy; systole, neck,
hour-glass.

condensation, compression, constraint, compactness; compendium &c.
596; squeezing &c. *v.*; strangulation;
corrugation; astringency, constrin-
gency; astringents, sclerotics; contrac-
tility, compressibility; coarctation.

inferiority in size.

V. become -small, – smaller; lessen,
decrease &c. 36; grow less, dwindle,
shrink, contract, narrow, shrivel, collapse, wither, lose flesh, wizen, fall
away, waste, wane, ebb; decay &c.
(*deteriorate*) 659.

be smaller than, fall short of; not
come up to &c. (*be inferior*) 34.

render smaller, lessen, diminish, contract, draw in, narrow, coarctate; constrict, constringe; condense, compress,
boil down, deflate, exhaust, empty;
squeeze, corrugate, crush, crumple up,
warp, purse up, pack, stow; pinch,
tighten, strangle; cramp; dwarf, be-
dwarf; shorten &c. 201; circumscribe
&c. 229; restrain &c. 751; fold &c. 258.

pare, reduce, attenuate, rub down,
scrape, file, grind, chip, shave, shear.

Adj. contracting &c. *v.*; astringent;
shrunk, contracted &c. *v.*; strangulated,
tabid, wizened, stunted; tabescent;
marasmic; waning &c. *v.*; neap; compact.

unexpanded &c. (expand &c. 194);
inswept; contractile; compressible;
smaller &c. (small &c. 193).

---

197. Nearness.—N. nearness &c.
adj.; proximity, propinquity; vicinity,

to; longinquity, elongation; offing, background; removedness; parallax; reach, span, stride; drift.

out-post, -skirt; horizon, sky-line; aphelion; foreign parts, *ultima Thule, ne plus ultra*, antipodes; long range, giant's stride.

dispersion &c. 73.

V. be -distant &c. *adj.*; extend –, stretch –, reach –, spread –, go –, get –, stretch away- to; range, outrange, outreach.

remain at a distance; keep –, stand- -away, – off, – aloof, – clear of.

Adj. distant; far -off, – away; remote, telescopic, distal, wide of; stretching to &c. *v.*; yon, -der; ulterior; trans-marine, -pontine, -atlantic, -alpine; tramon- tane; ultra-montane, -mundane; hyper- borean, antipodean; inaccessible, out of the way; unapproach-ed, -able; incontiguous.

Adv. far -off, – away; afar, -off; off; away; a -long, – great, – good- way off; wide away, aloof; wide –, clear- of; out of -the way, – reach; abroad, yonder, farther, further, beyond; *outre mer*, over the border, far and wide, over the hills and far away; from pole to pole &c. (*over great space*) 180; to the -uttermost parts, – ends- of the earth; out of -hearing, – range, nobody knows where, *à perte de vue*, out of the sphere of, wide of the mark; a far cry to.

apart, asunder; wide -apart, – asun- der; *longo intervallo*; at arm's length.

-age; neighbourhood, adjacency; con- tiguity &c. 199.

short -distance, – step, – cut; ear- shot, close quarters, stone's throw; bow –, gun –, pistol- shot; hair's breadth, span; close-up.

purlieus, neighbourhood, vicinage, *environs, alentours*, suburbs, confines, *banlieue*, borderland; whereabouts.

bystander; neighbour, borderer.

approach &c. 286; convergence &c. 290; perihelion.

V. be -near &c. *adj.*; adjoin, hang about, trench on; border –, verge upon; stand by, approximate, tread on the heels of, cling to, clasp, hug; cuddle, huddle; hang upon the skirts of, hover over; burn; abut.

bring –, draw- -near &c. 286; con- verge &c. 290; crowd &c. 72; place -side by side &c. *adv.*

Adj. near, nigh; close –, near- at hand; close, neighbouring, propinquent, bordering upon; adjacent, adjoining, limitrophe; proxim-ate, -al; at hand, handy; near the mark, near run; home, intimate.

Adv. near, nigh; hard –, fast- by; close -to, – upon, – up; at the point of; next door to; within -reach, – call, – hearing, – earshot, – range; within an ace of; but a step, not far from, at no great distance; on the -verge, – brink, – skirts- of; in the -environs &c. *n.*; at one's -door, – feet, – elbow, – finger's end, – side; on the tip of one's tongue; under one's nose; within a -stone's throw &c. *n.*; in -sight, – presence- of; at close quarters; cheek by -jole, – jowl; beside, alongside, side by side, *tête-à-*

tête; in juxtaposition &c. (*touching*) 199; yard-arm to yard-arm; at the heels of; on the confines of, at the threshold, bordering upon, verging to; in the way.

about; here-, there-abouts; roughly, in round numbers; approxim- -ately, -atively; as good as, well nigh.

198. Interval.—N. interval, inter- space; separation &c. 44; break, gap, opening; hole &c. 260; chasm, *hiatus*, cæsura; inter-ruption, -regnum; in- terstice, *lacuna*, cleft, mesh, crevice, chink, rime, creek, cranny, crack, chap, slit, slot, fissure, scissure, rift, flaw, breach, fracture, rent, gash, cut, leak, dike, ha-ha.

199. Contiguity. — N. contiguity, contact, proximity, apposition, juxta- position, touching &c. *v.*; abutment, osculation; meeting, appulse, appulsion, *rencontre*, rencounter, syzygy, coinci- dence, conjunction, coexistence; adhe- sion &c. 46.

border-land; frontier &c. (*limit*) 233; tangent.

gorge, defile, ravine, cañon, *crevasse,* abyss, abysm; gulf; inlet, frith, strait, gully, gulch, nullah; pass; notch; furrow &c. 259; yawning gulf; *hiatus -maxime, – valde- deflendus;* parenthesis &c. (*interjacence*) 228; void &c. (*absence*) 187; incompleteness &c. 530.

V. gape &c. (*open*) 260.

Adj. with an interval, far between.

Adv. at intervals &c. (*discontinuously*) 70; *longo intervallo.*

V. be -contiguous &c. *adj.*; join, adjoin, abut on, march with, border; tick, graze, touch, meet, osculate, kiss, come in contact, coincide; coexist; adhere &c. 46.

Adj. contiguous; touching &c. *v.*; in -contact &c. *n.*; conterminous, end to end, osculatory; pertingent; tangential.

hand to hand; close to &c. (*near*) 197; with no -interval &c. 198.

2°. LINEAR DIMENSIONS

200. Length.—**N.** length, longitude, span, extent, mileage.

line, bar, rule, stripe, streak, spoke, radius.

lengthening &c. *v.*; pro-longation, -duction, -traction; ten-sion, -sure; extension.

[Measures of length] line, nail, inch, hand, palm, foot, cubit, yard, ell, fathom, rod, pole, perch, furlong, mile, league; chain, metre, kilo-, centi-, milli- &c. -metre.

pedometer, perambulator, odometer, odograph, speedometer, cyclometer, log, telemeter, range finder; scale &c. (*measurement*) 466.

V. be -long &c. *adj.*; stretch out, sprawl; extend –, reach –, stretch- to; make a long arm, 'drag its slow length along.'

render -long &c. *adj.*; lengthen, extend, elongate; stretch; pro-long, -duce, -tract; let –, pay –, draw –, spin- out; drawl.

enfilade, look along, view in perspective.

Adj. long, -some; lengthy, lank, wire-drawn, outstretched; lengthened &c. *v.*; sesquipedalian &c. (*words*) 577; interminable, no end of.

line-ar, -al; longitudinal, oblong.

as long as -my arm, – to-day and to-morrow; unshortened &c. (shorten &c. 201).

Adv. lengthwise, at length, longitudinally, endlong, along; *tandem;* in a line &c. (*continuously*) 69; in perspective.

from -end to end, – stem to stern, – head to foot, – the crown of the head to the sole of the foot, – top to toe, – head to heels; fore and aft.

201. Shortness.—**N.** shortness &c. *adj.*; brevity; littleness &c. 193; a span.

shortening &c. *v.*; abbrevia-tion, -ture; abridgment, concision, retrenchment, curtailment, decurtation; reduction &c. (*contraction*) 195; epitome &c. (*compendium*) 596.

abridger, abstractor, epitomiser.

elision, ellipsis; conciseness &c. (*in style*) 572.

V. be -short &c. *adj.*; render -short &c. *adj.*; shorten, curtail, abridge, abbreviate, take in, reduce; compress &c. (*contract*) 195; epitomize &c. 596.

retrench, cut short, obtruncate; scrimp, cut, chop up, hack, hew; cut –, pare- down; clip, snip, dock, lop, prune; shear, shave, mow, reap, crop; snub; truncate, pollard, stunt, nip, nip in the bud, check the growth of; [in drawing] foreshorten.

Adj. short, brief, curt; compendious, compact; stubby, scrimp; shorn, stubbed; stumpy, thickset, podgy, stocky, pug; squab, -by; squat, dumpy; little &c. 193; curtailed of its fair proportions; short by; oblate; concise &c. 572; summary.

Adv. shortly &c. *adj.*; in short &c. (*concisely*) 572.

202. Breadth. Thickness.—N. breadth, width, latitude, amplitude; diameter, bore, calibre, radius; superficial extent &c. (*space*) 180.

thickness, crassitude; corpulence &c. (*size*) 192; dilatation &c. (*expansion*) 194.

V. be -broad &c. *adj.*; become -, render- -broad &c. *adj.*; expand &c. 194; thicken, widen.

Adj. broad, wide, ample, extended; discous; fan-like; out-spread, -stretched; wide as a church-door.

thick, dumpy, squab, squat, thick-set, tubby; thick as a rope, stubby &c. 201.

---

203. Narrowness. Thinness.—N. narrowness &c. *adj.*; closeness, exility; exiguity &c. (*little*) 193.

line; hair's -, finger's -breadth; strip, streak, vein.

thinness &c. *adj.*; tenuity; emaciation, macilency, *marcor*.

shaving, slip &c. (*filament*) 205; threadpaper, skeleton, shadow, scrag, anatomy, spindle-shanks, barebones, lantern jaws, mere skin and bone.

middle constriction, stricture, neck, waist, isthmus, wasp, hour-glass; ridge, *ghaut*, pass; ravine &c. 198.

narrowing, coarctation, angustation, tapering; contraction &c. 195.

V. be -narrow &c. *adj.*; narrow, taper, contract &c. 195; render -narrow &c. *adj.*

Adj. narrow, close; slender, thin, fine; *svelte*; thread-like &c. (*filament*) 205; finespun, taper, slim, gracile, slight, slight-made; scant, -y; spare, delicate, incapacious; contracted &c. 195; unexpanded &c. (expand &c. 194); slender as a thread, capillary.

emaciated, lean, meagre, gaunt, macilent; lank, -y; weedy, skinny, scrawny, scraggy; starv-ed, -eling; attenuated, shrivelled, wizened, pinched, peaky, skeletal, spindling, spindle- -legged, -shanked; extenuated, tabid, marcid, bare-bone, raw-boned; herring-gutted; worn to a shadow, lean as a rake; thin as a -lath, - whipping post, - wafer; hatchet-faced; lantern-jawed.

---

204. Layer.—N. layer, stratum, course, bed, zone, *substratum*, floor, flag, stage, story, tier, slab, escarpment, table, tablet, panel, plaque; board, plank; trencher, platter.

plate; lam-ina, -ella; sheet, flake, foil, wafer, scale, coat, peel, pellicle, ply, thickness, membrane, film, leaf, slice, shive, cut, rasher, shaving, integument &c. (*covering*) 223.

stratification, lamination, scaliness, nest of boxes, coats of an onion.

V. slice, shave, pare, peel; plate, coat, veneer; cover &c. 223.

Adj. lamell-ar, -ated, -iform; laminated, -iferous; micaceous; schist-ose, -ous; scaly, filmy, membranous, flaky, squamous; folia-ted, -ceous; stratified, -form; tabular, discoid, spathic.

---

205. Filament.—N. filament, line; fibre, fibril; funicle, vein, hair, capillament, *cilium*, tendril, gossamer; hair-stroke; harl.

wire, string, thread, packthread, cotton, sewing-silk, twine, twist, whip-cord, cord, rope, cable, yarn, hemp, oakum, jute, wool, worsted.

strip, shred, slip, spill, list, band, fillet, *fascia*, ribbon, riband, tape, roll, lath, slat, strake, splinter, shiver, shaving.

beard &c. (*roughness*) 256; ramification; strand.

Adj. fil-amentous, -aceous, -iform; fibr-ous, -illous; thread-like, wiry, stringy, ropy; capill-ary, -iform; funicular, wire-drawn; anguilliform; flagelliform; hairy &c. (*rough*) 256; ligulate.

---

206. Height.—N. height, altitude, elevation, ceiling; eminence. pitch; loftiness &c. *adj.*; sublimity.

tallness &c. *adj.*; stature, procerity; prominence &c. 250.

---

207. Lowness.—N. lowness &c. *adj.*; debasement, depression; prostration &c. (*horizontal*) 213; depression &c. (*concave*) 252.

molehill; lowlands; bottomlands;

colossus &c. (*size*) 192; giant, grenadier, giraffe.

mount, -ain; hill, butte, monticle, fell, knap; cape; head-, fore-land; promontory; ridge, hog's back, dune; rising -, vantage- ground; down; moor, -land; Alp; up-, high-lands; heights &c. (*summit*) 210; knoll, hummock, hillock, barrow, mound, mole, *kopje*; steeps, bluff, cliff, craig, tor, peak, pike, clough; escarpment, edge, ledge, brae; dizzy height.

tower, pillar, column, pylon, obelisk, monument, steeple, spire, minaret, *campanile*, belfry, turret, roof, dome, cupola, pagoda, pyramid; sky scraper; Eiffel tower.

pole, pikestaff, maypole, flagstaff; mast, top -, topgallant- mast.

ceiling &c. (*covering*) 223.

high water; high -, flood -, spring- tide.

altimetry &c. (*angle*) 244; altimeter, height-finder, hypsometer, barograph.

V. be -high &c. *adj.*; tower, soar, command; hover; cap, culminate; overhang, hang over, impend, beetle; bestride, ride, mount; perch, surmount; cover &c. 233; overtop &c. (*be superior*) 33; stand on tiptoe.

become -high &c. *adj.*; grow, - higher, - taller; upgrow; rise &c. (*ascend*) 305.

render -high &c. *adj.*; heighten &c. (*elevate*) 307.

Adj. high, elevated, eminent, exalted, lofty, supernal; tall; gigantic &c. (*big*) 192; Patagonian; towering, beetling, soaring, hanging [gardens]; elevated &c. 307; upper; highest &c. (*topmost*) 210; monticolous, perching, hill-dwelling.

up-, moor-land; hilly, mountainous, alpine, sub-alpine, heaven-kissing; cloud-topt, -capt, -touching; aerial.

overhanging &c. *v.*; incumbent, overlying; super-incumbent, -natant, -imposed; prominent &c. 250.

tall as a -maypole, - poplar, - steeple; lanky &c. (*thin*) 203.

Adv. on high, high up, aloft, up, above, aloof, overhead; up -, above- stairs; in the clouds; on -tiptoe, - stilts, - the shoulders of; over head and ears; breast high.

over, upwards; from top to bottom &c. (*completely*) 52.

basement- ground-floor; *rez de chaussée* &c. 211; hold; feet, heels.

low water; low -, ebb -, neap -, spring- tide.

V. be -low &c. *adj.*; lie -low, - flat; underlie; crouch, slouch, wallow, grovel; lower &c. (*depress*) 308.

Adj. low, neap, debased; nether, -most; flat, level with the ground; lying low &c. *v.*; crouched, subjacent, squat, prostrate &c. (*horizontal*) 213.

Adv. under; be-, under-neath; below; down, -wards; adown, at the foot of; under-foot, -ground; down -, below-stairs; at a low ebb; below par.

---

208. Depth.—N. depth; deepness &c. *adj.*; profundity, depression &c. (*concavity*) 252.

hollow, pit, shaft, well, crater, abyss; gulf &c. 198; bowels of the earth, bottomless pit, hell.

soundings, depth of water, water, draught, submersion; plummet, sound, probe; sounding -rod, - line, - machine; lead; submarine, diving bell, bathysphere; diver.

V. be -deep &c. *adj.*; render -deep &c. *adj.*; deepen.

plunge &c. 310; sound, heave the lead, take soundings; dig &c. (*excavate*) 252.

209. Shallowness.—N. shallowness &c. *adj.*; shoals; mere scratch.

Adj. shallow, superficial; skin -, ankle -, knee- deep; just enough to wet one's feet; shoal, -y

Adj. deep, -seated; profound, sunk, buried; submerged &c. 310; sub-aqueous, -marine, -terranean, -terrene; underground.

bottom-, sound-, fathom-less; unfathom-ed, -able; abysmal; deep as a well, deep-sea.

knee-, ankle-deep.

Adv. beyond –, out of- one's depth; over head and ears, over one's head.

210. Summit.—N. summit, -y; top, vertex, apex, zenith, pinnacle, acme, acropolis, culmination, meridian, utmost height, *ne plus ultra*, height, pitch, maximum, climax, apogee; culminating –, crowning –, turning- point; turn of the tide, fountain head; water-shed, -parting; sky, pole.

tip, -top; crest, crow's nest, cap, truck, peak, nib; end &c. 67; crown, brow; head, nob, noddle, pate.

high places, heights.

top-, top-gallant mast, sky scraper; quarter –, hurricane- deck.

architrave, frieze, cornice, coping, coping-stone, zoophorus, capital, headpiece, capstone, epistyle, sconce, pediment, entablature; tympanum; ceiling &c. (*covering*) 223.

attic, loft, garret, house-top, upper story, roof.

V. culminate, cap, crown, top; overtop &c. (*be superior to*) 33.

Adj. highest &c. (high &c. 206); top; top-, upper-most; tip-top; culminating &c. *v.*; meridi-an, -onal; capital, head, polar, supreme, supernal, top-gallant.

Adv. a-top, at the top of – the tree, – the heap.

211. Base.—N. base, -ment; plinth, dado, wainscot, baseboard; foundation &c. (*support*) 215; substructure, *substratum*, sump, ground, earth, pavement, floor, paving, flag, carpet, ground-floor, deck; footing, groundwork, basis; hold, bilge, orlop deck.

bottom, nadir, foot, sole, toe, hoof, keel, kelson, root.

Adj. bottom; under-, nether-most; fundamental; founded –, based –, grounded –, built- on.

---

212. Verticality. — N. verticality; erectness &c. *adj.*; perpendicularity; right angle, normal; azimuth circle.

wall, palisade, precipice, cliff, steep, bluff.

elevation, erection; square, plumb-line, plummet.

V. be -vertical &c. *adj.*; stand -up, – on end, – erect, – upright; stick –, cock-up.

render -vertical &c. *adj.*; set –, stick –, raise –, cock- up; erect, rear, raise, pitch, raise on its legs.

Adj. vertical, upright, erect, perpendicular, normal, plumb, straight, bolt upright; rampant; straight –, standing-up &c. *v.*; rectangular, orthogonal.

Adv. vertically &c. *adj.*; up, on end; up –, right- on end; *à plomb*, endwise; on one's legs; at right angles.

213. Horizontality.—N. horizontality; flatness; level, plane; stratum &c. 204; dead -level, – flat; level plane.

recumbency; lying down &c. *v.*; reclination, decumbence; de-, discumbency; proneness &c. *adj.*; accubation, supination, resupination, prostration; azimuth.

plain, floor, platform, bowling-green; cricket-ground; court; gridiron; baseball diamond; hockey rink; tennis-, croquet-ground, – lawn; billiard table; terrace, estrade, esplanade, *parterre*, table-land, *plateau*, ledge.

spirit-, level; T-square.

V. be -horizontal &c. *adj.*; lie, recline, couch; lie -down, – flat, – prostrate; sprawl, loll; sit down.

render -horizontal &c. *adj.*; lay, – down, – out; level, flatten, even, raze, equalize, smooth, align; prostrate, knock down, floor, fell, ground.

Adj. horizontal, level, even, plane;

flat &c. 251; flat as a -billiard table, – bowling green; alluvial; calm, – as a mill-pond; smooth, – as glass.

re-, de-, pro-, ac-cumbent; lying &c. *v.*; prone, supine, couchant, jacent, prostrate.

Adv. horizontally &c. *adj.*; on -one's back. – all fours, – its beam ends.

214. Pendency.—N. pend-, dependency; suspension, hanging &c. *v.*

pendant, drop, tippet, tassel, lobe, tail, train, flap, lappet, skirt, pig-tail, queue, pendulum.

peg, knob, button, hook, nail, stud, ring, staple, tenterhook; davit; fastening &c. 45; spar, horse.

chande-, gase-, electro-lier.

V. be -pendent &c. *adj.*; hang, depend, swing, dangle, droop, sag; swag; daggle, flap, trail, flow.

suspend, hang, sling, hook up, hitch, fasten to, append.

Adj. pend-ent, -ulous; pensile; hanging &c. *v.*; dependent; suspended &c. *v.*; lowering, overhanging, beetling, decumbent; loose, flowing.

having a -peduncle &c. *n.*; pedunculate, tailed, caudate.

215. Support.—N. support, ground, foundation, base, basis; *terra firma*; bearing, fulcrum, *point d'appui*, caudex, purchase, footing, hold, *-locus standi*; landing, – stage, – place; stage, platform; block; rest, resting-place; groundwork, *substratum*, sustentation, subvention; floor &c. (*basement*) 211.

supporter; aid &c. 707; prop, stand, anvil, fulciment; hod, stay, shore, skid, rib, sprag, truss, bandage; sleeper; stirrup, stilts, shoe, sole, heel, splint, lap; bar, rod, boom, sprit, outrigger.

staff, stick, crutch, alpenstock, bourdon; *bâton*, maulstick, colstaff, cowlstaff, staddle; stalk, ped-icel, -icle, – uncle.

post, pillar, shaft, column, pilaster; pediment, pedestal; plinth, shank, leg, socle, zocle; buttress, jamb, mullion, abutment; pile, baluster, banister, stanchion, king post; balustrade.

frame, -work, body, *chassis*, *fuselage*; scaffold, skeleton, beam, rafter, girder, lintel, joist, cantilever, travis, trave, corner-stone. summer, transom; rung, round, step, sill.

columella, back-bone; key-stone; axle, -tree; axis; arch, ogive, mainstay.

trunnion, pivot, rowlock; peg &c. (*pendency*) 214; tie-beam &c. (*fastening*) 45; thole pin.

board, ledge, shelf, hob, bracket, trevet, trivet, arbor, rack, hatrack; mantel, -piece, -shelf; slab, console; counter, dresser; flange, corbel; table, trestle, teapoy; shoulder; perch; horse; easel, desk; retable, predella.

seat, throne, dais; divan, musnud; chair, bench, form, stool, camp-stool, sofa, settee, davenport, stall, miserere, arm –, easy –, elbow –, rocking- chair; couch, day bed, *fauteuil*, woolsack, ottoman, settle, squab, bench, box, dicky; saddle, pannel, pillion; side –, pack- saddle; pommel.

bed, berth, pallet, tester, crib, cot, bassinet, hammock, shakedown, camp bed, bunk, truckle-bed, cradle, litter, stretcher, bedstead; four-poster, French bed; bedding, mattress, *paillasse*; pillow, bolster; mat, rug, cushion.

stool, footstool, hassock, faldstool, *prie-dieu*; tabouret; tripod. Atlas, Persides, Atlantes, Caryatides, Hercules.

V. be -supported &c.; lie –, sit –, recline –, lean –, loll –, rest –, stand –, step –, repose –, abut –, beat –, be based &c.- on; have at one's back; be-stride, -straddle.

support, bear, carry, hold, sustain, shoulder; hold –, back –, bolster –, shore- up; up-hold, -bear; prop; under-prop, -pin, -set; bandage, &c. 43; brace, truss; cradle, pillow.

give –, furnish –, afford –, supply –, lend- -support, – foundations; bottom, found, base, ground, embed.

maintain, keep on foot; aid &c. 707.

Adj. support-ing, -ed, &c. *v.*; atlantean, columellar; sustentative, fundamental, basal.

Adv. astride on, astraddle; pick-a-back.

---

216. Parallelism.—N. parallelism; coextension, concentricity, collimation.

V. be –, lie- parallel to; collimate.

Adj. parallel; coextensive, collateral, concentric, concurrent.

Adv. alongside, abreast &c. (*laterally*) 236.

---

217. Obliquity.—N. obliquity, inclination, skew, slope, slant; crookedness &c. *adj.*; slopeness; leaning &c. *v.*; bevel, bezel, ramp, tilt; bias, list, twist, swag, cant, lurch; distortion &c. 243; bend &c. (*curve*) 245; tower of Pisa.

acclivity, rise, ascent, grade, gradient, *glacis*, rising ground, hill, bank, declivity, downhill, dip, fall, devexity; gentle –, rapid- slope; easy -ascent, – descent; shelving beach; *talus*; *montagne Russe*; *facilis descensus Averni*.

steepness &c. *adj.*; cliff, precipice &c. (*vertical*) 212; escarpment, scarp.

[Measure of inclination] clinometer, theodolite, level, sextant, quadrant, protractor; angle, sine, cosine, tangent &c. hypothenuse.

diagonal; zigzag, chevron.

V. be -oblique &c. *adj.*; slope, slant, lean, incline, shelve, stoop, decline, descend, bend, heel, careen, sag, swag, seel, slouch, cant, sidle.

render -oblique &c. *adj.*; sway, bias; slope, slant; incline, bend, crook; cant, tilt; distort &c. 243.

Adj. oblique, inclined; sloping &c. *v.*; tilted &c. *v.*; recumbent, clinal, skew, askew, slant, aslant, bias, plagiedral, indirect, wry, awry, ajee, crooked; knock-kneed &c. (*distorted*) 243; bevel, out of the perpendicular.

uphill, rising, ascending, acclivous; downhill, falling, descending; declining, declivous, devex, anticlinal; steep, abrupt, precipitous, breakneck.

diagonal; trans-verse, -versal; athwart, antiparallel; curved &c. 245.

Adv. obliquely &c. *adj.*; on –, all on- one side; askew, askant, askance, aslope, asquint, edgewise, at an angle; side-long, -ways; slope-, slant-wise; by a side wind.

218. Inversion.—N. in-, e-, sub-, re-, retro-, intro-version; contraposition &c. 237; contrariety &c. 14; reversal; turn of the tide.

overturn; somer-sault, -set; summerset; *culbute*; revulsion; *pirouette*.

transposition, transposal, anastrophy, *metastasis, hyperbaton, anastrophe, hysteron-proteron*, hypallage, *synchysis, tmesis*, parenthesis; *metathesis*; palindrome; Spoonerism.

pronation and supination.

V. be -inverted &c.; turn –, go –, wheel- -round, – about, – to the right about; turn –, go –, tilt –, topple-over; capsize, turn turtle.

in-, sub-, retro-, intro-vert; reverse; up-, over-turn, -set; turn -topsy turvy &c. *adj.*; *culbuter*; transpose, put the cart before the horse, turn the tables.

Adj. inverted &c. *v.*; wrong side -out, – up; inside out, upside down; bottom –, keel- upwards; supine, on one's head, topsy turvy, *sens dessus sens dessous.*

inverse; reverse &c. (*contrary*) 14; opposite &c. 237.

topheavy, unstable.

Adv. inversely &c. *adj.*; hirdie-girdie; heels over head, head over heels.

219. Crossing.—N. crossing &c. *v.*; inter-section, – lacement, – twinement, -digitation; decussation, transversion; convolution &c. 248.

reticulation, meshwork, network; inosculation, anastomosis, intertexture, mortise.

net, *plexus*, web, mesh, twill, skein, sleeve, felt, lace; wicker; mat, -ting; plait, trellis, wattle, lattice, grating, *grille*, gridiron, tracery, fretwork, filigree, reticle; tissue, netting, mokes.

cross, crucifix, rood, crisscross, crux; chain, wreath, braid, cat's cradle, knot; entanglement &c. (*disorder*) 59.

[woven fabrics] cloth, linen, muslin, cambric, drill, homespun, tweed, broadcloth &c.

V. cross, decussate; inter-sect, -lace, -twine, -twist, -weave, -digitate, -link.

twine, entwine, weave, inweave, twist, wreathe; anastomose, inosculate, dovetail, splice, link.

mat, plait, plat, braid, felt, twill; tangle, entangle, ravel; net, knot; dishevel, raddle.

Adj. crossing &c. *v.*; crossed, matted &c. *v.*; transverse.

cross, cruciform, crucial; reti-form, -cular, -culated; areolar, cancellated, mullioned, latticed, grated, barred, streaked; textile, secant, plexal; interfretted.

Adv. across, thwart, athwart, transversely, crosswise.

3°. CENTRICAL DIMENSIONS*

1. *General*

220. Exteriority. — N. exteriority; outside, exterior; surface, superficies; skin &c. (*covering*) 223; *superstratum*; disk, disc; face, facet.

excentricity; circumjacence &c. 227.

V. be -exterior &c. *adj.*; lie around &c. 227.

place -exteriorly, – outwardly, – outside; put –, turn- out.

Adj. exter-ior, -nal; extraneous, outer, -most; out-ward, -lying, -side, -door; round about &c. 227; extramural.

superficial, skin-deep; frontal, discoid.

extraregarding; eccentric; outstanding; extrinsic &c. 6.

Adv. externally &c. *adj.*; out, without, over, outwards, *ab extra*, out of doors; *extra muros.*

221. Interiority.—N. interiority; inside, interior, endocrine; interspace, subsoil, *substratum.*

contents &c. 190; substance, pith, marrow; backbone &c. (*centre*) 222; heart, bosom, breast, abdomen; vitals, viscera, entrails, bowels, belly, intestines, guts, chitterlings, womb, lap; gland, cell; internal organs, *penetralia*, recesses, innermost recesses; cave &c. (*concavity*) 252.

inhabitant &c. 188.

V. be -inside &c. *adj.*, – within &c. *adv.*

place –, keep- within; enclose &c. (*circumscribe*) 229; intern; embed &c. (*insert*) 300.

Adj. inter-ior, -nal; inner, inside, intimate, inward, intraregarding; in-, inner-most; deep-seated; visceral, intes-

* That is, Dimensions having reference to a centre.

in the open air; *sub -Jove, - dio*; *à la belle étoile, al fresco.*

------

tine, -tinal; inland; subcutaneous; interstitial &c. (*interjacent*) 228; inwrought &c. (*intrinsic*) 5; enclosed &c. *v.*

home, domestic, indoor, intramural, vernacular; endemic.

Adv. internally &c. *adj.*; inwards, within, in, inly; here-, there-, where-in; *ab intra*, withinside; in -, within- doors; at home, in the bosom of one's family.

222. Centrality.—N. centrality, centricalness, centre; middle &c. 68; focus &c. 74.

core, kernel; nucleus, nucleolus; heart, pole, axis, pivot, fulcrum, bull's eye; hub, nave, navel; *umbilicus*, spine, backbone, marrow, pith; hot-bed; concentration &c. (*convergence*) 290; centralization; symmetry.

centre of -gravity, - pressure, - percussion, - oscillation, - buoyancy &c. metacentre.

V. be -central &c. *adj.*; converge &c. 290.

render central, centralize, concentrate; bring to a focus.

Adj. centr-al, -ical; middle &c. 68; axial, pivotal, focal, umbilical, concentric; middlemost, nuclear, centric, centraidal; spinal, vertebral.

Adv. middle; midst; centrally &c. *adj.*

223. Covering.—N. covering, cover;
canopy, tilt, awning, baldachin, tent, marquee, *tente d'abri*, umbrella, parasol, sunshade; veil (*shade*) 424; shield &c. (*defence*) 717; hall.

roof, dome, cupola, mansard roof; ceiling; thatch, tile; pan-, pen-tile; tiling, shingles, slates, slating, leads; shed &c. (*abode*) 189.

224. Lining.—N. lining, inner coating; coating &c. (*covering*) 223; stalactite, -agmite.

filling, stuffing, wadding, padding, bushing.

wainscot, *parietes*, wall, brattice.

V. line, stuff, incrust, wad, pad, fill.

Adj. lined &c. *v.*

------

top, lid, covercle, door, *operculum*, eyelid, blind, curtain.

bandage, plaster, lint, wrapping, dossil, finger stall.

coverlet, counterpane, sheet, quilt, comforter, eiderdown; tarpaulin, blanket, rug, drugget, linoleum, oilcloth; housing.

in-, tegument; skin, pellicle, fleece, fell, fur, ermine, miniver, sable, sealskin &c.; fabrikoid; leather, morocco, calf, pigskin, elk, kid, cowhide &c.; shagreen, hide; pelt, -ry; cuticle, *dermis*, scarfskin, *epidermis*.

clothing &c. 225; mask &c. (*concealment*) 530.

peel, crust, bark, rind, *cortex*, husk, shell, coat.

capsule; ferrule; sheath, -ing; pod, cod; casing, case, theca; *elytron*; *involucrum*; wrapp-ing, -er, cellophane; envelope, vesicle; dermatology, conchology.

armour, -plate, armouring; veneer, facing; pavement; scale &c. (*layer*) 204; coating, paint, stain; varnish &c. (*resin*) 356a; anointing &c. *v.*; inunction; incrustation, superposition, obduction, ground, enamel, whitewash, plaster, stucco, rough cast, pebble dash, compo; rendering; cerement; ointment &c. (*grease*) 356.

V. cover; super-pose, -impose; over-lay, -spread; wrap &c. 225; incase; face, case, veneer, pave, paper; tip, cap, bind, revet.

coat, paint, varnish, pay, incrust, stucco, cement, dab, plaster, tar; wash; be-, smear; be-, daub; anoint, do over; gild, plate, electroplate, japan, lacquer, lacker, enamel, whitewash; lay it on thick.

over-lie, -arch; conceal &c. 528.

Adj. covering &c. *v.*; cutaneous, dermal, cortical, cuticular, tegumentary, skinny, scaly, squamous; covered &c. *v.*; imbricated, loricated, armour-plated, iron-clad; under cover, hooded, cloaked, cowled.

225. Investment.—N. investment; covering &c. 223; dress, clothing, raiment, drapery, costume, attire, guise, toilet, *toilette*, trim; habiliment; vesture, -ment; garment, garb, palliament, apparel, wardrobe, wearing apparel, clothes, things.

array; tailoring, millinery; best bib and tucker; finery &c. (*ornament*) 847; full dress &c. (*show*) 882; garniture; theatrical properties.

outfit, equipment, *trousseau*; uniform, khaki, regimentals; academicals, canonicals &c. 999; livery, gear, harness, turn out, accoutrement, caparison, suit, rigging, trappings, traps, slops, togs, toggery; masquerade.

dishabille, morning dress, lounge suit, tea-gown, *kimono*, *négligé*, dressing-gown, *peignoir*, wrapper, undress; shooting-coat; smoking-jacket, mufti; rags, tatters, old clothes; mourning, weeds; duds; slippers.

robe, tunic, dolman, *paletot*, habit, gown, coat, coatee, frock, blouse, *pelisse*, middy, sagum, *toga*, smock-frock; frock-, dress-, morning-, tail-coat; dress-suit, – clothes, swallow-tail coat, dinner-, Eton-jacket.

cloak, pall; mantle, mantlet, mantua, shawl, *pelisse*, veil, yashmak; cape, tippet, kirtle, plaid, muffler, comforter, Balaclava helmet, haik, huke, chlamys, mantilla, tabard, housing, horse-cloth, burnous, *roquelaure*; *houppelande*; sur-, top·, over-, great-coat; *surtout*, spencer, cardigan, sweater, blazer; mackintosh, waterproof, slicker, raincoat, oilskin, trench coat, ulster, monkey-, pea-, pilot-jacket, redingote; wraprascal, poncho, cardinal, pelerine, talma.

jacket, jumper, vest, jerkin, waistcoat, doublet, *camisole*, gabardine; stays, *corsage*, corset, corselet, bodice; stomacher; skirt, petticoat, slip, farthingale, kilt, jupe, crinoline, bustle, hobble skirt, *panier*, apron, pinafore; loin cloth.

trousers; breeches, trews, pantaloons, unmentionables, inexpressibles, overalls, pyjamas, smalls, small-clothes; tights, pants, shorts, drawers; knickerbockers, knickers, plus fours, bloomers, divided skirt; phil-, fill-ibeg.

226. Divestment.—N. divestment; taking off &c. *v.*

nudity; bareness &c. *adj.*; undress; dishabille &c. 225, altogether; nu-, denu-dation; decortication, depilation, excoriation, desquamation; moulting; exfoliation.

baldness, alopecia, acomia.

V. divest; uncover &c. (*cover* &c. 223); denude, bare, strip; undress, unclothe, disrobe &c. (dress, enrobe, &c. 225); uncoif; dismantle; uncase; put –, take –, cast- off; shed, doff; husk, peel, pare, decorticate, desquamate, excoriate, skin, scalp, flay, bark, expose, lay open; exfoliate, moult, mew; cast the skin.

Adj. divested &c. *v.*; bare, naked, nude; un-dressed, -draped, -clad, -clothed, -appareled; exposed; in dishabille; *décolleté*; bald, threadbare, ragged, callow, roofless.

in -a state of nature, – nature's garb, – buff, – native buff, – birthday suit; *in puris naturalibus*; with nothing on, stark naked; bald as a coot, bare as the back of one's hand; out at elbows; barefoot; bareback; leaf-, nap-, hairless, shaved, clean shaven, tonsured, beardless, bald-headed, acomous.

---

head-dress, -gear; cap, *béret*, tam o' shanter, glengarry, topee, sombrero; hat; cocked –, high –, tall –, top –, silk –, opera –, crush -hat, *gibus*, beaver, castor, bonnet, tile, wideawake, billy-cock; bowler; soft felt –, straw –, leghorn -hat, panama; toque; wimple; night-, mob-, skull-cap, biretta; hood, cowl, coif; capote, calach; scull-cap; kerchief, snood; head, *coiffure*; crown &c. (*circle*) 247; *chignon*, pelt, wig, front, peruke, periwig; caftan, turban, fez, *tarboosh*, taj, shako, csako, busby; *képi*, forage cap, bearskin; helmet &c. 717; mask, domino.

body clothes; linen; shirt, sark, smock, shift, *chemise*, *lingerie*; night-gown, -shirt; bed-gown, *sac de nuit*; jersey, guernsey; underclothing, -waistcoat.

neck-erchief, -cloth; tie, ruff, collar, cravat, stock, handkerchief, bandana, scarf; bib, tucker; dicky; boa; girdle &c. (*circle*) 247; cummerbund.

shoe, pump, brogue, boot, slipper, sandal, galoche, goloshes, arctics, rubber boots, overshoes, patten, clog, sabot; high-low; Blucher –, Wellington –, Hessian –, jack –, top- boot; Balmoral; legging, puttee, buskin, greave, galligaskin, moccasin, *gamache*, gambado, gaiter, spatter-dash, spat, antigropeles; stocking, hose, gaskins, trunk-hose, sock, hosiery.

glove, gauntlet, mitten, cuff, muffettee, wristband, sleeve.

swaddling cloth, baby-linen, *layette*; pocket-handkerchief.

shroud &c. 363.

clothier, tailor, milliner, *costumier*, sempstress, seamstress, snip; dress-, habit-, breeches-, shoe-maker; cordwainer, cobbler, Crispin, hosier, hatter; draper, linendraper, haberdasher, mercer.

V. invest; cover &c. 223; envelop, lap, involve; in-, en-wrap; wrap; fold –, wrap –, lap –, muffle- up; overlap; sheathe, swathe, swaddle, roll up in, shroud, circumvest.

vest, clothe, array, dress, dight, drape, robe, enrobe, attire, tire, garb, habilitate, apparel, accoutre, rig, fit out; bedizen, deck &c. (*ornament*) 847; perk; equip, harness, caparison; dress up.

wear; don; put –, huddle –, slip- on; mantle.

Adj. invested &c. *v.*; habited; dight, -ed; clad, *costumé*, shod, *chaussé*; *en grande tenue* &c. (*show*) 882.

sartorial.

227. Circumjacence.—N. circumjacence, -ambience; environment, encompassment; atmosphere, medium; surroundings, *entourage*.

outpost; border &c. (*edge*) 231; girdle &c. (*circumference*) 230; outskirts, *boulevards*, suburbs, purlieus, precincts, *faubourgs*, *environs*, *banlieue*, neighbourhood, vicinity.

V. lie -around &c. *adv.*; surround, beset, compass, encompass, environ, inclose, enclose, encircle, circle, embrace, circumvent, lap, gird; begird, girdle, engird; skirt, twine round; hem in &c. (*circumscribe*) 229; besiege, invest, blockade.

Adj. circum-jacent, -ambient, -fluent;

228. Interjacence.—N. inter-jacence, -currence, -venience, -location, -digitation, -penetration; permeation.

inter-jection, -polation, -lineation, -spersion, -calation; embolism.

inter-vention, -ference, -position; in-, ob-trusion; insinuation; insertion &c. 300; dovetailing; infiltration; intromission.

intermedi-um, -ary; go-between, agent, middleman, medium, bodkin, intruder, interloper; parenthesis, episode; fly-leaf.

partition, *septum*, diaphragm, midriff; party-wall, panel, vail, bulkhead, brattice, *cloison*; half-way house.

V. lie –, come –, get- between; inter-

ambient; surrounding &c. *v.*; circumferential, surburban.

Adv. around, about; without; on -every side, – all sides; right and left, all round, round about; in the neighbourhood.

----

vene, slide in, interpenetrate, permeate.

put between, introduce, intromit, import; throw –, wedge –, edge –, jam –, worm –, foist –, run –, plough –, work- in; inter-pose, -ject, -calate, -polate, -line, -leave, -sperse, -weave, -lard, -digitate; let in, dovetail, splice, mortise; insinuate, smuggle; infiltrate, ingrain.

interfere, put in an oar, thrust one's nose in; intrude, obtrude; have a finger in the pie; introduce the thin end of the wedge; thrust in &c. (*insert*) 300.

Adj. inter-jacent, -current, -venient, -vening &c. *v.*, -mediate, -mediary, -calary, -stitial, -costal, -mural, -planetary, -stellar; embolismal.

parenthetical, episodic; mediterranean; intrusive; embosomed; merged, mean, middle, medium, median.

Adv. between, betwixt; 'twixt; among, -st; amid, -st; 'mid, -st; in the thick of; betwixt and between; sandwich-wise; parenthetically, *obiter dictum*.

229. Circumscription.—N. circumscription, limitation, inclosure; confinement &c. (*restraint*) 751; circumvallation, encincture; envelope &c. 232.

V. circumscribe, limit, bound, confine, enclose; surround &c. 227; compass about; imprison &c. (*restrain*) 751; hedge –, wall –, rail- in; fence –, hedge- round; embar; picket, corral.

enfold, bury, incase, pack up, enshrine, inclasp; wrap up &c. (*invest*) 225; embosom.

Adj. circumscribed &c. *v.*; begirt, lapt; circumambient; buried –, immersed- in; embosomed, in the bosom of, imbedded, encysted, mewed up; imprisoned &c. 751; land-locked, in a ring fence.

230. Outline.—N. outline, circumference; peri-meter, -phery; ambit, circuit, lines, *tournure, contour*, profile, *silhouette*, lineaments; bounds, coastline.

zone, belt, girth, band, baldric, zodiac, girdle, tire, cingle, clasp, girt; *cordon* &c. (*inclosure*) 232; circlet &c. 247.

V. outline, delineate, *silhouette*, circumscribe &c. 229; profile, block out.

Adj. outlined &c. *v.*; circumferential, perimetric, peripheral.

231. Edge.—N. edge, verge, brink, brow, brim, margin, border, confines, skirt, rim, felloe, felly, flange, side, mouth; jaws, chops, chaps, *fauces*; lip, muzzle.

threshold, door, porch; portal &c. (*opening*) 260; coast, shore, strand, beach, bank, wharf, quay, dock.

frame, fringe, flounce, frill, list, trimming, edging, skirting, hem, selvedge, welt; furbelow, valance, exergue.

Adj. border, marginal, skirting; labial, labiated, marginated.

232. Inclosure.—N. inclosure, enclosure, envelope; case &c. (*receptacle*) 191; wrapper; girdle &c. 230.

pen, fold, croft, sty; pen-, in-, sheep-fold; paddock, pound, corral, kraal; yard, compound; net, seine net.

wall; hedge, -row; *espalier*; fence &c. (*defence*) 717; pale, paling, balustrade, rail, railing, gunwale; quickset hedge, park paling, circumvallation, *enceinte*, ring fence.

barrier, barricade; gate, -way; door, hatch, *cordon*; prison &c. 752.

dike, dyke, ditch, fosse, moat, trench.

V. inclose; circumscribe &c. 229.

233. Limit.—N. limit, boundary, bounds, confine, *enclave*, term, bourn, verge, kerb-stone, curbstone, but, pale; termin-ation, -us; stint, frontier, precinct, marches.

boundary line, landmark; line of -demarcation, – circumvallation; pillars of Hercules; Rubicon, turning-point; *ne plus ultra*; sluice, flood-gate.

V. limit, bound, confine, define, circumscribe, demarcate, delimit, encompass.

Adj. definite; contermin-ate, -able, terminable, limitable; terminal, frontier, border, bordering, boundary.

Adv. thus far, – and no further.

2. *Special*

234. Front.—N. front; fore, – part; foreground; forefront, face, disk, disc, frontage, *façade*, *proscenium*, facia, frontispiece; priority, anteriority; obverse [of a medal].

fore –, front- rank, first line; van, -guard; advanced guard; outpost, scout.

brow, forehead, visage, physiognomy, phiz, features, countenance, map, mug; rostrum, beak, bow, stem, prow, prore, jib, bowsprit; forecastle.

pioneer &c. (*precursor*) 64; metoposcopy.

V. be –, stand- in front &c. *adj.*; front, face, confront, breast, brave; bend forwards; come to the -front, – fore.

Adj. fore, forward, anterior, front, frontal.

Adv. before; in -front, – the van, – advance; ahead, right ahead; fore-, head-most; in the foreground; before one's -face, – eyes; face to face, *vis-à-vis*.

236. Laterality.—N. laterality; side, flank, beam, quarter, lee; hand; cheek, jowl, jole, wing; profile; temple, *parietes*, loin, haunch, hip.

gable, -end; broadside; lee side.

points of the compass; East, Orient, Levant; West, occident; orientation.

V. be -on one side &c. *adv.*; flank, outflank; sidle; skirt, border.

Adj. lateral, sidelong; collateral;

235. Rear.—N. rear, back, posteriority; rear -rank, – guard; background, *hinterland*.

occiput, nape, scruff, chine; heels; tail, rump, croup, buttock, posteriors, bottom, seat, backside, scut, breech, *dorsum*, loin; dorsal –, lumbar- region; hind quarters.

stern, poop, after-part, counter; postern, heel-, tail-piece, crupper.

wake; train &c. (*sequence*) 281.

reverse; other side of the shield.

V. be -behind &c. *adv.*; fall astern; bend backwards; bring up the rear; follow &c. 622; tail, shadow.

Adj. back, rear; hind, -er, -most, -ermost; post-ern, -erior; dorsal, after; caudal, lumbar; mizzen.

Adv. behind; in the -rear, – ruck, – back-ground; behind one's back; at the -heels, – tail, – back- of; back to back.

after, -most, aft, abaft, astern, sternmost, aback, rear-, hind-, back-ward.

---

237. Contraposition.—N. contraposition, opposition; polarity; inversion &c. 218; opposite side; antithesis; reverse, inverse; counterpart; antipodes; opposite poles, North and South.

V. be -opposite &c. *adj.*; subtend.

Adj. opposite; reverse, inverse; antipodal, subcontrary; fronting, facing, diametrically opposite.

Northern, Septentrional, Boreal, arc-

parietal, flanking, skirting; flanked; sideling.

many-sided; multi-, bi-, tri-, quadri-lateral.

East-ern, -ward, -erly; orient, -al, auroral, Levantine; West-ern, -ward, -erly; occidental, Hesperian; equatorial.

Adv. side-ways, -long; broadside on; on one side, abreast, abeam, alongside, beside, aside; by, – the side of; side by side; cheek by jowl &c. (*near*) 197; to -windward, – leeward; laterally &c. *adj.*; right and left; on her beam ends.

238. Dextrality. — N. dextrality; right, – hand; dexter, offside, starboard.

Adj. dextral, right-handed; ambidextral, dexterous, dextrorsal &c.

tic; Southern, Austral, antarctic, polar.

Adv. over, – the way, – against; against; face to face, *vis-à-vis*; as poles asunder.

---

239. Sinistrality.—N. sinistrality; left, – hand; *sinister*, nearside, larboard, port.

Adj. sinistral, sinister, sinistrorsal &c., left-handed, sinistromanual, sinistrous.

Section III. FORM

1°. General Form

240. Form.—N. form, figure, shape; con-formation, -figuration; make, formation, frame, construction, design, cut, set, build, trim, cut of one's jib; stamp, type, cast, mould; fashion; contour &c. (*outline*) 230; structure &c. 329.

feature, lineament, outline, turn; phase &c. (*aspect*) 448; posture, attitude, *pose.*

[Science of form] morphology.

[Similarity of form] isomorphism.

forming &c. *v.*; form-, figur-, efformation; sculpture.

V. form, shape, figure, fashion, efform, carve, cut, chisel, hew, cast; rough-hew, -cast; sketch; block –, hammer- out; trim; lick –, put- into shape; model, knead, work up into, set, mould, sculpture; cast, stamp; built &c. (*construct*) 161.

Adj. formed &c. *v.*

[Receiving form] plastic, fictile, full-fashioned &c.

[Giving form] plasmic &c.

[Similar in form] isomorphous &c.

241. [Absence of form.] Amorphism. —N. amorphism, informity, uncouthness; unlicked cub, rough diamond; *rudis indigestaque moles*; disorder &c. 59; deformity &c. 243.

disfigure-, deface-ment, deformation; mutilation.

V. [Destroy form] deface, disfigure, deform, mutilate, truncate; derange &c. 61.

Adj. shapeless, amorphous, malformed, formless; un-formed, -hewn, -fashioned, -shapen; rough, rude, Gothic, barbarous, rugged, in the rough; misshapen &c. 243.

---

242. [Regularity of form.] Symmetry. —N. symmetry, shapeliness, finish; beauty &c. 845; proportion, eurythmy, eurythmic, uniformity, parallelism; bi-, tri-, multi-lateral symmetry; centrality &c. 222.

243. [Irregularity of form.] Distortion.—N. dis-, de-, con-tortion; knot, mop, warp, buckle, screw, twist; crookedness &c. (*obliquity*) 217; grimace; deformity; mal-, malcon-formation; monstrosity, misproportion, want

arborescence, branching, ramification.

Adj. symmetrical, shapely, well set, finished; beautiful &c. 845; classic, chaste, severe.

regular, uniform, balanced; equal &c. 27; parallel, coextensive.

arbor-escent, -iform; dendr-iform, -oid; branching; ramous, ramose.

of symmetry, *anamorphosis*; ugliness &c. 846; teratology.

V. distort, contort, twist, warp &c. *n.*; wrest, writhe, make faces, deform, misshape.

Adj. distorted &c. *v.*; out of shape, irregular, unsymmetric, awry, wry, askew, crooked, sinuous; anamorphous; not -true, – straight; on one side, crump, deformed; mis-shapen, -begotten; mis-, ill-proportioned; ill-made; grotesque, crooked as a ram's horn; hump-, hunch-, bunch-, crook-backed; bandy; bandy-, bow-legged; bow-, knock-kneed; splay-, club-footed; taliped; round-shouldered; snub-nosed; curtailed of one's fair proportions; scalene, stumpy &c. (*short*) 201; gaunt &c. (*thin*) 203; bloated &c. 194.

Adv. all manner of ways.

2°. SPECIAL FORM

244. Angularity.—N. angular-ity, -ness; aduncity; angle, cusp, bend; fold &c. 258; notch &c. 257; fork, bifurcation.

elbow, knee, knuckle, ankle, groin, crotch, crutch, crane, fluke, scythe, sickle, zigzag, kimbo.

corner, nook, recess, niche, oriel.

right angle &c. (*perpendicular*) 212; obliquity &c. 217; angle of 45°, mitre; acute –, obtuse –, salient –, re-entrant –, spherical –, solid –, dihedral- angle.

angular -measurement, – elevation, – distance, – velocity; trigon-, goni-ometry; altimetry; clin-, graph-, goni-ometer; theodolite; transit circle; sextant, quadrant; dichotomy.

triangle, trigon, wedge; rectangle, square, lozenge, diamond; rhomb, -us; quadr-angle, -ilateral; parallelogram; quadrature; poly-, penta-, hexa-, hepta-, octa-, deca-gon.

Platonic bodies; cube, rhomboid; tetra-, penta-, hexa-, octa-, dodeca-, icosa-hedron; prism, pyramid; parallelopiped.

V. bend, fork, bifurcate, crinkle, divaricate, branch, ramify.

Adj. angular, bent, crooked, aduncous, uncinated, aquiline, jagged, serrated; falc-iform, -ated; furcular, furcated, forked, bifurcate, crotched; zigzag; dovetailed; knock-kneed, crinkled, akimbo, kimbo, geniculated; oblique &c. 217.

fusiform, wedge-shaped, cuneiform; tri-angular, -gonal, -lateral; quadr-angular, -ilateral; rectangular, square, foursquare, multilateral; polygonal &c. *n.*; cubical, rhomboidal, pyramidal.

245. Curvature.—N. curv-ature, -ity, -ation; incurv-ity, -ation; bend; flex-ure, -ion; conflexure; crook, hook, bought, bending; de-, inflexion; arcuation, devexity, turn; deviation, *détour*, sweep; curl, -ing; bough; recurv-ity, -ation; sinuosity &c. 248; aduncity.

curve, arc, arch, arcade, vault, dome, bow, crescent, *meniscus*, half-moon, lunule, horse-shoe, loop, crane-neck;

246. Straightness.—N. straightness, rectilinearity, directness; inflexibility &c. (*stiffness*) 323; straight –, right –, direct-, bee- line; short cut.

V. be -straight &c. *adj.*; have no turning; not -incline, – bend, – turn, – deviate- to either side; go straight; steer for &c. (*direction*) 278.

render straight, straighten, rectify; set –, put- straight; un-bend, -fold,

para-, hyper-bola; catenary, festoon; conch-, cardi-oid; caustic, instep; tracery.

V. be -curved &c. *adj.*; sweep, swag, sag; deviate &c. 279; turn; re-enter.

render -curved &c. *adj.*; bend, curve, incurvate; de-, in-flect; crook; turn, round, arch, arcuate, arch over, loop the loop, concamerate; bow, coil, curl, recurve, frizzle.

Adj. curved &c. *v.*; curvi-form, -lineal, -linear; devex, devious; recurv-ed, -ous; *retroussé*; crump; bowed &c. *v.*; vaulted; hooked; falc-iform, -ated; semicircular, crescentic; lun-iform, -ular; semi-lunar, meniscal; conchoidal; cord-iform, -ated; cardioid; heart-, bell-, pear-, fig-shaped; reniform; lenti-form, -cular; bow-legged &c. (*distorted*) 243; oblique &c. 217; circular &c. 247.

-curl &c. 248, -ravel &c. 219, -wrap.

Adj. straight; rectiline-ar, -al; direct, even, right, true, in a line; unbent &c. *v.*; un-deviating, -turned, -distorted, -swerving; straight as an arrow &c. (*direct*) 278; inflexible &c. 323.

---

247. [Simple circularity.] **Circularity.** —**N.** circularity, roundness; rotundity &c. 249.

circle, circlet, ring, washer, areola, hoop, roundlet, *annulus*, annulet, bracelet, armlet, armilla; ringlet; eye, loop, wheel; cycle, orb, orbit, rundle, zone, belt, *cordon*, band; sash, girdle, cestus, cincture, baldric, fillet, *fascia*, wreath, garland; crown, corona, coronet, chaplet, snood, necklace, collar; noose, lasso, lariat.

ellipse, oval, ovule; ellipsoid, cycloid; epi-cycloid, -cycle; semi-circle; quadrant, sextant, sector.

V. make -round &c. *adj.*; round.

go round; encircle &c. 227; describe -a circle &c. 311.

Adj. round, rounded, circular, annular, orbicular; oval, ovate; elliptic, -al; ovoid, egg-shaped; pear-shaped &c. 245; cycloidal &c. *n.*; spherical &c. 249.

---

248. [Complex circularity.] **Convolution.**—**N.** winding &c. *v.*; con-, in-, circum-volution; wave, undulation, tortuosity, anfractuosity; sinu-osity, -ation, sinuousness; meandering, circuit, circumbendibus, twist, twirl, windings and turnings, *ambages*; torsion; inosculation; reticulation &c. (*crossing*) 219.

coil, roll, curl, buckle, spire, spiral, helix, corkscrew, worm, volute, whorl, rundle; tendril; scollop, scallop, escalop; kink.

serpent, snake, eel, maze, labyrinth.

V. be -convoluted &c. *adj.*; wind, twine, turn and twist, twirl; wave, undulate, meander; inosculate; entwine, intwine; twist, coil, roll; wrinkle, curl, crisp, twill; frizz, -le; crimp, crape, indent, scollop, scallop; wring, intort; contort; wreathe &c. (*cross*) 219.

Adj. convoluted; winding, twisted &c. *v.*; tortile, tortive; wavy; und-ated, -ulatory; circling, snaky, snake-like, serpentine; serpent-, anguill-, verm-iform; vermicular; mazy, tortu-ous, anfractuous, sinuous, flexuous, wavy, sigmoidal.

involved, intricate, complicated, perplexed; labyrinth-ic, -ian, -ine; circuitous; peristaltic; dædalian, curly.

wreathy, frizzly, *crêpé*, buckled; ravelled &c. (*in disorder*) 59.

spiral, coiled, helical, turbinated.

Adv. in and out, round and round.

---

249. Rotundity.—**N.** rotundity; roundness &c. *adj.*; cylindricity; spher-icity, -oidity; globosity.

cylin-der, -droid; barrel, drum; roll, -er; *rouleau*, column, rolling-pin, rundle; chimney-pot, drain-pipe.

cone, conoid; pear-, egg-, bell-shape.

sphere, globe, ball, boulder, bowlder; spher-, ellips-, ge-, glob-oid; oblong –, oblate- spheroid; drop, spherule, globule, vesicle, bulb, bullet, pellet, *pelote,* clew, pill, marble, pea, knob, pommel, knot.

V. render -spherical &c. *adj.*; form into a sphere, sphere, roll into a ball; give -rotundity &c. *n.*; round.

Adj. rotund; round &c. *(circular)* 247; cylindr-ic, -ical, -oid; columnar, lumbriciform; conic, -al; spher-ical, -oidal; glob-ular, -ated, -ous, -ose; egg-, bell-, pear-shaped; ov-oid, -iform; gibbous; campaniform, -ulate, -iliform; fungiform, bead-like, moniliform, pyriform, bulbous; *teres atque rotundus*; round as -an orange, – an apple, – a ball, – a billiard ball, – a cannon ball.

3°. SUPERFICIAL FORM

250. Convexity. — N. convexity, prominence, projection, swelling, gibbosity, bilge, bulge, protuberance, protrusion; excrescency, camber.

intumescence; tumour, tumor; tubercle, -osity; excrescence; hump, hunch, bunch, gnarl.

tooth, knob, elbow, process, *apophysis,* condyle, bulb, node, nodule, nodosity, tongue, *dorsum,* boss, embossment, bump, clump; sugar-loaf &c. *(sharpness)* 253; bow; mamelon.

pimple, wen, wheal, *papula,* postule, pock, proud flesh, growth, goitre, *sarcoma,* caruncle, corn, bunion, wart, furnuncle, polypus, adenoid, fungus, fungosity, *exostosis,* bleb, blister, blain; boil &c. *(disease)* 655; bubble, blob.

papilla, nipple, teat, pap, breast, dug, mammilla; proboscis, nose, neb, beak, snout, nozzle, snozzle; Adam's apple; belly, paunch, corporation; withers, back, shoulder, lip, flange.

peg, button, stud, ridge, rib, jutty, trunnion, snag.

cupola, dome, bee-hive; arch, balcony, eaves; pilaster.

relief, relievo, *cameo; basso-, mezzo-, alto-rilievo;* low-, bas-, high-relief.

hill &c. *(height)* 206; cape, promontory, mull; fore-, head-land; point of land, naze, ness, mole, jetty, hummock, ledge, spur.

V. be -prominent &c. *adj.*; project, bulge, protrude, bag, belly, pout, bouge, bunch; jut –, stand –, stick –, poke- out; stick –, bristle –, start –, cock –, shoot- up; swell –, hang –, bend- over; beetle.

render -prominent &c. *adj.*; raise 307; emboss, chase.

251. Flatness.—N. flatness &c. *adj.*; smoothness &c. 255.

plane; level &c. 213; plate, platter, table, tablet, slab.

V. render flat, flatten, squash; level &c. 213.

Adj. flat, plane, even, flush, scutiform, discoid; level &c. *(horizontal)* 213; smooth; flat as -a pancake, – a fluke, – a flounder, – a board, – my hand.

252. Concavity.—N. concavity, depression, dip; hollow, -ness; indentation, *intaglio,* cavity, antrum, dent, dint, dimple, follicle, pit, *sinus, alveolus, lacuna;* excavation, trench, sap, mine, tunnel, burrow; trough &c. *(furrow)* 259; honeycomb.

cup, basin, crater, punch-bowl; cell &c. *(receptacle)* 191; socket, faucet.

valley, vale, dale, dell, gap, dingle, combe, bottom, slade, strath, glade, grove, glen, cave, cavern, cove; grot, -to; alcove, *cul-de-sac,* blind alley; gully &c. 198; arch &c. *(curve)* 245; bay &c. *(of the sea)* 343.

excavator, sapper, miner.

V. be -concave &c. *adj.*; retire, cave in.

render -concave &c. *adj.*; depress, hollow; scoop, – out; gouge, dig, delve, excavate, dent, dint, mine, sap, undermine, burrow, tunnel, stave in.

Adj. depressed &c. *v.*; concave, hollow, stove in; dished; spoon-like; retiring; retreating; cavernous; porous &c. *(with holes)* 260; cellular, spongy, spongious; honeycombed, alveolar; infundibul-ar, -iform; funnel-, bell-shaped; campaniform, capsular; vaulted, arched.

Adj. convex, prominent, protuberant, underhung, undershot; projecting &c. *v.*; bossed, bossy, nodular, bunchy; clav-ate, -ated; hummocky, *moutonné*, mammiform; papul-ous, -ose; hemispheric, bulbous; bowed, arched; bold; bellied; tuber-ous, -culous; tumorous; cornute, knobby, odontoid; lenti-form, -cular; gibbous.

salient, in relief, raised, *repoussé*; bloated &c. (*expanded*) 194.

---

253. Sharpness.—N. sharpness &c. *adj.*; acuity, acumination; spinosity.

point, spike, spine, *spiculum*, tine; needle, pin; tack, nail; prick, -le; spur, rowel, barb; spit, cusp; horn, antler; snag; tag; thorn, bristle.

nib, tooth, incisor, tusk; spoke, cog, ratchet.

crag, crest, *arête*, cone, peak, sugar-loaf, pike, *aiguille*; spire, pyramid, steeple.

beard, *chevaux de frise*, porcupine, hedgehog, brier, bramble, thistle; comb, awn, bur.

wedge; knife-, cutting- edge; blade, edge-tool, cutlery, knife, penknife, whittle, razor; scalpel, bistoury, lancet; chisel; ploughshare, coulter; hatchet, axe, pick-axe, mattock, pick, adze, bill; bill-hook, cleaver, cutter; skiver; scythe, sickle, scissors, shears; sword &c. (*arms*) 727; bodkin &c. (*perforator*) 262.

sharpener, hone, strop; grind-, whet-stone; steel, emery.

V. be -sharp &c. *adj.*; taper to a point; bristle with.

render -sharp &c. *adj.*; sharpen, point, aculeate, acuminate, whet, barb, spiculate, set, strop, grind.

cut &c. (*sunder*) 44.

Adj. sharp, keen; acute; aci-cular, -form; acu-leated, -minated; pointed; tapering; conical, pyramidal; mucron-ate, -ated; spindle-, needle-shaped; spiked, spiky, ensiform, peaked, salient, cusp-ed; -idate, -idated; corn-ute, -uted, -iculate; prickly; spiny, spinous; thorny, bristling, muricated, pectinated, studded, thistly, briery; craggy &c. (*rough*) 256; snaggy; digitated, two-edged, fusiform; denti-form, -culated; toothed; odontoid; star-like; stell-ated, -iform; arrow-headed; arrowy, barbed, spurred, sagittal; spear-shaped, hastate; horned; conical.

cutting; sharp-, knife-edged; sharp -, keen- as a razor; sharp as a needle; sharpened &c. *v.*; set.

254. Bluntness.—N. bluntness &c. *adj.*

V. be -, render- blunt &c. *adj.*; obtund, dull; take off the -point, - edge; turn.

Adj. blunt, obtuse, dull, bluff.

---

255. Smoothness.—N. smoothness &c. *adj.*; polish, gloss; lubric-ity, -ation.

down, velvet, silk, satin; slide; bowling green &c. (*level*) 213; glass, ice; asphalt, pavement, flags.

roller, steam-roller; iron, flat-iron, tailor's goose; sand-, emery-paper; burnisher, turpentine and bees-wax.

V. smooth, -en; plane; file; mow, shave; level, roll; macadamize; polish, burnish, planish, levigate, calender, glaze; iron, hot-press, mangle; lubricate &c. (*oil*) 332.

256. Roughness.—N. roughness &c. *adj.*; tooth, grain, texture, ripple; asperity, rugosity, salebrosity, corrugation, nodosity; arborescence &c. 242.

brush, hair, beard, shag, mane, whisker, mutton-chops, *moustache*, *mustachio*, imperial, Van Dyke, tress, lock, curl, ringlet, *fimbriæ*, *cilia*, *villi*; eyelashes, eye-brows, love-lock.

plum-age, -osity; plume, *panache*, crest; feather, tuft, tussock, fringe, toupee.

wool, velvet, plush, nap, pile, floss,

Adj. smooth; polished &c. *v.*; even; level &c. 213; plane &c. (*flat*) 251; sleek, glossy; silken, silky; lanate, downy, velvety; glabrous, slippery, glassy, lubricous, oily, soft; unwrinkled; smooth as -glass, – ice, – velvet, – oil; slippery as an eel; woolly &c. (*feathery*) 256.

fluff, fur, down; byssus, moss, bur.

V. be -rough &c. *adj.*; go against the grain.

render -rough &c. *adj.*; roughen, rough cast, knurl; ruffle, crisp, crumple, crinkle, corrugate, engrail; set on edge, stroke –, rub- the wrong way, rumple.

Adj. rough, uneven; scabrous, knotted; nodular; rug-ged, -ose, -ous; asperous, crisp, salebrous, gnarled, unpolished, unsmooth, rough-hewn; knurled, cross-grained, crag-gy, -ged; crankling, scraggy, jagged, unkempt, prickly &c. (*sharp*) 253; arborescent &c. 242; leafy, well-wooded; feathery; plum-ose, -igerous; tufted, fimbriated, hairy, bristly, ciliated, filamentous, hirsute; crin-ose, -ite; bushy, hispid, villous, pappous, bearded, pilous, shaggy, shagged; fringed, befringed; set-ous, -ose, -aceous; 'like quills upon the fretful porcupine'; rough as a -nutmeg grater, – bear.

downy, velvety, flocculent, woolly; lan-ate, -ated; lanugin-ous. -ose; tomentous.

Adv. against the grain, in the rough, on edge.

257. Notch.—N. notch, dent, nick, cut; indent, -ation; serration; dimple.

embrasure, battlement, machicolation; saw, tooth, crenelle, scallop, scollop, vandyke.

V. notch, nick, cut, pink, mill, score, dent, indent, jag, scarify, scotch, crimp, scollop, crenulate, vandyke.

Adj. notched &c. *v.*; crenate, -d; dentate, -d; denticulate, -d; toothed, palmated, serrated.

258. Fold.—N. fold, plicature, pleat, plait, ply, crease; tuck, gather; flexion, flexure, joint, elbow, doubling, duplicature, wrinkle, rimple, crinkle, crankle, crumple, rumple, rivel, ruck, ruffle, dog's ear, corrugation, frounce, flounce, lapel; pucker, crow's feet.

V. fold, double, plicate, pleat, plait, crease, wrinkle, crinkle, crankle, curl, smock, cockle up, crocker, rimple, rumple, frizzle, frounce, rivel, twill, corrugate, ruffle, crimple, crumple, pucker; turn –, double- -down, – under; tuck, ruck, hem, gather.

Adj. folded &c. *v.*

259. Furrow.—N. furrow, groove, rut, *sulcus*, scratch, streak, *striæ*, crack, score, incision, slit; chamfer, fluting.

channel, gutter, trench, ditch, dike, dyke, moat, fosse, trough, kennel; ravine &c. (*interval*) 198.

V. furrow &c. *n.*; flute, groove, carve, corrugate, plough; incise, chase, enchase, grave, engrave, etch, bite in, cross-hatch.

Adj. furrowed &c. *v.*; ribbed, striated, sulcated, fluted, canaliculated; bisulc-ous, -ate; trisulcate; corduroy.

260. Opening.—N. hole, foramen; puncture, blow-out, perforation; pin-, key-, loop-, port-, peep-, mouse-, pigeon-hole; eye, – of a needle; eyelet; slot.

opening; apert-ure, -ness; hiation,

261. Closure.—N. closure, occlusion. blockade; shutting up &c. *v.*; obstruction &c. (*hindrance*) 706; gag; embolism; contraction &c. 195; infarction; con-, ob-stipation; blind -alley, – corner; *cul-de-sac*, *cæcum*; imper-foration,

yawning, oscitancy, dehiscence, patefaction, pandiculation; gap, chasm &c. (*interval*) 198.

embrasure, window, casement, light; sky-, fan-light; lattice; bay-, bow-window; oriel; dormer, lantern.

out-, in-let; vent, vomitory; *embouchure*; orifice, mouth, sucker, muzzle, throat, gullet, placket, weasand, wizen, nozzle, *æsophagus*.

portal, porch, gate, ostiary, postern, wicket, trap-door, hatch, door; arcade; gate-, door-, hatch-, gang-way; lych-gate.

way, path &c. 627; thoroughfare; channel, passage, tube, pipe; water-pipe &c. 350; air-pipe &c. 351; vessel, tubule, canal, gut, fistula; adjutage, ajutage; chimney, smoke stack, flue, tap, funnel, gully, tunnel, main; mine, pit, adit, shaft; gallery.

alley, aisle, glade, lane, vista.

bore, calibre; pore; blind orifice.

por-ousness, -osity; sieve, cullender, colander; grater, shredder; cribble, riddle, screen; honeycomb.

apertion, perforation; piercing &c. *v.*; terebration, empalement, pertusion, puncture, acupuncture, penetration.

opener, key, master-key, *passe-partout*.

V. open, ope, gape, dehisce, yawn, bilge; fly open.

perforate, pierce, empierce, tap, bore, drill; mine &c. (*scoop out*) 252; tunnel; trans-pierce, -fix; enfilade, impale, spike, spear, gore, spit, stab, pink, puncture, lance, trepan, trephine, stick, prick, riddle, punch; stave in.

cut a passage through; make -way, – room- for.

un-cover, -close, -rip; lay –, cut –, rip –, throw- open.

Adj. open; perforated &c. *v.*; perforate; wide open, agape, ajar; un-closed, -stopped; oscitant, gaping, yawning; patent.

tubular, cannular, fistulous; per-vious, -meable; foraminous; vesi-, vas-cular; porous, follicular, cribriform, honeycombed, infundibular, riddled; tubul-ous, -ated, piped.

opening &c. *v.*; aperient.

Int. *open sesame!*

262. Perforator. — **N.** perforator, piercer, borer, auger, gimlet, stylet, drill, wimble, awl, bradawl, scoop, terrier, corkscrew, dibble, trocar, trepan, trephine, probe, bodkin, needle, stiletto, broach, reamer, rimer, warder, lancet; punch, -eon; spikebit, gouge; spear &c. (*weapon*) 727.

-viousness &c. *adj.*, -meability; stopper &c. 263; *operculum.*

V. close, occlude, plug; block –, stop –, fill –, bung –, cork –, button –, stuff –, shut –, dam- up, obturate; blockade; obstruct &c. (*hinder*) 706; bar, bolt, stop, seal, plumb; choke, throttle; ram down, tamp, dam, cram; trap, clinch; put to –, shut- the door; batten down the hatches.

Adj. closed &c. *v.*; shut, operculated; unopened.

unpierced, imporous, cæcal; imperforate, -vious, -meable; impenetrable; un-, im-passable; invious; path-, way-less; untrodden.

unventilated; air-, water-tight; hermetically sealed; tight, snug.

------

263. Stopper.—**N.** stopper, stopple; plug, cork, bung, spike, spill, stop-cock, tap; rammer; ram, -rod; piston; stop-gap; wadding, stuffing, padding, stopping, dossil, pledget, tompion, tourniquet, obturator; wad.

cover &c. 223; valve, slide valve; vent-peg, spigot.

janitor, door –, gate- keeper, porter, commissionaire, *concierge*, warder, beadle, Cerberus, usher, guard, sentry, sentinel; ostiary.

SECTION IV. MOTION

1°. MOTION IN GENERAL

264. [Successive change of place.*]
Motion.—**N.** motion, movement, move; motivity, motility, going &c. *v.*; unrest.

stream, current, flow, flux, run, course, stir; conduction, evolution; kinematics.

step, rate, pace, tread, stride, gait, clip, port, footfall, cadence, carriage, velocity, angular velocity; progress, locomotion; journey &c. 266; voyage &c. 267; transit &c. 270.

restlessness &c. (*changeableness*) 149; mobility; movableness, motive power; laws of motion; mobilization.

V. be -in motion &c. *adj.*; move, go, hie, gang, budge, stir, pass, flit; hover -round, – about; shift, slide, slither, glide; roll, – on; flow, stream, run, drift, sweep along; wander &c. (*deviate*) 279; walk &c. 266; change –, shift-one's -place, – quarters; dodge; keep -going, – moving.

put –, set- in motion; move; impel &c. 276; propel &c. 284; render movable, mobilize.

Adj. moving &c. *v.*;in motion;motile, transitional; motory, motive; shifting, movable, mobile, mercurial, unquiet; restless &c. (*changeable*) 149; nomadic &c. 266; erratic &c. 279.

Adv. under way; on the -move, – wing, – tramp, – march.

265. Quiescence.—**N.** rest; stillness &c. *adj.*; quiescence; stag-nation, -nancy; fixity, immobility, catalepsy; indisturbance; quietism.

quiet, tranquillity, calm; repose &c. 687; peace; dead calm, anticyclone; statue-like repose; silence &c. 403; not a -breath of air, – mouse stirring; sleep &c. (*inactivity*) 683.

pause, lull &c. (*cessation*) 142; stand, – still; standing still &c. *v.*; lock; dead -lock, – stop, – stand; full stop; fix; embargo.

resting-place; bivouac; home &c. (*abode*) 189; pillow &c. (*support*) 215; haven &c. (*refuge*) 666; goal &c. (*arrival*) 292.

V. be -quiescent &c. *adj.*; stand –, lie- still; keep quiet, repose, hold the breath.

remain, stay; stand, lie to, ride at anchor, remain *in situ*, mark time, tarry; bring –, heave –, lay- to; pull –, draw- up; hold, halt; stop, – short; rest, pause, anchor; cast –, come to an- anchor; rest on one's oars; repose on one's laurels, take breath; stop &c. (*discontinue*) 142.

stagnate, vegetate; *quieta non movere*; let -alone, – well alone; abide, rest and be thankful; keep within doors, stay at home, go to bed.

dwell &c. (*be present*) 186; settle &c. (*be located*) 184; alight &c. (*arrive*) 292.

stick, – fast; stand, – like a post; not stir a -peg, – step; be at a -stand &c. *n.*

quell, becalm, hush, stay, lull to sleep, lay an embargo on; put the brake on.

Adj. quiescent, still; motion-, move-less; fixed; stationary; at -rest, – a stand, – a stand-still, – anchor; stock-still; immotile; standing still &c. *v.*; sedentary, untravelled, stay-at-home; becalmed, stagnant, quiet; un-moved, -disturbed, -ruffled; calm, restful; cataleptic; immovable &c. (*stable*) 150; sleeping &c. (*inactive*) 683; silent &c. 403; still as -a statue, – a post, – a mouse, – death.

Adv. at a stand &c. *adj.*; *tout court*; at the halt.

Int. stop! stay! avast! halt! hold, – hard! whoa!

Phr. *requiescat in pace.*

---

* A thing cannot be said to *move* from one place to another, unless it passes in succession through every intermediate place; hence motion is only such a change of place as is *successive*. 'Rapid, swift, &c., as thought' are therefore incorrect expressions.

266. [Locomotion by land.] **Journey.**
—**N.** travel; travelling &c. *v.*; wayfaring, campaigning.

journey, excursion, expedition, tour, trip, grand tour, circuit, peregrination, discursion, ramble, pilgrimage, *trek*, course, ambulation, march, walk, hike, promenade, constitutional, stroll, saunter, tramp, jog-trot, turn, stalk, perambulation; noctambulation; somnambulism, sleep walking; outing, ride, drive, airing, jaunt.

equitation, horsemanship, riding, *manège*, ride and tie.

roving, vagrancy, pererration; marching and countermarching; nomadism; vagabond-ism, -age; gadding; flit, -ting; migration; e-, im-, de-, inter-migration.

plan, itinerary, guide; hand-, road-book; Baedeker, Murray, Bradshaw, time table.

procession, parade, cavalcade, caravan, file, *cortège*, column.

[Organs and instruments of locomotion] vehicle &c. 272; locomotive &c. 271; legs, feet, pegs, pins, trotters.

traveller &c. 268.

V. travel, journey, course; tour; take –, go- a journey; take –, go out for- -a walk &c. *n.*; have a run; take the air.

flit, take wing; migrate, emigrate, *trek*; rove, prowl, roam, range, patrol, pace up and down, traverse; scour –, traverse- the country; peragrate; per-, circum-ambulate; nomadize, wander, ramble, stroll, saunter, hover, go one's rounds, straggle; gad, – about; expatiate.

walk, march, step, tread, pace, plod, wend; promenade; trudge, tramp; stalk, stride, straddle, strut, foot it, stump, bundle, bowl along, toddle; paddle; tread –, follow –, pursue- a path.

267. [Locomotion by water, or air.] **Navigation.**—**N.** navigation; aquatics; boating, cruising, yachting; ship &c. 273; oar, scull, sweep, punt pole, paddle, – wheel, screw, propeller, stern wheel, sail, canvas.

natation, swimming; fin, flipper, fish's tail.

aerial navigation, air service, airways, airmanship, aero-donetics, -dynamics, -mechanics, -station, -statics, -nautics; ballooning, balloonry; balloon &c. 273; flying, flight, aviation, volitation; wing, pinion, *aileron*.

voyage, sail, cruise, passage, circumnavigation, *periplus*; head-, stern-, lee-way.

mariner, aeronaut &c. 269.

V. sail; put to sea &c. (*depart*) 293; take ship, get under way; spread -sail, – canvas; gather way, have way on; make –, carry- sail; plough the -waves, – deep, – main, – ocean; walk the waters.

navigate, warp, luff, scud, boom, kedge; drift, course, cruise, coast; hug the -shore, – land; circumnavigate.

ply the oar, row, paddle, pull, scull, punt, steam.

swim, float; buffet the waves, ride the storm, skim, *effleurer*, dive, wade.

fly, aviate, be wafted, hover, soar, drift, glide, plane, sideslip, *volplane*, pique, dive, spin, roll, loop, flutter; take -wing, – a flight; wing one's -flight, – way.

Adj. sailing &c. *v.*; seafaring, nautical, maritime, naval; sea-going, coasting; afloat; navigable, aquatic, natatory.

volitant, volant, aerostatic, aerial, aeronautic; alar, alate, pennate.

Adv. under -way, – sail, – canvas, – steam; on the wing.

---

take horse, ride, drive, trot, amble, canter, prance, fisk, frisk, *caracoler*; gallop &c. (*move quickly*) 274; motor, cycle, taxi; go by -car, – train, – tram, – bus, – plane.

peg –, jog –, wag –, shuffle- on; stir one's stumps; bend one's -steps, – course; make –, find –, wend –, pick –, thread –, plough- one's way; coast, slide, glide, skim, skate, ski; march in procession, file off, defile.

go –, repair –, resort –, hie –, betake oneself- to.

Adj. travelling &c. *v.*; ambulatory, itinerant, peripatetic, perambulatory, roving, rambling, gadding, discursive, vagrant, migratory, nomadic; circumforane-an, -ous; somnambular, nocti-, mundi-vagant; locomotive, automotive, self-moving.

way-faring, -worn; travel-stained.

Adv. on -foot, – horseback, – Shanks's mare; by the Marrowbone stage; *in transitu* &c. 270; *en route* &c. 282.

Int. come along!

268. Traveller.—N. traveller, wayfarer, voyager, itinerant, passenger.

tourist, excursionist, globe-trotter; explorer, adventurer, mountaineer, Alpine Club; peregrinator, wanderer, rover, straggler, rambler; bird of passage; gad-about, -ling; vagrant, scatterling, landloper, waifs and estrays, wastrel, stray; loafer; tramp, -er, hobo, beachcomber, vagabond, nomad, Bohemian, gipsy, Arab, Wandering Jew, Hadji, pilgrim, palmer; peripatetic; somnambulist, sleep walker, noctambulist; emigrant, fugitive, refugee, *émigré*.

runner, courier, King's messenger; Mercury, Iris, Ariel, comet.

pedestrian, walker, foot-passenger; cyclist; wheelman.

rider, horseman, equestrian, cavalier, jockey, rough rider, trainer, breaker, huntsman.

driver, coachman, whip, Jehu, charioteer, postilion, post-boy, carter, wagoner, drayman, truckman; cab-man, -driver; *voiturier*, *vetturino*, *condottiere*; engine-driver; stoker, fireman, guard, brakeman, conductor; chauffeur, automobilist, motorist, motor –, truck –, taxi- driver.

269. Mariner.—N. sailor, mariner, navigator, argonaut; sea-man, -farer. -faring man; yachtsman; tar, jack tar, salt, gob, sea-dog, shellback, able seaman, A.B.; man-of-war's man, bluejacket, marine, jolly; midshipman, middy, reefer; captain, commander, master mariner, skipper, mate; ship-, boat-, ferry-, water-, lighter-, barge-, longshore- man, hoveller; bargee, gondolier; oar-, -sman; rower; boat-, cock-swain; coxswain; steersman, helmsman, pilot; crew; lascar.

aerial navigator, aeronaut, balloonist, Icarus, aviator, pilot, observer, flyer, airman.

270. Transference.—N. transfer, -ence; trans-, e-location; displacement; *meta-stasis*, *-thesis*; removal; re-, a-motion; relegation; de-, as-portation; extradition, conveyance, draft; carrying, carriage; convection, -duction, -tagion, infection; transfusion; transfer &c. (*of property*) 783.

transit, transition; passage, ferry, gestation; portage, porterage, carting, cartage; shovelling &c. *v.*; vect-ion, -ure, -itation; shipment, freight, wafture; trans-mission, -port, -portation, -umption, -plantation, -lation; shift-, dodg-ing; dispersion &c. 73; transposition &c. (*interchange*) 148; traction &c. 285.

[Thing transferred] drift, alluvium, detritus, *moraine*; gift, legacy, bequest, lease; freight, mails, cargo, luggage, baggage, goods.

V. trans-fer, -mit, -port, -place, -plant; convey, assign, carry, bear, fetch and carry; carry –, ferry- over; hand, pass, forward; shift; conduct, convoy, bring, fetch, reach.

send, delegate, consign, mail, post, relegate, turn over to, pass the buck, deliver; ship, embark; waft; switch, shunt; transpose &c. (*interchange*) 148; displace &c. 185; throw &c. 284; drag &c. 285.

shovel, lade, dip, ladle, bale, decant, draft off, transfuse.

Adj. transferred &c. *v.*; drifted; movable; port-able, -ative; conductive; contagious, infectious.

transferable, assignable, conveyable, devisable, negotiable, transmissible.

Adv. from -hand to hand, – pillar to post.

on –, by- the way; on the -road, – wing; as one goes; *in transitu, en route, chemin faisant, en passant,* in mid-progress.

271. Carrier.—N. carrier, porter, red cap, bearer, messenger, postman, tranter, conveyer; stevedore; coolie; conductor, locomotive, tractor, caterpillar tractor, motor.

beast of burden, cattle, horse, steed, nag, palfrey, Arab, blood horse, thorough-bred, galloway, charger, courser, racer, hunter, jument, pony, filly, colt, foal, barb, roan, jade, hack, *bidet,* pad, cob, tit, punch, roadster, goer; race-, pack-, draft-, cart-, dray-, post-horse, mount; Shetland pony, sheltie; garran; jennet, genet, bayard, mare, stallion, gelding; stud.

Pegasus, Bucephalus, Rozinante.

ass, donkey, jackass, mule, hinny; sumpter -horse, – mule; reindeer; camel, dromedary, mehari, llama, elephant; carrier pigeon.

carriage &c. (*vehicle*) 272; ship &c. 273.

Adj. equine, asinine.

272. Vehicle.—N. vehicle, conveyance, carriage, car, caravan, van, furniture van, pantechnicon; wagon, wain, dray, cart, lorry.

carriole; sledge, sled, sleigh, bobsleigh, toboggan, *luge,* truck, tram; limber, tumbrel, pontoon; barrow; wheel-, hand- -barrow, – cart, trolley; perambulator; Bath –, wheel –, sedan-chair, jinriksha, rickshaw; ekka; chaise; palan-keen, -quin; litter, horse-litter, brancard, crate, hurdle, stretcher, ambulance; velocipede, hobby-horse, coaster, scooter, go-cart; cycle; bi-, tri-, quadri-cycle; tandem, safety; skate, roller skate; ski, snow-shoe.

equipage, turn-out; coach, chariot, *quadriga,* chaise, phaëton, break, brake, mail-phaëton, wagonette, drag, curricle, tilbury, whisky, landau, *barouche,* victoria, brougham, clarence, calash, *calèche,* britzska, *araba,* kibitka; berlin; sulky, *désobligeant,* sociable, *vis-à-vis, dormeuse;* jaunting –, outside- car; *tarantass;* runabout; shay.

post-chaise; diligence, stage; stage –, mail –, hackney –, glass- coach; stage-wagon; car, omnibus, bus, fly, *cabriolet,* cab, hansom, shofle, four-wheeler, growler, *droshki,* drosky.

dog-cart, trap, gig, whitechapel, buggy, four-in-hand, unicorn, random, tandem; shandredhan, *char-à-banc.*

automobile, motor-, auto-, touring-, racing-, cycle-, side-, steam-, electric-

273. Ship.—N. ship, vessel, sail; craft, bottom.

navy, marine, fleet, flotilla, squadron; shipping.

man of war &c. (*combatant*) 726; transport, tender, store-ship; merchant ship, merchantman; packet, liner; whaler, slaver, collier, coaster, tanker, freighter, freight steamer, cargo boat, lighter; fishing-, pilot- boat; trawler, drifter; cable ship; hulk; yacht; floating palace, ocean greyhound.

ship, bark, barque, brig, snow, hermaphrodite brig; brigantine, barquentine; schooner; topsail –, fore and aft –, three masted- schooner; *chasse-marée;* sloop, cutter, corvette, clipper, foist, yawl, dandy, ketch, smack, lugger, barge, hoy, cat-, -boat, buss; sail-er, -ing vessel, wind jammer; steam-er, -boat, -ship; mail –, paddle –, screw –, sternwheel- steamer; tug; train-ferry; line of steamers &c.

boat, pinnace, launch, motor-boat, picket-boat; hydroplane; life-, long-, jolly-, bum-, fly-, cock-, ferry-, canal-boat, dory, dugout, galliot; shallop, gig, funny, skiff, dingy, scow, cockle-shell, wherry, coble, punt, cog, lerret; eight-, four-, pair- oar; randan; outrigger; float, raft, pontoon; prame, ice-yacht.

state barge, bucentaur.

catamaran, coracle, gondola, carvel, caravel; felucca, caique, canoe; trireme;

car; motor-, -omnibus, – bus, – cab, – cycle; limousine, landaulette, cabriolet, *coupé*, *voiturette*, runabout, electromobile, taxi, -cab.

train; passenger –, express –, freight –, subway –, special –, corridor –, parliamentary –, luggage –, goods-train, *train de luxe*; 1st-, 2nd-, 3rd-class--train, – carriage, – compartment; Pullman –, sleeping-, club-, observation-, dining-, restaurant-car; mail-, luggage-, brake-van, coach, car, carriage; rolling stock; horse-box, cattle-truck.

tramcar, trolley-omnibus, trackless trolley.

shovel, spoon, spatula, ladle, hod, hoe; spade, spaddle, loy; spud; pitchfork.

Adj. vehicular.

---

galley, – foist; bilander, dogger, hooker, howker; argosy, carack; galliass, galleon; galliot, polacca, polacre, corsair, tartane, junk, lorcha, praam, proa, prahu, saick, sampan, xebec, dhow; dahabeah; nuggar, cayak, piroque; trireme.

submarine, submersible.

aircraft (*combatant*) &c. 726; flying machine, air mail, aero-, air-, mono-, bi-, tri-, hydro aero-plane, plane, cabin plane, transport plane, *avion*, flying boat, glider, *aviette*, helicopter; balloon, air-, fire-, gas-, Mongolfier-, pilot-, captive-, free-, kite-, dirigible- balloon, air-ship, *Zeppelin*, blimp; kite, parachute.

nacelle, car, gondola, aileron; hangar, airport, landing field, airdrome; catwalk, controls, rudder, tail.

Adj. marine, maritime, naval, nautical, seafaring, sea-, ocean-going, seaworthy.

aerial, aeronautical, air-worthy, flying &c. *n.*

Adv. afloat, aboard; on -board, – ship board, – board ship.

2°. Degrees of Motion

274. Velocity.—N. velocity, speed, celerity; swiftness &c. *adj.*; rapidity, eagle speed; expedition &c. (*activity*) 682; pernicity; acceleration; haste &c. 684.

spurt, rush, dash, race, steeplechase; smart –, lively –, swift &c. *adj.* –, rattling –, spanking –, strapping- -rate, – pace; round pace; flying, flight.

gallop, canter, trot, round trot, run, scamper; hand –, full- gallop; swoop.

lightning, light, electricity, wind; cannon-ball, rocket, arrow, dart, quicksilver; telegraph, express train; torrent; swallow flight.

eagle, antelope, courser, race-horse, gazelle, greyhound, hare, doe, squirrel. Mercury, Ariel, Camilla, Harlequin. [Measurement of velocity] speedometer, log, -line, tachometer.

V. move quickly, trip, fisk; speed, hie, hasten, sprint, spurt, post, spank, scuttle; scud, -dle; scurry; scour, – the plain; scamper; run, – like mad; fly, race, run a race, cut away, cut and run, shoot, tear, whisk, whiz, sweep, skim, brush; cut –, bowl- along; rush

275. Slowness.—N. slowness &c. *adj.*; languor &c. (*inactivity*) 683; drawl; creeping &c. *v.*, lentor.

retardation; slackening &c. *v.*; delay &c. (*lateness*) 133; claudication.

jog-, dog-trot, walk; mincing steps; slow -march, – time.

slow -goer, – coach, – back; lingerer, loiterer, sluggard, tortoise, snail; dawdle &c. (*inactive*) 683.

V. move -slowly, &c. *adv.*; creep, crawl, lag, slug, walk, drawl, linger, loiter, saunter; plod, trudge, stump along, lumber; trail; drag; dawdle &c. (*be inactive*) 683; grovel, worm one's way, steal along; jog –, rub –, bundle-on; toddle, waddle, wabble, slug; traipse, slouch, shuffle, halt, hobble, limp, claudicate, shamble; flag, falter, totter, stagger; mince, step short; march in -slow time, – funeral procession; take one's time; hang fire &c. (*be late*) 133.

retard, relax; slacken, check, moderate, rein in, curb; reef; strike –, shorten –, take in- sail; put on the drag, apply the brake; clip the wings; reduce the

&c. (*be violent*) 173; dash -on, – off, – forward; bolt; trot, gallop, bound, flit, spring, dart, boom; march in -quick, – double-time; ride hard, get over the ground, scorch.

hurry &c. (*hasten*) 684; accelerate, put on; quicken; quicken –, mend- one's pace; clap spurs to one's horse; make -haste, – rapid strides, – forced marches, – the best of one's way; put one's best leg foremost, stir one's stumps, wing one's way, set off at a score; carry –, crowd- sail; go off like a shot, go ahead, gain ground; outstrip the wind, fly on the wings of the wind.

keep -up, – pace- with; outstrip &c. 303.

Adj. fast, speedy, swift, rapid, quick, fleet; nimble, agile, expeditious; ex- press; active &c. 682; flying, galloping &c. *v.*; light-, nimble-footed; winged, eagle-winged, mercurial, electric, tele- graphic; light-legged, light of heel; swift as -an arrow &c. *n.*; quick as -lightning &c. *n.*, – thought.*

Adv. swiftly &c. *adj.*; with -speed &c. *n.*; apace; at -a great rate, – full speed, – railway speed; full -drive, – gallop; post-haste, in full sail, tantivy; trippingly; instantaneously &c. 113; like a shot.

under press of -sail, – canvas, – sail and steam; *velis et remis*, on eagle's wing, in double quick time; with -rapid, – giant- strides; *à pas de géant*; in seven league boots; whip and spur; *ventre à terre*; as fast as one's -legs, – heels- will carry one; as fast as one can lay feet to the ground, at the top of one's speed; by leaps and bounds; with haste &c. 684; in- high – gear, – speed.

Phr. *vires acquirit eundo.*

speed, decelerate; slacken -speed, – one's pace, lose ground; back -water, – pedal, put the engines astern, throttle down.

Adj. slow, slack; tardy; dilatory &c. (*inactive*) 683; gentle, easy; leisurely; deliberate, gradual; insensible, imper- ceptible; languid, sluggish, apathetic, phlegmatic, slow-paced, tardigrade, snail-like; creeping &c. *v.*

Adv. slowly &c. *adj.*; leisurely; *piano, adagio*; *largo, larghetto*; at half speed, under easy sail; at a -foot's, – snail's, – funeral- pace; slower than molasses in January; in slow time; with -mincing steps, – clipped wings; *haud passibus æquis*; in- low –, gear, – speed.

gradually &c. *adj.*; *gradatim*; by -degrees, – slow degrees, – inches, – little and little; step by step; inch by inch, bit by bit, little by little, *seriatim*; consecutively.

3°. Motion Conjoined with Force

276. Impulse.—N. impulse, impul- sion, impetus; momentum; push, pulsion, thrust, shove, jog, jolt, brunt, booming, boost, throw; explosion &c. (*violence*) 173; propulsion &c. 284.

percussion, concussion, collision, oc- cursion, clash, encounter, cannon, *carambole*, appulse, shock, crash, bump; impact; *élan*; charge &c. (*attack*) 716; beating &c. (*punishment*) 972.

blow, dint, stroke, knock, tap, rap, slap, smack, pat, dab; fillip; slam, bang; hit, whack, thwack, clout; cuff &c. 972; squash, dowse, whap, swap, punch, thump, swipe, jab, pelt, kick, punce, calcitration; *ruade*; arietation; cut, thrust, lunge, yerk.

277. Recoil.—N. recoil; re-, retro- action; revulsion; rebound, *ricochet*; re-percussion, -calcitration; kick, *contre- coup*; springing back &c. *v.*; elasticity &c. 325; reflexion, reflex, reflux; rever- beration &c. (*resonance*) 408; rebuff, repulse; return.

ducks and drakes; boomerang; spring; reactionist, reactionary.

V. recoil, resile, react; spring –, fly –, bound- back; rebound, reverberate, repercuss, recalcitrate, echo, *ricochet*.

Adj. recoiling &c. *v.*; re-fluent, -percussive, -calcitrant, -actionary; retroactive.

Adv. on the -recoil &c. *n.*

---

* See note on 264.

hammer, sledge-hammer, mall, maul, mallet, flail; ram, -mer; bat-tering-ram, monkey, pile-driver, punch, bat, tamper, tamping iron; cudgel &c. (*weapon*) 727; axe &c. (*sharp*) 253.

[Science of mechanical forces] mechanics, dynamics &c.

V. give an -impetus &c. *n.*; impel, push; start, give a start to, set going; drive, urge, boom; thrust, prod, foin; cant; elbow, shoulder, jostle, justle, hustle, hurtle, shove, jog, jolt, bean, encounter; run -, bump -, butt- against; knock -, run- one's head against; impinge.

strike, knock, hit, bash, tap, rap, bat, slap, flap, dab, pat, thump, beat, bang, slam, dash; punch, thwack, whack; hit -, strike- hard; swap, batter, dowse, baste; pelt, patter, skelter, buffet, belabour, tamp; fetch one a blow, swat; poke at, pink, lunge, yerk; kick, calcitrate; butt; strike at &c. (*attack*) 716; whip &c. (*punish*) 972; propel &c. 284.

come -, enter- into collision; collide; foul; fall -, run- foul of. throw &c. (*propel*) 284.

Adj. impelling &c. *v.*; im-pulsive, -pellent; booming; dynamic, -al; impelled &c. *v.*

4°. Motion with Reference to Direction

278. Direction.—**N.** direction, bear-ing, course, set, drift, tenor; tendency &c. 176; incidence; bending, trending &c. *v.*; dip, tack, aim, collimation; steer-ing, -age.

point of the compass, cardinal -, half -, quarter- points; North, East, South, West; N by E, ENE, NE by N, NE &c.; rhumb, azimuth, line of collimation.

line, path, road, range, quarter, line of march; a-, al-lignment; straight shot, bee-line.

V. tend -, bend -, point- towards; conduct -, go- to; point -to, - at; bend, trend, verge, incline, dip, determine.

steer -, make- -for, - towards; aim -, level- at; take aim; keep -, hold- a course; be bound for; bend one's steps towards; direct -, steer -, bend -, shape- one's course; align -, allign-one's march; go straight, - to the point; march -on, - on a point.

ascertain one's -direction &c. *n.*; *s'orienter*, see which way the wind blows; box the compass.

Adj. directed &c. *v.*, - towards; pointing towards &c. *v.*; bound for; aligned -, alligned- with; direct, straight; un-deviating, -swerving; straightforward; North, -ern, -erly, &c. *n.*

directable &c. *v.*

Adv. towards; on the -road, - high

279. Deviation. — **N.** deviation; swerving &c. *v.*; obliquation, warp, refraction; flection, flexion; sweep; de-flection, -flexure; declination.

diversion, digression, departure from, aberration, drift, sheer; divergence &c. 291; zigzag; *détour* &c. (*circuit*) 629.

[Desultory motion] wandering &c. *v.*; vagrancy, evagation; by-paths and crooked ways.

[Motion sideways, oblique motion] sidling &c. *v.*; *échelon*, leeway; knight's move (at chess).

V. alter one's course, deviate, depart from, turn, trend; bend, curve &c. 245; swerve, heel, bear off.

intervert; deflect; divert, - from its course; put on a new scent, shift, shunt, switch, wear, draw aside, crook, warp, short circuit.

stray, straggle; sidle, edge; diverge &c. 291; tralineate, digress, divagate, wander; wind, twist, meander, meander around Robin Hood's barn; veer, tack, sheer; turn -aside, - a corner, - away from; wheel, steer clear of; ramble, rove, drift; go -astray, - adrift; yaw, dodge; step aside, ease off, make way for, shy.

fly off at a tangent; glance off; turn, wheel -, face- about; turn -, face- to the right about; wabble &c. (*oscillate*) 314; go out of one's way &c. (*perform a circuit*) 629; lose one's way.

road- to; *versus*, to; hither, thither, whither; directly; straight, – forwards, – as an arrow; point blank; in a -direct, – straight- line -to, – for, – with; in a line with; full tilt at, as the crow flies.

before –, near –, close to –, against- the wind; windwards, in the wind's eye.

through, *via*, by way of; in all -directions, – manner of ways; *quaqua-versum*, from the four winds.

280. [Going before.] Precession.—N.
precession, leading, heading; preced-ence &c. 62; priority &c. 116; the lead, *le pas*; van &c. (*front*) 234; precursor &c. 64.

V. go -before, – ahead, – in the van, – in advance; precede, forerun; usher in, introduce, herald, head, take the lead; lead, – the way, – the dance; get –, have- the start; steal a march; get -before, – ahead, – in front of; outstrip &c. 303; take precedence &c. (*first in order*) 62.

Adj. foremost, first, leading &c. *v.*

Adv. in advance, before, ahead, in the van; fore-, head-most; in front.

Phr. *seniores priores*.

282. [Motion forwards; progressive motion.] Progression.—N.
progress, -ion, -iveness; advancing &c. *v.*; ad-vance, -ment; ongoing; flood-tide, headway; march &c. 266; rise; improve-ment &c. 658.

V. advance; proceed, progress; get -on, – along, – over the ground; gain ground; jog –, rub –, wag- on; go with the stream; keep –, hold on- one's course; go –, move –, come –, get –, pass –, push –, press- -on, – forward, – forwards, – ahead; press onwards, step forward; make –, work –, carve –, push –, force –, edge –, elbow- one's way; make -progress, – head, – way, – headway, – advances, – strides, – rapid strides &c. (*velocity*) 274; go –, shoot- ahead; distance; make up leeway.

Adj. advancing &c. *v.*; pro-gressive, -fluent; advanced.

Adj. deviating &c. *v.*; aberrant, errant; ex-, dis-cursive; devious, de-sultory, loose; rambling; stray, erratic, vagrant, undirected; circuitous, indi-rect, zigzag; crab-like.

Adv. astray from, round about, wide of the mark; to the right about; all manner of ways; circuitously &c. 629.

obliquely, sideling, like the move of the knight on a chessboard.

281. [Going after.] Sequence.—N.
sequence, run; coming after &c. (*order*) 63; (*time*) 117; following; pursuit &c. 622.

follower, attendant, satellite, shad-ow, dangler, train.

V. follow; pursue &c. 622; go –, fly- after.

attend, beset, dance attendance on, dog, be-dog; tread -in the steps of, – close upon; be –, go –, follow- in the -wake, – trail, – rear- of; trail, follow as a shadow, hang on the skirts of; tread –, follow- on the heels of, tag after.

lag, get behind.

Adj. following &c. *v.*

Adv. behind; in the -rear &c. 235, – train of, wake of; after &c. (*order*) 63, (*time*) 117.

283. [Motion backwards.] Regres-sion.—N.
regress, -ion; retro-cession, -gression, -gradation, -action; *reculade*; retreat, withdrawal, retirement, re-migration; recession &c. (*motion from*) 287; recess; crab-like motion.

re-fluence, -flux; backwater, regur-gitation, ebb, return; resilience; re-flexion (*recoil*) 277; *volte-face*.

counter -motion, – movement, – march; veering, tergiversation, re-cidivation, backsliding, fall, relapse; deterioration &c. 659.

turning-point &c. (*reversion*) 145.

V. re-cede, -grade, -turn, -vert, -treat, -tire; retro-grade, -cede; back, – down, – out, crawl; withdraw; rebound &c. 277; go –, come –, turn –, hark –, draw –, fall –, get –, put –, run- back; lose ground; fall –, drop- astern; back water, put about; veer, – round; double,

Adv. forward, onward; forth, on ahead, under way, *en route* for, on -one's way, – the way, – the road, – the high road- to; in -progress, – mid progress; *in transitu* &c. 270.

Phr. *vestigia nulla retrorsum.*

wheel, counter-march; ebb, regurgitate; jib, shrink, shy.

turn -tail, – round, – upon one's heel, – one's back upon; retrace one's steps, dance the back step; sound –, beat- a retreat; go home.

Adj. receding &c. *v.*; retro-grade, -gressive; re-gressive, -fluent, -flex, -cidivous, -silient; crab-like; reactionary &c. 277; counter-clockwise.

Adv. back, -wards; reflexively, to the right about; *à reculons, à rebours.*

Phr. *revenons à nos moutons,* as you were.

---

284. [Motion given to an object situated in front.] **Propulsion.—N.** pro-pulsion, -jection; *vis a tergo*; push &c. (*impulse*) 276; e-, jaculation; ejection &c. 297; throw₂ fling, toss, shot, discharge, shy.

[Science of propulsion] gunnery, ballistics, archery.

missile, projectile, ball, *discus*, javelin, hammer, quoit, brickbat, shot, bullet; arrow, shaft, gun &c. (*arms*) 727.

shooter, shot; gunner, gun-layer; archer, toxophilite; bow-, rifle-, marksman; good –, crack- shot; sharpshooter &c. (*combatant*) 726.

V. propel, project, throw, fling, cast, pitch, chuck, toss, jerk, heave, shy, hurl; flirt, fillip.

dart, lance, tilt; e-, jaculate; fulminate, bolt, drive, sling, pitchfork.

send; send –, let –, fire- off; discharge, shoot; launch, send forth, let fly; dash.

put –, set- in motion; set agoing, start; give -a start, – an impulse- to; push, impel &c. 276; trundle &c. (*set in rotation*) 312; expel &c. 297.

carry one off one's legs; put to flight.

Adj. propelled &c. *v.*; propelling &c. *v.*; pro-pulsive, -jectile.

285. [Motion given to an object situated behind.] **Traction.—N.** traction; drawing &c. *v.*; draught, pull, haul; rake; 'a long pull, a strong pull and a pull all together'; towage, haulage.

V. draw, pull, haul, lug, rake, drag, draggle, tug, tow, trail, trawl, train; take in tow.

wrench, jerk, twitch.

Adj. drawing &c. *v.*; tractive, tractile; ductile.

---

286. [Motion towards.] **Approach.— N.** approach, approximation, appropinquation; access; appulse; afflux, -ion; advent &c. (*approach of time*) 121; pursuit &c. 622; convergence &c. 290.

V. approach, approximate; near; get –, go –, draw- near; come, – near, – to close quarters; move –, set in- towards; drift; make up to; gain upon; pursue &c. 622; tread on the heels of; bear up; make the land; hug the -shore, – land.

Adj. approaching &c. *v.*; approximative; convergent; affluent; impending, imminent &c. (*destined*) 152.

287. [Motion from.] **Recession.—N.** recession, retirement, withdrawal; retreat; retrocession &c. 283; departure &c. 293; recoil &c. 277; flight &c. (*avoidance*) 623.

V. recede, go, move from, retire, ebb, withdraw, shrink; come –, move –, go –, get –, drift- away; depart &c. 293; retreat &c. 283; move –, stand –, sheer- off; swerve from; fall back, stand aside; run away &c. (*avoid*) 623.

remove, shunt, side track, switch off.

Adj. receding &c. *v.*

Adv. on the road.

Int. come hither! approach! here! come! come near!

288. [Motion towards, actively.] **Attraction.—N.** attract-ion, -iveness; pull; drawing to, pulling towards, adduction, magnetism, gravity, attraction of gravitation; lure, bait, decoy.

lode-stone, -star; magnet, siderite, magnetite.

V. attract; draw -, pull -, drag-towards; adduce.

lure, bait, decoy.

Adj. attracting &c. *v.*; attrahent, attractive, adducent, adductive.

290. [Motion nearer to.] **Convergence.** —**N.** con-vergence, -fluence, -course, -flux, -gress, -currence, -centration; appulse, meeting; corradiation.

assemblage &c. 72; resort &c. (*focus*) 74; asymptote.

V. converge, concur; come together, unite, meet, fall in with; close -with, – in upon; centre -round, – in; enter in; pour in.

gather together, unite, concentrate, bring into a focus.

Adj. converging &c. *v.*; con-vergent, -fluent, -current; centripetal; asymptotical.

292. [Terminal motion at.] **Arrival.** —**N.** arrival, advent; landing; de-, disem-barkation; reception, welcome, *vin d'honneur.*

home, goal, bourn; landing-place, -stage; resting -, stopping -place; destination, harbour, haven, port; terminal, terminus, railway station, depot, airport; halt, halting -place, – ground; anchorage &c. (*refuge*) 666.

return, recursion, remigration; meeting; ren-, en-counter.

completion &c. 729.

V. arrive; get to, come to; come; reach, attain; come up, – with, – to; overtake; make, fetch; complete &c. 729; join, rejoin.

light, alight, dismount; land, go ashore; debark, disembark; put -in, – into; visit, cast anchor, pitch one's tent; sit down &c. (*be located*) 184; get to one's journey's end; make the

289. [Motion from, actively.] **Repulsion.—N.** repulsion; driving from &c. *v.*; repulse; abduction.

V. repel; push -, drive - &c. 276. from; chase, dispel; retrude; abduce, abduct; send away, repulse, dismiss.

keep at arm's length, turn one's back upon, give the cold shoulder; send packing; send -off, – away- with a flea in one's ear, – about one's business.

Adj. repelling &c. *v.*; repellant, repulsive; abducent, abductive.

291. [Motion further off.] **Divergence.** —**N.** diverg-ence, -ency; divarication, ramification, radiation; separation &c. (*disjunction*) 44; dispersion &c. 73; deviation &c. 279; aberration, declination.

V. diverge, divaricate, radiate; ramify; branch -, glance -, file- off; fly off, – at a tangent; spread, scatter, disperse &c. 73; deviate &c. 279; part &c. (*separate*) 44; splay apart.

Adj. diverging &c. *v.*; divergent, radiant, centrifugal; aberrant.

293. [Initial motion from.] **Departure.—N.** departure, decession, decampment; embarkation; take-off; outset, start; removal; exit &c. (*egress*) 295; exodus, Hejira, flight.

leave-taking, *congé,* valediction, valedictory, adieu, farewell, good-bye, stirrup-cup.

starting -point, – post; point -, place- of -departure, – embarkation; port of embarkation.

V. depart; go, – away; take one's departure, set out; set -, march -, put -, start -, be -, move -, get -, whip -, pack -, go -, take oneself- off; start, issue, march out, debouch; go -, sally-forth; sally, set forward; be gone.

leave a place, quit, vacate, evacuate, abandon; go off the stage, make ones' exit; retire, withdraw, remove; go -one's way, – along, – from home; take -flight, – wing; spring, fly, flit, wing

land; be in at the death; come –,
get- -back, – home; return; come in
&c. (*ingress*) 294; make one's appearance &c. (*appear*) 446; drop in; detrain;
outspan.

come to hand; come -at, – across;
hit; come –, light –, pop –, bounce –,
plump –, burst –, pitch- upon; meet;
en- ren-counter; come in contact.

Adj. arriving &c. *v.*; homeward-
bound; terminal.

Adv. here, hither.

Int. welcome! hail! all hail! good-
day, – morrow; greetings! hullo! well!

one's flight; fly –, whip- away; take off,
hop off; embark; go -on board, – aboard;
set sail; put –, go- to sea; sail, take ship;
hoist blue Peter; get under way, weigh
anchor; strike tents, break camp,
decamp; walk one's chalks, make
tracks, cut one's stick; cut and run;
take leave; say –, bid- -good-bye &c.
n.; disappear &c. 449; abscond &c.
(*avoid*) 623; entrain, embus, emplane;
saddle –, harness –, hitch- up; inspan.

Adj. departing &c. *v.*; valedictory;
outward bound.

Adv. whence, hence, thence; with a
foot in the stirrup; on the -wing, –
move.

Int. begone! &c. (*ejection*) 297; to horse! all aboard! farewell!
adieu! good-bye, – day! *au revoir! auf wiedersehen!* fare you well!
so long! God -bless you, – speed! *bon voyage!*

---

294. [Motion into.] **Ingress.—N.**
ingress; entrance, entry; introgression;
influx; intrusion, inroad, incursion,
invasion, irruption; pene-, interpene-
tration; illapse, import, importation,
infiltration; immigration; admission
&c. (*reception*) 296; insinuation &c.
(*interjacence*) 228; insertion &c. 300.

inlet; way in; mouth, door &c.
(*opening*) 260; path &c. (*way*) 627;
conduit &c. 350; immigrant, visitor,
incomer, newcomer, colonist.

V. have the *entrée*; enter; go –,
come –, pour –, flow –, creep –, slip –,
pop –, break –, burst- -into, – in; set
foot on; burst –, break- in upon; invade,
intrude, butt in, horn in, crash; insinuate itself; inter-, penetrate; infiltrate;
find one's way –, wriggle –, worm
oneself- into.

give entrance to &c. (*receive*) 296;
insert &c. 300.

Adj. incoming, ingressive &c. *n.*;
inward bound.

Adv. inward.

295. [Motion out of.] **Egress.—N.**
egress, exit, issue; emer-sion, -gence;
disemboguement; out-break, -burst; e-,
pro-ruption; emanation; evacuation;
ex-, trans-udation; extravasation, perspiration, sweating, leakage, percola-
tion, distillation, oozing; gush &c.
(*water in motion*) 348; outpour, -ing;
effluence, effusion; efflux, -ion; drain;
dribbling &c. *v.*; defluxion; drainage;
out-come, -put; discharge &c. (*excretion*) 299.

export; expatriation; e-, re-migration; *débouche*; exodus &c. (*departure*)
293; emigrant, migrant, *émigré*, colonist.

outlet, vent, spout, tap, sluice, flood-
gate; pore; vomitory, out-gate, sally-
port; way out; mouth, door &c.
(*opening*) 260; path &c. (*way*) 627;
conduit &c. 350; air-pipe &c. 351.

V. emerge, emanate, issue; go –,
come –, move –, pass –, pour –, flow-
out of; pass off, evacuate; migrate.

ex-, trans-ude; leak; run, – out,
– through; per-, trans-colate; seep;
strain, distil; perspire, sweat, drain,
ooze; filter, filtrate; dribble, gush,

spout, flow out; well, – out; pour, trickle &c. (*water in motion*)
348; effuse, extravasate, disembogue, discharge itself, debouch;
come –, break- forth; burst- out, – through; find vent, escape &c. 671.

Adj. effused &c. *v.*; outgoing, outward bound.

Adv. outward.

296. [Motion into, actively.] **Reception.**—**N.** reception; admission, admittance, *entrée*, importation; initiation; intro-duction, -mission, -ception; immission, ingestion, imbibition, absorption, ingurgitation, inhalation; suction, sucking; eating, drinking &c. (*food*) 298; insertion &c. 300; interjection &c. 228.

V. give -entrance to, – admittance to, – the *entrée*; intro-duce, -mit; usher, admit, receive, import, initiate, bring in, open the door to, throw open, ingest, absorb, imbibe, inhale, infiltrate; let –, take –, suck- in; re-admit, -sorb, -absorb; snuff up; swallow, ingurgitate; engulf, engorge; gulp; eat, drink &c. (*food*) 298.

Adj. admit-ting &c. *v.*, -ted &c. *v.*; admissible; absorbent; introductory, introceptive, intromittent, initiatory.

---

297. [Motion out of, actively.] **Ejection.**—**N.** ejection, emission, effusion, rejection, expulsion, eviction, extrusion, trajection; discharge.

egestion, evacuation, vomition, disgorgement, voidance, eruption, eruptiveness; ruc-, eruc-tation, blood-letting, venesection, phlebotomy, paracentesis; tapping, drainage; clear-ance, -age, voidance; vomiting, excretion &c. 299.

deportation; banishment &c. (*punishment*) 972; rogue's march; relegation, extradition; dislodgment.

V. give -exit, – vent- to; let –, give –, pour –, send- out; des-, dis-patch; exhale, excern, excrete, disembogue, secrete, secern; extravasate, shed, void, evacuate, egest, emit; open the -sluices, – floodgates; turn on the tap; extrude, detrude; effuse, spend, expend; pour forth; squirt, spirt, spill, slop; perspire &c. (*exude*) 295; breathe, blow &c. (*wind*) 349.

tap, draw off; bale –, lade- out; let blood, broach.

eject, reject; expel, discard; cut, send to Coventry, boycott, ostracize; *chasser*; banish &c. (*punish*) 972; throw &c. 284 -out, – up, – off, – away, – aside; push &c. 276 -out, – off, – away, – aside; shovel –, sweep- -out, – away; brush –, whisk –, turn –, send- -off, – away; discharge; send –, turn –, cast- adrift; turn –, bundle- out; throw overboard; give the sack to; send -packing, – about one's business, – to the right about; strike off the roll &c. (*abrogate*) 756; turn out- neck and heels, – head and shoulders, – neck and crop; pack off; send away with a flea in the ear; send to Jericho; bow out, show the door to, dismiss, fire, sack.

turn out of -doors, – house and home; evict, oust; exorcise, un-house, -kennel; dislodge; un-, dis-people; depopulate; relegate, deport.

empty; drain, – to the dregs; sweep off; clear, – off, – out, – away; suck, draw off, extract; clean out, make a clean sweep of, clear decks, purge.

em-, dis-, disem-bowel; eviscerate, gut; unearth, root -out, – up; averruncate; weed –, get out; eliminate, get rid of, do away with, shake off; exenterate.

vomit, spew, puke, keck, retch; belch, – out, eruct, eructate; cast –, bring- up; disgorge; expectorate, salivate, clear the throat, hawk, spit, sputter, splutter, slobber, drool, drivel, slaver, slabber.

unpack, unlade, unload, unship; break bulk.

be let out; ooze &c. (*emerge*) 295.

Adj. emitt-ing, -ed &c. *v.*

begone! get you gone! get –, go- -away, – along, – along with you! go your way! away, – with! off with you! go, – about your business! be off! avaunt! aroynt! get out!

298. [Eating.] Food.—**N.** eating &c.
v.; deglutition, gulp, epulation, mastication, manducation, rumination, gastronomy, gastrology; panto-, hippo-, ichthyo-phagy &c.; gluttony &c. 957; carnivorousness, vegetarianism.

mouth, jaws, mandible, mazard, chops.

drinking &c. *v.*; potation, draught, libation; carousal &c. (*amusement*) 840; drunkenness &c. 959.

food, *pabulum*; aliment, nourishment, nutriment; susten-ance, -tation; nurture, subsistence, provender, feed, fodder, provision, ration, keep, commons, board; commissariat &c. (*provision*) 637; prey, forage, pasture, pasturage; fare, cheer; diet, -ary; regimen; belly timber, staff of life; bread, -and cheese; proteins, carbohydrates, vitamines.

comestibles, eatables, victuals, edibles, *ingesta*; grub, prog, tack, hard tack, meat; bread, -stuffs; cereals; viands, cates, delicacy, dainty, creature comforts, contents of the larder, flesh-pots; festal board; ambrosia; good -cheer, – living.

hors-d'œuvre; soup, pottage, *potage*, broth, *bouillon*, *consommé*, *purée*, *borsch*, stock, skilly, gumbo; fish, – cakes, – pie; joint, *rôti*, *pièce de résistance*, *relevé*, hash, *réchauffé*, stew, *ragoût*, fricassee, mince, *salim*, *goulash*, *bouillabaisse*, remove, *entrée*, *croquette*, *rissole*, sausage, curry, bubble and squeak; haggis, collops, giblets; poultry, game &c.; biscuit, bun, scone, rusk, pancake, pie, pastry, pasty, patty, *patisserie*, tart, turnover, *vol-au-vent*, *soufflé*, dumpling, pudding, duff, *compote*, fritters, cake, napoleon, *blancmange*, custard, jelly, jam, sweets &c. 396; *entremet*; oatmeal, porridge, hasty pudding, gruel; eggs, omelet, cheese, matzoon, savoury; vegetable, salad, *mayonnaise*, fruit; sauce, condiment &c. 393; kickshaws.

table, *cuisine*, bill of fare, *menu*, *table d'hôte*, ordinary, *à la carte*; cover.

meal, repast, feed, spread; mess; dish, plate, course, side dish; regale; regale-, refresh-, entertain-ment; refection, collation, picnic, feast, banquet, junket; breakfast; lunch, -eon; *déjeuner*, bever, tiffin, tea, dinner, supper, snack, whet, bait, dessert; pot-luck, *table d'hôte*, *déjeuner à la fourchette*; hearty –, square –, substantial –, full- -meal; blow out; light refreshment; pemmican.

mouthful, bolus, gobbet, tit-bit, morsel, sop, sippet.

drink, beverage, liquor, broth, soup; potion, dram, draught, drench, swill; nip, peg, sip, sup, gulp.

wine, champagne, spirits, *liqueur*, beer, porter, stout, ale, malt liquor, julep, Sir John Barleycorn, stingo, heavy wet, bitter, lager-beer, cider; grog, toddy, flip, purl, punch, negus, cup, bishop, posset, wassail; bitters, *apéritif*, high-ball, cocktail; whisky, rum, absinthe; gin &c. (*intoxicating liquor*) 959; coffee, chocolate, cocoa, tea, *maté*, the cup that cheers but not inebriates.

eating-house &c. 189.

299. Excretion.—**N.** excretion, discharge, emanation; ejection &c. 297; exhalation, exudation, extrusion, secretion, effusion, extravasation, *ecchymosis*, evacuation, cacation, defecation, dysentery, dejection, *fæces*, excrement; perspiration, sweat; sub-, exud-ation; *diaphoresis*; sewage.

saliva, spittle, rheum; ptyalism, salivation, catarrh, distemper; diarrhœa; *ejecta*, *egesta*, *sputum*, *sputa*; *excreta*; lava; *exuviæ* &c. (*uncleanness*) 653.

hemorrhage, bleeding; catamenia, menses; outpouring &c. (*egress*) 295; leucorrhea.

V. excrete &c. (*eject*) 297; emanate &c. (*come out*) 295.

Adj. excretory, fæcal, secretory; ejective, eliminant.

V. eat, feed, fare, devour, swallow, take; gulp, bolt, snap; fall to; despatch, dispatch; discuss; take -, get -, gulp-down; lay -, tuck- in; lick, pick, peck; gormandize &c. 957; bite, champ, munch, cranch, craunch, crunch, chew, masticate, nibble, gnaw, mumble.

live on; feed -, batten -, fatten -, feast- upon; browse, graze, crop, regale; carouse &c. (*make merry*) 840; eat heartily, do justice to, play a good knife and fork, banquet.

break -bread, - one's fast; breakfast, lunch, dine, take tea, sup.

drink, - in, - up, - one's fill; quaff, sip, sup; suck, - up; lap; swig; swill, tipple &c. (*be drunken*) 959; empty one's glass, drain the cup; toss -off, - one's glass; wash down, crack a bottle, wet one's whistle.

cater, purvey &c. 637.

Adj. eatable, edible, esculent, comestible, alimentary; cereal, cibarious; dietetic; culinary; nutri-tive, -tious; succulent; drinkable, pot-able, -ulent; bibulous.

omn-, carn-, herb-, frug-, gran-, gramin-, phyt-ivorus; ichthyophagous.

prandial.

300. [Forcible ingress.] **Insertion.—N.** insertion, implantation, intercalation, embolism, introduction; interpolation, insinuation &c. (*intervention*) 228; planting &c. *v.*; injection, inoculation, importation, infusion; forcible -ingress &c. 294; immersion; submersion, -gence; dip, plunge; bath &c. (*water*) 337; interment &c. 363.

V. insert; intro-duce, -mit; put -, run- into; import; inject; interject &c. 228; infuse, instil, inoculate, impregnate, imbue, imbrue.

graft, ingraft, bud, plant, implant; dovetail.

obtrude; thrust -, stick -, ram -, stuff -, tuck -, press -, drive -, pop -, whip -, drop -, put- in; impact; empierce &c. (*make a hole*) 260.

embed; immerse, immerge, merge; bathe, soak &c. (*water*) 337; dip, plunge &c. 310.

bury &c. (*inter*) 363.

insert &c.- itself; plunge *in medias res.*

Adj. inserted &c. *v.*

301. [Forcible egress.] **Extraction.—N.** extraction; extracting &c. *v.*; removal, elimination, extrication, eradication, evolution.

evulsion, avulsion; wrench; expression, squeezing; extirpation, extermination; ejection &c. 297; export &c. (*egress*) 295; distillation.

extractor, corkscrew, forceps, pliers.

V. extract, draw, pit; take -, draw -, pull -, tear -, pluck -, pick -, get- out; wring from, wrench; extort; root -, weed -, grub -, rake- up, - out; eradicate; pull -, pluck- up by the roots; averruncate; unroot; uproot, pull up, extirpate, dredge.

remove; educe, elicit; evolve, extricate; eliminate &c. (*eject*) 297; eviscerate &c. 297.

express, squeeze -, press- out; distil.

Adj. extracted &c. *v.*

---

302. [Motion through.] **Passage.—N.** passage, transmission; permeation; pene-, interpene-tration; transudation, infiltration; *osmosis*, osmose, endos-, exos-mose; intercurrence; ingress &c. 294; egress &c. 295; path &c. 627; conduit &c. 350; opening &c. 260; journey &c. 266; voyage &c. 267.

V. pass, - through; perforate &c. (*hole*) 260; penetrate, permeate, thread, thrid, enfilade; go -through, - across; go -, pass- over; cut across; ford, cross; pass and repass, work; make -, thread -, worm -, force- one's way; make -, force- a passage; cut one's way through;

find its -way, – vent; transmit, make way, clear the course; traverse, go over the ground.

Adj. passing &c. *v.*; intercurrent; osmotic &c. *n.*

Adv. *en passant* &c. *(transit)* 270.

303. [Motion beyond.] **Overstep.—**
N. trans-cursion, -ilience, -gression; infraction, intrusion; trespass; encroach-, infringe-ment; extravagation, transcendence; redundance &c. 641; ingress &c. 294.

V. transgress, surpass, pass; go- beyond, – by; show in –, come to the-front; shoot ahead of; steal a march –, gain- upon.

over-step, -pass, -reach, -go, -ride, -leap, -jump, -skip, -lap, -shoot the mark; out-strip, -leap, -jump, -go, -step, -run, -ride, -rival, -do; beat, – hollow; distance; leave in the -lurch, – rear; go one better, throw into the shade; exceed, transcend, surmount; soar &c. *(rise)* 305.

encroach, intrude, trespass, infringe, invade, trench upon, intrench on; strain; stretch –, strain- a point; pass the Rubicon.

Adj. surpassing &c. *v.*

Adv. beyond the mark, ahead.

304. [Motion short of.] **Shortcoming.**
—N. shortcoming, failure; delinquency; falling short &c. *v.*; de-fault, -falcation; leeway; labour in vain, no go.

incompleteness &c. 53; imperfection &c. 651; insufficiency &c. 640; non-completion &c. 730; failure &c. 732.

V. come –, fall –, stop- -short, – short of; not reach; want; keep within -bounds, – the mark, – compass.

break down, stick in the mud, collapse, come to nothing; fall -through, – to the ground, – down; cave in, end in smoke, fizzle out, miss the mark, fail; lose ground; miss stays, slump.

Adj. unreached; deficient; short, – of; *minus*; out of depth; perfunctory &c. *(neglect)* 460.

Adv. within -the mark, – compass, – bounds; behindhand; *re infectâ*; to no purpose; far from it.

Phr. the bubble burst.

305. [Motion upwards.] **Ascent.—N.**
ascent, ascension; rising &c. *v.*; rise, upgrowth; leap &c. 309; acclivity, hill &c. 217; stair, stairs, stair-case, -way, flight of -steps, – stairs; ladder, companion, – way; lift, elevator &c. 307.

rocket, lark; sky-rocket, -lark; Alpine Club.

V. ascend, rise, mount, arise, uprise; go –, get –, work one's way –, start –, spring –, shoot- up; zoom; aspire.

climb, clamber, ramp, scramble, swarm, *escalade*, surmount; scale, – the heights.

tower, soar, hover, spire, plane, swim, float, surge; leap &c. 309.

Adj. rising &c. *v.*; scandent, buoyant; super-natant, -fluitant; excelsior.

Adv. uphill.

306. [Motion downwards.] **Descent.**
—N. descent, descension, declension, declination; fall; falling &c. *v.*; drop, cadence; subsidence, lapse; come-down, downfall, tumble, slip, tilt, trip, lurch, cropper, *culbute*; titubation, stumble; fate of Icarus; dive, nose-dive, *volplané*.

avalanche, *débâcle*, landslip, slide.

declivity, dip, hill; decline, drop.

V. descend; go –, drop –, come-down; fall, gravitate, drop, slip, slide, glissade, dive, plunge, settle; decline, slump, set, sink, droop, come down a peg.

dismount, alight, light, get down; swoop; stoop &c. 308; fall prostrate, precipitate oneself; let fall &c. 308.

tumble, trip, stumble, titubate, lurch, pitch, swag, topple; topple –, tumble- -down, – over; tilt, sprawl, plump down, come a cropper.

Adj. descending &c. *v.*; descendent, declivitous; downcast; decur-rent, sive; labent, deciduous; nodding to its fall.

Adv. down, -hill, -wards.

307. Elevation.—N. elevation; raising &c. *v.*; erection, lift; sublevation, upheaval; sublimation, exaltation; prominence &c. (*convexity*) 250.

lever &c. 633; crane, derrick, windlass, capstan, winch, dredger, lift, elevator, escalator, dumb waiter.

V. heighten, elevate, raise, lift, erect; set –, stick –, perch –, perk –, tilt- up; rear, hoist, heave; up-lift, -raise, -rear, -bear, -cast, -hoist, -heave; buoy, weigh, mount, give a lift; exalt, sublimate; place –, set- on a pedestal.

take –, drag –, fish- up; dredge.

stand –, rise –, get –, jump- up; spring to one's feet; hold -oneself, – one's head- up; draw oneself up to his full height.

Adj. elevated &c. *v.*; standing up; stilted, attollent, rampant.

Adv. on -stilts, – the shoulders of, – one's legs, – one's hind legs.

---

309. Leap.—N. leap, jump, hop, spring, bound, vault, saltation.

dance, caper, gambol; curvet, caracole; *gam-bade, -bado*; capriole, demivolt; buck, – jump; hop, skip and jump.

kangaroo, jerboa, chamois, goat, frog, grasshopper, flea.

V. leap; jump -up, – over the moon; hop, spring, bound, vault, ramp, cut capers, gambol, trip, skip, dance, caper; curvet, *caracole*; foot it, bob, bounce, flounce, start, frisk &c. (*amusement*) 840; jump about &c. (*agitation*) 315; trip it on the light fantastic toe, dance oneself off one's legs.

Adj. leaping &c. *v.*; saltatory, frisky.

Adv. on the light fantastic toe.

308. Depression.—N. lowering &c. *v.*; depression; dip &c. (*concavity*) 252; abasement; detrusion; reduction.

over-throw, -set, -turn; upset; prostration, subversion, precipitation.

bow; courtesy, curtsy; genuflexion, *kowtow*, obeisance, *salaam*.

V. depress, lower; let –, take- -down, – down a peg; cast; let -drop, – fall; sink, debase, bring low, abase, slash, reduce, detrude, pitch, precipitate.

over-throw, -turn, -set; upset, subvert, prostrate, level, fell; cast –, take –, throw –, fling –, dash –, pull –, cut –, knock –, hew- down; raze, – to the ground; humiliate, trample in the dust, pull about one's ears.

sit, – down; couch, squat, crouch, stoop, bend, bow, courtsey, curtsy; bob, duck, dip, genuflect, kneel; *kowtow*, *salaam*, make obeisance, prostrate oneself; bend, bow- the -head, – knee; incline the head; bow down; cower; recline &c. (*be horizontal*) 213.

Adj. depressed &c. *v.*; at a low ebb; prostrate &c. (*horizontal*) 213; detrusive.

310. Plunge.—N. plunge, dip, dive, header; ducking &c. *v.*; submergence, immersion, diver.

V. plunge, dip, souse, duck; dive, plump; take a -plunge, – header, make a plunge; bathe &c. (*water*) 337.

sub-merge, -merse; immerse, douse, sink, engulf, send to -the bottom, – Davy Jones' locker.

get out of one's depth; go -to the bottom, – down like a stone; founder, welter, wallow.

---

311. [Curvilinear motion.] **Circuition.—N.** circuition, circulation; turn, curvet; excursion; circum-vention, -navigation, -ambulation; north-west passage; ambit, gyre, lap, circuit &c. 629.

turning &c. *v.*; wrench; evolution; coil, helix, spiral; corkscrew.

V. turn, bend, wheel; go –, put- about; heel; go –, turn -round, – to the right about; turn on one's heel; make –, describe- a -circle, – complete circle; encircle; go –, pass- through -180°, – 360°.

circum-navigate, -aviate, -ambulate, -vent; put a girdle round the earth, go the round, make the round of.

turn –, round- a corner; double a point.

wind, circulate, meander; whisk, twirl; twist &c. (*convolution*) 248; make a *détour* &c. (*circuit*) 629.

Adj. turning &c. *v.*; circuitous; circum-foraneous, -fluent; devious, roundabout, circum-ambient, -flex, -navigable.

Adv. round about.

312. [Motion in a continued circle.] **Rotation.**—**N.** rotation, revolution, gyration, circulation, roll; circum-rotation, -volution, -gyration; volutation, circination, turbination, *pirouette*, convolution.

verticity; whir, whirl, swirl, eddy, vortex, whirlpool, gurge; cyclone, tornado; surge; *vertigo*, dizzy round; Maelstrom, Charybdis; Ixion; wheel of Fortune.

313. [Motion in a reverse circle.] **Evolution.**—**N.** evolution, unfolding, development; eversion &c. (*inversion*) 218.

V. evolve; un-fold, -roll, -wind, -coil, -twist, -furl, -twine, -ravel; disentangle; develop.

Adj. evolving &c. *v.*; evolved &c. *v.*

wheel, screw, propeller, whirligig, rolling stone, windmill; top, teetotum, merry-go-round; roller; cog-, fly-wheel, spit; jack; caster.

axis, axle, spindle, spool, pivot, pin, hinge, pole, swivel, gimbals, arbor, bobbin, mandrel, shaft.

[Science of rotatory motion] trochilics, gyrostatics.

V. rotate; roll, – along; revolve, spin; turn, – round; circumvolve; circulate, gyre, gyrate, wheel, whirl, swirl, twirl, trundle, troll, bowl; slew round.

roll up, furl; wallow, welter; box the compass; spin like a -top, – teetotum.

Adj. rotating &c. *v.*; rota-tory, -ry; circumrotatory, trochilic, vertiginous, gyratory; vortic-al, -ose.

Adv. head over heels, round and round, like a horse in a mill.

314. [Reciprocating motion, motion to and fro.] **Oscillation.**—**N.** oscillation; vibration, libration; motion of a pendulum; nutation; undulation; pulsation; pulse; throb; seismic disturbance.

alternation; coming and going &c. *v.*; ebb and flow, flux and reflux, ups and downs; wave, vibratiuncle, swing, beat, shake, wag, see-saw, dance, lurch, dodge; fluctuation; vacillation &c. (*irresolution*) 605.

seismometer, vibroscope, seismograph.

V. oscillate; vi-, li-brate; alternate, undulate, wave; sway, rock, swing; pulsate, beat; wag, -gle; nod, bob, courtesy, curtsy; tick; play; chatter, wamble, wabble; teeter, dangle, swag.

fluctuate, dance, curvet, reel, quake; quiver, quaver, shake, flicker; wriggle; roll, toss, pitch; flounder, stagger, totter, waddle; move –, bob- up and down &c. *adv.*; pass and repass, ebb and flow, come and go, shuttle; vacillate &c. 605.

brandish, shake, flourish.

Adj. oscillating &c. *v.*; oscill-, undul-, puls-, libr-atory; vibrat-ory, -ile; pendulous, shutterwise, seismic.

Adv. to and fro, up and down, backwards and forwards, see-saw, zigzag, wibble-wabble, in and out, from side to side, like buckets in a well.

315. [Irregular motion.] **Agitation.**—**N.** agitation, stir, tremor, shake, ripple, jog, jolt, jar, jerk, shock, succussion, trepidation, quiver, quaver, dance; jactit-ation, -ance; shuffling &c. *v.*; twitter, flicker, flutter.

disquiet, perturbation, commotion, turmoil, turbulence; tumult, -uation; hubbub, rout, bustle, fuss, racket, *subsultus*, staggers, megrims, epilepsy, fits, twitching, vellication, St. Vitus' dance.

spasm, throe, throb, palpitation, convulsion, paroxysm; tetanus.

disturbance &c. (*disorder*) 59; restlessness &c. (*changeableness*) 149.

ferment, -ation; ebullition, effervescence, hurly burly, *cahotage*; tempest, storm, ground swell, heavy sea, whirlpool, vortex &c. 312; whirlwind &c. (*wind*) 349.

V. be -agitated &c.; shake; tremble, – like an aspen leaf; quiver, quaver, quake, shiver, twitter, twire, dither, dodder; twitch, writhe, toss, shuffle, tumble, stagger, bob, reel, sway; wag, -gle, wiggle; wriggle, – like an eel; squirm; dance, stumble, shamble, flounder, totter, flounce, flop, curvet, prance.

throb, pulsate, beat, palpitate, go pit-a-pat; flutter, flitter, flicker, bicker; bustle.

ferment, effervesce, foam; boil, – over; bubble, – up; simmer.

toss -, jump- about; jump like a parched pea; shake like an aspen leaf; shake to its -centre, – foundations; be the sport of the winds and waves; reel to and fro like a drunken man; move -, drive- from post to pillar and from pillar to post; keep between hawk and buzzard.

agitate, shake, convulse, toss, tumble, bandy, wield, brandish, flap, flourish, whisk, jerk, hitch, jolt; jog, -gle; jostle, buffet, hustle, disturb, stir, shake up, churn, jounce, wallop, whip, vellicate.

Adj. shaking &c. *v.*; agitated, tremulous; de-, sub-sultory; shambling; giddy-paced, saltatory, convulsive, jerky, unquiet, restless, all of a twitter.

Adv. by fits and starts; subsultorily &c. *adj.*; *per saltum*; hop, skip and jump; in -convulsions, – fits, pit-a-pat.

CLASS III

WORDS RELATING TO MATTER

SECTION I. MATTER IN GENERAL

316. Materiality.—N. material-ity, -ness; materialization; corpor-eity, -ality; substantiality, material existence, incarnation, flesh and blood, *plenum*; physical condition.

matter, body, substance, brute matter, stuff, element, principle, protoplasm, plasma, *parenchyma*, material, *substratum*, hyle, *corpus*, *pabulum*; frame.

object, article, thing, something; still life; stocks and stones; materials &c. 635.

[Science of matter] physics; somatology, -ics; natural –, experimental- philosophy; physical science, *philosophie positive*, materialism, hylism; materialist, physicist.

317. Immateriality.—N. immateriality, -ness; incorporeity, dematerialization, unsubstantiality, spirituality; inextension; astral plane.

personality; I, myself, me; *ego*, spirit &c. (*soul*) 450; astral body; immaterialism; spiritual-ism, -ist; subliminal –, subconscious- self.

V. disembody, spiritualize, dematerialize.

Adj. immateri-al, -ate; incorpor-eal, -al; asomatous, unextended; un-, disembodied; extramundane, supersensible, unearthly; pneumatoscopic; spiritual &c. (*psychical*) 450; aery.

personal, subjective.

V. materialize, incorporate, incarnate, substantiate, embody.

Adj. material, bodily; corpor-eal, -al; physical; somat-ic, -oscopic; sensible, tangible, ponderable, palpable, substantial; fleshly, incarnate.

objective, impersonal, neuter, unspiritual, materialistic.

318. World.—N. world, creation, nature, universe; earth, globe, wide world; *cosmos*; terraqueous globe, sphere; macro-, mega-cosm; music of the spheres.

heavens, sky, welkin, empyrean; starry -heaven, – host; firmament; vault –, canopy- of heaven; celestial spaces.

heavenly bodies, stars, luminaries, nebulæ; galaxy, milky way, galactic circle, *via lactea*.

sun, orb of day, Apollo, Phœbus; photo-, chromo-sphere; solar system; planet, -oid, asteroid; comet; satellite; moon, orb of night, Diana, Luna; aerolite, meteor; falling –, shooting- star; meteorite.

constellation, zodiac, signs of the zodiac, Charles's wain, Great Bear, Southern Cross, Orion's belt, Cassiopeia's chair, Pleiades &c.

colures, equator, ecliptic, orbit.

[Science of heavenly bodies] astronomy; urano-graphy, -logy; cosmo-logy, -graphy, -gony; *eidouranion*, orrery; geography; geodesy

&c. (*measurement*) 466; star-gazing, -gazer; astronomer; cosmogonist, geodesist, geographer; observatory.

Adj. cosmic, cosmical, mundane; terr-estrial, -estrious, -aqueous, -ene, -eous; telluric, earthly, geotic, geodetic, cosmogonal, under the sun; sub-lunary, -astral.

solar, heliacal; lunar; celestial, heavenly, empyreal, sphery; starry, stellar; sider-eal, -al; astral; nebular.

Adv. in all creation, on the face of the globe, here below, under the sun.

319. Gravity.—N. gravi-ty, -tation; weight; heaviness &c. *adj.*; specific gravity; ponderosity, pressure, load; bur-den, -then; ballast, counterpoise; lump -, mass -, weight- of.

lead, millstone, mountain, Ossa on Pelion.

weighing, ponderation, trutination; weights; avoirdupois -, troy -, apothecaries'- weight; grain, scruple, drachm, ounce, pound, lb., load, stone, hundred-weight, cwt., ton, quintal, carat, penny-weight, tod, gramme, kilogramme &c.

[Weighing instrument] balance, scales, steelyard, beam, weighbridge, spring balance, weighing machine.

[Science of gravity] statics.

V. be -heavy &c. *adj.*; gravitate, weigh, press, cumber, load.

[Measure the weight of] weigh, poise.

Adj. weighty; weighing &c. *v.*; heavy, - as lead; ponder-ous, -able; lump-ish, -y; cumber-, burden-some; cumbrous, unwieldy, massive. in-, superin-cumbent.

320. Levity.—N. levity; lightness &c. *adj.*; imponderability, imponderables, buoyancy, volatility.

feather, dust, mote, down, thistle-down, flue, cobweb, gossamer, straw, cork, bubble; float, buoy; ether, air.

leaven, ferment, barm, yeast, enzyme.

V. be -light &c. *adj.*; float, swim, be buoyed up.

render -light &c. *adj.*; lighten, levi-tate; leaven.

Adj. light, subtile, subtle, airy; im-ponder-ous, -able; astatic, weightless, ethereal, sublimated; uncompressed, volatile; buoyant, floating &c. *v.*; barmy, frothy; portable.

light as -a feather, - thistle down, - air.

fermenting &c. *n.*

Section II. INORGANIC MATTER

1°. Solid Matter

321. Density.—N. density, solidity; solidness &c. *adj.*; impenetra-, im-permea-bility; incompressibility; im-porosity; cohesion &c. 46; constipa-tion, consistence, spissitude.

specific gravity; hydro-, areo-meter.

condensation; solid-ation, -ification; consolidation; concretion, caseation, coagulation; petrifaction &c. (*harden-ing*) 323; crystallization, precipitation; deposit, precipitate, silt; inspissation; thickening &c. *v.*

indivisibility, indiscerptibility, in-dissolvableness.

solid body, mass, block, knot, lump; con-cretion, -crete, -glomerate; cake,

322. Rarity.—N. rarity; tenuity; absence of -solidity &c. 321; subtility; sponginess, compressibility.

rarefaction, expansion, dilatation, inflation, subtilization.

ether &c. (*gas*) 334.

V. rarefy, expand, dilate, subtilize, attenuate, thin.

Adj. rare, subtile, thin, fine, tenuous, compressible, flimsy, slight; light &c. 320; cavernous, spongy &c. (*hollow*) 252.

rarefied &c. *v.*; unsubstantial; un-com-pact, -pressed.

clot, stone, curd, coagulum, grume; bone, gristle, cartilage.

V. be -dense &c. *adj.*; become –, render- solid &c. *adj.*; solid-ify, -ate; concrete, set, take a set, consolidate, congeal, coagulate; curd, -le; fix, clot, cake, candy, precipitate, deposit, cohere, crystallize; petrify &c. (*harden*) 323.

condense, thicken, inspissate, incrassate; compress, squeeze, ram down, constipate.

Adj. dense, solid; solidified &c. *v.*; cohe-rent, -sive &c. 46; compact, close, serried, thickset; substantial, massive, lumpish; impenetrable, impermeable, imporous; incompressible; constipated; concrete &c. (*hard*) 323; knot-ted, -ty; gnarled; crystal-line, -lizable; thick, grumous, stuffy.

un-dissolved, -melted, -liquefied, -thawed.

in-divisible, -discerptible, -frangible, -dissolvable, -dissoluble, -soluble, -fusible.

323. Hardness.—N. hardness &c. *adj.*; rigidity, renitence, inflexibility, temper, callosity, durity.

induration, petrifaction; lapid-ification, -escence; vitri-, ossi-, corni-fication; crystallization.

stone, pebble, flint, marble, rock, fossil, crag, crystal, quartz, granite, adamant; bone, cartilage; heart of oak, block, board, deal board; iron, steel; cast –, wrought- iron; nail; brick, concrete; cement.

V. render -hard &c. *adj.*; harden, stiffen, indurate, petrify, temper, ossify, vitrify.

Adj. hard, rigid, stubborn, stiff, firm; starch, -ed; stark, unbending, unlimber, unyielding; inflexible, tense; indurate, -d; gritty, proof.

adamant-ine, -ean; concrete, stony, rocky, lithic, granitic, vitreous; crystalline; horny, corneous; bony; oss-eous, -ific; cartilaginous; hard as a -stone &c. *n.*; stiff as -buckram, – a poker.

324. Softness.—N. softness, pliableness &c. *adj.*; flexibility; pli-ancy, -ability; sequacity, malleability; flabbiness; duct-, tract-ility; extend-, extensibility; plasticity; inelasticity, flaccidity, laxity.

clay, wax, butter, dough, pudding; cushion, pillow, feather-bed, pad, down, padding, wadding.

mollification; softening &c. *v.*

V. render -soft &c. *adj.*; soften, mollify, mellow, relax, temper; mash, knead, squash, *massage.*

bend, yield, relent, relax, give.

Adj. soft, tender, supple; pli-ant, -able; flex-ible, -ile; lithe, -some; lissom, limber, plastic; ductile; tract-ile, -able; malleable, extensile, sequacious, inelastic, mollient.

yielding &c. *v.*; flabby, limp, flimsy.

flaccid, flocculent, downy; spongy, œdematous, medullary, doughy, argillaceous, mellow.

soft as -butter, – down, – silk; yielding as wax; tender as a chicken.

325. Elasticity. — N. elasticity, springiness, spring, resilience, renitency, buoyancy.

india-rubber, caoutchouc, guttapercha, whalebone, gum elastic.

V. be -elastic &c. *adj.*; spring back &c. (*recoil*) 277.

Adj. elastic, tensile, springy, ductile, resilient, renitent, buoyant.

326. Inelasticity.—N. want of –, absence of- elasticity &c. 325; inelasticity &c. (*softness*) 324.

Adj. inelastic &c. (*soft*) 324.

327. Tenacity.—N. tenacity, toughness, strength; cohesion &c. 46; sequacity; stubbornness &c. (*obstinacy*) 606; viscidity &c. 352.

leather; gristle, cartilage.

328. Brittleness.—N. brittleness &c. *adj.*; frag-, friab-, frangib-, fiss-ility; frailty; house of -cards, – glass.

V. be -brittle &c. *adj.*; live in a glass house.

V. be -tenacious &c. *adj.*; resist fracture.

Adj. tenacious, tough, cohesive, adhesive, strong, resisting, sequacious, stringy, gristly, cartilaginous, leathery, coriaceous, tough as whit-leather; stubborn &c. (*obstinate*) 606.

break, crack, snap, split, shiver, splinter, crumble, break short, burst, fly, give way; fall to pieces; crumble -to, – into- dust.

Adj. breakable, brittle, frangible, fragile, frail, friable, delicate, gimcrack, shivery, fissile; splitting &c. *v.*; lacerable, splintery, crisp, crimp, short, brittle as glass.

---

329. [Structure.] Texture.—N. structure, organization, anatomy, frame, mould, fabric, construction; frame-work, carcass, architecture; stratification, cleavage.

substance, stuff, *compages*, *parenchyma*; constitution, staple, organism.

[Science of structures] organ-, oste-, my-, splanchn-, neur-, angi-, aden-ology; angi-, aden-ography.

texture; inter-, con-texture; tissue, grain, web, surface; warp and -woof, – weft; tooth, nap &c. (*roughness*) 256; fineness –, coarseness- of grain.

[Science of textures] histology.

Adj. structural, organic; anatomic, -al.

text-ural, -ile; fine-, coarse-grained; fine, delicate, subtile, gossamery, filmy; coarse; home-spun; linsey-woolsey.

330. Pulverulence.—N. [State of powder.] pulverulence; sandiness &c. *adj.*; efflorescence; friability.

powder, dust, sand, shingle; sawdust; grit; attrition; meal, bran, flour, *farina*, spore, sporule; crumb, seed, grain; particle &c. (*smallness*) 32; thermion; limature, filings, *débris*, *detritus*, scobs, magistery, fine powder; *flocculi*.

smoke; cloud of -dust, – sand, – smoke; puff –, volume -of smoke; sand –, dust- storm.

[Reduction to powder] pulverization, comminution, attenuation, granulation, disintegration, subaction, contusion, trituration, levigation, abrasion, detrition, multure; limation; filing &c. *v.*

[Instruments for pulverization] mill, millstone, grater, rasp, file, pestle and mortar, nutmeg grater, teeth, molar, grinder, chopper, grindstone, kern, quern, muller.

V. come to dust; be -disintegrated, – reduced to powder &c.

reduce –, grind- to powder; pulverize, comminute, granulate, triturate, levigate; scrape, file, abrade, rub down, grind, grate, rasp, pound, bray, bruise; con-tuse, -tund; beat, crush, cranch, craunch, crunch, muller, scranch, crumble, disintegrate; attenuate &c. 195.

Adj. powdery, pulverulent, granular, mealy, floury, farinaceous, branny, furfuraceous, flocculent, dusty, sandy, sabulous; aren-ose, -arious, -aceous; gritty; efflorescent, impalpable.

pulverizable; friable, crumbly, shivery; pulverized &c. *v.*; attrite; in pieces.

331. Friction.—N. friction, attrition; rubbing &c. *v.*; erasure; con-frication, -trition; affriction, abrasion, arrosion, limature, frication, rub; elbow-grease; rosin; *massage*.

V. rub, scratch, abrade, scrape, scrub,

332. [Absence of friction. Prevention of friction.] **Lubrication.—N.** smoothness &c. 255; unctuousness &c. 355.

lubri-cation, -fication; anointment; oiling &c. *v.*

fray, rasp, graze, curry, scour, polish, rub out, erase, gnaw; file, grind &c. (*reduce to powder*) 330; *massage*.

set one's teeth on edge; rosin.

Adj. anatriptic, abrasive.

synovia; lubricant, graphite, glycerine, oil &c. 356; saliva; lather.

V. lubri-cate, -citate; oil, grease, lather, soap; wax.

Adj. lubricated &c. *v.*

2°. FLUID MATTER

1. *Fluids in General*

333. Fluidity.—N. fluidity, liquidity; liquidness &c. *adj.*; gaseity &c. 334; liquefaction &c. 334.

fluid, inelastic fluid; liquid, liquor; lymph, humour, juice, sap, serum, blood, serosity, gravy, rheum, ichor, sanies.

solu-bility, -bleness.

[Science of liquids] hydro-logy, -statics, -dynamics, hydraulics &c.

V. be -fluid &c. *adj.*; flow &c. (*water in motion*) 348; liquefy &c. 335.

Adj. liquid, fluid, serous, juicy, succulent, sappy; fluent &c. (*flowing*) 348.

liquefied &c. 335; uncongealed; soluble, hydrostatic &c. *n.*

334. Gaseity.—N. gaseity, gaseousness; vapourousness &c. *adj.*; flatulence, -lency; volatility, aeration, gasification.

elastic fluid, gas, air, vapour, ether, steam, fume, reek, *effluvium, flatus*; cloud &c. 353.

[Science of elastic fluids] pneumat-ics, -ostatics; aero-statics, -dynamics &c.

gas-, gaso-meter.

V. gassify, aerate, aerify; emit vapour &c. 336.

Adj. gaseous, aeriform, ethereal, aerial, airy, vaporous, volatile, evaporable; flatulent; aerostatic &c. *n.*

335. Liquefaction.—N. liquefaction; liquescen-ce, -cy, deliquescence; melting &c. (*heat*) 384; colliqu-ation, -efaction; thaw; de-, liquation; lixiviation, dissolution.

solution, apozem, lixivium, infusion, decoction, flux.

solvent, diluent, menstruum, alkahest, *aqua fortis*.

V. render -liquid &c. 333; liquefy, run, deliquesce; melt &c. (*heat*) 384; solve; dissolve, resolve; liquate; hold in solution; leach, lixiviate.

Adj. lique-fied &c. *v.*, -scent, -fiable; deliquescent, soluble, colliquative; solvent.

336. Vaporization. — N. vapor-, volatil-ization; gasification; e-, vaporation; distillation, cohobation, sublimation, exhalation; volatility.

vaporizer, still, retort, spray, atomizer; fumigation, steaming.

V. render -gaseous &c. 334; vaporize, volatilize; distil, sublime; evaporate, exhale, smoke, transpire, emit vapour, fume, reek, steam, fumigate.

Adj. volatilized &c. *v.*; reeking &c. *v.*; volatile; evaporable, vaporizable.

2. *Specific Fluids*

337. Water.—N. water; serum, serosity; lymph; rheum; diluent.

dilution, maceration, lotion; washing &c. *v.*; im-, mersion; humectation, infiltration, spargefaction, affusion, irrigation, *douche*, balneation, bath.

deluge &c. (*water in motion*) 348; high water, flood-, spring-tide.

338. Air.—N. air &c. (*gas*) 334; common -, atmospheric- air; atmosphere, stratosphere, isothermal layer, troposphere, Heaviside layer.

open, - air; sky, welkin; blue, - sky; cloud &c. 353.

weather, climate, rise and fall of the barometer, isobar.

V. be -watery &c. *adj.*; reek.

add water, water, wet; moisten &c. 339; dilute, dip, immerse; merge; im-, sub-merge; plunge, souse, duck, drown; soak, steep, macerate, pickle, wash, sprinkle, sparge, lave, bathe, affuse, splash, swash, douse, slosh, drench; dabble, slop, slobber, irrigate, inundate, deluge; syringe, inject, gargle; infiltrate, percolate.

Adj. watery, aqueous, aquatic, lymphatic; balneal, diluent; drenching &c. *v.*; diluted &c. *v.*; weak; wet &c. (*moist*) 339.

Phr. the waters are out.

339. Moisture.—N. moisture; moistness &c. *adj.*; hum-idity, -ectation; madefaction, dew; *serein*; marsh &c. 345; Hygromet-ry, -er.

V. moisten, wet; humect, -ate; sponge, damp, dampen, bedew; imbue, imbrue, infiltrate, saturate; seethe, sop; soak, drench &c. (*water*) 337.

be -moist &c. *adj.*; not have a dry thread; perspire &c. (*exude*) 295.

Adj. moist, damp; watery &c. 337; undried, humid, wet, dank, muggy, dewy; roric; roscid; juicy.

wringing wet; wet -through, - to the skin; saturated &c. *v.*

swashy, soggy, dabbled; reeking, seething, dripping, soaking, soft, sodden, sloppy, muddy; swampy &c. (*marshy*) 345; irriguous.

341. Ocean.—N. sea, ocean, main, deep, brine, salt water, waters, waves, billows, high seas, offing, great waters, watery waste, 'vasty deep,' briny ocean, herring pond, steamer track, the seven seas; wave, tide &c. (*water in motion*) 348.

hydrograph-y, -er, oceanography; Neptune, Thetis, Triton, Naiad, Nereid; sea-nymph, Siren, mer-maid, -man; trident, dolphin.

Adj. oceanic; mar-ine, -itime; pleagic, -ian; sea-going, -worthy; hydrographic.

Adv. at -, on- sea; afloat, on the high seas.

[Science of air] pneumatics, aero-logy, -scopy, -graphy; meteorology, climatology; eudio-, baro-, aero-meter; aneroid, baro-graph, -scope; weather-gauge, -glass, -cock.

exposure to the -air, - weather; ventilation; aero-station, -nautics, -naut &c. 265 and 269.

V. air, ventilate; fan &c. (*wind*) 349.

Adj. containing air, flatulent, effervescent; windy &c. 349.

atmospheric, airy; aeri-al, -form; pneumatic; meteorological; weatherwise.

Adv. in the open air, out of doors, *à la belle étoile, al fresco; sub -Jove, - dio.*

340. Dryness.—N. dryness &c. *adj.*; siccity, aridity, drought, ebb-, neaptide, low water.

drying, ex-, de-siccation; evaporation; dehydration; arefaction, dephlegmation, drainage.

drier, desiccator.

V. be -dry &c. *adj.*; render -dry &c. *adj.*; dry; dry -, soak- up; sponge, swab, wipe; ex-, de-siccate, dehydrate, anhydrate; drain, parch.

be fine, hold up.

Adj. dry, anhydrous, arid, waterless; dried &c. *v.*; undamped; juice-, sapless; sear; husky; rainless, without rain, fine; dry as -a bone, - dust, - a stick, - a mummy, - a biscuit; desiccated; dehydrated; water-proof, -tight.

342. Land.—N. land, earth, ground, dry land, *terra firma.*

continent, mainland, peninsula, delta; tongue -, neck- of land; isthmus; oasis; promontory &c. (*projection*) 250; highland &c. (*height*) 206.

coast, shore, scar, strand, beach; bank, lea; sea- board, -side, -shore, -bank, -coast, -beach; rock-, ironbound coast; loom of the land; derelict; innings; *alluvium*, alluvion.

soil, glebe, clay, loam, marl, cledge, chalk, gravel, mould, subsoil, clod, clot; rock, crag, cliff.

acres; real estate &c. (*property*) 780; landsman, land-lubber, farmer.

geography &c. 318; agriculture &c. 371.

V. land, come to land; set foot on -the soil, - dry land; come -, go- ashore.

Adj. earthy; continental, midland; littoral, riparian, ripuarian; alluvial; terrene &c. (*world*) 318; landed, predial, territorial.

Adv. ashore; on -shore, - land.

343. Gulf. Lake.—N. land covered with water, gulf, gulph, bay, inlet, bight, estuary, arm of the sea, fiord, armlet; frith, firth, ostiary, mouth; lagune, lagoon; indraught; cove, creek; natural harbour; roads; strait, narrows; Euripus; sound, belt, gut, kyles.

lake, loch, lough, mere, tarn, plash, broad, pond, pool, lin, puddle, well, artesian well, tank, sump; standing -, dead -, sheet of- water; fish -, mill-pond; race; ditch, dike, dyke, dam; reservoir &c. (*store*) 636.

Adj. lacustrine; land locked.

345. Marsh.—N. marsh, swamp, morass, marish, moss, fen, bog, quag-mire, slough, sump, wash; mud, squash, slush.

Adj. marsh, -y; swampy, boggy, plashy, poachy, quaggy, soft; muddy, sloppy, squashy, spongy; paludal; moor-ish, -y; fenny.

344. Plain.—N. plain, table land, mesa, face of the country; open -, champaign-country; basin, downs, waste, weary waste, desert, tundra, wild, steppe, pampas, savanna, prairie, champaign, heath, common, wold, veld; moor, -land, uplands, fell; bush; *plateau* &c. (*level*) 213; *campagna*.

meadow, mead, haugh, pasturage, park, field, lawn, green, plat, plot, grass-plat, greensward, sward, grass, turf, sod, heather; lea, ley, lay; grounds.

Adj. campestrian, champaign, allu-vial.

346. Island.—N. island, isle, islet, eyot, ait, holm, reef, atoll, breaker; archipelago; islander.

Adj. insular, sea-girt.

---

3. *Fluids in Motion*

347. [Fluid in motion.] **Stream.—N.** stream &c. (*of water*) 348, (*of air*) 349.

V. flow &c. 348; blow &c. 349.

348. [Water in motion.] **River.—N.** running water.

jet, spirt, squirt, spout, splash, swash, rush, gush, *jet d'eau*; sluice, chute.

water-spout, -fall; fall, cascade, force, foss; lin, -n; ghyll, Niagara; cata-ract, -dupe, -clysm; *débâcle*, in-undation, deluge.

rain, -fall; *serein*; shower, scud; downpour, cloud burst; driving -, pouring -, drenching- rain; hyeto-logy, -graphy; rainy season, monsoon; pre-dominance of Aquarius, reign of St. Swithin; mizzle, drizzle, *stillicidium*, plash; dropping &c. *v.*

stream, course, flux, flow, profluence; effluence &c. (*egress*) 295; defluxion; flowing &c. *v.*; current, tide, race.

spring; fount, -ain; rill, rivulet, gill,

349. [Air in motion.] **Wind.—N.** wind, draught, *flatus*, *afflatus*, air; breath, - of air; puff, whiff, zephyr; blow, drift; *aura*; stream, current; under-current.

gust, blast, breeze, squall, gale, half a gale, storm, tempest, hurricane, whirlwind, tornado, samiel, cyclone, typhoon; simoon; harmattan, monsoon, trade wind, sirocco, *mistral, bise, föhn,* tramontane, levanter; capful of wind; fresh -, stiff- breeze; keen blast; blizzard.

windiness &c. *adj.*; ventosity; rough -, dirty -, ugly -, stress of- weather; dirty-, windy-, mackerel- sky; mare's tail; thick -, black -, white- squall.

anemography, aerodynamics; wind-gauge, anemometer, weather-cock, vane.

gullet, rillet; stream-, brook-let; runnel, sike, burn, beck, brook, stream, river; reach; tributary.

body of water, torrent, rapids, flush, flood, swash, spate; spring -, high -, full-tide; bore; eagre, *hygre*; fresh, -et; undertow, indraught, reflux, under-current, eddy, vortex, gurge, whirlpool, Maelström, regurgitation, overflow; confluence, corrivation.

wave, billow, surge, swell, ripple; roller, ground swell, surf, breaker, white horses; comber, beach-comber; rough -, heavy -, cross -, long -, short -, chopping -, choppy- sea, choppiness; tidal wave.

[Science of fluids in motion] Hydro-dynamics; Hydraul-ics &c.; rain-gauge &c.

water-bearer, - carrier, Aquarius.

irrigation &c. (*water*) 337; pump; watering-pot, - cart; hydrant, stand-pipe, hose, sprinkler, drencher; fire-engine, squirt, syringe.

V. flow, run; meander; gush, pour, spout, roll, jet, well, issue; drop, drip, dribble, plash, squirt, spurt, spirtle, trill, trickle, distil, percolate; stream, overflow, inundate, deluge, flow over, splash, swash; guggle, murmur, babble, bubble, purl, gurgle, sputter, regurgitate; ooze, flow out &c. (*egress*) 295.

rain, - hard, - in torrents, - cats and dogs, - pitchforks; come down in sheets; pour with rain, drizzle, mizzle, spit, sprinkle, set in.

flow -, fall -, open -, drain- into; discharge itself, disembogue.

[Cause a flow] pour; pour out &c. (*discharge*) 297; shower down; irrigate, drench &c. (*wet*) 337; spill, splash.

[Stop a flow] stanch; dam, -up &c. (*close*) 261; obstruct &c. 706.

Adj. fluent; dif-, pro-, af-fluent; tidal; flowing &c. *v.*; meand-ering, -ry, -rous; fluvi-al, -atile; streamy, showery, rainy, drizzly, drizzling, pluvial, pluviose, stillicidous.

suf-, insuf-, per-, in-, af-flation; blowing, fanning &c. *v.*; ventilation.

sneezing &c. *v.*; sternutation; hic-cup, -cough; catching of the breath; breathing &c.

Eolus, Eurus, Boreas, Zephyr, cave of Eolus.

air-pump, lungs, bellows, blow-pipe, fan, blower; pulmotor, ventilator, punkah, aspirator, exhauster, ejector.

V. blow, waft; blow -hard, - great guns, - a hurricane &c. *n.*; whistle, roar, howl, ring in the shrouds; stream, issue.

respire, breathe, in-, ex-hale, puff; whif, -fle; gasp, wheeze; snuff, -le; sniff, -le; sneeze, cough, belch.

fan, ventilate; in-, per-flate; blow -, pump- up.

Adj. blowing &c. *v.*; windy, airy, æolian, flatulent; breezy, gusty, squally; stormy, tempestuous, blustering; bois-terous &c. (*violent*) 173.

pulmon-ic, -ary.

---

350. [Channel for the passage of water.] **Conduit.**—**N.** conduit, channel, duct, watercourse, race; head -, tail-race; adit, aqueduct, canal, trough, flume, gutter, pantile; dike, canyon, ravine, gorge, hollow, main, gully, moat, ditch, drain, sewer, culvert, *cloaca*, sough, kennel, siphon, *piscina*; pipe &c. (*tube*) 260; funnel; tunnel &c. (*passage*) 627; water -, waste- pipe; emunctory, gully-hole, artery, aorta, vein, blood vessel; lymphatic; throat, alimentary canal, intestine; pore, spout, scupper; ad-, a-jutage;

351. [Channel for the passage of air.] **Air-pipe.**—**N.** air-pipe, - shaft, - way, - passage, - tube; shaft, flue, chimney, funnel, vent, blow-hole, nostril, nozzle, throat, weasand, *trachea; bronch-us, -ia*; larynx, tonsils, wind-pipe, spiracle; venti-duct, -lator; louvre, Venetian blinds; blow-pipe &c. (*wind*) 349; pipe &c. (*tube*) 260.

hose; gar-, gur-goyle; penstock, weir; flood-, water-gate; sluice, lock, valve; rose; waterworks.

Adj. vascular &c. (*with holes*) 260.

3°. IMPERFECT FLUIDS

352. Semiliquidity.—N. semiliquidity; stickiness &c. *adj.*; visc-idity, -osity; gumm-, glutin-, muc-osity; spiss-, crass-itude; lentor; adhesiveness &c. (*cohesion*) 46.

inspiss-, incrass-ation; thickening, coagulation.

jelly, aspic, mucilage, gelatin, isinglass; colloid, mucus, phlegm; pituite, lava; glair, starch, gluten, albumen, milk, cream, protein; syrup, treacle; gum, size, glue, paste; wax, bee's-wax; emulsoid, emulsion, soup; squash, mud, slush, slime, ooze; moisture &c. 339; marsh &c. 345.

V. inspiss-, incrass-ate; coagulate, gelatinize, gelatinify, gel, jell, emulsify, thicken; mash, squash, churn, beat up.

Adj. semi-fluid, -liquid; half-melted, -frozen; milky, muddy &c. *n.*; lact-eal, -ean, -eous, -escent, -iferous; emulsive, curdled, thick, succulent, uliginous.

gelat-, album-, mucilag-, glut-inous; gelatine, mastic, amylaceous, ropy, clammy, clotted; vis-cid, -cous; sticky, tacky; slab, -by; lentous, pituitous; mu-cid, -culent, -cous.

354. Pulpiness.—N. pulpiness &c. *adj.*; pulp, paste, dough, sponge, curd, pap, rob, jam, pudding, mush, fool, poultice, grume.

Adj. pulpy &c. *n.*; pultaceous, grumous.

V. pulp, pulpify, mash.

353. [Mixture of air and water.] Bubble. [Cloud.]—N. bubble; foam, froth, head, fume, spume, lather, suds, spray, surf, yeast, barm, spindrift.

cloud, vapour, fog, mist, haze, steam; scud, rack, *nimbus*; *cumulus*, woolpack, *cirrus, stratus*; *cirro-, cumulo-stratus*; *cirro-cumulus*; mackerel sky, mare's tail, dirty sky.

[Science of clouds] nephelognosy, nephology.

effervescence, fermentation; bubbling &c. *v.*

nebula; cloudiness &c. (*opacity*) 426; nebulosity &c. (*dimness*) 422.

V. bubble, boil, foam, froth, spume, mantle, sparkle, guggle, gurgle; effervesce, ferment, fizzle; aerate; cloud, overcast, befog.

Adj. bubbling &c. *v.*; frothy, nappy, effervescent, sparkling, *mousseux*, up, fizzy, with a head on.

cloudy &c. *n.*; vaporous, nebulous, overcast; nubiferous, nephological; foggy, brumous.

355. Unctuousness.—N. unctuousness &c. *adj.*; unctuosity, lubricity; ointment &c. (*oil*) 356; anointment; lubrication &c. 332.

V. oil &c. (*lubricate*) 332.

Adj. unctuous, oily, oleaginous, adipose, sebaceous; fat, -ty; greasy; waxy, butyraceous, soapy, saponaceous, pinguid, lardaceous; slippery.

356. Oil.—N. oil, fat, butter, cream, grease, tallow, suet, lard, dripping, margarine, oleomargarine, exunge, blubber; glycerine, stearine, elaine, oleagine; soap; soft soap, wax, cerement; paraffin, spermaceti, adipocere; petroleum, mineral -, rock -, crystal- oil, kerosene, vegetable -, colza -, olive -, linseed -, cotton seed -, rape -, nut -, fusel- oil; animal -, neat's foot -, signal -, train- oil; ointment, unguent, liniment, salve, pomade, pomatum, brilliantine, spike -, nard.

356a. Resin.—N. resin, rosin, colophony; gum; lac, shellac, sealing-wax; amber, -gris; bitumen, pitch, tar, asphalt, -e, -um; varnish, copal, mastic, magilp, lacquer, japan.

V. varnish &c. (*overlay*) 223.

Adj. resinous, bituminous, pitchy, tarry.

SECTION III.　ORGANIC MATTER

1°. VITALITY

1. *Vitality in general*

357. Organization.—N. organized
-world, – nature; living –, animated-
nature; living beings; organic remains,
organism; fossils; animal and vegetable
kingdom, *fauna* and *flora*, biota.

prot-oplasm, -ein; albumen; structure &c. 329; organ-ization, -ism.

[Science of living beings] biology;
natural history,* organic –, bio-chemis-
try, anatomy, physiology, embryology,
morphology, evolution, Darwinism,
Lamarkism, zoology &c. 368; botany
&c. 369; naturalist, biologist &c.

Adj. organ-ic, -ized.

359. Life.—N. life; vi-tality, -ability;
animation; vital -spark, – flame, –
force.

respiration, wind; breath -of life, –
of one's nostrils; life-blood; Archeus;
existence &c. 1.

vivification, vitalization; revivification &c. 163; Prometheus; life to come
&c. (*destiny*) 152.

[Science of life] physiology, etiology,
embryology, biology; animal economy.

nourishment, staff of life &c. (*food*)
298.

V. be -alive &c. *adj.*; live, breathe,
respire; subsist &c. (*exist*) 1; walk the
earth; strut and fret one's hour upon
a stage; be spared.

see the light, be born, come into the
world; fetch –, draw- -breath, – the
breath of life; quicken; revive; come
to, – life.

give birth to &c. (*produce*) 161;
bring to life, put into life, vitalize;
vivi-fy, -ficate; reanimate &c. (*restore*)
660; keep -alive, – body and soul
together, – the wolf from the door;
support life.

have nine lives like a cat.

358. Inorganization. — N. mineral
-world, – kingdom; unorganized –,
inorganic –, brute –, inanimate- matter.
[Science of the mineral kingdom]
mineralogy; geo-logy, -gnosy, -scopy;
metall-urgy, -ography; lithology;
orycto-logy, -graphy.

V. turn to dust, pulverize.

Adj. in-organic, -animate; unorganized; azoic; mineral.

----

360. Death.—N. death, dying &c. *v.*;
de-cease, -mise; dissolution, departure,
obit, release, rest, *quietus*, fall; loss,
bereavement.

end &c. 67 –, cessation &c. 142 –, loss
–, extinction –, ebb- of -life &c. 359.

death-warrant, -watch, -rattle, -bed;
stroke –, agonies –, shades –, valley of
the shadow –, jaws –, hand- of death;
last -breath, – gasp, – agonies; dying
-day, – breath, – agonies; swan song,
chant du cygne; *rigor mortis*; Stygian
shore; crossing the bar, the great
adventure.

King -of terrors, – Death; Death,
Angel of Death; mortality; doom &c.
(*necessity*) 601.

euthanasia; happy release; break up
of the system; natural -death, – decay;
sudden –, violent- death; untimely end,
watery grave; suffocation, *asphyxia*;
heart failure; fatal disease &c. (*disease*)
655; death-blow &c. (*killing*) 361.

necrology, bills of mortality, obituary; death-song &c. (*lamentation*) 839.

V. die, expire, perish; meet one's
-death, – end; pass away, be taken;
yield –, resign- one's breath; resign

* The term *Natural History* is also used as relating to all the objects in Nature
whether organic or inorganic, and including therefore *Mineralogy, Geology,
Meteorology,* &c.

Adj. living, alive; in -life, – the flesh, – the land of the living; on this side of the grave, above ground, breathing, quick, animated, viable; lively &c. (*active*) 682; alive and kicking; tenacious of life.

vital; vivi-fying, -fied &c. *v.*; Promethean.

Adv. *vivendi causâ.*

one's -being, – life; end one's -days, – life, – earthly career; breathe one's last; cease to -live, – breathe; depart this life; be -no more &c. *adj.*; go –, drop –, pop -off; lose –, lay down –, relinquish –, surrender- one's life; drop –, sink- into the grave; close one's eyes; fall –, drop- dead, – down dead; break one's neck; give –, yield- up the ghost; be all over with one.

pay the debt to nature, shuffle off this mortal coil, take one's last sleep; go the way of all flesh; join the -greater number, – majority, – choir invisible, to life immortal awake; come –, turn- to dust; cross the Stygian ferry; go to -one's long account, – one's last home, – Davy Jones's locker, – the wall; receive one's death warrant, make one's will, die a natural death, go out like the snuff of a candle; come to an untimely end; catch one's death; go off the hooks, kick the bucket, peg out; go West; hop the twig, turn up one's toes; die a violent death &c. (*be killed*) 361; make the supreme sacrifice.

Adj. dead, lifeless; deceased, demised, departed, defunct; late, gone, no more; ex-, in-animate; out of the world, taken off, released; departed this life &c. *v.*; dead and gone; bereft of life, stone dead, dead as -a door nail, – a door post, – mutton, – a herring, – nits; launched into eternity, gathered to one's fathers, numbered with the dead, gone to a better land, behind the veil, beyond the grave, – mortal ken.

dying &c. *v.*; mori-bund, -ent, Acherontic; hippocratic; *in -articulo, – extremis*; in the -jaws, – agony- of death; going, – off; *aux abois*; on one's -last legs, – death bed; at -the point of death, – death's door, – the last gasp; near one's end, given over, booked, fey; with one foot in –, tottering on the brink of- the grave.

still-born; mortuary; deadly &c. (*killing*) 361.

Adv. *post -obit, – mortem.*

Phr. life -ebbs, – fails, – hangs by a thread; one's -days are numbered, – hour is come, – race is run, – doom is sealed; Death -knocks at the door, – stares one in the face; the breath is out of the body; the grave closes over one; *sic itur ad astra.*

361. [Destruction of life; violent death.] **Killing.**—**N.** killing &c. *v.*; homicide, manslaughter, murder, assassination, trucidation, occision; lynching, effusion of blood; blood, -shed; gore, slaughter, carnage, butchery; *battue*, gladiatorial combat.

massacre; *fusillade, noyade, pogrom*; thuggism; racketeering.

death blow, finishing stroke, *coup de grâce, quietus*; execution &c. (*capital punishment*) 972; judicial murder; martyrdom.

butcher, slayer, murderer, Cain, assassin, cut-throat, garrotter, *bravo*, thug, racketeer, gunman, mobster, gangster, Moloch, *matador, sabreur*; *guet-à-pens*; gallows, executioner &c. (*punishment*) 975; man-eater.

regicide, parricide, fratricide, infanticide, aborticide &c.

suicide, *felo de se, suttee, hara kiri*, Juggernaut; immolation, holocaust.

suffocation, strangulation, *garrotte*; hanging &c. *v.*

deadly weapon &c. (*arms*) 727; Aceldama; the potter's field, the field of blood.

fatal accident, violent death, casualty.

[Destruction of animals] slaughtering; phthiozoics;* sport, -ing; the chase, venery; hunting, coursing, shooting, fishing; pig-sticking; sports-, hunts-, fisher-man; hunter, Nimrod; slaughterer, knacker, slaughter-house, shambles, *abattoir*.

V. kill, put to death, slay, shed blood; murder, assassinate, butcher, slaughter; victimize, immolate; massacre; take away –, deprive of-life; make away with, put an end to; despatch, dispatch; burke settle, do, – to death, – for.

strangle, garrotte, hang, lynch, throttle, choke, stifle, suffocate, stop the breath, smother, asphyxiate, drown.

sabre; cut -down, – to pieces, – the throat; jugulate; stab, run through the body, bayonet; put to the -sword, – edge of the sword.

shoot, – dead; blow one's brains out; brain, knock on the head; stone, lapidate; give –, deal- a death blow; give a -*quietus*, – *coup de grâce*.

behead, bowstring &c. (*execute*) 972.

hunt, shoot &c. *n*.

cut off, nip in the bud, launch into eternity, send to one's last account, bump off, rub out, sign one's death warrant, strike the death knell of.

give no quarter, pour out blood like water; decimate; run amuck, wade knee-deep –, imbrue one's hands- in blood.

die a violent death, welter in one's blood; dash –, blow- out one's brains; commit suicide; kill –, -make away with –, put an end to- oneself.

Adj. killing &c. *v.*; murd-, slaught-erous; sanguin-ary, -olent; blood-stained, -thirsty; homicidal, red-handed; bloody, -minded; ensanguined, gory, sanguineous.

mortal, fatal, lethal; dead-, death-ly; mort-, leth-iferous; unhealthy &c. 657; internecine; suicidal.

sporting; piscator-ial, -y.

Adv. in at the death.

362. Corpse.—N. corpse, corse, carcass, bones, skeleton, dry-bones; defunct, relics, *relinquiæ*, remains, mortal remains, dust, ashes, earth, clay; mummy; carrion; food for- worms, – fishes; tenement of clay, this mortal coil.

shade, ghost, *manes*, apparition &c. 980.

organic remains, fossils.

Adj. cadaverous, corpse-like; unburied &c. 363.

363. Interment.—N. interment, burial, inhumation, sepulture, en-tombment; in-, humation; obs-, ex-equies; funeral, wake, pyre, funeral pile; cremation.

funeral -rite, – solemnity; knell, passing bell, tolling; dirge &c. (*lamentation*) 839; cypress; *obit*, dead march, muffled drum; coroner, mortician, undertaker, mute, mourner, professional mourner, pall-bearer; elegy; funeral -oration, – sermon; epitaph.

grave clothes, shroud, winding-sheet, cere-cloth; cerement.

coffin, shell, sarcophagus, urn, pall, bier, hearse, catafalque, cinerary urn.

grave, pit, sepulchre, tomb, vault, crypt, catacomb, mausoleum, *Golgotha*, house of death, narrow house, long home; cemetery, necropolis, boneyard; burial-place, -ground; grave-, church-yard; God's acre; mortuary, tope, cromlech, dolmen, menhir, barrow, tumulus, cairn;

* Bentham, 'Chrestomathia.'

ossuary; bone-, charnel-, dead-house; *Morgue*; lich-gate; crematorium.

sexton, grave-digger.

monument, memorial, cenotaph, shrine; grave-, head-, tomb-stone; *memento mori*; hatchment, stone, cross.

exhumation, disinterment; necropsy, autopsy, *post-mortem* examination.

V. inter, bury; lay in –, consign to- the -grave, – tomb; en-, in-tomb; inhume; lay out, prepare for burial, embalm, mummify; conduct a funeral, hold services; toll the knell; put to bed with a shovel.

exhume, disinter, unearth.

Adj. buried &c. *v.*; burial; fune-real, -brial; mortuary, sepulchral, cinerary; elegiac; necroscopic.

Adv. *in memoriam*; *post-obit, -mortem*; beneath –, under- the sod.

Phr. *hic jacet, ci-git, requiescat in pace.*

2. *Special Vitality*

364. Animality.—N. animal life; anima-tion, -lity, -lization; breath.

flesh, – and blood; corporeal nature; *physique*; strength &c. 159.

V. animalize, incorporate.

Adj. fleshly, incarnate, carnal, corporeal, human.

366. Animal.*—N. animal, – kingdom; *fauna*; brute creation.

beast, brute, creature, created being; creeping –, living- thing; dumb -animal, – creature.

flocks and herds, live stock; domestic –, wild- animals; game, *feræ naturæ*; beasts of the field, fowls of the air, denizens of the day.

vertebrate, bi-, quadru-ped, mammal, marsupial, bird, reptile, batrachian, amphibian, fish, crustacean, shell fish, articulate, mollusc, worm, insect, zoophyte; protozoon, animalcule &c. 193.

horse &c. (*beast of burden*) 271; cattle, kine, ox; bull, -ock; steer, stot; cow, milch-cow, calf, heifer, shorthorn; sheep; lamb, -kin; ewe –, pet- lamb; ewe, ram, tup; pig, swine, boar, hog, shoat, sow; tag, teg, wether.

dog, bitch, hound; pup, -py; whelp, cur, mutt, mongrel; house-, watch-, sheep-, shepherd's-, sporting-, fancy-, lap-, toy-, bull-, badger-dog; mastiff; blood-, grey-, stag-, deer-, fox-, otterhound; harrier, beagle, spaniel, pointer,

365. Vegetability.—N. vegetable life; vegeta-tion, -bility; herbage.

V. vegetate, germinate, sprout, shoot; cultivate.

Adj. vegetable &c. 367; rank, lush.

---

367. Vegetable.*— N. vegetable – kingdom; *flora*, verdure.

plant; tree, shrub, bush; creeper; vine; herb, -age; grass.

annual; per-, bi-, tri-ennial; exotic.

timber; primeval –, virgin- forest; wood, -lands; hurst, frith, holt, weald, park, chase, greenwood, brake, grove, copse, coppice, *bocage, tope*, clump of trees, thicket, spinet, spinney; under-. brush-wood; boscage, scrub; the oak and the ash and the bonny ivy tree.

bush, jungle, prairie; heath, -er; fern, bracken; furze, gorse, whin broom; grass, turf, grassland, greensward, green, lawn, meadow; pas-ture, -turage; turbary; sedge, rush, weed; fungus, mushroom, toadstool; lichen, moss, conferva, mould; seaweed &c.; growth, crop.

foliage, leafage, branch, bough, ramage; spray &c. 51; leaf, frond, flag, petal, shoot, tendril.

flower, blossom, bud, bloom, bine; flowering plant; tree, sapling, pollard; timber-, fruit-tree; palm-, gum-tree; pulse, legume.

* Extended lists of names of specific varieties of animals, vegetables, &c., are beyond the scope of this work; see Introduction, p. xxv.

setter, retriever; Newfoundland; water
-dog, – spaniel; pug, poodle; dachshund;
Pinscher; turnspit; terrier; fox –, Skye-
terrier; Dandie Dinmont; colley.

cat; puss, -y; kitten; grimalkin; gib-,
tom-cat; mouser; fox, Reynard, vixen,
stag, deer, hart, buck, doe, roe, antelope.

bird; poultry, fowl, cock, hen,
chicken, chanticleer, partlet, rooster,
dunghill cock, barn-door fowl; feathered -tribes, – songster; singing –, dicky- bird; canary; finch; auk, dodo, moa, roc, phœnix.

snake, serpent, viper, adder; newt, eft; asp, vermin.

Adj. animal, zoological.

equine, bovine, vaccine, canine, feline; fishy; piscator-y, -ial;
molluscous, vermicular.

Adj. veget-able, -ous; herb-aceous,
-al; botanic; sylvan, silvan; arbor- ary,
-eous, -escent, -ical; dendritic, dendriform; woody, grassy; ver-dant,-durous;
floral, mossy; lign-ous, -eous; wooden,
leguminous; end-, ex-ogenous.

368. [The science of animals.] **Zoology.**—**N.** zoo-logy, -nomy, -graphy,
-tomy; anatomy; comparative anatomy; animal –, comparative- physiology; morphology.

anthrop-, ornith-, ichthy-, herpet-,
ophi-, malac-, helminth-, entom-, oryct-,
paleont-ology; ichthy- &c. -otomy;
taxidermy.

zo- &c. -ologist.

Adj. zoological &c. n.

369. [The science of plants.] **Botany.**
—**N.** botany; phyto-graphy, -logy,
-tomy; vegetable physiology; herbori-
zation, dendr-, myc-, fung-, alg-ology;
flora, pomona; botanist &c.; botanic
garden &c. (*garden*) 371; *hortus siccus,
herbarium,* herbal.

herb-ist, -arist, -alist, -orist, -arian
&c.

V. botanize, herborize.

Adj. botanical &c. n.

370. [The economy or management
of animals.] **Cicuration.**—**N.** taming &c.
v.; cicuration, zoohygiantics; domestication, -ity; *manège*; veterinary art;
breeding, pisciculture, apiculture &c.

menagery, vivarium, zoological garden, zoo; bear-pit; aviary, apiary, hive;
aquarium, fishery, fish hatchery; duck-,
fish-pond; stud-farm; stock farm, dairy.

[Destruction of animals] phthisozo-
ics* &c. (*killing*) 361.

neat-, cow-, shep-herd, shepherdess;
grazier, drover, cowboy, cowkeeper;
trainer, breeder, groom, ostler &c. 746;
veterinary surgeon, vet, horse doctor;
farrier; keeper; game keeper.

cage &c. (*prison*) 752; hen-coop,
bird-cage, cauf; sheep-fold &c. (*inclosure*) 232.

V. tame, domesticate, acclimatize,
breed, tend, break in, train, corral,
round up; cage, bridle &c. (*restrain*)
751; ride &c. 266.

drive, yoke, harness, hitch; groom,

371. [The economy or management
of plants.] **Agriculture.**—**N.** agriculture, cultivation, husbandry, farming;
georgics, geoponics; tillage, tilth, agronomy, gardening, spade husbandry,
vintage; hort-, arbor-, silv-, citr-, vit-,
flor-iculture; intensive culture; landscape gardening; forestry, afforesta-
tion.

husbandman, horticulturist, citri-
culturist, gardener, florist; agricult-or,
-urist; yeoman, farmer, cultivator,
tiller of the soil, ploughman, sower,
reaper; woodcutter, backwoodsman,
forester; vine grower, vintager; Boer;
Triptolemus.

field, meadow, garden; botanic –,
winter –, ornamental –, flower –, kitchen –, truck –, market –, hop- garden;
nursery; green-, hot-, glass-house;
conservatory, cucumber frame, *cloche,*
bed, border, seed-plot; grass-plat,
lawn; park &c. (*pleasure ground*) 840;
parterre, shrubbery, plantation, avenue,

* Bentham.

curry-comb; milk; shear; hatch; incubate.

Adj. pastoral, bucolic; tame, domestic, domesticated, broken in, gentle,
docile.

---

arboretum, pinery, *pinetum*, orchard;
vineyard, vinery; orangery; farm &c.
(*abode*) 189.

V. cultivate; till, – the soil; farm,
garden; sow, plant; reap, mow, cut;
manure, dress the ground, dig, delve,
dibble, hoe, plough, plow, harrow, rake,
weed, lop and top, force, transplant,
thin out, bed out, prune, graft.

Adj. agr-icultural, -arian, -estic.

arable; predial, rural, rustic, country, bucolic, Bœotian; horti-
cultural.

372. Mankind.—N. man, -kind; human -race, – species, – nature;
humanity, mortality, flesh, generation.

[Science of man] anthropo-logy, -graphy, -sophy; ethno-logy, -graphy;
humanitarianism.

human being; person, -age; individual, creature, fellow creature,
mortal, body, somebody, one; such a –, some- one; soul, living soul;
earthling; party, head, hand; *dramatis personæ*.

people, persons, folk, public, society, world; community, – at large;
general public; nation, -ality; state, realm; common-weal, -wealth;
republic, body politic; million &c. (*commonalty*) 876; population &c.
(*inhabitant*) 188.

cosmopolite; lords of the creation; ourselves.

Adj. human, mortal, personal, individual, national, civic, public,
cosmopolitan; anthropoid.

373. Man.—N. man, male, he; manhood &c. (*adolescence*) 131; gentleman,
sir, master; yeoman, wight, swain,
fellow, guy, blade, *beau*, chap, gaffer,
good man; husband &c. (*married man*)
903; Mr., mister, *monsieur, sahib, Herr,
señor, signor*; boy &c. (*youth*) 129;
Adonis.

[Male animal] cock, drake, gander,
dog, boar, stag, hart, buck, horse,
entire horse, stallion; gib-, tom-cat;
he-, Billy-goat; ram, tup; bull, -ock;
capon, ox, gelding; steer, stot.

Adj. male, he, masculine; manly,
virile; un-womanly, -feminine.

---

374. Woman.—N. woman, she, female, petticoat, skirt, moll, broad.

feminality, feminity, muliebrity;
womanhood &c. (*adolescence*) 131;
feminism; gynecology, gyniatrics,
gynics.

womankind; the -sex, – fair; fair –,
softer- sex; weaker vessel; the distaff
side.

dame, madam, *madame*, mistress,
Mrs., lady, *mem-sahib, Frau, señora,
signora, donna, belle,* matron, dowager,
goody, gammer; good -woman, – wife;
squaw; wife &c. (*marriage*) 903; ma-
tron-age, -hood.

Venus, nymph, wench, *grisette*; little
bit of fluff; girl &c. (*youth*) 129.

inamorata (love) &c. 897; courtesan &c. 962.

spinster, old maid, virgin, bachelor girl, new woman, amazon.

[Female animal] hen, slut, bitch, sow, doe, roe, mare; she-, Nanny-
goat; ewe, cow; lioness, tigress; vixen.

gynecæum, harem, *seraglio, zenana, purdah.*

Adj. female, she; feminine, womanly, ladylike, matronly, maidenly;
womanish, effeminate unmanly, gynecic.

2°. Sensation

(1.) *Sensation in general*

375. Physical Sensibility.—**N.** sensibility; sensitiveness &c. *adj.*; physical sensibility, feeling, perceptivity, anaphylaxis, susceptibility, æsthetics; moral sensibility &c. 822.

sensation, impression, effect; consciousness &c. (*knowledge*) 490.

external senses.

V. be -sensible &c. *adj.* -of; feel, perceive.

render, -sensible &c. *adj.*; excite, stir, sharpen, cultivate, tutor.

cause sensation, impress; excite -, produce- an impression.

Adj. sens-ible, -itive, -uous; æsthetic, perceptive, sentient; conscious &c. (*aware*) 490; impressionable, responsive, alive to.

acute, sharp, keen, vivid, lively, impressive, thin-skinned.

Adv. to the quick.

---

376. Physical Insensibility.—**N.** insensibility, physical insensibility; obtuseness &c. *adj.*; palsy, paralysis, *anæsthesia, analgesia, narcosis, hypnosis,* twilight sleep, stupor, coma, trance, catalepsy; sleep &c. (*inactivity*) 683; moral insensibility &c. 823; numbness &c. 381.

anæsthetic agent, general -, local-anæsthetic, opium, ether, chloroform, cocaine, novocaine, chloral; nitrous oxide, laughing gas; refrigeration.

V. be -insensible &c. *adj.*; have a -thick skin, - rhinoceros hide.

render -insensible &c. *adj.*; blunt, pall, obtund, benumb, deaden, paralyze; anæsthetize, drug, dope; put under the influence of -chloroform &c. *n.*; hypnotize; stupefy, stun, narcotize.

Adj. insensible, unfeeling, senseless, comatose, dazed, impercipient, callous, thick-skinned, pachydermatous; hard, -ened; case-hardened; proof; obtuse, dull; anæsthetic; paralytic, palsied, numb, dead.

---

377. Physical Pleasure.—**N.** pleasure; physical -, sensual -, sensuous-pleasure; bodily enjoyment, animal gratification, sensuality; hedonism, luxuriousness &c. *adj.*; dissipation, round of pleasure; titillation, *gusto,* creature comforts, comfort, ease; pillow &c. (*support*) 215; luxury, lap of luxury; purple and fine linen; bed of -down, - roses; velvet, clover; cup of Circe &c. (*intemperance*) 954.

treat; diversion, divertisement, entertainment; refreshment, regale; feast; *délice;* dainty &c. 394; *bonne bouche.*

source of pleasure &c. 829; happiness &c. (*mental enjoyment*) 827.

V. feel -, experience -, receive-pleasure; enjoy, relish; luxuriate -, revel -, riot -, bask -, swim -, wallow-in; feast on; gloat -over, - on; smack the lips.

live -on the fat of the land, - in comfort &c. *adv.*; bask in the sunshine, *faire ses choux gras.*

give pleasure &c. 829.

---

378. Physical Pain.—**N.** pain; suffering, -ance; bodily - physical- -pain, - suffering; mental suffering &c. 828; dolour, ache; aching &c. *v.*; smart, shoot, -ing; twinge, twitch, gripe, head-, ear-, tooth-ache; *migraine,* neuralgia, neuritis, lumbago, gout, sciatica; hurt, cut; sore, -ness; discomfort, *malaise; tic douloureux.*

spasm, cramp; nightmare, *ephialtes;* crick, stitch, kink; thrill, convulsion, throe; throb &c. (*agitation*) 315; pang.

sharp -, piercing -, throbbing -, shooting -, gnawing -, burning- pain; anguish, agony.

torment, torture; rack; cruci-ation, -fixion; martyrdom; martyr, toad under a harrow, vivisection.

V. feel -, experience -, suffer -, undergo- pain &c. *n.*; suffer, ache, smart, bleed; tingle, shoot; twinge, twitch, lancinate; writhe, wince, make a wry face; sit on -thorns, - pins and needles.

give -, inflict- pain; pain, hurt, chafe, sting, bite, gnaw, gripe, stab, grind;

Adj. enjoying &c. *v.*; luxurious, voluptuous, sensual, hedonistic, comfortable, cosy, snug, in comfort, at ease.

agreeable &c. 829; grateful, refreshing, comforting, cordial, genial; sensuous; palatable &c. 394; sweet &c. (*sugar*) 396; fragrant &c. 400; melodious &c. 413; lovely &c. (*beautiful*) 845.

Adv. in -comfort &c. *n.*; on -a bed of roses &c. *n.*; at one's ease.

pinch, tweak; grate, gall, fret, prick, pierce, wring, convulse; torment, torture; rack, agonize; crucify; ex-, cruciate; break on the wheel, put to the rack; flag &c. (*punish*) 972; grate on the ear &c. (*harsh sound*) 410.

Adj. in -pain &c. *n.*, – a state of pain; pained &c. *v.*

painful; aching &c. *v.*; biting, poignant; sore, raw, tender, with exposed nerve.

(2.) *Special Sensation*

1. *Touch*

379. [Sensation of pressure.] **Touch.—N.** touch; tact, -ion, -ility; feeling; palp-ation, -ability; manipulation; brush, tick, graze, contact &c. 199.

[Organ of touch] hand, finger, fore-finger, thumb, paw, feeler, *antenna*.

V. touch, feel, handle, finger, thumb, paw, fumble, grope, grabble; twiddle, tweedle; pass –, run- the fingers over, massage, rub, knead; palpate, stroke, manipulate, wield; throw out a feeler.

Adj. tact-ual, -ile; tangible, palpable; lambent.

380. Sensations of Touch.—N. itching &c. *v.*; titillation, formication, *aura*.

V. itch, tingle, creep, thrill, sting; prick, -le; tickle, titillate.

Adj. itching &c. *v.*

381. [Insensibility to touch.] **Numbness.—N.** numbness &c. (*physical insensibility*) 376; pins and needles.

local anæsthetic, cocaine, novocaine &c.; morphia.

V. benumb &c. 376; freeze, dull, deaden.

Adj. numb; benumbed &c. *v.*; intangible, impalpable.

2. *Heat*

382. Heat.—N. heat, caloric; temperature, warmth, fervour, calidity; incal-, incand-, recal-, decal-escence; glow, flush, blush; fever, hectic.

phlogiston; fire, spark, scintillation, flash, flame, blaze; arc; bonfire; firework, pyrotechny; wild-fire; sheet of fire, lambent flame; devouring element; conflagration.

summer, dog-days, canicule; baking &c. 384 –, white –, tropical –, Afric –, Bengal –, summer –, blood- heat; heat wave, sirocco, simoon; broiling sun; isolation; warming &c. 384.

sun &c. (*luminary*) 423; fire worshipper &c. 991; furnace &c. 386.

geyser, hot spring, volcano.

[Science of heat] pyrology; therm-

383. Cold.—N. cold, -ness &c. *adj.*; frigidity, gelidity, algidity, inclemency, *fresco*.

winter; depth of –, hard- winter; Siberia, Nova Zembla; Ant-, arctic, North –, South- Pole.

ice; snow, – flake, – crystal, – drift; sleet; hail, -stone; rime, frost; hoar –, white –, hard –, sharp- frost; icicle, thick-ribbed ice; fall of snow, snow storm, heavy fall, *avalanche*; ice-berg, -floe; floe, berg; *glacier*; *nevée, serac*.

[Sensation of cold] chilliness &c. *adj.*; chill; shivering &c. *v.*; gooseskin, -flesh; *rigor*, horripilation, chattering of teeth; frostbite, chilblain.

V. be -cold &c. *adj.*; shiver, starve, quake, shake, tremble, shudder, didder,

ology, -otics; thermometer &c. 389.

V. be -hot &c. *adj.*; glow, incandesce, flush, sweat, swelter, bask, smoke, reek, stew, simmer, seethe, boil, burn, singe, scorch, scald, grill, broil, blaze, flame; smoulder; parch, fume, pant.

heat &c. (*make hot*) 384; thaw, fuse, melt, give.

Adj. hot, heated, warm, mild, genial, tepid, lukewarm, unfrozen; therm-al, -ic; calorific; ferv-ent, -id; ardent; aglow.

sunny, torrid, tropical, estival, canicular; close, sultry, stifling, stuffy, suffocating, oppressive; reeking &c. *v.*; baking &c. 384.

red -, white -, smoking -, burning &c. *v.* -, piping- hot; like -a furnace, - an oven; hot as -fire, - pepper; hot enough to roast an ox.

fiery; incand-, incal-escent; candent, ebullient, glowing, smoking; on fire; blazing &c. *v.*; in -flames, - a blaze; alight, afire, ablaze; un-quenched, -extinguished; smouldering; in a -heat, - glow, - fever, - perspiration, - sweat; sudorific; swelter-ing, -ed; blood-hot, -warm; warm as -a toast, - wool; recalescent, thermogenic, pyrotechnic, feverish, febrile, inflamed.

volcanic, plutonic, igneous; isother-mal, -mic, -al.

Phr. Not a breath of air.

quiver; perish with cold; chill &c. (*render cold*) 385.

Adj. cold, cool; chill, -y; gelid, frigid, algid; fresh, keen, bleak, raw, inclement, bitter, biting, niveous, cutting, nipping, piercing, pinching; clay-cold; starved &c. (*made cold*) 385; shivering &c. *v.*; aguish, *transi de froid*; frostbitten, -bound, -nipped.

cold as -a stone, - marble, - lead, - iron, - a frog, - charity, - Christmas; cool as -a cucumber, - custard.

icy, glacial, frosty, freezing, wintry, brumal, hibernal, boreal, arctic, antarctic, polar, Siberian, hyemal; hyperbore-an, -al; ice-bound; frozen out.

un-warmed, -thawed, -heated; isocheimal, -chimenal.

Adv. coldly, bitterly &c. *adj.*; *à pierre fendre.*

---

384. Calefaction.—N. increase of temperature; heating &c. *v.*; cale-, tepe-, torre-faction; melting, fusion; liquefaction &c. 335; burning &c. *v.*; kindling, combustion; in-, ac-cension; con-, cremation; scorification; cauter-y, -ization; ustulation, calcination; in-, cineration; cupellation; carbonization.

ignition, inflammation, adustion, flagration; de-, con-flagration; empyrosis, incendiarism; arson; *auto da fé*; suttee.

boiling &c. *v.*; coction, ebullition, estuation, elixation, decoction.

furnace &c. 386; blanket, flannel, fur, muffler, wrap; wadding &c. (*lining*) 224; clothing &c. 225.

match &c. (*fuel*) 388; incendiary, pyromaniac; *pétroleur, pétroleuse*; cauterant, caustic, lunar caustic, apozem, moxa.

sunstroke, *coup de soleil*; insolation, sunburn.

pottery, ceramics, crockery, porcelain, china; earthen-, stone-ware; pot,

385. Refrigeration.—N. refrigeration, infrigidation, reduction of temperature; cooling &c. *v.*; con-gelation, -glaciation; ice &c. 383; solidification &c. (*density*) 321; refrigerator &c. 387.

extincteur; fire, - engine, - extinguisher, - annihilator, - brigade, - man; sprinkler, hose, hydrant, standpipe.

incombusti-bility, -bleness &c. *adj.*

V. cool, fan, refrigerate, refresh, ice; congeal, freeze, glaciate; benumb, starve, pinch, chill, petrify, chill to the marrow, nip, cut, pierce, bite, make one's teeth chatter; damp, slack; quench; put -, stamp- out; extinguish.

go -, burn- out.

Adj. cooled &c. *v.*; frozen out; cooling &c. *v.*; frigorific.

incombustible; un-, unin-flammable; fire-proof.

---

mug, *terra-cotta*, brick, clinker; cinder, ash, *scoriæ*; embers, dress, slag, products of combustion, coke, carbon, charcoal.

inflamma-, combusti-bility.

[Transmission of heat] diathermancy, transcalency.

V. heat, warm, chafe, stive, foment; make -hot &c. 382; sun oneself, bask in the sun.

fire; set -fire to, – on fire; kindle, enkindle, light, ignite, strike a light; apply the -match, – torch- to; re-kindle, -lume; fan –, add fuel to- the flame; poke –, stir –, blow- the fire; make a bonfire of; burn at the stake.

melt, thaw, fuse; liquefy &c. 335.

burn, inflame, roast, toast, fry, grill, singe, parch, bake, torrefy, scorch; brand, cauterize, sear, burn in; corrode, char, carbonize, calcine, incinerate; smelt, cupel, scorify; reduce to ashes; burn to a cinder; commit –, consign- to the flames.

boil, digest, stew, cook, seethe, scald, parboil, simmer; do to rags.

take –, catch- fire; blaze &c. (*flame*) 382.

Adj. heated &c. *v.*; molten, sodden; *réchauffé*; heating &c. *v.*

inflammable, burnable, inflammatory, combustible; diatherm-al -anous; burnt &c. *v.*; volcanic.

386. Furnace.—N. furnace, blast furnace, fire-box, stove, incinerator, destructor, crematorium, crematory, kiln, oven, oast-house; hot-, bake-, wash-house; laundry; conservatory; hearth, focus; athanor, hypocaust, reverberatory; volcano; forge, fiery furnace; *tuyère*, brasier, salamander, heater, warming-pan, foot-warmer, hot-water bottle; radiator; boiler, geyser, caldron, seething caldron, pot; urn, kettle; chafing-dish; retort, crucible, alembic, still; saggar.

fire-place, -dog, -irons; hearth, ingle, grate, range, kitchener; kitchen range; oil-, gas-, electric, -cooker, -stove; fireless cooker; fire; galley; ca-, cam-boose; poker, tongs, shovel, hob, trivet; and-, grid-iron; frying-, stew-pan &c.

hot –, Turkish –, Russian –, vapour –, shower –, warm- bath; *calidarium, tepidarium, sudatorium*, sudatory; *hammam*.

387. Refrigerator.—N. refrigerator, -y; *frigidarium*; cold storage; refrigerating-plant, – machine; ice-house, -pail, -bag, -chest, -pack; cooler, damper; wine-cooler, freezing mixture.

388. Fuel.—N. fuel, firing, combustible, coal, wallsend, anthracite, bituminous coal, slack, culm, cannel coal, lignite, briquette, coke, carbon, charcoal; turf, peat, fire-wood, bobbing, faggot, log, yule log, ember, cinder &c. (*products of combustion*) 384; kindling wood, tinder, touch-wood; fumigator, sulphur, brimstone; incense; port-fire; fire-barrel, -ball, -brand.

fuel oil, gas, gasoline, electricity.

brand, torch, fuse; wick; spill, match, safety match, light, lucifer, congreve, vesuvian, vesta, fusee, locofoco; linstock; illuminant.

candle &c. (*luminary*) 423; oil &c. (*grease*), 356; petrol, gasoline, methylated –, spirit; gas, acetylene.

Adj. carbonaceous; combustible, inflammable.

V. stoke, fire, feed, add fuel to the flames.

389. Thermometer.—N. thermo-meter, -scope, -stat, -pile, differential thermometer; pyro-, calori-meter; radio micrometer &c.

3. *Taste*

390. Taste.—N. taste, flavour, gust, *gusto*, relish, savour; sapor, sapidity; twang, smack, smatch; after-taste, tang.

tasting; de-, gustation.

palate, tongue, tooth, stomach.

V. taste, savour, smatch, smack, flavour, twang; tickle the palate &c. (*savoury*) 394; smack the lips.

Adj. sapid, saporific; gusta-ble, -tory; strong; flavoured, spiced, savoury; palatable &c. 394.

391. Insipidity.—N. insipidity; taste-lessness &c. *adj.*

V. be -tasteless &c. *adj.*

Adj. void of -taste &c. 390; insipid; jejune; taste-, gust-, savour-less; in-gustible, mawkish, milk and water, weak, stale, flat, vapid, *fade*, wishy-washy, mild; untasted.

---

392. Pungency.—N. pungency, piquancy, poignancy, *haut-goût*, strong taste, twang, race, tang.

sharpness &c. *adj.*; acrimony, acridity; roughness &c. (*sour*) 397; unsavouriness &c. 395.

nitre, saltpetre; mustard, cayenne, caviare; seasoning &c. (*condiment*) 393; brine.

dram, cordial, nip, pick-me-up, bracer, potion.

nicotine, tobacco, snuff, quid; segar; cigar, -ette, gasper, fag; cheroot; weed; fragrant –, Indian- weed; pipe, clay pipe, churchwarden, brier, meerschaum, hookah, hubble-bubble.

V. be -pungent &c. *adj.*; bite the tongue.

render -pungent &c. *adj.*; season, spice, salt, pepper, pickle, brine, devil, curry.

smoke, chew, take snuff.

Adj. pungent, strong; high-, full-flavoured; high-tasted, -seasoned; gamy; sharp, stinging, rough, *piquant*, racy; biting, mordant; spicy; seasoned &c. *v.*; hot, – as pepper; peppery, vellicating, escharotic, meracious; acrid, acrimonious, bitter; rough &c. (*sour*) 397; unsavoury &c. 395.

salt, saline, brackish, briny; salt as -brine, – a herring, – Lot's wife.

---

393. Condiment.—N. condiment, flavouring, salt, mustard, pepper, cayenne, curry, seasoning, sauce, spice, cinnamon, chillies, relish, *sauce piquante*, caviare, pot-herbs, onion, garlic, pickle, chutney, nutmeg &c.

V. season &c. (*render pungent*) 392.

---

394. Savouriness.—N. savouriness &c. *adj.*; relish, zest.

tit-bit, dainty, delicacy, ambrosia, nectar, *bonne bouche*; game, turtle, venison.

V. taste good, be -savoury &c. *adj.*; tickle the -palate, – appetite; flatter the palate.

render -palatable &c. *adj.*

relish, like, smack the lips.

Adj. savoury, well-tasted, to one's taste, tasty, good, palatable, nice, dainty, delectable; tooth-ful, -some;

395. Unsavouriness.—N. unsavouri-ness &c. *adj.*; amaritude; acri-mony, -tude; roughness &c. (*sour*) 397; acerb-ity, austerity; gall and worm-wood, rue, quassia, aloes; sickener.

V. be -unpalatable &c. *adj.*; sicken, disgust, nauseate, pall, turn the stomach.

Adj. un-savoury, -palatable, -sweet; ill-flavoured, un-appetizing, -eatable, inedible; bitter, – as gall; acrid, acri-monious; rough.

offensive, repulsive, nasty; sickening

gustful, appetizing, lickerish, delicate, delicious, exquisite, rich, luscious, ambrosial.

Adv. *per amusare la bocca.*

Phr. *cela se laisse manger.*

396. Sweetness.—N. sweetness, dulcitude, saccharinity.

sugar, cane-, beet-sugar; saccharine, glucose, syrup, treacle, molasses, honey, manna; confection, -ary; sweets, grocery, conserve, preserve, *confiture*, jam, marmalade, julep; sugar-candy, -plum; licorice, liquorice, plum, lollipop, *bon bon*, *jujube*, comfit, sweetmeat, caramel, toffee, butterscotch.

nectar; hydromel, mead, metheglin, honeysuckle, *liqueur*, sweet wine.

pastry, pie, tart, puff, pudding, cake.

dulc-ification, -oration.

V. be -sweet &c. *adj.*

render -sweet &c. *adj.*; sugar, saccharize, sweeten; edulcorate; dulc-orate, -ify; candy; mull.

Adj. sweet, sugary; sacchar-ine, -iferous; dulcet, honied, candied, luscious, nectarious, melliferous; sweetened &c. *v.*

sweet as -a nut, – sugar, – honey.

&c. *v.*; nauseous; loath-, ful-some; unpleasant &c. 830.

397. Sourness.—N. sourness &c. *adj.*; acid, -ity; acetous fermentation; acerbity.

vinegar, verjuice, crab, alum.

V. be -, turn- -sour &c. *adj.*; set the teeth on edge.

render -sour &c. *adj.*; acid-ify, -ulate.

Adj. sour; acid, -ulous, -ulated; acerb; tart, crabbed; acet-ous, -ose; sour as vinegar, sourish, acescent, sub-acid; styptic, hard, rough; unripe, green.

4. *Odour*

398. Odour.—N. odour, smell, odorament, scent, effluvium; eman-, exhal-ation; fume, essence, trail, nidor, redolence.

sense of smell; scent; act of -smelling &c. *v.*

V. have an -odour &c. *n.*; smell, – of, – strong of; exhale; give out a -smell &c. *n.*; scent.

smell, scent; snuff, – up; sniff, nose, inhale.

Adj. odor-ous, -iferous; smelling, strong-scented; redolent, graveolent, nidorous, pungent.

[Relating to the sense of smell] olfactory, quick-scented.

399. Inodorousness.—N. inodorousness; absence –, want- of smell.

V. be -inodorous &c. *adj.*; not smell. deodorize.

Adj. inodor-ous, -ate; scentless; without –, wanting- smell &c. 398.

deodoriz-ed, -ing.

400. Fragrance. — N. fragrance, aroma, redolence, perfume, *bouquet*; sweet smell, aromatic perfume.

perfumery; incense; musk, frankincense; pastil, -le; myrrh, perfumes of Arabia, chypre; otto, ottar, attar; bergamot, balm, civet, *pot-pourri*, pulvil; nosegay, *boutonnière*; scent, -bag; *sachet*, scent-bottle, smelling bottle, *vinaigrette*; toilet water, *eau de Cologne*; thurible, censer, thurification.

perfumer; incense bearer.

401. Fetor.—N. fetor, fetidness; bad &c. *adj.*; -smell, – odour; stench, stink; mephitis, foul –, mal- odour; *empyreuma*; mustiness &c. *adj.*; rancidity; foulness &c. (*uncleanness*) 653.

stoat, polecat, skunk; assafœtida; fungus, garlic; stink-pot, -bomb.

V. have a -bad smell &c. *n.*; smell; stink, – in the nostrils, – like a polecat; smell -strong &c. *adj.*, – offensively.

Adj. fetid; strong-smelling; high, bad, strong, fulsome, offensive, noisome, rank, rancid, reasty, tainted, musty,

V. be -fragrant &c. *adj.*; have a -perfume &c. *n.*; smell sweet, scent, perfume, thurify, embalm.

Adj. fragrant, aromatic, redolent, spicy, balmy, scented; sweet-smelling, -scented; perfum-ed, -atory; thuriferous; fragrant as a rose, muscadine, ambrosial.

fusty, frouzy; olid, -ous; nidorous; smelling, stinking; putrid &c. 653; suffocating, mephitic; empyreumatic.

---

5. *Sound*

(i.) SOUND IN GENERAL

402. Sound.—**N.** sound, noise, strain; accent, twang, intonation, tone, tune; cadence; sonority, sonorousness &c. *adj.*; audibility; resonance &c. 408; voice &c. 580.

[Science of sound] acou-, acu-stics; catacoustics, cataphonics; phon-ics, -etics, -ology, -ography; dia-coustics, -phonics.

telephone, phonograph &c. 418.

V. produce sound; sound, make a noise; give out -, emit- sound; phonetize, phonate; resound &c. 408.

Adj. sounding; soniferous; sonorific; resonant, audible, acoustic, auditory, distinct; stertorous; phonic, sonant; phonetic.

403. Silence.—**N.** silence; stillness &c. (*quiet*) 265; peace, hush, lull, rest; muteness &c. 581; solemn -, awful -, dead -, deathlike- silence.

V. be -silent &c. *adj.*; hold one's tongue &c. (*not speak*) 585.

render -silent &c. *adj.*; silence, still, hush; stifle, muffle, gag, stop; muzzle, put to silence &c. (*render mute*) 581.

Adj. silent; still, -y; calm, quiet; noise-, sound-, speech-less; hushed &c. *v.*; mute &c. 581; aphonic.

soft, solemn, awful, deathlike, silent as the grave; inaudible &c. (*faint*) 405.

Adv. silently &c. *adj.*; sub silentio; in perfect silence.

Int. hush! 'sh! silence! soft! whist! tush! chut! tut! *pax!* mum's the word! hold your tongue! shut up! be silent! be quiet! stop that noise! hold your row! dry up! peace, be still!

Phr. one might hear a -feather, - pin- drop.

---

404. Loudness.—**N.** loudness, power; loud noise, din; clang, -or; clatter, noise, bombilation, roar, uproar, racket, static, grinders, hubbub, *fracas, charivari*, trumpet blast, blare, flourish of trumpets, fanfare, *tintamarre*, peal, swell, blast, alarum, boom; resonance &c. 408.

vociferation; pandemonium, hullaballoo &c. 411; lungs; Stentor; megaphone; siren.

artillery, cannon, gunfire, shellburst, bomb; thunder.

V. be -loud &c. *adj.*; peal, swell, clang, boom, thunder, fulminate, roar; resound &c. 408; speak up, shout &c. (*vociferate*) 411; bellow &c. (*cry as an animal*) 412; give tongue.

rend the -air, - skies; fill the air; din -, ring -, thunder- in the ear;

405. Faintness.—**N.** faintness &c. *adj.*; faint sound, whisper, breath; under-tone, -breath; murmur, hum, rustle, buzz, purr; plash; sough, moan, sigh, susurration; tinkle; 'still small voice.'

hoarseness &c. *adj.*; raucity.

silencer, soft pedal, damper, mute, *sourdine*.

V. whisper, breathe, murmur, purl, hum, gurgle, ripple, babble, flow; tinkle; mutter &c. (*speak imperfectly*) 583.

steal on the ear; melt in -, float on- the air.

muffle, mute, deaden, damp, stifle.

Adj. inaudible; scarcely -, just- audible; low, dull; stifled, muffled; hoarse, husky; gentle, soft, faint; floating; purling, flowing &c. *v.*;

pierce –, split –, rend- the -ears, – head; deafen, stun; *faire le diable à quatre*; make one's windows shake; awaken –, startle- the echoes; make the welkin ring.

Adj. loud, sonorous; high-, big-sounding; blatant; deep, full, powerful, noisy, clangorous, multisonous, *fortissimo*; thundering, deafening &c. *v.*; trumpet-tongued; ear-splitting, -rending, -deafening; piercing; obstreperous, rackety, uproarious; enough to wake the -dead, – seven sleepers.

shrill &c. 410; clamorous &c. (*vociferous*) 411; stentor-ian, -ophonic.

Adv. loudly &c. *adj.*; aloud; at the top of one's voice, lustily, in full cry.

Phr. the air rings with.

whispered &c. *v.*; liquid; soothing; dulcet &c. (*melodious*) 413.

Adv. in a whisper, with bated breath, *sotto voce*, between the teeth, aside; *pian-o, -issimo*; *à la sourdine*; *con sordine*; out of earshot, inaudibly &c. *adj.*

(ii.) Specific Sounds*

406. [Sudden and violent sounds.] **Snap.**—**N.** snap &c. *v.*; rapping &c. *v.*; de-, crepitation; smack, clap, report; thud; burst, explosion, discharge, detonation, blow-out, back-fire, firing, salvo, volley, pistol-shot.

squib, cracker, gun, rifle, pop-gun.

V. rap, snap, tap, knock; click; clash; crack, -le; crash; pop; slam, bang, clap, thump, plump; toot; back-fire, explode, burst on the ear.

Adj. rapping &c. *v.*

Int. crash! bang!

407. [Repeated and protracted sounds.] **Roll.**—**N.** roll &c. *v.*; drumming &c. *v.*; tattoo; ding-dong; tantara; rataplan; whirr; rat-a-tat; rub-a-dub; pit-a-pat; quaver, clutter, *charivari*, racket; cuckoo; repetition &c. 104; peal of bells, devil's tattoo; reverberation &c. 408.

drumfire, barrage.

machine gun.

V. roll, drum, rumble, rattle, clatter, rustle, roar, drone, patter, clack.

hum, trill, shake; chime, peal, toll; tick, beat.

drum –, din- in the ear.

Adj. rolling &c. *v.*; monotonous &c. (*repeated*), 104; like a bee in a bottle.

408. Resonance.—**N.** resonance; ring &c. *v.*; ringing &c. *v.*; tintinnabulation; reflection, reverberation, clangor.

low –, base –, bass –, flat –, grave –, deep –, pedal- note; bass; *basso, – profondo*; bari-, bary-tone; *contralto*.

V. re-sound, -verberate, -echo; ring, ding, sing, jingle, gingle, chink, clink; tink, -le; chime; gurgle &c. 405; plash, guggle, echo, ring in the ear.

408a. Non-resonance. — **N.** thud, thump, dead sound; non-resonance; muffled drums, cracked bell; silencer, damper; mute, *sourdine*.

V. sound dead; stop –, damp- the -sound, – reverberations; deaden, muffle.

Adj. non-resonant, dead, muted, muffled.

Adj. resounding &c. *v.*; resonant, tinnient, tintinnabulary; deep-toned, -sounding, -mouthed; hollow, sepulchral; gruff &c. (*harsh*) 410.

409. [Hissing sounds.] **Sibilation.**—**N.** sibilation; hiss &c. *v.*; sternutation; high note &c. 410.

goose, serpent, snake.

* [The author's classification of sounds has been retained, though it does not entirely accord with the theories of modern science.—Ed.]

V. hiss, buzz, whiz, rustle; fizz, -le, sizzle, swish; wheeze, whistle, snuffle; squash; sneeze.

Adj. sibilant; hissing &c. *v.*; wheezy.

410. [Harsh sounds.] **Stridor.—N.** creak &c. *v.*; creaking &c. *v.*; discord &c. 414; stridor; harshness, roughness, sharpness &c. *adj.*; cacophony.

acute –, high- note; *soprano*, treble, tenor, *alto*, falsetto, *voce di testa*; shriek, cry &c. 411.

piccolo, fife, penny -whistle, – trumpet.

V. creak, grate, jar, burr, pipe, twang, jangle, clank, clink; scream &c. (*cry*) 411; yelp &c. (*animal sound*) 412; buzz &c. (*hiss*) 409.

set the teeth on edge, *écorcher les oreilles*; pierce –, split- the -ears, – head; offend –, grate upon –, jar upon- the ear.

Adj. creaking &c. *v.*; strident, stridulous, harsh, coarse, hoarse, horrisonous, raucous, metallic, rough, gruff, grum, sepulchral.

sharp, high, acute, shrill, high-pitched; trumpet-toned; piercing, ear-piercing; cracked; discordant &c. 414; cacophonous.

411. Cry.—N. cry &c. *v.*; voice &c. (*human*) 580; bark &c. (*animal*) 412.

vociferation, outcry, hullaballoo, chorus, clamour, hue and cry, plaint; lungs; stentor.

V. cry, roar, shout, bawl, brawl, halloo, halloa, hail, hoop, whoop, yell, bellow, howl, scream, screech, screak, shriek, shrill, squeak, squeal, squall, whine, whinny, pule, pipe, yaup.

cheer, hurrah; hoot; grumble, moan, groan.

snore, snort; grunt &c. (*animal sounds*) 412.

vociferate; raise –, lift up- the voice; call –, sing –, cry- out; exclaim; rend the air; thunder –, shout- at the -top of one's voice, – pitch of one's breath; *s'égosiller*; strain the -throat, – voice, – lungs; give a -cry &c.

Adj. crying &c. *v.*; clam-ant, -orous; vociferous; stentorian &c. (*loud*) 404; open-mouthed.

412. [Animal sounds.] **Ululation.—N.** cry &c. *v.*; crying &c. *v.*; ululation, latration, belling; reboation; call, note; bark, howl, yelp; twittering, woodnote; insect cry, fritinancy, drone; screech; cuckoo.

V. cry, ululate, howl, roar, bellow, blare, rebellow, bark, yelp; bay, – the moon; yap, growl, yarr, yawl, snarl, howl; grunt, -le; snort, squeak; neigh, bray; mew, mewl; purr, caterwaul, pule; bleat, low, moo; troat, croak, crow, screech, caw, coo, gobble, quack, cackle, gaggle, guggle; chuck, -le; cluck; clack; cheep, chirp, chirrup, twitter, sing, cuckoo; pout, wail, hum, buzz; hiss, blatter; hoot.

Adj. crying &c. *v.*; blatant, latrant; re-, mugient; deep-, full-mouthed.

Adv. in full cry.

(iii.) MUSICAL SOUNDS

413. Melody. Concord.—N. melody, rhythm, measure; rhyme &c. (*poetry*) 597.

pitch, *timbre*, intonation, tone, over-tone.

scale, gamut; diapason; diatonic –, chromatic –, enharmonic- scale; key, clef, chords,

modulation, temperament, syncope, syncopation, preparation, suspension, resolution.

414. Discord.—N. discord, -ance; dissonance, cacophony, caterwauling; harshness &c. 410; consecutive fifths.

[Confused sounds] Babel, pande-monium; Dutch –, cat's- concert; marrow-bones and cleavers.

V. be -discordant &c. *adj.*; jar &c. (*sound harshly*) 410.

Adj. discordant; dis-, ab-sonant; out of tune, tuneless; un-musical, -tunable; un-, im-melodious; un-, in-harmonious;

staff, stave, line, space, brace; bar, rest; *appogia-to, -tura; acciaccatura,* shake, *arpeggio.*

note, musical note, notes of a scale; sharp, flat, natural; high note &c. (*shrillness*) 410; low note &c. 408; interval; semitone; second, third, fourth &c.; diatessaron.

breve, semibreve, minim, crotchet, quaver; semi-, demisemiquaver; sustained note, drone, burden.

tonic; key-, leading-, fundamental- note; supertonic, mediant, dominant; sub-mediant, -dominant, organ-, pedal-point; octave, tetrachord; major –, minor- -mode, – scale, – key; Doric mode, passage, phrase.

concord, harmony; unison, -ance; chime, homophony; euphon-y, -ism; tonality; consonance; concent; part.

orchestration, harmonization, – phrasing.

[Science of harmony] harmon-y, -ics; thorough-, fundamental-bass; counterpoint; faburden.

piece of music &c. 415; composer, harmonist, contrapuntist.

V. be -harmonious &c. *adj.*; harmonize, chime, symphonize, transpose; put in tune, tune, accord, string; score, arrange, orchestrate.

Adj. harmoni-ous, -cal; in -concord &c. *n.,* – tune, – concert; unisonant, concentual, symphonizing, isotonic, homophonous, assonant, consonant.

measured, rhythmical, diatonic, chromatic, enharmonic.

melodious, musical; tuneful, tunable; sweet, dulcet, canorous; mell-ow, -ifluous; soft; clear, – as a bell; silvery; euphon-ious, -ic, -ical; symphonious; enchanting &c. (*pleasure-giving*) 829; fine-, full-, silver-toned.

Adv. harmoniously &c. *adj.*

sing-song; cacophonous; jarring, harsh &c. 410.

---

415. Music.—N. music, classical –, modern –, descriptive- music; concert, recital; strain, tune, air, *motif*; melody &c. 413; *aria, arietta*; piece of music, *sonata; rond-o, -eau; pastorale, cavatina,* roulade, *fantasia, toccata, concerto,* overture, symphony, symphonic poem, tone poem, prelude, voluntary, *intermezzo,* variations, *cadenza;* cadence; fugue, canon, serenade, *nocturne, notturno,* rhapsody, romance, *aubade,* dithyramb; opera, operetta; oratorio; composition, movement; stave.

instrumental music; full-, orchestral- score; minstrelsy, tweedledum and tweedledee, band, orchestra &c. 416; concerted piece, *potpourri,* medley, *capriccio,* incidental music; improvisation; peal.

vocal music, vocalism; chaunt, chant; psalm, -ody; hymn; song &c. (*poem*) 597; canticle, canzonet, *cantata, bravura, coloratura;* lay, ballad, ditty, carol, barcarolle, pastoral, recitative, *recitativo, solfeggio,* tonic sol-fa.

Lydian measures; slow -music, – movement; *adagio* &c. *adv.*; minuet; siren strains, soft music, lullaby; *berceuse,* cradle song, dump; dirge &c. (*lament*) 839; pibroch; martial music, march, funeral-, dead- march; dance music; waltz &c. (*dance*) 840; rag-time, syncopation, jazz.

solo, duet, *duo, trio;* quartet; quintet, sextet, septet; part song, descant, glee, madrigal, catch, round, chorus, *chorale;* antiphon, -y; accompaniment, second –, alto –, tenor –, bass- part; score, thorough bass; counterpoint.

composer &c. 413; musician &c. 416.

V. compose, perform &c. 416; attune.

Adj. musical; instrumental, orchestral, vocal, choral, lyric, operatic; harmonious &c. 413.

Adv. *adagio; largo, larghetto, andan-te, -tino; alla capella; maestoso, moderato; allegr-o, -etto; spiritoso, vivace, veloce; prest-o, -issimo; pian-o, -issimo, fort-e, -issimo, sforzando; con brio; capriccioso; scherz-o, -ando; legato, sostenuto, staccato, crescendo, diminuendo, rallentando, affettuoso, arioso; parlante, cantabile; obbligato; pizzicato, tremolo, vibrato.*

416. Musician. [Performance of Music.]—**N.** musician, *artiste, virtuoso,* performer, player, minstrel; bard &c. (*poet*) 597; instrumental-, organ-, accompan-, pian-, violin-, flaut-, harp-ist; harper, fiddler, fifer, trumpeter, piper, drummer; catgut scraper.

band, orchestra, waits.

vocal-, melod-ist; singer, warbler; songst-, chaunt-er, -ress; *diva, cantatrice,* coloratura, soprano, mezzo-soprano, alto, contralto, tenor, baritone, bass, *basso, -profondo.*

choir, quire, chorister; chorus, – singer; choral society, festival, *eisteddfod.*

nightingale, philomel, thrush; siren; Orpheus, Apollo, the Muses, Erato, Euterpe, Terpsichore; tuneful -nine, – quire.

composer &c. 413.

performance, virtuosity, execution, touch, expression, solmization.

V. play, pipe, strike –, tune- up, sweep the chords, tickle –, paw-the ivories, vamp, tweedle, fiddle; strike the lyre, beat the drum; blow –, sound –, wind- the horn; grind the organ; touch the -guitar &c. (*instruments*) 417; thrum, strum, twang, drum, beat –, keep- time, conduct.

execute, perform; accompany; sing –, play- a second; compose, write music, set to music, arrange, harmonize, orchestrate.

sing, chaunt, chant, hum, warble, carol, chirp, chirrup, lilt, purl, quaver, trill, shake, twitter, whistle; sol-fa; intone.

have -an ear for music, – a musical ear, – a correct ear, – absolute pitch.

Adj. playing &c. *v.*; musical, lyric.

Adv. *adagio, andante* &c. (*music*) 415.

417. Musical Instruments.—**N.** musical instruments; band; string-, brass-, drum and fife-, military-, bugle-, German-, dance-, jazz-band; orchestra, string quartet; orchestrion, orchestrelle.

[Stringed instruments] mono-, poly-chord; harp, lyre, lute, archlute, thearbo; mandol-a, -in, -ine; guitar; *ukulele;* psaltery, zither; bandore, cither, -n; gittern, rebeck, *bandurria,* banjo, zither banjo, *balalaika, samisen;* plectrum.

viol, -in, Cremona, Stradivarius; fiddle, kit; *vielle, viola, – d'amore, – di gamba;* tenor, *violoncello,* cello; bass, bass-, base-viol; double-bass, *contrabasso, violone,* hurdy-gurdy; strings, catgut; bow, fiddlestick.

piano, -forte; grand –, concert grand –, baby –, upright –, cottage-piano; pianino, pianette; harpsi-, clavi-, clari-, mani-chord; *clavier,* spinet, virginals; dulcimer, *cymbalo;* Eolian harp; piano-organ, -player, electric piano, player-piano, pianola.

[Wind instruments] organ, church –, pipe –, American- organ; har-moni-um, -phon; accordion, seraphina, concertina; melodeon; barrel-organ; humming top.

flute, fife, piccolo, flageolet, penny-whistle, reed instrument; clari-net, -onet; bass clarionet; saxophone; basset horn, *corno di bassetto*; musette, shawm, oboe, hautboy, *cor Anglais*, *corno Inglese*, bassoon, double bassoon, *contrafagotto*; bag-, union-pipes; ocarina, Pandean pipes; calliope; sirene, pipe, pitch-pipe; sourdet; whistle, catcall.

horn, bugle, key bugle, cornet, *cornet-à-pistons*, cornopean, clarion, trumpet, trombone, ophicleide, serpent; English-, French-, bugle-, sax-, flugel-, alt-, helicon-, post-horn; sackbut, euphonium, bombardon, tuba, bass tuba.

[Vibrating surfaces] cymbal, bell, gong, peal of bells, *carillon*; tambour, -ine; drum, tom-tom, tab-or, -ret, -ourine, -orin; *sistrum*; *grand caisse*, bass-, big-, side-, kettle-drum; *tympani*; war drums; tymbal, timbrel, castanet, bones; musical-glasses, -stones; harmonica, sounding-board, rattle; gramophone, phonograph.

[Vibrating bars] reed, tuning-fork, triangle, Jew's harp, musical box, harmonicon, xylophone, marimba, *celeste*.

sord-ine, -et; *sourd-ine, -et*; mute.

(iv.) PERCEPTION OF SOUND

418. [Sense of sound.] **Hearing.—N.** hearing &c. *v.*; audition, auscultation; eavesdropping; audibility; acoustics &c. 402.

acute -, nice -, delicate -, quick -, sharp -, correct -, musical -ear; ear for music.

ear, auricle, lug, acoustic organs, auditory apparatus, ear-drum, tympanum; ear-, speaking-trumpet, megaphone; telephone, radiophone, stethoscope, phonograph, gramophone, microphone.

hearer, auditor, listener, eavesdropper; audi-tory, -ence.

V. hear, overhear; hark, -en; list, -en; give -, lend -, bend- an ear; give attention; catch a sound, prick up one's ears; give -a hearing, - audience- to.

hang upon the lips of, be all ear, listen with both ears, monitor.

become audible; meet -, fall upon -, catch -, reach- the ear; be heard; ring in the ear &c. (*resound*) 408.

Adj. hearing &c. *v.*; auditory, auricular, aural, auditive, acoustic.

Adv. *arrectis auribus*.

Int. hark, - ye! hear! list, -en! *Oyez!* attention! lend me your ears!

419. **Deafness.—N.** deafness, hardness of hearing, surdity; inaudibility.

V. be -deaf &c. *adj.*; have no ear; shut -, stop -, close- one's ears; turn a deaf ear to.

render deaf, stun, deafen.

Adj. deaf, earless, surd; hard -, dull- of hearing; deaf-mute, stunned, deafened; stone deaf; deaf as -a post, - an adder, - a beetle, - a trunk-maker.

inaudible &c. 405; out of hearing.

6. *Light*

(i.) LIGHT IN GENERAL

420. **Light.—N.** light, ray, beam, stream, gleam, streak, pencil; sun-, moon-beam; dawn, aurora.

day; sunshine; light of -day, - heaven; sun &c. (*luminary*) 432, day-, broad day-, noontide- light; noon-tide, -day; glare.

421. **Darkness.—N.** darkness &c. *adj.*; blackness &c. (*dark colour*) 431; obscurity, gloom, murk; dusk &c. (*dimness*) 422; tenebrosity, umbrageousness.

Cimmerian -, Stygian -, Egyptian-darkness; night; midnight; dead of -,

glow &c. *v.*; afterglow, sunset; glimmering &c. *v.*; glint; play –, flood- of light; phosphorescence, lambent flame.

flush, halo, glory, nimbus, aureole, *aureola.*

spark, *scintilla; facula;* sparkling &c. *v.*; emication, scintillation, flash, blaze, coruscation, fulguration; flame &c. *(fire)* 382; lightning, *ignis fatuus,* &c. *(luminary)* 423, radio-activity.

lustre, sheen, shimmer, reflection; gloss, tinsel, spangle, brightness, brilliancy, splendour; ef-, re-fulgence; ful-gor, -gidity; dazzlement, resplendence, transplendency; luminousness &c. *adj.*; luminosity; lucidity; renitency; radi-ance, -ation; irradiation, illumination, phosphorescence, luminescence.

radiation, radiant heat, infra-red rays, visible radiation, ultra-violet –, actinic- rays, actinism; X –, Roentgen-rays; phot-, heli-ography; optical instruments &c. 445.

[Science of light] optics; photo-logy, -metry; di-, cat-optrics.

[Distribution of light] *chiaroscuro, clair-obscur,* clear obscure, breadth, light and shade, black and white, tonality, half-tone, mezzotint.

reflection, refraction, dispersion, double refraction, polarization, diffraction, interference.

illuminant &c. 423.

V. shine, glow, glitter, phosphoresce; glis-ter, -ten; twinkle, gleam; flare, – up; glare, beam, shimmer, glimmer, flicker, sparkle, scintillate, coruscate, flash, fulgurate, blaze; be -bright &c. *adj.*; reflect light, daze, dazzle, bedazzle, radiate, shoot out beams.

clear up, brighten.

lighten, enlighten; light, – up; irradiate, shine upon; give –, hang out- a light; cast –, throw –, shed- -lustre, – light- upon; illum-e, -ine, -inate; relume, strike a light; kindle &c. *(set fire to)* 384.

Adj. shining &c. *v.*; lumin-ous, -iferous; luc-id, -ent, -ulent, -ific, -iferous; illumina̧ting, light, -some; bright, vivid, splendent, nitid, lustrous, shiny, brilliant, beamy, scintillant, radiant, lambent; sheen, -y; glossy,

witching time of- night; blind man's holiday; darkness -visible, – that can be felt; palpable, obscure; Erebus.

shade, shadow, umbra, penumbra; sciagraphy; *silhouette;* radiograph, skiagraph.

obscuration; ad-, ob-umbration; ob-tenebration, offuscation, caligation; extinction; eclipse, total eclipse; gathering of the clouds.

shading; distribution of shade; *chiaroscuro* &c. *(light)* 420.

noctivagation, noctograph, noctuary. obscurantist.

V. be -dark &c. *adj.*

darken, obscure, shade; dim; tone down, lower; over-cast, -shadow; cloud, eclipse; ob-, of-fuscate; ob-, ad-umbrate, cast into the shade; be-cloud, -dim, -darken; cast –, throw –, spread- a -shade, – shadow, – gloom.

extinguish; put –, blow –, snuff- out; doubt.

Adj. dark, -some, -ling; obscure, tenebrous, tenebrious, sombrous, pitch dark, pitchy; caliginous; black &c. *(in colour)* 431.

sunless, lightless &c. *(see* sun, light, &c. 423); sombre, dusky; unilluminated &c. *(see* illuminate &c. 420); nocturnal; dingy, lurid, gloomy; murk-y, -some; shady, umbrageous; overcast &c. *(dim)* 422; cloudy &c. *(opaque)* 426; darkened &c. *v.*

dark as -pitch, – a pit, – Erebus.

benighted; noctivag-ant, -ous.

Adv. in the -dark, – shade; at night.

422. Dimness.—N. dimness &c. *adj.*; darkness &c. 421; paleness &c. *(light colour)* 429.

half-light, *demi-jour;* partial -shadow, – eclipse; shadow of a shade; glimmer, -ing; nebulosity; cloud &c. 353; eclipse.

aurora, dusk, twilight, gloaming, blind man's holiday, shades of evening, crepuscule, cockshut time; break of day, daybreak, dawn.

moon-light, -beam, -shine; star-, owl's-, candle-, rush-, fire-light; farthing candle.

V. be –, grow- -dim &c. *adj.*; flicker, twinkle, glimmer; loom, lower; fade; darken; pale, – its ineffectual fire.

burnished, glassy, sunny, orient, meridian; noon-day, -tide; cloudless, clear; un-clouded, -obscured.

garish; re-, tran-splendent; re-, effulgent; ful-gid, -gent; relucent, splendid, blazing, in a blaze, ablaze, rutilant, meteoric, phosphorescent; aglow.

bright as silver; light -, bright- as -day, - noonday, - the sun at noonday.

optical, actinic; photo-genic, -graphic; heliographic, radioactive.

423. [Source of light &c.] Luminary.
—**N.** luminary; light &c. 420; flame &c. (*fire*) 382.

spark, *scintilla*; phosphorescence.

sun, orb of day, day star, Phœbus, Apollo, Helios, Phaethon, Hyperion, Ra, Aurora; star, orb, meteor; falling -, shooting- star; blazing -, dog- star; Sirius, canicula, Aldebaran; morning star, Lucifer, Phosphor, evening star; Hesperus, Venus, planet, moon &c. 318; constellation, galaxy; northern light, *aurora -borealis, - australis*, zodiacal light; mock sun, parhelion.

lightning; fork -, sheet -, summer- lightning, St. Elmo's fire; phosphorus; *ignis fatuus*; Jack o' -, Friar's- lantern; Will o' the wisp, fire-drake, *Fata Morgana*.

glow-worm, fire-fly.

radium, luminous paint.

[Artificial light] gas; gas -, lime -, electric -, head -, search -, spot -, flash -, flood -, foot-light; lamp, oil -, gas -, arc -, incandescent- lamp; flare; lant-ern, -horn; dark lantern, bull's eye, projector; candle, *bougie*, tallow -, wax- candle; dip, farthing dip; taper, rush-light; oil &c. (*grease*) 356; wick, burner; Argand, moderator, duplex; torch, *flambeau*, link, brand; cresset; gase-, chande-, electro-lier; candelabrum, *girandole*, sconce, lustre, candle-stick.

firework, fizgig; pyrotechnics; Roman candle, Véry light, star shell, parachute light; rocket, lighthouse &c. (*signal*) 550.

V. illuminate &c. (*light*) 420.

Adj. self-luminous, incandescent; phosphor-ic, -escent; luminescent, fluorescent, radiant &c. (*light*) 420.

425. Transparency. — **N.** transparen-ce, -cy; translucen-ce, -cy; diaphaneity; luc-, pelluc-, limp-idity.

transparent medium, glass, crystal, mica; lymph, water.

V. be -transparent &c. *adj.*; transmit light.

Adj. transparent, pellucid, lucid, diaphanous; trans-, tra-lucent; limpid, clear, serene, crystalline, clear as crys-

render -dim &c. *adj.*; dim, bedim, obscure.

Adj. dim, dull, lack-lustre, dingy, darkish, shorn of its beams; dark 421.

faint, shadowed forth; glassy; bleary; cloudy; misty &c. (*opaque*) 426; muggy, fuliginous; nebul-ous, -ar; obnubilated, overcast, crepuscular, twilight, muddy, lurid, leaden, dun, dirty; looming &c. *v.*

pale &c. (*colourless*) 429; confused &c. (*invisible*) 447.

424. Shade.—**N.** shade; awning &c. (*cover*) 223; parasol, sunshade, umbrella; screen, curtain, shutter, blind, gauze, veil, mantle, mask; cloud, mist, gathering of clouds; smoke screen; smoked glasses, coloured spectacles; blinkers, blinders.

umbrage, glade; shadow &c. 421.

V. draw a curtain; put up -, close- a shutter; veil &c. *v.*; cast a shadow &c. (*darken*) 421; screen, obstruct the view.

Adj. shady, umbrageous, bowery.

426. Opacity.—**N.** opacity; opaqueness &c. *adj.*

film; cloud &c. 353.

V. be -opaque &c. *adj.*; obstruct the passage of light; ob-, of-fuscate.

Adj. opaque, impervious to light.

dim &c. 422; turbid, thick, muddy, opacous, obfuscated, fuliginous, cloudy, hazy, foggy, vaporous, nubiferous, muggy.

tal, vitreous, transpicuous, glassy, hyaline.

smoky, fumid, murky, dirty.

_____

427. Semitransparency.—N. semitransparency, opalescence, milkiness, pearliness; gauze, muslin; film; mist &c. (*cloud*) 353; frosted glass.

Adj. semi-transparent, -pellucid, -diaphanous, -opacous, -opaque; opal-escent, -ine; pearly, milky, frosted, mat; misty.

(ii.) Specific Light

428. Colour.—N. colour, hue, tint, tinge, dye, complexion, shade, tincture, cast, livery, coloration, chromatism, glow, flush; tone, key.

pure –, positive –, primary –, primitive –, complementary- colour; three primaries; spectrum, chromatic dispersion; broken –, secondary –, tertiary-colour.

local colour, colouring, keeping, tone, value, aerial perspective.

[Science of colour] chromatics, spectrum analysis; prism, spectroscope.

pigment, colouring matter, paint, dye, wash, distemper, stain; medium; mordant; oil-paint &c. (*painting*) 556.

V. colour, dye, tinge, stain, tint, tinct, tone, paint, wash, ingrain, grain, illuminate, emblazon, imbue; paint &c. (*fine art*) 556; daub.

Adj. coloured &c. *v.*; colorific, tingent, tinctorial; chromatic, prismatic; full-, high-, deep-coloured; doubly-dyed; polychromatic.

bright, vivid, intense, deep; fresh, unfaded; rich, gorgeous; highly coloured; gay; variegated &c. 440.

gaudy, florid; garish; showy, flaunting, flashy; raw, crude; glaring, flaring; discordant, inharmonious.

mellow, harmonious, pearly, sweet, delicate, tender, refined.

429. [Absence of colour.] Achromatism.—N. achromatism; de-, discoloration; pall-or, -idity; paleness &c. *adj.*; etiolation; neutral tint, monochrome, black-and-white.

V. lose -colour &c. 428; fade, fly, go; become -colourless &c. *adj.*; turn pale, pale, whiten.

deprive of colour, decolorize, bleach, tarnish, achromatize, blanch, etiolate, wash out, tone down.

Adj. uncoloured &c. (*see* colour &c. 428); colourless, achromatic, hueless, pale, pallid; pale-, tallow-faced; faint, dull, cold, muddy, leaden, dun, wan, sallow, dead, dingy, ashy, ashen, ghastly, cadaverous, glassy, lack-lustre; discoloured &c. *v.*

light-coloured, fair, *blond*; white &c. 430.

pale as -death, – ashes, – a witch, – a ghost, – a corpse.

_____

430. Whiteness.—N. whiteness &c. *adj.*; argent.

albification, albescence, albinism, etiolation.

snow, paper, chalk, milk, lily, ivory, silver, alabaster; white lead, chinese –, flake –, ivory –, zinc- white, white-wash, -ning, whiting.

V. be -white &c. *adj.*

render -white &c. *adj.*; whiten-bleach, blanch, etiolate, whitewash, silver, frost.

Adj. white; milky, milk-, snow-white; snowy, niveous, candid, chalky; hoar,

431. Blackness.—N. blackness &c. *adj.*; darkness &c. (*want of light*) 421; swarthness, lividity, dark colour, tone, colour; *chiaroscuro* &c. 420.

nigrification, infuscation, denigration.

jet, ink, ebony, coal, pitch, soot, smudge, charcoal, sloe, raven, crow; negro, blackamoor, man of colour, nigger, darky, Ethiopian, black.

[Pigments] lamp –, ivory –, blue-black; writing –, printing –, printer's –, Indian- ink.

V. be -black &c. *adj.*

-y; frosted, silvery; argent, -ine; canescent.

whitish, creamy, pearly, ivory, fair, *blond*, ash-blond, platinum blond; blanched &c. *v.*; high in tone, light.

white as -a sheet, – driven snow, – a lily, – silver; like -ivory &c. *n.*

render -black &c. *adj.*; blacken, infuscate, denigrate; blot, -ch; smutch; smirch; darken &c. 421.

Adj. black, sable, swarthy, sombre, dark, inky, ebon, atramentous, jetty; coal-, jet-black; fuliginous, pitchy, sooty, swart, dusky, dingy, murky, Ethiopic; low-toned, low in tone; of the deepest dye.

black as -jet &c. *n.*, – my hat, – a shoe, – a tinker's pot, – November, – thunder, – midnight; nocturnal &c. (*dark*) 421; nigrescent; gray &c. 432; obscure &c. 421.

Adv. in mourning.

432. Gray.—N. gray &c. *adj.*; neutral tint, silver, pepper and salt, *chiaroscuro*, *grisaille*, grayness.

[Pigments] Payne's gray; black &c. 431.

Adj. gray, grey; steel –, iron- gray, dun, drab, dingy, leaden, livid, sombre, sad, pearly; silver, -y, -ed; ash-en, -y; ciner-eous, -itious; grizzl-y, -ed; dove-, slate-, stone-, mouse-, ash-coloured; mole; cool.

433. Brown.—N. brown &c. *adj.*

[Pigments] bistre, ochre, sepia, Vandyke brown.

Adj. brown, adust, bay, dapple, auburn, chestnut, nutbrown, cinnamon, hazel, fawn, puce, *écru*, russet, tawny, fuscous, chocolate, maroon, foxy, tan, brunette, whitey-brown; snuff-, liver-coloured; brown as -a berry, – mahogany; reddish brown; copper-, rust- coloured; henna, bronze, khaki; russet, roan, sorrel.

sun-burnt; tanned &c. *v.*

V. render -brown &c. *adj.*; tan, embrown, bronze.

Primitive Colours*

434. Redness.—N. red, scarlet, vermilion, cardinal, Post Office, red, carmine, crimson, pink, lake, *couleur de rose*, cherry red, maroon, carnation, *couleur de rose*, *rose du Barry*; magenta, damask; flesh -colour, – tint; colour; fresh –, high-colour; warmth; gules.

ruby, garnet, carbuncle; rose; rust, iron-mould.

[Dyes and pigments] cinnabar, cochineal; fuchsine; ruddle, madder, red-lead; Indian –, light –, Venetian- red; red ink, annotto.

redness &c. *adj.*; rub-escence, -icundity, -ification; erubescence, blush.

V. be –, become- -red &c. *adj.*; blush, flush, colour up, mantle, redden.

render -red &c. *adj.*; redden, rouge; rub-ify, -ricate; incarnadine; ruddle.

Adj. red &c. *n.*, -dish; rufous, ruddy, florid, incarnadine, sanguine, bloody, gory; ros-y, -eate; blowz-y, -ed; brunt; rubi-cund, -form;

Complementary Colours

435. Greenness.—N. green &c. *adj.*; blue and yellow; vert.

emerald, verd antique, verdigris, malachite, beryl, aquamarine, reseda.

[Pigments] *terre verte*, verditer, bice, chlorophyl.

greenness, verdure, verdancy; virid-ity, -escence.

Adj. green, verdant; glaucous, olive; porraceous; green as grass.

emerald –, pea –, grass –, apple –, sea –, olive –, bottle –, leaf- green.

greenish; vir-ent, -escent.

* The author's classification of colours has been retained, though it does not entirely accord with the theories of modern science: Complete lists of shades or pigments are beyond the scope of this work.

lurid, stammel, blood-red; russet, murrey, carroty, sorrel, lateritious.

rose-, ruby-, cherry-, claret-, wine-, plum-, flame-, flesh-, peach-, salmon-, brick-, brickdust-coloured, reddish brown &c. 433.

blushing &c. *v.*; erubescent; reddened &c. *v.*

red as -fire, – blood, – scarlet, – a turkeycock, – a lobster; warm, hot; foxy.

436. Yellowness.—N. yellow &c. *adj.*; or.

[Pigments] gamboge; cadmium –, chrome –, Indian –, lemon- yellow; orpiment, yellow ochre, Claude tint, aureolin.

crocus, saffron, topaz, gold.

jaundice; London fog; yellowness &c. *adj.*

Adj. yellow, aureate, gold, golden, gilt, gilded, flavous, citrine, fallow; fulv-ous, -id; sallow, luteous, fawny, creamy, sandy; xanth-ic, -ous; jaundiced.

gold-, citron-, saffron-, lemon-, sulphur-, amber-, straw-, primrose-, cream-coloured; flaxen, yellowish, buff.

yellow as a -quince, – guinea, – crow's foot.

437. Purple.—N. purple &c. *adj.*; blue and red, bishop's purple; aniline dyes, gridelin, amethyst; purpure.

livid-ness, -ity.

V. empurple.

Adj. purple, violet, plum-coloured, lavender, lilac, puce, *mauve*; livid.

438. Blueness.—N. blue &c. *adj.*; garter-blue; watchet.

[Pigments] ultramarine, smalt, cobalt, cyanogen; Prussian –, syenite-blue; bice, indigo, woad.

lapis lazuli, sapphire, turquoise.

blue-, bluish-ness; bloom.

Adj. blue, azure, cerulean; sky-blue, -coloured, -dyed; navy-blue, aquamarine, electric blue, royal blue, cyanic; bluish; atmospheric, retiring; cold.

439. Orange.—N. orange, red and yellow; gold; or; flame &c. colour, *adj.*

[Pigments] ochre, Mars orange, cadmium.

V. gild, warm.

Adj. orange; ochreous; orange-, gold-, flame-, copper-, brass-, apricot-coloured; warm, hot, glowing.

440. Variegation.—N. variegation; di-, tri-chroism; iridescence, irisation, play of colours, polychrome, maculation, spottiness, striæ.

spectrum, rainbow, iris, tulip, peacock, chameleon, butterfly, tortoise-shell; mackerel, – sky; zebra, leopard, mother-of-pearl, nacre, opal, marble, batik.

check, plaid, tartan, patchwork; mar-, par-quetry; mosaic, *tesseræ*, tesselation, chess-board, checkers, chequers; harlequin; Joseph's coat; tricolour; patches, bands, stripes, spots &c. of colour.

V. be -variegated &c. *adj.*; variegate, stripe, streak, checker, chequer; be-, speckle, fleck; be-, sprinkle; stipple, maculate, dot, bespot; tattoo, inlay, tesselate, damascene; embroider, braid, quilt.

Adj. variegated &c. *v.*; many-coloured, -hued; divers-, parti-coloured; di-, poly-chromatic; bi-, tri-, versi-colour; of all -the colours of the rainbow, – manner of colours; kaleidoscopic.

iridescent; opal-ine, -escent; prismatic, nacreous, pearly, shot, *gorge de pigeon, chatoyant,* irisated.

pied, piebald, skewbald; motley; mottled, marbled; pepper and salt, paned, dappled, clouded, cymophanous.

mosaic, tesselated, chequered, plaid; tortoiseshell &c. *n.*

spott-ed, -y; punctated, powdered; speckled &c. *v.*; freckled, flea-bitten, studded; fleck-ed, -ered; striated, barred, veined; brind-ed, -led; tabby; watered; grizzled; listed; embroidered &c. *v.*; dædal.

(iii.) Perceptions of Light

441. Vision.—**N.** vision, sight, optics, eye-sight.

view, look, espial, glance, ken, *coup d'œil*; glimpse, peep, glint; gaze, stare, leer; perlustration, contemplation; conspect-ion, -uity; regard, survey; in-, intro-spection; *reconnaissance*, speculation, watch, espionage, *espionnage*, autopsy; ocular -inspection, – demonstration; sight-seeing.

macrography, micrography.

point of view; view-, stand-point; gazebo, loop-hole, *belvedere*, watch-tower.

field of view; theatre, amphitheatre, arena, vista, horizon; commanding –, bird's eye –, panoramic- view; periscope.

visual organ, organ of vision; eye; naked –, unassisted- eye; eye-ball, retina, pupil, iris, cornea, white; optics, orbs; saucer –, goggle –, gooseberry-eyes.

short sight &c. 443; clear –, sharp –, quick –, eagle –, piercing –, penetrating--sight, – glance, – eye; perspicacity, discernment; catopsis.

eagle, hawk; cat, lynx; Argus.

evil eye; basilisk, cockatrice.

spectacles, telescope &c. 445.

V. see, behold, discern, perceive, have in sight, descry, sight, make out, discover, distinguish, recognize, spy, espy, ken; get –, have –, catch- a -sight, – glimpse- of; command a view of; witness, contemplate, speculate; cast –, set- the eyes on; be a -spectator &c. 444- of; look on &c. (*be present*) 186; see sights &c. (*curiosity*) 455; see at a glance &c. (*intelligence*) 498.

look, view, eye; lift up the eyes, open one's eye; look -at, – on, – upon, – over, – about one, – round; survey, scan, inspect; run the eye -over, – through; reconnoitre, glance -round, – on, – over; turn –, bend- one's looks upon; direct the eyes to, turn the eyes on, cast a glance, make eyes at.

observe &c. (*attend to*) 457; watch &c. (*care*) 459; see with one's own eyes; watch for &c. (*expect*) 507; peek, peep, peer, pry, take a peep; play at bo-peep.

look -full in the face, – hard at, – intently; strain one's eyes; fix –, rivet- the eyes upon; stare, gaze; pore over, gloat -over, – on; leer, ogle, glare; goggle; cock the eye, squint, gloat, look askance; give the glad eye.

Adj. seeing &c. *v.*; visual, ocular, -al; ophthalmic.

far-, clear-sighted &c. *n.*; eagle-, hawk-, lynx-, keen-, Argus-eyed.

visible &c. 446.

442. Blindness.—**N.** blindness, anopsia, cecity, excecation, *amaurosis*, cataract, ablepsy, prestriction; dim-sightedness &c. 443.

V. be -blind &c. *adj.*; not see; lose sight of; have the eyes bandaged; grope in the dark.

not look; close –, shut –, turn away –, avert- the eyes; look another way; wink &c. (*limited vision*) 443; shut the eyes –, be blind- to; wink –, blink- at.

render -blind &c. *adj.*; blind, -fold; hoodwink, dazzle; put one's eyes out; throw dust into one's eyes; *jeter de la poudre aux yeux*; screen from sight &c. (*hide*) 528.

Adj. blind; eye-, sight-, vision-less; dark; stone-, sand-, stark-blind; undiscerning; dim-sighted &c. 443.

blind as -a bat, – a buzzard, – a beetle, – a mole, – an owl; wall-eyed.

blinded &c. *v.*

Adv. blind-ly, -fold; darkly.

Adv. visibly &c. 446; in sight of, with one's eyes open.
at -sight, – first sight, – a glance, – the first blush; *primâ facie.*
Int. look! &c. (*attention*) 457.
Phr. the scales falling from one's eyes.

443. [Imperfect vision.] **Dim-sightedness.** [Fallacies of vision.]—**N.** dim –, dull –, half –, short –, near –, long –, double –, astigmatic –, failing- sight; dim &c. -sightedness; snow blindness; purblindness, lippitude; my-, presby-opia; confusion of vision; astigmatism, nystagmus; colour-blindness, dichromism, chromato-pseudo-blepsis, Daltonism; nyctalopy; *strabismus*, strabism, squint, cast in the eye, swivel eye, goggle eyes; obliquity of vision.

winking &c. *v.*; nictitation; blinkard, albino.

dizziness, swimming, scotomy; cataract; ophthalmia.

[Limitation of vision] eye shade, blinker, blinder; screen &c. (*hider*) 530.

[Fallacies of vision] *deceptio visûs*; refraction, distortion, illusion, false light, *anamorphosis*, virtual image, *spectrum, mirage*, looming, phasma; phant-asm, -asma, -om; vision; spectre, apparition, ghost; *ignis fatuus* &c. (*luminary*) 423; spectre of the Brocken; magic mirror; magic lantern &c. (*show*) 448; mirror, lens &c. (*instrument*) 445.

V. be -dim-sighted &c. *n.*; see double; have a -mote in the eye, – mist before the eyes, – film over the eyes; see through a -prism, – glass darkly; wink, blink, nictitate; squint; look ask-ant, -ance; screw up the eyes, glare, glower.

dazzle, glare, blur, swim, loom.

Adj. dim-sighted &c. *n.*; my-, presby-opic; astigmatic; moon-, mope-, blear-, goggle-, gooseberry-, one-eyed; blind of one eye, monoculous; half-, pur-, colour-blind; dichromatic.

blind as a bat &c. (*blind*) 442; winking &c. *v.*

444. Spectator.—**N.** spectator, beholder, observer, inspector, viewer, looker-on, onlooker, witness, eye-witness, bystander, passer by; sight-seer.

spy, scout; sentinel &c. (*warning*) 668.

V. witness, behold &c. (*see*) 441; look on &c. (*be present*) 186.

445. Optical Instruments.—**N.** optical instruments; lens, meniscus, magnifier, reading –, burning- glass; micro-, mega-, teino-scope; spectacles, glasses, barnacles, goggles, giglamps, eyeglass, *pince-nez*, monocle; periscopic lens; telescope, glass, lorgnette, binocular; spy-, opera-, field-glass, periscope, range finder.

mirror, reflector, speculum; looking-, pier-, cheval-, hand-glass.

prism; camera, *camera-lucida, -obscura*; projector, stereopticon, magic lantern &c. (*show*) 448; chro-, thau-matrope; stereo-, pseudo-, poly-, kaleido-scope.

photo-, opto-, erio-, actino-, luci-, radio-, spectro-meter; polari-, polemo-, spectro-scope, diffraction grating.

optics, optician, optometry, optometrist; microscop-y, -ist; photometry, photography; photographer.

446. Visibility.—**N.** visibility, perceptibility; conspicuousness, distinctness &c. *adj.*; conspicuity; appearance &c. 448; exposure; manifestation &c. 525; ocular -proof, – evidence, – demonstration; field of view &c. (*vision*) 441.

447. Invisibility.—**N.** invisibility, non-appearance, imperceptibility; indistinctness &c. *adj.*; mystery, delitescence.

concealment &c. 528; latency &c. 526.

V. be –, become- -visible &c. *adj.*; appear, emerge, open to the view; meet –, catch- the eye; present –, show –, manifest –, produce –, discover –, reveal –, expose –, betray- itself; stand -forth, – out; show; arise; peep –, peer –, crop- out; start –, spring –, show –, turn –, crop- up; glimmer, glitter, glow, loom; glare; burst forth, scintillate; burst upon the -view, – sight; heave in sight; come -in sight, – into view, – out, – forth, – forward; see the light of day; break through the clouds; make its appearance, show its face, materialize, appear to one's eyes, come upon the stage, enter; float before the eyes, speak for itself &c. (*manifest*) 525; attract the attention &c. 457; reappear; live in a glass house.

expose to view &c. 525.

Adj. visible, perceptible, perceivable, discernible, apparent; in -view, – full view, – sight; exposed to view, *en évidence*; unclouded.

obvious &c. (*manifest*) 525; plain, clear, distinct, definite; well-defined, -marked; in focus; recognizable, palpable, autoptical; glaring, staring, conspicuous; stereoscopic; in -bold, – strong, – high- relief.

periscopic, panoramic.

before –, under- one's eyes; before one, *à vue d'œil*, in one's eye, *oculis subjecta fidelibus*.

Adv. visibly &c. *adj.*; in sight of; before one's eyes &c. *adj.*; *veluti in speculum*.

V. be -invisible &c. *adj.*; be hidden &c. (*hide*) 528; lurk &c. (*lie hidden*) 526; escape notice.

render -invisible &c. *adj.*; conceal &c. 528; put out of sight.

not see &c. (*be blind*) 442; lose sight of.

Adj. invisible, imperceptible; un-, in-discernible; un-, non-apparent; out of –, not in- sight; *à perte de vue*; behind the -scenes, – curtain; view-, sight-less; in-, un-conspicuous; unseen &c. (*see* see &c. 441); covert &c. (*latent*) 526; eclipsed, under an eclipse.

dim &c. (*faint*) 422; mysterious, dark, obscure, confused; indistin-ct, -guishable; shadowy, indefinite, undefined; ill-defined, -marked; blurred, fuzzy, out of focus; misty &c. (*opaque*) 426; veiled &c. (*concealed*) 528; delitescent.

---

448. Appearance.—**N.** appearance, phenomenon, sight, spectacle, show, premonstration, scene, species, view, *coup d'œil*; look-out, out-look, prospect, vista, perspective, bird's-eye view, scenery, landscape, picture, *tableau*; display, exposure, *mise en scène*; scenery, *décor*; rising of the curtain.

phant-asm, -om &c. (*fallacy of vision*) 443.

pageant, *spectacle*; peep-, raree-, gallanty-show; *ombres chinoises*; projector, optical –, magic- lantern, phantasmagoria, dissolving views; cinema, -tograph; bio-scope. -graph; moving pictures, movies, film, screen &c.; pan-, di-, cosm-, ge-orama; *coup* –, *jeu- de théâtre*; pageantry &c. (*ostentation*) 882; insignia &c. (*indication*) 550.

aspect, phase, *phasis*, seeming; shape &c. (*form*) 240; guise, look,

449. Disappearance.—**N.** disappearance, evanescence, eclipse, occultation.

departure &c. 293; exit, vanishing point; dissolving views.

V. disappear, vanish, dissolve, fade, melt away, pass, go, avaunt; be -gone &c. *adj.*; leave -no trace, – 'not a rack behind'; go off the stage &c. (*depart*) 293; suffer –, undergo- an eclipse; be lost to –, retire from- -sight, – view.

lose sight of.

efface &c. 552.

Adj. disappearing &c. *v.*; evanescent; missing, lost; lost to -sight, – view; gone; *spurlos versenkt*.

Int. vanish! disappear! avaunt! &c. (*ejection*) 297.

---

complexion, colour, image, mien, air, cast, carriage, port, demeanour; presence, expression, first blush, face of the thing; point of view, light.

lineament, feature, trait, lines; out-line, -side; contour, *silhouette*, face, countenance, physiognomy, visage, phiz, mug, cast of countenance, profile, *tournure*, cut of one's jib, metoposcopy; outside &c. 220.

V. appear; be –, become- visible &c. 446; seem, look, show; present –, wear –, carry –, have –, bear –, exhibit –, take –, take on –, assume- the -appearance, – semblance- of; look like; cut a figure, figure; present to the view; show &c. (*make manifest*) 525.

Adj. apparent, seeming, ostensible; on view.

Adv. apparently; to all -seeming, – appearance; ostensibly, seemingly, as it seems, on the face of it, *primâ facie*; at the first blush, at first sight; in the eyes of; to the eye.

CLASS IV

Words relating to the INTELLECTUAL FACULTIES

CLASS IV

Words relating to the INTELLECTUAL FACULTIES

Division (I.) FORMATION OF IDEAS

Section I. Operations of Intellect in General

450. Intellect.—N. intellect, mind, understanding, reason, thinking principle; rationality; cogitative –, cognitive –, intellectual- faculties; faculties, senses, consciousness, observation, percipience, apperception, mentality, intelligence, intellection, intuition, association of ideas, instinct, flair, conception, judgment, wits, parts, capacity, intellectuality, reasoning power, brains, genius; wit &c. 498; ability &c. (*skill*) 698; wisdom &c. 498.

soul, spirit, ghost, inner man, heart, breast, bosom, *penetralia mentis, divina particula auræ,* heart's core; ego, psyche, pneuma, subconsciousness, subconscious, subliminal self; dual personality.

organ –, seat- of thought; *sensorium,* sensory, brain, gray matter; head, -piece; pate, noddle, skull, scull, *pericranium, cerebrum, cranium,* brain-pan, -box; sconce, upper story.

[Science of mind] metaphysics; psychics, psycho-logy, -metry, -genesis, -analysis, -physics, psychi-atry, -cal research, thought reading &c. 992; ideology; mental –, moral- philosophy; philosophy of the mind; pneumat-, phren-ology; no –, cranio-logy, -scopy.

ideal-ity, -ism; transcendental-, spiritual-ism; immateriality &c. 317.

metaphysician, psychologist &c.

V. note, notice, mark; take -notice, – cognizance- of; be -aware, – conscious- of; realize; appreciate; ruminate &c. (*think*) 451; fancy &c. (*imagine*) 515; conceive, reason, understand.

Adj. [Relating to intellect] intellectual, mental, rational, subjective, metaphysical, nooscopic, spiritual; ghostly; psych-ical, -ological; cerebral.

immaterial &c. 317; endowed with reason.

Adv. *in petto.*

450a. Absence or want of Intellect.— N. absence –, want- of -intellect &c. 450; imbecility &c. 499; brutality; brute -instinct, – force.

Adj. unendowed with reason.

---

451. Thought.—N. thought; exercitation –, exercise- of the intellect; reflection, cogitation, consideration, meditation, study, lucubration, speculation, deliberation, pondering; head-,

452. [Absence or want of thought.] **Incogitancy.—N.** incogitancy, vacancy, inunderstanding; inanity, fatuity &c. 499; thoughtlessness &c. (*inattention*) 458.

brain-work; cerebration; mentation, deep reflection; close study, application &c. (*attention*) 457.

abstract thought, abstraction, contemplation, musing; brown study &c. (*inattention*) 458; reverie, Platonism; depth of thought, workings of the mind, thoughts, inmost thoughts; self-counsel, -communing, -consultation.

association –, succession –, flow –, train –, current- of -thought, – ideas.

after –, mature- thought; reconsideration, second thoughts; retrospection &c. (*memory*) 505; excogitation; examination &c. (*inquiry*) 461; invention &c. (*imagination*) 515.

thoughtfulness &c. *adj*.

V. think, reflect, reason, cogitate, excogitate, consider, deliberate; bestow -thought, – consideration- upon; speculate, contemplate, meditate, ponder, muse, dream, ruminate; brood –, con- over; animadvert, study; bend –, apply- the mind &c. (*attend*) 457; digest, discuss, hammer at, weigh, perpend; realize, appreciate; fancy &c. (*imagine*) 515; trow.

take into consideration; take counsel &c. (*be advised*) 695; commune with –, bethink- oneself; collect one's thoughts; revolve –, turn over –, run over- in the mind; chew the cud –, sleep- upon; take counsel of –, advise with- one's pillow.

rack –, ransack –, crack –, beat –, cudgel- one's brains; set one's -brain, – wits- to work.

harbour –, entertain –, cherish –, nurture- an -idea &c. 453; take into one's head; bear in mind; reconsider.

occur; present –, suggest- itself; come –, get- into one's head; strike one, flit across the view, come uppermost, run in one's head; enter –, pass in –, cross –, flash on –, flash across –, float in –, fasten itself on –, be uppermost in –, occupy- the mind; have in one's mind.

make an impression; sink –, penetrate- into the mind; engross the thoughts.

Adj. thinking &c. *v*.; thoughtful, pensive, meditative, reflective, cogitative, museful, wistful, contemplative, speculative, deliberative, studious, sedate, introspective, Platonic, philosophical.

lost –, engrossed –, rapt –, absorbed- in thought &c. (*inattentive*) 458; deep musing &c. (*intent*) 457.

in the mind, under consideration, in contemplation.

Adv. all things considered; taking everything into account.

Phr. the mind being on the stretch; the -mind, – head- -turning, – running- upon.

V. not -think &c. 451; not think of; dismiss from the -mind, – thoughts &c. 451.

indulge in reverie &c. (*be inattentive*) 458.

put away thought; unbend –, relax –, divert- the mind.

Adj. vacant, unintellectual, unideal, unoccupied, unthinking, inconsiderate, thoughtless; absent &c. (*inattentive*) 458; diverted; irrational &c. 499; narrow-minded &c. 481.

un-thought of, -dreamt of, -considered; off one's mind; incogitable, not to be thought of, inconceivable.

---

453. [Object of thought.] **Idea.**—**N.** idea, notion, conception, thought, apprehension, impression, perception, image, sentiment, reflection, observation, consideration; abstract idea, principle; archetype.

view &c. (*opinion*) 484; theory &c.

454. [Subject of thought.] **Topic.**— **N.** subject of –, material for- thought; food for the mind, mental *pabulum*.

subject, -matter; matter, theme, topic, what it is about, *thesis*, text, business, affair, matter in hand, argument; motion, resolution; head, chap-

514; conceit, fancy; phantasy &c. (*imagination*) 515.

point of view &c. (*aspect*) 448; field of view.

---

ter; case, point; proposition, theorem; field of inquiry; moot point, problem, &c. (*question*) 461.

V. float -, pass- in the mind &c. 451.

Adj. thought of; uppermost in the mind; *in petto*.

Adv. under -discussion, – consideration, – advisement; in -question, – the mind; on -foot, – the carpet, – the *tapis*; before the house, relative to &c. 9.

Section II. Precursory Conditions and Operations

455. [The desire of knowledge.] **Curiosity.** — **N.** interest, thirst for knowledge; curi-osity, -ousness; inquiring mind; inquisitiveness.

sight-seer, quidnunc, newsmonger, Paul Pry, peeping Tom, eavesdropper; gossip &c. (*news*) 532; questioner, *enfant terrible*.

V. be -curious &c. *adj.*; take an interest in, stare, gape; prick up the ears, see sights, lionize; pry, speer; dig up.

Adj. curious, inquisitive, burning with curiosity, overcurious, nosey; inquiring &c. 461; prying; inquisitorial; agape &c. (*expectant*) 507; attentive &c. 457.

Phr. what's the matter? what next?

456. [Absence of curiosity.] **Incuriosity.**—**N.** incuriosity; incuriousness &c. *adj.*; *insouciance* &c. 866; indifference, apathy.

V. be -incurious &c. *adj.*; have no -curiosity &c. 455; take no interest in &c. 823; mind one's own business.

Adj. incurious, uninquisitive, uninterested, indifferent, bored; impassive &c. 823.

---

457. Attention.—**N.** attention; mindfulness &c. *adj.*; intent-ness, -iveness; thought &c. 451; adverten-ce, -cy; observ-ance, -ation; consideration, reflection, perpension; heed; particularity; notice, regard &c. *v.*; circumspection &c. (*care*) 459; study, scrutiny, once-over; in-, intro-spection; revision, -al.

active -, diligent -, exclusive -, minute -, close -, intense -, deep -, profound -, abstract -, laboured -, deliberate- -thought, – attention, – application, – study.

minuteness, attention to detail &c. 459.

absorption of mind &c. (*abstraction*) 458.

indication, calling attention to &c. *v.*

V. be -attentive &c. *adj.*; attend, advert to, observe, look, see, view, remark, notice, regard, take notice, mark; give -, pay- -attention, – heed- to; listen in, incline -, lend- an ear to; trouble one's head about; give a

458. Inattention.—**N.** in-attention, -consideration; inconsiderateness &c. *adj.*; oversight; inadverten-ce, -cy; non-observance, disregard.

supineness &c. (*inactivity*) 683; *étourderie*; want of thought; heedlessness &c. (*neglect*) 460; insouciance &c. (*indifference*) 866.

abstraction; absence -, absorption- of mind; preoccupation, distraction, reverie, brown study, deep musing, fit of abstraction, woolgathering.

V. be -inattentive &c. *adj.*; overlook, disregard; pass by &c. (*neglect*) 460; not -observe &c. 457; think little of.

close -, shut- one's eyes to; wink at; pay no attention to; dismiss -, discard -, discharge- from one's -thoughts, – mind; drop the subject, think no more of; set -, turn -, put- aside; turn -away from, – one's attention from, – a deaf ear to, – one's back upon.

abstract oneself, dream, indulge in reverie.

escape -notice, – attention; come in

thought –, animadvert- to; occupy oneself with; contemplate &c. (*think of*) 451; look -at, – to, – after, – into, – over; see to; turn –, bend –, apply –, direct –, give- the -mind, – eye, – attention- to; have -an eye to, – in one's eye; bear in mind; take into -account, – consideration; keep in -sight, – view; have regard to, heed, mind, take cognizance of, be engaged in, entertain, recognize; make –, take- note of; note.

examine cursorily; glance -at, – upon, – over; cast –, pass- the eyes over; run over, turn over the leaves, dip into, perstringe; skim &c. (*neglect*) 460; take a cursory view of.

examine, – closely, – intently; scan, scrutinize, consider; give –, bend- one's mind to; overhaul, revise, pore over; inspect, review, pass under review; take stock of; fix –, rivet –, focus –, devote- the -eye, – mind, – thoughts, – attention- on *or* to; hear –, think- out; mind one's business.

revert –, hark back- to; watch &c. (*expect*) 507, (*take care of*) 459; hearken –, listen- to; prick up the ears; have –, keep- the eyes open; come to the point.

meet with attention; fall under one's -notice, – observation; be -under consideration &c. (*topic*) 454.

catch –, strike- the eye; attract notice; catch –, awaken –, wake –, invite –, solicit –, attract –, claim –, excite –, engage –, occupy –, strike –, arrest –, fix –, engross –, absorb –, rivet- the- attention, – mind, – thoughts; be -present to, – uppermost in- the mind.

bring under one's notice; point -out, – to, – at, – the finger at; lay the finger on, indigitate, indicate; direct –, call- attention to; show; put a -mark &c. (*sign*) 550- upon; call soldiers to 'attention'; bring forward &c. (*make manifest*) 525.

Adj. attentive, mindful, heedful, observant, regardful; alive –, awake- to, alert; observing &c. *v.*; taken up –, occupied- with; engaged –, engrossed –, interested –, wrapped- in; absorbed, rapt; breathless; pre-occupied &c. (*inattentive*) 458; watchful &c. (*careful*) 459; intent on, open-eyed, breathless, undistracted, upon the stretch; on the watch &c. (*expectant*) 507 steadfast.

Int. see! look, – here, – out, – alive, – you, – to it! mark! lo!

at one ear and go out at the other; forget &c. (*have no remembrance*) 506.

call off –, draw off –, call away –, divert –, distract- the -attention, – thoughts, – mind; put out of one's head; dis-concert, -compose; put out, confuse, perplex, bewilder, moider, fluster, muddle, dazzle; throw a sop to Cerberus.

Adj. inattentive; un-observant, -mindful, -heeding, -discerning; inadvertent; mind-, regard-, respect-less; listless &c. (*indifferent*) 866; blind, deaf; flighty, hand over head; cur-, percur-sory; giddy-, scatter-, hare-brained; unreflecting, *écervelé*, inconsiderate, off-hand, thoughtless, dizzy, muzzy, brainsick; giddy, – as a goose; wild, harum-scarum, rantipole, high-flying; heed-, care-less &c. (*neglectful*) 460.

absent, absent-minded, abstracted, *distrait*; lost; lost –, wrapped- in thought, woolgathering; rapt, in the clouds, bemused; dreaming –, musing-on other things; pre-occupied; en-grossed &c. (*attentive*) 457; in a -reverie &c. *n.*; off one's guard &c. (*inexpectant*) 508; napping; dreamy.

disconcerted, put out &c. *v.*; rattled.

Adv. inattentively, inadvertently &c. *adj.*; per incuriam, sub silentio.

Int. stand -at ease, – easy!

Phr. the attention wanders; one's wits gone a -woolgathering, – bird's nesting; it never entered into one's head; the mind running on other things; one's thoughts being elsewhere; had it been a bear it would have bitten you.

___

behold! soho! hark, – ye! mind! halloo! observe! lo and behold!
attention! *nota bene*; N.B.; *, †; I'd have you to know; notice!
take notice! O yes! *Oyez!*

Phr. this is –, these are- to give notice.

459. Care. [Vigilance.]—**N.** care,
solicitude, heed; heedfulness &c. *adj.*;
scruple &c. (*conscientiousness*) 939.

watchfulness &c. *adj.*; vigilance,
surveillance, eyes of Argus, watch, vigil,
look out, watch and ward, *l'œil du
maître*.

alertness &c. (*activity*) 682; attention &c. 457; prudence &c., circumspection &c. (*caution*) 864; forethought
&c. 510; precaution &c. (*preparation*)
673; tidiness &c. (*order*) 58, (*cleanli-
ness*) 652; accuracy &c. (*exactness*) 494;
minuteness, attention to detail; meticu-
lousness, nicety, circumstantiality.

V. be -careful &c. *adj.*; reck; take
care &c. (*be cautious*) 864; pay attention to &c. 457; take care of; look –,
see- -to, – after; keep -an eye, – a
sharp eye- upon; keep -watch, – watch
and ward; mount guard, set watch,
watch; keep in -sight, – view; chaperon,
play gooseberry; mind, – one's business.

look -sharp, – about one; look with
one's own eyes; keep a -good, – sharp-
look-out; have all one's -wits, – eyes-
about one; watch for &c. (*expect*) 507;
stand to; keep one's eyes –, have the
eyes –, sleep with one eye- open.

take precautions &c. 673; protect
&c. (*render safe*) 664.

do one's best &c. 682; mind one's
Ps and Qs, speak by the card, pick
one's steps.

Adj. care-, regard-, heed-ful; taking
care &c. *v.*; particular; prudent &c.
(*cautious*) 864; considerate; thoughtful &c. (*deliberative*) 451; provident
&c. (*prepared*) 673; alert &c. (*active*)
682; sure-footed.

guarded, on one's guard; on the
-*qui vive*, – alert, – watch, – look-out;
awake, broad awake, vigilant; watch-,
wake-, wist-ful; Argus-, lynx- eyed;
wide awake &c. (*intelligent*) 498;
on the watch for &c. (*expectant*)
507.

tidy &c. (*orderly*) 58, (*clean*) 652;
accurate &c. (*exact*) 494; scrupulous

460. Neglect.—**N.** neglect; carelessness &c. *adj.*; trifling &c. *v.*; negligence;
omission, laches, default; remissness,
slackness, procrastination; supineness
&c. (*inactivity*) 683; inattention &c.
458; *nonchalance* &c. (*insensibility*) 823;
imprudence, recklessness &c. 863;
slovenliness &c. (*disorder*) 59, (*dirt*)
653; improvidence &c. 674; non-completion &c. 730; inexactness &c. (*error*)
495.

paraleipsis [in rhetoric].

trifler, slacker, waster, waiter on
Providence; Micawber.

V. be -negligent &c. *adj.*; take no
care of &c. (take care of &c. 459);
neglect; let -slip, – go; lay –, set –,
cast –, put- aside; keep –, leave- out of
sight; lose sight of.

overlook, disregard; pass -over, – by;
let pass; blink; wink –, connive- at;
gloss over; take no -note, – notice, –
thought, – account- of; pay no regard
to; *laisser aller*; allow to lie on the
table.

scamp; trifle, fribble; do by halves;
skimp; cut; slight &c. (*despise*) 930;
play –, trifle- with; slur; skim, – the
surface; *effleurer*; take a cursory view
of &c. 457.

slur –, slip –, skip –, jump- over;
pretermit, miss, skip, jump, omit, give
the go-by to, push aside, throw into
the background, shelve, sink; ignore,
shut one's eyes to, refuse to hear, turn
a deaf ear to; leave out of one's calculation; not -attend to &c. 457, – mind;
not trouble -oneself, – one's head-
-with, –about; forget &c. 506; be caught
napping &c. (*not expect*) 508; leave a
loose thread; let the grass grow under
one's feet.

render -neglectful &c. *adj.*; put –,
throw- off one's guard.

Adj. neglecting &c. *v.*; unmindful,
negligent, neglectful; heedless, careless,
thoughtless; perfunctory, remiss,
slack.

inconsiderate; un-, in-circumspect;

&c. (*conscientious*) 939; *cavendo tutus* &c. (*safe*) 664.

Adv. carefully &c. *adj.*; with care, gingerly.

Phr. *quis custodiet ipsos custodes?*

off one's guard; un-wary, -watchful, -guarded; offhand.

supine &c. (*inactive*) 683; inattentive &c. 458; *insouciant* &c. (*indifferent*) 823; imprudent, reckless &c. 863; slovenly &c. (*disorderly*) 59, (*dirty*) 653; inexact &c. (*erroneous*) 495; improvident &c. 674.

neglected &c. *v.*; un-heeded, -cared for, -perceived, -seen, -observed, -noticed, -noted, -marked, -attended to, -thought of, -regarded, -remarked, -missed; shunted, shelved.

un-examined, -studied, -searched, -scanned, -weighed, -sifted, -explored.

abandoned; buried in a napkin, hid under a bushel.

Adv. negligently &c. *adj.*; hand over head, anyhow; in an unguarded moment &c. (*unexpectedly*) 508; *per incuriam.*

Int. never mind, no matter, let it pass; it will be all the same a hundred years hence.

461. Inquiry. [Subject of Inquiry. Question.]—**N.** inquiry; request &c. 765; search, research, quest; pursuit &c. 622.

examination, review, scrutiny, investigation, indagation; per-quisition, -scrutation, -vestigation; inqu-est, -isition; exploration; *exploitation*, ventilation.

sifting; calculation, analysis, dissection, resolution, induction; Baconian method.

strict –, close –, searching –, exhaustive- inquiry; narrow –, strict-search; study &c. (*consideration*) 451. *scire facias, ad referendum*; trial.

questioning &c. *v.*; interroga-tion, -tory; third degree; interpellation; challenge, examination, cross-examination, catechism; feeler, Socratic method, zetetic philosophy; leading question; discussion &c. (*reasoning*) 476; questionnaire, questionary.

reconnoitering, *reconnaissance*; prying &c. *v.*; espionage, *espionnage*; domiciliary visit, peep behind the curtain; lantern of Diogenes.

question, query, problem, *desideratum*, point to be solved, porism; subject –, field- of -inquiry, – controversy; point –, matter- in dispute; moot-point; issue, question at issue; bone of contention &c. (*discord*) 713; plain –, fair –, open- question; enigma &c. (*secret*) 533; knotty point &c. (*difficulty*) 704; *quod-libet*; threshold of an inquiry.

inquirer, investigator, experimenter, inquisitor, inspector, querist,

462. Answer.—**N.** answer, response, reply, replication, *riposte*, rejoinder, surrejoinder, rebutter, surrebutter, counter-evidence &c. 468, counter-charge, defence, plea; retort, repartee; contradiction &c. 536; rescript, -ion; antiphon, -y; acknowledgment; password; echo.

discovery &c. 480a; solution &c. (*explanation*) 522; rationale &c. (*cause*) 153; clue &c. (*indication*) 550.

Œdipus; oracle &c. 513; return &c. (*record*) 551.

V. answer, respond, reply, rebut, retort, rejoin; give –, return for- answer; acknowledge, echo.

explain &c. (*interpret*) 522; solve &c. (*unriddle*) 522; discover &c. 480a; fathom, hunt out &c. (*inquire*) 461; satisfy, set at rest, determine.

Adj. answering &c. *v.*; respon-sive, -dent; oracular; antiphonal; conclusive.

Adv. because &c. (*cause*) 153; on the -scent, – right scent.

Int. *eureka!*

examiner, catechist; scrut-ator, -ineer; analyst; quidnunc &c.
(*curiosity*) 455.

V. make -inquiry &c. *n.*; inquire, seek, search, frisk, speer, look
-for, – about for, – out for; scan, reconnoitre, explore, sound,
rummage, ransack, pry, peer, look round; look –, go- -over, –
through; spy, over-haul.

scratch the head, slap the forehead.

look –, peer –, pry- into every hole and corner; look behind the
scenes; trace up; hunt –, fish –, dig –, ferret- out; unearth; leave no
stone unturned.

seek a -clue, – clew; hunt, track, trail, shadow, mouse, dodge,
trace; follow the -trail, – scent; pursue &c. 622; beat up one's
quarters; fish for; feel for &c. (*experiment*) 463.

investigate; take up –, institute –, pursue –, follow up –, conduct –, carry on –, prosecute- -an inquiry &c. *n.*; look -at, – into;
pre-examine; discuss, canvass, agitate.

examine, study, consider, calculate; dip –, dive –, delve –, go
deep- into; make sure of, probe, sound, fathom; probe to the
-bottom, – quick; scrutinize, analyze, anatomize, dissect, parse,
resolve, sift, winnow; view –, try- in all its phases; thresh out.

bring in question, subject to examination; put to the proof &c.
(*experiment*) 463; audit, tax, pass in review; take into consideration
&c. (*think over*) 451; take counsel &c. 695.

ask, question, demand; put –, pop –, propose –, propound –,
moot –, start –, raise –, stir –, suggest –, put forth –, ventilate –,
grapple with –, go into- a question.

put to the question, interrogate, catechize, pump, grill; cross-
question, -examine; dodge; require an answer; pick –, suck- the brains
of; feel the pulse.

be -in question &c. *adj.*; undergo examination.

Adj. inquiry &c. *v.*; inquisitive &c. (*curious*) 455; requisit-ive,
-ory; catechetical, inquisitorial, analytic; in -search, – quest- of;
on the look-out for, interrogative, zetetic; all-searching.

un-determined, -tried, -decided; in -question, – dispute, – issue,
– course of inquiry; under -discussion, – consideration, – investigation &c. *n.*, *sub judice*, moot, proposed; doubtful &c. (*uncertain*) 475.

Adv. what? why? wherefore? whence? whither? where? *quære?*
how -comes, – happens, – is- it? what is the reason? what's -the
matter, – up, – in the wind? what on earth? when? who?

463. Experiment.—**N.** experiment; essay &c. (*attempt*) 675; research
&c. (*investigation*) 461; trial, tentative method, *tâtonnement*.

verification, probation, *experimentum crucis*, proof, criterion, diagnostic, test, tryout, crucial test, acid test.

crucible, reagent, check, touchstone, pix; assay, ordeal; ring.

empiricism, rule of thumb.

feeler; pilot -, messenger- balloon, *ballon d'essai*; pilot engine; scout;
straw to show the wind.

speculation, random shot, leap in the dark.

analy-zer, -st; adventurer, explorer, sourdough, prospector; experi-
ment-er, -ist, -alist; assayer.

V. experiment; essay &c. (*endeavour*) 675; try, assay, sample; make
-an experiment, – trial of; give a trial to; put upon –, subject to- trial;
experiment upon; rehearse; put –, bring –, submit- to the -test, – proof;
prove, verify, test, touch, practise upon, try one's strength.

grope; feel –, grope- -for, – one's way; fumble; *tâttonner, aller à tâtons*; put –, throw- out a feeler; send up a pilot balloon; see how the -land lies, – wind blows; consult the barometer; feel the pulse; fish –, bob- for; cast –, beat- about for; angle, trawl, cast one's net, beat the bushes.

venture, try one's fortune &c. (*adventure*) 675; explore &c. (*inquire*) 461.

Adj. experimental; probat-ive, -ory, -ionary; analytic, docimastic; tentative; empirical; speculative, tentative.

under probation, on one's trial, on trial, on approval.

464. Comparison.—N. comparison, collation, contrast; identification. sim-ile, -ilitude; allegory &c. (*metaphor*) 521.

V. compare -to, – with; collate, confront; place side by side &c. (*near*) 197; set –, pit- against one another; contrast, balance.

identify, draw a parallel, parallel.

compare notes; institute a comparison; *parva componere magnis*.

Adj. comparative, relative; metaphorical &c. 521.

compared with &c. *v.*; comparable.

Adv. relatively &c. (*relation*) 9; as compared with &c. *v.*

465. Discrimination.—N. discrimination, distinction, differentiation, diagnosis, diorism; nice perception; perception –, appreciation- of difference; acuteness; estimation &c. 466; nicety, refinement; taste &c. 850; *critique*, judgement, tact; insight, discernment &c. (*intelligence*) 498; *nuances*.

V. discriminate, distinguish, differentiate, severalize; separate; draw the line, sift; separate –, winnow- the chaff from the wheat; split hairs.

465a. Indiscrimination.—N. indiscrimination; promiscuity; indistinctness, -ion; uncertainty &c. (*doubt*) 475; obtuseness.

V. not -indiscriminate &c. 465; overlook &c. (*neglect*) 460- a distinction; con-found, -fuse, jumble; swallow whole.

Adj. indiscriminate, undiscriminating, promiscuous; undistinguish-ed, -able, -ing; unmeasured.

estimate &c. (*measure*) 466; know -which is which, – one's stuff, – one's way about, – what is what, – 'a hawk from a handsaw.'

take into -account, – consideration; give –, allow- due weight to; weigh carefully.

Adj. discriminating &c. *v.*; dioristic, discriminative, critical, distinctive; nice.

Phr. *il y a fagots et fagots*; *rem acu tetigisti.*

466. Measurement.—N. measurement, admeasurement, mensuration, survey, valuation, appraisement, assessment, assize; estim-ate, -ation; dead reckoning; reckoning &c. (*numeration*) 85; gauging &c. *v.*

metrology, weights and measures, compound arithmetic.

measure, yard measure, standard, rule, foot-rule, chain, tape, staff, compass, callipers; dividers; gage, gauge, planimeter; meter, line, rod, check.

volt, kilowatt, ampere, candle power; horse power; axle load; foot pound.

flood –, high water- mark; Plimsoll mark; index &c. 550.

scale; gradu-ation, -ated scale; nonius; vernier &c. (*minuteness*) 193; pedo (*length*)- 200, sounding line &c. (*depth*) 208, thermo (*heat* &c. 389)-, baro (*air* &c. 338)-, dynamo (*power*)- 276, anemo (*wind* 349)-, gonio (*angle* 244)- meter; landmark &c. (*limit*) 233; balance &c. (*weight*) 310; optical instruments &c. 445.

co-ordinates, ordinate and abscissa, polar co-ordinates, latitude and longitude, declination and right ascension, altitude and azimuth.

geo-, stereo-, hypso-metry; metage; surveying, land surveying; geo-desy, -detics, -desia; ortho-, alti-metry; *cadastre.*

astrolabe, armillary sphere.

land, -surveyor; geometer, topographer, cartographer, hydrographer.

V. measure, meter, mete; value, assess, rate, appraise, estimate, form an estimate, set a value on; appreciate; standardize.

span, pace, step; apply the -compass &c. *n.*; gauge, plumb, probe, calliper, sound, fathom &c. 208; heave the -log, – lead; weigh &c. 319; survey.

take an average &c. 29; graduate.

Adj. measuring &c. *v.*; metric, -al; measurable; geodetical, cadastral, topographical.

Section III. MATERIALS FOR REASONING

467. Evidence [on one side.]—**N.** evidence; facts, premises, *data, præcognita,* grounds.

indication &c. 550; criterion &c. (*test*) 463.

testi-mony, -fication; attestation; deposition &c. (*affirmation*) 535; examination.

admission &c. (*assent*) 488; author-ity, warrant, credential, diploma, voucher, certificate, docket; record &c. 551; document, muniments; *pièce justificative*; deed, warranty &c. (*security*) 771; signature, seal &c. (*identification*) 550; exhibit, citation, reference.

witness, indicator; eye-, ear-witness; deponent; sponsor.

oral –, documentary –, hearsay –, external –, extrinsic –, internal –, intrinsic –, circumstantial –, cumula-tive –, *ex parte* –, presumptive –, collateral –, constructive- evidence; proof &c. (*demonstration*) 478; evidence in chief; finger prints, dactylogram.

secondary evidence; confirmation, corroboration, adminicle, support; rati-fication &c. (*assent*) 488; authentica-tion, verification; compurgation, wager of law, comprobation.

citation, reference.

V. be -evidence &c. *n.*; evince, show, betoken, tell of; indicate &c. (*denote*) 550; imply, involve, argue, bespeak, breathe.

have –, carry- weight; tell, speak

468. [Evidence on the other side, on the other hand.] **Counter-evidence.—N.** counter-evidence; evidence on the other -side, – hand; disproof; refuta-tion &c. 479; negation &c. 536; con-flicting evidence.

plea &c. 617; vindication &c. 937; counter-protest; *tu quoque* argument; other side –, reverse- of the shield.

V. countervail, oppose; run counter; rebut &c. (*refute*) 479; subvert &c. (*de-stroy*) 162; check, weaken; contravene; contradict &c. (*deny*) 536; tell another story, turn the -tables, – scale; alter the case; cut both ways; prove a negative.

audire alteram partem.

Adj. countervailing &c. *v.*; contra-dictory, in rebuttal.

un-attested, -authenticated, -sup-ported by evidence; supposititious, trumped up.

Adv. *per contra,* conversely, on the other hand.

469. Qualification.—N. qualification, limitation, modification, colouring.

allowance, grains of allowance, con-sideration, extenuating circumstances.

condition, proviso, exception; ex-emption; salvo, saving clause; discount &c. 813.

V. qualify, limit, modify, affect, temper, leaven, give a colour to, in-troduce new conditions.

allow –, make allowance- for; ad-

volumes; speak for itself &c. (*manifest*) 525.

rest –, depend- upon; repose on.

bear -witness &c. *n.*; give -evidence &c. *n.*; testify, depose, witness, vouch for; sign, seal, undersign, set one's hand and seal, sign and seal, deliver as one's act and deed, certify, attest; acknowledge &c. (*assent*) 488.

make absolute, confirm, ratify, corroborate, endorse, countersign, support, bear out, vindicate, uphold, warrant.

adduce, attest, cite, quote; refer –, appeal- to; call, – to witness; bring -forward, – into court; allege, plead; produce –, confront- witnesses; collect –, bring together –, rake up- evidence.

have –, make out- a case; establish, circumstantiate, authenticate, substantiate, verify, make good, quote chapter and verse; bring -home to, – to book.

Adj. showing &c. *v.*; evidential, indica-tive, -tory; deducible &c. 478; grounded –, founded –, based- on; first hand, authentic, verifiable; corroborative, confirmatory; significant, conclusive.

Adv. by inference; according to, witness, *a fortiori*; still -more, – less; *raison de plus*; in corroboration &c. *n.* of; *valeat quantum*; under -seal, – one's hand and seal.

mit exceptions, take into account. take exception, object.

Adj. qualifying &c. *v.*; conditional; extenuatory; exceptional &c. (*unconformable*) 83.

hypothetical &c. (*supposed*) 514; contingent &c. (*uncertain*) 475.

Adv. provided, – always; if, unless, but, yet; according as; conditionally, admitting, supposing; on the supposition of &c. (*theoretically*) 514; with the understanding, even, although, though, for all that, after all, at all events.

with grains of allowance, *cum grano salis*; *exceptis excipiendis*; wind and weather permitting; if possible &c. 470.

subject to; with this -proviso &c. *n.*

Degrees of Evidence

470. Possibility.—N. possibility, potentiality; what -may be, – is possible &c. *adj.*; compatibility &c. (*agreement*) 23.

practicability, feasibility; practicableness &c. *adj.*

contingency, chance &c. 156.

V. be -possible &c. *adj.*; stand a chance, have a leg to stand on; admit of, bear.

render -possible &c. *adj.*; put in the way of.

Adj. possible; on the -cards, – dice; *in posse*, within the bounds of possibility, conceivable, credible, imaginable; compatible &c. 23.

practicable, feasible, workable, performable, achievable; within -reach, – measurable distance; accessible, superable, surmountable; at-, ob-tainable; contingent &c. (*doubtful*) 475.

Adv. possibly, by possibility; perhaps, -chance, -adventure; may be, haply, mayhap.

471. Impossibility.—N. impossibility &c. *adj.*; what -cannot, – can never- be; sour grapes; infeasibility, impracticability, hopelessness &c. 859.

V. be -impossible &c. *adj.*; have no chance whatever.

attempt impossibilities; square the circle; discover the -philosopher's stone, – elixir of life, – secret of perpetual motion; wash a blackamoor white; skin a flint; make -a silk purse out of a sow's ear, – bricks without straw; have nothing to go upon; weave a rope of sand, build castles in the air, *prendre la lune avec les dents*, extract sunbeams from cucumbers, set the Thames on fire, milk a he-goat into a sieve, catch a weasel asleep, *rompre l'anguille au genou*, be in two places at once.

Adj. impossible; not -possible &c. 470; absurd, contrary to reason; unlikely, at variance with facts; unreasonable &c. 477; incredible &c. 485; beyond the bounds of -reason, – possi-

if possible, wind and weather permitting, God willing, *Deo volente*, D.V.

---

bility; from which reason recoils; visionary; inconceivable &c. (*improbable*) 473; prodigious &c. (*wonderful*) 870; un-, in-imaginable, unthinkable, not a Chinaman's chance.

impracticable, unachievable; un-, in-feasible; insuperable; un-, in-surmountable; unat-, unob-tainable; out of -reach, – the question; not to be -had, – thought of; beyond control; desperate &c. (*hopeless*) 859; incompatible &c. 24; inaccessible, uncomeatable, impassable impervious, innavigable, inextricable.

out of –, beyond- one's -power, – depth, – reach, – grasp; too much for; *ultra crepidam.*

Phr. the grapes are sour; *non possumus; non nostrum tantas componere lites.*

472. Probability.—N. probability, likelihood; likeliness &c. *adj.*

vraisemblance, verisimilitude, plausibility; colour, semblance, show of; presumption; presumptive –, circumstantial- evidence; credibility.

reasonable –, fair –, good –, favourable- -chance, – prospect; prospect, well-grounded hope; chance &c. 156.

V. be -probable &c. *adj.*; give –, lend- colour to; point to; imply &c. (*evidence*) 467; bid fair &c. (*promise*) 511; stand fair for; stand –, run- a good chance.

presume, infer, suppose, take for granted.

think likely, dare say, flatter oneself; expect &c. 507; count upon &c. (*believe*) 484.

Adj. probable, likely, hopeful, to be expected, in a fair way.

plausible, specious, ostensible, colourable, *ben trovato*, well-founded, reasonable, credible, easy of belief, presumable, presumptive, apparent.

Adv. probably &c. *adj.*; belike; in all -probability, – likelihood; very –, most- likely; as likely as not; like enough; ten &c. to one; apparently, seemingly, according to every reasonable expectation; *primâ facie*; to all appearance &c. (*to the eye*) 448.

Phr. the -chances, – odds- are; appearances –, chances- are in favour of; there is reason to -believe, – think, – expect; I dare say; all Lombard Street to a China orange.

473. Improbability.—N. improbability, unlikelihood; unfavourable –, bad –, little –, small –, poor –, scarcely any –, no –, not a ghost of a- chance; bare possibility; long odds; incredibility &c. 485.

V. be -improbable &c. *adj.*; have a -small chance &c. *n.*

Adj. improbable, unlikely, contrary to all reasonable expectation, implausible.

rare &c. (*infrequent*) 137; unheard of, inconceivable; un-, in-imaginable; incredible &c. 485; more than doubtful.

Int. not likely! no fear!

Phr. the chances are against.

---

474. Certainty.—N. certainty; necessity &c. 601; certitude, certainness, surety, assurance, sureness; dead –, moral- certainty; infallibleness &c. *adj.*; infallibility, reliability.

gospel, scripture, church, pope, court of final appeal; *res judicata, ultimatum.*

positiveness; dogmat-ism, -ist, -izer; *doctrinaire*, know-all, bigot, -ry; opin-

475. Uncertainty.—N. uncertainty, incertitude, doubt; doubtfulness &c. *adj.*; dubi-ety, -tation, -tancy, -ousness.

hesitation, suspense; perplexity, embarrassment, dilemma, quandary, Morton's fork, bewilderment; timidity &c. (*fear*) 860; indecision, vacillation &c. 605; *diaporesis*, indetermination.

vagueness &c. *adj.*; haze, fog; ob-

ionist, Sir Oracle; *ipse dixit*; zealot.

fact; positive –, matter of- fact; *fait accompli*.

V. be -certain &c. *adj.*; stand to reason.

render -certain &c. *adj.*; in-, en-, assure; clinch, make sure; determine, decide, set at rest, 'make assurance double sure'; know &c. (*believe*) 484; dismiss all doubt.

dogmatize, lay down the law.

Adj. certain, sure; assured &c. *v.*; solid, well-founded.

unqualified, absolute, positive, determinate, definite, clear, unequivocal, categorical, unmistakable, decisive, decided, ascertained.

inevitable, unavoidable, ineluctable, avoidless.

unerring, infallible; unchangeable &c. 150; to be depended on, trustworthy, reliable, bound.

un-impeachable, -deniable, -questionable; in-disputable, -contestable, -controvertible, -defeasible, -dubitable; irrefutable &c. (*proven*) 478; conclusive, without power of appeal, final.

indubious; without –, beyond a –, without a shade or shadow of- -doubt – question; past dispute; beyond all -question, – dispute; un-doubted, -contested, -questioned, -disputed; question-, doubt-less.

bigoted, fanatical, dogmatic, opinionat-ed, -ive, *doctrinaire*.

authoritative, authentic, official.

sure as -fate, – death and taxes, – a gun.

evident, self-evident, axiomatic; clear, – as day, – as the sun at noonday; obvious.

Adv. certainly &c. *adj.*; for certain, certes, sure, no doubt, doubtless, and no mistake, *flagrante delicto*, sure enough, to be sure, of course, as a matter of course, *à coup sur*, to a certainty, undoubtedly; in truth &c. (*truly*) 494; at -any rate, – all events; without fail; *coûte que coûte*; whatever may happen, if the worst come to the worst; come –, happen- what -may, – will; sink or swim; rain or shine.

Phr. *cela va sans dire*; there is -no question, – not a shadow of doubt;

scurity &c. (*darkness*) 421; ambiguity &c. (*double meaning*) 520; contingency, double contingency, possibility upon a possibility; conjecture; open question &c. (*question*) 461; *onus probandi*; blind bargain, pig in a poke, leap in the dark, something or other; needle in a bottle of hay; roving commission.

fallibility, unreliability, untrustworthiness, precariousness.

V. be -uncertain &c. *adj.*; wonder whether.

lose the -clue, – clew, – scent; miss one's way.

not know -what to make of &c. (*unintelligibility*) 519, – which way to turn, – whether one stands on one's head or one's heels; float in a sea of doubt, hesitate, flounder; lose -oneself, – one's head, – one's way, wander aimlessly; muddle one's brains.

render -uncertain &c. *adj.*; put out, pose, puzzle, perplex, embarrass; confuse, -found; bewilder, mystify, bother, moider, nonplus, addle the wits, throw off the scent; *ambiguas in vulgus spargere voces*; keep in suspense.

doubt &c. (*disbelieve*) 485; hang –, tremble- in the balance; depend.

Adj. uncertain; casual; random &c. (*aimless*) 621; changeable &c. 149.

doubtful, dubious; indecisive; unsettled, -decided, -determined; in suspense, open to discussion; controvertible; in question &c. (*inquiry*) 461; insecure, unstable.

vague; in-determinate, -definite; ambiguous, equivocal; undefin-ed, -able; confused &c. (*indistinct*) 447; mystic, mysterious, veiled, obscure, cryptic, oracular.

perplexing &c. *v.*; enigmatic, paradoxical, apocryphal, problematical, hypothetical; experimental &c. 463.

fallible, questionable, precarious, slippery, ticklish, debatable, disputable; un-reliable, -trustworthy.

contingent, – on, dependent on; subject to; dependent on circumstances; occasional; provisional.

unauth-entic, -enticated, -oritative; un-ascertained, -confirmed; undemonstrated; un-told, -counted.

in a -state of uncertainty, – cloud,

the die is cast &c. (*necessity*) 601.

_____

– fault, – a loss, – one's wit's end, – a *nonplus*; puzzled &c. *v.*; lost, abroad, *désorienté*; dis-tracted, -traught.

– maze; ignorant &c. 491; on the horns of a dilemma; afraid to say; out of one's reckoning, astray, adrift; at -sea,

Adv. *pendente lite*; *sub spe rati.*

Phr. Heaven knows; who can tell? who shall decide when doctors disagree?

Section IV. Reasoning Processes

476. Reasoning. — N. reasoning; ratio-cination, -nalism; dialectics, in-duction, generalization.

discussion, comment; ventilation; inquiry &c. 461.

argumentation, controversy, debate; polemics, wrangling; contention &c. 720; logomachy; dis-putation, -cepta-tion; paper war.

art of reasoning, logic.

process –, train –, chain- of reason-ing; de-, in-duction; synthesis, analysis.

argument; case, plea, *plaidoyer*, opening; *lemma*, proposition, terms, premises, postulate, *data*, starting point, principle; inference &c. (*judg-ment*) 480.

pro-, syllogism; enthymeme, sorites, dilemma, *perilepsis, a priori* reasoning, *reductio ad absurdum*, horns of a di-lemma, *argumentum ad hominem*, com-prehensive argument.

reasoner, logician, dialectician; dis-putant; controver-sialist, -tist; wrang-ler, arguer, debater, polemic, casuist, rationalist; scientist.

logical sequence; good case; correct –, just –, sound –, valid –, cogent –, logical –, forcible –, persuasive –, per-suasory –, consectary –, conclusive &c. 478 –, subtle- reasoning; force of argu-ment; strong -point, – argument.

arguments, reasons, pros and cons.

V. reason, argue, discuss, debate, dispute, wrangle; bandy -words, – arguments; chop logic; hold –, carry on- an argument; controvert &c. (*deny*) 536; canvass; comment –, moralize-upon; consider &c. (*examine*) 461.

open a -discussion, – case; join –, be at- issue; moot; come to the point; stir –, agitate –, ventilate –, torture- a question; try conclusions; take up a -side, – case.

477. [The absence of reasoning.] **Intuition.** [False or vicious reasoning; show of reason.] **Sophistry.—N.** intui-tion, instinct, association; presenti-ment; rule of thumb.

sophistry, paralogy, perversion, casu-istry, jesuitry, equivocation, evasion, mental reservation; chicane, -ry; quid-dit, quiddity; mystification; special pleading; speciousness &c. *adj.*; non-sense &c. 497; word-, tongue-fence.

false –, vicious- reasoning; *petitio principii, ignoratio elenchi; post hoc ergo propter hoc; non sequitur, ignotum per ignotius.*

misjudgment &c. 481; false teaching &c. 538.

sophism, solecism, paralogism; quib-ble, quirk, *elenchus*, elench, fallacy, *quodlibet*, subterfuge, subtlety, quillet; inconsistency, antilogy; 'a mockery, a delusion and a snare'; claptrap, mere words; 'lame and impotent conclusion.'

meshes –, cobwebs- of sophistry; flaw in an argument; weak point, bad case.

over-refinement; hair-splitting &c. *v.*

sophist, casuist, paralogist.

V. judge -intuitively, – by intuition; hazard a proposition, talk at random.

reason -ill, – falsely &c. *adj.*; paralo-gize; misjudge &c. 481.

pervert, quibble; equivocate, mysti-fy, evade, elude; gloss over, varnish; misteach &c. 538; mislead &c. (*error*) 495; cavil, refine, subtilize, split hairs; misrepresent &c. (*lie*) 544.

beg the question, reason in a circle, cut blocks with a razor, beat about the bush, play fast and loose, blow hot and cold, prove that black is white and white black, travel out of the record, *parler à tort et à travers*, put oneself out of court, not have a leg to stand on.

Adj. intuitive, instinctive, impulsive;

contend, take one's stand upon, insist, lay stress on; infer &c. 480.

follow from &c. (*demonstration*) 478.

Adj. rational; reasoning &c. *v.*; rationalistic; argumentative, controversial, dialectic, polemical; discursory, -ive; disputatious.

debatable, controvertible.

logical; in-, de-ductive; synthetic, analytic; relevant &c. 23.

Adv. for, because, hence, whence, seeing that, since, sith, then, thence, so; for -that, – this, – which- reason; for-, inasmuch as; whereas, *ex concesso*, considering, in consideration of; there-, where-fore; consequently, *ergo*, thus, accordingly; *a fortiori*.

in -conclusion, – fine; finally, after all, *au bout du compte*, on the whole, taking one thing with another.

rationally &c. *adj.*

independent of –, anterior to- reason; gratuitous, hazarded; unconnected.

unreasonable, illogical, false, unsound, invalid; unwarranted, not following; inconsequent, -ial; inconsistent, incongruous; abson-ous, -ant; unscientific; untenable, inconclusive, incorrect; fall-acious, -ible; groundless, unproved.

deceptive, sophistical, sophisticated, casuistical, jesuitical; illus-ive, -ory; specious, hollow, plausible, *ad captandum*, evasive; irrelevant &c. 10.

weak, feeble, poor, flimsy, loose, vague, irrational; nonsensical &c. (*absurd*) 497; foolish &c. (*imbecile*) 499; frivolous, pettifogging, quibbling; fine-spun, over-refined.

at the end of one's tether, *au bout de son latin*.

Adv. intuitively &c. *adj.*; by intuition; illogically &c. *adj.*

Phr. *non constat*; that goes for nothing.

---

478. Demonstration.—N. demonstration, proof; conclusiveness &c. *adj.*; *apodixis*, probation, comprobation.

logic of facts &c. (*evidence*) 467; *experimentum crucis* &c. (*test*) 463; argument &c. 476; irrefragability.

V. demonstrate, prove, establish, make good; show; evince &c. (*be evidence of*) 467; verify &c. 467; settle the question, reduce to demonstration, set the question at rest.

make out, – a case; prove one's point, have the best of the argument; draw a conclusion &c. (*judge*) 480.

follow, – of course; stand to reason; hold -good, – water.

Adj. demonstra-ting &c. *v.*, -tive, -ble; probative, unanswerable, conclusive; apodictic, -al; irre-sistible, -futable, -fragable, undeniable.

categorical, decisive, crucial.

demonstrated &c. *v.*; proven; un-confuted, -answered, -refuted; evident &c. 474.

deducible, consequential, consectary, inferential, following.

Adv. of course, in consequence, consequently, as a matter of course.

Phr. *probatum est*; there is nothing more to be said, Q.E.D., it must follow.

479. Confutation.—N. con-, re-futation; answer, complete answer; disproof, conviction, redargution, invalidation; expos-ure, -ition; clincher; retort; *reductio ad absurdum*; knock down –, *tu quoque*- argument.

V. con-, re-fute; parry, negative, disprove, redargue, expose, show the fallacy of, rebut, defeat; demolish &c. (*destroy*) 162; over-throw, -turn; scatter to the winds, explode, invalidate; silence; put –, reduce- to silence; clinch -an argument, – a question; give one a set down, stop the mouth, shut up; have, – on the hip; get the better of; confound, convince.

not leave a leg to stand on, cut the ground from under one's feet.

be confuted &c.; fail; expose –, show- one's weak point.

Adj. confut-ing, -ed &c. *v.*; capable of refutation; re-, con-futable.

condemned -on one's own showing, – out of one's own mouth.

Phr. the argument falls to the ground, *cadit quæstio*, it does not hold water, '*suo sibi gladio hunc jugulo.*'

[155]

Section V. Results of Reasoning

480. Judgment. [Conclusion.]—**N.** result, conclusion, upshot; deduction, inference, ergotism, illation; corollary, porism; moral.

estimation, valuation, appreciation, judication; di-, ad-judication; arbitrament, -ement, -ation; assessment, ponderation.

award, estimate; review, criticism, *critique*, notice, report.

decision, determination, judgment, finding, verdict, sentence, decree, – nisi, – absolute, – interlocutory; dictum; *res judicata*.

plébiscite, referendum, voice, casting vote; vote &c. (*choice*) 609; opinion &c. (*belief*) 484; good judgment &c. (*wisdom*) 498.

judge, jurist, umpire; arbi-ter, -trator; assessor, referee; censor, reviewer, critic; *connoisseur*; commentator &c. 524; inspector, inspecting officer.

V. judge, conclude; come to –, draw –, arrive at- a conclusion; ascertain, determine, make up one's mind.

deduce, derive, gather, collect, draw an inference, make a deduction, weet, ween.

form an estimate, estimate, size up, appreciate, value, count, assess, rate, rank, account; regard, consider, think of; look upon &c. (*believe*) 484.

settle; pass –, give- an opinion; decide, try, pronounce, rule; pass -judgment, – sentence; sentence, doom; find; give –, deliver- judgment; adjud-ge, -icate; arbitrate, award, report; bring in a verdict; make absolute, set a question at rest; confirm &c. (*assent*) 488.

comment, criticize; review, pass under review &c. (*examine*) 457; investigate &c. (*inquire*) 461.

hold the scales, sit in judgment; try –, hear- a cause.

Adj. judging &c. *v.*; judicious &c. (*wise*) 498; determinate, conclusive, censorious, critical &c. 932.

Adv. on the whole, all things considered.

481. Misjudgment. — **N.** misjudgment, obliquity of –, warped- judgment; mis-calculation, -computation, -conception &c. (*error*) 495; hasty conclusion.

prejud-gment, -ication, -ice; foregone conclusion; pre-notion, -vention, -conception, -dilection, -possession, -apprehension, -sumption, -sentiment; fixed –, preconceived- idea; *idée fixe*; *mentis gratissimus error*; fool's paradise.

esprit de corps, party spirit, race –, class- prejudice, partisanship, clannishness, *prestige*.

bias, warp, twist; hobby, fad, whim, craze, quirk, crotchet, partiality, infatuation, blind side, mote in the eye.

one-sided –, partial –, narrow –, confined –, superficial- -views, – ideas, – conceptions, – notions; narrow mind; bigotry &c. (*obstinacy*) 606; *odium theologicum*; pedantry; hypercriticism. *doctrinaire* &c. (*positive*) 474.

V. mis-judge, -estimate, -think, -conjecture, -conceive &c. (*error*) 495; fly in the face of facts; mis-calculate, -reckon, -compute.

overestimate &c. 482; underestimate &c. 483.

pre-, fore-judge; pre-suppose, -sume, -judicate; dogmatize; have a -bias &c. *n.*; have only one idea; *jurare in verba magistri*, run away with the notion; jump –, rush- to a conclusion; look only at one side of the shield; view -with jaundiced eye, – through distorting spectacles; not see beyond one's nose; *dare pondus fumo*; get the wrong sow by the ear &c. (*blunder*) 699.

give a -bias, – twist; bias, warp, twist; pre-judice, -possess.

Adj. misjudging &c. *v.*; ill-judging, wrong-headed; prejudiced, prejudicial, &c. *v.*; jaundiced; short-sighted, purblind; partial, one-sided, superficial.

narrow-minded; confined, insular, provincial, parochial, illiberal, intolerant, narrow, besotted, infatuated, fanatical, cracked, warped, *entêté*, positive, dogmatic, dictatorial; conceited; opin-, opini-ative; opinion-ed, -ate, -ative, -ated; self-opinioned, wedded to an opinion, *opiniâtre*; bigoted &c. (*obstinate*) 606; crotchety, fussy, impracticable; unreason-able, -ing; stupid &c. 499; credulous &c. 486.

misjudged &c. *v.*

Adv. *ex parte.*

Phr. nothing like leather; the wish the father to the thought.

480a. [Result of search or inquiry.] **Discovery.—N.** discovery, invention, detection, disenchantment, disclosure, find, ascertainment, revelation.

trover &c. 775.

V. discover, find, determine, evolve; fix upon; find -, trace -, make -, hunt -, fish -, worm -, ferret -, root- out; fathom; bring -, draw- out; educe, elicit, bring to light, invent; dig -, grub -, fish- up; unearth, disinter.

solve, resolve; un-riddle, -ravel, -lock; pick -, open- the lock; find a -clue, - clew- to; interpret &c. 522; disclose &c. 529.

trace, get at; hit it, have it; lay one's -finger, - hands- upon; spot; get -, arrive- at the -truth &c. 494; put the saddle on the right horse, hit the right nail on the head.

be near the truth, burn; smoke, scent, sniff, smell a rat.

open the eyes to; see -through, - daylight, - in its true colours, - the cloven foot; detect; catch, - tripping.

pitch -, fall -, light -, hit -, stumble -, pop- upon; come across; meet -, fall in- with.

recognize, realize, verify, make certain of, identify.

Int. *eureka!*

482. Overestimation.—N. overestimation &c. *v.*; exaggeration &c. 549; vanity &c. 880; optim-, pessim-ism, -ist; megalomania.

much -cry and little wool, - ado about nothing; storm in a teacup; fine talking, rodomontade, gush, hot air, gas, bombast.

egotism &c. 880; boasting &c. 884.

V. over-estimate, -rate, -value, -prize, -weigh, -reckon, -strain, -praise; estimate too highly, attach too much importance to, make mountains of molehills, catch at straws; strain, magnify; exaggerate &c. 549; set too high a value upon; think -, make- -much, - too much- of; outreckon.

extol, - to the skies; make the -most, - best, - worst- of, eulogize, panegyrize, gush, puff, boost; make two bites of a cherry.

have too high an opinion of oneself &c. (*vanity*) 880.

Adj. overestimated &c. *v.*; oversensitive &c. (*sensibility*) 822; inflated, puffed up, exaggerated &c. 549.

Phr. all his geese are swans; *parturiunt montes.*

483. Underestimation.—N. underestimation; depreciation &c. (*detraction*) 934; pessim-ism, -ist; undervaluing &c. *v.*; modesty &c. 881.

V. under-rate, -estimate, -value, -reckon; depreciate; disparage &c. (*detract*) 934; not do justice to; mis-, dis-prize; ridicule &c. 856; slight &c. (*despise*) 930; neglect &c. 460; slur over, under-state.

make -light, - little, - nothing, - no account- of; minimize, belittle, run down, think nothing of; set -no store by, - at naught; shake off as dewdrops from the lion's mane.

Adj. depreciat-ing, -ed, -ive, -ory, &c. *v.*; un-appreciated, -valued, -prized; pejorative.

484. Belief.—N. belief; credence; credit; assurance; faith, trust, troth, confidence, presumption, sanguine expectation &c. (*hope*) 858; dependence on, reliance on.

persuasion, conviction, convincement, plerophory, self-conviction; certainty &c. 474; opinion, mind, view; conception, thinking; impression &c. (*idea*) 453; surmise &c. 514; conclusion &c. (*judgment*) 480.

tenet, dogma, principle, way of thinking; popular belief &c. (*assent*) 488.

firm –, implicit –, settled –, fixed –, rooted –, deep-rooted –, staunch –, unshaken –, steadfast –, inveterate –, calm –, sober –, dispassionate –, impartial –, well-founded- -belief, – opinion &c.; *uberrima fides*.

system of opinions, school, doctrine, articles, canons; declaration –, profession- of faith; tenets, *credenda*, creed; thirty-nine articles &c. (*orthodoxy*) 983*a*; catechism; assent &c. 488; *propaganda* &c. (*teaching*) 537.

credibility &c. (*probability*) 472.

V. believe, credit; give -faith, – credit, – credence- to; see, realize; assume, receive; set down –, take- for; have –, take- it; consider, esteem, presume.

count –, depend –, calculate –, pin one's faith –, reckon –, lean –, build –, rely –, rest- upon; lay one's account for; make sure of.

make oneself easy -about, – on that score; take on -trust, – credit; take for -granted, –gospel; allow –, attach-some weight to.

know, – for certain; have –, make-no doubt; doubt not; be – rest- -assured &c. *adj.*; persuade –, assure –, satisfy-oneself; make up one's mind.

give one credit for; confide –, believe –, put one's trust- in; place –, repose- implicit confidence in; take -one's word for, – at one's word; place reliance on, rely upon, swear by, regard to.

think, hold; take, – it; opine, be of opinion, conceive, trow, ween, fancy, apprehend; have –, hold –, possess –, entertain –, adopt –, imbibe –, embrace

485. Unbelief. Doubt.—N. un-, dis-, mis-belief; discredit, miscreance; infidelity &c. (*irreligion*) 989; dissent &c. 489; change of -opinion &c. 484; retraction &c. 607.

doubt &c. (*uncertainty*) 475; skepticism, misgiving, demur; dis-, mis-trust; misdoubt, suspicion, jealousy, scruple, qualm; *onus probandi*.

incredib-ility, -leness; incredulity; unbeliever &c. 487.

V. dis-believe, -credit; not -believe &c. 484; misbelieve; refuse to admit &c. (*dissent*) 489; refuse to believe &c. (*incredulity*) 487.

doubt; be -doubtful &c. (*uncertain*) 475; doubt the truth of; be -skeptical as to &c. *adj.*; diffide; dis-, mis-trust; suspect, smoke, scent, smell a rat; have –, harbour –, entertain- -doubts, – suspicions; have one's doubts.

demur, stick at, pause, hesitate, scruple, waver, stop and consider.

hang in -suspense, – doubt.

throw doubt upon, raise a question; bring –, call- in question; question, challenge, query; dispute; deny &c. 536; cavil; cause –, raise –, start –, suggest –, awake- a -doubt, – suspicion; ergotize.

startle, stagger; shake –, stagger-one's faith, – belief.

Adj. unbelieving; incredulous –, skeptical- as to; distrustful –, shy –, suspicious- of; doubting &c. *v.*

doubtful &c. (*uncertain*) 475; disputable; unworthy –, undeserving- of -belief &c. 484; questionable; sus-pect, -picious; open to -suspicion, – doubt; staggering, hard to believe, incredible, not to be believed, inconceivable.

fallible &c. (*uncertain*) 475; undemonstrable; controvertible &c. (*untrue*) 495.

Adv. *cum grano salis.*

Phr. *fronti nulla fides*; *nimium ne crede colori*; 'timeo Danaos et dona ferentes'; credat Judæus Apella*; let those believe who may.

–, get hold of –, hazard –, foster –, nurture –, cherish- -a belief, – an opinion &c. *n.*

view –, consider –, take –, hold –, conceive –, regard –, esteem –, deem –, look upon –, account –, set down- as; surmise &c. 514.

get –, take- it into one's head; come round to an opinion; swallow &c. (*credulity*) 486.

cause to -be believed &c. *v.*; satisfy, persuade, have the ear of, gain the confidence of, assure; con-vince, -vict, -vert; put across, sell; wean, bring round; bring –, put –, win- over; indoctrinate &c. (*teach*) 537; cram down the throat; produce –, carry- conviction; bring –, drive- home to.

go down, find credence, pass current; be -received &c. *v.*, – current &c. *adj.*; possess –, take hold of –, take possession of- the mind.

Adj. believing &c. *v.*; certain, sure, assured, positive, cocksure, satisfied, confident, unhesitating, convinced, secure.

under the impression; impressed –, imbued –, penetrated- with.

confiding, trustful, suspectless; unsusp-ecting, -icious; void of suspicion; credulous &c. 486; wedded to.

believed &c. *v.*; accredited, putative; unsuspected.

worthy of –, deserving of –, commanding- -belief, – confidence; credible, reliable, trusted, trustworthy, to be depended on, undoubted; satisfactory; probable &c. 472; fiduci-al, -ary; persuasive, impressive.

relating to belief, doctrinal.

Adv. in the -opinion, – eyes- of; *me judice*; me-seems, -thinks; to the best of one's belief; I -dare say, – doubt not, – have no doubt, – am sure; in my opinion; sure enough &c. (*certainty*) 474; depend –, rely- upon it; be –, rest- assured; I'll warrant you &c. (*affirmation*) 535.

---

486. Credulity.—N. credul-ity, -ousness &c. *adj.*; gull-, cull-ibility; gross credulity, infatuation; self-delusion, -deception; blind reasoning; superstition; one's blind side; bigotry &c. (*obstinacy*) 606; hyper-orthodoxy &c. 984; misjudgment &c. 481.

credulous person &c. (*dupe*) 547.

V. be -credulous &c. *adj.*; *jurare in verba magistri*; follow implicitly; swallow, – whole, gulp down; take on trust; take for -granted, – gospel; run away with -a notion, – an idea; jump –, rush- to a conclusion; think the moon is made of green cheese; take –, grasp- the shadow for the substance; catch at straws.

impose upon &c. (*deceive*) 545.

Adj. credulous, gullible; easily -deceived &c. 545; simple, green, soft, childish, silly, stupid; over-credulous, -confident; infatuated, superstitious; confiding &c. (*believing*) 484.

Phr. the wish the father to the thought; *credo quia impossibile.*

487. Incredulity.—N. incredul-ousness, -ity; skepticism, pyrrhonism; want of faith &c. (*irreligion*) 989.

suspiciousness &c. *adj.*; scrupulosity; suspicion &c. (*unbelief*) 485; dissent &c. 489.

unbeliever, skeptic, aporetic; atheist, agnostic, infidel, disbeliever, misbeliever, pyrrhonist &c. 989; heretic &c. (*heterodox*) 984.

V. be -incredulous &c. *adj.*; distrust &c. (*disbelieve*) 485; refuse to believe; shut one's -eyes, – ears- to; turn a deaf ear to; hold aloof; ignore; *nullis jurare in verba magistri.*

Adj. incredulous, skeptical, unbelieving, inconvincible; hard –, shy- of belief; suspicious, scrupulous, distrustful, heterodox &c. 984.

488. Assent.—N.

assent, -ment; acquiescence, admission; nod; ac-, con-cord, -cordance; agreement &c. 23; affirm-ance, -ation; recognition, acknowledgment, avowal; confession, – of faith.

unanimity, common consent, *consensus*, acclamation, chorus, *vox populi*; popular –, current- -belief, – opinion; public opinion; concurrence &c. (*of causes*) 178; co-operation &c. (*voluntary*) 709.

ratification, confirmation, corroboration, approval, acceptance, *visa*; indorsement &c. (*record*) 551.

consent &c. (*compliance*) 762.

affirmant, consenter, covenantor, subscriber, endorser, upholder.

V. assent; give –, yield –, nod- assent; acquiesce; agree &c. 23; receive, accept, accede, accord, concur, lend oneself to, consent, coincide, reciprocate, go with; be -at one with &c. *adj.*; go along –, chime in –, strike in –, close- with; echo, enter into one's views, agree in opinion; vote –, give one's voice- for; recognize; subscribe –, conform –, defer- to; say -yes, – ditto, – amen, – aye- to.

acknowledge, own, admit, allow, avow, confess; concede &c. (*yield*) 762; come round to; abide by; permit &c. 760.

come to –, arrive at- -an understanding, – terms, – an agreement.

con-, af-firm; ratify, approve, endorse, countersign; visa; corroborate &c. 467.

go –, swim- with the stream, float with the current; be in the fashion, join in the chorus; be in every mouth.

Adj. assenting &c. *v.*; of one -accord, – mind; of the same mind, at one with, agreed, acquiescent, content; willing &c. 602.

un-contradicted, -challenged, -questioned, -controverted.

carried –, agreed- -*nem. con.* &c. *adv.*; unanimous; agreed on all hands, carried by acclamation.

affirmative &c. 535.

Adv. yes, yea, ay, aye, true; good; well; very -well, – true; well and good; granted; *placet*; even –, just- so; to be sure, surely, 'thou hast said'; truly, exactly, precisely,

489. Dissent.—N.

dissent; discordance &c. (*disagreement*) 24; difference –, diversity- of opinion.

non-conformity &c. (*heterodoxy*) 984; protestantism, recusancy, schism; disaffection; secession &c. 624; recantation &c. 607.

dissension &c. (*discord*) 713; discontent &c. 832; cavilling.

protest; contradiction &c. (*denial*) 536; non-compliance &c. (*rejection*) 764; disapprobation &c. 932; hartal.

dissent-ient, -er; non-juror, -content; recusant, sectary, schismatic, protestant, non-conformist, separatist, non-co-operator, conscientious objector, passive resister.

V. dissent, demur; call in question &c. (*doubt*) 485; differ in opinion, disagree; say -no &c. 536; refuse -assent, – to admit; cavil, protest, raise one's voice against, make bold to differ; repudiate; contradict &c. (*deny*) 536; agree to differ.

have no notion of, differ *toto cœlo*; revolt -at, – from the idea.

shake the head, shrug the shoulders; look -askance, – askant.

secede; recant &c. 607.

Adj. dissenting &c. *v.*; negative &c. 536; diss-ident, -entient; unconsenting &c. (*refusing*) 764; non-content, -juring; protestant, recusant; uncon-vinced, -verted.

unavowed, unacknowledged; out of the question.

discontented &c. 832; unwilling &c. 603; extorted.

sectarian, denominational, schismatic, heterodox, intolerant.

Adv. no &c. 536; at -variance, – issue- with; under protest; *non placet*.

Int. God forbid! not for the world; not on your life; I beg to differ; I'll be hanged if; never tell me; your humble servant, pardon me; tell that to the marines.

Phr. many men many minds; *quot homines tot sententiæ*; *tant s'en faut*; *il s'en faut bien*.

that's just it, indeed, certainly, certes, *ex concesso*; of course, unquestionably, assuredly, no doubt, doubtless, undoubtedly.

be it so; so -be it, – let it be, so mote it be; amen; with all my heart; willingly &c. 602.

affirmatively, in the affirmative.

with one -consent, – voice, – accord; unanimously, *unâ voce*, by common consent, in chorus, to a man, *nem. con.*; *nemine -contradicente*, – *dissentiente*; without a dissentient voice; as one man, one and all, on all hands.

490. Knowledge.—N. knowledge; cogn-izance, -ition, -oscence; acquaintance, experience, ken, privity, insight, familiarity; com-, ap-prehension; recognition; appreciation &c. (*judgment*) 480; intuition; consci-ence, -ousness; perception, precognition; acroamatics.

light, enlightenment; glimpse, inkling; side light; glimmer, -ing; dawn; scent, suspicion; impression &c. (*idea*) 453; discovery &c. 480*a*.

system –, body- of knowledge; science, philosophy, pansophy; theory, Etiology; circle of the sciences; pandect, doctrine, body of doctrine; cy-, ency-clopædia; school &c. (*system of opinions*) 484.

tree of knowledge; republic of letters &c. (*language*) 560.

erudition, learning, lore, scholarship, reading, letters; literature; booklearning, bookishness; biblio-mania, -latry; information, general information; store of -knowledge &c.; education &c. (*teaching*) 537; culture, attainments; acqui-rements, -sitions; accomplishments, proficiency; practical knowledge &c. (*skill*) 698; higher education, liberal education; dilettantism; rudiments &c. (*beginning*) 66.

deep –, profound –, solid –, accurate –, acroatic –, acroamatic –, vast –, extensive –, encyclopædical- -knowledge, – learning; omniscience, pantology.

march of intellect; progress –, advance- of -science, – learning; schoolmaster abroad.

V. know, ken, scan, wot; wot –, be aware &c. *adj.*- of; ween, weet, trow, have, possess.

conceive; ap-, com-prehend; take, realize, understand, appreciate; fathom, make out; recognize, discern, perceive, see, get a sight of, experience.

491. Ignorance. — N. ignorance, nescience, *tabula rasa*, crass ignorance, *ignorance crasse*; unacquaintance; unconsciousness &c. *adj.*; dark-, blindness; incomprehension, inexperience, simplicity.

unknown quantities, x, y, z.

sealed book, *terra incognita*, virgin soil, unexplored ground; dark ages.

[Imperfect knowledge] smattering, superficiality, half-learning, sciolism, glimmering; bewilderment &c. (*uncertainty*) 475; incapacity.

[Affectation of knowledge] pedantry; charlatan-ry, -ism.

V. be -ignorant &c. *adj.*; not -know &c. 490; know -not, – not what, – nothing of; have no -idea, – notion, – conception; not have the remotest idea; not know chalk from cheese.

ignore, be blind to; keep in ignorance &c. (*conceal*) 528.

see through a glass darkly; have a -film over the eyes, – glimmering &c. *n.*; wonder whether; not know what to make of &c. (*unintelligibility*) 519; not pretend –, not take upon oneself- to say.

Adj. ignorant, nescient; un-knowing, -aware, -acquainted, -apprized, -witting, -weeting, -conscious; wit-, weetless; a stranger to; unconversant.

un-informed, -cultivated, -versed, -instructed, -taught, -initiated, -tutored, -schooled, -guided, -enlightened; Philistine; behind the age.

shallow, superficial, green, rude, empty, half-learned, illiterate; un-read, -informed, -educated, -learned, -lettered, -bookish; empty-headed; low-brow; pedantic.

in the dark; be-nighted, -lated; blind-ed, -fold; hoodwinked; misinformed; *au bout de son latin*, at the

know full well; have –, possess- some knowledge of; be -*au courant* &c. *adj.*; have -in one's head, – at one's fingers' ends; know by -heart, – rote; be master of; *connaître le dessous des cartes*, know what's what &c. 698.

see one's way; learn, discover &c. 480*a*.

come to one's knowledge &c. (*information*) 527.

Adj. knowing &c. *v.*; cognitive; acroamatic.

aware –, cognizant –, conscious- of; acquainted –, made acquainted- with; privy –, no stranger- to; *au -fait*, – *courant*; in the secret; up –, alive- to; sensible of; behind the -scenes, – curtain; let into; apprized –, informed- of; undeceived.

proficient –, versed –, read –, forward –, strong –, at home- in; conversant –, familiar- with.

erudite, instructed, learned, lettered, educated; high-brow; well-conned, -informed, -read, -grounded, -educated; enlightened, shrewd, insightful, *savant*, blue, bookish, scholastic, solid, profound, deep-read, book-learned; accomplished &c. (*skilful*) 698; omniscient; self-taught, -educated.

known &c. *v.*; ascertained, well-known, recognized, received, notorious, noted; proverbial; familiar, – as household words, to every schoolboy; hackneyed, trite, commonplace.

knowable, cogn-oscible, -izable.

Adv. to –, to the best of- one's knowledge.

Phr. one's eyes being opened &c. (*disclosure*) 529.

end of his tether; at fault; at sea &c. (*uncertain*) 475; caught tripping.

un-known, -apprehended, -explained, -ascertained, -investigated, -explored, -heard of, -perceived; concealed &c. 528; novel.

Adv. ignorantly &c. *adj.*; unawares; for -anything, – aught- one knows; not that one knows.

Int. God –, Heaven –, the Lord –, nobody- knows.

Phr. a little learning is a dangerous thing.

_____

492. Scholar—N. scholar, *connoisseur*, *savant*, pundit, schoolman, professor, graduate, wrangler, moonshee; academ-ician, -ist; fellow, don, post graduate, advanced student; master –, bachelor- of arts; doctor, licentiate, gownsman; philo-sopher, -math; scientist, clerk; soph, -ist, -ister; linguist, classicist; glosso-, etymo-, philologist; philologer; lexico-, glosso-grapher; scholiast, commentator, annotator, grammarian; *littérateur, literati, dilettanti, illuminati*; Mezzofanti, admirable Crichton, Mæcenas.

book-worm, *helluo librorum*, biblio-phile, -maniac; blue-stocking, *bas-bleu*; big-wig, learned Theban.

learned –, literary- man; *homo multarum literarum*; man of -learning, – letters, – education; high-brow, intelligentsia.

antiquar-ian, -y; archæologist; sage &c. (*wise man*) 500.

pedant, *doctrinaire*; pedagogue, Dr. Pangloss; pantologist.

teacher &c. 540; schoolboy &c. (*learner*) 541.

Adj. learned &c. 490; brought up at the feet of Gamaliel.

493. Ignoramus.—N. ignoramus, illiterate, moron, dunce, numskull; wooden spoon; no scholar.

sciolist, smatterer, dabbler, half-scholar; *charlatan*; wiseacre.

novice, griffin; greenhorn &c. (*dupe*) 547; tyro &c. (*learner*) 541.

lubber &c. (*bungler*) 701; fool &c. 501; pedant &c. 492.

Adj. bookless, shallow, simple, dense, dumb, thick, dull, ignorant &c. 491.

_____

494. [Object of knowledge.] Truth.
—N. fact, reality &c. (*existence*) 1;
plain matter of fact; nature &c. (*principle*) 5; truth, verity; gospel; orthodoxy &c. 983a; authenticity; veracity &c. 543.

accuracy, exactitude; exact-, precise-ness &c. *adj.*; precision, delicacy; rigour, mathematical precision, punctuality; clockwork precision &c. (*regularity*) 80.

orthology; *ipsissima verba*; letter of the law, realism.

plain -, honest -, sober -, naked -, unalloyed -, unqualified -, stern -, exact -, intrinsic- truth; *nuda veritas*; the very thing; not an -illusion &c. 495; real Simon Pure; unvarnished tale; the truth, the whole truth and nothing but the truth; just the thing.

V. be -true &c. *adj.*, – the case; stand the test; have the true ring; hold -good, – true, – water; conform to rule.

render -, prove- -true &c. *adj.*; substantiate &c. (*evidence*) 467.

get at the truth &c. (*discover*) 480a.

Adj. real, actual &c. (*existing*) 1; veritable, true; certain &c. 474; substantially -, categorically- true &c.; true -to the letter, – to life, – to scale, – the facts, – as gospel; unimpeachable; veracious &c. 543; unre-, uncon-futed; un-ideal, -imagined; realistic.

exact, accurate, definite, precise, well defined, just, right, correct, strict, severe; close &c. (*similar*) 17; literal; rigid, rigorous; scrupulous &c. (*conscientious*) 939; religiously exact, punctual, mathematical, scientific; faithful, constant, unerring; curious, particular, punctilious, meticulous, nice, delicate, fine.

genuine, authentic, legitimate, pukka; orthodox &c. 983a; official, *ex officio*.

pure, natural, sound, sterling; unsophisticated, -adulterated, -varnished, -coloured; in its true colours.

well-grounded, -founded; solid, substantial, tangible, valid; undis-torted, -guised; un-affected, -exaggerated, -romantic, -flattering.

Adv. truly &c. *adj.*; verily, indeed, in reality; as a matter of fact; beyond

495. Error.—N. error, fallacy; misconception, -apprehension, -understanding; inexactness &c. *adj.*; laxity; misconstruction &c. (*misinterpretation*) 523; miscomputation &c. (*misjudgment*) 481; *non-sequitur* &c. 477; misstatement, -report; anachronism; malapropism.

mistake; miss, fault, blunder, boner, bloomer, howler, *quid pro quo*, cross purposes, oversight, misprint, *erratum*, *corrigendum*, slip, blot, flaw, loose thread; trip, stumble &c. (*failure*) 732; botchery &c. (*want of skill*) 699; slip of the -tongue, – pen; *lapsus -linguæ*, – *calami*, clerical error; bull &c. (*absurdity*) 497.

il-, de-lusion; false -impression, – idea; bubble; self-deceit, -deception; warped notion; mists of error; superstition, exploded notion.

heresy &c. (*heterodoxy*) 984; hallucination &c. (*insanity*) 503; false light &c. (*fallacy of vision*) 443; dream &c. (*fancy*) 515; fable &c. (*untruth*) 546; bias &c. (*misjudgment*) 481; misleading &c. *v.*

V. be -erroneous &c. *adj.*

cause error; mis-lead, -guide; lead -astray, – into error; beguile, misinform &c. (*misteach*) 538; delude; give a false -impression, – idea; falsify, garble, misstate; deceive &c. 545; lie &c. 544.

err; be -in error &c. *adj.*, – mistaken &c. *v.*; be deceived &c. (*duped*) 547; mistake, receive a false impression, deceive oneself; fall into -, lie under -, labour under- -an error &c. *n.*; be in the wrong, blunder; mis-apprehend, -conceive, -understand, -reckon, -count, -calculate &c. (*misjudge*) 481.

play -, be- at cross purposes &c. (*misinterpret*) 523.

trip, stumble; lose oneself &c. (*uncertainty*) 475; go astray; fail &c. 732; take the wrong sow by the ear &c. (*mismanage*) 699; put the saddle on the wrong horse; reckon without one's host; take the shadow for the substance &c. (*credulity*) 486; dream &c. (*imagine*) 515.

Adj. erroneous, untrue, false, devoid of truth, fallacious, faulty, apocryphal,

-doubt, – question; with truth &c. (*veracity*) 543; certainly &c. (*certain*) 474; actually &c. (*existence*) 1; in effect &c. (*intrinsically*) 5.

exactly &c. *adj.*; *ad amussim*; *verbatim*, – *et literatim*; word for word, literally, *literatim*, *totidem verbis*, *sic*, to the letter, chapter and verse, *ipsissimis verbis*; *ad unguem*; to an inch; to a -nicety, – hair, – tittle, – turn, – T; *au pied de la lettre*; neither more nor less; in -every respect, – all respects; *sous tous les rapports*; at -any rate, – all events; strictly speaking.

Phr. the -truth, – fact- is; *rem acu tetigisti*.

---

scent; in the wrong box; at cross purposes, all in the wrong, all abroad, at sea.

Adv. more or less.

unreal, ungrounded, groundless; unsubstantial &c. 4; heretical &c. (*heterodox*) 984; unsound; illogical &c. 477; wrong.

in-, un-exact; in-accurate, -correct; indefinite &c. (*uncertain*) 475.

illus-ive, -ory; delusive; mock; ideal &c. (*imaginary*) 515; spurious &c. 545; deceitful &c. 544; perverted.

controvertible, unsustain-able, -ed; unauthenticated, untrustworthy.

exploded, refuted, discarded.

in –, under an- error &c. *n.*; mistaken &c. *v.*; tripping &c. *v.*; out, – in one's reckoning; aberrant; beside –, wide of the- -mark, – truth; astray &c. (*at fault*) 475; on -a false, – the wrong- all in the wrong, all

---

496. Maxim.—**N.** maxim, aphorism; apo-, apoph-thegm; *dictum*, saying, gnome, adage, saw, proverb, epigram; sentence, *mot*, motto, word, by-word, precept, moral, phylactery, *protasis*, brocard.

axiom, postulate, theorem, *scholium*, truism.

reflection &c. (*idea*) 453; conclusion &c. (*judgment*) 480; golden rule &c. (*precept*) 697; principle, *principia*; profession of faith &c. (*belief*) 484; formula.

wise –, sage –, received –, admitted –, recognized- maxim &c.; true –, common –, hackneyed –, trite –, commonplace- saying &c.

Adj. aphoristic, proverbial, phylacteric; axiomatic, gnomic.

Adv. as -the saying is, – they say.

---

497. Absurdity.—**N.** absurd-ity, -ness &c. *adj.*; imbecility &c. 499; alogy, nonsense, paradox, inconsistency; stultiloqu-y, -ence, futility.

blunder, muddle, bull; Irish-, Hibernic-ism; slip-slop; anticlimax, bathos; sophism &c. 477.

farce, burlesque, *galimatias*, *amphigouri*, rhapsody; farrago &c. (*disorder*) 59; extravagance, romance; sciomachy.

joke, catch, sell, pun, verbal quibble, macaronic.

jargon, fustian, twaddle &c. (*no meaning*) 517; exaggeration &c. 549; moonshine, stuff; mare's nest.

vagary, tomfoolery, mummery, monkey- trick, practical joke, *boutade*, *escapade*.

V. play the fool &c. 499; stultify, blunder, muddle; joke; talk nonsense, *parler à tort et à travers*; *battre la campagne*; be -absurd &c. *adj.*

Adj. absurd, nonsensical, preposterous, egregious, senseless, farcical, inconsistent, ridiculous, extravagant, quibbling, futile; macaronic, punning, paradoxical.

foolish &c. 499; sophistical &c. 477; unmeaning &c. 517; without rhyme or reason; fantastic.

Int. fiddle-de-dee! pish! pish and tush! pho! stuff and nonsense! rubbish! rot! bosh! in the name of the Prophet—figs!

Phr. *credat Judæus Apella*; tell it to the marines.

Faculties

498. Intelligence. Wisdom.—**N.** intelligence, capacity, comprehension,

499. Imbecility. Folly.—**N.** want of -intelligence &c. 498, – intellect &c.

understanding; intellect &c. 450; nous, parts, sagacity, mother wit, wit, *esprit*, gumption, quick parts, grasp of intellect; acuteness &c. *adj.*; acumen, subtlety, penetration; perspica-cy, -city; discernment, long-headedness, due sense of, good judgment; discrimination &c. 465; craftiness, cunning &c. 702; refinement &c. (*taste*) 850.

head, brains, gray matter, headpiece, upper story, long head; eagle -eye, – glance; eye of a -lynx, – hawk.

wisdom, sapience, sense; good –, common –, plain –, horse- sense; clear thinking; rationality, reason; reasonableness &c. *adj.*; judgment; solidity, depth, profundity, calibre; enlarged views; reach –, compass- of thought; enlargement of mind.

genius, inspiration, *geist*, fire of genius, heaven-born genius, soul; talent &c. (*aptitude*) 698.

[Wisdom in action] prudence &c. 864; vigilance &c. 459; tact &c. 698; foresight &c. 510; sobriety, self-possession, *aplomb*, ballast, mental -poise, – balance.

a bright thought, inspiration, brainwave, not a bad idea.

V. be -intelligent &c. *adj.*; have all one's wits about one; understand &c. (*intelligible*) 518; catch –, take in- an idea; take a -joke, – hint.

see -through, – at a glance, – with half an eye, – far into, – through a millstone; penetrate; discern &c. (*descry*) 441; foresee &c. 510.

discriminate &c. 465; know what's what &c. 698; listen to reason.

Adj. [Applied to persons] intelligent, quick of apprehension, keen, acute, alive, brainy, awake, bright, quick, sharp; quick-, keen-, clear-, sharp-eyed, -sighted, -witted; wide awake; canny, shrewd, astute; clear-headed; far-sighted &c. 510; discerning, perspicacious, penetrating, piercing; argute; nimble-, needle-witted; sharp as a needle; alive to &c. (*cognizant*) 490; clever &c. (*apt*) 698; arch &c. (*cunning*) 702; *pas si bête*; acute &c. 682.

wise, sage, sapient, sagacious, reasonable, rational, sound, in one's right

450; shallow-, silli-, foolish-ness &c. *adj.*; imbecility, incapacity, vacancy of mind, poverty of intellect, clouded perception, poor head, apartments to let; stup-, stol-idity; hebetude, dull understanding, meanest capacity; short-sightedness; incompetence &c. (*unskilfulness*) 699.

one's weak side; bias &c. 481; infatuation &c. (*insanity*) 503.

simplicity, puerility, babyhood; dotage, anility, second childishness, senile dementia, fatuity; idio-cy, -tism; drivelling.

folly, frivolity, desipience, irrationality, trifling, ineptitude, nugacity, inconsistency, lip-wisdom, conceit; sophistry &c. 477; giddiness &c. (*inattention*) 458; eccentricity &c. 503; extravagance &c. (*absurdity*) 497; rashness &c. 863.

act of folly &c. 699.

V. be -imbecile &c. *adj.*; have no -brains, – sense &c. 498.

trifle, drivel, *radoter*, dote; ramble &c. (*madness*) 503; play the -fool, – monkey, – goat, take leave of one's senses; not see an inch beyond one's nose; stultify oneself &c. 699; talk nonsense &c. 497.

Adj. [Applied to persons] un-intelligent, -intellectual, -reasoning; mind-, wit-, reason-, brain-less; having no -head &c. 498; not -bright &c. 498; inapprehensible.

weak-, addle-, puzzle-, blunder-, muddle-, muddy-, pig-, beetle-, maggoty-, gross-headed; beef-, fat- -witted, -headed.

weak-, feeble-minded; dull-, shallow-, rattle-, lack-brained; half-, nit-, short-, dull-, blunt-witted; shallow-, clod-, addle-pated; dim-, short-sighted; thick-skulled; weak in the upper story.

shallow, *borné*, weak, wanting, soft, nutty, sappy, spoony; dull, – as a beetle; stupid, heavy, insulse, obtuse, blunt, stolid, doltish, asinine; inapt &c. 699; prosaic &c. 843.

child-ish, -like; infant-ine, -ile; baby-, bab-ish; puerile, anile; simple &c. (*credulous*) 486.

fatuous, idiotic, imbecile, moronic,

mind, sensible, *abnormis sapiens*, judicious, strong-minded.

un-prejudiced, -biassed, -bigoted, -prepossessed; un-dazzled, -perplexed; of unwarped judgment, impartial, equitable, fair, broad-minded.

cool; cool-, long-, hard-, strong-headed; long-sighted, calculating, thoughtful, reflecting; solid, deep, profound.

oracular; heaven-directed, -born.

prudent &c. (*cautious*) 864; sober, staid, solid; considerate, politic, wise in one's generation; watchful &c. 459; provident &c. (*prepared*) 673; in advance of one's age; wise as -a serpent, – Solomon, – Solon.

[Applied to actions] wise, sensible, reasonable, judicious; well-judged, -advised; prudent, politic; expedient &c. 646.

---

500. Sage.—N. sage, wise man; pundit; master -mind, – spirit of the age; longhead, thinker, philosopher.

authority, oracle, mentor, luminary, shining light, *esprit fort*, *magnus Apollo*, Solon, Solomon, Nestor, Magi, 'second Daniel.'

man of learning &c. 492; expert &c. 700; wizard &c. 994.

[Ironically] wiseacre, bigwig.

Adj. wise, learned; authoritative, oracular; erudite &c. 490; venerable, reverenced, revered, *emeritus*.

---

drivelling; blatant, babbling; vacant; sottish; bewildered &c. 475.

blockish, unteachable; Bœot-ian, -ic; bovine; un-gifted, -discerning, -enlightened, -wise, -philosophical; apish.

foolish, silly, senseless, irrational, insensate, nonsensical, inept; maudlin.

narrow-minded &c. 481; bigoted &c. (*obstinate*) 606; giddy &c. (*thoughtless*) 458; rash &c. 863; eccentric &c. (*crazed*) 503.

[Applied to actions] foolish, unwise, indiscreet, injudicious, improper, unreasonable, without reason, ridiculous, silly, stupid, asinine; ill-imagined, -advised, -judged, -devised; inconsistent, irrational, unphilosophical; extravagant &c. (*nonsensical*) 497; sleeveless, idle; useless &c. 645; inexpedient &c. 647; frivolous &c. (*trivial*) 643; absurd &c. 497.

Phr. *Davis sum non Œdipus.*

501. Fool.—N. fool, idiot, tomfool, wiseacre, simpleton, Simple Simon, nit-wit, witling, dizzard, donkey, ass; ninny, -hammer; moron, dolt, booby, Tom Noddy, looby, hoddy-doddy, noddy, nonny, noodle, nizy, owl; goose, -cap; *imbécile*; gaby, *radoteur*, nincompoop, *badaud*, zany; trifler, babbler; pretty fellow; natural, *niais*.

child, baby, infant, innocent, milksop, sop.

oaf, lout, loon, lown, dullard, doodle, calf, colt, buzzard, block, put, stick, stock, numps, tony.

bull-, dunder-, addle-, block-, dull-, logger-, jolt-, jolter-, beetle-, gross-, thick-, giddy-head; num-, thickskull; lack-, shallow-brain; half-, lack-wit; dunder-pate; fat-head, poor stick.

sawney, gowk; clod, -hopper; clod-, clot-poll, -pate; bull-calf; men of Bœotia, wise men of Gotham.

un sot à triple étage, sot; jobbernowl, changeling, mooncalf, *gobemouche*.

dotard, driveller; old -fogey, – woman; crone, grandmother.

greenhorn &c. (*dupe*) 547; dunce &c. (*ignoramus*) 493; lubber &c. (*bungler*) 701; madman &c. 504.

one who -will not set the Thames on fire, – did not invent gunpowder; *qui n'a pas inventé la poudre*; no conjuror.

502. Sanity.—N. sanity; soundness &c. *adj.*; rationality, normality, sobriety, lucidity, lucid interval; senses, sober senses, sound mind, *mens sana*.

503. Insanity.—N. disordered -reason, – intellect; diseased –, unsound –, abnormal- mind; derangement, unsoundness.

V. be -sane &c. *adj.*; retain one's senses, – reason.

become -sane &c. *adj.*; come to one's senses, sober down.

render -sane &c. *adj.*; bring to one's senses, sober.

Adj. sane, rational, reasonable, *compos mentis*, of sound mind; sound, -minded.

self-possessed; sober, -minded.

in one's -sober senses, – right mind; in possession of one's faculties.

Adv. sanely &c. *adj.*

insanity, lunacy; madness &c. *adj.*; mania, *rabies, furor*, mental alienation, paranoia, aberration; *amentia*, dementation, -tia, -cy; *dementia præcox*; *morosis*, idiocy, phrenitis, frenzy, raving, incoherence, wandering, delirium, calenture of the brain, delusion, hallucination; lycanthropy, brain storm, *delirium tremens*, D.T's.

vertigo, dizziness, swimming; sunstroke, *coup de soleil*, siriasis.

fanaticism, infatuation, craze; oddity, eccentricity, twist, monomania; klepto-, dipso-mania; hypochondriasis &c. (*low spirits*) 837; *melancholia*, hysteria.

screw –, tile –, slate- loose; bee in one's bonnet, rats in the upper story.

dotage &c. (*imbecility*) 499.

V. be –, become- -insane &c. *adj.*; lose one's senses, – reason, – faculties, – wits; go –, run- mad, run amuck; rave, dote, ramble, wander; drivel &c. (*be imbecile*) 499; have a -screw loose &c. *n.*, – devil; *avoir le diable au corps*; lose one's head &c. (*be uncertain*) 475.

derange, render –, drive- -mad &c. *adj.*; madden, dementate, addle the wits, derange the head, infatuate, befool; turn -the brain, – one's head.

Adj. insane, mad, lunatic; crazy, crazed, *aliéné, non compos mentis*; not right, cracked, touched; bereft of reason; unhinged, deranged, unsettled in one's mind; insensate, reasonless, beside oneself, demented, daft; phren-, fren-zied, -etic; possessed, – with a devil; far gone, maddened, moonstruck; shatterpated; barmy; mad-, scatter-, shatter-, crack-brained; off one's head; bug-house, *loco*.

maniacal; manic, manic-depressive; delirious, light-headed, incoherent, rambling, doting, wandering; frantic, raving, stark staring mad, amok, amuck.

corybantic, dithyrambic; rabid, giddy, vertiginous, dizzy, wild, haggard, mazed; flighty; distr-acted, -aught; bewildered &c. (*uncertain*) 475.

mad as a -March hare, – hatter; of -unsound mind &c. *n.*; touched –, wrong –, not right- in one's -head, – mind, – wits, – upper story; out of one's -mind, – senses, – wits; not in one's right mind.

fanatical, infatuated, odd, eccentric; hypp-ed, -ish.

imbecile, silly &c. 499.

Adv. like one possessed.

Phr. the mind having lost its balance; the reason under a cloud; *tête -exaltée, -montée*.

504. Madman.—N. madman, lunatic, maniac, bedlamite, candidate for Bedlam, raver, madcap; energumen; paranoiac; auto-, mono-, pyro-, megalo-, dipso-, klepto-maniac; hypochondriac &c. (*low spirits*) 837.

dreamer &c. 515; rhapsodist, seer, high-flier, enthusiast, crank, eccentric, nut, fanatic, *fanatico; exalté*; knight errant, Don Quixote.

idiot &c. 501.

Section VI. EXTENSION OF THOUGHT

1°. *To the Past*

505. Memory.—N. memory, remembrance; reten-tion, -tiveness; tenacity; *veteris vestigia flammæ*; tablets of the memory; readiness.

reminiscence, recognition, recurrence, recollection, rememoration; retrospect, -ion; after-thought.

suggestion &c. (*information*) 527; prompting &c. *v.*; hint, reminder, token of remembrance, *memento, souvenir,* keepsake, relic, *memorandum*; remembrancer, flapper; memorial &c. (*record*) 551; commemoration &c. (*celebration*) 883.

things to be remembered, *memorabilia.*

art of -, artificial- memory; *memoria technica*; mnemo-nics, -technics; phrenotypics; Mnemosyne; memorandum-, note-, engagement-, prompt-book.

retentive -, tenacious -, green -, trustworthy -, capacious -, faithful -, correct -, exact -, ready -, prompt-memory.

V. remember, mind; retain the -memory, - remembrance- of; keep in view.

have -, hold -, bear -, carry -, keep -, retain- in *or* in the -thoughts, - mind, - memory, - remembrance; be in -, live in -, remain in -, dwell in -, haunt -, impress- one's -memory, - thoughts, - mind.

sink in the mind; run in the head; not be able to get it out of one's head; be deeply impressed with; rankle &c. (*revenge*) 919.

recur to the mind; flash -on the mind, - across the memory.

recognize, recollect, bethink oneself, recall, call up, conjure up, retrace; look -, trace- -back, - backwards; think -, look back- upon; review; call -, recall -, bring- to mind; remembrance; carry one's thoughts back; rake up the past.

suggest &c. (*inform*) 527; prompt; put -, keep- in mind; remind; fan the embers; call -, summon -, rip- up; renew; *infandum renovare dolorem*; task -, tax -, jog -, flap -, refresh -, rub up -, awaken- the memory; pull by the sleeve; bring back to the memory, put in remembrance, memorialize.

get -, have -, learn -, know -, say -, repeat- by -heart - rote; drive -, get- into -one's head; say one's lesson; repeat, - as a parrot; have at one's fingers' ends.

506. Oblivion.—N. oblivion; forgetfulness &c. *adj.*; obliteration &c. 552, of -, insensibility &c. 823 to- the past.

short -, treacherous -, loose -, slippery -, failing- memory; decay -, failure -, lapse- of memory; memory like a sieve; waters of -Lethe, - oblivion, *amnesia.*

pardon, acquittal, amnesty, oblivion; absolution.

V. forget; be -forgetful &c. *adj.*; fall -, sink- into oblivion; have -a short memory &c. *n.*, - no head.

forget one's own name, have on the tip of one's tongue, come in at one ear and go out at the other.

slip -, escape -, fade from -, die away from- the memory; lose, - sight of.

unlearn; efface &c. 552 -, discharge- from the memory; consign to -oblivion, - the tomb of the Capulets; think no more of &c. (*turn the attention from*) 458; cast behind one's back, wean one's thoughts from; let bygones be bygones &c. (*forgive*) 918.

Adj. forgotten &c. *v.*; unremembered, past recollection, bygone, out of mind; buried -, sunk- in oblivion; clean forgotten; gone out of one's -head, - recollection.

forgetful, oblivious, mindless, heedless, Lethean; insensible &c. 823- to the past.

Phr. *non mi ricordo*; the memory -failing, - deserting one, - being at (*or* in) fault.

commit to memory; memorize; con, – over; fix –, rivet –, imprint –, impress –, stamp –, grave –, engrave –, store –, treasure up –, bottle up –, embalm –, enshrine- in the memory; load –, store –, stuff –, burden- the memory with.

redeem from oblivion; keep the memory -alive, – green; *tangere ulcus*; keep up the memory of; commemorate &c. (*celebrate*) 883.

make a note of &c. (*record*) 551.

Adj. remember-ing, -ed &c. *v.*; mindful, reminiscential; retained in the memory &c. *v.*; pent up in one's memory; fresh; green, – in remembrance, still vivid; unforgotten, present to the mind; within one's -memory &c. *n.*; indelible; not to be forgotten, unforgettable, enduring; uppermost in one's thoughts; memorable &c. (*important*) 642.

Adv. by -heart, – rote; without book, *memoriter*.

in memory of; *in memoriam*; suggestive.

Phr. *manet altâ mente repostum; forsan et hæc olim meminisse juvabit.*

2°. To the Future

507. Expectation.—N. expect-ation, -ance, -ancy; anticipation, reckoning, calculation; contingency; foresight &c. 510.

contemplation, prospection, look out; prospect, perspective, horizon, vista; destiny &c. 152.

suspense, waiting, abeyance; curiosity &c. 455; anxious –, ardent –, eager –, breathless –, sanguine- expectation; torment of Tantalus.

presumption, hope &c. 858; trust &c. (*belief*) 484; prognostication, auspices &c. (*prediction*) 511.

V. expect; look -for, – out for, – forward to; hope for, anticipate; have in -prospect, – contemplation; keep in view; contemplate, promise oneself; not -wonder &c. 870 -at, – if.

wait –, tarry –, lie in wait –, watch –, bargain- for; keep a -good, – sharp- look-out for; await; stand at 'attention,' abide, bide one's –, mark- time, watch.

foresee &c. 510; prepare for &c. 673; forestall &c. (*be early*) 132; count upon &c. (*believe in*) 484; think likely &c. (*probability*) 472; make one's mouth water.

lead one to expect &c. (*predict*) 511; have in store for &c. (*destiny*) 152.

prick up one's ears, hold one's breath.

Adj. expectant; expecting &c. *v.*; in -expectation &c. *n.*; on the watch &c. (*vigilant*) 459; open -eyed, -mouthed;

508. Inexpectation.—N. in-, non-expectation; false expectation &c. (*disappointment*) 509; miscalculation &c. 481; unforeseen contingency, the unforeseen, the unexpected.

surprise, sudden burst, thunderclap, blow, shock; bolt out of the blue; eye-opener; wonder &c. 870.

V. not -expect &c. 507; be taken by surprise; start; miscalculate &c. 481; not bargain for; come –, fall- upon.

be -unexpected &c. *adj.*; come -unawares &c. *adv.*; turn up, pop, drop from the clouds; come –, burst –, flash –, bounce –, steal –, creep- upon one; come –, burst- like a thunderclap, -bolt; take –, catch- -by surprise, – unawares, – napping.

pounce –, spring a mine- upon.

surprise, startle, take aback, electrify, stun, stagger, take away one's breath, throw off one's guard; astonish &c. (*strike with wonder*) 870.

Adj. non-expectant; surprised &c. *v.*; un-warned, -aware; off one's guard; inattentive &c. 458.

un-expected, -anticipated, -prepared for, -looked for, -foreseen, -hoped for; dropped from the clouds; beyond –, contrary to –, against- expectation; out of one's reckoning; unheard of &c. (*exceptional*) 83; startling; sudden &c. (*instantaneous*) 113.

Adv. abruptly, unexpectedly, plump, pop, *à l'improviste*, unawares; without

agape, gaping, all agog; on -tenter-
hooks, – tiptoe, – the tiptoe of expectation; *aux aguets*; ready; curious &c.
455; looking forward to; prepared for;
on the rack.

expected &c. *v.*; long expected, foreseen; in prospect &c. *n.*; prospective;
in -one's eye, – view, – the horizon;
impending &c. (*destiny*) 152.

-notice, – warning, – saying 'by your
leave'; like a -thief in the night, –
thunderbolt; in an unguarded moment;
suddenly &c. (*instantaneously*) 113.

Int. heyday! &c. (*wonder*) 870.

Phr. little did one -think, – expect;
nobody would ever -suppose, – think,
– expect; who would have thought?

Adv. expectantly; in the event of; on the watch &c. *adj.*; with
-breathless expectation &c. *n.*, – bated breath, – eyes, – ears strained;
arrectis auribus; on edge.

Phr. we shall see; *nous verrons*.

509. [Failure of expectation.] **Disappointment.—N.** disappointment,
disillusionment; blighted hope, balk; blow; slip 'twixt cup and lip;
non-fulfilment of one's hopes; sad -, bitter- disappointment; trick of
fortune; afterclap; false -, vain- expectation; miscalculation &c. 481;
fool's paradise; much cry and little wool.

V. be disappointed; look -blank, – blue; look -, stand- -aghast &c.
(*wonder*) 870; find to one's cost; laugh on the wrong side of one's
mouth; find one a false prophet.

disappoint; crush -, dash -, balk -, disappoint -, blight -, falsify -,
defeat -, not realize- one's -hope, – expectation; balk, jilt, bilk; play one
-false, – a trick; dash the cup from the lips; tantalize; dumb-found,
-founder; disillusion, -ize; dissatisfy, disgruntle.

Adj. disappointed &c. *v.*; disconcerted, aghast; out of one's reckoning; disgruntled.

Phr. the mountain brought forth a mouse; *nascitur ridiculus mus*;
parturiunt montes; *diis aliter visum*, the bubble burst; one's countenance
falling.

510. Foresight.—N. foresight, prospicience, prevision, longsighted-
ness; anticipation; providence &c. (*preparation*) 673.

fore-thought, -cast; pre-deliberation, -surmise; foregone conclusion
&c. (*prejudgment*) 481; prudence &c. (*caution*) 864.

foreknowledge; *prognosis*; pre-cognition, -science, -notion, -sentiment;
second sight; sagacity &c. (*intelligence*) 498.

prospect &c. (*expectation*) 507; foretaste; prospectus &c. (*plan*) 626.

V. foresee; look -forwards to, – ahead, – beyond; scent from afar;
feel in one's bones; look -, pry -, peep- into the future.

see one's way; see how the -land lies, – wind blows, – cat jumps.

anticipate; expect &c. 507; be beforehand &c. (*early*) 132; predict
&c. 511; fore-know, -judge, -cast; surmise; have an eye to the -future,
– main chance; *respicere finem*; keep a sharp look-out &c. (*vigilance*)
459; forewarn &c. 668.

Adj. foreseeing &c. *v.*; prescient; anticipatory; far-seeing, -sighted;
sagacious &c. (*intelligent*) 498; weather-wise; provident &c. (*prepared*)
673; prospective &c. 507.

Adv. against the time when.

511. Prediction.—N. prediction, announcement; program, programme
&c. (*plan*) 626; premonition &c. (*warning*) 668; *prognosis*, prophecy,
vaticination, Mantology, prognostication, premonstration, augur-y,
-ation; a-, ha-riolation; fore-, a-boding; bode-, abode-ment; omin-ation,

-ousness; auspices, forecast; sign, presage, prognostic; omen &c. 512; horoscope, nativity; sooth, -saying; fortune-telling; divination; crystal gazing, necromancy &c. 992; prophet &c. 512.

[Divination by the stars] astrology, horoscopy, astromancy, judicial astrology.*

[Place of prediction] *adytum.*

prefigur-ation, -ement; prototype, type.

V. predict, prognosticate, prophesy, vaticinate, divine, foretell, sooth-say, augurate, tell fortunes; cast a -horoscope, – nativity; advise; forewarn &c. 668.

presage, augur, bode; a-, fore-bode, -cast; fore-, be-token; pre-figure, -show; portend; fore-show, -shadow, shadow forth, typify, ominate, signify, point to, precurse.

usher in, herald, premise, announce; lower.

hold out –, raise –, excite- -expectation, – hope; bid fair, promise, lead one to expect; be the -precursor &c. 64.

Adj. predicting &c. *v.*; predictive, prophetic, fatidical, vaticinal, oracular, Sibylline, haruspical, weatherwise.

ominous, presageful, portentous; augur-ous, -al, -ial; auspici-al, -ous; prescious, monitory, extispicious, premonitory, precursory, significant of, pregnant with, big with the fate of.

Phr. 'coming events cast their shadows before.'

512. Omen.—N. omen, portent, presage, prognostic, augury, auspice; sign &c. (*indication*) 550; herald, forerunner, harbinger &c. (*precursor*) 64.

bird of ill omen; signs of the times; gathering clouds; warning &c. 668.

prefigurement &c. 511.

513. Oracle.—N. oracle; prophet, -ess; seer, soothsayer, augur, fortune-teller, palmist, medium, clairvoyant, crystal gazer, witch, geomancer, *aruspex*; a-, ha-ruspice; Sibyl; Python, -ess; Pythia; Pythian –, Delphian- oracle; Monitor, Sphinx, Tiresias, Cassandra, Sibylline leaves; Zadkiel, Old Moore; sorcerer &c. 994; interpreter &c. 524.

Section VII. Creative Thought

514. Supposition.—N. supposition, assumption, postulation, condi-tion, pre-supposition, hypothesis, postulate, *postulatum*, theory, *data*; pro-, position; *thesis*, theorem; proposal &c. (*plan*) 626.

---

* The following terms, expressive of different forms of divination, have been col-lected from various sources, and are here given as a curious illustration of bygone superstitions:

Divination *by oracles*, Theomancy; *by the Bible*, Bibliomancy; *by ghosts*, Psycho-mancy; *by spirits seen in a magic lens*, Cristallomantia; *by shadows or manes*, Scio-mancy; *by appearances in the air*, Aeromancy, Chaomancy; *by the stars at birth*, Genethliacs; *by meteors*, Meteoromancy; *by winds*, Austromancy; *by sacrificial ap-pearances*, Aruspicy (or Haruspicy), Hieromancy, Hieroscopy; *by the entrails of animals sacrificed*, Hieromancy; *by the entrails of a human sacrifice*, Anthropomancy; *by the entrails of fishes*, Ichthyomancy; *by sacrificial fire*, Pyromancy; *by red-hot iron*, Sidero-mancy; *by smoke from the altar*, Capnomancy; *by mice*, Myomancy; *by birds*, Orniscopy, Ornithomancy; *by a cock picking up grains*, Alectryomancy (or Alectoromancy); *by fishes*, Ophiomancy; *by herbs*, Botanomancy; *by water*, Hydromancy; *by fountains*,

bare –, vague –, loose- -supposition, – suggestion; conceit; conjecture; guess, – work; rough guess, shot; conjecturality; surmise, suspicion, inkling, suggestion, suggestiveness, association of ideas, hint; presumption &c. (*belief*) 484; divination, speculation.

theorist, speculator, doctrinarian, hypothesist.

V. suppose, conjecture, surmise, suspect, guess, divine; theorize; pre-sume, -surmise, -suppose; assume, fancy, wis, take it; give a guess, speculate, believe, dare say, take it into one's head, take for granted.

put forth; pro-pound, -pose; moot; hypothesize; start, put a case, submit, move, make a motion; hazard –, throw out –, put forward- a - suggestion, – conjecture.

allude to, suggest, hint, put it into one's head.

suggest itself &c. (*thought*) 451; run in the head &c. (*memory*) 505; marvel –, wonder- -if, – whether.

Adj. supposing &c. *v.*; given, mooted, postulatory; assumed &c. *v.* supposit-ive, -itious; gratuitous, speculative, conjectural, hypothetical, suppositional, theoretical, academic, supposable, presumptive, putative.

suggestive, allusive, stimulating.

Adv. if, – so be; an; on the -supposition &c. *n.*; *ex hypothesi*; in -case, – the event of; *quasi*, as if, provided; perhaps &c. (*by possibility*) 470; for aught one knows.

515. Imagination.—N. imagination; originality; invention; fancy; inspiration; *verve*; empathy.

warm –, heated –, excited –, sanguine –, ardent –, fiery –, boiling –, wild –, bold –, daring –, playful –, lively –, fertile- -imagination, – fancy.

'mind's eye'; 'such stuff as dreams are made of.'

ideal-ity, -ism; romanticism, utopianism, castle-building; dreaming; frenzy; ecs-, ex-tasy; calenture &c. (*delirium*) 503; reverie, brown study, trance; somnambulism.

conception, *vorstellung*, excogitation, 'a fine frenzy,' poetic frenzy, divine afflatus; cloud-, dream-land; flight –, fumes- of fancy; 'thick-coming fancies'; creation –, coinage- of the brain; imagery, word painting.

conceit, maggot, figment, myth, dream, vision, shadow, chimera; phan-tasm, -tasy; fantasy, fancy; whim, -sey; vagary, rhapsody, romance, *extravaganza*; air-drawn dagger, bugbear, nightmare; flying Dutchman, great sea-serpent, man in the moon, castle in the air, *château en Espagne*; Utopia, Atlantis, happy valley, millennium, fairy land; land of Prester John, kingdom of Micomicon; work of fiction &c. (*novel*) 594; poetry &c. 597; drama &c. 599; Arabian nights; *le pot au lait*; dream of Alnaschar &c. (*hope*) 858; day –, golden- dream.

illusion &c. (*error*) 495; phantom &c. (*fallacy of vision*) 443; *Fata*

Pegomancy; *by a wand*, Rhabdomancy; *by dough of cakes*, Crithomancy; *by meal*, Aleuromancy, Alphitomancy; *by salt*, Halomancy; *by dice*, Cleromancy; *by arrows*, Belomancy; *by a balanced hatchet*, Axinomancy; *by a balanced sieve*, Coscinomancy; *by a suspended ring*, Dactyliomancy; *by dots made at random on paper*, Geomancy; *by precious stones*, Lithomancy; *by pebbles*, Pessomancy; *by pebbles drawn from a heap*, Psephomancy; *by mirrors*, Catoptromancy; *by writings in ashes*, Tephramancy; *by dreams*, Oneiromancy; *by the hand*, Palmistry, Chiromancy; *by nails reflecting the sun's rays*, Onychomancy; *by finger rings*, Dactylomancy; *by numbers*, Arithmancy; *by drawing lots*, Sortilege; *by passages in books*, Stichomancy; *by the letters forming the name of the person*, Onomancy, Nomancy; *by the features*, Anthroposcopy; *by the mode of laughing*, Geloscopy; *by ventriloquism*, Gastromancy; *by walking in a circle*, Gyromancy; *by dropping melted wax into water*, Ceromancy; *by currents*, Bletonism.

Morgana &c. (*ignis fatuus*) 423; vapour &c. (*cloud*) 353; stretch of the imagination &c. (*exaggeration*) 549.

idealist, romanticist, visionary; mopus; romancer, dreamer; somnambulist; rhapsodist &c. (*fanatic*) 504.

V. imagine, fancy, conceive; ideal-, real-ize; dream, – of; 'give to airy nothing a local habitation and a name.'

create, originate, devise, invent, coin, fabricate; improvise, strike out something new.

set one's wits to work; strain –, crack- one's invention; rack –, ransack –, cudgel- one's brains; excogitate.

give -play, – the reins, – a loose- to the -imagination, – fancy; empathize; indulge in reverie.

conjure up a vision; fancy –, represent –, picture –, figure- to oneself; envisage.

float in the mind; suggest itself &c. (*thought*) 451.

Adj. imagined &c. *v.*; *ben trovato*; air-drawn, -built.

imagin-ing &c. *v.*, -ative; original, inventive, creative, fertile, productive; ingenious.

romantic, high-flown, flighty, extravagant, fanatic, enthusiastic, Utopian, Quixotic; preposterous, rhapsodical.

ideal, unreal; in the clouds, *in nubibus*; unsubstantial &c. 4; illusory &c. (*fallacious*) 495; fictitious, theoretical, hypothetical.

fabulous, legendary; myth-ic, -ological; chimerical; imagin-, visionary; notional; fan-cy, -ciful, -tastic, -tastical; whimsical; fairy, -like.

dreamy, entranced, vaporous.

DIVISION (II.) COMMUNICATION OF IDEAS
Section I. NATURE OF IDEAS COMMUNICATED

516. [Idea to be conveyed.] **Meaning.** [Thing signified.]—**N.** meaning; signific-ation, -ance; sense, expression; im-, pur-port; drift, tenor, implication, connotation, essence, force, spirit bearing, colouring; scope.

matter; subject, -matter; argument, text, sum and substance; gist &c. 5.

general –, broad –, substantial –, colloquial –, literal –, plain –, simple –, accepted –, natural –, unstrained –, true &c. (*exact*) 494 –, honest &c. 543 –, *primâ facie* &c. (*manifest*) 525- meaning.

literality; literal interpretation; after acceptation; allusion &c. (*latency*) 526; suggestion &c. (*information*) 527; synonym; figure of speech &c. 521; acceptation &c. (*interpretation*) 522.

V. mean, signify, express, connote, denote; im-, pur-port; convey, imply, breathe, indicate, bespeak, bear a sense; tell –, speak- of; touch on; point –, allude- to; drive at; involve &c. (*latency*) 526; declare &c. (*affirm*) 535.

517. [Absence of meaning.] **Unmeaningness.**—**N.** unmeaningness &c. *adj.*; scrabble, scribble, scrawl, daub, (*painting*), strumming (*music*).

empty sound, dead letter, *vox et præterea nihil*; 'a tale told by an idiot, full of sound and fury, signifying nothing'; 'sounding brass and a tinkling cymbal.'

nonsense, jargon, gibberish, jabber, mere words, hocus-pocus, fustian, rant, bombast, balderdash, palaver, patter, flummery, *verbiage*, babble, *bavardage*, *baragouin*, platitude, *niaiserie*; inanity; rigmarole, rodomontade; truism; *nugæ canoræ*; twaddle, twattle, fudge, trash; stuff, – and nonsense; bosh, rubbish, rot, drivel, moonshine, wish-wash, fiddle-faddle, flapdoodle; absurdity &c. 497; vagueness &c. (*unintelligibility*) 519.

V. mean nothing; be -unmeaning &c. *adj.*; twaddle, quibble, rant, gabble, scrabble &c. *n.*

Adj. unmeaning; meaning-, sense-less;

understand by &c. (*interpret*) 522.

Adj. meaning &c. *v.*; expressive, suggestive, meaningful, allusive; signific-ant, -ative, -atory; pithy; full of –, pregnant with- meaning.

declaratory &c. 535; intelligible &c. 518; literal, metaphrastic; synonymous; tantamount &c. (*equivalent*) 27; implied &c. (*latent*) 526; explicit &c. 525; literal &c. 562.

Adv. to that effect; that is to say &c. (*being interpreted*) 522.

literally; evidently, from the context.

518. Intelligibility.—N. intelligibility, clearness, clarity, explicitness &c. *adj.*; lucidity, perspicuity; legibility, plain speaking &c. (*manifestation*) 525; precision &c. 494; a word to the wise.

V. be -intelligible &c. *adj.*; speak -for itself, – volumes; tell its own tale, lie on the surface.

render -intelligible &c. *adj.*; popularize, simplify, clear up; elucidate &c. (*explain*) 522.

understand, comprehend; take, – in; catch, grasp, recognize, follow, collect, master, make out; see -with half an eye, – daylight; – one's way; enter into the ideas of; – come to an understanding.

Adj. intelligible; clear, – as -day, – crystal, – noonday; lucid; per-, transpicuous; luminous, transparent; comprehensible.

easily understood, easy to understand, for the million, intelligible to the meanest capacity, popularized.

plain, distinct, explicit, clear-cut; positive; definite &c. (*precise*) 494.

graphic, vivid, telling; expressive &c. (*meaning*) 516; illustrative &c. (*explanatory*) 522.

un-ambiguous, -equivocal, -mistakable &c. (*manifest*) 525, -confused; legible, recognizable; obvious &c. 525.

Adv. in plain -terms, – words, – English.

Phr. he that runs may read &c. (*manifest*) 525.

nonsensical; void of -sense &c. 516.

in-, un-expressive; vacant, fatuous; not significant; insignificant.

trashy, washy, inane, vague, trumpery, trivial, fiddle-faddle, twaddling, quibbling.

unmeant, not expressed; tacit &c. (*latent*) 526.

inexpressible, undefinable, incommunicable.

Int. rubbish! &c. 497.

519. Unintelligibility.—N. unintelligibility, incomprehensibility, imperspicuity; inconceivableness, vagueness &c. *adj.*; obscurity; ambiguity &c. 520; doubtful meaning; uncertainty &c. 475; perplexity &c. (*confusion*) 59; spinosity; *obscurum per obscurius*; mystification &c. (*concealment*) 528; latency &c. 526; transcendentalism.

paradox; enigma, riddle &c. (*secret*) 533; *dignus vindice nodus*; sealed book; steganography, freemasonry.

pons asinorum, asses' bridge; double –, high- Dutch, Greek, Hebrew; jargon &c. (*unmeaning*) 517.

obscurantist.

V. be -unintelligible &c. *adj.*; require -explanation &c. 522; have a doubtful meaning, pass comprehension.

render -unintelligible &c. *adj.*; conceal &c. 528; darken &c. 421; confuse &c. (*derange*) 61; perplex &c. (*bewilder*) 475.

not -understand &c. 518; lose, – the clue; miss; not know what to make of, be able to make nothing of, give it up; not be able to -account for, – make either head or tail of; be at sea &c. (*uncertain*) 475; wonder &c. 870; see through a glass darkly &c. (*ignorance*) 491.

not understand one another; play at cross purposes &c. (*misinterpret*) 523.

Adj. un-intelligible, -accountable, -decipherable, -discoverable, -knowable, -fathomable; in-cognizable, -explicable, -scrutable; inap-, incomprehensible; insol-vable, -uble; impenetrable.

illegible, indecipherable, as Greek to one, unexplained, paradoxical; enigmatic, -al; puzzling, baffling.

obscure, dark, muddy, clear as mud, seen through a mist, dim, nebulous, shrouded in mystery; undiscernible &c. (*invisible*) 447; misty &c. (*opaque*) 426; hidden &c. 528; latent &c. 526.

indefinite &c. (*indistinct*) 447; perplexed &c. (*confused*) 59; undetermined, vague, loose, ambiguous; mysterious; mystic, -al; transcendental; occult, recondite, esoteric, abstruse, crabbed.

incon-ceivable, -ceptible; searchless; above –, beyond –, past-comprehension; beyond one's depth; unconceived.

inexpressible, undefinable, incommunicable, unutterable, ineffable, unpronounceable.

520. [Having a double sense.] **Equivocalness.—N.** equivocalness &c. *adj.*; double -meaning &c. 516; ambiguity, *double entendre*, pun, para-gram, *calembour*, quibble, *équivoque*, anagram; conundrum &c. (*riddle*) 533; word-play &c. (*wit*) 842; homonym, -y; amphibo-ly, -logy; am-biloquy.

Sphinx, Delphic oracle.

equivocation &c. (*duplicity*) 544; white lie, mental reservation &c. (*concealment*) 528.

V. be -equivocal &c. *adj.*; have two -meanings &c. 516; equivocate &c. (*palter*) 544.

Adj. equivocal, ambiguous, amphibolous, homonymous; double-tongued &c. (*lying*) 544.

521. Metaphor.—N. figure of speech; *façon de parler*, way of speaking, colloquialism.

phrase &c. 566; figure, trope, metaphor, tralatition, metonymy, enallage, *catachresis, synecdoche, autonomasia*; irony, satire, figurative-ness &c. *adj.*; image, -ry; *metalepsis*, type, anagoge, simile, personifica-tion, *prosopopæia*, allegory, apologue, parable, fable; allusion, adum-bration; application; euphemism; euphuism.

V. employ -metaphor &c. *n.*; personify, allegorize, adumbrate, shadow forth, apply, allude –, refer- to.

Adj. metaphorical &c. *n.*; figurative, catachrestical, typical, tralati-tious, parabolic, allegorical, allusive, anagogical; ironical; colloquial.

Adv. so to -speak, – say, – express oneself; as it were.

Phr. *mutato nomine de te fabula narratur.*

522. Interpretation.—N. interpreta-tion, definition; explan-, explic-ation; solution, answer; rationale; plain –, simple –, strict- interpretation; mean-ing &c. 516.

translation; rend-ering, -ition; red-dition; literal –, free- translation; key, crib; secret; clew &c. (*indication*) 550; Rosetta stone.

exegesis; ex-pounding, -position; Hermeneutics; comment, -ary; infer-ence &c. (*deduction*) 480; illustration, exemplification; gloss, annotation, *scholium*, note; e-, di-lucidation, enucle-ation; *éclaircissement, mot de l'énigme*.

symptomat-, semei-ology; metopo-scopy, physiognomy; diagnosis, prog-

523. Misinterpretation. — N. mis-interpretation, -apprehension, -under-standing, -acceptation, -construction, -application; *catachresis*; cross -read-ing, – purposes; mistake &c. 495.

misrepresentation, perversion, exag-geration &c. 549; false -colouring, – construction; abuse of terms; parody, travesty; falsification &c. (*lying*) 544.

V. mis-interpret, -apprehend, -under-stand, -conceive, -judge, -doubt, -spell, -translate, -construe, -apply; mistake &c. 495.

misrepresent, pervert; garble &c. (*falsify*) 544; distort, detort; travesty, play upon words; stretch –, strain –, wrest- the -sense, – meaning; explain

nosis; paleography &c. (*philology*) 560.

accept-ion, -ation, -ance; light, reading, lection, construction, version.

equivalent, – meaning &c. 516; synonym; para-, meta-phrase; convertible terms, apposition; dictionary &c. 562; polyglot.

V. interpret, explain, define, construe, translate, render; do –, turn-into; transfuse the sense of.

find out &c. 480*a*- -the meaning &c. 516- of; read; spell –, figure –, make- out; decipher, decode, unravel, disentangle, puzzle out; find the key of, enucleate, resolve, solve; read between the lines.

account for; find –, tell- the cause &c. 153- of; throw –, shed- -light, – new light, – a fresh light- upon; clear up, elucidate.

illustrate, exemplify; unfold, expound, comment upon, annotate; popularize &c. (*render intelligible*) 518.

take –, understand –, receive –, accept- in a particular sense; understand by, put a construction on, be given to understand.

Adj. explanatory, expository; explica-tive, -tory; exegetical; hermeneutic, interpretive, illustrative, elucidative, annotative, scholiastic.

polyglot; literal; para-, meta-phrastic; cosignificative, synonymous; equivalent &c. 27.

Adv. in -explanation &c. *n.*; that is to say, *id est, videlicet,* to wit, namely, in other words.

literally, strictly speaking; in -plain, – plainer- -terms, – words, – English; more simply.

away; put a -bad, – false- construction on; give a false colouring, look through -rose coloured –, – dark – spectacles.

be –, play- at cross purposes.

Adj. misinterpreted &c. *v.*; untranslat-ed, -able.

Adv. at cross purposes.

---

524. Interpreter.—N. interpreter, translator, ex-positor, -pounder, -ponent, -plainer; demonstrator.

scholiast, commentator, annotator; meta-, para-phrast.

spokesman, speaker, mouthpiece, prolocutor; diplomat &c. 758.

guide, courier, dragoman, *valet de place, cicerone,* showman; oneiro-critic; Œdipus; oracle &c. 513.

Section II. Modes of Communication

525. Manifestation.—N. manifestation; unfolding; plainness &c. *adj.*; plain speaking; expression; showing &c. *v.*; exposition, demonstration, *séance*; exhibition, production; display, showing off &c. 882, premonstration. [Thing shown] exhibit, show.

indication &c. (*calling attention to*) 457; publicity &c. 531; disclosure &c. 529; openness &c. (*honesty*) 543, (*artlessness*) 703; *épanchement,* prominence.

V. make –, render- -manifest &c. *adj.*; bring -forth, – forward, – to the front, – into view; give notice; express; represent, set forth, exhibit; show, – up; expose; produce; hold up –, expose- to view; set –, place –, lay-

526. Latency.—N. latency, inexpression; hidden –, occult- meaning; occultness, occultism, mysticism, mystery, cabala, symbolism, anagoge; silence &c. (*taciturnity*) 585; concealment &c. 528; more than meets the -eye, – ear; Delphic oracle; *le dessous des cartes,* undercurrent.

allusion, insinuation, implication; innuendo &c. 527; adumbration; 'something rotten in the state of Denmark.'

snake in the grass &c. (*pitfall*) 667; secret &c. 533.

darkness, invisibility, imperceptibility.

latent influence, power behind the throne; friend at court, wire puller.

before -one, – one's eyes; tell to one's face; trot out, put through one's paces, unfold, show off, show forth, unveil, bring to light, display, demonstrate, unroll; lay open; draw –, bring- out; bring out in strong relief; call –, bring- into notice; hold up the mirror; wear one's heart upon his sleeve; show one's -face, – colours; manifest oneself; speak out; make no -mystery, – secret- of; unfurl the flag; proclaim &c. (*publish*) 531.

indicate &c. (*direct attention to*) 457; disclose &c. 529; elicit &c. 480a; interpret &c. 522.

be -manifest &c. *adj.*; appear &c. (*be visible*) 446; transpire &c. (*be disclosed*) 529; speak for itself, stand to reason; stare one in the face; loom large, appear on the horizon, rear its head; give -token, – sign, – indication of; tell its own tale &c. (*intelligible*) 518; go without saying.

Adj. manifest, apparent; salient, striking, demonstrative, prominent, in the foreground, notable, pronounced.

flagrant; notorious &c. (*public*) 531; arrant; stark staring; unshaded, glaring.

defin-ed, -ite; distinct, conspicuous &c. (*visible*) 446; obvious, evident, incontestable, unmistakable, not to be mistaken, plain, clear, palpable, self-evident, autoptical; intelligible &c. 518; clear as -day, – daylight, – noonday; plain as -a pikestaff, – the sun at noonday, – the nose on one's face, – the way to the parish church.

ostensible; open, – as day; overt, patent, express, explicit; naked, bare, literal, downright, undisguised, exoteric.

unreserved; frank, plain spoken &c. (*artless*) 703; barefaced, brazen, bold, shameless, daring, flaunting, loud.

manifested &c. *v.*; disclosed &c. 529; expressible, capable of being shown, producible; in-, un-concealable.

Adv. manifestly, openly &c. *adj.*; before one's eyes, under one's nose, to one's face, face to face, above board, *cartes sur table*, on the stage, in plain sight, in open court, in the open, – streets; at the cross roads; in market overt; in the face of -day, – heaven; in -broad –, open- daylight; without reserve; at first blush, *primâ facie*, on the face of; in set terms.

Phr. *cela saute aux yeux*; he that runs may read; you can see it with half an eye; it needs no ghost to tell us; the meaning lies on the surface; *cela va sans dire*; *res ipsa loquitur*.

V. be -latent &c. *adj.*; lurk, smoulder, underlie, make no sign; escape -observation, – detection, – recognition; lie hid &c. 528.

laugh in one's sleeve; keep back &c. (*conceal*) 528.

involve, imply, implicate, connote, import, understand, allude to, infer, leave an inference; symbolize; whisper &c. (*conceal*) 528.

Adj. latent; lurking &c. *v.*; secret &c. 528; occult, symbolic, mystic; implied &c. *v.*; dormant.

un-apparent, -known, -seen &c. 441; in the background; invisible &c. 447; indiscoverable, dark; impenetrable &c. (*unintelligible*) 519; un-spied, -suspected.

un - said, - written, - published, -breathed, -talked of, -told &c. 527, -sung, -exposed, -proclaimed, -disclosed &c. 529, -pronounced, -mentioned, -expressed; not expressed, tacit.

un-developed, -solved, -explained, -traced, -discovered &c. 480a, -tracked, -explored, -invented.

indirect, crooked, inferential; by -inference, – implication; implicit; constructive; allusive, covert, muffled; steganographic; under-stood, -hand, -ground; concealed &c. 528; delitescent.

Adv. by a side wind; *sub silentio*; in the background; behind -the scenes, – one's back, – the veil; below the surface; on the tip of one's tongue; secretly &c. 528; between the lines; by a mutual understanding.

Phr. 'thereby hangs a tale.' 'that is another story.'

---

527. Information.—**N.** information, enlightenment, acquaintance, knowledge &c. 490; publicity &c. 531.

communication, intimation; not-ice, -ification; e-, an-nunciation; announcement; representation, round robin, presentment.

case, estimate, specification, report, advice, monition; news &c. 532; return &c. (*record*) 551; account &c. (*description*) 594; statement &c. (*affirmation*) 535.

mention; acquainting &c. *v.*; instruction &c. (*teaching*) 537; outpouring; intercommunication, communicativeness.

informant, authority, teller, announcer, annunciator, harbinger, herald, intelligencer, commentator, columnist, reporter, exponent, mouthpiece; informer, keek, eavesdropper, delator, detective, sleuth; *mouchard*, spy, stool pigeon, newsmonger; messenger &c. 534; *amicus curiæ*.

valet de place, *cicerone*, pilot, guide; guide-, hand-book; *vade mecum*; manual; map, plan, chart, gazetteer; itinerary &c. (*journey*) 266.

hint, suggestion, wrinkle, innuendo, inkling, whisper, passing word, word in the ear, subaudition, cue, by-play; gesture &c. (*indication*) 550; gentle – broad- hint; *verbum sapienti*; word to the wise; insinuation &c. (*latency*) 526.

V. tell; inform, – of; acquaint, – with; impart, – to; make acquainted with, bring to the ears of, apprise, advise, enlighten, awaken.

let fall, mention, express, intimate, represent, communicate, make known; publish &c. 531; notify, signify, specify, convey the knowledge of.

let one –, have one to- know; serve notice, give one to understand; give notice; set –, lay –, put- before; point out, put into one's head; put one in possession of; instruct &c. (*teach*) 537; direct the attention to &c. 457.

an-nounce, -nunciate; report, – progress; bring –, send –, leave –, write- word; tele-graph, -phone; ring –, call- up; wire; retail, render an account; give an account &c. (*describe*) 594; state &c. (*affirm*) 535.

528. Concealment.—**N.** concealment; hiding &c. *v.*; occultation, mystification.

seal of secrecy; screen &c. 530; disguise &c. 530; masquerade; masked battery; hiding place &c. 530; cipher, code, crypt-, stegan-ography; invisible –, sympathetic- ink; palimpsest; freemasonry.

stealth, -iness; obreption; slyness &c. (*cunning*) 702.

latit-ancy, -ation; seclusion &c. 893; privacy, secrecy, secretness; *incognita*.

reticence; reserve; mental –, reservation, aside; *arrière pensée*, suppression, evasion, white lie, misprision; silence &c. (*taciturnity*) 585; suppression of truth &c. 544; underhand dealing; close-, secretive-ness &c. *adj.*; mystery.

latency &c. 526; snake in the grass; secret &c. 533.

V. conceal, hide, secrete, stow away, put out of sight; lock –, seal –, bottle- up.

cover, screen, cloak, veil, shroud; screen from -sight, – observation; draw the veil; draw –, close- the curtain; curtain, shade, eclipse, throw a veil over; be-cloud, -fog, -mask; mask, disguise; ensconce, muffle, smother; whisper.

keep -from, – back, – to oneself; keep -snug, – close, – secret, – dark; bury; sink, suppress; keep -from, – out of- -view, – sight; keep in –, throw into- the -shade, – background; cover up one's tracks; stifle, hush up, withhold, reserve; fence with a question; ignore &c. 460.

code, codify, use a cipher.

keep -a secret, – one's own counsel; hold one's tongue &c. (*silence*) 585; make no sign, not let it go further; not breathe a -word, – syllable- about; not let the right hand know what the left is doing; hide one's light under a bushel, bury one's talent in a napkin.

keep –, leave- in -the dark, – ignorance; blind, – the eyes; blindfold, hoodwink, mystify; puzzle &c. (*render uncertain*) 475; bamboozle &c. (*deceive*) 545.

be -concealed &c. *v.*; suffer an eclipse;

disclose &c. 529; show cause; explain &c. (*interpret*) 522.

hint; give an inkling of; **give -,** drop -, throw out- a hint; insinuate; allude -, make allusion- to; glance at; tip off, tip the wink &c. (*indicate*) 550; suggest, prompt, give the cue, breathe; whisper, - in the ear.

give a bit of one's mind; **tell one plainly,** - once for all; speak volumes.

un-deceive, -beguile; set right, correct, open the eyes of, disabuse.

be -informed of &c.; know &c. 490; learn &c. 539; get scent of, gather from; awaken -, open one's eyes- to; become -alive, - awake- to; keep posted; hear, overhear, understand.

come to one's -ears, - knowledge; reach one's ears.

Adj. informed &c. *v.*; *communiqué*; reported &c. *v.*; published &c. 531; advisory.

expressive &c. 516; explicit &c. (*open*) 525, (*clear*) 518; plain-spoken &c. (*artless*) 703.

declara-, nuncupa-, exposi-tory; declarative, enunciative, communicat-ive, -ory; oral.

Adv. from information received; according to -rumour, - report; in the air; from what one can gather.

Phr. a little bird told me.

retire from sight, couch; hide oneself; lie -hid, - in ambush, - low, - *perdu*, - snug, - close; seclude oneself &c. 893; lurk, sneak, skulk, slink, pussy-foot, prowl; steal -into, - out of, - by, - along; play at -bopeep, - hide and seek; hide in holes and corners.

Adj. concealed &c. *v.*; hidden; veiled, secret, recondite, mystic, cabalistic, occult, dark; cryptic, -al; private, privy, *in petto*, auricular, clandestine, close, inviolate.

behind a -screen &c. 530; under -cover, - an eclipse; in -ambush, - hiding, - disguise; in a -cloud, - fog, - mist, - haze, - dark corner; in the -shade, - dark; clouded, wrapt in clouds; invisible &c. 447; buried, under-ground, *perdu*; incommunicado; secluded &c. 893.

un-disclosed &c. 529, -told &c. 527; covert &c. (*latent*) 526; mysterious &c. (*unintelligible*) 519.

irrevealable, inviolable; confidential; esoteric; not to be spoken of.

obreptitious, furtive, stealthy, feline; skulking &c. *v.*; surreptitious, under-hand, hole and corner; sly &c. (*cunning*) 702; secretive, evasive, noncom-mittal, reserved, reticent, uncommunicative, buttoned up; close, - as wax; taciturn &c. 585.

Adv. secretly &c. *adj.*; in -secret, - private, - one's sleeve, - holes and corners; in the dark &c. *adj.*

januis clausis, with closed doors, *à huis clos*; hugger-mugger, *à la dérobée*; under the -cloak of, - rose, - table; *sub rosâ, en tapinois*, in the background, aside, on the sly, with bated breath, *sotto voce*, in a whisper, without beat of drum, *à la sourdine*.

in -, strict- confidence; confidentially &c. *adj.*; between -our-selves, - you and me; *entre nous, inter nos*, under the seal of secrecy; in -code, - cipher.

underhand, by stealth, like a thief in the night; stealthily &c. *adj.*; behind -the scenes, - the curtain, - one's back, - a screen &c. 530; *incognito; in camerâ*.

Phr. it -must, - will- go no further; 'tell it not in Gath,' nobody the wiser.

529. Disclosure.—N. disclosure; retection; unveiling &c. *v.*; deterration, revealment, revelation; divulgence, expos-ition, -ure; *exposé*; whole truth; tell-tale &c. (*news*) 532.

acknowledgment, avowal; confession, -al; shrift.

530. Ambush. [Means of conceal-ment.]—**N.** hiding-place; secret -place, - drawer; recess, hole, funk hole, holes and corners; closet, crypt, *adytum*, ab-ditory, *oubliette*, safe, - deposit.

am-bush, -buscade; stalking horse; lurking-hole, -place; secret path,

bursting of a bubble; *dénouement.*

V. dis-close, -cover, -mask; draw –, draw aside –, lift –, raise –, lift up –, remove –, tear- the -veil, – curtain; un-mask, -veil, -fold, -cover, -seal, -kennel; take off –, break- the seal; lay -open, – bare; expose; open, – up; bare, bring to light; evidence; make - clear, – evident, – manifest; evince.

divulge, reveal, break; let into the secret; reveal the secrets of the prison-house; tell &c. (*inform*) 527; breathe, utter, blab, peach; let -out, – fall, – drop, – the cat out of the bag; betray; tell tales, – out of school; come out with; give -vent, – utterance- to; open the lips, blurt out, vent, whisper about; speak out &c. (*make manifest*) 525; make public &c. 531; unriddle &c. (*find out*) 480a; split; blow the gaff; break the news.

acknowledge, allow, concede, grant, admit, own, confess, avow, throw off all disguise, turn inside out, make a clean breast; show one's -hand, – cards; unburden –, disburden- one's -mind, – con-science, – heart; open –, lay bare –, tell a piece of- one's mind; unbosom oneself, own to the soft impeachment; say –, speak- the truth; turn -King's, –Queen's, –State's- evidence.

raise –, drop –, lift –, remove –, throw off- the mask; expose; debunk; lay open; un-deceive, -beguile; disabuse, set right, correct, open the eyes of; *désillusionner.*

be -disclosed &c.; transpire, come to light; come in sight &c. (*be visible*) 446; become known, escape the lips; come –, ooze –, creep –, leak –, peep –, crop- out; show its -face, – colours; discover &c. itself; break through the clouds, flash on the mind.

Adj. disclosed &c. *v.*

Int. out with it!

Phr. the murder is out; a light breaks in upon one; the scales fall from one's eyes; the eyes are opened.

backstairs; retreat &c. (*refuge*) 666.

screen, cover, shade, blinker; veil, curtain, blind, *purdah,* cloak, cloud.

mask, vizor, visor, disguise, masquer-ade dress, domino; *camouflage.*

pitfall &c. (*source of danger*) 667; trap &c. (*snare*) 545.

V. ambush, ambuscade, lie in ambush &c. (*hide oneself*) 528; lie in wait for; set a trap for &c. (*deceive*) 545.

Adv. *aux aguets.*

531. Publication.—N. publication; public -announcement &c. 527; promulgation, propagation, proclamation, pronouncement, encyclical, *pronunciamento;* circulation, indiction, edition, imprint, impression, printing; hue and cry.

publicity, notoriety, currency, flagrancy, cry, *bruit; vox populi;* report &c. (*news*) 532.

the Press, fourth estate, public press, newspaper, periodical, journal, gazette; house organ, trade publication, tabloid; daily, weekly, monthly, quarterly, annual, magazine, monograph, book; review; news sheet, special edition, supplement, feature, rotogravure, comic strips; leaflet, pamphlet; telegraphy; publisher &c. *v.*

circular, – letter; manifesto, advertisement, puff, placard, bill, *affiche,* broadside, poster; notice &c. 527; programme.

V. publish; make -public, – known &c. (*information*) 527; speak –, talk- of; broach, utter; put forward; circulate, propagate, promulgate; spread –, abroad; rumour, diffuse, disseminate, evulgate; put –, give –, send- forth; emit, edit, get out; issue; cover, report; bring –, lay –, drag- before the public; give -out, – to the world; put –, bandy –, hawk –, buzz –, whisper –, bruit –, blaze- about; drag into the -open day, – limelight; voice.

proclaim, herald, blazon; blaze –, noise- abroad; sound a trumpet; trumpet –, thunder- forth; give tongue; announce with -beat of drum, – flourish of trumpets; proclaim -from the housetops, – at Charing Cross, at the cross roads; declare, declaim.

advertise, placard; post, – up; *afficher*, publish in the Gazette, send round the crier.

raise a -cry, – hue and cry, – report; set news afloat.

telegraph, cable, wireless, broadcast.

be -published &c.; be –, become- public &c. *adj.*; come out; go –, fly –, buzz –, blow- about; get -about, – abroad, – afloat, – wind; find vent; see the light; go forth, take air, acquire currency, pass current; go -the rounds, – the round of the newspapers, – through the length and breadth of the land; *virum volitare per ora*; pass from mouth to mouth; spread; run –, spread- like wildfire.

Adj. published &c. *v.*; current &c. (*news*) 532; in circulation, public; notorious; flagrant, arrant; open &c. 525; trumpet-tongued; encyclical, promulgatory; exoteric.

Adv. publicly &c. *adj.*; in open court, with open doors; in the limelight.

Int. *Oyez!* O yes! notice!

Phr. notice is hereby given; this is –, these are- to give notice.

532. News.—N. news; information &c. 527; piece –, budget- of -news, – information; report, story, yarn, copy, filler, intelligence, tidings; stop press news.

word, advice, *aviso*, message; dis-, des-patch; radio, telegram, cable, wireless telegram, radio-gram, marconigram, communication, errand, embassy; *bulletin*.

rumour, hearsay, *on dit*, flying rumour, news stirring, cry, buzz, *bruit*, fame; talk, *ouï-dire*, scandal, eavesdropping; town –, table- talk; tittle-tattle; *canard*, topic of the day, idea afloat.

fresh –, stirring –, old –, stale- news; glad tidings; old –, stale- story.

533. Secret.—N. secret; dead –, profound- secret; *arcanum*, mystery; latency &c. 526; Asian mystery; sealed book, secrets of the prison-house; *le dessous des cartes*.

enigma, riddle, puzzle, nut to crack, conundrum, charade, rebus, logograph; mono-, ana-gram; acrostic, cross-word puzzle; Sphinx; *crux criticorum*.

maze, labyrinth, Hyrcynian wood.

problem &c. (*question*) 461; paradox &c. (*difficulty*) 704; unintelligibility &c. 519; *terra incognita* &c. (*ignorance*) 491.

Adj. secret &c. (*concealed*) 528.

narrator &c. (*describe*) 594; news-, scandal-monger; tale-bearer; tell-tale, gossip, tattler, busy-body, chatterer; informer.

V. transpire &c. (*be disclosed*) 529; rumour &c. (*publish*) 531.

Adj. many-tongued; rumoured; publicly –, currently- -rumoured, – reported; rife, current, floating, afloat, going about, in circulation, in everyone's mouth, all over the town.

Adv. as the story -goes, – runs; as they say, it is said.

534. Messenger.—N. messenger, envoy, emissary, legate; nuncio, internuncio; intermediary; ambassador &c. (*diplomatist*) 758.

marshal, flag-bearer, herald, crier, trumpeter, bellman, pursuivant, *parlementaire, apparitor*.

courier, runner, dawk, *estafette*; Hermes, Mercury, Iris, Ariel.

postman, letter carrier, telegraph boy, messenger boy, district messenger; despatch rider, commissionaire, errand-boy.

mail; post, -office; letter-bag; mail -boat, – train, – coach, – van, aerial mail; tele-graph, -phone; cable, wire; carrier-pigeon; wireless tele-graph, -phone; radiotele-graph, -phone.

journalist, newspaperman, reporter; gentleman –, representative- of the press; sob sister; penny-a-liner; special –, war –, own- correspondent; spy, scout; informer &c. 527.

535. Affirmation.—N. affirm-ance, -ation; statement, allegation, assertion, predication, declaration, word, averment.

asseveration, adjuration, swearing, oath, affidavit; deposition &c. (*record*) 551; avouchment, assurance; protest, -ation; profession; acknowledgment &c. (*assent*) 488; pledge.

vote, voice, suffrage, ballot.

remark, observation; position &c. (*proposition*) 514; saying, *dictum*, sentence, *ipse dixit*.

emphasis, positiveness, peremptoriness; dogmatism &c. (*certainty*) 474; dogmatist &c. 887.

V. assert; make -an assertion &c. *n.*; have one's say; say, affirm, predicate, declare, state, represent; protest, profess.

put -forth, – forward; advance, allege, propose, propound, enunciate, enounce, broach, set forth, hold out, maintain, contend, pronounce, pretend.

depose, depone, aver, avow, avouch, asseverate, swear; make –, take one's- oath; make –, swear –, put in- an affidavit; take one's Bible oath, kiss the book, vow, *vitam impendere vero*; swear till -one is black in the face, – all's blue; be sworn, call Heaven to witness; vouch, warrant, certify, assure, swear by bell, book and candle.

swear by &c. (*believe*) 484; insist –, take one's stand- upon; emphasize, lay stress on; assert -roundly, – positively; lay down, – the law; raise one's voice, dogmatize, have the last word; rap out; repeat; re-assert, -affirm.

announce &c. (*information*) 527; acknowledge &c. (*assent*) 488; attest &c. (*evidence*) 467; adjure &c. (*put to one's oath*) 768.

Adj. asserting &c. *v.*; declaratory, predicatory, pronunciative, affirmative, *soi-disant*; positive; certain &c. 474; express, explicit &c. (*patent*) 525; absolute, emphatic, flat, broad, round, pointed, marked, distinct, decided, confident, assertive, insistent, trenchant, dogmatic, definitive, formal, solemn, categorical, peremptory; unretracted; predicable, affirmable.

536. Negation.—N. ne-, abne-gation; denial; dis-avowal, -claimer; abjuration; contra-diction, -vention; recusation, protest; rebuttal; recusancy &c. (*dissent*) 489; flat –, emphatic- -contradiction, – denial; *démenti*.

qualification &c. 469; repudiation &c. 610; retractation &c. 607; confutation &c. 479; refusal &c. 764; prohibition &c. 761.

V. deny; contra-dict, -vene; controvert, give denial to, gainsay, negative, shake the head.

dis-own, -affirm, -claim, -avow; recant &c. 607; revoke &c. (*abrogate*) 756.

dispute, impugn, traverse, rebut, join issue upon; bring –, call- in question &c. (*doubt*) 485.

deny -flatly, – peremptorily, – emphatically, – absolutely, – wholly, – entirely; give the lie to, belie.

repudiate &c. 610; set aside, ignore &c. 460; rebut &c. (*confute*) 479; qualify &c. 469; refuse &c. 764.

Adj. denying &c. *v.*; denied &c. *v.*; contradictory; negat-ive, -ory; revocatory; recusant &c. (*dissenting*) 489; at issue upon.

Adv. no, nay, not, nowise; not a -bit, – whit, – jot; not -at all, – in the least, – so; no such thing; nothing of the -kind, – sort; quite the contrary, *tout au contraire*, far from it; *tant s'en faut*; on no account, in no respect; by -no, – no manner of- means; negatively.

Phr. there never was a greater mistake; I know better; *non hæc in fœdera*.

Adv. affirmatively &c. *adj.*; in the affirmative.

with emphasis, *ex cathedrâ*, without fear of contradiction.

I must say, indeed, i' faith, let me tell you, why, give me leave to say, marry, you may be sure, I'd have you to know; upon my -word, – honour; by my troth, egad, I assure you; by -jingo, – Jove, – George, – &c.; troth, seriously, sadly, in –, in sober- -sadness, – truth, – earnest; of a truth, truly, pardi, perdy; in all conscience, upon oath; be assured &c. *(belief)* 484; yes &c. *(assent)* 488; I'll -warrant, – warrant you, – engage, – answer for it, – be bound, – venture to say, – take my oath; in fact, as a matter of fact, forsooth, joking apart; so help me God; not to mince the matter.

Phr. quoth he; *dixi*.

537. Teaching.—N. teaching &c. *v.*; instruction; edification; education; pedagogy; tuition; tutor-, tutel-age; direction, guidance.

qualification, preparation; train-, school-ing &c. *v.*; discipline; exer-cise, -citation; drill, practice.

persuasion, proselytism, propagandism, *propaganda*; in-doctrination, -culcation, -oculation.

explanation &c. *(interpretation)* 522; lesson, lecture, sermon, homily; apologue, parable; discourse, prelection, preachment, disquisition.

exercise, task; *curriculum*; course, – of study; grammar, three R's, initiation, A. B. C. &c. *(beginning)* 66.

elementary –, primary –, secondary –, grammar school –, high school –, college –, university –, technical –, liberal –, classical –, religious –, denominational –, moral –, secular- education; technical –, vocational- training; university extension lectures; propædeutics, moral tuition; evening classes, correspondence course.

physical education, gymnastics, calisthenics, eurythmics; *sloyd*.

V. teach, instruct, edify, school, tutor; cram, prime, coach; enlighten &c. *(inform)* 527.

in-culcate, -doctrinate, -oculate, -fuse, -stil, -fix, -graft, -filtrate; imbue, -pregnate, -plant; graft, sow the seeds of, disseminate, propagandize.

give an idea of; put -up to, – in the way of; set right.

sharpen the wits, enlarge the mind; give new ideas, open the eyes, bring forward, 'teach the young idea how to shoot'; improve &c. 658.

538. Misteaching.—N. mis-teaching, -information, -intelligence, -guidance, -direction, -persuasion, -instruction, -leading &c. *v.*; perversion, false teaching; sophistry &c. 477; college of Laputa; the blind leading the blind.

V. mis-inform, -teach, -direct, -guide, -instruct, -correct; pervert; put on a false –, throw off the- scent; deceive &c. 545; mislead &c. *(error)* 495; misrepresent; lie &c. 544; *ambiguas in vulgum spargere voces*, preach to the wise, teach one's grandmother to suck eggs.

render unintelligible &c. 519; bewilder &c. *(uncertainty)* 475; mystify &c. *(conceal)* 528; unteach.

Adj. misteaching &c. *v.*; unedifying.

Phr. *piscem natare doces*.

539. Learning.—N. learning; acquisition of -knowledge &c. 490, – skill &c. 698; acquirement, attainment; edification, scholarship, erudition; lore; information; self-instruction; study, reading, perusal; inquiry &c. 461.

ap-, prenticeship; pupil-age, -arity; tutelage, novitiate, matriculation.

docility &c. *(willingness)* 602; aptitude &c. 698.

V. learn; acquire –, gain –, receive –, take in –, drink in –, imbibe –, pick up –, gather –, get –, obtain –, collect –, glean- -knowledge, – information, – learning.

acquaint oneself with, master; make oneself -master of, – acquainted with; grind, cram; get –, coach- up; learn by -heart, – rote.

read, spell, peruse; con –, pore –; thumb- over; wade through; dip into;

expound &c. (*interpret*) 522; lecture; prelect; read –, give- a -lesson,– lecture, – sermon, – discourse; hold forth, preach; sermon-, moral-ize; point a moral.

train, discipline; bring up, – to; educate, form, ground, prepare, qualify, drill, exercise, practice, habituate, familiarize with, nurture, dry-nurse, breed, rear, take in hand; break, – in; tame; pre-instruct; initiate; inure &c. (*habituate*) 613.

put to nurse, send to school.

direct, guide; direct attention to &c. (*attention*) 457; impress upon the -mind, – memory; beat into, – the head; convince &c. (*belief*) 484.

Adj. teaching &c. *v.*; taught &c. *v.*; educational; scholastic, academic, doctrinal; disciplinal; instructive, didactic, hortative, pedagogic, tutorial.

Phr. the schoolmaster abroad.

540. Teacher.—N. teacher, trainer, instructor, institutor, master, tutor, don, director, Corypheus, dry nurse, coach, grinder, crammer; governor, bear-leader; governess, duenna; disciplinarian.

professor, lecturer, reader, prelector, prolocutor, preacher; Boanerges; pastor &c. (*clergy*) 996; schoolmaster, dominie, usher, pedagogue, abecedarian; schoolmistress, dame, monitor, proctor, pupil-teacher.

expositor &c. 524; preceptor, guide; mentor &c. (*adviser*) 695; pioneer, apostle, missionary, propagandist, moonshee; example &c. (*model for imitation*) 22.

professorship &c. (*school*) 542. tutelage &c. (*teaching*) 537.

Adj. professorial, tutorial &c. 537.

run the eye -over, – through; turn over the leaves.

study; be -studious &c. *adj.*; consume the midnight oil, mind cne's book.

go to -school, – college, – the university; serve -an (*or* one's) apprenticeship, – one's time; learn one's trade; be -informed &c. 527; be -taught &c. 537.

Adj. studious; schol-astic, -arly; teachable; docile &c. (*willing*) 602; apt &c. 698, industrious &c. 682; learned, erudite.

Adv. at one's books; *in statu pupillari* &c. (*learner*) 541.

---

541. Learner.—N. learner, scholar, student, *alumnus*, *élève*, pupil; ap-, prentice; articled clerk; school-boy, -girl, beginner, tyro, abecedarian, alphabetarian.

recruit, novice, neophyte, tenderfoot, inceptor, *débutant*, catechumen, probationer; undergraduate; freshman, frosh; sophomore, junior, senior; junior –, senior- soph; sophister, questionist, fellow-, commoner, pensioner, exhibitioner, sizar, scholar, fellow, advanced –, post graduate –, research- student.

class, form, grade, standard, remove; pupilage &c. (*learning*) 539.

disciple, follower, apostle, proselyte; fellow student, school-mate, -fellow, class mate, condisciple.

Adj. *in statu pupillari*, in leading strings, sophomoric.

542. School.—N. school, academy, university, *alma mater*, college, seminary, Lyceum; instit-ute, -ution, *conservatoire*; *palæstra*, *gymnasium*.

day –, boarding –, public –, preparatory –, elementary –, primary –, infant –, dame's –, grammar –, middle class –, Board –, County –, Council –, parochial –, denominational –, Sunday –, National –, British and Foreign –, collegiate –, secondary –, continuation –, night –, correspondence –, secretarial –, military –, law –, medical –, business –, technical- school; technical –, training- college; Polytechnic; training ship; *Kindergarten*, nursery, *crèche*, reformatory.

pulpit, desk, reading desk, ambo, class-, lecture-room, theatre, amphitheatre, forum, stage, rostrum, platform, hustings, tribune.

school –, horn –, text- book; grammar, primer, abecedary, rudiments, manual, *vade mecum*, Lindley Murray, Cocker.

professor-, lecture-, reader-ship; chair; schoolmaster &c. 540.

School Board, Council of Education; *propaganda*.

Adj. scholastic, academic, collegiate; educational.

Adv. *ex cathedrâ*.

---

543. Veracity.—N. veracity; truthfulness, frankness &c. *adj*.; truth, sooth, sincerity, candour, honesty, fidelity; plain dealing, *bona fides*; love of truth; probity &c. 939; ingenuousness &c. (*artlessness*) 703.

the truth the whole truth and nothing but the truth; honest –, sobertruth &c. (*fact*) 494; unvarnished tale; light of truth.

V. speak –, tell- the truth; speak by the card; paint in its –, show oneself in one's-true colours; make a clean breast &c. (*disclose*) 529; speak one's mind &c. (*be blunt*) 703; not -lie &c. 544, – deceive &c. 545.

Adj. truthful, true; ver-acious, -edical; scrupulous &c. (*honourable*) 939; sincere, candid, frank, open, straightforward, unreserved; open-, true-, simple- hearted; honest, trustworthy; undissembling &c. (dissemble &c. 544); guileless, pure; unperjured, true blue, as good as one's word; unaffected, unfeigned, *bonâ fide*; outspoken, ingenuous &c. (*artless*) 703; undisguised &c. (*real*) 494.

Adv. truly &c. (*really*) 494; on oath; in plain words &c. 703; in –, with –, of a –, in good –, very- truth; as the -dial to the sun, – needle to the pole; honour bright; troth; in good -sooth, – earnest; unfeignedly, with no nonsense, in sooth, sooth to say, *bonâ fide*, *in foro conscientiæ*; without equivocation; *cartes sur table*, from the bottom of one's heart; by my troth &c. (*affirmation*) 535.

544. Falsehood. — N. false-hood, -ness; fals-ity, -ification; misrepresentation; deception &c. 545; untruth &c. 546; guile; bad faith; lying &c. *v*.; misrepresentation; mendacity, perjury, false swearing; forgery, invention, fabrication; subreption; covin.

perversion –, suppression- of truth; *suppressio veri*; perversion, distortion, false colouring; exaggeration &c. 549; prevarication, equivocation, shuffling, fencing, evasion, fraud; *suggestio falsi* &c. (*lie*) 546; mystification &c. (*concealment*) 528; simulation &c. (*imitation*) 19; dis-simulation, -sembling; deceit.

sham; pretence, pretending, malingering.

lip-homage, – service; mouth honour; hollowness; mere -show, – outside, eye-wash, window dressing; duplicity, double dealing, insincerity, hypocrisy, cant, humbug, casuistry; jesuit-ism, -ry; pharisaism; Machiavelism, 'organized hypocrisy'; crocodile tears, mealymouthedness, quackery; charlatan-ism, -ry; gammon; bun-kum, -come; flam, bam, flim-flam, cajolery, flattery; Judas kiss; perfidy &c. (*bad faith*) 940; *il volto sciolto i pensieri stretti*.

unfairness &c. (*dishonesty*) 940; artfulness &c. (*cunning*) 702; misstatement &c. (*error*) 495.

V. be -false &c. *adj*., – a liar &c. 548; speak -falsely &c. *adv*.; tell -a lie &c. 546; lie, fib; lie like a trooper; swear falsely, forswear, perjure oneself, bear false witness.

---

mis-state, -quote, -cite, -report, -represent; belie, falsify, pervert, distort; put a false construction upon &c. (*misinterpret*) 523.

prevaricate, equivocate, quibble; palter, – to the understanding; *répondre en Normand*; trim, shuffle, fence, mince the truth, beat about the bush, blow hot and cold, play fast and loose.

garble, gloss over, disguise, give a colour to; give –, put- a -gloss, – false colouring- upon; colour, varnish, cook, dress up, embroider: varnish right and puzzle wrong, exaggerate &c. 549.

invent, fabricate; trump –, get- up; forge, hatch, concoct; romance &c. (*imagine*) 515; cry 'wolf!'

dis-semble, -simulate; feign, assume, put on, pretend, make believe; play -false, – a double game; coquet; act –, play- a part; affect &c. 855; simulate, pass off for; counterfeit, fake, sham, make a show of; malinger; swing the lead; say the grapes are sour.

cant, play the hypocrite, sham Abraham, *faire pattes de velours*, put on the mask, clean the outside of the platter, lie like a conjuror; hang out –, hold out –, sail under- false colours; 'commend the poisoned chalice to the lips'; *ambiguas in vulgus spargere voces*; deceive &c. 545.

Adj. false, deceitful, mendacious, unveracious, fraudulent, untruthful, dishonest; faith-, truth-, troth-less; un-fair, -candid; evasive; un-, dis-ingenuous; hollow, insincere, *Parthis mendacior*; forsworn.

canting; hypocrit-, jesuit-, pharisa-ical; tartuffish; Machiavelian; double-tongued, -faced, -handed, -minded, -hearted, -dealing; two-faced, bare-faced; Janus-faced; smooth-faced, -spoken, -tongued; plausible; mealy-mouthed; affected &c. 855.

collus-ive, -ory; artful &c. (*cunning*) 702; perfidious &c. 940, spurious &c. (*deceptive*) 545; untrue &c. 546; falsified &c. *v.*; covinous.

Adv. falsely &c. *adj.*; *à la Tartufe*, with a double tongue; out of whole cloth; slily &c. (*cunning*) 702.

545. Deception.—N. deception; falseness &c. 544; untruth &c. 546; impos-ition, -ture; fraud, deceit, guile; fraudulen-ce, -cy; covin; knavery &c. (*cunning*) 702; misrepresentation &c. (*falsehood*) 544.

delusion, gullery, bluff, spoof, *blague*; juggl-ing, -ery; sleight of hand, legerdemain; presti-giation, -digitation; magic &c. 992; conjur-ing, -ation; hocus pocus, jockeyship; trickery, coggery, hanky-panky, chicanery, pettifogging, sharp practice; *supercherie*, cozenage, circumvention, ingannation, collusion; treachery &c. 940; practical joke.

trick, cheat, wile, ruse, blind, feint, plant, bubble, fetch, catch, chicane, juggle, reach, hocus, bite; thimble-rig, card-sharping, artful dodge, machination, swindle, hoax; tricks upon travellers; confidence trick; stratagem &c. (*artifice*) 702; theft &c. 791.

snare, trap, pitfall, decoy, gin; sprin-ge, -gle; noose, hook; bait, decoy-duck, tub to the whale, baited trap, *guet-à-pens*; cobweb, net, meshes, toils, mouse-trap, bird-lime; ambush &c. 530; trap-door, sliding panel, false bottom; spring-net, -gun; mask, -ed battery; mine; booby trap.

Cornish hug; wolf in sheep's clothing &c. (*deceiver*) 548; disguise, -ment; false colours, masquerade, mummery, borrowed plumes; *pattes de velours*.

mockery &c. (*imitation*) 19; copy &c. 21; counterfeit, sham, brummagem, make-believe, forgery, fraud, fake; lie &c. 546; 'a mockery, a delusion, and a snare,' hollow mockery.

whited –, painted- sepulchre; tinsel, paste, false jewellery, scagliola, ormolu, German silver, Britannia metal, paint; jerry building; man of straw.

illusion &c. (*error*) 495; *ignis fatuus* &c. 423; mirage &c. 443.

V. deceive, take in; defraud, cheat, jockey, do, cozen, diddle, nab, gyp, chouse, double cross, play one false, bilk, cully, jilt, bite, pluck, swindle, victimize; abuse; mystify; blind one's eyes; blindfold, hoodwink, spoof, bluff; throw dust into the eyes, 'keep the word of promise to the ear and break it to the hope,' 'draw a herring across the trail.'

impose –, practise –, play –, put –, palm –, foist- upon; snatch a verdict.

circumvent, overreach; out-reach, -wit, -manœuvre; steal a march upon, give the go-by to, leave in the lurch.

set –, lay- a -trap, – snare- for; bait the hook, forelay, spread the toils, lime; decoy, waylay, lure, beguile, delude, inveigle; tra-, tre-pan; kidnap; lei-, hook-in; trick; en-, in-trap, -snare, entoil, benet; nick, springe; catch, – in a trap; sniggle, entangle, illaqueate, hocus, practise on one's credulity, dupe, gull, hoax, fool, befool, bamboozle; hum, -bug; gammon, stuff up, dope, sell; play a -trick, – practical joke- upon one; balk, trip up, throw a tub to a whale; fool to the top of one's bent, send on -a wild goose chase, – a fool's errand; make -game, – a fool, – an April fool, – an ass- of; trifle with, cajole, flatter; come over &c. (*influence*) 615; gild the pill, make things pleasant, divert, put a good face upon; dissemble &c. 544.

cog, – the dice, play with marked cards; live by one's wits, play at hide and seek; obtain money under false pretences &c. (*steal*) 791; conjure, juggle, practise chicanery; gerrymander.

play –, palm –, foist –, fob- off.

lie &c. 544; misinform &c. 538; mislead &c. (*error*) 495; betray &c. 940; be -deceived &c. 547.

Adj. deceived &c. *v.*; deceiving &c. *v.*; cunning &c. 702; prestigi-ous, -atory; decept-ive, -ious; deceitful, covinous; delus-ive, -ory; illus-ive, -ory; elusive, insidious, *ad captandum vulgus.*

untrue &c. 546; mock, sham, make-believe, counterfeit, faked, pseudo, spurious, so-called, pretended, feigned, trumped up, bogus, scamped, fraudulent, tricky, factitious, artificial, bastard; surreptitious, illegitimate, contraband, adulterated, sophisticated; unsound, rotten at the core; colourable; disguised; meretricious; tinsel, pinchbeck, plated; catch-penny; Brummagem; simulated &c. 544.

Adv. under -false colours, – the garb of, – cover of; over the left.

Phr. *fronti nulla fides.*

546. Untruth.—N. untruth, falsehood, lie, story, thing that is not, fib, bounce, crammer, taradiddle, whopper.

forgery, fabrication, invention; mis-statement, -representation; per-version, falsification, gloss, *suggestio falsi*; exaggeration &c. 549.

fiction; fable, nursery tale; romance &c. (*imagination*) 515; untrue –, false –, trumped up- -story, – statement; thing devised by the enemy; *canard*; shave, sell, hum, yarn, traveller's tale, Canterbury tale, cock and bull story, fairy tale, clap-trap.

myth, moonshine, bosh, all my eye, -and Betty Martin, mare's nest, farce.

irony; half truth, white lie, pious fraud; mental reservation &c. (*concealment*) 528.

pretence, pretext; false -plea &c. 617; subterfuge, evasion, shift, shuffle, make-believe; sham &c. (*deception*) 545.

profession, empty words; Judas kiss &c. (*hypocrisy*) 544; disguise &c. (*mask*) 530.

V. have a false meaning; not ring true.

pretend, sham, feign, counterfeit, make believe.

Adj. untrue, false, trumped up; void of -, without- foundation; far

from the truth, false as dicer's oaths; unfounded, *ben trovato*, invented,
fabulous, fabricated, forged; fict-, fact-, supposit-, surrept-itious; e-,
il-lusory; ironical; satirical; evasive; *soi-disant* &c. (*misnamed*) 565.

Phr. *se non e vero e ben trovato.*

547. Dupe.—N. dupe, gull, gudgeon,
gobemouche, cull, cully, victim, sucker,
pigeon, April fool; laughing stock &c.
857; Cyclops, simple Simon, flat, mug,
greenhorn; fool &c. 501; puppet, cat's
paw.

V. be -deceived &c. 545, – the dupe
of; fall into a trap; swallow –, nibble
at- the bait; bite; catch a Tartar.

Adj. credulous &c. 486; mistaken
&c. (*error*) 495.

548. Deceiver.—N. deceiver &c.
(deceive &c. 545); dissembler, hypocrite; sophist, Pharisee, Jesuit, Maw-
worm, Pecksniff, Joseph Surface, Tartufe, Janus; serpent, snake in the grass,
cockatrice, Judas, wolf in sheep's
clothing; Molly Maguire; jilt; shuffler.

liar &c. (lie &c. 544); story-teller,
perjurer, false-witness, *menteur à triple
étage*, Scapin.

impostor, pretender, capper, decoy,
fraud, *soi-disant*, humbug; adventurer;
Cagliostro, Fernam Mendez Pinto; ass in lion's skin &c. (*bungler*)
701; actor &c. (*stage player*) 599.

quack, *charlatan*, mountebank, saltimbanco, *saltimbanque*, empiric, quacksalver, medicaster.

conjuror, juggler, magician, necromancer, trickster, prestidigitator, medium, jockey; crimp; decoy-duck, stool pigeon; rogue, knave,
cheat; swindler &c. (*thief*) 792; jobber.

549. Exaggeration.—N. exaggeration; expansion &c. 194; hyperbole,
stretch, strain, colouring; high colouring, caricature, *caricatura*; extravagance &c. (*nonsense*) 497; Baron Munchausen; men in buckram, yarn,
fringe, embroidery, traveller's tale; Pelion upon Ossa.

storm in a teacup; much ado about nothing &c. (*over-estimation*) 482;
puffery &c. (*boasting*) 884; rant &c. (*turgescence*) 577.

figure of speech, *façon de parler*; stretch of -fancy, – the imagination;
flight of fancy &c. (*imagination*) 515.

false colouring &c. (*falsehood*) 544; aggravation &c. 835.

V. exaggerate, magnify, pile up, aggravate; amplify &c. (*expand*)
194; overestimate &c. 482; hyperbolize; over-charge, -state, -draw,
-lay, -shoot the mark, -praise; make -much, – the most- of; strain, – a
point; stretch, – a point; go great lengths; spin a long yarn; draw –,
shoot with- a long-bow; deal in the marvellous.

out-Herod Herod, run riot, talk at random.

heighten, overcolour; colour -highly, – too highly; embroider, *broder*;
flourish; colour &c. (*misrepresent*) 544; puff &c. (*boast*) 884.

Adj. exaggerated &c. *v.*; overwrought; bombastic &c. (*magniloquent*)
577; hyperbolical, on stilts; fabulous, extravagant, preposterous, egregious, *outré*, high-flying.

Adv. hyperbolically &c. *adj.*

Section III. MEANS OF COMMUNICATING IDEAS
1.° *Natural Means*

550. Indication.—N. indication; symbol-ism, -ization; semeio-logy,
-tics; sign of the times.

lineament, feature, *trait*, characteristic, trick, diagnostic; divining-
rod; cloven hoof; footfall; means of recognition; earmark.

sign, symbol; ind-ex, -ice, -icator; point, -er; marker; exponent, note, token, symptom.

type, figure, emblem, cipher, device; representation &c. 554; epigraph, motto, posy.

gest-ure, -iculation; pantomime; wink, glance, leer; nod, shrug, beck; touch, nudge; grip; dactylo-logy, -nomy; freemasonry, telegraphy, chirology, by-play, dumb-show; cue; hint &c. 527; clue, clew, key, scent, track &c. 551.

signal, -post; rocket, blue light; watch-fire, -tower; telegraph, semaphore, flag-staff; cresset, fiery cross; calumet; heliograph, signal-, flash-lamp.

mark, line, stroke, dash, score, stripe, streak, scratch, tick, dot, point, notch, nick, blaze; asterisk, red letter, Italics, heavy type, inverted commas, quotation marks, sublineation, underlining, jotting; print; impr-int, -ess, -ession; note, annotation, mark of exclamation.

[For identification] badge, criterion; counter-check, -mark, -sign, -foil; duplicate, tally; label, tab, ticket, stub, billet, letter, counter, *tessera*, card, bill, check; witness, voucher; stamp; *cachet*; trade -, Hall- mark; broad arrow; signature; address -, visiting- card; *carte de visite*; credentials &c. (*evidence*) 467; passport, identity book; attestation; hand, - writing, sign-manual; cipher; monogram, - mark, seal, sigil, signet; autograph, -y; paraph, brand; superscription; in-, endorsement; title, heading, rubric, docket; *mot -de passe, - du guet*; *passe-parole*; shibboleth; watch-, catch-, pass-word; open *sesame*.

insignia; banner, -et, -ol; bandrol; flag, colours, streamer, standard, eagle, labarum, oriflamb, *oriflamme*; figure-head; ensign; pen-non, -nant, -dant; burgee, blue Peter, jack, ancient, gonfalon, union-jack; tricolour, stars and stripes; bunting.

heraldry, crest; coat of -, arms; armorial bearings, hatchment; e-, scutcheon; shield, supporters; livery, uniform; cockade, *epaulette*, brassard, chevron; garland, chaplet, love-knot, fillet, favour.

[Of locality] beacon, cairn, post, staff, flagstaff, hand, pointer, vane, cock, weathercock; guide-, hand-, finger-, directing-, sign-post; pillars of Hercules, pharos, signal fire; land-, sea-mark; lighthouse, balize; pole-, load-, lode-star; cynosure, guide; address, direction, name; sign, -board.

[Of the future] warning &c. 668; omen &c. 512; prefigurement &c. 511. [Of the past] trace record &c. 551. [Of danger] warning &c. 668; alarm &c. 669. [Of authority] sceptre &c. 747. [Of triumph] trophy &c. 733. [Of quantity] gauge &c. 466. [Of distance] mile-stone, -post. [Of disgrace] brand, fool's cap, stigma, mark of Cain. [For detection] check, tell-tale; test &c. (*experiment*) 463.

notification &c. (*information*) 527; advertisement &c. (*publication*) 531.

word of command, call; bugle-, trumpet-call; reveille, taps; bell, alarum, cry; battle -, rallying- cry.

church, bell, angelus, sacring bell; muezzin.

exposition &c. (*explanation*) 522; proof &c. (*evidence*) 463; pattern &c. (*prototype*) 22.

V. indicate; be the -sign &c. *n.*- of; denote, betoken; argue, testify &c. (*evidence*) 467; bear the -impress &c. *n.*- of; con-note, -notate.

represent, stand for; typify &c. (*prefigure*) 511; symbolize.

put -an indication, - a mark, - &c. *n.*; note, mark, tick, blaze, stamp, earmark; set one's seal upon; label, ticket, docket; dot, spot, score, dash, trace, chalk; print; im-print, -press, surprint; engrave, stereotype, electrotype.

make a -sign &c. *n.*; signalize; give –, hang out- a signal; beck, -on; gesture; nod; wink, glance, leer, nudge, shrug, tip the wink; gesticulate; raise –, hold up- the -finger, – hand; saw the air, suit the action to the word.

wave –, unfurl –, hoist –, hang out- a banner &c. *n.*; wave -the hand, – a kerchief; give the cue &c. (*inform*) 527; show one's colours; give –, sound- an alarm; beat the drum, sound the trumpets, raise a cry.

sign, seal, attest &c. (*evidence*) 467; underline &c. (*give importance to*) 642; call attention to &c. (*attention*) 457; give notice &c. (*inform*) 527.

Adj. indicat-ing &c. *v.*, -ive, -ory; de-, con-notative; diacritical, representative, typical, symbolic, pantomimic, pathognomonic, symptomatic, ominous, characteristic, demonstrative, diagnostic, exponential, emblematic, armorial; individual &c. (*special*) 79.

known –, recognizable- by; indicated &c. *v.*; pointed, marked.

[Capable of being denoted] denotable; indelible.

Adv. in token of; symbolically &c. *adj.*; in dumb show.

Phr. *ecce signum; ex ungue leonem, ex pede Herculem.*

---

551. Record.—**N.** trace, vestige, relic, remains; scar, *cicatrix*; foot-step, -mark, -print; track, mark, wake, trail, spoor, scent, *piste.*

monument, hatchment, escutcheon, slab, tablet, trophy, achievement; obelisk, pillar, column, monolith, cromlech, dolmen; memorial; *memento* &c. (*memory*) 505; testimonial, medal, ribbon, order; commemoration &c. (*celebration*) 883.

record, note, minute; *dossier*; register, -try; census, roll &c. (*list*) 86; cartulary, diptych, Domesday book; entry, memorandum, indorsement, inscription, copy, duplicate, docket; notch &c. (*mark*) 550; muniment, deed &c. (*security*) 771; document; deposition, *procès-verbal*; affidavit; certificate &c. (*evidence*) 467.

552. [Suppression of sign.] Obliteration.—**N.** obliteration; erasure, rasure; effacement; cancel, -lation; cassation; circumduction; deletion, blot; *tabula rasa.*

V. efface, obliterate, erase, rase, expunge, cancel; blot –, take –, rub –, scratch –, strike –, wipe –, wash –, sponge- out; wipe –, rub- off; wipe away; deface, render illegible; draw the pen through, apply the sponge.

be -effaced &c.; leave no -trace &c. 449; 'leave not a rack behind.'

Adj. obliterated &c. *v.*; out of print; printless; leaving no trace; intestate; un-recorded, -registered, -written.

Int. *dele*; out with it!

---

note-, memorandum-, pocket-, commonplace-book; portfolio; scoring-board, -sheet; bulletin board; card index, file; pigeon-holes, *excerpta, adversaria*, jottings, dottings.

gazette, -er; newspaper, magazine &c. 531; alman-ac, -ack; calendar, ephemeris, noctuary, diary, log, journal, account-, cash-, day-book, ledger.

archive, scroll, state-paper, Congressional Record, return, bluebook; statistics &c. 86; *compte rendu*; Acts –, Transactions –, Proceedings- of; Hansard's Debates; chronicle, annals; legend; history, biography &c. 594.

registration; en-, in-rolment; tabulation; entry, booking; signature &c. (*identification*) 550; recorder &c. 553; journalism.

drawing, photograph &c. 554; phonograph –, gramophone-record; music roll.

V. record; put –, place- upon record; go on record; chronicle, calendar, hand down to posterity; keep up the memory of &c. (*remember*) 505; commemorate &c. (*celebrate*) 883; report &c. (*inform*) 527; commit to –, reduce to- writing; put –, set down- -in writing, – in black and white; put –, jot –, take –, write –, note –, set- down; note, minute, put on paper; take –, make- a -note, – minute, – memorandum; make a return.

mark &c. (*indicate*) 550; sign &c. (*attest*) 467.

enter, book; post, – up; insert, make an entry of; mark –, tick-off; register, list, docket, enroll, inscroll; file &c. (*store*) 636.

Adv. on record.

553. Recorder.—N. recorder, notary, clerk; regis-trar, -trary, -ter; prothonotary; amanuensis, secretary, scribe, stenographer, remem-brancer, book-keeper, *custos rotulorum*, Master of the Rolls.

annalist; histori-an, -ographer; chronicler, journalist, reporter, col-umnist; biographer &c. (*narrator*) 594; antiquary &c. (*antiquity*) 122; memorialist.

draughtsman &c. 559; engraver 558; photographer, cinematographer, camera man.

Recording instrument, recorder, camera, phonograph, gramophone, dictaphone, telegraphone, telautograph, printing telegraph, tape ma-chine, ticker, time recorder, cash register, turnstile, speedometer, voting machine, seismograph, photostat.

554. Representation.—N. represent--ation, -ment; imitation &c. 19; illus-tration, delineation, depictment, por-trayal; imagery, portraiture, iconog-raphy; design, -ing; art, fine arts; painting &c. 556; sculpture &c. 557; engraving &c. 558; photography, radi-ography, skiagraphy.

person-ation, -ification; impersona-tion; drama &c. 599.

555. Misrepresentation.—N. mis-representation, distortion, exaggera-tion; daubing &c. *v.*; bad likeness, daub, sign-painting; scratch, carica-ture; *anamorphosis*.

V. misrepresent, distort, overdraw, travesty, parody, burlesque, exagger-ate, caricature, daub.

Adj. misrepresented &c. *v.*

picture, drawing, sketch, draught, draft; tracing; copy &c. 21; photo-, helio-graph; daguerreo-, talbo-, calo-, helio-type; cabinet, *carte-de-visite*, snapshot; X-ray photo-graph; radio-gram, -graph, skia-graph, -gram.

image, likeness, icon, portrait; striking –, speaking- likeness; very image; effigy, fac-simile.

figure, – head; puppet, doll, *figurine*, aglet, manikin, lay-figure, model, *marionnette*, *fantoccini*, bust; waxwork, statue, -tte, auto-maton, Robot.

hieroglyphic, anaglyph; dia-, mono-gram, -graph.

map, plan, chart; ground plan, projection, elevation; ichno-, carto-graphy; atlas; outline, scheme; view &c. (*painting*) 556.

artist, draughtsman &c. 559.

V. represent, delineate; depict, -ure; portray; picture; take –, catch- a likeness &c. *n.*; hit off, photograph, daguerreotype; figure; shadow -forth, – out; adumbrate; body forth; describe &c. 594; trace, copy; mould.

dress up; illustrate, symbolize.

paint &c. 556; carve &c. 557; engrave &c. 558.

person-ate, -ify; impersonate; assume a character; pose as; act;

play &c. (*drama*) 599; mimic &c. (*imitate*) 19; hold the mirror up to nature.

Adj. represent-ing &c. *v.*, -ative; illustrative; represented &c. *v.*; imitative, figurative.

like &c. 17; graphic &c. (*descriptive*) 594.

556. Painting.—N. painting; depicting; drawing &c. *v.*; design; perspective, skiagraphy; *chiaroscuro* &c. (*light*) 420; composition; treatment, values, atmosphere, tone, technique.

historical –, portrait –, miniature –, landscape –, marine –, flower –, scene- painting; scenography.

school, style; the grand style, high art, *genre*, portraiture; ornamental art &c. 847.

mono-, poly-chrome; *grisaille*.

pallet, palette; easel; brush, pencil, stump; blacklead, charcoal, crayons, chalk, pastel; paint &c. (*colouring matter*) 428; water-, body-, oil-colour; oils, oil-paint; varnish &c. 356a; *gouache*, tempera, distemper, fresco, water-glass; enamel; encaustic painting; *graffito, gesso*; mosaic; tapestry.

picture, painting, piece, *tableau*, canvas; oil &c.- painting; fresco, cartoon; easel –, cabinet- picture; drawing, draught, draft; pencil &c. –, watercolour- drawing; sketch, outline; study.

portrait &c. (*representation*) 554; whole –, full –, half- length; kitcat, head; miniature; shade, *silhouette*; profile.

landscape, sea-piece, -scape; view, scene, prospect; interior; bird's-eye view; pan-, di-orama; still life.

picture –, art- gallery; *studio, atelier*.

V. paint, design, limn, draw, sketch, pencil, scratch, shade, stipple, hatch, dash off, chalk out, square up; colour, dead-colour, wash, varnish; draw in -pencil &c. *n.*; paint in -oils &c. *n.*; stencil; depict &c. (*represent*) 554.

Adj. painted &c. *v.*; pictorial, graphic, picturesque, decorative; classical, romantic, pre-Raphaelite, modern, cubist, futurist, vorticist.

pencil, oil &c. *n.*

Adv. in -pencil &c. *n.*

Phr. *fecit, delineavit.*

557. Sculpture.—N. sculpture, insculpture; carving &c. *v.*; statuary ceramics, plastic arts.

high –, low –, bas- relief; relievo; *basso-, alto-, mezzo-relievo; intaglio* anaglyph; medal, -lion; *cameo*.

marble, bronze, *terra cotta*; ceramic ware, pottery, porcelain, china, earthenware, faïence, enamel, *cloisonné*.

statue &c. (*image*) 554; cast &c. (*copy*) 21; glyptotheca.

V. sculpture, carve, cut, chisel, model, mould; cast.

Adj. sculptured &c. *v.*; in relief, anaglyptic, ceroplastic, ceramic; parian; marble &c. *n.*

558. Engraving.—N. engraving, chalcography; line –, mezzotint –, stipple –, chalk- engraving; dry-point, bur; etching, aquatinta; plate –, copper-plate –, steel –, wood-, process-, photo-engraving; xylo-, ligno-, glypto-, cero-, litho-, chromolitho-, photolitho-, zinco-, glypho- -graphy, -graph.

impression, print, engraving, plate; steel-, copper-plate; etching; mezzo-, aqua-, litho-tint; cut, woodcut, block; stereo-, grapho-, auto-, helio-type; half-tone; *photogravure, rotogravure*.

graver, *burin*, etching-point, style; plate, stone, wood-block, negative; die, punch, stamp.

printing; plate –, copper-plate –, intaglio –, anastatic –, lithographic –, colour –, three colour- printing; type-printing &c. 591.

illustr-, illumin-ation; *vignette*, initial letter, *cul de lampe*, tail-piece.

V. engrave, grave, stipple, scrape, etch; bite, – in; lithograph &c. *n.*; print.

Adj. insculptured; engraved &c. *v.*

Phr. *sculpsit, imprimit.*

559. Artist.—N. artist; painter, limner, drawer, sketcher, delineator; cartoon-, caricatur-ist, designer, engraver; draughtsman; copyist; enamel-ler, -list.

historical –, landscape –, genre –, marine –, flower –, portrait –, miniature –, scene –, sign- painter; engraver; Apelles; sculptor, carver, chaser, modeller, lapidary, *figuriste*, statuary; Phidias, Praxiteles; Royal Academician.

photographer, retoucher.

2°. *Conventional Means*
1. *Language generally*

560. Language.—N. language; phraseology &c. 569; speech &c. 582; tongue, lingo, vernacular, slang; mother –, vulgar –, native- tongue; household words; King's *or* Queen's English; idiom; dialect &c. 563.

volapuk, esperanto, ido, occidental, Ro.

confusion of tongues, Babel, *pasigraphie*; pantomime &c. (*signs*) 550; *onomatopœia*.

phil-, gloss-, glott-ology; linguistics, chrestomathy; paleo-logy; -graphy; comparative grammar.

literature, letters, polite literature, *belles lettres*, muses, humanities, *literæ humaniores*, republic of letters, dead languages, classics; genius of a language; scholarship &c. (*knowledge*) 490.

linguist &c. (*scholar*) 492.

V. speak, say, express by words &c. 566.

Adj. lingu-al, -istic; dialectic; vernacular, current, colloquial, slangy; bilingual, polyglot; literary.

561. Letter.—N. letter; character; hieroglyphic &c. (*writing*) 590; type &c. (*printing*) 591; capitals; majus-, minus-cule; alphabet, ABC, abecedary, Christ-cross-row.

consonant, vowel, diphthong; mute, surd; sonant, liquid, labial, dental, palatal, guttural.

syllable; mono-, dis-, poly-syllable; affix, prefix, suffix.

spelling, orthography; phon-ography, -etic spelling; ana-, meta-grammatism.

cipher, monogram, anagram; double –, acrostic.

V. spell.

Adj. literal; alphabetical, abecedarian; syllabic; uncial &c. (*writing*) 590; phonetic, voiced, mute &c. *n.*

562. Word.—N. word, term, vocable; name &c. 564; phrase &c. 566; root, etymon; derivative; part of speech &c. (*grammar*) 567.

dictionary, vocabulary, word book,

563. Neology.—N. neolo-gy, -gism; new-fangled expression; barbarism; caconym; archaism, black letter, monk-ish Latin; corruption; missaying, an-tiphrasis.

lexicon, index, glossary, thesaurus, *gradus, delectus,* concordance.

etymology, lexicology, derivation; phonology, orthoepy; gloss-, termin-, orism-ology; paleology &c. (*philology*) 560; comparative philology.

lexicograph-er, -y; glossographer &c. (*scholar*) 492; etymologist; logolept.

verbosity, verbiage, loquacity &c. 584.

Adj. verbal, literal; titular, nominal. [Similarly derived] conjugate, paronymous; derivative.

Adv. verbally &c. *adj.*; *verbatim* &c. (*exactly*) 494.

paronomasia, play upon words; word-play &c. (*wit*) 842; *double-entente* &c. (*ambiguity*) 520; palindrome, paragram, clinch; abuse of -language, – terms.

dialect, brogue, *patois,* provincialism, broken English, *lingua franca*; Brit-, Gall-, Scott-, Hibern-icism; Americanism; Gipsy lingo, Romany, pidgin English.

dog Latin, macaronics, gibberish, confusion of tongues, Babel; jargon.

colloquialism &c. (*figure of speech*) 521; by-word; technicality, lingo, slang, cant, *argot,* St. Giles's Greek, thieves' Latin, peddler's French, flash tongue, Billingsgate, Wall Street slang.

pseudonym &c. (*misnomer*) 565; Mr. So-and-so; what d'ye call 'em, what's his name; thingum-my, -bob; *je ne sais quoi.*

neologist, coiner of words.

V. coin words.

Adj. neologic, -al; rare; archaic; obsolete &c. (*old*) 124; colloquial, dialectic, slang, cant.

---

564. Nomenclature. — N. nomenclature; naming &c. *v.*; nuncupation, nomination, baptism; orismology; *onomatopœia*; antonomasia.

name; appella-tion, -tive; designation; title; head, -ing, caption; denomination; by-name, epithet.

style, proper name; præ-, ag-, cognomen; patronymic, surname; cognomination; compellation, description; empty -title, – name; handle to one's name; namesake, eponym.

synonym, antonym.

term, expression, noun; by-word; convertible terms &c. 522; technical term; cant &c. 563.

V. name, call, term, denominate, designate, style, entitle, intitule, clepe, dub, christen, baptize, nickname, characterize, specify, define, distinguish by the name of; label &c. (*mark*) 550.

be -called &c. *v.*; take –, bear –, go (*or* be known) by –, go (*or* pass) under –, rejoice in- the name of.

Adj. named &c. *v.*; hight, yclept, known as; what one may -well, – fairly, – properly, – fitly- call.

nuncupa-tory, -tive; cognominal, titular, nominal; orismological.

565. Misnomer.—N. misnomer; *lucus a non lucendo*; Mrs. Malaprop; what d'ye call 'em &c. (*neologism*) 563.

nickname, *sobriquet,* by-name, handle, moniker; assumed -name, – title; *alias; nom de -guerre, – plume, – théâtre*; pseudonym, pen name, stage name.

V. mis-name, -call, -term; nickname; assume -a name, – an alias.

Adj. misnamed &c. *v.*; pseudonymous; *soi-disant*; self-called, -styled, -christened; so-called.

nameless, anonymous; without a –, having no- name; innominate, unnamed.

Adv. in no sense.

---

566. Phrase.—N. phrase, expression, set phrase; sentence, paragraph; figure of speech &c. 521; idi-om, -otism; turn of expression.

paraphrase &c. (*synonym*) 522; periphrase &c. (*circumlocution*) 573; motto &c. (*proverb*) 496.

phraseology &c. 569.

V. express, phrase; word, – it; give -words, – expression- to; voice; arrange in –, clothe in –, put into –, express by- words; couch in terms; find words to express; speak by the card.

Adj. expressed &c. *v.*; idiomatic.

Adv. in -round, – set, – good, set- terms; in set phrases.

567. Grammar.—**N.** grammar, accidence, syntax, *praxis*, analysis, paradigm, punctuation; parts of speech; inflexion, case, declension, conjugation; *jus et norma loquendi*; Lindley Murray &c. (*school-book*) 542; correct style; philology &c. (*language*) 560.

V. parse, analyze; decline, conjugate; punctuate.

Adj. grammatical; syntactic; inflexional.

568. Solecism.—**N.** solecism; bad -, false –, faulty- grammar; slip, error; slip of the -pen, – tongue; *lapsus calami-, – linguæ; faux pas*; slip-slop; bull.

V. use -bad, – faulty- grammar; solecize, commit a solecism; murder the -King's, – Queen's- English; break Priscian's head.

Adj. ungrammatical; in-correct, -accurate; faulty, improper, incongruous, abnormal.

569. Style.—**N.** style, diction, phraseology, wording; manner, strain; composition; mode of expression, choice of words, literary power, ready pen, pen of a ready writer; command of language &c. (*eloquence*) 582; authorship; *la morgue littéraire*.

V. express by words &c. 566; write.

Various Qualities of Style

570. Perspicuity.—**N.** perspicuity &c. (*intelligibility*) 518; plain speaking &c. (*manifestation*) 525; defin-iteness, -ition; exactness &c. 494; perspicuousness, logical acuteness.

Adj. lucid &c. (*intelligible*) 518; explicit &c. (*manifest*) 525; exact &c. 494.

571. Obscurity.—**N.** obscurity &c. (*unintelligibility*) 519; involution; hard words; ambiguity &c. 520; vagueness &c. 475, inexactness &c. 495; what d'ye call 'em &c. (*neologism*) 563; cloudiness, confusion.

Adj. obscure &c. *n.*; crabbed, involved, confused.

572. Conciseness.—**N.** conciseness &c. *adj.*; brevity, 'the soul of wit,' laconism; Tacitus; ellipsis; syncope; abridgment &c. (*shortening*) 201; compression &c. 195; epitome &c. 596; monostitch; portmanteau word, telescope word, protogram.

V. be -concise &c. *adj.*; condense &c. 195; abridge &c. 201; abstract &c. 596; come to the point.

Adj. concise, brief, short, terse, close; to the point, exact; neat, compact, condensed, pointed; laconic, curt, pithy, trenchant, summary; pregnant; compendious &c. (*compendium*) 596; succinct; elliptical, epigrammatic, crisp, sententious.

Adv. concisely &c. *adj.*; briefly,

573. Diffuseness.—**N.** diffuseness &c. *adj.*; amplification &c. *v.*; dilating &c. *v.*; verbosity, *verbiage,* wordiness, cloud of words, *copia verborum*; flow of words &c. (*loquacity*) 584.

poly-, tauto-, batto-, perisso-logy; pleonasm, exuberance, redundance; thrice-told tale; prolixity; circumlocution, *ambages*; periphra-se, -sis; roundabout phrases; episode; expletive; penny-a-lining; padding, drivel, twaddle, rigmarole; richness &c. 577.

V. be -diffuse &c. *adj.*; run out on, descant, expatiate, enlarge, dilate, amplify, expand, inflate, pad; launch –, branch- out; rant.

maunder, prose; harp upon &c. (*repeat*) 104; dwell on, insist upon.

summarily; in -brief, – short, – a word, – few words, – a nutshell; for shortness sake; to -come to the point, – make a long story short, – cut the matter short, – be brief; it comes to this, the long and the short of it is.

digress, ramble, *battre la campagne,* beat about the bush, perorate, spin a long yarn, protract; spin –, swell –, draw- out, drivel.

Adj. dif-, pro-fuse; wordy, verbose, largiloquent, copious, exuberant, effusive, pleonastic, lengthy; long, -some, -winded, -spun, -drawn out; diffusive, spun out, protracted, prolix, prosing, maundering; circumlocutory, periphrastic, ambagious, roundabout; digressive; dis-, ex-cursive; rambling, episodic; flatulent, frothy.

Adv. diffusely &c. *adj.*; at large, *in extenso*; about it and about it.

574. Vigour.—N. vigour, power, force; boldness, raciness &c. *adj.*; spirit, point, antithesis, piquancy; *verve*, glow, fire, warmth, ardour, enthusiasm; 'thoughts that breathe and words that burn'; strong language; punch; gravity, sententiousness; elevation, loftiness, sublimity.

eloquence; command of -words, – language.

Adj. vigorous, nervous, powerful, forcible, trenchant, mordant, biting, incisive, impressive; sensational.

spirited, lively, glowing, sparkling, racy, bold, slashing; pungent, *piquant,* full of point, pointed, pithy, antithetical; sententious.

lofty, elevated, sublime, grand, weighty, ponderous; eloquent; vehement, petulant, impassioned; poetic.

Adv. in -glowing, – good set, – no measured- terms.

575. Feebleness.—N. feebleness &c. *adj.*

Adj. feeble, bald, tame, meagre, insipid, nerveless, jejune, vapid, trashy, cold, frigid, poor, dull, dry, languid; pros-ing, -y, -aic; unvaried, monotonous, weak, frail, washy, wishy-washy, sloppy; sketchy, slight; careless, slovenly, loose, lax; slip-shod, -slop; inexact; dis-jointed, -connected; puerile, childish; flatulent; rambling &c. (*diffuse*) 573.

576. Plainness.—N. plainness &c. *adj.*; simplicity, severity; plain -terms, – English; Saxon English; household words.

V. speak plainly; call a spade 'a spade'; plunge *in medias res*; come to the point.

Adj. plain, simple; un-ornamented, -adorned, -varnished; home-ly, -spun; neat; severe, chaste, pure, Saxon; commonplace, matter of fact, natural, prosaic, sober, unimaginative.

dry, unvaried, monotonous &c. 575.

Adv. in plain -terms, – words, – English, – common parlance; point blank.

577. Ornament. — N. ornament; floridness &c. *adj.*; turg-idity, -escence; altiloquence &c. *adj.*; orotundity; declamation, teratology; well-rounded periods; elegance &c. 578.

inversion, antithesis, alliteration, *paronomasia*; figurativeness &c. (*metaphor*) 521.

flourish; flowers of -speech, – rhetoric; euph-uism, -emism.

big-, high-sounding words; macrology, *sesquipedalia verba*, sesquipedalianism; Alexandrine; inflation, pretension; rant, bombast, fustian, bunkum, balderdash, prose run mad; fine writing; Minerva press.

phrasemonger; euph-uist, -emist.

V. ornament, overlay with ornament, overcharge; smell of the lamp.

Adj. ornamented &c. *v.*; beautified &c. 847; ornate, florid, rich, flowery; euph-uistic, -emistic; sonorous; high-, big-sounding; inflated, swelling, tumid; turg-id, -escent; pedantic, pompous, stilted;

high-flown, -flowing; sententious, rhetorical, declamatory; grandiose; grand-, magn-, alt-iloquent; sesquipedal, -ian; Johnsonian, mouthy; bombastic; fustian; frothy, flashy, flaming, flamboyant.

antithetical, alliterative; figurative &c. 521; artificial &c. (*inelegant*) 579.

Adv. *ore rotundo*; with rounded phrase.

578. Elegance.—N. elegance, purity, grace, ease, felicity, distinction, gracefulness, refinement, readiness &c. *adj.*; concinnity, euphony, numerosity, balance, rhythm, symmetry, proportion; restraint; good taste, propriety.

well rounded –, well turned –, flowing- periods; the right word in the right place; antithesis &c. 577.

purist, stylist.

V. point an antithesis, round a period.

Adj. elegant, polished, classical, Attic, correct, Ciceronian, artistic; chaste, pure, Saxon, academical.

graceful, easy, readable, fluent, flowing, tripping; unaffected, natural, unlaboured; mellifluous; euph-onious, -emistic; rhythmical, balanced, symmetrical.

felicitous, happy, neat; well –, neatly- -put, – expressed.

579. Inelegance. — N. inelegance; vulgarity, bad taste; stiffness &c. *adj.*; unlettered Muse; barbarism; slang &c. 563; solecism &c. 568; mannerism &c. (*affectation*) 855; euphuism; fustian &c. 577; cacophony; want of balance; words that -break the teeth, – dislocate the jaw.

V. be -inelegant &c. *adj.*

Adj. inelegant, graceless, ungraceful, unpolished; harsh, abrupt; dry, stiff, cramped, formal, *guindé*; forced, laboured, awkward; artificial, mannered, ponderous; turgid &c. 577; affected, euphuistic; barbarous, uncouth, grotesque, rude, crude, halting; vulgar, offensive to ears polite.

---

2. *Spoken Language*

580. Voice.—N. voice; vocality; organ, lungs, bellows; good –, fine –, powerful &c. (*loud*) 404 –, musical &c. 413- voice; intonation; tone &c. (*sound*) 402- of voice.

vocalization; cry &c. 411; strain, utterance, prolation; exclam-, ejacul-, vocifer-ation; enunci-, articul-ation; articulate sound, distinctness; clearness, – of articulation; stage whisper; delivery; attack.

accent, -uation; emphasis, stress; broad –, strong –, pure –, native –, foreign- accent; pronunciation.

[Word similarly pronounced] homonym.

orthoepy; euphony &c. (*melody*) 413.

gastri-, ventri-loquism; ventriloquist; polyphon-ism, -ist.

[Science of voice] phonology &c. (*sound*) 402.

V. sing, speak, utter, breathe, voice; give -utterance, – tongue; cry &c.

581. Aphony.—N. aphony, *aphonia*; dumbness &c. *adj.*; obmutescence; absence –, want- of voice; dysphony; silence &c. (*taciturnity*) 585; raucity; harsh &c. 410 –, unmusical &c. 414- voice; *falsetto*, 'childish treble'; mute, dummy, deaf mute.

V. keep silence &c. 585; speak -low, – softly; whisper &c. (*faintness*) 405.

silence; render -mute, – silent &c. 403; muzzle, muffle, suppress, smother, gag, strike dumb, dumb-found, -founder; drown the voice, put to silence, stop one's mouth, cut one short. stick in the throat.

Adj. aphon-ous, -ic, dumb, mute; deaf-mute, – and dumb; mum; tongue-tied; breath-, tongue-, voice-, speech-, word-less; mute as a -fish, – stockfish, – mackerel; silent &c. (*taciturn*) 585; muzzled; in-articulate, -audible.

croaking, raucous, hoarse, husky,

(*shout*) 411; ejaculate, rap out; vocalize, prolate, articulate, enunciate, enounce, pronounce, accentuate, aspirate, deliver, mouth; emit, murmur, whisper, – in the ear, croon, yodel.

Adj. vocal, phonetic, oral; ejaculatory, articulate, distinct, stertorous; enunciative; accentuated, aspirated; euphonious &c. (*melodious*) 413.

582. Speech.—N. speech, faculty of speech; locution, talk, parlance, verbal intercourse, prolation, oral communication, word of mouth, *parole*, palaver, prattle; effusion.

oration, recitation, delivery, say, address, speech, lecture, harangue, sermon, *tirade*, screed, formal speech, salutatory, peroration; prelection; speechifying; soliloquy &c. 589; allocution &c. 586; interlocution &c. 588.

oratory; elo-cution, -quence; rhetoric, declamation; grandi-, multi-loquence; burst of eloquence; facundity; talkativeness; flow –, command-of -words, – language; *copia verborum*; power of speech, gift of the gab; *usus loquendi*.

speaker &c. *v.*; spokesman; pro-, inter-locutor; mouthpiece, Hermes; ora-tor, -trix, -tress; Demosthenes, Cicero; rhetorician; stump –, platform-orator, tub-thumper; elocutionist; speech-maker, patterer, *improvisatore*.

V. speak, – of; say, utter, pronounce, deliver, give utterance to; utter –, pour- forth; breathe, let fall, come out with; rap –, blurt- out; have on one's lips; have at the -end, – tip- of one's tongue.

break silence; open one's -lips, – mouth; lift –, raise- one's voice; give –, wag the- tongue; talk, outspeak; put in a word or two.

hold forth; make –, deliver- -a speech &c. *n.*; speechify, harangue, declaim, stump, flourish, spout, rant, recite, lecture, preach, sermonize, discourse, be on one's legs; have –, say- one's say; expatiate &c. (*speak at length*) 573; speak one's mind.

soliloquize &c. 589; tell &c. (*inform*) 527; speak to &c. 586; talk together &c. 588.

be -eloquent &c. *adj.*; have -a tongue in one's head, – the gift of the gab &c. *n.*

pass –, escape- one's lips; fall from the -lips, – mouth.

Adj. speaking &c., spoken &c. *v.*; oral, lingual, phonetic, not written, unwritten, outspoken; elo-quent, -cutionary; orat-, rhet-orical; declamatory; grandiloquent &c. 577; talkative &c. 584.

dry, hollow, sepulchral, hoarse as a raven.

Adv. with -bated breath, – the finger on the lips; *sotto voce*; in a -low tone, – cracked voice, – broken voice; in an aside.

Phr. *vox faucibus hæsit.*

---

583. [Imperfect Speech.] Stammering.—N. inarticulateness; stammering &c. *v.*; hesitation &c. *v.*; impediment in one's speech; aphasia, titubancy, traulism; whisper &c. (*faint sound*) 405; lisp, drawl, tardiloquence; nasal -tone, – accent; twang; *falsetto* &c. (*want of voice*) 581; broken -voice, – accents, – sentences.

brogue &c. 563; slip of the tongue, *lapsus linguæ.*

V. stammer, stutter, hesitate, falter, hammer; balbu-tiate, -cinate; haw, hum and haw, be unable to put two words together.

mumble, mutter; maund, -er; whisper &c. 405; mince, lisp; jabber, gabble, gibber; sp-, spl-utter; muffle, mump; drawl, mouth; croak; speak -thick, – through the nose; snuffle, clip one's words; murder the -language, – King's (*or* Queen's) English; mis-pronounce, -say.

Adj. stammering &c. *v.*; inarticulate, guttural, nasal; tremulous.

Adv. *sotto voce* &c. (*faintly*) 405.

Adv. orally &c. *adj.*; by word of mouth, *vivâ voce*, from the lips of.
Phr. quoth -, said- he &c.

584. Loquacity. — N. loquac-ity, -iousness; talkativeness &c. *adj.*; garrulity; multiloquence, much speaking, effusion, wordiness.

jaw; gab, -ble; jabber, chatter; prate, prattle, cackle, clack; twaddle, twattle, rattle; *caquet, -terie*; blabber, *bavardage*, bibble-babble, gibble-gabble; small talk &c. (*converse*) 588.

fluency, flippancy, volubility, flowing tongue; flow, - of words; *flux de -bouche, - mots, - paroles; copia verborum, cacoëthes loquendi*; verbosity &c. (*diffuseness*) 573; gift of the gab &c. (*eloquence*) 582.

talker; chatter-er, -box; babbler &c. *v.*; rattle; ranter; sermonizer, proser, driveller; wind bag; gossip &c. (*converse*) 588; magpie, jay, parrot, poll, Babel; *moulin à paroles*.

V. be -loquacious &c. *adj.*; talk glibly, pour forth, patter; prate, palaver, prose, chatter, prattle, clack, jabber, jaw; rattle, - on; twaddle, twattle; babble, gabble; out-talk; talk oneself -out of breath, - hoarse; maunder, gush, blatter; talk a donkey's hind leg off; expatiate &c. (*speak at length*) 573; gossip &c. (*converse*) 588; din in the ears &c. (*repeat*) 104; talk -at random, - nonsense &c. 497; be hoarse with talking.

Adj. loquacious, talkative, conversational, garrulous, linguacious, multiloquous; chattering &c. *v.*; chatty &c. (*sociable*) 892; declamatory &c. 582; open-mouthed.

fluent, voluble, glib, flippant; long-tongued, -winded &c. (*diffuse*) 573.

Adv. trippingly on the tongue; glibly &c. *adj.*
Phr. the tongue running -fast, - loose, - on wheels.

585. Taciturnity.—N. silence, muteness, obmutescence; taciturnity, pauciloquy, costiveness, curtness; reserve, reticence &c. (*concealment*) 528; *aposiopesis*.

man of few words.

V. be -silent &c. *adj.*; keep silence; hold one's -tongue, - peace, - jaw; not speak &c. 582; say nothing; seal -, close -, put a padlock on- the -lips, - mouth; put a bridle on one's tongue; keep one's tongue between one's teeth; make no sign, not let a word escape one; keep a secret &c. 528; not have a word to say; lay -, place- the finger on the lips; render mute &c. 581.

stick in one's throat.

Adj. silent, mute, mum; silent as -a post, - a stone, - the grave &c. (*still*) 403; dumb &c. 581.

taciturn, sparing of words; close, - mouthed, - tongued; laconic, costive, inconversable, curt; reserved; reticent &c. (*concealing*) 528.

Int. tush! silence! mum! hush! *chut!* hist! tut! &c. 403.

---

586. Allocution. — N. allocution, alloquy, address; speech &c. 582; apostrophe, interpellation, appeal, invocation, salutation; word in the ear.

[Feigned dialogue] dialogism.

platform &c. 542; audience &c. (*interview*) 588.

V. speak to, address, accost, make up to, apostrophize, appeal to, invoke; hail, salute; call to, halloo.

take -aside, - by the button, button-hole; talk to in private.

lecture &c. (*make a speech*) 582.

Int. soho! halloo! hey! hist! hi!

587. Response &c., *see* Answer 462;

---

588. Interlocution.—N. interlocution; collocution, colloquy, converse, conversation, confabulation, talk, discourse, verbal intercourse; communion, oral communication, commerce; dia-, duo-, tria-logue.

causerie, chat, chit-chat; small –, table –, teatable –, town –, village –, idle- talk; tattle, gossip, tittle-tattle; babble, -ment; *tripotage*, cackle, prittle-prattle, *on dit*; talk of the -town, – village.

conference, parley, interview, audience, *pourparler*; *tête-à-tête*; reception, *conversazione*; congress &c. (*council*) 696; pow-wow.

hall of audience, *durbar*, coliseum, assembly hall, auditorium.

palaver, debate, logomachy, war of words, controversy.

talker, gossip, tattler; Paul Pry; tabby; chatterer &c. (*loquacity*) 584; interlocutor &c. (*spokesman*) 582; conversation-ist, -alist; dialogist.

'the feast of reason and the flow of soul'; *mollia tempora fandi*.

V. talk together, converse, confabulate; hold –, carry on –, join in –, engage in- a conversation; put in a word; shine in conversation; bandy words; parley; palaver; chat, gossip, tattle; prate &c. (*loquacity*) 584.

discourse –, confer –, commune –, commerce- with; hold -converse, – conference, – intercourse; talk it over; be closeted with; talk with one -in private, – *tête-à-tête*.

Adj. conversing &c. *v.*; interlocutory; convers-ational, -able; discursive, -çoursive; chatty &c. (*sociable*) 892; colloquial, *tête-à-tête*, confabulatory.

589. Soliloquy.—N. soliloquy, monologue, apostrophe.

solilo-quist, -quizer, monologist.

V. soliloquize; say –, talk- to oneself; say aside, think aloud, apostrophize.

Adj. soliloquizing &c. *v.*

Adv. aside.

---

3. *Written Language*

590. Writing.—N. writing &c. *v.*; chiro-, stelo-, cero-graphy, graphology; stylography; pen-craft, -script, -manship; quill-driving; typewriting.

writing, manuscript, MS., *literæ scriptæ*; these presents.

stroke –, dash- of the pen; *coup de plume*; line; pen and ink.

letter &c. 561; uncial writing, cuneiform character, arrow-head, Ogham, Runes, futhorc; hieroglyphic, hieratic, demotic; script; contraction.

short-hand; steno-, brachy-, tachy-graphy; secret writing, writing in cipher; crypt-, stegan-ography; phono-, pasi-, poly-, logo-graphy.

copy; tran-, re-script; draft, rough –, fair- copy; handwriting; signature, sign-manual; auto-, mono-, holo-graph; hand, fist; mark.

calligraphy; good –, running –,

591. Printing.—N. printing; block –, type- printing, lino-, mono-type; plate printing &c. (*engraving*) 558; the press &c. (*publication*) 531; composition.

print, letterpress, text, matter, standing type; context, note, page, column; over-running; head-, foot-line, title.

typography; stereo-, electro-, apro-type; type, black letter, heavy type, font, fount; pi, pie; capitals &c. (*letters*) 561; diamond, pearl, nonpareil, minion, brevier, bourgeois, long primer, small pica, pica, english, great primer.

folio &c. (*book*) 593; copy, impression, pull, proof, galley –, author's –, page- proof, revise.

printer, compositor, reader; printer's devil.

V. print; compose; put –, go- to press; pass –, see- through the press;

flowing -, cursive -, legible -, copper-plate -, round -, bold- hand.

cacography, *griffonage, barbouillage*; bad -, cramped -, crabbed -, illegible-hand; scribble &c. *v.*; *pattes de mouche*; ill-formed letters; pot-hooks and hangers.

stationery; pen, quill, goose-quill, reed; stylographic-, fountain-pen; pencil, style, stylus; paper, foolscap, parchment, vellum, papyrus, pad, tablet, block, note book, slate, marble, pillar, table, black board.

ink-bottle, -pot, -stand, -well, -horn; typewriter.

transcription &c. (*copy*) 21; inscription &c. (*record*) 551; super-scription &c. (*indication*) 550.

composition, authorship; *cacoethes scribendi.*

writer, scribe, amanuensis, scrivener, secretary, clerk, penman, copyist, transcriber, quill-driver; writer for the press &c. (*author*) 593.

shorthand writer, stenographer; typewriter, typist.

V. write, pen; copy, engross; write out, - fair; transcribe; scribble, scrawl, scrabble, scratch; interline; stain paper; write down &c. (*record*) 551; sign &c. (*attest*) 467; take down, - in shorthand; typewrite, type.

compose, indite, draw up, redact, draft, formulate; dictate; in-scribe, throw on paper, dash off; concoct.

take -up the pen, - pen in hand; shed -, spill -, dip one's pen in- ink.

Adj. writing &c. *v.*; written &c. *v.*; in -writing, - black and white; under one's hand.

uncial, Runic, cuneiform, hieroglyphical &c. *n.*

Adv. *currente calamo*; pen in hand.

publish &c. 531; bring out; appear in -, rush into- print.

Adj. printed &c. *v.*; in type; typo-graphical &c. *n.*

---

592. Correspondence. — N. corre-spondence, letter, epistle, note, *billet*, post-, letter-card, missive, circular, form letter; favour, *billet-doux*; des-, dis-patch; *bulletin*, communication &c. 532; these presents; rescript, -ion; post &c. (*messenger*) 534; letter writer, correspondent.

V. correspond, - with; write -, send a letter- to; keep up a correspondence; drop a line to; despatch; communicate with; circularize.

Adj. epistolary.

---

593. Book.—N. book, -let; writing, work, volume, tome, opuscule; tract, -ate; *livret*; *brochure, libretto*, hand-book, treatise, text-book, codex, man-ual, pamphlet, monograph, enchiridion, circular, publication; book of poems; novel; chap-book.

part, issue, number, *livraison*; album, portfolio; periodical, serial, magazine, *ephemeris*, annual, journal.

paper, bill, sheet, broadsheet, screed; leaf, -let; fly-leaf, page; quire, ream.

chapter, section, head, article, para-graph, passage, clause, supplement, appendix; *feuilleton*.

folio, quarto, octavo; duo-, sexto-, octo-decimo.

en-, cyclopædia, dictionary, lexicon, thesaurus, concordance, anthology, bibliography; compilation, compendium, catalogue &c. 86; library, bibliotheca; the press &c. (*publication*) 531.

writer, author, *littérateur*, essayist, journalist, publicist; scribe, penman, war -, special -, correspondent; pen, scribbler, the scrib-bling race; ghost, hack, literary hack, Grub-street writer; writer for -, gentleman of -, representative of- the press; reporter, penny-a-liner; editor, sub-editor; playwright &c. 599; poet &c. 597.

bookseller, publisher; biblio-pole, -polist, -grapher; librarian; book -collector, – worm.

book -shop, – club, circulating –, lending –, public- library; publishing house.

knowledge of books, bibliography; book-learning &c. (*knowledge*) 490.

594. Description.—N. description, account, statement, report; *exposé* &c. (*disclosure*) 529; specification, particulars, scenario, plot; state –, summary- of facts; brief &c. (*abstract*) 596; return &c. (*record*) 551; *catalogue raisonné* &c. (*list*) 86; guide-book &c. (*information*) 527.

delineation &c. (*representation*) 554; sketch, vignette; monograph; minute –, detailed –, particular –, circumstantial –, graphic- account; narration, recital, rehearsal, relation.

histori-, chron-ography; historic Muse, Clio; history; bi-, autobi-ography; necrology, obituary.

narrative, history; memoir, memorials; annals &c. (*chronicle*) 551; tradition, legend, saga, epic, epos, story, tale, historiette; personal narrative, journal, letters, life, adventures, fortunes, experiences, confessions; anecdote, ana, *trait*.

work of fiction, short story, novelette, novel, romance, penny dreadful, shilling shocker, Minerva press; fairy –, nursery- tale; fable, allegory, parable, apologue.

relator &c. *v.*; *raconteur*; historian &c. (*recorder*) 553; biographer, fabulist, novelist, story teller, romancer, teller of tales, spinner of yarns, anecdotist.

V. describe; set forth &c. (*state*) 535; draw a picture, picture; portray &c. (*represent*) 554; characterize, particularize; narrate, relate, recite, recount, sum up, run over, recapitulate, rehearse, fight one's battles over again.

unfold &c. (*disclose*) 529- a tale; tell; give –, render- an account of; report, make a report, draw up a statement.

detail; enter into –, descend to- -particulars, – details.

Adj. descriptive, graphic, narrative, epic, suggestive, well-drawn; historic; auto-, biographical, realistic, expository, tradition-al, -ary; legendary; fabulous, mythical; anecdotic, storied; described &c. *v.*

595. Dissertation.—N. dissertation, treatise, essay; *thesis*, theme; tract, -ate, -ation, excursus; discourse, memoir, disquisition, lecture, sermon, homily, pandect.

commentary, review, *critique*, criticism, article; lead-er, -ing article, editorial; argument, running commentary.

investigation &c. (*inquiry*) 461; study &c. (*consideration*) 451; discussion &c. (*reasoning*) 476; exposition &c. (*explanation*) 522.

commentator, critic, essayist, pamphleteer; publicist, reviewer, leader writer, editor, annotator.

V. dissert –, descant –, write –, touch- upon a subject; dissertate; treat of –, take up –, ventilate –, discuss –, deal with –, go into –, canvass –, handle –, do justice to- a subject; comment, criticize, interpret &c. 522.

Adj. dis-cursive, -coursive; disquisitional, disquisitionary; expository, critical.

596. Compendium.—N. compend, -ium; abstract, *précis*, epitome, *multum in parvo*, analysis, pandect, digest, sum and substance, brief, abridgment, summary, *aperçu*, draft, minute, note; synopsis, text-book, *conspectus*, outlines, syllabus, contents, heads, prospectus.

album; scrap –, note –, memorandum –, commonplace- book; extracts, *excerpta*, cuttings; fugitive -pieces, – writings; *spicilegium*, flowers, anthology, miscellany, *collectanea, analecta*; compilation.

recapitulation, *résumé*, review.

abbrevia-tion, -ture; contraction; shortening &c. 201; compression &c. 195.

V. abridge, abstract, epitomize, summarize; make –, prepare –, draw –, compile- an abstract &c. *n.*

recapitulate, review, skim, run over, sum up.

abbreviate &c. (*shorten*) 201; condense &c. (*compress*) 195; compile &c. (*collect*) 72; edit, blue pencil.

Adj. compendious, synoptic, analectic, analytical; abridged &c. *v.*

Adv. in -short, – epitome, – substance, – few words.

Phr. it lies in a nutshell.

---

597. Poetry.—N. poetry, poetics, poesy, Muse, Calliope, tuneful Nine, Parnassus, Helicon, Pierides, Pierian spring, afflatus, inspiration.

versification, rhyming, making verses; prosody, scansion, orthometry.

poem; epic, – poem; epopee, *epopæa*, ode, epode, idyl, lyric, eclogue, pas-toral, bucolic, georgic, dithyramb, anacreontic, sonnet, roundelay, *rondel, rondoletto, rondeau, rondo,* triolet; madrigal, canzonet, *cento*, monody, elegy, palinode; rhapsody.

dramatic –, lyric- poetry; opera; posy, anthology.

song, ballad, lay; love –, drinking –, war –, folk –, sea- song; lullaby; music &c. 415; nursery rhymes.

[Bad poetry] doggerel, Hudibrastic verse, prose run mad; maca-ronics; macaronic –, leonine- verse; runes.

canto, stanza, distich, verse, line, couplet, triplet, quatrain, sestet; *strophe, antistrophe*, refrain, chorus, burden.

verse, rhyme, assonance, crambo, metre, measure, foot, numbers, strain, rhythm; accentuation &c. (*voice*) 580; iambus, dactyl, spondee, trochee, anapæst &c.; hex-, pent-ameter; Alexandrine; blank verse, alliteration.

elegiacs &c. *adj.*; elegiac &c. *adj.* -verse, – metre, – poetry.

poet, – laureate; laureate; minor poet, bard, lyrist, scald, trouba-dour, *trouvère*; minstrel; minne-, meister-singer; *improvisatore*; versifier, sonneteer; ballad monger; rhym-er, -ist, -ester; poetaster.

V. poetize, sing, versify, make verses, rhyme, scan.

Adj. poetic, -al; lyric, -al; tuneful; epic; dithyrambic &c. *n.*; metrical; a-, catalectic; elegiac, iambic, trochaic, spondaic, ana-pæstic; Ionic, Sapphic, Alcaic, Pindaric.

598. Prose.—N. prose, – writer, pros-aism, -aist, -er.

V. prose, write prose.

write -prose, – in prose.

Adj. pros-y, -aic; unpoetical.

rhymeless, unrhymed, in prose, not in verse.

---

599. The Drama.—N. the -drama, – stage, – theatre, – play; theat-ricals, dramaturgy, histrionic art, buskin, sock, *cothurnus*, Melpomene and Thalia, Thespis.

play, drama, stage-play, piece, five-act play, tragedy, comedy, opera, comic opera, *vaudeville, comedietta, lever de rideau*, curtain raiser, inter-lude, afterpiece, exode, farce, *divertissement, extravaganza*, burletta, harlequinade, pantomime, mimodrama, burlesque, *opéra bouffe*, musical comedy, review, revue, intimate revue, variety, cabaret entertainment, *ballet, spectacle*, masque, *drame, comédie drame*; melo-drama, -drame; *comédie larmoyante*, emotional drama, sensation drama, tragi-, farcical-comedy; mono-drame, -logue; duologue; trilogy; charade, *proverbe*; mystery, miracle –, morality- play.

act, scene, *tableau*; in-, intro-duction; pro-, epi-logue, curtain; *libretto*, book, script.

performance, representation, show, *mise en scène*, stagery, *jeu de théâtre*, stage-craft; acting; gesture &c. 550; impersonation &c. 554; stage business, gag, patter, buffoonery.

theatre; play-, opera-house; house; music hall; *cabaret*; amphi-theatre, circus, hippodrome; puppet-show, *fantoccini*; *marionnettes*, Punch and Judy.

cinema, -tograph-, picture –, theatre, the pictures, the movies, the talkies.

auditory, *auditorium*, front of the house, stalls, boxes, balcony, dress –, upper- -circle, – boxes, amphitheatre, pit, gallery; *foyer*; green-room; dressing rooms, *coulisses*.

flat; drop, – scene; wing, screen, side-scene; transformation scene, curtain, act-drop, safety –, fire- curtain; *proscenium*, forestage.

stage, revolving stage, scene, the boards; star –, grave –, trap, mezzanine floor; flies; gridiron, floats, battens, footlights; lime –, spot –, flood –, bunch-lights; scenery, set, *décor*; orchestra;

theatrical -costume, – properties, props.

part, *rôle*, character, cast, *dramatis personæ*; *répertoire*.

actor, player; stage –, strolling- player; old –, stager, performer; mime, -r; *artiste*; com-, trag-edian, straight man; *tragédienne*, Thespian, Roscius, star.

pantomimist, clown, harlequin, *buffo*, buffoon, *farceur, grimacier*, pantaloon, columbine; *Pierrot, Pierrette*; punch, -inello; *pulcinell-o, -a*; mute, *figurante*, general utility; super, -numerary, extra.

mummer, guiser, guisard, gysart, masque.

mountebank, Jack Pudding; tumbler, posture-master, acrobat, equilibrist, juggler, contortionist; *danseuse, ballerina*, ballet -dancer, – girl, *coryphée*; *bayadère, geisha*; chorus -singer, – girl.

company; first tragedian, *prima donna*, lead, leading lady, pro-tagonist; *jeune premier*; juvenile lead, *débutant, -e*; light –, genteel –, low- -comedy, – comedian; *soubrette*, walking gentleman, *amoroso*, heavy, heavy father, *ingénue, jeune veuve, commère, compère*.

property man, *costumier*, machinist, stage hand, electrician, prompter, call-boy; director, manager; stage –, acting –, business- manager; *entrepreneur, impresario*, producer, press agent.

dramatic -author, – writer; play-writer, -wright; dramatist, mimo-grapher; dramatic critic.

V. act, play, perform; stage, produce, put on the stage; personate &c. 554; mimic &c. (*imitate*) 19; enact; play –, act –, go through –, perform- a part; rehearse, spout, gag, rant; 'strut and fret one's hour upon a stage'; tread the -stage, – boards; come out; star.

Adj. dramatic; theatric, -al; scenic, histrionic, anctorial, comic, tragic, buskined, farcical, tragi-comic, melodramatic, operatic; stagey spec-tacular; stagestruck.

Adv. on the -stage, – boards; before -the floats, – an audience; in the limelight, behind the footlights; behind the scenes.

CLASS V

WORDS RELATING TO THE VOLUNTARY POWERS*

CLASS V

Words relating to THE VOLUNTARY POWERS*

Division (I.) INDIVIDUAL VOLITION

Section I. Volition in General

1°. Acts of Volition

600. Will.—N. will, volition, conation†, velleity; will and pleasure, free-will; freedom &c. 748; discretion; choice, inclination, intent, purpose, option &c. (*choice*) 609; voluntariness; spontane-ity, -ousness; originality.

pleasure, wish, desire, mind; frame of mind &c. (*inclination*) 602; intention &c. 620; predetermination &c. 611; self-control &c. determination &c. (*resolution*) 604; will-power.

V. will, list; see –, think- fit; determine &c. (*resolve*) 604; settle &c. (*choose*) 609; volunteer.

have a will of one's own; do what one chooses &c. (*freedom*) 748; have it all one's own way; have one's -will, – own way.

use –, exercise- one's discretion; take -upon oneself, – one's own course, – the law into one's own hands; do -of one's own accord, – upon one's own -responsibility, – authority; take the bit between one's teeth; take responsibility; originate &c. (*cause*) 153.

Adj. voluntary, volitive, volitional, wilful; free &c. 748; optional; discretion-al, -ary; volitient; dictatorial.

minded &c. (*willing*) 602; prepense &c. (*predetermined*) 611; intended &c. 620; autocratic; unbidden &c. (bid &c. 741); spontaneous; original &c. (*causal*) 153.

Adv. voluntarily &c. *adj.*; at -will, – pleasure; à -volonté, – discrétion; al piacere; ad -libitum, – arbitrium; as -one thinks proper, – it seems good to.

601. Necessity.—N. involuntariness; instinct, blind –, natural- impulse; inborn –, innate- proclivity; the force of circumstances.

necessi-ty, -tation, necessarianism; obligation; compulsion &c. 744; subjection &c. 749; stern –, hard –, dire –, imperious –, inexorable –, iron –, adverse- -necessity, – fate; what must be.

desti-ny, -nation; fatality, fate, *kismet*, doom, foredoom, election, predestination; pre-, fore-ordination; lot, fortune; fatalism, determinism; inevitableness &c. *adj.*; spell &c. 993.

star, -s; planet, -s; astral influence; sky, Fates, Norns, *Parcæ*, Sisters three, Clotho, Lachesis, Atropos; book of fate; God's will, will of Heaven; wheel of Fortune, Ides of March, Hobson's choice.

last -shift, – resort; *dernier ressort*; *pis aller* &c. (*substitute*) 147; necessaries &c. (*requirement*) 630.

necess-arian, -itarian; fatalist, determinist; automaton.

V. lie under a necessity; be -fated, – doomed, – destined &c., – in for, – under the necessity of; have no -choice, – alternative; be- obliged –, forced –, driven –, one's -fate &c. *n.*to; be -pushed to the wall, – driven into a corner, – unable to help, – drawn irresistibly.

destine, doom, foredoom, devote; pre-destine, -ordain; cast a spell &c. 992; necessitate; compel &c. 744.

* Conative powers or faculties (Hamilton).   †Hamilton.

of one's own -accord, – free will; *proprio* –, *suo* –, *ex mero- motu*; out of one's own head; by choice &c. 609; purposely &c. (*intentionally*) 620; deliberately &c. 611.

Phr. *stet pro ratione voluntas; sic volo sic jubeo.*

Adj. necessary; needful &c. (*requisite*) 630.

fated; destined &c. *v.*; fateful; elect; spell-bound.

compulsory &c. (*compel*) 744; uncontrollable, inevitable, unavoidable, irresistible, irrevocable, inexorable, binding; avoid-, resist-less; written in the book of fate.

involuntary, instinctive, automatic, blind, mechanical; un-conscious, -witting, -thinking; unintentional &c. (*undesigned*) 621; impulsive &c. 612.

Adv. necessarily &c. *adv.*; of -necessity, – course; *ex necessitate rei*; needs must; perforce &c. 744; *nolens volens*; will he nil he, willy nilly, *bon gré mal gré*, willing or unwilling, *coûte que coûte*, forcefully. *faute de mieux*; by stress of; if need be.

Phr. it cannot be helped; there is no- help for, – helping- it; it -will, – must, – must needs- be, – be so, – have its way; the die is cast; *jacta est alea; che sarà sarà*; 'it is written'; one's- days are numbered, – fate is sealed; *Fata obstant; diis aliter visum.*

---

602. Willingness.—N. willingness, voluntariness &c. *adj.*; willing mind, heart.

disposition, inclination, leaning, *animus*; frame of mind, humour, mood, vein; bent &c. (*turn of mind*) 820; *penchant* &c. (*desire*) 865; aptitude &c. 698.

doc-ility, -ibleness, tractability; persuasi-bleness, -bility; pliability &c. (*softness*) 324.

geniality, cordiality; goodwill; alacrity, readiness, earnestness, forwardness, enthusiasm; zeal, eagerness &c. (*desire*) 865.

assent &c. 488; compliance &c. 762; pleasure &c. (*will*) 600.

labour of love, self-appointed task; volunteer, -ing, gratuitous service; unpaid worker, amateur.

V. be -willing &c. *adj.*; incline, lean to, mind, propend; had as lief; lend –, give –, turn- a willing ear; have -a, – half a, – a great- mind to; hold –, cling- to; desire &c. 865.

see –, think- -good, – fit, – proper; acquiescence &c. (*assent*) 488; comply with &c. 762.

swallow –, nibble at- the bait; gorge the hook; swallow hook, line and sinker; have –, make- no scruple of; make no bones of; jump –, catch- at; meet half way; volunteer, offer oneself &c. 763.

---

603. Unwillingness.—N. unwillingness &c. *adj.*; indispos-ition, -edness; disinclination, aversation, aversion; nolleity, nolition; renitence; reluctance; indifference &c. 866; backwardness &c. *adj.*; slowness &c. 275; want of -alacrity, – readiness; indocility &c. (*obstinacy*) 606.

scrupul-ousness, -osity; qualms of conscience, delicacy, demur, scruple, qualm, shrinking, recoil; hesitation &c. (*irresolution*) 605; fastidiousness &c. 868.

averseness &c. (*dislike*) 867; dissent &c. 489; refusal &c. 764.

slacker, scrimshanker, *embusqué*, unwilling worker, forced labor.

V. be -unwilling &c. *adj.*; nill; dislike &c. 867; grudge, begrudge; not be able to find it in one's heart to, not have the stomach to.

demur, stick at, scruple, stickle; hang fire, run rusty, slack, shirk, scamp, give up, fight shy of, not pull fair; recoil, shrink, swerve; hesitate &c. 605; avoid &c. 623.

oppose &c. 708; dissent &c. 489; refuse &c. 764.

Adj. unwilling; not in the vein, loth, shy of, disinclined, indisposed, averse, reluctant, not content; adverse &c. (*opposed*) 708; laggard, backward, remiss, slack, slow to; renitent; indifferent &c. 866; scrupulous; squeamish

Adj. willing, minded, fain, disposed, inclined, favourable; favourably-minded, -inclined, -disposed; nothing loth; in the -vein, – mood, – humour, – mind.

ready, forward, enthusiastic, earnest, eager; bent upon &c. (*desirous*) 865; predisposed, propense.

docile; persua-dable, -sible; suasible, easily persuaded, facile, easy-going; amenable; tractable &c. (*pliant*) 324; genial, gracious, cordial, hearty; content &c. (*assenting*) 488.

voluntary, gratuitous, spontaneous; unasked &c. (ask &c. 765); unforced &c. (*free*) 748.

Adv. willingly &c. *adj.*; fain, freely, as lief, heart and soul; with -pleasure, – all one's heart, – open arms; with -good, – right good- will; *de bonne volonté, ex animo; con amore*, heart in hand, nothing loth, without reluctance, of one's own accord, graciously, with a good grace, without demur.

à la bonne heure; by all -means, – manner of means; to one's heart's content; yes &c. (*assent*) 488.

Int. sure, -ly! of course!

&c. (*fastidious*) 868; repugnant &c. (*dislike*) 867; rest-iff, -ive; demurring &c. *v.*; unconsenting &c. (*refusing*) 764; involuntary &c. 601; grudging, irreconcilable.

Adv. unwillingly &c. *adj.*; grudgingly, with a heavy heart; with -a bad, – an ill- grace; against –, sore against- -one's wishes, – one's will, – the grain; *invitâ Minervâ; à contre cœur; malgré soi*; in spite of -one's teeth, – oneself; *nolens volens* &c. (*necessity*) 601; perforce &c. 744; under protest; no &c. 536; not for the world, far be it from me; not if I can help it; if I must I must.

---

604. Resolution.—N. determination, will; iron –, unconquerable- will; will of one's own, decision, resolution, backbone, grit; strength of -mind, – will; resolve &c. (*intent*) 620; *intransigeance*; firmness &c. (*stability*) 150; energy, manliness, vigour; game, pluck; resoluteness &c. (*courage*) 861; zeal &c. 682; *aplomb*; desperation; devot-ion, -edness.

mastery over self; self-control, -command, -mastery, -possession, -reliance, -government, -restraint, -conquest, -denial; moral -courage, – strength, – fibre; perseverance &c. 604a; tenacity; obstinacy &c. 606; bull-dog; British lion.

V. have -determination &c. *n.*; know one's own mind; be -resolved &c. *adj.*; make up one's mind, will, resolve, determine; decide &c. (*judgment*) 480; form –, come to- a -determination, – resolution, – resolve; conclude, fix, seal, determine once for all, bring to a crisis, drive matters to an extremity; take a decisive step &c. (*choice*) 609; take upon oneself &c. (*undertake*) 676.

devote oneself –, give oneself up- to; throw away the scabbard, kick down

605. Irresolution.—N. irresolution, infirmity of purpose, indecision; in-, un-determination, loss of will power; unsettlement; uncertainty &c. 475; demur, suspense; hesi-tating &c. *v.*, -tation, -tancy; vacillation; ambivalence; changeableness &c. 149; fluctuation; alternation &c. (*oscillation*) 314; caprice &c. 608; lukewarmness.

fickleness, levity, *légèreté*; pliancy &c. (*softness*) 324; weakness; timidity &c. 860; cowardice &c. 862; half measures.

waverer, ass between two bundles of hay; shuttlecock, butterfly; time-server, opportunist, turn coat.

V. be -irresolute &c. *adj.*; hang –, keep- in suspense; leave '*ad referendum*'; think twice about, pause; dawdle &c. (*inactivity*) 683; remain neuter; dilly dally, hesitate, boggle, hover, wobble, shilly-shally, hum and haw, demur, not know one's own mind; debate, balance; dally –, coquet- with; will and will not, *chasser-balancer*; go half-way, compromise, make a compromise; be thrown off one's balance, stagger like a drunken man; be afraid &c. 860; let 'I dare not' wait upon 'I would'; falter, waver.

the ladder, nail one's colours to the mast, set one's back against the wall, set one's teeth, put one's foot down, burn one's bridges, take one's stand; stand firm &c. (*stability*) 150; steel oneself; stand no nonsense, not listen to the voice of the charmer.

buckle to; put –, lay –, set- one's shoulder to the wheel; put one's heart into; run the gantlet, make a dash at, take the bull by the horns; beard the lion in his den; rush –, plunge- *in medias res*; go in for; insist upon, make a point of; set one's heart, – mind- upon.

stick at nothing; make short work of &c. (*activity*) 682; not stick at trifles; go -all lengths, – the whole hog; persist &c. (*persevere*) 604a; go down with colours flying, die game; go through fire and water, ride in the whirlwind and direct the storm.

Adj. resolved &c. *v.*; determined; strong-willed, -minded; resolute &c. (*brave*) 861; self-possessed, plucky, tenacious; decided, definitive, peremptory; un-hesitating, -flinching, -shrinking; firm, cast iron, indomitable, game to the backbone; inexorable, relentless, not to be -shaken, – put down; *tenax propositi*; inflexible &c. (*hard*) 323;

vacillate &c. 149; change &c. 140; retract &c. 607; fluctuate; alternate &c. (*oscillate*) 314; keep off and on, play fast and loose; blow hot and cold &c. (*caprice*) 608.

shuffle, palter, blink; trim.

Adj. irresolute, infirm of purpose, double-minded, half-hearted; un-decided, -resolved, -determined; drifting; shilly-shally; fidgety, tremulous; wobbly; hesitating &c. *v.*; off one's balance; at a loss &c. (*uncertain*) 475.

vacillating &c. *v.*; unsteady &c. (*changeable*) 149; unsteadfast, fickle, unreliable, irresponsible, unstable, without ballast; capricious &c. 608; volatile, frothy; light, -some, -minded; giddy; fast and loose.

weak, feeble-minded, frail; timid &c. 860; cowardly &c. 862; facile; pliant &c. (*soft*) 324; unable to say 'no,' easy-going.

revocable, reversible.

Adv. irresolutely &c. *adj.*; irresolvedly; in faltering accents; off and on; from pillar to post; see-saw &c. 314.

Int. 'how happy could I be with either!'

---

obstinate &c. 606; steady &c. (*persevering*) 604a; unbending, unyielding, irrevocable; firm as a rock; grim.

earnest, serious; set –, bent –, intent- upon.

steeled –, proof- against; *in utrumque paratus.*

Adv. resolutely &c. *adj.*; in –, in good- earnest; seriously, joking apart, earnestly, heart and soul; on one's metal; manfully, like a man, with a high hand; with a strong hand &c. (*exertion*) 686.

at any -rate, – risk, – hazard, – price, – cost, – sacrifice; at all -hazards, – risks, – events; cost what it may; *coûte que coûte*; *à tort et à travers*; once for all; neck or nothing; rain or shine; with colours nailed to the mast.

Phr. *spes sibi quisque.*

604a. Perseverance.—N. perseverance; continuance &c. (*inaction*) 143; permanence &c. (*absence of change*) 141; firmness &c. (*stability*) 150.

constancy, steadiness; singleness –, tenacity- of purpose; persistence, plodding, patience; sedulity &c. (*industry*) 682; pertina-cy, -city, -ciousness; iteration &c. 104.

bottom, game, pluck, stamina, backbone, grit; indefatiga-bility, bleness; bulldog courage.

V. persevere, persist; hold -on, – out; die in the last ditch, be in at the death; stick –, cling –, adhere- to; stick to one's text, keep on; keep to –, maintain- one's -course, – ground; bear –, keep –, hold-up; plod; stick to work &c. (*work*) 686; continue &c. 143; follow up; die -in harness, – at one's post.

Adj. persevering, constant; stead-y, -fast; un-deviating, -wavering, -faltering, -swerving, -flinching, -sleeping, -flagging, -drooping; steady as time; uninter-, un-remitting; plodding; industrious &c. 682; strenuous &c. 686; pertinacious; persist-ing, -ent.

solid, sturdy, staunch, stanch, true to oneself; unchangeable &c. 150; unconquerable &c. (*strong*) 159; indomitable, game to the last, indefatigable, untiring, unwearied, never tiring.

Adv. through -evil report and good report, – thick and thin, – fire and water; *per fas et nefas*; without fail, sink or swim, at any price, *vogue la galère*; in sickness and in health.

Phr. never say die; *vestigia nulla retrorsum*.

606. Obstinacy.—N. obstinateness &c. *adj.*; obstinacy, tenacity; perseverance &c. 604*a*; immovability; old school; inflexibility &c. (*hardness*) 323; obdur-acy, -ation; dogged resolution; resolution &c. 604; ruling passion; blind side.

self-will, contumacy, perversity; pervica-cy, -city; indocility.

bigotry, intolerance, dogmatism; opinia-try, -tiveness; fixed idea &c.; intractability, incorrigibility; (*prejudgment*) 481; fanaticism, zealotry, infatuation, monomania, opinionativeness.

mule; opin-ionist, -ionatist, -iator, -ator; stickler, dogmatist, die-hard, bitter-ender; bigot; zealot, enthusiast, fanatic.

V. be -obstinate &c. *adj.*; stickle, take no denial, fly in the face of facts; opinionate, be wedded to an opinion, hug a belief; have one's own way &c. (*will*) 600; persist &c. (*persevere*) 604*a*; have –, insist on having- the last word.

die -hard, – fighting, fight -against destiny, – to the last ditch; not yield an inch, stand out.

Adj. obstinate, tenacious, stubborn, obdurate, case-hardened; inflexible &c. (*hard*) 323; immovable, not to be moved; inert &c. 172; unchangeable &c. 150; inexorable &c. (*determined*) 604; mulish, obstinate as a mule, pig-headed.

dogged; sullen, sulky; un-moved, -influenced, -affected.

wilful, self-willed, perverse; res-ty, -tive, -tiff; pervicacious, wayward, refractory, unruly; head-y, -strong; *entêté*; contumacious; cross-grained.

607. Tergiversation.—N. change of -mind, – intention, – purpose; afterthought.

tergiversation, recantation; palinode, -ody; renunciation; abjur-ation, -ement; defection &c. (*relinquishment*) 624; going over &c. *v.*; apostasy; retract-ion, -ation; withdrawal, disavowal &c. (*negation*) 536; revo-cation, -kement; reversal; repentance &c. 950; *redintegratio amoris*.

coquetry, flirtation; vacillation &c. 605; back-sliding, recidivation.

turn-coat, -tippet; rat, apostate, renegade, mugwump; con-, per-vert; proselyte, deserter; backslider, recidivist; black leg.

time-server, -pleaser; timist, Vicar of Bray, trimmer, ambidexter; weathercock &c. (*changeable*) 149; Janus.

V. change one's -mind, – intention, – purpose, – note; abjure, renounce; withdraw from &c. (*relinquish*) 624; wheel –, turn –, veer- round; turn a *pirouette*; go over –, pass –, change –, skip- from one side to another; go to the right about; box the compass, shift one's ground, go upon another tack; back down, crawl, crawfish.

apostatize, change sides, go over, rat; recant, retract; revoke; rescind &c. (*abrogate*) 756; recall, forswear, abjure, unsay; come -over, – round- to an opinion.

draw in one's horns, eat one's words; eat –, swallow- the leek; swerve, flinch, back out of, retrace one's steps, think better of it; come back –, return- to one's first love; turn over a new leaf &c. (*repent*) 950.

arbitrary, dogmatic, opinionated, positive, bigoted; prejudiced &c. 481; prepossessed, infatuated; stiff-backed, -necked, -hearted; hard-mouthed, hidebound; unyielding; im-pervious, -practicable, -persuasible; unpersuadable; in-, un-tractable; incorrigible, deaf to advice, impervious to reason; crotchety &c. 608.

Adv. obstinately &c. *adj.*

Phr. *non possumus*; no surrender.

---

trim, shuffle, play fast and loose, blow hot and cold, coquet, flirt, hold with the hare but run with the hounds; straddle; *nager entre deux eaux*; wait to see how the -cat jumps, – wind blows.

Adj. changeful &c. 149; irresolute &c. 605; ductile, slippery as an eel, trimming, ambidextrous, timeserving; coquetting &c. *v.*

revocatory, reactionary.

Phr. 'a change came o'er the spirit of my dream.'

608. Caprice.—N. caprice, fancy, humour; whim, -sey, -wham; crotchet, *capriccio*, quirk, freak, maggot, fad, vagary, prank, fit, flimflam, *escapade*, *boutade*, wild-goose chase; capriciousness &c. *adj.*; kink.

V. be -capricious &c. *adj.*; have a maggot in the brain; take it into one's head, strain at a gnat and swallow a camel; blow hot and cold; play -fast and loose, – fantastic tricks.

Adj. capricious; erratic, eccentric, fitful, hysterical; full of -whims &c. *n.*; maggoty; inconsistent, fanciful, fantastic, whimsical, crotchety, particular, humoursome, freakish, skittish, wanton, wayward; contrary; captious; arbitrary; unrestrained, undisciplined; not amenable to reason; uncomfortable &c. 83; penny wise and pound foolish; fickle &c. (*irresolute*) 605; frivolous, sleeveless, giddy, volatile.

Adv. by fits and starts, without rhyme or reason, at one's own sweet will.

Phr. *nil fuit unquam sic impar sibi*; the deuce is in him.

609. Choice.—N. choice, option; discretion &c. (*volition*) 600; preoption; alternative; dilemma; *embarras de choix*; adoption, co-optation; novation; decision &c. (*judgment*) 480.

election, poll, ballot, vote, voice, suffrage, plumper, cumulative vote; *plebiscitum*, *plébiscite*, *vox populi*; *referendum*, electioneering; voting &c. *v.*; franchise; ballot box; slate, ticket.

selection, excerption, gleaning, eclecticism; *excerpta*, gleanings, cuttings, scissors and paste; pick &c. (*best*) 650.

preference, prelation; predilection &c. (*desire*) 865.

V. offer for one's choice, set before; hold out –, present –, offer- the alternative; put to the vote.

use –, exercise –, one's- -discretion, – option; adopt, take up, embrace, espouse; choose, elect, co-opt; take –, make- one's choice; make choice of, fix upon.

vote, poll, hold up one's hand; divide.

settle; decide &c. (*adjudge*) 480; list

609a. Absence of Choice.—N. no –, Hobson's- choice; first come, first served; necessity &c. 601; not a pin to choose &c. (*equality*) 27; any, the first that comes.

neutrality, indifference; indecision &c. (*irresolution*) 605.

V. be -neutral &c. *adj.*; have no choice; waive, not vote; abstain –, refrain- from voting; leave undecided; make a virtue of necessity.

Adj. neu-tral, -ter; indifferent; undecided &c. (*irresolute*) 605.

Adv. either &c. (*choice*) 609.

610. Rejection.—N. rejection, repudiation, exclusion; declination; refusal &c. 764.

V. reject; set –, lay- aside; give up; decline &c. (*refuse*) 764; exclude, except, eliminate; pluck, spin; cast.

repudiate, scout, set at naught; fling –, cast –, thrown –, toss- -to the winds, – to the dogs, – overboard, – away; send to the right about; dis-

&c. (*will*) 600; make up one's mind &c. (*resolve*) 604.

select; pick, – and choose; pick –, single- out, excerpt; cull, glean, winnow; sift –, separate –, winnow- the chaff from the wheat; pick up, pitch upon; pick one's way; indulge one's fancy.

set apart, reserve, mark out for; mark &c. 550.

prefer; have -rather, – as lief; fancy &c. (*desire*) 865; be persuaded &c. 615.

take a -decided, – decisive- step; commit oneself to a course; pass –, cross- the Rubicon; cast in one's lot with; take for better or for worse.

Adj. optional; co-optative; discretional &c. (*voluntary*) 600; on approval.

eclectic; choosing &c. *v.*; preferential; chosen &c. *v.*; choice &c. (*good*) 648.

Adv. optionally &c. *adj.*; at pleasure &c. (*will*) 600; either, – the one or the other; or; at the option of; whether or not; once for all; for one's money.

by -choice, – preference; in preference; rather, before.

claim &c. (*deny*) 536; discard &c. (*eject*) 297, (*have done with*) 678.

Adj. rejected &c. *v.*; reject-aneous, -itious; not -chosen &c. 609, – to be thought of; out of the question.

Adv. neither, – the one nor the other; no &c. 536.

Phr. *non hæc in fœdera.*

---

611. Predetermination. — N. premeditation, -deliberation, -determination, -destination; foreordination; foregone conclusion; *parti pris*; resolve, propendency; intention &c. 620; project &c. 626.

V. pre-determine, -destine, -meditate, -resolve, -concert; foreordain; resolve beforehand.

Adj. pre-pense, -meditated &c. *v.*, -designed; advised, studied, designed, calculated; aforethought; intended &c. 620; foregone.

well-laid, -devised, -weighed; maturely .considered; cut and dried; cunning.

Adv. advisedly &c. *adj.*; with premeditation, deliberately, all things considered, with eyes open, in cold blood; intentionally &c. 620.

613. Habit.—N. habit, -ude; assuetude, -faction; wont; run, way.

common –, general –, natural –, ordinary –, habitual- -course, – run, – state- of things; matter of course; beaten -path, – track, – ground.

prescription, custom, use, usage, immemorial usage, practice; tradition; prevalence, observance; conventional-

612. Impulse.—N. impulse, sudden thought; *impromptu*, improvisation; inspiration, hunch, flash, spurt.

improvisatore, improvisatrice, improviser, extemporizer; creature of impulse.

V. flash on the mind.

say what comes uppermost; improvise, extemporize; rise to the occasion; spurt.

Adj. extemporaneous, impulsive, indeliberate; improvis-ed, -ate, -atory; un-, unpre-meditated; *improvisé*; unprompted, -guided; natural, unguarded; spontaneous &c. (*voluntary*) 600; instinctive &c. 601.

Adv. extem-pore, -poraneously; offhand, *impromptu, à l'improviste*; improviso; on the spur of the -moment, – occasion.

614. Desuetude.—N. desuetude, disusage; disuse &c. 678; want of -habit, – practice; inusitation; newness to; new brooms.

infraction of usage &c. (*unconformity*) 83; non-prevalence; 'a custom more honoured in the breach than the observance.'

V. be -unaccustomed &c. *adj.*; leave

ism, -ity; mode, fashion, vogue; *etiquette* &c. (*gentility*) 852; order of the day, cry; conformity &c. 82.

habitué, addict.

one's old way, old school, consuetude, *veteris vestigia flammæ*; *laudator temporis acti*.

rule, standing order, precedent, routine; red-tape, -tapism; pipe-clay; rut, groove.

cacoëthes; bad –, confirmed –, inveterate –, intrinsic &c. 5- habit; addiction, trick.

training &c. (*education*) 537; seasoning, hardening, inurement; radication; second nature, acclimatization; knack &c. (*skill*) 698.

V. be -wont &c. *adj.*

fall into a custom &c. (*conform to*) 82; tread –, follow- the beaten -track, – path; *stare super antiquas vias*; move in a rut, run on in a groove, go round like a horse in a mill, go on in the old jog-trot way.

habituate, inure, harden, season, caseharden; accustom, familiarize; naturalize, acclimatize; keep one's hand in; train &c. (*educate*) 537.

get into the -way, – knack- of; learn &c. 539; cling –, adhere- to; repeat &c. 104; acquire –, contract –, fall into- a -habit, – trick; addict oneself –, take- to; accustom oneself to.

be -habitual &c. *adj.*; prevail; come into use, become a habit, take root; gain –, grow- upon one.

Adj. habitual; ac-, customary; prescriptive; accustomed &c. *v.*; traditional; of -daily, – every-day- occurrence; wonted, usual, general, ordinary, common, frequent, every-day, household, jog-trot; well-trodden, -known; familiar, vernacular, trite, commonplace, banal, bromidic, conventional, regular, set, stock, official, established, stereotyped; pre-vailing, -valent; current, received, acknowledged, recognized, accredited; of course, admitted, understood.

conformable &c. 82; according to -use, – custom, – routine; in -vogue, – fashion; fashionable &c. (*genteel*) 852.

wont; used – given – addicted –, attuned –, habituated &c. *v.*- to; in the habit of; *habitué*; at home in &c. (*skilful*) 698; seasoned; permeated –, imbued- with; devoted –, wedded- to; never free from.

hackneyed, fixed, rooted, deep-rooted, ingrafted, permanent, inveterate, besetting; naturalized; ingrained &c. (*intrinsic*) 5.

Adv. habitually &c. *adj.*; always &c. (*uniformly*) 16.

as -usual, – is one's wont, – things go, – the world goes, – the sparks fly upwards; *more -suo, – solito*.

as a rule, for the most part; generally &c. *adj.*; most often, – frequently.

Phr. *cela s'entend*.

off –, cast off –, break off –, wean oneself of –, violate –, break through –, infringe- -a habit, – a custom, – a usage; break one's fetters; disuse &c. 678; wear off.

Adj. un-accustomed, -used, -wonted, -seasoned, -inured, -habituated, -trained; new; green &c. (*unskilled*) 699; fresh, original, unhackneyed.

unusual &c. (*unconformable*) 83; unconventional, non-observant; disused &c. 678.

Adv. just for once.

2°. *Causes of Volition*

615. Motive.—N. motive, springs of action.

reason, ground, call, principle; main-

615a. Absence of Motive.—N. absence of motive; caprice &c. 608; chance &c. (*absence of design*) 621.

spring, *primum mobile*, key-stone; the why and the wherefore; *pro* and *con*, reason why; secret –, ulterior- motive, *arrière-pensée*; intention &c. 620.

inducement, consideration; attraction &c. 288; loadstone; magnet, -ism, -ic force; allect-ation, -ive; temptation, enticement, *agacerie*, allurement, witchery; bewitch-ment, -ery; charm; spell &c. 993; fascination, blandishment, cajolery; seduc-tion, -ement; honeyed words, voice of the tempter, son of the Sirens; forbidden fruit, golden apple.

persuasi-bility, -bleness; attractability; impress-, suscept-ibility; softness; persuas-, attract-iveness; tantalization.

influence, prompting, dictate, instance; impuls-e, -ion; incit-ement, -ation; press, instigation; provocation &c. (*excitation of feeling*) 824; inspiration; per-, suasion; encouragement, advocacy; exhortation, advice &c. 695; solicitation &c. (*request*) 765; lobbying.

incentive, stimulus, spur, fillip, whip, goad, rowel, provocative, whet, dram.

bribe, lure; decoy, – duck; bait, trail of a red herring; bribery and corruption; sop, – for Cerberus.

prompter, tempter; seduc-er, -tor; suggester, coaxer, wheedler; instigator, firebrand, incendiary; Siren, Circe; *agent provocateur*; lobbyist.

V. induce, move; draw, – on; bring in its train, give an -impulse &c. *n.-* to; inspire; put up to, prompt, call up; attract, beckon.

stimulate &c. (*excite*) 824; spirit up, inspirit; a-, rouse; ecphorize; animate, incite, provoke, instigate. set on, actuate; act –, work –, operate- upon; encourage; pat –, clap- on the -back, – shoulder.

influence, weigh with, bias, sway, incline, dispose, predispose, turn the scale, inoculate; lead, – by the nose; have –, exercise- influence- -with, – over, – upon; go –, come- round one; turn the head, magnetize.

persuade; prevail -with, – upon; overcome, carry; bring -round, – to one's senses; draw –, win –, gain –, come –, talk- over; procure, enlist, engage; invite, court.

tempt, seduce, overpersuade, entice, allure, captivate, fascinate, intrigue, bewitch, carry away, charm, conciliate, wheedle, coax, lure, suggest; inveigle; tantalize; cajole &c. (*deceive*) 545.

tamper with, bribe, suborn, grease the palm, bait with a silver hook, gild the pill, make things pleasant, put a sop into the pan, throw a sop to, bait the hook.

V. have no motive; scruple &c. (*be unwilling*) 603.

Adj. without rhyme or reason; aimless &c. (*chance*) 621.

Adv. capriciously; out of mere caprice.

616. Dissuasion.—N. dissuasion, dehortation, expostulation, remonstrance; deprecation &c. 766.

discouragement, damper, wet blanket; warning.

cohibition &c. (*restraint*) 751; curb &c. (*means of restraint*) 752; check &c. (*hindrance*) 706.

reluctance &c. (*unwillingness*) 603; contraindication.

V. dissuade, dehort, cry out against, remonstrate, expostulate, warn, contra-indicate.

disincline, indispose, shake, stagger; dispirit; dis-courage, -hearten, -enchant; deter; hold –, keep- back &c. (*restrain*) 751; render -averse &c. 603; repel; turn aside &c. (*deviation*) 279; wean from; act as a drag &c. (*hinder*) 706; throw cold water on, damp, cool, chill, blunt, calm, quiet, quench; deprecate &c. 766.

Adj. dissuading &c. *v.*; dissuasive; dehortatory, expostulatory; monit-ive, -ory.

dissuaded &c. *v.*; uninduced &c. (induce &c. 615); unpersuadable &c. (*obstinate*) 606; averse &c. (*unwilling*) 603; repugnant &c. (*dislike*) 867.

enforce, force; impel &c. (*push*) 276; propel &c. 284; whip, lash, goad, spur, prick, urge; egg –, hound –, hurry- on; drag &c. 285; exhort; advise &c. 695; call upon &c., press &c. (*request*) 765; advocate.

set -an example, – the fashion; keep in countenance; back up.

be -persuaded &c.; yield to temptation, come round; concede &c. (*consent*) 762; obey a call; follow -advice, – the bent, – the dictates of; act on principle.

Adj. impulsive, motive; suas-, persuas-, hortat-ive, -ory; protreptical; inviting, tempting &c. *v.*; seductive, attractive, irresistible; fascinating &c. (*pleasing*) 829; provocative &c. (*exciting*) 824.

induced &c. *v.*; disposed; persuadable &c. (*docile*) 602; spellbound; instinct –, smitten- with; inspired &c. *v.*- by.

Adv. because, therefore &c. (*cause*) 155; from -this, – that- motive; for -this, – that- reason; for; by reason –, for the sake –, on the score –, on account- of; out of, from, as, forasmuch as.

for all the world; on principle.

617. [Ostensible motive, ground, or reason assigned.] **Plea.—N.** plea, pretext; allegation, advocation; ostensible -motive, – ground, – reason; excuse &c. (*vindication*) 937; colour; gloss, guise.

loop-, starting-hole; how to creep out of, salvo, come off.

handle, peg to hang on, room, *locus standi*; stalking-horse, *cheval de bataille*, cue.

pretence &c. (*untruth*) 546; put off, subterfuge, dust thrown in the eyes; blind; moonshine; mere –, shallow- pretext; lame -excuse, – apology; tub to a whale; false plea, sour grapes; makeshift, shift, white lie; special pleading &c. (*sophistry*) 477; soft sawder &c. (*flattery*) 933.

V. plead, allege; shelter oneself under the plea of; excuse &c. (*vindicate*) 937; gloss over; lend a colour to; furnish a -handle &c. *n.*; make a -pretext, – handle- of; use as a plea &c. *n.*; take one's stand upon, make capital out of; pretend &c. (*lie*) 544.

Adj. ostensible &c. (*manifest*) 525; excusing; alleged, apologetic; pretended &c. 545.

Adv. ostensibly; under -colour, – the plea, – the pretence- of.

3°. Objects of Volition

618. Good.—N. good, benefit, advantage; improvement &c. 658; interest, service, behoof, behalf; weal; main chance, *summum bonum*, common weal; 'consummation devoutly to be wished'; gain, boot; profit, harvest.

boon &c. (*gift*) 784; good turn; blessing, benison; world of good; piece of good -luck, – fortune; nuts, prize, windfall, godsend, waif, treasure trove.

good fortune &c. (*prosperity*) 734; happiness &c. 827.

[Source of good] goodness &c. 648; utility &c. 644; remedy &c. 662; pleasure-giving &c. 829.

Adj. commendable &c. 931; useful &c. 644; good &c., beneficial &c. 648.

619. Evil.—N. evil, ill, harm, hurt, mischief, nuisance; machinations of the devil, Pandora's box, ills that flesh is heir to.

blow, buffet, stroke, scratch, bruise, wound, gash, mutilation; mortal -blow, – wound; *immedicabile vulnus*; damage, loss &c. (*deterioration*) 659.

disadvantage, prejudice, drawback.

disaster, accident, casualty; mishap &c. (*misfortune*) 735; bad job, devil to pay; calamity, bale, woe, catastrophe, tragedy; ruin &c. (*destruction*) 162; adversity &c. 735.

mental suffering &c. 828. [Evil spirit] demon &c. 980. [Cause of evil] bane &c. 663. [Production of evil]

V. benefit, profit, advantage, serve, help, avail; do good to, gain, prosper, flourish.

Adv. well, aright, satisfactorily, favourably, not amiss; all for the best; to one's -advantage &c. *n.*; in one's -favour, – interest &c. *n.*

Phr. so far so good.

badness &c. 649; painfulness &c. 830; evil doer &c. 913.

outrage, wrong, injury, foul play; bad –, ill- turn; disservice; spoliation &c. 791; grievance, crying evil.

V. be in trouble &c. (*adversity*) 735; harm, injure, hurt, do disservice to.

Adj. disastrous, bad &c. 649; awry, out of joint; disadvantageous, injurious, harmful.

Adv. amiss, wrong, ill, to one's cost.

Section II. Prospective Volition*
1°. *Conceptional Volition*

620. Intention.—N. intent, -ion, -ionality; purpose; *quo animo*; project &c. 626; undertaking &c. 676; predetermination &c. 611; design, ambition.

contemplation, mind, *animus*, view, purview, proposal; study; look out.

final cause; *raison d'être*; *cui bono*; object, aim, end; 'the be all and the end all'; drift &c. (*meaning*) 516; tendency &c. 176; destination, mark, point, butt, goal, target, bull's-eye, quintain; prey, quarry, game.

decision, determination, resolve; set –, settled- purpose; *ultimatum*; resolution &c. 604; wish &c. 865; *arrière-pensée*; motive &c. 615.

[Study of final causes] teleology.

V. intend, purpose, design, mean; have to; propose to oneself; harbour a design; have in -view, – contemplation, – one's eye, – *petto*; have an eye to.

bid –, labour- for; be –, aspire –, endeavour- after; be –, aim –, drive –, point-, level - at; take aim; set before oneself; study to.

take upon oneself &c (*undertake*) 676; take into one's head; meditate, contemplate; think – dream –, talk-of; premeditate &c. 611; compass, calculate; dest-ine, -inate; propose.

project &c. (*plan*) 626; have a mind to &c. (*be willing*) 602; desire &c. 865; pursue &c. 622.

Adj. intended &c. *v.*; intentional, advised, express, determinate; prepense &c. 611; bound for; intending &c. *v.*; minded, disposed, inclined;

621. [Absence of purpose in the succession of events.] **Chance.†—N.** chance &c. 156; lot, fate &c. (*necessity*) 601; luck; good luck &c. (*good*) 618; bad luck &c. 735; wheel of fortune; mascot; swastika.

speculation, venture, stake, flutter, flier, gamble, game of chance; mere –, random- shot; blind bargain, leap in the dark; pig in a poke &c. (*uncertainty*) 475; fluke, pot-luck.

drawing lots; sorti-legy, -tion; *sortes, – Virgilianæ*; *rouge et noir*, hazard, *roulette*, pitch and toss, chuck-farthing, cup-tossing, heads or tails, cross and pile, wager; bet, -ting; risk, stake, plunge; gambling; the turf.

stock exchange, bourse, board of trade, curb exchange.

gaming-, gambling-, betting-house; hell; betting ring, totalisator; dice, – box; dicer; gam-bler, -ester, plunger, stock operator, manipulator, punter; man of the turf; adventurer, speculator; bookmaker, layer, backer.

V. chance &c. (*hap*) 156; stand a chance &c. (*be possible*) 470.

toss up; cast –, draw- lots; leave –, trust- -to chance, – to the chapter of accidents; tempt fortune; chance it, take one's chance; run –, incur –, encounter- the -risk, – chance; stand the hazard of the die.

speculate, try one's luck, set on a cast, raffle, put into a lottery, buy a pig in a poke, shuffle the cards.

risk, venture, hazard, stake; lay, – a wager; make a bet, wager, bet, gamble,

* That is, volition having reference to a future object.   † See note on 156.

bent upon &c. (*earnest*) 604; at stake, on the -anvil, – *tapis*; in -view; – prospect, – the breast of; *in petto*; teleological.

Adv. intentionally &c. *adj.*; advisedly, wittingly, knowingly, designedly, purposely, on purpose, by design, studiously, pointedly; with -intent &c. *n.*; deliberately &c. (*with premeditation*) 611; with one's eyes open, in cold blood.

for; with -a view, – an eye- to; in order -to, – that; to the end –, with the intent- that; for the purpose –, with the view –, in contemplation –, on account- of.

in pursuance of, pursuant to; *quo animo*; to all intents and purposes.

622. [Purpose in action.] **Pursuit.**— **N.** pursuit; pursuing &c. *v.*; prosecution; pursuance; enterprise &c. (*undertaking*) 676; business &c. 625; adventure &c. (*essay*) 675; quest &c. (*search*) 461; scramble, hue and cry, game; hobby.

chase, hunt, *battue*, race, steeplechase, hunting, coursing; ven-ation, -ery; fox-chase; sport, -ing; shooting, angling, fishing, hawking.

pursuer; hunt-er, -sman; sportsman, Nimrod, the field; hound &c. 366.

V. pursue, prosecute, follow; run –, make –, be –, hunt –, prowl- after; shadow; carry on &c. (*do*) 680; engage in &c. (*undertake*) 676; set about &c. (*begin*) 66; endeavour &c. 675; court &c. (*request*) 765; seek &c. (*search*) 461; aim at &c. (*intention*) 620; follow the trail &c. (*trace*) 461; fish for &c. (*experiment*) 463; press on &c. (*haste*) 684; run a race &c. (*velocity*) 274.

chase, give chase, course, dog, hunt, hound, stalk; tread –, follow- on the heels of &c. (*sequence*) 281.

rush upon; rush headlong &c. (*violence*) 173; ride –, run- full tilt at; make a leap –, jump –, snatch- at; run down; start game.

tread a path; take –, hold- a course; shape –, direct –, bend- one's -steps, – course; play a game; fight –, elbow- one's way; follow up; take -to, – up; go in for; ride one's hobby.

Adj. pursuing &c. *v.*; in quest of &c.

game, play for; play at chuck-farthing.

Adj. fortuitous &c. 156; unintentional, -ded; accidental; not meant; un-designed, -purposed; unpremeditated &c. 612; never thought of.

indiscriminate, promiscuous; undirected, random; aim-, drift-, design-, purpose-, cause-less; without purpose. possible &c. 470.

Adv. casually &c. 156; unintentionally &c. *adj.*; unwittingly.

en passant, by the way, incidentally; as it may happen; at -random, – a venture, – haphazard; as luck would have it, by -chance, – good fortune; un-, -luckily.

———

623. [Absence of pursuit.] **Avoidance.** —**N.** abst-ention, -inence; forbearance; refraining &c. *v.*; inaction &c. 681; neutrality.

avoidance, evasion, elusion; seclusion &c. 893.

avolation, flight; escape &c. 671; retreat &c. 287; recoil &c. 277; departure &c. 293; rejection &c. 610.

shirker &c. *v.*; slacker; truant; fugitive, refugee; runa-way, -gate; renegade; deserter.

V. abstain, refrain, spare, not attempt; not do &c. 681; maintain the even tenor of one's way.

eschew, keep from, let alone, have nothing to do with; keep –, stand –, hold- -aloof, – off; take no part in, have no hand in.

avoid, shun; steer –, keep- clear of; fight shy of; keep -one's, – at a respectful- distance; keep –, get- out of the way; evade, elude, turn away from; set one's face against &c. (*oppose*) 708; deny oneself.

shrink; hang –, hold –, draw- back; recoil &c. 277; retire &c. (*recede*) 287; flinch, blink, blench, shy, shirk, dodge, parry, make way for, give place to.

beat a retreat; turn -tail, – one's back; take to one's heels; run, -away, – for one's life; cut and run; be off, – like a shot; fly, flee; fly –, flee –, run away- from; take –, take to- flight; desert, elope; make –, scamper –, sneak –, shuffle –, sheer- off; break –,

(*inquiry*) 461; in -pursuit, – full cry, – hot pursuit; on the scent.

Adv. in pursuance of &c. (*intention*) 620; after.

Int. tally-ho! yoicks! so-ho!

_____

burst –, tear oneself –, slip –, slink –, steal- -away, – away from; slip cable, part company, turn on one's heel; sneak out of, play truant, give one the go by, give leg bail, take French leave, slope, decamp, flit, bolt, abscond, levant, skedaddle, absquatulate, cut one's stick, walk one's chalks, show a light pair of heels, make oneself scarce; escape &c. 671; go away &c. (*depart*) 293; abandon &c. 624; reject &c. 610.

lead one a -dance, – a merry chase, – pretty dance; throw off the scent, play at hide and seek.

Adj. unsought, unattempted; avoiding &c. *v.*; neutral; shy of &c. (*unwilling*) 603; elusive, evasive, distant; fugitive, runaway; shy, wild.

Adj. lest, in order to avoid.

Int. forbear! keep –, hands- off! *sauve qui peut!* devil take the hindmost!

624. Relinquishment.—N. relinquish-, abandon-ment; desertion, defection, secession, withdrawal; cave of Adullam; *nolle prosequi.*

discontinuance &c. (*cessation*) 142; renunciation &c. (*recantation*) 607; abrogation &c. 756; resignation &c. (*retirement*) 757; desuetude &c. 614; cession &c. (*of property*) 782.

V. relinquish, give up, abandon, desert, forsake, leave in the lurch; depart –, secede –, withdraw- from; back – out of, – down from, leave, go back on one's word, quit, take leave of, bid a long farewell; vacate &c. (*resign*) 757.

renounce &c. (*abjure*) 607; forego, have done with, drop; write off; disuse &c. 678; discard &c. 782; wash one's hands of; drop all idea of; *nolle-pros.*; lose interest in.

break –, leave- off; desist; stop &c. (*cease*) 142; hold –, stay- one's hand; quit one's hold; give over, shut up shop.

throw up the -game, – cards; give up the -point, – argument; pass to the order of the day, move the previous question, table the motion.

Adj. unpursued; relinquished &c. *v.*; relinquishing &c. *v.*

Int. avast &c.! (*stop*) 142.

625. Business.—N. business, occupation, employment; pursuit &c. 622; what one is doing-, – about; affair, concern, matter, case, undertaking.

matter in hand, irons in the fire; thing to do, *agendum*, task, work, job, chore, errand, transaction, commission, mission, charge, care; duty &c. 926.

part, *rôle*, cue; province, function, look-out, department, capacity, sphere, orb, field, line; walk, – of life; beat, round, routine; race, career.

office, place, post, incumbency, living; situation, appointment, billet, berth, employ; service &c. (*servitude*) 749; engagement; undertaking &c. 676.

vocation, calling, profession, *métier*, cloth, faculty; industry, art; industrial arts; craft, mystery, handicraft; trade &c. (*commerce*) 794.

exercise; work &c. (*action*) 680; avocation; press of business &c. (*activity*) 682.

V. pass -, employ -, spend- one's time in; employ oneself -in, – upon;

occupy –, concern- oneself with; make it one's -business &c. *n.*; undertake &c. 676; enter a profession; betake oneself to, turn one's hand to;
have to do with &c. (*do*) 680.

drive a trade; carry on –, do –, transact- -business, – a trade &c. *n.*;
keep a shop; ply one's task, – trade; labour in one's vocation; pursue
the even tenor of one's way; attend to -business, – one's work.

officiate, serve, act; act –, play- one's part; do duty; serve –, discharge –, perform- the -office, – duties, – functions- of; hold –, fill- -an
office, – a place, – a situation; hold a portfolio.

be -about, – doing, – engaged in, – employed in, – occupied with, –
at work on; have one's hands in, have in hand; have on one's -hands,
– shoulders; bear the burden; have one's hands full &c. (*activity*) 682.

be -in the hands of, – on the stocks, – on the anvil; pass through
one's hands.

Adj. business-like; work-a-day; professional; official, functional;
busy &c. (*actively employed*) 682; on –, in- -hand, – one's hands; afoot;
on -foot, – the anvil; going on; acting.

Adv. in the course of business, all in a day's work; professionally
&c. *adj.*

626. Plan.—N. plan, scheme, design, project; propos-al, -ition; suggestion; resolution, motion; precaution &c. (*provision*) 673; deep-laid
&c. (*premeditated*) 611- plan &c.; racket.

system &c. (*order*) 58; organization &c. (*arrangement*) 60; germ &c.
(*cause*) 153; Five Year Plan.

sketch, skeleton, outline, draught, draft, *ébauche, brouillon*; rough
-cast, – draft, – draught, – copy; copy; proof, revise.

forecast, *programme*, prospectus, scenario; *carte du pays*; card; bill,
protocol; order of the day, list of agenda, *memorandum*; bill of fare &c.
(*food*) 298; base of operations; platform, plank.

rôle; policy &c. (*line of conduct*) 692.

contrivance, invention, expedient, receipt, nostrum, artifice, device,
gadget; stratagem &c. (*cunning*) 702; trick &c. (*deception*) 545; alternative, loophole, shift &c. (*substitute*) 147; last shift &c. (*necessity*) 601.

measure, step; stroke, – of policy; master stroke; trump-, court-card;
cheval de bataille, great gun; *coup*, – *d'état*; clever –, bold –, good-
-move, – hit, – stroke; bright -thought, – idea, great idea.

intrigue, cabal, plot, frame-up, conspiracy, complot, machination;
under-, counter-plot.

schem-ist, -atist; strategist, machinator, schemer; projector, author,
builder, artist, promoter, designer &c. *v.*; conspirator; *intrigant* &c.
(*cunning*) 702.

V. plan, scheme, design, frame, contrive, project, forecast, sketch;
conceive, devise, invent &c. (*imagine*) 515; set one's wits to work
&c. 515; spring a project; fall –, hit- upon; strike –, chalk –, cut –,
lay –, map-out; lay down a plan; shape –, mark- out a course; prede-
termine &c. 611; concert, preconcert, preestablish; prepare &c. 673;
hatch, – a plot; concoct; take -steps, – measures.

cast, recast, systematize, organize; arrange &c. 60; digest, mature.

plot; counter-plot, -mine; dig a mine; lay a train; intrigue &c.
(*cunning*) 702.

Adj. planned &c. *v.*; strategic, -al; planning &c. *v.*; in course of preparation &c. 673; under consideration; on the -*tapis*, – carpet, – table.

627. Method. [Path.]—N. method, way, manner, wise, gait, form, mole, fashion, tone, guise; *modus operandi*; procedure &c. (*line of conduct*) 692.

path, road, route, course; line of -way, – road; trajectory, orbit, track, beat, tack.

steps; stair, -case; flight of stairs, ladder, stile.

bridge, viaduct, gauntry, pontoon, stepping stone, plank, gangway, catwalk, drawbridge; pass, ford, ferry, tunnel, subway, elevated; pipe &c. 260.

door; gateway &c. (*opening*) 260; channel, passage, avenue, means of access, approach, perron, adit, entrance; artery, lane, alley, aisle, lobby, corridor, cloister; back- door, -stairs; secret passage; covert-way.

road-, path-, stair-way; thoroughfare; highway, pike, turnpike, trail, parkway, *boulevard*; turnpike –, royal –, coach- road; broad –, King's –, Queen's- highway; beaten -track, – path; horse –, bridle- road, – track, – path; pathway; walk, *trottoir*, foot-path, pavement, flags, side-walk; by –, cross- -road, – path, – way; cut; short -cut &c. (*mid-course*) 628; *carrefour*; private –, occupation- road; highways and byways; rail-, tram-road, -way; funicular, ropeway, causeway; defile, cutting; canal &c. (*conduit*) 350; street &c. (*abode*) 189.

Adv. how; in what -way, – manner; by what mode; so, in this way, after this fashion, on these lines.

one way or another, anyhow; somehow or other &c. (*instrumentality*) 631; by way of; *viâ*; *in transitu* &c. 270; on the high road to.

Phr. *hæ tibi erunt artes.*

---

628. Mid-course.—**N.** middle-, mid-course; moderation, mean &c. 29; middle &c. 68; *juste milieu*, *mezzo termine*, golden mean, *aurea mediocritas*.

straight &c. (*direct*) 278 -course, – path; short –, cross- cut; short-circuit; great circle sailing.

neutrality; half –, half and half-measures; compromise.

V. keep in –, steer –, preserve- -a middle, – an even- course; go straight &c. (*direct*) 278.

go half way, compromise, make a compromise.

Adj. neutral, average, even, impartial, moderate, straight &c. (*direct*) 278.

629. Circuit.—**N.** circuit, round-about way, digression, divagation, *détour*, circum-ambience, -ambulation, bendibus, *ambages*, loop; winding &c. (*circuition*) 311; zigzag &c. (*deviation*) 279.

V. perform –, make- a circuit; go -round about, – out of one's way; make a *détour*; meander &c. (*deviate*) 27; circumambulate.

lead a pretty dance; beat about, – the bush; make two bites of a cherry.

Adj. circuitous, indirect, round-about; zig-zag &c. (*deviating*) 279; circum-ambient, -ambulatory.

Adv. by -a side wind, – an indirect course; in a roundabout way; from pillar to post.

---

630. Requirement.—**N.** requirement, need, wants, necessities; neces-saries, – of life; stress, exigency, pinch, *sine quâ non*, matter of necessity; case of -need, – life or death.

needfulness, essentiality, necessity, indispensability, urgency, pre-requisite.

requisition &c. (*request*) 765, (*exaction*) 741; run upon; demand –, call- for.

desideratum &c. (*desire*) 865; want &c. (*deficiency*) 640.

charge, claim, command, injunction, requisition, mandate, order, *ultimatum*.

V. require, need, want, have occasion for, entail; not be able to -do without, – dispense with; prerequire.

render necessary, necessitate, create a necessity for, call for, put in requisition; make a requisition &c. (*ask for*) 765, (*demand*) 741.

stand in need of; lack &c. 640; desiderate; desire &c. 865; be -necessary &c. *adj.*

Adj. required &c. *v.*; requisite, needful, necessary, imperative, essential, indispensable, prerequisite; called for; in -demand, – request.

urgent, exigent, pressing, instant, crying, absorbing.

in want of; destitute of &c. 640.

Adv. *ex necessitate rei* &c. (*necessarily*) 601; of –, out of stern- necessity; at a pinch.

Phr. there is no time to lose; it cannot be -spared, – dispensed with.

2° *Subservience to Ends*

1. *Actual Subservience*

631. Instrumentality.—N. instrumentality; aid &c. 707; subservien-ce, -cy; mediation, inter-vention, -mediacy, medium, inter-medium, -mediary, vehicle, hand; agency &c. 170.

minister, handmaid, servant, slave, maid, valet; midwife, *accoucheur*, obstetrician; go-between; cat's paw; stepping-stone.

key; master –, pass –, latch- key; 'open sesame'; passport, *passe partout*, safe-conduct; influence.

instrument &c. 633; expedient &c. (*plan*) 626; means &c. 632.

V. subserve, minister, tend, mediate, intervene; come –, go- between, interpose; pull the strings; be -instrumental &c. *adj.*; pander to.

Adj. instrumental; useful &c. 644; ministerial, subservient, mediatorial; inter-mediate, -vening; conducive.

Adv. through, by, *per*; where-, there-, here-by; by the -agency &c. 170- of; by dint of; by –, in- virtue of; through the -medium &c. *n.*-of; along with; on the shoulders of; by means of &c. 632; by –, with--the aid &c. (*assistance*) 707- of.

per fas et nefas, by fair means or foul; somehow, – or other; by hook or by crook.

632. Means.—N. means, resources, revenue, wherewithal, ways and means, income; capital &c. (*money*) 800; stock in trade &c. 636; provision &c. 637; a shot in the locker; appliances &c. (*machinery*) 633; means and appliances; conveniences; cards to play; expedients &c. (*measures*) 626; two strings to one's bow; sheet anchor &c. (*safety*) 666; aid &c. 707; medium &c. 631.

V. find –, have –, possess- means &c. *n.*; provide the wherewithal.

Adj. instrumental &c. 631; mechanical &c. 633.

Adv. by means of, with; by -what, – all, – any, – some- means; where-, here-, there-with; wherewithal.

how &c. (*in what manner*) 627; through &c. (*by the instrumentality of*) 631; with –, by- the aid &c. (*assistance*) 707- of; by the -agency &c. 170- of.

633. Instrument.—N. machinery, mechanism, engineering.

instrument, organ, tool, implement, utensil, contrivance, machine, motor, engine, lathe, gin, mill, pump.

gear; tack-le, -ling, trice, rigging, gear, apparatus, appliances; plant, *matériel*; harness, trappings, fittings, accoutrements; equip-ment, -age;

appointments, furniture, upholstery; chattels; paraphernalia &c. (*belongings*) 780; *impedimenta*.

mechanical powers; lever, -age; mechanical advantage; crow, -bar; handspike, gavelock, jemmy, arm, limb, wing; oar, paddle; pulley, sheave; parbuckle; wheel and axle; wheel-, clock-work; wheels within wheels; pinion, gear wheel, spur –, bevel- gearing, chains, belting, crank, winch, capstan, windlass, crane, derrick, hoist, lift &c. 307; cam; pedal; wheel &c. (*rotation*) 312; inclined plane; wedge; screw; jack; spring, mainspring.

handle, hilt, haft, shaft, heft, shank, blade, trigger, tiller, helm, treadle, key; turnscrew, screwdriver, spanner, wrench.

hammer &c. (*impulse*) 276; edge tool &c. (*cut*) 253; borer &c. 262; vice, teeth &c. (*hold*) 781; nail, rope &c. (*join*) 45; peg &c. (*hang*) 214; support &c. 215; spoon &c. (*vehicle*) 272; arms &c. 727; oar &c. (*navigation*) 267.

Adj. instrumental &c. 631; mechanical, machinal, automatic, self-acting; brachial.

634. Substitute.—N. substitute &c. 147; deputy &c. 759; proxy, alternative, understudy.

635. Materials.—N. material, raw material, stuff, stock, staple; building materials, bricks and mortar; metal; stone; clay, brick; crockery &c. 384; compo, -sition; reinforced –, ferro-, concrete; cement; wood, ore, timber; gravel, cobbles, macadam, asphalt, tarmac.

materials; supplies, munition, fuel, grist, household stuff; *pabulum* &c. (*food*) 298; ammunition &c. (*arms*) 727; contingents; relay, reinforcement; baggage &c. (*personal property*) 780; means &c. 632.

Adj. raw &c. (*unprepared*) 674; wooden &c. *n.*

636. Store.—N. stock, fund, mine, vein, lode, quarry; spring; fount, -ain; well, -spring; milch-cow.

stock in trade, supply; heap &c. (*collection*) 72; treasure; reserve, *corps de réserve*, reserve fund, nest-egg, savings, *bonne bouche*.

crop, harvest, mow, vintage; yield, product, gleanings.

store, accumulation, hoard, rick, stack; lumber; relay &c. (*provision*) 637.

store-house, -room, -closet; depository, *dépôt*, cache, safe deposit, vault, pantechnicon, re-pository, -servatory, -pertory; *repertorium*; promptuary, warehouse, *entrepôt*, magazine, dump, buttery, larder, pantry, panary, lanary, still-room, spence; crib, garner, granary, silo, barn; bunker; thesaurus; bank &c. (*treasury*) 802; armoury; arsenal; dock; gallery, museum, library, conservatory, hot-house; menag-ery, -erie, aquarium, zoological gardens.

reservoir, cistern, tank, sump, pond, mill-pond; gasometer.

budget, quiver, bandolier, portfolio; coffer &c. (*receptacle*) 191.

conservation; storing &c. *v.*; storage.

dictionary &c. 562; list &c. 86.

V. store; put –, lay –, set- by; stow away; set –, lay- apart; store –, hoard –, treasure –, lay –, heap –, put –, garner –, save- up; *cache*; accumulate, amass, hoard, fund, garner, save, bank.

conserve, reserve; keep –, hold- back; husband, – one's resources.

deposit; stow, stack, load, dump; harvest; heap, collect &c. 72; lay -in, – down, – by, store &c. *adj.*; keep, file [papers]; lay in &c. (*provide*) 637; preserve &c. 670; put by for a rainy day.

Adj. stored &c. *v.*; in -store, – reserve, – ordinary; spare, super-numerary.

637. Provision.—N. provision, sup-ply; grist, – to the mill; subvention &c. (*aid*) 707; resources &c. (*means*) 632.

providing &c. *v.*; purveyance; rein-forcement; commissary, commissariat.

rations; iron –, emergency- rations; provender &c. (*food*) 298; *viaticum*; ensilage.

caterer, purveyor, commissary, quar-termaster, steward, housekeeper, man-ciple, feeder, batman, victualler, store-keeper, grocer, provision merchant, green-, grocer, *comprador, restaurateur*; sutler &c. (*merchant*) 797; innkeeper, publican, confectioner, baker, butcher, wine merchant, vintner.

V. provide; make -provision, – due provision for; lay in, – a stock, – a store.

sup-ply, -peditate; furnish; find, – one in; arm.

cater, victual, provision, purvey, for-age; beat up for; stock, – with; make good, replenish; fill, – up; recruit, feed, ration.

have in -store, – reserve; keep, – by one, – on foot; have to fall back upon; store &c. 636; provide against a rainy day &c. (*economy*) 817.

639. Sufficiency.—N. sufficiency, adequacy, enough, withal, *quantum sufficit*, satisfaction, competence; no less.

mediocrity &c. (*average*) 29.

fill; fulness &c. (*completeness*) 52; plen-itude, -ty; abundance; copiousness &c. *adj.*; amplitude, galore, lots, pro-fusion; full measure; 'good measure pressed down, shaken together and running over.'

luxuriance &c. (*fertility*) 168; afflu-ence &c. (*wealth*) 803; fat of the land; 'a land flowing with milk and honey'; cornucopia; horn of -plenty, – Amal-thæa; mine &c. (*stock*) 636.

outpouring; flood &c. (*great quantity*) 31; tide &c. (*river*) 348; repletion &c. (*redundance*) 641; satiety &c. 869; rich man &c. 803.

638. Waste.—N. consumption, ex-penditure, exhaustion; dispersion &c. 73; ebb; leakage &c. (*exudation*) 295; loss &c. 776; wear and tear; waste; prodigality &c. 818; misuse &c. 679; wasting &c. *v.*; rubbish &c. (*useless*) 645.

mountain in labour.

V. spend, expend, use, consume, swallow up, exhaust, deplete; impov-erish; spill, drain, empty; disperse &c. 73.

cast –, throw –, fling –, fritter- away; burn the candle at both ends, waste; squander &c. 818.

'waste its sweetness on the desert air'; cast -one's bread upon the waters, – pearls before swine; employ a steam engine to crack a nut, waste powder and shot, break a butterfly on a wheel; labour in vain &c. (*useless*) 645; cut a whetstone with a razor, pour water into a sieve; tilt at windmills.

leak &c. (*run out*) 295; run to waste; ebb; melt away, run dry, dry up.

Adj. wasted &c. *v.*; at a low ebb.

wasteful &c. (*prodigal*) 818; penny wise and pound foolish.

Phr. *magno conatu magnas nugas; le jeu n'en vaut pas la chandelle.*

640. Insufficiency.—N. insufficiency; inadequa-cy, -teness; incompetence &c. (*impotence*) 158; deficiency &c. (*incom-pleteness*) 53; imperfection &c. 651; shortcoming &c. 304; paucity; stint; scantiness &c. (*smallness*) 32; none to spare; bare subsistence.

scarcity, dearth; want, need, lack, poverty, exigency; inanition, starva-tion, famine, drought.

dole, pittance, mite; short -allow-ance, – commons; half-rations; ban-yan –, fast- day, Lent.

emptiness, poorness &c. *adj.*; deple-tion, vacancy, flaccidity; ebb-tide; low water; 'a beggarly account of empty boxes'; indigence &c. (*poverty*) 804; insolvency &c. (*non-payment*) 808; poor man &c. 804; bankrupt &c. 808.

V. be -insufficient &c. *adj.*; not -suf-

V. be -sufficient &c. *adj.*; suffice, do, just do, satisfy, pass muster; have -enough &c. *n.*; eat –, drink –, have-one's fill; roll –, swim- in; wallow in &c. (*superabundance*) 641.

abound, exuberate, teem, flow, stream, rain, shower down; pour, – in; swarm; bristle with.

render -sufficient &c. *adj.*; replenish &c. (*fill*) 52.

Adj. sufficient, enough, adequate, up to the mark, commensurate, competent, satisfactory, valid, tangible.

measured; moderate &c. (*temperate*) 953.

full &c. (*complete*) 52; ample; plen-ty, -tiful, -teous; plenty as blackberries; copious, abundant; abounding &c. *v.*; replete, enough and to spare, flush; choke-full; well-stocked, -provided; liberal; unstint-ed, -ing; stintless; without stint; un-sparing, -measured; lavish &c. 641; wholesale.

rich; luxuriant &c. (*fertile*) 168; affluent &c. (*wealthy*) 803; wantless; big with &c. (*pregnant*) 161.

un-exhausted, -wasted; exhaustless, inexhaustible.

Adv. sufficiently, amply &c. *adj.*; full; in -abundance &c. *n.*; with no sparing hand; to one's heart's content, *ad libitum*, without stint.

Phr. cut and come again.

fice &c. 639; come short of &c. 304; run dry.

want, lack, need, require; *caret*; be in want &c. (*poor*) 804; live from hand to mouth.

render- insufficient &c. *adj.*; drain of resources; impoverish &c. (*waste*) 638; stint &c. (*begrudge*) 819; put on short -commons, – allowance.

do -insufficiently &c. *adv.*; scotch the snake.

Adj. insufficient, inadequate; too -little &c. 32; not -enough &c. 639; unequal to; incompetent &c. (*impotent*) 158; 'weighed in the balance and found wanting'; perfunctory &c. (*neglect*) 460; deficient &c. (*incomplete*) 53; wanting &c. *v.*; imperfect &c. 651; ill-furnished, -provided, -stored, -off.

slack, at a low ebb; empty, vacant, bare; short –, out –, destitute –, devoid –, bereft &c. 789 –, denuded- of; dry, drained.

un -provided, -supplied, -furnished; un-replenished, -fed; un-stored, -treasured; empty-handed.

meagre, poor, thin, scrimp, sparing, spare, stinted, stunted; skimpy; starv-ed, -eling; half-starved, emaciated, famine-stricken, famished, under-fed, undernourished; jejune.

scant &c. (*small*) 32; scarce; not to be had, – for love or money, – at any price; scurvy; stingy &c. 819; at the end of one's tether; without -resources &c. 632; in want &c. (*poor*) 804; in debt &c. 806.

Adv. insufficiently &c. *adj.*; in default –, for want- of; failing.

641. Redundance.—N. redundance; too -much, – many; super-abundance, -fluity, -fluence, -saturation; nimiety, transcendency, exuberance, profuseness; profusion &c. (*plenty*) 639; repletion, enough in all conscience, *satis superque*, lion's share; more than -enough &c. 639; plethora, engorgement, congestion, load, surfeit, sickener; turgescence &c. (*expansion*) 194; over-dose, -measure, -supply, -flow; inundation &c. (*water*) 348; *avalanche.*

accumulation &c. (*store*) 636; heap &c. 72; drug, – in the market; glut; crowd; burden.

excess; sur-, over-plus, epact; margin; remainder &c. 40; duplicate; surplusage, expletive; work of –, supererogation; *bonus, bonanza.*

luxury; intemperance &c. 954; extravagance &c. (*prodigality*) 818; exorbitance, lavishment.

pleonasm &c. (*diffuseness*) 573; too many irons in the fire; embarrassment of riches; money to burn.

V. super-, over-abound; know no bounds, swarm; meet one at every turn; creep –, bristle- with; overflow; run –, flow –, well –, brim-over; run riot; over-run, -stock, -lay, -charge, -dose, -feed, -burden, -load, -do, -whelm, -shoot the mark &c. (*go beyond*) 303; surcharge, supersaturate, gorge, glut, load, drench, whelm, inundate, deluge, flood; drug, – the market.

choke, cloy, accloy, suffocate; pile up, lay it on, – with a trowel, lay on thick; impregnate with; lavish &c. (*squander*) 818.

send –, carry- coals to Newcastle, – owls to Athens; teach one's grandmother to suck eggs; *pisces natare docere*; kill the slain, 'gild refined gold,' 'paint the lily'; butter one's bread on both sides, put butter upon bacon; employ a steam-engine to crack a nut &c. (*waste*) 638.

exaggerate &c. 549; wallow in; roll in &c. (*plenty*) 639; remain on one's hands, hang heavy on hand, go a begging.

Adj. redundant; too -much, – many; exuberant, inordinate, super-abundant, excessive, overmuch, replete, profuse, lavish; prodigal &c. 818; exorbitant; overweening; extravagant; overcharged &c. *v.*; super-saturated, drenched, overflowing; running -over, – to waste, – down.

crammed –, filled- to overflowing; gorged, stuffed, ready to burst; dropsical, turgid, plethoric, full-blooded; obese &c. 194; voluminous.

superfluous, unnecessary, needless, supervacaneous, uncalled for, to spare, in excess; over and above &c. (*remainder*) 40; *de trop*; adscititious &c. (*additional*) 37; supernumerary &c. (*reserve*) 636; on one's hands, spare, duplicate, supererogatory, expletive; *un peu fort*.

Adv. over, too, over and above; over –, too- much; too far; without -, beyond -, out of- measure; with . . . to spare; over head and ears; up to one's -eyes, – ears; *extra*; beyond the mark &c. (*transcursion*) 303; over one's head.

Phr. it never rains but it pours.

2. *Degree of Subservience*

642. Importance.—N. importance, consequence, moment, prominence, consideration, mark, materialness.

import, significance, concern; emphasis, interest.

greatness &c. 31; superiority &c. 33; notability &c. (*repute*) 873; weight &c. (*influence*) 175; value &c. (*goodness*) 648; usefulness &c. 644.

gravity, seriousness, solemnity; no -joke, – laughing matter; pressure, urgency, stress; matter of life and death. *memorabilia, notabilia*, great doings; red-letter day.

great -thing, – point; main chance, 'the be all and end all,' cardinal point, outstanding feature; substance, gist &c. (*essence*) 5; sum and substance, *gravamen*, head and front; important -, principal -, prominent -, essential-part; half the battle; *sine quâ non*; breath of one's nostrils &c. (*life*) 359; cream, salt, core, kernel, heart, nucleus;

643. Unimportance.—N. unimportance, insignificance, nothingness, immateriality.

triviality, trivia, fribble, levity, frivolity; paltriness &c. *adj.*; poverty; smallness &c. 32; vanity &c. (*uselessness*) 645; matter of -indifference &c. 866; no object; side issue.

nothing, – to signify, – worth speaking of, – particular, – to boast of, – to speak of; small -, no great -, trifling &c. *adj.* -matter; mere -joke, – nothing; hardly -, scarcely- anything; nonentity, cipher, figurehead; no great shakes, *peu de chose*; child's play; small beer.

toy, plaything, popgun, paper pellet, gimcrack, gewgaw, bauble, trinket, *bagatelle*, kickshaw, knicknack, whimwham, trifle, 'trifles light as air.'

trumpery, trash, rubbish, stuff, *fatras*, frippery; 'leather or prunello'; chaff, drug, froth, bubble, smoke, cob-

key, -note, -stone; corner stone; trump-card &c. (*device*) 626; salient points.

top-sawyer, first fiddle, *prima donna*, chief, big-wig; triton among the minnows.

V. be -important &c. *adj.*, – somebody, – something; import, signify, matter, be an object; carry weight &c. (*influence*) 175; make a figure &c. (*repute*) 873; be in the ascendant, come to the front, lead the way, take the lead, play first fiddle, throw all else into the shade; lie at the root of; deserve –, merit –, be worthy- -of notice, – regard, – consideration.

attach –, ascribe –, give- importance &c. *n.*- to; value, care for; set store -upon, – by; mark &c. 550; mark with a white stone, underline; write –, put –, print- in -italics, – capitals, – large letters, – large type, – letters of gold; accentuate, emphasize, lay stress on.

make -a fuss, – a stir, – a piece of work, – much ado- about; make -of, – much of.

Adj. important; of -importance &c. *n.*; momentous, material; to the point; not to be -overlooked, – despised, – sneezed at; egregious; weighty &c. (*influential*) 175; of note &c. (*repute*) 873; notable, prominent, salient, signal; memorable, remarkable; worthy of -remark, – notice; never to be forgotten; stirring, eventful.

grave, serious, earnest, noble, grand, solemn, impressive, commanding, imposing.

urgent, pressing, critical, instant.

paramount, essential, vital, all-absorbing, radical, cardinal, chief, main, prime, primary, principal, leading, capital, foremost, overruling; of vital &c. importance.

in the front rank, first-rate, A1; superior &c. 33; considerable &c. (*great*) 31; marked &c. *v.*; rare &c. 137.

significant, telling, trenchant, emphatic, pregnant; *tanti*.

Adv. materially &c. *adj.*; in the main; above all, *par excellence*, to crown all.

------

web; weed; refuse &c. (*inutility*) 645; scum &c. (*dirt*) 653.

joke, jest, snap of the fingers; fudge &c. (*unmeaning*) 517; fiddlestick, – end; pack of nonsense, mere farce.

straw, pin, fig, continental, button, rush; bulrush, feather, halfpenny, farthing, brass farthing, doit, pepper-corn, jot, rap, pinch of snuff, old song.

minutiæ, details, minor details, small fry; dust in the balance, feather in the scale, drop in the ocean, flea-bite, molehill; fingle-fangle.

nine days' wonder, *ridiculus mus*; flash in the pan &c. (*impotence*) 158; much ado about nothing &c. (*overestimation*) 482; storm in a teacup.

V. be -unimportant &c. *adj.*; not -matter &c. 642; go for –, matter –, signify- -little, – nothing, – little or nothing; not matter a -straw &c. *n.*

make light of &c. (*underestimate*) 483; catch at straws &c. (*overestimate*) 482.

Adj. unimportant; of -little, – small, – no- -account, – importance &c. 642; immaterial; un-, non-essential; not vital; irrelevant, incidental, indifferent.

subordinate &c. (*inferior*) 34; *médiocre* &c. (*average*) 29; passable, fair, respectable, tolerable, commonplace; uneventful, mere, common; ordinary &c. (*habitual*) 613; inconsiderable, so-so, insignificant, inappreciable, nugatory.

trifling, trivial; slight, slender, light, flimsy, frothy, idle; puerile &c. (*foolish*) 499; airy, shallow; weak &c. 160; powerless &c. 158; frivolous, petty, niggling; pid-, ped-dling; fribble, inane, ridiculous, farcical; fini-cal, -kin; fiddle-faddle, namby-pamby, wishy-washy, milk and water.

poor, paltry, pitiful; contemptible &c. (*contempt*) 930; sorry, mean, meagre, shabby, miserable, wretched, vile, scrubby, scrannel, weedy, niggardly, scurvy, putid, beggarly, worthless, twopenny-halfpenny, cheap, trashy, catchpenny, gimcrack, trumpery, one-horse; toy.

not worth -the pains, – while, – mentioning, – speaking of, – a thought, – a curse, – a straw, – rap &c. *n.*; beneath –, unworthy of- -notice, – regard, – consideration, – contempt; *de lanâ caprinâ*; vain &c. (*useless*) 645.

Adv. slightly &c. *adj.*; rather, somewhat, pretty well, fairly well, tolerably.

for aught one cares.

Int. no matter! pish! tush! tut! pshaw! pugh! pooh, -pooh! fudge! bosh! humbug! fiddle-stick, – end! fiddlededee! never mind! *n'importe!* what -signifies, – matter, – boots it, – of that, –'s the odds! a fig for! stuff! nonsense! stuff and nonsense!

Phr. *magno conatu magnas nugas*; *le jeu n'en vaut pas la chandelle*; it -matters not, – does not signify; it is of no -consequence, – importance.

---

644. Utility.—N. utility; usefulness &c. *adj.*; efficacy, efficiency, adequacy; service, use, stead, avail; help &c. (*aid*) 707; applicability &c. *adj.*; subservience &c. (*instrumentality*) 631; function &c. (*business*) 625; value; worth &c. (*goodness*) 648; money's worth; productiveness &c. 168; *cui bono* &c. (*intention*) 620; utilization &c. (*use*) 677; step in the right direction.

common weal, public good; utilitarianism &c. (*philanthropy*) 910.

V. be -useful &c. *adj.*; avail, serve; subserve &c. (*be instrumental to*) 631; conduce &c. (*tend*) 176; answer –, serve- -one's turn, – a purpose.

act a part &c. (*action*) 680; perform –, discharge- -a function &c. 625; do –, render- -a service, – good service, – yeoman's service; bestead, stand one in good stead; be the making of; help &c. 707.

bear fruit &c. (*produce*) 161; bring grist to the mill; profit, remunerate; benefit &c. (*do good*) 648.

find one's -account, – advantage- in; reap the benefit of &c. (*be better for*) 658.

render useful &c. (*use*) 677.

Adj. useful; of -use &c. *n.*; serviceable, usable, proficuous, good for; subservient &c. (*instrumental*) 631; conducive &c. (*tending*) 176; subsidiary &c. (*helping*) 707.

advantageous &c. (*beneficial*) 648; profitable, gainful, remunerative, worth one's salt; in-, valuable; prolific &c. (*productive*) 168.

adequate; ef-ficient, -ficacious; effect-ive, -ual; practicable, expedient &c. 646.

645. Inutility.—N. inutility; uselessness &c. *adj.*; inefficacy, futility; inep-, inap-titude; unsubservience; inadequacy &c. (*insufficiency*) 640; inefficiency &c. (*incompetence*) 158; unskilfulness &c. 699; disservice; unfruitfulness &c. (*unproductiveness*) 169; labour -in vain, – lost, – of Sisyphus; lost -trouble, – labour; work of Penelope; sleeveless errand, wild goose chase, mere farce.

tautology &c. (*repetition*) 104; supererogation &c. (*redundance*) 641.

vanitas vanitatum, vanity, inanity, worthlessness, nugacity; triviality &c. (*unimportance*) 643.

caput mortuum, waste paper, dead letter; blunt tool.

litter, rubbish, lumber, odds and ends, cast-off clothes; button-top; shoddy; rags, orts, trash, refuse, sweepings, scourings, off-scourings, dross, slag, waste, rubble, dottle, drast, *débris*; stubble, leavings; broken meat; dregs &c. (*dirt*) 653; weeds, tares; rubbish heap, dust hole; *rudera*, deads.

fruges consumere natus &c. (*drone*) 683.

V. be -useless &c. *adj.*; go a begging &c. (*redundant*) 641; fail &c. 732.

seek –, strive- after impossibilities; use vain efforts, labour in vain, roll the stone of Sisyphus, beat the air, lash the waves, *battre l'eau avec un bâton, donner un coup d'épée dans l'eau*, fish in the air, milk the ram, drop a bucket into an empty well, sow the sand; bay the moon; preach –, speak- to the winds; whistle jigs to a milestone; kick against the pricks, *se battre contre des moulins*; lock the stable door

applicable, available, ready, handy, at hand, tangible; commodious, adaptable; of all work.

Adv. usefully &c. *adj.*; *pro bono publico.*

---

when the steed is stolen &c. (*too late*) 135; hold a farthing candle to the sun; cast pearls before swine &c. (*waste*) 638; carry coals to Newcastle &c. (*redundance*) 641; wash a blackamoor white &c. (*impossible*) 471.

render -useless &c. *adj.*; dis-mantle, -mast, -mount, -qualify, -able; unrig; cripple, lame &c. (*injure*) 659; spike guns, clip the wings; put out of gear.

Adj. useless, inutile, inefficacious, futile, unavailing, bootless; inoperative &c. 158; inadequate &c. (*insufficient*) 640; in-, un-sub-servient; inept, inefficient &c. (*impotent*) 158; of no -avail &c. (*use*) 644; ineffectual &c. (*failure*) 732; incompetent &c. (*unskilful*) 699; 'stale, flat and unprofitable'; superfluous &c. (*redundant*) 641; dispensable; thrown away &c. (*wasted*) 638; abortive &c. (*immature*) 674.

worth-, value-less; unsaleable; not worth a straw &c. (*trifling*) 643; dear at any price.

vain, empty, inane; gain-, profit-, fruit-less; un-serviceable, -profitable; ill-spent; unproductive &c. 169; *hors de combat*; barren, sterile, impotent, unproductive; effete, past work &c. (*impaired*) 659; obsolete &c. (*old*) 124; fit for the -dust-hole, - wastepaper basket; good for nothing; of no earthly use; not worth -having, - powder and shot; leading to no end, uncalled for; un-necessary, -needed, superfluous.

Adv. uselessly &c. *adj.*; to -little, - no, - little or no- purpose.

Int. *cui bono?* what's the good!

---

646. [Specific subservience.] **Expedience.—N.** expedien-ce, -cy; desirableness, -bility &c. *adj.*; fitness &c. (*agreement*) 23; utility &c. 644; propriety; advantage; opportunism, pragmatism.

high time &c. (*occasion*) 134.

V. be -expedient &c. *adj.*; suit &c. (*agree*) 23; befit; suit -, befit- the -time, - season, - occasion.

conform &c. 82.

Adj. expedient; desir-, advis-, acceptable; convenient; worth while, meet; fit, -ting; due, proper, eligible, seemly, becoming; befitting &c. *v.*; opportune &c. (*in season*) 134; *in loco*; suitable &c. (*accordant*) 23; applicable &c. (*useful*) 644; practical, effective, pragmatical; suitable, handy.

Adv. in the right place; conveniently &c. *adj.*; in the nick of time.

Phr. *operæ pretium est.*

---

647. Inexpedience.—N. inexpedien-ce, -cy; undesira-bleness, -bility &c. *adj.*; discommodity, impropriety; unfitness &c. (*disagreement*) 24; inutility &c. 645; inconvenience, inadvisability; disadvantage.

V. be -inexpedient &c. *adj.*; come amiss &c. (*disagree*) 24; embarrass &c. (*hinder*) 706; put to inconvenience; pay too dear for one's whistle.

Adj. inexpedient, undesirable; un-, in-advisable; objectionable; troublesome, in-apt, -eligible, -admissible, -convenient; in-, dis-commodious; disadvantageous; inappropriate, unsuitable, unfit &c. (*inconsonant*) 24.

ill-contrived, -advised; unsatisfactory; unprofitable &c., unsubservient &c. (*useless*) 645; inopportune &c. (*unseasonable*) 135; out of -, in the wrong- place; improper, unseemly.

clumsy, awkward; cum-brous, -bersome; lumbering, unwieldy, hulky; un-manageable &c. (*impracticable*) 704; impedient &c. (*in the way*) 706. unnecessary &c. (*redundant*) 641.

Phr. it will never do.

648. [Capability of producing good. Good qualities.] **Goodness.—N.** goodness &c. *adj.*; excellence, merit; virtue &c. 944; value, worth, price.

super-excellence, -eminence; superiority &c. 33; perfection &c. 650; *coup de maître*; master-piece, *chef d'œuvre*, prime, flower, cream, *élite*, pick, A1, none such, *nonpareil*, *crême de la crême*, flower of the flock, cock of the roost, salt of the earth; champion.

tid-bit; gem, – of the first water; *bijou*, precious stone, jewel, pearl, diamond, ruby, brilliant, treasure; good thing; *rara avis*, one in a thousand.

beneficence &c. 906; good man &c. 948.

V. be -beneficial &c. *adj.*; produce –, do- -good &c. 618; profit &c. (*be of use*) 644; benefit; confer a -benefit &c. 618.

be the making of, do a world of good, make a man of.

produce a good effect; do a good turn, confer an obligation; improve &c. 658.

do no harm, break no bones.

be -good &c. *adj.*; excel, transcend &c. (*be superior*) 33; bear away the bell.

stand the -proof, – test; pass -muster, – an examination.

challenge comparison, vie, emulate, rival.

Adj. harm-, hurt-less; unobnoxious; in-nocuous, -nocent, -offensive.

beneficial, valuable, of value; serviceable &c. (*useful*) 644; advantageous, profitable, edifying; salutary &c. (*healthful*) 656.

favourable; propitious &c. (*hope-giving*) 858; fair.

good, – as gold; excellent; better; superior &c. 33; above par; nice, fine; genuine &c. (*true*) 494.

best, choice, select, picked, elect, eximious, *recherché*, rare, priceless; unpara-goned, -lleled &c. (*supreme*) 33; superlatively &c. 33- good; super-fine, -excellent; bonzer; of the first water; first-rate, -class; high-wrought; exquisite, very best, crack, prime, tip-top, gilt-edged, capital, cardinal; standard &c. (*perfect*) 650; inimitable.

admirable, estimable; praiseworthy &c. (*approve*) 931; pleasing &c. 829; *couleur de rose*, precious, of great price;

649. [Capability of producing evil. Bad qualities.] **Badness.—N.** hurtfulness &c. *adj.*; virulence.

evil doer &c. 913; bane &c. 663; plague-spot &c. (*insalubrity*) 657; evil star, ill wind; snake in the grass, skeleton in the closet; *amari aliquid*, thorn in the side; Jonah, jinx, hoodoo.

malignity; malevolence &c. 907; tender mercies [ironically].

ill-treatment, annoyance, molestation, abuse, oppression, persecution, outrage; misusage &c. 679; injury &c. (*damage*) 659.

badness &c. *adj.*; peccancy, abomination; painfulness &c. 830; pestilence &c. (*disease*) 655; guilt &c. 947; depravity &c. 945.

V. be -hurtful &c. *adj.*; cause –, produce –, inflict –, work –, do- evil &c. 619; damnify, endamage, hurt, harm, scathe; injure &c. (*damage*) 659; pain &c. 830.

wrong, aggrieve, oppress, persecute; trample –, tread –, bear hard –, put-upon; overburden; weigh -down, – heavy on; victimize; run down; molest &c. 830.

maltreat, abuse; ill-use, -treat; thwart, buffet, bruise, scratch, maul; smite &c. (*scourge*) 972; do -violence, – harm, – a mischief; stab, pierce, outrage.

do –, make- mischief; bring –, get-into trouble.

destroy &c. 162.

Adj. hurt-, harm-, scath-, bane-, baleful; injurious, deleterious, detrimental, noxious, pernicious, mischievous, full of mischief, mischief-making, malefic, malignant, nocuous, noisome; prejudicial; dis-serviceable, -advantageous; wide-wasting.

unlucky, sinister; obnoxious, untoward, disastrous.

oppressive, burdensome, onerous; malign &c. (*malevolent*) 907.

corrupting &c. (corrupt &c. 659); virulent, venomous, envenomed, corrosive; poisonous &c. (*morbific*) 657; deadly &c. (*killing*) 361; destructive &c. (*destroying*) 162; inauspicious &c. 859.

bad, ill, arrant, as bad as bad can be, dreadful; hor-rid, -rible; dire; rank,

costly &c. (*dear*) 814; worth -its weight in gold, – a Jew's eye, – a king's ransom; matchless, peerless, invaluable, inestimable, precious as the apple of the eye.

tolerable &c. (*not very good*) 651; up to the mark, un-exceptionable, -objectionable; satisfactory, tidy.

in -good, – fair- condition; fresh; unspoiled; sound &c. (*perfect*) 650.

Adv. beneficially &c. *adj.*; well &c. 618.

---

peccant, foul, fulsome; rotten, – at the core.

vile, base, villainous; mean &c. (*paltry*) 643; injured &c., deteriorated &c. 659; unsatisfactory, exception, -able, indifferent; below par &c. (*imperfect*) 651; ill-contrived, -conditioned; wretched, sad, grievous, deplorable, lamentable; piti-ful, -able, woeful &c. (*painful*) 830.

evil, wrong; depraved &c. 945; shocking; reprehensible &c. (*disapprove*) 932.

hateful, – as a toad; abominable, detestable, execrable, cursed, accursed, confounded; damn-ed, -able; infernal; diabolic &c. (*malevolent*) 907.

inadvisable &c. (*inexpedient*) 647; unprofitable &c. (*useless*) 645; incompetent &c. (*unskilful*) 699; irremediable &c. (*hopeless*) 859.

Adv. badly &c. *adj.*; wrong, ill; to one's cost; where the shoe pinches.

Phr. bad is the best; the worst come to the worst.

650. Perfection. — N. perfection; perfectness &c. *adj.*; indefectibility; impecc-ancy, -ability.

pink, *beau idéal*, phœnix, paragon; pink –, acme- of perfection; *ne plus ultra*; summit &c. 210.

cygne noir; philosopher's stone; chrysolite, Koh-i-noor, black tulip.

model, standard, pattern, mirror, admirable Crichton; trump; very prince of.

master-piece, -stroke, super-excellence &c. (*goodness*) 648; transcendence &c. (*superiority*) 33.

V. be -perfect &c. *adj.*; transcend &c. (*be supreme*) 33.

bring to perfection, perfect, ripen, mature; consummate, complete &c. 729; put in trim &c. (*prepare*) 673; put the finishing touch to.

Adj. perfect, faultless, ideal; indefective, -ficient, -fectible; immaculate, spotless, impeccable; free from -imperfection &c. 651; un-blemished, -injured &c. 659; sound, – as a roach; in perfect condition; scathless, intact, harmless; seaworthy &c. (*safe*) 644; right as a trivet; *in seipso totus teres atque rotundus*; consummate &c. (*complete*) 52; finished &c. 729; complete in itself.

best &c. (*good*) 648; model, standard; inimitable, unparagoned, unparalleled &c. (*supreme*) 33; superhuman, divine;

651. Imperfection.—N. imperfection; imperfectness &c. *adj.*; defic.ency; inadequacy &c. (*insufficiency*) 640; peccancy &c. (*badness*) 649; immaturity &c. 674.

fault, defect, weak point; screw loose; rift within the lute; fly in the ointment; flaw &c. (*break*) 70; gap &c. 198; twist &c. 243; taint, attainder; bar sinister, hole in one's coat; blemish &c. 848; weakness &c. 160; half-blood, touch of the tar brush; shortcoming &c. 304; drawback; seamy side.

mediocrity; no great -shakes, – catch; not much to boast of.

V. be -imperfect &c. *adj.*; have a -defect &c. *n.*; lie under a disadvantage; spring a leak.

not –, barely- pass muster; fall short &c. 304.

Adj. imperfect; not -perfect &c. 650; de-ficient, -fective; faulty, unsound, mutilated, tainted; out of -order, – tune; cracked, leaky; sprung; warped &c. (*distort*) 243; lame; injured &c. (*deteriorated*) 659; peccant &c. (*bad*) 649; frail &c. (*weak*) 160; inadequate &c. (*insufficient*) 640; crude &c. (*unprepared*) 674; incomplete &c. 53; found wanting; below par; shorthanded; below –, under- its full -strength, – complement.

indifferent, middling, ordinary, medi-

beyond all praise &c. (*approbation*) 931; *sans peur et sans reproche*.

Adv. to perfection, to the limit; perfectly &c. *adj.*; *ad unguem*; clean, - as a whistle.

ocre; average &c. 29; so-so; *così-così*, milk and water; tolerable, fair, passable; pretty -well, - good; rather -, moderately- good; good -, well- enough; decent; not -bad, - amiss; inobjectionable, admissible, bearable, only better than nothing.

secondary, inferior; second-rate, -best, one-horse.

Adv. almost &c.; to a limited extent, rather &c. 32; pretty, moderately; only; considering, all things considered, enough.

Phr. *surgit amari aliquid.*

---

652. Cleanness.—N. cleanness &c. *adj.*; purity; cleaning &c. *v.*; purification, defecation &c. *v.*; purgation, lustration; de-, abs-tersion; epuration, mundation, ablution, lavation, colature; disinfection &c. *v.*; drain-, sewerage.

lavatory, bath, -room; swimming pool, natatorium; public baths; hot -, cold -, Turkish -, Swedish -, Russian -, vapour- bath; *hammam*, laundry, washhouse; washerwoman, laundress, laundryman; scavenger, cleaner, sweeper, goodie; crossing sweeper, white wings, dustman, sweep.

brush; broom, besom, carpet-sweeper, vacuum-cleaner, mop, squilgee, rake, shovel, sieve, riddle, screen, filter; scraper, strigil.

napkin, *serviette*, cloth, table-, carving-cloth, table-linen, napery, maukin, handkerchief, towel, sudary; doyley, doily, duster, sponge, mop, swab.

cover, drugget, mat, doormat.

soap, wash, lotion, detergent, cathartic, purgative; purifier &c. *v.*; dentifrice, tooth-powder, -paste; mouth wash; disinfectant.

V. be -, render- clean &c. *adj.*

clean, -se; mundify, rinse, wring, flush, full, wipe, mop, sponge, scour, swab, scrub, holystone, brush up.

wash, shampoo, lave, launder, buck; abs-, de-terge; clear, purify; de-purate, -spumate, -fecate; purge, expurgate; Bowdlerize; elutriate, lixiviate, edulcorate, clarify, refine, rack; fil-ter, -trate; drain, strain.

disinfect, sterilize, pasteurize, fumigate, ventilate, deodorize; whitewash.

sift, winnow, screen, riddle, pick, weed, comb, rake, brush, sweep.

653. Uncleanness.—N. uncleanness &c. *adj.*; impurity; immundi-ty, -city; impurity &c. [of mind] 961.

defilement, contamination &c. *v.*; defœdation; soil-ure, -iness; abomination; leaven; taint, -ure; fetor &c. 401.

decay; putre-scence, -faction; corruption; mould, must, mildew, dry-rot, *mucor*, rubigo, caries.

slovenry; slovenliness &c. *adj.*; squalor.

dowdy, drab, slut, malkin, slattern, sloven, slammerkin, scrub, draggletail, mudlark, dustman, sweep; beast.

dirt, filth, soil, slop; dust, cobweb, flue; smoke, soot, smudge, smut, grime, raff.

sordes, dregs, grounds, lees; sedi-, settle-ment; heel-tap; dross, -iness; mother, precipitate, *scoriæ*, ashes, cinders, recrement, slag; scum, froth.

hog-wash, swill, ditch-, dish-, bilge-water; rinsings, cheese-parings; sweepings &c. (*useless refuse*) 645; off-, out-scourings; off-scum; *caput mortuum*, *residuum*, sprue, feculence, clinker, draff; scurf, -iness; *exuviæ*, morphew; fur, -fur; dandruff; tartar.

riffraff; vermin, louse, cootie, flea, bug.

mud, mire, quagmire, *alluvium*, silt, sludge, slime, slush, slosh.

spawn, offal, garbage, carrion; *excreta* &c. 299; slough, peccant humour, pus, matter, suppuration, *lienteria*; *fæces*, excrement, ordure, dung; sew-, sewer-age; muck, coprolite; guano, manure, compost.

dunghill, *coluvies*, mixen, midden, bog, laystall, sink, w.c., water-, earth-closet, latrine, privy, jakes, John's; cess, -pool; sump, sough, *cloaca*, drain,

rout –, clear –, sweep &c.- out; make a clean sweep of.

Adj. clean, -ly; pure; immaculate; spot-, stain-, taint-less; without a stain, un-stained, -spotted, -soiled, -sullied, -tainted, -infected, -adulterated; aseptic; sweet, – as a nut.

neat, spruce, tidy, trim, gimp, clean as a new penny, like a cat in pattens; cleaned &c. *v.*; kempt.

Adv. neatly &c. *adj.*; clean as a whistle.

———

sewer, common sewer; Cloacina; dusthole.

sty, pig-sty, lair, den, Augean stable, sink of corruption; slum, rookery.

V. be –, become- unclean &c. *adj.*; rot, putrefy, fester, rankle, reek; stink &c. 401; mould, -er; go -bad &c. *adj.*

render -unclean &c. *adj.*; dirt, -y; soil, smoke, tarnish, slaver, spot, smear, daub, blot, blur, smudge, smutch, smirch; d-, dr-abble, -aggle; spatter, slubber; be-smear &c., -mire, -slime, -grime, -foul; splash, stain, distain, maculate, sully, pollute, defile, debase, contaminate, taint, leaven; corrupt &c. (*injure*) 659; cover with -dust &c. *n.*; drabble in the mud.

wallow in the mire; slob-, slab-ber.

Adj. unclean, dirty, filthy, grimy; soiled &c. *v.*; not to be handled with kid gloves; dusty, snuffy, smutty, sooty, smoky; thick, turbid, dreggy; slimy.

uncleanly, slovenly, untidy, sluttish, dowdy, slatternly, draggle-tailed; un-combed, -kempt, -scoured, -swept, -wiped, -washed, -strained, -purified; squalid.

nasty, coarse, foul, impure, offensive, abominable, beastly, reeky, reechy; fetid &c. 401.

mouldy, lentiginous, musty, mildewed, rusty, moth-eaten, mucid, rancid, bad, gone bad, touched, fusty, reasty, rotten, corrupt, tainted, high, fly-blown, maggoty; putr-id, -escent, -efied; purulent, carious, peccant, fec-al, -ulent; stercoraceous, excrementitious; scurfy, impetiginous; gory, bloody; rotting &c. *v.*; rotten as -a pear, – cheese.

crapulous &c. (*intemperate*) 954; gross &c. (*impure in mind*) 961.

654. Health.—**N.** health, sanity; soundness &c. *adj.*; vigour; good –, perfect –, excellent –, rude –, robust-health; bloom, *mens sana in corpore sano*; Hygeia; incorrupti-on, -bility; good state –, clean bill- of health, eupepsia.

V. be in health &c. *adj.*; bloom, flourish.

keep -body and soul together, – on one's legs; enjoy -good, – a good state of- health; have a clean bill of health.

return to health; recover &c. 660; get better &c. (*improve*) 658; take a -new, – fresh- lease of life; convalesce, be convalescent, recruit; restore to health; cure &c. (*restore*) 660.

Adj. health-y, -ful; in -health &c. *n.*; well, sound, strong, fit, hearty, hale, fresh, blooming, green, whole; florid, flush, hardy, stanch, staunch,

655. Disease.*—**N.** disease; illness, sickness &c. *adj.*; ailing &c. *v.*; 'the ills that flesh is heir to'; morb-idity, -osity; infirmity, ailment, indisposition; complaint, disorder, malady; distemper, -ature.

visitation, attack, seizure, stroke, fit, epilepsy, apoplexy, shock, shell-shock.

delicacy, loss of health, valetudinarianism, invalidism, cachexy; *cachexia*, atrophy, *marasmus*; indigestion, *dyspepsia*; decay &c. (*deterioration*) 659; malnutrition, decline, consumption, palsy, paralysis, prostration; occupational diseases.

taint, pollution, infection, contagion, septicity, septicæmia, blood poisoning, pyæmia, epi-, en-demic; murrain, plague, pestilence, virus, pox.

sore, ulcer, abscess, fester, boil; pimple &c. (*swelling*) 250; carbuncle,

———

* Extended lists of different diseases are beyond the scope of this work.

brave, robust, vigorous, weather-proof; convalescent.

un-scathed, -injured, -maimed, -marred, -tainted; sound of wind and limb, safe and sound; without a scratch.

on one's legs; sound as a -roach, – bell; fresh as -a daisy, – a rose, – April; picture of health; bursting with health; fit as a fiddle; hearty as a buck; in -fine, – high- feather; in -good case, – full bloom; in fine fettle; pretty bobbish, tolerably well, as well as can be expected.

sanitary &c. (*health-giving*) 656; sanatory &c. (*remedial*) 662.

gathering, whitlow, imposthume, peccant humour, issue; rot, canker, cancer, *carcinoma, caries,* mortification, corruption, gangrene, *sphacelus,* leprosy, eruption, rash, breaking out, venereal disease.

fever, calenture; inflammation.

fatal &c. (*hopeless*) 859- -disease &c.; dangerous illness, galloping consumption, churchyard cough; general breaking up, break up of the system.

[Disease of mind] neurasthenia; idiocy &c. 499; insanity &c. 503.

martyr to disease; cripple; 'the halt, the lame and the blind'; valetudinar-y, -ian; invalid, patient, case; sick-room, -chamber, hospital &c. 662.

[Science of disease] path-, eti-, nos-ology, therapeutics, diagnosis, prognosis.

V. be -ill &c. *adj.*; ail, suffer, labour under, be affected with, complain of; droop, flag, languish, halt; sicken, peak, pine, waste away, fail, lose strength; gasp.

keep one's bed; feign sickness &c. (*falsehood*) 544, malinger.

lay -by, – up; take –, catch- -a disease &c. *n.*, – an infection; be stricken by; break out.

Adj. diseased; ailing &c. *v.*; ill, – of; taken ill, seized with; indisposed, unwell, sick, squeamish, poorly, seedy; affected –, afflicted-with illness; laid up, confined, bed-ridden, invalided, in hospital, on the sick list; out of -health, – sorts; valetudinary.

un-sound, -healthy; sickly, morbose, healthless, infirm, chlorotic, unbraced, drooping, flagging, lame, halt, crippled, halting.

morbid, tainted, vitiated, peccant, contaminated, poisoned, septic, tabid, mangy, leprous, cankered; rotten, – to, – at- the core; withered, palsied, paralytic, tuberculous; dyspeptic.

touched in the wind, broken-winded, spavined, gasping; *hors de combat* &c. (*useless*) 645.

weak-ly, -ened &c. (*weak*) 160; decrepit; decayed &c. (*deteriorated*) 659; incurable &c. (*hopeless*) 859; in declining health; cranky; in a bad way, in danger, prostrate; moribund &c. (*death*) 360.

morbific, epidemic &c. 657.

---

656. Salubrity.—N. salubrity, salubriousness; healthiness &c. *adj.*

fine -air, – climate; eudiometer.

[Preservation of health] *hygiène*; valetudinarian, -ism, preventorium, sanitarian; *sanitarium, sanitorium,* immunity.

V. be -salubrious &c. *adj.*; agree with, be good for; assimilate &c. 23.

Adj. salu-brious, -tary, -tiferous, wholesome; health-y, -ful; sanitary, prophylactic, benign, bracing, tonic,

657. Insalubrity.—N. insalubrity; unhealthiness &c. *adj.*; non-naturals; plague spot; malaria &c. (*poison*) 663; death in the pot, contagion.

Adj. insalubrious; un-healthy, -wholesome; noxious, noisome, foul; morbi-fic, -ferous; mephitic, septic, azotic, deleterious; pesti-lent, -ferous, -lential; virulent, venomous, envenomed, poisonous, toxic, narcotic.

contagious, infectious, catching, taking, communicable, epidemic, zymotic;

invigorating, good for, nutritious, hyg-eian, -ienic.

in-noxious, -nocuous, -nocent; harmless, uninjurious, uninfectious; immune.

sanative &c. (*remedial*) 662; restorative &c. (*reinstate*) 660; useful &c. 644.

658. Improvement.—N. improvement; a-, melioration; betterment; mend, amendment, emendation; mending &c. *v.*; advancement; advance &c. (*progress*) 282; ascent &c. 305; promotion, preferment; elevation &c. 307; increase &c. 35.

cultiv-, civiliz-ation; menticulture, culture, march of intellect; eugenics, euthenics, meliorism, telesis.

reform, -ation; revision, radical reform; second thoughts, correction, *limæ labor*, refinement, elaboration; purification &c. 652; repair &c. (*restoration*) 660; recovery &c. 660.

revise; revised –, new- edition.

reformer, radical, progressive.

V. improve; be –, become –, get-better; mend, amend.

advance &c. (*progress*) 282; ascend &c. 305; increase &c. 35; fructify, ripen, mature; pick up, come about, rally, take a favourable turn; turn -over a new leaf, – the corner; raise one's head, sow one's wild oats; recover &c. 660.

be -better &c. *adj.*, – improved by; turn to -right, – good, – best- account; profit by, reap the benefit of; make -good use of, – capital out of; place to good account; take advantage of.

render better, improve, emend, make over, better; a-, meliorate; correct.

improve –, refine- upon; rectify; enrich, mellow, elaborate, fatten.

promote, cultivate, advance, forward, enhance; bring -forward, – on; foster &c. 707; invigorate &c. (*strengthen*) 159.

touch –, rub –, brush –, furbish –, bolster –, vamp –, brighten –, warm-up; polish, cook, make the most of, set off to advantage; prune; repair &c. (*restore*) 660; put in order &c. (*arrange*) 60.

review, revise, edit, redact; make -corrections, – improvements &c. *n.*; doctor &c. (*remedy*) 662; purify &c. 652.

sporadic, endemic, pandemic, epizoötic.

innutritious, indigestible, ungenial; uncongenial &c. (*disagreeing*) 24.

deadly &c. (*killing*) 361.

---

659. Deterioration.—N. deterioration, debasement; want, ebb; recession &c. 287; retrogradation &c. 283; decrease &c. 36.

degenera-cy, -tion, -teness; degradation; deprav-ation, -ement; depravity &c. 945; demoralization, retrogression.

impairment, inquination, injury, damage, loss, detriment, delaceration, outrage, havoc, inroad, ravage, scath; perversion, prostitution, vitiation, discoloration, oxidation, pollution, defœdation, poisoning, venenation, leaven, contamination, canker, corruption, adulteration, alloy.

decl-ine, -ension, -ination; decadence, -cy; falling off &c. *v.*; caducity, decreptitude, senility.

decay, dilapidation, ravages of time, wear and tear; cor-, e-rosion; mouldi-, rotten-ness; moth and rust, dry-rot, blight, marasmus, atrophy, collapse; disorganization; *délabrement* &c. (*destruction*) 162.

wreck, mere wreck, honeycomb, *magni nominis umbra*.

V. be –, become--worse,–deteriorated &c. *adj.*; have seen better days, deteriorate, degenerate, fall off; wane &c. (*decrease*) 36; ebb; retrograde &c. 283; decline, droop; go down &c. (*sink*) 306; go -downhill, – on from bad to worse, – farther and fare worse; jump out of the frying pan into the fire.

run to -seed, – waste; swale, sweal; lapse, be the worse for; break, – down; spring a leak, crack, start; shrivel &c. (*contract*) 195; fade, go off, wither, moulder, rot, rankle, decay, go bad; go to –, fall into- decay; 'fall into the sear and yellow leaf,' rust, crumble, shake; totter, – to its fall; perish &c. 162; die &c. 360.

[Render less good] deteriorate; weaken &c. 160; put back; taint, infect, contaminate, poison, empoison,

relieve, refresh, revive, infuse new blood into, recruit, re-invigorate, renew, revivify, freshen, build -afresh, – anew; uplift, inspire.

re-form, -model, -organise; new model, civilize.

view in a new light, think better of, appeal from Philip drunk to Philip sober.

palliate, mitigate; lessen &c. 36- an evil.

Adj. improving &c. *v.*; progressive, improved &c. *v.*; better, – off, – for; all the better for; better advised.

reform-, emend-atory; reparatory &c. (*restorative*) 660; remedial &c. 662.

corrigible, improvable, curable, accultural.

Adv. on -consideration, – reconsideration, – second thoughts, – better advice; *ad melius inquirendum*; on the -mend, – up grade.

---

envenom, canker, corrupt, exulcerate, pollute, vitiate, inquinate; de-, embase; denaturalize, leaven; de-flower, -bauch, -file, -prave, -grade; stain &c. (*dirt*) 653; discolour; alloy, adulterate, sophisticate, tamper with, prejudice.

pervert, prostitute, demoralize, brutalize; render vicious &c. 945; compromise.

embitter, ex-, acerbate, aggravate.

injure, impair, labefy, damage, harm, hurt, shend, scathe, spoil, mar, despoil, dilapidate, waste; overrun; ravage; pillage &c. 791.

wound, stab, pierce, maim, lame, surbate, cripple, hough, hamstring, hit between wind and water, scotch, mangle, mutilate, disfigure, blemish, deface, warp.

blight, rot; cor-, e-rode, eat away; wear -away, – out; gnaw, – at the root of; sap, mine, undermine, shake, sap the foundations of, break up; dis-organize, -mantle, -mast; destroy &c. 162.

damnify &c. (*aggrieve*) 649; do one's worst; knock down; deal a blow to; play -havoc, – sad havoc, – the mischief, – the deuce, – the very devil- -with, – among; decimate.

Adj. unimproved &c. (improve &c. 658); deteriorated &c. *v.*; altered, – for the worse; injured &c. *v.*; sprung; withering, spoiling, &c. *v.*; on the -wane, – decline; tabid; degenerate; worse; the –, all the- worse for; out of -repair, – tune; imperfect &c. 651; the worse for wear; battered; weather-ed, -beaten; stale, *passé*, shaken, dilapidated, frayed, faded, wilted, shabby, second-hand, secondrate, threadbare; worn, – to- -a thread, – a shadow, – the stump, rags; reduced, – to a skeleton, skeletonized; far gone.

decayed &c. *v.*; moth-, worm-eaten; mildewed, rusty, mouldy, spotted, seedy, time-worn, moss-grown; discoloured; effete, wasted, crumbling, mouldering, rotten, cankered, blighted, tainted; depraved &c. (*vicious*) 945; decrep-id, -it; broken down; done, – for, – up; worn out, used up; fit for the -dust-hole, – wastepaper basket; past work &c. (*useless*) 645.

at a low ebb, in a bad way, on one's last legs, washed -up, – out; undermined, deciduous; nodding to its fall &c. (*destruction*) 162; tottering &c. (*dangerous*) 665; past cure &c. (*hopeless*) 859; fatigued &c. 688; backward, retrograde &c. (*retrogressive*) 283; deleterious &c. 649; behind the times.

Adv. on the down grade; beyond hope.

Phr. out of the frying pan into the fire; *ægrescit medendo*.

---

660. Restoration.—N. restor-ation, -al; re-instatement, -placement, -habilitation, -establishment, -construction; reproduction &c. 163; re-novation, -newal; reviv-al, -escence; refreshment

661. Relapse.—N. relapse, lapse; falling back &c. *v.*; retrogradation &c. (*retrogression*) 283; deterioration &c. 659.

[Return to, or recurrence of a bad

&c. 689; re-suscitation, -animation, -vivification, -viction; Phœnix; reorganization.

renaissance, renascence, rebirth, second youth, rejuvenation, rejuvenescence, new birth; regenera-tion, -cy, -teness; palingenesis, reconversion, resurgence, resurrection.

redress, retrieval, reclamation, recovery; convalescence; resumption, *résumption.*

recurrence &c. (*repetition*) 104; *réchauffé, rifacimento.*

cure, recure, sanation; healing &c. *v.*; redintegration; rectification, instauration.

repair, reparation, mending; recruiting &c. *v.*; cicatrization; disinfection; tinkering.

reaction; redemption &c. (*deliverance*) 672; restitution &c. 790; relief &c. 834.

mender, repairer, renewer; tinker, cobbler; doctor &c. 662; *vis medicatrix* &c. (*remedy*) 662.

curableness.

V. return to the original state; recover, rally, revive; come -to, - round, - to oneself; pull through, weather the storm, be oneself again; get -well, - round, - the better of, - over, - about; rise from -one's ashes, - the grave; resurge, resurrect; survive &c. (*outlive*) 110; resume, reappear; come to, - life again; live -, rise- again; relive.

heal, skin over, cicatrize; right itself.

restore, put back, place *in statu quo*; re-instate, -place, -seat, -habilitate, -establish, -estate, -install.

re-construct, -build, -organize, -constitute; reconvert; re-new, -novate; recondition; regenerate; rejuvenate.

re-deem, -claim, -cover, -trieve; rescue &c. (*deliver*) 672.

redress, recure; cure, heal, remedy, doctor, physic, medicate; break of; bring round, set on one's legs.

re-suscitate, -vive, -animate, -vivify, -call to life; reproduce &c. 163; warm up; reinvigorate, refresh &c. 689.

redintegrate, make whole; recoup &c. 790; make -good, - all square; rectify; put -, set- -right, - to rights, - straight; set up, correct; put in order &c. (*arrange*) 60; refit, recruit; fill up, - the ranks; reinforce.

repair, mend; put in -repair, - thorough repair, - complete repair; retouch, botch, vamp, tinker, doctor, cobble; do -, patch -, plaster -, vamp- up; darn, fine-draw, heel-piece; stop a gap, stanch, staunch, caulk, calk, careen, splice, bind up wounds.

Adj. restored &c. *v.*; *redivivus,* convalescent; in a fair way; none the worse; rejuvenated, renascent.

restoring &c. *v.*; restorative, recuperative; sana-, repara-tive, -tory; curative, remedial.

restor-, recover-, san-, remedi-, retriev-, cur-able.

Adv. *in statu quo*; as you were.

Phr. *revenons à nos moutons.*

state] backsliding, recidivation, recrudescence.

V. relapse, lapse; fall -, slide -, sinkback; have a relapse; return; retrograde &c. 283; recidivate; fall off &c. 659- again.

---

662. Remedy.—N. remedy, help, redress; antidote, anti-toxin, anti-,

663. Bane.—N. bane, curse, thorn in the -side, -flesh, bugbear, *bête noire*;

counter-poison, prophylactic, antiseptic, germicide, bactericide, corrective, restorative, stimulant, pick-me-up, tonic; sedative &c. 174; palliative; febrifuge; alter-ant, -ative; specific; emetic, carminative; narcotic &c. *adj.*; Nepenthe, Mithridate.

cure; radical –, perfect –, certain-cure; sovereign remedy.

physic, medicine, patent medicine, Galenicals, simples, drug, potion, draught, dose, pill, bolus, lozenge, tablet, tabloid, capsule; electuary; linct-us, -ure; medicament.

nostrum, receipt, recipe, prescription; catholicon, panacea, elixir, *elixir vitæ*, philosopher's stone; balm, balsam, cordial, theriac, ptisan.

salve, ointment, cerate, oil, lenitive, lotion, cosmetic; plaster; epithem, embrocation, liniment, cataplasm, sinapism, arquebusade, traumatic, vulnerary, pepastic, poultice, collyrium, depilatory.

compress, pledget; bandage &c. (*support*) 215.

treatment, medical treatment, regimen; diet-ary, -etics; *vis medicatrix, – naturæ; médecine expectante;* seton, blood-letting, bleeding, venesection, phlebotomy, cupping, leeches; operation, surgical operation; tonsillectomy, appendectomy; injection, electrolysis, massage.

pharma-cy, -cology, -ceutics; acology; materia medica, pharmacopœia, therapeutics, therapy, posology, pathology &c. 655; homœ-, hetero-, all-, hydr-opathy; cold water –, open air- cure; dietetics; sur-, chirur-gery, osteopathy; healing art, leechcraft, practice of medicine; ortho-pædy, -praxy; dentistry, midwifery, obstetrics, gynæcology.

faith -cure, – healing, Christian science; psycho-therapy, -analysis, psychiatry.

hospital, infirmary, clinic; pest-, lazar-house; lazaretto, lazaret; lock hospital; *maison de santé; ambulance;* dispensary; *sanatorium, sanitarium,* spa, baths, pump-room, well; *hospice;* Red Cross; nursing home; asylum.

doctor, physician, surgeon; medical –, general- practitioner, consultant, specialist; medical attendant; medical student, medico; chemist, apothecary, pharmacopolist, druggist; leech; Æsculapius, Hippocrates, Galen; *accoucheur,* gynæcologist, midwife, oculist, aurist, dentist; operator; osteopath, bonesetter; nurse, monthly nurse, sister; dresser; *masseur, masseuse.*

V. apply a -remedy &c. *n.*; doctor, dose, physic, nurse, minister to, attend, dress the wounds, plaster, bandage, poultice; heal, cure, work a cure, kill or cure, remedy, stay (disease), snatch from the jaws of death; prevent &c. 706; relieve &c. 834; palliate &c. 658;

evil &c. 619; hurtfulness &c. (*badness*) 649; painfulness &c. (*cause of pain*) 830; scourge &c. (*punishment*) 975; *damnosa hereditas;* white elephant.

sting, fang, thorn, tang, bramble, briar, nettle.

poison, leaven, virus, venom; intoxicant; arsenic, Prussic acid, antimony, tartar emetic, strychnine, nicotine, cyanide of potassium, corrosive sublimate; curare; hyoscine &c.; poison-, mustard-, tear-gas; carbon di-, mon-oxide; ptomaine poisoning, botulism; miasm, mephitis, malaria, azote, sewer gas; pest, stench &c. 401.

rust, worm, moth, moth and rust, fungus, mildew; dry-rot; canker, -worm; cancer; torpedo; viper &c. (*evil-doer*) 913; demon &c. 980.

hemlock, hellebore, nightshade, *belladonna,* henbane, aconite; Upas tree.

drugs, dope, opium, morphia, morphine, cocaine, heroin, hashish, bhang. [Science of poisons] Toxicology.

Adj. baneful &c. (*bad*) 649; poisonous &c. (*unwholesome*) 657.

restore &c. 660; drench with physic; consult, operate, extract, deliver; bleed, cup, let blood, transfuse; electrolyse; psycho-analyse.

Adj. remedial; restorative &c. 660; corrective, palliative, healing; sana-tory, -tive; prophylactic; salutiferous &c. (*salutary*) 656; medic-al, -inal; therapeutic, surgical, chirurgical, orthopedic, epulotic, paregoric, tonic, corroborant, analeptic, balsamic, anodyne, hypnotic, neurotic, narcotic, sedative, lenitive, demulcent, emollient; depuratory; deter-sive, -gent; abstersive, disinfectant, febrifugal, alternative; traumatic, vulnerary.

dietetic, alimentary; nutrit-ious, -ive; peptic; alexi-pharmic, -teric; remedi-, cur-able.

3. *Contingent Subservience*

664. Safety.—N. safety, security, impregnability; invulnera-bility, -bleness &c. *adj.*; danger -past, – over; storm blown over; coast clear; escape &c. 671; means of escape, safety-valve; safeguard, palladium, sheet anchor, rock, tower of strength.

guardian-, ward-, warden-ship; tutelage, custody, safe keeping; preservation &c. 670; protection, auspices.

safe-conduct, escort, convoy; guard, shield &c. (*defence*) 717; guardian angel, tutelary -god, – deity, – saint; *genius loci.*

protector, guardian; ward-en, -er; preserver, custodian, *duenna, chaperon,* third person.

watch-, ban-dog; Cerberus; watch-, patrol-, police-man, constable, peeler, bobby, copper, cop, bull, flat-foot, detective, armed guard; sentinel, sentry, scout &c. (*warning*) 668; garrison; guard-ship.

[Means of safety] refuge &c., anchor &c. 666; precaution &c. (*preparation*) 673; quarantine, *cordon sanitaire.* [Sense of security] confidence &c. 858.

V. be -safe &c. *adj.*; keep one's head above water, tide over, save one's bacon; ride out –, weather- the storm; light upon one's feet; bear a charmed life; escape &c. 671; possess nine lives.

make –, render- -safe &c. *adj.*; protect, watch over; take care of &c. (*care*) 459; preserve &c. 670; cover, screen, shelter, shroud, flank, ward; guard &c. (*defend*) 717; secure &c. (*restrain*) 751; intrench, fence round &c. (*circumscribe*) 229; house, nestle, ensconce; take charge of.

665. Danger.—N. danger, peril, insecurity, jeopardy, risk, hazard, venture, precariousness, slipperiness; instability &c. 149; defencelessness &c. *adj.*

exposure &c. (*liability*) 177; vulnerability; vulnerable point, heel of Achilles; forlorn hope &c. (*hopelessness*) 859.

[Dangerous course] leap in the dark &c. (*rashness*) 863; road to ruin, *facilis descensus Averni*, hair-breadth escape.

cause for alarm; source of danger &c. 667. [Approach of danger] rock –, breakers- ahead; storm brewing; clouds -in the horizon, – gathering; warning &c. 668; alarm &c. 669. [Sense of danger] apprehension &c. 860.

V. be -in danger &c. *adj.*; be exposed to –, run into –, incur –, encounter- -danger &c. *n.*; run a risk; lay oneself open to &c. (*liability*) 177; lean on –, trust to- a broken reed; feel the ground sliding from under one, have to run for it; have the -chances, – odds- against one.

hang by a thread, totter; tremble on the -verge, – brink; sleep –, stand -on a volcano; sit on a barrel of gunpowder, live in a glass house.

bring –, place –, put- in -danger &c. *n.*; endanger, expose to danger, imperil; jeopard, -ize, compromise; sail too near the wind &c. (*rash*) 863; put one's head in the lion's mouth.

adventure, risk, hazard, venture, stake, set at hazard; run the gauntlet &c. (*dare*) 861; engage in a forlorn hope.

threaten &c. 909- danger; run one

escort, convoy; garrison; watch, mount guard, patrol, scout, spy.

make assurance double sure &c. (*caution*) 864; take up a loose thread; take precautions &c. (*prepare for*) 673; take in a reef; double reef topsails.

seek safety; take –, find- shelter &c. 666; run into port.

Adj. safe, secure, sure; in -safety, – security; have an anchor to windward; on the safe side; under the -shield of, – shade of, – wing of, – shadow of one's wing; under -cover, – lock and key; out of -danger, – the meshes, – harm's way; in -harbour, – port; on sure ground, at anchor, high and dry, above water, on *terra firma*; unthreatened, -molested; protected &c. *v.*; *cavendo tutus*; panoplied &c. (*defended*) 717.

snug, sea-, air-worthy; weather-, water-, fire-, bomb-proof.

defensible, tenable, proof against, invulnerable; un-assailable, -attackable; im-pregnable, -perdible; founded on a rock; inexpugnable.

safe and sound &c. (*preserved*) 670; harmless; scathless &c. (*perfect*) 650; unhazarded; not -dangerous &c. 665.

protecting &c. *v.*; guardian, tutelary; preservative &c. 670; trustworthy &c. 939.

Adv. *ex abundanti cautelâ*; with impunity.

Phr. all's well; all clear; *salva res est*; *suave mari magno*; safety first.

———

hard; lay a trap for &c. (*deceive*) 545.

Adj. in -danger &c. *n.*; endangered &c. *v.*; fraught with danger; danger-, hazard-, peril-, parl-, pericul-ous; un-safe, unprotected &c. (safe, protect &c. 664); insecure, untrustworthy, unreliable; built upon sand, on a sandy basis.

defence-, fence-, guard-, harbour-less; unshielded; vulnerable, expugnable, unsheltered, exposed; open to &c. (*liable*) 177.

aux abois, at bay; on -the wrong side of the wall, – a lee shore, – the rocks.

at stake, in question; precarious, aleatory, critical, ticklish; slip-pery, -py; hanging by a thread &c. *v.*; with a halter round one's neck; between -the hammer and the anvil, – Scylla and Charybdis, – two fires; on the -edge, – brink, – verge of a- -precipice, – volcano; in the lion's den, on slippery ground, under fire; not out of the wood.

un-warned, -admonished, -advised; unprepared &c. 674; off one's guard &c. (*inexpectant*) 508.

tottering; un-stable, -steady; shaky, top-heavy, tumble-down, ramshackle, crumbling, waterlogged; help-, guide-less; in a bad way; reduced to –, at the last extremity; trembling in the balance; nodding to its fall &c. (*destruction*) 162.

threatening &c. 909; ominous, ill-omened; alarming &c. (*fear*) 860; explosive; poisonous &c. 657.

adventurous &c. (*rash*) 863, (*bold*) 861.

Int. stop! look out! beware! take care!

Phr. *incidit in Scyllam qui vult vitare Charybdim*; *nam tua res agitur paries dum proximus ardet.*

666. [Means of safety.] **Refuge.**—**N.** refuge, sanctuary, retreat, fastness; stronghold, keep, last resort; ward; prison &c. 752; asylum, ark, home, almshouse, refuge for the destitute; hiding-place &c. (*ambush*) 530; *sanctum sanctorum* &c. (*privacy*) 893.

roadstead, anchorage; breakwater, mole, port, haven; harbour, – of refuge; sea-port; pier, jetty, embankment, quay.

667. [Source of danger.] **Pitfall.**—**N.** rocks, reefs, coral reef, sunken rocks, snags; sands, quicksands, Goodwin sands, sandy foundation; slippery ground; breakers, shoals, shallows, bank, shelf, flat, lee shore, iron-bound coast; rock –, breakers- ahead; derelict.

precipice; abyss, chasm, pit, crevasse; maelstrom, whirlpool, eddy, vortex, rapids, current, bore, tidal wave; storm, squall, hurricane, whirl-

covert, shelter, abri, screen, lee-wall, wing, shield, umbrella; splash-, dash-board, mudguard.

wall &c. (*inclosure*) 232; fort &c. (*defence*) 717.

anchor, kedge; grap-nel, -pling iron; sheet-, mushroom-anchor, main-stay; support &c. 215; check &c. 706; ballast.

jury-mast; vent-peg; safety -valve, – lamp; lightning conductor.

means of escape &c. (*escape*) 671; life-boat, swimming belt, cork jacket; life preserver, breeches buoy; parachute, plank, stepping-stone.

safeguard &c. (*protection*) 664.

V. seek –, take –, find- refuge &c. *n.*; seek –, find- safety &c. 664; throw oneself into the arms of; claim sanctuary; take to the -hills, – woods; make port, reach shelter, bar –, bolt –, lock -the door, – gate; let the portcullis down; raise the drawbridge.

wind; volcano; ambush &c. 530; pit-fall, trap-door; trap &c. (*snare*) 545.

sword of Damocles; wolf at the door, snake in the grass, viper in one's bosom, death in the pot; latency &c. 526.

ugly customer, dangerous person, *le chat qui dort*; firebrand, hornet's nest.

Phr. *latet anguis in herbâ*; *proximus ardet Ucalegon.*

---

668. Warning.—**N.** warning, caution, *caveat*; notice &c. (*information*) 527; premoni-tion, -shment; prediction &c. 511; contraindication; symptom; lesson, dehortation; admonition, monition; alarm &c. 669.

handwriting on the wall, *tekel upharsin*, yellow flag; fog-signal, -horn; siren; monitor, warning voice, Cassandra, signs of the times, Mother Carey's chickens, stormy petrel, bird of ill omen, gathering clouds, clouds in the horizon, cloud no bigger than a man's hand, death-watch.

watch-tower, beacon, signal-post; light-house &c. (*indication of locality*) 550.

sent-inel, -ry; watch, -man; watch and ward; watch-, ban-, house-dog; patrol, vedette, picket, bivouac, scout, spy, spial; advanced –, rear-guard, lookout, flagman.

cautiousness &c. 864.

V. warn, caution; fore-, pre-warn; ad-, pre-monish; give -notice, – warning; menace &c. (*threaten*) 909; put on one's guard; sound the alarm &c. 669; croak.

beware, ware; take -warning, – heed at one's peril; watch out for; keep watch and ward &c. (*care*) 459.

Adj. warning &c. *v.*; premonitory, monitory, cautionary; admoni-tory, -tive; ominous, threatening, lowering, minatory, symptomatic.

warned &c. *v.*; on one's guard &c. (*careful*) 459, (*cautious*) 864.

Adv. *in terrorem* &c. (*threat*) 909.

Int. beware! ware! take care! mind –, take care-what you are about; mind! look out!

Phr. *ne reveillez pas le chat qui dort; fœnum habet in cornu.*

669. [Indication of danger.] **Alarm.**—**N.** alarm; alarum, larum, alarm bell, tocsin, *alerte*, beat of drum, sound of trumpet, note of alarm, hue and cry, signal of distress, S.O.S.; blue-lights; war-cry, -whoop; warning &c. 668; fog-signal, -horn; siren; yellow flag; danger signal; red -light, – flag; fire -bell, – alarm; burglar alarm, police whistle, watchman's rattle.

false alarm, cry of wolf; bug-bear, -aboo.

V. give –, raise –, sound –, beat- the *or* an -alarm &c. *n.*; alarm; warn &c. 668; ring the tocsin; *battre la générale*; cry wolf.

Adj. alarming &c. *v.*

Int. *sauve qui peut! qui vive?* who goes there?

670. Preservation.—N. preservation; safe keeping; conservation &c. (*storage*) 636; maintenance, upkeep, support, sustentation, conservatism; *vis conservatrix*; salvation &c. (*deliverance*) 672; drying &c. *v.*

[Means of preservation] prophylaxis; preserv-er, -ative; canned goods; cold pack; hygi-astics, -antics; cover, drugget; *cordon sanitaire*.

[Superstitious remedies] charm &c. 993.

V. preserve, maintain, keep, sustain, support; keep -up, – alive; not willingly let die; shore –, bank- up; nurse; save, rescue; be –, make--safe &c. 664; take care of &c. (*care*) 459; guard &c. (*defend*) 717.

stare super antiquas vias; hold one's own; hold –, stand- -one's ground &c. (*resist*) 719.

embalm, dry, cure, smoke, salt, pickle, season, kyanize, bottle, pot, tin, can; husband &c. (*store*) 636.

Adj. preserving &c. *v.*; conservative; prophylactic; preserva-tory, -tive; hygienic.

preserved &c. *v.*; un-impaired, -broken, -injured, -hurt, -singed, -marred; safe, – and sound; intact, with a whole skin, without a scratch.

Phr. *nolumus leges Angliæ mutari*.

671. Escape.—N. escape, scape; avolation, elopement, flight, get-away; evasion &c. (*avoidance*) 623; retreat; narrow –, hairbreadth-escape; close –, near- shave; come off, impunity.

[Means of escape] loophole &c. (*opening*) 260; path &c. 627; secret -door, – passage; refuge &c. 666; vent, – peg; safety-valve; draw-bridge, fire-escape.

reprieve &c. (*deliverance*) 672; liberation &c. 750.

refugee &c. (*fugitive*) 623.

V. escape, scape; make –, effect –, make good- one's escape, make a get-away; get -off, – clear off, – well out of; *échapper belle*, save one's bacon; weather the storm &c. (*safe*) 664; escape scot-free.

elude &c., make off &c. (*avoid*) 623; march off &c. (*go away*) 293; give one the slip; slip through the -hands, – fingers; slip the collar, wriggle out of; break -loose, – from prison; break –, slip –, get- away; find -vent, – a hole to creep out of.

Adj. escap-ing, -ed &c. *v.*; stolen away, fled.

Phr. the bird has flown.

672. Deliverance.—N. deliverance, extrication, rescue; repriev-e, -al; respite; ransom; liberation &c. 750; truce, armistice; redemption, salvation; riddance; gaol delivery; exemption, day of grace; redeemableness.

V. deliver, extricate, rescue, save, redeem, ransom, free, liberate, release, set free, redeem, emancipate; bring -off, – through; *tirer d'affaire*, get the wheel out of the rut; snatch from the jaws of death, come to the rescue; rid; retrieve &c. (*restore*) 660; be –, get- rid of.

Adj. saved &c. *v.*; extric-, redeem-, rescu-able.

Phr. to the rescue!

3°. *Precursory Measures*

673. Preparation.—N. preparation; providing &c. *v.*; provi-sion, -dence; anticipation &c. (*foresight*) 510; pre-caution, -concertation, -disposition;

674. Non-Preparation. — N. non-, absence of –, want of- preparation; unpreparedness; inculture, inconcoction, improvidence.

forecast &c. (*plan*) 626; rehearsal, note of preparation.

[Putting in order] arrangement &c. 60; clearance; adjustment &c. 23; tuning; equipment, outfit, accoutrement, armament, array.

ripening &c. *v.*; maturation, evolution; elaboration, concoction, digestion; gestation, hatching, incubation, sitting.

groundwork, datum, first stone, cradle, stepping-stone; foundation, scaffold &c. (*support*) 215; scaffolding, *échafaudage*.

[Preparation -of men] training &c. (*education*) 537; inurement &c. (*habit*) 613; novitiate; [– of food] cook-ing, -ery; brewing, culinary art; [– of the soil] till-, plough-, sow-ing; semination, cultivation.

[State of being prepared] prepared-, readi-, ripe-, mellow-ness; maturity; *un impromptu fait à loisir*.

[Preparer] preparer, teacher, coach, trainer, pioneer; *avant-courrier*, *·coureur*; sappers and miners, paviour, navvy; packer, stevedore; warming-pan; precursor &c. 64.

V. prepare; get –, make- ready; make preparations, settle preliminaries, get up, sound the note of preparation; address oneself to.

set –, put- in order &c. (*arrange*) 60; forecast &c. (*plan*) 626; prepare –, plough –, dress- the ground; till –, cultivate- the soil; predispose, sow the seed, lay a train, dig a mine; lay –, fix- the -foundations, – basis, -groundwork; dig the foundations, erect the scaffolding; lay the first stone &c. (*begin*) 66.

rough-hew; cut out work; block –, hammer- out; lick into shape &c. (*form*) 240.

elaborate, mature, ripen, mellow, season, bring to maturity; nurture &c.

(*aid*) 707; hatch, cook, brew; temper; anneal, smelt; dry, cure &c. 670.

equip, arm, man; fit-out, -up; furnish, rig, dress, garnish, betrim, accoutre, array, fettle, fledge; dress –, furbish –, brush –, vamp- up; refurbish; sharpen one's tools, trim one's foils, set, prime, attune; whet the -knife, – sword; wind –, screw- up; adjust &c. (*fit*) 27; put in -trim, – train, – gear, – working order, – tune, – a groove for, – harness; pack, stow away, store.

immaturity, crudity; rawness &c. *adj.*; abortion; disqualification.

[Absence of art] nature, state of nature; virgin soil, unweeded garden; rough diamond, neglect &c. 460.

rough copy &c. (*plan*) 626; germ &c. 153; raw material &c. 635.

improvisation &c. (*impulse*) 612.

V. be -unprepared &c. *adj.*; want –, lack- preparation; lie fallow; *s'embarquer sans biscuits*; live from hand to mouth.

[Render unprepared] dismantle &c. (*render useless*) 645; undress &c. 226.

extemporize, improvise.

surprise, pay a surprise visit, take by surprise, drop in upon, take unawares; take pot-luck.

Adj. un-prepared &c. [prepare &c. 673]; without -preparation &c. 673; incomplete &c. 53; rudimental, embryonic, abortive; immature, unripe, raw, green, crude; coarse; rough, -cast, -hewn; in the rough; un-hewn, -formed, -fashioned, -wrought, -laboured, -blown, -cooked, -boiled, -concocted, -cut, -polished.

callow, un-hatched, -fledged, -nurtured, -licked, -taught, -educated, -cultivated, -trained, -tutored, -drilled, -exercised; precocious, premature; un-, in-digested; un-mellowed, -seasoned, -leavened.

fallow; un-sown, -tilled; natural, in a state of nature; undressed; in dishabille, *en déshabille, en négligé*.

un-, dis-qualified; unfitted; ill-digested; un-begun, -ready, -arranged, -organized, -furnished, -provided, -equipped, -trimmed; out of -gear, – order; dismantled &c. *v.*

shiftless, improvident, unthrifty, thoughtless, unguarded; happy-go-lucky; caught napping &c. (*inexpectant*) 508; unpremeditated &c. 612.

Adv. extempore &c. 612.

———

train &c. (*teach*) 537; inure &c. (*habituate*) 613; breed; prepare &c.- for; rehearse; make provision for; take -steps, – measures, – precautions; provide, – against; beat up for recruits; open the door to &c. (*facilitate*) 705.

set one's house in order, make all snug; clear -decks, – for action; close one's ranks; shuffle the cards.

prepare oneself; serve an apprenticeship &c. (*learn*) 539; lay oneself out for, get into harness, gird up one's loins, buckle on one's armour, *reculer pour mieux sauter*, prime and load, shoulder arms, get the steam up, put the horses to.

guard –, make sure- against; forearm, make sure, prepare for the evil day, have a rod in pickle, provide against a rainy day, feather one's nest; lay in provisions &c. 637; make investments; keep on foot.

be -prepared, – ready &c. *adj.*; hold oneself in readiness, watch and pray, keep one's powder dry; lie in wait for &c. (*expect*) 507; anticipate &c. (*foresee*) 510; *principiis obstare*; *veniente occurrere morbo.*

Adj. preparing &c. *v.*; in -preparation, – course of preparation, – agitation, – embryo, – hand, – train; afoot, afloat; on -foot, – the stocks, – the anvil; under consideration &c. (*plan*) 626; brewing, hatching, forthcoming, brooding; in -store for, – reserve.

precautionary, provident; prepara-tive, -tory; provisional, in-choate, under revision; preliminary &c. (*precedent*) 62.

prepared &c. *v.*; in readiness; ready, – to one's hand, – made, cut and dried; ready for use, reach me down; made to one's hand, handy, on the table, made to order; in gear; in working -order, – gear; snug; in practice.

ripe, mature, mellow; practised &c. (*skilled*) 698; laboured, elaborate, highly-wrought, smelling of the lamp, worked up.

in -full feather, – best bib and tucker; in –, at- harness; in – the saddle, – arms, – battle array, – war paint; up in arms; armed -at all points, – to the teeth, – *cap-à-pie*; sword in hand; booted and spurred.

in utrumque –, *semper- paratus*; on the alert &c. (*vigilant*) 459; at one's post.

Adv. in -preparation, – anticipation of; afoot, astir, abroad; abroach.

675. Essay.—N. essay, trial, endeavour, aim, attempt; venture, adventure, speculation, *coup d'essai*, *début*; probation &c. (*experiment*) 463.

V. try, essay; experiment &c. 463; endeavour, strive; tempt, tackle, take on, attempt, make an attempt; venture, adventure, speculate, take one's chance, tempt fortune; try one's -fortune, – luck, – hand; use one's endeavour; feel –, grope –, pick- one's way.

try hard, push, make a bold push, use one's best endeavour; do one's best &c. (*exertion*) 686.

Adj. essaying &c. *v.*; experimental &c. 463; tentative, empirical, probationary.

Adv. experimentally &c. *adj.*; on trial, at a venture; by rule of thumb. if one may be so bold.

676. Undertaking.—N. undertaking; compact &c. 769; engagement &c. (*promise*) 768; enter-, em-prise; venture &c. 675; pilgrimage; matter in hand &c. (*business*) 625; move; first move &c. (*beginning*) 66.

V. undertake; engage –, embark- in; launch –, plunge- into; volunteer; apprentice oneself to; engage &c. (*promise*) 768; contract &c. 769; take upon -oneself, – one's shoulders; devote oneself to &c. (*determination*) 604.

take -up, – in hand; tackle; set –, go- about; set –, fall- -to, – to work; launch forth; set up shop; put in -hand, – execution; set forward; break the neck of a business, be in for; put one's hand to; betake oneself to, turn one's hand to, go to do; begin &c. 66; broach, institute, &c. (*originate*) 153; put –, lay- one's -hand to the plough, – shoulder to the wheel.

have in hand &c. (*business*) 625; have many irons in the fire &c. (*activity*) 682.

Adj. undertaking &c. *v.*; on the anvil &c. 625; adventurous, venturesome.

Int. here goes!

677. Use.—N. use; employ, -ment; exer-cise, -citation; appli-cation, -ance; adhibition, disposal; consumption; agency &c. (*physical*) 170; usufruct; usefulness &c. 644; recourse, resort, avail, pragmatism.

[Conversion to use] utilization, serv-ice, wear.

[Way of using] usage.

V. use, make use of, employ, put to use; apply, put in -action, – operation, – practice; set -in motion, – to work.

ply, work, wield, handle, manipulate; play, – off; exert, exercise, practise, avail oneself of, profit by; resort –, have recourse –, recur –, take –, betake oneself- to; take -up with, – advantage of; lay one's hands on, try.

render useful &c. 644; mould; turn to -account, – use; convert to use, utilize, administer; work up; call –, bring- into play; put into requisition; call –, draw- forth; press –, enlist- into the service; bring to bear upon, devote, dedicate, consecrate, apply, adhibit, dispose of; make a -handle, – cat's paw- of.

fall back upon, make a shift with; make the -most, – best- of.

use –, swallow- up; consume, absorb, expend; tax, task, wear, put to task.

Adj. in use; used &c. *v.*; well-worn, -trodden.

useful &c. 644; subservient &c. (*instrumental*) 631; utilitarian; pragmatical.

678. Disuse.—N. forbearance, abstinence; disuse; relinquishment &c. 782; desuetude &c. (*want of habit*) 614.

V. not use; do without, dispense with, let alone, not touch, forbear, abstain, spare, waive, neglect; keep back, reserve.

lay -up, – by, – on the shelf, – up in a napkin; shelve; set –, put –, lay-aside; disuse, leave off, have done with; supersede; discard &c. (*eject*) 297; dismiss, give warning.

throw aside &c. (*relinquish*) 782; make away with &c. (*destroy*) 162; cast –, heave –, throw- overboard; cast to the -dogs, – winds; dismantle &c. (*render useless*) 645.

lie –, remain- unemployed &c. *adj.*

Adj. not used &c. *v.*; un-employed, -applied, -disposed of, -spent, -exercised, -touched, -trodden, -essayed, -gathered, -culled; uncalled for, not required.

disused &c. *v.*; done with; run down, used up, cast off.

679. Misuse.—N. mis-use, -usage, -employment, -application, -appropriation.

abuse, profanation, prostitution, desecration; waste &c. 638.

V. mis-use, -employ, -apply, -appropriate.

desecrate, abuse, profane, prostitute; waste &c. 638; over-task, -tax, -work; squander &c. 818.

cut a whetstone with a razor, employ a steam-engine to crack a nut; catch at a straw.

Adj. misused &c. *v.*

Section III. Voluntary Action

1°. *Simple Voluntary Action*

680. Action.—N. action, performance; doing &c. *v.*; perpetration; exercise, -citation; movement, operation, evolution, work; labour &c. (*exertion*) 686; *praxis*, execution; procedure &c. (*conduct*) 692; handicraft; business &c. 625; agency &c. (*power at work*) 170.

deed, act, overt act, stitch, touch, gest; transaction, job, doings, dealings, proceeding, measure, step, manœuvre, bout, passage, move, stroke, blow; *coup, – de main, – d'état; tour de force* &c. (*display*) 882; feat, exploit, stunt; achievement &c. (*completion*) 729; handiwork, workmanship, craftsmanship; manufacture; stroke of policy &c. (*plan*) 626.

actor &c. (*doer*) 690.

V. do, perform, execute; achieve &c. (*complete*) 729; transact, enact; commit, perpetrate, inflict; exercise, prosecute, carry on, work, practise, play.

employ oneself, ply one's task; officiate, have in hand &c. (*business*) 625; labour &c. 686; be at work; pursue a course; shape one's course &c. (*conduct*) 692.

act, operate; take -action, – steps; strike a blow, lift a finger, stretch forth one's hand; take in hand &c. (*undertake*) 676; put oneself in motion; put in practice; carry into execution &c. (*complete*) 729; act upon.

be -an actor &c. 690; take –, act –, play –, perform- a part in; participate in; have a -hand in, – finger in the pie; have to do with; be a -party to, – participator in; bear –, lend- a hand; pull an oar, run in a race; mix oneself up with &c. (*meddle*) 682.

be in action; come into operation &c. (*power at work*) 170.

Adj. doing &c. *v.*; acting; in action; in harness; on duty; at work; in operation &c. 170; up to one's ears in work, in the midst of things.

Adv. in the -act, – midst of, – thick of; red-handed, *in flagrante delicto*; while one's hand is in.

681. Inaction.—N. inaction, passiveness, abstinence from action; non-interference; Fabian –, conservative-policy; neglect &c. 460; stagnation, vegetation; loafing.

inactivity &c. 683; rest &c. (*repose*) 687; quiescence &c. 265; want of –, in- occupation; unemployment; idle hours, time hanging on one's hands, *dolce far niente*; sinecure.

V. not -do, – act, – attempt; be -inactive &c. 683; abstain from doing, do nothing, hold, spare; not -stir, – move, – lift- a -finger, – foot, – peg; fold one's -arms, – hands; leave –, let- alone; let -be, – pass, – things take their course, – it have its way, – well alone; *quieta non movere; stare super antiquas vias;* rest and be thankful, live and let live; lie –, rest- upon one's oars; *laisser -aller, – faire;* stand aloof; refrain &c. (*avoid*) 623; keep oneself from doing; remit –, relax- one's efforts; desist &c. (*relinquish*) 624; stop &c. (*cease*) 142; pause &c. (*be quiet*) 265.

wait, lie in wait, bide one's time, take time, tide it over.

cool –, kick- one's heels; loaf, while away the -time, – tedious hours; pass –, fill up –, beguile- the time; talk against time; waste time &c. (*inactive*) 683.

lie -by, – on the shelf, – in ordinary, – idle, – to, – fallow; keep quiet, slug; have nothing to do, whistle for want of thought; twiddle one's thumbs.

undo, do away with; take -down, – to pieces; destroy &c. 162.

Adj. not doing &c. *v.*; not done &c. *v.*; undone; passive; un-occupied, -employed; out of -employ, – work, – a job; fallow; *désœuvré.*

Adv. *re infectâ*, at a stand, *les bras croisés*, with folded arms; with the hands -in the pockets, – behind one's back; *pour passer le temps.*

Int. so let it be! stop! &c. 142; hands off!

Phr. nothing doing; *cunctando restituit rem.*

682. Activity.—N. activity; brisk-ness, liveliness &c. *adj.*; animation, life, vivacity, spirit, verve, dash, energy, go.

nimbleness, agility; smartness, quick-ness &c. *adj.*; velocity &c. 274; alacrity, promptitude; des-, dis-patch; expedi-tion; haste &c. 684; punctuality &c. (*early*) 132.

eagerness, zeal, ardour, *perfervidum ingenium, empressement,* earnestness, intentness; *abandon*; vigour &c. (*physi-cal energy*) 171; devotion &c. (*resolu-tion*) 604; exertion &c. 686.

industry, assiduity; assiduousness &c. *adj.*; sedulity; laboriousness; drudg-ery &c. (*labour*) 686; painstaking, diligence; perseverance &c. 604a; in-defatigation; habits of business.

vigilance &c. 459; wakefulness; sleep-, rest-lessness; *pervigilium, in-somnia*; racketing.

movement, bustle, hustle, stir, fuss, ado, bother, pottering; fidget, -iness; flurry &c. (*haste*) 684.

officiousness; dabbling, meddling; inter-ference, -position, -meddling, but-ting in, intrusiveness; tampering with, intrigue.

press of business, no sinecure, plenty to do, many irons in the fire, great doings, busy hum of men, battle of life, thick of -things, – the action; the mad-ding crowd.

housewife, busy bee; new brooms; sharp fellow, blade; hustler, devotee, enthusiast, fan, zealot, fanatic; med-dler, intermeddler, intriguer, busybody, kibitzer, pickthank.

V. be -active &c. *adj.*; busy oneself in; stir, -about, – one's stumps; bestir –, rouse- oneself; speed, hasten, peg away, lay about one, bustle, fuss; raise –, kick up- a dust; push; make a -push, – fuss, – stir; go ahead, push forward; flight –, elbow- one's way; make prog-ress &c. 282; toil &c. (*labour*) 686; drudge, plod, persist &c. (*persevere*) 604a; keep -up the ball, – the pot boiling.

look sharp; have all one's eyes about one &c. (*vigilance*) 459; rise, arouse oneself, get up early, hustle, push; be about, keep moving, steal a march, kill two birds with one stone; seize the opportunity &c. 134; lose no time, not

683. Inactivity.—N. inactivity; in-action &c. 681; inertness &c. 172; obstinacy &c. 606.

lull &c. (*cessation*) 142; quiescence &c. 265; rust, -iness.

idle-, remiss-ness &c. *adj.*; sloth, indolence, indiligence; otiosity, daw-dling &c. *v.*

dullness &c. *adj.*; languor; segni-ty, -tude; lentor; sluggishness &c. (*slow-ness*) 275; procrastination &c. (*delay*) 133; torp-or, -idity, -escence; stupor &c. (*insensibility*) 823; somnolence; drowsiness &c. *adj.*; nodding &c. *v.*; oscit-ation, -ancy; pandiculation, hyp-notism, lethargy; heaviness, heavy eye-lids, sand in the eyes.

sleep, slumber; sound –, heavy –, balmy- sleep; Morpheus, dreamland; coma, trance, catalepsy, hypnosis, ecstasis, dream, hibernation, nap, doze, snooze, *siesta,* wink of sleep, forty winks, snore; Hypnology.

dull work; pottering; relaxation &c. (*loosening*) 47; Castle of Indolence.

[Cause of inactivity] lullaby, *ber-ceuse*; anæsthetic, sedative &c. 174; torpedo.

idler, drone, droil, dawdle, mopus; do-little, *fainéant,* dummy, sleeping partner; afternoon farmer; truant &c. (*runaway*) 623; lounger, *lazzarone,* floater, loafer, tramp, beggar, cadger; lub-ber, -bard; slow-coach &c. (*slow*) 275; opium –, lotus- eater; slug; lag-, slug-gard, lie-abed; slumberer, dor-mouse, marmot; waiter on Providence, *fruges consumere natus.*

V. be -inactive &c. *adj.*; do nothing &c. 681; move slowly &c. 275; let the grass grow under one's feet; take one's time, dawdle, poke, drawl, droil, lag, hang back, slouch; loll, -op; lounge, loaf, loiter; go to sleep over; sleep at one's post, *ne battre que d'une aile.*

take -it easy, – things as they come; lead an easy life, vegetate, swim with the stream, eat the bread of idleness; loll in the lap of -luxury, – indolence; waste –, consume –, kill –, lose- time; burn daylight, waste the precious hours.

idle –, trifle –, fritter –, fool- away time; spend –, take- time in; ped-, pid-dle; potter, putter, dabble, faddle,

lose a moment, make the most of one's time, not suffer the grass to grow under one's feet, improve the shining hour, make short work of; dash off; make haste &c. 684; do one's best, take pains &c. (*exert oneself*) 686; do –, work- wonders.

have -many irons in the fire, – one's hands full, – much on one's hands; have other -things to do, – fish to fry; be busy; not have a moment -to spare, – that one can call one's own.

have one's fling, run the round of; go all lengths, stick at nothing, run riot.

outdo; over-do, -act, -lay, -shoot the mark; make a toil of a pleasure.

have a hand in &c. (*act in*) 680; take an active part, put in one's oar, have a finger in the pie, mix oneself up with, trouble one's head about, intrigue; agitate.

tamper with, meddle, moil; inter-meddle, -fere, -pose; obtrude; poke –, thrust- one's nose in, butt in.

Adj. active; brisk, – as a lark, – as a bee; lively, animated, vivacious; alive, – and kicking; frisky, spirited, stirring.

nimble, – as a squirrel; agile; light-, nimble-footed; featly, tripping.

quick, prompt, yare, instant, ready, alert, spry, sharp, smart, slick, go-ahead; fast &c. (*swift*) 274; quick as a lamplighter, expeditious; awake, broad awake; wide awake &c. (*intelligent*) 498.

forward, eager, ardent, strenuous, zealous, enterprising, pushing, in earnest; resolute &c. 604.

industrious, assiduous, diligent, sedulous, notable, painstaking; intent &c. (*attention*) 457; indefatigable &c. (*persevering*) 604a; unwearied; unsleeping, sleepless, never tired; plodding, hard-working &c. 686; business-like, workaday.

bustling; restless, – as a hyæna; fussy, fidgety, pottering; busy, – as a hen with one chicken.

working, labouring, at work, on duty, in harness; up in arms; on one's legs, at call; up and -doing, – stirring.

busy, occupied; hard at -work, – it; up to one's ears in, full of business, busy as a bee.

meddling &c. *v.*; meddlesome, pushing, officious, overofficious, *intrigant*.

astir, stirring; a-going, -foot; on foot; in full swing; eventful; on the alert &c. (*vigilant*) 459.

fribble, fiddle-faddle; dally, dilly-dally.

sleep, slumber, be asleep; hibernate; oversleep; sleep like a -top, – log, – dormouse; sleep -soundly, – heavily; doze, drowze, snooze, nap; take a -nap &c. *n.*; dream; snore; settle –, go –, go off- to sleep; drop off; fall –, drop-asleep; close –, seal up- -the -eyes, – eyelids; weigh down the eyelids; get sleepy, nod, yawn; go to bed, turn in.

languish, expend itself, flag, hang fire; relax.

render -idle &c. *adj.*; sluggardize; mitigate &c. 174.

Adj. inactive; motionless &c. 265; unoccupied &c: (*doing nothing*) 681.

indolent, lazy, slothful, idle, otiose, lusk, remiss, slack, inert, torpid, slug-gish, languid, supine, heavy, dull, leaden, lumpish; exanimate, soulless; listless; dron-y, -ish; lazy as Ludlam's dog.

dilatory, laggard; lagging &c. *v.*; slow &c. 275; rusty, flagging; lacka-daisical, maudlin, fiddle-faddle; potter-ing &c. *v.*; shilly-shally &c. (*irresolute*) 605.

sleeping &c. *v.*; asleep; fast –, dead –, sound- asleep; in a sound sleep; sound as a top, dormant, comatose; in the -arms, – lap- of Morpheus.

sleep-y, -ful; dozy, drowsy, somno-lent, torpescent; lethargic, -al; heavy, – with sleep; napping; somni-fic, -ferous; sopor-ous, -ific, -iferous; hyp-notic; balmy, dreamy; un-, una-wak-ened.

sedative &c. 174.

Adv. inactively &c. *adj.*; at leisure &c. 685.

Phr. the eyes begin to draw straws.

Adv. actively &c. *adj.*; with -life and spirit, – might and main &c. 686, – haste &c. 684, – wings; full tilt, *in mediis rebus.*

Int. be –, look- -alive, – sharp! move –, push- on! keep moving! go ahead! stir your stumps! *age quod agis!*

Phr. *carpe diem* &c. (*opportunity*) 134; *nulla dies sine lineâ*; *nec mora nec requies*; no sooner said than done &c. (*early*) 132; catch a weasel asleep.

---

684. Haste.—N. haste, urgency; des-, dis-patch; acceleration, spurt, spirt, forced march, rush, dash; velocity &c. 274; precipit-ancy, -ation, -ousness &c. *adj.*; impetuosity; *brusquerie*; hurry, scurry, scuttle, drive, scramble, push, hustle, bustle, fuss, fidget, flurry, flutter, splutter.

V. haste, hasten; make -haste, – a dash &c. *n.*; hurry –, dash –, whip –, push –, press- -on, – forward; hurry, skurry, scuttle along, bundle on, dart to and fro, bustle, flutter, scramble; plunge, – headlong; run, race, speed; dash off; rush &c. (*violence*) 173.

bestir oneself &c. (*be active*) 682; lose -no time, – not a moment, – not an instant; make short work of; make the best of one's -time, – way.

be -precipitate &c. *adj.*; jump at; be in -haste, – a hurry &c. *n.*; have -no time, – not a moment- -to lose, – to spare; work -under pressure, – against time.

quicken &c. 274; accelerate, expedite, put on, precipitate, urge, whip, spur, flog, goad.

Adj. hasty, hurried, *brusque*; scrambling, cursory, precipitate, headlong, furious, boisterous, impetuous, hot-headed; feverish, fussy; pushing.

in -haste, – a hurry &c. *n.*; in -hot, – all- haste; breathless, pressed for time, hard pressed, urgent.

Adv. with -haste, – all haste, – breathless speed; in haste &c. *adj.*; apace &c. (*swiftly*) 274; amain; all at once &c. (*instantaneously*) 113; at short notice &c., immediately &c. (*early*) 132; posthaste; by -express, – telegraph, – wire, – wireless, – air mail.

hastily, precipitately &c. *adj.*; helter-skelter, hurry-skurry, holus-bolus; slap-dash, -bang; full-tilt, -drive; heels over head, head and shoulders, headlong, *à corps perdu.*

by -fits and starts, – spurts; hop, skip and jump.

Phr. *sauve qui peut*, devil take the hindmost, no time to be lost; no sooner said than done &c. (*early*) 132; a word and a blow.

Int. hurry up! look alive! get a move on! buck up! double march! rush! urgent!

685. Leisure.—N. leisure; spare -time, – hours, – moments; vacant hour; time, – to spare, – on one's hands; holiday &c. (*rest*) 687; *otium cum dignitate*, ease.

V. have -leisure &c. *n.*; take one's -time, – leisure, – ease; repose &c. 687; move slowly &c. 275; while away the time &c. (*inaction*) 681; be -master of one's time, – an idle man; *desipere in loco.*

Adj. leisurely; slow &c. 275; deliberate, quiet, calm, undisturbed; at -leisure, – one's ease, – a loose end.

Phr. time hanging heavy on one's hands.

---

686. Exertion.—N. exertion, effort, strain, tug, pull, stress, force, pressure, throw, stretch, struggle, spell, spurt, spirt; stroke –, stitch- of work.

687. Repose.—N. repose, rest, silken repose; sleep &c. 683.

relaxation, breathing time; halt, pause &c. (*cessation*) 142; respite.

'a strong pull, a long pull and a pull all together'; dead lift; heft; gymnastics, sports; exer-cise, -citation; wear and tear; ado; toil and trouble; uphill -, hard -, warm- work; harvest time.

labour, work, toil, travail, manual labour, sweat of one's brow, swink, operoseness, drudgery, slavery, fagging, hammering; *limæ labor.*

trouble, pains, duty; resolution &c. 604; energy &c. (*physical*) 171.

V. exert oneself; exert -, tax- one's energies; use exertion.

labour, work, toil, moil, sweat, fag, drudge, slave, drag a lengthened chain, wade through, strive, strain; make -, stretch- a long arm; pull, tug, ply; ply -, tug at- the oar; do the work; take the labouring oar.

bestir oneself (*be active*) 682; take trouble, trouble oneself.

work hard; rough it; put forth -one's strength, - a strong arm; fall to work, bend the bow; buckle to, set one's shoulder to the wheel &c. (*resolution*) 604; work like a -Briton, - horse, - carthorse, - galley-slave, - coalheaver; labour -, work- day and night; redouble one's efforts; do double duty; work double -hours, - tides; sit up, burn the -midnight oil, - candle at both ends; stick to &c. (*persevere*) 604a; work -, fight- one's way; lay about one, hammer at.

take pains; do one's -best, - level best, - utmost; do -the best one can, - all one can, - all in one's power, - as much as in one lies, - what lies in one's power; use one's -best, - utmost- endeavour; try one's -best, - utmost; play one's best card; put one's -best, - right- leg foremost; have one's whole soul in one's work, put all one's strength into, strain every nerve; spare no -efforts, - pains; go all lengths; go through fire and water &c. (*resolution*) 604; move heaven and earth, leave no stone unturned.

Adj. labouring &c. *v.*

laborious, operose, elaborate; strained; toil-, trouble-, burden-, weari-some; uphill; herculean, gymnastic, athletic, palestric.

hardworking, painstaking, strenuous, energetic.

hard at work, on the stretch.

Adv. laboriously &c. *adj.*; lustily; with -might and main, - all one's might, - a strong hand, - sledge-hammer, - much ado; to the best of one's abilities, *totis viribus, vi et armis, manibus pedibusque,* tooth and nail, *unguibus et rostro,* hammer and tongs, heart and soul; through thick and thin &c. (*perseverance*) 604a.

by the sweat of one's brow, *suo Marte.*

day of rest, *dies non,* Sabbath, Lord's day, holiday, red-letter day, vacation, recess.

V. repose; rest, - and be thankful; take -rest, - one's ease.

relax, unbend, slacken; take breath &c. (*refresh*) 689; rest upon one's oars; pause &c. (*cease*) 142; stay one's hand.

lie down; recline, - on a bed of down, - on an easy chair; go to -rest, - bed, - sleep &c. 683.

take a holiday, shut up shop; lie fallow &c. (*inaction*) 681.

Adj. reposing &c. *v.*; unstrained.

Adv. at rest.

------

688. Fatigue.—N. fatigue; weariness &c. 841; yawning, drowsiness &c. 683; lassitude, tiredness, fatigation, exhaustion; sweat.

anhelation, shortness of breath, panting; faintness; collapse, prostration,

689. Refreshment.—N. bracing &c. *v.*; recovery of -strength &c. 159; restoration, revival &c. 660; repair, refection, refocillation, refreshment, regalement, bait; relief &c. 834.

V. brace &c. (*strengthen*) 159; rein-

swoon, fainting, *deliquium*, syncope, lipothymy.

V. be -fatigued &c. *adj.*; yawn &c. (*get sleepy*) 683; droop, sink, flag; lose -breath, – wind; gasp, pant, puff, blow, drop, swoon, faint, succumb.

fatigue, tire, weary, bore, irk, fag, jade, harass, exhaust, knock up, wear out, prostrate.

tax, task, strain; over-task, -work, -burden, -tax, -strain.

Adj. fatigued &c. *v.*; weary &c. 841; drowsy &c. 683; drooping &c. *v.*; haggard; toil-, way-worn; footsore, surbated, weatherbeaten; faint; done –, used –, knocked- up; exhausted, prostrate, spent; over-tired, -spent, -fatigued; forspent; unre-freshed, -stored.

worn, – out; battered, shattered, pulled down, seedy, altered.

breath-, wind-less; short of –, out of -breath, – wind; blown, puffing and blowing; short-breathed; anhelous; broken-, short-winded.

ready to drop, more dead than alive, dog -tired, – weary, walked off one's legs, tired to death, on one's last legs, played out, *hors de combat*.

fatiguing &c. *v.*; tire-, irk-, weari-some; weary; trying.

vigorate; air, freshen up, refresh, recruit; repair &c. (*restore*) 660; fan, refocillate.

breathe, respire; draw –, take –, gather –, take a long –, regain –, re-cover- breath; get better, raise one's head; recover –, regain –, renew- one's strength &c. 159; perk up.

come to oneself &c. (*revive*) 660; feel like a giant refreshed.

Adj. refreshing &c. *v.*; recuperative &c. 660.

refreshed &c. *v.*; un-tired, -wearied.

----

690. Agent.—**N.** doer, actor, agent, performer, perpetrator, operator; execu-tor, -trix; practitioner, worker, stager.

bee, ant, working bee, labouring oar, shaft horse, servant –, maid-of all work, general servant, factotum.

workman, artisan; crafts-, handicrafts-man; mechanic, operative; working –, labouring- man; hewers of wood and drawers of water, labourer, navvy; hand, man, day labourer, journeyman, hack; mere -tool &c. 633; porter, docker, stevedore, beast of burden, drudge, fag.

maker, artificer, artist, wright, manufacturer, architect, contractor, builder, mason, bricklayer, smith, forger, Vulcan; black-, tin-smith; carpenter; ganger, platelayer.

machinist, mechanician, engineer, electrician, plumber, gasfitter &c.

semp-, sem-, seam-stress; needle-, char-, work-woman; tailor, cord-wainer.

minister &c. (*instrument*) 631; servant &c. 746; representative &c. (*commissioner*) 758, (*deputy*) 759.

co-worker, fellow-worker, party to, participator in, co-operator, col-league, associate, collaborator, *particeps criminis*, *dramatis personæ*; *personnel*.

Phr. '*quorum pars magna fui.*'

----

691. Workshop.—**N.** work-shop, -house; laboratory; manufactory, mill, factory, armoury, arsenal, mint, forge, loom; cabinet, *studio*, *bureau*, *atelier*; hive, – of industry; nursery; hot-house, -bed; kitchen, kitchenette; dock, -yard; slip, yard, wharf; found-ry, -ery; furnace; vineyard, orchard, farm, kitchen garden.

melting pot, crucible, alembic, caldron, mortar, *matrix*.

2°. *Complex Voluntary Action*

692. Conduct.—N. dealing, transaction &c. (*action*) 680; business &c. 625.

tactics, game, policy, polity; general-, statesman-, seaman-ship; strate-gy, -gics; plan &c. 626.

husbandry; house-keeping, -wifery; stewardship; *ménage*; regimen, *régime*; econom-y, -ics; political economy; management; government &c. (*direction*) 693.

execution, manipulation, treatment, campaign, career, life, course, walk, race.

conduct; behaviour; de-, com-portment; carriage, *maintien*, demeanour, guise, bearing, manner, mien, air, observance.

course –, line- of -conduct, – action, – proceeding; *rôle*; process, ways, practice, procedure, *modus operandi*; method &c., path &c. 627.

V. transact, execute; des-, dis-patch; proceed with, discharge; carry -on, – through, – out, – into effect; work out; go –, get- through; enact; put into practice; officiate &c. 625.

behave –, comport –, demean –, carry –, bear –, conduct –, acquit- oneself.

run a race, lead a life, play a game; take –, adopt- a course; steer –, shape- one's course; play one's- -part, – cards; shift for oneself; paddle one's own canoe.

conduct; manage &c. (*direct*) 693.

deal –, have to do- with; treat, handle a case; take -steps, – measures.

Adj. conducting &c. *v.*; strategical, business-like, practical, economic, executive.

693. Direction.—N. direction; manage-ment, -ry; government, gubernation, conduct, legislation, regulation, guidance; steer-, pilot-age; reins, – of government; helm, rudder, controls, joy stick, needle, compass, binnacle; guiding –, load –, lode –, pole- star; cynosure.

super-vision, -intendence; *surveillance*, oversight; eye of the master; control, charge, auspices; board of control &c. (*council*) 696; command &c. (*authority*) 737.

premier-, senator-ship; director &c. 694; chair, seat, portfolio.

statesmanship; state-, king-craft.

minis-try, -tration; administration; steward-, proctor-ship; agency.

V. direct, manage, govern, conduct; order, prescribe, cut out work for; head, lead; lead –, show- the way; take the lead, lead on; regulate, guide, steer, pilot; take –, be at- the helm; have –, handle –, hold –, take- the reins, handle the ribbons; drive, tool; tackle.

super-intend, -vise; overlook, control, keep in order, look after, see to, oversee, legislate for; administer, ministrate; patronize; have the -care, – charge- of; have –, take- the direction; pull the -strings, – wires; rule &c. (*command*) 737; have –, hold- -office, – the portfolio; preside, – at the board; take –, occupy –, be in- the chair; pull the stroke oar.

Adj. directing &c. *v.*; executive, supervisory, hegemonic.

Adv. at the -helm, – head of, in charge of; under the auspices of.

694. Director.—N. director, manager, governor, rector, comptroller; super-intendent, -visor; intendant; over-seer, -looker; foreman, boss, straw boss; supercargo, husband, inspector, visitor, ranger, surveyor, ædile, moderator, monitor, taskmaster; master &c. 745; leader, ring- leader, demagogue, corypheus, conductor, fugleman, precentor, bell- wether, agitator.

[250]

guiding star &c. (*guidance*) 693; adviser &c. 695; guide &c. (*information*) 527; pilot; helmsman; steers-man, -mate; man at the wheel; wire-puller.

driver, whip, Jehu, charioteer; coach-, car-, cab-man, jarvey; postilion, *vetturino*, muleteer, teamster; whipper in; engineer, engine driver, motorman, *chauffeur*.

head, – man; principal, president, speaker; chair, -man; captain &c. (*master*) 745; superior; dean; mayor &c. (*civil authority*) 745; vice-president, prime minister, premier, vizier, grand vizier; dictator.

officer, functionary, minister, official, red-tapist, bureaucrat; man –, Jack- in office; office-bearer; person in authority &c. 745.

statesman, strategist, legislator, lawgiver, politician, administrator, statist, statemonger; Minos, Draco; arbiter &c. (*judge*) 967; king maker, power behind the throne.

board &c. (*council*) 696.

secretary, – of state; Reis Effendi; vicar &c. (*deputy*) 759; steward, factor; agent &c. 758; bailiff, middleman; ganger, clerk of works; landreeve; factotum, major-domo, seneschal, housekeeper, shepherd, *croupier*; proctor, procurator, curator, librarian.

Adv. *ex officio.*

695. Advice.—N. advice, counsel, adhortation; word to the wise; suggestion, submonition, recommendation, advocacy, consultation.

exhortation &c. (*persuasion*) 615; expostulation &c. (*dissuasion*) 616; admonition &c. (*warning*) 668; guidance &c. (*direction*) 693.

instruction, charge, injunction.

adviser, prompter; counsel, -lor; monitor, mentor, Nestor, *magnus Apollo*, senator; teacher &c. 540.

guide, manual, chart &c. (*information*) 527.

physician, leech, archiater; arbiter &c. (*judge*) 967.

refer-ence, -ment; consultation, conference, parley, *pourparler* &c. 696.

V. advise, counsel; give -advice, – counsel, – a piece of advice; suggest, prompt, submonish, recommend, prescribe, advocate; exhort &c. (*persuade*) 615.

enjoin, enforce, charge, instruct, call; call upon &c. (*request*) 765; dictate.

expostulate &c. (*dissuade*) 616; admonish &c. (*warn*) 668.

advise with; lay heads –, consult- together; compare notes; hold a council, deliberate, be closeted with.

confer, consult, refer to, call in; take –, follow- advice; follow implicitly; be advised by, have at one's elbow, take one's cue from.

Adj. recommendatory; hortative &c. (*persuasive*) 615; dehortatory &c. (*dissuasive*) 616; admonitory &c. (*warning*) 668; consultative.

Int. go to!

696. Council.—N. council, committee, subcommittee, *comitia*, court, chamber, cabinet, board, bench, staff; consultation.

senate, *senatus*, parliament, house, – of Lords, – Peers, – Commons, legislature, legislative assembly, federal council, chamber of deputies, directory, *reichsrath*, *rigsdag*, *cortes*, storthing, witenagemote, *junta*, divan, *musnud*, sanhedrim, Amphictyonic council; *duma*, *zemstvo*, *soviet*, *cheka*, *ogpu*; *Dail Eireann*; caput, consistory, chapter, syndicate; court of appeal &c. (*tribunal*) 966; board of -control, – works; vestry; county –, borough –, district –, parish –, town- council, local board.

cabinet -, privy- council, royal commission; cockpit, convocation, synod, congress, congregation, convention, diet, states-general, aulic council.

League of Nations, assembly, *caucus*, conclave, *clique*, conventicle; meeting, sitting, *séance*, conference, session, hearing, palaver, *pourparler*, *durbar*, pow-wow, house; *quorum*.

senator; member, - of parliament; councillor, M.P., representative of the people.

Adj. senatorial, curule, parliamentary.

697. Precept.—N. precept, direction, instruction, charge; prescript, -ion; *recipe*, receipt; golden rule; maxim &c. 496.

commandment, rule, ruling, canon, law, code, *corpus juris*, *lex scripta*, common -, unwritten -, canon-law; the Ten Commandments; act, statute, convention, rubric, stage direction, regulation; form, -ula, -ulary; technicality; nice point.

order &c. (*command*) 741.

698. Skill.—N. skill, skilfulness, ad-dress; dexter-ity, -ousness; adroitness, expertness &c. *adj.*; proficiency, com-petence, craft, callidity, facility, knack, trick, sleight; master-y, -ship; excel-lence, panurgy; ambidext-erity, -rous-ness; sleight of hand &c. (*deception*) 545.

sea-, air-, marks-, horse-manship; tight-, rope-dancing.

accomplish-, acquire-, attain-ment; art, science; techn-icality, -ology, -ique; practical -, technical- knowledge; tech-nocracy; finish, technic.

knowledge of the world, world wis-dom, *savoir-faire*; tact; mother wit &c. (*sagacity*) 498; discretion &c. (*caution*) 864; *finesse*; craftiness &c. (*cunning*) 702; management &c. (*conduct*) 692; *ars celare artem*; self-help.

cleverness, talent, ability, ingenuity, capacity, parts, talents, faculty, en-dowment, *forte*, turn, gift, genius, flair, feeling; intelligence &c. 498; sharpness, readiness &c. (*activity*) 682; invention &c. 515; apt-ness, -itude; turn -, capa-city -, genius- for; felicity, capability, *curiosa felicitas*, qualification, habili-tation.

proficient &c. 700.

masterpiece, *coup de maître*, *chef-d'œuvre*, *tour de force*; good stroke &c. (*plan*) 626.

V. be -skilful &c. *adj.*; excel in, be master of; have -a turn for &c. *n.*

know -what's what, - a hawk from a handsaw, - what one is about, - on

699. Unskilfulness.—N. unskilful-ness &c. *adj.*; want of -skill &c. 698; incompeten-ce, -cy; in-ability, -felicity, -dexterity, -experience; clumsiness; dis-qualification, unproficiency; quackery.

folly, stupidity &c. 499; indiscretion &c. (*rashness*) 863; thoughtlessness &c. (*inattention*) 458, (*neglect*) 460.

mis-management, -conduct; im-policy; maladministration; mis-rule, -government, -application, -direction, -feasance.

absence of rule, rule of thumb; bungling &c. *v.*; failure &c. 732; screw loose; too many cooks.

blunder &c. (*mistake*) 495; *étourderie*, *gaucherie*, act of folly, *balourdise*; botch, -ery; bad job, sad work.

sprat sent out to catch a whale, much ado about nothing, wildgoose chase.

bungler &c. 701; fool &c. 501.

layman, amateur.

V. be -unskilful &c. *adj.*; not see an inch beyond one's nose; blunder, bungle, boggle, fumble, muff, botch, bitch, flounder, loppet, stumble, trip; hobble &c. 275; put one's foot in it; make a -mess, - hash, - sad work- of; overshoot the mark.

play -tricks with, - Puck; mis-manage, -conduct, -direct, -apply, -send.

stultify -, make a fool of -, commit-oneself; act foolishly; play the fool; put oneself out of court; lose one's -head, - cunning.

begin at the wrong end; do things

which side one's bread is buttered, – what's o'clock, – a thing or two; have cut one's -eye, – wisdom- teeth.

see -one's way, – where the wind lies, – which way the wind blows; have -all one's wits about one, – one's hand in; *savoir vivre*; *scire quid valeant humeri quid ferre recusent.*

look after the main chance; cut one's coat according to one's cloth; live by one's wits; exercise one's discretion, feather the oar, sail near the wind; stoop to conquer &c. (*cunning*) 702; play one's -cards well, – best card; hit the right nail on the head, put the saddle on the right horse.

take advantage of, make the most of; profit by &c. (*use*) 677; make a hit &c. (*succeed*) 731; make a virtue of necessity; make hay while the sun shines &c. (*occasion*) 134.

Adj. skilful, dexterous, adroit, expert, apt, slick, handy, quick, deft, ready, resourceful, gain; smart &c. (*active*) 682; proficient, good at, up to, at home in, master of, a good hand at, *au fait*, thoroughbred, masterly, crack, accomplished; conversant &c. (*knowing*) 490.

experienced, practised, skilled; up -, well up- in; in -practice, – proper cue; competent, efficient, qualified, capable, fitted, fit for, up to the mark, trained, initiated, prepared, primed, finished.

clever, able, ingenious, felicitous, gifted, talented, endowed, cute, inventive &c. 515; shrewd, sharp &c. (*intelligent*) 498; cunning &c. 702; alive to, up to snuff, not to be caught with chaff; discreet.

neat-handed, fine-fingered, ambidextrous, sure-footed; cut out -, fitted- for.

technical, artistic, scientific, dædalian, shipshape; workman-, business-, statesman-like.

Adv. skillfully &c. *adj.*; well &c. 618; artistically; with -skill, – consummate skill; *secundum artem, suo Marte*; to the best of one's abilities &c. (*exertion*) 686; like a machine.

by halves &c. (*not complete*) 730; make two bites of a cherry; play at cross purposes; strain at a gnat and swallow a camel &c. (*caprice*) 608; put the cart before the horse; lock the stable door when the horse is stolen &c. (*too late*) 135.

not know -what one is about, – one's own interest, – on which side one's bread is buttered; stand in one's own light, quarrel with one's bread and butter, throw a stone in one's own garden, kill the goose which lays the golden eggs, pay dear for one's whistle, cut one's own throat, burn one's fingers; knock -, run- one's head against a stone wall; fall into a trap, catch a Tartar, bring the house about one's ears; have too many -eggs in one basket (*imprudent*) 863, – irons in the fire.

mistake &c. 495; take the shadow for the substance &c. (*credulity*) 486; be in the wrong box, aim at a pigeon and kill a crow; take -, get- the wrong sow by the ear, – the dirty end of the stick; put -the saddle on the wrong horse, – a square peg into a round hole, – new wine into old bottles.

cut a whetstone with a razor; hold a farthing candle to the sun &c. (*useless*) 645; fight with -, grasp at- a shadow; catch at straws, lean on a broken reed, reckon without one's host, pursue a wildgoose chase; go on a fool's -, sleeveless- errand; go further and fare worse; loose -, miss- one's way; fail &c. 732.

Adj. un-skilful &c. 698; unskilled, inexpert; bungling &c. *v.*; awkward, clumsy, unhandy, lubberly, *gauche*, *maladroit*; left-, heavy-handed; slovenly, slatternly; gawky.

adrift, at fault.

in-, un-apt; inhabile; un-tractable, -teachable; giddy &c. (*inattentive*) 458; inconsiderate &c. (*neglectful*) 460; stupid &c. 499; inactive &c. 683; incompetent; un-, dis-, ill-qualified; unfit; quackish; raw, green, inexperienced, rusty, out of practice.

un-accustomed, -used, -trained &c. 537, -initiated, -conversant &c. (*ignorant*) 491; shiftless; unbusinesslike, unpractical; unstatesmanlike.

un-, ill-, mis-advised; ill-devised, -imagined, -judged, -contrived, -conducted; un-, mis-guided; misconducted, foolish, wild; infelicitous; penny wise and pound foolish &c. (*inconsistent*) 608.

Phr. one's fingers being all thumbs; the right hand forgets its cunning.

il se noyerait dans une goutte d'eau.

incidit in Scyllam qui vult vitare Charybdim; out of the frying pan into the fire.

---

700. Proficient.—**N.** proficient, expert, adept, dab; *connoisseur* &c. (*scholar*) 492; master, -hand; top-sawyer, *prima donna*, first fiddle, *chef de cuisine*; protagonist; past master; profess-or, -ional, specialist.

picked man; medallist, prizeman.

veteran; old -stager, – campaigner, – soldier, – file, – hand; man of -business, – the world.

nice –, good –, clean- hand; practised –, experienced- -eye, – hand; marksman; good –, dead –, crack- shot; rope-dancer, funambulist, acrobat, contortionist; cunning man; conjuror &c. (*deceiver*) 548; wizard &c. 994.

genius; master-mind, – head, – spirit.

cunning –, sharp -blade, – fellow; jobber; cracksman &c. (*thief*) 792; politician, tactician, diplomat, -ist, strategist.

pantologist, admirable Crichton, Jack of all trades; prodigy of learning; walking encyclopædia; mine of information.

701. Bungler.—**N.** bungler; blunder-er, -head; marplot, fumbler, lubber, lout, oaf, duffer, stick, clown; bad –, poor- -hand, – shot; butter-fingers.

no conjuror, flat, muff, slow coach, looby, lubber, swab; clod, yokel, hick, awkward squad, novice, greenhorn, jaywalker, *blanc-bec.*

land lubber; fresh water –, fair weather- sailor; horse-marine; fish out of water, ass in lion's skin, jackdaw in peacock's feathers; quack &c. (*deceiver*) 548; Lord of Misrule.

sloven, slattern, trapes.

Phr. *il n'a pas inventé la poudre*; h will never set the Thames on fire.

---

702. Cunning.—**N.** cunning, craft; cunningness, craftiness &c. *adj.*; subtlety, artificiality; manœuvring &c. *v.*; temporization; circumvention.

chicane, -ry; sharp practice, knavery, jugglery; concealment &c. 528; nigger in the woodpile; guile, duplicity &c. (*falsehood*) 544; foul play.

diplomacy, politics; Machiavellism; jobbery, back-stairs influence, gerrymandering.

art, -ifice; device, machination; plot &c. (*plan*) 626; manœuvre, stratagem, dodge, artful dodge, wile; trick, -ery &c. (*deception*) 545; *ruse*, – *de guerre*; *finesse*, side-blow, thin end of the wedge, shift, go by, subterfuge, evasion; white lie &c. (*untruth*) 546; juggle, *tour de force*; tricks -of the trade, – upon travellers; imposture, deception; *espièglerie*; net, trap &c. 545.

Ulysses, Machiavel, sly boots, fox,

703. Artlessness.—**N.** artlessness &c. *adj.*; nature, simplicity; innocence &c. 946; *bonhomie, naïveté, abandon,* candour, sincerity; singleness of -purpose, – heart; honesty &c. 939; plain speaking; *épanchement.*

rough diamond, matter of fact man; *le palais de vérité; enfant terrible.*

V. be -artless &c. *adj.*; look one in the face; wear one's heart upon his sleeves for daws to peck at; think aloud; speak -out, – one's mind; be free with one, call a spade a spade.

Adj. artless, natural, pure, native, simple, plain, inartificial, untutored, unsophisticated, *ingénu*, unaffected, *naïve*; sincere, frank; open, – as day; candid, ingenuous, guileless, unsuspicious, childlike; honest &c. 939; innocent &c. 946; Arcadian; undesigning, straightforward, unreserved, unvarnished, above-board; simple-, single-

reynard; Scotch-, Yorkshire-man; Jew, Yankee; intriguer, *intrigant*, schemer, trickster.

V. be -cunning &c. *adj.*; have cut one's eye-teeth; contrive &c. (*plan*) 626; live by one's wits; manœuvre; intrigue, gerrymander, *finesse*, double, temporize, stoop to conquer, *reculer pour mieux sauter*, circumvent, steal a march upon; overreach &c. 545; throw off one's guard; surprise &c. 508; out-do, get the better of, snatch from under one's nose; snatch a verdict; waylay, undermine, introduce the thin end of the wedge; play -a deep game, – tricks with; have an axe to grind; *ambiguas in vulgum spargere voces*; flatter, make things pleasant.

Adj. cunning, crafty, artful; skilful &c. 698; subtle, feline, vulpine; cunning as a -fox, – serpent; deep, – laid; profound; designing, contriving; intriguing &c. *v.*; strategic, diplomatic, politic, Machia-vellian, time-serving; artificial; trick-y, -sy; wily, sly, slim, insidious, stealthy, foxy; underhand &c. (*hidden*) 528; subdolous; deceitful &c. 545; double-tongued, -faced; shifty; crooked; arch, pawky, shrewd, acute; sharp, – as a needle; canny, astute, leery, knowing, up to snuff, too clever by half, not to be caught with chaff.

Adv. cunningly &c. *adj.*; slily, on the sly, by a side wind.

Phr. diamond cut diamond.

minded; frank-, open-, single-, simple-hearted; open and above-board.

free-, plain-, out-spoken; blunt, downright, direct, matter of fact, un-poetical; unflattering.

Adv. in plain -words, – English; without mincing the matter; not to mince the matter &c. (*affirmation*) 535.

Phr. *Davus sum non Œdipus; liberavi animam meam.*

Section IV. ANTAGONISM

1°. *Conditional Antagonism*

704. Difficulty.—N. difficulty; hard-ness &c. *adj.*; impracticability &c. (*impossibility*) 471; tough –, hard –, uphill- work; hard –, Herculean –, Augean- task; task of Sisyphus, Sisy-phean labour, tough job, teaser, rasper, dead lift.

dilemma, embarrassment; perplexity &c. (*uncertainty*) 475; involvement; in-tricacy; entanglement &c. 59; cross fire; awkwardness, delicacy, ticklish card to play, deadlock, knot, Gordian knot, *dignus vindice nodus*, net, meshes, maze; coil &c. (*convolution*) 248; crooked path.

nice –, delicate –, subtle –, knotty-point; vexed question, *vexata quæstio*, poser; puzzle &c. (*riddle*) 533; para-dox; hard –, nut to crack; bone to pick, *crux, pons asinorum*, where the shoe pinches.

nonplus, quandary, strait, pass, pinch, pretty pass, stress, brunt; criti-

705. Facility. — N. facility, ease; easiness &c. *adj.*; capability; feasibility &c. (*practicability*) 470; flexibility, pli-ancy &c. 324; smoothness &c. 255; convenience.

plain –, smooth –, straight- sailing; mere child's play, holiday task.

smooth water, fair wind; smooth – royal- road; clear -coast, – stage; *tabula rasa; full play* &c. (*freedom*) 748.

disen-cumbrance, -tanglement; de-oppilation; permission &c. 760.

V. be -easy &c. *adj.*; go on –, run-smoothly; have -full play &c. *n.*; go –, run- on all fours; obey the helm, work well.

flow –, swim –, drift –, go- with the--stream, – tide; see one's way; have -it all one's own way, – the game in one's own hands; walk over the course, win -at a canter, – hands down; make -light of, – nothing of; be at home in &c. (*skilful*) 698.

cal situation, crisis; trial, rub, emergency, exigency, scramble.

scrape, hobble, slough, quagmire, hot water, hornet's nest; sea –, peck- of troubles; pretty kettle of fish; pickle, stew, *imbroglio*, mess, muddle, botch, fuss, bustle, ado; false position; set fast, stand; dead -lock, – set; fix, horns of a dilemma, *cul de sac*; hitch; stumbling block &c. (*hindrance*) 706.

V. be -difficult &c. *adj.*; run one hard, go against the grain, try one's patience, put one out; put to one's -shifts, – wit's end; go hard with –, try- one; pose, perplex &c. (*uncertain*) 475; bother, nonplus, gravel, bring to a dead lock; be -impossible &c. 471; be in the way of &c. (*hinder*) 706.

meet with –, labour under –, get into –, plunge into –, struggle with –, contend with –, grapple with- difficulties; labour under a disadvantage; be -in difficulty &c. *adj.*

fish in troubled waters, buffet the waves, swim against the stream, scud under bare poles.

have -much ado with, – a hard time of it; come to the -push, – pinch; bear the brunt.

grope in the dark, lose one's way, weave a tangled web, walk among eggs.

get into a -scrape &c. *n.*; bring a hornet's nest about one's ears; be put to one's shifts; flounder, boggle, struggle; not know which way to turn &c. (*uncertain*) 475; get -tangled up, – wound up; *perdre son latin*; stick - at, – in the mud, – fast; come to a -stand, – dead lock; hold the wolf by the ears.

render -difficult &c. *adj.*; encumber, embarrass, ravel, entangle; put a spoke in the wheel &c. (*hinder*) 706; lead a pretty dance.

Adj. difficult, not easy, hard, tough; trouble-, toil-, irk-some; operose, laborious, onerous, arduous, Herculean, formidable; sooner –, more easily- said than done; difficult –, hard- to deal with; ill-conditioned, crabbed; not -to be handled with kid gloves, – made with rosewater.

awkward, unwieldy, unmanageable; intractable, stubborn &c. (*obstinate*) 606; perverse, refractory, plaguy, trying, thorny, rugged; knot-ted, -ty; invious; path-, track-less; labyrinthine &c. (*convoluted*) 248; intricate, complicated &c. (*tangled*) 59; impracticable &c. (*impossible*) 471; not -feasible &c. 470; desperate &c. (*hopeless*) 859.

embarrassing, perplexing &c. (*uncertain*) 475; delicate, ticklish,

render -easy &c. *adj.*; facilitate, smooth, ease; popularize; lighten, – the labour; free, clear; dis-encumber, -embarrass, -entangle, -engage; deobstruct, unclog, extricate, unravel; untie –, cut- the knot; disburden, unload, exonerate, emancipate, free from, deoppilate; humour &c. (*aid*) 707; lubricate &c. 332; relieve &c. 834.

leave -a hole to creep out of, – a loophole, – the matter open; give -the reins to, – full play, – full swing; make way for; open the -door to, – way; prepare –, smooth –, clear- the -ground, – way, – path, – road; pave the way, bridge over; permit &c. 760.

Adj. easy, facile; feasible &c. (*practicable*) 470; easily -managed, – accomplished; within reach, accessible, easy of access, for the million, open to.

manageable, wieldy; towardly, tractable; submissive; yielding, ductile; pliant &c. (*soft*) 324; glib, slippery; smooth &c. 255; on -friction wheels, – velvet; convenient.

un-, dis-burdened, -encumbered, -embarrassed; exonerated; un-loaded, -obstructed, -trammelled, - impeded, -restrained &c. (*free*) 748; at ease, light.

at –, quite at- home; in -one's element, – smooth water.

Adv. easily &c. *adj.*; readily, smoothly, swimmingly, *ad lib.*, on easy terms, single-handed.

Phr. touch and go.

Int. all clear!

---

critical; beset with –, full of –, surrounded by –, entangled by –, encompassed with- difficulties.

under a difficulty; in -difficulty, – hot water, – the suds, – a cleft stick, – a fix, – the wrong box, – a scrape &c. *n.*, – deep water, – a fine pickle; *in extremis*; between -two stools, – Scylla and Charybdis; surrounded by -shoals, – breakers, – quicksands; at cross purposes; not out of the wood.

reduced to straits; hard –, sorely- pressed; run hard; pinched, put to it, straitened; hard -up, – put to it, – set; put to one's shifts; puzzled, at a loss &c. (*uncertain*) 475; at -the end of one's tether, – one's wit's end, – a nonplus, – a standstill; gravelled, nonplussed, stranded, aground; stuck –, set- fast; up a tree, at bay, *aux abois*, driven -into a corner, – from post to pillar, – to extremity, – to one's wit's end, – to the wall; *au bout de son latin*; out of one's -depth, – reckoning; put –, thrown -out.

accomplished with difficulty; hard-fought, -earned.

Adv. with -difficulty, – much ado; hardly &c. *adj.*; uphill; against the -stream, – grain; *à rebours*; *invitâ Minervâ*; in the teeth of; at –, upon- a pinch; at long odds.

Phr. ay there's the rub; *hic labor hoc opus*; things are come to a pretty pass.

2°. *Active Antagonism*

706. Hindrance. — N. prevention, preclusion, obstruction, stoppage; prohibition; inter-ruption, -ception, -clusion; hindrance, impedition; retardment, -ation; constriction; embarrassment, oppilation; coarctation, stricture, restriction; anchor &c. 666; restraint &c. 751 & 752; inhibition &c. 761; blockade &c. (*closure*) 261; picketing.

inter-ference, -position; obtrusion; dis-couragement, -countenance, -approval, -approbation; opposition &c. 708.

impediment, let, obstacle, obstruction, knot, knag; check, hitch, *contretemps*, *impasse*, screw loose, grit in the oil.

bar, stile, barrier; turn-stile, -pike; gate, portcullis; bulwark, parapet, barricade &c. (*defence*) 717; wall, dead wall, breakwater, groyne; bulkhead, block, buffer; stopper &c. 263; boom, dam, weir, burrock.

drawback, objection; stumbling-block, -stone; lion in the path; snag; snags and sawyers.

en-, in-cumbrance; clog, skid, shoe, spoke; brake, drag, – chain, – weight; stay, stop; preventive, prophylactic; contraception; load, burden, fardel,

707. Aid.—N. aid, -ance; assistance, help, opitulation, succour; support, lift, advance, furtherance, promotion; coadjuvancy &c. (*co-operation*) 709.

patronage, championship, countenance, favour, interest, advocacy, auspices.

sustentation, subvention, subsidy, bounty, alimentation, nutrition, nourishment, maintenance; manna in the wilderness; food &c. 298; means &c. 632.

ministr-y, -ation; subministration; accommodation.

relief, rescue; help at a dead lift; supernatural aid; *deus ex machinâ*.

supplies, reinforcements, succours, contingents, recruits; support &c. (*physical*) 215; adjunct, ally &c. (*helper*) 711.

V. aid, assist, help, succour, lend one's aid; come to the aid &c. *n.*- of; contribute, subscribe to; bring –, give –, furnish –, afford –, supply- -aid &c. *n.*; render assistance; give –, stretch –, lend –, bear –, hold out- a -hand, – helping hand; give one a -lift, – cast, – turn; take -by the hand, – in tow; help a lame dog over a stile, lend wings to.

onus, millstone round one's neck, *impedimenta*; dead weight; lumber, pack; nightmare, Ephialtes, incubus, old man of the sea; remora.

difficulty &c. 704; insuperable &c. 471- obstacle; estoppel; ill wind; head wind &c. (*opposition*) 708; trammel, tether &c. (*means of restraint*) 752; hold back, counterpoise; damper, wet blanket, hinderer, marplot, kill-joy, dog in the manger, interloper; trail of a red herring; opponent &c. 710.

V. hinder, impede, impedite, embarrass.

keep -, stave -, ward- off; picket; obviate; a-, ante-vert; turn aside, draw off, prevent, forefend, nip in the bud; retard, slacken, check, let; counter-act, -check; preclude, debar, foreclose, estop; inhibit &c. 761; shackle &c. (*restrain*) 751; restrict, restrain, cohibit.

obstruct, filibuster, stop, stay, bar, bolt, lock; block, – up; belay, barricade; block –, stop- the way; dam up &c. (*close*) 261; put on the -brake &c. *n.*; scotch –, lock –, put a spoke in- the wheel; put a stop to &c. 142; traverse, contravene; inter-rupt, -cept; oppose &c. 708; hedge -in, – round; cut off; interclude.

inter-pose, -fere, -meddle &c. 682.

cramp, hamper; clog, – the wheels; cumber; en-, in-cumber; handicap; choke; saddle -, load- with; overload, lay; lumber, trammel, tie one's hands, put to inconvenience; in-, discommode; discompose; hustle, drive into a corner; choke off.

run -, fall- foul of; cross the path of, break in upon.

thwart, frustrate, disconcert, balk, foil, baffle, snub, override, circumvent; defeat &c. 731; spike guns &c. (*render useless*) 645; spoil, mar, clip the wings of; cripple &c. (*injure*) 659; put an extinguisher on; damp; dishearten &c. (*dissuade*) 616; discountenance, throw cold water on, spoil sport; lay -, throw- a wet blanket on; cut the ground from under one, take the wind out of one's sails, undermine; be -, stand- in the way of; act as a drag; hang like a millstone round one's neck.

relieve, rescue; set -up, – agoing, – on one's legs; bear –, pull- through; give new life to, be the making of; reinforce, recruit; set –, put –, push-forward; give -a lift, – a shove, – an impulse- to; promote, further, forward, advance; speed, expedite, quicken, hasten.

support, sustain, uphold, prop, hold up, bolster.

cradle, nourish; nurture, nurse, dry nurse, suckle, put out to nurse; manure, cultivate, force; foster, cherish, foment; feed –, fan- the flame.

serve; do service to, tender to, pander to; ad-, sub-, minister to; tend, attend, wait on; take care of &c. 459; entertain; smooth the bed of death.

oblige, accommodate, consult the wishes of; humour, cheer, encourage.

second, stand by; back, – up; pay the pipe:, abet; work –, make interest –, stick up –, take up the cudgels- for; take up –, espouse –, adopt- the cause of; advocate, beat up for recruits, press into the service; squire, give moral support to, keep in countenance, countenance, patronize; lend -oneself, – one's countenance- to; smile –, shine-upon; favour, befriend, take up, take in hand, enlist under the banners of; side with &c. (*co-operate*) 709.

be of use to; subserve &c. (*instrument*) 631; benefit &c. 648; render a service &c. (*utility*) 644; conduce &c. (*tend*) 176.

Adj. aiding &c. *v.*; auxiliary, adjuvant, helpful; coadjuvant &c. 709; subservient, ministrant, ancillary, accessory, subsidiary.

at one's beck; friendly, amicable, favourable, propitious, well-disposed; neighbourly; obliging &c. (*benevolent*) 906.

Adv. with –, by- -the aid &c. *n.*- of; on –, in- behalf of; in -aid, – the service, – the name, – favour, – furtherance- of; on account of; for the sake of, on the part of; *non obstante*.

Int. help! save us! to the rescue! S.O.S.!

Adj. hindering &c. *v.*; obstr-uctive, -uent; impedi-tive, -ent; intercipient; prophylactic &c. (*remedial*) 662.

in the way of, unfavourable; onerous, burdensome; cumb-rous, -ersome; obtrusive.

hindered &c. *v.*; wind-bound, water-logged, heavy laden; hard pressed.

unassisted &c. (*see* assist &c. 707); single-handed, alone; deserted &c. 624.

708. Opposition.—N. opposition, antagonism; oppug-nancy, -nation; impugnation; contravention; counteraction &c. 179; counterplot.

cross-fire, under-current, head-wind.

clashing, collision, conflict, lack of harmony, contest.

competition, two of a trade, rivalry, emulation, race; war to the knife.

absence of -aid &c. 707; resistance &c. 719; restraint &c. 751; hindrance &c. 706.

V. oppose, counteract, run counter to; withstand &c. (*resist*) 719; control &c. (*restrain*) 751; hinder &c. 706; antagonize, oppugn, fly in the face of, go dead against, kick against, fall foul of; set -, pit- against; face, confront, cope with; make a -stand, – dead set-against; set -oneself, one's face- against; protest –, vote –, raise one's voice-against; disfavour, turn one's back upon; set at naught, slap in the face, slam the door in one's face.

be –, play- at cross purposes; counter-work, -mine; thwart, overthwart.

stem, breast, encounter; stem –, breast- the -tide, – current, – flood; buffet the waves; beat up –, make head- against; grapple with; kick against the pricks &c. (*resist*) 719; contend &c. 720 –, do battle &c. (*warfare*) 722- -with, – against.

contra-dict, -vene; belie; go –, run –, beat –, militate- against; come in conflict with.

emulate &c. (*compete*) 720; rival, spoil one's trade.

Adj. oppos-ing, -ed &c. *v.*; adverse, antagonistic; ambivalent; contrary &c. 14; at variance &c. 24; at issue, at war with; in opposition; 'agin the Government.'

un-favourable, -friendly; hostile, inimical, cross, unpropitious.

709. Co-operation.—N. co-operation; coadju-vancy, -tancy; coagency, co-efficiency; concert, concurrence, complicity, participation; union &c. 43; amalgamation, combination &c. 48; collusion.

association, alliance, colleagueship, jointstock, copartnership, trust, cartel, pool, ring, combine, interlocking directorate; confederation &c. (*party*) 712; federation, coalition, fusion; a long pull, a strong pull and a pull all together; log-rolling, freemasonry.

unanimity &c. (*assent*) 488; *esprit de corps*, party spirit; clan-, partisan-ship; reciprocity, concord &c. 714.

V. co-operate, co-adjute, concur; conduce &c. 178; combine, cartelize, unite one's efforts; keep –, draw –, pull –, club –, hang –, hold –, league –, band –, be banded- together; stand –, put-shoulder to shoulder; act in concert, join forces, fraternize, cling to one another, conspire, concert, lay one's heads together; confederate, be in league with; collude, understand one another, play into the hands of, hunt in couples.

side –, take side –, go along –, go hand in hand –, join hands –, make common cause –, strike in –, unite –, join –, mix oneself up –, take part –, play along –, cast in one's lot- with; join –, enter into- partnership with; rally round, follow the lead of; come to, pass over to, come into the views of; be –, row –, sail- in the same boat; sail on the same tack.

be a party to, lend oneself to; participate; have a -hand in, – finger in the pie; take –, bear- part in; second &c. (*aid*) 707; take the part of, play the game of; espouse a -cause, – quarrel.

Adj. co-operating &c. *v.*; in -co-operation &c. *n.*, – league &c. (*party*) 712;

in hostile array, front to front, with crossed bayonets, at daggers drawn; up in arms; resistant &c. 719.

competitive, emulous.

Adv. against, *versus*, counter to, in conflict with, at cross purposes.

against the -grain, – current, – stream, – wind, – tide; with a head-wind; with the wind -ahead, – in one's teeth.

in spite, in despite, in defiance; in the -way, – teeth, – face- of; across; a-, over-thwart; where the shoe pinches.

though &c. 30; even; *quand même; per contra.*

Phr. *nitor in adversum.*

coadju-vant, -tant; hand and glove with.

favourable &c. 707- to; un-opposed &c. 708.

Adv. as one man &c. (*unanimously*) 488; shoulder to shoulder; in co-operation with.

---

710. Opponent.—N. opponent, antagonist, adversary; adverse party, opposition; enemy &c. 891; assailant.

oppositionist, obstructive; obscurantist; brawler, wrangler, brangler, disputant, extremist, irreconcilable, die-hard, bitter-ender.

malcontent; Jacobin, Fenian &c. 742; demagogue, reactionist.

passive resister, conscientious objector.

rival, competitor, contestant.

---

711. Auxiliary.—N. auxiliary; re-cruit; assistant; adju-vant, -tant; adjunct; help, -er, -mate, -ing hand; midwife; colleague, partner, mate, *confrère*, co-operator; coadju-tor, -trix; collaborator.

ally; friend &c. 890, confidant, *fidus Achates*, pal, chum, buddy, *alter ego.*

confederate; ac-, complice; accessory, – after the fact; *particeps criminis.*

aide-de-camp, secretary, clerk, associate, marshal; right-hand; candle-, bottle-holder; hand-maid; servant &c. 746; puppet, cat's-paw, stooge, dependent, creature, jackal; tool, *âme damnée*; satellite, adherent, parasite.

votary, disciple; secta-rian, -ry; seconder, backer, upholder, supporter, abettor, advocate, partisan, champion, patron, friend at court, mediator.

friend in need, Jack at a pinch, *deus ex machinâ*, guardian angel, fairy godmother; special providence, tutelary genius.

---

712. Party.—N. party, faction, side, denomination, class, communion, set, crowd, crew, band, horde, posse, phalanx; regiment &c. 726; family, clan &c. 166.

Tories, Conservatives, Unionists, Whigs, Liberals, Radicals, Labour party, Socialists, Communists &c.; Republicans, Democrats, Farmer-Labor; *Fascisti*, Revolutionaries &c. 742.

community, body, fellowship, sodality, solidarity; con-, fraternity; sorority; brother-, sister-hood.

Freemasons, Knights Templars, Odd Fellows, Ku Klux Klan &c.

knot, gang, *clique*, ring, circle; *coterie*, club, *casino.*

corporation, corporate body, guild; establishment, company; co-partnership; firm, house; joint concern, joint-stock company, trust, investment trust, combine &c. 709.

society, association; instit-ute, -ution; union; trade-union; league, syndicate, alliance, *Verein, Bund, Zollverein*, combination; league –, alliance- offensive and defensive; coalition; federation; confedera -tion, -cy; junto, cabal, *camarilla, camorra, brigue*; freemasonry; party spirit &c. (*co-operation*) 709.

staff; cast, *dramatis personæ*.

V. unite, join; club together &c. (*co-operate*) 709; cement –, form- a party &c. *n*.; associate &c. (*assemble*) 72.

Adj. in -league, – partnership, – alliance &c. *n*.

bonded –, banded –, linked &c. (*joined*) 43- together; embattled; confederated, federative, joint, corporate, leagued, fraternal, masonic, cliquish.

Adv. hand in hand, side by side, shoulder to shoulder, *en masse*, in the same boat.

---

713. Discord.—N. disagreement &c. 24; dis-cord, -accord, -sidence, -sonance; jar, clash, shock; jarring, jostling &c. *v*.; screw loose.

variance, difference, dissension, misunderstanding, cross purposes, odds, *brouillerie*; division, split, rupture, disruption, division in the camp, house divided against itself, rift within the lute; disunion, breach; schism &c. (*dissent*) 489; feud, faction.

quarrel, dispute, rippet, spat, tiff, *tracasserie*, squabble, altercation, words, high words; wrangling &c. *v*.; jangle, brabble, cross questions and crooked answers, snip-snap; family jars.

polemics; litigation; strife &c. (*contention*) 720; warfare &c. 722; outbreak, open rupture; breaking off of negotiations, recall of ambassadors; declaration of war.

broil, brawl, row, racket, hubbub, rixation; embroilment, embranglement, *imbroglio*, *fracas*, breach of the peace, piece of work, scrimmage, rumpus; breeze, squall; riot, disturbance &c. (*disorder*) 59; commotion &c. (*agitation*) 315; bear garden, Donnybrook Fair.

subject of dispute, ground of quarrel, battle ground, disputed point; bone -of contention, – to pick; apple of discord, *casus belli*; question at issue &c. (*subject of inquiry*) 461; vexed question, *vexata quæstio*, brand of discord.

troublous times; cat-and-dog life; contentiousness &c. *adj*.; enmity &c. 889; hate &c. 898; Kilkenny cats; disputant &c. 710; strange bedfellows.

V. be -discordant &c. *adj*.; disagree, come amiss &c. 24; clash, jar, jostle, pull different ways, conflict, have no measures with, misunderstand one another; differ; dissent &c. 489; have a -bone to pick, – crow to pluck- with.

fall out, quarrel, dispute; litigate; controvert &c. (*deny*) 536;

714. Concord.—N. concord, accord, harmony, symphony, homology; agreement &c. 23; sympathy &c. (*love*) 897; response; union, unison, unity; bonds of harmony; peace &c. 721; unanimity &c. (*assent*) 488; league &c. 712; happy family.

rapprochement; *réunion*; amity &c. (*friendship*) 888; reciprocity; alliance, *entente cordiale*, good understanding, conciliation, arbitration, peacemaker &c. 724.

V. agree &c. 23; accord, harmonize with; fraternize; be -concordant &c. *adj*.; go hand in hand; blend –, tone in- with; run parallel &c. (*concur*) 178; understand one another; pull together &c. (*co-operate*) 709; put up one's horses together, sing in chorus.

side –, sympathize –, go –, chime in –, fall in- with; come round; be pacified &c. 723; assent &c. 488; enter into the -ideas, – feelings- of; reciprocate.

hurler avec les loups; go –, swim- with the stream.

pour oil on troubled waters, keep in good humour, render accordant, put in tune; come to an understanding, meet half-way; keep the –, remain at- peace.

Adj. concordant, congenial; agreeing &c. *v*.; in- accord &c. *n*.; harmonious, united, cemented; banded together &c. 712; allied; friendly &c. 888; fraternal; conciliatory; at one with; of one mind &c. (*assent*) 488.

at peace, in still water; tranquil &c. (*pacific*) 721.

Adv. with one voice &c. (*assent*) 488; in concert with, hand in hand; on one's side, unanimously.

---

squabble, wrangle, jangle, brangle, bicker, nag; spar &c. (*contend*) 720; have -words &c. *n.* with; fall foul of.

split; break -, break squares -, part company- with; declare war, try conclusions; join -, put in- issue; pick a quarrel, fasten a quarrel on; sow -, stir up- -dissension &c. *n.*; embroil, estrange, entangle, disunite, widen the breach; set -at odds, - together by the ears; set -, pit- against; rub up the wrong way.

get into hot water, fish in troubled waters, brawl; kick up a -row, - dust; turn the house out of window.

Adj. discordant; disagreeing &c. *v.*; out of tune, dissonant, inharmonious, harsh, grating, jangling, ajar, on bad terms; dissentient &c. 489; inconsistent, contradictory, incongruous, discrepant; un--reconciled, -pacified.

quarrelsome, unpacific; gladiatorial, controversial, polemic, disputatious; factious; liti-gious, -gant; pettifogging.

at odds, at loggerheads, at daggers drawn, at variance, at issue, at cross purposes, at sixes and sevens, at feud, at high words; up in arms, together by the ears, in hot water, embroiled.

torn, disunited.

Phr. *quot homines tot sententiæ*; no love lost between them, *non nostrum tantas componere lites.*

715. Defiance.—**N.** defiance; daring &c. *v.*; dare, challenge, *cartel*; threat &c. 909; war-cry, -whoop.

V. defy, dare, beard; brave &c. (*courage*) 861; bid defiance to; set at -defiance, - naught; hurl defiance at; dance the war dance; snap the fingers at, laugh to scorn; disobey &c. 742.

show -fight, - one's teeth, - a bold front; bluster, look big, stand akimbo; double -, shake- the fist; threaten &c. 909.

challenge, call out; throw -, fling- down the -gauntlet, - gage, - glove.

Adj. defiant; defying &c. *v.*; with arms akimbo; rebellious, insolent; reckless, greatly daring.

Adv. in -defiance, - the teeth- of; under one's very nose.

Int. do your worst! come if you dare! come on! marry come up! hoity toity!

Phr. *noli me tangere; nemo me impune lacessit.*

716. Attack.—**N.** attack; assault, - and battery; onset, onslaught, charge.

aggression, drive, offence; incursion, inroad, invasion; irruption; outbreak; *estrapade, ruade; coup de main*, sally, *sortie, camisade*, raid, foray; run -at, - against; dead set at.

storm, -ing; boarding, *escalade*; siege, investment, obsession, bombardment, cannonade; air raid.

fire, volley; platoon -, file -, rapid-fire; *fusillade*; sharp-shooting, sniping; broadside; raking -, cross -, machine gun- fire; volley of grapeshot, *feu d'enfer*; salvo.

cut, thrust, lunge, pass, *passado, carte* and *tierce*, home thrust; *coup de pied*; kick, punch &c. (*impulse*) 276.

717. Defence.—**N.** defence, protection, guard, ward; shielding &c. *v.*; propugnation; preservation &c. 670; guardianship.

self-defence, -preservation; resistance &c. 719.

safeguard &c. (*safety*) 664; screen &c. (*shelter*) 666, (*concealment*) 530; barrage; fortification; muni-tion, -ment; bulwark, fosse, moat, ditch, intrenchment, trench, dugout, gas mask; dike, dyke; parapet, parados, sunk fence, embankment, mound, mole, bank; earth- field-work, gabions; fence, wall, dead wall, contravallation; paling &c. (*inclosure*) 232; palisade, haha, stockade, *stoccado, laager, sangar*; barri-er, -cade; boom; portcullis, *chevaux de*

battue, razzia, Jacquerie, dragonnade; devastation &c. 162.

assailant, aggressor, invader.

base of operations, point of attack.

V. attack, assault, assail; set –, fall-upon; charge, impugn, break a lance with, enter the lists.

assume –, take- the offensive; be –, become- the aggressor; strike the first blow, fire the first shot, throw the first stone at; lift a hand –, draw the sword-against; take up the cudgels; advance –, march- against; march upon, invade, harry; come on, show fight.

strike at, poke at, thrust at; aim –, deal- a blow at; give –, fetch- one a -blow, – kick; have a -cut, – shot, – fling, – shy- at; be down –, pounce-upon; fall foul of, pitch into, launch out against; bait, slap on the face; make a -thrust, – pass, – set, – dead set- at; dunt; bear down upon.

close with, come to close quarters, bring to bay.

ride full tilt against; let fly at, dash at, run a tilt at, rush at, tilt at, run at, fly at, hawk at, have at, let out at; make a -dash, – rush at; attack tooth and nail; strike home; drive –, press-one hard; be hard upon, run down, strike at the root of.

lay about one, run amuck.

fire -upon, – at, – a shot at; shoot at, pop at, level at, let off a gun at; open fire, pepper, bombard, shell, pour a broadside into; fire -a volley, – red-hot shot; spring a mine.

throw -a stone, – stones- at; stone, lapidate, pelt; hurl -at, – against, – at the head of.

beset, besiege, beleaguer; lay siege to, invest, open the trenches, plant a battery, sap, mine; storm, board, scale the walls.

cut and thrust, bayonet, butt; kick, strike &c. (*impulse*) 276; whip &c. (*punish*) 972.

Adj. attacking &c. *v.*; aggressive, offensive, obsidional.

up in arms; on the warpath; over the top.

Adv. on the offensive.

Int. 'up and at them!'

---

frise; aba-, abat-, abba-tis; *vallum*, circumvallation, battlement, rampart, scarp; e-, counter-scarp; glacis, case-mate.

mine, countermine.

buttress, abutment; shore &c. (*support*) 215.

breastwork, *banquette*, curtain, mant-let, bastion, demilune, redan, ravelin; advanced –, horn –, out- work, lunette; barb-acan, -ican; redoubt; fort-elage, -alice; lines; coast defence.

loop-hole, machicolation; sally-port, postern gate.

hold, stronghold, fastness; asylum &c. (*refuge*) 666; keep, donjon, fort-ress, citadel; capitol, castle; tower, – of strength; fort, barracoon, pah, sconce, martello tower, peel-house, block-house, rath; wooden walls; turret, barbette.

buffer, corner-stone, fender, apron, mask, gauntlet, thimble, carapace, armour, shield, buckler; target, targe, ægis, breastplate, cuirass, plastron, habergeon, mail, coat of mail, brigan-dine, hauberk, lorication, helmet, helm, basinet, sallet, salade, heaume, morion, murrion, armet, cabaset, vizor, cas-quetel, siege-cap, head-piece, casque, steel helmet, tin hat; *pickelhaube*, csako; shako &c. (*dress*) 225; bearskin; panoply; truncheon &c. (*weapon*) 727.

garrison, picket, piquet; defender, protector; guardian &c. (*safety*) 664; trabant, body guard, champion; knight-errant, Paladin; propugner.

V. defend, forfend, fend; shield, screen, shroud; fence round &c. (*cir-cumscribe*) 229; fence, intrench; guard &c. (*keep safe*) 664; guard against; take care of &c. (*vigilance*) 459; bear harm-less; keep –, ward –, beat- off; hinder &c. 706.

parry, repel, propugn, put to flight; give a warm reception to [*ironical*]; hold –, keep- at -bay, – arm's length.

stand –, act- on the defensive; show fight; maintain –, stand- one's ground; stand by; hold one's own; bear –, stand- the brunt; fall back upon, hold, stand in the gap.

Adj. defending &c. *v.*; defensive; mural; armed, – at all points, – *cap-à-pie*, – to the teeth; panoplied, accoutred, harnessed; iron-plated, -clad; loop-holed, castellated, machicolated, casemated; defended &c. *v.*; proof against, bomb-, bulletproof; protective.

Adv. defensively; on the -defence, – defensive; in defence; at bay, *pro aris et focis.*

Int. no surrender! *il ne passeront pas!*

Phr. defence not defiance.

718. Retaliation. — N. retaliation, reprisal, retort; counter-stroke, -blast, -plot, -project; retribution, *lex talionis*; reciprocation &c. (*reciprocity*) 12.

requital, desert, tit for tat, give and take, blow for blow, *quid pro quo*, a Roland for an Oliver, measure for measure, an eye for an eye, diamond cut diamond, the biter bit, a game at which two can play; boomerang.

recrimination &c. (*accusation*) 938; revenge &c. 919; compensation &c. 30; reaction &c. (*recoil*) 277.

V. retaliate, retort, turn upon; pay -off, – back; pay in -one's own, – the same- coin; cap; reciprocate &c. 148; turn the tables upon, return the compliment; give -a *quid pro quo* &c. *n.*, – as much as one takes; give and take, exchange -blows, – fisticuffs; be -quits, – even- with; pay off old scores.

serve one right, be hoist on one's own petard, throw a stone in one's own garden, catch a Tartar.

Adj. retaliating &c. *v.*; retalia-tory, -tive; retributive, recriminatory, reciprocal.

Adv. in retaliation; *en revanche.*

Phr. *mutato nomine de te fabula narratur; par pari refero; tu quoque;* you're another; *suo sibi gladio hunc jugulo.*

719. Resistance. — N. resistance, stand, front, oppugnation; opposition &c. 708; renitence, reluctation, recalcitration, recalcitrance; repugnance; kicking &c. *v.*

repulse, rebuff.

insurrection &c. (*disobedience*) 742; strike; turn -, lock -, barring- out; *levée en masse, Jacquerie*; riot &c. (*disorder*) 59.

V. resist; not -submit &c. 725; repugn, reluctate, withstand; stand up -, strive -, bear up -, be proof -, make head- against; stand, – firm, – one's ground, – the brunt of, – out; hold -one's ground, – one's own, – out.

breast the -wave, – current; stem the -tide, – torrent; face, confront, grapple with; show a bold front &c. (*courage*) 861; present a front; make a -, take one's- stand.

kick, – against; recalcitrate, kick against the pricks; oppose &c. 708; fly in the face of; lift the hand against &c. (*attack*) 716; rise up in arms &c. (*war*) 722; strike, turn out; draw up a round robin &c. (*remonstrate*) 932; revolt &c. (*disobey*) 742; make a riot.

prendre le mors aux dents; take the bit between the teeth; sell one's life dearly, die hard, keep at bay; repel, repulse.

Adj. resisting &c. *v.*; resist-ive, -ant; refractory &c. (*disobedient*) 742; recalcitrant, re-nitent, -pulsive, -pellant; up in arms.

proof against; unconquerable &c. (*strong*) 159; stubborn, unconquered; indomitable &c. (*persevering*) 604a; unyielding &c. (*obstinate*) 606.

Int. hands off! keep off!

720. Contention. — N. contention, strife; contest, -ation; struggle; belligerency; opposition &c. 708.

controversy, polemics; debate &c. (*discussion*) 476; war of words, logomachy, litigation; paper war, ink slinging; high words &c. (*quarrel*) 713; sparring &c. *v.*

721. Peace.—N. peace; amity &c. (*friendship*) 888; harmony &c. (*concord*) 714; tranquillity &c. (*quiescence*) 265; truce &c. (*pacification*) 723; pacificism; pipe -, calumet- of peace.

piping time of peace, quiet life; neutrality.

V. be at peace; keep the peace &c.

competition, rivalry; corrival-ry, -ship; agonism, *concours*, match, race, horse-racing, heat, steeple chase, point-to-point race, handicap; boat race, regatta; field-day; sham fight, Derby day; turf, sporting, bull-fight, tauro-machy, *gymkhana*, rodeo, Olympiad.

wrestling, *ju-jitsu*, pugilism, boxing, fisticuffs, spar, mill, set-to, scrap, round, bout, event; prize-fighting; quarter-staff, single stick; gladiatorship, gymnastics; athletic-s, – sports; games of skill &c. 840.

shindy; *fracas* &c. (*discord*) 713; clash of arms; tussle, scuffle, broil, fray; affray, -ment; velitation; col-, luctation; brabble, *brigue*, scramble, *mêlée*, scrimmage, stramash, bush-fighting.

free –, stand up –, hand to hand –, running- fight.

conflict, skirmish; ren-, en-counter; *rencontre*, collision, affair, brush, fight; battle, – royal; combat, action, engagement, joust, tournament; tilt, -ing; tourney, list; pitched battle, guerilla warfare.

death-struggle, struggle for life or death, Armageddon; hard knocks, sharp contest, tug of war.

naval -engagement, – battle; *naumachia*, sea-fight.

duel, -lo; single combat, monomachy, satisfaction, *passage d'armes*, passage of arms, affair of honour; triangular duel; hostile meeting, digladiation; appeal to arms &c. (*warfare*) 722.

deeds –, feats- of arms; pugnacity; combativeness &c. *adj.*; bone of contention &c. 713.

V. contend; contest, strive, struggle, scramble, wrestle; spar, square; exchange -blows, – fisticuffs; scrap, mix with, fib, justle, tussle, tilt, box, stave, fence; skirmish; fight &c. (*war*) 722; wrangle &c. (*quarrel*) 713.

contend &c. –, grapple –, engage –, close –, buckle –, bandy –, try conclusions –, have a brush &c. *n.* –, tilt- with; encounter, fall foul of, pitch into, clapperclaw, run a tilt at; oppose &c. 708; reluct.

join issue, come to blows, be at loggerheads, set-to, come to the scratch, exchange shots, measure swords, meet hand to hand; take up the -cudgels, – glove, – gauntlet; enter the lists; couch one's lance; give satisfaction; appeal to arms &c. (*warfare*) 722.

lay about one; break the peace.

compete –, cope –, vie –, race- with; outvie, emulate, rival; run a race; contend &c. –, stipulate –, stickle- for; insist upon, make a point of.

Adj. contending &c. *v.*; together by the ears, at loggerheads, at war, at issue.

competitive, rival; belligerent; contentious, combative, bellicose, unpeaceful; warlike &c. 722; quarrelsome &c. 901; pugnacious; pugilistic, gladiatorial; palestric, -al.

Phr. *a verbis ad verbera*; a word and a blow.

(*concord*) 714; make peace &c. 723.

Adj. pacific; peace-able, -ful; calm, tranquil, untroubled, halcyon; blood-less; neutral.

Phr. the storm blown over; the lion lies down with the lamb.

---

722. Warfare.—N. warfare; fighting &c. *v.*; hostilities; war, arms, the sword; Mars, Bellona, grim visaged war, *horrida bella*, Armageddon.

appeal to -arms, – the sword; ordeal

723. Pacification.—N. pacification, conciliation; reconcil-iation, -ement; shaking of hands, accommodation, ar-rangement, adjustment; terms, com-promise; amnesty, deed of release.

–, wager- of battle; *ultima ratio regum*, arbitrament of the sword.

battle array, campaign, crusade, expedition; mobilization; state of siege; battle-field &c. (*arena*) 728; warpath.

art of war, tactics, strategy, castra-metation; general-, soldier-ship; aerial–, submarine –, naval –, chemical- warfare; military evolutions, ballistics, gunnery; chivalry; poison gas; gunpowder, shot, – and shell.

battle, tug of war &c. (*contention*) 720; service, campaigning, active service, tented field; fiery cross, trumpet, clarion, bugle, pibroch, slogan; war-cry, -whoop; battle cry, beat of drum, rappel, tom-tom; word of command; pass-, watch-word.

war to the -death, – knife; *guerre à -mort, – outrance*; open –, internecine –, civil- war.

V. arm; raise –, mobilize- troops; raise up in arms; take up the cudgels &c. 720; take up –, fly to –, appeal to--arms, – the sword; draw –, unsheathe-the sword; dig up the hatchet; go to –, declare –, wage –, let slip the dogs of-war; cry havoc; kindle –, light- the torch of war; raise one's banner, send round the fiery cross; hoist the black flag; throw –, fling- away the scabbard; enrol, enlist, join up; take the field; take the law into one's own hands; do –, give –, join –, engage in –, go to- battle; flesh one's sword; set to, fall to, engage, measure swords with, draw the trigger, cross swords; come to -blows, – close quarters; fight; combat; contend &c. 720; battle –, break a lance- with.

serve; see –, be on- -service, – active service; campaign; wield the sword, shoulder a musket, smell powder, be under the fire; spill –, imbrue the hands in- blood; be on the warpath.

carry on -war, – hostilities; keep the field; fight the good fight; go over the top; cut one's way through; fight -it out, – like devils, – one's way, – hand to hand; sell one's life dearly.

Adj. conten-ding, -tious &c. 720; armed, – to the teeth, – cap-à-pie; sword in hand; in –, under –, up in- arms; at war with; bristling with arms; in -battle array, – open arms, – the field; embattled.

unpacific, unpeaceful; belligerent, combative, armigerous, bellicose, martial, warlike; mili-tary, -tant; soldier-like, -ly; chivalrous; strategical, internecine.

Adv. *flagrante bello*, in the -thick of the fray, – cannon's mouth; at the -sword's point, – point of the bayonet.

Int. *væ victis!* to arms! to your tents O Israel!

Phr. the battle rages.

peace-offering; olive-branch; overtures; pipe –, calumet –, preliminaries-of peace.

truce, armistice; suspension of -arms, – hostilities; breathing-time; convention; *modus vivendi*; flag of truce, white flag, *parlementaire, cartel*.

hollow truce, *pax in bello*; drawn battle.

V. pacify, tranquillize, compose; allay &c. (*moderate*) 174; reconcile, propitiate, placate, conciliate, meet half-way, hold out the olive-branch, heal the breach, make peace, restore harmony, bring to terms.

settle –, arrange –, accommodate--matters, – differences; set straight; make up a quarrel, *tantas componere lites*; come to -an understanding, – terms; bridge over, hush up; make -it, – matters- up; shake hands.

raise a siege; put up –, sheathe- the sword; bury the hatchet, lay down one's arms, turn swords into ploughshares; smoke the calumet of peace, close the temple of Janus; keep the peace &c. (*concord*) 714; be -pacified &c.; come round.

Adj. conciliatory, pacificatory; composing &c. v.; pacified &c. v.

Phr. *requiescat in pace.*

724. Mediation.—N. media-tion, -torship, -tization; inter-vention, -position, -ference, -meddling, -cession; parley, negotiation, arbitration; flag of truce &c. 723; good offices, peace-offering; diploma-tics, -cy; compromise &c. 774.

mediator, intercessor, peacemaker, make-peace, negotiator, go-between; diplomatist &c. (*consignee*) 758; moderator, propitiator, umpire, arbitrator.

V. media-te, -tize; inter-cede, -pose, -fere, -vene; step in, negotiate; meet half-way; arbitrate; *magnas componere lites*.

Adj. mediatory, propitiatory, diplomatic.

725. Submission.—N. submission, yielding, acquiescence, compliance; non-resistance; obedience &c. 743; submissiveness, deference.

surrender, cession, capitulation, resignation.

obeisance, homage, kneeling, genuflexion, courtesy, curtsy, *salaam*, *kowtow*, prostration.

V. succumb, submit, yield, bend, resign, defer to, accede.

lay down -, deliver up- one's arms; hand over one's sword; lower -, haul down -, strike- one's flag, - colours; deliver the keys of the city.

surrender, - at discretion; cede, capitulate, come to terms, retreat, beat a retreat; draw in one's horns &c. (*humility*) 879; give -way, - ground, - in, - up; cave in; suffer judgment by default; bend, - to one's yoke, - before the storm; reel back; bend -, knuckle- -down, - to, - under; knock under.

humble oneself; eat -dirt, - the leek, - humble pie; bite -, lick- the dust; be -, fall- at one's feet; craven; crouch before, throw oneself at the feet of; swallow the -leek, - pill; kiss the rod; turn the other cheek; *avaler des couleuvres*, gulp down.

obey &c. 743; kneel to, bow to, pay homage to, cringe to, truckle to; bend the -neck, - knee; kneel, fall on one's knees, bow submission, courtesy, curtsy, *kowtow*; make obeisance.

pocket the affront; make -the best of, - a virtue of necessity; grin and abide, shrug the shoulders, resign oneself; submit with a good grace &c. (*bear with*) 826.

Adj. surrendering &c. *v.*; submissive, resigned, crouching; down-trodden; down on one's marrow bones; on one's bended knee; weak-kneed, un-, non-resisting; pliant &c. (*soft*) 324; undefended.

untenable, indefensible; humble &c. 879.

Phr. have it your own way; it can't be helped; amen &c. (*assent*) 488.

726. Combatant.—N. combatant; disputant, controversialist, polemic, litigant, belligerent; competitor, rival, corrival; fighter, assailant, aggressor; champion, Paladin; moss-trooper, swashbuckler, fire-eater, duellist, bully, bludgeon-man, rough, fighter, fighting-man, prize-fighter, pugilist, pug, boxer, bruiser, the fancy, gladiator, athlete, wrestler; fighting-, game-cock; swordsman, *sabreur*.

warrior, soldier, Amazon, man-at-arms, armigerent; campaigner, veteran; red-coat, military man, *rajpoot*, brave.

armed force, troops, soldiery, military, forces, sabaoth, the army, standing army, regulars, the line, troops of the line, militia, territorials, yeomanry, volunteers, trainband, fencible; auxiliary -, reserve- forces; reserves, *posse comitatus*, national guard, *gendarme*, beefeater; guards, -man; yeoman of the guard, life guards, household troops.

janissary; myrmidon; Mama-, Mame-luke; spahee, *spahi*, Cossack,

Croat, Pandour; irregular, free lance, *franc-tireur, bashi-bazouk, guerilla, condottiere*; mercenary.

levy, draught, commando; *Land-wehr, -sturm*; conscript, recruit, rookie, cadet, raw levies.

private, – soldier; Tommy Atkins, rank and file, peon, trooper, doughboy, sepoy, *askari, légionnaire,* legionary, food for powder, cannon fodder; officer &c. (*commander*) 745; subaltern, ensign, shave-tail, standard bearer, non-com; spear-, pike-man; halberdier, lancer; musketeer, carabineer, rifleman, sharpshooter, yager, skirmisher; grenadier, fusileer; archer, bowman.

horse and foot; horse –, foot- soldier; cavalry, horse, artillery, horse –, field –, heavy –, mountain- artillery, infantry, light horse, *voltigeur, Uhlan,* mounted rifles, dragoon, hussar, trooper; light –, heavy-dragoon; heavy; *cuirassier*; gunner, cannoneer, bombardier, artilleryman, matross; sapper, – and miner; engineer; light infantry, rifles, *chasseur, zouave*; military train, supply and transport, coolie.

army, – corps, *corps d'armée*, host, division, column, wing, detachment, *escadrille*, garrison, flying column, brigade, regiment, *corps*, battalion, squadron, company, platoon, battery, subdivision, section, squad; piquet, picket, guard, rank, file; legion, phalanx, cohort; cloud of skirmishers; impi.

war-horse, charger, *destrier*.

armoured -train, – car; tank.

marine, man of war's man &c. (*sailor*) 269; navy, first line of defence, wooden walls; naval forces, fleet, flotilla, armada, squadron.

man-of-war, warship; H.M.S., U.S.S.; capital ship; line-of-battle ship, battle ship; super-, dreadnought, battle –, armoured –, protected – light- cruiser; scout, flotilla leader; destroyer, torpedo boat; submarine, submersible, U-boat; submarine chaser, eagle boat, mystery ship, Q-boat; mine-layer, -sweeper; ship of the line, iron-clad, turret-ship, ram, Monitor, floating battery; first-rate, frigate, sloop of war, corvette, gunboat, bomb-vessel, fire-boat; flag ship, guard ship, cruiser; airplane carrier; privateer; tender; depôt –, parent- ship; store –, troop- ship; transport, catamaran.

aircraft &c. 273, air force, scout, fighter, bomber, troop carrier, aerial patrol, seaplane, flying boat, torpedo plane; airship, Zeppelin; rigid –, semi-rigid –, non-rigid- airship; dirigible –, free –, captive –, kite –, observation- balloon.

anti-aircraft guns, searchlights, sound locators; catapult.

727. Arms.—N. arm, -s; weapon, deadly weapon; arma-ment, -ture; panoply, stand of arms; armour &c. (*defence*) 717; armoury &c. (*store*) 636.

ammunition; powder, – and shot; explosive; propellant; gun-powder, -cotton; dynam-, melin-, cord-, lydd-ite; trinitrotoluene, T.N.T., ammonal; cartridge; ball cartridge, *cartouche*, fire-ball; dud, black Maria; 'villainous saltpetre'; poison –, mustard –, lachrymatory –, tear- gas.

sword, sabre, broadsword, cutlass, falchion, scimitar, cimeter, brand, whinyard, bilbo, glaive, glave, rapier, skean, Toledo, Ferrara, tuck, claymore, creese, kris, *kukri*, dagger, dirk, hanger, poniard, stiletto, stylet, dudgeon, bayonet; sword-bayonet, -stick; side arms, foil, blade, steel; axe, bill; pole-, battle-axe; gisarm, halberd, partisan, tomahawk, bowie-knife; at-, att-, yat-aghan; yatachan; good –, trusty –, naked-sword; cold –, naked- steel.

club, mace, truncheon, staff, bludgeon, cudgel, life-preserver, shil-lelagh, sprig; hand-, quarter-staff; bat, cane, stick, knuckle-duster, sand bag.

gun, piece; fire-arms; artillery, ordnance; siege –, battering-train; park, battery; cannon, gun of position, heavy –, siege –, field –, moun-tain –, anti-aircraft –, breech loading –, quick firing- gun; field piece, mortar, trench mortar, mine thrower, howitzer, carronade, culverin, basilisk; falconet, jingal, swivel, *pederero, bouche à feu*; smooth bore, rifled cannon; Armstrong –, Lancaster –, Paixhan –, Whitworth –, Parrott –, Krupp –, Gatling –, Maxim –, Vickers –, Hotchkiss –, Lewis –, machine- gun; tommy gun, Thompson's submachine gun; *mitrailleu-r, -se*; pompom; blow pipe.

small arms; musket, -ry, firelock, flintlock, fowling-piece, shot gun, rifle, *fusil*, caliver, carbine, blunderbuss, musketoon, Brown Bess, matchlock, harquebuss, *arquebuse*, haguebut; petronel; smallbore; breech-, muzzle-loader; Miniè –, Enfield –, Westley Richards –, Snider –, Springfield –, Martini-Henry –, Lee-Metford –, Lee-Enfield –, Mauser –, Männlicher –, magazine –, repeating- rifle; needle-gun, *chassepot*; pis-tol, -et; revolver, automatic pistol, automatic; wind-, air-gun; flame –, gas-projector.

bow, cross-bow, arbalest, balister, catapult, sling; battering-ram &c. (*impulse*) 276; gunnery; ballistics &c. (*propulsion*) 284.

missile, bolt, projectile, shot, pellet, ball; grape; grape –, canister –, bar –, cannon –, langrel –, langrage –, round –, chain- shot; explosive; incendiary –, expanding –, soft-nosed –, dum-dum- bullet; slug, stone, brickbat; hand –, rifle- grenade; high explosive –, incendiary –, star –, gas- shell; depth –, gas –, incendiary –, stink- bomb; petard, torpedo, carcass, rocket; congreve, – rocket; shrapnel, *mitraille*; thunderbolt; mine, land mine, infernal machine.

pike, lance, spear, spontoon, javelin, assagai, throwing stick, dart, djerrid, arrow, reed, shaft, bolt, boomerang, harpoon, gaff.

728. Arena.—N. arena, field, platform; scene of action, theatre; walk, course; hustings; stage, boards &c. (*playhouse*) 599; amphi-theatre; Coli-, Colos-seum; Flavian amphitheatre, hippodrome, circus, race-course, track, *stadium, corso*, turf, cockpit, bear-garden, play-ground, playing fields, *gymnasium, palæstra*, ring, lists; tilt-yard, -ing ground; *Campus Martius, Champ de Mars*; aerodrome, airport, air base, flying field.

theatre –, seat- of war; battle-field, -ground; field of -battle, – slaughter; no man's land; Aceldama, camp; the enemy's camp; trysting-place &c. (*place of meeting*) 74.

Section V. Results of Voluntary Action

729. Completion.—N. completion; accomplish-, achieve-, fulfil-ment; per-formance, execution; des-, dis-patch; consummation, culmination, climax; finish, conclusion, effectuation; close &c. (*end*) 67; terminus &c. (*arrival*) 292; winding up; *finale, dénouement*, catastrophe, issue, upshot, result; final –, last –, crowning –, finishing- -touch, – stroke; last finish, *coup de grâce*;

730. Non-Completion.—N. non-com-pletion, -fulfilment; shortcoming &c. 304; incompleteness &c. 53; drawn -battle, – game; work of Penelope, task of Sisyphus.

non-performance, inexecution; neg-lect &c. 460.

V. not -complete &c. 729; leave -unfinished &c. *adj.*, – undone; neglect &c. 460; let -alone, – slip; lose sight of.

crowning of the edifice; coping-, key-stone; missing link &c. 53; superstructure, *ne plus ultra*, work done, *fait accompli*.

elaboration; finality; completeness &c. 52.

V. effect, -uate; accomplish, achieve, compass, consummate, hammer out; bring to -maturity, – perfection; perfect, complete; elaborate.

do, execute, make; go –, get- through; work out, enact; bring -about, – to bear, – to pass, – through, – to a head.

des-, dis-patch; knock –, finish –, polish- off; make short work of; dispose of, set at rest; perform, discharge, fulfil, realize; put in -practice, – force; carry -out, – into effect, – into execution; make good; be as good as one's word.

do thoroughly, not do by halves, go the whole hog; drive home; be in at the death &c. (*persevere*) 604a; carry through, play out, exhaust, deliver the goods, fill the bill.

finish, bring to a close &c. (*end*) 67; wind up, stamp, clinch, seal, set the seal on, put the seal to; give the -final touch &c. *n.* to; put the -last, – finishing- hand to; crown, – all; cap.

ripen, culminate; come to a -head, – crisis; come to its end; die -a natural death, – of old age; run -its course, – one's race; touch –, reach –, attain- the goal; reach &c. (*arrive*) 292; get in the harvest.

Adj. completing, final; conclu-ding, -sive; crowning &c. *v.*; exhaustive, complete, mature, perfect, consummate.

done, completed &c. *v.*; done for, sped, wrought out; highly wrought &c. (*preparation*) 673; thorough &c. 52; ripe &c. (*ready*) 673.

Adv. completely &c. (*thoroughly*) 52; to crown all, out of hand.

Phr. the race is run; *actum est*; *finis coronat opus*; *consummatum est*; *c'en est fait*; it is all over; the game is played out, the bubble has burst.

fall short of &c. 304; do things by halves; scotch the snake, not kill it; hang fire; be slow to; collapse &c. 304.

Adj. not completed &c. *v.*; incomplete &c. 53; uncompleted, unfinished, unaccomplished, unperformed, unexecuted; sketchy, addle.

in progress, in hand; going on, proceeding; on one's hands; on the fire; on the stocks; in preparation; lacking the finishing touch.

Adv. *re infectâ*.

-----

731. Success.—N. success, -fulness; speed; advance &c. (*progress*) 282.

trump card; hit, stroke; lucky –, fortunate –, good- -hit, – stroke; bold –, master- stroke; *coup de maître*, checkmate; half the battle, prize; profit &c. (*acquisition*) 775; best seller.

continued success; good fortune &c. (*prosperity*) 734; time well spent.

advantage over; edge; upper-, whip-hand; ascendancy, mastery; expugnation, conquest, victory, subdual; subjugation &c. (*subjection*) 749.

triumph &c. (*exultation*) 884; proficiency &c. (*skill*) 698; conqueror, victor, winner, champion; master of the -situation, – position.

V. succeed; be -successful &c. *adj.*;

732. Failure. — N. failure; non-success, -fulfilment; dead failure, successlessness; abortion, miscarriage; *brutum fulmen* &c. 158; labour in vain &c. (*inutility*) 645; no go; inefficacy; inefficaciousness &c. *adj.*; vain –, ineffectual –, abortive- -attempt, – efforts; flash in the pan, 'lame and impotent conclusion'; frustration; slip 'twixt cup and lip &c. (*disappointment*) 509.

blunder &c. (*mistake*) 495; fault, omission, miss, oversight, slip, trip, stumble, claudication, footfall; false –, wrong- step; *faux pas*, titubation, *bévue*, *faute*, lurch; botchery &c. (*want of skill*) 699; scrape, jam, mess, muddle, foozle, *fiasco*, breakdown.

mishap &c. (*misfortune*) 735; split,

gain one's -end, – ends; crown with success.

gain –, attain –, carry –, secure –, win- -a point, – an object; put over; make a go of; manage to, contrive to; accomplish &c. (*effect, complete*) 729; do –, work- wonders.

come off -well, – successfully, – with flying colours; make short work of; take –, carry- by storm; bear away the bell; win -one's spurs, – the battle; win –, carry –, gain- the -day, – prize, – palm; climb on the bandwagon; have -the best of it, – it all one's own way, – the game in one's own hands, – the ball at one's feet, – one on the hip; walk over the course; carry all before one, remain in possession of the field; score a success, win hands down.

speed; make progress &c. (*advance*) 282; win –, make –, work –, find- one's way; strive to some purpose; prosper &c. 734; drive a roaring trade; make profit &c. (*acquire*) 775; reap -, gather- the -fruits, – benefit of, – harvest; make one's fortune, get in the harvest, turn to good account; turn to account &c. (*use*) 677.

triumph, be triumphant; gain –, obtain- -a victory, – an advantage; chain victory to one's car.

surmount –, overcome –, get over- -a difficulty, – an obstacle &c. 706; *se tirer d'affaire*; make head against; stem the -torrent, – tide, – current; weather -the storm, – a point; turn a corner, keep one's head above water, tide over; master; get –, have –, gain- the -better of, – best of, – upper hand, – ascendancy, – whip hand, – start of; distance; surpass &c. (*superiority*) 33.

defeat, conquer, vanquish, discomfit; over-come, · throw, -power, -master, -match, -set, -ride, -reach; out-wit, -do, -flank, -manœuvre, -general, -vote; take the wind out of one's adversary's sails; beat, – hollow; rout, lick, drub, floor, worst; put -down, – to flight, – to the rout, – *hors de combat*, – out of court.

silence, quell, nonsuit, checkmate, upset, confound, nonplus, trump; baffle &c. (*hinder*) 706; circumvent, elude; trip up, – the heels of; drive

collapse, smash, blow, explosion.

repulse, rebuff, defeat, rout, over-throw, discomfiture; beating, drubbing; *quietus*, nonsuit, subjugation; check-, fool's-mate.

fall, downfall, ruin, perdition; wreck &c. (*destruction*) 162; death-blow; bankruptcy &c. (*non-payment*) 808.

losing game, *affaire flambée.*

victim, prey; bankrupt.

V. fail; be -unsuccessful &c. *adj.*; not -succeed &c. 731; make -vain efforts &c. *n.*; do –, labour –, toil- in vain; lose one's labour, take nothing by one's motion; bring to naught, make nothing of; wash a blackamoor white &c. (*impossible*) 471; roll the stone of Sisyphus &c. (*useless*) 645; do by halves &c. (*not complete*) 730; lose ground &c. (*recede*) 283; flunk; fall short of &c. 304.

miss, – one's aim, – the mark, – one's footing, – stays; slip, trip, stumble; make a -slip &c. *n.*, – blunder &c. 495, – mess of, – botch of; bitch it, mis-carry, abort, go up like a rocket and come down like the stick, reckon with-out one's host; get the wrong sow by the ear &c. (*blunder, mismanage*) 699.

limp, halt, hobble, titubate; fall, tumble; lose one's balance; fall -to the ground, – between two stools; flounder, falter, stick in the mud, run aground, split upon a rock; run –, knock –, dash- one's head against a stone wall; break one's back; break down, sink, drown, founder, have the ground cut from under one; get into -trouble, – a mess, – a scrape; come to grief &c. (*adversity*) 735; go to -the wall, – the dogs, – pot; lick –, bite- the dust; be -defeated &c. 731; have the worst of it, lose the day, come off second best, lose; fall a prey to; succumb &c. (*submit*) 725; not have a leg to stand on.

come to nothing, end in smoke; fall -to the ground, – through, – dead, – still-born, – flat; slip through one's fingers; hang –, miss- fire; flash in the pan, collapse; topple down &c. (*descent*) 305; go to wrack and ruin &c. (*destruction*) 162.

go amiss, go wrong, go cross, go hard with, go on a wrong tack; go on –,

-into a corner, – to the wall; run hard, put one's nose out of joint.

settle, do for; break the -neck of, – back of; capsize, sink, shipwreck, drown, swamp; subdue; subjugate &c. (*subject*) 749; reduce; make the enemy bite the dust; victimize, roll in the dust, trample under foot, put an extinguisher upon.

answer, – the purpose; avail, prevail, take effect, do, turn out well, work well, take, tell, bear fruit; hit -it, – the mark, – the right nail on the head; nick it; turn up trumps, make a hit; find one's account in.

Adj. succeeding &c. *v.*; successful; prosperous &c. 734; triumphant; flushed –, crowned- with success; victorious; set up; in the ascendant; unbeaten &c. (*see* beat &c. *v.*); well-spent; felicitous, effective, in full swing.

Adv. successfully &c. *adj.*; with flying colours, in triumph, swimmingly; *à merveille*, beyond all hope; to some –, good- purpose; to one's heart's content.

Phr. *veni vidi vici*, the day being one's own, one's star in the ascendant; *omne tulit punctum.*

come off –, turn out –, work- ill; take -a wrong, – an ugly- turn; gang agley.

be all -over with, – up with; explode; dash one's hopes &c. (*disappoint*) 509; defeat the purpose; upset the apple cart; sow the wind and reap the whirlwind, jump out of the frying pan into the fire.

Adj. unsuccessful, successless; failing, tripping &c. *v.*; at fault; unfortunate &c. 735.

abortive, addle, still-born; fruitless, sterile, bootless; ineffect-ual, -ive; inefficient &c. (*impotent*) 158; inefficacious; lame, hobbling, *décousu*; insufficient &c. 640; unavailing &c. (*useless*) 645; of no effect.

aground, grounded, swamped, stranded, cast away, wrecked, foundered, capsized, shipwrecked, nonsuited; foiled; defeated &c. 731; struck –, borne –, broken- down; down-trodden; over-borne, -whelmed; all up with; beaten to a frazzle.

lost, undone, ruined, broken; bankrupt &c. (*not paying*) 808; played out; done -up, – for; dead beat, ruined root and branch, *flambé*, knocked on the head; destroyed &c. 162.

frustrated, thwarted, crossed, unhinged, disconcerted, dashed; thrown -off one's balance, – on one's back, – on one's beam ends; unhorsed, in a sorry plight; hard hit.

stultified, befooled, dished, hoist on one's own petard; victimized, sacrificed.

wide of the mark &c. (*error*) 495; out of one's reckoning &c. (*inexpectation*) 508; left in the lurch; thrown away &c. (*wasted*) 638; unattained; uncompleted &c. 730.

Adv. unsuccessfully &c. *adj.*; to little or no purpose, in vain, *re infectâ*.

Phr. the bubble has burst, the game is up, all is lost; the devil to pay; *parturiunt montes* &c. (*disappointment*) 509.

---

733. Trophy.—**N.** trophy; medal, prize, palm; ribbon, blue ribbon, *cordon bleu*; citation; cup; laurel, -s; bays, crown, chaplet, wreath, civic crown; Victoria Cross, V.C., *Croix de Guerre*, Iron Cross; Distinguished Service Cross, Medal of Honor, Congressional Medal; insignia &c. 550; feather in one's cap &c. (*honour*) 873; decoration &c. 877; garland, triumphal arch.

triumph &c. (*celebration*) 883; flying colours &c. (*show*) 882.

monumentum ære perennius.

---

734. Prosperity.—**N.** prosperity, welfare, well-being; affluence &c. (*wealth*) 803; success &c. 731; thrift, roaring

735. Adversity.—**N.** adversity, evil &c. 619; failure &c. 732; bad –, ill –, evil –, adverse –, hard- -fortune, – hap,

trade; chicken in every pot, the full dinner pail; good –, smiles of- fortune; blessings, godsend.

luck; good –, run of- luck; sunshine; fair -weather, – wind; palmy –, bright –, halcyon- days; piping times, tide, flood, high tide.

Saturnia regna, Saturnian age; golden -time, – age; bed of roses; fat of the land, milk and honey, loaves and fishes, fleshpots of Egypt.

made man, lucky dog, *enfant gâté*, spoiled child of fortune.

upstart, *parvenu, nouveau riche*, profiteer, skipjack, mushroom.

V. prosper, thrive, flourish; be -prosperous &c. *adj.*; drive a roaring trade; go on -well, – smoothly, – swimmingly; sail before the wind, swim with the tide; run -smooth, – smoothly, – on all fours.

rise –, get on- in the world; work –, make- one's way; look up; lift –, raise- one's head, make one's -fortune, – pile, feather one's nest.

flower, blow, blossom, bloom, fructify, bear fruit, fatten, batten.

keep oneself afloat; keep –, hold- one's head above water; light –, fall- on one's -legs, – feet; drop into a good thing; bear a charmed life; bask in the sunshine; have a -good, – fine- time of it; have a run, – of luck; have the -good fortune &c. *n.* to; take a favourable turn; live -on the fat of the land, – in clover.

Adj. prosperous; thriving &c. *v.*; in a fair way, buoyant; well -off, – to do, – to do in the world; set up, at one's ease; rich &c. 803; in good case; in -full, – high- feather; fortunate, lucky, in luck; born -with a silver spoon in one's mouth, – under a lucky star; on the sunny side of the hedge.

auspicious, propitious, providential. palmy, halcyon; agreeable &c. 829; *couleur de rose.*

Adv. prosperously &c. *adj.*; swimmingly; as good luck would have it; beyond all -expectation, – hope, – one's wildest dreams.

Phr. one's star in the ascendant, all for the best, one's course runs smooth.

––––––––

– luck, – lot; frowns of fortune; evil -dispensation, – star, – genius; ups and downs of life, broken fortunes; hard -case, – lines, – life; sea –, peck- of troubles; hell upon earth; slough of despond; jinx.

trouble, humiliation, hardship, curse, blight, blast, load, pressure.

pressure of the times, iron age, evil day, time out of joint; hard –, bad –, sad- times; rainy day, cloud, dark cloud, gathering clouds, ill wind; visitation, infliction; affliction &c. (*painfulness*) 830; bitter -pill, – cup; care, trial; the sport of fortune.

mis-hap, -chance, -adventure, -fortune; disaster, calamity, catastrophe; accident, casualty, cross, reverse, check, *contretemps*, rub, pinch, setback.

losing game; falling &c. *v.*; fall, down-fall, come-down; ruin-ation, -ousness; undoing; extremity; ruin &c. (*destruction*) 162.

V. be -ill off &c. *adj.*; go hard with; fall on evil, – days; go on ill; not -prosper &c. 734.

go -downhill, – to rack and ruin &c. (*destruction*) 162, – to the dogs; fall, – from one's high estate; decay, sink, decline, go down in the world; have seen better days; bring down one's grey hairs with sorrow to the grave; come to grief; be all -over, – up- with; bring a -wasp's, – hornet's- nest about one's ears.

Adj. unfortunate, unblest, unhappy, unlucky; im-, un-prosperous; luck-, hap-less; out of luck; in trouble, in a bad way, in an evil plight; under a cloud; clouded; ill –, badly- off; in adverse circumstances; poor &c. 804; behindhand, down in the world, decayed, undone; on the road to ruin, on its last legs, on the wane; in one's utmost need.

planet-struck, devoted; born -under an evil star, – with a wooden ladle in one's mouth; ill-fated, -starred, -omened; inconspicuous, ominous, doomed, unpropitious.

adverse, untoward; disastrous, calamitous, ruinous, dire, deplorable.

Adv. if the worst come to the worst, as ill luck would have it, from bad to worse, out of the frying pan into the fire.

Phr. one's star is on the wane; one's luck -turns, – fails; the game is up, one's doom is sealed, the ground crumbles under one's feet, *sic transit gloria mundi, tant va la cruche à l'eau qu'à la fin elle se casse.*

736. Mediocrity.—N. moderate –, average- circumstances; respectability; middle classes, *bourgeoisie*; mediocrity; golden mean &c. (*midcourse*) 628, (*moderation*) 174.

V. jog on; go –, get on- -fairly, – quietly, – peaceably, – tolerably, – respectably; steer a middle course &c. 628.

Adj. middling, so-so, fair, medium, moderate, mediocre, second-, third- &c. -rate.

Division (II). INTERSOCIAL VOLITION*

Section I. General Intersocial Volition

737. Authority.—N. authority; influence, patronage, power, preponderance, credit, *prestige*, prerogative, jurisdiction; right &c. (*title*) 924.

divine right, dynastic rights, authoritativeness; absolut-eness, -ism; despotism, tyranny; *jus nocendi.*

command, empire, sway, rule; domin-ion, -ation; sovereignty, supremacy, suzerainty; lord-, head-ship; chiefdom; seignior-y, -ity, hegemony, patriarchate, patriarchy; master-y, -ship, -dom; government &c. (*direction*) 693; dictation, control.

hold, grasp; grip, -e; reach; iron sway &c. (*severity*) 739; fangs, clutches, talons; rod of empire &c. (*sceptre*) 747.

reign, regnancy, *régime*, dynasty; director-, dictator-ship; protector-ate, -ship; caliphate, pashalic, electorate; presiden-cy, -tship; administration; pro-, consulship; prefecture; seneschalship; magistra-ture, -cy; raj.

empire; monarchy; king-hood, -ship; royalty, regality, autocracy, monocracy, arist-archy, -ocracy; oligarchy, democracy, demogogy; republic, -anism, federalism; socialism, collectivism; communism, bolshevism, syndicalism; mob law, mobocracy, ochloc-

738. [Absence of authority.] **Laxity. —N.** laxity; lax-, loose-, slack-ness; toleration &c. (*lenity*) 740; freedom &c. 748.

anarchy, interregnum; relaxation; loosening &c. *v.*; remission; dead letter, *brutum fulmen*, misrule; licence, licentiousness; insubordination &c. (*disobedience*) 742; lynch law &c. (*illegality*) 964; nihilism.

[Deprivation of power] dethronement, deposition, usurpation, abdication.

V. be -lax &c. *adj.*; *laisser -faire, – aller*; hold a loose rein; give -the reins to, – rope enough, – a loose to; tolerate; relax; misrule.

go beyond the length of one's tether; have one's -swing, – fling; act without -instructions, – authority; act on one's own responsibility, usurp authority.

dethrone, depose; abdicate.

Adj. lax, loose; slack; remiss &c. (*careless*) 460; weak.

relaxed; licensed; reinless, unbridled; anarchical; unauthorized &c. (*unwarranted*) 925.

racy, ergatocracy; *vox populi, imperium in imperio*; bureaucracy; beadle-, bumble-dom; stratocracy; martial law, military -power, – government; feodality, feudal system, feudalism.

Thearchy, diarchy; du-, tri-, heter-archy; du-, tri-umvirate; auto-cracy, -nomy; limited monarchy; constitutional -government, – monarchy; home rule, autonomy; self-government, -determination; representative government; Soviet government.

* Implying the action of the will of one mind over the will of another.

gyn-archy, -ocracy, -æocracy; petticoat government, matri-archate, matriarchy.

[Vicarious authority] commission &c. 755; deputy &c. 759; per-mission &c. 760.

country, state, realm, commonwealth, canton, constituency, toparchy, municipality, polity, body politic, *posse comitatus.*

person in authority &c. (*master*) 745; judicature &c. 965; cabinet &c. (*council*) 696; usurper; seat of -government, – authority; head-quarters.

[Acquisition of authority] accession; installation &c. 755; usur-pation.

V. authorize &c. (*permit*) 760; warrant &c. (*right*) 924; dictate &c. (*order*) 741; have –, hold –, possess –, exercise –, exert –, wield--authority &c. *n.*

be -at the head of &c. *adj.*; hold –, be in –, fill an- office; hold –, occupy- a post; be -master &c. 745.

rule, sway, command, control, administer; govern &c. (*direct*) 693; lead, preside over, reign; possess –, be seated on –, occupy-the throne; sway –, wield- the sceptre; wear the crown.

have –, get- the -upper, – whip- hand; gain a hold upon, pre-ponderate, dominate, boss, rule the roost; over-ride, -rule, -awe; lord it over, hold in hand, keep under, make a puppet of, lead by the nose, hold in the hollow of one's hand, turn round one's little finger, bend to one's will, hold one's own, wear the breeches; have -the ball at one's feet, – it all one's own way, – the game in one's own hand, – on the hip, – under one's thumb; be master of the situation; take the lead, play first fiddle, set the fashion; give the law to; carry with a high hand; lay down the law; 'ride in the whirl-wind and direct the storm'; rule with a rod of iron &c. (*severity*) 739.

ascend –, mount- the throne, take the reins, – into one's hand; assume -authority &c. *n.*, – the reins of government; take –, assume the- command.

be -governed by, – in the power of; be under -the rule of, – the domination of.

Adj. ruling &c. *v.*; regnant, at the head, dominant, paramount, supreme, predominant, preponderant, in the ascendant, influential; gubernatorial; imperious; authoritative, executive, administrative, clothed with authority, official, *ex officio*, ministerial, bureaucratic, departmental, imperative, peremptory, overruling, absolute; hege-monic, -al; arbitrary; compulsory &c. 744; stringent.

regal, sovereign; royal, -ist; monarchical, kingly; imperial, -istic; princely; feudal; aristo-, auto-cratic; oligarchic &c. *n.*; democratic, republican, dynastic.

at one's command; in one's -power, – grasp; under control; authorized &c. (*due*) 924.

Adv. in the name of, by the authority of, *de par le Roi*, in virtue of; under the auspices of, in the hands of.

at one's pleasure; by a -dash, – stroke- of the pen; *ex mero motu*; *ex cathedrâ.*

Phr. the grey mare the better horse; 'every inch a king.'

---

739. Severity.—N. severity; strict-ness, formalism, harshness &c. *adj.*; rigour, stringency, austerity; inclem-

740. Lenity. — N. leni-ty, -ence, -ency; moderation &c. 174; toler-ance, -ation; mildness, gentleness; favour;

ency &c. (*pitilessness*) 914*a*; arrogance &c. 885.

arbitrary power; absolut-, despot-ism; dictatorship, autocracy, tyranny, domineering, oppression; assumption, usurpation; inquisition, reign of terror, martial law; iron -heel, – rule, – hand, – sway; tight grasp; brute -force, – strength; coercion &c. 744; strong –, tight- hand.

hard -lines, – measure; tender mercies [ironical]; sharp practice; bureaucracy, red tape; pipe-clay, officialism.

tyrant, disciplinarian, martinet, stickler, formalist, bashaw, despot, hard master, Draco, oppressor, inquisitor, extortioner, harpy, vulture, bird of prey.

V. be -severe &c. *adj.*

assume, usurp, arrogate, take liberties; domineer, bully &c. 885; tyrannize, inflict, wreak, stretch a point, put on the screw; be hard upon; bear –, lay- a heavy hand on; be –, come- down upon; ill-treat; deal -hardly with, – hard measure to; rule with a rod of iron, chastise with scorpions; dye with blood; oppress, override; trample –, tread- -down, – upon, – under foot; crush under an iron heel, ride roughshod over; rivet the yoke; hold –, keep- a tight hand; force down the throat; coerce &c. 744; give no quarter &c. (*pitiless*) 914*a*.

Adj. severe; strict, hard, harsh, dour, rigid, stiff, stern, rigorous, uncompromising, exacting, exigent, *exigeant*, inexorable, inflexible, obdurate, austere, relentless, Spartan, Draconian, stringent, strait-laced, puritanical, prudish, searching, unsparing, ironhanded, hard-headed, peremptory, absolute, positive, arbitrary, imperative; co-ercive &c. 744; tyrannical, despotic, masterful, extortionate, grind-ing, withering, oppressive, inquisitorial; inclement &c. (*ruthless*) 914*a*; cruel &c. (*malevolent*) 907; haughty, arrogant &c. 885.

Adv. severely &c. *adj.*; with a -high, – strong, – tight, – heavy-hand.

at the point of the -sword, – bayonet.

Phr. *Delirant reges plectuntur Achivi.*

indulgen-ce, -cy; clemency, mercy, forbearance, quarter; compassion &c. 914.

V. be -lenient &c. *adj.*; tolerate, bear with; *parcere subjectis*, give quarter.

indulge, allow one to have his own way, spoil.

Adj. lenient; mild, – as milk; gentle, soft; tolerant, indulgent, easy-going; clement &c. (*compassionate*) 914; for-bearing; complaisant, long-suffering.

---

741. Command.—N. command, order, ordinance, act, *fiat*, bidding, *dictum*, hest, behest, call, beck, nod.

des-, dis-patch; message, direction, injunction, charge, instructions; appointment, fixture.

demand, exaction, imposition, requisition, claim, reclamation, re-vendication; *ultimatum* &c. (*terms*) 770; request &c. 765; requirement.

dictation; dict-, mand-ate; *caveat*, decree, decree -nisi, – absolute, *senatus consultum*; precept; pre-, re-script; writ, ordination, bull, edict, decretal, dispensation, prescription, brevet, placet, ukase, *firman*, hatti-sheriff, warrant, passport, *mittimus, mandamus*, summons, subpœna, *nisi prius*, interpellation, citation; word, – of command; *mot d'ordre*; bugle –, trumpet- call; beat of drum, tattoo; order of the day; enact-ment &c. (*law*) 963; *plébiscite* &c. (*choice*) 609.

V. command, order, decree, enact, ordain, dictate, direct, give orders.

prescribe, set, appoint, mark out; set –, prescribe –, impose- a task; set to work, put in requisition &c. 926.

bid, enjoin, charge, call upon, instruct; require, – at the hands of; exact, impose, tax, task; demand; insist on &c. (*compel*) 744.

claim, lay claim to, revendicate, reclaim.

cite, summon; call –, send- for; subpœna; beckon.

issue a command; make –, issue –, promulgate- -a requisition, – a decree, – an order &c. *n.*; give the -word of command, – word, – signal; call to order; give –, lay down- the law; assume the command &c. (*authority*) 737; remand.

be -ordered &c.; receive an order &c. *n.*

Adj. commanding &c. *v.*; authoritative &c. 737; decret-ory, -ive, -al; imperative, jussive, decisive, final.

Adv. in a commanding tone; by a -stroke, – dash- of the pen; by order, at beat of drum, on the first summons; at the word of command.

Phr. the decree is gone forth; *sic volo sic jubeo; le Roi le veut.*

---

742. Disobedience.—N. disobedience, insubordination, contumacy; infraction, -fringement; violation, non-compliance; non-observance &c. 773.

revolt, rebellion, mutiny, outbreak, rising, uprising, putsch, insurrection, *émeute*; riot, tumult &c. (*disorder*) 59; strike &c. (*resistance*) 719; barring out; defiance &c. 715.

mutinousness &c. *adj.*; mutineering; sedition, treason; high –, petty –, misprision of- treason; *premunire*; *lèse-majesté*; violation of law &c. 964; defection, secession, revolution, *sabotage*, bolshevism, *Sinn Fein.*

insurgent, mutineer, rebel, revolter, rioter, traitor, *carbonaro, sansculottes*, red republican, communist, Fenian, chartist, *frondeur*; seceder, runagate, brawler, anarchist, demagogue; suffragette; Spartacus, Masaniello, Wat Tyler, Jack Cade; bolshevist, bolshevik, maximalist, ringleader.

V. disobey, violate, infringe; shirk; set at defiance &c. (*defy*) 715; set authority at naught, run riot, fly in the face of, bolt, take the law into one's own hands; kick over the traces.

turn –, run- restive; champ the bit; strike &c. (*resist*) 719; rise, – in arms; secede; mutiny, rebel.

Adj. disobedient; uncompl-ying, -iant; unsubmissive, unruly, ungovernable; insubordinate, impatient of control; rest-iff, -ive; refractory, contumacious; recusant &c. (*refuse*) 764; recalcitrant; resisting &c. 719; lawless, mutinous, seditious, insurgent, riotous, revolutionary.

disobeyed, unobeyed; unbidden.

743. Obedience.—N. obedience; observance &c. 772; compliance; submission &c. 725; subjection &c. 749; non-resistance; passiveness, passivity, resignation.

allegiance, loyalty, fealty, homage, deference, devotion, fidelity, constancy.

submiss-ness, -iveness; ductility &c. (*softness*) 324; obsequiousness &c. (*servility*) 886.

V. be -obedient &c. *adj.*; obey, bear obedience to; submit &c. 725; comply, answer the helm, come at one's call; do -one's bidding, – what one is told, – suit and service; attend to orders, serve -devotedly, – loyally, – faithfully.

follow, – the lead of, – to the world's end; serve &c. 746; play second fiddle.

Adj. obedient; compl-ying, -iant; law-abiding, loyal, faithful, leal, devoted; at one's -call, – command, – orders, – beck and call; under -beck and call, – control.

restrainable; resigned, passive; submissive &c. 725; henpecked; pliant &c. (*soft*) 324.

unresist-ed, -ing.

Adv. obediently &c. *adj.*; in compliance with, in obedience to.

Phr. to hear is to obey; as –, if- you please; at your service.

---

744. Compulsion.—**N.** compulsion, coercion, coaction, constraint, eminent domain, duress, enforcement, press, conscription.

force; brute -, main -, physical- force; the sword, *ultima ratio*; club -, mob -, lynch- law; *argumentum baculinum*, *le droit du plus fort*, martial law.

restraint &c. 751; necessity &c. 601; *force majeure*; Hobson's choice; the spur of necessity.

V. compel, force, make, drive, coerce, constrain, enforce, necessitate, oblige.

force upon, press; cram -, thrust -, force- down the throat; say it must be done, make a point of, insist upon, take no denial; put down, dragoon.

extort, wring from; put -, turn- on the screw; drag into; bind, - over; pin -, tie- down; require, tax, put in force; commandeer; restrain &c. 751.

Adj. compelling &c. *v.*; coercive, coactive; inexorable &c. 739; compuls-ory, -atory; obligatory, stringent, peremptory, binding.

forcible, not to be trifled with; irresistible &c. 601; compelled &c. *v.*; fain to.

Adv. by -force &c. *n.*, - force of arms; on compulsion, perforce; *vi et armis*, under the lash; at the point of the -sword, - bayonet; forcibly; by a strong arm.

under protest, in spite of one's teeth; against one's will &c. 603; *nolens volens* &c. (*of necessity*) 601; by stress of -circumstances, - weather; under press of; *de rigueur*.

---

745. Master.—**N.** master, *padrone*; lord, - paramount; command-er, -ant; captain; chief, -tain; *sahib*, sirdar, sachem, sheik, head, senior, governor, *duce*, ruler, dictator; leader &c. (*director*) 694.

lord of the ascendant; cock of the -walk, - roost; grey mare; mistress.

potentate; liege, - lord; suzerain, sovereign, monarch, autocrat, despot, tyrant, oligarch, overlord.

crowned head, emperor, king, anointed king, majesty, *imperator*, protector, president, stadtholder, judge.

cæsar, kaiser, czar, sultan, grand Turk, caliph, imaum, shah, padishah, sophi, mogul, great mogul, khan, cham; lama, tycoon, mikado, inca, cazique; domn; vaivode; wai-, way-wode; landamman; seyyid, cacique.

prince, duke &c. (*nobility*) 875; archduke, doge, elector; seignior; mar-, land-grave; rajah, emir, nizam, nawab, negus.

empress, queen, sultana, czarina, princess, infanta, duchess, margravine, begum, maharani.

regent, viceroy, exarch, palatine,

746. Servant.—**N.** subject, liegeman; servant, retainer, follower, henchman, servitor, domestic, menial, help, lady help, *employé*, *attaché*; official.

retinue, suite, *cortège*, staff, court.

attendant, squire, usher, page, buttons, donzel, footboy; dog robber; train-, cup-bearer; waiter, busboy, tapster, butler, livery servant, lackey, footman, flunkey, valet, *valet de chambre*; boots; scout, gyp; equerry, groom; jockey, hostler, ostler, tiger, orderly, messenger, cad, gillie, caddie; *wallah*; journeyman, herdsman, swineherd.

bailiff, castellan, seneschal, chamberlain, *major-domo*, groom of the chambers.

secretary; under -, assistant- secretary; clerk; clerical staff, stenographer, subsidiary; agent &c. 758; subaltern; under-ling, -strapper; man.

maid, -servant, waitress; handmaid; *confidente*, lady's maid, abigail, *soubrette*; nurse, *bonne*, *ayah*; nurse-, nursery-, house-, parlour-, waiting-, chamber-, kitchen-, scullery-, between -, laundry -, dairy-maid; *femme -*, *fille de chambre*; *camarista*; *chef de cuisine*,

khedive, hospodar, beglerbeg, three-tailed bashaw, pasha, pashaw, bashaw, bey, beg, dey, scherif, tetrarch, satrap, mandarin, subhadar, nabob, maharajah; burgrave; laird &c. (*proprietor*) 779; High Commissioner.

the -authorities, – powers that be, – government; staff, *état major*, aga, official, man in office, person in authority.

[Naval authorities] admiral, -ty, – of the fleet; rear-, vice-, port-admiral; senior-, naval officer, S.N.O., commodore, captain, commander, lieutenant-commander, lieutenant, sub-lieutenant, midshipman, warrant –, petty- officer, leading seaman; skipper, mate, master.

[Military authorities] marshal, field-marshal, *maréchal*; general, -issimo; commander-in-chief, *seraskier*, *hetman*; lieutenant-, major-general; commandant; colonel, lieutenant-colonel, major, captain, centurion, skipper, lieutenant, second-lieutenant, officer, staff-officer, *aide de camp*, brigadier, brigade-major, adjutant, *jemidar*, ensign, cornet, cadet, subaltern, warrant officer, quartermaster, noncommissioned officer, N.C.O.; sergeant, -major; top-sergeant, colour sergeant; corporal, -major; lance-, acting-corporal; drum major; shavetail.

[Air authorities] air -marshal, – commodore; group captain, squadron leader, wing commander, flight lieutenant, flying –, pilot-officer.

[Civil authorities] judge &c. 967; mayor, -alty; prefect, chancellor, archon, provost, magistrate, syndic; alcalde, alcaid; burgomaster, *corregidor*, seneschal, alderman, warden, constable, portreeve; lord mayor, sheriff; officer &c. (*executive*) 965.

cordon bleu, cook, scullion, Cinderella; maid –, servant- of all work, tweeny, general servant, girl, slavey; laundress, bed-maker, goodie, char-woman &c. (*worker*) 690.

serf, vassal, slave, negro, helot; bondsman, -woman; bondslave; *âme damnée*, *odalisque*, ryot, *adscriptus glebæ*; vill-ain, -ein; bead-, bede-sman; sizar; pension-er, -ary; client; dependant, -ent; hanger on, stooge, satellite; parasite &c. (*servility*) 886; led captain; *protégé*, ward, hireling, mercenary, puppet, creature.

badge of slavery; bonds &c. 752.

V. serve; minister to, wait –, attend –, dance attendance –, pin oneself-upon; squire, tend, hang on the sleeve of, char, do for; fag; valet.

Adj. in the train of; in one's -pay, – employ; at one's call &c. (*obedient*) 743; in bonds.

———

747. [Insignia of authority.] **Sceptre.—N.** sceptre, regalia, rod of empire, sword of state, mace, *fasces*, wand; staff, – of office; *bâton*, truncheon; flag &c. (*insignia*) 550; ensign –, emblem –, badge –, insignia- of authority, rank marks, brassard, badge, sash; cocked –, brass- hat.

epaulette, aiguilette, crown, star, eagle, bar, double bar, pip, stripe, chevron, curl, ring, anchor, shoulder-strap, tab.

throne, chair, musnud, divan, dais, woolsack.

toga, pall, mantle, robes of state, ermine, purple.

crown, coronet, diadem, tiara, triple crown, mitre, crozier, cardinal's hat &c.; cap of maintenance; decoration; title &c. 877; portfolio.

key, signet, seals, talisman; helm; reins &c. (*means of restraint*) 752.

———

748. Freedom.—N. freedom, liberty, independence; licence &c. (*permission*) 760; facility &c. 705.

scope, range, latitude, play; free –, full- -play, – scope; free stage and no

749. Subjection. — N. subjection; depend-ence, -ance, -ency; subordination; thrall, thraldom, enthralment, subjugation, bondage, serfdom; feudal--ism, -ity; vassalage, villenage; slavery,

favour; swing, full swing, elbow-room, margin, rope, wide berth; Liberty Hall.

franchise, denization; free -, freed-, livery- man; denizen.

autonomy, self-government, home-rule, self-determination, liberalism, free trade; non-interference &c. 706.

immunity, exemption; emancipation &c. (*liberation*) 750; en-, af-franchisement; rights, privileges.

free land, freehold; allodium; frank-almoigne, mortmain.

independent, free-lance, -thinker, -trader.

V. be -free &c. *adj.*; have -scope &c. *n.*, - the run of, - one's own way, - a will of one's own, - one's fling; do what one -likes, - wishes, - pleases, - chooses; go at large, feel at home, paddle one's own canoe; stand on one's -legs, - rights; shift for oneself.

take a liberty; make -free with, - oneself quite at home; use a freedom; take -leave, - French leave.

set free &c. (*liberate*) 750; give the reins to &c. (*permit*) 760; allow -, give-scope &c. *n.* to; give a horse his head.

make free of; give the -freedom of, - franchise; en-, af-franchise.

laisser -faire, - *aller*; live and let live; leave to oneself; leave -, let- alone; mind one's own business.

Adj. free, - as air; out of harness, independent, at large, loose, scot free; left -alone, - to oneself.

in full swing; uncaught, unconstrained, unbuttoned, unconfined, unrestrained, unchecked, unprevented, unhindered, unobstructed, unbound, uncontrolled, untrammelled.

unsubject, ungoverned, unenslaved, unenthralled, unchained, unshackled, unfettered, unreined, unbridled, uncurbed, unmuzzled, unimpeded.

unrestricted, unlimited, unconditional; absolute; discretionary &c. (*optional*) 600.

unassailed, unforced, uncompelled.

unbiassed, unprejudiced, uninfluenced, spontaneous.

free and easy; at -, at one's- ease; *dégagé*, quite at home; wanton, rampant, irrepressible, unvanquished.

exempt; freed &c. 750; freeborn; autonomous, freehold, allodial; *gratis* &c. 815.

unclaimed, going a begging.

Adv. freely &c. *adj.*; *ad libitum* &c. (*at will*) 600.

enslavement, involuntary servitude.

service; servi-tude, -torship; tendence, employ, tutelage, clientship; liability &c. 177; constraint &c. 751; oppression &c. (*severity*) 739; yoke &c. (*means of restraint*) 752; submission &c. 725; obedience &c. 743.

V. be -subject &c. *adj.*; be -, lie- at the mercy of; depend -, lean -, hangupon; fall -a prey to, - under; play second fiddle.

be a -mere machine, - puppet, - football; not dare to say one's soul is his own; drag a chain.

serve &c. 746; obey &c. 743; submit &c. 725.

break in, tame; subject, subjugate; master &c. 731; tread -down, - under foot; weigh down; drag at one's chariot wheels; reduce to -subjection, - slavery; en-, in-, be-thral; enslave, lead captive; take into custody &c. (*restrain*) 751; rule &c. 737; drive into a corner, hold at the sword's point; keep under; hold in -bondage, - leading strings, - swaddling clothes.

Adj. subject, dependent, subordinate; feud-al, -atory; in subjection to, under control; in -leading strings, - harness; subjected, enslaved &c. *v.*; constrained &c. 751; subservient, servile, fawning, slavish, obsequious, cringing; down-trodden; over-borne, -whelmed; under the lash, on the hip, led by the nose, henpecked; the -puppet, - sport, - plaything- of; under one's -orders, - command, - thumb; like dirt under one's feet; a slave to; at the mercy of; in the -power, - hands, - clutches- of; at the feet of; at one's beck and call &c. (*obedient*) 743; liable &c. 177; parasitical; stipendiary.

Adv. under.

---

750. Liberation.—**N.** liberation, disengagement, release, disenthrallment, enlargement, emancipation; af-, enfranchisement; manumission; discharge, dismissal.

deliverance &c. 672; redemption, extrication, acquittance, absolution; acquittal &c. 970; escape &c. 671.

V. liberate, free; set -free, – clear, – at liberty; render free, emancipate, release; en-, af-franchise; manumit; enlarge; dis-band, -charge, -miss, -enthral; let -go, – loose, – out, – slip; cast -, turn- adrift; deliver &c. 672; absolve &c. (*acquit*) 970; reprieve.

unfetter &c. 751; untie &c. 44; loose &c. (*disjoin*) 44; loosen, relax; un-bolt, -bar, -close, -cork, -clog, -hand, -bind, -latch, -chain, -harness; dis-engage, -entangle; clear, extricate, unloose.

gain –, obtain –, acquire- one's -liberty &c. 748; get -rid, – clear- of; deliver oneself from; shake off the yoke, slip the collar; break -loose, – prison; tear asunder one's bonds, cast off trammels; escape &c. 671.

Adj. at -liberty, – large, free, liberated &c. *v.*; out of harness &c. 748; adrift.

Int. unhand me! let me go!

---

751. Restraint.—**N.** restraint; hindrance &c. 706; coercion &c. (*compulsion*) 744; cohibition, constraint, repression; discipline, control, self-restraint &c. 604.

confinement; durance, duress; im-, prisonment; incarceration, coarctation, entombment, mancipation, durance vile, thrall, -dom, limbo, captivity; blockade; quarantine; detention.

arrest, -ation; custody, keep, care, charge, ward, restringency.

curb &c. (*means of restraint*) 752; *lettres de cachet.*

limitation, restriction, protection, monopoly; prohibition &c. 761; economic pressure.

prisoner &c. 754.

V. restrain, check; put –, lay- under restraint; en-, in-, be-thral; restrict; debar &c. (*hinder*) 706; constrain; coerce &c. (*compel*) 744; curb, control; hold –, keep- -back, – from, – in, – in check, – within bounds; hold in -leash, – leading strings; withhold.

keep under; repress, suppress; smother; pull in, rein in; hold, – fast; keep a tight hand on; prohibit &c. 761; in-, co-hibit.

enchain; fasten &c. (*join*) 43; fetter, shackle; en-, trammel; bridle, muzzle, gag, pinion, manacle, handcuff, tie one's hands, hobble, bind hand and foot; swathe, swaddle; pin –, peg- down; tether, picket; tie, – up, – down; secure; forge fetters.

confine; shut –, clap –, lock –, box –, mew –, bottle –, cork –, seal –, button- up; shut –, hem –, bolt –, wall –, rail- in; impound, pen, coop; enclose &c. (*circumscribe*) 229; cage; in-, en-cage; close the door upon, cloister; imprison, immure; incarcerate, entomb; clap –, lay- under hatches; put in -irons, – a strait waistcoat; throw –, cast- into prison; put into bilboes.

arrest; take -up, – charge of, – into custody; take –, make- -prisoner, – captive; captivate; lead -captive, – into captivity; send –, commit- to prison; commit; give in -charge, – custody; subjugate &c. 749.

Adj. re-, con-strained; imprisoned &c. *v.*; pent up; jammed in, wedged in; under -restraint, – lock and key, – hatches; serving –, doing- time; in swaddling clothes; on *parole*; in custody &c. (*prisoner*) 754; cohibitive; coactive &c. (*compulsory*) 744.

stiff, restringent, straitlaced, hide-bound.

ice-, wind-, weather-bound; 'cabined, cribbed, confined'; in Lob's pound, laid by the heels.

Adv. in captivity, under arrest, behind the bars, in -prison, – jail, – durance vile.

752. [Means of restraint.] Prison.—N. prison, -house; jail, gaol, cage, coop, den, death house, condemned –, cell; stronghold, fortress, keep, donjon, dungeon, *Bastille, oubliette,* bridewell, house of correction, hulks, toll-booth, panopticon, penitentiary, guard-room, clink, can, stir, tronk, jug, lock-up, hold; round –, watch –, station –, sponging-house; station; house of detention, black hole, pen, fold, pound; enclosure &c. 232; penal settlement; chain gang; debtors' prison; reformatory; federal penitentiary, state prison; criminal lunatic asylum; bilboes, stocks, limbo, quod.

Dartmoor, Newgate, Fleet, Marshalsea; King's (*or* Queen's) Bench; Sing Sing, Dannemora.

bond; strap, bandage, splint, tourniquet; irons, pinion, gyve, fetter, shackle, trammel, manacle, handcuff, bracelets, darbies, strait waist-coat, strait-jacket.

yoke, collar, halter, harness; muzzle, gag, bit, brake, curb, snaffle, bridle; rein, -s; ribbons, lines, bearing-rein; martingale, leading string; tether, picket, band, guy, chain; cord &c. (*fastening*) 45.

bolt, bar, lock, padlock, rail, wall; paling, palisade; fence; barrier, barricade.

brake, drag &c. (*hindrance*) 706.

753. Keeper.—N. keeper, custodian, *custos,* ranger, warder, jailer, gaoler, turnkey, castellan, guard; watch, -dog, -man; Charley; sen-try, -tinel; watch and ward; *concierge,* coast-guard, *guarda costa,* gamekeeper.

escort, body guard, convoy.

protector, governor, duenna; guardian; governess &c. (*teacher*) 540; nurse, *bonne, ayah, amah.*

754. Prisoner.—N. prisoner, captive, *détenu,* close prisoner.

jail-bird, ticket-of-leave man.

V. stand committed; be -imprisoned &c. 751.

Adj. imprisoned &c. 751; in -prison, – quod, – durance vile, – limbo, – custody, – charge, – chains; under -lock and key, – hatches; on *parole;* detained at his Majesty's pleasure.

755. [Vicarious authority.] Commission.—N. commission, delegation; con-, as-signment; procuration; deputation, legation, mission, embassy; agency, agentship; power of attorney, proxy; clerkship.

errand, charge, *brevet,* diploma, *exequatur,* permit &c. (*permission*) 760.

appointment, nomination, return; charter; ordination; installation, inauguration, investiture; accession, coronation, enthronement.

vicegerency; regency, regentship.

viceroy &c. 745; consignee &c. 758; deputy &c. 759.

V. commission, delegate, depute; consign, assign; charge; in-, en-trust; turn over to; commit, – to the hands of; authorize &c. (*permit*) 760.

put in commission, accredit, engage, hire, bespeak, appoint, name, nominate, return, ordain; install, induct,

756. Abrogation.—N. abrogation, annulment, nullification; cancelling &c. *v.;* cancel; revo-cation, -kement; repeal, rescission, defeasance.

dismissal, *congé,* demission; depos-al, -ition; sack; dethronement; disestablish-, disendow-ment; deconsecration.

aboli-tion, -shment; dissolution.

counter-order, -mand; repudiation, retractation; recantation &c. (*tergiversation*) 607.

V. abrogate, annul, cancel; destroy &c. 162; abolish; revoke, repeal, rescind, reverse, retract, recall; over-rule, -ride; set aside; disannul, dissolve, quash, nullify, declare null and void; dis-establish, -endow; deconsecrate.

disclaim &c. (*deny*) 536; ignore, repudiate; recant &c. 607; divest oneself, break off.

counter-mand, -order; do away with; sweep –, brush- away; throw -over-

inaugurate, invest, crown; en-roll, -list.

employ, empower; give power of attorney to; set –, place- over; send out.

be commissioned, be accredited; represent, stand for; stand in the -stead, – place, – shoes- of.

Adj. commissioned &c. *v.*

Adv. *per procuratione.*

board, – to the dogs; scatter to the winds, cast behind.

dismiss, discard; cast –, turn- -off, – out, – adrift, – out of doors, – aside, – away; send -off, – away, – about one's business; discharge, get rid of, fire out, fire &c. (*eject*) 297; jilt.

cashier; break; oust; set down, unseat, -saddle; un-, de-, disen-throne; depose, uncrown; unfrock, strike off the roll; dis-bar, -bench.

be -abrogated &c.; receive its quietus.

Adj. abrogated &c. *v.*; *functus officio.*

Int. get along with you! begone! go about your business! away with!

---

757. Resignation.—N. resignation, retirement, abdication, renunciation, abjuration, disclaimer, abandonment, relinquishment.

V. resign; give –, throw- up; lay down, throw up the cards, wash one's hands of, abjure, renounce, forego, disclaim, abandon, relinquish, retract, demit; deny &c. 536.

abrogate &c. 756; desert &c. (*relinquish*) 624; get rid of &c. 782.

abdicate; vacate, – one's seat; accept the stewardship of the Chiltern Hundreds; retire; tender –, send in –, hand in- one's resignation.

Adj. abdicant, renunciatory &c. *v.*

Phr. 'Othello's occupation's gone.'

---

758. Consignee.—N. consignee, trustee, nominee, committee.

delegate; commiss-ary, -ioner; emissary, envoy, commissionaire; messenger &c. 534.

diplomatist, diplomat, *corps diplomatique*, embassy; am-, em-bassador; representative, resident, consul, legate, nuncio, internuncio, *chargé d'affaires, attaché.*

vicegerent &c. (*deputy*) 759; plenipotentiary.

functionary, placeman, curator; treasurer &c. 801; agent, factor, bailiff, steward, clerk, secretary, attorney, solicitor, proctor, broker, underwriter, commission agent, auctioneer, one's man of business; factotum &c. (*director*) 694; caretaker.

negotiator, go between; middleman; under agent, *employé*; servant &c. 746.

salesman; commercial, – traveller; bagman, *commis-voyageur*, touter.

newspaper –, own –, war –, special- correspondent; reporter.

---

759. Deputy.—N. deputy, substitute, vice, proxy, *locum tenens*, delegate, representative, next friend, surrogate, secondary.

regent, vicegerent, vizier, minister, vicar; premier &c. (*director*) 694; chancellor, prefect, provost, warden, lieutenant, archon, consul, proconsul; viceroy &c. (*governor*) 745; commissioner &c. 758; plenipotentiary, *alter ego.*

team, eight, eleven; champion.

V. be -deputy &c. *n.*; stand –, appear –, hold a brief –, answer- for; represent; stand –, walk- in the shoes of; stand in the stead of.

substitute, ablegate, accredit; commission, empower, delegate &c. 755.

Adj. acting; vice, -regal; accredited to.

Adv. in behalf of, by proxy.

Section II. Special Intersocial Volition

760. Permission.—N. permission, leave; allow-, suffer-ance; toler-ance, -ation; liberty, law, licence, concession, grace; indulgence &c. (*lenity*) 740; favour, dispensation, exemption, release; connivance; vouchsafement.

authorization, warranty, accordance, admission.

permit, warrant, *brevet*, precept, sanction, authority, *firman*; pass, -port; furlough, licence, *carte blanche*, ticket of leave; grant, charter, patent.

V. permit; give -permission &c. *n.*, - power; let, allow, admit; suffer, bear with, tolerate, recognize; concede &c. 762; accord, vouchsafe, favour, humour, gratify, indulge, stretch a point; wink at, connive at; shut one's eyes to.

grant, empower, charter, enfranchise, privilege, confer a privilege, license, authorize, warrant; sanction; entrust &c. (*commission*) 755.

give -*carte blanche*, - the reins to, - scope to &c. (*freedom*) 748; leave -alone, - it to one, - the door open; open the -door to, - floodgates; give a loose to.

let off; absolve &c. (*acquit*) 970; release, exonerate, dispense with.

ask -, beg -, request- -leave, - permission.

761. Prohibition.—N. pro-, in-hibition; *veto*, disallowance; interdict, -ion; injunction; embargo, ban, *verboten*, taboo, proscription; *index expurgatorius*; restriction &c. (*restraint*) 751; hindrance &c. 706; forbidden fruit.

V. pro-, in-hibit; forbid, put one's *veto* upon, disallow; bar; debar &c. (*hinder*) 706, forefend.

keep -in, - within bounds; restrain &c. 751; cohibit, withhold, limit, circumscribe, clip the wings of, restrict, narrow; interdict, taboo; put -, place- under -an interdiction, - the ban; proscribe, censor; exclude, shut out; shut -, bolt -, show- the door; warn off; dash the cup from one's lips; forbid the banns.

Adj. prohibit-ive, -ory; interdictive; proscriptive; restrictive, exclusive; forbidding &c. *v.*

prohibited &c. *v.*; not -permitted &c. 760; unlicensed, contraband, under the ban of; illegal &c. 964; unauthorized, not to be thought of.

Adv. on no account &c. (*no*) 536.

Int. forbid it heaven! &c. (*deprecation*) 766.

hands -, keep- off! hold! stop! avast!
Phr. that will never do.

Adj. permitting &c. *v.*; permissive, indulgent; permitted &c. *v.*; patent, chartered, permissible, allowable, lawful, legitimate, legal; legalized &c. (*law*) 963; licit; unforbid, -den; unconditional.

Adv. permissibly; by -, with -, on- -leave &c. *n.*; *speciali gratiâ*; under favour of; *pace*; *ad libitum* &c. (*freely*) 748, (*at will*) 600; by all means &c. (*willingly*) 602; yes &c. (*assent*) 488.

---

762. Consent.—N. consent; assent &c. 488; acquiescence; approval &c. 931; compliance, agreement, concession; yield-ance, -ingness; accession, acknowledgment, acceptance, agnition.

settlement, ratification, confirmation, adjustment.

permit &c. (*permission*) 760; promise &c. 768.

V. consent; assent &c. 488; yield assent, admit, allow, concede, grant, yield; come -over, - round; give in to, acknowledge, agnize, give consent, comply with, acquiesce, agree to, fall in with, accede, accept, embrace an offer, close with, take at one's word, have no objection.

satisfy, meet one's wishes, settle, come to terms &c. 488; not -refuse &c. 764; turn a willing ear &c. (*willingness*) 602; jump at; deign, vouchsafe; promise &c. 768.

Adj. consenting &c. *v.*; agreeable, compliant; agreed &c. (*assent*) 488; unconditional.

Adv. yes &c. (*assent*) 488; by all means &c. (*willingly*) 602; if -, as-you please; be it so, so be it, well and good, of course.

763. Offer.—**N.** offer, proffer, presentation, tender, bid, overture; propos-al, -ition; motion, invitation; candidature; offering &c. (*gift*) 784.

V. offer, proffer, present, tender; bid; propose, move; make -a motion, – advances; start; invite, hold out, place- at one's disposal, – in one's way, put forward.

hawk about; offer for sale &c. 796; press &c. (*request*) 765; lay at one's feet.

offer -, present- oneself; volunteer, come forward, be a candidate; stand -, bid- for; seek; be at one's service; go a begging; bribe &c. (*give*) 784.

Adj. offer-ing, -ed &c. *v.*; in the market, for sale, to let, disengaged, on hire.

764. Refusal.—**N.** refusal, rejection; non-, in-compliance; denial; declining &c. *v.*; declension; peremptory -, flat -, point blank- refusal; repulse, rebuff; discountenance.

recusancy, renunciation, abnegation, negation, protest, disclaimer; dissent &c. 489; revocation &c. 756.

V. refuse, reject, deny, decline; nill, negative; refuse -, withhold- one's assent; shake the head; close the -hand, – purse; grudge, begrudge, be slow to, hang fire.

be deaf to; turn -a deaf ear to, – one's back upon; set one's face against, discountenance, not hear of, have nothing to do with, wash one's hands of, stand aloof, forswear, set aside, cast behind one; not yield an inch &c. (*obstinacy*) 606.

resist, cross; not -grant &c. 762; repel, repulse; shut -, slam- the door in one's face; rebuff; send -back, – to the right about, – away with a flea in the ear; deny oneself, not be at home to; discard &c. (*repudiate*) 610; rescind &c. (*revoke*) 756; disclaim, protest; dissent &c. 489.

Adj. refusing &c. *v.*; rest-ive, -iff; recusant; uncomplying, non-compliant, unconsenting, uncomplaisant, protestant; not willing to hear of, deaf to.

refused &c. *v.*; ungranted, out of the question, not to be thought of, impossible.

Adv. no &c. 536; on no account, not for the world; no thank you.

Phr. *non possumus*; [ironically] your humble servant; *bien obligé*.

765. Request.—**N.** requ-est, -isition; claim &c. (*demand*) 741; petition, suit, prayer; begging letter, round-robin.

motion, overture, application, canvass, address, appeal, apostrophe; imprecation; rogation; proposal, proposition.

orison &c. (*worship*) 990; incantation &c. (*spell*) 993.

mendicancy; asking, panhandling, begging &c. *v.*; postulation, solicitation, invitation, entreaty, importunity, supplication, instance, impetration, imploration, obsecration, obtestation, invocation, interpellation.

V. request, ask; beg, crave, sue, pray, petition, solicit, invite, pop the question, make bold to ask; beg -leave, – a boon; apply to, call to, put to; call -upon, – for; make -, address -, prefer -, put up- a -request, – prayer, – petition;

766. [Negative request.] Deprecation.—**N.** deprecation, expostulation; remonstrance; intercession, mediation.

V. deprecate, protest, expostulate, enter a protest, intercede for.

Adj. deprecatory, expostulatory, intercessory, mediatorial.

deprecated, protested.

un-, unbe-sought; unasked &c. (*see* ask &c. 765).

Int. cry you mercy! God forbid! forbid it Heaven! Heaven -forefend, – forbid! far be it from! hands off! &c. (*prohibition*) 761.

make -application, – a requisition; ask –, trouble- one for; claim &c. (*demand*) 741; offer up prayers &c. (*worship*) 990; whistle for.

beg hard, entreat, beseech, plead, supplicate, implore, apostrophize; conjure, adjure; obtest; cry to, kneel to, appeal to; invoke, evoke; impetrate, imprecate, ply, press, urge, beset, importune, dun, tax, clamour for; cry -aloud, – for help; fall on one's knees; throw oneself at the feet of; come down on one's marrow-bones.

beg from door to door, send the hat round, go a begging; mendicate, mump, cadge, panhandle, beg one's bread.

dance attendance on, besiege, knock at the door.

bespeak, canvass, tout, make interest, court; seek, bid for &c. (*offer*) 763; publish the banns.

Adj. requesting &c. *v.*; precatory; suppli-ant, -cant, -catory; invoc-, imprec-, rog-atory; postulant, mendicant.

importunate, clamorous, urgent; solicitous; cap in hand; on one's -knees, – bended knees, – marrow-bones.

Adv. prithee, do, please, pray; be so good as, be good enough; have the goodness, vouchsafe, will you, I pray thee, if you please.

Int. for -God's, – heaven's, – goodness', – mercy's- sake.

767. Petitioner.—N. petitioner, solicitor, applicant; suppli-ant, -cant; suitor, candidate, claimant, postulant, aspirant, competitor, bidder; place -, pot- hunter; prizer.

beggar, mendicant, mumper, sturdy beggar, cadger, panhandler.

canvasser, barker, touter &c. 768.

sycophant, parasite &c. 886.

Section III. Conditional Intersocial Volition

768. Promise.—N. promise, undertaking, word, troth, plight, pledge, *parole*, word of honour, vow; oath &c. (*affirmation*) 535; profession, assurance, warranty, guarantee, insurance, obligation; contract &c. 769.

engagement, pre-engagement: affiance; betroth, -al, -ment; marriage -compact, – vow.

V. promise; give a -promise &c. *n.*; undertake, engage; make -, form- an engagement; enter -into, – on- an engagement; bind -, tie -, pledge -, commit -, take upon- oneself; vow; swear &c. (*affirm*) 535, give -, pass -, pledge -, plight- one's -word, – honour, – credit, – troth; betroth, plight faith; take the vows.

assure, warrant, guarantee, vouch for, avouch, covenant &c. 769; attest &c. (*bear witness*) 467.

hold out an expectation; contract an obligation; become -bound to, – sponsor for; answer -, be answerable- for; secure; give security &c. 771; underwrite.

adjure, administer an oath, put to one's oath, swear a witness.

Adj. promising &c. *v.*; promissory; votive; under hand and seal; upon -oath, – affirmation.

promised &c. *v.*; affianced, pledged, bound; committed, compromised; in for it.

Adv. as one's head shall answer for; upon my honour.

Phr. in for a penny, in for a pound.

768a. Release from engagement.—N. release &c. (*liberation*) 750.

Adj. absolute; unconditional &c. (*free*) 748.

769. Compact.—N. compact, contract, agreement, bargain, deal, transaction; affidation; pact, -ion; bond, covenant, indenture.

stipulation, settlement, convention; compromise, *cartel.*

protocol, treaty, *concordat, Zollverein, Sonderbund,* charter, *Magna Charta,* Pragmatic Sanction.

negotiation &c. (*bargaining*) 794; diplomacy &c. (*mediation*) 724; negotiator &c. (*agent*) 758.

ratification, completion, signature, seal, sigil, signet.

V. contract, covenant, agree for, engage &c. (*promise*) 768.

treat, negotiate, stipulate, make terms; bargain &c. (*barter*) 794.

make –, strike- a bargain; come to -terms, – an understanding; compromise &c. 774; set at rest; close, – with; conclude, complete, settle; confirm, ratify, clench, subscribe, underwrite; en-, in-dorse; put the seal to; sign, seal &c. (*attest*) 467; indent.

take one at one's word, bargain by inch of candle.

Adj. contractual, agreed &c. *v.*; conventional; under hand and seal; signed, sealed and delivered.

Phr. *caveat emptor.*

770. Conditions.—N. conditions, terms; articles, – of agreement.

clauses, provisions; proviso &c. (*qualification*) 469; covenant, stipulation, obligation, *ultimatum, sine quâ non; casus fœderis.*

V. make –, come to- -terms &c. (*contract*) 769; make it a condition, stipulate, insist upon, make a point of; bind, tie up.

Adj. conditional, provisional, guarded, fenced, hedged in.

Adv. conditionally &c. (*with qualification*) 469; provisionally, *pro re natâ*; on condition; with a reservation.

771. Security.—N. security; guaran-ty, -tee; gage, warranty, bond, tie, pledge, plight, mortgage, debenture, hypothecation, bill of sale, lien, pignus, pawn, pignoration; real security; bottomry; collateral, vadium.

stake, deposit, earnest, handsel, caution.

promissory note; bill, – of exchange; I.O.U.; personal security, covenant, specialty; *parole* &c. (*promise*) 768.

acceptance, indorsement, signature, execution, stamp, seal.

spon-sor, -sion, -sorship; surety, bail; mainpernor, hostage.

recognizance; deed –, covenant- of indemnity.

authentication, verification, warrant, certificate, voucher, docket, doquet; record &c. 551; probate, attested copy.

receipt; ac-, quittance; discharge, release.

muniment, title-deed, instrument; deed, – poll; assurance, insurance, indenture; charter &c. (*compact*) 769; charter-poll; paper, parchment, settlement, will, testament, last will and testament, codicil.

V. give -security, – bail, – substantial bail; go bail; pawn, impawn, hock, spout, mortgage, hypothecate, impignorate.

guarantee, warrant, assure; accept, indorse, underwrite, insure.

execute, stamp; sign, seal &c. (*evidence*) 467.

let, sett; grant –, take –, hold- a lease; hold in pledge; lend on security &c. 787.

Adj. secure, -ed; pledged &c. *v.*; in pawn, on deposit.

772. Observance.—N. observance, performance, compliance; obedience

773. Non-observance. — N. non-observance &c. 772; evasion, inob-

&c. 743; fulfilment, satisfaction, discharge; acquit-tance, -tal.

adhesion, acknowledgment; fidelity &c. (*probity*) 939; exact &c. 494- observance.

V. observe, comply with, respect, acknowledge, abide by; cling to, adhere to, be faithful to, act up to; meet, fulfil; carry -out, - into execution; execute, perform, keep, satisfy, discharge; do one's office.

perform -, fulfill -, discharge -, acquit oneself of- an obligation; make good; make good -, keep- one's -word, - promise; redeem one's pledge; keep faith with, stand to one's engagement.

Adj. observant, faithful, true, loyal; honourable &c. 939; true as the -dial to the sun, - needle to the pole; punct-ual, -ilious; meticulous; literal &c. (*exact*) 494; as good as one's word.

Adv. faithfully &c. *adj.*

servance, failure, omission, neglect, laches, laxity, informality.

infringement, infraction; violation, transgression.

retractation, repudiation, nullification; protest; forfeiture.

lawlessness; disobedience &c. 742; bad faith &c. 940.

V. fail, neglect, omit, elude, evade, give the go by to, cut, set aside, ignore; shut -, close- one's eyes to, avoid.

infringe, transgress, pirate, violate, break, trample under foot, do violence to, drive a coach and six through.

discard, protest, repudiate, fling to the winds, set at naught, nullify, declare null and void; cancel &c. (*wipe off*) 552.

retract, go back from, be off, forfeit, go from one's word, palter; stretch -, strain- a point.

Adj. violating &c. *v.*; lawless, transgressive; elusive, evasive; lax, casual; non-observant.

unfulfilled &c. (*see* fulfil &c. 772).

---

774. Compromise.—N. com-promise, -mutation, -position; middle term, *mezzo termine*; compensation &c. 30; adjustment, mutual concession.

V. com-promise, -mute, -pound; take the mean; split the difference, meet one half way, give and take; come to terms &c. (*contract*) 769; submit to -, abide by- arbitration; patch up, bridge over, fix up, arrange; adjust, - differences; agree; make -the best of, - a virtue of necessity; take the will for the deed.

Section IV. POSSESSIVE RELATIONS*

1°. *Property in general*

775. Acquisition.—N. acquisition; gaining &c. *v.*; obtainment; procuration, -ement; purchase, descent, inheritance; gift &c. 784.

recovery, retrieval, revendication, replevin; redemption, salvage, trover; find, *trouvaille*, foundling.

gain, thrift; money-making, -grubbing; lucre, filthy lucre, loaves and fishes, the main chance, pelf; emolument &c. 973; wealth &c. 803.

profit, earnings, winnings, innings, clean-up, pickings, perquisite, net profit; income &c. (*receipt*) 810; proceeds, -duce, -duct; out-come, -put;

776. Loss.—N. loss; de-, perdition; forfeiture, lapse.

privation, bereavement; deprivation &c. (*dispossession*) 789; riddance.

V. lose; incur -, experience -, meet with- a loss; miss; mislay, let slip, allow to slip through the fingers, squander; be without &c. (*exempt*) 777a; forfeit.

get rid of &c. 782; waste &c. 638.

be lost, lapse.

Adj. losing &c. *v.*; not having &c. 777a.

shorn of, deprived of; denuded, bereaved, bereft, *minus*, cut off; dispos-

* That is, relations which concern property.

return, fruit, crop, harvest, tilth; second crop, aftermath; benefit &c. (*good*) 618.

sweepstakes, trick, prize, pool.

[Fraudulent acquisition] subreption; theft, stealing &c. 791.

V. acquire, get, gain, win, earn, obtain, procure, gather, annex; collect &c. 72; pick, – up; glean, take &c. 789.

find; come –, pitch –, light- upon; scrape -up, – together; get in, reap and carry, net, bag, sack, bring home, secure, come across, derive, draw, get in the harvest.

profit; make –, draw- profit; turn to -profit, – account; make -capital out of, – money by; obtain a return, reap the fruits of; reap –, gain- an advantage; turn -a penny, – an honest penny; make the pot boil, bring grist to the mill; make –, coin –, raise- money; raise -funds, – the wind; fill one's pocket &c. (*wealth*) 803.

treasure up &c. (*store*) 636; realize, clear; produce &c. 161; take &c. 789.

get back, recover, regain, retrieve, revendicate, replevy, redeem, come by one's own.

come -by, – in for; receive &c. 785; inherit; step into, – a fortune, – the shoes of; succeed to.

get -hold of, – between one's finger and thumb, – into one's hand, – at; take –, come into –, enter into- possession.

be -profitable &c. *adj.*; pay, answer.

accrue &c. (*be received*) 785.

Adj. acquir-ing, -ed &c. *v.*; acquisitive; productive, profitable, advantageous, gainful, remunerative, paying, lucrative.

sessed &c. 789; rid of, quit of; out of pocket.

lost &c. *v.*; long lost; irretrievable &c. (*hopeless*) 859; irredentist; off one's hands.

Int. farewell to! adieu to! good riddance!

---

777. Possession.—N. possession, seisin; ownership &c. 780; occupancy; hold, -ing; tenure, tenancy, feodality, dependency; villenage; socage, chivalry, knight service.

exclusive possession, impropriation, monopoly, corner; retention &c. 781; pre-possession, -occupancy; nine points of the law.

future possession, heritage, inheritance, heirship, reversion, fee, seigniority, feud, fief.

bird in hand, *uti possidetis*, *chose* in possession.

V. possess, have, hold, occupy, enjoy; be -possessed of &c. *adj.*; have -in hand &c. *adj.*; own &c. 780; command.

inherit; come -to, – in for.

engross, monopolize, forestall, regrate, impropriate, have all to oneself, corner; have a firm hold of &c. (*retain*) 781; get into one's hand &c. (*acquire*) 775.

belong to, appertain to, pertain to; be -in one's possession &c. *adj.*; vest in.

Adj. possessing &c. *v.*; worth; possessed of, seized of, master of, in possession of; endowed –, blest –, instinct –, fraught –, laden –, charged –, instilled –, with.

possessed &c. *v.*; on hand, by one; in hand, in store, in stock; in one's -hands, – grasp, – possession; at one's -command, – disposal; one's own &c. (*property*) 780.

unsold; unshared.

777a. Exemption.—N. exemption; exception, immunity, privilege, release &c. 927a; absence &c. 187.

V. not -have &c. 777; be -without &c. *adj.*

Adj. exempt from, devoid of, without, unpossessed of, unblest with, immune from.

not -having &c. 777; unpossessed; untenanted &c. (*vacant*) 187; without an owner.

unobtained, unacquired.

778. [Joint possession.] Participation.—N. participation; co-, joint-tenancy; possession –, tenancy- in common; joint –, common- stock; co-, partnership; communion; community of -possessions, – goods; communalism, communism, socialism, collectivism; co-operation &c. 709; profit sharing.

snacks, co-portion, picnic, hotchpotch; co-heirship, -parceny, -parcenary; gavelkind.

participator, sharer; co-, partner; shareholder; co-, joint-tenant; tenants in common; co-heir, -parcener.

communist, socialist.

V. par-ticipate, -take; share, – in; come in for a share; go -shares, – snacks, – halves; share and share alike.

have –, possess –, be seized- -in common, – as joint tenants &c. *n.* join in; have a hand in &c. (*co-operate*) 709.

Adj. partaking &c. *v.;* communistic, socialistic, co-operative, profit sharing.

Adv. share and share alike.

779. Possessor.—N. possessor, holder; occup-ant, -ier; tenant; person –, man- -in possession &c. 777; renter, lodger, lessee, under-lessee; zemindar, ryot; tenant -on sufferance, – at will, – from year to year, – for years, – for life.

owner; propriet-or, -ress, -ary; impropriator, master, mistress, lord.

land-holder, -owner, -lord, -lady; lord -of the manor, – paramount; heritor, laird, vavasour, landed gentry, mesne lord.

cestui-que-trust, beneficiary, mortgagor.

grantee, feoffee, relessee, devisee; legat-ee, -ary.

trustee; holder &c.- of the legal estate; mortgagee.

right –, rightful- owner.

[Future possessor] heir, – apparent; – presumptive; heiress; inherit-or, -ress, -rix; reversioner, remainder-man.

780. Property.—N. property, possession, *suum cuique, meum et tuum.*

owner-, proprietor-, lord-ship; seignority; empire &c. (*dominion*) 737.

interest, stake, estate, right, title, claim, demand, holding; tenure &c. (*possession*) 777; vested –, contingent –, beneficial –, equitable-interest; use, trust, benefit; legal –, equitable- estate; seisin.

absolute interest, paramount estate, freehold; fee, – simple, – tail; estate -in fee, – in tail, – tail; estate in tail -male, – female, – general.

limitation, term, lease, settlement, strict settlement, particular estate; estate -for life, – for years, – *pur autre vie;* remainder, reversion, expectancy, possibility.

dower, dowry, *dot,* jointure, marriage portion, appanage, inheritance, heritage, patrimony, alimony; legacy &c. (*gift*) 784.

assets, belongings, means, resources, circumstances; wealth &c. 803; money &c. 800; what one -is worth, – will cut up for; estate and effects.

landed –, real- -estate, – property; realty; land, -s; subdivision; plot, site; tenements; hereditaments; corporeal –, incorporeal- heredita- ments; acres; ground &c. (*earth*) 342; acquest; messuage.

territory, state, kingdom, principality, realm, empire, protectorate, margravate, dependancy, colony, sphere of influence, mandate.

manor, honour, domain, demesne; farm, ranch, plantation, *hacienda*; allodium &c. (*free*) 748; fieff, feoff, feud, zemindary, dependency.

free-, copy-, lease-holds; chattels real; fixtures, plant, heirloom easement; folkland; right of -common, – user.

personal -property, – estate, – effects; personalty, chattels, goods, effects, movables; stock, – in trade; things, traps, rattle-traps, para- phernalia; equipage &c. 633.

parcels, appurtenances.

impedimenta; lug-, bag-gage; bag and baggage; pelf; cargo, lading.

rent-roll; income &c. (*receipts*) 810.

patent, copyright; *chose* in action; credit &c. 805; debt &c. 806.

V. possess &c. 777; be the -possessor &c. 779- of· own; have for one's own, – very own; come in for, inherit; enfeoff.

savour of the realty.

be one's -property &c. *n.*; belong to; ap-, pertain to.

Adj. one's own; landed, predial, manorial, allodial, seigniorial; free-, copy-, lease-hold; feu-, feo-dal; hereditary, entailed, personal.

Adv. to one's -credit, – account; to the good.

to one and -his heirs for ever, – the heirs of his body, – his heirs and assigns, – his executors, administrators and assigns.

---

781. Retention.—N. retention; re- taining &c. *v.*; keep, detention, custody; tenacity, firm hold, grasp, gripe, grip, iron grip.

fangs, teeth, claws, talons, nail, hook, tentacle, *tenaculum*; bond &c. (*vincu- lum*) 45.

clutches, tongs, forceps, pincers, nippers, pliers, tweezers, vise.

paw, hand, finger, wrist, fist, neaf, neif.

bird in hand; captive &c. 754.

V. retain, keep; hold, – fast, – tight, – one's own, – one's ground; clinch, clench, clutch, grasp, gripe, hug, have a firm hold of.

secure, withold, detain; hold –, keep- back; keep close; husband &c. (*store*) 636; reserve; have –, keep- in stock &c. (*possess*) 777; entail, tie up, settle.

Adj. retaining &c. *v.*; retentive, tenacious.

unforfeited, undeprived, undisposed, uncommunicated.

incommunicable, inalienable; in mortmain; in strict settlement.

Phr. *uti possidetis.*

---

782. Relinquishment. — N. relin- quishment, abandonment &c. (*of a course*) 624; renunciation, expropria- tion, dereliction; cession, surrender, dispensation; resignation &c. 757; riddance.

derelict &c. *adj.*; jetsam; waif, foundling, orphan.

V. relinquish, give up, surrender, yield, cede; let -go, – slip; spare, drop, resign, forego, renounce, abjure, aban- don, expropriate, give away, dispose of, part with; lay -aside, – apart, – down, – on the shelf &c. (*disuse*) 678; set –, put- aside; make away with, cast be- hind; discard, cast off, dismiss; maroon.

give -notice to quit, – warning; super- sede; be –, get- -rid of, – quit of; eject &c. 297.

rid –, disburden –, divest –, dispos- sess- oneself of; wash one's hands of; divorce, desert; disinherit, cut off.

cast –, throw –, pitch –, fling- -away, – aside, – overboard, – to the dogs; cast –, throw –, sweep- to the winds; put –, turn –, sweep- away; jettison. quit one's hold.

Adj. relinquished &c. *v.*; cast off, derelict; unowned, unappropriated, unculled; left &c. (*residuary*) 40; divorced; disinherited.

Int. away with!

2°. *Transfer of Property*

783. Transfer.—N. transfer, conveyance, assignment, alienation, abalienation; demise, limitation; conveyancing; transmission &c. (*transference*) 270; enfeoffment, bargain and sale, lease and release; exchange &c. (*interchange*) 148; barter &c. 794; substitution &c. 147.

succession, reversion; shifting -use, – trust; devolution.

V. transfer, convey; alien, -ate; assign; grant &c. (*confer*) 784; consign; make –, hand- over; pass, hand, transmit, negotiate; hand down; exchange &c. (*interchange*) 148.

change -hands, – from one to another; devolve, succeed; come into possession &c. (*acquire*) 775; take over.

abalienate; disinherit; dispossess &c. 789; substitute &c. 147.

Adj. alienable, negotiable, transferable, reversional.

Phr. estate coming into possession.

784. Giving.—N. giving &c. *v.*; bestowal, donation; present-ation, -ment; accordance; con-, cession; delivery, consignment, dispensation, communication, endowment; invest-ment,-iture; award.

almsgiving, charity, liberality, generosity; philanthropy &c. 910.

[Thing given] gift, donation, present, *cadeau*; fairing; free gift, boon, favour, benefaction, grant, offering, oblation, sacrifice, immolation.

grace, act of grace, *bonus, bonanza*.

allowance, contribution, subscription, subsidy, tribute, subvention.

bequest, legacy, devise, will, dotation, appanage; dowry; voluntary -settlement, – conveyance &c. 783; amortization.

alms, largess, bounty, dole, sportule, donative, help, oblation, offertory, Peter's pence, *honorarium*, gratuity, Maundy money, Christmas box, Easter offering, vail, tip, *douceur*, drink money, *pourboire, trinkgeld, backsheesh*; fee &c. (*recompense*) 973; consideration.

bribe, bait, ground-bait; peace-offering, handsel.

giver, grantor &c. *v.*; donor, feoffer, settlor; almoner; testator; investor, subscriber, contributor; fairy godmother; Santa Claus, benefactor &c. 816.

V. deliver, hand, pass, put into the hands of; hand –, make –, deliver –, pass –, turn- over.

present, give away, dispense, dispose of; give –, deal –, dole –, mete –, fork –, shell –, squeeze- out.

pay &c. 807; render, impart, communicate.

785. Receiving.—N. receiving &c. *v.*; acquisition &c. 775; reception &c. (*introduction*) 296; suscipiency, acceptance, admission.

re-, ac-cipient; assignee, devisee; lega-tee, -tary; grantee, feoffee, donee, relessee, lessee.

sportulary, stipendiary; beneficiary; pension-er, -ary; almsman.

income &c. (*receipt*) 810.

V. receive; take &c. 789; acquire &c. 775; admit.

take in, catch, touch; pocket; put into one's -pocket, – purse; accept; take off one's hands.

be received; come -in, – to hand; pass –, fall- into one's hand; go into one's pocket; fall to one's -lot, – share; come –, fall- to one; accrue; have -given &c. 784 to one.

Adj. receiving &c. *v.*; re-, suscipient.

received &c. *v.*; given &c. 784; second-hand.

not given, unbestowed &c. (*see* give, bestow &c. 784).

concede, cede, yield, part with, shed cast; spend &c. 809.

give, bestow, confer, grant, accord, award, assign.

entrust, consign, vest in.

make a present; allow, contribute, subscribe, donate, furnish its quota.

invest, endow, settle upon; bequeath, leave, devise.

furnish, supply, help; ad-, minister to; afford, spare; accommodate –, indulge –, favour- with; shower down upon; lavish, pour on, thrust upon; tip, bribe; tickle –, grease- the palm; offer &c. 763; sacrifice, immolate.

Adj. giving &c. *v.*; given &c. *v.*; allow-ed, -able; concessional; communicable; charitable, eleemosynary, sportulary, tributary; *gratis* &c. 815.

786. Apportionment.—N. apportion-, allot-, consign-, assign-, appointment; appropriation; dis-pensation, -tribution; allocation, division, deal; repartition; administration.

dividend, portion, contingent, share, allotment, lot, cut, split, measure, dose; dole, meed, pittance; *quantum*, ration; ratio, proportion, quota, *modicum*, mess, allowance.

V. apportior., divide; cut, split, divvy; distribute, administer, dispense; billet, allot, detail, cast, share, mete; portion –, parcel –, dole- out; deal, carve.

partition, assign, appropriate, appoint.

come in for one's share &c. (*participate*) 778.

Adj. apportioning &c. *v.*; respective.

Adv. respectively, each to each.

787. Lending.—N. lending &c. *v.*; loan, advance, accommodation, feneration; mortgage &c. (*security*) 771; investment.

mont de piété, pawnshop, hock shop, spout, my uncle's.

lender, pawnbroker, money lender, usurer, Jew, Shylock.

V. lend, advance, loan, accommodate with; lend on security; pawn &c. (*security*) 771.

intrust, invest; place –, put- out to interest; sink, risk.

let, demise, lease, sett, under-, sub-let.

Adj. lending &c. *v.*; lent &c. *v.*; un-borrowed &c. (*see* borrowed &c. 788).

Adv. in advance; on -loan, – security.

788. Borrowing. — N. borrowing pledging, pawning.

borrowed plumes; plagiarism &c. (*thieving*) 791.

replevin.

V. borrow, desume; pawn.

hire, rent, farm; take a -lease, – demise; take –, hire- by the -hour, – mile, – year &c.

raise –, take up- money; float bonds; raise the wind; fly a kite, borrow of Peter to pay Paul; run into debt &c. (*debt*) 806.

make use of, plagiarize, pirate.

replevy.

789. Taking.—N. taking &c. *v.*; reception &c. (*taking in*) 296; deglutition &c. (*taking food*) 298; appropriation, prehension, prensation; capture, caption; ap-, de-prehension; abreption, seizure; ab-duction, -lation; subtraction &c. (*subduction*) 38; abstraction, a-demption.

790. Restitution.—N. restitution, return; ren-, red-dition; reinstatement, restoration; reinvestment, recuperation; repatriation; rehabilitation &c. (*reconstruction*) 660; reparation, atonement, indemnity, compensation, recompense.

release, replevin, redemption; recov-

dispossession; depriv-ation, -ement; bereavement; divestment; disherison; distraint, distress; sequestration, confiscation, attachment, execution; eviction &c. 297.

rapacity, extortion, vampirism, predacity, blood-sucking; theft &c. 791.

resumption; repris-e, -al; recovery &c. 775.

clutch, swoop, wrench; grip &c. (retention) 781; haul, take, catch; scramble.

taker, captor, capturer; vampire; extortioner.

V. take, catch, hook, nab, bag, sack, pocket, put into one's pocket, scrounge; receive; accept.

reap, crop, cull, pluck; gather &c. (get) 775; draw.

ap-, im-propriate; assume, possess oneself of; take possession of; commandeer; lay -, clap- one's hands on; help oneself to; make free with, dip one's hands into, lay under contribution; intercept; scramble for; deprive of.

take -, carry -, bear- -away, - off; abstract; hurry off -, run away- with; abduct; steal &c. 791; ravish; seize; pounce -, spring-upon; swoop -to, - down upon; take by -storm, - assault; snatch, reave.

snap up, nip up, whip up, catch up; kidnap, crimp, capture, lay violent hands on.

get -, lay -, take -, catch -, lay fast -, take firm- hold of; lay by the heels, take prisoner; fasten upon, grip, grapple, embrace, gripe, clasp, grab, clutch, collar, throttle, take by the throat, claw, clinch, clench, make sure of.

catch at, jump at, make a grab at, snap at, snatch at; reach, make a long arm, stretch forth one's hand.

take -from, - away from; deduct &c. 38; retrench &c. (curtail) 201; dispossess, ease one of, snatch from one's grasp; tear -, tear away -, wrench -, wrest -, wring- from; extort; deprive of, bereave; disinherit, cut off with a shilling.

oust &c. (eject) 297; divest; levy, distrain, confiscate; sequest-er, -rate, accroach; usurp; despoil, strip, fleece, shear, displume, impoverish, eat out of house and home; drain, - to the dregs; gut, dry, exhaust, swallow up; absorb &c. (suck in) 296; draw off; suck, - like a leech, - the blood of.

retake, resume; recover &c. 775.

Adj. taking &c. v.; privative, prehensile; pred-aceous, -al, -atory, -atorial; rap-acious, -torial; ravenous: parasitic; all-devouring, -engulfing.

bereft &c. 776.

Adv. at one fell swoop.

Phr. give an inch and take an ell.

ery &c. (getting back) 775; remitter, reversion.

V. return, restore; recondition; give -, carry -, bring- back; render, - up; give up; let go, unclutch; dis-, re-gorge; regurgitate; recoup, reimburse, repay, indemnify, reinvest, remit, rehabilitate; repair &c. (make good) 660.

redeem, recover &c. (get back) 775; take back again; revest, revert.

Adj. restoring &c. v.; recuperative &c. 660; in full restitution, to compensate for.

Phr. suum cuique.

---

791. Stealing.—N. stealing &c. v.; theft, thievery, robbery, latrociny, direption; abstraction, appropriation; plagiar-y, -ism; rape, kidnapping, depredation; raid, hold up.

spoliation, plunder, pillage; sack, -age; rapine, *brigandage*, highway robbery, foray, *razzia*; black-mail; piracy, privateering, buccaneering; filibuster-ing, -ism; burglary; house-breaking; cattle-stealing, -rustling, -lifting.

peculation, embezzlement; fraud &c. 545; larceny, petty larceny, pilfering, shop-lifting.

thievishness, rapacity, kleptomania, Alsatia; den of -Cacus, – thieves.

licence to plunder, letters of marque.

V. steal, thieve, rob, purloin, pilfer, filch, lift, prig, bag, nim, crib, cabbage, palm; abstract; appropriate, plagiarize.

convey away, carry off, abduct, kidnap, shanghai, impress, crimp; make –, walk –, run- off with; run away with; spirit away; seize &c. (*lay violent hands on*) 789.

plunder, pillage, rifle, sack, loot, ransack, spoil, spoliate, despoil, strip, sweep, gut, forage, levy black-mail, pirate, pickeer, maraud, lift cattle, rustle, poach, smuggle, run.

stick –, hold- up.

swindle, peculate, embezzle; sponge, mulct, rook, bilk, pluck, pigeon, skin, fleece, diddle; defraud &c. 545; obtain under false pretences; live by one's wits.

rob –, borrow of- Peter to pay Paul; set a thief to catch a thief.

disregard the distinction between *meum* and *tuum*.

Adj. thieving &c. *v.*; thievish, light-fingered; fur-acious, -tive; piratical; pred-aceous, -al, -atory, -atorial; raptorial &c. (*rapacious*) 789.

stolen &c. *v.*

Phr. *sic vos non vobis.*

792. Thief.—N. thief, robber, *homo trium literarum*, pilferer, rifler, filcher, plagiarist.

spoiler, depredator, pillager, marauder; harpy, shark, land-shark, falcon, moss-trooper, bushranger, Bedouin, brigand, freebooter, bandit, thug, dacoit, pirate, corsair, viking, Paul Jones; buccan-eer, -ier; piqu-, pick-eerer; rover, ranger, privateer, filibuster; rapparee, wrecker, picaroon; smuggler, poacher, plunderer; racketeer.

highwayman, Dick Turpin, Claude Duval, Macheath, knight of the road, footpad, sturdy beggar; abductor, kidnapper.

cut-, pick-purse; pick-pocket, light-fingered gentry; sharper; card-, skittle-sharper; crook; thimble-rigger; rook, Greek, blackleg, leg, welsher, defaulter; Autolycus, Cacus, Barabbas, Jeremy Diddler, Robert Macaire, artful dodger, trickster; swell mob, *chevalier d'industrie*; shop-lifter.

swindler, peculator; forger, coiner, counterfeiter, shoful; fence, receiver of stolen goods, duffer; smasher.

burglar, housebreaker; cracks-, mags-man; Bill Sikes, Jack Sheppard, Jonathan Wild, Raffles, cat burglar.

793. Booty.—N. booty, spoil, plunder, prize, loot, graft, swag, pickings, boodle; *spolia opima*, prey; blackmail; stolen goods.

Adj. looting &c. *n.*; manubial, spoliative.

3°. *Interchange of Property*

794. Barter.—N. barter, exchange, scorse, truck system; interchange &c. 148.

a Roland for an Oliver; *quid pro quo*; com-mutation, -position.

trade, commerce, mercature, buying and selling, bargain and sale; traffic, business, nundination, custom, shopping; commercial enterprise, speculation, jobbing, stock-jobbing, *agiotage*, brokery, arbitrage.

dealing, transaction, negotiation, bargain.

free trade.

V. barter, exchange, truck, scorse, swop; interchange &c. 148; commutate &c. (*substitute*) 147; compound for.

trade, traffic, buy and sell, give and take, nundinate; carry on -, ply -, drive- a trade; be in -business, - the city; keep a shop, deal in, employ one's capital in.

trade -, deal -, have dealings- with; transact -, do- business with; open -, keep- an account with.

bargain; drive -, make- a bargain; negotiate, bid for; dicker, haggle, higgle; chaffer, huckster, cheapen, beat down; stickle, - for; out-, under-bid; ask, charge; strike a bargain &c. (*contract*) 769.

speculate, give a sprat to catch a herring; buy in the cheapest and sell in the dearest market; rig the market.

Adj. commercial, mercantile, trading; interchangeable, marketable, staple, in the market, for sale.

wholesale, retail.

Adv. across the counter; on 'change.

795. Purchase.—N. purchase, emption; buying, purchasing, shopping; pre-emption, refusal.

coemption, bribery; slave trade.

buyer, purchaser, *emptor*, vendee; patron, employer, client, customer, *clientèle*.

V. buy, purchase, invest in, procure; rent &c. (*hire*) 788; repurchase, buy in.

keep in one's pay, bribe, suborn; pay &c. 807; spend &c. 809.

make -, complete- a purchase; buy over the counter; pay cash for.

shop, market, go a shopping.

Adj. purchased &c. *v.*

Phr. *caveat emptor.*

796. Sale.—N. sale, vent, disposal; auction, roup, Dutch auction; custom &c. (*traffic*) 794.

vendi-bility, -bleness.

seller, salesman; peddler, smous; vender, vendor, consignor; merchant &c. 797; auctioneer.

V. sell, vend, dispose of, effect a sale; sell -over the counter, - by auction &c. *n.*; dispense, retail; deal in &c. 794; sell -off, - out; turn into money; realize; bring -to, - under- the hammer; put up to auction; auction, offer -, put up- for sale; hawk, peddle, bring to market; offer &c. 763; undersell; dump, unload.

let; mortgage &c. (*security*) 771.

Adj. under the hammer, in the market, for sale.

saleable, marketable, vendible, in demand, having a ready sale; unsaleable &c., unpurchased, unbought; on one's hands.

97. Merchant.—N. merchant, trader, dealer, monger, chandler, salesman; changer; regrater; shop-keeper, -man; trades-man, -people, -folk.

retailer; chapman, hawker, huckster, higgler; peddler, smous, pedlar, *colporteur*, cadger, Autolycus; sutler, *vivandière*; coster-man, -monger; market woman; cheap jack; caterer &c. 637; tallyman.

money-broker, -changer, -lender; stock-broker, -jobber; cambist, usurer, moneyer, banker.

jobber; broker &c. (*agent*) 758; buyer &c. 795; seller &c. 796.

concern; firm &c. (*partnership*) 712.

798. Merchandise. — N. merchandise, ware, commodity, effects, goods, article, stock, produce, staple commodity; stock in trade &c. (*store*) 636; cargo &c. (*contents*) 190.

799. Mart.—N. mart; market, -place, *forum*; fair, bazaar, staple; stock –, exchange; 'change, *bourse*, Wall Street, Rialto, hall, guildhall; toll-booth, custom-house; Tattersalls.

shop, stall, booth; wharf; office, chambers, counting-house, *bureau*; coun-, comp-ter.

ware-house, -room; *dépôt*, interposit, *entrepôt*, *emporium*, establishment; store &c. 636.

open market, market-overt.

4°. *Monetary Relations*

800. Money.—N. money -matters, – market; finance; accounts &c. 811; funds, treasure; capital, stock; assets &c. (*property*) 780; wealth &c. 803; supplies, ways and means, wherewithal, sinews of war, almighty dollar, needful, cash.

sum, amount; balance, -sheet; sum total; proceeds &c. (*receipts*) 810.

currency, circulating medium, specie; coin, – of the realm; piece, hard cash, dollar, sterling coin; pounds shillings and pence; £ s. d., guineas; pocket, breeches pocket, purse; money in hand; the best, ready, – money; filthy lucre, shekels, roll, jack, rhino, blunt, dust, bawbees, brass, dibs, dough, mopus, tin, salt, chink, oof, spondulics, pile, wads.

precious metals, gold, silver, copper, nickel; bullion, bar, ingot, nugget.

petty cash; pocket-, pin-money; small –, change; small coin, loose cash; doit, stiver, rap, mite, farthing, *sou*, penny, shilling, bob, tanner, tester, groat, guinea, ducat; *rouleau*; *wampum*; good –, round –, lump-sum; power –, mint –, tons- of money; plum, lac of rupees, millions, money-bags, miser's hoard, stocking, mine of wealth &c. 803.

[Science of coins] numismatics, chrysology.

paper-money; money –, postal –, Post Office- order; note, – of hand; bank –, treasury- note; Bradbury; promissory note; I O U., bond; bill, – of exchange; draft, check, order, warrant, *coupon*, debenture, exchequer bill, *assignat*, greenback, gold –, silver- certificate.

copper, nickel, dime, quarter, two bits, half a dollar, dollar, buck, simoleon, fiver, tenner, a twenty, a sawbuck, a century, a grand; eagle, double eagle.

gold standard, bimetallism, fiat money; rate of –, exchange; in-, de-flation.

remittance &c. (*payment*) 807; credit &c. 805; liability &c. 806; solvency &c. 803.

draw-er, -ee; oblig-or, -ee; moneyer, coiner, counterfeiter, forger.

false –, bad- money; base –, counterfeit- coin, flash note, slip, kite; Bank of Elegance.

argumentum ad crumenam.

V. amount to, come to, mount up to; touch the pocket; draw, – upon; endorse &c. (*security*) 771; issue, utter, circulate; discount &c. 813.

forge, counterfeit, coin, circulate –, pass- bad money.

Adj. monetary, pecuniary, crumenal, fiscal, financial, sumptuary, numismatical; sterling; solvent &c. 803.

801. Treasurer.—**N.** treasurer; bursar, -y; purser, purse-bearer; cash-keeper, banker; depositary; questor, receiver, steward, trustee, chartered –, accountant; Accountant-General, almoner, liquidator, paymaster, cashier, teller; cambist; money-changer &c. (*merchant*) 797.

financier, Chancellor of the Exchequer, minister of finance; Secretary of the Treasury, Director of the Budget, Controller of Currency.

802. Treasury.—**N.** treasury, bank, exchequer, almonry, fisc, hanaper, bursary; safe; strong-box, -hold, -room; coffer; chest &c. (*receptacle*) 191; depository &c. 636; till, -er; cash-box, -register, purse, pocket-book, wallet; money-bag, -belt, -box; *porte-monnaie.*

purse-strings; pocket, breeches pocket.

sinking fund; stocks; government –, public –, parliamentary- -stocks, – funds, – securities, bonds; gilt-edged securities; Consols, Liberty bonds, government bonds, *crédit mobilier.*

803. Wealth.—**N.** wealth, riches, fortune, handsome fortune, opulence, affluence; good –, easy- circumstances; independence; competence &c. (*sufficiency*) 639; solvency, soundness, solidity.

provision, livelihood, maintenance; alimony, dowry; means, resources, substance; property &c. 780; command of money.

income &c. 810; capital, money; round sum &c. (*treasure*) 800; mint of money, mine of wealth, *El Dorado,* Pactolus, Golconda, Potosi, *bonanza;* philosopher's stone.

long –, full –, well lined –, heavy-purse; purse of Fortunatus.

pelf, Mammon, lucre, filthy lucre; loaves and fishes; fleshpots of Egypt.

rich –, moneyed –, warm- man; man of substance; capitalist, millionaire, Nabob, Crœsus, Midas, Plutus, Dives, Timon of Athens; Timo-, Pluto-cracy; Danaë.

V. be -rich &c. *adj.;* roll –, wallow-in -wealth, – riches; have money to burn.

afford, well afford; command -money, – a sum; make both ends meet, hold one's head above water.

become -rich &c. *adj.;* fill one's -pocket &c. (*treasury*) 802; feather one's nest, clean up –, make- a fortune; make money &c. (*acquire*) 775.

enrich, imburse.

worship -Mammon, – the golden calf.

Adj. wealthy, rich, affluent, opulent, moneyed, monied, worth -a great deal,

804. Poverty.—**N.** poverty, indigence, penury, pauperism, destitution, want; need, -iness; lack, necessity, privation, distress, difficulties, wolf at the door.

bad –, poor –, needy –, embarrassed –, reduced –, straitened- circumstances; slender –, narrow- means; straits; hand to mouth existence, *res angusta domi,* low water, impecuniosity.

beggary; mendi-cancy, -city; broken –, loss of- fortune; insolvency &c. (*non-payment*) 808.

empty -purse, – pocket; light purse; beggarly account of empty boxes.

poor man, pauper, mendicant, mumper, beggar, starveling; *pauvre diable.*

V. be -poor &c. *adj.;* want, lack, starve, live from hand to mouth, have seen better days, go down in the world, be on one's uppers, come upon the parish; go to -the dogs, – wrack and ruin; not have a -penny &c. (*money*) 800, – shot in one's locker; beg one's bread; *tirer le diable par la queue;* run into debt &c. (*debt*) 806.

render -poor &c. *adj.;* impoverish; reduce, – to poverty; pauperize, fleece, ruin, bring to the parish.

Adj. poor, indigent; poverty -stricken; badly –, poorly –, ill- off; poor as -a rat, – a church mouse, – Job's turkey, – Job; fortune-, dower-, money-, penni-less; unportioned, unmoneyed; impecunious; broke, flat; out –, short-of -money, – cash; without –, not worth- a rap &c. (*money*) 800; *qui n'a pas le sou,* out of pocket, hard up; out at

– much; well -to do, – off; warm; well –, provided for.

made of money; rich as Crœsus; rolling in -riches, – wealth.

flush, – of -cash, – money, – tin; in -funds, – cash, – full feather; solvent, solid, sound, pecunious, out of debt, all straight; able to pay 20s in the £.

Phr. one's ship coming in.

-elbows, – heels; seedy, bare-footed; beggar-ly, -ed; destitute; fleeced, strapped, stripped; bereft, bereaved; reduced.

in -want &c. *n.*; needy, necessitous, distressed, pinched, straitened; put to one's -shifts, – last shifts; unable to -keep the wolf from the door, – make both ends meet; embarrassed, under hatches; involved &c. (*in debt*) 806; insolvent &c. (*not paying*) 808.

Adv. *in formâ pauperis.*

Phr. *zonam perdidit.*

805. Credit.—N. credit, trust, tick, score, tally, account.

letter of credit, circular note; duplicate; mortgage, lien, debenture, paper credit, floating capital; draft; securities.

creditor, lender, lessor, mortgagee; dun; usurer.

V. keep –, run up- an account with; entrust, credit, accredit.

place to one's -credit, – account; give –, take- credit; fly a kite.

Adj. credit-ing, -ed; accredited.

Adv. on -credit &c. *n.*; to the -account, – credit- of.

806. Debt.—N. debt, obligation, liability, indebtment, debit, score.

arrears, deferred payment, deficit, default; insolvency &c. (*non-payment*) 808; bad debt.

interest; usance, usury; premium; floating -debt, – capital.

debtor, debitor; mortgagor; defaulter &c. 808; borrower.

V. be -in debt &c. *adj.*; owe; incur –, contract- a debt &c. *n.*; run up -a bill, – a score, – an account; go on tick, put on the cuff; borrow &c. 788; run –, get- into debt; outrun the constable.

answer –, go bail- for; back one's note.

Adj. indebted; liable, chargeable, answerable for.

in -debt, – embarrassed circumstances, – difficulties; incumbered, involved; involved –, plunged –, deep –, over head and ears- in debt; deeply involved; fast tied up; insolvent &c. (*not paying*) 808; *minus,* out of pocket.

unpaid; unrequieted, unrewarded; owing, due, in arrear, outstanding.

807. Payment.—N. pay-, defrayment; discharge; ac-, quittance; settlement, clearance, liquidation, satisfaction, reckoning, arrangement.

acknowledgment, release; receipt, – in full, – in full of all demands; voucher.

repayment, reimbursement, retribution; pay &c. (*reward*) 973; money paid &c. (*expenditure*) 809.

ready money &c. (*cash*) 800; stake, remittance, instalment.

payer, liquidator &c. 801.

V. pay, defray, make payment; pay -down, – on the nail, – ready money, – at sight, – in advance; cash, honour a bill, acknowledge; redeem; pay in kind.

808. Non-payment.—N. non-payment; default, defalcation; protest, repudiation; application of the sponge; whitewashing.

insolvency, bankruptcy, failure; overdraft, overdrawn account; insufficiency &c. 640; run upon a bank.

waste paper bonds; dishonoured –, protested- bills; bogus cheque.

bankrupt, insolvent debtor, lame duck, man of straw, welsher, stag, defaulter, absconder, levanter.

V. not -pay &c. 807; fail, break, stop payment; become -insolvent, – bankrupt; be gazetted.

protest, dishonour, repudiate, nullify.

pay under protest; button up one's

pay one's -way, – shot, – footing; pay -the piper, – sauce for all, – costs; do the needful; come across; shell –, fork- out; come down with, – the dust; tickle –, grease- the palm; expend &c. 809; put –, lay- down.

discharge, settle, quit, acquit oneself of; account –, reckon –, settle –, be even –, be quits- with; strike a balance; settle –, balance –, square- accounts with; quit scores; foot the bill; wipe –, clear- off old scores; satisfy; pay in full; satisfy –, pay in full of- all demands; clear, liquidate; pay -up, – old debts.

disgorge, make repayment; repay, refund, reimburse, retribute; make compensation &c. 30.

Adj. paying &c., paid &c. v.; owing nothing, out of debt, all straight, clear of -debt, – encumbrance; unowed, never indebted.

Adv. to the tune of; on the nail; money –, cash- down; cash on delivery.

pockets, draw the purse strings; apply the sponge; pay over the left shoulder, get whitewashed; swindle &c. 791; run up bills, fly kites.

Adj. not paying; in debt &c. 806; behindhand, in arrear; beggared &c. (*poor*) 804; unable to make both ends meet; *minus*; worse than nothing.

insolvent, bankrupt, in the gazette, gazetted, ruined.

unpaid &c. (*outstanding*) 806; *gratis* &c. 815; unremunerated.

---

809. Expenditure.—N. expenditure, money going out; out-goings, -lay; expenses, disbursement; prime cost &c. (*price*) 812; circulation; run upon a bank.

[Money paid] payment &c. 807; pay &c. (*remuneration*) 973; bribe &c. 973; fee, footing, garnish; subsidy; tribute, Peter's pence; contingent, quota; donation &c. 784.

pay in advance, earnest, handsel, deposit, instalment.

investment; purchase &c. 795.

V. expend, spend; run –, get- through; pay, disburse; open –, loose –, untie- the purse strings; lay –, shell –, fork- out; bleed; make up a sum, invest, sink money.

fee &c. (*reward*) 973; pay one's way &c. (*pay*) 807; subscribe &c. (*give*) 784; subsidize, bribe.

Adj. expend-ing, -ed &c. v.; sumptuary, liberal &c. 816; open-handed, lavish &c. 818; extensive &c. 814.

810. Receipt.—N. receipt, accountable –, conditional –, binding –, return-receipt; value received, money coming in; income, incomings, innings, revenue, return, proceeds; gross receipts, net profit; earnings &c. (*gain*) 775.

rent, – roll; rent-al, -age; rack-rent.

premium, *bonus*; sweepstakes, tontine,'prize, drawing.

pension, annuity; jointure &c. (*property*) 780; alimony, pittance; emolument &c. (*remuneration*) 973.

V. receive &c. 785; take money; draw –, derive- from; get, be in receipt of, acquire &c. 775; take &c. 789.

bring in, yield, afford, pay, return; accrue &c. (*be received from*) 785.

Adj. receiv-ing, -ed &c. v.; profitable &c. (*gainful*) 775.

---

811. Accounts.—N. accounts, accompts; commercial –, monetary- arithmetic; statistics &c. (*numeration*) 85; money matters, finance, budget, bill, score, reckoning, account.

books, account book, ledger; day –, cash –, pass- book; journal; debtor and creditor –, cash –, petty cash –, running- account; account-current; balance, – sheet; *compte rendu*, account settled.

book-keeping, audit; double –, single- entry; reckoning &c. 85.

chartered –, certified public –, accountant; auditor, actuary, book-keeper; financier &c. 801; accounting party.

V. keep accounts, enter, post, book, credit, debit, carry over; take stock; balance -, make up -, square -, settle -, wind up -, cast up -, add up -, tot up- accounts; make accounts square.

bring to book, audit, tax, surcharge and falsify.

falsify -, garble -, cook -, doctor- an account.

Adj. monetary &c. 800; account-able, -ing; statistical.

812. Price.—**N.** price, amount, cost, expense, prime cost, charge, figure, demand, damage, fare, hire; wages &c. (*remuneration*) 973.

dues, duty, toll, tax, impost, cess, sess, tallage, levy, capitation-, poll-, income-, sur-, sales-, super-tax; gabel, *gabelle*; gavel, *octroi*, custom, tariff, excise, assessment, taxation, benevolence, tithe, tenths, exactment, ransom, salvage; broker-, wharf-, lighter-, ton-, freight-age.

worth, rate, value, valuation, appraisement, money's worth, par value; penny &c. -worth; price current, market price, quotation; what it will -fetch &c. *v.*

bill &c. (*account*) 811; shot.

V. bear -, set -, fix- a price; appraise, assess, price, charge, demand, ask, require, exact, run up; distrain; run up a bill &c. (*debt*) 806; have one's price; liquidate.

amount to, come to, mount up to; stand one in.

fetch, sell for, cost, bring in, yield, afford.

Adj. priced &c. *v.*; to the tune of, *ad valorem*; mercenary, venal.

Phr. no penny. no paternoster; *point d'argent, point de Suisse*, no longer pipe, no longer dance, no song, no supper.

one may have it for.

813. Discount.—**N.** discount, abatement, concession, reduction, depreciation, allowance, qualification, set off, drawback, poundage, *agio*, percentage; rebate, -ment; backwardation, contango; salvage; tare and tret.

V. discount, bate; a-, re-bate; deduct, reduce, mark down, take off, allow, give, make allowance; tax, depreciate.

Adj. discounting &c. *v.*

Adv. at a discount, below par.

814. Dearness. — **N.** dearness &c. *adj.*; high -, famine -, fancy- price; overcharge; extravagance; exorbitance, extortion; heavy pull upon the purse; Pyrrhic victory.

V. be -dear &c. *adj.*; cost -much, - a pretty penny; rise in price, look up.

overcharge, bleed, fleece, skin, extort.

pay -too much, - through the nose, - too dear for one's whistle.

Adj. dear; high, -priced; of great price, expensive, costly, precious, worth a Jew's eye, dear bought; unreasonable, extravagant, exorbitant, extortionate.

at a premium; not to be had, - for love or money; beyond -, above- price; priceless, of priceless value.

Adv. dear, -ly; at great -, heavy-cost; *à grands frais*.

Phr. prices looking up; *le jeu ne vaut pas la chandelle*.

815. Cheapness.—**N.** cheapness, low price; depreciation; bargain; good penny &c.- worth, *bon marché*.

[Absence of charge] gratuity; free -quarters, - seats, - admission, - warren; pass, Annie Oakley; run of one's teeth; nominal price, peppercorn rent; labour of love.

drug in the market.

V. be -cheap &c. *adj.*; cost little; come down -, fall- in price.

buy for -a mere nothing, - an old song; have one's money's worth; cheapen, beat down.

Adj. cheap; low, - priced; moderate, reasonable; in-, un-expensive; well -, worth the money; *magnifique et pas cher*; good -, cheap- at the price; dirt -, dog- cheap; cheap, -as dirt, - and nasty; catchpenny.

reduced, marked down, half-price, depreciated, unsaleable.

gratuitous, *gratis*, free, for love,

– nothing; cost-, expense-less; without charge, not charged, un-taxed; scot –, shot –, rent- free; free of -cost, – expense; honor-ary, unbought, unpaid, complimentary.

Adv. for a mere song; at -cost price, – prime cost, – a reduction, – a bargain; on the cheap.

816. Liberality.—N. liberality, gener-osity, munificence; bount-y, -eousness, -ifulness; hospitality; charity &c. (*be-neficence*) 906.

benefactor, free giver, Lady Bounti-ful.

V. be -liberal &c. *adj.*; spend –, bleed- freely; shower down upon; open one's purse strings &c. (*disburse*) 809; spare no expense, give -with both hands, – *carte blanche.*

Adj. liberal, free, generous; charit-able &c. (*beneficent*) 906; hospitable; bount-iful, -eous; handsome; unspar-ing, ungrudging; open-, free-, full-handed; open-, large-, free-hearted; munificent, princely, unstinting.

overpaid.

Adv. liberally, ungrudgingly, with open hand.

---

818. Prodigality.—N. prodi-gality, -gence; unthriftiness, waste, -fulness; profus-ion, -eness; extravagance; squan-dering &c. *v.*; lavishness; malversation.

prodigal; spend-, waste-thrift; losel, play-boy, spender, squanderer, locust.

V. be -prodigal &c. *adj.*; squander, lavish, sow broadcast; pour forth like water; pay through the nose &c. (*dear*) 814; spill, waste, dissipate, exhaust, drain, eat out of house and home, overdraw, outrun the constable; run -out, – through; misspend; throw -good money after bad, – the helve after the hatchet; burn the candle at both ends; make ducks and drakes of one's money; squander one's substance, spend money like water; fool –, potter –, muddle –, fritter –, throw- away one's money; pour water into a sieve, kill the goose that lays the golden eggs; *manger son blé en herbe.*

Adj. prodigal, profuse, thriftless, un-thrifty, improvident, wasteful, losel,

817. Economy.—N. economy, fru-gality; thrift, -iness; prudence, care, husbandry, good housewifery, saving-ness, retrenchment.

savings; prevention of waste, save-all; cheese parings and candle ends; parsimony &c. 819.

V. be -economical &c. *adj.*; econo-mize, save; retrench; cut- down ex-penses, – one's coat according to one's cloth, make both ends meet, keep within compass, meet one's expenses, pay one's way; keep one's head above water; husband &c. (*lay by*) 636; save –, invest- money; put out to interest; provide –, save- -for, – against- a rainy day; feather one's nest; look after the main chance.

Adj. economical, frugal, careful, thrifty, saving, chary, spare, sparing; parsimonious &c. 819.

underpaid.

Adv. sparingly &c. *adj.*; *ne quid nimis.*

819. Parsimony. — N. parsimony, parcity; parsimoniousness, stinginess &c. *adj.*; stint; illiberality, avarice, tenacity, avidity, rapacity, extortion, venality, cupidity; selfishness &c. 943; *auri sacra fames.*

miser, niggard, churl, screw, tight-wad, skinflint, crib, codger, muckworm, money-grubber, pinchfist, scrimp, lick-penny, hunks, curmudgeon, *Harpagon*, Silas Marner, harpy, extortioner, Jew, usurer.

V. be -parsimonious &c. *adj.*; grudge, begrudge, stint, skimp, pinch, gripe, screw, dole out, hold back, withhold, starve, famish, live upon nothing, skin a flint.

drive a -bargain, – hard bargain; cheapen, beat down; stop one hole in a sieve; have an itching palm, grasp, grab.

Adj. parsimonious, penurious, stingy, miserly, mean, shabby, peddling, scrubby, pennywise, near, niggardly,

extravagant, lavish, dissipated, over liberal; full-handed &c. (*liberal*) 816.

penny wise and pound foolish.

Adv. with an unsparing hand; money burning one's pocket; recklessly profuse.

Int. hang the expense!

----

frugal to excess; close; fast-, close-, strait-handed; close-, hard-, tight-fisted; tight, sparing; chary; grudging, griping &c. *v.*; illiberal, ungenerous, churlish, hidebound, sordid, mercenary, venal, covetous, usurious, avaricious, greedy, extortionate, rapacious.

Adv. with a sparing hand.

CLASS VI

Words relating to the SENTIENT and MORAL POWERS.

CLASS VI

WORDS RELATING TO THE SENTIENT AND MORAL POWERS.

~~~~~~~~

SECTION I. AFFECTIONS IN GENERAL

820. Affections.—N. affections, character, qualities, disposition, nature, spirit, tone; temper, -ament; *diathesis*, idiosyncrasy; cast –, habit –, frame- of -mind, – soul; predilection, turn; natural –, turn of mind; bent, bias, predisposition, proneness, proclivity; propen-sity, -sedness, -sion, -dency; vein, humour, mood, grain, mettle; sympathy &c. (*love*) 897.

soul, heart, breast, bosom, inner man; heart's -core, – strings, – blood; heart of hearts, *penetralia mentis*; secret and inmost recesses of the –, cockles of one's- heart; inmost -heart, – soul; back-bone.

passion, pervading spirit; ruling –, master- passion; *furore*; fulness of the heart, heyday of the blood, flesh and blood, flow of soul, force of character.

V. have –, possess- -affections &c. *n.*; be of a -character &c. *n.*; be -affected &c. *adj.*; breathe.

Adj. affected, characterized, formed, moulded, cast; at-, tempered; framed; pre-, disposed; prone, inclined; having a -bias &c. *n.*; tinctured –, imbued –, penetrated –, eaten up- with.

inborn, inbred, ingrained, in the grain, congenital, inherent, bred in the bone; deep-rooted, ineffaceable, inveterate; pathoscopic.

Adv. in one's -heart &c. *n.*; at heart; heart and soul &c. 821; in the -vein, – mood.

821. Feeling.—N. feeling; suffering &c. *v.*; endurance, tolerance, sufferance, supportance, experience, response; sympathy &c. (*love*) 897; impression, inspiration, affection, sensation, emotion, pathos, deep sense.

fire, warmth, glow, unction, *gusto*, vehemence; ferv-our, -ency; heartiness, cordiality; earnestness, eagerness; *empressement*, ardour, zeal, passion, enthusiasm, *verve*, *furore*, fanaticism; excitation of feeling &c. 824; fulness of the heart &c. (*disposition*) 820; passion &c. (*state of excitability*) 825; ecstasy &c. (*pleasure*) 827.

blush, suffusion, flush; hectic; tingling, thrill, kick, turn, shock; agitation &c. (*irregular motion*) 315; quiver, heaving, flutter, flurry, fluster, twitter, tremor; throb, -bing; pulsation, palpitation, painting; trepid-, perturb-ation; ruffle, hurry of spirits, pother, stew, ferment.

V. feel; receive an -impression &c. *n.*; be -impressed with &c. *adj.*; entertain –, harbour –, cherish- -feeling &c. *n.*

respond; catch the -flame, – infection; enter the spirit of.

bear, suffer, support, sustain, endure, brook, thole, aby; abide &c.

(*be composed*) 826; experience &c. (*meet with*) 151; taste, prove; labour
–, smart- under; bear the brunt of, brave, stand.

swell, glow, warm, flush, blush, change colour, mantle; turn -colour,
– pale, – red, – black in the face; blench, crimson, whiten, pale, tingle,
thrill, heave, pant, throb, palpitate, go pit-a-pat, tremble, quiver,
flutter, twitter; stagger, reel; shake &c. 315; be -agitated, – excited
&c. 824; look -blue, – black; wince, draw a deep breath.

impress &c. (*excite the feelings*) 824.

Adj. feeling &c. *v.*; sentient; sensuous; sensor-ial, -y; emo-tive,
-tional; of –, with- feeling &c. *n.*

warm, quick, lively, smart, strong, sharp, acute, cutting, piercing,
incisive; keen, – as a razor; trenchant, pungent, racy, *piquant*, poignant, caustic.

impressive, deep, profound, indelible; deep-, home-, heart-felt;
swelling, soul-stirring, deep-mouthed, heart-expanding, electric, thrilling, rapturous, ecstatic.

earnest, wistful, eager, breathless; fer-vent, -vid; gushing, passionate, warmhearted, hearty, cordial, sincere, zealous, enthusiastic, glowing, ardent, burning, red-hot, fiery, flaming; boiling, – over.

pervading, penetrating, absorbing; rabid, raving, feverish, fanatical,
hysterical; impetuous &c. (*excitable*) 825; overmastering.

impressed –, moved –, touched –, affected –, penetrated –, seized –,
imbued &c. 820- with; devoured by; wrought up &c. (*excited*) 824;
struck all of a heap; rapt; in a -quiver &c. *n.*; enraptured &c. 829.

Adv. heart and soul, from the bottom of one's heart, *ab imo pectore*,
de profundis, at heart, *con amore*, heartily, devoutly, over head and ears.

Phr. the heart -big, – full, – swelling, – beating, – pulsating, – throbbing, – thumping, – beating high, – melting, – overflowing, – bursting,
– breaking.

822. Sensibility. — N. sensi-bility,
-bleness, -tiveness; moral sensibility;
impress-, affect-ibility; suscepti-ble-
ness, -bility, -vity; mobility; viva-city,
-ciousness; tender-, soft-ness; senti-
mental-ity, -ism.

excitability &c. 825; fastidiousness
&c. 868; physical sensibility &c. 375.

sore -point, – place; where the shoe
pinches.

V. be -sensible &c. *adj.*; have a
-tender, – warm, – sensitive- heart.

take to –, treasure up in the- heart;
shrink.

'die of a rose in aromatic pain';
touch to the quick.

Adj. sensi-ble, -tive; impressi-ble,
-onable; suscepti-ve, -ble; alive to,
impassion-able, -ed; gushing; warm-,
tender-, soft-hearted; tender –, as a
chicken; soft, sentimental, romantic;
enthusiastic, highflying, spirited, mettlesome, vivacious, lively, expressive,
mobile, tremblingly alive; excitable

823. Insensibility.—N. insensi-bility,
-bleness; moral insensibility; inertness,
inertia, *vis inertiæ*; impassi-bility,
-bleness; inappetency, apathy, phlegm,
dulness, hebetude, supineness, lukewarmness, insusceptibility, unimpress-
ibility.

cold -fit, – blood, – heart; cold-,
cool-ness; frigidity, *sang-froid*; stoicism,
imperturbation &c. (*inexcitability*) 826;
nonchalance, unconcern, dry eyes;
insouciance &c. (*indifference*) 866;
recklessness &c. 863; callousness; heart
of stone, stock and stone, marble,
deadness.

torp-or, -idity; obstupefaction, lethargy, coma, trance; sleep &c. 683;
suspended animation; stup-or, -efac-
tion; paralysis, palsy; numbness &c.
(*physical insensibility*) 376.

neutrality; quietism, vegetation.

V. be -insensible &c. *adj.*; have a
rhinoceros hide; show -insensibility
&c. *n.*; not -mind, – care, – be affected

&c. 825; over-sensitive, without skin, thin-skinned; fastidious &c. 868.

Adv. sensibly &c. *adj.*; to the -quick, - inmost core.

———————

by; have no desire for &c. 866; have -, feel -, take- no interest in; *nil admirari*; not care a -straw &c. (*unimportance*) 643 for; disregard &c. (*neglect*) 460; set at naught &c. (*make light of*) 483; turn a deaf ear to &c. (*inattention*) 458; vegetate.

render -insensible, - callous; blunt, obtund, numb, benumb, paralyze, chloroform, deaden, hebetate, stun, stupefy; brut-ify, -alize.

inure; harden, - the heart; steel, case-harden, sear.

Adj. insensible, unconscious; impassi-ve, -ble; blind to, deaf to, dead to; un-, in-susceptible; unimpress-ionable, -ible; passion-, spirit-, heart-, soul-less; unfeeling, unmoral.

apathetic; leuco-, phlegmatic; dull, frigid; cold, -blooded, -hearted; unemotional; cold as charity; flat, obtuse, inert, supine, sluggish, torpid; sleepy &c. (*inactive*) 683; languid, half-hearted, tame; numb, -ed; comatose; anæsthetic &c. 376; stupefied, chloroformed, palsy-stricken.

indifferent, lukewarm; Laodicean; careless, mindless, regardless; inattentive &c. 458; neglectful &c. 460; disregarding.

unconcerned, *nonchalant, pococurante, insouciant, sans souci*; un-ambitious &c. 866.

un-affected, -ruffled, -impressed, -inspired, -excited, -moved, -stirred, -touched, -shocked, -struck; unblushing &c. (*shameless*) 885; unanimated; vegetative.

callous, thick-skinned, pachydermatous, impervious; hard, -ened; inured, case-hardened; steeled -, proof- against; imperturbable &c. (*inexcitable*) 826; unfelt.

Adv. insensibly &c. *adj.*; *æquo animo*; without being -moved, - touched, - impressed; in cold blood; with -dry eyes, - withers unwrung.

Phr. never mind; it is of no consequence &c. (*unimportant*) 643; it cannot be helped; nothing coming amiss; it is all -the same, - one- to.

824. Excitation.—N. excitation of feeling; mental -, excitement; suscitation, galvanism, stimulation, piquancy, provocation, inspiration, calling forth, infection; interest, animation, agitation, perturbation; subjugation, fascination, intoxication; en-, ravishment; entrancement, high pressure.

unction, impressiveness &c. *adj.*; emotional appeal; melodrama; psychological moment, crisis; sensationalism.

trial of temper, *casus belli*; irritation &c. (*anger*) 900; passion &c. (*state of excitability*) 825; thrill &c. (*feeling*) 821; repression of feeling &c. 826.

V. excite, affect, touch, move, impress, strike, interest, intrigue, animate, inspire, impassion, smite, infect; stir -, fire -, warm- the blood; set astir; a-, wake; a-, waken; call forth; e-, pro-voke; raise up, summon up, call up, wake up, blow up, get up, light up; raise; get up steam, rouse, arouse, stir, fire, kindle, enkindle, apply the torch, set on fire, inflame, illuminate.

stimulate; ex-, suscitate; inspirit; spirit up, stir up, work up; infuse life into, give new life to; bring -, introduce- new blood; quicken;

sharpen, whet; work upon &c. (*incite*) 615; hurry on, give a fillip, put on one's mettle.

fan the -fire, – flame; blow the coals, stir the embers; fan, – into a flame; foster, heat, warm, foment, raise to a fever heat; keep -up, – the pot boiling; revive, rekindle; rake up, rip up.

stir –, play on –, come home to- the feelings; touch -a string, – a chord, – the soul, – the heart; go to one's heart, penetrate, pierce, go through one, touch to the quick, open the wound; possess –, pervade –, penetrate –, imbrue –, absorb –, affect –, disturb- the soul.

absorb, rivet the attention; sink into the -mind, – heart; prey on the mind; intoxicate; over-whelm, -power; *bouleverser*, upset, turn one's head.

fascinate; enrapture &c. (*give pleasure*) 829.

agitate, perturb, ruffle, fluster, flutter, shake, disturb, faze, startle, shock, stagger; give one a -shock, – turn; strike -dumb, – all of a heap; stun, astound, electrify, galvanize, petrify.

irritate, sting; cut, – to the -heart, – quick; try one's temper; fool to the top of one's bent, pique; infuriate, madden, make one's blood boil; lash into fury &c. (*wrath*) 900.

be -excited &c. *adj.*; flash up, flare up; catch the infection; thrill &c. (*feel*) 821; mantle; work oneself up; seethe, boil, simmer, foam, fume, flame, rage, rave; run mad &c. (*passion*) 825.

Adj. excited &c. *v.*; wrought up, on the *qui vive*, astir, sparkling; in a -quiver &c. 821, – fever, – ferment, – blaze, – state of excitement; in hysterics; black in the face, over-wrought; hot, red-hot, flushed, feverish; all -of a twitter, – of a flutter, – of a dither, – in a pucker; with -quivering lips, – tears in one's eyes.

flaming; boiling, – over; ebullient, seething; foaming, – at the mouth; fuming, raging, carried away by passion, wild, raving, frantic, mad, distracted, distraught, beside oneself, out of one's wits, amuck, ready to burst, *bouleversé*, demoniacal.

lost, *éperdu*, tempest-tossed; haggard; ready to sink.

stung to the quick, up, on one's high ropes.

exciting &c. *v.*; impressive, warm, glowing, fervid, swelling, imposing, spirit-stirring, thrilling; high-wrought; soul-stirring, -subduing; heart-swelling, -thrilling; agonizing &c. (*painful*) 830; telling, sensational, melodramatic, hysterical; over-powering, -whelming; more than flesh and blood can bear.

piquant &c. (*pungent*) 392; spicy, appetizing, provocative, *provoquant*, tantalizing.

Adv. till one is black in the face.

Phr. the heart -beating high, – going pit-a-pat, – leaping into one's mouth; the blood -being up, – boiling in one's veins; the eye -glistening, – 'in a fine frenzy rolling'; the head turned.

---

825. [Excess of sensitiveness.] **Excitability.—N.** excitability, impetuosity, vehemence; boisterousness &c. *adj.*; turbulence; impatience, intolerance, non-endurance; irritability &c. (*irascibility*) 901; itching &c. (*desire*) 865; wincing; disquiet, -ude; restlessness; fidge-ts, -tiness; agitation &c. (*irregular motion*) 315.

826. [Absence of excitability, or of excitement.] **Inexcitability.—N.** inexcit-, imperturb-, inirrit-ability; even temper, tranquil mind, dispassion; tolerance, toleration, patience.

passiveness &c. (*physical inertness*) 172; hebet-ude, -ation; impassibility &c. (*insensibility*) 823; stupefaction.

coolness, calmness &c. *adj.*; compo-

trepidation, perturbation, ruffle, hurry, -skurry, fuss, flurry; fluster, flutter; pother, stew, ferment; whirl; thrill &c. (*feeling*) 821; state –, fever- of excitement; transport.

passion, excitement, flush, heat; fever, -heat; fire, flame, fume, blood boiling; tumult; effervescence, ebulli- tion; boiling, – over; whiff, gust, storm, tempest; scene, breaking out, burst, fit, paroxysm, explosion; out-break, -burst; agony.

violence &c. 173; fierceness &c. *adj.*; rage, fury, *furor, furore,* desperation, madness, distraction, raving, delirium, brain storm; frenzy, hysterics; intoxi- cation; tearing –, raging- passion, towering rage; anger &c. 900.

fascination, infatuation, fanaticism; Quixot-ism, -ry; *tête montée.*

V. be -impatient &c. *adj.*; not be able to -bear &c. 826; bear ill, wince, chafe, champ the bit; be in a -stew &c. *n.*; be out of all patience, fidget, fuss, not have a wink of sleep; toss, – on one's pillow.

lose one's temper &c. 900; break –, burst –, fly- out; go –, fly- -off, – off the handle, – off at a tangent; explode; flare up, flame up, fire up, burst into a flame, take fire, fire, burn; boil, – over; foam, fume, rage, rave, rant, tear; go –, run- -wild, – mad; go into hysterics; run -riot, – amuck; *battre la campagne, faire le diable à quatre,* play the deuce; raise -Cain, – the devil.

Adj. excitable, easily excited, in an excitable state; highly strung; irritable &c. (*irascible*) 901; impatient, intol- erant.

feverish, febrile, hysterical; delirious, mad, moody, maggoty-headed.

unquiet, mercurial, electric, galvanic, hasty, hurried, restless, fidgety, fussy; chafing &c. *v.*

startlish, mettlesome, high mettled, skittish.

vehement, demonstrative, violent, wild, furious, fierce, fiery, hot-headed, mad-cap.

over-zealous, enthusiastic, impas- sioned, fanatical; rabid &c. (*eager*) 865.

rampant, clamorous, uproarious, tur-

sure, placidity, indisturbance, imper- turbation, *sang-froid,* tranquillity, se- renity; quiet, -ude; peace of mind, mental calmness.

staidness &c. *adj.*; gravity, sobriety, Quakerism; philosophy, equanimity, stoicism, command of temper; self- possession, -control, -command, -re- straint; presence of mind.

submission &c. 725; resignation; suffer-, support-, endur-, long-suffer-, forbear-ance; longanimity; fortitude; patience -of Job, – 'on a monument,' – 'sovereign o'er transmuted ill'; moder- ation; repression –, subjugation- of feeling; restraint &c. 751.

tranquillization &c. (*moderation*) 174.

V. be -composed &c. *adj.*

laisser -faire, – *aller;* take things -easily, – as they come; take it easy, run on, live and let live; take -easily, – coolly, – in good part; *æquam serva e mentem.*

bear, – well, – the brunt; go through, support, endure, brave, disregard.

tolerate, suffer, stand, bide; abide, aby; bear –, put up –, abide- with; acquiesce; submit &c. (*yield*) 725; submit with a good grace; resign –, reconcile- oneself to; brook, digest, eat, swallow, pocket, stomach; make -light of, – the best of, – a virtue of necessity; put a good face on, keep one's countenance; carry -on, – through; check &c. 751- oneself.

compose, appease &c. (*moderate*) 174; propitiate; repress &c. (*restrain*) 751; render insensible &c. 823; over- come –, allay –, repress- one's -excit- ability &c. 825; master one's feelings.

make -oneself, – one's mind- easy; set one's mind at -ease, – rest.

calm –, cool- down; thaw, grow cool.

be -borne, – endured; go down.

Adj. in-, un-excitable; imperturbable; unsusceptible &c. (*insensible*) 823; un-, dis-passionate; cold-blooded, inirri- table; enduring &c. *v.*; stoical, Platonic, philosophic, staid, stayed; sober, – minded; grave; sober –, grave- as a judge; sedate, demure, cool-, level- headed; steady.

easy-going, peaceful, placid, calm; quiet, – as a mouse; tranquil, serene;

bulent, tempestuous, tumultuary, boisterous.

impulsive, impetuous, passionate; uncontroll-ed, -able; ungovernable, irrepressible, stanchless, inextinguishable, burning, simmering, volcanic, ready to burst forth.

excit-ed, -ing &c. 824.

Int. pish! pshaw!

Phr. *noli me tangere.*

cool, – as -a cucumber, – custard; undemonstrative.

temperate &c. (*moderate*) 174; composed, collected; un-excited, -stirred, -ruffled, -disturbed, -perturbed, -impassioned; unoffended; unresisting.

meek, tolerant; patient, – as Job; submissive &c. 725; tame; content, resigned, chastened, subdued, lamb-like; gentle, – as a lamb; *suaviter in modo*; mild, – as mother's milk; soft as peppermint; armed with patience, bearing with, clement, forbearant, long-suffering.

Adv. 'like patience on a monument smiling at grief'; *æquo animo*, in cold blood &c. 823; more in sorrow than in anger.

Int. patience! and shuffle the cards.

Section II. PERSONAL AFFECTIONS*
1°. Passive Affections

827. Pleasure.—N. pleasure, gratification, enjoyment, fruition; ob-, delectation; relish, zest; *gusto* &c. (*physical pleasure*) 377; satisfaction &c. (*content*) 831; complacency.

well-being; good &c. 618; snugness, comfort, ease; cushion &c. 215; *sans souci*, mind at ease.

joy, gladness, delight, glee, cheer, sunshine; cheerfulness &c. 836.

treat, refreshment; frolic, fun, lark, gambol, merry-making; amusement &c. 840; luxury &c. 377; hedonism.

mens sana in corpore sano.

happiness, felicity, bliss; beati-tude, -fication; enchantment, transport, rapture, ravishment, ecstasy; *summum bonum*; paradise, elysium &c. (*heaven*) 981; third –, seventh- heaven; unalloyed -happiness &c.

honeymoon; palmy –, halcyon- days; golden -age, – time; *Saturnia regna*, Eden, Arcadia, happy valley, Agapemone; Cockaigne.

V. be pleased &c. 829; feel –, experience- pleasure &c. *n.*; joy; enjoy –, hug- oneself; be in -clover &c. 377, – elysium &c. 981; tread on enchanted ground; fall –, go- into raptures.

feel at home, breathe freely, bask in the sunshine.

be -pleased &c. 829- with; receive –, derive- pleasure &c. *n.*- from; take -pleasure &c. *n.*- in; delight in, rejoice

828. Pain. — N. mental suffering, pain, dolour; suffer-ing, -ance; ache, smart &c. (*physical pain*) 378; passion.

displeasure, dissatisfaction, discomfort, discomposure, disquiet; *malaise*; inquietude, uneasiness, vexation of spirit; taking; discontent &c. 832.

dejection &c. 837; weariness &c. 841.

annoyance, irritation, worry, infliction, visitation; plague, bore; bother, -ation; stew, vexation, mortification, chagrin, *esclandre*; *mauvais quart d'heure.*

care, anxiety, solicitude, trouble, trial, ordeal, fiery ordeal, shock, blow, cark, dole, fret, burden, load.

concern, grief, sorrow, distress, affliction, woe, bitterness, gloom, heartache; heavy –, aching –, bleeding –, broken-heart; heavy affliction, gnawing grief. unhappiness, infelicity, misery, tribulation, wretchedness, desolation; despair &c. 859; extremity, prostration, depth of misery.

nightmare, *ephialtes*, incubus.

anguish, agony; throe, tor-ture, -ment; crucifixion, martyrdom; pang, twinge, stab; the rack, the stake; purgatory &c. (*hell*) 982.

hell upon earth; iron age, reign of terror; slough of despond &c. (*adversity*) 735; peck –, sea- of troubles; ills that flesh is heir to &c. (*evil*) 619;

* Or those which concern one's own state of feeling.

in, indulge in, luxuriate in; gloat over &c. (*physical pleasure*) 377; enjoy, relish, like; love &c. 897; take -to, – a fancy to; have a liking for; enter into the spirit of.

take in good part.

treat oneself to, solace oneself with.

Adj. pleased &c. 829; not sorry; glad, -some; pleased as Punch.

happy, blest, blessed, blissful, beatified; happy as -a king, – the day is long; thrice happy, *ter quaterque beatus*; enjoying &c. *v.*; joyful &c. (*in spirits*) 836; hedonic.

in -a blissful state, – paradise &c. 981, – raptures, – ecstasies, – a transport of delight.

comfortable &c. (*physical pleasure*) 377; at ease; content &c. 831; *sans souci*, in clover.

overjoyed, entranced, enchanted; enraptured; en-, ravished; transported; fascinated, captivated.

with -a joyful face, – sparkling eyes.

pleasing &c. 829; ecstatic, beat-ic, -ific; painless, unalloyed, without alloy, cloudless.

Adv. happily &c. *adj.*; with pleasure &c. (*willingly*) 60; with -glee &c. *n.*

Phr. one's heart leaping with joy.

---

miseries of human life; unkindest cut of all.

sufferer, victim, prey, martyr, object of compassion, wretch, shorn lamb.

V. feel –, suffer –, experience –, undergo –, bear –, endure- pain &c. *n.*; smart, ache &c. (*physical pain*) 378; suffer, bleed, ail; be the victim of; bear –, take up- the cross.

labour under afflictions; quaff the bitter cup, have a bad time of it; fall on evil days &c. (*adversity*) 735; go hard with, come to grief, fall a sacrifice to, drain the cup of misery to the dregs, sup full of horrors.

sit on thorns, be on pins and needles, wince, fret, chafe, worry oneself, be in a taking, fret and fume, take -on, – to heart.

grieve; mourn &c. (*lament*) 839; yearn, repine, pine, droop, languish, sink; give way; despair &c. 859; break one's heart; weigh upon the heart &c. (*inflict pain*) 830.

Adj. in –, in a state of –, full of- pain &c. *n.*; suffering &c. *v.*; pained, afflicted, worried, displeased &c. 830; aching, griped, sore &c. (*physical pain*) 378; on the rack, in limbo; between hawk and buzzard.

un-comfortable, -easy; ill at ease; in a -taking, – way; disturbed; discontented &c. 832; out of humour &c. 901a; weary &c. 841.

heavy laden, stricken, crushed, a prey to, victimized, ill-used.

unfortunate &c. (*hapless*) 735; to be pitied, doomed, devoted, accursed, undone, lost, stranded.

unhappy, infelicitous, poor, wretched, miserable, woe-begone; cheerless &c. (*dejected*) 837; careworn.

concerned, sorry; sorrow-ing, -ful; cut up, chagrined, horrified, horror-stricken; in –, plunged in –, a prey to- grief &c. *n.*; in tears &c. (*lamenting*) 839; steeped to the lips in misery; heart-stricken, -broken, -scalded; broken-hearted; in despair &c. 859.

Phr. 'the iron entered into our soul'; '*hæret lateri lethalis arundo*'; one's heart bleeding.

---

829. [Capability of giving pleasure; cause or source of pleasure.] **Pleasurableness.**—**N.** pleasurable-, pleasant-, agreeable-ness &c. *adj.*; pleasure giving, jocundity, delectability; amusement &c. 840.

attraction &c. (*motive*) 615; attractiveness, -ability; invitingness &c. *adj.*; charm, fascination, captivation, en-

830. [Capability of giving pain; cause or source of pain.] **Painfulness.** —**N.** painfulness &c. *adj.*; trouble, care &c. (*pain*) 828; trial; af-, in-fliction; cross, blow, stroke, burden, load, curse; bitter -pill, – draught, – cup; waters of bitterness.

annoyance, grievance, nuisance, vexation, mortification, sickener; bore,

chantment, witchery, seduction, winsomeness, winning ways, amenity, amiability, sweetness.

loveliness &c. (*beauty*) 845; sunny –, bright- side; sweets &c. (*sugar*) 396; goodness &c. 648; manna in the wilderness, land flowing with milk and honey.

treat; regale &c. (*physical pleasure*) 377; dainty; tit-, tid-bit; nuts, *sauce piquante*.

V. cause –, produce –, create –, give –, afford –, procure –, offer –, present –, yield- pleasure &c. 827.

please, charm, delight; gladden &c. (*make cheerful*) 836; take, captivate, fascinate; enchant, entrance, enrapture, transport, bewitch; en-, ravish.

bless, beatify; satisfy; gratify, – desire &c. 865; slake, satiate, quench; indulge, humour, flatter, tickle; tickle the palate &c. (*savoury*) 394; regale, refresh; enliven; treat; amuse &c. 840; take –, tickle –, hit- one's fancy; meet one's wishes; win –, gladden –, rejoice –, warm the cockles of- the heart; do one's heart good.

attract, allure &c. (*move*) 615; stimulate &c. (*excite*) 824; interest, intrigue.

make things pleasant, popularize, gild the pill, sweeten.

Adj. causing pleasure &c. *v.*; pleasure-giving; pleas-ing, -ant, -urable; agreeable, cushy; grat-eful, -ifying; leef, lief, acceptable; welcome, – as the roses in May; welcomed; favourite; to one's -taste, – mind, – liking, – heart's content; satisfactory &c. (*good*) 648.

refreshing; comfortable; cordial; genial; glad, -some; sweet, delectable, nice, dainty; delic-ate, -ious; dulcet; luscious &c. 396; palatable &c. 394; luxurious, voluptuous; sensual &c. 377.

attractive &c. 615; inviting, prepossessing, engaging; win-ning, -some; taking, fascinating, captivating, killing; seduc-ing, -tive; alluring, enticing; appetizing &c. (*exciting*) 824; cheering &c. 836; bewitching; interesting, absorbing, enchanting, entrancing, enravishing.

charming; delightful, felicitous, exquisite; lovely &c. (*beautiful*) 845;

bother, pother, hot water, sea of troubles, hornet's nest, plague, pest.

cancer, ulcer, sting, thorn; canker &c. (*bane*) 663; scorpion &c. (*evil-doer*) 913; dagger &c. (*arms*) 727; scourge &c. (*instrument of punishment*) 975; carking –, canker worm of- care.

mishap, misfortune &c. (*adversity*) 735; désagrément, esclandre, rub.

source of -irritation, – annoyance; wound, sore subject, skeleton in the closet; thorn in -the flesh, – one's side; where the shoe pinches, gall and wormwood.

sorry sight, heavy news, provocation; affront &c. 929; head and front of one's offending.

infestation, molestation; malignity &c. (*malevolence*) 907.

V. cause –, occasion –, give –, bring –, induce –, produce –, create –, inflict-pain &c. 828; pain, hurt, wound.

pinch, prick, gripe &c. (*physical pain*) 378; pierce, lancinate, cut.

hurt –, wound –, grate upon –, jar upon- the feelings; wring –, pierce –, lacerate –, break –, rend- the heart; make the heart bleed; tear –, rend-the heart-strings; draw tears from the eyes.

sadden; make -unhappy &c. 828; plunge into sorrow, grieve, fash, afflict, distress; cut -up, – to the heart.

displease, annoy, incommode, discommode, discompose, trouble, disquiet, disturb, thwart, cross, perplex, molest, tease, rag, tire, irk, vex, mortify, wherret, worry, plague, bother, pester, bore, pother, harass, harry, badger, heckle, bait, beset, infest, persecute, importune, be troublesome.

wring, harrow, torment, torture; put to the -rack, – question; break on the wheel, rack, scarify; cruci-ate, -fy; convulse, agonize; barb the dart; plant a -dagger in the breast, – thorn in one's side.

irritate, provoke, sting, nettle, try the patience, pique, fret, rile, tweak the nose, chafe, gall; sting –, wound –, cut- to the quick; aggrieve, affront, enchafe, enrage, ruffle, sour the temper; give offence &c. (*resentment*) 900.

ravishing, rapturous; heartfelt, thrilling, ecstatic; beat-ic, -ific; seraphic;
empyrean; elysian &c. (*heavenly*) 981.
palmy, halcyon, Saturnian.

Phr. *decies repetita placebit.*

————————

maltreat, bite, snap at, assail, bully;
smite &c. (*punish*) 972.

sicken, disgust, revolt, nauseate, disenchant, repel, offend, shock, stink in
the nostrils; go against -, turn- the
stomach; make one sick, set the teeth
on edge, go against the grain, grate on
the ear; stick in one's -throat, - gizzard;
rankle, gnaw, corrode, horrify, appal,
freeze the blood; chill the spine; make
the -flesh creep, - hair stand on end;
make the blood -curdle, - run cold; make one shudder.

haunt, - the memory; weigh -, prey- on the -heart, - mind,
- spirits; bring one's grey hairs with sorrow to the grave; add a
nail to one's coffin.

Adj. causing pain, hurting &c. *v.*; hurtful &c. (*bad*) 649; painful;
dolor-ific, -ous; unpleasant; un-, dis-pleasing; disagreeable, unpalatable, bitter, distasteful; uninviting; unwelcome; undesir-able, -ed;
obnoxious; unacceptable, unpopular, thankless.

unsatisfactory, untoward, unlucky, uncomfortable.

distressing; afflict-ing, -ive; joy-, cheer-, comfort-less; dismal,
disheartening; depress-ing, -ive; dreary, melancholy, grievous,
piteous; woeful, rueful, mournful, deplorable, pitiable, lamentable;
sad, affecting, touching, pathetic.

irritating, provoking, stinging, annoying, aggravating, mortify-
ing, galling; unaccommodating, invidious, vexatious; trouble-,
tire-, irk-, weari-some; plagu-ing, -y; awkward.

importunate; teas-, pester-, bother-, harass-, worry-, torment-,
cark-ing.

in-toler-, -suffer-, -support-able; un-bear-, -endur-able; past bearing; not to be -borne, - endured; more than flesh and blood can
bear; enough to -drive one mad, - provoke a saint, - make a parson
swear, - try the patience of Job.

shocking, terrific, grim, appalling, crushing; dreadful, fearful,
frightful; thrilling, tremendous, dire; heart-breaking, -rending,
-wounding, -corroding, -sickening; harrowing, rending.

odious, hateful, execrable, repulsive, repellent, abhorrent; horri-d,
-ble, -fic, -fying; offensive; nause-ous, -ating; disgust-, sicken-,
revolt-ing; nasty; loath-some, -ful; fulsome; vile &c. (*bad*) 649;
hideous &c. 846.

sharp, acute, sore, severe, grave, hard, harsh, cruel, biting, acrimonious, caustic; cutting, corroding, consuming, racking, excruciating, searching, searing, grinding, grating, agonizing; envenomed.

ruinous, disastrous, calamitous, tragical; desolating, withering;
burdensome, onerous, oppressive; cumb-rous, -ersome.

Adv. painfully &c. *adj.*; with -pain &c. 828; deuced.

Int. *hinc illæ lachrymæ!* woe is me!

Phr. *surgit amari aliquid*; the place being too hot to hold one;
the iron entering into the soul.

————————

831. Content.—N. content, -ment,
-edness; complacency, satisfaction, entire satisfaction, ease, heart's ease,
peace of mind; serenity &c. 826; cheer-

832. Discontent. — N. discontent,
-ment; dissatisfaction; dissent &c. 489;
labour unrest.

disappointment, mortification; cold

fulness &c. 836; ray of comfort; comfort &c. (*well-being*) 827.

re-, conciliation; resignation &c. (*patience*) 826.

waiter on Providence.

V. be -content &c. *adj.*; rest -satisfied, – and be thankful; take the good the gods provide, let well alone, feel oneself at home, hug oneself, lay the flattering unction to one's soul.

take -up with, – in good part; assent &c. 488; be reconciled to, make one's peace with; get over it; take -heart, – comfort; put up with &c. (*bear*) 826.

render -content &c. *adj.*; set at ease, comfort; set one's -heart, – mind- at -ease, – rest; speak peace; conciliate, reconcile, win over, propitiate, disarm, beguile; content, satisfy; gratify &c. 829.

be -tolerated &c. 826; go down, – with; do.

Adj. content, -ed; satisfied &c. *v.*; at -ease, – one's ease, – home; with the mind at ease, *sans souci, sine curâ*, easy-going, not particular; conciliatory; unrepining, of good comfort; resigned &c. (*patient*) 826; cheerful &c. 836.

un-afflicted, -vexed, -molested, -plagued; serene &c. 826; at rest; snug, comfortable; in one's element.

satisfactory, satisfying, ample, sufficient, adequate, tolerable.

Adv. to one's heart's content; *à la bonne heure*; all for the best.

Int. amen &c. (*assent*) 488; very well, so much the better, well and good; it –, that- will do; it cannot be helped.

Phr. nothing comes amiss.

comfort; regret &c. 833; repining, taking on &c. *v.*; inquietude, vexation of spirit, soreness; heart-burning, -grief; querulousness &c. (*lamentation*) 839; hypercriticism.

malcontent, grumbler, growler, croaker, *laudator temporis acti*; censurer, complainer, faultfinder, murmurer, Adullamite, Diehard, Bitterender.

the Opposition, cave of Adullam, indignation meeting, 'winter of our discontent.'

V. be -discontented &c. *adj.*; quarrel with one's bread and butter; repine; regret &c. 833; wish one at the bottom of the Red Sea; take -on, – to heart; shrug the shoulders; make a wry –, pull a long- face; knit one's brows; look -blue, – black, – black as thunder, – blank, – glum.

take -in bad part, – ill; fret, chafe, make a piece of work; grumble, croak, grouse; lament &c. 839.

cause -discontent &c. *n.*; dissatisfy, disappoint, mortify, put out, disconcert; cut up; dishearten.

Adj. discontented; dissatisfied &c. *v.*; unsatisfied, ungratified; dissident; dissentient &c. 489; malcontent, exigent, exacting, hypercritical.

repining &c. *v.*; regretful &c. 833; down in the mouth &c. (*dejected*) 837.

in -high dudgeon, – a fume, – the sulks, – the dumps, – bad humour; glum, sulky; sour, – as a crab; soured, sore; out of -humour, – temper.

disappointing &c. *v.*; unsatisfactory.

Int. so much the worse!

Phr. that –, it- will never do.

833. Regret.—N. regret, repining; home sickness, nostalgia; *mal –, maladie-du pays*; lamentation &c. 839, contrition, compunction, penitence &c. 950.

bitterness, heart-burning.

laudator temporis acti &c. (*discontent*) 832.

V. regret, deplore; bewail &c. (*lament*) 839; repine, cast a longing lingering look behind; rue, – the day; repent &c. 950; *infandum renovare dolorem.*

prey –, weigh –, have a weight- on the mind; leave an aching void.

Adj. regretting &c. *v.*; regretful; home-sick.

regretted &c. *v.*; much to be regretted, regrettable; lamentable &c. (*bad*) 649.

Int. what a pity! hang it!
Phr. 'tis -pity, – too true.

834. Relief.—**N.** relief; deliverance; refreshment &c. 689; easement, softening, alleviation, mitigation, palliation &c. 174; soothing, lullaby; cradle song, *berceuse.*

solace, consolation, comfort, encouragement.

lenitive, restorative &c. (*remedy*) 662; poultice &c. *v.*; cushion &c. 215; crumb of comfort, balm in Gilead; aspirin.

V. relieve, ease, alleviate, mitigate, palliate, soothe, addulce; salve; soften, – down; foment, stupe, poultice; assuage, allay.

cheer, comfort, console; encourage, bear up, pat on the back, give comfort, set at ease; enliven, gladden –, cheer- the heart.

remedy; cure &c. (*restore*) 660; refresh; pour -balm into, – oil on.

smooth the ruffled brow of care, temper the wind to the shorn lamb, lay the flattering unction to one's soul.

disburden &c. (*free*) 705; take off a load of care.

be relieved; breathe more freely, draw a long breath; take comfort; dry –, wipe- the -tears, – eyes.

Adj. relieving &c. *v.*; consolatory, soothing; assua-ging, -sive; bal-my, -samic; lenitive, palliative; anodyne &c. (*remedial*) 662; curative &c. 660.

835. Aggravation.—**N.** aggravation, heightening; exacerbation; exasperation; overestimation &c. 482; exaggeration &c. 549.

V. aggravate, render worse, heighten, embitter, sour; ex-, acerbate; exasperate, envenom; tease, provoke, enrage.

add fuel to the -fire, – flame; fan the flame &c. (*excite*) 824; go from bad to worse &c. (*deteriorate*) 659.

Adj. aggravated &c. *v.*; worse, unrelieved; aggravable; aggravating &c. *v.*

Adv. out of the frying pan into the fire, from bad to worse, worse and worse.

Int. so much the worse!

---

836. Cheerfulness.—**N.** cheerfulness &c. *adj.*; geniality, gaiety, *l'allegro,* cheer, good humour, spirits; high –, animal –, flow of- spirits; glee, high glee, light heart; sunshine of the -mind, – breast; *gaieté de cœur, bon naturel.*

liveliness &c. *adj.*; life, alacrity, vivacity, animation, *allégresse*; jocundity, joviality, jollity; levity; jocularity &c. (*wit*) 842.

mirth, merriment, hilarity, exhilaration; laughter &c. 838; merry-making &c. (*amusement*) 840; heyday, rejoicing &c. 838; marriage bells.

nepenthe, Euphrosyne.

optimism &c. (*hopefulness*) 858; self-complacency.

V. be -cheerful &c. *adj.*; have the ... at ease, smile, put a good face ... keep up one's spirits; view -the ... ide of the picture, – things *en ... le rose*; *ridentem dicere verum,*

837. Dejection.—**N.** dejection; dejectedness &c. *adj.*; depression, prosternation; lowness –, depression- of spirits; weight –, oppression –, damp- on the spirits; low –, bad –, drooping –, depressed- spirits; heart sinking; heaviness –, failure- of heart.

heaviness &c. *adj.*; infestivity, gloom; weariness &c. 841; tædium vitæ, disgust of life; *mal du pays* &c. (*regret*) 833.

melancholy; sadness &c. *adj.*; *il penseroso, melancholia,* dismals, mumps, mopes, lachrymals, dumps, blues, blue devils, doldrums, vapours, megrims, spleen, horrors, hypochondriasis, pessimism; despondency, slough of Despond; disconsolateness &c. *adj.*; hope deferred, blank despondency.

prostration, – of soul; broken heart; despair &c. 859; cave of -despair, – Trophonius.

cheer up, brighten up, light up, bear up; chirp, take heart, cast away care, drive dull care away, perk up.

rejoice &c. 838; carol, chirrup, lilt; frisk, rollick, give a loose to mirth.

cheer, enliven, elate, exhilarate, gladden, inspirit, animate, raise the spirits, inspire; put in good humour; cheer -, rejoice- the heart; delight &c. (*give pleasure*) 829.

Adj. cheerful; happy &c. 827; cheery, -ly; of good cheer, smiling; blithe; in -, in good- spirits; in high -spirits, - feather; happy as -the day is long, - a king; gay, - as a lark; *allegro*; light, -some, -hearted; buoyant, *débonnaire*, bright, free and easy, airy; janty, jaunty, canty; spright-ly, -ful; spry; spirit-ed, -ful; lively; animated, breezy, vivacious; brisk, - as a bee; sparkling; sportive; full of -play, - spirit; all alive.

sunny, palmy; hopeful &c. 858.

merry, - as a -cricket, - grig, - marriage bell; joyful, joyous, jocund, jovial; jolly, - as a thrush, - as a sandboy; blithesome; glee-ful, -some; hilarious, rattling.

winsome, bonny, hearty, buxom.

play-ful, -some; *folâtre*, playful as a kitten, tricksy, frisky, frolicsome; gamesome; jocose, jocular, waggish; mirth-, laughter-loving; mirthful, rollicking.

elate, -d; exulting, jubilant, flushed; rejoicing &c. 838; cock-a-hoop.

cheering, inspiriting, exhilarating; cardiac, -al; pleasing &c. 829; flourishing, halcyon.

Adv. cheerfully &c. *adj.*

Int. never say die! come! cheer up! hurrah! &c. 838; 'hence loathed melancholy!' begone dull care! away with melancholy!

demureness &c. *adj.*; gravity, solemnity; long -, grave- face.

hypochondriac, seek-sorrow, self-tormentor, *heautontimorumenos*, *malade imaginaire*, *médecin tant pis*; croaker, pessimist; mope, mopus.

[Cause of dejection] affliction &c. 830; sorry sight; *memento mori*; damper, wet blanket, Job's comforter; death's head, skeleton at the feast.

V. be -dejected &c. *adj.*; grieve; mourn &c. (*lament*) 839; take on, give way, lose heart, despond, droop, sink.

lower, look downcast, frown, pout; hang down the head; pull -, make- a long face; laugh on the wrong side of the mouth; grin a ghastly smile; look -blue, - like a drowned man; lay -, take- to heart.

mope, brood over; fret; sulk; pine, - away; yearn; repine &c. (*regret*) 833; despair &c. 859.

refrain from laughter, keep one's countenance; be -, look- grave &c. *adj.*; repress a smile, keep a straight face.

depress; dis-courage, -hearten; dispirit; damp, dull, deject, lower, sink, dash, knock down, unman, prostrate, break one's heart; frown upon; cast a -gloom, - shade- on; sadden; damp -, dash -, wither- one's hopes; weigh -, lie heavy -, prey- on the -mind, - spirits; damp -, depress- the spirits.

Adj. cheer-, joy-, spirit-less; uncheerful, -y; unlively; unhappy &c. 828; melancholy, dismal, sombre, dark, gloomy, adust, *triste*, clouded, murky, lowering, frowning, lugubrious, Acherontic, funereal, mournful, lamentable, dreadful.

dreary, flat; dull, - as -a beetle, - ditchwater; depressing &c. *v.*

'melancholy as a gib cat'; oppressed with -, a prey to- melancholy; downcast, -hearted; down -in the mouth, - on one's luck; heavy-hearted; in the -dumps, - suds, - sulks, - doldrums; in doleful dumps, in bad humour; sullen; mumpish, dumpish; mopish, moping; moody, glum; sulky &c. (*discontented*) 832; out of -sorts, - humour, - heart, - spirits; ill at ease, low-spirited, in low spirits, a cup too low; weary &c. 841; dis-couraged, -heartened; desponding; chop-, jaw-, crest-fallen.

sad, pensive, *penseroso*, tristful; dole-some, -ful; woebegone, lachrymose, in tears, melancholic, hypped, hypochondriacal, bilious, jaundiced, atrabilious, saturnine, splenetic; lackadaisical.

serious, sedate, staid, stayed; grave, – as -a judge, – an undertaker, – a mustard pot; sober, solemn, demure; grim; grim-faced, -visaged; rueful, wan, long-faced.

disconsolate; un-, in-consolable; forlorn, comfortless, desolate, désolé, sick at heart; soul-, heart-sick; au désespoir; in despair &c. 859; lost.

overcome; broken-, borne-, bowed-down; heart-stricken &c. (mental suffering) 828; cut up, dashed, sunk; unnerved, unmanned; down-fallen, -trodden; broken-hearted; care-worn.

Adv. with -a long face, – tears in one's eyes; sadly &c. adj.

Phr. the countenance falling; the heart -failing, – sinking within-one.

838. [Expression of pleasure.] **Re-joicing.**—**N.** rejoicing, exultation, triumph, jubilation, heyday, flush, revelling; merry-making &c. (amusement) 840; jubilee &c. (celebration) 883; pæan, Te Deum &c. (thanksgiving) 990; congratulation &c. 896; applause &c. 971.

smile, simper, smirk, grin; broad –, sardonic- grin.

laughter, giggle, titter, crow, cheer, chuckle, snicker, snigger, shout; Homeric laughter, horse –, hearty- laugh; guffaw; burst –, fit –, shout –, roar –, peal- of laughter; cachinnation.

risibility; derision &c. 856.

Momus; Democritus the Abderite; rollicker; Laughter holding both his sides.

V. rejoice; thank –, bless- one's stars; congratulate –, hug- oneself; rub –, clap- one's hands; smack the lips, fling up one's cap; dance, skip, caleer; sing, carol, chirrup, chirp; hurrah; cry for –, leap with- joy; exult &c. (boast) 884; triumph; hold jubilee &c. (celebrate) 883; make merry &c. (sport) 840; sing a pæan of joy.

smile, simper, smirk; grin, – like a Cheshire cat; mock, laugh in one's sleeve; laugh, – outright; giggle, titter, snigger, crow, smicker, chuckle, snicker, cackle; burst -out, – into a fit of laughter; shout, split, roar.

shake –, split –, hold both- one's sides; roar –, die- with laughter.

raise laughter &c. (amuse) 840.

Adj. rejoicing &c. v.; jubilant, exultant, triumphant; flushed, elated; laughing &c. v.; risible; ready to -burst, – split, – die with laughter; convulsed with laughter.

839. [Expression of pain.] **Lamentation.**—**N.** lament, -ation; wail, complaint, plaint, murmur, mutter, grumble, groan, moan, whine, whimper, sob, sigh, suspiration, heaving, deep sigh.

cry &c. (vociferation) 411; scream, howl; outcry, wail of woe, frown, scowl.

tear; weeping &c. v.; flood of tears, fit of crying, lachrymation, melting mood, weeping and gnashing of teeth.

plaintiveness &c. adj.; languishment; condolence &c. 915.

mourning, weeds, willow, cypress, crêpe, crape, deep mourning; sackcloth and ashes; knell &c. 363; dump, death-song, dirge, coronach, keen, nenia, requiem, elegy, epicedium; threne; mon-, thren-ody; jeremiad; ululation.

mourner, professional mourner, keener; grumbler &c. (discontent) 832; Niobe; Heraclitus.

V. lament, mourn, deplore, grieve, weep over; be-wail, -moan; keen; condole with &c. 915; fret &c. (suffer) 828; wear –, go into –, put on- mourning; wear -the willow, – sackcloth and ashes; infandum renovare dolorem &c. (regret) 833; give sorrow words.

sigh; give –, heave –, fetch- a sigh; 'waft a sigh from Indus to the pole'; sigh 'like furnace'; wail.

cry, weep, sob, greet, blubber, pipe, snivel, bibber, whimper, pule; pipe one's eye; drop –, shed- -tears, – a tear; melt –, burst- into tears; fondre en larmes; cry -oneself blind, – one's eyes out.

scream &c. (cry out) 411; mew &c. (animal sounds) 412; groan, moan,

laughable &c. (*ludicrous*) 853.

Int. hip, hip, -hurrah! huzza! aha! hail! tolderolloll! tra-la la! Heaven be praised! *io triumphe! tant mieux!* so much the better.

Phr. the heart leaping with joy.

whine, yammer; roar; roar –, bellow-like a bull; cry out lustily, rend the air, yell.

frown, scowl, make a wry face, grimace, gnash one's teeth, wring one's hands, tear one's hair, beat one's breast, roll on the ground, burst with grief.

complain, murmur, mutter, grumble, growl, clamour, make a fuss about, croak, grunt, maunder; deprecate &c. (*disapprove*) 932.

cry out before one is hurt, complain without cause.

Adj. lamenting &c. *v.*; in mourning, in sackcloth and ashes; crying, sorrowing, -ful &c. (*unhappy*) 828; mourn-, tear-ful; lachrymose; plaint-ive, -ful, quer-ulous, -imonious; in the melting mood.

in tears, with tears in one's eyes; with -moistened, – watery-eyes; bathed –, dissolved- in tears; 'like Niobe all tears.'

elagiac, epicedial, threnetic.

Adv. *de profundis; les larmes aux yeux.*

Int. heigh-ho! alas! alack! O dear! ah –, woe is- me! lackadaisy! well –, lack –, alack- a day! well-a-way! alas the day! *O tempora! O mores!* what a pity! *miserabile dictu!* O lud lud! too true!

Phr. tears -standing in, – starting from- the eyes; eyes -suffused, – swimming, – brimming –, overflowing- with tears.

---

840. Amusement.—N. amuse-, entertain-ment; diver-sion, -tissement; reaction, relaxation, solace; pastime, *passetemps*, sport; labour of love; pleasure &c. 827.

fun, frolic, merriment, whoopee, jollity; jovial-ity, -ness; heyday; laughter &c. 838; jocos-ity, -eness; droll-, buffoon-, tomfool-ery; mummery, masquing, pleasantry; wit &c. 842; quip, quirk.

play; game, – at romps; gambol, romp, prank, antic, rig, lark, spree, skylarking, vagary, trick, monkey trick, *gambade, fredaine, escapade, échappée,* bout, *espièglerie;* practical joke &c. (*ridicule*) 856.

dance; round –, square –, solo –, step –, tap –, clog –, skirt –, sand –, folk –, morris- dance, *pas seul,* step, turn, *chassé,* cut, shuffle, double shuffle; hop, reel, rigadoon, saraband, hornpipe, bolero, fandango, pavan, tarantella, minuet, waltz, polka; galop, -ade; Schottische, *pas de quatre,* Boston, one-, two-step, rumba, tango, maxixe, fox-, turkey-trot, shimmy, ragtime, cakewalk, jazz, blues, Charleston; jig, breakdown, fling, strathspey; *alle-*

841. Weariness.—N. weariness, defatigation, boredom, *ennui;* lassitude &c. (*fatigue*) 688; drowsiness &c. 683.

disgust, nausea, loathing, sickness; satiety &c. 869; *tædium vitæ* &c. (*dejection*) 837.

wearisome-, tedious-ness &c. *adj.*; dull work, tedium, monotony, twice told tale.

bore, button-hole, proser, wet blanket; heavy hours, 'the enemy' [time].

V. weary; tire &c. (*fatigue*) 688; bore; bore –, weary –, tire- -to death, – out of one's life, – out of all patience; set –, send- to sleep.

pall, sicken, nauseate, disgust.

harp on the same string; drag its -slow, – weary- length along.

never hear the last of; be -tired &c. *adj.* -of, – with; yawn; die with *ennui.*

Adj. wearying &c. *v.*; wearing; weari-, tire-, irk-some; uninteresting, stupid, bald, devoid of interest, dry, monotonous, dull, arid, tedious, humdrum, mortal, flat; pros-y, -ing; slow; soporific, somniferous, dormitive.

disgusting &c. *v.*; unenjoyed.

weary; tired &c. *v.*; drowsy &c. (*sleepy*) 683; uninterested, flagging,

mande; gavot, -te; mazurka, morisco; quadrille, lancers, country dance, *cotillon*, polonaise, Sir Roger de Coverley, Swedish dance; *ballet* &c. (*drama*) 599; ball; *bal, – masqué, – costumé*; masquerade, fancy dress ball; *thé dansant*; Terpsichore, choreography, Russian ballet, classical dancing; eurythmics; nautch dance, *danse du ventre*, cancan.

festivity, merry-making; party &c. (*social gathering*) 892; *fête*, festival, gala, *ridotto*; revel-s, -ry, -ling; carnival, brawl, saturnalia, high jinks; feast, banquet &c. (*food*) 298; regale, *symposium*, wassail; carous-e, -al; jollification, junket, wake, pic-nic, *fête champêtre*, garden party, gymkhana, regatta, track meet, field-day, jamboree, treat.

round of pleasures, dissipation, a short life and a merry one, racketing, holiday making, high jinks.

rejoicing &c. 838; jubilee &c. (*celebration*) 883.

bonfire, fireworks, *feu-de-joie*, rocket, catherine wheel, roman candle &c.

holiday; gala –, red letter –, play- day; high days and holidays; high –, Bank- holiday; May –, Derby- day; Saint –, Easter –, Whit- Monday; King's birthday, Empire Day; *mi-carême*; *Bairam*; wayzgoose, bean feast, beano.

place of amusement, theatre &c. 599; concert-, ball-, assembly-room; music-hall, cinema, movies, talkies, vaudeville; hippodrome, circus, rodeo; *casino, kursaal*; winter garden; park, pleasance, arbour; garden &c. 371; pleasure-, play-, cricket-, football-, polo-, croquet-, archery-, hunting-ground; golf links, race course, stadium, gridiron, bowl, speedway, racing track, ring; gymnasium, swimming pool; shooting gallery; tennis-, racket-court; bowling-green, -alley; croquet-lawn, rink, skating rink; roller-coaster, roundabout, carousel, merry-go-round; swing; *montagne russe*; switchback, scenic railway &c.

game, – of -chance, – skill; athletic sports, gymnastics; fencing; archery, rifle-shooting; tournament, pugilism &c. (*contention*) 720; sporting &c. 622; horse-racing, the turf; aquatics &c. 267; skating, roller skating; ski-running, -joring, -jumping, bobsleighing, luging, tobogganing, winter sports; sliding; cricket, tennis, lawn –, table –, deck- tennis, rackets, fives, squash, ping pong, trap bat and ball, battledore and shuttlecock, badminton, *la grâce*; pall mall, tip-cat, croquet, golf, curling, hockey, basketball, soccer, football, Rugby, Association, *pallone*, polo; tent-pegging, tilting at the ring, quintain, greasy pole; quoits, *discus*; throwing the hammer, putting the -weight, – shot, tossing the caber; knurr and spell; leap-frog, hop, skip and jump; French and English, tug of war; blind man's buff, hunt the slipper, hide-and-seek, kiss in the ring; snapdragon; cross questions and crooked answers; jig-saw puzzle; rounders, base-ball, *la crosse* &c.; angling; swimming, diving, water-polo.

billiards, pool, pyramids, snooker, bagatelle; bowls, skittles, ninepins, kail, American bowls.

cards; bridge, auction, contract, whist, rubber; round game, coon-can, loo, cribbage, *bésique*, pinocle, euchre, drole, *écarté*, skat, picquet, all-fours, quadrille, ombre, reverse, Pope Joan, commit;

used up, worn out, *blasé*, life-weary, weary of life; sick of.

Adv. wearily &c. *adj.*; *usque ad nauseam.*

Phr. time hanging heavily on one's hands; *toujours perdrix; crambe repetita.*

bo-, boa-ston; *vingt-et-un*; *quinze*, thirty-one, put-and-take, speculation, connections, brag, cassino, lottery, commerce, snip-snap-snorem, lift smoke, blind hookey, Polish bank, poker, banker; faro; Earl of Coventry, Napoleon, nap, patience, pairs; old maid, fright, beggar-my-neighbour; *baccarat, chemin de fer, monté, roulette.*

chess, draughts, backgammon, dominoes, checkers, mah jong, merelles, nine men's morris, go-bang, solitaire; game of –, fox and-goose; loto; &c.*

morra; gambling &c. (*chance*) 621.

toy, plaything, bauble; doll &c. (*puppet*) 554; teetotum; knick-knack &c. (*trifle*) 643; magic lantern &c. (*show*) 448; peep-, puppet-, raree-, gallanty-show; marionettes, Punch and Judy; toy-shop; 'quips and cranks and wanton wiles, nods and becks and wreathed smiles.'

sportsman, gamester, gambler &c. 621; reveller, master of the -ceremonies, – revels; *arbiter elegantiarum.*

V. amuse, entertain, divert, enliven; tickle, – the fancy; titillate, raise a smile, put in good humour; cause –, create –, occasion –, raise –, excite –, produce –, convulse with- laughter; set the table in a roar, be the death of one.

recreate, solace, cheer, rejoice; please &c. 829; interest; treat, regale.

amuse oneself; game; play, – a game, – pranks, – tricks; sport, disport, toy, wanton, revel, junket, feast, carouse, banquet, make merry; drown care; drive dull care away; frolic, gambol, frisk, romp; caper; dance &c. (*leap*) 309; keep up the ball; run a rig, sow one's wild oats, have one's fling, paint the town red, take one's pleasure; see life; *desipere in loco*, play the fool.

make –, keep- holiday; go a Maying.

while away –, beguile- the time; kill time, dally.

Adj. amusing, entertaining, diverting &c. *v.*; recreative, lusory; pleasant &c. (*pleasing*) 829; laughable &c. (*ludicrous*) 853; witty &c. 842; fest-ive, -al; jovial, jolly, jocund, roguish, rompish; sporting; playful, – as a kitten; sportive, ludibrious.

amused &c. *v.*; 'pleased with a feather, tickled with a straw.'

Adv. 'on the light fantastic toe,' at play, in sport.

Int. *vive la bagatelle! vogue la galère!*

Phr. *Deus nobis hæc otia fecit; dum vivimus vivamus.*

---

842. Wit.—N. wit, -tiness; attic -wit, – salt; atticism; salt, *esprit*, point, fancy, whim, humour, drollery, pleasantry.

farce, buffoonery, fooling, tomfoolery; harlequinade &c. 599; broad -farce, – humour; fun, *espièglerie*; *vis comica.*

jocularity; jocos-ity, -eness; facetiousness; wagg-ery, -ishness; whimsicality; comicality &c. 853.

smartness, ready wit, banter, *badi-*

843. Dulness.—N. dulness, heaviness, flatness; infestivity &c. 837; stupidity &c. 499; want of originality, dearth of ideas.

prose, matter of fact; heavy book, *conte à dormir debout*; platitude.

V. be -dull &c. *adj.*; prose, platitudinize, take *au sérieux*, be caught napping.

render -dull &c. *adj.*; damp, depress, throw cold water on, lay a wet blanket on; fall flat upon the ear; hang fire.

---

* A curious list of games is given in Sir Thomas Urquhart's translation of Rabelais' *Life of Gargantua*, book i. chapter 22.

nage, *persiflage*, retort, repartee, *quid pro quo*; ridicule &c. 856.

facetiæ, quips and cranks; jest, joke, capital joke; standing -jest, – joke; conceit, quip, quirk, crank, quiddity, *concetto*, *plaisanterie*, brilliant idea; merry –, bright –, happy- thought; sally; flash, – of wit, – of merriment; scintillation; *mot*, – *pour rire*; witticism, smart saying, *bon mot*, *jeu d'esprit*, epigram; jest book; dry joke, *quodlibet*, cream of the jest.

word-play, *jeu de mots*; play -of, – upon- words; pun, -ning; *double entente* &c. (*ambiguity*) 520; quibble, verbal quibble; conundrum &c. (*riddle*) 533; anagram, acrostic, double acrostic, *nugæ canoræ*, trifling, idle conceit, *turlupinade*.

old joke, Joe Miller, chestnut, hoary-headed jest.

V. joke, jest, cut jokes; crack a joke; perpetrate a -joke, – pun; make -fun of, – merry with; set the table in a roar &c. (*amuse*) 840; scintillate.

retort, flash back; banter &c. (*ridicule*) 856; *ridentem dicere verum*; joke at one's expense.

Adj. witty, attic, salty; quick-, nimble-witted; keen, clever, smart, brilliant, pungent, jocular, jocose, funny, waggish, facetious, whimsical, humorous, gilbertian; playful &c. 840; merry and wise; pleasant, sprightly, *spirituel*, sparkling, epigrammatic, full of point, *ben trovato*; comic &c. 853.

Adv. in joke, in jest, in sport, in play.

Adj. dull, – as ditch water; dry, insipid, jejune; unentertaining, uninteresting, unlively, unimaginative; heavisome, heavy-gaited; insulse; dry as dust; pros-y, -ing, -aic; matter of fact, commonplace, banal, pointless; 'weary, flat, stale and unprofitable.'

stupid, slow, flat, sluggish, ponderous, humdrum, monotonous; melancholic &c. 837; stolid &c. 499; plodding.

Phr. *Davus sum non Œdipus.*

---

844. Humorist.—N. humorist, wag, wit, reparteeist, epigrammatist, gag man, punster; *bel esprit*, life of the party; wit-snapper, -cracker, -worm; joker, jester, jokesmith, Joe Miller, *drôle de corps*, *gaillard*, spark, *persiffleur*, banterer.

buffoon, *farceur*, merry-andrew, mime, tumbler, acrobat, mountebank, charlatan, posturemaster, harlequin, punch, *pulcinella*, scaramouch, clown; wearer of the -cap and bells, – motley; motley fool; pantaloon, gipsy; jack -pudding, – in the green, – a dandy; zany; mad-cap, pickle-herring, witling, caricaturist, *grimacier*.

2°. Discriminate Affections

845. Beauty.—N. beauty, the beautiful, *le beau ideal*, loveliness.

[Science of the perception of beauty] Callæsthetics.*

form, elegance, grace, beauty unadorned; symmetry &c. 242; comeliness, fairness &c. *adj.*; pulchritude, polish, gloss; good -effect, – looks; *belle tournure*; bloom, brilliancy, radiance, splendour, gorgeousness, magnificence; sublimi-ty, -fication.

846. Ugliness.—N. ugliness &c. *adj.*; deformity, inelegance; disfigurement &c. (*blemish*) 848; want of symmetry, inconcinnity; distortion &c. 243; squalor &c. (*uncleanness*) 653.

forbidding countenance, vinegar aspect, hanging look, wry face, '*spretæ injuria formæ*.'

eyesore, object, figure, sight, fright, spectre, scarecrow, hag, harridan, satyr, witch, toad, baboon, monster,

* Whewell, 'Philosophy of the Inductive Sciences.'

concinnity, delicacy, . refinement; charm, *je ne sais quoi*, style, *chic*, swank.

Venus, – of Milo; Aphrodite, Hebe, the Graces, Peri, Houri, Cupid, Apollo, Hyperion, Adonis, Antinous, Narcissus; Helen of Troy.

peacock, butterfly; flower, flow'ret gay, rose, lily, asphodel; garden; flower of, pink of; *bijou*; jewel &c. (*ornament*) 847; work of art.

pleasurableness &c. 829.

beautifying; landscape gardening; decoration &c. 847; calisthenics.

V. be -beautiful &c. *adj.*; shine, beam, bloom; become one &c. (*accord*) 23; set off, grace, flatter one.

render -beautiful &c. *adj.*; beautify; polish, burnish; gild &c. (*decorate*) 847; set out.

'snatch a grace beyond the reach of art.'

Adj. beaut-iful, -eous; handsome; pretty; lovely, graceful, elegant; delicate, dainty, refined, exquisite; fair, personable, comely, seemly; bonny; good-looking; well-favoured, -made, -formed, -proportioned; proper, shapely; symmetrical &c. (*regular*) 242; harmonious &c. (*colour*) 428; sightly.

fit to be seen, passable, not amiss.

goodly, dapper, tight, jimp; gimp; janty, jaunty; natty, quaint, trim, tidy, neat, spruce, smart, tricksy.

bright, -eyed; rosy-, cherry-cheeked; rosy, ruddy; blooming, in full bloom.

brilliant, shining; beam-y, -ing; sparkling, swanky, splendid, resplendent, dazzling, glowing; glossy, sleek.

showy, specious; rich, gorgeous, superb, magnificent, grand, fine, sublime, imposing; majestic 873.

artistic, -al; æsthetic; pict-uresque, -orial; *fait à peindre*, paintable; well-composed, -grouped, -varied; curious.

Caliban, Æsop, '*monstrum horrendum informe ingens cui lumen ademptum.*'

V. be -ugly &c. *adj.*; look ill, grin horribly a ghastly smile, make faces.

render -ugly &c. *adj.*; deface; dis-, de-figure; deform, spoil, distort &c. 243; blemish &c. (*injure*) 659; soil &c. (*render unclean*) 653.

Adj. ugly, – as -sin, – a toad, – a scarecrow, – a dead monkey; plain, bald &c. 226; homely &c. (*unadorned*) 849; ordinary, unornamental, inartistic; unsightly, unseemly, uncomely, unshapely, unlovely; sightless, seemless; not fit to be seen; unbeaut-eous, -iful; beautiless; shapeless &c. (*amorphous*) 241; course; garish, over-decorated &c. 882.

mis-shapen, -proportioned; monstrous; gaunt &c. (*thin*) 203; dumpy &c. (*short*) 201; curtailed of its fair proportions; ill-made, -shaped, -proportioned; crooked &c. (*distorted*) 243; hard-featured, -visaged; ill-, hard-, evil-favoured; ill-looking; unprepossessing.

graceless, inelegant; ungraceful, ungainly, uncouth; stiff; rugged, rough, gross, rude, awkward, clumsy, slouching, rickety; gawky; lump-ing, -ish; lumbering; hulk-y, -ing; unwieldy.

squalid, haggard; grim, -faced, -visaged; grisly, ghastly; ghost-, death-like; cadaverous, gruesome.

frightful, hideous, odious, uncanny, forbidding, repellant, repulsive; horri-d, -ble; shocking &c. (*painful*) 830.

foul &c. (*dirty*) 653; dingy &c. (*colourless*) 429; gaudy &c. (*colour*) 428; disfigured &c. *v.*; discoloured (*blemished*) &c. 848.

enchanting &c. (*pleasure-giving*) 829; attractive &c. (*inviting*) 615; becoming &c. (*accordant*) 23; ornamental &c. 847.

undeformed, undefaced, unspotted; spotless &c. (*perfect*) 650.

---

847. Ornament. — N. ornament, -ation, -al art; ornat-ure, -eness; adorn-ment, decoration, embellishment; architecture.

garnish, polish, varnish, French pol-

848. Blemish.—N. blemish, disfigurement, deformity; defect &c. (*imperfection*) 651; flaw; injury &c. (*deterioration*) 659; spots on the sun; eyesore.

ish, gilding, japanning, lacquer, ormolu, enamel.

cosmetics, rouge, powder, lipstick, lip salve, mascara; manicure, nail polish; permanent –, Marcel –, finger-wave.

pattern, diaper, powdering, panelling, graining, pargeting, inlay, detail; texture &c. 329; richness; tracery, moulding, beading, reeding, fillet, listel, strapwork, *coquillage*, flourish, *fleur-de-lis*, arabesque, fret, *anthemion*; egg and -tongue, – dart; *astragal*, zigzag, *acanthus, cartouche*; pilaster &c. (*projection*) 250; cyma, ogee.

em-, broidery, needlework; knitting, crochet, tatting, brocade, *brocatelle*, beads, bugles; galloon, lace, gimp, *guipure*, fringe, trapping, border, edging, insertion, *motif*, trimming; *passementerie*; drapery, hanging, tapestry, arras; millinery, ermine.

wreath, festoon, garland, lei, chaplet, flower, nosegay, *bouquet*, posy, 'daisies pied and violets blue.'

tassel, knot; shoulder-knot, *épaulette*, epaulet, aigulet, *aiguillette*, frog; star, rosette, bow; feather, plume, *panache*, *aigrette*.

jewel, -ry, -lery; bijoutry; *bijou*, *-terie*; diadem, tiara; pendant, trinket, locket, necklace, armilla, bracelet, bangle, armlet, anklet, ear-, nose- ring, carcanet, chain, *châtelaine*, albert, brooch, torque.

gem, precious stone; diamond, brilliant, beryl, aquamarine, alexandrite, cat's eye, emerald, calcedony, chrysoprase, cornelian, jasper, bloodstone, agate, heliotrope; girasol, -e; onyx, plasma; sard, -onyx; garnet, lapis-lazuli, opal, peridot, chrysolite, sapphire, ruby; spinel, -le; balais; oriental –, topaz; turquois, -e; zircon, jacinth, hyacinth, carbuncle, amethyst; moonstone; pearl, coral.

finery, frippery, gewgaw, gimcrack, knick-knack, tinsel, spangle, sequin, *clinquant*, pinch-beck, paste; excess of ornament &c. (*vulgarity*) 851; gaud, pride, ostentation; frills and furbelows.

illustration, illumination, *vignette*; *fleuron*; head-, tail-piece; *cul-de-lampe*; flowers of rhetoric &c. 577; work of art, article of vertu, *bric-à-brac*, curio, *bibelot*.

V. ornament, embellish, enrich, decorate, adorn, beautify, adonize.

smarten, furbish, polish, gild, varnish, whitewash, enamel, japan, lacquer, paint, grain.

garnish, trim, dizen, bedizen, prink, prank; trick –, fig- out; deck, bedeck, dight, bedight, array; dress, – up, preen, spruce up,

stain, blot, slur; spot, -tiness; speck, -le; blur, freckle, mole, *macula*, patch, blotch, birthmark, blain, maculation, tarnish, smudge, smear; dirt &c. 653; bruise, black eye, scar, wem; pustule; excrescence, pimple &c. (*protuberance*) 250.

V. disfigure &c. (*injure*) 659; speckle; render ugly &c. 846.

Adj. pitted, freckled, discoloured, bloodshot, bruised, disfigured; stained &c. n.; imperfect &c. 651; injured &c. (*deteriorated*) 659.

849. Simplicity. — N. simplicity; plain-, homeli-ness; undress, nudity, nakedness, beauty unadorned, chastity, chasteness.

V. be -simple &c. *adj.*

render -simple &c. *adj.*; simplify, chasten, strip of ornament.

Adj. simple, plain; home-ly, -spun; ordinary, household.

natural, unaffected; free from -affectation, – ornament; *simplex munditiis*; *sans façon, en déshabillé*, nude, naked.

chaste, inornate, severe.

un-adorned, -ornamented, -decked, -garnished, -arranged, -trimmed, -varnished.

bald, flat, dull, blank.

titivate; spangle, bespangle, powder; embroider, work; chase, tool, emboss, fret; emblazon, blazon, illuminate; illustrate.

become &c. (*accord with*) 23.

Adj. ornamented, beautified &c. *v.*; ornate, rich, gilt, begilt, tesselated, enamelled, inlaid; festooned; topiary.

smart, gay, tricksy, flowery, glittering; new-gilt, -spangled; fine, – as -a Mayday queen, – fivepence, – a carrot fresh scraped; pranked out, bedight, well-groomed.

in full dress &c. (*fashion*) 852; *en grande -tenue, – toilette*; in best bib and tucker, in Sunday best, *endimanché*; dressed to advantage.

showy, flashy; gaudy &c. (*vulgar*) 851; garish; gorgeous.

ornamental, decorative; becoming &c. (*accordant*) 23.

---

850. [Good taste.] **Taste.**—**N.** taste; good –, refined –, cultivated- taste; delicacy, refinement, fine feeling, gust, *gusto*, tact, *finesse*; nicety &c. (*discrimination*) 465; polish, elegance, grace.

virtu; dilettanteism, virtuosity; fine art; cul-ture, -ivation.

[Science of taste] æsthetics.

man of -taste &c.; *connoisseur*, judge, critic, *conoscente*, *virtuoso*, *amateur*, *dilettante*, Aristarchus, Corinthian, *arbiter elegantiarum*, stagirite, euphemist.

'caviare to the general.'

V. appreciate, judge, criticize, discriminate &c. 465.

Adj. in good taste; tasteful, tasty; unaffected, pure, chaste, classical, attic; cultivated, refined; dainty; æsthetic, artistic; elegant &c. 578; euphemistic.

to one's -taste, – mind; after one's fancy; *comme il faut*; *tiré à quatre épingles*.

Adv. elegantly &c. *adj.*

Phr. *nihil tetigit quod non ornavit.*

852. Fashion.—**N.** fashion, style, *ton, bon ton*, society; good –, polite-society; drawing room, civilized life, civilization, town, *beau monde*, high life, court; world; fashionable –, gay-world; Vanity Fair; show &c. (*ostentation*) 822.

manners, breeding &c. (*politeness*) 894; air, demeanour &c. (*appearance*) 448; *savoir faire*; gentlemanliness, gentility, decorum, propriety, *bienséance*; conventions –, dictates- of society; Mrs. Grundy; convention, -ality; punctilio; form, -ality; etiquette, point of

851. [Bad taste.] **Vulgarity.**—**N.** vulgar-ity, -ism; barbar-, Vandal-, Gothic-ism; *mauvais goût*, bad taste; Babbittry; *gaucherie*, awkwardness, want of tact; ill-breeding &c. (*discourtesy*) 895; ungentlemanly behaviour.

coarseness &c. *adj.*; indecorum, misbehaviour.

low-, homeli-ness; low life, *mauvais ton*, rusticity; boorishness &c. *adj.*; brutality; rowdy-, ruffian-, blackguardism; ribaldry; slang &c. (*neology*) 563.

bad joke, *mauvaise plaisanterie*.

[Excess of ornament] gaudi-, tawdriness; false ornament; finery, frippery, trickery, tinsel, gewgaw, *clinquant*.

rough diamond, tomboy, hoyden, cub, unlicked cub; clown &c. (*commonalty*) 876; Hun, Goth, Vandal, Bœotian; vulgarian; snob, cad, bounder, gent; *parvenu* &c. 876; frump, dowdy; slattern &c. 653.

V. be -vulgar &c. *adj.*; misbehave; talk –, smell of the- shop.

Adj. in bad taste, vulgar, unrefined, gutter.

coarse, indecorus, ribald, gross; unseemly, unbeseeming, unpresentable; *contra bonos mores*; ungraceful &c. (*ugly*) 846.

dowdy; slovenly &c. (*dirty*) 653; ungenteel, shabby genteel; low &c. (*plebeian*) 876; uncourtly; uncivil &c. (*discourteous*) 895; ill-bred, -mannered; underbred; ungentleman-ly, -like; unladylike, unfeminine; wild, – as an unbacked colt.

unkempt, uncombed, untamed, unlicked, unpolished, uncouth, plebeian;

etiquette; custom &c. 613; mode, vogue, style, go; rage &c. (*desire*) 865; prevailing taste, *dernier cri*, dress &c. 225.

man –, woman- of -fashion, – the world; height –, pink –, star –, glass –, leader- of fashion; *arbiter elegantiarum* &c. (*taste*) 850; upper ten thousand &c. (*nobility*) 875; *élite* &c. (*distinction*) 873.

V. be -fashionable &c. *adj.*, – the rage &c. *n.*; have a run, pass current.

follow –, conform to –, fall in with-the fashion &c. *n.*; go with the stream &c. (*conform*) 82; *savoir -vivre*, – *faire*; keep up appearances, behave oneself.

set the –, bring into- fashion; give a tone to –, cut a figure in- society, rub shoulders with nobility, keep one's carriage.

incondite; heavy, rude, awkward; home-ly, -spun, -bred; provincial, hick, countrified, rustic, uncultivated, fresh-water; boorish, clownish; savage, brut-ish, blackguard, rowdy, snobbish; barbar-ous, -ic; Gothic, unclassical doggerel, heathenish, tramontane, out-landish; Bohemian.

obsolete &c. (*antiquated*) 124; un-fashionable, old-fashioned, out of date; new-fangled &c. (*unfamiliar*) 83; fan-tastic, odd &c. (*ridiculous*) 853.

particular; affected &c. 855; mere-tricious; extravagant, monstrous, hor-rid; shocking &c. (*painful*) 830.

gaudy, tawdry, bedizened, tricked out, gingerbread; obtrusive, flaunting, loud, flashy, garish, showy.

Adj. fashionable; in -fashion &c. *n.*; *à la mode*, *comme il faut*; admitted –, admissible- in -society &c. *n.*; presentable, decorous, punctilious, conventional &c. (*customary*) 613; genteel; well-bred, -mannered, -behaved, -spoken; gentleman-like, -ly; ladylike; civil, polite &c. (*courteous*) 894.

polished, refined, thoroughbred, courtly; *distingué*, aristocratic, unembarrassed, poised, *dégagé*; ja-, jau-nty; dashing, fast, showy, high toned, toney.

modish, stylish, in the latest style, *recherché*; new-fangled &c. (*unfamiliar*) 83.

in -court, – full, – evening- dress; *en grande tenue* &c. (*ornament*) 847.

Adv. fashionably &c. *adj.*; for fashion's sake.

853. Ridiculousness.—N. ridiculousness &c. *adj.*; comical-, odd-ity &c. *adj.*; extravagance, drollery.

farce, comedy; burlesque &c. (*ridicule*) 856; buffoonery &c. (*fun*) 840; frippery; doggerel verses; Irish bull, Hibernianism, Hibernicism; Spoonerism; absurdity &c. 497; bombast &c. (*unmeaning*) 517; anti-climax, bathos; monstrosity &c. (*unconformity*) 83; laughing stock &c. 857.

V. be -ridiculous &c. *adj.*; pass from the sublime to the ridiculous; make one laugh; play the fool, make a fool of oneself, commit an absurdity.

play a joke on, make a -fool of, – sucker of, – monkey of.

Adj. ridiculous, ludicrous; comic, -al; droll, funny, laughable, *pour rire*, grotesque, farcical, odd; whimsical, – as a dancing bear; fanciful, fantastic, queer, rum, quizzical, waggish, quaint, *bizarre*; eccentric &c. (*unconformable*) 83; strange, outlandish, out of the way, *baroque*, *rocaille*, rococo; awkward &c. (*ugly*) 846.

absurd, extravagant, *outré*, monstrous, preposterous, bombastic, inflated, stilted, burlesque, mock heroic.

drollish; serio-, tragic-comic; gimcrack, contemptible &c. (*unim-portant*) 643; doggerel; ironical &c. (*derisive*) 856; risible.

Phr. '*risum teneatis amici?*' *rideret Heraclitus.*

854. Fop.—N. fop, fine gentleman; swell; dand-y, -iprat; exquisite, coxcomb, toff, beau, macaroni, blade, blood, buck, man about town, fast man; fribble, jemmy, spark, popinjay, puppy, prig, *petit maître*; jacka-napes, -dandy; man milliner; Jemmy Jessamy, carpet-knight, masher, Dundreary, Johnnie, dude.

belle, fine lady, *coquette*, flirt.

855. Affectation.—N. affectation; affectedness &c. *adj.*; acting a part &c. *v.*; pretence &c. (*falsehood*) 544, (*ostentation*) 882; boasting &c. 884.

charlatanism, quakery, shallow profundity, humbug, pretension, airs, pedantry, purism, precisianism, euphuism, prunes and prisms; teratology &c. (*altiloquence*) 577.

mannerism, *simagrée*, grimace.

conceit, foppery, dandyism, man millinery, coxcombry, puppyism.

stiffness, formality, buckram; prudery, demureness, coquetry, mock modesty, *minauderie*, sentimentalism; *mauvaise honte*, false shame.

affector, performer, actor; pedant, pedagogue, *doctrinaire*, purist, euphuist, mannerist; shoneen; *grimacier*; lump of affectation, *précieuse ridicule*, *bas bleu*, blue stocking, poetaster; prig, hypocrite; charlatan &c. (*deceiver*) 548; *petit maître* &c. (*fop*) 854; flatterer &c. 935; *coquette*, prude, puritan; precisian, formalist.

V. affect, act a part, put on; give oneself airs &c. (*arrogance*) 885; boast &c. 884; coquet; simper, mince, attitudinize, strike a pose, pose; flirt a fan; over-act, -play, -do.

Adj. affected, full of affectation, pretentious, pedantic, stilted, stagey, theatrical, big-sounding, *ad captandum*, canting, insincere.

not natural, unnatural; self-conscious; *maniéré*; artificial; over-wrought, -done, -acted; euphuistic &c. 577.

stiff, starch, formal, prim, smug, demure, *tiré à quatre épingles*, quakerish, puritanical, prudish, pragmatical, priggish, conceited, cox-comical, foppish, dandified; fini-cal, -kin, -cky, mincing, simpering, namby-pamby, sentimental, languishing.

856. Ridicule.—N. ridicule, derision; sardonic -smile, – grin; irrision; snigger; scoffing &c. (*disrespect*) 929; mockery, quiz, banter, irony, *persiflage*, raillery, chaff, *badinage*; quizzing &c. *v.*

squib, satire, skit, quip, quib, grin.

parody, burlesque, travesty; farce &c. (*drama*) 599; caricature, take-off.

buffoonery &c. (*fun*) 840; practical joke, horseplay.

V. ridicule, deride; laugh at, grin at, smile at; snigger; laugh in one's sleeve; banter, rally, chaff, joke, twit, quiz, poke fun at, jolly, roast, rag; fleer; play –, play tricks- upon; fool, – to the top of one's bent; show up.

satirize, parody, caricature, burlesque, travesty.

turn into ridicule; make merry with; make -fun, – game, – a fool, – an April fool- of; rally; scoff &c. (*disrespect*) 929.

raise a laugh &c. (*amuse*) 840; play the fool, make a fool of oneself. be ridiculous &c. 853.

Adj. deris-ory, -ive; mock; sarcastic, ironical, quizzical, burlesque, Hudibrastic; scurrilous &c. (*disrespectful*) 929.

Adv. in -ridicule &c. *n.*

857. [Object and cause of ridicule.] **Laughing-stock.**—**N.** laughing-, jesting-, gazing-stock; butt, game, fair game; April fool &c. (*dupe*) 547.

original, oddity; queer –, odd- fish; quiz, square toes; old –, fogey *or* fogy.

monkey; buffoon &c. (*jester*) 844; pantomimist &c. (*actor*) 599.

jest &c. (*wit*) 842.

3°. PROSPECTIVE AFFECTIONS

858. Hope.—**N.** hope, -s; desire &c. 865; fervent hope, sanguine expectation, trust, confidence, reliance; faith &c. (*belief*) 484; affiance, assurance; secur-eness, -ity; reassurance.

good -omen, – auspices; promise, well-grounded hopes; good –, bright-prospect; clear sky.

as-, pre-sumption; anticipation &c. (*expectation*) 507.

hopefulness, buoyancy, optimism, enthusiasm, heart of grace, aspiration; optimist, utop-ian, -ist; Pollyanna.

castles in the air, *châteaux en Espagne*, hope chest, *le pot au lait*, Utopia, millennium; day –, golden-dream; dream of Alnaschar; airy hopes, fool's paradise; *mirage* &c. (*fallacies of vision*) 443; fond hope.

beam –, ray –, gleam –, glimmer –, dawn –, flash –, star- of hope; cheer; bit of blue sky, silver lining of the cloud, bottom of Pandora's box, balm in Gilead.

anchor, sheet-anchor, main-stay; staff &c. (*support*) 215; heaven &c. 981.

V. hope, trust, confide, rely on, put one's trust in, lean upon; pin one's -hope, – faith- upon &c. (*believe*) 484.

feel –, entertain –, harbour –, in-dulge –, cherish –, feed –, foster –, nourish –, encourage –, cling to –, live in- hope &c. *n.*; see land; feel –, rest- -assured, – confident &c. *adj.*

presume; promise oneself; expect &c. (*look forward to*) 507.

hope for &c. (*desire*) 865; anticipate.

be -hopeful &c. *adj.*; look on the bright side of, view on the sunny side, make the best of it, hope for the best; put -a good, – a bold, – the best- face upon; keep one's spirits up; take heart, – of grace; be of good -heart, – cheer; flatter oneself, lay the flattering unction to one's soul.

859. [Absence, want, or loss of hope.] **Hopelessness.**—**N.** hopelessness &c. *adj.*; despair, desperation; despondency &c. (*dejection*) 837; pessimism.

hope deferred, dashed hopes; vain expectation &c. (*disappointment*) 509.

airy hopes &c. 858; forlorn hope; bad -job, – business; *enfant perdu*; gloomy –, black spots in the- horizon; slough of Despond, cave of Despair.

Job's comforter; bird of -bad, – ill-omen.

V. despair; lose –, give up –, aban-don –, relinquish- -all hope, – the hope of; give -up, – over; yield to despair; falter; despond &c. (*be dejected*) 837; *jeter le manche après la cognée.*

inspire –, drive to- despair &c. *n.*; disconcert; dash –, crush –, shatter –, destroy- one's hopes; hope against hope.

Adj. hopeless, desperate, despairing, in despair, *au désespoir*, forlorn; in-consolable &c. (*dejected*) 837; broken-hearted.

out of the question, not to be thought of; impracticable &c. 471; past -hope, – cure, – mending, – recall; at one's last gasp &c. (*death*) 360; given -up, – over.

incurable, cureless, immedicable, re-mediless, beyond remedy; incorrigible; irre-parable, -mediable, -coverable, -versible, -trievable, -claimable, -deem-able, -vocable; ruined, undone; im-mitigable.

unpromising, unpropitious; inauspi-cious, ill-omened, threatening, clouded over, lowering, ominous.

Phr. '*lasciate ogni speranza voi ch' entrate*'; its days are numbered; the worst come to the worst.

860. Fear.—**N.** fear, timidity, diffi-dence, want of confidence; apprehen-sive-, fearful-ness &c. *adj.*; solicitude,

catch at a straw, hope against hope, count one's chickens before they are hatched.

give –, inspire –, raise –, hold out- hope &c. *n.*; raise expectations; en- courage, hearten, cheer, assure, re- assure, buoy up, embolden; promise, bid fair, augur well, be in a fair way, look up, flatter, tell a flattering tale.

Adj. hoping &c. *v.*; in -hopes &c. *n.*; hopeful, confident; secure &c. (*certain*) 484; sanguine, in good heart, buoyed up, buoyant, elated, flushed, exultant, enthusiastic; utopian.

unsus-pecting, -picious; fearless, free –, exempt from- -fear, – suspicion, – distrust, – despair; undespairing, self- reliant.

probable, on the high road to; within sight of -shore, – land; promising, propitious; of –, full of- promise; of good omen; auspicious, *de bon augure*; reassuring; encouraging, cheering, in- spiriting, looking up, bright, roseate, *couleur de rose*, rose-coloured.

Adv. hopefully &c. *adj.*

Int. God speed! good luck!

Phr. *nil desperandum*; never say die, *dum spiro spero, latet scintillula forsan*, all is for the best, *spero meliora*; the wish being father to the thought; 'hope told a flattering tale'; *rusticus expectat dum defluat amnis*.

---

anxiety, care, apprehension, misgiving; mistrust &c. (*doubt*) 485; suspicion, qualm; hesitation &c. (*irresolution*) 605.

nervous-, restless-ness &c. *adj.*; in-, dis-quietude; flutter, trepidation, fear and trembling, perturbation, tremor, quivering, shaking, trembling, throb- bing heart, palpitation, ague fit, cold sweat; abject fear &c. (*cowardice*) 862; mortal funk, heart-sinking, despond- ency; despair &c. 859.

fright; affright, -ment; alarm, pavor, dread, awe, terror, horror, dismay, consternation, panic, scare, stampede [of horses].

intimidation, terrorism, reign of terror.

[Object of fear] bug-bear, -aboo; scarecrow; hobgoblin &c. (*demon*) 980; daymare, nightmare, Gorgon, Medusa, mormo, ogre, Hurlothrumbo, raw head and bloody bones, fee faw fum, *bête noire, enfant terrible*.

alarmist &c. (*coward*) 862.

V. fear, stand in awe of; be -afraid &c. *adj.*; have -qualms &c. *n.*; appre- hend, sit upon thorns, eye askance; distrust &c. (*disbelieve*) 485.

hesitate &c. (*be irresolute*) 605; falter, funk, cower, crouch; skulk &c. (*coward- ice*) 862; let 'I dare not' wait upon 'I would'; take -fright, – alarm; start, wince, flinch, shy, shrink; fly &c. (*avoid*) 623.

tremble, shake; shiver, – in one's shoes; shudder, flutter; shake –, tremble- -like an aspen leaf, – all over; quake, quaver, quiver, quail; get the wind up.

grow –, turn- pale; blench, stand aghast; not dare to say one's soul is one's own.

inspire –, excite- -fear, – awe; raise apprehensions; give –, raise –, sound- an alarm; alarm, startle, scare, cry 'wolf,' disquiet, dismay; fright, -en; affright, terrify; astound; frighten from one's propriety; frighten out of one's -wits, – senses, – seven senses; awe; strike -all of a heap, – an awe into, – terror; harrow up the soul, appal, unman, petrify, horrify.

make one's -flesh creep, – hair stand on end, – blood run cold, – teeth chatter; chill one's spine; take away –, stop- one's breath; make one -tremble &c.

haunt, obsess, beset; prey –, weigh- on the mind.

put in -fear, – bodily fear; terrorize, intimidate, cow, daunt, over- awe, abash, deter, discourage; browbeat, bully; threaten &c. 909.

Adj. fearing &c. *v.*; frightened &c. *v.*; in -fear, – a fright &c. *n.*; haunted with the -fear &c. *n.*- of.

afraid, fearful; tim-id, -orous; nervous, diffident, coy, faint-hearted, tremulous, shaky, afraid of one's shadow, apprehensive, restless, fidgety; more frightened than hurt.

aghast; awe-, horror-, terror-, panic- -struck, -stricken; frightened to death, white as a sheet; pale, – as -death, – ashes, – a ghost; breathless, in hysterics.

inspiring fear &c. *v.*; alarming; formidable, redoubtable; perilous &c. (*danger*) 665; portentous; fear-ful, -some; dread, -ful; fell; dire, -ful; shocking; terri-ble, -fic; tremendous; horri-d, -ble, -fic; ghastly; awful, awe-inspiring, eerie, weird; revolting &c. (*painful*) 830.

Adv. *in terrorem.*

Int. 'angels and ministers of grace defend us!'

Phr. *ante tubam trepidat; horresco referens,* one's heart failing one, *obstupui steteruntque comæ et vox faucibus hæsit.*

---

861. [Absence of fear.] **Courage.—N.** courage, bravery, valour; resolute-, bold-ness &c. *adj.*; spirit, daring, gallantry, intrepidity; contempt –, defiance- of danger; derring-do; audacity; rashness &c. 863; dash; defiance &c. 715; confidence, self-reliance.

man-liness, -hood; nerve, pluck, mettle, game; heart, – of grace; spunk, gameness, grit, face, virtue, hardihood, fortitude; firmness &c. (*stability*) 150; heart of oak; bottom, backbone &c. (*perseverance*) 604a.

resolution &c. (*determination*) 604; tenacity, bull-dog courage.

prowess, heroism, chivalry.

exploit, feat, achievement; heroic -deed, – act; bold stroke.

man, – of mettle; hero, demigod, paladin, heroine, Amazon, Hector, Joan of Arc; lion, tiger, panther, bulldog; game-, fighting-cock; bully, fire-eater &c. 863; dare-devil.

V. be -courageous &c. *adj.*; dare, venture, make bold; face –, front –, affront –, confront –, brave –, defy –, despise –, mock- danger; look in the face; look -full, – boldly, – danger- in the face; face; meet, – in front; brave, beard; defy &c. 715.

take –, muster –, summon up –, pluck up- courage; nerve oneself, take heart; take –, pluck up- heart of grace; hold up one's head, screw one's courage to the sticking place; come -to, – up to- the scratch; stand, – to one's guns, – fire, – against; bear up, – against; hold out &c. (*persevere*) 604a.

put a bold face upon; show –,

862. [Excess of fear.] **Cowardice.—N.** cowardice, pusillanimity; cowardliness &c. *adj.*; timidity, effeminacy.

poltroonery, baseness; dastard-ness, -y; abject fear, funk; Dutch courage; fear &c. 860; white feather, faint heart.

coward, poltroon, dastard, sneak, recreant; shy –, dunghill- cock; coistril, milksop, white-liver, nidget, cur, craven, one that cannot say 'Boo' to a goose; Bob Acres, Jerry Sneak.

alarm-, terror-, pessim-ist; runagate &c. (*fugitive*) 623; shirker.

V. quail &c. (*fear*) 860; be -cowardly &c. *adj.*, – a coward &c. *n.*; funk; cower, skulk, sneak; flinch, shy, fight shy, slink, turn tail; run away &c. (*avoid*) 623; show the white feather, have cold feet, show a yellow streak.

Adj. coward, -ly; fearful, shy; tim-id, -orous; skittish; poor-spirited, spiritless, soft, effeminate.

weak-minded; infirm of purpose &c. 605; weak-, faint-, chicken-, lily-, pigeon-hearted; yellow; white-, lily-, milk-livered; milksop, smock-faced; unable to say 'Boo' to a goose.

dastard, -ly; base, craven, sneaking, dunghill, recreant; unwar-, unsoldier-like.

'in face a lion but in heart a deer.' unmanned; frightened &c. 860.

Int. *sauve qui peut!* devil take the hindmost!

Adv. in fear and trembling, in fear of one's life, in a blue funk.

Phr. *ante tubam trepidat,* one's courage oozing out.

---

present- a bold front, face the music; envisage; show fight.

bell the cat, take the bull by the horns, beard the lion in his den, march up to the cannon's mouth, go through fire and water, run the gauntlet, go over the top.

give –, infuse –, inspire- courage; reassure, encourage, embolden, inspirit, cheer, hearten, nerve, put upon one's mettle, rally, raise a rallying cry; pat on the back, make a man of, keep in countenance.

Adj. courageous, brave; val-iant, -orous; gallant, intrepid; spirit-ed, -ful; high-spirited, -mettled; mettlesome, game, plucky; man-ly, -ful; resolute; stout, -hearted; iron-, lion-hearted; heart of oak; Penthesilean.

bold, – spirited; daring, audacious; fear-, daunt-, dread-, awe-less; un-daunted, -appalled, -dismayed, -awed, -blenched, -abashed, -alarmed, -flinching, -shrinking, -blenching; apprehensive; confident, self-reliant; bold as -a lion, – brass.

enterprising, adventurous; ventur-ous, -esome; dashing, chival-rous; soldierly &c. (*warlike*) 722; heroic.

fierce, savage; pugnacious &c. (*bellicose*) 720.

strong-minded, hardy, doughty; firm &c. (*stable*) 150; determined &c. (*resolved*) 604; dogged, indomitable &c. (*persevering*) 604a.

up to, – the scratch; upon one's mettle; reassured &c. *v.*; un-feared, undreaded.

Phr. one's blood being up.

---

863. Rashness.—N. rashness &c. *adj.*; temerity, want of caution, im-prudence, indiscretion; over-confidence, presumption, audacity.

precipit-ancy, -ation; impetuosity; levity; foolhardi-hood, -ness; heed-, thought-lessness &c. (*inattention*) 458; carelessness &c. (*neglect*) 460; despera-tion; Quixotism, knight-errantry; fire-eating.

gam-ing, -bling; blind bargain, leap in the dark, fool's paradise; too many eggs in one basket.

desperado, rashling, mad-cap, dare-devil, Hotspur, fire-eater, bully, *bravo*, Hector, scapegrace, *enfant perdu*; Don Quixote, knight-errant, Icarus; adven-turer; gam-bler, -ester; dynamitard.

V. be -rash &c. *adj.*; stick at nothing, play a desperate game; run into danger &c. 665; play with -fire, – edge tools.

carry too much sail, sail too near the wind, ride at single anchor, go out of one's depth.

take a leap in the dark, buy a pig in a poke.

donner tête baissée; knock one's head against a wall &c. (*be unskilful*) 699; rush on destruction; kick against the

864. Caution.—N. caution; cautious-ness &c. *adj.*; discretion, prudence, cautel, heed, circumspection, calcula-tion, deliberation; safety first.

foresight &c. 510; vigilance &c. 459; warning &c. 668.

coolness &c. *adj.*; self-possession, -command; presence of mind, *sang froid*; well-regulated mind; worldly wisdom, Fabian policy.

V. be -cautious &c. *adj.*; take -care, – heed, – good care; have a care; mind, – what one is about; be on one's guard &c. (*keep watch*) 459; make assurance double sure; ca' canny.

bespeak &c. (*be early*) 132.

think twice, look before one leaps, keep one's weather eye open, count the cost, look to the main chance, cut one's coat according to one's cloth; feel one's -ground, – way; see how the land lies &c. (*foresight*) 510; wait to see how the cat jumps; bridle one's tongue; *reculer pour mieux sauter* &c. (*prepare*) 673; let well alone, let sleeping dogs lie, *ne pas réveiller le chat qui dort*.

keep out of -harm's way, – troubled waters; keep at a respectful distance, stand aloof; keep –, be- on the safe side.

pricks, tempt Providence, go on a forlorn hope.

count one's chickens before they are hatched; reckon without one's host; catch at straws; trust to –, lean on- a broken reed.

Adj. rash, incautious, indiscreet, injudicious; imprudent, improvident, temerarious; uncalculating; heedless; careless &c. (*neglectful*) 460; without ballast, heels over head; giddy &c. (*inattentive*) 458; wanton, reckless, wild, madcap; desperate, devil-may-care.

hot-blooded, -headed, -brained; head-long, -strong; break-neck; foolhardy; harebrained; precipitate, impulsive.

over-confident, -weening; ventur-esome, -ous; adventurous, Quixotic; fire-eating, cavalier; free-and-easy.

off one's guard &c. (*inexpectant*) 508.

Adv. post haste, *à corps perdu*, hand over head, *tête baissée*, head-foremost; happen what may.

Phr. neck or nothing, the devil being in one.

husband one's resources &c. 636.

caution &c. (*warn*) 668.

Adj. cautious, wary, guarded; on one's guard &c. (*watchful*) 459; *cavendo tutus*; *in medio tutissimus*.

care-, heed-ful; cautelous, stealthy, chary, shy of, circumspect, prudent, canny, safe, non-committal, discreet, politic; sure-footed &c. (*skilful*) 698.

unenterprising, unadventurous, cool, steady, self-possessed; over-cautious.

suspicious, leery, vigilant.

Adv. cautiously, gingerly &c. *adj.*

Int. have a care! look out! *cave canem!*

Phr. *timeo Danaos; festina lente.*

---

865. Desire.—N. desire, wish, fancy, fantasy; want, need, exigency.

mind, inclination, leaning, bent, *animus*, partiality, *penchant*, predilection; propensity &c. 820; willingness &c. 602; liking, love, fondness, relish.

longing, hankering; solicitude, anxiety; yearning, coveting; aspiration, ambition, vaulting ambition; eagerness, zeal, ardour, *empressement*, breathless impatience, over-anxiety; solicitude, impetuosity &c. 825.

appet-ite, -ition, -ence, -ency; sharp appetite, keenness, hunger, stomach, twist; thirst, -iness; drouth, mouth-watering; itch, -ing; prurience, *cacoëthes*, cupidity, lust, concupiscence.

edge of -appetite, – hunger; torment of Tantalus; sweet –, lickerish- tooth; itching palm; longing –, wistful –, sheep's- eye.

avidity; greed, -iness; covetous-, ravenous-ness &c. *adj.*; grasping, craving, canine appetite, rapacity; voracity &c. (*gluttony*) 957.

passion, rage, *furore*, mania, *manie*; inextinguishable desire; dips-, klept-, mon-omania.

[Person desiring] desirer, lover, *ama-

866. Indifference.—N. indifference, neutrality; coldness &c. *adj.*; unconcern, *insouciance, nonchalance*; want of -interest, – earnestness; anorexy, inappetency; apathy &c. (*insensibility*) 823; supineness &c. (*inactivity*) 683; disdain &c. 930; recklessness &c. 863; inattention &c. 458.

V. be -indifferent &c. *adj.*; stand neuter; take no interest in &c. (*insensibility*) 823; have no -desire &c. 865, – taste, – relish- for; not care for; care nothing -for, – about; not care a -straw &c. (*unimportance*) 643 -about, – for; not mind.

set at naught &c. (*make light of*) 483; spurn &c. (*disdain*) 930.

Adj. indifferent, cold, frigid, luke-warm; cool, – as a cucumber; unconcerned, *insouciant*, phlegmatic, *pococurante*, easy-going, devil-may-care, careless, listless, lackadaisical, feckless; half-hearted; un-ambitious, -aspiring, -desirous, -solicitous, -attracted.

un-attractive, -alluring, -desired, -desirable, -cared for, -wished, -valued, all one to.

insipid &c. 391; vain.

Adv. for aught one cares.

teur, votary, devotee, aspirant, solicitant, candidate; cormorant &c. 957; sycophant.

[Object of desire] *desideratum*; want &c. (*requirement*) 630; 'consummation devoutly to be wished'; attraction, magnet, allurement, fancy, temptation, seduction, lure, fascination, *prestige*, height of one's ambition, idol; whim, -sey; maggot; hobby, -horse.

Fortunatus's cap, wishing cap, love potion.

V. desire; wish, – for; be -desirous &c. *adj.*; have a -longing &c. *n.*; hope &c. 858.

care for, affect, like, list; take to, cling to, take a fancy to; fancy; prefer &c. (*choose*) 609.

have -an eye, – a mind- to; find it in one's heart &c. (*be willing*) 602; have a fancy for, set one's eyes upon; cast a sheep's eye –, look sweet- upon; take into one's head, have at heart, be bent upon; set one's -cap at, – heart upon, – mind upon; covet.

want, miss, need, lack, desiderate, feel the want of; would fain -have, – do; would be glad of.

be -hungry &c. *adj.*; have a good appetite, play a good knife and fork; hunger –, thirst –, crave –, lust –, itch –, hanker –, run mad- after; raven –, die- for; burn to.

desiderate; sigh –, cry –, gape –, gasp –, pine –, pant –, languish –, yearn –, long –, be on thorns –, hope- for; aspire after; catch at, grasp at, jump at.

woo, court, solicit; fish –, spell –, whistle –, put up- for; ogle.

cause –, create –, raise –, excite –, provoke- desire; whet the appetite; appetize, titillate, allure, attract, take one's fancy, tempt; hold out -temptation, – allurement; tantalize, make one's mouth water, *faire venir l'eau à la bouche*.

gratify desire &c. (*give pleasure*) 829.

Adj. desirous; desiring &c. *v.*; orectic, appetitive; inclined &c. (*willing*) 602; partial to; fain, wishful, optative; anxious, wistful, curious; at a loss for, sedulous, solicitous.

craving, hungry, sharp-set, peckish,

Int. never mind.

867. Dislike.—N. dis-like, -taste, -relish, -inclination, -placency.

reluctance; backwardness &c. (*unwillingness*) 603.

repugnance, disgust, queasiness, turn, nausea, loathing; avers-eness, -ation, -ion; abomination, antipathy, abhorrence, horror; mortal –, rooted- -antipathy, – horror; hatred, detestation; hate &c. 898; animosity &c. 900; hydrophobia.

sickener; gall and wormwood &c. (*unsavoury*) 395; shuddering, cold sweat.

V. dis-, mis-like, -relish; mind, object to; have rather not, not care for; have –, conceive –, entertain –, take- -a dislike, – an aversion- to; have no -taste, – stomach- for.

shun, avoid &c. 623; eschew; withdraw –, shrink –, recoil- from; not be able to -bear, – abide, – endure; shrug the shoulders at, shudder at, turn up the nose at, look askance at; make a -mouth, – wry face, – grimace; make faces.

loathe, nauseate, abominate, detest, abhor; hate &c. 898; take amiss &c. 900; have enough of &c. (*be satiated*) 869.

cause –, excite- dislike; disincline, repel, sicken; make –, render- sick; turn one's stomach, nauseate, wamble, disgust, shock, stink in the nostrils; go against the -grain, – stomach; stick in the throat; make one's blood run cold &c. (*give pain*) 830; pall.

Adj. disliking &c. *v.*; averse to, loth, adverse; shy of, sick of, out of conceit with; disinclined; heart-, dog-sick; queasy.

disliked &c. *v.*; uncared for, unpopular; out of favour; repulsive, repugnant, repellent; abhorrent, insufferable, fulsome, nauseous; loath-some, -ful; offensive; disgusting &c. *v.*; disagreeable &c. (*painful*) 830; unsavoury &c. 395.

Adv. *usque ad nauseam.*

Int. faugh! foh! ugh!

868. Fastidiousness.—N. fastidiousness &c. *adj.*; nicety, meticulosity,

ravening, with an empty stomach, esurient, lickerish, thirsty, athirst, parched
with thirst, pinched with hunger, famished, dry, drouthy; hungry as a
-hunter, – hawk, – horse, – church
mouse.

greedy, – as a hog; over-eager, voracious; ravenous, – as a wolf; open-
mouthed, covetous, rapacious, grasping, extortionate, exacting, sordid,
alieni appetens; insati-able, -ate; unquenchable, quenchless; omnivorous.

unsatisfied, unsated, unslaked.

eager, avid, keen; burning, fervent,
ardent; agog; all agog; breathless;
impatient &c. (*impetuous*) 825; bent –,
intent –, set- -on, – upon; mad after,
enragé, rabid, dying for, devoured by
desire.

aspiring, ambitious, vaulting, sky-
aspiring.

desirable; popular; desired &c. *v.*; in
demand; pleasing &c. (*giving pleasure*)
829; appeti-zing, -ble; tantalizing.

Adv. wistfully &c. *adj.*; fain.

Int. would -that, – it were! O for!
esto perpetua! if only!

Phr. the wish being father to the
thought; *sua cuique voluptas*; *hoc erat
in votis*, the mouth watering, the fingers
itching; *aut Cæsar aut nullus.*

hypercriticism, difficulty in being
pleased, *friandise*, epicurism, *omnia
suspendens naso.*

discrimination, discernment, good
taste, perspicacity.

epicure, gourmet.

[Excess of delicacy] prudery, prud-
ishness, primness.

V. be -fastidious &c. *adj.*; split hairs,
discriminate, have a sweet tooth.

mince the matter; turn up one's nose
at &c. (*disdain*) 930; look a gift horse
in the mouth, see spots on the sun.

Adj. fastidious, meticulous, exacting,
nice, delicate, *délicat*, finical, finicky,
difficult, dainty, lickerish, squeamish,
thin-skinned; s-, queasy; hard -, diffi-
cult- to please; querulous, particular,
over-particular, straitlaced, prudish,
prim, scrupulous; censorious &c. 932;
hypercritical, discriminating, discerning, perspicacious.

Phr. *noli me tangere.*

869. Satiety.—N. satiety, satisfaction, saturation, repletion, glut, surfeit; weariness &c. 841.

spoiled child; *enfant gâté*; too much
of a good thing, *toujours perdrix*;
crambe repetita.

V. sate, satiate, satisfy, saturate;
cloy, quench, slake, pall, glut, gorge,
surfeit; bore &c. (*weary*) 841; tire &c.
(*fatigue*) 688; spoil.

have -enough of, – quite enough of, – one's fill, – too much of; be
-satiated &c. *adj.*

Adj. satiated &c. *v.*; overgorged; *blasé*, used up, sick of, heart-sick.

Int. enough! hold! *eheu jam satis!*

4°. Contemplative Affections

870. Wonder.—N. wonder, marvel;
astonish-, amaze-, wonder-, bewilderment; amazedness &c. *adj.*; admiration, awe; stup-or, -efaction; stound,
fascination; sensation; surprise &c.
(*inexpectation*) 508; cynosure.

note of admiration; thaumaturgy
&c. (*sorcery*) 992.

V. wonder, marvel, admire; be -sur-
prised &c. *adj.*; start; stare; open -,
rub -, turn up- one's eyes; gloar; gape,
open one's mouth, hold one's breath;

871. [Absence of wonder.] **Expectance.—N.** expectan-ce, -cy &c. (*expectation*) 507; calmness, composure, tranquillity, serenity, coolness, imperturb-
ability &c. 826.

nine days' wonder.

V. expect &c. 507; not -be surprised,
– wonder &c. 870; *nil admirari*, make
nothing of.

Adj. expecting &c. *v.*; unamazed,
astonished at nothing; *blasé* &c. (*weary*)
841; unimaginative, calm, serene, im-

look –, stand- -aghast, – agog; look blank &c. (*disappointment*) 509; *tomber des nues*; not believe one's -eyes, – ears, – senses.

not be able to account for &c. (*unintelligible*) 519; not know whether one stands on one's head or one's heels.

surprise, astonish, amaze, astound; dumbfound, -er; startle, dazzle; strike, – with -wonder, – awe; electrify; stun, stupefy, petrify, confound, bewilder, flabbergast; stagger, throw on one's beam ends, fascinate, turn the head, take away one's breath, strike dumb; make one's -hair stand on end, – tongue cleave to the roof of one's mouth; make one stare.

take by surprise &c. (*be unexpected*) 508.

be -wonderful &c. *adj.*; beggar –, baffle- description; stagger belief.

Adj. surprised &c. *v.*; aghast, all agog, breathless, agape; openmouthed; awe-, thunder-, moon-, planet-struck; spell-bound; lost in -amazement, – wonder, – astonishment; struck all of a heap, unable to believe one's senses, like a duck in thunder.

wonderful, wondrous; surprising &c. *v.*; unexpected &c. 508; unheard of; mysterious &c. (*inexplicable*) 519; miraculous; *foudroyant*.

in-describable, -expressible, -effable; un-utterable, -speakable.

monstrous, prodigious, stupendous, marvellous; in-conceivable, -credible; in-, un-imaginable; strange &c. (*uncommon*) 83; passing strange.

striking &c. *v.*; over-whelming; wonder-working.

Adv. wonderfully &c. *adj.*; fearfully; for a –, in the name of-wonder; strange to say; *mirabile -dictu, – visu*; to one's great surprise.

with -wonder &c. *n.*, – gaping mouth, – open eyes, – upturned eyes; eyes starting out of one's head.

Int. lo, – and behold! O! hey-day! halloo! what! indeed! really! surely! humph! hem! good -lack, – heavens, – gracious! – lord! by jove! gad so! well a day! dear me! only think! lack-a-daisy! my -stars, – goodness! gracious goodness! goodness gracious! mercy on us! heavens and earth! God bless me! bless -us, – my heart! odzookens! *O gemini!* adzooks! hoity-toity! strong! Heaven save –, bless- the mark! can such things be! zounds! 'sdeath! what -on earth, – in the world! who would have thought it! &c. (*inexpectation*) 508; fancy! did you ever? you don't say so! what do you say to that! how now! where am I? well I'm blowed! &c.

Phr. *vox faucibus hæsit*; one's hair standing on end.

perturbable &c. 826; expected &c. *v.*; foreseen.

common, ordinary &c. (*habitual*) 613.

Int. no wonder; of course; why not?

———

872. Prodigy.—N. prodigy, phenomenon; wonder, -ment; genius, marvel, miracle; freak, monster &c. (*unconformity*) 83; curiosity, lion, infant prodigy, sight, spectacle; *jeu –, coup- de théâtre*; gazing-stock; sign; portent &c. 512.

bursting of a -shell, – bomb; volcanic eruption, peal of thunder; thunder-clap, -bolt.

what no words can paint; wonders of the world; *annus mirabilis*; *dignus vindice nodus*.

5°. Intrinsic Affections*

873. Repute.—N. distinction, mark, name, figure; repute, reputation, char-

874. Disrepute.—N. disrepute, discredit; ill-, bad- -repute, -name, -odour,

* Or personal affections derived from the opinions or feelings of others.

acter; good –, high- repute; note, notability, notoriety, *éclat*, 'the bubble
reputation,' vogue, celebrity; fame,
famousness; renown; popularity, *aura
popularis*; esteem, approval, approbation &c. 931; credit, *succès d'estime*,
prestige, talk of the town; name to
conjure with.

glory, honour; lustre &c. (*light*) 420;
illustriousness &c. *adj.*

account, regard, respect; reputable-
ness &c. *adj.*; respectability &c. (*probity*) 939; good -name, – report; fair
name.

dignity; stateliness &c. *adj.*; solemnity, grandeur, splendour, nobility,
majesty, sublimity.

rank, standing, brevet rank, precedence, *pas*, station, place, *status*; position, – in society; order, degree, *locus
standi*, caste, condition.

greatness &c. *adj.*; eminence; height
&c. 206; importance &c. 642; pre-,
super-eminence; high mightiness, primacy; top of the -ladder, – tree.

elevation; ascent &c. 305; super-,
ex-altation; dignification, aggrandizement.

dedication, consecration, enthronement, canonization, apotheosis, deification, celebration, enshrinement, glorification.

hero, man of mark, great card, celebrity, worthy, lion, *rara avis*, notability, somebody; man of rank &c.
(*nobleman*) 875; pillar of the -state,
- society, – church.

chief &c. (*master*) 745; first fiddle
&c. (*proficient*) 700; scholar &c. 492;
cynosure, mirror; flower, pink, pearl;
paragon &c. (*perfection*) 650; choice
and master spirits of the age; *élite*;
star, sun, constellation, galaxy.

ornament, honour, feather in one's
cap, halo, aureole, nimbus; halo –,
blaze- of glory; blushing honours;
laurels &c. (*trophy*) 733.

memory, posthumous fame, niche in
the temple of fame; immor-tality, -tal
name; *magni nominis umbra*.

V. be conscious of glory; be proud
of &c. (*pride*) 878; exult &c. (*boast*)
884; be vain of &c. (*vanity*) 880.

be -distinguished &c. *adj.*; shine &c.

-favour; disapprobation &c. 932; in-
gloriousness, derogation; a-, de-base-
ment; abjectness &c. *adj.*; degradation,
dedecoration; 'a long farewell to all
one's greatness'; odium, obloquy, opprobrium, ignominy.

dishonour, disgrace; shame, humiliation; scandal, baseness, vileness;
perfidy, turpitude &c. (*improbity*) 940;
infamy.

tarnish, taint, defilement, pollution.
stain, blot, spot, blur, stigma, brand,
reproach, imputation, slur.

crying –, burning- shame; *scandalum
magnatum*, badge of infamy, blot in
one's escutcheon; bend –, bar- sinister;
champain, point champain; by-word
of reproach; Ichabod.

argumentum ad verecundiam; sense
of shame &c. 879.

V. be -inglorious &c. *adj.*; incur
-disgrace &c. *n.*; have –, earn- a bad
name; put –, wear- a halter round one's
neck; disgrace –, expose- oneself.

play second fiddle; lose caste; pale
one's ineffectual fire; recede into the
shade; fall from one's high estate; keep
in the background &c. (*modesty*) 881;
be conscious of disgrace &c. (*humility*)
879; look -blue, – foolish, – like a fool;
cut a -poor, – sorry- figure; laugh on
the wrong side of the mouth; make a
sorry face, go away with a flea in one's
ear, slink away.

cause -shame &c. *n.*; shame, disgrace,
put to shame, dishonour; throw –,
cast –, fling –, reflect- dishonour &c.
n. upon; be a -reproach &c. *n.* to; derogate from.

tarnish, stain, blot, sully, taint; discredit; degrade, debase, defile; beggar;
expel &c. (*punish*) 972.

impute shame to, brand, post, stigmatize, vilify, defame, slur, cast a slur
upon, hold up to shame, send to Coventry; tread –, trample- under foot;
show up, drag through the mire, heap
dirt upon; reprehend &c. 932.

bring low, put down, snub; take
down a peg, – lower, – or two.

obscure, eclipse, outshine, take the
shine out of; throw –, cast- into the
shade; overshadow; leave –, put- in
the background; push into a corner,

(*light*) 420; shine forth, figure; make –, cut- a -figure, – dash, – splash.

rival, surpass; out-shine, -rival, -vie, -jump; emulate, vie with, eclipse; throw –, cast- into the shade; over-shadow.

live, flourish, glitter, scintillate, flaunt; gain –, acquire- honour &c. *n.*; play first fiddle &c. (*be of importance*) 642; bear the -palm, – bell; lead the way; take -precedence, – the wall of; gain –, win- -laurels, – spurs, – golden opinions &c. (*approbation*) 931; gradu-ate, take one's degree, pass one's exami-nation, win a -scholarship, – fellowship.

make -a, – some- -noise, – noise in the world; leave one's mark, exalt one's horn, star, have a run, be run after; enjoy popularity, come -into vogue, – to the front; raise one's head.

enthrone, signalize, immortalize, deify, exalt to the skies; hand one's name down to posterity.

consecrate; dedicate to, devote to; enshrine, inscribe, blazon, lionize, blow the trumpet, crown with laurel.

confer –, reflect- honour &c. *n.* on; shed a lustre on; redound to one's honour, ennoble.

give –, do –, pay –, render- honour to; honour, accredit, pay regard to, dignify, glorify; sing praises to &c. (*approve*) 931; look up to; exalt, aggran-dize, elevate, nobilitate.

Adj. distinguished, *distingué*, noted; of -note &c. *n.*; honoured &c. *v.*; popu-lar; fashionable &c. 852.

put one's nose out of joint; put out, – of countenance.

upset, throw off one's centre; dis-compose, disconcert; put to the blush &c. (*humble*) 879.

Adj. disgraced &c. *v.*; blown upon; shorn of -its beams, – one's glory; overcome, down-trodden; loaded with -shame &c. *n.*; in -bad repute &c. *n.*; out of -repute, – favour, – fashion, – countenance; at a discount; under -a cloud, – an eclipse; unable to show one's face; in the -shade, – back-ground; out at elbows, down in the world, down and out.

inglorious; nameless, renownless, ob-scure, unknown to fame; un-noticed, -noted, -honoured, -glorified.

shameful; dis-graceful, -creditable, -reputable; despicable; questionable; unbecoming, unworthy; derogatory; degrading, humiliating, *infra digni-tatem*, dedecorous; scandalous, infa-mous, too bad, unmentionable; ribald, opprobrious; arrant, shocking, outra-geous, notorious, shady.

ignominious, scrubby, dirty, abject, vile, beggarly, pitiful, low, mean, shabby; base &c. (*dishonourable*) 940.

Adv. to one's shame be it spoken.

Int. fie! shame! for shame! *proh pudor! O tempora! O mores!* ough! *sic transit gloria mundi!*

in good odour; in –, in high- favour; reput-, respect-, credit-able.

remarkable &c. (*important*) 642; notable, notorious; celebrated, renowned, in every one's mouth, talked of; fam-ous, -ed; far-famed; conspicuous, to the front; foremost; in the -front rank, – ascendant.

imperishable, deathless, immortal, never fading, *ære perennius*; time-honoured.

illustrious, glorious, splendid, brilliant, radiant; bright &c. 420; full-blown; honorific.

eminent, prominent; high &c. 206; in the zenith; at the -head of, – top of the tree; peerless, of the first water; superior &c. 33; super-, pre-eminent.

great, dignified, proud, noble, honourable, worshipful, lordly, grand, stately, august, princely, imposing, solemn, transcendent, majestic, sacred, sublime, heaven-born, heroic, *sans peur et sans reproche*; sacrosanct.

Int. hail! all hail! *ave! viva! vive!* long life to! glory –, honour- be to!

Phr. one's name -being in every mouth, – living for ever; *sic itur ad astra, fama volat, aut Cæsar aut nullus*; not to know him argues oneself unknown; none but himself could be his parallel, *palmam qui meruit ferat.*

875. Nobility.—N. nobility, rank, condition, distinction, optimacy, blood, *pur sang*, birth, high descent, order; quality, gentility; blue blood of Castile; *ancien régime.*

high life, *haut monde*; upper -classes, – ten thousand; *élite*, aristocracy, great folks; fashionable world &c. (*fashion*) 852; salariat.

peer, -age; house of -lords, – peers; lords, – temporal and spiritual; *noblesse*; baronage, knightage; noble, -man; lord, -ling; grandee, *magnifico, hidalgo*; don, -ship; aristocrat, swell, three-tailed bashaw; gentleman, squire, squireen, patrician, laureate.

gentry, gentlefolk; squirarchy, better sort, *magnates, primates, optimates.*

king &c. (*master*) 745; prince, crown prince, *Dauphin*; duke; marquis, -ate; earl, viscount, baron, thane, banneret; baronet, -cy; knight, -hood; count, armiger, laird; sig-, seig-nior; esquire, boyar, margrave, vavasour, sheik, emir, ameer, scherif, *pasha*, effendi, sahib.

queen &c. 745; princess, begum, duchess, marchioness; countess &c.; lady, dame.

personage –, man- of -distinction, – mark, – rank; nota-bles, -bilities; celebrity, big-wig, magnate, great man, star; *magni nominis umbra*; 'every inch a king'; grand Panjandrum.

V. be -noble &c. *adj.*

Adj. noble, exalted; of -rank &c. *n.*; princely, titled, patrician, aristocratic; high-, well-born; of gentle blood; genteel, *comme il faut*, gentlemanlike, courtly &c. (*fashionable*) 852; highly respectable.

Adv. in high quarters.

877. Title.—N. title, honour; knighthood &c. (*nobility*) 875.

royal –, serene- highness, excellency, grace; lordship, worship, Rt. Hon., rever-ence, -end; esquire, sir; madam, *madame*; master, mistress, Mr., Mrs., *signor, señor, Mein Herr, mynheer*;

876. Commonalty.—N. commonalty, democracy; obscurity; low -condition, – life, – society, – company; *bourgeoisie*; mass of -the people, – society; Brown, Jones, and Robinson; Tom, Dick, and Harry; lower –, humbler- -classes, – orders; vulgar –, common- herd; rank and file, *hoc genus omne*; the -many, – general, – crowd, – people, – populace, – multitude, – million, – masses, – mobility, – peasantry; king Mob; proletariat, *fruges consumere nati*, great unwashed; man in the street.

mob; rabble, – rout; chaff, rout, horde, *canaille*; scum –, *residuum* –, dregs- of -the people, – society; swinish multitude, *fæx populi*; *profanum* –, *ignobile- vulgus*; vermin, riff-raff, tag-rag and bobtail; small fry.

commoner, one of the people, democrat, plebeian, republican, proletary, *prolétaire, roturier*, Mr. Snooks, *bourgeois, épicier*, Philistine, cockney; *grisette, demi-monde.*

peasant, countryman, boor, carle, churl; vill-ain, -ein; serf, kern, tyke, tike, chuff, ryot, fellah; long-shore-man; swain, clown, hind; clod, -hopper; hobnail, yokel, hick, rube, cider squeezer, bog-trotter, bumpkin; plough-man, -boy; rustic, chawbacon, tiller of the soil; hewers of wood and drawers of water, groundling; gaffer, loon, put, cub, Tony Lumpkin, looby, lout, under-ling; *gamin*, guttersnipe, street arab, mudlark; rough, rowdy, ruffian, roughneck; pot-wallopper, slubberde-gullion; vulgar –, low- fellow; cad, curmudgeon.

upstart, *parvenu, nouveau-riche*, skip-jack; nobody, – one knows; *hesterni quirites, pessoribus orti; bourgeois gentil-homme, novus homo*, snob, gent, mush-room, no one knows who, adventurer; man of straw.

beggar, panhandler, gaberlunzie, muckworm, mudlark, *sans-culotte*, raff, tatterdemalion, caitiff, ragamuffin, Pariah, outcast of society, tramp, weary Willie, bum, vagabond, *chiffon-*

your –, his- honour; handle to one's name.

decoration, laurel, palm, wreath, garland, bays, medal, ribbon, riband, blue ribbon, *cordon*, cross, crown, coronet, star, garter; feather, – in one's cap; chevron, epaulet, *épaulette*, colours, cockade; livery; order, arms, armorial bearings, shield, scutcheon, crest, reward &c. 973.

nier, rag-picker, Cinderella, cinder-wench, scrub, jade; boots, gossoon.

Goth, Vandal, Hottentot, savage, barbarian, Yahoo; unlicked cub, rough diamond.

barbar-ousness, -ism; Bœotia.

V. be -ignoble &c. *adj.*, – nobody &c. *n.*

Adj. ignoble, common, mean, low, base, vile, sorry, scrubby, beggarly, below par; no great shakes &c. (*unimportant*) 643; home-ly, -spun; vulgar, low-minded; snobbish, *parvenu*.

plebeian, proletarian; of -low, – mean- -parentage, – origin, extraction; low-, base-, earth-born, low bred; mushroom, dunghill, risen from the ranks; unknown to fame, obscure, untitled.

rustic, uncivilized; lout-, boor-, clown-, churl-, brut-, raff-ish; rude, unlicked, unpolished.

barbar-ous, -ian, -ic, -esque; cockney, born within sound of Bow bells.

underling, menial, servile, subaltern.

Adv. below the salt.

---

878. Pride.—N. dignity, self-respect, *mens sibi conscia recti.*

pride; haughtiness &c. *adj.*; high notions, *hauteur*; vainglory, crest; arrogance &c. (*assumption*) 885; pomposity &c. 882.

proud man, highflier; fine -gentleman, – lady; *grande dame.*

V. be -proud &c. *adj.*; put a good face on; look one in the face; stalk abroad, perk oneself up; presume, swagger, strut; rear –, lift up –, hold up- one's head; hold one's head high, look big, take the wall, 'bear like the Turk no rival near the throne,' carry with a high hand; ride the –, mount on one's- high horse; set one's back up, bridle, toss the head; give oneself airs &c. (*assume*) 885; boast &c. 884.

pride oneself on; glory in, take a pride in; pique –, plume –, hug- oneself; stand upon, be proud of; put a good face on; not -hide one's light under a bushel, – put one's talent in a napkin; not think small beer of oneself &c. (*vanity*) 880.

Adj. dignified; stately; proud, -crested; lordly, baronial; lofty-minded; high-souled, -minded, -mettled, -handed, -plumed, -flown, -toned.

879. Humility.—N. hum-ility, -bleness; meek-, low-ness; lowli-ness, -hood; abasement, self-abasement, -effacement; submission &c. 725; resignation.

condescension; affability &c. (*courtesy*) 894.

modesty &c. 881; verecundity, blush, suffusion, confusion; sense of -shame, – disgrace; humiliation, mortification; let –, set- down.

V. be -humble &c. *adj.*; deign, vouchsafe, condescend; humble –, demean- oneself; stoop, – to conquer; carry coals; submit &c. 725; submit with a good grace &c. (*brook*) 826; yield the palm.

lower one's -tone, – note; sing small, draw in one's horns, sober down; hide one's -face, – diminished head; not dare to show one's face, take shame to oneself, not have a word to say for oneself; feel –, be conscious of- -shame, – disgrace; drink the cup of humiliation to the dregs; eat -humble pie, – one's words, – dirt; be humiliated, receive a snub.

blush -for, – up to the eyes; redden, change colour; colour up; hang one's head, look foolish, feel small.

render humble; humble, humiliate;

haughty, paughty, insolent, lofty, high, mighty, swollen, puffed up, flushed, blown; vain-glorious; purse-proud, fine; proud as -a peacock, Lucifer; bloated with pride.

supercilious, disdainful, bumptious, magisterial, imperious; high -handed, – and mighty; overweening, consequential; arrogant &c. 885; unblushing &c. 880.

stiff, -necked; starch; perked –, stuck- up; in buckram, straitlaced; prim &c. (*affected*) 855.

on one's -high horses, – tight ropes, – high ropes; on stilts; *en grand seigneur*.

Adv. with head erect, with one's nose in the air.

Phr. *odi profanum vulgus et arceo.*

let –, set –, take –, tread –, frowndown; snub, abash, abase, make one sing small, strike dumb; teach one -his distance, – his place; take down a peg, – lower; throw –, cast- into the shade &c. 874; stare –, put- out of countenance; put to the blush; confuse, ashame, mortify, disgrace, crush; send away with a flea in one's ear.

get a set down.

Adj. humble, lowly, meek; modest &c. 881; humble-, sober-minded; unoffended; submissive &c. 725; servile &c. 886.

condescending; affable &c. (*courteous*) 894.

humbled &c. *v.*; bowed down, resigned; abashed, ashamed, dashed; out of countenance; down in the mouth; down on one's -knees, – marrow-bones; humbled in the dust, brow-beaten; chap-, crest-fallen; dumbfoundered, flabbergasted, struck all of a heap.

shorn of one's glory &c. (*disrepute*) 874.

Adv. with -downcast eyes, – bated breath, – bended knee; on all fours, on one's feet.

under correction, with due deference.

Phr. I am your -obedient, – very humble- servant; my service to you.

---

880. Vanity.—N. vanity; conceit, -edness; self-conceit, -complacency, -confidence, -sufficiency, -esteem, -love, -approbation, -praise, -glorification, -laudation, -gratulation, -applause, -admiration; *amour-propre*; selfishness &c. 943.

airs, pretensions, mannerism; egotism; prigg-ism, -ishness; coxcombery, gaudery, vainglory, elation; pride &c. 878; ostentation &c. 882; assurance &c. 885.

vox et præterea nihil; *cheval de bataille.*

ego-ist, -tist; peacock, coxcomb &c. 854; Sir Oracle &c. 887.

V. be -vain &c. *adj.*, – vain of; pique oneself &c. (*pride*) 878; lay the flattering unction to one's soul.

have -too high, – an overweening-opinion of -oneself, – one's talents; blind oneself as to one's own merit; not think -small beer, – *vin ordinaire*-of oneself; put oneself forward; fish

881. Modesty.—N. modesty; humility &c. 879; diffidence, timidity; retiring disposition, unobtrusiveness, bashfulness &c. *adj.*; *mauvaise honte*; blush, -ing; verecundity; self-knowledge.

reserve, constraint; demureness &c. *adj.*; blushing honours.

V. be -modest &c. *adj.*; retire, reserve oneself; give way to; draw in one's horns &c. 879; hide one's face.

keep -private, – in the background, – one's distance; pursue the noiseless tenor of one's way, 'do good by stealth and blush to find it fame,' hide one's light under a bushel, cast a sheep's eye.

Adj. modest, diffident; humble &c. 879; timid, timorous, bashful; shy, nervous, skittish, coy, sheepish, shamefaced, blushing, over-modest.

unpreten-ding, -tious; un-obtrusive, -assuming, -ostentatious, -boastful, -aspiring; poor in spirit.

for compliments; give oneself airs &c. (*assume*) 885; boast &c. 884.

render -vain &c. *adj.*; inspire with -vanity &c. *n.*; inflate, puff up, turn up, turn one's head.

Adj. vain, – as a peacock; conceited, assured, overweening, pert, forward, perky; vain-glorious, high-flown; ostentatious &c. 882; puffed up, inflated, flushed.

self-satisfied, -confident, -sufficient, -flattering, -admiring, -applauding, -glorious, -opinionated; *entêté* &c. (*wrong-headed*) 481; wise in one's own conceit, pragmatical, overwise, pretentious, priggish; egotistic, -al; *soi-disant* &c. (*boastful*) 884; arrogant &c. 885.

un-abashed, -blushing; un-constrained, -ceremonious; free and easy.

Adv. vainly &c. *adj.*

Phr. how we apples swim!

out of countenance &c. (*humbled*) 879.

reserved, constrained, demure.

Adv. humbly &c. *adj.*; quietly, privately; without -ceremony, – beat of drum; *sans façon.*

---

882. Ostentation.—N. ostentation, display, show, flourish, parade, *étalage*, pomp, array, state, solemnity; dash, splash, glitter, strut, swank, side, swagger, pomposity; preten-se, -sions; showing off; fuss.

magnificence, splendour; *coup d'œil*; grand doings.

coup de théâtre; stage -effect, – trick; clap-trap; *mise en scène*; *tour de force*; *chic*.

demonstration, flying colours; tomfoolery; flourish of trumpets &c. (*celebration*) 883; pageant, -ry; spectacle, exhibition, procession; turn –, set- out; grand function; *fête*, gala, field-day, review, march past, promenade, insubstantial pageant.

dress; court –, full –, evening –, ball –, fancy- dress; tailoring, millinery, man-millinery, frippery; foppery, equipage.

ceremon-y, -ial; ritual; form, -ality; etiquette; punct-o, -ilio, -iliousness; starched-, stateli-ness.

mummery, solemn mockery, mouth honour.

attitudinarian; fop &c. 854.

V. be -ostentatious &c. *adj.*; come –, put oneself- forward; attract attention, star it.

make –, cut- a -figure, – dash, – splash; strut, blow one's own trumpet; figure, – away; make a show, – display; glitter.

show -off, – one's paces; parade, march past; display, exhibit, put forward, hold up; trot –, hang- out; sport, brandish, blazon forth; dangle, – before the eyes.

cry up &c. (*praise*) 931; *prôner*, flaunt, emblazon, prink, set off, mount, have framed and glazed.

put a good, – smiling- face upon; clean the outside of the platter &c. (*disguise*) 544.

Adj. ostentatious, showy, dashing, pretentious; ja-, jau-nty; grand, pompous, palatial; high-sounding; turgid &c. (*big-sounding*) 577; garish, gorgeous; gaudy, – as a -peacock, – butterfly, – tulip; flaunting, flashing, flaming, glittering; gay &c. (*ornate*) 847; colourful.

splendid, magnificent, sumptuous.

theatrical, dramatic, spectacular, scenic, ceremonial, ritual, -istic.

solemn, stately, majestic, formal, stiff, ceremonious, punctilious, starch-ed, -y.

en grande tenue, in best bib and tucker, in Sunday best, *endimanché*.

Adv. with -flourish of trumpet, – beat of drum, – flying colours, – a brass band.

ad captandum vulgus.

883. Celebration.—N. celebration, solemnization, jubilee, diamond jubilee, commemoration, ovation, pæan, triumph, jubilation.

triumphal arch, bonfire, salute; salvo, – of artillery; *feu de joie*, flourish of trumpets, *fanfare*, colours flying, illuminations, fireworks.

inauguration, installation, presentation; *début*, coming out, birth-day anniversary, bi-, ter-, centenary; silver –, golden –, diamond-wedding, -day; coronation; Lord Mayor's show; harvest home, red letter day, festival; trophy &c. 733; *Te Deum* &c. (*thanksgiving*) 990; fête &c. 882; holiday &c. 840.

V. celebrate, keep, signalize, do honour to, commemorate, solemnize, hallow, mark with a red letter, hold high festival, maffick.

pledge, drink to, toast, hob and nob.

inaugurate, install, instate, induct, chair.

rejoice &c. 838; kill the fatted calf, hold jubilee, roast an ox, fire a salute.

Adj. celebrating &c. *v.*; commemorative, celebrated, immortal.

Adv. in -honour, – commemoration, – celebration of.

Int. hail! all hail! *io* -*pæan*, – *triumphe!* 'see the conquering hero comes!'

884. Boasting.—N. boasting &c. *v.*; boast, vaunt, crake; preten-ce, -sions; puff, -ery; flourish, *fanfaronnade*; gasconade; bluff, swank, brag, -gardism; bravado, bunkum, Buncombe; highfalutin; jact-itation, -ancy; bounce, rant, bluster; venditation, vapouring, rodomontade, bombast, fine talking, tall talk, magniloquence, teratology, heroics; jingoism, Chauvinism; exaggeration &c. 549; gas, hot air.

vanity &c. 880; *vox et præterea nihil*; much cry and little wool, *brutum fulmen*.

exultation; glorification; flourish of trumpets; triumph &c. 883.

boaster; bragg-art, -adocio; hot air merchant; Gascon, *fanfaron*, pretender, fourflusher, *soi-disant*; windbag, blowhard, bluffer; chau-vinist; blusterer &c. 887; charlatan, jack-pudding, trumpeter; puppy &c. (*fop*) 854.

V. boast, make a boast of, brag, vaunt, puff, show off, flourish, crake, crack, trumpet, strut, swagger, vapour, bluff; draw the long bow.

exult, crow over, neigh, chuckle, triumph; glory, gloat, jubilate; throw up one's cap; talk big, *se faire valoir*, *faire claquer son fouet*, take merit to oneself, make a merit of, sing *Io triumphe*, holloa before one is out of the wood.

Adj. boasting &c. *v.*; magniloquent, flaming, Thrasonic, stilted, gas-conading, braggart, boastful, pretentious, *soi-disant*; vain-glorious &c. (*conceited*) 880.

elate, -d; jubilant, triumphant, exultant; in high feather; flushed, – with victory; cock-a-hoop; on stilts.

vaunted &c. *v.*

Adv. vauntingly &c. *adj.*; with a brass band.

Phr. 'let the galled jade wince.'

885. [Undue assumption of superiority.] **Insolence.—N.** insolence; haughtiness &c. *adj.*; arrogance, airs; overbearance, brashness, bumptiousness, contumely, disdain; domineering &c. *v.*; tyranny &c. 739.

impertinence; cheek, nerve, sauce; sauciness &c. *adj.*; flippancy, dicacity, petulance, procacity, bluster; swagger, -ing &c. *v.*; bounce; terrorism; jingoism, chauvinism.

as-, pre-sumption; beggar on horseback; usurpation.

impudence, assurance, audacity, self-assertion, hardihood, front, face, brass; shamelessness &c. *adj.*; effrontery, hardened front, face of brass.

assumption of infallibility.

malapert, saucebox &c. (*blusterer*) 887.

V. be -insolent &c. *adj.*; bluster, vapour, swagger, swell, give oneself airs, snap one's fingers, kick up a dust; swear &c. (*affirm*) 535; rap out oaths; roister.

arrogate; as-, pre-sume; make -bold, – free; take a liberty, give an inch and take an ell.

domineer, bully, dictate, hector; lord it over, bulldoze; *traiter de haut, regarder de haut en bas*; exact; snub, huff, beard, fly in the face of; put to the blush; bear –, beat- down; browbeat, intimidate; trample –, tread- -down, – under foot; dragoon, ride roughshod over, terrorize.

out-face, -look, -stare, -brazen, -brave; stare out of countenance; brazen out; lay down the law; teach one's grandmother to suck eggs; assume a lofty bearing; talk –, look- big; put on big looks, act the *grand seigneur*; mount –, ride- the high horse; toss the head, carry with a high hand.

tempt Providence, want snuffing.

Adj. insolent, haughty, arrogant, imperious, magisterial, dictatorial, arbitrary; high-handed, high and mighty; contumelious, supercilious, overbearing, intolerant, domineering; overweening, high-flown.

flippant, pert, cavalier, saucy, forward, impertinent, fresh, malapert.

precocious, assuming, would-be, bumptious.

bluff; brazen-, browed-faced, shameless, aweless, unblushing, unabashed; bold-, bare-faced; dead –, lost- to shame.

886. Servility.—N. servility; slavery &c. (*subjection*) 749; obsequiousness &c. *adj.*; subserviency; abasement; pros-tration, -ternation; genuflexion &c. (*worship*) 990; fawning &c. *v.*; tuft-hunting, time-serving, flunkeyism; sycophancy &c. (*flattery*) 933; humility &c. 879.

sycophant, parasite, yes-man; toad, -y, -eater; tuft-hunter; snob, flunkey, lap-dog, spaniel, lick-spittle, smell-feast, *Græculus esuriens*, hanger on, stooge, *cavaliere servente*, led captain, carpet knight; time-server, fortune-hunter, Vicar of Bray, Sir Pertinax Mac Sycophant, pick-thank; flatterer &c. 935; doer of dirty work; *âme damnée*, tool; reptile; slave &c. (*servant*) 746; courtier; sponge, jackal; truckler.

V. cringe, bow, stoop, kneel, bend the knee; fall on one's knees, prostrate oneself; worship &c. 990.

sneak, crawl, crouch, cower, truckle to, grovel, fawn, toady, lick the feet of, kiss the hem of one's garment.

pay court to; feed –, fatten –, batten- on; dance attendance on, pin oneself upon, hang on the sleeve of, *avaler des couleuvres*, keep time to, fetch and carry, do the dirty work of.

go with the stream, follow the crowd, worship the rising sun, hold with the hare and run with the hounds.

Adj. servile, obsequious; supple, – as a glove; soapy, oily, pliant, cringing, fawning, slavish, grovelling, sniveling, mealy-mouthed; beggarly, sycophantic, parasitical; abject, prostrate, down on one's marrow-bones; base, mean, sneaking; crouching &c. *v.*

Adv. hat –, cap- in hand.

impudent, audacious, presumptuous, free and easy, devil-may-care, rollicking; janty, jaunty; roistering, blustering, hectoring, swaggering, vapouring; thrasonic, fire-eating, 'full of sound and fury.'

Adv. insolently, with a high hand; *ex cathedrâ*.

Phr. one's bark being worse than his bite.

887. Blusterer.—N. bluster-, swagger-, vapour-, roister-, brawl-er; brazen-face; *fanfaron*; braggart &c. (*boaster*) 884; bully, terrorist, rough, rough-neck; hooligan, hoodlum, larrikin, ruffian; Mo-hock, -hawk; drawcansir, swashbuckler, Captain Boabdil, Sir Lucius O'Trigger, Thraso, Pistol, Parolles, Bombastes Furioso, Hector, Chrononhotonthologos; jingo; desperado, dare-devil, fire-eater; fury &c. (*violent person*) 173; rowdy.

puppy &c. (*fop*) 854; prig; Sir Oracle, dogmatist, *doctrinaire*, stump orator, jack-in-office; saucebox, malapert, jackanapes, minx; bantam-cock.

Section III. SYMPATHETIC AFFECTIONS

1°. Social Affections

888. Friendship. — N. friendship, amity; friendliness &c. *adj.*; brotherhood, fraternity, sodality, confraternity, sorosis, sisterhood; harmony &c. (*concord*) 714; peace &c. 721.

firm -, staunch -, intimate -, familiar -, bosom -, cordial -, tried -, devoted -, lasting -, fast -, sincere -, warm -, ardent- friendship.

cordiality, fraternization, *entente cordiale*, good understanding, *rapprochement*, sympathy, fellow-feeling, response, welcomeness; *camaraderie*.

affection &c. (*love*) 897; favouritism; goodwill &c. (*benevolence*) 906; partiality.

acquaintance, familiarity, intimacy, intercourse, fellowship, knowledge of; introduction.

V. be -friendly &c. *adj.*, - friends &c. 890, - acquainted with &c. *adj.*; know; have the ear of; keep company with &c. (*sociality*) 892; hold communication -, have dealings -, sympathize- with; have a leaning to; bear good will &c. (*benevolence*) 906; love &c. 897; make much of; befriend &c. (*aid*) 707; introduce to.

set one's horses together; hold out -, extend- the right hand of -friendship, - fellowship; become -friendly &c. *adj.*; make -friends &c. 890 with; break the ice, be introduced to; make -, pick -, scrape- acquaintance with; get into favour, gain the friendship of.

shake hands with, fraternize, embrace; receive with open arms, throw oneself into the arms of; meet half way, take in good part.

Adj. friendly; amic-able, -al; well affected, unhostile, neighbourly, brotherly, fraternal, sisterly, sympathetic, harmonious, hearty, cordial, warm-hearted, devoted.

889. Enmity.—N. enmity, hostility; unfriendliness &c. *adj.*; discord &c. 713.

alienation, estrangement; dislike &c. 867; hate &c. 898; antagonism.

heartburning; animosity &c. 900; malevolence &c. 907.

V. be -inimical &c. *adj.*; keep -, hold- at arm's length; be at loggerheads; bear malice &c. 907; fall out; take umbrage &c. 900; harden the heart, alienate, estrange.

Adj. inimical, unfriendly, hostile; at -enmity, - variance, - swords points, - daggers drawn, - open war with; up in arms against; in bad odour with.

on bad -, not on speaking- terms; cool; cold, -hearted; estranged, alienated, disaffected, irreconcilable.

friends -, well -, at home -, hand in hand- with; on -good, – friendly, – amicable, – cordial, – familiar, – intimate- -terms, – footing; on -speaking, – visiting- terms; in one's good -graces, – books.

acquainted, familiar, intimate, thick, hand and glove, hail fellow well met, free and easy; welcome.

Adv. amicably &c. *adj.*; with open arms; *sans cérémonie*; arm in arm.

890. Friend.—N. friend, – of one's bosom, intimate acquaintance, neighbour, well-wisher; *alter ego*; best –, bosom –, fast- friend; *amicus usque ad aras*; *fidus Achates*; *persona grata*.

favourer, *fautor*, patron, backer, Mæcenas; tutelary saint, good genius, advocate, partisan, sympathiser; ally; friend in need &c. (*auxiliary*) 711.

associate, compeer, comrade, mate, companion, *confrère*, *camarade*, *confidante*, colleague; old –, crony; side-kick; chum, buddy, bunkie, roommate, pal; play-fellow, -mate; classmate, schoolfellow; bed-fellow, -mate; maid of honour.

compatriot; fellow –, countryman, – townsman.

shop-, ship-, mess-mate; fellow –, boon –, pot- companion; co-partner.

Arcades ambo, Pylades and Orestes, Castor and Pollux, Nisus and Euryalus, Damon and Pythias, *par nobile fratrum*.

host, Amphitryon, Boniface; guest, visitor, frequenter, *habitué*; *protégé*.

892. Sociality.—N. soci-ality, -ability, -ableness &c. *adj.*; social intercourse; consociation; inter-course, -community; consort-, companion-, fellow-, comrade-ship; clubbism; *esprit de corps*.

conviviality; good -fellowship, – company, *camaraderie*; joviality, jollity, *savoir-vivre*, festivity, festive board, merry-making; loving cup; hospitality, heartiness; cheer.

welcome, -ness; greeting; hearty –, warm –, welcome- reception; urbanity &c. (*courtesy*) 894; intimacy, familiarity.

good –, jolly- fellow, good mixer, Rotarian; *bon enfant*.

social –, family- circle; circle of acquaintance, *coterie*, society, company.

social -gathering, – *réunion*; assembly &c. (*assemblage*) 72; party, entertainment, reception, *levée*, at home, *conversazione*, *soirée*, *matinée*, evening –, morning –, afternoon –, garden –, dinner –, tea –, cocktail- party; symposium, sing-song; kettle-, drum; *partie carrée*, dish of tea, *ridotto*, rout, house-

891. Enemy.—N. enemy; antagonist, foeman; open –, bitter- enemy; opponent &c. 710; back friend.

public enemy, enemy to society, traitor, anarchist &c. 743.

Phr. every hand being against one.

———

893. Seclusion. Exclusion.—N. seclusion, privacy; retirement; concealment; reclusion, recess; snugness &c. *adj.*; delitescence; rustication, *rus in urbe*; solitude; solitariness &c. (*singleness*) 87; isolation; loneliness &c. *adj.*; estrangement from the world, anchoritism, voluntary exile; aloofness.

cell, hermitage; convent &c. 1000; *sanctum sanctorum*; study, library, den; hide-out.

depopulation, desertion, desolation; wilderness &c. (*unproductive*) 169; howling wilderness; rotten borough, Old Sarum.

exclusion, excommunication, banishment, exile, ostracism, proscription; cut, – direct; dead cut.

inhospit-ality, -ableness &c. *adj.*; un-, dis-sociability; domesticity, Darby and Joan.

recluse, hermit, eremite, cenobite; anchor-et, -ite; Simon Stylites; Troglodyte, Timon of Athens, Santon, *solitaire*, ruralist, disciple of Zimmermann, closet cynic, Diogenes; outcast, Pariah,

warming; ball, prom, hop, dance, *thé dansant*; festival &c. (*amusement*) 840; wedding breakfast; 'the feast of reason and the flow of soul.'

visit, -ing; round of visits; call, morning call; interview &c. (*interlocution*) 588; assignation; tryst, -ing place; appointment.

club &c. (*association*) 712.

V. be -sociable &c. *adj.*; know; be -acquainted &c. *adj.*; associate -, sort -, keep company -, walk hand in hand -with; eat off the same trencher, club together, consort, bear one company, join; make acquaintance with &c. (*friendship*) 888; make advances, fraternize, embrace; intercommunicate.

be -, feel -, make oneself- at home with; make free with; crack a bottle with; take pot luck with, receive hospitality, live at free quarters.

visit, pay a visit; interchange -visits, - cards; call -at, - upon; leave a card; drop in, look in; look one up, beat up one's quarters.

entertain; give a -party &c. *n.*; be at home, see one's friends, hang out, keep open house, do the honours; receive, - with open arms; welcome; give a warm reception &c. *n.* to; kill the fatted calf.

Adj. sociable, companionable, clubbable, clubby, conversable, cosy, cosey, chatty, conversational; homiletical.

convivial; fest-ive, -al; jovial, jolly, hospitable.

welcome, - as the roses in May; *fêté*, entertained.

free and easy, hail fellow well met, familiar, on visiting terms, acquainted.

social, neighbourly; international, cosmopolitan, gregarious.

Adv. *en famille*, in the family circle; *sans -façon, - cérémonie*, arm in arm.

894. Courtesy.—**N.** courtesy; respect &c. 928; good -manners, - behaviour; - breeding; manners; politeness &c. *adj.*; *bienséance*, urbanity, comity, gentility; gentle -, breeding; polish, presence, cultivation, culture; civili-ty, -zation; amenity, suavity; good -temper, - humour; amiability, easy temper, complacency, soft tongue,

castaway, outsider, pilgarlic; wastrel, foundling, orphan.

V. be -, live- secluded &c. *adj.*; keep -, stand -, hold oneself- -aloof, - in the background; keep snug; shut oneself up; deny -, seclude- oneself; creep into a corner, rusticate, *aller planter ses choux*; retire, - from the world; hermetize, take the veil; abandon &c. 624.

cut, - dead; refuse to -associate with, - acknowledge; look cool -, turn one's back -, shut the door- upon; repel, blackball, excommunicate, exclude, exile, expatriate; banish, outlaw, maroon, ostracize, proscribe, cut off from, send to Coventry, keep at arm's length, draw a cordon round; boycott, blockade, lay an embargo on, isolate.

depopulate; dis-, un-people.

Adj. secluded, sequestered, retired, delitescent, private, bye; out of the -world, -way; in a backwater; 'the world forgetting by the world forgot.'

snug, domestic, stay-at-home.

unsociable; un-, dis-social; inhospitable, cynical, inconversable, unclubbable, *sauvage*, eremetic.

solitary; lone-ly, -some; isolated, single.

excluded, estranged; unfrequented; uninhabit-able, -ed; tenantless; un-tenanted, -occupied; abandoned; deserted, - in one's utmost need; unfriended; kith-, friend-, home-less; lorn, forlorn, desolate.

un-visited, -introduced, -invited, -welcome; under a cloud, left to shift for oneself, derelict, outcast, outside the gates.

banished &c. *v.*; under an embargo.

Phr. *noli me tangere.*

---

895. Discourtesy.—**N.** discourtesy; ill-breeding; ill -, bad -, ungainly- manners; insuavity; grouchiness; uncourteousness &c. *adj.*, tactlessness; rusticity, inurbanity; illiberality, incivility, displacency.

disrespect &c. 929; procacity, impudence; barbar-ism, -ity; misbehaviour, brutality, blackguardism, conduct un-

mansuetude; condescension &c. (*humility*) 879; affability, complaisance, *prévenance*, amiability, gallantry, chivalry; pink of -politeness, – courtesy.

compliment; fair –, soft –, sweet-words; honeyed phrases, flattering remarks, ceremonial; salutation, reception, presentation, introduction, *accueil*, greeting, recognition; welcome, *abord*, respects, *devoir*, regards, remembrances; kind -regards, – remembrances; love, best love, duty; deference.

obeisance &c. (*reverence*) 928; bow, courtesy, curtsy, scrape, *salaam*, *kowtow*, bowing and scraping; kneeling; genuflexion &c. (*worship*) 990; obsequiousness &c. 886; capping, shaking hands &c. *v.*; grip of the hand, embrace, hug, squeeze, *accolade*, loving cup, *vin d'honneur*, pledge; love token &c. (*endearment*) 902; kiss, buss, salute.

mark of recognition, nod; 'nods and becks and wreathed smiles'; valediction &c. 293; condolence &c. 915.

V. be -courteous &c. *adj.*; show -courtesy &c. *n.*

mind one's P's and Q's, behave oneself, be all things to all men, conciliate, speak one fair, take in good part; make –, do- the amiable; look as if butter would not melt in one's mouth; mend one's manners.

receive, do the honours, usher, greet, hail, bid welcome; welcome, – with open arms; shake hands; hold out –, press –, squeeze- the hand; bid God speed; speed the parting guest; cheer, serenade.

salute; embrace &c. (*endearment*) 902; kiss, – hands; drink to, pledge, hob and nob; move to, nod to; smile upon.

uncover, cap; touch –, take off- the hat; doff the cap; pull the forelock; present arms; make way for; bow; make one's bow; scrape, curtsy, courtesy; bob a -curtsy, – courtesy; kneel; bow –, bend- the knee; salaam, *kowtow*.

visit, wait upon, present oneself, pay one's respects, pay a visit &c. (*sociability*) 892; dance attendance on &c. (*servility*) 886; pay attentions to; do homage to &c. (*respect*) 928.

becoming a gentleman, *grossièreté, brusquerie*; vulgarity &c. 851.

churlishness &c. *adj.*; spinosity, perversity; moroseness &c. (*sullenness*) 901*a*.

bad-, ill-temper; sternness &c. *adj.*; austerity; moodishness, captiousness &c. 901; cynicism; tartness &c. *adj.*; acrimony, acerbity, virulence, asperity.

scowl, black looks, frown; short answer, rebuff; hard words, contumely; unparliamentary language, personality.

bear, bruin, brute, grouch, blackguard, beast; unlicked cub; frump, cross-patch; saucebox &c. 887.

V. be -rude &c. *adj.*; insult &c. 929; treat with discourtesy; take a name in vain; make -bold, – free- with; take a liberty; stare out of countenance, ogle, point at, put to the blush.

cut; turn -one's back upon, – on one's heel; give the cold shoulder; keep at -a distance, – arm's length; look -cool, – coldly, – black- upon; show the door to, send away with a flea in the ear.

lose one's temper &c. (*resentment*) 900; sulk &c. 901*a*; frown, scowl, glower, pout; snap, snarl, growl.

render -rude &c. *adj.*; brut-alize, -ify.

Adj. dis-, un-courteous; uncourtly; ill-bred, -mannered, -behaved, -conditioned; unbred; unmanner-ly, ed; im-, un-polite; un-polished, -civilized, -genteel; ungentleman-like, -ly; unladylike; blackguard; vulgar &c. 851; dedecorous; foul-mouthed, -spoken; abusive.

un-civil, -gracious, -ceremonious; cool; pert, forward, obtrusive, impudent, rude, saucy, precocious; insolent &c. 885.

repulsive; un-complaisant, -accommodating, -neighbourly, -gallant; inaffable; un-gentle, -gainly; rough, rugged, bluff, blunt, gruff; churl-, boor-, bear-ish; brutal, *brusque*; stern, harsh, austere; cavalier.

tart, sour, crabbed, sharp, short, trenchant, sarcastic, crusty, biting, caustic, virulent, bitter, acrimonious, venomous, contumelious; snarling &c, *v.*; surly, – as a bear; perverse; grim.

prostrate oneself &c. (*worship*) 990. give -, send- one's duty &c. *n.* to.

render -polite &c. *adj.*; polish, civilize, humanize.

Adj. courteous, polite, civil, mannerly, urbane; well-behaved, -mannered, -bred, -brought up, gently bred, of gentle -breeding, - manners, good-mannered, polished, civilized, cultivated; refined &c. (*taste*) 850; gentlemanlike &c. (*fashion*) 852; gallant, chivalrous, on one's good behaviour.

fine -, fair -, soft- spoken; honey-mouthed, -tongued; oily, unctuous, bland, suave; obliging, conciliatory, complaisant, complacent; obsequious &c. 886.

ingratiating, winning; gentle, mild; good-humoured, cordial, gracious, amiable, tactful, addressful, affable, genial, friendly, familiar; neighbourly.

Adv. courteously &c. *adj.*; with a good grace; with -open, - outstretched- arms; *à bras ouverts*; *suaviter in modo*, in good humour.

Int. hail! welcome! well met! *ave!* all hail! good -day, - morning &c., - morrow! God speed! *pax vobiscum!* may your shadow never be less! *chin-chin!*

sullen &c. 901*a*; peevish &c. (*irascible*) 901.

Adv. discourteously &c. *adj.*; with -discourtesy &c. *n.*, - a bad grace.

---

896. Congratulations.—**N.** con-, gratulation; felicitation; salute &c. 894; condolence &c. 915; compliments of the season; good -, best-wishes.

V. con-, gratulate; felicitate, compliment; give -, wish one- joy; tender -, offer- one's congratulations; wish -many happy returns of the day, - a merry Christmas and a happy new year.

congratulate oneself &c. (*rejoice*) 838.

Adj. con-, gratulatory.

---

897. Love.—**N.** love; fondness &c. *adj.*; liking; inclination &c. (*desire*) 865; regard, dilection, admiration, fancy.

affection, sympathy, fellow-feeling; tenderness &c. *adj.*; heart, brotherly love; benevolence &c. 906; attachment.

yearning, tender passion, *affaire de coeur*, *amour*, gallantry, passion, flame, devotion, fervour, enthusiasm, transport of love, rapture, enchantment, infatuation, adoration, idolatry.

narcissism, Œdipus complex, Electra complex.

Cupid, Venus, Eros; myrtle; true lover's knot; love -token, - suit, - affair, - tale, - story; the old story, plighted love; courtship &c. 902; *amourette.*

maternal love.

attractiveness, charm; popularity; favourite &c. 899.

lover, suitor, follower, admirer, adorer, wooer, amoret, beau, sweet-

898. Hate.—**N.** hate, hatred, vials of hate; Hymn of Hate.

dis-affection, -favour; alienation, estrangement, coolness; enmity &c. 889; animosity &c. 900.

umbrage, pique, grudge; dudgeon, spleen; bitterness, - of feeling; ill -, bad- blood; acrimony; malice &c. 907; implacability &c. (*revenge*) 919.

repugnance &c. (*dislike*) 867; odium, unpopularity; loathing, detestation, antipathy; object of -hatred, - execration; abomination, aversion, *bête noire*; enemy &c. 891; bitter pill; source of annoyance &c. 830.

V. hate, detest, abominate, abhor, loathe; recoil -, shudder- at; shrink from, view with horror, hold in abomination, revolt against, execrate; scowl &c. 895; disrelish &c. (*dislike*) 867.

owe a grudge; bear -spleen, - a grudge, - malice &c. (*malevolence*) 907; conceive an aversion to.

heart, inamorato, swain, young man, flame, love, truelove; leman, Lothario, gallant, paramour, *amoroso, cavaliere servente*, captive, *cicisbeo*; *caro sposo*, Don Juan, sheik, ladies' man, squire of dames, Knave of Hearts.

inamorata, lady-love, idol, darling, duck, Dulcinea, angel, goddess, *cara sposa*; mistress.

betrothed, affianced, *fiancée*.

flirt, *coquette*; amorette; pair of turtle doves; abode of love, *agapemone*.

V. love, like, affect, fancy, care for, take an interest in, be partial to, sympathize with; be -in love &c. *adj.*-with; have –, entertain –, harbour –, cherish- a -love &c. *n.* for; regard, revere; take to, bear love to, be wedded to; set one's affections on; make much of, feast one's eyes on; hold dear, prize, treasure; hug, cling to, cherish, pet, caress &c. 902.

burn; adore, idolize, love to distraction, *aimer eperdument*; dote -on, – upon.

take a fancy to, fall for, be stuck on, look sweet upon; become -enamoured &c. *adj.*; fall in love with, lose one's heart; desire &c. 865.

excite love; win –, gain –, secure –, engage- the -love, – affections, – heart; take the fancy of; have a place in –, wind round- the heart; attract, attach, endear, charm, fascinate, captivate, bewitch, seduce, enamour, enrapture, turn the head.

get into favour; ingratiate –, insinuate –, worm- oneself; propitiate, curry favour with, pay one's court to, make a date with, *faire l'aimable*, set one's cap at, flirt, coquet.

Adv. loving &c. *v.*; fond of; taken –, struck- with; smitten, bitten; attached to, wedded to; enamoured; charmed &c. *v.*; in love; love-sick; over head and ears in love.

affectionate, tender, sweet upon, sympathetic, loving, fond, amorous, amatory; erotic, uxurious, ardent, passionate, rapturous, devoted, motherly.

loved &c. *v.*; beloved; well –, dearly- beloved; dear, precious, darling, pet, little; favourite, popular.

congenial; to –, after- one's -mind, – taste, – fancy, – own heart.

in one's good -graces &c. (*friendly*) 888; dear as the apple of one's eye, nearest to one's heart.

lovable, adorable; lovely, sweet; attractive, seductive, winning; charming, engaging, interesting, enchanting, captivating, fascinating, intriguing, bewitching; amiable, like an angel, angelic, seraphic.

excite –, provoke- hatred &c. *n.*; be -hateful &c. *adj.*; stink in the nostrils; estrange, alienate, repel, set against, sow dissension, set by the ears, envenom, incense, irritate, rile, ruffle, vex; horrify &c. 830.

Adj. hating &c. *v.*; abhorrent; averse from &c. (*disliking*) 867; set against.

bitter &c. (*acrimonious*) 895; implacable &c. (*revengeful*) 919.

un-loved, -beloved, -lamented, -deplored, -mourned, -cared for, -endured, -valued; disliked &c. 867.

crossed in love, forsaken, rejected, love-lorn, jilted.

obnoxious, hateful, odious, abominable, repulsive, offensive, shocking; disgusting &c. (*disagreeable*) 830.

invidious, spiteful; malicious &c. 907.

insulting, irritating, provoking.

[Mutual hate] at -daggers drawn, – swords points; not on speaking terms &c. (*enmity*) 889.

Phr. no love lost between.

---

899. Favourite.—N. favourite, pet, cosset, minion, idol, jewel, spoiled child, *enfant gâté*; led captain; crony; fondling; apple of one's eye, man after one's own heart; *persona grata*.

love, dear, darling, duck, honey, jewel; mopsey, moppet; sweetheart &c. (*love*) 897.

general –, universal- favourite; idol of the people; matinée idol, movie –, radio- star.

900. Resentment.—N. resentment, displeasure, animosity, anger, wrath, indignation; vexation, exasperation, bitter resentment, wrathful indignation.

pique, umbrage, huff, miff, soreness, dudgeon, acerbity, virulence, bitterness, acrimony, asperity, spleen, gall; heart-burning, -swelling; rankling.

ill –, bad- -humour, – temper; irascibility &c. 901; ill blood &c. (*hate*) 898; revenge &c. 919.

excitement, irritation; warmth, bile, choler, ire, fume, pucker, dander, ferment, ebullition; towering -passion, – rage, *acharnement*, angry mood, taking, pet, tiff, passion, fit, tantrums.

burst, explosion, paroxysm, storm, rage, fury, desperation; violence &c. 173; fire and fury; vials of wrath; gnashing of teeth, hot blood, high words.

scowl &c. 895; sulks &c. 901*a*.

[Cause of umbrage] affront, provocation, offence; indignity &c. (*insult*) 929; grudge, crow to pluck, sore subject; red rag to a bull; *casus belli*.

Furies, Erinys, Eumenides, Alecto, Megæra, Tisiphone.

buffet, slap in the face, box on the ear, rap on the knuckles.

V. resent; take -amiss, – ill, – to heart, – offence, – umbrage, – huff, – exception; take in -ill part, – bad part, – dudgeon; *ne pas entendre raillerie*; breathe revenge, cut up rough.

fly –, fall –, get- into a -rage, – passion; bridle –, bristle –, froth –, fire –, flare- up; open –, pour out- the vials of one's wrath.

pout, knit the brow, frown, scowl, lower, snarl, growl, gnarl, gnash, snap; redden, colour; look -black, – black as thunder, – daggers; bite one's thumb; show –, grind- one's teeth; champ the bit.

chafe, mantle, fume, kindle, fly out, take fire; boil, – over; boil with -indignation, – rage; rage, storm, foam; vent one's -rage, – spleen; lose one's temper, stand on one's hind legs, stamp the foot, kick up a row, fly off the handle, cut up rough; stamp –, quiver –, swell –, foam- with rage; burst with anger; raise Cain, breathe fire and fury.

have a fling at; bear malice &c. (*revenge*) 919.

cause –, raise- anger; affront, offend; give -offence, – umbrage; anger; hurt the feelings; insult, discompose, fret, ruffle, nettle, heckle, huff, pique; excite &c. 824; irritate, stir the blood, stir up bile; sting, – to the quick; rile, provoke, chafe, wound, incense, inflame, enrage, aggravate, add fuel to the flame, fan into a flame, widen the breach, envenom, embitter, exasperate, infuriate, kindle wrath; stick in one's gizzard; rankle &c. 919.

put out of humour; put one's -monkey, – back- up; set –, get- one's back up; raise one's -gorge, – dander, – choler; work up into a passion; make -one's blood boil, – the ears tingle; throw into a ferment, madden, drive one mad; lash into -fury, – madness; fool to the top of one's bent; set by the ears.

bring a hornet's nest about one's ears.

Adj. angry, wrath, irate; ire-, wrath-ful; cross &c. (*irascible*) 901; sulky &c. 901*a*; bitter, virulent; acrimonious &c. (*discourteous*) &c. 895; violent &c. 173.

warm, burning; boiling, – over; fuming, raging; foaming, – at the mouth; convulsed with rage.

offended &c. *v.*; waxy, *acharné*; wrought, worked up; indignant, hurt, sore, peeved; set against.

fierce, wild, rageful, furious, mad with rage, fiery, infuriate, rabid, savage; relentless &c. 919.

flushed with -anger, – rage; in a -huff, – stew, – fume, – pucker, – passion, – rage, – fury; on one's high ropes, up in arms; in high dudgeon.

Adv. angrily &c. *adj.*; in the height of passion; in the heat of -passion, – the moment.

Int. *tantæne animis cœlestibus iræ!* marry come up! zounds! 'sdeath!

Phr. one's -blood, – back, – monkey- being up; *fervens difficili bile jecur*; the gorge rising, eyes flashing fire; the blood -rising, – boiling; *hæret lateri lethalis arundo*.

901. Irascibility.—N. irascibility, temper; crossness &c. *adj.*; susceptibility, procacity, petulance, irritability, tartness, acerbity, protervity; pugnacity &c. (*contentiousness*) 720.

excitability &c. 825; bad –, fiery –, crooked –, irritable &c. *adj.*- temper; *genus irritabile*, hot blood.

ill humour &c. (*sullenness*) 901a; asperity &c., churlishness &c. (*discourtesy*) 895.

huff &c. (resentment) 900; a word and a blow.

Sir Fretful Plagiary; brabbler, Tartar; shrew, vixen, virago, termagant, dragon, scold, Xanthippe; porcupine; spit-fire; fire-eater &c. (*blusterer*) 887; fury &c. (*violent person*) 173.

V. be -irascible &c. *adj.*; have a -temper &c. *n.*, – devil in one; fire up &c. (*be angry*) 900.

Adj. irascible; bad-, ill-tempered; irritable, susceptible; excitable &c. 825; thin-skinned &c. (*sensitive*) 822; fretful, fidgety; on the fret.

hasty, over-hasty, quick, warm, hot, testy, touchy, techy, tetchy; like -touchwood, – tinder; huffy; pet-tish, -ulant; waspish, snapp-y, -ish, peppery, fiery, passionate, choleric, shrewish, 'sudden and quick in quarrel.'

querulous, captious, mood-y, -ish; quarrelsome, contentious, disputatious; pugnacious &c. (*bellicose*) 720; cantankerous, exceptious; restive &c. (*perverse*) 901a; churlish &c. (*discourteous*) 895.

cross, – as -crabs, – two sticks, – a cat, – a dog, – the tongs; like a bear with a sore head; fractious, peevish, *acariâtre*.

in a bad temper; sulky &c. 901a; angry &c. 900.

resent-ful, -ive; vindictive &c. 919.

Int. pish!

901a. Sullenness.—N. sullenness &c. *adj.*; morosity, spleen; churlishness &c. (*discourtesy*) 895; irascibility &c. 901.

moodiness &c. *adj.*; perversity; obstinacy &c. 606; torvity, spinosity; crabbedness &c. *adj.*

ill –, bad- -temper, – humour; sulks, dudgeon, mumps, doleful dumps, doldrums, fit of the sulks, *bouderie*, black looks, scowl; huff &c. (*resentment*) 900.

V. be -sullen &c. *adj.*; sulk; frown, scowl, lower, glower, grouse, grouch, crab, gloam, pout, have a hang-dog look, glout.

Adj. sullen, sulky; ill-tempered, -humoured, -affected, -disposed; in -an ill, – a bad, ·· a shocking- -temper, – humour; out of -temper, –

humour; knaggy, **torvous**, crusty, **crabbed; sore as a** boil; surly &c.
(*discourteous*) 895.

moody; spleen-ish, -ly; splenetic, cankered.

cross, -grained; perverse, wayward, humoursome; restive; cantankerous, refractory, intractable, exceptious, sinistrous, deaf to reason, unaccommodating, rusty, crust, froward.

dogged &c. (*stubborn*) 606.

grumpy, glum, grim, grum, morose, frumpish; in the -sulks &c. *n.*; out of sorts; scowl-, glower-, growl-ing.

peevish &c. (*irascible*) 901.

902. [Expression of affection or love.] **Endearment.—N.** endearment, caress; blandish-, blandi-ment; *épanchement*, fondling, billing and cooing, dalliance.

embrace, salute, kiss, buss, smack, osculation, deosculation; amorous glances; ogle, side glance, sheep's eyes.

courtship, wooing, suit, addresses, the soft impeachment; lovemaking; an affair; serenading; caterwauling.

flirting &c. *v.*; flirtation, gallantry; coquetry, spooning.

true lover's knot, plighted love, engagement, bethrothal; love -tale, – token, – letter; *billet-doux*, valentine.

honeymoon; Strephon and Chloe, 'Arry and 'Arriet.

V. caress, fondle, pet, dandle, nurse; pat, – on the -head, – cheek; chuck under the chin, smile upon, coax, wheedle, cosset, coddle, cocker; make -of, – much of, pamper; cherish, foster, kill with kindness.

clasp, hug, cuddle; fold –, strain- in one's arms; nestle, nuzzle, neck, embrace, kiss, buss, smack, blow a kiss; salute &c. (*courtesy*) 894.

bill and coo, spoon, toy, dally, flirt, coquet; galli-, gala-vant; philander; make love; pay one's -court, – addresses, – attentions- to; serenade; court, woo; set one's cap at; be –, look- sweet upon; ogle, cast sheep's eyes upon; *faire les yeux doux*.

fall in love with, win the affections &c. (*love*) 897; die for.

propose; make –, have- an offer; pop the question; plight one's -troth, – faith; become -engaged, – betrothed.

Adj. caressing &c. *v.*; 'sighing like furnace'; love-sick, spoony.

caressed &c. *v.*

903. Marriage.—N. marriage, matrimony, wedlock, union, intermarriage, *vinculum matrimonii*, nuptial tie, knot.

married state, coverture, bed, cohabitation.

match; betrothment &c. (*promise*) 768; wedding, nuptials, Hymen, bridal; e-, spousals; leading to the altar &c. *v.*; nuptial benediction, *epithalamium.*

torch –, temple- of Hymen; hymeneal altar; honeymoon.

bride, bridegroom; brides-maid, -man.

best –, grooms-man, page, usher.

married -man, – woman, – couple; neogamist, Benedick, partner, spouse, mate, yokemate; husband, man, con-

904. Celibacy.—N. celibacy, singleness, single blessedness; bachelor-hood, -ship; miso-gamy, -gyny.

virginity, *pucelage*; maiden-hood, -head.

unmarried man, bachelor, Cœlebs, agamist, old bachelor; miso-gamist, -gynist; celibate.

unmarried woman, spinster; maid, -en; virgin, *feme sole*, old maid; bachelor girl; nun &c.

V. live single; keep bachelor hall.

Adj. un-married, -wedded; wife-, spouse-less; single, virgin, celibate.

905. Divorce.—N. divorce, -ment; separation; judicial separation, separ-

sort, baron; old –, good- man; wife of one's bosom; help-meet, -mate, rib, better half, grey mare, old woman, good wife; feme, – coverte; squaw, lady; matron, -age, -hood; man and wife; wedded pair, Darby and Joan.

affinity, soul-mate.

mono-, bi-, di-, deutero-, tri-, poly-gamy; mormonism; poly-andry; Turk, Bluebeard.

unlawful –, left-handed –, companionate –, morganatic –, ill-assorted- marriage; *mésalliance*; *mariage de convenance*; an affair.

match-maker, marriage broker, matrimonial agent.

V. marry, wive, take to oneself a wife; be -married, – spliced; go –, pair- off; wed, espouse, lead to the hymeneal altar, take 'for better, for worse,' give one's hand to, bestow one's hand upon; remarry; intermarry.

marry, join, handfast; couple &c. (*unite*) 43; tie the nuptial knot; give -away, – in marriage; affy, affiance; betroth &c. (*promise*) 768; publish –, bid- the banns; be asked in church.

Adj. married &c. *v.*; one, – bone and one flesh.

marriageable, nubile.

engaged, betrothed, affianced.

matrimonial, marital, conjugal, connubial, wedded; nuptial, hymeneal, spousal, bridal.

Phr. the grey mare the better horse.

ate maintenance; *separatio a -mensâ et thoro, – vinculo matrimonii.*

widowhood, viduage, viduity, weeds.

widow, -er; relict; dowager; *divorcée*; cuckold.

V. live -separately, – apart; separate, divorce, disespouse, put away; wear the horns.

2°. Diffusive Sympathetic Affections

906. Benevolence.—N. benevolence, Christian charity; God's -love, – grace; good-will; philanthropy &c. 910; un-selfishness &c. 942.

good -nature, – feeling, – wishes; kind-, kindli-ness &c. *adj.*; lovingkind-ness, benignity, brotherly love, charity, humanity, fellow-feeling, sympathy; goodness –, warmth- of heart; *bon-homie*; kind-heartedness; amiability, milk of human kindness, tenderness; love &c. 897; friendship &c. 888.

toleration, consideration, generosity; mercy &c. (*pity*) 914.

charitableness &c. *adj.*; bounty, alms-giving; good works, beneficence, the luxury of doing good.

acts of kindness, a good turn; good –, kind- -offices; – treatment.

good Samaritan, sympathizer, well-wisher, philanthropist, *bon enfant*; altruist.

V. be -benevolent &c. *adj.*; have one's heart in the right place, bear good will; wish -well, – God speed;

907. Malevolence.—N. malevolence; bad intent, -ion; un-, dis-kindness; ill -nature, – will, – blood; bad blood; enmity &c. 889; hate &c. 898; malig-nity; malice, – aforethought, – pre-pense; maliciousness &c. *adj.*; spite, despite; resentment &c. 900.

uncharitableness &c. *adj.*; incom-passionateness &c. 914a; gall, venom, rancour, rankling, virulence, mordac-ity, acerbity; churlishness &c. (*dis-courtesy*) 895.

hardness of heart, heart of stone, obduracy; cruelty; cruelness &c. *adj.*; brutality, savagery; fer-ity, -ocity; barbarity, inhumanity, immanity, truc-ulence, ruffianism; evil eye, cloven -foot, – hoof; Inquisition; torture.

ill –, bad- turn; affront &c. (*disre-spect*) 929; outrage, atrocity; ill usage; intolerance, bigotry, persecution; ten-der mercies [ironical]; 'unkindest cut of all.'

V. be -malevolent &c. *adj.*; bear –, harbour- -spleen, – a grudge, – mal-

view –, regard- with an eye of favour; take in good part; take –, feel- an interest in; be –, feel- interested- in; sympathize with, feel for; fraternize &c. (*be friendly*) 888.

enter into the feelings of others, do as you would be done by, meet half-way.

treat well; give comfort, smooth the bed of death; do -good, – a good turn; benefit &c. (*goodness*) 648; render a service, be of use; aid &c. 707.

Adj. benevolent; kind, -ly; well-meaning; amiable; obliging, accommodating, indulgent, considerate, gracious, complacent, good-humoured.

warm-, soft-, kind-, tender-, large-, broad-hearted; merciful &c. 914; philanthropic &c. 910; charitable, beneficent, humane, benign, benignant; bount-eous, -iful &c. 816.

good-, well-natured; spleenless; sympath-izing, -etic; complaisant &c. (*courteous*) 894; kindly, well-meant, -intentioned.

fatherly, motherly, brotherly, sisterly; pat-, mat-, frat-ernal; friendly &c. 888.

Adv. with -a good intention, – the best intentions.

Int. God speed! much good may it do!

---

ice; betray –, show- the cloven foot.

hurt &c. (*physical pain*) 378; annoy &c. 830; injure, harm, wrong; do -harm, – an ill office- to; outrage; disoblige, malign, plant a thorn in the breast.

molest, worry, harass, haunt, harry, bait, tease, throw stones at; play the devil with; hunt down, dragoon, hound; persecute, oppress, grind; maltreat; ill-treat, -use.

wreak one's malice on, do one's worst, break a butterfly on the wheel; dip –, imbrue- one's hands in blood; have no mercy &c. 914a.

Adj. male-, unbene-volent; unbenign; ill-disposed, -intentioned, -natured, -conditioned, -contrived; evil-minded, -disposed.

malicious; malign, -ant; rancorous; de-, spiteful; mordacious, caustic, bitter, envenomed, acrimonious, virulent; un-amiable, -charitable; maleficent, venomous, grinding, galling.

harsh, disobliging; un-kind, -friendly, -gracious; treacherous; inofficious; invidious; uncandid; churlish &c. (*uncourteous*) 895; surly, sullen &c. 901a.

cold, -blooded, -hearted; hard-, flint-, marble-, stony-hearted; hard of heart, unnatural; ruthless &c. (*unmerciful*) 914a; relentless &c. (*revengeful*) 919.

cruel; brut-al, -ish; savage, – as a -bear, – tiger; ferine, feral, ferocious; inhuman; barbarous, fell, untamed, tameless, truculent, incendiary; bloodthirsty &c. (*murderous*) 361; atrocious.

fiend-ish, -like; demoniacal; diabolic, -al; devilish, infernal, hellish, Satanic.

Adv. malevolently &c. *adj.*; with -bad intent &c. *n.*

908. Malediction.—N. malediction, malison, curse, imprecation, denunciation, execration, anathema, ban, proscription, excommunication, commination, thunders of the Vatican, fulmination, *maranatha*, aspersion, vilification, vituperation, scurrility.

abuse; foul –, bad –, strong –, unparliamentary- language, Limehouse; Billingsgate, sauce, evil speaking; cursing &c. *v.*; profane swearing, oath.

threat &c. 909; more bark than bite; invective &c. (*disapprobation*) 932.

V. curse, accurse, imprecate, damn, swear at; slang; curse with bell, book and candle; invoke –, call down- curses on the head of; devote to destruction.

execrate, beshrew, scold; anathematize &c. (*censure*) 932; hold up to execration, denounce, proscribe, excommunicate, fulminate, thunder against; threaten &c. 909; curse up hill and down dale.

curse and swear; swear, – like a trooper; fall a cursing, rap out an oath, damn, cuss.

Adj. curs-ing, -ed &c. *v.*; maledictory.

Int. woe to! beshrew! *ruat cœlum!* ill –, woe- betide! confusion seize! damn! confound! blast! curse! devil take! hang! out with! a plague –, out- upon! aroynt! *honi soit!*

Phr. *delenda est Carthago.*

909. Threat.—N. threat, menace; defiance &c. 715; abuse, minacity, intimidation; fulmination; commination &c. (*curse*) 908; gathering clouds &c. (*warning*) 668.

V. threat, -en; menace; snarl, growl, gnarl, mutter, bark, bully. defy &c. 715; intimidate &c. 860; keep –, hold up –, hold out- *in terrorem*; shake –, double –, clinch- the fist at; thunder, talk big, fulminate, use big words, bluster, look daggers.

Adj. threatening, menacing; mina-tory, -cious; comminatory, abusive; *in terrorem*; ominous &c. (*predicting*) 511; defiant &c. 715; under the ban.

Int. *væ victis!* at your peril! do your worst!

910. Philanthropy. — N. philan-thropy; altruism, humanit-y, -arian-ism; universal benevolence; *deliciæ humani generis*; cosmopolitanism, utilitarianism, the greatest happiness of the greatest number, social science, sociology.

common weal, public welfare, socialism, communism.

patriotism, civism, nationality, love of country, *amor patriæ*, public spirit.

chivalry, knight errantry; generosity &c. 942.

philanthropist, altruist &c. 906; utilitarian, Benthamite, socialist, communist, cosmopolite, citizen of the world, *amicus humani generis*; knight errant; patriot.

Adj. philanthropic, altruistic, humanitarian, utilitarian, cosmopolitan; public-spirited, patriotic; humane, large-hearted &c. (*benevolent*) 906; chival-ric, -rous, generous &c. 942.

Adv. *pro -bono publico, – aris et focis.*

Phr. *'humani nihil a me alienum puto.'*

911. Misanthropy.—N. misanthropy, incivism; egotism &c. (*selfishness*) 943; moroseness &c. 901a; cynicism; defeatism.

misanthrope, misanthropist, egotist, cynic, man-hater, Timon, Diogenes. woman-hater, misogynist.

Adj. misanthropic, antisocial, unpatriotic; egotistical &c. (*selfish*) 943; morose &c. 901a.

912. Benefactor. — N. benefactor, saviour, good genius, tutelary saint, patron, guardian angel, fairy godmother, good Samaritan; *pater patriæ*; salt of the earth &c. (*good man*) 948; auxiliary &c. 711.

913. [Maleficent being.] Evil-doer. —N. evil- -doer, – worker; wrong doer &c. 949; mischief maker, marplot; oppressor, tyrant; firebrand, incendiary, pyromaniac, anarchist, destroyer, Hun, *Boche*, Vandal, iconoclast; communist; terrorist, *apache*, gunman, gangster, racketeer.

savage, brute, ruffian, barbarian, semi-barbarian, caitiff, desperado; Mo-hock, -hawk; bludgeon man, bully, rough, hooligan, larrikin, dangerous classes, ugly customer; thief &c. 792.

cockatrice, scorpion, hornet; viper, adder; snake, – in the grass;

serpent, cobra, asp, rattlesnake, anaconda; canker-, wire-worm; locust, Colorado beetle; torpedo; bane &c. 663.

cannibal; Anthropophag-us, -ist; bloodsucker, vampire, ogre, ghoul, gorilla; vulture; gyr-, ger-falcon.

wild beast, tiger, hyæna, butcher, hangman; cut-throat &c. (*killer*) 361; blood-, sleuth-, hell-hound.

hag, hellhag, beldam, Jezebel.

monster; fiend &c. (*demon*) 980; homicidal maniac, devil incarnate, demon in human shape; Frankenstein's monster.

harpy, siren, vampire; Furies, Eumenides &c. 900.

Attila, scourge of the human race.

Phr. *fœnum habet in cornu.*

3°. Special Sympathetic Affections

914. Pity.—N. pity, compassion, commiseration; bowels, – of compassion; condolence &c. 915; sympathy, fellow-feeling, tenderness, yearning, forbearance, humanity, mercy, clemency, exorability; leniency &c. (*lenity*) 740; charity, ruth, long-suffering.

melting mood; *argumentum ad misericordiam*; quarter, grace, *locus pœnitentiæ*.

sympathizer, champion, partisan.

V. pity; have –, show –, take- pity &c. *n.*; commiserate, compassionate; condole &c. 915; sympathize; feel –, be sorry –, yearn- for; weep, melt, thaw, enter into the feelings of.

forbear, relent, relax, give quarter, wipe the tears, *parcere subjectis*, give a *coup de grâce*, put out of one's misery; be cruel to be kind.

raise –, excite- pity &c. *n.*; touch, soften; melt, – the heart; appeal to one's better feelings; propitiate, disarm.

ask for -mercy &c. *n.*; supplicate &c. (*request*) 765; cry for quarter, beg one's life, kneel; deprecate.

Adj. pitying &c. *v.*; pitiful, compassionate, sympathetic, touched.

merciful, clement, ruthful; humane; humanitarian &c. (*philanthropic*) 910; tender, – hearted, – as a chicken; soft, – hearted; unhardened; lenient &c. 740; exorable, forbearing; melting &c. *v.*; weak.

Int. for pity's sake! mercy! have –, cry you- mercy! God help you! poor -thing, – dear, – fellow! woe betide! *quis talia fando temperet a lachrymis!*

Phr. one's heart bleeding for; *haud ignara mali miseris succurrere disco.*

914a. Pitilessness.—N. pitilessness &c. *adj.*; inclemency; inexorability, hardness of heart; inflexibility; severity &c. 739; malevolence &c. 907.

V. have no –, shut the gates of- mercy &c. 914; give no quarter.

Adj. piti-, merci-, ruth-, bowel-less; unpitying, unmerciful, inclement; in-, un-compassionate; inexorable, inflexible; harsh &c. 739; cruel &c. 907; unrelenting &c. 919.

915. Condolence.—N. condolence; lamentation &c. 839; sympathy, consolation.

V. condole with, console, sympathize &c. 914, share one's misery; feel for; express –, testify- pity; afford –, supply- consolation; lament &c. 839- with; send one's condolences.

4°. Retrospective Sympathetic Affections

916. Gratitude. — **N.** gratitude, thankfulness, gratefulness, feeling of obligation.

acknowledgment, recognition thanksgiving, giving thanks.

thanks, praise, benediction; pæan; *Te Deum* &c. (*worship*) 990; grace, – before, – after- meat; thank-offering. requital.

V. be -grateful &c. *adj.*; thank; give –, render –, return –, offer –, tender- thanks &c. *n.*; acknowledge, requite.

feel –, be –, lie- under an obligation; *savoir gré*; not look a gift horse in the mouth; never forget, overflow with gratitude; thank –, bless- one's stars; fall on one's knees.

Adj. grateful, thankful, obliged, beholden, indebted to, under obligation.

Int. thanks! many thanks! gramercy! much obliged! thank you! thank Heaven! Heaven be praised!

917. Ingratitude.—**N.** ingratitude, thanklessness, oblivion of benefits; unthankfulness.

'benefits forgot'; thankless -task, – office.

V. be -ungrateful &c. *adj.*; forget benefits; look a gift horse in the mouth.

Adj. un-grateful, -mindful, -thankful; thankless, ingrate, wanting in grati- tude, insensible of benefits.

forgotten; un-acknowledged, -thank- ed, -requited, -rewarded; ill-requited.

Int. thank you for nothing! *'et tu Brute !'*

918. Forgiveness.—**N.** forgiveness, pardon, condonation, grace, remission, absolution, amnesty, oblivion; indul- gence; reprieve.

conciliation; reconciliation &c. (*paci- fication*) 723; propitiation.

excuse, exoneration, quittance, re- lease, indemnity; bill –, act –, cove- nant –, deed- of indemnity; exculpa- tion &c. (*acquittal*) 970.

longanimity, placability, forbear- ance; *amantium iræ*; *locus pœni- tentiæ*.

V. forgive, – and forget; pardon, condone, think no more of, let bygones be bygones, shake hands; forget an injury, bury the hatchet; clean the slate.

excuse, pass over, overlook; wink at &c. (*neglect*) 460; bear with; allow –, make allowances- for; let one down easily, not be too hard upon, pocket the affront; blot out one's transgres- sion.

let off, remit, absolve, give absolu- tion, reprieve; acquit &c. 970.

beg –, ask –, implore- pardon &c. *n.*; conciliate, propitiate, placate; make up a quarrel &c. (*pacify*) 723; let the wound heal.

919. Revenge.—**N.** revenge, -ment; vengeance; avenge-ment, -ance; sweet revenge, *vendetta*, death-feud, eye for an eye, blood for blood, a Roland for an Oliver; retaliation &c. 718; day of reckoning.

rancour, vindictiveness, implacabil- ity; malevolence &c. 907; ruthlessness &c. 914a.

avenger, vindicator, Nemesis, Eume- nides.

V. re-, a-venge; take –, have one's- revenge; breathe -revenge, – vengeance; wreak one's -vengeance, – anger; give no quarter.

have -accounts to settle, – a crow to pluck, – a rod in pickle; pay off old scores.

keep the wound green; harbour -revenge, – vindictive feeling; bear malice; rankle, – in the breast; have at one's mercy.

Adj. revenge-, venge-ful; vindictive, rancorous; pitiless &c. 914a; ruthless, rigorous, avenging, retaliative.

unforgiving, unrelenting; inexorable, stony-hearted, implacable; relent-, re- morse-less.

æternum servans sub pectore vulnus; rankling, immitigable.

Adj. forgiving, placable, conciliatory. forgiven &c. *v.*; un-resented, -avenged, -revenged.

Adv. cry you mercy.

Phr. *veniam petimusque damusque vicissim*; more in sorrow than in anger.

Phr. *manet -cicatrix, – altâ mente repostum.*

revenge is sweet.

---

920. Jealousy.—N. jealous-y, -ness; jaundiced eye, heartburning; green-eyed monster; yellows; Juno.

V. be -jealous &c. *adj.*; view with -jealousy, – a jealous eye.

Adj. jealous, – as a Barbary pigeon; jaundiced, yellow-eyed, horn-mad.

921. Envy.—N. envy; enviousness &c. *adj.*; rivalry; *jalousie de métier.*

V. envy, covet, lust after, crave, burst with envy, regard with envious eyes.

Adj. envious, invidious, covetous; *alieni appetens.*

SECTION IV. MORAL AFFECTIONS

1°. MORAL OBLIGATIONS

922. Right.—N. right; what -ought to, – should- be; fitness &c. *adj.*; *summum jus.*

justice, equity; equitableness &c. *adj.*; propriety; fair play, impartiality, measure for measure, give and take, *lex talionis*, square deal.

Astræa, Nemesis, Themis.

scales of justice, even-handed justice, retributive justice, *suum cuique*; clear stage –, fair field- and no favour; Queensberry rules.

morals &c. (*duty*) 926; law &c. 963; honour &c. (*probity*) 939; virtue &c. 944.

V. be -right &c. *adj.*; stand to reason.

see -justice done, – one righted, – fair play; do justice to; recompense &c. (*reward*) 973; hold the scales even, give and take; serve one right, put the saddle on the right horse; give -every one, – the devil- his due; *audire alteram partem.*

deserve &c. (*be entitled to*) 924.

Adj. right, good; just, reasonable; fit &c. 924; equ-al, -able, -itable; even-handed, fair, – and square.

legitimate, justifiable, rightful; as it -should, – ought to- be; lawful &c. (*permitted*) 760, (*legal*) 963.

deserved &c. 924.

Adv. rightly &c. *adj.*; in -justice, – equity, – reason.

without -distinction of, – regard to, – respect to- persons; upon even terms.

Int. all right!

923. Wrong. — N. wrong; what -ought not to, – should not- be; *malum in se*; unreasonableness, grievance; shame.

injustice; unfairness &c. *adj.*; iniquity, foul play, partiality, leaning; favour, -itism; nepotism, party spirit, partisanship; undueness &c. 925; unlawfulness &c. 964.

robbing Peter to pay Paul &c. *v.*; the wolf and the lamb; vice &c. 945.

a custom more honoured in the breach than the observance.

V. be -wrong &c. *adj.*; cry to heaven for vengeance.

do -wrong &c. *n.*; be -inequitable &c. *adj.*; favour, lean towards; encroach; impose upon; reap where one has not sown; give an inch and take an ell; rob Peter to pay Paul.

Adj. wrong, -ful; bad, too bad; unjust, -fair; in-, un-equitable; unequal, partial, one-sided.

objectionable; un-reasonable, -allowable, -warrantable, -justifiable; not cricket, not playing the game; improper, unfit; unjustified &c. 925; illegal &c. 964; iniquitous, criminal; immoral &c. 945; injurious &c. 649.

in the wrong, – box.

Adv. wrongly &c. *adj.*

Phr. it will not do; this is too bad.

924. Dueness.—**N.** due, -ness; right, privilege, prerogative, prescription, title, claim, pretension, demand, birthright.

immunity, licence, liberty, franchise; vested -interest, – right; licitness.

sanction, authority, warranty, charter; warrant &c. (*permission*) 760; constitution &c. (*law*) 963; tenure; bond &c. (*security*) 771.

deserts, merits, dues.

claimant, appellant; plaintiff &c. 938.

V. be -due &c. *adj.* to, – the due &c. *n.* of; have -right, – title, – claim- to; be entitled to; have a claim upon; belong to &c. (*property*) 780.

deserve, merit, be worthy of, richly deserve.

demand, claim; call upon –, come upon –, appeal to- for; re-vendicate, -claim; exact; insist -on, – upon; challenge; take one's stand, make a point of, require, lay claim to, assert, assume, arrogate, make good; substantiate; vindicate a -claim, – right; make out a case.

give –, confer- a right; sanction, entitle; authorize &c. 760; sanctify, legalize, ordain, prescribe, allot.

give every one his due &c. 922; pay one's dues; have one's -due, – rights; stand upon one's rights.

use a right, assert, enforce, put in force, lay under contribution.

Adj. having a right to &c. *v.*; entitled to; claiming; deserving, meriting, worthy of.

privileged, allowed, sanctioned, warranted, authorized; ordained, prescribed, constitutional, chartered, enfranchised.

925. [Absence of right.] **Undueness** —**N.** undueness &c. *adj.*; *malum prohibitum*; impropriety; illegality &c. 964.

falseness &c. *adj.*; emptiness –, invalidity- of title; illegitimacy.

loss of right, disfranchisement, forfeiture.

usurpation, assumption, tort, violation, breach, encroachment, presumption, seizure, stretch, exaction, imposition, lion's share.

usurper, pretender, Carlist; impostor.

V. be -undue &c. *adj.*; not be -due &c. 924.

infringe, encroach, trench on, exact; arrogate, – to oneself; give an inch and take an ell; stretch –, strain- a point; usurp, violate, do violence to; sail under false colours.

dis-franchise, -entitle, -qualify; invalidate.

relax &c. (*be lax*) 738; misbehave &c. (*vice*) 945; misbecome.

Adj. undue; unlawful &c. (*illegal*) 964; unconstitutional, *ultra vires*; illicit; un-authorized, -warranted, -allowed, -sanctioned, -justified; un-, dis-entitled, -qualified; un-privileged, -chartered.

illegitimate, bastard, spurious, false; usurped, tortious.

un-deserved, -merited, -earned; unfulfilled.

forfeited, disfranchised.

improper; un-meet, -fit, -befitting, -seemly; un-, mis-becoming; seemless; *contra bonos mores*; not the thing, out of the question, not to be thought of; preposterous, pretentious, would- be.

---

prescriptive, presumptive; absolute, indefeasible; un-, in-alienable; imprescriptible, inviolable, unimpeachable, unchallenged; sacrosanct.

due to, merited, deserved, condign, richly deserved, *emeritus*.

allowable &c. (*permitted*) 760; lawful, licit, legitimate, legal; legalized &c. (*law*) 963.

square, unexceptionable, right; equitable &c. 922; due, *en règle*; fit, -ting; correct, proper, meet, befitting, becoming, seemly; decorous; creditable, up to the mark, right as a trivet; just –, quite- the thing; *selon les règles*.

Adv. duly, *ex officio*, *de jure*; by -right, – divine right; as is -fitting, – proper, – fitting and proper; *jure divino, Dei gratiâ*, in the name of.

Phr. *civis Romanus sum*.

926. Duty.—**N.** duty, what ought to be done, moral obligation, account-ableness, liability, *onus*, responsibility; bounden –, imperative- duty; call, – of duty.

allegiance, fealty, tie; engagement &c. (*promise*) 768; part; function, calling &c. (*business*) 625.

morality, morals, decalogue; case of conscience; conscientiousness &c. (*probity*) 939; conscience, inward monitor, still small voice within, sense of duty, tender conscience.

dueness &c. 924; propriety, fitness, seemliness, amenableness, decorum; the -thing, – proper thing; the -right, – proper- thing to do.

[Science of morals] eth-ics, -ology; deon-, are-tology; moral –, ethical-philosophy; casuistry, polity.

observance, fulfilment, discharge, performance, acquittal, satisfaction, redemption; good behaviour.

V. be -the duty of, – incumbent &c. *adj.* on, – responsible &c. *adj.*; behoove, become, befit, beseem; belong –, pertain- to; fall to one's lot; devolve on; lie -upon, – on one's head, – at one's door; rest -with, – on the shoulders of.

take upon oneself &c. (*promise*) 768; be –, become- -bound to, – sponsor for; be responsible for; incur a -responsibility &c. *n.*; be –, stand –, lie- under an obligation; have to answer for, owe it to oneself.

impose a -duty &c. *n.*; enjoin, require, exact; bind, – over; saddle with, prescribe, assign, call upon, look to, oblige.

927. Dereliction of Duty.—**N.** dere; liction of duty; fault &c. (*guilt*) 947- sin &c. (*vice*) 945; non-observance, -performance, -co-operation; neglect, carelessness, laziness, incompetence, eye-service, relaxation, infraction, violation, transgression, failure, evasion, indolence; dead letter.

slacker, loafer, striker, non-co-operator.

V. violate; break, – through; infringe; set -aside, – at naught; trample -on, – under foot; slight, neglect, evade, renounce, forswear, repudiate; wash one's hands of; escape, transgress, fail.

call to account &c. (*disapprobation*) 932.

927a. Exemption.—**N.** exemption, freedom, irresponsibility, immunity, liberty, licence, release, exoneration, excuse, dispensation, absolution, franchise, renunciation, discharge; exculpation &c. 970; *ægrotat*.

V. be -exempt &c. *adj.*

exempt, release, acquit, discharge, quit-claim, remise, remit; free, set at liberty, let off, pass over, spare, excuse, dispense with, give dispensation, license; stretch a point; absolve &c. (*forgive*) 918; exonerate &c. (*exculpate*) 970; save the necessity.

Adj. exempt, free, immune, at liberty, scot free; released &c. *v.*; unbound, unencumbered; irresponsible, unaccountable, not answerable; excusable.

---

enter upon –, perform –, observe –, fulfil –, discharge –, adhere to –, acquit oneself of –, satisfy- -a duty, – an obligation; act one's part, redeem one's pledge, do justice to, be at one's post; do duty; do one's duty &c. (*be virtuous*) 944.

be on one's good behaviour, mind one's P's and Q's.

Adj. obligatory, binding; imperative, peremptory; stringent &c. (*severe*) 739; behooving &c. *v.*; incumbent –, chargeable- on; under obligation; obliged –, bound –, tied- by; saddled with.

due –, beholden –, bound –, indebted- to; tied down; compromised &c. (*promised*) 768; in duty bound.

amenable, liable, accountable, responsible, answerable.

right, meet &c. (*due*) 924; moral, ethical, casuistical, conscientious, ethological.

Adv. with a safe conscience, as in duty bound, on one's own responsibility, at one's own risk, *suo periculo*; *in foro conscientiæ*; *quamdiu se bene gesserit*; at one's post, on duty.

Phr. *dura lex sed lex.*

2°. MORAL SENTIMENTS

928. Respect.—**N.** respect, regard, consideration; courtesy &c. 894; attention, deference, reverence, honour, esteem, estimation, veneration, admiration; approbation &c. 931.

homage, fealty, obeisance, genuflexion, kneeling, prostration; obsequiousness &c. 886; salaam, *kowtow*, bow, presenting arms, salute.

respects, regards, duty, *devoirs*, *égards*.

devotion &c. (*piety*) 987.

V. respect, regard; revere, -nce; hold in reverence, honour, venerate, hallow; esteem &c. (*approve of*) 931; think much of; entertain –, bear- respect for; have a high opinion of; look up to, defer to; pay -attention, – respect &c. *n.*- to; do –, render- honour to; do the honours, hail; show courtesy &c. 894; salute, present arms; do –, pay- homage to; pay tribute to, kneel to, bow to, bend the knee to; fall down before, prostrate oneself, kiss the hem of one's garment; worship &c. 990.

keep one's distance, make room, observe due decorum, stand upon ceremony.

command –, inspire- respect; awe, impose, overawe, dazzle.

Adj. respecting &c. *v.*; respectful, deferential, decorous, reverential, obsequious, ceremonious, bare-headed, cap in hand, on one's knees; prostrate &c. (*servile*) 886.

respected &c. *v.*; in high -esteem, – estimation; time-honoured, venerable, *emeritus*.

Adv. in deference to; with -all, – due, – the highest- respect; with submission.

saving your -grace, – presence; *salva sit reverentia*; *pace tanti nominis*.

Int. hail! all hail! *esto perpetua!* may your shadow never be less!

929. Disrespect. — **N.** dis-respect, -esteem, -estimation, -favour, -repute; low estimation; disparagement &c. (*dispraise*) 932, (*detraction*) 934.

irreverence; slight, neglect; *spretæ injuria formæ*; superciliousness &c. (*contempt*) 930.

vilipendency, contumely, affront, dishonour, insult, indignity, outrage, discourtesy &c. 895; practical joking; scurrility, scoffing, sibilation; ir-, derision; mockery, irony &c. (*ridicule*) 856; sarcasm.

hiss, hoot, gibe, flout, jeer, scoff, gleek, taunt, sneer, quip, fling, wipe, slap in the face.

V. hold in disrespect &c. (*despise*) 930; misprize, disregard, slight, undervalue, depreciate, trifle with, set at naught, pass by, push aside, overlook, turn one's back upon, laugh in one's sleeve; be -disrespectful &c. *adj.*, – discourteous &c. 895; treat with -disrespect &c. *n.*; set down, browbeat.

dishonour, desecrate; insult, affront, outrage.

speak slightingly of; disparage &c. (*dispraise*) 932; vilipend, call names; throw –, fling- dirt; drag through the mud, point at, indulge in personalities; make -mouths, – faces; bite the thumb; take –, pluck- by the beard; toss in a blanket, tar and feather.

have –, hold- in derision; deride, scoff, sneer, laugh at, snigger, ridicule, gibe, mock, jeer, taunt, twit, niggle, gleek, gird, flout, fleer; roast, turn into ridicule; guy, burlesque &c. 856; laugh to scorn &c. (*contempt*) 930; smoke; fool; make -game, – a fool, – an April fool- of; play a practical joke; rag; lead one a dance, run the rig upon, have a fling at, scout, hiss, hoot, mob.

Adj. disrespectful; aweless, irreverent; disparaging &c. 934; insulting &c. *v.*; supercilious &c. (*scornful*) 930; rude, derisive, contemptuous, sarcastic; scurri-le, -lous; contumelious.

un-respected, -worshipped, -envied, -saluted; un-, dis-regarded.

Adv. disrespectfully &c. *adj.*

930. Contempt.—N. contempt, disdain, scorn, sovereign contempt; despi-sal, -ciency; vilipendency, contumely; slight, sneer, spurn, by-word.

contemptuousness &c. *adj.*; scornful eye; smile of contempt; derision &c. (*disrespect*) 929.

[State of being despised] despisedness.

V. despise, contemn, scorn, disdain, feel contempt for, view with a scornful eye, disregard, slight, not mind; pass by &c. (*neglect*) 460.

look down upon; hold -cheap, – in contempt, – in disrespect; think -nothing, – small beer- of; make light of; underestimate &c. 483; esteem -slightly, – of small or no account; take no account of, care nothing for; set no store by; not care a -straw &c. (*unimportance*) 643; set at naught, laugh in one's sleeve, snap one's fingers at, shrug one's shoulders, turn up one's nose at, pooh-pooh, damn with faint praise; sneeze –, whistle –, sneer- at; curl up one's lip, toss the head, *traiter de haut*; laugh at &c. (*be disrespectful*) 929.

point the finger of –, hold up to –, laugh to- scorn; scout, hoot, flout, hiss, scoff at.

turn -one's back, – a cold shoulder- upon; tread –, trample- -upon, – under foot; spurn, kick; fling to the winds &c. (*repudiate*) 610; send away with a flea in the ear.

Adj. contemptuous; disdain-, scorn-ful; withering, contumelious, supercilious, cynical, haughty, bumptious, cavalier; derisive.

contemptible, despicable; pitiable; pitiful &c. (*unimportant*) 643; despised &c. *v.*; down-trodden; unenvied.

Adv. contemptuously &c. *adj.*

Int. a fig for &c. (*unimportant*) 643; bah! never mind! away with! hang it! fiddle-de-dee!

931. Approbation.—N. approbation; approv-al, -ement; sanction, advocacy; nod of approbation; esteem, estimation, good opinion, golden opinions, admiration; love &c. 897; appreciation, regard, account, popularity, *kudos*, credit; repute &c. 873.

commendation, praise; laud, -ation; good word; meed –, tribute- of praise; encomium; eulog-y, -ium; *éloge*, panegyric; homage, hero worship; benediction, blessing, benison.

applause, plaudit, clap; clapping, – of hands; accl-aim, -amation; cheer; pæan, hosannah; shout –, peal –, chorus –, thunders- of -applause &c.; Kentish fire; Prytaneum; blurb.

V. approve; think -good, – much of, well of, – highly of; esteem, value, prize; set great store -by, – on.

do justice to, appreciate; honour, hold in esteem, look up to, admire; like &c. 897; be in favour of, wish God speed; hail, – with satisfaction.

stand –, stick- up for; uphold, hold

932. Disapprobation.—N. disapprobation, -val; improbation; dis-esteem, -valuation, -placency; odium; dislike &c. 867; dissent &c. 489.

dis-praise, -commendation; blame, censure, obloquy; detraction &c. 934; disparagement, depreciation; denunciation; condemnation &c. 971; ostracism; boycott; black-list, -ball; *index -expurgatorius, – librorum prohibitorum*.

animadversion, reflection, stricture, objection, exception, criticism; sardonic -grin, – laugh; sarcasm, insinuation, innuendo; bad –, poor –, left-handed- compliment.

satire; sneer &c. (*contempt*) 930; taunt &c. (*disrespect*) 929; cavil, carping, censoriousness; hypercriticism &c. (*fastidiousness*) 868.

reprehension, remonstrance, expostulation, reproof, reprobation, admonition, increpation, reproach; rebuke, reprimand, castigation, jobation, lecture, curtain lecture, blow up, wigging, dressing, – down; rating, scolding, trim-

up, countenance, sanction; clap –, pat-
on the back; keep in countenance, endorse, give credit, recommend; mark
with a white -mark, – stone.

commend, praise; be-, laud; compliment, pay a tribute, bepraise; clap,
– the hands; applaud, cheer, acclaim,
acclamate, encore; panegyrize, eulogize, cry up, *prôner*, puff; extol, – to
the skies; magnify, glorify, exalt, boost,
swell, make much of; flatter &c. 933;
bless, give a blessing to; have –, say- a
good word for; speak -well, – highly,
– in high terms- of; sing –, sound –,
chaunt –, resound- the praises of; sing
praises to; cheer –, applaud- to the
-echo, – very echo.

redound to the -honour, – praise, –
credit- of; do credit to; deserve -praise
&c. *n.*; recommend itself; pass muster.

be -praised &c.; receive honourable
mention; be in -favour, – high favour-
with; ring with the praises of, win
golden opinions, gain credit, find favour
with, stand well in the opinion of;
laudari a laudato viro.

Adj. approving &c. *v.*; in favour of;
lost in admiration.

commendatory, complimentary, ben-
edictory, laudatory, panegyrical, eulo-
gistic, encomiastic, acclamatory, lavish
of praise, uncritical.

approved, praised &c. *v.*; un-cen-
sured, -impeached; popular, in good
odour; in high esteem &c. (*respected*)
928; in –, in high- favour.

deserving –, worthy of- praise &c. *n.*;
praiseworthy, commendable, of estimation; good &c. 648; meritorious, estimable, creditable, plausible, unimpeachable; beyond all praise.

Adv. commendably, with credit, to
admiration; well &c. 681; with three
times three.

Int. hear, hear! well done! *brav-o! -a!
-i! bravissimo! euge! macte virtute!* so far
so good, that's right, quite right; *optime!* one cheer more; may your shadow never be less! *esto perpetua!* long
life to! *viva! evviva!* God speed! *valete
et plaudite! encore! bis!*

Phr. *probatum est.*

---

ming; correction, set down, rap on the
knuckles, *coup de bec*, rebuff; slap, – on
the face; home thrust, hit; frown, scowl,
black look.

diatribe; jeremiad; *tirade*, philippic.

clamour, outcry, hue and cry; hiss,
-ing; sibilation, cat-call; execration &c.
908.

chiding, upbraiding &c. *v.*; exprobration, abuse, vituperation, invective,
objurgation, contumely, personal remarks; hard –, cutting –, bitter- words.

evil-speaking; bad language &c. 908;
personality.

V. disapprove; dislike &c. 867; lament &c. 839; object to, take exception to; be scandalized at, think ill
of; view with -disfavour, – dark eyes,
– jaundiced eyes; *nil admirari*, disvalue, improbate.

frown upon, look grave; bend –,
knit- the brows; shake the head at,
shrug the shoulders; turn up the nose
&c. (*contempt*) 930; look -askance, –
black upon; look with an evil eye;
make a wry -face, – mouth- at; set
one's face against.

dis-praise, -commend, -parage; deprecate, speak ill of, not speak well of,
slate, condemn &c. (*find guilty*) 971.

blame; lay –, cast- blame upon;
censure, *fronder*, reproach, pass censure
on, reprobate, impugn.

remonstrate, expostulate, recriminate.

reprehend, chide, admonish; bring –,
call- -to account, – over the coals, – to
order; take to task, reprove, lecture,
bring to book; read a -lesson, – lecture-
to; rebuke, correct.

reprimand, chastise, castigate, lash,
blow up, trounce, trim, *laver la tête*,
overhaul; give it one, – finely; gibbet.

accuse &c. 938; impeach, denounce;
hold up to -reprobation, – execration;
expose, brand, gibbet, stigmatize;
show –, pull –, take- up; cry 'shame'
upon; be outspoken; raise a hue and
cry against.

execrate &c. 908; exprobrate, speak
daggers, vituperate; abuse, – like a
pickpocket; scold, rate, objurate, upbraid, fall foul of; jaw; rail, – at, – in
good set terms; bark at; anathematize,

call names; call by -hard, – ugly- names; a-, re-vile; vili-fy, -pend; bespatter; backbite; clapperclaw; rave –, thunder –, fulminate-against; load with reproaches; lash with the tongue.

exclaim –, protest –, inveigh –, declaim –, cry out –, raise one's voice- against.

decry; cry –, run –, frown- down; clamour, hiss, hoot, mob, ostracize; draw up –, sign- a round robin; black-ball, -list.

animadvert –, reflect- upon; glance at; cast -reflection, – re-proach, – a slur- upon; insinuate, damn with faint praise; 'hint a fault and hesitate dislike'; not to be able to say much for.

scoff at, point at; twit, taunt &c. (*disrespect*) 929; sneer at &c. (*despise*) 930; satirize, lampoon; defame &c. (*detract*) 934; depre-ciate, find fault with, criticize, cut up; pull –, pick- to pieces; take exception; cavil; peck –, nibble –, carp- at; be -censorious &c. *adj.*; pick -holes, – a hole, – a hole in one's coat; make a fuss about.

take –, set- down; snub, snap one up, give a rap on the knuckles; throw a stone -at, – in one's garden; have a -fling, – snap- at; have words with, pluck a crow with; give one a -wipe, – lick with the rough side of the tongue.

incur blame, excite disapprobation, scandalize, shock, revolt; get a bad name, forfeit one's good opinion, be under a cloud, come under the ferule, bring a hornet's nest about one's ears.

take blame, stand corrected; have to answer for.

Adj. disapproving &c. *v.*; scandalized.

disparaging, condemnatory, damnatory, denunciatory, reproach-ful, abusive, objurgatory, clamorous, vituperative; defamatory &c. 934.

satirical, sarcastic, sardonic, cynical, dry, sharp, cutting, biting, severe, virulent, withering, trenchant, hard upon; censorious, criti-cal, captious, carping, hypercritical; fastidious &c. 868; sparing of –, grudging- praise.

disapproved, chid &c. *v.*; in bad odour, blown upon, unapproved; unblest; at a discount, exploded; weighed in the balance and found wanting.

blameworthy, reprehensible &c. (*guilt*) 947; to –, worthy of-blame, answerable, uncommendable, exceptionable, not to be thought of, bad &c. 649; vicious &c. 945.

un-lamented, -bewailed, -pitied.

Adv. with a wry face; reproachfully &c. *adj.*

Int. it is too bad! it -won't, – will never- do! marry come up! Oh! come! 'sdeath!

forbid it Heaven! God –, Heaven- forbid! out –, fie- upon it! away with! tut! *O tempora! O mores!* shame! fie, – for shame! out on you!

tell it not in Gath!

933. Flattery.—N. flattery, adula-tion, gloze; bland-ishment, -iloquence; cajolery; fawning, wheedling &c. *v.*; captation, coquetry, sycophancy, ob-sequiousness, flunkeyism, toad-eating, tuft-hunting; snobbishness.

incense, honeyed words, flummery; bun-kum, -combe; blarney, *placebo*, but-

934. Detraction.—N. detraction, dis-paragement, depreciation, vilification, obloquy, scurrility, scandal, defama-tion, aspersion, traducement, slander, calumny, obtrectation, evil-speaking, backbiting, *scandalum magnatum*.

personality, libel, squib, lampoon, skit, pasquinade; *chronique scandaleuse*.

ter; soft -soap, – sawder; rose water.

voice of the charmer, mouth honour; lip-homage; euphemism; unctuousness &c. *adj.*

V. flatter, praise to the skies, puff; wheedle, cajole, glaver, coax; fawn, – upon; humour, gloze, soothe, pet, coquet, slaver, butter; be-spatter, -slubber, -plaster, -slaver; lay it on thick, overpraise; earwig, cog, collogue; truckle –, pander *or* pandar –, pay court- to; court; creep into the good graces of; curry favour with, hang on the sleeve of; fool to the top of one's bent; lick the dust.

lay the flattering unction to one's soul, gild the pill, make things pleasant.

overestimate &c. 482; exaggerate &c. 549.

Adj. flattering &c. *v.*; adulatory; mealy-, honey-mouthed; honeyed; smooth, – tongued; soapy, oily, unctuous, blandiloquent, specious; fine-, fair-spoken; plausible, servile, sycophantic, fulsome; courtier-ly, -like.

Adv. *ad captandum.*

---

935. Flatterer.—N. flatterer, adulator; eu-logist, -phemist; optimist, encomiast, *laudator*, whitewasher, booster.

toad-y, -eater; sycophant, courtier, pickthank, Sir Pertinax MacSycophant; *flâneur, prôneur*; puffer, touter, *claqueur*; claw-back, ear-wig, doer of dirty work; parasite, hanger on &c. (*servility*) 886.

---

937. Vindication.—N. vindication, justification, warrant; exoneration, exculpation; acquittal &c. 970; whitewashing.

extenuation; pallia-tion, -tive; softening, mitigation.

reply, defence; recrimination &c. 938.

apology, gloss, varnish; plea &c. 617; salvo; excuse, extenuating circumstances; allowance, – to be made; *locus pœnitentiæ.*

apologist, vindicator, justifier; defendant &c. 938.

justifiable charge, true bill.

sarcasm, cynicism; criticism (*disapprobation*) 932; invective &c. 932; envenomed tongue; *spretæ injuria formæ.* detractor &c. 936.

V. detract, derogate, decry, depreciate, disparage; run –, cry- down; minimize, make light of; belittle, sneer at &c. (*contemn*) 930; criticize, pull to pieces, pick a hole in one's coat, asperse, cast aspersions, blow upon, bespatter, blacken; vili-fy, -pend; avile; give a dog a bad name, brand, malign, backbite, libel, lampoon, traduce, slander, defame, calumniate, bear false witness against; speak ill of behind one's back.

'damn with faint praise, assent with civil leer; and without sneering, others teach to sneer.'

fling dirt &c. (*disrespect*) 929; anathematize &c. 932; dip the pen in gall, view in a bad light.

Adj. detracting &c. *v.*; defamatory, detractory, derogatory; disparaging, libellous; scurril-e, -ous; abusive; foulspoken, -tongued, -mouthed; slanderous; calumni-ous, -atory; sar-castic, -donic; satirical, cynical.

---

936. Detractor.—N. detractor, reprover; cens-or, -urer; cynic, critic, caviller, carper, wordcatcher.

defamer, backbiter, slanderer, knocker, Sir Benjamin Backbite, lampooner, satirist, traducer, libeller, calumniator, dearest foe, dawplucker, Thersites; Zoilus; good-natured –, candid- friend [satirically]; reviler, vituperator, castigator; shrew &c. 901.

disapprover, *laudator temporis acti.*

---

938. Accusation. — N. accusation, charge, imputation, slur, inculpation, exprobration, delation; crimination; in-, ac-, re-crimination; *tu quoque* argument; invective &c. 932.

de-nunciation, -nouncement; libel, challenge, citation, arraignment; im-, ap-peachment; indictment, bill of indictment, true bill; lawsuit &c. 969; condemnation &c. 971.

gravamen of a charge, head and front of one's offending, *argumentum ad hominem*; scandal &c. (*detraction*) 934; *scandalum magnatum.*

V. justify, warrant; be an -excuse &c. *n.*- for; lend a colour, furnish a handle; vindicate; ex-, dis-culpate; acquit &c. 970; clear, set right, exonerate, whitewash.

extenuate, palliate, excuse, soften, apologize, varnish, slur, gloze; put a -gloss, – good face- upon; mince; gloss over, bolster up, help a lame dog over a stile.

advocate, defend, plead one's cause; stand –, stick –, speak- up for; contend –, speak- for; bear out, keep in countenance, support; plead &c. 617; say in defence; plead ignorance; confess and avoid, propugn, put in a good word for.

take the will for the deed, make allowance for, do justice to; give -one, – the Devil- his due.

make good; prove -the truth of, – one's case; be justified by the event.

Adj. vindicat-ed, -ing &c. *v.*; vindicat-ive, -ory; palliative; exculpatory; apologetic.

excusable, defensible, pardonable; veni-al, -able; specious, plausible, justifiable.

Phr. '*honi soit qui mal y pense.*'

accuser, prosecutor, plaintiff, complainant, petitioner; relator, informer; appellant.

accused, defendant, prisoner, panel, co-, respondent; litigant.

V. accuse, charge, tax, impute, twit, taunt with, reproach.

brand with reproach; stigmatize, slur; cast a -stone at, – slur on; incriminate; inculpate, implicate; call to account &c. (*censure*) 932; take to -blame, – task; put in the black book.

inform against, indict, denounce, arraign; im-, ap-peach; have up, show up, pull up; challenge, cite, lodge a complaint; prosecute, bring an action against &c. 969.

charge –, saddle- with; lay to one's -door, – charge; lay the blame on, bring home to; cast –, throw- in one's teeth; cast the first stone at.

have –, keep- a rod in pickle for; have a crow to pluck with.

trump up a charge.

Adj. accusing &c. *v.*; accusat-ory, -ive; imputative, denunciatory; re-, criminatory.

accused &c. *v.*; suspected; under -suspicion, – a cloud, – *surveillance*; in -custody, – detention; in the -lock up, – watch house, – house of detention.

accusable, imputable; in-defensible, -excusable; un-pardonable, -justifiable; vicious &c. 945.

Int. look at home; *tu quoque* &c. (*retaliation*) 718.

3°. Moral Conditions

939. Probity.—N. probity, integrity, rectitude; uprightness &c. *adj.*; honesty, faith; honour; good faith, *bona fides*; purity, clean hands.

fairness &c. *adj.*; fair play, justice, equity, impartiality, principle; grace.

constancy; faithfulness &c. *adj.*; fidelity, loyalty; incorrupt-ion, -ibility.

trustworthiness &c. *adj.*; truth, candour, singleness of heart; veracity &c. 543; tender conscience &c. (*sense of duty*) 926.

punctil-iousness, -io; delicacy, nicety; scrupul-osity, -ousness &c. *adj.*; scruple; point, – of honour; punctuality.

dignity &c. (*repute*) 873; respectability, -bleness &c. *adj.*; gentleman; man of -honour, – his word; *fidus*

940. Improbity. N. improbity; dishon-esty, -our; deviation from rectitude; disgrace &c. (*disrepute*) 874; fraud &c. (*deception*) 545; lying &c. 544; bad –, Punic- faith; *mala –, Punica- fides*; infidelity; faithlessness &c. *adj.*; Judas kiss, betrayal; scrap of paper.

breach of -promise, – trust, – faith; prodition, disloyalty, divided allegiance, treason, high treason; apostacy &c. (*tergiversation*) 607; non-observance &c. 773.

shabbiness &c. *adj.*; villainy; baseness &c. *adj.*; abjection, debasement, turpitude, moral turpitude, laxity, trimming, shuffling.

perfidy; perfidiousness &c. *adj.*;

Achates, preux chevalier, galantuomo;
truepenny, trump, brick; true Briton,
white man, sportsman.

court of honour, a fair field and no
favour; *argumentum ad verecundiam.*

V. be -honourable &c. *adj.*; deal
-honourably, – squarely, – impartially,
– fairly; speak the truth &c. *(veracity)*
543; tell the truth and shame the devil,
vitam impendere vero; show a proper
spirit, make a point of; do one's duty
&c. 944; play the game.

redeem one's pledge &c. 926; keep –,
be as good as- one's -promise, – word;
keep faith with, not fail.

give and take, *audire alteram partem,*
give the devil his due, put the saddle
on the right horse.

redound to one's honour.

Adj. upright; honest, – as daylight;
veracious &c. 543; virtuous &c. 944;
honourable; fair, right, just, equitable,
impartial, even-handed, square; fair –,
open- and aboveboard.

constant, – as the northern star;
faithful, loyal, staunch; true, – blue,
– to one's colours, – to the core, – as
the needle to the pole; true-hearted,
trust-y, -worthy; as good as one's
word, to be depended on, incorruptible.

manly, straightforward &c. *(ingenuous)* 703; frank, candid, open-hearted.

conscientious, tender - conscienced,
right-minded; high-principled, -mind-
ed; scrupulous, religious, strict; nice,
punctilious, correct, punctual; respect-,
reput-able; gentlemanlike.

inviol - able, - ate; un - violated,
-broken, -betrayed; un-bought, -bribed.

innocent &c. 946; pure; stainless; un-stained, -tarnished, -sullied,
-tainted, -perjured; uncorrupt, -ed;
unde-filed, -praved, -bauched; *integer
vitæ scelerisque purus; justus et tenax
propositi.*

chivalrous, jealous of honour, *sans
peur et sans reproche*; high-spirited.

supra-mundane, unworldly, over-
scrupulous.

Adv. honourably &c. *adj.*; *bona fide;*
on the square, in good faith, honour bright, *foro conscientiæ*, with
clean hands; by fair means.

treachery, double-dealing; unfairness
&c. *adj.*; knavery, roguery, rascality,
foul-play; jobb-ing, -ery; Tammany,
graft; venality, nepotism; corruption,
job, shuffle, fishy transaction, barratry;
sharp practice, heads I win, tails you
lose; mouth-honour &c. (*flattery*) 933.

V. be -dishonest &c. *adj.*; play false;
break one's -word, – faith, – promise;
jilt, betray, forswear; shuffle &c. (*lie*)
544; live by one's wits, sail near the
wind; play with marked cards.

disgrace –, dishonour –, demean –,
degrade- oneself; derogate, stoop,
grovel, sneak, lose caste; sell oneself,
go over to the enemy; seal one's
infamy.

Adj. dishon-est, -ourable; un-con-
scientious, -scrupulous; fraudulent &c.
545; knavish; disgraceful &c. (*disreputable*) 874; wicked &c. 945.

false-hearted, disingenuous; unfair,
one-sided; double, -tongued, -faced;
time-serving, crooked, tortuous, insidious, Machiavellian, dark, slippery;
questionable; fishy; perfidious, treacherous, perjured.

infamous, arrant, foul, base, vile,
low, ignominious, blackguard.

contemptible, abject, mean, shabby,
little, paltry, dirty, scurvy, scabby,
sneaking, grovelling, scrubby, rascally,
pettifogging; beneath one; not cricket.

low-minded, -thoughted; base-
minded.

undignified, indign; unbe-coming,
-seeming, -fitting; de-rogatory, -grad-
ing; *infra dignitatem*; ungentleman-ly,
-like; un-knightly, -chivalric, -manly,
-handsome; recreant, inglorious.

corrupt, venal; debased, mongrel.

faithless, of bad faith, false, unfaith-
ful, disloyal; untrustworthy; trust-,
troth-less; lost to shame, dead to
honour.

Adv. dishonestly &c. *adj.*; *malâ fide,*
like a thief in the night, by crooked
paths; by foul means.

Int. *O tempora! O mores!*

---

941. Knave.—N. knave, rogue, villain; Scapin, rascal; Lazarillo de
Tormes; bad man &c. 949; blackguard &c. 949.

traitor, betrayer, arch-traitor, conspirator, stool pigeon, Judas, Catiline; reptile, serpent, snake in the grass, wolf in sheep's clothing, sneak, Jerry Sneak, tell-tale, squealer, mischief-maker, trimmer; renegade &c. (*tergiversation*) 607; truant, recreant; sycophant &c. (*servility*) 886.

942. Disinterestedness.—N. disinterestedness &c. *adj.*; generosity; liberal-ity, -ism; altruism; benevolence &c. 906; elevation, loftiness of purpose, exaltation, magnanimity; chival-ry, -rous spirit; heroism, sublimity.

self-denial, -abnegation, -effacement, -sacrifice, -immolation, -control &c. (*resolution*) 604; stoicism, devotion, martyrdom, *suttee*.

labour of love.

V. be -disinterested &c. *adj.*; make a sacrifice, lay one's head on the block; put oneself in the place of others, do as one would be done by, do unto others as we would men should do unto us.

Adj. disinterested; unselfish; self-denying, -sacrificing, -devoted; generous.

handsome, liberal, noble; noble-, high-minded; princely, great, high, elevated, lofty, exalted, spirited, stoical, magnanimous; great-, large-hearted, chivalrous, heroic, sublime.

un-bought, -bribed; uncorrupted &c. (*upright*) 939.

943. Selfishness.—N. selfishness &c. *adj.*; self-love, -indulgence, -worship, -interest; ego-tism, -ism; egocentrism, narcissism; *amour propre* &c. (*vanity*) 880; nepotism.

worldliness &c. *adj.*; world wisdom. illiberality; meanness &c. *adj.*

time-server; tuft-, fortune-hunter; self-seeker; jobber, worldling; egotist, egoist, monopolist, nepotist, profiteer; temporizer, trimmer; dog in the manger, charity that begins at home.

V. be -selfish &c. *adj.*; please -, indulge -, coddle- oneself; consult one's own -wishes, - pleasure; look after one's own interest; feather one's nest; take care of number one, have an eye to the main chance, know on which side one's bread is buttered; give an inch and take an ell; wangle.

Adj. selfish; self-seeking, -indulgent, -interested; wrapt up -, centred- in self; egotistic, -al; egoistical; egocentric.

illiberal, mean, ungenerous, narrow-minded; mercenary, venal; covetous &c. 819.

unspiritual; earthly, -minded; mundane; worldly, -minded, -wise; time-serving.

interested; *alieni appetens sui profusus.*

Adv. ungenerously &c. *adj.*; to gain some private ends; from selfish -, interested- motives.

Phr. *après nous le déluge.*

944. Virtue.—N. virtue; virtuous-ness &c. *adj.*; morality; moral recti-tude; integrity &c. (*probity*) 939; nobleness &c. 873.

morals; ethics &c. (*duty*) 926; cardinal virtues.

merit, worth, desert, excellence, credit; self-control &c. (*resolution*) 604; self-denial &c. (*temperance*) 953.

well-doing; good -actions, - behaviour; discharge -, fulfilment -, performance- of duty; well-spent life; innocence &c. 946.

V. be -virtuous &c. *adj.*; practise virtue &c. *n.*; do -, fulfil -, perform -,

945. Vice. — N. vice; evil -doing, - courses; wrong doing; wickedness, viciousness &c. *adj.*; iniquity, peccability, demerit; sin, Adam; old -, offending- Adam.

immorality, impropriety, indecorum, scandal, laxity, looseness of morals; want of -principle, - ballast; obliquity, backsliding, infamy, demoralization, pravity, depravity, pollution; hardness of heart; brutality &c. (*malevolence*) 907; corruption &c. (*debasement*) 659; knavery &c. (*improbity*) 940; profligacy; lust &c. 961; flagrancy, atrocity; cannibalism.

discharge- one's duty; redeem one's pledge &c. 926; act well, – one's part; fight the good fight; acquit oneself well; command –, master- one's passions; keep -straight, – in the right path.

set -an, – a good- example; be on one's -good, – best- behaviour.

Adj. virtuous, good; innocent &c. 946; meritorious, deserving, worthy, desertful, correct; dut-iful, -eous; moral; right, -eous, -minded; well-intentioned, creditable, laudable, commendable, praiseworthy; above –, beyond- all praise; excellent, admirable; sterling, pure, noble.

exemplary; match-, peer-less; saintly, -like; heaven-born, angelic, seraphic, godlike.

Adv. virtuously &c. *adj.*; *e merito.*

---

infirmity; weakness &c. *adj.*; weakness of the flesh, frailty, imperfection; error; weak side; foible; fail-ing, -ure; crying –, besetting- sin; defect, deficiency, shortcoming; cloven foot.

lowest dregs of vice, sink of iniquity, Alsatian den; *gusto picaresco.*

fault, crime; criminality &c. (*guilt*) 947.

sinner &c. 949.

V. be -vicious &c. *adj.*; sin, commit sin, do amiss, err, transgress; misdemean –, forget –, misconduct- oneself; mis-do, -behave; fall, lapse, slip, trip, offend, trespass; deviate from the -line of duty, – path of virtue &c. 944; take a wrong course, go astray; hug a -sin, – fault; sow one's wild oats.

render -vicious &c. *adj.*; demoralize, brutalize; corrupt &c. (*degrade*) 659.

Adj.* vicious; sinful; sinning &c. *v.*; wicked, iniquitous, bad, immoral, unrighteous, wrong, criminal; naughty, incorrect; undut-eous, -iful.

unprincipled, lawless, disorderly, *contra bonos mores*, indecorous, unseemly, improper; dissolute, profligate, scampish; unworthy; worth-, desert-less; disgraceful, recreant; reprehensible, blameworthy, uncommendable; dis-creditable, -reputable.

base, sinister, scurvy, foul, gross, vile, black, grave, facinorous, felonious, nefarious, shameful, scandalous, infamous, villainous, of a deep dye, heinous; flag-rant, -itious; atrocious, incarnate, accursed.

Mephistophelian, satanic, diabolic, hellish, infernal, stygian, fiend-ish, -like, hell-born, demoniacal, devilish.

mis-created, -begotten; demoralized, corrupt, depraved.

evil-minded, -disposed; ill-conditioned; malevolent &c. 907; heart-, grace-, shame-, virtue-less; abandoned, lost to virtue; unconscionable; sunk –, lost –, deep –, steeped- in iniquity.

incorrigible, irreclaimable, obdurate, reprobate, past praying for; culpable, reprehensible &c. (*guilty*) 947.

unjustifiable; in-defensible, -excusable; inexpiable, unpardonable, irremissible.

weak, frail, lax, infirm, imperfect, indiscreet; demoralizing, degrading.

Adv. wrong; sinfully &c. *adj.*; without excuse.

Int. *O tempora! O mores!*

---

946. Innocence. — N. innocence; guiltlessness &c. *adj.*; incorruption, impeccability.

clean hands, clear conscience, *mens sibi conscia recti.*

innocent, new born babe, lamb, dove.

V. be -innocent &c. *adj.*; *nil conscire sibi nullâ pallescere culpâ.*

947. Guilt.—N. guilt, -iness; culpability; crimin-ality, -ousness; deviation from rectitude &c. (*improbity*) 940; sinfulness &c. (*vice*) 945; peccability.

mis-conduct, -behaviour, -doing, -deed; malpractice, fault, sin, error, transgression; dereliction, delinquency; indiscretion, lapse, slip, trip, *faux pas,*

---

* Most of these adjectives are applicable both to the act and to the agent.

acquit &c. 970; exculpate &c. (*vindicate*) 937.

Adj. innocent, not guilty; unguilty; guilt-, fault-, sin-, stain-, blood-, spotless; clear, immaculate; *rectus in curiâ*; un-spotted, -blemished, -erring; undefiled &c. 939; unhardened, Saturnian; Arcadian &c. (*artless*) 703.

in-, un-culpable; unblam-ed, -able; blameless, inerrable, above suspicion; irrepr-oachable, -ovable, -ehensible; un-exceptionable, -objectionable, -impeachable; salvable; venial &c. 937.

harmless; in-offensive, -noxious, -nocuous; dove-, lamb-like; pure, harmless as doves; innocent as -a lamb, – the babe unborn; more sinned against than sinning.

virtuous &c. 944; un-reproved, -impeached, -reproached.

Adv. innocently &c. *adj.*; with clean hands; with a -clear, – safe- conscience.

948. Good Man. — **N.** good man, worthy.

good woman, goddess, *madonna*, virgin.

model, paragon &c. (*perfection*) 650; good example; hero, demigod, seraph, angel; innocent &c. 946; saint &c. (*piety*) 987; benefactor &c. 912; philanthropist &c. 910; Aristides.

brick, trump, rough diamond, ugly duckling.

salt of the earth; one in ten thousand; one of the best.

Phr. *si sic omnes!*

peccadillo; flaw, blot, omission; fail-ing, -ure.

offence, trespass; mis-demeanour, -feasance, -prision; tort; mal-efaction, -feasance, -versation; crime, felony.

enormity, atrocity, outrage; deadly –, mortal –, unpardonable- sin; died without a name.

corpus delicti.

Adj. guilty, to blame, culpable, pec-cable, in fault, censurable, reprehensible, blameworthy, uncommendable, illaudable; weighed in the balance and found wanting; exceptionable, objectionable.

Adv. *in flagrante delicto*; red-handed, in the very act.

949. Bad Man.—**N.** bad man, wrongdoer, worker of iniquity; evil-doer &c. 913; sinner; the -wicked &c. 945; bad example.

rascal, scoundrel, villain, miscreant, caitiff; wretch, reptile, viper, serpent, cockatrice, basilisk, urchin; tiger, monster; devil &c. (*demon*) 980; devil incarnate; demon in human shape, Nana Sahib; hell-hound, -cat; rake-hell.

bad woman, jade, Jezebel, adultress, &c. 962.

scamp, scapegrace, rip, runagate, ne'er-do-well, reprobate, *roué*, rake; limb; one who has sold himself to the devil, fallen angel, *âme damnée, vaurien*, *mauvais sujet*, loose fish, sad dog; lost –, black- sheep; castaway, recreant, defaulter; prodigal &c. 818; libertine &c. 962.

rough, rowdy, ugly customer, ruffian, hoodlum, bully; Jonathan Wild; hangman; incendiary; thief &c. 792; murderer &c. 361.

culprit, delinquent, criminal, malefactor, misdemeanant; felon; convict, jail-bird, ticket-of-leave man; outlaw.

blackguard, *polisson*, loafer, sneak; raps-, ras-callion; cullion, mean wretch, varlet, kern, *âme-de-boue, drôle*; cur, dog, hound, whelp, mongrel; lown, loon, runnion, outcast, vagabond; rogue &c. (*knave*) 941; scum of the earth, riff-raff; *Arcades ambo.*

Int. sirrah!

950. Penitence.—**N.** penitence, contrition, compunction, repentance, remorse; regret &c. 833.

self-reproach, -reproof, -accusation,

951. Impenitence.—**N.** impenitence, irrepentance, recusance.

hardness of heart, seared conscience, induration, obduracy.

-condemnation, -humiliation; stings -, pangs -, qualms -, prickings -, twinge -, twitch -, touch -, voice- of conscience; compunctious visitings of nature.

acknowledgment, confession &c. (*disclosure*) 529; apology &c. 952; recantation &c. 607; penance &c. 952; resipiscence.

awakened conscience, deathbed repentance, *locus pœnitentiæ*, stool of repentance, cutty stool.

penitent, Magdalen, prodigal son, returned prodigal, a sadder and a wiser man.

V. repent, be sorry for; be -penitent &c. *adj.*; rue; regret &c. 833; think better of; recant &c. 607; knock under &c. (*submit*) 725; plead guilty; sing -*miserere*, – *de profundis*; cry *peccavi*; own oneself in the wrong; acknowledge, confess &c. (*disclose*) 529; humble oneself; beg pardon &c. (*apologize*) 952; turn over a new leaf, put on the new man, turn from sin; reclaim; repent in sackcloth and ashes &c. (*do penance*) 952; learn by experience.

Adj. penitent; repenting &c. *v.*; repentant, contrite; conscience-smitten, -stricken; self-accusing, -convicted.

penitenti-al, -ary; chastened, reclaimed; not hardened; unhardened.

Adv. *meâ culpâ.*

Phr. *peccavi*; *erubuit*; *salva res est*; *vous l'avez voulu, Georges Dandin.*

V. be -impenitent &c. *adj.*; steel -, harden- the heart; die -game, – and make no sign.

Adj. impenitent, uncontrite, obdurate; hard, -ened; seared, recusant; unrepentant; relent-, remorse-, grace-, shrift-less.

lost, incorrigible, irreclaimable.

unre-claimed, -formed; unrepented, unatoned.

---

952. Atonement.—N. atonement, reparation; compromise, composition; compensation &c. 30; quittance, quits; indemni-ty, -fication; expiation, redemption, reclamation, conciliation, propitiation.

amends, apology, *amende honorable*, satisfaction; peace -, sin -, burnt- offering; scapegoat, sacrifice.

penance, fasting, maceration, sackcloth and ashes, white sheet, shrift, flagellation, lustration; purga-tion, -tory.

V. atone, – for; expiate; propitiate; make -amends, – good; reclaim, redeem, repair, ransom, absolve, purge, shrive, do penance, stand in a white sheet, repent in sackcloth and ashes.

set one's house in order, wipe off old scores, make matters up; pay the -forfeit, – penalty.

apologize, beg pardon, express regret, *faire amende honorable*, give satisfaction; come -, fall- down on one's -knees, – marrow bones.

Adj. propitiatory, expiatory; sacrific, -ial, -atory; piacul-ar, -ous.

4°. Moral Practice

953. Temperance.—N. temperance moderation, sobriety, soberness.

forbearance, abnegation; self-denial, -restraint, -control &c. (*resolution*) 604.

frugality; vegetarianism, teetotalism, total abstinence, prohibition; abst-inence, -emiousness, asceticism &c. 955; system of -Pythagoras, – Cornaro; Pythagorism, Stoicism.

954. Intemperance.—N. intemperance; sensuality, animalism, carnality; pleasure; effeminacy, silkiness; luxur-y, -iousness; lap of -pleasure, – luxury.

indulgence; high-, free- living, inabstinence, self-indulgence; voluptuousness &c. *adj.*; epicur-ism, -eanism; sybaritism.

vegetarian; Pythagorean, gymnoso-phist; teetotaler &c. 958; abstainer.

V. be -temperate &c. *adj.*; abstain, forbear, refrain, deny oneself, spare; know when one has had enough; take the pledge; look not upon the wine when it is red.

Adj. temperate, moderate, sober, frugal, sparing; abst-emious, -inent; within compass; measured &c. (*sufficient*) 639.

Pythagorean; vegetarian; teetotal, pussy-foot.

dissipation; licentiousness &c. *adj.*; debauchery; crapulence.

revel-s, -ry; debauch, carousal, jolli-fication, drinking bout, wassail, Satur-nalia, orgies; excess, too much; intoxi-cation &c. 959.

Circean cup; drug habit &c. 663.

V. be -intemperate &c. *adj.*; indulge, exceed; live -well, – high, – on the fat of the land; give a loose to -indulgence &c. *n.*; dine not wisely but too well; wallow in -voluptuousness &c. *n.*; plunge into dissipation.

revel, rake, live hard, run riot, sow one's wild oats; slake one's -appetite, – thirst; swill; pamper.

Adj. intemperate, inabstinent, intoxicated &c. 958; sensual, self-indulgent; voluptuous, luxurious, licentious, wild, dissolute, rakish, fast, debauched.

brutish, crapulous, swinish, piggish, hoggish, bestial.

Paphian, Epicurean, Sybaritical; bred –, nursed- in the lap of luxury; indulged, pampered, full-fed.

954a. Sensualist.—**N.** Sybarite, voluptuary, Sardanapalus, man of pleasure, carpet knight; epicure, -an; *gourm-et, -and*; gormandizer, gutling, glutton, pig, hog; votary –, swine- of Epicurus; sensualist; Heliogabalus; free –, hard- liver; libertine &c. 962; hedonist.

955. Asceticism.—**N.** asceticism, puritanism, sabbatarianism; cyni-cism, austerity; total abstinence.

mortification, maceration, sackcloth and ashes, flagellation; penance &c. 952; fasting &c. 956; martyrdom.

ascetic; anchor-et, -ite; martyr; *Heautontimorumenos*; hermit &c. (*recluse*) 893; puritan, sabbatarian, cynic.

Adj. ascetic, austere, puritanical; cynical; over-religious.

956. Fasting. — **N.** fasting; exro-phagy; famishment, starvation; bant-ing.

fast, *jour maigre*; fast –, banyan-day; Lent, quadragesima; Rama-dan, -zan; spare –, meagre- diet; lenten -diet, – entertainment; *soupe maigre*, short -rations, – commons; Barmecide feast; hunger strike.

V. fast, starve, clem, famish, perish with hunger; dine with Duke Hum-phrey; make two bites of a cherry.

Adj. lenten, quadragesimal; unfed; starved &c. *v.*; half-starved; fasting &c. *v.*; hungry &c. 865.

957. Gluttony.—**N.** gluttony; greed; greediness &c. *adj.*; voracity.

epicurism; good –, high- living; edacity, gulosity, crapulence; gutt-, guzz-ling; over-indulgence.

good cheer, blow out; feast &c. (*food*) 298; gastronomy.

epicure, *bon vivant, gourmand*; glut-ton, cormorant, hog, belly-god, Apicius, gastronome, gormandizer.

V. gormandize, gorge; over-gorge, -eat- oneself; engorge, eat one's fill, cram, stuff, stodge, glut, satiate; gutt-le, guzz-le; bolt, devour, gobble up; gulp &c. (*swallow food*) 298; raven, eat out of house and home.

have the stomach of an ostrich;

play a good knife and fork &c. (*appetite*) 865.
pamper, indulge.

Adj. gluttonous, greedy; gormandizing &c. *v.*; edacious, omnivorous, crapulent, swinish, voracious, devouring.
pampered; over-fed, -gorged.

958. Sobriety.—**N.** sobriety; teetotalism, temperance &c. 953.

water-drinker; teetotal-er, -ist; abstainer, Good Templar, Rechabite, band of hope; prohibitionist, pussyfoot.
V. take the pledge.
Adj. sober, – as a judge; dry, on the water wagon.

959. Drunkenness.—**N.** drunkenness &c. *adj.*; intemperance; drinking &c. *v.*; inebri-ety, -ation; ebri-ety, -osity; befuddlement; insobriety; intoxication; temulency, bibacity, wine-bibbing; com-, potation; deep potations, bacchanals, *bacchanalia*, libations.
oino-, dipso-mania; *delirium tremens*, d.t.; alcohol, -ism.

drink; alcoholic drinks, alcohol, booze; gin, blue ruin, grog, brandy, port wine; punch, -bowl; cup, rosy wine, flowing bowl; drop, – too much; dram; beer, wine, spirits &c. (*beverage*) 298; cocktail, nip, peg; stirrup cup.

drunkard, sot, toper, tippler, bibber, wine-bibber; hard –, gin –, dram- drinker; soak, soaker, sponge, tun; love-, toss-pot; thirsty soul, reveller, carouser; Bacchanal, -ian; Bacch-al, -ante; devotee to Bacchus, dipsomaniac.

V. get –, be- drunk &c. *adj.*; see double; take a -drop, – glass- too much; drink, tipple, tope, booze, bouse, guzzle, swill, soak, sot, lush, bib, swig, carouse; sacrifice at the shrine of Bacchus; take to drinking; drink -hard, – deep, – like a fish; have one's swill, drain the cup, splice the main brace, take a hair of the dog that bit you.

liquor, – up; wet one's whistle, take a whet; lift one's elbow; crack a –, pass the- bottle; toss off &c. (*drink up*) 298; go to the -ale, – public-house.

make one -drunk &c. *adj.*; inebriate, fuddle, fuzzle, get into one's head.

Adj. drunk, tipsy; intoxicated; inebri-ous, -ate, -ated; in one's cups; in a state of -intoxication &c. *n.*; temulent, -ive; fuddled, mellow, cut, boosy, fou, fresh, merry, elevated, squiffy; plastered, befuddled, sozzled; flush, -ed; flustered, disguised, groggy, beery; topheavy; potvaliant, glorious; potulent; over-come, -taken; whittled, screwed, tight, primed, oiled, corned, raddled, sewed up, lushy, nappy, muddled, muzzy, bosky, obfuscated, maudlin; crapulous, dead –, blind- drunk.

inter pocula; in –, the worse for- liquor, having had a drop too much, half seas over, three sheets in the wind; under the table, blind to the world, one over the eight.

drunk as -a piper, – a fiddler, – a lord, – Chloe, – an owl, – David's sow, – a wheelbarrow.

drunken, bibacious, bibulous, sottish; given –, addicted- to -drink, – the bottle; toping &c. *v.*; wet.
Phr. *nunc est bibendum*.

960. Purity.—**N.** purity; decency, decorum, delicacy; continence, chastity, honesty, virtue, modesty, shame; pudicity, *pucelage*, virginity.
vestal, virgin, Joseph, Hippolytus; Lucretia, Diana; prude.

961. Impurity.—**N.** impurity; uncleanness &c. (*filth*) 653; immodesty; grossness &c. *adj.*; indelicacy, indecency; impudicity; obscenity, ribaldry, smut, bawdry, *double entendre*, *équivoque*; Aretinism; pornography.

Adj. pure, undefiled, modest, delicate, decent, decorous; *virginibus puerisque*; chaste, continent, virtuous, honest, Platonic.

_____

concupiscence, lust, carnality, flesh, salacity; pruriency, lechery, lasciviency, lubricity, lewdness.

incontinence, intrigue, *faux pas*; *amour, -ette*; gallantry; debauchery, libertinism, *libertinage*, fornication; *liaison*; wenching, venery, dissipation.

seduction; defloration, defilement, abuse, violation, rape; incest.

social evil, harlotry, stupration, whoredom, concubinage, cuckoldom, adultery, advoutry, *crim. con.*; free love.

seraglio, harem, zenana; brothel, bagnio, stew, bawdy-house, *lupanar*, house of ill fame, *bordel*, kip.

V. be -impure &c. *adj.*; intrigue; debauch, defile, assault, attack, seduce; prostitute; abuse, violate, deflower; commit -adultery &c. *n.*

Adj. impure; unclean &c. (*dirty*) 653; not to be mentioned to ears polite; immodest, shameless; in-decorous, -delicate, -decent; loose, suggestive, *risqué*, coarse, gross, broad, free, equivocal, smutty, fulsome, ribald, obscene, bawdy, pornographic.

concupiscent, prurient, lickerish, rampant, lustful; carnal, -minded; lewd, lascivious, lecherous, libidinous, erotic, ruttish, salacious; Paphian; voluptuous; incestuous.

unchaste, light, wanton, licentious, adulterous, debauched, dissolute; of -loose character, – easy virtue; frail, gay, riggish, incontinent, meretricious, rakish, gallant, dissipated; no better than she should be; on the -town, – streets, – *pavé*, – loose.

adulterous, incestuous, bestial.

962. Libertine.—**N.** libertine; voluptuary &c. 954*a*; rake, debauchee, loose fish, rip, rake-hell, fast man; *intrigant*, gallant, seducer, fornicator, lecher, satyr, goat, whoremonger, *paillard*, adulterer, gay deceiver, Lothario, Don Juan, Blue-beard.

adulteress, advoutress, courtesan, prostitute, strumpet, tart, hustler, chippy, broad, harlot, whore, punk, *fille de joie*; woman, – of the town; street-walker, Cyprian, miss, piece; frail sisterhood, fallen woman; demirep, wench, trollop, trull, baggage, hussy, drab, bitch, jade, skit, rig, quean, mopsy, slut, minx, harridan; woman -of easy virtue &c. (*unchaste*) 961; wanton, fornicatress; Jezebel, Messalina, Delilah, Thaïs, Phryne, Aspasia, Lais, *lorette, cocotte, petite dame, grisette*; demi-monde; white slave.

concubine, mistress, fancy woman, kept woman, doxy, *chère amie, bona roba*.

pimp; pand-er, -ar; bawd, *conciliatrix*, procuress, mackerel; wittol.

5°. Institutions

963. Legality.—**N.** legality; legitimacy, -teness, legitimization.

legislature; law, code, *corpus juris*, constitution, pandect, charter, act, enactment, statute, rule; canon &c. (*precept*) 697; ordinance, institution; regulation; by-, bye-law, rescript; decree &c. (*order*) 741; *ordonnance*;

964. [Absence or violation of law.] **Illegality.**—**N.** lawlessness; breach –, violation- of law; disobedience &c. 742; unconformity &c. 83.

arbitrariness &c. *adj.*; antinomy, violence, brute force, despotism, outlawry.

mob –, lynch –, club –, Lydford –,

standing order; *plébiscite* &c. (*choice*) 609.

legal process; form, -ula, -ality; rite; arm of the law; *habeas corpus*.

[Science of law] jurisprudence, nomology; legislation, codification.

equity, common law; *lex* -, *lex non-scripta*, unwritten law; law of nations, international law, *jus gentium*; *jus civile*; civil -, criminal -, canon -, statute -, ecclesiastical- law; *lex mercatoria*.

constitutional-ism, -ity; justice &c. 922.

V. legalize, legitimize; enact, ordain; decree &c. (*order*) 741; pass a law; legislate; codify, formulate; authorize.

Adj. legal, legitimate; according to law; vested, constitutional, chartered, legalized; lawful &c. (*permitted*) 760; statut-able, -ory; legislat-orial, -ive.

Adv. legally &c. *adj.*; in the eye of the law; *de jure*.

---

martial -, drumhead- law; *coup d'état*; *le droit du plus fort*; *argumentum baculinum*.

illegality, informality, unlawfulness, illegitimacy, bar sinister.

trover and conversion; smuggling, boot-legging, rum-running, poaching; simony.

speakeasy, speakie, blind pig.

V. offend against -, violate- the law; set the law at defiance, ride rough-shod over, drive a coach and six through a statute; make the law a dead letter, take the law into one's own hands.

smuggle, run, poach.

Adj. illegal; prohibited &c. 761; not allowed, unlawful, illegitimate, illicit, contraband, actionable.

unchartered, unconstitutional; unwarrant-ed, -able; unauthorized; informal, unofficial; in-, extra-judicial.

lawless, arbitrary; despotic, -al; summary, irresponsible; un-answerable, -accountable.

null and void; a dead letter.

Adv. illegally &c. *adj.*; with a high hand, in violation of law.

965. Jurisdiction. [Executive.]—**N.** jurisdiction, judicature, administration of justice, soc; executive, commission of the peace; magistracy &c. (*authority*) 737.

judge &c. 967; tribunal &c. 966; municipality, corporation, bailiwick, shrievalty; lord lieutenant; lord -, mayor, city manager, alderman &c. 745; sheriff, bailie, shrieve, chief -, constable; police, - force; constabulary, bumbledom.

officer; proctor, high -, commissioner; bailiff, tipstaff, bum-bailiff, catchpoll, beadle; police-man, -constable, -sergeant; *sbirro, alguazil, gendarme*, kavass, *lictor*, macebearer, *huissier*, bedel.

press-gang; exciseman, gauger, custom-house officer, *douanier*.

coroner, edile, ædile, portreeve, paritor; *posse comitatus*.

V. judge, sit in judgment.

Adj. executive, administrative, municipal; inquisitorial, causidical; judic-atory, -iary, -ial; juridical.

Adv. *coram judice*.

966. Tribunal.—**N.** tribunal, court, board, bench, judicatory, curia; court ot -justice, - law, - arbitration; inquisition; guild.

justice -, judgment -, mercy- seat; woolsack; bar, - of justice; dock; forum, hustings, *bureau*, drum-head; jury-, witness-box.

senate-house, town-hall, theatre; House of -Lords, - Commons.

assize, eyre; ward-, burgh-mote; superior courts of Westminster; court of -record, - oyer and terminer, - assize, - appeal, - error; High court of -Judicature, - Appeal; Judicial Committee of the Privy Council; Star-Chamber; Court of -Chancery, - King's *or* Queen's Bench, - Exchequer, - Common Pleas, - Probate, - Arches, - Admiralty, - Criminal Appeal; Lords Justices' -, Rolls -, Vice Chancellor's -,

Stannary –, Divorce –, Palatine –, ecclesiastical –, county –, police-court; sessions; quarter –, petty- sessions; court -leet, – baron, – of pie poudre, – of common council; board of green cloth.

court-martial; drum-head court-martial; *durbar*, divan; Areopagus; *rota*.

Adj. judicial &c. 965; appellate; curial.

967. Judge.—N. judge; justi-ce, -ciar, -ciary; chancellor; justice –, judge- of assize; recorder, common serjeant; puisne –, assistant –, county court- judge; conservator –, justice- of the peace, J.P.; court &c. (*tribunal*) 966; grand –, petty –, coroner's- jury; panel, juror, juryman; twelve men in a box; magistrate, police magistrate, stipendiary, the great unpaid, beak; his -worship, – honour, – lordship; deemster, moderator.

Lord -Chancellor, – Justice; Master of the Rolls, Vice-Chancellor; Lord Chief -Justice, – Baron; Mr. Justice; Baron, – of the Exchequer.

jurat, assessor; arbi-ter, -trator; umpire; refer-ee, -endary; revising barrister; domesman; censor &c. (*critic*) 480; official –, receiver.

archon, tribune, prætor, *ephor*, syndic, *podestà*, mullah, ulema, mufti, cadi, kadi; Rhadamanthus.

litigant &c. (*accusation*) 938.

V. adjudge &c. (*determine*) 480; try a -case, – prisoner.

Adj. judicial &c. 965.

Phr. 'a Daniel come to judgment.'

968. Lawyer.—N. lawyer, jurist, legist, civilian, pundit, publicist, jurisconsult, legal adviser, advocate; barrister, – at law; counsel, -lor; King's *or* Queen's counsel; K.C.; Q.C.; silk gown, leader; junior, – counsel; stuff gown, serjeant-at-law, bencher; tubman; judge &c. 967.

bar, legal profession, gentleman of the long robe; junior –, outer –, inner- bar; Inns of Court; equity draftsman, conveyancer, pleader, special pleader.

solicitor, attorney, proctor; notary, – public; scrivener, cursitor; writer, – to the signet; S.S.C.; limb of the law; pettifogger.

V. practise -at, – within- the bar; plead; call –, be called- -to, – within- the bar; take silk.

Adj. learned in the law; at the bar; forensic.

969. Lawsuit.—N. lawsuit, suit, action, cause, petition; litigation; dispute &c. 713.

citation, arraignment, prosecution, impeachment; accusation &c. 938; presentment, true bill, indictment.

apprehension, arrest; committal; imprisonment &c. (*restraint*) 751.

writ, summons, subpœna, *latitat, nisi prius; habeas corpus.*

pleadings; declaration, bill, claim; *procès-verbal*, bill of right, information, *corpus delicti*; affidavit, state of facts; answer, replication, plea, demurrer, rebutter, rejoinder; surre-butter, -joinder.

suitor, party to a suit; litigant &c. 938; libellant.

hearing, trial; verdict &c. (*judgment*) 480; appeal, – motion; writ of error; *certiorari*.

case, decision, precedent, ruling; decided case, reports.

V. go to –, appeal to the- law; bring to -justice, – trial, – the bar; put on trial, pull up; accuse &c. 938; prefer –, file- a claim &c. *n.*; take the law of, inform against.

serve with a writ, cite, apprehend, arraign, sue, prosecute, bring an action against, indict, impeach, attach, distrain, commit; arrest; summon, -s; give in charge &c. (*restrain*) 751.

empanel a jury, implead, join issue; close the pleadings; set down for hearing.

try, hear a cause; sit in judgment; adjudicate &c. 480.

Adj. litigious &c. (*quarrelsome*) 713; *qui tam*; *coram* –, *sub- judice.*

Adv. *pendente lite.*

Phr. *adhuc sub judice lis est.*

---

970. Acquittal. — N. acquit-tal, -ment; clearance, exculpation, exoneration; discharge &c. (*release*) 750; *quietus,* absolution, compurgation, reprieve, respite; pardon &c. (*forgiveness*) 918.

[Exemption from punishment] impunity, immunity.

V. acquit, exculpate, exonerate, clear; absolve, whitewash, assoil, discharge, release; liberate &c. 750.

reprieve, respite; pardon &c. (*forgive*) 918; let off, – scot free.

Adj. acquitted &c. *v.*; un-condemned, -punished, -chastised; recommended to mercy.

---

971. Condemnation.—N. condemnation, conviction, proscription, damnation; death warrant; penalty &c. 974.

attain-der, -ture, -tment.

V. condemn, convict, cast, bring home to, find guilty, damn, doom, sign the death warrant, sentence, pass sentence on, attaint, confiscate, proscribe, sequestrate; non-suit.

disapprove &c. 932; accuse &c. 938.

stand condemned.

Adj. condem-, dam-natory; condemned &c. *v.*; non-suited &c. (*failure*) 732; self-convicted.

Phr. *mutato nomine de te fabula narratur.*

---

972. Punishment.—N. punishment, punition; chast-isement, -ening; correction, castigation.

discipline, infliction, trial; judgment; penalty &c. 974; retribution; thunderbolt, Nemesis; requital &c. (*reward*) 973; penology; retributive justice.

lash, scaffold &c. (*instrument of punishment*) 975; imprisonment &c. (*restraint*) 751; chain gang; transportation, banishment, expulsion, deportation, exile, involuntary exile, ostracism; penal servitude, hard labour; galleys &c. 975; beating &c. *v.*; flagellation, fustigation, gantlet, *strappado, estrapade, bastinado, argumentum baculinum,* stick law, rap on the knuckles, box on the ear; blow &c. (*impulse*) 276; stripe, cuff, kick, buffet, pummel; slap, – in the face; wipe, douse; *coup de grâce*; torture, rack; picket, -ing; *dragonnade*; capital punishment, extreme penalty; execution; hanging &c. *v.*; de-capitation, -collation; *garrot-te, -to*; electrocution, lethal chamber; crucifixion, impalement; martyrdom, *auto-da-fé; noyade; hara-kiri,* happy despatch.

V. punish; chast-ise, -en; castigate, correct, inflict punishment, administer correction, deal retributive justice.

visit upon, pay; pay –, serve- out; settle with, get even with, get one's own back; do for; make short work of, give a lesson to, strafe, serve one right, make an example of; have a rod in pickle for; give it one.

strike &c. 276; deal a blow to, administer the lash, smite; slap, – the face; smack, cuff, box the ears, spank, thwack, thump, beat, lay on, swinge, buffet; thresh, thrash, pummel, drub, leather, trounce, baste, belabour; lace, – one's jacket; dress, give a -dressing, – down; trim, warm, wipe, tund, cob, bang, strap, comb, lash, lick, larrup, whallop, whop, flog, scourge, whip, birch, cane, give the stick, switch, flagellate, horsewhip, *bastinado*, towel, rub down with an oaken towel, rib roast, dust one's jacket, fustigate, pitch into, lay about one, beat black and blue; beat to a -mummy, – jelly; give a black eye; hit on the head; sandbag.

tar and feather; pelt, stone, lapidate; mast-head, keelhaul.

execute; bring to the -block, – gallows; behead; de-capitate, -collate; guillotine; hang, turn off, gibbet, bowstring, hang, draw and quarter; shoot; decimate; burn; electrocute; break on the wheel, crucify; em-, im-pale; flay; lynch; put to death.

torture; put -on, – to- the rack; picket.

banish, exile; trans-, de-port; expel, ostracize; rusticate; drum out; dismiss, -bar, -bench; strike off the roll, unfrock; post.

suffer, – for, – punishment; be -flogged, – hanged &c.; come to the gallows, dance upon nothing, die in one's shoes; be rightly served.

Adj. punishing &c. *v.*; penal; puni-tory, -tive; inflictive, castigatory; punished &c. *v.*

Int. *à la lanterne!*

---

973. Reward.—**N.** reward, recompense, remuneration, prize, meed, guerdon, reguerdon; indemni-ty, -fication, price; quittance; compensation; reparation, *ersatz*, assythment, redress; retribution, reckoning, acknowledgment, requital, amends, sop; atonement; consideration, return, *quid pro quo*; salvage, perquisite; vail &c. (*donation*) 784; *douceur*, bribe, bait, baksheesh, tip; hush-, smart-money; blackmail; carcelage; *solatium*.

allowance, salary, stipend, wages; pay, -ment; emolument; tribute; batta, shot, scot; premium, fee, *honorarium*; hire.

crown &c. (*decoration of honour*) 877.

V. re-ward, -compense, -pay, -quite; re-, munerate; compensate; fee, tip, bribe; pay one's footing &c. (*pay*) 807; make amends, indemnify, atone; satisfy, acknowledge.

get for one's pains, reap the fruits of.

Adj. remunerat-ive, -ory; munerary, compensatory, retributive, reparatory.

974. Penalty.—**N.** penalty; retribution &c. (*punishment*) 972; pain, pains and penalties; *peine forte et dure*; penance &c. (*atonement*) 952; the devil to pay.

fine, mulct, amercement; forfeit, -ure; escheat, damages, deodand, sequestration, confiscation, *premunire*.

V. penalize, fine, mulct, amerce, sconce, confiscate; sequest-rate, -er; escheat; estreat, forfeit.

975. [Instrument of punishment.] **Scourge.**—**N.** scourge, rod, cane, stick; ra-, rat-tan; birch, – rod; rod in pickle; switch, ferule, cudgel, truncheon; rubber hose.

whip, lash, strap, thong, cowhide, knout; cat, – o'-nine-tails, *sjambok*, quirt; rope's end.

pillory, stocks, whipping-post; cuck-, duck-ing stool; brank; triangle, wooden horse, maiden, thumbscrew, boot, rack, wheel, iron heel; treadmill, crank, galleys.

scaffold; block, axe, *guillotine*; stake; cross; gallows, gibbet, Tyburn tree; drop, noose, rope, halter, bowstring; electric chair, lethal chamber.

house of correction &c. (*prison*) 752.

gaol-, jail-er; executioner; hang-, heads-man; Jack Ketch; lyncher.

Section V. RELIGIOUS AFFECTIONS

1°. Superhuman Beings and Regions

976. Deity.—N. Deity, Divinity; God-head, -ship; Omnipotence, Providence.

[Quality of being divine] divin-eness, -ity.

God, Lord, Jehovah, *Deus*; The -Almighty, – Supreme Being, – First Cause; *Ens Entium*; Author –, Creator- of all things; Author of our being; The -Infinite, – Eternal; The All-powerful, -wise, -merciful, -holy; The Omni-potent, -scient.

[Attributes and perfections] infinite -power, – wisdom, – goodness, – justice, – truth, – love, – mercy; omni-potence, -science, -presence; unity, immutability, holiness, glory, majesty, sovereignty, infinity, eternity.

The -Trinity, – Holy Trinity, – Trinity in Unity, – Triune God; Three in One and One in Three.

God the Father; The -Maker, – Creator, – Preserver.

[Functions] creation, preservation, divine government; The-ocracy, -archy; providence; ways –, dealings –, dispensations –, visitations- of Providence.

God the Son, Jesus, Christ; The -Messiah, – Anointed, – Saviour, – Redeemer, – Mediator, – Intercessor, – Advocate, – Judge; The Son of -God, – Man, – David; The Only Begotten; The Lamb of God, The Word; Em-, Im-manuel; The -King of Kings and Lord of Lords, – King of Glory, – Prince of Peace, – Good Shepherd, – Way, – Truth, – Life, – Bread of Life, – Light of the World; The -Lord our, – Sun of- Righteousness.

The -Incarnation, – Hypostatic Union, – Word made Flesh.

[Functions] salvation, redemption, atonement, propitiation, mediation, intercession, judgment.

God the Holy Ghost, The Holy Spirit, Paraclete; The -Comforter, – Consoler, – Spirit of Truth, – Dove.

[Functions] inspiration, unction, regeneration, sanctification, consolation.

eon, æon, special providence, *Deus ex machinâ*; *Avatar*.

V. create, uphold, preserve, govern &c.

atone, redeem, save, propitiate, mediate &c.

predestinate, elect, call, ordain, bless, justify, sanctify, glorify &c.

Adj. almighty, holy, hallowed, sacred, divine, heavenly, celestial; messianic; sacrosanct; all-powerful, -wise, -seeing, -knowing; omnipotent, omniscient; supreme.

super-human, -natural; ghostly, spiritual, hyperphysical, unearthly; the-istic, -ocratic, deistic; anointed.

Adv. *jure divino*, by divine right; *Deo volente*, D.V.

---

977. [Beneficent spirits.] Angel.—N.
angel, archangel; heavenly host, choir invisible, host of heaven, sons of God; Michael, Gabriel &c.; seraph, -im; cherub, -im; ministering spirit, morn-

978. [Maleficent spirits.] Satan.—N.
Satan, the Devil, Lucifer, Ahrimanes, Belial; Sammael, Zamiel, Beelzebub, the Prince of the Devils; Mephistopheles, his satanic majesty.*

* The slang expressions 'the -deuce, – dickens, – old Gentleman; old -Nick, – Scratch, – Horny, – Harry, – Gooseberry,' have not been inserted in the text.

ing star; saint, *Madonna*; Our Lady, the Blessed Virgin, the Virgin Mary.

Adj. angelic, seraphic, cherubic.

---

the tempter; the evil -one, – spirit; the -author of evil, – wicked one, – old Serpent; the Prince of -darkness, – this world, – the power of the air; the -foul, – arch- fiend; the devil incarnate; the -common enemy, – angel of the bottomless pit; Abaddon, Apollyon, Mammon.

fallen angels, unclean spirits, devils; the -rulers, – powers- of darkness; inhabitants of Pandemonium; demon &c. 980.

diabolism; devil-ism, -ship, -dom, -ry, -worship; *diablerie*; satanism, manicheism; the cloven foot; black magic &c. 992.

Adj. satanic, diabolic, devilish, infernal, hell-born.

*Heathen, Mythological and other fabulous Deities and Powers**

979. Jupiter.—**N.** god, -dess; heathen gods and goddesses; Pantheon; Jupiter, Jove, Zeus, Apollo, Mars, Mercury, Neptune, Vulcan, Bacchus, Pluto, Saturn, Cupid, Eros, Pan; Juno, Ceres, Proserpina, Dina, Minerva, Pallas, Athenae, Venus, Aphrodite, Vesta; The Fates &c. 601.

Allah, Brahma, Vishnu, Siva, Shiva, Krishna, Juggernaut, Buddha; Ra, Isis, Osiris; Belus, Bel, Baal, Asteroth &c.; Thor, Odin; Mumbo Jumbo; good –, tutelary- genius; demiurge, familiar, – spirit; Sibyl; fairy, fay; sylph, -id; Ariel, peri, nymph, nereid, dryad, oread, sea-maid, Banshee, Benshie, Ormuzd; Oberon, Titania, Mab, hamadryad, naiad, mermaid, kelpie, Ondine, nix, nixie, sprite; denizens of the air; pixy &c. (*bad spirit*) 980.

mythology; heathen –, fairy- mythology; Lemprière, folklore.

Adj. fairy-, sylph-like; sylphic.

---

980. Demon.—**N.** demon, -ry, -ism, -ology; evil genius, fiend, familiar, – spirit, devil; bad –, unclean- spirit; cacodemon, incubus, Frankenstein's monster, succubus and succuba, Titan, Shedim, Mephistopheles, Asmodeus, Moloch, Belial, Ahriman, fury, The Furies &c. 900; harpy; Friar Rush.

vampire, ghoul; af-, ef-freet; afrite; ogre, -ss; gnome, gin, djinn, imp, deev, *lamia*; bo-gie, -gle; nis, kobold, flibbertigibbet, fairy, brownie, pixy, elf, dwarf, urchin, Puck, Robin Goodfellow; lepre-, cluri-chaune; troll, dwerger, sprite, oaf, changeling, bad fairy, nixe, pigwidgeon, Will-o'-the-wisp; Erl King.

[Supernatural appearance] ghost, spectre, apparition, genie, spirit, shade, shadow, vision, phantom &c. 443; materialization (*spiritualism*) 992; hob-, goblin; wraith, spook, werwolf, boggart, banshee, *loup-garou*, *lemures*; evil eye.

nisse, necks; mer-man, -maid, -folk; siren, Lorelei; satyr, faun.

Adj. supernatural, weird, uncanny, unearthly, spectral; ghost-ly, -like; elf-in, -like; fiend-ish, -like; impish, demoniacal; haunted.

981. Heaven.—**N.** heaven; kingdom of -heaven, – God; heavenly kingdom; throne –, presence- of God; inheritance of the saints in light.

Paradise, Eden, abode of the blessed; Holy City, New Jerusalem; celestial bliss, glory.

[Mythological -heaven] Olympus; [– paradise] Elysium, Elysian fields, Arcadia, bowers of bliss, garden of the Hesperides, Islands of the Blessed;

982. Hell.—**N.** hell, bottomless pit, place of torment; habitation of fallen angels; Pandemonium, Abaddon, Domdaniel.

hell fire; everlasting -fire, – torment; lake of fire and brimstone; fire that is never quenched, worm that never dies.

purgatory, limbo, gehenna, abyss.

[Mythological hell] Tartarus, Hades, Avernus, Styx, Stygian creek, pit of Acheron, Cocytus, Phlegethon, Lethe;

* Only a selection of those best known to literature is included.

happy hunting-ground; third –, seventh- heaven; Valhalla (Scandinavian); Nirvana (Buddhist).

future state, eternity, eternal life, life after death, eternal home, resurrection, translation; resuscitation &c. 660; apotheosis, deification.

Adj. heavenly, celestial, supernal, unearthly, from on high, paradisiacal, beatific, elysian, Olympian, Arcadian.

infernal regions, *inferno*, shades below, realms of Pluto.

Pluto, Rhadamanthus, Erebus, Charon, Cerberus; Tophet.

Adj. hellish, infernal, stygian.

2°. RELIGIOUS DOCTRINES

983. [Religious Knowledge.] **Theology.**—**N.** Theology (natural and revealed); Theo-gony, -sophy; Divinity; Hagio-logy, -graphy; Caucasian mystery; monotheism; religion; religious -persuasion, – sect, – denomination; cult; creed &c. (*belief*) 484; articles –, declaration –, profession –, confession- of faith.

theolog-ue, -ian; divine, schoolman, canonist, monotheist.

Adj. theological, religious; canonical; denominational; sectarian &c. 984.

983a. Orthodoxy.—**N.** orthodoxy; strictness, soundness, religious truth, true faith; truth &c. 494.

Christian-ity, -ism; Catholic-ism, -ity; 'the faith once delivered to the saints'; hyperorthodoxy &c. 984; iconoclasm.

the Holy –, the Orthodox- Church; Catholic –, Universal –, Apostolic –, Established- Church; temple of the Holy Ghost; Church –, body –, members –, disciples –, followers- of Christ; Christian, – community; true believer; canonist &c. (*theologian*) 983; Christendom, collective body of Christians, the Church Militant.

canons &c. (*belief*) 484; thirty-nine articles; Apostles' –, Nicene –, Athanasian- Creed; Church Catechism; textuary.

Adj. orthodox, sound, literal, strict, faithful, catholic, schismless, Christian, evangelical, scriptural, divine, monotheistic; true &c. 494.

984. Heterodoxy. [Sectarianism.]—**N.** heterodoxy; error &c. 495; false doctrine, heresy, schism; schismanticism, -alness; recusancy, backsliding, apostasy; atheism &c. (*irreligion*) 989.

bigotry &c. (*obstinacy*) 606; fanaticism, iconoclasm; hyperorthodoxy, precisianism, bibliolatry, hagiolatry, sabbatarianism, puritanism; idolatry &c. 991; superstition &c. (*credulity*) 486; dissent &c. 489.

sectar-ism, -ianism; nonconformity; secularism; syncretism, religious sects; the clash of creeds.

protestant-, advent-, Arian-, Erastian-, Calvin-, quaker-, method-, anabapt-, Pusey-, tractarian-, ritual-, Origen-, Sabellian-, Socinian-, De-, The-, mon-, material-, positiv-, latitudinarian-ism &c.

High –, Low –, Broad –, Free-Church; ultramontanism; monasticism; pap-ism, -istry; papacy; Anglican-, Catholic-, Roman-ism; popery, Scarlet Lady, Church of Rome, Greek Church; Christian Science, The Church of Christ Scientist.

pagan-, heathen-, ethic-ism; mythology; animism; poly-, di-, tri-, pan-theism; dualism; heathendom.

Juda-, Gentil-, Mahometan-, Islam-, Turc-, Brahmin-, Hindoo-, Buddh-, Lama-, Confucian-, Shinto-, Sabian-, Gnostic-, Soofee-, Hylothe-, Mormon-ism.

Theosophy; Spiritualism, Occultism.

heretic, antichrist; pagan, heathen; pai-, pay-nim; *giaour*; gentile; pan-, poly-theist; idolator; misbeliever, apostate, backslider.

bigot &c. (*obstinacy*) 606; fanatic, dervish, abdal, iconoclast.

latitudinarian, limitarian, Deist, Theist, Unitarian; positivist, materialist; agnostic, sceptic &c. 989.

schismatic; sectar-y, -ian, -ist; seceder, separatist, recusant, dissenter; non-conformist, -juror; Huguenot, Protestant; orthodox dissenter, Congregationalist, Independent; Episcopalian, Presbyterian; Lutheran, Calvinist, Quaker, Methodist, Wesleyan; Ana-, Baptist; Dunker; Mormon, Latter-day Saint, Irvingite, Sandemanian, Glassite, Erastian; Sub-, Supra-lapsarian; Gentoo, Antinomian, Swedenborgian, Adventist, Plymouth Brother; Theosophist &c.

Catholic, Roman Catholic, Romanist, papist, ultramontane; Old Catholic, tractarian, Anglican, Puseyite, ritualist; Puritan.

Jew, Hebrew, Rabbist; Mahometan, Mohammedan, Mussulman, Moslem, Islamite, Osmanli; Brahm-in, -an; Parsee, Sofi, Soofee; Buddhist; Zoroastrian, Magi, Gymnosophist, fire-worshipper, Sabian, Gnostic, Sadducee, Rosicrucian &c.

Adj. heterodox, heretical; un-orthodox, -scriptural, -canonical; antiscriptural, apocryphal; un-, anti-christian; schismatic, recusant, iconoclastic; sectarian; dis-senting, -sident; secular &c. (*lay*) 997.

pagan; heathen, -ish; ethnic, -al; gentile, painim; pan-, poly-theistic; agnostic, sceptic.

Judaical, Mohammedan, Moslem, Brahminical, Buddhist &c. *n.* Romish, Protestant &c. *n.*

bigoted &c. (*prejudiced*) 481, (*obstinate*) 606; superstitious &c. (*credulous*) 486; fanatical; idolatrous &c. 991; visionary &c. (*imaginative*) 515.

---

985. Revelation.—N. revelation, inspiration, *afflatus*.

Word, – of God; Scripture; the -Scriptures, – Bible, – Book of Books; Holy -Writ, – Scriptures; inspired writings, Gospel.

Old Testament, Septuagint, Vulgate, Pentateuch; Octateuch; the -Law, – Jewish Law, – Prophets; major –, minor- Prophets; Hagio-grapha, -logy; Hierographa; Apocrypha.

New Testament; Gospels, Evangelists, Acts, Epistles, Apocalypse, Revelations.

Talmud; Mishna, Masorah.

prophet &c. (*seer*) 513; evangelist, apostle, disciple, saint; the –, the Apostolical- fathers; Holy Men of old, inspired -writers, – penmen.

Adj. scriptural, biblical, sacred, prophetic; evangel-ical, -istic; apostolic, -al; inspired, theopneustic, apocalyptic, ecclesiastical, canonical, textuary.

986. Pseudo-Revelation.*—N. the -Koran, – Alcoran; Ly-king, Shaster, Vedas, Zendavesta, Vedidad, Purana, Edda; Go-, Gau-tama; Book of Mormon.

[False prophets and religious founders] Buddha, Zoroaster, Zerdhusht, Confucius, Mahomet.

[Idols] golden calf &c. 991; Baal, Moloch, Dagon.

---

* See note on page 378.

3°. RELIGIOUS SENTIMENTS

987. Piety.—N. piety, religion, theism, faith; religiousness, holiness &c. *adj.*; saintship; religionism; sanctimony &c. (*assumed piety*) 988; reverence &c. (*respect*) 928; humility, veneration, devotion; prostration &c. (*worship*) 990; grace, unction, edification; sancti-ty, -tude; consecration.

spiritual existence, odour of sanctity, beauty of holiness.

theopathy, beatification, adoption, regeneration, conversion, justification, sanctification, salvation, inspiration, bread of life; Body and Blood of Christ.

believer, convert, theist, Christian, devotee, pietist; the -good, – righteous, – just, – believing, – elect; Saint, *Madonna*.

the children of -God, – the kingdom, – light.

V. be -pious &c. *adj.*; have -faith &c. *n.*; believe, receive Christ; revere &c. 928; worship &c. 950; be -converted &c.

convert, edify, sanctify, hallow, keep holy, beatify, regenerate, inspire, consecrate, enshrine.

Adj. pious, religious, devout, devoted, reverent, godly, heavenly minded, humble; pure, – in heart; holy, spiritual, pietistic; saint-ly, -like; seraphic, sacred, solemn.

believing, faithful, Christian, Catholic.

elected, adopted, justified, sanctified, regenerated, inspired, consecrated, converted, unearthly, not of the earth.

988. Impiety.—N. impiety; sin &c. 945; irreverence; profan-eness &c. *adj.*, -ity, -ation; blasphemy, desecration, sacrilege; scoffing &c. *v.*

[Assumed piety] hypocrisy &c. (*falsehood*) 544; pietism, cant, pious fraud; lip-devotion, -service, -reverence; misdevotion, formalism, austerity; sanctimon-y, -iousness &c. *adj.*; pharisaism, precisianism; sabbat-ism, -arianism; *odium theologicum*, sacerdotalism; bigotry &c. (*obstinacy*) 606, (*prejudice*) 481.

hardening, backsliding, declension, perversion, reprobation apostacy, recusancy.

sinner &c. 949; scoffer, blasphemer; sacrilegist; worldling; hypocrite &c. (*dissembler*) 548; Scribes and Pharisees; Tartufe, Maw-worm.

bigot; saint [ironically]; Pharisee, sabbatarian, formalist, methodist, puritan, pietist, precisian, religionist, devotee, ranter, fanatic, wowser.

the -wicked, – evil, – unjust, – reprobate; son of -men, – Belial, – the wicked one; children of darkness.

V. be -impious &c. *adj.*; profane, desecrate, blaspheme, revile, scoff; swear &c. (*malediction*) 908; commit sacrilege.

snuffle; turn up the whites of the eyes; idolize.

Adj. impious; irreligious &c. 989; desecrating &c. *v.*; profane, irreverent, sacrilegious, blasphemous.

un-hallowed, -sanctified, -regenerate; hardened, perverted, reprobate.

hypocritical &c. (*false*) 544; canting, pietistical, sanctimonious, unctuous, pharisaical, over-righteous, righteous over much.

bigoted, fanatical &c. 481 & 606; priest-ridden.

Adv. under the -mask, cloak, – pretence, – form, – guise- of religion.

989. Irreligion.—N. irreligion, indevotion; ungodliness &c. *adj.*; laxity, quietism, apathy, indifference, passivity.

scepticism, doubt; un-, dis-belief; incredul-ity, -ousness &c. *adj.*; want of -faith, – belief; pyrrhonism; doubt &c. 485; agnosticism.

atheism, deism; hylotheism; materialism; positivism; nihilism.

infidelity, freethinking, antichristianity, rationalism.

atheist, anti-christian, sceptic, unbeliever, deist, infidel, pyr-rhonist; *giaour*, heathen, alien, gentile, Nazarene; *esprit fort*, free-thinker, latitudinarian, rationalist; materialist, positivist, nihilist, agnostic.

V. be -irreligious &c. *adj.*; disbelieve, lack faith; doubt, question &c. 485.

dechristianize; serve Mammon, love darkness better than light.

Adj. irreligious; in-, un-devout; devout-, god-, grace-less; un-godly, -holy, -sanctified, -hallowed; atheistic, without God.

sceptical, free-thinking; un-believing, -converted; incredulous, faithless, lacking faith; deistical; un-, anti-christian.

worldly, mundane, earthly, carnal, unspiritual; worldly &c.-minded.

Adv. irreligiously &c. *adj.*

4°. Acts of Religion

990. Worship.—N. worship, adoration, devotion, aspiration, latria, homage, service, humiliation; kneeling, genuflexion, prostration.

prayer, invocation, supplication, rogation, intercession, orison, holy breathing; petition &c. (*request*) 765; collect, litany, Lord's prayer, paternoster, *Ave Maria*, rosary; bead-roll; latria, dulia, hyperdulia, vigils; revival; cult.

thanksgiving; giving -, returning- thanks; grace, praise, glorifica-tion, benediction, doxology, hosanna; h-, allelujah; *Te Deum, non nobis Domine, nunc dimittis*; pæan.

psalm, -ody; hymn, plainsong, chant, chaunt, response, anthem, motet; antiphon, -y.

oblation, sacrifice, incense, libation; burnt -, votive -, thank-offering; offertory, collection.

discipline; self-discipline, -examination, -denial; fasting.

divine service, office, duty; morning prayer; mass, matins, evensong, vespers, compline; holy day &c. (*rites*) 998.

worshipper, congregation, communicant, celebrant.

V. worship, lift up the heart, aspire; revere &c. 928; adore, do serv-ice, pay homage; humble oneself, kneel; bow -, bend- the knee; fall -down, - on one's knees; prostrate oneself, bow down and worship, recite the rosary.

pray, invoke, supplicate; put -, offer- up -prayers, - petitions; beseech &c. (*ask*) 765; say one's prayers, tell one's beads.

return -, give- thanks; say grace, bless, praise, laud, glorify, magnify, sing praises; give benediction, lead the choir, intone, chant, sing.

propitiate, offer sacrifice, fast, deny oneself; vow, offer vows, give alms.

work out one's salvation; go to church; attend -service, - mass; communicate &c. (*rite*) 998.

Adj. worshipping &c. *v.*; devout, devotional, reverent, pure, solemn; fervid &c. (*heartfelt*) 821.

Int. h-, allelujah! hosanna! glory be to God! O Lord! pray God that! God -grant, - bless, - save, - forbid! *sursum corda.*

991. Idolatry.—N. idol-atry, -ism; demon-ism, -olatry; idol -, demon -, devil -, fire- worship; zoolatry, fetishism, Mari-, Bibli-, ecclesi-, heli-olatry.

deification, apotheosis, canonization; hero worship.

sacrifices, hecatomb, holocaust; human sacrifices, immolation, mactation, infanticide, self-immolation, *suttee.*

idol, golden calf, graven image, fetish, *avatar,* Juggernaut, joss, *lares et penates;* Baal &c. 986.

idolater &c. *n.*

V. worship -idols, – pictures, – relics; put on a pedestal, bow down to, prostrate oneself before, make sacrifice to; deify, canonize, idolize.

Adj. idolatrous.

992. Sorcery.—N. sorcery; superstition; occult -art, – sciences; black –, magic; the black art, necromancy, theurgy, thaumaturgy; demon-ology, -omy, -ship; *diablerie,* bedevilment; witch-craft, -ery; glamour; fetis-hism, -ism; ghost dance; hoodoo, voodoo; Shamanism [Esquimaux], vampirism; conjuration; bewitchery, exorcism, enchantment, incantation, obsession, possession, mysticism, second sight, mesmerism, animal magnetism; od –, odylic- force; electro-biology, *clairvoyance;* spiritualism, spirit-rapping, table-turning; thought reading, telepathy, thought transference, automatic writing, *planchette,* ouija board; crystal gazing; spirit manifestation, materialization, astral body, ectoplasm &c.

divination &c. (*prediction*) 511; sortilege, ordeal, *sortes Virgilianæ;* hocus-pocus &c. (*deception*) 545; oracle &c. 513.

V. practice -sorcery &c. *n.*; cast a -horoscope, – nativity; conjure, exorcise, charm, enchant; be-witch, -devil; overlook, look on with the evil eye; entrance, mesmerize, magnetize; fascinate &c. (*influence*) 615; taboo; wave a wand; rub the -ring, – lamp; cast a spell; call up spirits, – from the vasty deep; raise spirits from the dead; raise –, lay- ghosts; command genii.

Adj. magic, -al; mystic, weird, cabalistic, talismanic, phylacteric, incantatory; charmed &c. *v.*

993. Spell.—N. spell, charm, incantation, exorcism, weird, cabala, exsufflation, cantrap, runes, abracadabra, hocus-pocus, open *sesame,* counter-charm, Ephesian letters, bell, book and candle, Mumbo-jumbo, evil-eye, fee-faw-fum.

talisman, amulet, periapt, telesm, phylactery, philtre, wish-bone, merry-thought, mascot, scarab, swastika; fetish; *agnus Dei.*

wand, caduceus, rod, divining rod, lamp of Aladdin, magic carpet, seven-league boots; magic ring; wishing –, Fortunatus's- cap.

994. Sorcerer.—N. sorcerer, magician; thaumat-, the-urgist; conjuror, necromancer, seer, wizard, witch; fairy &c. 980; *lamia,* hag, warlock, charmer, exorcist, voodoo, mage, diviner, dowser; cunning –, medicine- man, witch doctor; Shaman, figure-flinger, ecstatica, medium, *clairvoyant,* mesmerist, hypnotist; *deus ex machinâ;* astrologer; soothsayer &c. 513.

Katerfelto, Cagliostro, Merlin, Comus, Mesmer, Rosicrucian; Hecate, Circe, Lilith, siren, weird sisters; witch of Endor.

5°. RELIGIOUS INSTITUTIONS

995. Churchdom.—N. church, -dom; ministry, apostleship, priesthood, prelacy, hierarchy, church government, christendom, pale of the church.

clerical-, sacerdotal-, episcopalian-, ultramontan-ism; Theocracy; ecclesiolog-y, -ist; priestcraft, *odium theologicum.*

monach-ism, -y; monasticism, monkhood.

[Ecclesiastical offices and dignities] pontificate, primacy, arch-bishopric, archiepiscopacy; prelacy; bishop-ric, -dom; episcop-ate, -acy; see, diocese; deanery, stall; canon-ry, -icate; prebend, -aryship; benefice, incumbency, glebe, advowson, living, cure, – of souls; rector-ship; vicar-iate, -ship; pastor-ate, -ship; deacon-ry, -ship; -curacy; chaplain, -cy, -ship; cardinal-ate, -ship; abbacy, presbytery.

holy orders, ordination, institution, consecration, induction, reading in, preferment, translation, presentation.

popedom, papacy; the -Vatican, – apostolic see, – see of Rome; re-ligious sects &c. 984.

council &c. 696; conclave, college of cardinals, convocation, synod, consistory, chapter, vestry, presbytery; sanhedrim, *congé d'élire*; ecclesiastical courts, consistorial court, court of Arches.

V. call, ordain, induct, prefer, translate, consecrate, present, elect, bestow.

take -orders, – the veil, – vows.

Adj. ecclesi-astical, -ological; clerical, sacerdotal, priestly, prelatical, pastoral, ministerial, capitular, theocratic; hierarchical, archiepiscopal; episcopal, -ian; canonical; mon-astic, -achal; monkish; abbati-al, -cal; pontifical, papal, apostolic; ultramontane, priest-ridden.

---

996. Clergy.—N. clergy, clericals, ministry, priesthood, presbytery, the cloth, the pulpit.

clergyman, divine, ecclesiastic, churchman, priest, presbyter, hiero-phant, pastor, shepherd, minister, clerk in holy orders; father, – in Christ; *padre, abbé, curé*; patriarch; reverend; black coat; confessor; sky pilot.

997. Laity.—N. laity, flock, fold, congregation, assembly, brethren, people.

temporality, secularization.

layman, civilian; parishioner, cate-chumen; secularist.

V. secularize.

Adj. secular, lay, laical, civil, tem-poral, profane.

---

dignitaries of the church; ecclesi-, hier-arch; eminence, reverence, elder, primate, metropolitan, archimandrite, archbishop, bishop, prelate, diocesan, suffragan, dean, subdean, archdeacon, prebendary, canon, rural dean, rector, parson, vicar, perpetual curate, residentiary, beneficiary, incumbent, chaplain, curate, – in charge; deacon, -ess; preacher; lay reader, lecturer; capitular; missionary, propagan-dist, Jesuit, revivalist, field preacher.

churchwarden, sidesman; clerk, precentor, choir; almoner, *suisse*, verger, beadle, sexton, sacristan; acol-yth, -othyst, -yte; thurifer; chorister, choir boy.

[Roman Catholic priesthood] Pope, *Papa*, Holy Father, pontiff, high priest, cardinal; ancient –, flamen; confessor, penitentiary; spiritual director.

cenobite, conventual, abbot, prior, monk, friar, lay brother, beadsman, mendicant, pilgrim, palmer; canon-regular, -secular; Jesuit, Franciscan, Friars minor, Minorites; Observant, Capuchin, Dominican, Carmelite; Augustinian; Gilbertine; Austin-, Black-, White-, Grey-, Crossed-, Crutched-Friars; Bonhomme, Carthusian, Benedictine, Cistercian, Trappist, Cluniac, Premonstratensian, Maturine; Templar. Hospitaller.

abb-, prior-, canon-ess; mother superior; *religieuse*, nun, sister, *beguine*, novice, postulant.

[Under the Jewish dispensation] prophet, priest, high priest, Levite; Rabbi, -n; scribe.

[Mohammedan &c.] mullah, ulema, imauam, sheik; so-fi, -phi; mufti, hadji, muezzin, dervish; fa-kir, -quir; brahmin, gooroo, druid, bonze, santon, abdal, Lama, talapoin, caloyer &c.

V. take orders &c. 995.

Adj. the –, the very –, the Right- Reverend; ordained, in orders, called to the ministry.

998. Rite.—N. rite; ceremon-y, -ial; ordinance, observance, function, duty; form, -ulary; solemnity, sacrament; incantation &c. (*spell*) 993; service, psalmody &c. (*worship*) 990; liturgies.

ministration; preach-ing, -ment; predication, sermon, homily, exhortation, lecture, discourse, pastoral.

baptism, christening, chrism, immersion; baptismal regeneration; font; circumcision.

confirmation; imposition –, laying on- of hands; churching, purification, ordination &c. (*churchdom*) 995; excommunication.

Eucharist, Lord's supper, communion; the –, the holy- sacrament; celebration, high celebration; *missa cantata*; offertory; introit; consecration; con-, tran-substantiation; real presence; elements, bread and wine; mass; high –, low –, dry- mass.

matrimony &c. 903; burial &c. 363; visitation of the sick.

seven sacraments, impanation, extreme unction, last rites, *viaticum*, invocation of saints, canonization, transfiguration, auricular confession; fasting; maceration, flagellation, sackcloth and ashes; penance &c. (*atonement*) 952; absolution; telling of beads, reciting the rosary, processional; thurification, incense, holy water, aspersion.

relics, rosary, beads, reliquary, host, cross, rood, crucifix, pax, pix, pyx, *agnus Dei*, censer, thurible, patera, urceole; chalice, patten, Holy Grail, sangrail; seven-branch candle stick, monstrance, sacring bell.

ritual, rubric, canon, ordinal; liturgy, prayer-book, book of common prayer, pietas, euchology, litany, lectionary; missal, breviary, massbook, bead-roll.

psalter; psalm –, hymn- book; hymn-al, -ology; psalmody.

ritual-, ceremonial-ism; sabbat-ism, -arianism; ritualist, sabbatarian.

holyday, feast, fast; Sabbath, Passover, Pentecost; Advent, Christmas, Noel, Epiphany, Lent, Shrove Tuesday, Ash Wednesday, Maundy Thursday; Passion –, Holy- week; Good Friday, Easter, Ascension Day, Whitsuntide; Trinity Sunday, Corpus Christi; All-Saints' –, – Souls'- Day; Candle-, Lam-, Martin-, Michael-mas; hogmanay; Rama-dan, -zan; Bairam &c. &c.

V. perform service, do duty, minister, officiate, baptize, dip, sprinkle; confirm, lay hands on; give –, administer –, take –, receive –. attend –, partake of- the -sacrament, – communion; communicate; celebrate mass; administer –, receive- extreme unction; anele, shrive, absolve, confess; do penance; genuflect; cross oneself, make the sign of the cross.

excommunicate, ban with bell, book and candle.

preach, sermonize, predicate, lecture.

Adj. ritual, -istic; ceremonial, liturgic; baptismal, eucharistical; paschal.

999. Canonicals.—N. canonicals, vestments; robe, gown, Geneva gown, frock, pallium, surplice, cassock, dalmatic, scapulary, cope. scarf, tunicle, chasuble, alb, *alba*, stole; fan-on, -nel; tonsure, cowl, hood; calo-te, -tte; bands; capouch, amice, orarium, ephod; apron, lawn sleeves, pontificals, pall; mitre, tiara, triple crown; shovel –, cardinal's-hat; biretta; crosier; pastoral staff; costume &c. 225.

1000. Temple.—**N.** place of worship; house of -God, – prayer.

temple, cathedral, minister, church, kirk, chapel, meeting-house, bethel, tabernacle, conventicle, *basilica*, fane, holy place, chantry, oratory.

synagogue; mosque; marabout; pantheon; pagoda; joss-house; dagobah, tope; kiosk.

parsonage, rectory, vicarage, manse, deanery, glebe, church house; Vatican; bishop's palace; Lambeth.

altar, shrine, sanctuary, Holy of Holies, *sanctum sanctorum*, sacrarium, -isty; communion –, holy –, Lord's- table; table of the Lord; pyx; baptistery, font; piscina, stoup; aumbry; sedile; reredos; rood -loft, – screen; jube.

chancel, quire, choir, nave, aisle, transept, lady chapel, vestry, crypt, cloisters, porch; triforum, clerestory, churchyard, *golgotha*, calvary, Easter sepulchre; stall, pew, sitting; pulpit, ambo, lectern, reading-desk, confessional, prothesis, credence, baldachin, *baldacchino*; jesse, apse, belfry; chapter-house; presbytery.

monastery, priory, abbey, friary, convent, nunnery, cloister.

Adj. claustral, cloistered; monast-ic, -erial; conventual.

INDEX

INDEX

N.B.: The numbers refer to the headings under which the words or phrases occur. When the same word or phrase may be used in various senses, the several headings under which it, or its synonyms, will be found, according to those meanings, are indicated by the words printed in Italics. These words in Italics are not intended to explain the meaning of the word or phrase to which they are annexed, but only to assist in the required reference.

When the word given in the Index is itself the title or heading of a category, the number of reference is printed in blacker type, thus: **abode 189.**

---

come – 658
get – *public* 531
  recover 660
go – *turn* 311
going – *news* 532
not know what
  one is – 699
put –
  turn round 283
round – 311
send – one's busi-
  ness 756
set – 676
turn – *invert* 218
what it is – 454
what one is – 625
– it and about it
  573
– to 121
– to be 152
above 206
– all 33, 642
– board
  manifest 525
  artless 703
  fair 939
– comprehension
  519
– ground 359
– the mark 33
– par 31, 648
– praise 944
– price 814
– stairs 206
– suspicion 946
– water *safe* 664
above-mentioned
  preceding 62
  repeated 104
  prior 116
abracadabra 993
Abraham,
  sham – 544
abrasion
  paring 38
  filing 330, 331
abreast 216, 236
abreption 789
abri 666
– tente d' – 233
abridge *lessen* 36
  shorten 201
– *in writing* 572,
  596
abridgment
  compendium 596
abroach 673
abroad
  extraneous 57
  distant 196
  uncertain 475

get – *public* 531
abrogation 756
abrupt *sudden* 113
  violent 173
  steep 217
  unexpected 508
  style 579
abruption 44
abscess 655
abscissa 466
abscission
  retrenchment 38
  division 44
abscond
  escape 623
  not pay 808
absence 187
– of choice 609a
– of influence
  175a
– of intellect 450a
– of mind 458
– of motive 615a
absentee 187
absinthe 298
absolute
  not relative 1
  great 31
  complete 52
  certain 474
  affirmative 535
  authoritative 737
  severe 739
  free 748
  unalienable 924
make – 467, 480
– interest 980
absolution 978
absolutism 506, 739
absolve
  liberate 750
  forgive 918
  exempt 927a
  shrive 952
  acquit 970
absonant 414, 477
absorb *combine* 48
  take in 296
  consume 677
– the mind 457,
  458
– the soul 824
– ed in thought
  451
absorbing 630, 821,
  829
absquatulate 623
abstain 623
  disuse 678
  temperance 953
– from action 681

– from voting 609a
abstainer 953, 958
abstemious 953
absterge 652
abstersive 662
abstinence [*see*
  abstain]
total – 953, 955
abstract
  separate 44
  abridge 596
  take 789
  steal 791
in the – *apart* 44
  alone 87
– idea 453
– oneself
  inattention 458
– thought 451
  attention 457
abstracted
  inattentive 458
abstruse 519
absurdity
  impossible 471
  nonsense **497**
  ridiculous 853
abundant *great* 31,
  63
  enough 639
abundanti cautelâ,
  ex – 664
abuse *deceive* 545
  ill-treat 649
  misuse 679
  malediction 908
  threat 909
  upbraid 932
  violate 961
– of language 563
– of terms 523
abusive 895, 934
abut *near* 197 *touch*
  199, 215
abutment 717
aby *remain* 141
  endure 821, 826
abysmal *deep* 208
abyss *space* 180
  depth 208
  interval 198
  danger 667
  hell 982
A.C. 106
academic
  teaching 537, 542
  theory 514
academical
  style 578
academicals
  225 *robes*

academician 492
  Royal – 559
academy 542
acanthus 847
a capite ad calcem
  52
acariâtre 901
acarpous 169
acatalectic 597
acaudal 38
accede 488, 725, 762
accelerate
  early 132
  stimulate 173
  velocity 274
  hasten 684
accension 384
accent *sound* 402
  tone of voice 580
  rhythm 597
accentuate 642
accentuated 580
accept *assent* 488
  consent 762
  receive 785
  take 789
acceptable 646, 829
acceptance 771
acceptation 522
acception 522
access 286
  easy of – 705
  means of – 627
accessible 470, 705
accession
  adjunct 39
  increase 35
  addition 37
  - *to office* 737, 755
  consent 762
accessory
  extrinsic 6
  additive 37
  adjunct 39
  accompanying 88
  aid 707
  auxiliary 711
acciaccatura 413
accidence 567
accident *event* 151
  chance 156
  disaster 619
  misfortune 735
  fatal – 361
accidental
  extrinsic 6
  fortuitous 156
  undesigned 621
accidents,
  trust to the chap-
  ter of – 621

relevant 23
receivable 296
tolerable 651
– in society 852
admit
  composition 54
  include 76
  let in 296
  assent 488
  acknowledge 529
  permit 760
  concede 762
  accept 785
  – exceptions 469
  – of 470
admitted
  customary 613
  – maxim &c. 496
admixture 41
admonish
  warn 668
  advise 695
  reprove 932
ado *activity* 682
  exertion 686
  difficulty 704
  make much –
    about 542
  much – about
    nothing
  overestimate 482
  unimportant 643
  unskilful 699
adolescence 131
Adonis 845
adonize 847
adopt
  naturalize 184
  choose 609
  – a cause *aid* 707
  – a course 692
  – an opinion 484
adoption
  religious 987
adore 897, 990
adorn 847
adown 207
adrift *unrelated* 10
  disjoined 44
  dispersed 73
  uncertain 475
  unapt 699
  free 750
  go – *deviate* 279
  turn – *disperse* 73
  liberate 750
  dismiss 756
adroit 698
adscititious
  extrinsic 6
  added 37

redundant 641
adscriptus glebæ
  746
adulation 933
adulator 935
Adullam, cave of –
  624, 832
Adullamite 832
adult 131
adulterate *mix* 41
  deteriorate 659
adulterated 545
adulterer 962
adultery 961
adumbrate
  darkness 421
  allegorize 521
  represent 554
adumbration
  semblance 21
  allusion 526
aduncity 244, 245
adust
  colour 433
  gloomy 837
adustion 384
advance *increase* 35
  course 109
  progress 282
  assert 535
  improve 658
  aid 707
  succeed 731
  lend 787
  in – *precedence* 62
  front 234
  precession 280
  in – of 33
  in – of one's age
    498
  – against 716
  – of learning &c.
    490
advanced 282
  – in life 128
  – guard 234
  – student 541
  – work 717
advances, make –
  offer 763
  social 892
advantage
  superiority 33
  influence 175
  good 618
  expedience 646
  mechanical – 633
  dressed to – 847
  find one's – in 644
  gain an – 775
  set off to – 658

take – of 677, 698
  – over *success* 731
advantageous
  beneficial 648
  profitable 775
advene 37
advent
  futurity 121
  event 151
  approach 286
  arrival 292
Advent 998
adventism 984
adventitious 6, 156
adventive 156
adventure *event* 151
  chance 156
  pursuit 622
  danger 665
  trial 675
  the great – 360
adventurer
  traveller 268
  deceiver 548
  experimenter 463
  gambler 621
  rash 863
  ignoble 876
adventures 594
adventurous
  undertaking 676
  bold 861
  rash 863
adversaria 551
adversary 710
adverse
  contrary 14
  opposed 708
  unprosperous 735
  disliking 867
  – party 710
adversity 735
advert 457
advertise 531
advice *notice* 527
  news 532
  counsel **695**
advisable 646
advise *predict* 511
  inform 527
  counsel 695
  – with one's pillow
    451
advised *predeter-*
  mined 611
  intended 620
  better – 658
adviser 540, 695
advocacy 931
advocate
  prompt 615

recommend 695
  aid 707
  auxiliary 711
  friend 890
  vindicate 937
  counsellor 968
Advocate, the – 976
advocation 617
advoutress 962
advoutry 961
advowson 995
adynamic 160
adytum *room* 191
  prediction 511
  secret place 530
adze 253
adzooks 870
ædile 965
ægis 717
ægrescit medendo
  659
ægrotat 927*a*
æolian 349
  – harp 417
æon 976
æquam servare
  mentem 826
æquo animo 823,
  826
ærate 334, 353
ære perennius 873
aerial 273
  elevated 206
  flying 267
  gas 334
  air 338
  – navigation 267
  – navigator 269
  – mail 534
  – patrol 726
  – perspective 428
  – warfare 722
aerie 189
aerify 334
aerodonetics 267
aerodrome 728
aerodynamics 267,
  334, 349
aerolite 318
aerology 338
aeromancy 511
aeromechanics 267
aerometer 338
aeronaut 269
aeronautical 273
aeronautics 267,
  338
aeroplane 273
aerostat *balloon* 273
aerostatics 267, 334
aerostation 338

increase 35
vehemence 173
exaggerate 549
render worse 659
distress 835
exasperate 900
aggravating 830
aggravation 835
aggregate 50, 72, 84
aggregation 46
aggression 716
aggressor 726
aggrieve 649, 830
aggroup 72
aghast
  disappointed 509
  fear 860
  wonder 870
agile 274, 682
agio 813
agiotage 794
agitate *move* 315
  inquire 461
  activity 682
  excite the feelings
  824
  – *a question* 476
agitation [*see* agi-
  tate]
  changeableness
  149
  energy 171
  motion **315**
  in – *preparing* 673
agitator *leader* 694
aglet 554
agley, gang – 732
aglow 382, 420
agnate 11
agnition 762
agnomen 564
agnostic 487
agnosticism 984,
  989
agnus Dei 993, 998
ago 122
  not long – 123
agog *expectant* 507
  desire 865
  wonder 870
agoing 682
  set – 707
agonism 720
agonizing 824, 830
agony 378, 828
  – of death 360
  – of excitement
  825
agrarian 371
agree *accord* 23
  concur 178

assent 488
concord 714
consent 762
compact 769
compromise 774
  – in opinion 488
  – with *salubrity*
  656
agreeable
  comfortable 82
  physically 377
  mentally 829
agreeably to 82
agreement 23 [*see*
  agree]
  compact 769
agrestic 371
agriculture 371
agronomy 371
aground *fixed* 150
  in difficulty 704
  failure 732
ague-fit 860
aguets, aux –
  expectation 507
  ambush 530
aguish *cold* 383
ah me! 839
aha! *rejoicing* 838
ahead 234, 280
  go – *progression*
  282
  shoot – *transcur-*
  sion 303
  activity 682
  rock – 665, 667
Ahrimanes 987, 980
aid 707, 906
  by the – of 631,
  632
aide-de-camp 711,
  745
aidless 160
aigrette 847
aiguille 253
aiguillette 747, 847
aigulet 847
ail 655, 828
aileron 267, 273
ailment 655
aim 278, 620, 675
  – a blow at 716
aimable 894
  faire l' – 897
aimer éperdument
  897
aimless *without*
  motive 615a
  chance 621
air *unsubstantial* 4
  broach 66

lightness 320
gas 334
atmospheric **338**
wind 349
tune 415
appearance 448
refresh 689
demeanour 692
fashionable 852
beat the – 645
fill the – 404
fine – *salubrity* 656
fish in the – 645
fowls of the – 366
in the – 527
rend the – 404
take – 531
air-balloon 273
air base 728
air-commodore 745
aircraft 273, 726
air-drawn 515
airdrome 273
air-force 726
air-gun 727
airing 266
air-mail 273
airman 269
airmanship 698
air-marshal 745
air-passage 351
air-pipe 351
airport 273, 292,
  728
air-pump 349
air-raid 716
airs *affectation* 855
  pride 878
  vanity 880
  arrogance 885
air-shaft 351
air service 267
airship 273, 726
air-tight 261
airways 267
airworthy 273, 664
airy [*see* air]
  windy 349
  unimportant 643
  gay 836
  – *hopes* 858, 859
  give to – nothing
  a local habita-
  tion &c. 515
aisle *passage* 260
  way 627
  in a church 1000
ait 346
ajar *open* 260
  discordant 713
ajee 217

ajutage 260, 350
akimbo *angular* 244
  stand – 715
akin *related* 9
  *consanguineous*11
  similar 17
al fresco 220
alabaster *white* 430
alack! 839
alacrity *willing* 602
  active 682
  cheerful 836
Aladdin's lamp 993
alar 267
alarm *warning* 668
  notice of danger
  669
  fear 860
  cause for – 665
  give an – *indicate*
  550
alarmist 862
alarum 114, 550, 669
alas! 839
alate 267
alb 999
albeit 30
albert
  chain 847
albification 430
albinescence 430
albinism 430
albino 443
album 593, 596
albumen
  semi-liquid 352
  protein 357
Alcaic 597
alcaid 745
alcalde 745
alcazar 189
alchemy 144
alcohol 995
Alcoran 986
alcove 191, 252
Aldebaran 423
alderman 745
ale 298
alea, jacta est – 601
aleatory 665
Alecto 173
alectromancy 511
alehouse 189
  go to the – 959
alembic
  conversion 144
  vessel 191
  furnace 386
  laboratory 691
alentours 197
alert *watchful* 457,

459
active 682
alerte 669
aleuromancy 511
Alexandrine
  ornate style 577
  verse 597
alexandrite 848
alexipharmic 662
alexiteric 662
algebra 85
algid 383
algology 369
algorithm 85
alguazil 965
alias
  otherwise 18
  pseudonym 565
alibi 187
alien *irrelevant* 10
  foreign 57
  transfer 783
  gentile 989
alienable 783
alienate
  transfer 783
  estrange 44, 889
  set against 898
alienation
  mental – 503
alieni appetens
  grasping 865
  envious 921
  selfish 943
alienism 54
align 278
alight *stop* 265
  arrive 292
  descend 306
  on fire 382
alike 17
  share and share –
  778
aliment *food* 298
alimentary 662
  – canal 350
alimentation
  aid 707
alimony
  property 780
  provision 803
  income 810
aliquot 51, 84
aliter visum, diis –
  601
alive
  living 359
  intelligent 498
  active 682
  cheerful 836
  be – with 102

keep – *continue*
  143
keep the memory
  – 505
look – 684
  – to *attention* 457
  cognizant 490
  informed 527
  able 698
  sensible 822
alkahest 335
all *whole* 50
  complete 52
  generality 78
  – absorbing 642
in – ages 112
  – aboard 495
  – agog 865
  – in all 50
  – along 106
  – along of 154
  – but 32
  – colours 440
  – considered 451,
  480
  – day long 110
  – devouring 190
in – directions 278
  – engrossing 190
at – events *com-*
  pensation 30
  qualification 469
  true 494
  resolve 604
  – fours *easy* 705
  cards 840
  – in good time 152
  – hail! *welcome* 292
  honour to 873
  celebration 883
  courtesy 894
  – hands *everybody*
  78
on – hands 488
  – of a dither 824
  – of a heap 72
  – knowing 976
  – manner of *differ-*
  ence 15
  multiform 81
with – one's might
  686
  – at once 113
  – one 27, 866
  – out 52
  – over *end* 67
  universal 78
  destruction 162
  space 180
at – points 52
  – in one's power

686
– powerful
  mighty 159
  God 976
in – quarters 180
with – respect 928
in – respects 52,
  494
  – right! 922
  – Saints' day 998
  – searching 461
  – seeing 976
on – sides 227
  – sorts *diverse* 16a
  mixed 41
  multiform 81
  – talk 4
  – things to all
  men 894
  – the time 106
at – times 136
  – together 50
  – ways 243, 279
  – wise 976
  – the world and
  his wife 78
of – work
  useful 644
  maid – 746
Allah 979
allay
  moderate 174
  pacify 723
  relieve 834
  – excitability 826
allective 615
allege *evidence* 467
  assert 535
  plea 617
allegiance 743, 926
allegory 464, 521,
  594
allegro *music* 415
  cheerful 836
allelujah 990
allemande 840
all-embracing 76
alleviate 174, 834
alley *court* 189
  passage 26
  way 627
alliance *relation* 9
  kindred 11
  physical co-opera-
  tion 178
  voluntary co-oper-
  ation 709
  party 712
  union 714
allied to *like* 17
alligation 43

allign 278
alliteration
  similarity 17
  style in writing
  577
  poetry 597
allocation 60, 786
allocution **586**
allodium *free* 748
  property 780
allopathy 662
alloquy 586
allot *arrange* 60
  distribute 786
  due 924
allow *assent* 488
  admit 529
  permit 760
  consent 762
  give 784
  – to have one's
  own way 740
allowable 760, 924
allowance
  qualification 469
  gift 784
  allotment 786
  discount 813
  salary 973
  with grains of –
  485
  make – for *forgive*
  918
  vindicate 937
alloy *mixture* 41
  combination 48
  debase 659
allude *hint* 514
  mean 516
  refer to 521
  latent 526
  inform 527
allure *move* 615
  create desire 865
alluring 829
allusive
  relative 9
alluvial *level* 213
  land 342
  plain 344
alluvium
  deposit 40
  land 342
  soil 653
ally *combine* 48
  auxiliary 711
  friend 891
alma mater 542
almanac
  list 86
  chronometry 114

amice 999
amicus –. curiæ 527
– humani generis
910
– usque ad aras
890
amidships 68
amidst 41, 228
amiss 619
come – *disagree* 24
mistime 135
inexpedient 647
do – 945
nothing comes –
823
take – 867, 900
amity *concord* 714
peace 721
friendship 888
ammunition 635,
727
amnesia 506
amnesty 506, 723,
918
amnis, rusticus ex-
pectat dum de-
fluat – *hope* 858
amœbæan 63
amok 503
among 41, 228
amor patriæ 910
amore, con – 602,
821
amoroso 599
amorous 897
– glances 902
amorphous 83, 241
amorphism **241**
amortization 784
amotion 270
amount
quantity 25
degree 26
sum of money 800
price 812
gross – 50
– to 27, 85
amour 897, 961
– propre 880
ampere 466
amphibian 366
amphibious 83
amphibology 520
Amphictyonic
council 696
amphigouri 497
amphitheatre
prospect 441
school 542
theatre 599
arena 728

Amphitryon 890
amphora 191
ample *much* 31
spacious 180
large 192
broad 202
copious 639
amplify
expand 194
exaggerate 549
diffuse style 573
amplitude
quantity 25
degree 26
size 192
breadth 202
enough 639
ampoulé 191
ampulla 191
amputate 38
amuck 824
run – 503
amulet 247, 993
amusare la bocca,
per – 394
amuse 829, 840
amusement **840**
place of – 840
amussim, ad – 494
amylaceous 352
an *if* 514
ana 594
Anabaptist 984
anabasis 35
anachronism
false time **115**
inopportune 135
error 495
anacoluthon 70
anaconda 913
anacreontic 597
anæmia 160
anæsthesia 376,
381, 683
anaglyph 554, 557
anagoge 521, 526
anagram
double sense 520
secret 533
letter 561
wit 842
analecta 596
analeptic 662
analgesia 376
analogy 9, 17
analogous 12
analysis
decomposition 49
arrangement 60
algebra 85

inquiry 461
experiment 463
reasoning 476
grammar 567
compendium 596
analyst 461, 463
anamorphosis
distortion 243
optical 443
misrepresentation
555
anapæst 597
anaphylaxis 375
anarchist
destroyer 165
disobedient 742
evil-doer 913
anarchy 59, 738
anastatic printing
558
anastomosis 43, 219
anastrophe 218
anathema 908
anathematize 908
censure 932
detract 934
anatomize *dissect* 44
investigate 461
anatomy
dissection 44
leanness 203
texture 329
anatomy
science 357
comparative – 368
anatriptic 331
ancestral
bygone 122
old 124
aged 128
ancestry 166
anchor
connection 45
stop 265
safeguard 666
badge 747
hope 858
at – *fixed* 150
stationed 184
safe 664
cast – *settle* 184
arrive 292
have an – to wind-
ward 664
sheet – *means* 632
anchorage
location 184
roadstead 189
refuge 866
anchored 150

anchorite 893, 955
ancien régime 875
ancient *old* 124
flag 550
– times 122
ancientness 122
ancillary 707
and 37, 88
andante 415
andiron 386
androgynous 83
anecdote 594
anele 998
anemography 349
ἀνεμώλια βάζειν 497
anemometer
wind 349
measure 466
anent 9
aneroid 338
anew *again* 104
newly 123
anfractuosity 248
angel
object of love 897
good person 948
supernatural
being **977**
fallen –
bad man 949
devil 978
guardian –
safety 664
auxiliary 711
benefactor 912
– of Death 362
– 's visits 137
angelic 944
angels and minis-
ters of grace de-
fend us! 860
angelus 550
anger 900
more in sorrow
than in – 826,
918
angiology 329
angle 244
try 463
at an – 217
Anglicanism 984
angling 622, 840
anguille au genou,
rompre l' – 158,
471
anguilliform 205,
248
anguis in herbâ 667
anguish
physical 378

moral 828
angular 244
– velocity 264
angularity 244
angusta domi, res
– 804
angustation 203
anhelation 688
anhydrate 340
anhydrous 340
aniline dyes 437
anility 128, 499
animadvert
consider 451
attend to 457
reprehend 932
animal 366
female – 374
– cries 412
– economy 359
– gratification 377
– life 364
– physiology 368
– spirits 836
– and vegetable
kingdom 357
animalcule 193, 366
animalism
sensuality 954
animality 364
animate
induce 615
excite 824
enliven 836
animation
life 359
animality 364
activity 682
vivacity 836
suspended – 823
animism 984
animo, ex – 602
quo – 620
animosity
dislike 867
enmity 889
hatred 898
anger 900
animus
willingness 602
intention 620
desire 865
ankle 244
– deep 208, 209
anklet 847
ankylosis 150
annalist 114, 553
annals
chronology 114
record 551
account 594

anneal 673
annex
addition 37
adjunct 39
junction 43
acquire 775
Annie Oakley 815
annihilate 2, 162
anniversary 138
anno 106
Anno Domini
era 106
old age 124
annotation 522, 550
annotator 524
scholar 492
interpreter 524
editor 595
annotto 434
announce
predict 511
inform 527
publish 531
assert 535
announcer 527
annoy
molest 649, 907
disquiet 830
annoyance 828
source of – 830
annual *periodic* 138
plant 367
book 593
annuity 810
annul 162, 750
annular 247
annunciate 527
annus magnus 108
anodyne
lenitive 174
remedial 662
relief 834
anoint *coat* 223
lubricate 332
oil 355
anointed
deity 976
king 745
anomaly 59, 83
disorder 59
irregularity 83
anon 132
anonymous 565
anopsia 442
anorexy 866
another
different 15
repetition 104
– story 468, 526
go upon – tack 607
– time 119

answer
to an inquiry **462**
confute 479
solution 522
succeed 731
pecuniary profit
775
pleadings 969
require an – 461
– for *deputy* 759
promise 768
go bail 806
I'll – for it 535
– the helm 745
– the purpose 731
– to *correspond* 9
– one's turn 644
answerable
agreement 23
liable 177
bail 806
duty 926
censurable 932
ant 690
Antæus 159, 192
antagonism
difference 14
physical 179
voluntary 708
enmity 889
antagonist 710, 891
antagonistic 24
antarctic 237
antecedence 62, 116
antecedent 64
antechamber 191
ante Christum 106
antedate 115
antediluvian 124
antemundane 124
antenna 379
anteposition 62
anterior
in order 62
in time 116
in place 234
– to *reason* 477
anteroom 191
antevert 706
anthem 990
anthemion 847
anthology
book 533
collection 596
poem 597
anthracite 388
anthropoid 372
anthropology
zoology 368
mankind 372

anthropomancy 511
anthropophagi 913
anthroposcopy 511
anthroposophy 372
antic 840
anti-aircraft gun
564, 727
antichambre,
faire – 133
antichristian 984,
989
antichronism 115
anticipate
anachronism 115
priority 116
future 121
early 132
expect 507
foresee 510
prepare 673
hope 858
in – 116
anticlimax
decrease 36
bathos 497, 853
anticlinal 217
anticyclone 265
antidote 662
antigropelos 225
antilogarithm 84
antilogy 477
antimony 663
Antinomian 984
antinomy 964
Antinous 845
antiparallel 217
antipathy 867, 898
antiphon *music* 415
answer 462
worship 990
antiphrasis 563
antipodes
difference 14
distance 196
contraposition
237
antipoison 660
antiquary
past times 122
scholar 492
historian 553
antiquas vias,
stare super –
613, 670
antiquated 128
antique 124
antiquity 122
antiscriptural 984
antiseptic 652, 662
antisocial 911
antistrophe 597

antithesis	**aphorism** 496	*appeal* 765	**appertain**
contrast 14	**aphrodite** 845, 979	**apothecary** 662	*related to* 9
difference 15	**apiary** 370	–'s weight 319	*component* 56
opposite 237	**apiculture** 370	**apothegm** 496	*belong* 777
style 574, 577	**Apicius** 957	**apotheosis**	*property* 780
antitoxin 662	**apiece** 79	*resuscitation* 163	**appetite** 865
antitype 22	**apish** 19, 499	*canonization* 873	tickle the –
antler 253	**aplanatic** 429	*heaven* 981	*savoury* 394
antonomasia	**aplomb**	*hero worship* 991	**appetizing** 865
metaphor 521	*stability* 150	**apozem** 335, 384	*exciting* 824
nomenclature 564	*self-possession*	**appal** 830, 860	**applaud** 931
antonym 14	498	**appanage**	**apple** – of discord
antrum 252	*resolution* 604	*property* 780	713
anvil *support* 215	**Apocalypse** 985	*gift* 784	golden –
on the –	**Apocrypha** 985	**apparatus** 633	*allurement* 615
intended 620	**apocryphal**	**apparel** 225	– of one's eye *good*
in hand 625	*uncertain* 475	**apparent**	648
preparing 673	*erroneous* 495	*visible* 446	*love* 897
anxiety *pain* 828	*heterodox* 984	*appearing* 448	*favorite* 899
fear 860	**apodictic** 478	*probable* 472	– off another tree
desire 865	**apodosis** 67	*manifest* 525	15
anxious expectation	**apogee** 210	heir – 779	how we –s swim!
507	**apograph** 21	**apparition**	880
any *some* 25	**Apollo** *sun* 318	*fallacy of vision*	**apple-green** 435
part 51	*music* 416	443	**apple-pie order** 58
no choice 609a	*luminary* 423	*spirit* 980	**appliance** *use* 677
at – *price* 604a	*beauty* 845	**apparitor** 534	–s *means* 632
at – *rate*	*god* 979	**appeach** 938	*machinery* 633
certain 474	*magnus* – 500, 695	**appeal** 586, 765	**applicable** *relevant*
true 494	**Apollyon** 978	court of – 966	23
at all hazards 604	**apologue**	– to arms 722	*useful* 644
anybody 78	*metaphor* 521	– motion 969	*expedient* 646
anyhow 460, 627	*teaching* 537	– from Philip	**applicability** 9
anything one	*description* 594	drunk to Philip	**applicant** 767
knows, for – 491	**apology** *excuse* 617	sober 658	**application** *study*
aorist 109, 119	*vindication* 937	– to *call to witness*	457
aorta 350	*penitence* 950	467	*metaphor* 521
apace *early* 132	*atonement* 952	– to for (*claim*) 924	*use* 677
swift 274	**apophthegm** 496	**appear** 446, 525	*request* 765
apache 913	**apophysis** 250	– for 759	**apply,** *use* 677
apart 44, 87	**apoplexy** 158, 655	– in print 591	– a match 384
set – 636	**aporetic** 487	**appearance** **448**	– the match to **a**
wide – 196	**aposiopesis** 585	make one's – 292	train 66
apartment 191	**apostasy**	to all – 448	– the mind 457
–s 189	*recantation* 607	*probable* 472	– a remedy 662
–s to let	*dishonour* 940	**appearances**	**appoggiatura** 413
imbecile 499	*heterodoxy* 984	keep up – 852	**appointment**
apathetic 275	**apostate**	**appease** 174	*employment* 625
apathy	*convert* 144	**appellant** 924, 938	*order* 741
indifference 465	*turncoat* 607	**appellate** 966	*charge* 755
insensibility 823	*impiety* 988	**appellation** 564	*assignment* 786
irreligion 989	**apostle** *teacher* 540	**append** *add* 37	*interview* 892
ape *imitate* 19	*disciple* 541	*sequence* 63	**appointments**
Apelles 559	*inspired* 985	*hang* 214	*gear* 633
aperçu 596	–'s creed 983a	**appendage** 39	**apportion** *arrange*
aperture 260	**apostolic** 985	**appendectomy** 662	60
apex 210	– church 983a	**appendix**	*disperse* 73
aphasia 583	– see 995	*adjunct* 39	*allot* 786
aphelion 196	**apostrophe**	*sequel* 65	**apportionment** **786**
aphonic 403	*address* 586	*end* 67	**appositeness** 9
aphony 581	*soliloquy* 589	*book* 593	**apposition**

ment 24
topic 454
discussion 476
meaning 516
have the best of
an – 478
argumentum
– baculinum
compel 744
lawless 964
punish 972
– ad crumenam
800
– ad hominem
reasoning 476
accuse 938
– ad verecundiam
939
Argus-eyed 441, 459
argute 498
aria 415
arianism 984
arid 340
unproductive 169
uninteresting 841
Ariel *courier* 268
swift 274
messenger 534
spirit 979
arietation 276
arietta 415
aright *well* 618
Ariman [*see* Ahri-
manes]
ariolation 511
arioso 415
aris et focis, pro –
defence 717
philanthropy 910
arise *exist* 1
begin 66
happen 151
mount 305
appear 446
– from 154
Aristarchus 850
Aristides
good man 948
aristocracy
power 737
fashion 852
nobility 875
ἄριστον μέτρον 628
Arithmancy 511
arithmetic 85
ark *abode* 189
asylum 666
arm *part* 51
power 157
instrument 633
provide 637

prepare 673
war 722
weapon 727
make a long – 200
– chair 215
– in arm
together 88
friends 888
sociable 892
– of the law 963
– of the sea 343
armada 726
Armageddon 720,
722
armament 673, 727
armed 717
– at all points 673
– force 726
– guard 664
armet 717
armful 25
armiger 875
armigerent 726
armigerous 722
armilla 247, 847
armillary sphere
466
armipotent 157
armistice
cessation 142
respite 672
pacification 723
armless 158
armlet *ring* 247
gulf 343
ornament 847
armorial bearings
550, 877
armour *cover* 223
defence 717
arms 727
buckle on one's –
673
– plated 223
armoured
– car 726
– cruiser 726
– train 726
armoury *store* 636
workshop 691
arm's length
at – 196
keep at –
repel 289
defence 717
enmity 889
seclusion 893
discourtesy 895
arms 727 [*see* arm]
heraldry 550
war 722

honours 877
clash of – 720
deeds of – 720
with folded – 681
in – *infant* 129
throw oneself into
the – of 666, 880
under – 722
up in – *active* 682
discord 713
resistance 719
resentment 900
enmity 889
Armstrong gun 727
army *collection* 72
multitude 102
troops 726
aroma 400
around 227
lie – 220
arouse *move* 615
excite 824
– oneself 682
aroynt *begone* 297
malediction 908
arquebusade 662
arquebuse 727
arraign 938, 969
arrange
set in order 60
plan 626
compromise 774
– with creditors
807
– itself 58
arrange – *matters*
pacify 723
– music 413, 416
– in a series 69
– under 76
arrangement 23, **60**
[*see* arrange]
order 58
temporary – 111
arrant *identical* 31
manifest 525
notorious 531
bad 649
disreputable 874
base 940
arras 847
array *order* 58, 60
series 69
assemblage 72
multitude 102
dress 225
prepare 673
adorn 847
ostentation 882
battle – 722
arrear, in – 53, 808

arrears *debt* 806
arrectis auribus
hear 418
expect 507
arrest *stop* 142
restrain 751
in law 969
– the attention 457
arrière-pensée
after-thought 65
mental reservation
528
motive 615
set purpose 620
arrival 292
arrive *happen* 151
reach 292
complete 729
– at a conclusion
480
– at the truth 480*a*
arrogant *severe* 739
proud 878
insolent 885
arrogate 885, 924
– to oneself
undue 925
arrondissement 181
arrosion 331
arrow *swift* 274
missile 284
arms 727
broad – 550
arrow-head
form 253
writing 590
'Arry and 'Arriet
902
ars celare artem
698
arsenal *store* 636
workshop 661
arsenic 663
arson 384
art *representation*
554
business 625
skill 698
cunning 702
fine – 850
work of – 845, 847
– gallery 556
artery 350, 627
artes, hæ tibi
erunt – 627
artesian well 343
artful 544, 702
– dodge 545, 702
article *thing* 3
part 51
matter 316

<table>
<tr><td>

chapter 593
review 595
goods 798
articled clerk 541
articles
thirty-nine – 983*a*
– of agreement
770
– of faith 484, 983
articulate 366
articulation
junction 43
speech 580
articulo, in –
transient 111
dying 360
artifice 626, 702
artificer 690
artificial
fictitious 545
cunning 702
affected 855
– language 579
artillery
explosion 404
arms 727
artilleryman 726
artisan 690
artist *painter* &c.
559
contriver 626
agent 690
artiste *music* 416
drama 599
artistic *skilful* 698
beautiful 845
taste 850
– language 578
artlessness 703
aruspex 513
aruspicy 511
arundo, hæret
lateri lethalis –
828
as *motive* 615
– broad as long 27
– can be 52
– good as 27
– if *similar* 17
suppose 514
– little as may be
32
– it may be
circumstance 8
event 151
chance 156
– much again 90
– soon as 120
– they say 496, 532
– things are 7
– things go 151,

</td><td>

613
– to 9
– usual 82
– it were 17, 521
– you were 141,
283
– well as 37
– the world wags
151
ascend *be great* 31
increase 35
rise 305
improve 658
ascendancy
power 157
influence 175
success 731
ascendant
lord of the – 745
in the –
influence 175
important 642
success 731
authority 737
repute 873
one's star in the –
prosperity 734
ascension
[see ascend]
calefaction 384
– Day 998
ascent
[see ascend]
gradient 217
rise **305**
glory 873
ascertain *fix* 150
determine 480
ascertained 474,
490
ascertainment 480*a*
asceticism 955
ascititious
intrinsic 6
additional 37
supplementary 52
ascribe 155
aseptic 652
ash 384
– coloured 432
– blond 430
ashen 429
Ash Wednesday
998
ashamed 879
ashes *corpse* 362
dirt 653
lay in – 162
pale as – 429, 860
rise from one's –
660

</td><td>

ashore 342
go – *arrive* 292
ashy 429
Asian mystery 533
aside *laterally* 236
whisper 405
private 528
say – 589
set &c. – *displace*
185
neglect 460
negative 536
reject 610
disuse 678
abrogate 756
discard 782
step – 279
asinine *ass* 271
fool 499
ask *inquire* 461
request 765
for sale 794
price 812
– leave 760
askance 217
eye – *fear* 860
look – *vision* 441,
443
dissent 489
dislike 867
disapproval 932
askari 726
asked in church 903
askew 217, 243
aslant 217
asleep 683
aslope 217
Asmodeus 980
asomatous 317
asp *animal* 366
evil-doer 913
Aspasia 962
aspect *feature* 5
state 7
situation 183
appearance 448
aspen leaf
shake like an –
315, 860
asperity
roughness 256
discourtesy 895
anger 900
irascibility 901
asperse 934
aspersion
malediction 908
rite 998
asphalte
smooth 255
resin 356*a*

</td><td>

material 635
asphodel 845
aspic 352
asphyxia 360
asphyxiate 361
aspirant 767, 865
aspirate 580
aspirator 349
aspire *rise* 305
hope 858
desire 865
worship 990
aspirin 834
asportation 270
asquint 217
ass *beast of burden*
271
fool 501
make an – of
delude 545
– between two
bundles of
hay 605
–'s bridge 519
– in lion's skin
cheat 548
bungler 701
assafœtida 401
assagai 727
assail 716, 830
assailant 710, 726
assassin, –ate 361
assault 716, 961
take by – 789
assay 463
asseguay 727
assemblage 72
assembly
council 696
society 892
religious 997
assembly hall 588
assembly room 189
assent *belief* 484
agree **488**
willing 602
consent 762
content 831
assert 535, 924
assess *measure* 466
determine 480
tax 812
assessor
judge 967
assets 780, 800
asseverate 535
assiduity 110
assiduous 682
assign
commission 755
transfer 270, 783

</td></tr>
</table>

give 784
allot 786
− as cause 155
− a duty 926
− places 60
assignat 800
assignation 892
place of − 74
assignee *donee* 785
assimilate
  uniform 16
  resemble 17
  imitate 19
  agree 23
  transmute 144
assist 707
  − at 186
assistant 711
assister *be present*
  186
assize *measure* 466
  tribunal 966
  justice of − 967
associate *mix* 41
  unite 43
  collect 72
  accompany 88
  colleague 690
  auxiliary 711
  friend 890
  − with 892
association
  [*see* associate]
  relation 9
  combination 48
  co-operation 709
  partnership 712
  − of ideas
  intellect 450
  thought 451
  intuition 477
  hint 514
  − football 840
assoil *acquit* 970
assonance
  music 413
  poetry 597
assort *arrange* 60
assortment 72, 75
assuage 174, 834
assuetude 613
assume *believe* 484
  suppose 514
  falsehood 544
  take 789
  insolent 885
  right 924
  − authority 737
  − a character 554
  − command 741
  − a form 144

− the offensive 716
assumed name 565
assumption
  [*see* assume]
  severity 739
  hope 858
  usurpation 925
assurance
  speculation 156
  certainty 474
  belief 484
  assertion 535
  promise 768
  security 771
  hope 858
  vanity 880
  insolence 885
  make − double
    sure *safe* 664
  caution 864
assuredly
  assent 488
assythment 973
astatic 320
asterisk 550
astern 235
  put the engines −
    275
  fall − 283
asteroid 318
Asteroth 979
asthenia 160
astigmatism 443
astir 682
  set − 824
astonish 870
astonished
  − at nothing 871
astonishing
  great 31
astound *excite* 824
  fear 860
  surprise 870
astra, sic itur ad −
  360, 873
Astræa 922
astraddle 215
astragal 847
astral 318
  − body 717, 992
  − influence 601
  − plane 317
astray 475, 495
  go − *deviate* 279
  sin 945
astriction 43
astride 215
astringent 195
astrolabe 466
astrologer 994

astrology 511
astromancy 511
astronomy 318
astute 498, 702
asunder 44, 196
  as poles − 237
asylum *hospital* 663
  retreat 666
  defence 717
asymptote 290
at, be − 620
  up and − them!
    716
ataghan 727
atavism 144, 163
ataxia 158
atelier 556, 691
athanasia 112
Athanasian creed
  983*a*
athanor 386
atheism 989
atheist 487
Athenae 979
Athens, owls to −
  641
athirst 865
athlete *strong* 159
  gladiator 726
athletic *strong* 159
  strenuous 686
  − sports
  contest 720
  games 840
athwart
  oblique 217
  crossing 219
  opposing 708
Atkins, Tommy 726
Atlantis 515
Atlas *arrangement*
  60
  list 86
  strength 159
  support 215
  maps 554
atmosphere *circumambience*
  227
  air 338
  painting 556
atmospheric blue
  438
atoll 346
atom *small* 32, 193
atomic energy 157
atomizer 336
atoms
  crush to − 162
atomy 193

atonement
  restitution 790
  expiation **952**
  amends 973
  religious 976
atony 160
atrabilious 837
atramentous 431
atrium 191
atrocity
  malevolence 907
  vice 945
  guilt 947
atrophy
  shrinking 195
  disease 655
  decay 659
atropos 601
attach *join* 43
  love 897
  legal 969
  − importance to
    642
attaché
  employé 746
  diplomatic 758
  − case 191
attack *singing* 580
  disease 655
  assault **716**
  debauch 961
attaghan 727
attain *arrive* 292
  succeed 731
  − majority 131
attainable 470
attainder
  taint 651
  at law 971
attainment
  knowledge 490
  learning 539
  skill 698
attar 400
attempter 41, 174
attempered 820
attempt 675
  vain − 732
  − impossibilities
    471
attend
  accompany 88
  be present 186
  follow 281
  apply the mind
    457
  medically 662
  aid 707
  serve 746
  − to business 625
  − to orders 743

autoptical 446, 535
autotype 558
autumn 126
auxiliary 711
  additional 34
  helpful 707
  – forces 726
avail *benefit* 618
  useful 644
  succeed 731
  of no – 645
  – oneself of 677
avalanche *fall* 306
  snow 383
  redundance 641
avaler les couleu-
  vres 725, 886
avant-courier 64,
  673
avant-propos 64
avarice 819
avast! *stop* 142, 265
  desist 624
  forbid 761
avatar *change* 140
  deity 976
  idol 991
avaunt! 297, 449
ave! *honour* 873
  courtesy 894
Ave maria 990
avenge 919
avenue
  plantation 371
  way 627
aver 535
average *mean* 29,
  628
  médiocre 651
  – circumstances
  736
  take an – 466
Averni, facilis de-
  scensus – 217,
  665
Avernus 982
averruncate 297,
  301
aversion *unwilling-*
  ness 603
  dislike 867
  hate 898
avert 706
  – the eyes 442
aviary 370
aviation 267
aviator 269
avidity *avarice* 819
  desire 865
airette 273
avile 932, 934

avion 273
aviso 532
avocation 625
avoidance 623
avoidless 474, 601
avoirdupois 319
avolation 623, 671
avouch 535, 768
avow *assent* 488
  disclose 529
  assert 535
avulsion 44, 301
avuncular 11
await *future* 121
  be kept waiting
  133
  impend 152
  expect 507
awake *attentive* 457
  careful 459
  intelligent 498
  active 682
  – to life immortal
  360
awaken *inform* 527
  excite 824
  – the attention 457
  – the memory 505
award *adjudge* 480
  give 784
aware 490
away 187, 196
  break – 623
  fly – 293
  move – 287
  take – from 789
  get &c. – 671
  throw &c. –
  eject 297
  reject 610
  waste 638
  relinquish 782
  – from *unrelated* 10
  – with! 930, 932
  do – with *undo* 681
  abrogate 756
awe *fear* 860
  wonder 870
  respect 928
aweless *fearless* 861
  insolent 885
  disrespectful 329
awful 31, 860
  – silence 403
awhile 111
awkward
  inelegant 579
  inexpedient 647
  unskilful 699
  difficult 704
  painful 830

  ugly 846
  vulgar 851
  ridiculous 853
  – squad 701
awl 262
awn 253
awning 223, 424
awry *oblique* 217
  distorted 243
  evil 619
axe *edge tool* 253
  impulse 276
  weapon 727
  for beheading 975
  have an – to grind
  702
Axinomancy 511
axiom 496
axiomatic 474
axis *support* 215
  centre 222
  rotation 312
axle 312
  wheel and – 633
axle load 466
axletree 215
ay 488
ayah 746, 753
aye *ever* 112
  yes 488
azimuth
  horizontal 213
  direction 278
  measurement 466
  – circle 212
azoic 358
azote 663
azotic 657
azure 438
azygous *single* 87

B

Baal 979, 986
Babbittry 851
babble *rivulet* 348
  faint sound 405
  unmeaning 517
  talk 584, 588
babbler 501
babbling
  foolish 499
babe 129
  innocent as the –
  unborn 946
Babel *confusion* 59
  discord 414
  tongues 560
  jargon 563
  loquacity 584

baboon 846
baby *infant* 129
  fool 501
  – linen 225
babyhood 127
babyish 499
baccarat 840
bacchanals 959
Bacchus 979
  drink 959
bachelor 904
  – of arts 492
  – girl 374
bacillus 193
back *rear* 235
  shoulder 250
  aid 707
  behind one's –
  latent 526
  hidden 528
  come – 292
  give – 790
  fall – *relapse* 661
  go – 283
  go – from *retract*
  773
  have at one's – 215
  hold – *avoid* 623
  keep – *reserve* 636
  look – 505
  on one's – *impo-*
  tent 158
  horizontal 213
  failure 732
  pat on the –
  incite 615
  encourage 861
  approve 931
  pay – *retaliate* 718
  put – *deteriorate*
  659
  restore 660
  send – 764
  take – again 790
  carry one's
  thoughts – 505
  some time – 122
  spring – 277
  trace – 505
  turn – 283
  turn one's – 283
  turn one's – upon
  repel 289
  inattention 458
  avoid 623
  oppose 508
  seclusion 893
  discourtesy 895
  disrespect 929
  contempt 930
  set one's – against

balanced 150, 242
balbucinate 583
balbutiate 583
balcony 250
  theatre 599
bald *bare* 226
  style 575
  uninteresting 841
  ugly 846
  plain 849
baldachin 223, 1000
balderdash 517, 577
baldric 230, 247
bale *bundle* 72
  load 190
  ladle 270
  evil 619
  – *out* 297
baleful 649
balister 727
balize 550
balk *disappoint* 509
  deceive 545
  hinder 706
Balkanize 713
ball *globe* 249
  missile 284
  shot 727
  dance 840
  party 892
  – *at one's feet* 731,
  737
  keep up the – 143,
  682
ballad 415, 597
  – *monger* 597
ballast
  compensation 30
  weight 319
  wisdom 498
  safety 666
  without – *rash* 863
  vicious 945
ballerina 599
ballet 599, 840
ballet-dancer 599
ballistics
  projectiles 284
  war 722
  arms 727
ballon d'essai 463
balloon 273, 726
balloonist 269
balloonry 267
ballot 535, 609
ball-room 840
balm *moderate* 174
  fragrance 400
  remedy 662
  relief 834
Balmoral *boot* 225

balmy
  sleep 683
balneal 337
balourdise 699
balsam 662
balsamic
  salubrious 834
balustrade
  support 215
  inclosure 232
bam 544
bambino 129
bamboozle 545
ban *exclude* 55
  prohibit 761
  denounce 908
  under the – 909
  – with bell, book,
    and candle 998
banal 613, 843
band *ligature* 45
  assemblage 72
  filament 205
  belt 230
  ring 247
  music 415, 416,
  417
  party 712
  shackle 752
  – *of hope* 958
  – *together* 709
  – *with* 720
bandage 43, 45
  support 215
  cover 223
  remedy 662
  restraint 752
  the eyes -d 442
bandana 225
bandbox 191
banded together
  178, 712
bandit 792
bandog 664, 668
bandolier 636
bandore 417
bandrol 550
bands 999
bandurria 417
bandy
  exchange 148
  agitate 315
  – *about* 531
  – *legged* 243
  – *words* 476, 588
bane 619, **663**
baneful 649
bang *impel* 276
  sound 406
  beat 972
bangle 847

banish *eject* 297
  seclude 893
  punish 972
banister 215
banjo 417
bank *acclivity* 217
  side of lake 342
  store 636
  sand 667
  fence 717
  money 802
  sea – 342
  – *of elegance* 800
  – *holiday* 840
  – *up* 670
banker 797, 801
  game 840
bank-note 800
bankruptcy 732, 808
banlieue 197, 227
banner 550
  enlist under the -s
  of 707
  raise one's – 722
banneret 875
banns
  forbid the – 761
  publish the –
  ask 765
  marriage 903
banquet 298, 840
banquette 717
banshee 979, 980
bantam cock 887
banter 842, 856
banterer 844
banting 956
bantling 129, 167
banyan *stint* 640
  fast 956
baptism *name* 564
  rite 998
Baptist 984
baptistery 1000
bar *except* 38
  exclude 55
  hotel 189
  line 200
  support 215
  inclosure 232
  close 261
  music 413
  hindrance 706
  insignia 747
  prison 752
  prohibit 761
  ingot 800
  tribunal 966
  legal profession
  968
  – *sinister flaw* 651

  disrepute 874
  illegal 964
  crossing the – 360
Barabbas 792
baragouin 517
barb *spike* 253
  nag 271
  – the dart *pain* 830
barbacan 717
barbarian
  uncivilized 876
  evil-doer 913
barbaric 851, 876
barbarism
  neology 563
  bad style 579
  vulgarity 851
  discourtesy 895
barbarous
  unformed 241
  plebeian 876
  maleficent 907
barbette 717
barbican 717
barbouillage 590
barcarolle 415
bard 416, 597
bare *mere* 32
  nude 226
  manifest 525
  disclose 529
  scanty 640
  – *back* 226
  – *bone* 203
  – *faced* *deceitful*
  544, *insolent* 885
  – *foot* 226, 804
  - *headed* 928
  scud under - poles
  704
  - *possibility* 473
  - *supposition* 514
bargain
  compact 769
  barter 794
  cheap 815
  into the - 37
  - *for* 507
  - *and sale transfer*
  of property 783
barge 273
bargee 269
baritone 408
bark *rind* 223
  strip 226
  ship 273
  yelp 412
  - *at threaten* 909
  censure 932
  more - than bite
  908

worse than bite 885
barker 767
barleycorn
  little 193
Barleycorn, Sir
  John - 298
barm *leaven* 320
  bubbles 353
Barmecide feast
  956
barmy 320, 503
barn 189
barnacles 445
barndoor fowl 366
barograph 206, 338
barometer *air* 338
  measure 466
  consult the – 463
baron *peer* 875
  husband 903
  court – 966
  – of the Exchequer
  967
baronet 875
baronial 878
baroque 853
baroscope 338
barouche 272
barque 273
barrack 189
barracoon 717
barrage 407, 717
barratry 940
barred 219, 440
barrel 191, 249
  – organ 417
barren 169, 645
barricade *fence* 232
  obstacle 706
  defence 717
  prison 752
barrier [see barri-
cade]
barring *save* 38
  excluding 55
  except 83
  – out *resist* 719
  disobey 742
barrister 968
  revising – 967
barrow
  mound 206
  vehicle 272
  grave 363
barter
  reciprocate 12
  interchange 148
  commerce **794**
barytone 408
basal 215

bas-bleu
  scholar 492
  affectation 855
base
  site 183
  lowest part **211**
  support 215
  bad 649
  cowardly 862
  shameful 874
  servile 886
  dishonourable 940
  vicious 945
  – ball 840
  – born 876
  – coin 800
  – note 408
  – of operations
  plan 626
  attack 716
  – viol 417
baseball diamond
  213
baseboard 211
based on *ground of*
  belief 467
baseless 2, 4
basement *cellar* 191
  lowest part 207,
  211
bash 276
bashaw 739, 745
bashful 881
bashi bazouk 726
basilica 1000
basilisk *sight* 441
  cannon 737
  serpent 949
basin *dock* 189
  vessel 191
  hollow 252
  plain 344
basinet 717
basis
  lowest part 211
  support 215
  preparation 673
bask *physical enjoy-*
  ment 377
  warmth 382
  prosperity 734
  moral enjoyment
  827
basket 191
  – of 190
bas-relief 250, 557
bass *music* 415
  – note 408
  – viol 417
basset horn 417
bassinet 191, 215

bassoon 417
basso-profondo 408
basso-rilievo 250,
  557
bastard 545, 925
baste *beat* 276
  punish 972
Bastille 752
bastinado 972
bastion 717
bat 276, 727
batch 25, 72
bate *diminish* 36
  subtract 38
  reduce price 813
bated breath
  with – *faint sound*
  405
  expecting 507
  hiding 528
  whisper 581
  humble 879
bath 337, 652
  public –s 652
  warm – 386
  – room 191, 652
Bath chair 272
bathe *immerse* 300
  plunge 310
  water 337
bathos 497
bathysphere 208
batik 440
batman 637
bâton *support* 215
  sceptre 747
batrachian 366
betta 973
battalion 726
batten
  feed 298
  stage lighting 599
  – down the
  hatches 261
  – on 886
batter *destroy* 162
  beat 276
battered 659, 688
battering-ram 276
battering-train 727
battery *electric* 153
  artillery 726
  guns 727
  floating – 726
  plant a – 716
battle 720, 722
  half the – 642
  win the – 731
  – array *order* 60
  prepare 673
  war 722

– axe 727
– cruiser 726
– cry 550, 722
– field *arena* 728
– ground *discord*
  713
– ship 726
– with *oppose* 708
battledore and
  shuttlecock
  interchange 148
  game 840
battlement 257, 717
battre
– la campagne
  nonsense 497
  diffuse style 573
  excitable 825
– l'eau avec un
  bâton 645
– le fer sur l'en-
  clume 134
– la générale 669
se – contre des
  moulins 645
ne – que d'une aile
  683
battology
  repeat 104
  diffuse style 373
battue *pursuit* 622
  attack 716
  kill 361
bauble 643, 840
bavardage 517, 584
bawd 962
bawdy, – house 961
bawl 411
bawn 189
bay *concave* 252
  gulf 343
  cry 412
  brown 433
  at – *danger* 665
  difficulty 704
  defence 717, 719
  bring to – 716
  – the moon 645
  – window 260
bayadére 599
bayard 271
bayonet *kill* 361
  attack 716
  weapon 727
  crossed –s 708
  at the point of the
  – *war* 722
  severity 739
  coercion 744
bays *trophy* 733
  crown 877

bazaar 799
B.C. 106
be 1
 – all and end all
  whole 50
  intention 620
  importance 642
 – off *depart* 293
  eject 297
  retract 773
 – it so 488
 – that as it may 30
beach 231, 342
beach comber 268
beacon 550, 663
bead 249
beadle *janitor* 263
  law officer 965
  church 996
beadledom 737
beadroll *list* 86
  prayers 990
  ritual 998
beads
  ornament 847
  tell one's – 990,
  998
beadsman
  servant 746
  clergy 996
beagle 366
beak *face* 234
  nose 250
  magistrate 967
beaker 161
beam *support* 215
  plank 236
  weigh 319
  light 420
 on – ends
  powerless 158
  horizontal 213
  side 236
  fail 732
  wonder 870
beaming
  beautiful 845
bean 276
beanfeast 840
bear *produce* 161
  sustain 215
  carry 270
  admit of 470
  suffer 821
  endure 826
 bring to – 677
 more than flesh
  and blood can –
  824
 unable to –
  excited 825

dislike 867
 – away 789
 – away the bell
  648, 731
 – the brunt 704,
  717
 – the burden 625
 – the cross 828
 – company 88
 – down 173, 885
 – down upon 716
 – false witness 544
 – fruit *produce* 161
  useful 644
  success 731
  prosper 734
 – a hand 680
 – hard upon 649
 – harmless 717
 – ill 825
 – off *deviate* 279
 – on 215
 – oneself 692
 – out *evidence* 467
  vindicate 937
 – pain 828
 – the palm 33
 – a sense 516
 – through 707
 – up *approach* 286
  persevere 604a
  relieve 834
  cheerful 836
 – up against 719,
  861
 – upon
  relevant 9, 23
  influence 175
 – with
  tolerate 740
  permit 760
  take coolly 826
  forgive 918
bear
  savage 907
  surly 895
 had it been a – it
  would have bit-
  ten you 458
 – garden
  disorder 59
  discord 713
  arena 728
 – leader 540
 – pit 370
 – skin *cap* 225
  helmet 717
 – with a sore back
  901
bearable 651
beard *hair* 205

prickles 253
  rough 256
  defy 715
  brave 861
  insolence 885
 pluck by the –
  disrespect 929
 – the lion 604
beardless 127, 226
bearer 271, 363
bearing *relation* 9
  support 215
  direction 278
  meaning 516
  demeanour 692
 – rein 706, 752
bearings
  circumstances 8
  situation 183
  armorial – 550
beast *animal* 366
  unclean 653
  discourteous 895
 – of burden 271,
  690
beat *be superior* 33
  periodic 138
  region 181
  impulse 276
  surpass 303
  oscillate 314
  agitation 315
  crush 330
  sound 407
  line of pursuit 625
  path 627
  overcome 731
  strike 972
 – about
  circuit 629
 – the air 645
 – against 708
 – one's breast 839
 – about the bush
  try for 463
  evade the point 477
  prevaricate 544
  diffuse style 573
 – down *destroy* 162
  cheapen 794, 819
  insolent 885
 – of drum
  music 416
  publish 531
  alarm 669
  wear 722
  command 741
  pomp 882
 without – of
  drum 528
 – into *teach* 537

 – off 717
 – a retreat
  retire 283
  avoid 623
  submit 725
 – time *clock* 114
  music 416
 – up *churn* 352
 – up against
  oppose 708
 – up for *cater* 637
 – up one's quarters
  seek 461
  visit 892
 – up for recruits
  prepare 673
  aid 707
beaten track
  habit 613
  way 627
 leave the – 83
 tread the – 82
beatic 827
beatific 829, 981
beatification 827,
  987
beating high
 the heart – 824
beatitude 827
beau *man* 373
  fop 854
  admirer 897
 – idéal 650, 845
 – monde 852
beautify 845, 847
beautiless 846
beauty 845
beaver *hat* 225
becalm 265
because *cause* 153
  attribution 155
  answer 462
  reasoning 476
  motive 615
bechance 151
beck *rill* 348
  sign 550
  mandate 741
 at one's – *aid* 707
  obey 743
beckon *sign* 550
  motive 615
  call 741
becloud *dark* 421
  hide 528
become
  change to 144
  accord with 23
  behove 926
 – of 151
becoming

bespeak *early* 132
　evidence 467
　indicate 516
　engage 755
　ask for 765
bespeckle 440
bespot 440
besprinkle 41, 440
best 648, 650
　all for the –
　　good 618
　　prosper 734
　　content 831
　　hope 858
　bad is the – 649
　do one's –
　　care 459
　　try 675
　　activity 682
　　exertion 686
　have the – of it 731
　make the – of it
　　over-estimate 482
　　use 677
　　submit 725
　　compromise 774
　　take easily 826
　　hope 858
　the – 800
　to the – of one's
　　belief 484
　– bib and tucker
　　prepared 673
　　ornament 847
　　ostentation 882
　– friends 890
　– intentions 906
　– man 903
　– part 31, 50
　– seller 731
　make the – of
　　one's time 684
bestead 644
bestial 954, 961
bestir oneself
　activity 682
　haste 684
　exertion 686
bestow 784
　– one's hand 903
　– thought 451
bestraddle 215
bestrew 73
bestride 206, 215
bet 621
betake oneself to
　journey 266
　business 625
　use 677
bête, pas si – 498
bête noire *bane* 663

fear 860
　hate 898
bethel 1000
bethink 451, 505
bethral 749, 751
betide 151
betimes 132
betoken
　evidence 467
　predict 511
　indicate 550
betray *disclose* 529
　deceive 545
　dishonour 940
　– itself *visible* 446
betrayer 941
betrim 673
betroth 768, 903
betrothed 897
better *good* 648
　improve 658
　appeal to one's –
　　feelings 914
　get – *health* 654
　improve 658
　refreshment 689
　restoration 660
　get the – of, 479,
　　702, 731
　think – of 658, 950
　seen – days
　　deteriorate 659
　　adversity 735
　　poor 804
　– half 903
　only – than noth-
　　ing 651
　– sort 875
　for – for worse
　　choice 609
　　marriage 903
between 228
　– cup and lip 111
　far – 198
　lie – 228
　– the lines 526
　vibrate – two ex-
　　tremes 149
　– ourselves 528
　– two fires 665
　– maid 746
betwixt 228
bevel 217
　– gearing 653
bever 298
beverage 298
bévue 732
bevy 72, 102
bewail *regret* 833
　lament 839
beware 665, 668

bewilder
　put out 458
　uncertainty 475
　astonish 870
bewitch
　fascinate 615
　please 829
　excite love 897
　exorcise 992
bey 745
beyond *superior* 33
　distance 196
　go – 303
　– compare 31, 33
　– control 471
　– one's depth 208,
　　519
　– expression 31
　– one's grasp 471
　– hope 731, 534
　– the mark 303,
　　641
　– measure 641
　– possibility 471
　– praise
　　perfect 650
　　approbation 931
　　virtue 944
　– price 814
　– question 474, 494
　– reason 471
　– remedy 859
　– seas 57
bezel 217
bhang 663
bias *influence* 175
　tendency 176
　slope 217
　prepossession 481
　disposition 820
bib *pinafore* 225
　drink 959
bibber *weep* 839
　tope 959
bibble-babble 584
bibelot 847
bibendum, nunc
　est – 959
Bible 895
　– oath 535
biblioclasm 162
bibliography 593
bibliolatry
　learning 490
　heterodoxy 984
　idolatry 991
bibliomancy 511
bibliomania 490
bibliomaniac 492
bibliophile 492
bibliopole 593

bibliotheca 593
bibulous 298, 959
bicameral 90
bicapital 90
bice 435, 438
bicentenary 98,
　138, 883
bicker *flutter* 315
　quarrel 713
bicolour 440
biconjugate 91
bicuspid 91
bicycle 272
bid *order* 741
　offer 763
　– the banns 903
　– defiance 715
　– fair *tend* 176
　　probable 472
　　promise 511
　　hope 858
　– a long farewell
　　624
　– for *intend* 620
　　offer 763
　　request 765
　　bargain 794
bidder 767
bide *wait* 133
　remain 141
　take coolly 806
　– one's time 133
　watch 507
　inactive 681
bidet 271
biennial
　periodic 138
　plant 367
bienséance 852, 894
bier 363
bifacial 90
bifarious 90
bifid 91
bifold 90
biform 90
bifurcate 91, 244
big *in degree* 31
　in size 192
　wide 194
　look – *defy* 715
　　proud 878
　　insolent 885
　talk – 885, 909
　– sounding
　　loud 404
　　words 577
　　affected 855
　– swollen 194
　– with 161
　– with the fate of
　　511

bigamy 903
biggin 191
bight 343
bigot *positive* 474
  prejudice 481
  obstinate 606
  heterodox 984
  impious 988
bigotry 907
bigwig *scholar* 492
  sage 500
  nobility 875
bijou *goodness* 648
  beauty 845
  ornament 847
bilander 273
bilateral 90, 236
bilbao 727
bilboes 752
  put into – 751
bile 900
bilge *base* 211
  convex 250
  yawn 260
  – water 653
bilious 837
bilingual 560
bilk
  disappoint 509
  cheat 545
  steal 791
bill *list* 86
  hatchet 253
  placard 531
  ticket 550
  paper 593
  plan 626
  weapon 727
  money order 800
  money account
    811
  charge 812
  in law 969
  true – 969
  – and coo 902
  – of exchange 771
  – of fare *food* 298
    plan 626
  – of indictment
    938
  –s of mortality 360
  – of sale 771
billet *locate* 184
  ticket 550
  apportion 786
billet *epistle* 592
  – doux 902
billfold 191
billhook 253
billiard – ball 249
  – room 191

– table *flat* 213
billiards 840
Billingsgate 563,
  908
billion 98
billow *sea* 348
  river 341
billy-cock 225
billy-goat 373
bimetallism 800
bin 191
binary 89
bind *connect* 43
  cover 223
  compel 744
  condition 770
  obligation 926
  – hand and foot
    751
  – oneself 768
  – over 744
  – up wounds 660
binding 681, 744
bine 367
binnacle 693
binocular 445
binomial 89
biogenesis 161
biograph 448
biography 594
biology 357, 359
bioscope 448
biota 357
biparous 89
bipartite 44, 91
biplane 273
biplicity 89
biquadrate 96
birch *flog* 972
  – rod 975
bird 366
  kill two –s with
    one stone 682
  –'s eye view 441,
    448
  –s of a feather 17
  the – has flown
    187, 671
  – in hand 777, 781
  – of ill omen
    omen 512
    warning 668
    hopeless 859
  – of passage 268
  – of prey 739
  a little – told me
    527
birdcage 370
birdlime *glue* 45
  trap 545
biretta 999

birth *beginning* 66
  production 161
  paternity 166
  nobility 875
  – place 153
  – right 924
birthday 138, 883
  – suit 226
birthmark 848
bis *repeat* 104
  approval 931
biscuits, s'embar-
  quer sans – 674
bise 349
bisection 68, **91**
bishop *punch* 298
  clergy 996
  –'s palace 1000
  –'s purple 437
bishopric 995
bisque 33
bissextile 138
bistoury 253
bistre 433
bisulcate 259
bit
  small quantity 32
  part 51
  interval 106
  curb 752
  just a – 26
  – by bit
  by degrees 26
  by instalments 51
  in detail 79
  slowly 275
  – between the
    teeth 600, 719
bitch *animal* 366
  female 374
  clumsy 699
  fail 732
  impure 962
bite *eat* 298
  physical pain 378
  cold 385
  cheat 545
  dupe 547
  etch 558
  mental pain 830
  – the dust 725
  – in 259
  – the thumb 900,
    929
  – the tongue 392
biter bit 718
biting *pain* 378
  cold 383
  pungent 392
  painful 830
  discourteous 895

censorious 932
bitten 897
bitter *beer* 298
  cold 383
  taste 392, 395
  painful 830
  acrimonious 895
  hate 898
  angry 900
  malevolent 907
  – end 67
  – ender 606, 710,
    832
  – pill 735
  – words 932
bitterly *greatly* 31
bitterness
  [*see* bitter]
  pain 828
  regret 833
bitumen 356*a*
bituminous coal
  388
bivouac
  encamp 184
  camp 189
  repose 265
  watch 668
bi-weekly 138
bizarre 83, 853
blab 529
blabber 584
black *colour* 431
  crime 945
  look – *feeling* 821
  discontent 832
  angry 900
  – art 992
  – and blue
    beat 972
  – board 590
  – book 938
  – eye 848, 972
  – in the face
    swear 535
    excitement 821,
      824
  – flag 722
  – hole *crowd* 72
    prison 752
  – lead 556
  – letter *old* 124
    barbarism 563
    print 591
  – list 932
  – looks
    discourteous 895
    sullen 901*a*
    disapprove 932
    magic 998
  – mail *theft* 791

severe 739
hands in – *cruel* 907
in the – 5
life – 359
new – 658, 824
spill – *war* 722
– for blood 919
– boil *excite* 824, 825
anger 900
– run cold 830, 860
– heat 382
– horse 271
– hound 913
– letting 297, 662
– poisoning 655
– red 434
– stained 361
– sucker 789, 913
– thirsty *murderous* 361
cruel 907
– up *excited* 824
angry 900
bloodless 160
peace 721
virtue 946
bloody [*see* blood]
red 434
unclean 653
cruel 907
bloom *youth* 127
flower 367
blue 438
health 654
prosperity 734
bloomer 495
bloomers 225
blooming 654, 845
blossom
flower 154, 161, 367
prosperity 734
blot *blacken* 431
error 495
obliterate 552
dirty 653
blemish 848
disgrace 874
guilt 947
– out *destroy* 162
forgive 918
blotch 848
blouse 225
blow *expand* 194
knock 276
wind 349
unexpected 508

disappointment 509
evil 619
action 680
get wind 688
failure 732
prosper 734
pain 828, 830
come to –s 720, 722
deal a – at 716
deal a – to 972
death – 360, 361
– for blow 718
– one's brains out 361
– the coals 824
– down 162
– the fire 384
– the gaff 529
– hole 351
– the horn 416
– hot and cold *lie* 544
irresolute 605
tergiversation 607
caprice 608
– a kiss 902
– off *disperse* 73
– out *food* 298
darken 421
gorge 957
– over *past* 122
– pipe 349, 727
– the trumpet 873
– one's own trumpet 882
– up *destroy* 162
eruption 173
inflate 194
wind 349
excite 824
objurgate 932, 934
blower 349
blowhard 884
blown [*see* blow]
fatigued 688
proud 878
storm – over 664, 721
– upon 874, 932
blow-out 406
blowzy *swollen* 194
red 434
blubber *fat* 356
cry 839
Blucher boot 225
bludgeon 727
– man 726, 913
blue *sky* 338
colour 438

learned 490
bit of – hope 858
look –
disappointed 509
feeling 821
discontent 832
disrepute 874
out of the – 508
swear till all's – 535
true – 543, 939
– book 86, 551
– blood 875
– devils 837
– jacket 269
– light 550, 669
– pencil 174, 596
– moon 110
– Peter 293, 550
– and red 437
– ribbon 733, 877
– ruin 959
– stocking *scholar* 492
affectation 855
– and yellow 435
Bluebeard
marriage 903
libertine 962
blueness **438**
blues 837, 840
bluff *violent* 173
high cliff 206
blunt 254
deceive 545
boasting 884
insolent 885
discourteous 895
blunder *error* 495
absurdity 497
awkward 699
failure 732
– upon 156
blunderbuss 727
blunderhead 701
blunderheaded 499
blunt *weaken* 160
inert 172
moderate v. 174
obtuse 254
benumb 376
damp v. 616
plain-spoken 703
cash 800
deaden 823
discourteous 895
– tool 645
– witted 499
bluntness **254**
blur
imperfect vision

443
dirt 653
blemish 848
stigma 874
blurb 931
blurred
invisible 447
blurt out 529, 582
blush *flush* 382
redden 434
feel 821
humbled 879
modest 881
at first – *see* 441
appear 448
manifest 525
put to the –
humble 897
browbeat 885
discourtesy 895
blushing honours 873, 881
bluster *violent* 173
defiant 715
boasting 884
insolent 885
threaten 909
blusterer **887**
blustering [*see* bluster]
windy 349
Bo to a goose, not say – 862
boa 225
boanerges 540
boar 366, 373
board *layer* 204
support 215
food 298
hard 323
council 696
attack 716
tribunal 966
festive – 892
go by the – 158, 162
go on – 293
on – 186, 273
preside at the – 693
– of trade 621
– school 542
boarding-house 189
boarder 188
boards 599, 728
boast 884
not much to – of 651
boasting **884**
boaston 840
boat 273

in the same – 88
– race 720
boating 267
boatman 269
boatswain 269
bob *depress* 308
leap 309
oscillate 314
agitate 315
money 800
– a curtsy 894
– for *fish* 463
Bobadil, Captain –
887
bobbed
hair 53
bobbin 312
bobbing *fuel* 388
bobbish 654
bobby *police* 664
bobsleigh 272
bobsleighing 840
bobtailed 53
bocage 367
**bocca, per amusare
la** – 394
Boche 913
boddice 225
bode 511
bodega 189
bodily
substantially 3
wholly 50
material 316
– enjoyment 377
– fear 860
– pain 378
bodkin
go between 228
perforator 262
body *substance* 3
whole 50
assemblage 72
frame 215
matter 316
party 712
in a – *together* 88
– and blood of
Christ 987
– clothes 225
– colour 556
– of doctrine 490
– forth 554
– guard 717, 753
– of knowledge
490
– politic
mankind 372
authority 737
keep – and soul
together 654

– of water 438
Bœotian *rustic* 371
stupid 499
fool 501
vulgar 851
ignoble 876
Boer 371
bog 345, 653
– trotter 876
boggart 980
boggle *hesitate* 605
awkward 699
difficulty 704
bogie 980
truck 272
bogle 980
bogus 545
Bohemian
unconventional 83
nomad 268
ungenteel 851
boil *violence* 173
effervesce 315
bubble 353
heat 382, 384
ulceration 655
excitement 824,
825
anger 900
– down 195
boiler 386
boisterous
violent 173
hasty 684
excitable 825
bold *prominent* 250
unreserved 525
vigorous 574
brave 861
make – with 895
show a – front 715,
861
– faced 885
– push *essay* 675
– relief *visible* 446
– stroke *plan* 626
success 731
bole 50
bolero 840
bollard 45
bolshevik 144, 146
bolshevist 737, 742
bolster *support* 215
repair 658
aid 707
– up *vindicate* 937
bolt *sift* 42
fasten 43
fastening 45
close 261
move rapidly 274

propel 284
run away 623
escape 671
hindrance 706
shaft 727
disobey 742
shackle 752
thunder – 872
– the door 761
– food 298, 957
– in 751
– upright 212
bolthead 191
bolus *mouthful* 298
remedy 662
bomb 404, 727
– proof 664, 717
– vessel 726
bombard 716
bombardier 726
bombardon 417
bombast
unmeaning 517
magniloquence
577
ridiculous 853
boasting 884
exaggeration 549
Bombastes Furioso
887
bomber
aeroplane 726
bombilation 404
bon de – *augure*
858
– *enfant social* 892
kindly 906
– *gré mal gré* 601
– *marché* 815
– *mot* 842
– *naturel* 836
– *ton* 852
– *vivant* 957
– *voyage* 293
bona – *fides*
veracity 543
probity 939
– *roba* 962
bonanza 641, 784
wealth 803
bonbon 396
bond *relation* 9
tie 45
compact 769
security 771
money 800
right 924
– of union 9, 45
government – 802
Liberty – 802
bondage 749

bonded together
712
bonds [*see* bond]
fetters 752
funds 802
in – *service* 746
tear asunder one's
– 750
– of harmony 714
bondsman 746
bone *strength* 159
dense 321
hard 323
bred in the – 5
feel it in one's –
510
– of contention
713, 720
one – and one flesh
903
– to pick *difficulty*
704
discord 713
– setter 662
bonehouse 363
boner 495
bones [*see* bone]
corpse 362
music 417
break no – 648
make no – 602,
705
boneyard 363
bonfire 382
festivity 840
celebration 883
make a – of 384
bonhomie 703, 906
bonhomme 996
Boniface 890
bonne 746, 753
– *bouche end* 67
pleasant 377
savoury 394
saving 636
à la – *heure* 602,
831
de – *volonté* 602
bonnet 225
bonny 836, 845
bono: cui –
intention 620
utility 644
inutility 645
pro – *publico* 644,
910
bonus *extra* 641
gift 784
money 810
bony 323
bonze 996

bonzer 648
booby 501
– trap 545
boodle 793
book *register* 86
publication 531
   record 551
   volume **593**
   script 599
   enter accounts 811
at one's –s 539
bring to –
   evidence 467
   account 811
   reprove 932
mind one's – 539
school – 542
without –
   by heart 505
– of Books 985
– club 593
– of fate 601
– learning 490
– shop 593
book-case 191
booked *dying* 360
bookish 490
bookkeeper 553
bookkeeping 811
bookless
   unlearned 493
bookmaking 156
bookseller 593
bookworm 492, 593
boom
   support 215
   sail 267
   rush 274
   impulse 276
   sound 404
   obstacle 706
   defence 717
boomerang
   recoil 277
   retribution 718
   weapon 727
boon 784
   beg a – 765
– companion 890
boor *clown* 876
boorish 851, 895
boost 276, 482, 931
booster 935
boot *box* 191
   dress 225
   advantage 618
   punishment 975
   to – *added* 37
– legging 964
booted and spurred
   673

booth 189, 799
bootless 645, 732
boots *dress* 225
   servant 746
   low person 876
   what – it? 643
booty **793**
booze 959
bo-peep 441, 528
bordel 961
border *edge* 231
   limit 233
   flower bed 371
   ornament 847
– upon 197, 199
bore *diameter* 202
   hole 260
   tide 348, 667
   fatigue 688
   trouble 828
   plague 830
   weary 841
bored 456
boreal
   Northern 237
   cold 383
Boreas 349
boredom 841
borer 262
born 359
– so 5
– under an evil
   star 735
– under a lucky
   star 734
borne 826
– down *failure* 732
   defection 837
borné 499
borough 181, 189
   rotten – 893
– council 696
borrow 19, 788
– of Peter &c. 147
borrowed plumes
   deception 545
borrower 806
borrowing 788
bosh *absurdity* 497
   unmeaning 517
   untrue 546
   trifling 643
bosky 959
bosom *breast* 221
   mind 450
   affections 820
   in the – of 229
– of one's family
   221
– friend 890

boss 250, 694, 737
   straw – 694
boston 840
botanic garden 369,
   371
Botanomancy 511
Botany 367, **369**
botch *bungle* 59
   mend 660
   unskilful 699
   difficulty 704
   fail 732
both 89
   listen with – ears
   418
   burn the candle at
   – ends 641
   butter one's bread
   on – sides 641
bother
   uncertainty 475
   bustle 682
   difficulty 704
   trouble 828
   harass 830
bothy 189
bottle
   receptacle 191
   preserve 670
   bee in a – 407
   crack a – 298
   pass the – 959
   smelling – 400
– green 435
– holder
   auxiliary 177
   mediator 724
– up *remember* 505
   hide 528
   restrain 751
bottom
   lowest part 211
   support 215
   posterior 235
   combe 252
   ship 273
   pluck 604a
   courage 861
   at – 5
   at the – of
   cause 153
   go to the – 310
   probe to the – 461
   from the – of one's
   heart *veracity*
   543
   feeling 821
– upwards 218
– land 180, 207
bottomless 208
– pit 982

angel of the – pit
   978
bottomry 771
botulism 663
bouche:
   bonne – *end* 67
   savoury 394
   saving 636
   pleasant 829
– à feu 727
bouderie 901a
boudoir 191
bouffe, opera 599
bouge 250
bough *part* 51
   curve 245
   tree 367
bought *flexure* 245
bougie 423
boulder 249
boulevards 227
bouleversement
   revolution 146
   destruction 162
   excite 824
bouillabaise 298
bouillon 298
bounce *violence* 173
   jump 309
   lie 546
   boast 884
   insolence 885
– upon 292, 508
bouncing *large* 192
bound
   circumscribe 229
   swift 274
   leap 309
   certain 474
   I'll be – 535
– back *recoil* 277
– by 926
– for *direction* 278
   destination 620
– to *promise* 768
   responsible 926
boundary 233
bounden duty 926
bounder 851
boundless 105, 180
bounds 230, 233
   keep within –
   moderation 174
   shortcoming 304
   restrain 751
   prohibit 761
– of possibility 470
bountiful 816, 906
   Lady – 816
bounty *gift* 784
bouquet

breach *crack* 44
 gap 198
 quarrel 713
 violation 925
 custom honoured
  in the – 614
 – of faith 940
 – of law 83, 964
 – of the peace 713
bread 298
 beg – 765
 selfish 943
 quarrel with –
  and butter 699
 – of idleness 683
 – of life *Christ* 976
 piety 987
 – upon the waters
  638
 – and wine 998
breadbasket 191
breadth 202
 chiaroscuro 420
break
 fracture 44
 discontinuity 70
 change 140
 gap 198
 carriage 272
 crumble 328
 disclose 529
 cashier 756
 violate 773, 927
 bankrupt 808
 – away 623
 – bread 298
 – bulk 297
 – camp 293
 – of day *morning*
  125
 twilight 422
 – down *destroy*
  162
 fall short 304
 decay 659
 fail 732
 dance 840
 – one's fetters 614
 – forth 295
 – ground 66
 – a habit 614
 – the heart *pain*
  828, 830
 dejection 837
 – the ice 888
 – in *ingress* 294
 domesticate 370
 teach 537
 tame 749
 – in upon *derange*
  61

inopportune 135
 hinder 706
 – a lance 716, 722
 – a law 83
 – loose 671, 750
 – one's neck
 powerless 158
 die 360
 – the neck of
 task 676
 success 731
 – the news 529
 – no bones 648
 – of 660
 – off *cease* 142
 relinquish 624
 abrogate 756
 – out *begin* 66
 violent 173
 disease 655
 excited 825
 – the peace 173,
  720
 – Priscian's head
  568
 – prison 750
 – the ranks 61
 – short 328
 – silence 582
 – the teeth 579
 – the thread 70
 – through the
  clouds *visible*
  446
 disclose 529
 – through a cus-
  tom 614
 – up *disjoin* 44
 decompose 49
 end 67
 révolution 146
 destroy 162
 – up of the system,
  360, 665
 – on the wheel
 physical pain 378
 mental pain 830
 punishment 972
 – with 713
 – with the past
  146
 – word *deceive* 525
 improbity 940
breaker
 of horses 268
 reef 346
 wave 348
breakers 348, 667
 surrounded by –
  704
 – ahead 665

breakfast 298
breakneck
 precipice 217
 rash 863
breakwater
 refuge 666
 obstruction 706
breast *interior* 221
 confront 234
 convex 250
 mind 450
 oppose 708
 soul 820
 at the – 129
 in the – of 620
 – the current 719
 – high 206
breastplate 717
breastwork 717
breath *instant* 113
 breeze 349
 life 359
 animality 364
 faint sound 405
 with bated – 581
 hold – *quiet* 265
 expect 507
 wonder 870
 not a – of air 265,
  382
 out of – 688
 in the same – 120
 shortness of – 688
 take – 265, 689
 take away one's –
 unexpected 508
 fear 860
 wonder 870
breathe *exist* 1
 blow 349
 live 359
 faint sound 405
 evince 467
 mean 516
 inform 527
 disclose 529
 utter 580
 speak 582
 refresh 689
 – freely 827, 834
 – one's last 360
 not – a word 528
breathing time 687,
  723
breathless
 voiceless 581
 out of breath 688
 feeling 821
 fear 860
 eager 865
 wonder 870

 – attention 457
 – expectation 507
 – impatience 865
 – speed 684
bred in the bone 820
breech 235
 – loader 727
breeches 225
 wear the – 737
 – buoy 666
 – maker 225
 – pocket
 money 800, 802
breed *kind* 75
 multiply 161
 progeny 167
 animals 370
 rear 537
breeding 161, 852,
  894
breeze *wind* 349
 discord 713
breezy 836
brethren 997
breve 413
brevet
 warrant 741
 commission 755
 permit 760
 – rank 873
breviary 998
brevier 591
brevity 201, 572
brew 41, 673
brewing
 impending 152
 storm – 665
bribe *equivalent* 30
 tempt 615
 offer 763
 gift 784
 buy 795
 expenditure 809
 reward 973
bric-à-brac 847
brick *hard* 323
 pottery 384
 material 635
 trump 939, 948
 make -s without
  straw 471
 – colour 434
brickbat 727
bricklayer 690
bride 903
bridewell 752
bridge 45, 627
 – over *join* 43
 facilitate 705
 make peace 723
 compromise 774

cards 840
bridle *restrain* 751
  rein 752
  – road 627
  – one's tongue
    585, 864
  – up 900
brief *time* 111
  space 201
  concise 572
  compendium 596
  hold a – for 759
  – case 191
briefly *anon* 132
brier
  sharp 253
  pipe 390
  bane 663
brig 273
brigade 726
brigadier 745
brigand 792
brigandage 791
brigandine 717
brigantine 273
bright *shine* 420
  colour 428
  intelligent 498
  cheery 836
  beauty 845
  glory 873
  – days 734
  – eyed 845
  – prospect 858
  – side 829
  look at the – side
    836, 858
  – thought
  sharp 498
  good stroke 626
  wit 842
brighten up
  furbish 658
brigue 712, 720
brilliant
  shining 420
  good 648
  wit 842
  beautiful 845
  gem 847
  glorious 873
  – idea 842
brilliantine 356
brim 231
  – over 641
brimful 52
brimstone 388
brindled 440
brine 341, 392
bring 270
  – about 153, 729

– back 790
– back to the
    memory 505
– to bear upon
  relation 9
  action 170
– into being 161
– to a crisis 604
– forth 161
– forward
  evidence 467
  manifest 525
  teach 537
  improve 658
– grey hairs to the
    grave 735, 830
– grist to the mill
    644
– home 775
– home to 155
– in *receive* 296
  income 810
  price 812
– to life 359
– to light 480a
– low 874
– to maturity 673,
    729
– to mind 505
– under one's
    notice 457
– off 672
– out
  discover 480a
  manifest 525
  publish 591
– over
  persuade 484
– to perfection
    677
– into play 677
– to a point 74
– in question 461
– up the rear 235
– round
  persuade 615
  restore 660
– to terms 723
– to *convert* 144
  halt 265
– together 72
– in its train 88
– to trial 969
– up *develop* 161
  vomit 297
  educate 537
– in a verdict 480
– word 527
brink 231
  on the –
  almost 32

coming 121
  near 197
  – of the grave 360
briny 392
  – ocean 341
brio *music* 415
  active 682
brisk *prompt* 111
  energetic 171
  active 682
  cheery 836
bristle 253
  – up *stick up* 250
  angry 900
  – with 639, 641
  – with arms 722
bristly 256
Britannia metal
    545
Briticism 563
British 188
  – lion 604
Briton, true – 939
  work like a – 686
brittleness 328
britzska 272
broach *begin* 66
  found 153
  reamer 262
  tap 297
  publish 531
  assert 535
broad *general* 78
  space 202
  lake 343
  emphatic 535
  indelicate 961,
    962
  – accent 580
  – awake 459, 682
  – daylight 420,
    525
  – farce 842
  – grin 838
  – highway 627
  – hint 527
  – meaning 516
  – minded 498
broadcast
  disperse 73
  spread 78
  publish 531
  sow – 818
broadcloth 219
broadhearted 906
broadsheet 593
broad-shouldered
    159
broadside 236
  publication 531
  cannonade 716

broadsword 727
Brobdingnagian
    192
brocade 847
brochure 593
Brocken, spectre of
    the 443
broder 549
brogue *boot* 225
  dialect 563
broidery 847
broil *heat* 382
  fry 384
  fray 713, 720
broke *poor* 804
broken
  discontinuous 70
  weak 160
  – colour 428
  – down
  decrepit 659
  failing 732
  dejected 837
  – English 563
  – fortune 735, 804
  – heart 828, 837
  hopeless 859
  – reed 160, 665
  – meat 645
  – voice 581, 583
  – winded
  disease 655
  fatigue 688
broker 758, 797
brokerage *pay* 812
brokery 794
bromidic 613
bronchia 351
bronze *alloy* 41
  brown 433
  sculpture 557
brooch 847
brood 102, 167
  – over 451, 847
brooding
  preparing 673
brook *stream* 348
  bear 821, 826
broom 652
broth 298
brothel 961
brother *kin* 11
  similar 17
  equal 27
brotherhood 712
brotherly
  friendship 888
  love 897
  benevolence 906
brougham 272
brought to bed 161

brouillerie 713
brouillon 626
brow *top* 210
  edge 231
  front 234
browbeat
  intimidate 860
  swagger 885
  disrespect 929
  —en *humbled* 879
brown 433
  — Bess 727
  — *study* 451, 458
Brown, Jones and
  Robinson 876
brownie 980
browse 298
bruin 895
bruise *powder* 330
  hurt 619
  injure 649
  blemish 848
bruiser 726
bruit
  report 531, 532
brumal 126, 383
brumous 353
Brummagem 545
brunette 433
brunt *beginning* 66
  impulse 276
  bear the —
  difficulty 704
  defence 717
  endure 821, 826
brush *rough* 256
  rapid motion 274
  graze 379
  clean 652
  fight 720
  paint — 556
  — *away reject* 297
  abrogate 756
  — up *clean* 652
  furbish 658
  prepare 673
brushwood 367
brusque *violent* 173
  haste 684
  discourtesy 895
brutal *vulgar* 851
  rude 895
  savage 907
brutalize
  [*see* brutal]
  corrupt 659
  deaden 823
  vice 945
brute *animal* 366
  rude 895
  maleficent 913

— force
  strength 159
  violence 173
  animal 450a
  severe 739
  compulsion 744
  lawless 964
  — *matter* 316, 358
Brute, et tu 917
brutish [*see* brute]
  vulgar 851
  ignoble 876
  intemperate 954
brutum fulmen
  impotent 158
  failure 732
  lax 738
  boast 884
bubble
  unsubstantial 4
  transient 111
  little 193
  convexity 250
  light 320
  water 348
  air **353**
  error 495
  deceit 545
  trifle 643
  — burst
  fall short 304
  disappoint 509
  fail 732
  — *reputation* 873
  — and squeak 298
  — up *agitation* 315
buccaneer 791, 792
bucentaur 273
Bucephalus 271
buck *stag* 366
  male 373
  wash 652
  money 800
  fop 854
  — basket 191
  — jump 309
  — up 684
bucket 191
  kick the — 360
  drop — in empty
    well 645
  like —s in well 314
buckle *tie* 43
  fastening 45
  distort 243
  curl 248
  — on one's armour
    673
  — to 604, 686
  — with *grapple* 720
buckler 717

buckram 855, 878
  men in — 549
bucolic
  pastoral 370
  poem 597
bud 367
  beginning 66
  germ 153
  expand 194
  graft 300
  — from 154
Buddha 979, 986
Buddhism 984
budding *young* 127
buddy 711, 890
budge 264
budget *heap* 72
  bag 191
  store 636
  finance 811
  — of news 532
buff 436
  blind man's — 840
  native — 226
buffer
  hindrance 706
  defence 717
buffet 191
  strike 276
  agitate 315
  evil 619
  bad 649
  affront 900
  smite 972
  — the waves 704,
    708
  bar 189
buffo 599
buffoon *actor* 599
  humorist 844
  butt 857
buffoonery 840, 842
bug 653
bugaboo 669, 860
bugbear
  imaginary 155
  bane 663
  alarm 669
  fear 860
buggy 272
bugle
  instrument 417
  war-cry 722
  ornament 847
  — call 550, 741
build *construct* 161
  form 240
  — anew 658
  — upon a rock 150
  — up *compose* 54
  — upon *belief* 484

builder 626, 690
building material
  635
buildings 189
built on *basis* 211
bulb 249, 250
bulge 250
bulk 50, 192
  — large 31
bulkhead 228, 706
bull *animal* 366
  male 373
  error 495
  absurdity 497
  solecism 568
  police 664
  ordinance 741
  — in a china shop
    59
  like a — at a gate
    173
  take the — by the
    horns 604, 861
Bull, John — 188
bullcalf 501
bulldog *animal* 366
  pluck 604, 604a
  courage 861
bulldoze 885
bullet *ball* 249
  arms 727
  missile 284
bulletin 532, 592
  — board 551
bullfight 720
bullhead 501
bullion 800
bullseye *centre* 222
  lantern 423
  aim 620
bully *fighter* 726
  maltreat 830
  frighten 860
  courage 861
  rashness 863
  bluster 885
  blusterer 887
  threaten 909
  evil doer 913
  bad man 949
bulrush
  worthless 643
bulwark 706, 717
bum 876
bumbailiff 965
bumbledom 737,
  965
bumboat 273
bump 250, 276
  — off 361
bumper 52

- appetite 865
canister 191
canker *disease* 655
  deterioration 659
  bane 663
  pain 830
canned goods 670
cannel coal 388
cankered
  sullen 901a
cankerworm 663
  evil-doer 913
  care 830
cannibal 913
cannibalism 945
cannon
  collision 276
  loud 404
  arms 727
  - fodder 726
  -'s mouth *war* 722
  courage 861
cannonade 716
cannonball 249, 274
cannoneer 726
cannot 271
cannular 260
canny 498, 702
  ca' - 864
canoe 273
  paddle one's own
  - 748
canon *rule* 80
  ravine 198
  music 415
  belief 484
  precept 697
  priest 996
  rite 998
  - law 697
canonical
  regular 82
  inspired 985
  ecclesiastical 995
canonicals **999**
canonist 983
canonization
  repute 873
  deification 991
  rite 998
canonry 995
canopy 223
  - of heaven 318
canorous 413
cant *oblique* 217
  jerk 276
  hypocrisy 544
  neology 563
  impiety 988
cantabile 415
cantankerous 901,

901a
cantata 415
  missa - 998
cantatrice 416
canteen 189, 191
canter 266, 274
  win at a - 705
canterbury
  receptacle 191
Canterbury tale
  546
cantharides 171
canticle 415
cantilever 215
canting 855
cantle 51
cantlet 32, 51
canto 597
canton 181, 737
cantonment 184,
  189
cantrap 993
canty 836
canvas *sail* 267
  picture 556
  under press of -
  274
canvass
  investigate 461
  discuss 476
  dissert 595
  solicit 765
canvasser 767
canyon 350
canzonet 415, 597
caoutchouc 325
cap *be superior* 33
  height 206
  summit 210
  cover 223
  hat 225
  retaliate 718
  complete 929
  salute 894
  fling up one's -
  838
  Fortunatus's - 993
  set one's - at 897,
  902
  - and bells 844
  - fits 23
  - in hand
  request 765
  servile 886
  respect 928
  - of maintenance
  747
capability
  endowment 5
  power 157
  skill 698

facility 705
capacious *space* 180
  - memory 505
capacity
  endowment 5
  power 157
  space 180
  size 192
  intellect 450
  wisdom 498
  office 625
  talent 698
cap-à-pie
  complete 52
  armed -
    prepared 673
    defence 717
    war 722
caparison 225
cape *height* 206
  cloak 225
  projection 250
capella, alla - 415
caper *leap* 309
  dance 840
capful *quantity* 25
  small 32
  - of wind 349
capillament 205
capillary
  hairlike 205
  thin 203
capital *city* 189
  top 201
  letter 561
  important 642
  excellent 648
  money 800
  wealth 803
  make - out of
    pretext 617
    acquire 775
  print in -s 642
  - messuage 189
  - punishment 972
  ship 726
capitalist 803
capitation 85
  - tax 812
capitol 189, 717
capitular 995, 996
capitulate 725
capnomancy 511
capon 373
caponize 38, 158
capote 225
capouch 999
capper 548
capriccio *music* 415
  whim 608
caprice **608**

out of - 615a
capricious
  irregular 139
  changeable 149
  irresolute 605
  whimsical 608
capriole 309
capsize 218, 731
capsized 732
capstan 307, 633
capstone 210
capsular 252
capsule *vessel* 190
  tunicle 223
  medicine 662
captain 269, 745
captandum, ad -
  sophistry 477
  deception 545
  affectation 855
  ostentation 882
  flattery 933
captation 933
captious
  capricious 608
  irascible 901
  censorious 932
caption
  taking 789
  beginning 66
  heading 564
captivate
  induce 615
  restrain 751
  please 829
captivated 827
captivating 829, 897
captive
  prisoner 754
  adorer 897
  lead - 749
  make - 751
  - balloon 273
captivity 751
capture 789
Capuchin 996
caput 696
  - mortuum 645,
  653
caquet 584
car 272
carabineer 726
carack 273
caracole 309
caracoler 266
caraffe 191
caramel 396
carambole 276
carapace 717
cara sposa 897
carat 309

cartes sur table
525, 543
Carthago, delenda
est – 908
Carthusian 996
cartilage
dense 321
hard 323
tough 327
cartography 466,
554
cartoon 21, 556
cartoonist 559
cartouche
ammunition 727
ornament 847
cartridge 727
cartulary 86, 551
caruncle 250
carve *cut* 44
make 161
form 240
sculpture 557
apportion 786
– one's way 282
carvel 273
carver 559
caryatides 215
Cary's chickens,
Mother – 668
cascade 348
case *state* 7
box 191
sheath 223
topic 454
argument 476
specification 527
grammar 567
affair 625
patient 655
law-suit 969
be the – 1, 494
in good – 654, 734
in –
circumstance 8
event 151
supposition 514
make out a – 467,
924
– in point 23, 82
caseation 321
caseharden
strengthen 159
habituate 613
case-hardened
callous 376, 823
obstinate 606
casemate 189, 717
casement 260
casern 189
cash *money* 800

pay 807
in – 803
pay – for 795
– account 811
– book 551
– box 802
– down 807
– register 85, 553,
802
cashier *dismiss* 756
treasurer 801
casing 223
casino 712; 840
cask 191
casket 191
casque 717
Cassandra 513, 668
cassation 552
casserole 191
Cassiopeia's chair
318
cassock 999
cast *mould* 21
small quantity 32
spread 73
tendency 176
form 240
throw 284
tinge 428
aspect 448
drama 599
reject 610
plan 626
company 712
give 784
allot 786
condemn 971
give one a – 707
set on a – 621
– about for 463
– accounts 811
– adrift *disperse* 73
eject 297
liberate 750
dismiss 756
– anchor 265, 292
– aside 460
– aspersions 934
– away 610, 638
lost 732
– behind one
forget 506
refuse 764
relinquish 782
– away care 836
– off clothes 645
– of countenance
448
– of the dice 156
– in a different

mould 18
– dishonour &c.
upon 874
– to the dogs 162
– down 308, 837
– in the eye 443
– the eyes back
122
– eyes on 441
– the eyes over
457
– a gloom 837
– off a habit 614
– iron 323
resolute 604
– in one's lot with
609
– lots 621
– lustre upon 420
– of mind 820
– a nativity 511,
992
– one's net 463
– off *divest* 226
disused 678
dismiss 756
relinquish 782
– over-board 678
– the parts 60
– reflection upon
932
– in the same
mould 17
– a shade 421
– the skin 226
– a slur 874
accuse 938
– a spell 992
– off trammels 750
– up *add* 85
happen 151
eject 297
castanet 417
castaway *exile* 893
reprobate 949
caste 75, 873
lose – 940
castellan 746, 753
castellated 717
caster *cruet* 191
wheel 312
castigate 932, 972
castigator 936
casting 21
casting – vote 480
– weight 28, 30
castle *at chess* 148
abode 189
defence 717
– in the air
impossible 471

imagination 515
hope 858
Castle of Indolence
683
castor *hat* 225
Castor and Pollux
89, 890
castrametation
189, 722
castrate *subduct* 38
impotent 158
casual *extrinsic* 6
chance 156
uncertain 475
lax 773
casualty *event* 151
killed 361
evil 619
misfortune 735
casuist 476
casuistry
sophistry 477
falsehood 544
duty 926
casus belli
quarrel 713
irritation 824,
900
casus foederis 770
cat *nine lives* 359
animal 366
keen sight 441
fall on one's feet
734
cross 901
gib –, tom – *male*
373
rain –s and dogs
348
let – out of bag
529
– boat 273
– burglar 792
– call *whistle* 417
disapproval 932
–'s cradle 219
– and dog life 713
as the – jumps
event 151
see how the –
jumps 510
fickleness 607
caution 864
– o' nine tails 975
– in pattens 652
–'s paw *dupe* 547
instrumental 631
use 677
auxiliary 711
catabasis 36
catachresis 521, 523

concord 714
cemetery 363
cenobite 893, 996
cenotaph 363
censer 998
censor
 moderate 174
 critic 480
 ban 761
 detractor 936
censorious 480, 932
censurable 947
censure 932
censurer 936
census 85, 86
 record 551
centaur 83, 366
centenarian 130
centenary
 hundred 98
 period 138
 celebration 883
centesimal 99
cento 597
centrality 222
centralize
 combine 48
centre 68, 222
 – *round* 72, 290
centrifugal 291
centripetal 290
centroidal 222
centuple 98
centurion 745
century
 hundred 98
 period 108
 long time 110
 money 800
ceramic
 bake 384
 – *ware* 557
cerate 662
Cerberus
 janitor 263
 custodian 664
 hades 932
 sop for – 615
cereal 298
cerebration 451
cerebrum 450
cere-cloth 363
cerement
 covering 223
 wax 356
 burial 363
ceremonious 928
ceremony
 parade 882
 courtesy 894
 rite 998

Ceres 979
cerise 434
cerography 558,
 590
Ceromancy 511
ceroplastic 557
certain *special* 79
 indefinite number
 100
 sure 474
 belief 484
 true 494
 make – of 480a
 of a – age 128
 to a – degree 32
certainly *yes* 488
certainness 474
certainty **474**
certes 474, 488
certificate
 evidence 467
 record 551
 security 771
certify 467, 535
certiorari 969
certitude 474
cerulean 438
cess *tax* 812
 sewer 653
cessation **142**
cession
 surrender 725
 of property 782
 gift 784
cesspool 653
cestui-que trust 779
cestus 45, 247
chafe
 physical pain 378
 warm 384
 irritate 825
 mental pain 828,
 830
 discontent 832
 incense 900
chaff *trash* 643
 ridicule 856
 vulgar 876
 not to be caught
 with – 698, 702
 winnow – from
 wheat 609
chaffer 794
chafing-dish 386
chagrin 828
chain *fasten* 43
 vinculum 45
 series 69
 measure 200
 interlinking 219
 measure 466

gearing 633
imprison 752
ornament 847
drag a – 749
drag a lengthened
 – 686
in –s 754
chain gang 752, 972
chain-shot 727
chair *support* 215
 vehicle 272
 professorship 542
 throne 747
 celebration 883
 president 694
 in the – 693
chairman 694
chaise 272
chalcography 558
chalet 189
chalice 191, 998
chalk *earth* 342
 white 430
 mark 550
 drawing 556
 – from cheese 14,
 491
 – out *plan* 626
challenge
 question 461
 doubt 485
 claim 924
 defy 715
 accuse 938
 – comparison 648
cham 745
chamber *room* 191
 council 696
 mart 799
 sick – 655
chamberlain 746
chambermaid 746
chameleon 149, 440
chamfer 259
chamois 309
champ 298
 – the bit *disobedi-*
 ent 742
 chafe 825
 angry 900
champagne 298
champaign 344
champain 874
Champ de Mars
 728
champêtre, fête –
 840
champion
 best 648
 auxiliary 711
 defence 717

combatant 726
representative 759
sympathizer 914
championship 707
chance **156, 621**
 be one's – 151
 game of – 840
 great – 472
 small – 473
 stand a – 177, 470
 take one's – 675
 –s against one 665
 whirligig of – 156
 as – would have it
 152
chancel 1000
chancellor
 president 745
 deputy 759
 judge 967
 – of the exchequer
 801
chancery
 court of – 966
 – suit *delay* 133
chandelier 214, 423
chandelle, le jeu
 n'en vaut pas la
 – 638, 643
 dear 814
chandler 797
change
 alteration **140**
 mart 799
 small coin 800
 inter– 148
 radical – 146
 sudden – 146
 – about 149
 – colour 821
 – for 147
 – hands 783
 – of mind 607
 – of opinion 485
 – of place 264
changeableness
 149, 605
changeful
 fickle 607
changeling
 substitute 147
 fool 501
changeless 16
changer 797
channel
 furrow 259
 opening 260
 conduit 350
 way 627
chant *song* 415
 sing 416

worship 990
chant du cygne 360
chanter 416
chanticleer 366
chantry 1000
chaomancy 511
chaos 59
chap *crack* 198
  jaw 231
  fellow 373
  – book 593
chapel 1000
chaperon
  accompany 88
  watch 459
  protect 664
chapfallen 878
chaplain 995, 996
chaplet *circle* 247
  garland 550
  trophy 733
  ornament 847
chapman 797
chapter *part* 51
  topic 454
  book 593
  council 696
  church 995
  – of accidents
    156, 621
  – house 1000
  – and verse 467,
    494
char *burn* 384
  serve 746
char-à-banc 272
character
  nature 5
  state 7
  class 75
  oddity 83
  letter 561
  drama 599
  disposition 820
  reputation 873
characteristic
  intrinsic 5
  special 79
  tendency 176
  mark 550
characterize 564,
  594
characterized 820
charade 533, 599
charcoal *fuel* 384,
  388
  black 431
  drawing 556
charge *fill* 52
  contents 190
  business 625

requisition 630
  direction 693
  advice 695
  precept 697
  attack 716
  order 741
  custody 751
  commission 755
  bargain for 794
  price 812
  accusation 938
  in – prisoner 754
  justifiable – 937
  take – of 664
  take in – 751
  – on *attribute* 155
  – with 155, 777
chargé d'affaires
  758
chargeable *debt* 806
  – on *duty* 926
charger
  carrier 271
  fighter 726
Charing Cross, pro-
  claim at – 531
chariot 272
  drag at one's –
    wheels 749
charioteer 268, 694
charity *give* 784
  liberal 816
  beneficent 906
  pity 914
  Christian – 906
  cold as – 823
  – that begins at
    home 943
charivari 404, 407
charlatan
  ignoramus 493
  imposter 548
  mountebank 844
  boaster 884
charlatanism
  ignorance 491
  falsehood 544
  affectation 855
Charles's wain 318
Charleston 840
Charley 753
charm *motive* 615
  please 829
  beauty 845
  love 897
  conjure 992
  spell 993
  bear a –ed life 644,
    734
charmer 994
  voice of the – 933

not listen to voice
  of – 604
charnel-house 363
Charon 982
chart 527, 554
charter
  commission 755
  permit 760
  compact 769
  security 771
  privilege 924
chartered
  legal 963
  – accountant 801,
    811
  – libertine 962
Chartist 742
charwoman 690,
  746
chary
  economical 817
  stingy 819
  cautious 864
Charybdis 312, 665
chase *emboss* 250
  furrow 259
  drive away 289
  killing 361
  forest 367
  pursue 622
  ornament 847
  wild goose – 645
chaser 559
chasm *interval* 198
  opening 260
chassé 840
chassemarée 273
chassepot 727
chasser 297
  – balancer 605
chasseur 726
chassis 215
chaste
  shapely 242
  language 576, 578
  simple 849
  good taste 850
  pure 960
chasten
  moderate 174
  punish 972
chastened
  subdued spirit
    826
  penitent 950
chastise 932, 972
  – with scorpions
    739
chasuble 999
chat 588
chat qui dort 667,

668
château 189
  – en Espagne 858
chatelaine 847
chatoyant 440
chattels 633, 789
chatter 314, 584
chatterbox 584
chattering of teeth
  cold 383
chatty 584, 892
chauffeur 268
chaunt
  song 415
  sing 416
  worship 990
chaussé 225
Chauvinism 884,
  885
chawbacon 876
cheap 643, 815
  hold – 930
  – jack 797
cheapen *haggle* 794
  begrudge 819
cheapness **815**
cheat 545, 548
check
  numerical 85
  stop 142
  moderate 174
  counteract 179
  slacken 275
  plaid 440
  experiment 463
  measure 466
  evidence 468
  ticket 550
  dissuade 616
  hinder 706
  misfortune 735
  restrain 751
  money order 800
  – the growth 201
  – oneself 826
checkered 149
checkers 440, 840
checkmate
  stop 142
  success 731
  failure 732
check-roll 86
check-string
  pull the – 142
cheek *side* 236
  impertinence 885
  – by jowl *with* 88
  near 197
cheeks *dual* 89
cheep 412
cheer *repast* 298

unanimity 488
poetry 597
opera 599
concord 714
– girl 599
chose
– in action 780
– in possession 777
chouse 545
choux gras, faire ses – 377
chrestomathy 560
chrism 998
Christ 976
  Church of – 893*a*
  receive – 987
Christ-cross-row 561
christen 564, 998
Christendom 983*a*, 995
Christian 983*a*, 987
– charity 906
– science 662, 984
Christmas 138, 998
Christmas-box 784
chromatic
  colour 428
– scale *music* 413
chromato-pseudoblepsis 443
chromatrope 445
chrome 436
chromolithograph 558
chromosphere 318
chronic 110
chronicle
  measure time 114
  annals 551
chronicler 553
chronography
  measure time 114
  description 594
chronology 114
chronometry 114
Chrononhotonthologos 887
chrysalis 129
chrysoprase 847
chrysolite 847
  perfection 650
chrysology 800
chubby 192
chuck *throw* 284
  animal cry 412
– it 142
– under chin 902
chuck-farthing 621
chuckle

animal cry 412
laugh 838
exult 884
chuff 876
chum 711, 890
chunk 51
Church
  infallible 474
  orthodox 983*a*
  Christendom 995
  temple 1000
  dignitaries of – 996
  go to – 990
  High –, Low – &c. 984
– of Christ 983*a*
– bell 550
– house 1000
churchdom 995
churching 998
churchman 996
churchwarden 996
  pipe 392
churchyard 363, 1000
– cough 655
churl *boor* 876
churlish
  niggard 819
  rude 895
  sulky 901*a*
  malevolent 907
churn 315, 352
chut! *silent* 403
  taciturn 585
chute 348
chutney 393
chypre 400
cibarious 298
cicatrix 551
  manet – 919
cicatrize 660
Cicero 582
cicerone 524, 527
ciceronian 578
cicisbeo 897
cicuration 370
cider 298
cider squeezer 876
ci-devant 122
cigar 392
ci-git 363
cilia 205, 256
cimeter 727
Cimmerian 421
cinch 45
cincture 247
cinder
  combustion 384
  dirt 653

Cinderella
  servant 746
  commonalty 876
cinema 448, 599, 840
cinematograph 448
cinematographer 553
cinerary 363
cineration 384
cinereous 432
cingle 230
cinnabar 434
cinnamon 393, 433
cinque 98
cipher
  unsubstantial 4
  number 84
  compute 85
  zero 101
  concealment 528
  mark 550
  letter 561
  unimportant 643
  writing in – 590
Circe 615, 994
– an cup 377, 954
circination 312
circle *region* 181
  embrace 227
  form 247
  party 712
  describe a – 311
  great – sailing 628
– of acquaintance 892
– of the sciences 490
circlet 247
circling 248
circuit *region* 181
  outline 230
  winding 248
  tour 266
  indirect path 311
  indirect course **629**
circuition 311
circuitous 279, 311
– method 629
circular *round* 247
  publication 531
  letter 592
  pamphlet 593
– note 805
circularity 247
circularize 592
circulate
  circuit 311
  rotate 312
  publish 531

circulating medium 800
circulation
  [*see* circulate]
  in – *news* 532
– of money 809
circumambient 227, 229, 311, 629
circumambulate
  travel 266
  go round 311, 629
circumaviate 311
circumbendibus 248, 629
circumcision 44, 998
circumduction 552
circumference 230
circumferential 227
circumflex 311
circumfluent
  lie round 227
  move round 311
circumforaneous
  travelling 266
  circuition 311
circumfuse 73
circumgyration 312
circumjacence 227
circumlocution 573
circumnavigate
  navigation 267
  circuition 311
circumrotation 312
circumscribe
  surround 229
  limit 233, 761
circumscription **229**
circumspection
  attention 457
  care 459
  caution 459
circumstance
  phase 8
  event 151
circumstances
  property 780
  bad – 804
  depend on – 475
  good – 803
  under the – 8
circumstantial 8
– account 594
– evidence 467
  probability 472
circumstantiality 459
circumstantiate 467
circumvallation
  enclosure 229, 232

defence 717
line of − 233
circumvent
  environ 227
  move round 311
  cheat 545
  cunning 702
  hinder 706
  defeat 731
circumvest 225
circumvolution
  winding 248
  rotation 312
circus
  buildings 189
  drama 599
  arena 728
  amusement 840
cirrus 353
cistern
  receptacle 191
  store 636
Cistercian 996
cit 188
citadel 717
citation 467, 733
cite
  quote as example 82
  as evidence 467
  summon 741
  accuse 938
  arraign 969
cithern 417
citizen 188
− of the world 910
citriculture 371
citrine 436
city 189
  in the − 794
city manager 965
civet 400
civic 372
civil *courteous* 894
  laity 997
  − authorities 745
  − crown 733
  − law 963
  − war 722
civilian *lawyer* 968
  layman 997
civilization
  improvement 658
  fashion 852
  courtesy 894
civilized life 852
civism 910
clack *clatter* 407
  animal cry 412
  talkative 584
clad 225

claim *requisition* 630
  demand 741
  property 780
  right 924
  lawsuit 969
  − the attention 457
claimant
  petitioner 767
  right 924
clair-obscur 420
clairvoyance 992
clairvoyant 513, 994
clamant 411
clamber 305
clammy 352
clamorous
  [*see* clamour]
  loud 404
  excitable 825
clamour *cry* 411
  wail 839
  − against 932
  − for 765
clamp *fasten* 43
  fastening 45
clan *race* 11
  class 75
  family 166
  party 712
clandestine 528
clangor 404
clank 410
clannishness 481
clanship 709
clap *explosion* 406
  applaud 931
  thunder −
  prodigy 872
  − the hands
  rejoice 838
  − on 31
  − on the shoulder 615
  − together 43
  − up *imprison* 751
clapperclaw
  contention 720
  censure 932
claptrap
  pretence 546
  display 882
claquer 935
  faire − son fouet 884
clarence 272
claret colour 434
clarify 652
clarinet 417
clarion *music* 417

war 722
clarity 518
clash *disagree* 24
  cross 179
  concussion 276
  sound 406
  oppose 708
  discord 713
  − of arms 720
clasp *fasten* 43
  fastening 45
  stick 46
  come close 197
  belt 230
  embrace 902
class *arrange* 60
  category **75**
  learners 541
  party 712
  − prejudice 481
  − room 542
classic *old* 124
  symmetry 242
classical
  elegant writing 578
  taste 850
  − art 556
  − dancing 840
  − education 537
  − music 415
classicist 492
classics 560
classify 60
classmate 890
clatter 404, 407
claudication
  slowness 275
  failure 732
clause *part* 51
  passage 593
  condition 770
clausis, januis − 528
claustral 110
clavate 250
clavichord 417
clavier 417
claw *hook* 781
  grasp 789
  − back 935
clay *soft* 324
  earth 342
  corpse 362
  material 635
  − pipe 392
clay-cold 383
claymore 727
clean
  entirely 52
  perfect 650

unstained 652
− bill of health 654
− breast
  disclose 529
− forgotten 506
− hand
  proficient 700
with − hands
  honesty 939
  innocence 946
− out *empty* 297
− shaven 226
− sweep
  revolution 146
  destruction 162
clean-up 775
clear *simple* 42
  sound 413
  light 420
  transparent 425
  visible 446
  certain 474
  intelligible 518
  manifest 525
  easy 705
  liberate 750
  profit 775
  vindicate 937
  innocent 946
  acquit 975
all − 664, 705
coast − 664
get − off 671
keep − of 623
make − 529
− for action
  prepare 673
− articulation 580
− conscience 946
− the course 302
− cut 518
− the ground
  facilitate 705
− of *distant* 196
− off *pay* 807
− out *empty* 297
  clean 652
− sighted
  vision 441
  shrewd 498
− sky *hope* 858
− stage
  occasion 134
  easy 705
  right 922
− thinking 498
− the throat 297
− up *light* 420
  intelligible 518
  interpret 522
clearheaded 498

lofty 206	*weapon* 727	*combine* 48	game – 861
inattentive 458	*sociality* 892	**coalheaver**	– boat 273
dreaming 515	– law	work like a – 686	– and bull story
under a –	*compulsion* 744	**coalition** 43, 709,	546
insane 503	*lawless* 964	712	– the eye 441
adversity 735	– together	**coaming** 232	– of the roost
disrepute 874	*co-operate* 709	**coaptation** 23	*best* 648
secluded 893	**clubby** 892	**coarctation**	*master* 745
censured 932	**club car** 272	*decrease* 36	– up *vertical* 212
accused 938	**clubfooted** 243	*contraction* 195	*convex* 250
– burst 348	**cluck** 412	*narrow* 203	**cockade** *badge* 550
–capt 206	**clue** 550	*impede* 706	*title* 877
– of dust 330, 353	seek a – 461	*restraint* 751	**cock-a-hoop**
–s gathering	**clump**	**coarse** *harsh* 410	*gay* 836
dark 421	*assemblage* 72	*dirty* 653	*exulting* 884
danger 665	*projecting mass*	*unpolished* 674	**Cockaigne** 827
warning 668	250	*garish* 846	**cockatrice**
– no bigger than a	– of trees 367	*vulgar* 851	*monster* 83
man's hand 668	**clumsy**	*impure* 961	*piercing eye* 548
– of skirmishers	*unfit* 647	– grain 329	*evil-doer* 913
726	*awkward* 699	**coast** *border* 231	*miscreant* 949
– of smoke 353	*ugly* 846	*slide* 266	**cockcrow** 125
– of words 573	**Cluniac** 996	*navigate* 267	**cocked hat** 225, 745
clouded	**clurichaune** 980	*land* 342	**cocker** *fold* 258
variegated 440	**cluster** 72	– defence 717	*caress* 902
dejected 837	**clutch** *retain* 781	– line 230	**Cocker**
hopeless 859	*seize* 789	**coaster** 273	*school book* 542
– perception 499	**clutches** 737	**coastguard** 753	according to – 82
cloudiness 571	in the – of 749	**coat** *layer* 204	**cockle** *fold* 258
cloudland 515	**clutter** 407	*paint* 223	– of one's heart
cloudless	**coacervation** 72	*habit* 225	820
light 420	**coach**	cut – according to	**cockleshell** 273
happy 827	*carriage* 272	cloth 698	**cockloft** 191
cloudy *dim* 422,	*teach* 537	– of arms 550	**cockney**
426	*tutor* 540, 673	– of mail 717	*Londoner* 188
clough 206	– painter 540	**coating, inner –**	*plebeian* 876
clout 276	– road 627	224	**cockpit** *hold* 191
cloven 91	drive a – and six	**coax** *persuade* 615	*council* 696
cloven foot	through 964	*endearment* 902	*arena* 728
mark 550	– up 539	*flatter* 933	**cockshut**
malevolence 907	**coachhouse** 191	**cob** *horse* 271	*morning* 125
vice 945	**coachman** 268, 694	*punish* 972	*evening* 126
Satan 978	**coaction** 744	**cobalt** 438	*dusk* 422
see the – 480*a*	**coadjutant** 709	**cobble** *mend* 660	**cock-sparrow** 193
show the – 907	**coadjutor** 711	**cobbler** 225	**cocksure** 484
clover	**coadjuvancy** 709	**cobbles** 635	**cockswain** 269
luxury 377	**coagency** 178, 709	**coble** 273	**cocktail** 298, 959
prosperity 734	**coagmentation** 72	**cobra** 913	– party 892
comfort 827	**coagulate**	**cobweb** *light* 320	**cocoa** 298
clown	*cohere* 46	*fiction* 545	**cocotte** 962
pantomime 599	*density* 321	*flimsy* 643	**coction** 384
bungler 702	*semi-liquid* 352	*dirt* 653	**Cocytus** 982
buffoon 844	**coal** 388	–s of antiquity	**cod** *shell* 223
vulgar 851	call over the –s	124	**coddle** 902
rustic 876	932	–s of sophistry	– oneself 943
cloy 641, 869	carry –s 879	477	**code** *conceal* 528
club	– black 431	**cocaine** 376, 381,	*precept* 697
place of meeting	carry –s to New-	663	*law* 963
74	castle 641	**cochineal** 434	**codex** 593
house 189	**coalesce**	**cock** *bird* 366	**codger** 819
association 712	*identity* 13	*male* 373	**codicil** *sequel* 65

comfit 396
comfort
  pleasure 377
  delight 827
  content 831
  relief 834
  give – 906
comfortable
  pleasing 829
comforter
  covering 223
Comforter 976
comfortless
  painful 830
  dejected 837
comic *wit* 842
  ridiculous 853
  – opera 599
  – strips 531
coming [see come]
  impending 152
  – events
    prediction 511
  – out 883
  – time 121
comitia 696
comity 894
comma 142
  inverted –s 550
command *high* 206
  requisition 630
  authority 737
  order **741**
  possess 777
  at one's –
    obedient 743
  – belief 484
  – of language
    writing 574
    speaking 582
  – of money 803
  – one's passions
    944
  – respect 928
  – one's temper
    826
  – a view of 441
commandant 745
commander 269
commandeer 744,
  789
commanding
  [see command]
  important 642
commando 726
commandment 697
comme deux
  gouttes d'eau 17
comme il faut
  taste 850
  fashion 852

genteel 875
commemorate 883
commence 66
commencement de
  la fin *end* 67
  destruction 162
commend 931
  – the poisoned
    chalice 544
commendable 944
commensurate
  accordant 23
  numeral 85
  adequate 639
comment
  reason 476
  judgment 480
  interpretation 522
  criticize 595
commentary 595
commentator 492,
  524, 527
commerce
  conversation 588
  barter 794
  cards 840
commercial 811
  – arithmetic 811
  – traveller 758
commère 599
commination 908,
  909
commingle 41
comminute 330
commiserate 914
commissariat 637
commissary
  provisions 637
  consignee 758
commission
  task 625
  delegate **755**, 759
  Royal – 696
  – of the peace 965
commissioner 758
commissionaire
  doorkeeper 263
  messenger 534
  consignee 758
commissure 43
commis-voyageur
  758
commit *do* 680
  delegate 755
  cards 840
  arrest 969
  – an absurdity 853
  – oneself to a
    course 609
  – to the flames
    384

– to memory 505
– oneself
  clumsy 699
  promise 768
  – to prison 751
  – sin 945
  – to writing 551
committee
  council 696
  consignee 758
  (*director* 694)
commix 41
commode 191
commodious 644
commodity 798
commodore 745
common
  general 78
  ordinary 82
  plain 344
  habitual 613
  trifling 643
  base 876
  in – *related* 9
  participate 778
  right of – 780
  short –s 640
  tenant in – 778
  make – cause 709
  – consent 488
  – council 966
  – course 613
  – herd 876
  – law *old* 124
  law 697, 963
  – measure 84
  – origin 153
  – parlance 576
  – place 82
  – place book
    record 551
  compendium 596
  – saying 496
  – sense 498
  – sewer 653
  – stock 778
  – weal
    mankind 372
    good 681
    utility 644
    philanthropy 910
Common Pleas
  Court of – 966
commonalty **876**
commoner 876
commonplace
  usual 82
  known 490
  plain 576
  habit 613
  unimportant 643

dull 843
commons 298
commonwealth
  territory 181
  community 372
  authority 737
commorant 188
commotion 315
communalism 778
commune
  township 181
commune with 588
  – oneself 451
communibus annis
  29
communicant 990
communicate
  join 43
  tell 527
  correspond 592
  give 784
  sacrament 998
communication
  news 532
  of disease 657
  oral – 582, 588
communion
  discourse 588
  society 712
  participation 778
  sacrament 998
  hold – with 888
  – table 1000
communiqué 527
communism 737
communist
  party 712
  rebel 742
  participation 778
  philanthropy 910
  evil doer 913
community
  party 712
  – at large 372
  – of goods 778
commutation
  compensation 30
  substitution 147
  interchange 148
  compromise 774
  barter 794
commutual 12
compact
  joined 43
  united 87
  receptacle 191
  small 193
  compressed 195
  compendious 201
  dense 321
  bargain **769**

compages
whole 50
structure 329
compagination 43
companion *match*
17
accompaniment
88
ladder 305
friend 890
companionable 892
companionship 892
companionway 305
company
assembly 72
actors 599
party, partner-
ship 712
troop 726
sociality 892
bear – 88
in – with 88
comparable 9
comparative 464
degree 26
– *anatomy* 368
comparatively 32
compare 464
– *notes* 695
comparison 464
compartition 44
compartment
part 51
region 181
place 182
cell 191
carriage 272
compass
degree 26
space 180
surround 227
measure 466
intend 620
guidance 693
achieve 729
box the –
azimuth 278
rotation 312
keep within –
moderation 174
fall short 304
economy 817
points of the – 236
in a small – 193
– *about* 229
– *of thought* 498
compassion 914
object of – 828
compatible
consentaneous 23
possible 470

compatriot
inhabitant 188
friend 890
compeer *equal* 27
friend 890
compel 744
compellation 564
compendency 43
compendious 201
compendium 596
book 593
compensate
make up for 30
requite 973
compensation 30
compère 599
competence
power 157
sufficiency 639
skill 698
wealth 803
competition
opposition 708
contention 720
competitor
opponent 710
combatant 726
candidate 767
compilation
collect 72
book 593
compendium 596
compile 54
complacent
pleased 827
content 831
courteous 894
kind 906
complain 839
complainant 938
complaint
illness 655
murmur 839
lodge a – 938
– *without cause*
839
complaisant
lenient 740
courteous 894
kind 906
complement
adjunct 39
remainder 40
part 52
arithmetic 84
complementary
correlation 12
colour 428
complete
entire 52
accomplish 729

compact 769
– *answer* 479
– *circle* 311
in a – *degree* 31
completeness 52
completion 729
complex 59
complexion
state 7
colour 428
appearance 448
compliance
conformity 82
obedience 743
consent 762
observance 772
complicate
derange 61
complicated
disorder 59
convolution 248
complice 711
complicity 709
compliment
courtesy 894, 896
praise 931
poor – 932
–s *of season* 896
complimentary
free 815
complot 626
comply [*see* compli-
ance]
compo *coating* 223
material 635
component 56
componere lites
723, 724
comport
– *oneself* 692
– *with* 23
compos mentis 502
compose
make up 54, 56
produce 161
moderate 174
music 416
write 590
printing 591
pacify 723
assuage 826
composed
self-possessed 826
composer
music 413
composite 41
composition 54
[*see* compose]
combination 48
piece of music 415
picture 556

style 569
writing 590
building material
635
compromise 774
barter 794
atonement 952
compositor
printer 591
compost 653
composure 826, 871
compotation 959
compote 298
compound
mix 41
combination 48
limited space 182
enclosure 232
compromise 774
– *arithmetic* 466
– *for substitute* 147
barter 794
comprador 637
comprehend
compose 54
include 76
know 490
understand 518
comprehension [*see*
comprehend]
intelligence 498
comprehensive 76
complete 50
general 78
wide 192
– *argument* 476
compress
contract 195
curtail 201
condense 321
remedy 662
compressible 322
comprise 76
comprobation
evidence 467
demonstration 478
compromise
dally with 605
mid-course 628
taint 659
danger 665
pacify 723
compact 769
compound **774**
atone 952
compromised
promised 768
compter 799
compte rendu
record 551
accounts 811

comptroller 694
compulsion **744**
compunction 833,
    950
compurgation
    evidence 467
    acquittal 970
compute 85
comrade 890
comradeship 892
con think 451
    get by heart 505
    learn 539
conation 600
conatu magnas
    nugas, magno –
    waste 638
    unimportance 643
conatus 176
concamerate 245
concatenation
    junction 43
    continuity 69
concavity **252**
conceal
    invisible 447
    hide 528
    cunning 702
concealment **528,**
    893
concede
    assent 488
    admit 529
    permit 760
    consent 762
    give 784
conceit idea 453
    folly 499
    supposition 514
    imagination 515
    wit 842
    affectation 855
    vanity 880
conceited
    dogmatic 481
conceivable 470
conceive begin 66
    beget 161
    teem 168
    believe 484
    understand 490
    imagine 515
    plan 626
concent 413
concentrate
    assemble 72
    centrality 222
    converge 290
concentric 216, 222
conception
    [see conceive]

intellect 450
idea 453
concern
    relation 9
    event 151
    business 625
    importance 642
    firm 797
    grief 828
    – oneself with 625
concert
    agreement 23
    synchronism 120
    music 415
    act in – 709
    in – musical 413
    concord 714
    – measures 626
concertina 417
concerto 415
concert-room 840
concession
    permission 760
    consent 762
    compromise 774
    giving 784
    discount 813
concesso, ex –
    reasoning 476
    assent 488
concetto 842
conchoid 245
conchology 223
concierge 163, 753
conciliate
    talk over 615
    pacify 723
    satisfy 831
    courtesy 894
    atonement 952
conciliatory [see
    conciliate]
    concord 714
    forgiving 918
conciliatrix 962
concinnity
    agreement 23
    style 578
    beauty 845
conciseness **572**
concision 201
conclave
    assembly 72
    council 696
    church 995
conclude
    end 67
    infer 480
    resolve 604
    complete 729
    compact 769

conclusion
    [see conclude]
    sequel 65
    germination 161
    judgment 480
    try –s 476
    forgone – 611
    hasty – 481
conclusive
    [see conclude]
    answer 462
    evidence 467
    certain 474
    proof 478
    – reasoning 476
concoct lie 544
    write 590
    plan 626
    prepare 673
concomitant
    accompany 88
    same time 120
    concurrent 178
concord agree 23
    music **413**
    assent 488
    harmony **714**
concordance 562
    book 593
concordant 173
concordat 769
concordia discors
    24, 59
concours 720
concourse
    assemblage 72
    convergence 290
concremation 384
concrete existent 3
    mass 46
    definite 79
    density 321
    hardness 323
    materials 635
concubinage 961
concubine 926
concupiscence 865,
    961
concur
    co-exist 120
    causation 178
    converge 290
    assent 488
    concert 709
concurrence **178,**
    216
concussion 276
condemnation 932,
    971
condemned cell 752
condense

compress 195
dense 321
condensed
    concise 572
condescend 879
condign 924
condiment **393**
condisciple 541
condition state 7
    modification 469
    supposition 514
    term 770
    repute 873
    rank 875
    in – plump 192
    in good – 648
    on – 770
    in perfect – 650
    physical – 316
conditional 8
conditions **770**
condolence 914, **915**
condone 918
condottiere
    traveller 268
    fighter 726
conduce
    contribute 153
    tend 176
    concur 178
    avail 644
conducive 631
conduct
    transfer 270
    music 416
    procedure **692**
    lead 693
    safe –
    passport 631
    safety 664
    – a funeral 363
    – an inquiry 461
    – to 278
conduction 264
conductor 269
    conveyer 271
    director 694
    lightning – 666
conduit **350**
conduplicate 89
condyle 250
cone round 249
    pointed 253
confabulation 588
confection 396
    confectionary 396
confectioner 637
confederacy
    co-operation 709
    party 712
confederate 711

confer *advise* 695
  give 784
  – benefit 648
  – power 157
  – privilege 760
  – right 924
  – with 588
conference [*see* confer]
  council 696
confess *assent* 488
  avow 529
  penitence 950, 998
  – and avoid 937
confession [*see* confess]
  auricular – 998
  – of faith 983
confessional 1000
confessions
  biography 594
confessor 996
confidant 711
confidante
  servant 746
  friend 890
confidence
  trust 484
  hope 858
  courage 861
  in – 528
  – trick 545
confident 535
configuration 240
confine
  region 182
  circumscribe 229
  limit 231, 233
  imprison 751
confined
  narrow judgment 481
  ill 655
confinement
  childbed 161
confines of
  on the – 197
confirm
  corroborate 467
  assent 488
  consent 762
  compact 769
  rite 998
confirmed 150
  – habit 613
confiscate *take* 789
  condemn 971
  penalty 974
confiture 396
conflagration 382,

384
conflexure 245
conflict
  opposition 708
  discord 713
  contention 720
conflicting
  contrary 14
  counteracting 179
  – evidence 468
confluence
  junction 43
  convergence 290
  river 348
conflux
  assemblage 72
  convergence 290
conform *assent* 488
  – to rule 494
conformable 23, 178
conformation 54, 240
conformity **82**, 178
confound
  disorder 61
  destroy 162
  not discriminate 465a
  perplex 475
  defeat 731
  astonish 870
  curse 908
confounded
  great 31
  bad 649
confraternity
  party 712
  friendship 888
confrère
  colleague 711
  friend 890
confrication 331
confront *face* 234
  compare 464
  oppose 708
  resist 719
  – danger 861
  – witnesses 467
confucianism 984
Confucius 986
confuse *derange* 61
  perplex 458
  obscure 519
  not discriminate 465a
  abash 879
confused *disorder* 59
  invisible 447
  uncertain 475

style 571
confusion
  [*see* confuse]
  – seize 908
  – of tongues 560, 563
  – of vision 443
  – worse-con-founded 59
confutation **479**
congé 293, 756
  – d'élire 995
congeal *dense* 321
  cold 385
congeneric
  similar 17
  included 76
congenial
  related 9
  agreeing 23
  concord 714
  love 897
congenital 5, 820
congeries 72
congestion 641
conglaciation 385
conglobation 72
conglomerate
  cohere 46
  assemblage 72
  council 696
  dense 321
conglutinate 46
congratulate 896
  – oneself 838
congratulation **896**
congregation
  assemblage 72
  worshippers 990
  laity 997
Congregationalist 984
congress
  assembly 72
  convergence 290
  conference 588
  council 698
Congressional Medal 733
Congressional Record 551
congreve *fuel* 388
  – rocket 727
congruous
  agreeing 23
  (*expedient* 646)
conical *round* 249
  pointed 253
conjecture 475, 514
conjoin 43
conjoint 48

conjointly 37
conjugal 903
conjugate
  words 562
  grammar 567
  – in all its tenses &c. 104
conjugation
  junction 43
  pair 89
  phase 144
  grammar 567
conjunction 43
  in – with 37
conjuncture
  contingency **8**
  occasion 134
conjure *deceive* 545
  entreat 765
  sorcery 992
  name to – with 873
  – up *recall* 505
  – up a vision 505
conjuror
  deceiver 548
  sorcerer 994
connaître les dessous des cartes 490
connate
  intrinsic 5
  kindred 11
  cause 153
connatural
  uniform 16
  similar 17
connect *relate* 9
  link 43
connection
  [*see* connect]
  kin 11
  in – with 9
connections
  cards 840
connective 45
conned, well – 490
connive
  overlook 460
  co-operate 709
  allow 760
connoisseur
  critic 480
  scholar 492
  taste 850
connotate 550
connote 516, 550
  imply 526
connubial 903
connuted 9
conoscente 850

conquer 731
conquered
 (*failure* 732)
conquering hero
 comes 883
conqueror 731
consanguinity **11**
consciarecti, mens—
 pride 878
 innocence 946
conscience
 knowledge 490
 moral sense 926
 in all – *great* 31
 affirmation 535
 awakened – 950
 qualms of – 603
 clear – 946
 stricken – 950
 tender – 926
 honour 939
conscientious 926
 scrupulous 939
 – objector 489
conscious
 intuitive 450
 knowledge 490
 – of disgrace 874
 – of glory 873
conscript 726
conscription 744
consecrate *use* 677
 dedicate 873
 sanctify 987
 holy orders 995
consecration
 rite 998
consectory 478
 – reasoning 476
consecution 63
consecutive
 following 63
 continuous 69
 – fifth 414
consecutively
 slowly 275
consensus 488
 – of opinion 23
consent *assent* 488
 compliance **762**
 with one – 178
consentaneous
 agreeing 23
 (*expedient* 646)
consequence
 event 151
 effect 154
 importance 642
 in – 478
 of no – 643
 take the –s 154

consequent 63
consequential
 deducible 478
 arrogant 878
consequently
 reasoning 476
 effect 154
conservation
 permanence 141
 storage 636
 preservation 670
conservatism 141,
 670
conservative 141,
 712
 – policy 681
conservatoire 542
conservator
 of the peace 967
conservatory
 receptacle 191
 floriculture 371
 furnace 386
 store 636
conserve 396, 636
consider *think* 451
 attend to 457
 examine 461
 adjudge 480
 believe 484
considerable
 in degree 31
 in size 192
 important 642
considerate
 careful 459
 judicious 498
 benevolent 906
consideration
 purchase money
 147
 thought 451
 idea 453
 attention 457
 qualification 469
 inducement 615
 importance 642
 gift 784
 benevolence 906
 respect 928
 requital 973
 deserve – 642
 in – of
 compensation 30
 reasoning 476
 on – 658
 take into –
 thought 451
 attention 457
 under –
 topic 454

 inquiry 461
 plan 626
considered, all
 things –
 collectively 50
 judgment 480
 premeditation 611
 imperfection 651
consign
 transfer 270
 commission 755
 property 783
 give 784
 – to the flames 384
 – to oblivion 506
 – to the tomb 363
consignee **758**
consignor 796
consignment
 commission 755
 gift 784
 apportionment
 786
consilience 178
consist
 – in 1
 – of 54
consistence
 density 321
consistency
 uniformity 16
 agreement 23
consistently with
 82
consistory
 council 696
 church 995
consolation
 relief 834
 condole 915
 religious 976
console
 table 215
Consoler
 the – 976
consolidate
 unite 46, 48
 condense 321
consols 802
consommé 298
consonant
 agreeing 23
 musical 413
 letter 561
consort
 accompany 88
 associate 892
 spouse 903
 – with 23
consortium 23
consortship 892

conspection 441
conspectus 596
conspicuous
 visible 446
 famous 873
conspiracy 626
conspirator 626
 traitor 941
conspire
 concur 178
 co-operate 709
constable
 policeman 664
 governor 745
 officer 965
constant
 fixed 5
 uniform 16
 continuous 69
 regular 80
 continual 112
 frequent 136
 regular 138
 immutable 150
 exact 494
 persevering 604a
 obey 743
 faithful 939
 – flow 69
constellation
 stars 318
 luminary 423
 glory 873
consternation 860
constipation
 closure 261
 density 321
constituency 181,
 737
constituent 51, 56
constitute
 compose 54, 56
 produce 161
constitution
 nature 5
 state 7
 composition 54
 structure 329
 charter 924
 law 963
constitutional
 walk 226
 – government **737**
constrain
 compel 744
 restrain 751
 abash 881
constraint 195
constrict 195, 706
constringe 195
construct 161

aid 707
give 784
contribution 784
  lay under – 789,
  924
contrition
  abrasion 331
  regret 833
  penitence 950
contrivance 633
contrive
  produce 161
  plan 626
  – to *succeed in* 731
contriving
  cunning 702
control
  power 157
  influence 175
  regulate 693
  authority 737
  restrain 751
  board of – 696
  under –
    obedience 743
    subjection 749
controller of
  currency 801
controls 273, 693
controversial
  discussion 476
  discordant 713
controversialist
  476, 726
controversy
  disagreement 24
  discussion 476
  debate 588
  contention 720
controvert
  deny 536
controvertible
  uncertain 475
  debatable 476
  untrue 495
contumacy
  obstinacy 606
  disobedience 742
contumely
  arrogance 885
  rudeness 895
  disrespect 929
  scorn 930
  reproach 932
contund 330
contuse 330
conundrum *pun*
  520
  riddle 533
  wit 842
convalescence 654,

660
convection 270
convenance
  mariage de – 903
convene 72
conveniences 632
convenient 646, 705
convent 1000
conventicle
  assembly 72
  council 696
  chapel 1000
convention
  agreement 23
  assembly 72
  rule 80
  council 696
  precept 697
  treaty of peace
   723
  compact 769
  –s *of society* 852
conventional 82,
  613
conventual 996,
  1000
convergence 290
convergent 286
conversable
  talk 588
  sociable 892
conversant
  know 490
  skilful 698
conversation 588
conversational
  loquacious 584
  interlocution 588
  sociable 892
conversazione 588,
  892
converse
  reverse 14
  talk 588
conversely 468
conversion 144
  trover and – 964
convert
  change to 140, 144
  opinion 484
  tergiversation 607
  religion 987
  – to *use* 677
convertible 13, 27
  – terms 522
convexity 250
convey
  transfer 270
  mean 516
  assign 783
  – away 791

– the knowledge
  of 527
conveyance
  [*see* convey]
  vehicle 272
conveyancer 968
conveyancing 783
convict
  convince 484
  condemned 949
  condemn 971
convicted, self –
  950
conviction
  confutation 479
  belief 484
  prove guilty 971
convince
  belief 484
  confute 479
  teach 537
convivial 892
convocate 72
convocation
  council 696
  church 995
convoke 72
convolution
  coil 248
  rotation 312
convoy
  accompany 88
  transfer 270
  guard 664
  escort 753
convulse
  derange 61
  violent 173
  agitate 315
  bodily pain 378
  mental pain 830
convulsed with
  – *laughter* 838
  – *rage* 900
convulsion
  [*see* convulse]
  disorder 59
  revolution 146
  in –s 325
coo 412
cook *heat* 384
  falsify 544
  improve 658
  prepare 673
  servant 746
  too many –s 699
  – *accounts* 811
cool *moderate* 174
  cold 383
  refrigerate 385
  grey 432

dissuade 616
cautious 864
indifferent 866
unamazed 871
unfriendly 889
discourteous 895
look – upon
  unsocial 893
take –ly 826
– down 826
– one's heels
  kept waiting 133
  inaction 681
cooler 387
coolheaded
  judicious 498
  unexcitable 826
coolie
  bearer 271
  military 726
coolness
  insensibility 823
  estrangement 898
coon-can 840
coop *abode* 189
  restrain 751
  prison 752
co-operation
  physical 178
  voluntary 709
  participation 778
co-operator 690, 711
co-optation 609
co-ordinate
  equal 27
  arrange 60
  measure 466
cootie 653
cop 664
copal 356a
coparcener 778
copartner
  accompanying 88
  participator 778
  associate 890
copartnership
  co-operation 709
  party 712
cope *equal* 27
  oppose 708
  contend 720
  canonicals 999
copia verborum
  diffuse 573
  loquacious 584
coping stone
  top 210
  completion 729
copious
  diffuse style 573
  abundant 639

coportion 778
copper *money* 800
　policeman 664
copper-coloured
　433, 439
copper-plate
　engraving 558
　writing 590
coppice 367
coprolite 653
copse 367
copula 45
copulation 43
copy
　imitate 19
　facsimile **21**
　prototype 22
　news 532
　record 551
　represent 554
　write 590
　for the press 591
　plan 626
　– *book* 22
copyhold 780
copyist
　imitator 19
　artist 559
　writer 590
copyright 780
coquet *lie* 544
　change the mind
　607
　affected 855
　endearment 902
　flattery 933
　– *with*
　irresolute 605
coquette
　affected 854, 855
　flirt 897
coquillage 847
coracle 273
coral 847
　– *reef* 667
coram judice
　jurisdiction 965
　lawsuit 969
cor Anglais 417
corbeille 191
corbel 215
cord *tie* 45
　filament 205
cordage 45
cordated 245
cordial
　pleasure 377
　dram 392
　willing 602
　remedy 662
　feeling 821

grateful 829
friendly 888
courteous 894
cordiform 245
cordite 727
cordon
　inclosure 232
　circularity 247
　decoration 877
　– *bleu* 733, 746
　– *sanitaire*
　safety 664
　preservation 670
corduroy 259
cordwainer
　shoemaker 225
　artificer 690
core *gist* 5
　source 153
　centre 222
　gist 642
　true to the – 939
coriaceous 327
Corinthian 850
co-rival
　[*see* corrival]
cork *plug* 263
　lightness 320
　– *jacket* 666
　– *up close* 261
　restrain 751
corking pin 45
corkscrew
　spiral 248
　perforator 262
　circuition 311
cormorant
　desire 865
　gluttony 957
corn
　projection 250
Cornaro 953
cornea 441
corned 959
cornelian 847
corneous 323
corner *place* 182
　receptacle 191
　angle 244
　monopoly 777
　– *creep into a* –
　893
　in a dark – 528
　drive into a – 706
　push into a – 874
　rub off –s 82
　– *turn a* – 311
　turn the – 658
　– *stone*
　support 215
　importance 642

defence 717
cornet *music* 417
　officer 745
cornice 210
corniculate 253
cornification 323
Cornish hug 545
corno 417
cornopean 417
cornucopia 639
cornute
　projecting 250
　sharp 253
corollary
　adjunct 39
　deduction 480
corona 247
coronach 839
coronation
　enthronement 755
　celebration 883
coroner 363, 965
　–'s jury 967
coronet *hoop* 247
　insignia 747
　title 877
corporal
　corporeal 316
　officer 745
corporate 43
　– *body* 712
corporation
　bulk 192
　convex 250
　association 712
　jurisdiction 965
corporeal 3, 316,
　364
　– *hereditaments*
　780
corporeity 316
corps *assemblage* 72
　troops 726
　à – *perdu*
　haste 684
　rash 863
　– *de reserve* 636
corpse **362**
corpulence 192
corpus 316
　– Christi 998
　– delicti
　guilt 947
　lawsuit 969
　– *juris*
　precept 697
　law 963
corpuscle
　small 32
　little 193
corradiation

focus 74
convergence 290
corral 232, 370
correct
　orderly 58
　true 494
　inform 527
　disclose 529
　improve 658
　repair 660
　due 924
　censure 932
　honourable 939
　virtuous 944
　punish 972
　– *ear* 416, 418
　– *memory* 505
　– *reasoning* 476
　– *style*
　grammatical 567
　elegant 578
correction
　[*see* correct]
　house of – 752
　under – 879
corrective 662
corregidor 745
correlation
　relation 9
　reciprocity **12**
correspondence
　correlation 12
　similarity 17
　agreement 23
　writing **592**
　– *course* 537
correspondent
　messenger 534
　journalist 593
　consignee 758
corresponding
　similar 17
　agreeing 23
corridor *region* 181
　place 191
　passage 627
　– *train* 272
corrigendum 495
corrigible 658
corrival 726
corrivalry 720
corrivation 348
corroborant 662
corroboration
　evidence 467
　assent 488
corrode *burn* 384
　erode 659
　afflict 830
corrosive
　[*see* corrode]

creditable *right* 924
creditor 805
credo quia
  impossibile 486
credulity **486**
credulous person
  dupe 547
creed *belief* 484
  theology 983
  Apostles' – 983*a*
creek *interval* 198
  water 343
creel 191
creep *crawl* 275
  tingle 380
  (*inactivity* 683)
  – in 294
  – into a corner 893
  – into the good
    graces of 933
  – out 529
  – upon one 508
  -- with
    multitude 102
    redundance 641
creeper 367
creeping
  sensation 380
  – thing 366
creese 727
cremation
  of corpses 363
  burning 384
crematorium 363,
  386
crematory 386
crême de la crême
  648
Cremona 417
crenate 257
crenelle 257
crenulate 257
creole 57
crêpé 248, 839
crepidam, ultra –
  471
crepitation 406
crepuscule
  dawn 125
  dusk 422
crescendo
  increase 35
  musical 415
crescent
  growing 35
  street 189
  curve 245
cresset 423, 550
crest *supremacy* 33
  summit 210
  pointed 253

tuft 256
sign 550
armorial 877
pride 878
on the – 33
crest-fallen
  dejected 837
  humble 879
crevasse 198, 667
crevice 198
crew *assemblage* 72
  inhabitants 188
  mariners 269
  party 712
crib *bed* 215
  key 522
  granary 636
  steal 791
  parsimony 819
cribbage 840
cribbed, confined,
  cabined – 751
cribble 260
cribriform 260
Crichton,
  Admirable –
  scholar 492
  perfect 650
  proficient 700
crick *pain* 378
cricket *game* 840
  not – 940
  – ground 213
crier 534
  send round the –
    531
crim. con. 961
crime 945, 947
criminal 923, 945
  culprit 949
  – law 963
  court of – appeal
    966
criminality 947
criminate 938
crimp *crinkle* 248
  notch 257
  brittle 328
  deceiver 548
  take 789
  steal 791
crimple 258
crimson 434, 821
cringe *submit* 725
  subject 749
  servility 886
crinite 256
crinkle *angle* 244
  convolution 248
  roughen 256
  fold 258

crinoline 225
cripple *disable* 158
  weaken 160
  injure 659
crippled
  disease 655
crisis
  conjuncture 8
  present time 118
  opportunity 134
  event 151
  strait 704
  excitement 824
  bring to a – 604
  come to a – 729
crisp *rumpled* 248
  rough 256
  brittle 328
  style 572
Crispin 225
criss-cross 219
cristallomantia 511
criterion *test* 463
  evidence 467
  indication 550
crithomancy 511
critic *judge* 480
  taste 850
  detractor 936
critical
  contingent 8
  opportune 134
  discriminating
    465
  important 642
  dangerous 665
  difficult 704
  censorious 932
criticism
  judgment 480
  dissertation 595
  disapprobation
    932
  detraction 934
critique
  [*see* criticism]
croak *cry* 412
  hoarseness 581
  stammer 583
  warning 668
  discontent 832
  lament 839
croaker 832, 837
Croat 726
crochet 847
crock 191
crockery 384
crocodile tears 544
crocus *yellow* 436
Crœsus 803
croft 189, 232

Croix de Guerre 733
cromlech 363, 551
crone *veteran* 130
  fool 501
crony *friend* 890
  favourite 899
crook *curve* 245
  deviation 279
  thief 792
crooked
  sloping 217
  distorted 243
  angular 244
  latent 526
  crafty 702
  ugly 846
  dishonourable 940
  – path 704
  – temper 901
  – ways 279
croon 580
crop
  stomach 191
  harvest 154
  shorten 201
  eat 298
  vegetable 367
  store 636
  gather 775
  take 789
  second – 167, 775
  – out *visible* 446
  disclose 529
  – up *begin* 66
  take place 151
  reproduction 163
cropper *fall* 306
croquet *game* 840
  – ground *level* 213
croquette 298
crosier 747, 999
cross *mix* 41
  across 219
  pass 302
  grave 363
  oppose 708
  failure 732
  disaster 735
  refuse 764
  pain 830
  decoration 877
  fretful 901
  punishment 975
  rites 998
  fiery – 722
  proclaim at the –
    roads 531
  red – 662
  –ed bayonets 708
  – breed 63
  – cut 628

CUB

cub *young* 129
  vulgar 851
  clown 876
  unlicked – 241
cubby-hole 191
cube
  three dimensions
    92, 93
  form 244
cubicle 191
cubist 556
cubit 200
cucking stool 975
cuckold 905
cuckoldom 961
cuckoo
  imitation 19
  repetition 104
  sound 407
  cry 412
cuddle 196, 902
cudgel *beat* 276
  weapon 727
  punish 975
  take up the –s
  aid 707
  attack 716
  contention 720
  – one's brains
    think 451
    imagine 515
cue *hint* 527
  watchword 550
  plea 617
  rôle 625
  take one's – from
    695
  in proper – 698
cuff *sleeve* 225
  blow 276
  punishment 972
cui bono 644, 645
cuique voluptas
  sui – 865
cuirass 717
cuirassier 726
cuisine 298
  batterie de – 957
culbute
  inversion 218
  fall 306
cul-de-lampe
  engraving 558
  ornament 847
cul-de-sac
  concave 252
  closed 261
  difficulty 704
culinary 298
  – art 673
cull *dupe* 547

CUP

choose 609
  take 789
cullender 260
cullibility 486
cullion 949
cully *deceive* 545,
    547
culm 388
culminate
  maximum 33
  height 206
  top 210
  complete 729
culpability *vice* 945
  guilt 947
culprit 949
cult 983
cultivate *till* 365,
    371
  sharpen 375
  improve 658
  prepare 673
  aid 707
cultivated
  courteous 894
  – taste 850
cultivator 371
culture
  knowledge 490
  improvement 658
  taste 850
  politeness 894
culverin 727
culvert 350
cum multis aliis 37,
    102
cumber *load* 319
  obstruct 706
cumbersome
  incommodious
    647
  disagreeable 830
cummerbund 225
cumulative 72
  increasing 35
  assembled 72
  – evidence 467
  – vote 609
cumulus 353
cunctando restituit
  rem 681
cunctation 133
cuneiform 244
  – character 590
cunning
  prepense 611
  sagacious 698
  artful **702**
  – fellow 700
  – man 994
cup *vessel* 191

CUR

hollow 252
  beverage 298
  remedy 662
  trophy 733
  tipple 959
  between – and lip
    111
  in one's –s 959
  – that cheers &c.
    298
  – of humiliation
    879
  dash the – from
    one's lips 509
  – too low 837
cupbearer 746
cupboard 191
cupellation 384
Cupid *beauty* 845
  love 897
  gods 979
cupidity
  avarice 819
  desire 865
cupola *height* 206
  roof 223
  dome 250
cup-tossing 621
cur *dog* 366
  coward 862
  sneak 949
curable 658, 660,
    662
curacy 995
curare 663
curate 996
curative 660
curator 694, 758
curb *moderate* 174
  slacken 275
  dissuade 616
  restrain 751
  shackle 752
curb exchange 621
curbstone 233
curd *density* 321
  pulp 354
  (*cohere* 46)
curdle *condense* 321
  (*cohere* 46)
  make the blood –
    830
curdled 352
cure *reinstate* 660
  remedy 662
  preserve 670
  benefice 995
curé 996
cureless 859
curfew 126
curia 966

CUR

curio 847
curiosa felicitas 698
curiosity
  unconformity 83
  inquiring **455**
  phenomenon 872
curious
  exceptional 83
  inquisitive 455
  true 494
  beautiful 845
  desirous 865
curiously *very* 31
curl *bend* 245
  convolution 248
  hair 256
  cockle up 258
  badge 747
  – up one's lip 930
curling *game* 840
curmudgeon
  miser 819
  plebeian 876
currency
  publicity 531
  money 800
current *existing* 1
  usual 78
  present 118
  happening 151
  flow 264
  of water 348
  of air 349
  rife 531, 532
  language 560
  habit 613
  danger 667
  account – 811
  against the – 708
  go with the – 82
  pass –
    believed 484
    fashion 852
  stem the – 708
  – belief 488
  – of events 151
  – of ideas 451
  – of time 109
currente calamo
    590
curricle 272
curriculum 537
curry *food* 298
  rub 331
  condiment 392,
    393
  – favour with
    love 897
    flatter 933
curry-comb 370
curse *bane* 663

adversity 735	custody *safe* 664	*misuse* 679	branch 162
painful 830	*captive* 751	– both ways 468	– up rough 900
malediction 908	*retention* 781	– capers 309	– and run 274
cursed *bad* 649	in – *prisoner* 754	– according to	*depart* 293
cursitor 968	*accused* 938	cloth	*escape* 623
cursive 590	take into – 751	*economy* 817	– short *stop* 142
cursory	custom *old* 124	*caution* 864	*destroy* 162
transient 111	*habit* 613	– and come again	*shorten* 201
inattentive 458	*barter* 794	*repeat* 104	*silence* 581
hasty 684	*sale* 796	*enough* 639	– one's stick
take a – view of	*tax* 812	– dead 893	*depart* 283
457	*fashion* 852	– direct 893	*avoid* 623
neglect 460	– honoured in	– down *destroy* 162	– one's own throat
curst 901*a*	breach 614	*shorten* 201	699
curt *short* 201	**customary**	*fell* 308	– and thrust 716
concise 572	[see custom]	*kill* 361	– in two 91
taciturn 585	*regular* 80	– down expenses	– up *divide* 44
curtail *retrench* 38	**customer** 795	817	*destroy* 162
shorten 201	**custom-house** 799	– and dried	*pained* 828
–ed of its fair pro-	– *officer* 965	*arranged* 60	*give pain* 830
portions	**custos** 753	*prepared* 673	*discontented* 832
distorted 243	– rotulorum 553	– a figure	*dejected* 837
ugly 846	**cut** *divide* 44	*appearance* 448	*censure* 932
curtain 223	*bit* 51	*fashion* 852	what one will – up
shade 424	*discontinuity* 70	*repute* 873	for 780
hide 528, 530	*interval* 198	*display* 882	– one's way
theatre 599	*curtail* 201	– the first turf 66	through 302
fortification 717	*layer* 204	– the ground from	**cutaneous** 223
behind the –	*form* 240	under one	**cute** 698
invisible 447	*notch* 257	*confute* 479	**cuticle** 223
inquiry 461	*blow* 276	*hinder* 706	**cutlass** 727
knowledge 490	*eject* 297	– to the heart 824,	**cutlery** 253
close the – 528	*reap* 371	830	**cut-purse** 792
raise the – 529	*physical pain* 378	– ice with	**cutter** 273
rising of the – 448	*cold* 385	*influence* 175	**cut-throat**
– lecture 932	*neglect* 460	– of one's jib 448	*killer* 361
– raiser 66, 599	*carve* 557	– jokes 842	*evil-doer* 913
curtsy	*engraving* 558	– the knot 705	**cutting** *sharp* 253
stoop 308, 314	*road* 627	– off *subduct* 38	*cold* 383
submit 725	*attack* 716	*disjoin* 44	*path* 627
polite 894	*portion* 786	*kill* 361	*affecting* 821
curule 696	*affect* 824	*impede* 706	*painful* 830
curvature 245	*mental pain* 830	*bereft* 776	*reproachful* 932
curvet *leap* 309	*dance step* 840	*secluded* 893	**cuttings**
turn 311	*decline acquaint-*	– off with a shil-	*excerpta* 596
oscillate 314	*ance* 893	ling 789	*selections* 609
agitate 315	*discourtesy* 895	– open 260	**cutty stool** 950
curvilinear 245	*tipsy* 959	– out *surpass* 33	**cwt.** 98, 319
– motion 311	– short 628	*stop* 142	**cyanogen** 438
cushion *pillow* 215	unkindest – of all	*substitute* 147	**cyanide of potas-**
soft 324	*pain* 828	*plan* 626	**sium** *poison* 663
relief 834	*malevolence* 907	– out for 698	**cycle** *time* 106
cushy 829	– across 302	– out work	*period* 138
cusp *angle* 244	– adrift 44	*prepare* 673	*circle* 247
sharp 253	– along 274	*direct* 693	*ride* 266
cuspidor 191	have a – at 716	– to pieces	*vehicle* 272
cuss 908	– away 274	*destroy* 162	– car 272
custard 298	– a whetstone with	*kill* 361	**cyclist** 268
custodes? quis cus-	a razor	– a poor figure 874	**cycloid** 247
todiet – 459	*sophistry* 477	– to the quick 830	**cyclometer** 200
custodian 753	*waste* 638	– up root and	**cyclone**

rotation 312
wind 349
cyclopædia
  knowledge 490
  book 593
Cyclopean
  strong 159
  huge 192
Cyclops
  monster 83
  mighty 159
  huge 192
  dupe 547
cygne
  chant du – 360
  – noir 650
cylindric 249
cyma 847
cymbal 417
cymbalo 417
cymophanous 440
cynic
  misanthrope 911
  detractor 936
  ascetic 955
  closet – 893
cynical
  contemptuous 930
  censorious 932
  detracting 934
cynicism
  discourtesy 895
  contempt 930
cynosure *sign* 550
  direction 693
  wonder 870
  repute 873
Cynthia of the
  minute 149
cypher [*see* cipher]
cypress
  interment 363
  mourning 839
Cyprian 962
cyst 191
czar 745

D

da capo 104
dab *small* 32
  paint 223
  slap 276
  clever 700
dabble *water* 337
  dirty 653
  meddle 682
  fribble 683
dabbled *wet* 339
dabbler 493

dachshund 366
dacoit 792
dactyl 597
dactylogram 467
dactyliomancy 511
dactylonomy
  numeration 85
  symbol 550
dad 166
daddy 166
dado 211
dædal
  variegated 440
dædalion
  convoluted 248
  artistic 698
daft 503
dagger 727
  look –s *anger* 900
  threat 909
  air drawn – 515
  plant – in breast
  give pain 830
  speak –s 932
  at –s drawn
  opposed 708
  discord 713
  enmity 889
  hate 898
daggle *hang* 214
  dirty 653
dagobah 1000
Dagon 986
daguerreotype
  represent 554
  paint 556
dahabeah 273
Dail Eireann 696
daily
  frequent 136
  periodic 138
  – occurrence
  normal 82
  habitual 613
  – paper 531
dainty *food* 298
  savoury 394
  pleasing 829
  delicate 845
  tasty 850
  fastidious 868
dairy 191, 370
  – maid 946
dais *support* 215
  throne 747
daisy
  fresh as a – 654
  – pied 847
dale 252
dally *delay* 133
  irresolute 605

inactive 683
amuse 840
fondle 902
dalmatic 999
Daltonism 443
dam *parent* 166
  close 261
  pond 343
  obstruct 706
damage *evil* 619
  injure, spoil 659
  price 812
damages 974
damascene 440
damask 434
dame
  woman 374
  teacher 540
  lady 875
damn
  malediction 908
  condemn 971
  – with faint
    praise 932, 934
damnable 649
damnatory
  disapprove 932
  condemn 971
damnify
  damage 649
  spoil 659
damnosa hereditas
  663
Damocles
  sword of – 667
Damon and
  Pythias 890
damozel 129
damp
  moderate 174
  moist 339
  cold 385
  sound 405
  dissuade 616
  hinder 706
  depress 837
  dull 843
  – the sound 408*a*
damper 387
damsel
  youth 129
  female 374
Dan to Beersheba
  52, 180
Danaë 803
Danaos, timeo –
  doubt 485
  caution 864
dance
  jump 309
  oscillate 314

agitate 315
rejoice 838
sport 840
sociality 892
lead the – 175
lead one a –
  run away 623
  circuit 629
  difficult 704
  practical joke 929
St. Vitus' – 315
– attendance
  waiting 133
  follow 281
  servant 746
  petition 765
  servility 886
– the back step
  283
– upon nothing
  972
– the war dance
  715
dance-band 417
dance-music 415
dander 900
Dandie Dinmont
  366
dandiprat 193
dandle 902
dandruff 653
dandy
  ship 273
  fop 854
dandyism 855
danger 665
  in – *liable* 177
  source of – 667
  – past 664
  – signal 669
dangerous
  [*see* danger]
  – classes 913
  – illness 655
  – person 667
dangle *hang* 214
  swing 314
  display 882
dangler 281
Daniel *sage* 500
  judge 967
dank 339
Dannemora 752
danseuse 599
dapper
  little 193
  elegant 845
dapple 433
dappled 440
darbies
  handcuffs 752

Darby and Joan
  secluded 893
  married 903
dare *defy* 715
  face danger 861
  – not 860
  – say *probable* 472
  believe 484
  suppose 514
dare-devil
  courage 861
  rash 863
  bluster 887
daring 861
  unreserved 525
  – imagination 515
dark
  obscure 421
  dim 422
  black 431
  blind 442
  invisible 447
  unintelligible 519
  latent 526
  joyless 837
  insidious 940
  in the –
  ignorant 491
  leap in the –
  experiment 463
  chance 621
  rash 863
  keep – *hide* 528
  – ages 491
  – cloud 735
  view with – eyes
  932
  – lantern 423
darkly
  see through a
  glass – 443
darkness [*see* dark]
  421
  children of – 988
  love – better than
  light 989
  powers of – 978
darky 431
darling *beloved* 897
  favourite 899
darn 660
dart *swift* 274
  propel 284
  missile 727
  – to and fro 684
Dartmoor 752
Darwinism 357
dash
  small quantity 32
  mix 41
  swift 276

fling 284
mark 550
courage 861
cut a – *repute* 873
display 882
– at *resolution* 604
attack 716
– board 666
– cup from lips 761
– down 308
– hopes
disappoint 509
fail 732
dejected 837
despair 859
– on 274
– off *paint* 556
write 590
active 682
haste 684
– of the pen 590
dashed [*see* dash]
humbled 879
dashing
fashionable 852
brave 861
ostentatious 882
dastard 862
data *evidence* 467
reasoning 476
supposition 514
date *time* 106
chronology 114
datum 673
daub *cover* 223
paint 428
misrepresent 555
dirt 653
daughter 167
daunt 860
dauntless 861
Dauphin 875
davenport 191, 215
davit 214
Davus sum non
  Œdipus
unintelligent 499
artless 703
dull 843
Davy Jones' locker
  310
dawdle *tardy* 133
slow 275
inactive 683
dawk 534
dawn
precursor 64
begin 66
priority 116
morning 125
light 420

dim 422
glimpse 490
dawplucker 936
day
  period 108
  present time 118
  light 410
  all – 110
  clear as –
  certain 474
  intelligible 518
  manifest 525
  close of – 126
  decline of – 126
  denizens of the –
  366
  good old –'s 122
  have had its – 124
  one fine – 119
  open as – 703
  order of the – 613
  red letter – 642
  see the light of –
  446
  – after day
  diuturnal 110
  frequent 136
  – by day
  repeatedly 104
  time 106
  periodic 138
  – after the fair
  135
  –s gone by 122
  – of judgment 121
  happy as the – is
  long 827, 836
  – and night
  frequent 136
  labour – and night
  686
  –s numbered
  transient 111
  death 360
  – one's own 731
  – of rest 686
  – star 423
  – after to-morrow
  121
  – before yesterday
  122
  –s of week 138
  all in –'s work 625
daybed 215
daybook *record* 551
  accounts 811
daybreak
  morning 125
  dim 422
day-dream
  fancy 515

hope 858
day-labourer 690
daylight 125, 420
  see – *intelligible*
  518
  – saving 114
daymare 859
daze 420
dazed 376
dazzle
  light 420
  blind 422, 443
  put out 458
  astonish 870
  awe 928
dazzling
  [*see* dazzle]
  beautiful 845
de: – die in diem
  time 106
  periodic 138
  – facto 1
  – fond en comble
  52
  – novo 104
  – omnibus rebus
  81
  – profundis 821
deacon 996
deaconry 995
dead *complete* 52
  inert 172
  colourless 429
  lifeless 360
  insensible 376
  – against
  contrary 14
  oppose 708
  more – than alive
  688
  – asleep 683
  – beat
  powerless 158
  – certainty 474
  – colour 556
  – cut 893
  – drunk 959
  – failure 732
  – flat 213
  – heat 27
  – languages 560
  – letter
  impotent 158
  unmeaning 517
  useless 645
  laxity 738
  exempt 927
  illegal 964
  – level 16
  – lift *exertion* 686
  difficulty 704, 706

kill 361
play havoc 659
punish 972
decipher 522
decision
  judgment 480
  resolution 604
  intention 620
  law case 969
decisive
  certain 474
  proof 478
  commanding 741
  take a – step 609
deck *floor* 211
  beautify 847
declaim 531, 582
  – against 932
declamatory
  style 577
  speech 582
declaration
  affirmation 535
  law pleadings 969
  – of faith
  belief 484
  theology 983
  – of war 713
declaratory
  meaning 516
  inform 527
declare
  publish 531
declension
  [*see* decline]
  grammar 567
  backsliding 988
declensions 5
declination
  [*see* decline]
  deviation 279
  measurement 466
  rejection 610
decline *decrease* 36
  old 124
  weaken 160
  descent 306
  grammar 567
  be unwilling 603
  reject 610
  disease 655
  become worse 659
  adversity 735
  refuse 764
  – of day 126
  – of life 128
declivity *slope* 217
  descent 306
decoction 335, 384
decode 522
decollate 972

décolleté 226
decoloration 429
decomposition 49
deconsecrate 756
decontrol 158
décor 448, 599
decoration
  insignia 747
  ornament 847
  title 877
decorative 556
decorous
  [*see* decorum]
  fashionable 862
  proper 924
  respectful 928
decorticate 226
decorum
  fashion 852
  duty 926
  purity 960
décousu
  discontinuous 70
  failure 732
decoy *attract* 288
  deceive 545
  deceiver 548
  entice 615
decrease 36, 195
decree
  judgment 480
  order 741
  law 963, 969
decrement
  decrease 36
  thing deducted **40a**
  contraction 195
decrepit *old* 128
  weak 158, 160
  disease 655
  decayed 659
decrepitate 406
decrescendo 36
decretal 741
decry *underrate* 483
  censure 932
  detract 934
decumbent 213
decuple 98
decursive 306
decurtation 201
decussation 219
dedecorous
  disreputable 874
  discourteous 895
dedicate *use* 677
  inscribe 873
deduce *deduct* 38
  infer 480
deducible
  evidence 467

proof 478
deduct *retrench* 38
  deprive 789
  subtract 813
deduction
  [*see* deduce]
  decrement **40a**
  reasoning 476
deed *evidence* 467
  record 551
  act 680
  security 771
  –s of arms 720
  – without a name
  947
deem 484
deemster 967
deep *great* 31
  profound 208
  sea 341
  sonorous 404
  cunning 702
  plough the – 267
  – colour 428
  – in debt 806
  – game 702
  – knowledge 490
  – mourning 839
  – note 408
  – potations 959
  – reflection 451
  – sense 821
  – sigh 839
  – study 457
  in – water 704
deepen 35
deep-dyed
  intense 171
  black 431
  vicious 945
deep-felt 821
deep-laid *plan* 626
deep-mouthed
  resonant 408
  bark 412
  thrilling 821
deep-musing 458
deep-read 490
deep-rooted
  stable 150
  strong 159
  belief 484
  habit 613
  affections 820
deep-sea 208
deep-seated 208,
  221
deer 366
  in heart a – 862
deev 980
deface

destroy form 241
  obliterate 552
  injure 659
  render ugly 846
defalcation
  incomplete 53
  contraction 195
  shortcoming 304
  non-payment 808
defame *shame* 874
  censure 932
  detract 934
defamer 936
defatigation 841
default
  incomplete 53
  shortcoming 304
  neglect 460
  insufficiency 640
  debt 806
  non-payment 808
  in – of 187
  judgment by – 725
defaulter *thief* 792
  non-payer 808
  rogue 949
defeasance 756
defeat
  confute 479
  succeed 731
  failure 732
  – one's hope 509
defeatism 911
defecate 652
defecation 299
defect
  decrement **40a**
  incomplete 53
  imperfect 651
  failing 945
defection
  relinquishment
  624
  disobedience 742
defective
  incomplete 53
  insufficient 640
  imperfect 651
defence
  plea 462
  resist **717**
  vindication 937
  first line of – 726
defenceless
  impotent 158
  weak 160
  exposed 665
defendant 938
defensible *safe* 664
  excusable 937
defensive alliance

712
defer 133
  – to *assent* 488
  submit 725
  respect 928
deference
  obedience 743
  humility 879
  courtesy 894
  respect 928
defiance 715, 909
  threat 909
  in – *opposition* 708
  set at – *disobey* 742
  – of danger 861
deficiency
  [see deficient]
  vice 945
deficient
  inferior 34
  incomplete 53
  shortcoming 304
  insufficient 640
  imperfect 651
deficit
  incompleteness 53
  debt 806
defigure 846
defile
  interval 198
  march 266
  dirt 653
  spoil 659
  shame 874
  impure 961
define
  specify 79
  limit 233
  explain 522
  name 564
definite
  [see define]
  visible 446
  certain 474
  exact 494
  intelligible 518
  manifest 525
  perspicuous 570
definition
  interpretation 521
definitive *final* 67
  affirmative 535
  decided 604
deflagration 384
deflate 195
deflation
  currency 800
deflect
  curve 245
  deviate 279
deflower

spoil 659
violate 961
defluxion
  egress 295
  flowing 348
defœdation 653, 659
deform 241
deformity
  distortion 243
  ugliness 846
  blemish 848
defraud *cheat* 545
  swindle 791
defray 807
deft *suitable* 23
  clever 698
defunct 360, 362
defy 715
  disobey 742
  threaten 909
  – *danger* 861
dégagé *free* 748
  fashion 852
degenerate 659
deglutition 298
degradation
  deterioration 659
  shame 874
  dishonour 940
degree 26
  term 71
  honour 873
  by –s 26
  by slow –s 275
degustation 390
dehiscence 260
dehort
  dissuade 616
  advise 695
dehydrate 340
Dei gratiâ 924
deification 873, 981
deify
  honour 873
  idolatry 991
deign
  condescend 762
  consent 879
Deism
  heterodoxy 984
  irreligion 989
Deity 976
  tutelary – 664
dejection
  excretion 299
  melancholy **837**
déjeúner 298
délabrement 162
delaceration 659
delation 938

delator 527
delay 133
dele 552
delectable
  savoury 394
  agreeable 829
delectation 827
delectus 562
delegate
  transfer 270
  commission 755
  consignee 758
  deputy 759
delenda est Carthago
  destroy 162
  curse 908
delete 162
deleterious
  pernicious 649
  unwholesome 657
deletion 552
deletory
  destructive 162
deliberate
  slow 275
  think 451
  attentive 457
  leisure 685
  advise 695
  cautious 864
deliberately
  [see deliberate]
  late 133
  with premedi-
  tation 611
delicacy *weak* 160
  slender 203
  dainty 298
  brittleness 328
  texture 329
  savoury 394
  colour 428
  exact 494
  scruple 603
  ill health 655
  difficult 704
  pleasing 829
  beauty 845
  taste 850
  fastidious 868
  honour 939
  pure 960
  delicate ear 418
délice 377
delicious *taste* 394
  pleasing 829
delicti, corpus –
  guilt 947
  lawsuit 969
delicto, in

flagrante – 947
delight
  pleasure 827
  pleasing 829
Delilah 962
delimit 233
delineate
  outline 230
  represent 554
  describe 594
delineator 559
delineavit 556
delinquency 304, 947
delinquent 949
deliquation 335
deliquesce 36
deliquescence 335
deliquium
  paralysis 158
  fatigue 688
delirant reges plectuntur Achivi 739
delirium
  raving 503
  passion 825
  – *tremens* 503, 959
delitescence
  invisible 447
  latency 526
  seclusion 893
deliver
  transfer 270
  utter 580, 582
  birth 662
  rescue 672
  liberate 750
  give 784
  relieve 834
  – as one's act and deed 467
  – the goods 729
  – judgment 480
  – a speech 582
deliverance 672
delivery
  [see deliver]
  bring forth 161
  cash on – 807
dell 252
Delphic oracle
  prophetic 513
  equivocal 520
  latent 526
delta 342
delude *error* 495
  deceive 545
deluge *crowd* 72
  water 337

flood 348
redundance 641
delusion
[see delude]
insane 503
self – *credulous* 486
delve *dig* 252
till 371
– into *inquire* 461
demagogue
director 694
malcontent 710
rebel 742
demagogy 737
demand
inquire 461
order 741
ask 765
price 812
claim 924
in – *require* 630
desire 865
saleable 796
demarcation 233
dematerialize 317
demean oneself
conduct 692
humble 879
dishonour 940
demeanour
aid 448
conduct 692
fashion 852
demency 503
dementia 503
demerit 945
demesne
abode 189
property 780
demi- 91
demigod *hero* 861
angel 948
demigration 266
demijohn 191
demi-jour 422
demi-lune 717
demi-monde
plebeian 876
licentious 962
démenti 536
demirep 962
demise *death* 360
transfer 783
lease 787
demisemiquaver 413
demission 756
demit 757
demiurge
deity 979

demivolt 309
demobilize 73
democracy *rule* 737
commonalty 876
Democrats
party 712
Democritus 838
demoiselle 129
demolish 479
demon *violent* 173
bane 663
devil **980**
– in human shape 913, 949
– *worship* 991
demoniacal
malevolent 907
furious 824
wicked 945
demonology
demons 980
sorcery 992
demonstration
number 85
proof **478**
manifest 525
ostentation 882
ocular – 441, 446
demonstrative
manifest 525
indicative 550
vehement 825
demonstrator 524
demoralize
unnerve 158
spoil 659
vicious 945
Demosthenes 582
demotic 590
demulcent
mild 174
soothing 662
demur
disbelieve 485
dissent 489
unwilling 603
hesitate 605
without – 602
demure
grave 826
sad 837
affected 855
modest 881
demurrage 132
demurrer 969
den *abode* 189
study 191, 893
sty 653
prison 752
– of thieves 791

denary 98
denaturalize
corrupt 659
denaturalized
abnormal 83
dendriform 242, 367
dendrology 369
denial
negation 536
refusal 764
self – 953
denigrate 431
denization 748
denizen
inhabitant 188
freeman 748
–s of the air 979
–s of the day 366
Denmark, rotten in the state of – 526
denomination
class 75
name 564
sect 712
religious – 983
denominational
dissent 489
theological 983
– education 537
denominator 84
denote
specify 79
mean 516
indicate 550
dénouement
end 67
result 154
disclosure 529
completion 729
denounce
curse 908
disapprove 932
accuse 938
dense
crowded 72
ignorant 493
density **321**
dent 252, 257
dental 561
denticulated 253, 257
dentifrice 652
dentistry 662
denude 226
denuded *loss* 776
– of
insufficient 640
denunciation
[see denounce]
deny *dissent* 489

negative 556
refuse 764
– oneself
avoid 623
seclude 893
temperate 953
ascetic 990
Deo volente 470, 976
deobstruct 705
deodand 974
deodorize 399
clean 652
deontology 926
deoppilation 705
deorganization 61
deosculation 902
depart 293
– from
deviate 15, 279
relinquish 624
– this life 360
departed
non-existent 2
department
class 75
region 181
business 625
departure 293
new – 66
point of – 293
depend *hang* 214
contingent 475
– upon
be the effect of 154
evidence 467
trust 484
– on circumstances 475
depended on, to be –
certain 474
reliable 484
honourable 939
dependency 777, 780
dependent
effect 154
liable 177
hanging 214
puppet 711
servant 746
subject 749
deperdition 776
dephlegmation 340
depict 554, 556
describe 594
depilation 226
depilatory 662
depletion 638, 640
deplorable *bad* 649

agree to – 489
beg to – 439
– in opinion 489
– toto cœlo
  contrary 14
  dissimilar 18
  dissent 489
difference 15
  [*see* differ]
  numerical 84
  perception of –
    465
  split the – 774
  – engine 85
different 15
  multiform 81
  – time **119**
differentia 15
differential 15, 84
  – calculus 85
differentiate 79, 465
differentiation
  calculation 85
  discrimination
    465
difficult 704
  – to please 868
difficulties
  poverty 804
  in – 806
difficulty 704
  question 461
diffide 485
diffident 860, 881
diffluent 348
diffraction 470
  – grating 445
diffuse *mix* 41
  disperse 73
  publish 531
  style 573
diffuseness 104, **573**
dig *deepen* 208
  excavate 252
  till 371
  – out 461
  – the foundations
    673
  – up 455, 480*a*
digamy 903
digest *arrange* 60
  boil 384
  think 451
  compendium 596
  plan 626
  prepare 673
  brook 826
diggings 189
dight *dress* 225
  ornament 847
digit 84

digitate 44
digitated 253
digladiation 720
dignify 873
dignitary
  clergy 996
dignity
  glory 873
  pride 878
  honour 939
dignus vindice
  nodus
  unintelligible 519
  difficulty 704
  prodigy 872
digress
  deviate 279
  style 573
digression
  circuit 629
dihedral 89
  – angle 244
diis alitur visum
  disappointment
    509
  necessity 601
dijudication 480
dike *gap* 198
  fence 232
  furrow 259
  gulf 343
  conduit 350
  defence 717
dilaceration 44
dilapidation 659
dilate
  increase 35
  swell 194
  widen 202
  rarefy 322
  expatiate 573
dilatory
  slow 275
  inactive 683
dilection 89
dilemma
  uncertain 475
  logic 476
  choice 609
  difficulty 704
dilettante 492, 850
dilettantism
  knowledge 490
diligence
  coach 272
diligent
  active 682
  – thought 457
dilly-dally
  irresolution 605
  inactivity 683

dilucidation 522
diluent 335
dilute *weaken* 160
  water 337
diluvian 124
dim *dark* 421
  faint 422
  invisible 447
  unintelligible 519
dime 800
dimension 192
dimidiate 91
diminish
  lessen 36
  contract 195
  – the number 103
diminutive 32, 193
diminuendo
  decreasingly 36
  music 415
dimness **422**
dimple 252, 257
dimsightedness **443**
  unwise 499
din 404
  – in the ear
  repeat 104
  drum 407
  loquacity 584
dine 298
  – with Duke
    Humphrey 87
ding 408
ding-dong
  repeat 104
  chime 407
dining-car 272
dining-room 191
dingle 252
dingy *boat* 273
  dark 421, 422
  colourless 429
  black 431
  gray 432
dinner 298
  – jacket 225
  – party 892
dint *power* 157
  concavity 252
  blow 276
  by – of
  instrumentality
    631
dio, sub – 220, 338
diocesan 996
diocese 181, 995
Diogenes
  recluse 893
  cynic 911
  lantern of –
  inquiry 461

dioptrics 420
diorama *view* 448
  painting 556
diorism 465
dip *slope* 217
  concavity 252
  ladle 270
  direction 278
  insert 300
  descent 306
  plunge 310
  water 337
  candle 423
  baptize 998
  – one's hands into
  take 789
  – into
  glance at 457
  inquire 461
  learn 539
diphthong 561
diploma
  evidence 467
  commission 755
diplomacy
  artfulness 702
  mediation 724
  negotiation 769
diplomatist
  messenger 534
  expert 700
  consignee 758
dipper 191
dipsomania
  insanity 503
  desire 865
  drunkenness 959
dipsomaniac 504
diptych 86, 551
dire *hateful* 649
  disastrous 735
  grievous 830
  fearful 860
direct
  straight 246
  teach 537
  artless 703
  command 741
  – attention to **457**
  – one's course
  motion 278
  pursuit 622
  – the eyes to 441
direction
  [*see* direct]
  tendency **278**
  indication 550
  management **693**
  precept 697
directly *soon* 132
director

teacher 540
theatre 599
manager **694**
master 745
– of the budget
801
directorship 737
directory *list* 86
council 696
diremption 44
direption 791
dirge
funeral 363
song 415
lament 839
dirigible balloon
273, 726
dirk 727
dirt 653
throw –
defame 874
disrespect 929
– cheap 815
like – under one's
feet 749
dirty *dim* 222
opaque 426
unclean 653
disreputable 874
dishonourable 940
– end of stick 699
– sky 353
– weather 349
do – work
servile 886
flatterer 935
diruption 162
disability
impotence 158
disable 158
weaken 160
disabuse 527, 529
disaccord 713
disadvantage
evil 619
inexpedience 647
at a – 34
lie under a – 651
disadvantageous
647, 649
disaffection
dissent 489
enmity 889
hate 898
disaffirm 536
disagreeable 830,
867
disagreement
difference 15
incongruity **24**
dissent 489

discord 713
disallow 761
disannul 756
disappearance 449
disappointment
balk **509**
fail 732
discontent 832
disapprobation 706,
932
disapprover 936
disarm *disable* 158
weaken 160
reconcile 831
propitiate 914
disarrange 61
disarray
disorder 59
undress 226
disaster *evil* 619
failure 732
adversity 735
calamity 830
disastrous *bad* 649
disavow 536
disband
separate 44
disperse 73
liberate 750
disbar
abrogate 756
punish 972
disbarment 55
disbelief 485, 487
religious 989
disbench 756, 972
disbowel 297
disbranch 44
disburden
facilitate 705
– one's mind 529
– oneself of 782
disburse 809
disc 220, 234
discard *eject* 297
relinquish 624
disuse 678
abrogate 756
refuse 764
repudiate 773
surrender 782
– from one's
thoughts 458
discarded 495
disceptation 476
discern *see* 441
know 490
discernible 446
discernment 498,
868
discerption 44

discharge
violence 173
propel 284
emit 297
excrete 299
sound 406
acquit oneself 692
complete 729
liberate 750
abrogate 756
pay 807
exempt 927a
acquit 970
– a duty 926, 944
– a function
business 625
utility 644
– itself *egress* 295
river 348
– from the mem-
ory 506
– from the mind
458
– an obligation
772
discind 44
disciple *pupil* 541
votary 711
Christian 985
disciplinarian
master 540
martinet 739
discipline
order 58
teaching 537
training 673
restraint 751
punishment 972
religious 990
disclaim *deny* 536
repudiate 756
abjure 757
refuse 764
disclosure 480a, **529**
discoid *layer* 204
frontal 220
flat 251
discoloration 429
discoloured
shabby 659
ugly 846
blemish 848
discomfit 731
discomfiture 732
discomfort
physical 378
mental 828
discommend 932
discommode
hinder 706
annoy 830

discommodious
645, 647
discompose
derange 61
put out 458
hinder 706
pain 830
disconcert 874
anger 900
discomposure 828
disconcert
derange 61
distract 458
disappoint 509
hinder 706
discontent 832
confuse 879
disconcerted
hopeless 859
disconformity 83
discongruity 24
disconnected
style 575
disconnection
irrelation 19
disjunction 44
discontinuity 70
disconsolate 837
discontent 832
discontinuance
cessation 142
relinquishment
624
discontinuity 70
discord
difference 15
disagreement 24
of sound **414**
of colour 428
dissension **713**
discount
decrease 36
decrement 40a
money 813
at a –
disrepute 874
disapproved 932
discountenance
disfavour 706
refuse 764
discourage
dissuade 616
sadden 837
frighten 860
discourse
teach 537
speech 582
talk 588
dissert 595
sermon 998
discourtesy 895

discous 202
discover
  perceive 441
  solve 462
  find 480a
  disclose 529
  – *itself*
  be seen 446
discovery 480a
discredit
  disbelief 485
  dishonour 874
discreditable
  vicious 945
discreet *careful* 459
  cautious 864
discrepancy 15
discrepant 24, 713
discrete
  separate 44, 70
  single 87
discretion *will* 600
  choice 609
  skill 698
  caution 864
  surrender at – 725
  use – 609
  years of – 131
discrétion à – 600
discrimination
  difference 15
  nice perception
  465
  wisdom 498
  taste 850
  fastidiousness 868
disculpate 937
discumbency 213
discursion 266
discursive
  moving 264
  migratory 266
  wandering 279
  argumentative 476
  diffuse style 573
  conversable 588
  disserting 595
discus 840
discuss *eat* 298
  reflect 451
  inquire 461
  reason 476
  dissert 595
discussion
  [*see* discuss]
  open to – 475
  under – 461
disdain
  indifference 866
  fastidious 868
  arrogance 885

  pride 878
  contempt 930
disease **655**
  occupational – 655
  –d mind 503
disembark 292
disembarrass 705
disembody
  decompose 49
  disperse 73
  spiritualize 317
disembogue
  emit 295
  eject 297
  flow out 348
disembowel 297,
  301
disembroil 60
disenable 158
disenchant
  discover 480a
  dissuade 616
  displease 830
disencumber 705
disendow 756
disengage
  detach 44
  facilitate 705
  liberate 750
disengaged
  to let 763
disentangle
  separate 44
  arrange 60
  unroll 313
  decipher 522
  facilitate 705
  liberate 750
disenthral 750
disenthrone 756
disentitle 925
disespouse 905
disestablish
  displace 185
  abrogate 756
disesteem 929, 932
disfavour
  oppose 708
  hate 898
  disrespect 929
  view with – 932
disfigure
  deface 241
  injure 659
  deform 846
  blemish 848
disfranchise 925
disgorge *emit* 297
  flow out 348
  restore 790
  pay 807

disgrace
  shame 874
  dishonour 940
  sense of – 879
disgraceful
  vice 945
disgruntle 509
disguise
  unlikeness 18
  conceal 528
  mask 530
  falsify 544
  untruth 546
disguised in drink
  959
disgust *taste* 395
  offensive 830
  weary 841
  dislike 867
  hatred 898
  – of life 837
dish *destroy* 162
  plate 191
  food 298
  – of tea 892
dishabille
  undress 225
  unprepared 674
dishearten
  dissuade 616
  pain 830
  discontent 832
  deject 837
dished 252, 732
disherison 789
dishevel
  loose 47
  untidy 59
  disorder 61
  disperse 73
  intermix 219
dishonest *false* 544
  base 940
dishonour
  disrepute 874
  disrespect 929
  baseness 940
  – bills 808
dish-water 653
disillusion 509
disincline
  dissuade 616
  dislike 867
disinclined 603
disinfect
  purify 652
  restore 660
disinfectant 662
disingenuous
  false 544
  dishonourable 940

disinherit
  relinquish 782
  transfer 783
  deprive 789
disintegrate
  separate 44
  decompose 49
  pulverize 330
disinter *exhume* 363
  discover 480a
disinterested **942**
disjecta membra
  separate 44
  disorder 59
  dispersed 73
  – *poetæ* 597
disjoin 44
disjointed
  disorder 59
  powerless 158
  style 575
disjunction **44**
disjunctive 70
diskindness 907
dislike **867**
  reluctance 603
  hate 898
dislocate
  separate 44
  put out of joint 61
dislocated
  disorder 59
dislodge
  displace 185
  eject 297
disloyal 940
dismal
  depressing 830
  dejected 837
dismantle
  destroy 162
  divest 226
  render useless 645
  injure 659
  disuse 678
dismask 529
dismast
  render useless 645
  injure 659
  disuse 678
dismay 860
dismember
  separate 44
  disperse 73
dismiss
  send away 289
  discharge 297
  discard 678
  liberate 750
  abrogate 756
  relinquish 782

abrogate 756
dissolving views
448, 449
dissonance
disagreement 24
unmusical 414
discord 713
dissuasion 616
dissyllable 561
distaff
– *side* 374
distain *dirty* 653
ugly 846
distal 196
distance 196
overtake 282
go beyond 303
defeat 731
angular – 244
keep at a –
discourtesy 895
keep one's –
avoid 623
modest 881
respect 928
teach one his – 879
– *of time*
long time 110
past 122
distaste 867
distasteful 830
distemper 299, 428
colour 428
painting 556
disease 655
distend 194
distended 192
distich 89, 597
distil *come out* 295
extract 301
evaporate 336
drop 348
distinct
disjoined 44
audible 402
visible 446
intelligible 518
manifest 525
express 535
articulate 580
distinction
difference 15
discrimination
465
style 578
fame 873
rank 875
– without a differ-
ence 27
distinctive 15
– *feature* 79

distinctness 15
distingué 852, 873
distinguish
perceive 441
discriminate 465
– by the name of
564
distinguishable 15
distinguished
superior 33
repute 873
**Distinguished
Service Cross**
733
distortion
obliquity 217
twist **243**
of vision 443
misinterpret 523
falsehood 544
misrepresent 555
ugly 846
distract 458
distracted
confused 475
insane 503
excited 824
distraction
passion 825
love to – 897
distrain *take* 789
appraise 812
attach 969
distrait 458
distraught 824
distress
distraint 789
poverty 804
affliction 828
cause pain 830
signal of – 669
distressingly
excessively 31
distribute
arrange 60
disperse 44, 73
allot 786
district 181
– *council* 696
distrust
disbelief 485
fear 860
distrustful 487
disturb
derange 61
change 140
agitate 315
excite 824
distress 828, 830
disturbance 59
disunion

discord 24
separation 44
disorder 59
discord 713
disuse
desuetude 614
relinquish 624
unemploy **678**
disused
old 124
disvalue 932
ditch
inclosure 232
trench 259
water 343
conduit 350
defence 717
to the last – 606
ditch-water 653
ditheism 984
dither 315
dithyramb
music 415
poetry 597
dithyrambic 503
ditto 13, 104
say – to 488
ditty 415
– *box* 191
diurnal 138
diuturnity 110
diva 416
divagate 279, 629
divan *sofa* 215
council 696
throne 747
tribunal 966
divaricate *differ* 15
bifurcate 91
diverge 291
dive *swim* 267
fly 267
plunge 306, 310
– *into inquire* 461
divellicate 44
diver 208
divergence
difference 15
variation 20a
disagreement 24
deviation 279
separation **291**
divers *different* 15
multiform 81
many 102
– *coloured* 440
diverse 15
diversify
very 20a
change 140
diversion

change 140
deviation 279
pleasure 377
amusement 840
diversity
difference 15
irregular 16a
dissimilar 18
multiform 81
– *of opinion* 489
divert *turn* 279
deceive 545
amuse 840
– the mind 452,
458
divertissement
diversion 377
drama 599
amusement 840
Dives 803
divest *denude* 226
take 789
– *oneself of*
abrogate 756
relinquish 782
divestment 226
divide *differ* 15
separate 44
part 51
arrange 60
arithmetic 85
bisect 91
vote 609
apportion 786
dividend *part* 51
number 84
portion 786
**divina particula
auræ** 450
divination
prediction 511
sorcery 992
divine *predict* 511
guess 514
perfect 650
of God 976, 983,
983a
clergyman 996
divine afflatus 515
– *right*
authority 737
due 924
– *service* 990
diving 840
diving-bell 208
diving-rod 550,
993
Divinity *God* 976
theology 983
divisible
number 84

division
[*see* divide]
part 51
class 75
arithmetic 85
discord 713
military 726
divisor 84
divorce
separation 44
relinquish 782
matrimonial **905**
Divorce Court 966
divulge 529
divulsion 44
divvy 786
dixi 535
dizen 847
dizzard 501
dizzy
dimsighted 443
confused 458
vertigo 503
– height 206
– round 312
djerrid 727
djinn 980
do *fare* 7
suit 23
produce 161
cheat 545
act 680
complete 729
succeed 731
I beg 765
all one can – 686
plenty to – 682
thing to – 625
– away with
destroy 162
eject 297
abrogate 756
– battle 722
– one's bidding
743
– business 625
– to death 361
– as done by 906,
942
– for *destroy* 162
kill 361
conquer 731
serve 746
punish 972
– good 906
– harm 907
– honour 873
– into
translate 522
– justice to 595
– like 19

– little 683
– no harm 648
– nothing 681
– nothing but 136
– one's office 772
– as others do 82
– over 223
– as one pleases
748
– a service
useful 644
aid 707
– up 660
have to – with
680, 692
– without 678
– the work 686
– wrong 923
docere, pisces na-
tare – 641
docile *domesticated*
370
learning 539
willing 602
docimastic 463
dock *diminish* 36
cut off 38
port 189
shorten 201
edge 231
store 636
tribunal 966
docked
incomplete 53
docker 690
docket
list 86
evidence 467
note 550
record 551
security 771
dockyard 691
doctor
learned man 492
restore 660
remedy 662
after death the –
135
– accounts 811
when –s disagree
475
doctrinaire
positive 474
pedant 492
affectation 855
blusterer 887
doctrinal 537
doctrinarian 514
doctrine *tenet* 484
knowledge 490
document 551

documentary
evidence 467
dodder 315
doddering 128
dodecahedron 244
dodge *change* 140
shift 264
deviate 279
oscillate 314
pursue 461
avoid 623
stratagem 702
dodger, artful – 792
dodo 366
extinct as the –
122
doe *swift* 274
deer 366
female 374
doer
originator 164
agent 690
doff 226
– the cap 894
dog *follow* 281
animal 366
male 373
pursue 622
wretch 949
cast to the –s
destroy 162
reject 610
disuse 678
abrogate 756
relinquish 782
fire – 386
go, to the –s
destruction 162
fail 732
adversity 735
poverty 804
sea – 269
watch –
safety 664
warning 668
keeper 753
hair of – that bit
you 959
let sleeping –s lie
141
– in manger 706,
943
–tired 686
–s of war 722
dog-cart 272
dog-cheap 815
dog-days 382
doge 745
dogged
obstinate 606
valour 861

sullen 901*a*
dogger 273
doggerel
verse 597
ridiculous 851,
853
dog-hole 189
dog-Latin 563
dogma *tenet* 484
theology 983
dogmatic
certain 474
positive 481
assertion 535
obstinate 606
dogmatist 887
dog's ear 258
dog robber 746
dog-sick 867
dog-star 423
dog-trot 275
dog-weary 688
doily 852
doing
up and – 682
what one is – 625
doings
events 151
actions 680
conduct 692
doit *trifle* 643
coin 800
dolce far niente 681
doldrums
dejection 837
sulks 901*a*
dole
small quantity 32
scant 640
give 784
allot 786
parsimony 819
grief 828
doleful 837
– dumps 901*a*
doll *small* 193
image 554
dollar 800
dolman 225
dolmen 363, 551
dolorem, infandum
renovare – 833
dolorous 830
dolour
physical 378
moral 828
dolphin 341
dolt 501
doltish 499
domain
class 75

region 181
property 780
Domdaniel 982
dome high 206
  roof 223
  curvature 245
  convex 250
Domesday book
  list 86
  record 551
domesman 967
domestic
  inhabitant 188
  home 189
  interior 221
  servant 746
  secluded 893
  – animals 366
domesticate
  locate 184
  acclimatize 613
  – animals 370
domicile 189
domiciled 186
domiciliary 188
  – visit 461
dominant 175
  note in music 413
domination 737
dominical 998
domineer
  tyrannize 739
  insolence 885
Domini, anno – 106
Dominican 996
Dominie 540
dominion 181, 737
domino dress 225
  mask 530
  game 840
domn 745
don put on 225
  scholar 492
  teacher 540
  noble 875
Don Juan 897
donation 784
done finished 729
  work – 729
  – for spoilt 659
  failure 732
  – up
  impotent 158
  tired 688
  have – with
  cease 142
  relinquish 624
  disuse 678
donee 785
donjon 717, 752
donkey ass 271

fool 501
talk a –'s hind leg
  off 584
donna 374
Donnybrook Fair
  disorder 59
  discord 713
donor 784
donzel 746
doodle 501
doom end 67
  fate 152
  destruction 162
  death 360
  judgment 480
  necessity 601
  sentence 971
  – sealed
  death 360
  adversity 735
doomed 735, 828
doomsday
  end 67
  future 121
  till – 112
door entrance 66
  cover 223
  brink 231
  barrier 232
  opening 260
  passage 627
  at one's – 197
  beg from door to –
  765
  bolt the – 666
  close the – upon
  751
  death's – 360
  keep within –s 265
  lie at one's – 926
  lock the – 666
  open a – to
  liable 177
  open the – to
  receive 296
  facilitate 705
  permit 760
  show the – to
  eject 297
  discourtesy 895
  – mat 652
doorkeeper 263
doorway 260
dope 376, 545, 663
doquet
  security 771
Dorado, El – 803
Doric mode 413
dormant
  inert 172
  latent 526

asleep 683
dormer 260
dormeuse 272
dormir debout,
  conte à – 843
dormitive 841
dormitory 191
dormouse 683
dorp 189
dorsal 235
dorser 191
dorsum 235, 250
dory 273
dose quantity 25
  part 51
  medicine 662
  apportion 786
dosser 191
dossier bundle 72
  record 551
dossil 223, 263
dot small 32
  place 182
  little 193
  variegate 440
  mark 550
  dowry 780
  on the – 113
dotage 128, 499
dotard 130, 501
dotation 784
dottle 40, 645
dote drivel 499, 503
  – upon 897
douanier 965
double
  similar 17
  increase 35
  duplex 90
  substitute 147
  fold 258
  turn 283
  finesse 702
  march at the – 274
  see –
  dim sight 443
  drunk 959
  – acrostic
  letters 561
  wit 842
  – dutch 518
  – entry 811
  – the fist 909
  – march 684
  – meaning 520
  – a point 311
  in – quick time
  274
  – reef topsails 664
  – sure 474
  work – tides 686

– up
  render powerless
  158
double bar 747
double-bass 417
doublecross 545
double-dealing
  lie 544
  cunning 940
double-distilled 171
double-dyed 428
double-eagle 800
double-edged 90,
  171
double entendre
  ambiguity 520
  impure 961
double-faced
  lie 544
  cunning 702, 940
double-headed 90
double-minded 605
double-shotted 171
doublet 225
double-tongued
  lie 544
  cunning 702, 940
doubt
  uncertain 475
  disbelieve **485**
  sceptic 989
doubtful 475
  more than – 473
  – meaning
  unintelligible 519
doubtless
  certain 474
  belief 484
  assent 488
douceur 784, 973
douche 337
dough 324, 354, 800
doughty 861
dour 739
douse
  immerse 310
  splash 337
  blow 972
Dove
  Holy Ghost 976
dove
  innocent 946
  roar like sucking –
  174
dovecote 189
dovetail
  agree 23
  join 43
  intersect 219
  intervene 228
  angle 244

insert 300
dowager 374, 905
dowdy 653, 851
dower 780, 803, 810
dowerless 804
down
  below 207
  light 320
  bear – upon 716
  bed of –
    pleasure 377
    repose 687
  come – 306
  get – 306
  go –
    sink 306
    calm 826
  keep – 36
  money – 807
  take –
    lower 308
    rebuff 874
    humble 879
  – on one's mar-
    row-bones 886
  – in the mouth 837
  – and out 874
  – in price 815
  go – like a stone
    310
  be – upon
    attack 716
    severe 739
  downcast 306, 837
  – eyes 879
downfall
  destruction 162
  fall 306
  failure 732
  misfortune 735
downhill 217, 306
  go –
    adversity 735
downpour 348
downright
  absolute 31
  manifest 525
  sincere 703
downs 206, 344
down-trodden
  submission 725
  vanquished 732
  subject 749
  dejected 837
  disrepute 874
  contempt 930
downwards 306
downy
  smooth 255
  plumose 256
  soft 324

dowry 780, 784
dowse 276
dowser 994
doxology 990
doxy 897
doyer 128
doyley 652
doze 683
dozen 98
drab *colour* 432
  slut 653
  hussy 962
drabble 653
drachm 319
Draco 694, 739
draff 653
draft [*see also*
  draught]
  multitude 102
  drawing 554, 556
  write 590
  abstract 596
  plan 626
  cheque 800
  credit 805
  – off *displace* 185
  transfer 270
draft-horse 271
drag *carriage* 272
  crawl 275
  traction 285
  impediment 706
  put on the – 275
  – a chain
    tedious 109, 110
    exertion 686
    subjection 749
  – into
    implicate 54
    compel 744
  – through mire
    disrepute 874
    disrespect 929
  – on *tedious* 110
  – into open day
    531
  – towards
    attract 288
  – slow length
    long 200
    weary 841
draggle 285, 653
  – tail 59
drag-net
  all sorts 78
dragoman 524
dragon *monster* 83
  violent 173
  animal 366
  irascible 901
dragonnade

attack 716
  punish 972
dragoon
  soldier 726
  compel 744
  insolent 885
  worry 907
drain
  flow out 295
  empty 297
  dry 340
  conduit 350
  waste 638
  clean 652
  unclean 653
  exhaust 789
  dissipate 818
  – the cup
    drink 298
    drunken 959
  – the cup of
    misery 828
  – into 348
  – pipe 249
  – of resources 640
drake *male* 373
  fire – 423
dram *drink* 298
  pungent 392
  stimulus 615
  – drinking 959
drama **599**
dramatic 599
  ostentation 882
  – author 599
  – critic 599
  – poetry 597
dramatis personæ
  mankind 372
  play 599
  agents 690
  party 712
drapery 225, 847
drast 645
drastic 171
draught
  [*see also* draft]
  depth 208
  traction 285
  drink 298
  stream of air 349
  delineation 554,
    556
  plan 626
  physic 662
  troops 726
  – off 73
draughts
  game 840
draughtsman
  artist 559

draw *equality* 27
  compose 54
  pull 285
  delineate 554, 556
  – aside 279
  – off the attention
    458
  – back
    deduction 40a
    regret 283
    avoid 623
  – breath
    refresh 689
    feeling 821
    relief 834
  – a cheque 800
  – a curtain 424
  – down 153
  – forth 677
  – from 810
  – on futurity 132
  – in one's horns
    tergiversation 607
    humility 879
  – in 195
  – an inference 480
  – the line 465
  – lots 621
  – near *time* 121
  approach 286
  – off *eject* 297
  hinder 706
  take 789
  – on *time* 121
  event 151
  induce 615
  – out
    protract 110
    late 133
    prolong 200
    extract 301
    discover 480a
    exhibit 525
    diffuse style 573
  – over *induce* 615
  – a parallel 9
  – the pen through
    552
  – a picture 594
  – profit 775
  – and quarter 972
  – the sword
    attack 716
    war 722
  – the teeth of 158
  – together
    assemble 72
    co-operate 709
  – towards 288
  – up *order* 58
  stop 265

write 590
- up a statement 594
- upon *money* 800
- the veil 528
drawback *evil* 619
  imperfection 651
  hindrance 706
  discount 813
drawbar 45
drawbridge
  way 627
  escape 671
  raise the - 666
drawcansir 887
drawee 800
drawer
  receptacle 191
  artist 559
  - of water 690
drawers
  dress 225
drawhead 45
drawing
  delineation 554, 556
  prize 810
drawing-room
  assembly 72
  room 191
  fashion 852
drawl *prolong* 200
  creep 275
  in speech 583
  sluggish 683
drawn *equated* 27
  - battle
  - irresistibly 601
  pacification 723
  incomplete 730
dray 272
  - horse 271
drayman 268
dread 860
dreadful *great* 31
  bad 649
  dire 830
  depressing 837
  fearful 860
dreadless 861
dreadnought
  warship 726
dream
  unsubstantial 4
  error 495
  fancy 515
  sleep 683
  golden - 858
  - of *think* 451
  intend 620
  - on other things

458
dreamer
  madman 504
  imaginative 515
dreamy
  unsubstantial 4
  inattentive 458
  sleepy 683
dreary
  monotonous 16
  solitary 87
  melancholy 830, 837
dredge *collect* 72
  extract 301
  raise 307
dregs
  remainder 40
  refuse 645
  dirt 653
  - of the people 876
  - of vice 945
drench *drink* 298
  water 337
  redundance 641
  - with physic 662
drencher 248
drenching rain 348
dress
  uniformity 16
  agree 23
  equalize 27
  clothes 225
  prepare 673
  ornament 847
  ostentation 882
  full - 852
  - circle 599
  - the ground 371
  - up *falsehood* 544
  represent 554
  - wounds 662
  - to advantage 847
dress-coat 225
dresser
  sideboard 215
  surgeon 662
dressing 932, 972
  - room 191, 599
dressing-gown 225
dressmaker 225
dribble 295, 348
driblet 25, 32
drift
  accumulate 72
  distance 196
  motion 264
  flying 267
  float 267
  transfer 270

  direction 278
  deviation 279
  approach 286
  wind 349
  meaning 516
  intention 620
  snow - 383
drifter 273
drifting 605
driftless 621
drill *fabric* 219
  bore 260
  auger 262
  teach 537
  prepare 673
  - hall 191
drink
  swallow 296
  liquor 298
  tipple 959
  - one's fill
  enough 639
  - in *imbibe* 296, 298
  - in learning 539
  - to *celebrate* 883
  courtesy 894
drinking-bout 954
drink-money 784
drip 295, 348
dripping *wet* 330
  fat 356
drive *airing* 266
  impel 276
  propel 284
  break in 370
  urge 615
  haste 684
  direct 693
  attack 716
  compel 744
  - at *mean* 516
  intend 620
  - a bargain
  barter 794
  parsimony 819
  - care away 836
  - a coach and six through 83
  - into a corner
  difficult 704
  hinder 706
  defeat 731
  subjection 749
  - to despair 859
  - matters to an extremity 604
  - from *repel* 289
  - one hard 716
  - home 729
  - in 300

- to the last 133
- out 297
- trade
  business 625
  barter 794
drivel *slobber* 297
  imbecile 499
  mad 503
  rubbish 517
driveller 501, 584
driver 268
  director 694
driving rain 348
drizzle 348
droil 683
droit du plus fort 744
drôle *cards* 840
drole 949
  - de corps 844
drollery
  amusement 840
  wit 842
  ridiculous 853
dromedary 271
drone *slow* 275
  sound 407, 412, 413
  inactive 683
drool 297
droop
  weak 160
  hang 214
  sink 306
  disease 655
  decline 659
  flag 688
  sorrow 828
  dejection 837
drop *small quantity* 32
  discontinue 142
  powerless 158
  bring forth 161
  spherule 249
  emerge 295
  fall 306
  trickle 348
  relinquish 624
  discard 782
  gallows 975
  let - 308
  ready to -
  fatigue 688
  - asleep 683
  - astern 283
  - from the couds 508
  - dead 360
  - by drop
  by degrees 26

in parts 51
– in the bucket 32
– in upon 674
– into a good
  thing 734
– into the grave
  360
– a hint 527
– all idea of 624
– in *arrive* 292
immerse 300
sociality 892
– the mask 529
– off *decrease* 36
die 360
sleep 683
– in the ocean
trifling 643
– the subject 458
– too much 959
dropping fire 70
drop-scene 599
dropsical 194, 641
droshki 272
dross
remainder 40
slag 384
trash 643, 645
dirt 653
drought
dryness 340
insufficiency 640
drouth *desire* 865
drove
assemblage 72
multitude 102
drover 370
drown
affusion 337
kill 361
ruin 731, 732
– *care* 840
– the voice 581
drowsy *slow* 275
sleepy 683
weary 841
drub
defeat 731, 732
punish 972
drudge *labour* 686
worker 682, 690
drug
render insensible
  376
superfluity 641
trash 643
remedy 662
bane 663
– in the market
  815
drugget

cover 223
clean 652
preserve 670
druggist 662
druid 996
drum
repeat 104
cylinder 249
sound 407
music 417
party 892
beat of –
signal 550
alarm 669
war 722
command 741
parade 882
ear – 418
muffled –
funeral 363
non-resonance
  408a
– and fife band 417
– *fire* 407
– *out* 972
drum-head 964,
  966
drum-major 745
drummer 416
drunken 959
reel like a – man
  315
drunkenness 959
dry *arid* 340
style 575, 576, 579
hoarse 581
scanty 640
preserve 670
exhaust 789
tedious 841
dull 842
thirsty 865
cynical 932
teetotal 958
run – 640
with – eyes 823
– dock 189
– joke 842
– land 342
– the tears 834
– up 340, 638
dryad 979
dry-as-dust
antiquarian 122
dull 843
dryness 340
dry-nurse
teach 537
teacher 540
aid 707
dry-point 558

dry-rot
dirt 653
decay 659
bane 663
dualism 984
duality 89
duarchy 737
dub 564
dubious 475
ducat 800
duce 745
duchess 745, 875
duchy 181
duck *stoop* 308
plunge 310
water 337
darling 897, 899
play –s and
  drakes
recoil 277
prodigality 818
–'s egg
zero 101
– in thunder 870
ducking-stool 975
duckling 127
duck-pond 370
duct 350
ductile
elastic 323
flexible 324
trimming 607
easy 705
docile 743
dud 158, 727
dude 854
duds 225
dudgeon
dagger 727
discontent 832
churlishness 895
hate 898
anger 900
sullenness 901a
due
expedient 646
owing 806
proper 924, 926
give his – to
right 922
vindication 937
fair 939
in – course 109
– *occasion* 134
– respect 928
– sense of 498
– time
soon 132
– to
cause and effect
  154, 155

give – weight 465
duel 720
duellist 726
dueness 924
duenna
teacher 540
guardian 664
keeper 753
dues 812
duet 415
duff 298
duffer
bungler 701
smuggler 792
dug 250
dug-out
old man 130
boat 273
defence 717
duke *ruler* 745
noble 875
dulce domum 189
dulcet
sweet 396
sound 405
melodious 413
agreeable 829
dulcify 174, 396
dulcimer 417
Dulcinea 897
dulcorate 396
dulia 990
dull *weak* 160
inert 172
moderate 174
blunt 254
insensible 376,
  381
sound 405
dim 422
colourless 429
ignorant 493
stolid 499
style 575
inactive 683
unapt 699
callous 823
dejected 837
weary 841
prosing 843
simple 849
– of hearing 419
– sight 443
dullard 501
dullness 843
duly 924
duma 696
dumb 581
– animal 366
– show 550
– waiter 307

strike –
ignorant 493
astonish 870
humble 879
dumbfounder
disappoint 509
silence 581
astonish 870
humble 879
dummy
substitute 147
impotent 158
speechless 581
inactive 683
dump *music* 415
store 636
lament 839
undersell 796
dumpling 298
dumps
discontent 832
dejection 837
sulk 901a
dumpy *little* 193
short 201
thick 202
dun *dim* 422
colourless 429
grey 432
importune 765
creditor 805
dunce
ignoramus 493
fool 501
dunderhead 501
dune 206
dung 653
dungeon 752
dunghill
dirt 653
cowardly 862
baseborn 876
– *cock* 366
Dunker 984
dunt 716
duo 415
duodecimal 99
duodecimo
little 193
book 593
duodenary 98
duologue
interlocution 588
drama 599
dupe
credulous 486
deceive 545
deceived **547**
duplex 90, 189
duplicate
imitate 19

copy 21
double 90
tally 550
record 551
redundant 641
pawn 805
duplication
imitation 19
doubling **90**
repetition 104
duplicature
fold 258
duplicity
duality 89
falsehood 544
dura lex sed lex 926
durable
long time 110
stable 150
durance 141, 751
in – 754
duration 106
contingent – **108a**
infinite – 112
durbar
conference 588
council 696
tribunal 966
duress
compulsion 744
restraint 751
during 106
– *pleasure &c.*
108a
durity 323
dusk
evening 126
half-light 422
dusky
dark 421
black 431
dust *levity* 320
powder 330
corpse 362
trash 643
dirt 653
money 800
come to –
die 360
come down with
the – 807
humbled in the –
879
kick up a – 885
level with the –
162
lick the –
submit 725
fail 732
make to bite the –
731

turn to –
deorganized 358
die 360
– in the balance
643
throw – in the
eyes
blind 442
deceive 545
plead 617
– one's *jacket* 972
duster 652
dust-bin, dust-hole
191, 645
fit for the –
useless 645
dirty 653
spoilt 659
dustman
cleaner 652
dust-storm 330
dusty
powder 330
dirt 653
Dutch
double – 519
high – 519
– *auction* 796
– *courage* 862
Dutchman, flying
515
dutiful 944
duty
business 625
work 686
tax 812
courtesy 894
obligation **926**
respect 928
worship 990
rite 998
do one's –
virtue 944
on – 680, 682
duumvirate 737
Duval, Claude –
792
D.V. 470, 976
dwarf
lessen 36
small 193
elf 980
dwell
reside 186
abide 265
– upon
descant 573
dweller 188
dwelling 184, 189
dwindle *lessen* 36
shrink 195

dyad 89
dye 428
dying 360
dyke [*see* dike]
dynamic energy
157
dynamics 276
dynamitard 863
dynamite 727
dynamo 153
dynasty 737
dysentery 299
dyspepsia 655
dysphony 581

E

each 79
– to each 786
– other 12
– in his turn 148
eager
willing 602
active 682
ardent 821
desirous 865
– *expectation* 507
eagle
standard 550
money 800
– boat 726
– eye *sight* 441
intelligence 498
– winged *swift* 274
insignia 747
eagre 348
ean 161
ear 418
corn 154
come to one's –s
527
din in the –
loud 404
drum 407
all – 418
have the – of
belief 484
friendship 888
lend an –
hear 418
attend 457
meet the – 418
nice – 418
no – 419
offend the – 410
pick up the –s
attention 457
expectation 507
put about one's –s
308

quick – 418
reach one's –s 527
ring in the – 408
set by the –s
  discord 713
  hate 898
  resentment 900
split the –s 404
together by the –s
  discord 713
  contention 720
up to one's –s
  redundance 641
  active 680, 682
willing – 602
word in the – 586
– for music 416,
  418
in at one – out at
  the other
  inattention 458
  forget 506
not for –s polite
  961
make the –s tingle
  anger 900
– ache 378
ear-drum 418
earl 875
earless 419
earliness 132
early 132
get up – 682
earmark 550
earn 775
earnest *willing* 602
  determined 604
  emphatic 642
  pledge 771
  pay in advance
    809
  eager 821
in –
  affirmation 535
  veracious 543
  strenuous 682
ear-piercing 410
ear-ring 847
ear-shot 197
out of – 405
ear-splitting 404
earth *ground* 211
  world 318
  land 342
  corpse 362
what on –
  inquiry 461
  wonder 870
– closet 653
earthenware
  baked 384

sculpture 557
earthling 372
earthly 318
end of one's –
  career 360
of no – use 645
earthly-minded
  943, 989
earthquake 146,
  173
earthwork 717
earwig *flatter* 933,
  935
ear-witness 467
ease *bodily* 377
  style 578
  leisure 685
  facility 705
  mental 827
  content 831
at one's –
  prosperous 734
mind at –
  cheerful 836
set at – *relief* 834
take one's – 687
– off *deviate* 297
– one of *take* 789
easel *support* 215
  painting 556
– picture 556
easement
  property 780
  relief 834
easily
  [*see easy*]
let one down – 918
– accomplished
  705
– deceived 486
– persuaded 602
East 236, 278
Easter *period* 138
  rite 998
– Monday
  holiday 840
– offering
  gift 784
– sepulchre 1000
easy *gentle* 275
  style 578
  facile 705
make oneself –
  about 484
take it –
  inactive 683
  inexcitable 826
– ascent 217
– of belief 472
– chair
  support 215

repose 687
– circumstances
  803
– going
  willing 602
  irresolute 605
  lenient 740
  inexcitable 826
  contented 831
  indifferent 866
– sail
  moderate 174
  slow 275
– temper 894
– terms 705
– to understand
  518
– virtue 961
eat *food* 298
  tolerate 826
– dirt 725, 879
– one's fill
  enough 639
  gorge 957
– heartily 298
– one's words 879
– out of house and
  home *take* 789
  prodigal 818
  gluttony 957
– of the same
  trencher 892
– one's words 607
eatables 298
eaten up with 820
eau, battre l' – 645
faire venir l' – à la
  bouche 865
mettre de l' – dans
  son vin 174
eaves 250
eavesdropper 455,
  527
eavesdropping 418,
  532
ébauche 626
ebb *decrease* 36
  contract 195
  regress 283
  recede 287
  waste 638
  spoil 659
low – 36
  low 207
  depression 308
  insufficient 640
– and flow 314
– of life 360
ebb-tide *low* 207
  dry 340
ebony 431

ebriety 959
ebullient
  violent 173
  hot 382
  excited 824
ebullition
  energy 171
  violence 173
  agitation 315
  heating 384
  excitation 825
  anger 900
écarté 840
ecce
  – iterum Crispinus
    104
  – signum 550
eccentric 220
  irregular 83
  foolish 499
  crazed 503, 504
  capricious 608
ecchymosis 299
ecclesiastic
  church 995
  clergy 996
ecclesiastical
  canonical 985
  – court 966
  – law 963
ecclesiolatry 991
écervelé 458
échafaudage 673
échappée 840
échapper belle 671
échelon 279
echo *imitate* 19
  copy 21
  repeat 104
  reflection 277
  resonance 408
  answer 462
  assent 488
applaud to the –
  931
awake –es 404
éclaircissement 522
éclat 873
eclectic 609
eclipse *surpass* 33
  disappearance
    449
  hide 528
  outshine 873, 874
partial – *dim* 422
total – *dark* 421
under an –
  invisible 447
  out of repute 874
ecliptic 318
eclogue 597

economic pressure
751
economy
  order 58
  conduct 692
  frugality **817**
  animal – 359
écorcher les oreilles
410
ecphorize 615
écru 433
ecstasis 683
ecstasy
  frenzy 515
  transport 821
  rapture 827
ecstatic 829
ecstatica 994
ectoplasm 992
ectype 21
ecumenical 78
edacity 957
Edda 986
eddy
  whirlpool 348
  current 312
  danger 667
Eden 827
edge *energy* 171
  height 206
  brink **231**
  sidle 279
  advantage 731
  cutting – 253
  on – 256, 507
  take the – off 174
  – of hunger 865
  – in 228
  – one's way 282
edge-tools 253
  play with – 863
edgewise 217
edging
  obliquity 217
  border 231
  ornament 847
edible 298
edict 741
edification
  building 161
  teaching 537
  learning 539
  piety 987
edifice 161
edifying *good* 648
edile 965
edit
  publication 531
  condense 596
  revise 658
edition, new – 658

editor 593
educate 537
educated 490
  self – 490
education
  teaching 537
  knowledge 490
  man of – 492
  higher – 490
educational 537,
  542
educe *extract* 301
  discover 480a
educt 40
eduction 40a
edulcorate 396, 652
eel 248
  wriggle like an –
  315
eerie 860
efface
  delete 162
  disappear 449
  obliterate 552
  – from the
    memory 506
effect
  consequence **154**
  product 161
  impression 375
  complete 729
  carry into – 692
  with crushing –
    162
  in – 5
  take – 731
  to that – 516
effective
  capable 157
  useful 644
effectuation 729
expedient 646
effects 780, 798
effectual 731
effectually 52
effectuate 729
effeminate
  weak 160
  womenlike 374
  timorous 862
  sensual 954
effeminize 158
effendi 875
effervesce
  energy 171
  violence 173
  agitate 315
  bubble 353
  excited 825
effervescent 338
effete *old* 128

weak 160
useless 645
spoiled 659
efficacious
  [*see* efficient]
efficient
  power 157
  agency 170
  utility 644
  skill 698
effigy 21, 554
effleurer *skim* 267,
  460
efflorescence 330
effluxion of time
  109
effluence *egress* 295
  flow 348
effluvium 334, 398
efflux 295
efformation 240
effort 686
effreet 980
effrontery 885
effulgence 420
effuse
  pour out 295, 297
  excrete 299
  speech 582
  loquacity 584
effusion of blood
  361
effusive 573
eft 366
eftsoons 117
egad 535
égards 928
egesta 299
egestion 297
egg *beginning* 66
  cause 153
  food 298
  walk among –s
  704
  too many –s in
    one basket
  unskilful 699
  (*imprudent* 863)
  – and dart
  ornament 847
  – on 615
egg-shaped 247,
  249
ego *intrinsic* 5
  speciality 79
  immaterial 317
  non – 6
egocentrism 943
egotism
  vanity 880
  cynicism 911

selfishness 943
egregious
  exceptional 83
  absurd 497
  exaggerated 549
  important 642
egregiously 31, 33
egress **295**
Egyptian darkness
  421
eheu! fugaces
  labuntur anni
  111
eiderdown 223
eidouranion 318
Eiffel tower 206
eight *number* 98
  boat 273
  representative 759
eisteddfod 72, 416
eighty 98
either *choice* 609
  happy with – 605
ejaculate
  propel 284
  utter 580
ejection 185, **297**
ejecta 299
ejector 349
eke *also* 37
  – out *complete* 52
  spin out 110
ekka 272
El Dorado 803
elaborate
  improve 658
  prepare 673
  laborious 686
  work out 729
elaine 356
élan 276
elapse 109, 122
elastic fluid 334
elasticity
  power 157
  strength 159
  energy 171
  spring **325**
elate *cheer* 836
  rejoice 838
  hope 858
  vain 880
  boast 884
elbow *angle* 244
  projection 250
  push 276
  at one's –
  near 197
  advice 695
  lift one's –

drink 959
out at –s
  undress 226
  poor 804
  disrepute 874
  one's way
  progress 282
  pursuit 622
  active 682
elbow-chair 215
elbow-grease 331
elbow-room 180,
  748
elder *older* 124
  aged 128
  veteran 130
  clergy 996
elect *choose* 609
  good 648
  predestinate 976
  pious 987
  clergy 996
election
  numerical 84
  necessity 601
electioneering 609
elector 745
electorate 737
Electra complex
  897
electric
  swift 274
  sensation 821
  excitable 825
  car 272
  – blue 438
  – chair 974
  – light 423
  – piano 417
electrician 599, 690
electricity 157, 388
electrify
  unexpected 508
  excite 824
  astonish 870
electro-biology 992
electrocution 972
electrolier 214, 423
electrolyze 49
electro-magnetism
  157
electromobile 272
electron 32
electroplate 223
electrotype 21, 591
electuary 662
eleemosynary 784
elegance
  in style 578
  beauty 845
  taste 859

Bank of – 800
elegy *interment* 363
  poetry 597
  lament 839
element
  component 56
  beginning 66
  cause 153
  matter 316
  in one's –
  facility 705
  content 831
  devouring – 382
  out of its – 195
elementary 42
  – education 537
  – school 542
elements
  Eucharist 998
elench 477
elephant
  large 192
  carrier 271
  white – *bane* 663
elevated
  tipsy 959
elevation
  height 206
  vertical 212
  raising **307**
  plan 554
  – of style 574
  improvement 658
  glory 873
  – of mind 942
  angular – 244
élève 541
eleven 98
  representative 759
eleventh hour
  evening 126
  late 133
  opportune 134
elf *infant* 129
  little 193
  imp 980
elicit *cause* 153
  draw out 301
  discover 480a
  manifest 525
eligible 646
Elijah's mantle 63
eliminant 299
eliminate
  subduct 38
  simplify 42
  exclude 55
  weed 103
  extract 301
  reject 610
elision 44, 201

élite *best* 648
  distinguished 873
  aristocratic 875
elixation 384
elixir 662
  – of life 471
elk 223
ell 200
  take an –
  take 789
  insolence 885
  wrong 923
  undue 925
  selfish 943
ellipse 247
ellipsis *shorten* 201
  style 572
ellipsoid 247, 249
elocation 185, 270
elocution 582
éloge 931
elongation 196, 200
elopement 623, 671
eloquence 572, 582
else 37
elsewhere 187
elucidate 522
elude
  sophistry 477
  avoid 623
  escape 671
  succeed 731
  palter 773
elusive 545
elusory 546
elutriate 652
elysian 829, 981
Elysium 827, 981
elytron 223
Elzevir edition 193
emaciation 195,
  203, 640
emanate 151
  go out of 295
  excrete 299
  – from 544
emanation 398
emancipate
  facilitate 705
  free 748, 750
emasculate
  impotent 158
embalm
  interment 363
  perfume 400
  preserve 670
  – in the memory
  505
embankment
  esplanade 189
  refuge 666

fence 717
embar 229
embargo
  stoppage 265
  prohibition 761
  exclusion 893
embark
  transfer 270
  depart 293
  – in *begin* 66
  engage in 676
embarquer sans
  biscuits, s' – 674
embarras de
  – choix 609
embarrass 641,
  704, 706
embarrassed 804,
  806
embarrassing 475
embase 659
embassy
  errand 532
  commission 755
  consignee 758
embattled
  arranged 60
  leagued 712
  war array 722
embed
  locate 184
  base 215
  enclose 221
  insert 300
embellish 847
embers 384
embezzle 791
embitter
  deteriorate 659
  aggravate 835
  acerbate 900
emblazon
  colour 428
  ornament 847
  display 882
emblem 550, 747
embody
  join 43
  combine 48
  form a whole 50
  compose 54
embolden
  hope 858
  encourage 861
embolism 228, 261,
  300
embonpoint 192
embosomed
  lodged 184
  interjacent 228
  circumscribed 229

emboss *convex* 250
  ornament 847
embouchure 260
embowel 297
embrace
  cohere 46
  compose 54
  include 76
  enclose 227
  choose 609
  take 789
  friendship 888
  sociality 892
  courtesy 894
  endearment 902
  – *an offer* 760
embrangle 61
embranglement 713
embrasure 257, 260
embrocation 662
embroider
  variegate 440
  lie 544
  ornament 847
embroidery
  adjunct 39
  exaggeration 549
embroil *derange* 61
  discord 713
embroilment 59
embrown 433
embryo
  beginning 66
  cause 153
  in – *destined* 152
  preparing 673
embryology 357
embryonic 193, 674
embus 293
embusqué 603
emendation 658
emerald *green* 435
  jewel 847
emerge 295, 446
emergency
  circumstance 8
  event 151
  difficulty 704
emeritus 500, 928
emersion 295, 446
emery
  sharpener 253
  – *paper*
  smooth 255
emetic *remedy* 662
émeute 742
emication 420
emigrant 57, 268
emigrate 266, 295
emigré 268, 295
eminence

height 206
fame 873
church dignitary
  996
eminent domain
  744
eminently 33
emir 745, 875
emissary
  messenger 534
  consignee 758
emission 297
emit *eject* 297
  publish 531
  voice 580
  – *vapour* 336
Emmanuel 976
emmet 193
emollient 662
emolument
  acquisition 775
  receipt 810
  remuneration 973
emotion 821
  –*al appeal* 824
  –*al drama* 599
empale 260, 972
empanel 86, 969
empathy 515
emperor 745
emphasis 580
emphatic 535, 642
emphatically 31
empierce
  perforate 260
  insert 300
empire 737, 789
  – *day* 840
empiric 548
empirical 463, 675
empiricism 463
emplane 293
employ
  business 625
  use 677
  servitude 749
  commission 755
  in one's – 746
  – *one's capital in*
    794
  – *oneself* 680
  – *one's time in*
    625
employé
  servant 746
  agent 758
employer 795
empoison 659
emporium 799
empower
  power 157

commission 755
accredit 759
permit 760
empress 745
empressement
  activity 682
  emotion 821
  desire 865
emprise 676
emption 795
emptor 795
  caveat – 769
empty *clear* 185
  vacant 187
  deflate 195
  drain 297
  ignorant 491
  waste 638
  deficient 640
  useless 645
  beggarly account
    of – *boxes*
    poverty 804
  – *one's glass* 298
  – *purse* 804
  – *sound* 517
  – *stomach* 865
  – *title name* 564
  undue 925
  – *words* 546
empty-handed 640
empty-headed 4,
  491
empurple 437
empyrean *sky* 318
  blissful 829
empyreuma 41
empyrosis 384
emulate *imitate* 19
  goodness 648
  rival 708
  compete 720
  glory 873
emulsion 352
emunctory 350
en – bloc 50
  – *masse* 50
  – *passant*
    parenthetical 10
    transient 111
  à propos 134
  – *rapport* 9
  – *règle order* 58
  conformity 82
  – *route*
  journey 266
  progress 282
enable 157
enact *drama* 599
  action 680
  conduct 692

complete 729
order 741
law 963
enallage 521
enamel *coating* 223
  painting 556
  ornament 847
enameller 559
enamour 897
encage 751
encamp 184, 189
encampment 184
encaustic 556
enceinte
  with child 161
  region 181
  inclosure 232
enchafe 830
enchain 751
enchant *please* 829
enchanted 827
enchanting 845,
  897
enchantment
  sorcery 992
enchase 43, 259
enchiridion 593
enchorial 188
encincture 229
encircle 76, 227,
  311
enclave *close* 181
  boundary 233
enclose 227, 229
enclosure
  region 181
  envelope 232
  fence 752
encomiast 935
encomium 931
encompass 227, 233
  –*ed with difficul-*
    ties 704
encore 104, 931
encounter
  undergo 151
  clash 276
  meet 292
  withstand 708
  contest 720
  – *danger* 665
  – *risk* 621
encourage
  animate 615
  aid 707
  comfort 834
  hope 858
  embolden 861
encroach
  transcursion 303
  do wrong 923

infringe 925
encumber 704, 706
encumbrance
  clear of – 807
encyclical 531
encyclopædia 490,
  593
  walking – 700
encyclopædical
  general 78
  – knowledge 490
encysted 229
end
  termination 67
  effect 154
  object 620
  at an – 142
  come to its – 729
  one's journey's –
    292
  on – 212
  put an – to
    destroy 162
    kill 361
  begin at the
    wrong – 699
  – one's days 360
  –s of the earth 196
  – to end *space* 180
  touching 199
  length 200
  – of life 360
  – in smoke 732
  – of one's tether
    sophistry 477
    ignorant 491
    insufficient 640
    difficult 704
endamage 649
endanger 665
endear 897
endearment 902
endeavour
  pursue 622
  attempt 675
  use one's best –
    686
  – after 620
endemic
  special 79
  interior 221
  disease 657
endimanché 847,
  882
endless
  multitudinous
    102
  infinite 105
  perpetual 112
endlessly 16
endlong 200

endocrine 221
endogenous 367
endorse
  evidence 467
  assent 488
  compact 769
  – *a bill* 800
  approve 931
endorsement 550
endosmose 302
endow
  confer power 157
endowed with
  possessed of 777
endowment
  intrinsic 5
  power 157
  talent 698
  gift 784
endrogynous 83
endue 157
endure *time* 106
  last 110
  persist 143
  continue 141
  undergo 151
  feel 821
  submit to 826
  unable to – 867
  – for ever 112
  – *pain* 828
enduring
  indelible 505
endwise 212
enemy *time* 841
  foe 891
  the common – 978
  thing devised by
    the – 546
  – to society 891
energumen 504
energy *power* 157
  strength 159
  physical 171
  resolution 604
  activity 682
enervate 158, 160
enfant, bon – 906
  – gâté
  prosperity 734
  satiety 869
  favorite 899
  – perdu
  hopeless 859
  reckless 863
  – terrible
  curiosity 455
  artless 703
  object of fear 860
enfeeble 160
enfeoff 780, 783

Enfield rifle 727
enfilade
  lengthwise 200
  pierce 260
  pass through 302
enfold 229
enforce *urge* 615
  advise 695
  compel 744
  require 924
enfranchise
  free 748
  liberate 750
  permit 760
enfranchised 924
engage
  bespeak 132
  induce 615
  undertake 676
  do battle 722
  commission 755
  promise 768
  compact 769
  I'll –
  affirmation 535
  – the attention
    457
  – with 720
engaged
  marriage 903
  be – 135
  – in *attention* 457
engagement
  business 625
  battle 720
  betrothal 902
engaging
  pleasing 829
  amiable 897
engender 161
engine 153, 633
engine-driver 268
engineer 690, 694,
    726
engineering 633
engird 227
English 188
  broken – 563
  king's – 560
  murder the king's
    – 568
  plain –
  intelligible 518
  interpreted 522
  style 576
  – horn 417
engorge
  swallow 296
  gluttony 957
engorgement
  too much 641

engrail 256
engrave
  furrow 259
  mark 550
  – in the memory
    505
engraver 559
engraving 21, 22,
    558
engross *write* 590
  possess 777
  – the thoughts
    thought 451
    attention 457
engrossed in
    thought 451
engulf
  destroy 162
  plunge 310
  swallow up 296
enhance
  increase 35
  improve 658
enharmonic 413
enigma
  question 461
  secret 533
enigmatic
  uncertain 475
  unintelligible 517
  obscure 519
enigme, mot d' –
    522
enjoin *advise* 695
  command 741
  prescribe 926
enjoy
  physically 377
  possess 777
  morally 827
  – health 654
  – popularity 873
  – a state 7
enkindle *heat* 384
  excite 824
enlarge
  increase 35
  swell 194
  in writing 573
  liberate 750
  – the mind 537
enlarged views 498
enlighten
  illumine 420
  inform 527
  teach 537
enlightened
  knowledge 490
enlist *engage* 615
  war 722
  commission 755

under the ban-
  ners of 707
– into the service
  677
enliven
  delight 829
  cheer 836
  amuse 840
enmity 889
ennoble 873
ennui 841
enormity
  crime 947
enormous *great* 31
  big 192
  – *number* 102
enough *much* 31
  no more! 142
  sufficient 639
  moderately 651
  satiety 869
  know when one
    has had – 953
  – in all conscience
    641
  – to drive one
    mad 830
  – and to spare 639
enounce 535, 580
enrage 830, 900
enragé 865
enrapture
  excite 824
  beatify 829
  love 897
enraptured 827
enravish 829
enravished 827
enravishment 824
enrich
  improve 658
  wealth 803
  ornament 847
enrobe 225
enroll *list* 86
  record 551
  – *troops* 722
  commission 755
ens *essence* 1
Ens Entium 976
ensample 22
ensanguined 361
ensconce
  conceal 528
  safety 664
ensconced
  located 184
ensemble 50
enshrine
  circumscribe 229
  repute 873

sanctify 987
– in the memory
  505
ensiform 253
ensign
  standard 550
  officer 726
  master 745
  – of authority 747
ensilage 637
enslave 749
ensnare 545
ensue *follow* 63, 117
  happen 151
ensure 474
entablature 210
entail *cause* 153
  tie up property
    781
entangle
  interlink 43
  derange 61
  ravel 219
  entrap 545
  embroil 713
entangled
  disorder 59
  – by difficulties
    704
entend, cela s' – 613
entente
  agreement 23
  alliance 714
  friendship 888
enter *go in* 294
  appear 446
  note 551
  accounts 811
  – into the compo-
    sition of 56
  – into details
    special 79
    describe 594
  – into an engage-
    ment 768
  – into the feelings
    of 914
  – into the ideas of
    understand 518
    concord 714
  – in *converge* 290
  – the lists
    attack 716
    contention 720
  – the mind 451
  – a profession 625
  – into the spirit of
    feel 821
    delight 827
  – upon 66
  – into one's views

  488
enterprise
  pursuit 622
  undertaking 676
  commercial – 794
enterprising
  active 171, 682
  courageous 861
entertain
  bear in mind 457
  support 707
  amuse 840
  sociality 892
  – doubts 485
  – feeling 821
  – an idea 451
  – an opinion 484
entertainment 840
  pleasure 377
  repast 298
entêté 481, 606
enthral
  subjection 749
  restraint 751
enthrone 873
enthronement 755
enthusiasm
  language 574
  willingness 602
  feeling 821
  hope 858
  love 897
enthusiast
  madman 504
  obstinate 606
  active 682
enthusiastic
  imaginative 515
  sensitive 822
  excitable 825
  sanguine 858
enthymeme 476
entice 615
enticing 829
entire *whole* 50
  complete 52
  continuous 69
  – horse 373
entirely *much* 31
entitle *name* 564
  give a right 924
entity 1
entoil 545
entomb *inter* 363
  imprison 751
Entomology 368
entourage 88, 183,
  227
entozoon 193
entrails 221
entrammel 751

entrance
  beginning 66
  ingress 294
  way 627
  enrapture 827,
    829
  magic 992
  give – to 296
entranced 515
entrancement 824
entrap 545
entrain 293
entre nous 528
entreat 765
entrée
  reception 296
  dish 298
  give the – 296
  have the – 294
  – dish 191
entremet 298
entrepôt 636, 799
entrepreneur 599
entre-sol 191
entrust
  commission 755
  give 784
  credit 805
entry *beginning* 66
  ingress 294
  record 551
entwine *join* 43
  intersect 219
  convolve 248
enucleate 522
enumerate 85
  – among 76
enumeration 86
enunciate
  inform 527
  affirm 535
  voice 580
envelop 225
envelope 223, 232
envenom
  deprave 659
  exasperate 835
  hate 898
  anger 900
envenomed
  bad 649
  insalubrious 657
  painful 830
  malevolent 907
  – tongue 934
environ 227
environment 183
environs 197
  in such and such –
    183
envisage 515, 861

envoy
messenger 534
consignee 758
envy 921
enwrap 225
enzyme 320
Eolian harp 417
Eolus 349
eon 976
épanchement
manifest 525
artless 703
endearment 902
epact 641
épaulette
badge 550, 747
ornament 847
decoration 877
éperdu 824
épergne 191
ephemeral 111
ephemeris
calendar 114
record 551
book 593
Ephesian letters
993
ephialtes
physical pain 378
hindrance 706
mental pain 828
ephod 999
ephor 967
epic 594, 597
epicedium 839
epicene 81, 83
épicier 876
epicure
fastidious 868
sybarite 954a
glutton 957
epicurean 954
Epicurus, system
of – 954
epicy-cle, -cloid
247
epidemic
general 78
disease 655
insalubrity 657
epidermis 223
epigenesis 161
epigram 496, 842
epigrammatic 572
epigrammatist 844
epigraph 550
epilepsy 315, 655
epilogue
sequel 65
end 67
drama 599

èpingles, tiré à
quatre – 855
Epiphany 998
episcopal 995
Episcopalian 984
episcopate 995
episode
adjunct 39
discontinuity 70
interjacence 228
episodic
irrelative 10
style 573
epistle 592
Epistles 985
epistrophe 104
epistyle 210
epitaph 363
epithalamium 903
epithem 662
epithet 564
epitome
miniature 193
short 201
concise 572
epizoötic 657
epoch *time* 106
instant 113
date 114
present time 118
epode 597
eponym 564
epopœa 597
epos 594
epulation 298
epulotic 662
epuration 652
equable 16, 922
equal *even* 27
equitable 922
– *chance* 156
– *times* 120
– *to power* 157
equality 13, **27**
equalize 213
equanimity 826
equate 27, 30
equations 85
equator 68, 318
equatorial 68, 236
equerry 746
equestrian 268
equibalanced 27
equidistant 68
equilibration 27
equilibrist 599
equilibrium 27
equine *carrier* 271
horse 366
equinox 125, 126
equip 225, 673

equipage
vehicle 272
instruments 633
display 882
equiparent 27
equipment 633
equipoise &c. 27, 30
equiponderate 30
equitable *wise* 498
just 922
due 924
honourable 939
– *interest* 780
equitation 266
equity *right* 922
honour 939
law 963
in – 922
– *draftsman* 968
equivalent
identical 13
equal 27
compensation 30
substitute 147
translation 522
equivocalness
dubious 475
double meaning
520
impure 961
equivocate
sophistry 477
palter 520
lie 544
equivocation
[*see* equivocate]
without – 543
équivoque
double meaning
520
impure 961
era *time* 106, 108
date 114
eradicate
destroy 162
extract 301
erase *destroy* 162
obliterate 331, 552
Erastian 984
erasure 552
Erato 416
ere 116
– *long* 132
– *now* 116
past 122
Erebus *dark* 421
hell 982
erect *build* 161
vertical 212
raise 307
with head – 878

– the scaffolding
673
erewhile 116, 122
ergatocracy 737
ergo 476
ergotism 480
ergotize 485
eriometer 445
Erinys 900
Erl King 980
ermine
badge of authority
747
ornament 847
erode 36, 659
Eros 897, 979
erosion 36
erotic 897, 961
err – *in opinion* 495
– *morally* 945
errand
message 532
business 625
commission 755
errand-boy 534
errant 279
erratic
irregular 139
changeable 149
wandering 279
capricious 608
erratum 495
erroneous 495
error *fallacy* **495**
vice 945
guilt 947
court of – 966
writ of – 969
ersatz 973
erst 122
erubescence 434
erubuit salva res
est 95
eruct 297
eructate 297
erudition 490, 539
eruption
upheaval 146
violence 173
egress 295, 297
disease 655
volcanic – 872
escadrille 726
escalade
mounting 305
attack 716
escalator 307
escalop 248
escapade
absurdity 497
freak 608

prank 840
escape
flight **671**
liberate 750
evade 927
means of – 664, 666
– the lips
disclosure 529
speech 582
– the memory 506
– notice &c.
invisible 447
inattention 458
latent 526
escarp 717
escarpment
stratum 204
height 206
oblique 217
escharotic
caustic 171
pungent 392
eschatology 67
escheat 144, 974
eschew
avoid 623
dislike 867
esclandre 828, 830
escort
accompany 88
safeguard 664
keeper 753
escritoire 191
esculent 298
escutcheon 550
esoteric
private 79
concealed 528
Espagne, château en – *fancy* 515
hope 858
espalier 232
especial 79
especially 33
espial 441
espiéglerie
cunning 702
fun 840
wit 842
espionnage 441, 461
esplanade
houses 189
flat 213
espouse
choose 609
marriage 903
– a cause *aid* 707
co-operate 709
esprit

shrewdness 498
wit 842
bel – 844
– de corps
bias 481
co-operation 709
sociality 892
(*party* 712)
– fort
thinker 500
irreligious 989
espy 441
esquire 875, 877
essay
experiment 463
dissertation 595
endeavour **675**
essayist 593, 595
esse 1
essence
nature 5
scent 398
essential
intrinsic 5
great 31
required 630
important 642
essentially
intrinsically 5
substantially 3
essential stuff 5
establish
settle 150
create 161
place 184
evidence 467
demonstrate 478
– *equilibrium* 27
established
permanent 141
habit 613
– *church* 983a
establishment
party 712
shop 799
estafette 534
estaminet 189
estate *condition* 7
property 780
come to man's – 131
esteem
believe 484
repute 873
approve 931
in high – 928
estimable 648
estimate
measure 466
adjudge 480
information 527

– too highly 482
estimation
[*see* esteem, estimate]
estime
succès d' – 873
estival 382
esto perpetua!
perpetuity 112
permanence 141
desire 865
estop 706
estrade 213
estrange
alienate 44, 889
discord 713
hate 898
estranged
secluded 893
estrapade
attack 716
punishment 972
estreat 974
estuary 343
estuation 384
esurient 865
et – cætera
add 37
include 76
plural 100
– hoc genus omne
similar 17
include 76
multiform 81
étalage 882
état major 745
etch *furrow* 259
engraving 558
eternal 112
– home 981
Eternal, the – 976
eterne 112
eternify 112
eternity 112
an – 110
launch into – 360, 361
ether
lightness 320
rarity 322
vapour 334
anæsthetic 376
ethereal 4
ethicism 984
ethics 926
Ethiopian 431
–'s skin 150
Ethiopian's skin *unchangeable* 150
ethnology 372
ethnic 984

ethology 926
ethos 5
etiolate 429, 430
etiology *causes* 155, 359
knowledge 490
disease 655
etiquette
custom 613
fashion 832
ceremony 882
étoile, à la belle –
out of doors 220
in the air 338
Eton jacket 225
étourderie
inattention 458
unskilfulness 699
etymological 560
etymology 562
etymon *origin* 153
verbal 562
Eucharist 998
euchology 998
euchre 840
eudiometer
air 338
salubrity 656
euge! 931
eugenics 658
eulogist 935
eulogize 482
eulogy 931
Eumenides *fury* 900
evil-doers 913
revenge 919
eunuch 158
eupepsia 654
euphemism
metaphor 521
style 577, 578
flattery 933
euphemist
man of taste 850
flatterer 935
euphony 413, 578
Euphrosyne 836
euphuism
metaphor 521
elegant style 577
affected style 579
affectation 855
Eurasian 41
eureka! 462, 480a
Euripus 343
Eurus 349
eurythmics 537, 840
eurythmy 242
Euterpe 416

[479]

euthanasia 360
euthenics 658
evacuate
  quit 293
  excrete 295
  emit 297
evacuation 299
evade *sophistry* 477
  avoid 623
  not observe 773
  exempt 927
evagation 279
evanescent
  small 32
  transient 111
  little 193
  disappearing 449
evangelical 983*a*,
  985
Evangelists 985
evanid 160
evaporable 334
evaporate
  unsubstantial 4
  transient 111
  vaporize 336
evaporation 340
evasion
  sophistry 477
  concealment 528
  falsehood 544
  untruth 546
  avoidance 623
  escape 671
  cunning 702
  non-observance
    773
  dereliction 927
eve 126
  on the – of
  transient 111
  prior 116
  future 121
evection 61
even
  uniform 16
  equal 27
  still more 33
  regular 138
  level 213
  straight 246
  flat 251
  smooth 255
  although 469
  in spite of 708
  – course 628
  – now 118
  – so
  for all that 30
  yes 488
  – temper 826

– terms 922
– tenor
  uniform 16
  order 58
  continuity 58
  pursue the –
    tenor
  continue 143
  avoid 623
  business 625
  be – with
  retaliate 718
  pay 807
  get – with 972
even-handed 922,
  939
evening 126
  shades of – 422
  – classes 537
  – star 423
evenness 16
evensong 126, 990
event 151
  bout 720
  in the – of
  circumstance 8
  expectation 507
  supposition 514
  justified by the –
    937
eventful 151
  remarkable 642
  stirring 682
eventide 126
eventual 121
eventuality 151
eventually
  effect 154
ever 16, 112
  did you – ? 870
  – and anon 136
  – changing 149
  – recurring 104
ever so 31
  – little 32
  – long 110
  – many 102
evergreen
  continuous 69
  lasting 110
  always 112
  fresh 123
everlasting 112
  – life 152
  – fire 982
evermore 112
eversion 218
evert 140
every 78
  – hand against
    one 891

– day
  conformity 82
  frequent 136
  habit 613
  – description 81
  – inch 50
  in – mouth
  assent 488
  news 532
  repute 873
  – other 138
  in – quarter 180
  in – respect 494
  on – side 227
  at – turn 186
  – whit 52
everybody 78
everyone 78
  – his due 922
  – in his turn 148
everywhere 180,
  186
evict 297
evidence 467
  disclose 529
  ocular – 446
évidence, en – 446
evident
  concrete 3
  visible 446
  certain 474
  manifest 525
evidently 516
evil *harm* **619**
  badness 649
  impious 988
  – day
  prepare for – 673
  adversity 735
  – eye *vision* 441
  malevolence 907
  disapprobation
    932
  demon 980
  sorcery 992
  spell 993
  – favoured 846
  – fortune 735
  – genius 980
  – hour 135
  – one 978
  – plight 735
  through – report
    &c. 604*a*
  – star 649
evil-doer **913**
evil-doing 945
evil-minded 907,
  945
evil-speaking
  malediction 908

  censure 932
  detraction 934
evince *show* 467
  prove 478
  disclose 529
eviscerate 297, 301
eviscerated 4
evoke *cause* 153
  call upon 765
  excite 824
evolution
  numerical 85
  production 161
  motion 264
  extraction 301
  circuition 311
  turning out **313**
  organization 357
  training 673
  action 680
  military –s 722
evolve
  discover 480*a*
  evolved from 154
  [*and see*
    evolution]
evulgate 531
evulsion 301
evivva! 931
ewe 366, 374
  – lamb 366
ewer 191
ex
  – animo 602
  – cathedra 542
  – officio 494, 924
  – parte 467
  – pede Herculem
    82
  – post facto 122,
    133
  – tempore
  instant 113
  occasion 134
exacerbate
  increase 35
  exasperate 173
  aggravate 659,
    835
exact *similar* 17
  special 79
  true 494
  style 572
  require 741
  tax 812
  insolence 885
  claim 924, 926
  – meaning 516
  – memory 505
  – observance 772
  – truth 494

exacting
severe 739
discontented 832
grasping 865
fastidious 868
exaction
[*see* exact]
undue 925
exactly
just so 488
exaggeration
increase 35
expand 194
overestimate 482
magnify **549**
misrepresent 555
exalt
increase 35
elevate 307
extol 931
– one's horn 873
exalté 504
tête –e 503
exalted *high* 206
repute 873
noble 875
magnanimous
942
examination
[*see* examine]
evidence 467
undergo – 461
examine 457, 461
example
pattern 22
instance 82
bad – 949
good – 948
make an – of 974
set a good – 944
exanimate
dead 360
supine 360
exarch 745
exasperate
exacerbate 173
aggravate 835
enrage 900
excavate 252
excecation 442
exceed *surpass* 33
remain 40
transgress 303
intemperance 954
excel *surpass* 33
– in *skilful* 698
excellence 648, 944
excellence, par –
642
excellency 877
excelsior 305

except *subduct* 38
exclude 55
reject 610
exception
unconformity 83
qualification 469
exemption 777a
disapproval 932
take –
qualify 469
resent 900
exceptionable
bad 649
guilty 947
exceptional
original 20
extraneous 57
unconformable 83
in an – *degree* 31
exceptious 901,
901a
exceptis
excipiendis 469
excern 297
excerpt 609
excerpta *parts* 51
compendium 596
selections 609
excerption 609
excess
remainder 40
redundance 641
intemperance 954
excessive 31
exchange
reciprocity 12
interchange 148
transfer 783
barter 794
mart 799
bill of – 771
rate of – 800
– *blows* &c.
retaliation 718
battle 720
Exchequer 802
Baron of – 967
Court of – 966
– bill 800
excise 812
exciseman 965
excision 38
excitability **825**,
901
excitation 824
excite *energy* 171
violence 173
– *morally* 824
– *attention* 457
– *desire* 865
– *hope* 811

– an impression
375
– *love* 897
excited fancy 515
excitement 824, 825
anger 900
exclaim 411
– *against* 932
exclamation 580
mark of – 550
exclude
leave out 42, 55
reject 610
prohibit 761
banish 893
exclusion **55, 57**
exclusive
simple 42
omitting 55
special 79
irregular 83
forbidding 761
– of 38
– *possession* 777
– *thought* 457
excogitate 451, 515
excommunicate
banish 893
curse 908
rite 998
excoriate 226
excrement
excretion 299
dirt 653
excrescence
projection 250
blemish 848
excreta
excretion 299
dirt 653
excretion 297, **299**
excruciating 378,
830
exculpate
forgive 918
vindicate 937
acquit 970
excursion 266, 311
excursionist 268
excursive
deviating 279
- *style* 573
excursus 595
excuse *plea* 617
forgive 918
exempt 927a
vindicate 793
execrable 649, 830
execrate 898, 908
execution
music 416

action 680
conduct 692
signing 771
observance 772
punishment 972
carry into –
complete 729
put in –
undertaking 676
executioner 975
executive
conduct 692
direction 693
authority 737
judicature 965
executor 690
to one and his –s
&c., *property*
780
exegetical 522
exemplar 22
exemplary 944
exemplify
quote 82
illustrate 522
exempt *free* 748
dispensation 927a
– from *absent* 187
unpossessed 777a
exemption
exception 83
qualification 469
deliverance 692
permission 760
non-possession
777a
non-liability **927a**
exenterate 297
exequatur 755
exequies 363
exercise
operation 170
teach 537
task 625
use 677
act 680
exert 686
– *authority* 737
– *discretion* 600
– the intellect 451
– *power* 157
exergue 231
exert *use* 677
– *authority* 737
– *oneself* 686
exertion 171, **686**
exfoliate 226
exhalation
ejection 297
excretion 299
vapour 336

breath 349
odour 398
exhaust
 paralyze 158
 empty 195
 waste 638
 fatigue 688
 complete 729
 drain 789
 squander 818
exhausted
 inexistent 2
exhauster 349
exhaustive
 complete 52
 – inquiry 461
exhaustless
 infinite 105
 enough 639
exhibit *evidence* 467
 show 525
 display 882
exhilarate 836
exhort
 persuade 615
 advise 695
exhortation 998
exhume
 past times 122
 disinter 363
exigeant 739
exigency *crisis* 8
 requirement 630
 dearth 640
 difficulty 704
 need 865
exigent
 exacting 739
 discontented 832
exiguous 103, 193
exile
 transport 185
 banish 893
 punish 972
 voluntary – 893
exility 203
eximious 648
existence *being* 1
 thing 3
 – *in time* 118
 – *in space* 186
 come into – 151
exit
 departure 293
 egress 295
 disappear 449
 give – to 297
ἐξοχήν, κατ᾽ –
 supreme 33
 important 642
exode 599

[482]

exodus 293
exogenous 367
exonerate
 disburden 705
 release 760
 forgive 918
 exempt 927a
 vindicate 937
 acquit 970
exorable 914
exorbitant
 enormous 31
 redundant 641
 dear 814
exorcise 297
exorcism 992, 993
exorcist 994
exordium 64, 66
exosmose 302
exostosis 250
exoteric 525, 531
exotic *alien* 10
 exceptional 83
 plant 367
expand *increase* 35
 swell 194
 - *in breadth* 202
 rarefy 322
 - *in writing* 573
expanse 180, 192
expansion **194**
expatiate
 range 266
 - *in writing* &c.
 573
 - *in discourse* 584
expatriate 295, 893
expect
 look forward to
 507
 hope 858
 not wonder 871
 future 121
 reason to – 472
expectance **871**
expectancy 780
expectante,
 médecine –
 wait 133
 remedy 662
expectation **507**
 beyond – 508
 hold out an – 768
expected
 as well as can be –
 654
expectorate 297
expedience **646**
expedient
 plan 626
 means 632

useful 646
 temporary – 147
expedite *early* 132
 quickening 274
 hasten 684
 aid 707
expedition
 [*see* expedite]
 march 266
 activity 682
 war 722
expel *push* 284
 eject 297
 punish 972
expend *waste* 638
 use 677
 pay 809
 – *itself* 683
expenditure **809**
expense *price* 812
 joke at one's –
 842
 spare no – 816
expenseless 815
expenses 809
expensive 814
experience
 meet with 151
 knowledge 490
 undergo 821
 learn by – 950
experienced 698
 – eye &c. 700
experiences
 narrative 594
experiment **463,**
 675
Experimental
 Philosophy 316
experimentum
 crucis *test* 463
 proof 478
expert 698, 700
expiate 952
expire *end* 67
 run its course 109
 die 360
expired *past* 122
explain 462, 522
 – *away* 523
explainer 524
expletive 573, 641
explication 522
explicit *clear* 518
 potent 525
explode *burst* 173
 confute 479
 failure 732
 passion 825
exploded *past* 122
 antiquated 124

error 495
 blown upon 932
exploit 680, 861
exploitation 461
explore 461, 463
explorer 268
explosion
 [*see* explode]
 revolution 146
 violence 173
 sound 406
 anger 900
explosive
 dangerous 665
 ammunition 727
exponent
 numerical 84
 interpreter 524
 informant 527
 index 550
export 295
expose *denude* 226
 confute 479
 disclose 529
 censure 932
 – to danger 665
 – oneself
 disreputable 874
 – to view
 visible 446
 manifest 525
exposé
 disclosure 529
 description 594
exposed to
 liable 177
exposition [*see*
 expose]
 explanation 522
expositor 524, 540
expository
 explaining 522
 informing 527
 describing 594
 disserting 595
expostulate
 dissuade 616
 advise 695
 deprecate 766
 reprehend 932
exposure [*see*
 expose]
 appearance 448
 – to weather 338
expound
 interpret 522
 teach 537
expounder 524
express
 rapid 274
 squeeze out 301

186
up to one's –s
  641
have one's –s
  about one 459
– askance 860
–s draw straws 683
an – for an – 718,
  919
– glistening 824
in the – of the law
  963
– of the master
  693
– of a needle 260
–s open
  attention 457
  care 459
  intention 620
–s opened
  disclosure 529
–s out 442
eye-ball 441
eyebrows 256
eyeglass 445
eyelashes 256
eyeless 442
eyelet 260
eyelid 223
eye-shade 443
eye-sight 441
eyesore 846, 848
eye-teeth
  have cut one's –
  adolescence 131
  skill 698
  cunning 702
eye-wash 544
eye-witness
  spectator 444
  evidence 467
eyot 346
eyre 966
eyry 189

F

Fabian policy
  delay 133
  inaction 681
  caution 864
fable *error* 495
  metaphor 521
  fiction 546
  description 590
fabric *state* 7
  effect 154
  texture 329
fabricate
  composition 54

make 161
invent 515
falsify 544
fabrication *lie* 546
fabula narratur, de
  te – *retaliate* 718
  condemn 971
fabulist 594
fabulous
  enormous 31
  imaginary 515
  untrue 546
  exaggerated 549
faburden 413
façade 234
face *exterior* 220
  covering 223
  front 234
  aspect 448
  oppose 708
  resist 719
  brave 861
  impudence 885
  change the – of
  146
  fly in the – of
  disobey 742
  put a good – upon
  sham 545
  calm 826
  cheerful 836
  hope 858
  pride 878
  display 882
  vindicate 93
  in the – of
  presence 186
  opposite 708
  look in the –
  see 441
  proud 878
  make –s
  distort 243
  ugly 846
  disrespect 929
  on the – of
  manifest 525
  show –
  present 186
  visible 446
  not show –
  disreputable 874
  bashful 879
  to one's – 525
  wry – 378
  – about 279
  set one's – against
  708
  – of the country
  344
  on the – of the

earth
  space 180
  world 318
– to face *front* 234
  contraposition
  237
  manifest 525
– of the thing
  appearance 448
facet 220
facetiæ 842
facetious 842
facia 234
facile *willing* 602
  irresolute 605
  easy 705
facile princeps 33
facilis descensus
  Averni
  sloping 217
  danger 665
facilitate 705
facility *skill* 698
  easy **705**
facing *covering* 223
facinorous 945
façon de parler 521,
  549
fac-simile 21, 554
fact *existence* 1
  event 151
  certainty 474
  truth 494
  in – 535
faction 712, 713
factious 24
factitious 545, 546
factor
  numerical 84
  director 694
  consignee 758
factory 691
factotum
  agent 690
  manager 694
  employé 758
facts *evidence* 467
  summary of – 594
  at variance with –
  471
facula 420
faculties 450
  in possession of
  one's – 502
faculty
  power 157
  profession 625
  skill 698
facundity 582
fad 481, 608
faddle 683

fade *vanish* 4
  transient 111
  become old 124
  droop 160
  grow dim 422
  lose colour 429
  disappear 449
  spoil 659
– from the
  memory 506
fade 391
fadge 23
fæces 299, 653
fæx populi 876
fag *cigarette* 392
  labour 686
  fatigue 688
  drudge 690, 746
– end
  remainder 40
  end 67
faggot 72, 388
fagots et fagots 15,
  465
faïence 557
fail *droop* 160
  shortcoming 304
  be confuted 479
  illness 655
  not succeed 732
  not observe 773
  not pay 808
  dereliction 927
failing [see fail]
  incomplete 53
  insufficient 640
  vice 945
  guilt 947
  – heart 837
  – luck 735
  – memory 506
  – sight 443
  – strength 160
failure **732**
  heart – 360
fain *willing* 602
  compulsive 744
  wish 865
fainéant 683
faint
  small in degree 32
  impotent 158
  weak 160
  sound 405
  dim 422
  colour 429
  swoon 688
– heart *fear* 860
  cowardice 862
  damn with –
  praise 930, 932,

pleased 827
fascination [*see*
  fascinate]
infatuation 825
desire 870
fascine 72
Fascisti 712
fas et nefas, per –
  604*a*, 631
fash 830
fashion
state 7
form 240
custom 613
method 627
ton **852**
after a –
  middling 32
after this – 617
follow the – 82
be in the – 488
man of – 852
set the –
influence 175
authority 737
for –'s sake 852
fast *joined* 43
steadfast 150
rapid 274
fashionable 852
intemperate 954
not eat 956
worship 990
rite 998
stick – 704
– asleep 683
– by 197
– day 956
– friend 890
– and loose
sophistry 477
falsehood 544
irresolute 605
tergiversation 607
caprice 608
– man *fop* 854
libertine 962
fasten *join* 43
hang 214
restrain 751
– on the mind 451
– a quarrel upon
  713
– upon 789
fastening 45
fast-handed 819
fastidious
censorious 932
fastidiousness **868**
fasting
insufficiency 640

worship 990
penance 952
abstinence **956**
fastness
asylum 666
defence 717
fat *corpulent* 192
expansion 194
unctuous 355
oleaginous 356
kill the –ted calf
celebration 883
sociality 892
– in the fire
disorder 59
violence 173
– of the land
pleasure 377
enough 639
prosperity 734
intemperance 95
fata – Morgana
occasion 134
ignis fatuus 423
– obstant 601
fatal 361
– disease 655
fatalism 601
fatality 601
fate *end* 67
necessity 601
chance 621
be one's – 156
sure as – 474
Fates 601, 979
fat-head 501
father *eldest* 128
paternity 166
priest 996
Apostolical –s 985
gathered to one's
  –s 360
heavy – 599
– upon 155
Father, God the –
  976
fatherland 189
fatherless 158
fatherly 906
fathom
length 200
investigate 461
solve 462
measure 466
discover 480*a*
knowledge 490
fathomless 208
fatidical 511
fatigation 688
fatigue **688**
fatras 643

fatten
expand 194
improve 658
prosperous 734
– on *parasite* 886
– upon
feed 298
fatuity 4, 499
fatuous 517
fat-witted 499
faubourg 227
fauces 231
faucet 252
faugh! 867
fault
break 70
error 495
imperfection 651
failure 732
vice 945
guilt 947
at –
uncertain 475
ignorant 491
unskilful 699
find – with 932
faultless 650, 946
faulty 495, 651
faun 980
fauna 366
faut: comme il –
taste 850
fashion 852
il s'en – bien 489
tant s'en – 536
faute 732
– de mieux
substitution 147
necessity 601
fauteuil 215
fautor 890
faux pas
error 568
failure 732
misconduct 947
intrigue 961
favour
resemble 16
badge 550
letter 592
aid 707
indulgence 740
permit 760
gift 784
partiality 923
appearances in –
  of 472
get into –
friendship 888
love 897
in – *repute* 873

approbation 931
in – of
approve 931
under – of 760
view with – 906
– with 784
favourable
occasion 134
willing 602
good 648
aid 707
– prospect 472
– to 709
take a – turn
improve 658
prosperity 734
favourably
well 618
favourer 890
favourite
pleasing 829
beloved 897, **899**
favouritism
friendship 888
wrong 923
fawn *colour* 433
cringe 749, 886
flatter 993
fay 979
fealty
obedience 743
duty 926
respect 928
fear **860**
fearful
painful 830
timid 862
fearfully 31, 870
fearless *hope* 858
courage 861
fearsome 860
feasible 470, 705
feast *period* 138
repast 298
pleasure 377
revel 840
rite 998
– one's eyes 897
feast of reason
conversation 588
– and flow of soul
sociality 892
feat *action* 680
courage 861
– of arms 720
– of strength 159
feather
class 75
tuft 256
light 320
trifle 643

ornament 847
  decoration 877
in full –
  prepared 673
  prosperous 734
  rich 803
hear a – drop 403
in high –
  health 654
  cheerful 884
pleased with a –
  840
– in one's cap
  honour 873
  decoration 877
– one's nest
  prepare 673
  prosperity 734
  wealth 803
  economy 817
  selfish 943
– the oar 698
– in the scale 643
feather-bed 324
feathered tribes
  366
feathery 256
featly 682
feature
  character 5
  component 56
  form 240
  appearance 448
  press 531
  lineament 550
– in 56
features
  face 234
febrifuge 662
febrile 382, 825
fecal 653
fecit 556
feckless 866
feculence 653
fecund 168
fecundate 161
federal council 696
– penitentiary 752
federalism 737
federation 48, 709,
  712
fee *possession* 777
  property 780
  pay 809
  reward 973
feeble *weak* 160
  illogical 477
feeble-minded 497,
  605
feebleness
  style **575**

feed *eat* 298
  supply 637
– the flame 707
fee-faw-fum
  bugbear 860
  spell 993
feel *sense* 375
  touch 379
  emotion 821
– for *try* 463
  benevolence 906
  pity 914
  condole with 915
– the pulse 461
– the want of 865
– one's way
  essay 675
  caution 864
feeler 379
  inquiry 461
  experiment 463
feeling 698, **821**
feet *low* 207
  walkers 266
at one's –
  near 197
  subjection 749
  humility 879
fall at one's –
  submit 725
fall on one's –
  prosper 734
lick the – of
  servile 886
light upon one's –
  safe 664
spring to one's –
  307
throw oneself at
  the – of
  entreat 765
feign 544, 546
feigned 545
feint 545
felicitas, curiosa –
  698
felicitate 896
felicitous
  agreeing 23
– *style* 578
  skilful 698
  successful 731
  pleasant 829
felicity 827
feline *cat* 366
  stealthy 528
  cunning 702
fell *destroy* 162
  mountain 206
  lay flat 21
  skin 223

  lay low 308
  moor 344
  dire 860
  malevolent 907
fellah 876
felloe 231
fellow *similar* 17
  equal 27
  companion 88
  dual 89
  man 373
  scholar 492, 541
fellow-commoner
  541
fellow-companion
  890
fellow-countryman
  890
fellow-creature 372
fellow-feeling
  friendship 888
  love 897
  benevolence 906
  pity 914
fellowship
  partnership 712
  distinction 873
  friendship 888
  companionship
  890
  good – 892
fellow-student 541
fellow-worker 690
felly 231
felo-de-se 361
felon 949
felonious 945
felony 947
felt *texture* 219
  heart– 821
felucca 273
female 374
feme coverte 903
feme sole 904
feminality
  weakness 160
  woman 374
feminine 374
feminism 374
femme de chambre
  746
fen 345
fence *enclose* 232
  evade 544
  defence 717
  fight 720
  prison 752
  thief 792
– round 229
– with a question
  528

fenced 770
fenceless 665
fencible 726
fencing 840
feneration 787
fend 717
fender 717
Fenian 710, 742
fenum habet in
  cornu 668, 913
feodal 780
feodality 737, 777
feoff *property* 780
feoffee 779, 785
feoffer 784
feræ naturæ 366
feral 907
ferine 907
ferment
  disorder 59
  energy 171
  violence 173
  agitation 315
  lightness 320
  effervesce 353
  emotion 821
  excitement 824,
  825
  anger 900
fermentation,
  acetous – 397
fern 367
ferocity 173, 907
Ferrara
  sword 727
ferret out 461, 480*a*
ferro-concrete 635
ferrule 223
ferry 270, 627
ferry-boat 273
ferry-man 269
fertile 161, 168
– imagination 515
ferule 975
  come under the –
  932
fervent *hot* 382
  desirous 865
– hope 858
fervid *hot* 382
  heartfelt 821
  excited 824
fervour *heat* 382
  animation 821
  love 897
festal *eating* 298
  social 892
fester 653, 655
festina lente 864
festival
  music 416

celebration 883
festivity 840, 892
festoon 245, 847
fetch *bring* 270
  arrive 292
  evasion 545
  sell for 812
  – one a blow
   strike 276
   attack 716
  – and carry
   servile 886
  – a sigh 839
fête 840, 882
fêté 892
fetishism 992
fetid 401
fetish 991, 993
fetter 751, 752
fettle 673
  state 5
  prepare 673
  in fine – 159, 654
feu
  – d'enfer 716
  – de joie
  amusement 840
  celebration 883
feud *discord* 713
  possess 777
  property 780
  death – 919
feudal 737, 780
feudatory 749
feuilleton 593
fever *heat* 382
  disease 655
  excitement 825
feverish *hurry* 684
  animated 821
  excited 824
few
  a – 100
  – and far between
   70
  – words
  concise 572
  taciturn 585
  compendium 596
fewness 103
fey 360
fez 225
fiancée 897
fiasco 732
fiat 741
  – money 800
fib *falsehood* 544,
  546
  thump 720
fibre *link* 45
  filament 205

moral – 60
fickle 149, 605
fictile 240
fiction *untruth* 546
  work of – 594
fictitious 515, 546
fiddle 416, 417
fiddle-de-dee
  absurd 497
  unimportant 643
  contempt 930
fiddlefaddle
  unmeaning 517
  trifle 643
  dawdle 683
fiddler 416
fiddlestick 417
  – end 643
fidelity
  veracity 543
  obedience 743
  observance 772
  honour 939
fidget *changes* 149
  activity 682
  hurry 684
  excitability 825
fidgety
  irresolute 605
  fearful 860
  irascible 901
fiducial 156
fiduciary 484
fidus Achates
  auxiliary 711
  associate 743
  friend 890
fie *disreputable* 874
  – upon it
  censure 932
fief 777
field *opportunity*
  134
  scope 180
  region 181
  plain 344
  agriculture 371
  business 625
  arena 728
  property 780
  the – *hunting* 622
  beasts of the – 366
  playing –s 728
  the potter's – 361
  take the – 722
  – artillery 726
  the – of blood 361
  – of inquiry
  topic 454
  inquiry 461
  – of view

vista 441
  idea 453
field-day
  contention 720
  amusement 840
  display 882
field-glass 445
field-marshal 745
field-piece 727
field-preacher 996
field-work 717
fiend 913, 980
fiend-like
  malevolent 907
  wicked 945
  fiend 980
fierce *violent* 173
  passion 825
  daring 861
  angry 900
fiery *violent* 173
  hot 382
  strong feeling 821
  excitable 825
  angry 900
  irascible 901
  – cross 550, 722
  – furnace 386
  – imagination 515
  – ordeal 828
fife 417
fifer 416
fifth 98, 99
fifty 98
fig
  unimportance 643
  in the name of the
   prophet –s! 497
  – out 847
fight
  contention 720
  warfare 722
  show –
  defence 717
  courage 861
  – one's battles
   again 594
  – against destiny
   606
  – the good fight
   944
  – it out 722
  – shy *avoid* 603,
   623
  coward 862
  – one's way
  pursue 622
  active 682
  exertion 686
fighter 726
fighting-cock 726,

861
fighting-man 726
figment 515
figurante 599
figurate number 84
figuration 240
figurative
  metaphorical 521
  representing 554
  – *style* 577
figure
  number 84
  form 240
  appearance 448
  metaphor 521
  indicate 550
  represent 554
  price 812
  ugly 846
  cut a –
  repute 873
  display 882
  poor – 874
  – to oneself 515
  – of speech 521
  – out 522
  exaggeration 549
figure-flinger 994
figure-head 4, 550,
  554, 643
figurine 554
figuriste 559
filaceous 205
filament 205
filamentous 256
filch 791
filcher 762
file *subduct* 38
  arrange 60
  row 69
  assemblage 72
  list 86
  reduce 195
  smooth 255
  pulverize 330
  record 551
  store 636
  soldiers 726
  – a claim &c. 969
  – off *march* 266
  diverge 291
file-fire 716
filial 167
filiation
  consanguinity 11
  attribution 155
  posterity 167
filibuster 133, 706,
  792
filibustering 791
filiform 205

fire-ball *fuel* 388
  arms 727
fire-balloon 273
fire-barrel 388
fire-bell 669
fire-boat 726
fire-brand
  fuel 388
  instigator 615
  dangerous man 667
  incendiary 913
fire-brigade 385
fire-curtain 599
fire-drake 423
fire-eater
  fighter 726
  blusterer 887
fire-eating
  rashness 863
  insolence 885
fire-engine 348
fire-escape 671
fire-extinguisher 385
fire-fly 423
fireless cooker 386
fire-light 422
firelock 727
fireman *stoker* 268
  extinguisher 385
fire-place 386
fire-proof 385, 644
fireside 189
firewood 388
firework
  fire 382
  luminary 423
  celebration 883
  amusement 840
fire-worship 991
fire-worshipper 984
firing *fuel* 388
  explosion 406
firkin 191
firm
  junction 43
  stable 150
  hard 323
  resolute 604
  partnership 712
  merchant 797
  brave 861
  stand – 719
  – as a rock 604
  – belief 484
  – hold 781
firmament 318
firman 741, 760
first 66
  – blush

morning 125
  leading 280
  vision 441
  appearance 448
  manifest 525
  – blow 716
  – cause 976
  – that comes 609a
  – fiddle
  importance 642
  proficient 700
  authority 737
  – come first
    served 609a
  – and foremost 66
  – impression 66
  – and last 87
  – line 234
  come back to –
    love 607
  – move 66
  – opportunity 132
  at – sight 448
  – stage 66
  – stone
    preparation 673
    attack 716
  on the – summons 741
  of the – water
    best 648
    repute 873
first-born 124, 128
first-fruits 154
first-hand 20, 467
firstlings 128, 154
first-rate
  important 642
  excellent 648
  man-of-war 726
firth 343
fisc 802
fiscal 800
fish *food* 298
  sport 361, 622
  animal 366
  food for –es 362
  other – to fry
    ill-timed 135
    busy 682
  queer – 857
  – in the air 645
  – for compliments 880
  – for *seek* 4
    experiment 463
    desire 865
  – hatchery 370
  – out *inquire* 461
    discover 480a
  – in troubled

waters
  difficult 704
  discord 713
  – up *raise* 307
  find 480a
  – out of water
  disagree 24
  unconformable 83
  displaced 185
  bungler 701
fisherman 361
fishery 370
fishing *kill* 361
  pursue 622
fishing-boat 273
fishpond 343, 370
fish-trail 267
fishy transaction 940
fisk 266, 274
fissile 328
fission 44
fissure 44
  chink 198
fist
  handwriting 590
  grip 781
  shake the –
  defy 515
  threat 909
fisticuffs 720
fistula 260
fit *state* 7
  agreeing 23
  equal 27
  paroxysm 173
  agitation 315
  caprice 608
  expedient 646
  healthy 654
  disease 655
  excitement 825
  anger 900
  right 922
  due 924
  duty 926
  in –s 315
  think – 600
  – of abstraction 458
  – of crying 839
  – for 698
  – out *dress* 225
  prepare 673
  – to be seen 845
  by –s and starts
  irregular 59
  discontinuous 70
  agitated 315
  capricious 608
  haste 684

fitful
  irregular 139
  changeable 149
  capricious 608
fittings 633
five **98**
  division by – 99
  – act play 599
  – and twenty 98
Five Year Plan 626
fiver 800
fives *game* 840
fix *join* 43
  arrange 60
  establish 150
  place 184
  immovable 265
  solidify 321
  resolve 604
  difficulty 704
  – the eyes upon 441
  – the foundations 673
  – the memory 505
  – the time 114
  – the thoughts 457
  – up 774
  – upon *discover* 480a
  choose 609
fixed *intrinsic* 5
  permanent 141
  stable 150
  quiescent 265
  habitual 613
  – idea 481
  – opinion 484
  – periods 138
fixity 141
fixity of purpose 141
fixture
  appointment 741
  property 780
fizgig 423
fizz 409
fizzle 353
  – out 304
flabelliform 194
flabbergast 870, 879
flabby 324
flabbiness 324
flaccid *weak* 160
  soft 324
  empty 640
flag *weak* 160
  flat stone 204
  floor 211

way of all – 360
weakness of the –
 945
– and blood
 substance 3
 materiality 316
 animality 364
 affections 820
make the – creep
 pain 830
 fear 860
flesh-colour 434
flesh-pots 298
– of Egypt 734,
 803
fleshly 316
fleur-de-lis 847
fleuron 847
flexible 324, 705
flexion
 curvature 245
 fold 258
 deviation 279
flexuous 248
flexure 245, 258
flibbertigibbet 980
flicker
 changing 149
 waver 314
 flutter 315
 light 420
 dim 422
flickering 139
flier 621
flies *theatre* 599
flight *flock* 102
 volitation 267
 swiftness 274
 departure 293
 avoidance 623
 escape 671
– lieutenant 745
put to –
 propel 284
 repel 717
 vanquish 731
– of fancy 515
– of stairs 305,
 627
– of time 109
flighty *inattentive*
 458
 mad 503
 fanciful 515
flim-flam 544, 608
flimsy *unsubstan-*
 tial 4
 weak 160
 rarity 322
 soft 324
 sophistical 477

trifling 643
flinch *swerve* 607
 avoid 623
 fear 860
 cowardice 862
fling *propel* 284
 jig 840
 jeer 929
have one's –
 active 682
 laxity 738
 freedom 748
 amusement 840
– aside 782
have a – at
 attack 716
 resent 900
 disrespect 929
 censure 932
– away *reject* 610
 waste 638
 relinquish 782
– down 308
– to the winds
 destroy 162
 not observe 773
flint *hard* 323
flint-hearted 907
flintlock 727
flip *beverage* 298
flippant *fluent* 584
 pert 885
flipper *paddle* 267
flirt *propel* 284
 coquet 607, 854
 love 897
 endearment 902
– a fan 855
flit *elapse* 109
 changeable 149
 move 264
 travel 266
 swift 274
 depart 293
 run away 623
flitter
 small part 32
 changeable 149
 flutter 315
flitting 111
float *establish* 150
 navigate 267
 boat 273
 buoy up 305
 lightness 320
before the –s
 on the stage 599
– on the air 405
– before the eyes
 446
– bonds 788

– in the mind
 thought 451
 imagination 515
floater 683
floating
 [see float]
 rumoured 532
– battery 726
– capital 805
– debt 806
– dock 189
flocculent
 woolly 256
 soft 324
 pulverulent 330
flock
 assemblage 72
 multitude 102
 laity 997
–s and herds 366
– together 72
floe *ice* 383
flog 972
 hasten 684
flood *much* 31
 crowd 72
 river 348
 abundance 639
 redundance 641
 prosperity 734
stem the – 708
– of light 420
– of tears 839
flood-gate
 limit 233
 egress 295
 conduit 350
open the –s
 eject 297
 permit 760
flood-light 423,
 599
flood-mark 466
flood-tide
 increase 35
 complete 52
 height 206
 advance 282
 water 337
floor *level* 204
 base 211
 horizontal 213
 support 215
 overthrow 731
ground – 191
flop 315
Flora 369
floral 367
florescence 154
floriculture 371
florid *colour* 428

 red 434
– *style* 577
 health 654
florist 371
floss 256
flotilla 273, 726
flotsam and jetsam
 73
flounce
 trimming 231
 jump 309
 agitation 315
flounder
 change 149
 toss 315
 uncertain 475
 bungle 699
 difficulty 704
 fail 732
flour 330
flourish
 brandish 314, 315
 exaggerate 549
 language 577
 speech 582
 prosper 618
 healthy 654
 prosperous 734
 ornament 847
 repute 873
 display 882
 boast 884
– of trumpets
 loud 404
 cheerfulness 836
 publish 531
 ostentation 882
 celebrate 883
 boast 884
flout 929, 936
flow *course* 109
 hang 214
 motion 264
 stream 348
 murmur 405
 abundance 639
– from
 result 154
– of ideas 451
– in 294
– into *river* 348
– out 295
– over 641
– of soul
 conversation 588
 affections 820
 cheerful 836
 social 892
– with the tide
 705
– of time 109

– implicitly 486, 695
– the lead of
  co-operate 709
– suit *imitate* 19
– the trail 461
– up
  continue 143
  persevere 604a
follower
  [*see* follow]
  successor 65
  learn 541
  servant 746
  lover 897
folly
  building 189
  irrationality **499**
  act of –
    mismanagement 699
foment
  stimulate 173
  warm 384
  promote 707
  excite 824
  relieve 834
fond 897
  – *hope* 858
fondle 902
fondling 899, 902
fondness
  desire 865
fondre en larmes 839
fons et origo 153
font *origin* 153
  type 591
  rite 998
  altar 1000
food 298
  preparation of – 673
  – for the mind 454
  – for powder 726
fool 501
  pudding 354
  deceive 545
  ridicule 856
  disrespect 929
  make a – of
    oneself
  bungle 699
  motley – 844
  play the –
  folly 499
  amusement 840
  –'s errand
  deceived 545
  unskilful 699
  –'s mate 732

–'s paradise
  unsubstantial 4
  misjudgment 481
  disappoint 509
  hope 858
  rash 863
  – to the top of
    one's bent
  excite 824
  anger 900
  flatter 933
  – away money 818
  – away time 683
foolhardy 863
fooling 842
foolish 499
  act –ly 699
  look –
    disrepute 874
    shame 879
foolscap 550, 559
foot
  length 200
  stand 211
  metre 597
  at the – of 207
  keep on –
    continue 143
    support 251
    provide 637
    prepare 673
  not stir a – 681
  on – *existing* 1
    during 106
    journey 266
    topic 454
    business 625
    preparing 673
    active 682
  put one's – down
    resolved 604
  put one's – in
    undertake 676
    bungle 699
  set – on land 342
  trample under – 930
  – the bill 807
  – by foot 51
  one – in the grave
    age 128
    death 360
  it *journey* 266
  dance 309
  at –'s pace 275
foot-ball
  subjection 749
  game 840
footboy 746
footfall
  motion 264

indication 550
  stumble 732
footing
  circumstances 8
  rank 71
  influence 175
  situation 183
  foundation 211
  support 215
  payment 809
  friendly – 888
  get a –
    location 184
  be on a –
    state 7
  pay one's – 807
footlights 599
footman 746
footmark 551
footpad 792
foot-passenger 268
footpath 627
foot pound 466
footprint 551
foot-soldier 726
foot-warmer 386
footsore 688
footstep 551
footstool 215
foozle 732
fop 854
foppery 882
foppish 855
for *cause* 155
  tendency 176
  reason 476
  motive 615
  intention 620
  preparation 673
  have –
    price **812**
  – all that
    notwithstanding 30
  qualification 469
  – all the world
    like 17
  – aught one
    knows 156
  – better for worse 78
  – ever 112
  – example 82
  – form's sake 82
  – good
    complete 52
    diuturnity 110
    permanence 141
  – the most part
    great 31
    general 78

special 79
  – the nonce 118
  – nothing 815
  – a season 106
  – a time 111
  – the time being 106
forage
  food 298
  provision 637
  steal 791
forage-cap 225
foramen 260
foraminous 260
forasmuch as
  relating to 9
  cause 155
  reason 476
  motive 615
foray *attack* 716
  robbery 791
forbear
  avoid 623
  spare 678
  lenity 740
  sufferance 826
  pity 914
  abstain 953
  forbearance 918
forbid 761
  God –
    dissent 489
    deprecation 766
    censure 932
    prayer 990
forbidden fruit
  seduction 615
  prohibition 761
forbidding
  ugly 846
force *corps* 72
  power 157
  strength 159
  agency 170
  energy 171
  violence 173
  cultivate 371, 707
  cascade 348
  - *of style* 574
  urge 615
  exertion 686
  compulsion 744
  armed – 726
  brute – 964
  put in – 924
  – of argument 476
  – of arms 744
  – of character 820
  – down the throat
    severe 739
    compel 744

– majeure 744
– open 173
– one's way
  progression 282
  passage 302
forced *irrelative* 10
- *style* 579
be – to 601
– labor 603
– march 744
forcefully 601
forceps
  extraction 301
  grip 781
forces 726
forcible [*see* force]
ford 302, 627
fore 234
fore and aft
  complete 52
  lengthwise 200
– schooner 273
fore part 234
forearm 673
forebears 166
forebode 511
forecast
  foresight 510
  prediction 511
  plan 626
foreclose 706
foredoom 152, 601
forefathers 166
forefend
  prohibit 761
forefinger 379
forego
  relinquish 624
  renounce 757
  surrender 782
foregoing 62, 116
foregone
  past 122
– conclusion
  prejudged 481
  predetermined
  611
foreground 234
in the –
  manifest 525
forehead 234
foreign
  alien 10
  extraneous 57
– accent 580
– parts 196
foreigner 57
forejudge
  prejudge 481
  foresight 510
foreknow 510

foreland 206, 254
forelay 545
fore ock
pull the – 894
take time by the –
  early 132
  occasion 134
foreman 694
foremost
  superior 33
  beginning 66
  front 234
  in advance 280
  important 642
  reputed 873
forenoon 125
forensic 968
foreordain 152
foreordination 601,
  611
forerun 62, 116, 280
forerunner 64, 512
foresee 507, 510
foreseen 871
foreshadow 152,
  511
foreshorten 201
foreshow 511
foresight 116, **510**
  caution 864
forest 367
forestage 599
forestry 371
forestall
  prior 116
  early 132
  possession **777**
foretaste 510
foretell 511
forethought 459,
  510
foretoken 511
forewarn 511, 668
foreword 64
forfeit *fail* 773
  lose 776
  penalty 974
– one's good
  opinion 932
forfeiture
  disfranchisement
  925
forfend 706, 717
forgather 72
forge *imitate* 19
  produce 161
  furnace 386
  trump up 544
  workshop 691
– fetters 751
forged

false 546
forger
  maker 690
  thief 792
forgery
  deception 545
forget 506
hand – cunning
  699
– benefits 917
– injury 918
– oneself 945
forgive 918
forgo
  relinquish 624
  renounce 757
  surrender 782
forgotten
  past 122
  ingratitude 917
not to be – 505
– by the world
  893
fork *bifid* 91
  pointed 244
– lightning 423
– out
  give 784
  pay 807
  expenditure 809
forlorn
  dejected 837
  hopeless 859
  deserted 893
– hope
  danger 665
  rashness 863
form *state* 7
  likeness 21
  make up 54
  order 58
  arrange 60
  convert 144
  produce 161
  bench 215
  shape **240**
  educate 537
  pupils 541
  manner 627
  beauty 845
  fashion 852
  etiquette 882
  law 963
  rite 998
– letter 592
– part of 56
– a party 712
– a resolution 604
formal [*see* form]
  regular 82
  definitive 535

- *style* 579
  affected 855
  stately 882
– speech 582
formalism 739, 988
formalist 82
formality [*see*
  formal]
  ceremony 852
  affectation 855
  law 963
formation
  composition 54
  production 161
  shape 240
formative 153
formed [*see* form]
  attempered 820
former
  in order 62
  prior in time 116
  past 122
formication 380
formidable 704, 860
formless 241
formula *rule* 80
  arithmetic 84
  maxim 496
  precept 697
  law 963
formulary 998
formulate 590
fornication 961
fornicator 962
foro conscientiæ
  veracity 543
  duty 926
  probity 939
forsake 624
forsaken 898
forsooth 535
forspent 688
forswear *lie* 544
  tergiversation 607
  refuse 764
  transgress 927
  improbity 940
fort 666, 717
fort
le droit du plus –
  compulsion 744
  illegality 964
un peu – 641
fortalice 717
forte 415, 698
fortelage 717
forth 282
come –
  egress 295
  visible 446
go – *depart* 293

the decree has
gone – 741
forthcoming 152,
673
forthwith 132
fortification 717
fortify 159
fortiori, a – 467, 476
fortissimo 404
fortiter in re 171
fortitude 826, 861
fortnightly 138
fortress 717, 752
fortuitous
  extrinsic 6
  chance 156
  undersigned 621
  – concourse of
   atoms 59
fortunate
  opportune 134
  successful 731
  prosperous 734
Fortunatus's – cap
  wish 865
  spell 993
  – purse 803
fortune *chance* 156
  fate 601
  wealth 803
  be one's – 151
  clean up a – 803
  evil – 621, 735
  good – 734
  make one's –
  succeed 731
  wealth 803
  tempt –
  hazard 621
  essay 675
  trick of – 509
  try one's – 675
  wheel of – 601, 621
fortune-hunter 886,
943
fortuneless 804
fortune-teller 513
fortune-telling 511
fortunes of
  narrative 594
forty 98
  – winks 683
forum 799
  school 542
  tribunal 966
forward *early* 132
  transmit 270
  advance 282
  willing 602
  improve 658
  active 682

help 707
vain 880
insolent 885
uncourteous 895
bend – 234
come –
  in sight 446
  offer 763
  display 882
look – to 507
move – 282
press – *haste* 684
put – *aid* 507
  offer 763
put oneself – 880
set – 676
– in *knowledge* 490
foss 348
fosse
  inclosure 232
  ditch 259
  defence 717
fossil
  ancient 124
  hard 323
  organic 357
  dry bones 362
foster *aid* 707
  excite 824
  caress 902
  – a belief 484
fou 959
foudroyant 870
foul
  collide 276
  bad 649
  dirty 653
  unhealthy 657
  ugly 846
  base 940
  vicious 945
  fall – of
  oppose 708
  quarrel 713
  attack 716
  fight 720
  censure 932
  run – of
  impede 706
  – fiend 978
  – means 940
  – language
  malediction 908
  – odour 401
  – play *evil* 619
  cunning 702
  wrong 923
  improbity 940
foul-mouthed 895
foul-spoken 934
found 153, 215

foundation
  beginning 66
  stability 150
  base 211
  support 215
  lay the –s 673
  sandy – 667
  shake to its –s 315
founded
  well – 472
  – on *base* 211
  evidence 467
founder
  originator 164
  sink 310
  fail 732
  religious –s 986
foundery 691
founding 22
foundling
  trover 775
  derelict 782
  outcast 893
fount *type* 591
fountain
  source 153
  river 348
  store 636
  – head 210
  – pen 590
four 95
  on all –s 13, 23
  horizontal 213
  easy 705
  prosperous 734
  humble 879 ·
  – in hand 272
  – score &c. 98
  – square 244
  – times 96
  from the – winds
   278
fourflusher 884
fourfold 96
four-oar 273
four-poster 215
fourth 96, 97
  musical 413
  – estate 531
four-wheeler 272
fowl 366
fowling-piece 727
fox *animal* 366
  cunning 702
  – chase 622
fox-trot 840
foxy *colour* 433, 434
  cunning 720
foyer 191, 599
fracas
  disorder 59

noise 404
discord 713
contention 720
fraction *part* 51
  numerical 84
  less than one **100a**
fractious 901
fracture
  disjunction 44
  discontinuity 70
  fissure 198
fragile 160, 328
fragment
  small 32, 193
  part 51, 100a
fragrance 400
fragrant weed 392
frail *weak* 160
  brittle 328
  feeble 575
  irresolute 605
  imperfect 651
  failing 945
  impure 961
  – sisterhood 962
frais, à grands –
  481
frame
  condition 7
  make 161
  support 215
  border 231
  form 240
  substance 316
  structure 329
  contrive 626
  cucumber – 371
  have –d and
   glazed 822
  – of mind
  inclination 602
  disposition 820
frame-up 626
framework
  support 215
  structure 329
franchise
  voting 609
  freedom 748
  right 924
  exemption 927a
Franciscan 996
franc-tireur 726
frangible 160, 328
frank *open* 525
  sincere 543
  artless 703
  honourable 939
frankalmoigne 748
Frankenstein 913,
980

frankincense 400
frantic
  violent 173
  delirious 503
  excited 824
fraternal
  brother 11
  concord 714
  friendly 888
fraternity
  [*see* fraternal]
  party 712
fraternize
  co-operate 48, 709
  agree 714
  sympathize 888
  associate 892
fratricide 361
Frau 374
fraud
  falsehood 544
  deception 545
  pretender 548
  dishonour 940
  pious – 988
fraught *full* 52
  pregnant 161
  possessing 777
  – with danger 665
fray *rub* 331
  battle 720
  in the thick of
    the – 722
frayed 659
frazzle
  beaten to a – 732
freak 608, 872
  – of Nature 83
freckle 848
freckled 440
fredaine 840
free
  detached 44, 47
  unconditional 52
  liberate 672
  unobstructed 705
  at liberty 748, 750
  gratis 815
  liberal 816
  insolent 885
  exempt 927a
  impure 961
  – balloon 273
  – and easy
  cheerful 836
  adventurous 863
  vain 880
  insolent 885
  friendly 888
  sociable 892
  – fight 720

– from
  simple 42
  never – from 613
  – gift 784
  – from imperfec-
    tion 650
  – lance 726
  – land 748
  – liver 954a
  – love 961
  make – of 748
  – play 170, 748
  – quarters
  cheap 815
  hospitality 892
  – space 180
  – stage 748
  – trade
  commerce 794
  – translation 522
  – will 600
  make – with
  frank 703
  take 789
  sociable 892
  uncourteous 895
freebooter 792
freeborn 748
freedman 748
freedom 748
free-handed 816
freehold 780
freely
  willingly 602
freeman 748
freemasonry
  unintelligible 519
  secret 528
  sign 550
  co-operation 709
  party 712
free-spoken 703
freethinker 989
freeze
  benumb 381
  cold 385
  – the blood 830
freezing 383
  – mixture 387
freight *lade* 184
  cargo 190
  transfer 270
freightage 812
freighter 273
freight train 272
French
  peddler's – 563
  – and English 840
  – horn 417
  – leave *avoid* 623
  freedom 748

– polish 847
frenetic 503
frenzy
  madness 503
  imagination 515
  excitement 825
frequency 136
frequent
  in number 104
  in time 136
  in space 186
  habitual 613
  visit 892
fresco *cold* 383
  painting 556
  al –
  out of doors 220
  in the air 338
fresh *additional* 37
  new 123
  flood 348
  cold 383
  colour 428
  remembered 505
  unaccustomed 614
  good 648
  healthy 654
  impertinent 885
  tipsy 959
  – breeze 349
  – colour 434
  – news 532
freshen 658, 689
freshet 348
freshman 541
freshwater 851
freshwater sailor
  701
fret *suffer* 378
  grieve 828
  gall 830
  discontent 832
  sad 837
  ornament 847
  irritate 900
  – and fume 828
fretful 901
fret-work 219
friable 328, 330
friandise 868
friar 996
  –'s lantern 423
  – Rush 980
  Black –s 996
friary 1000
fribble
  slur over 460
  trifle 643
  dawdle 683
  fop 854
fricassee 298

frication 331
friction *force* 157
  obstacle 179
  rubbing **331**
  on – wheels 705
friend 711, **890**
  candid – 936
  next – 759
friendless 893
friendly 714, **894**
friends, be – 888
  see one's – 892
friendship 9, 888
frieze 210
frigate 726
fright
  cards 840
  alarm 860
frightful 31, 830,
  846
frightfully 31
frightfulness 860
frigid
  cold 383
  - *style* 575
  callous 823
  indifferent 866
frigidarium 387
frigorific 385
frill 231, 248
  frills and furbe-
  lows 847
fringe
  border 231
  lace 256
  exaggeration 549
  ornament 847
frippery
  trifle 643
  ornament 847
  finery 851
  ridiculous 853
  ostentation 882
frisk *prance* 266
  leap 309
  search 461
  gay 836
  amusement 840
frisky 682, 836
frith *chasm* 198
  strait 343
  forest 367
fritinancy 412
fritter *small* 32
  – away *lessen* 36
  waste 638
  – away time 683
fritters 298
frivolous
  unreasonable 477
  foolish 499

fetid 401
bad 649
abhorrent 867
adulatory 933
impure 961
fulvid 436
fulvous 436
fumble
derange 61
handle 379
grope 463
awkward 699
fumbler 701
fume
violent 173
exhalation 334, 336
froth 353
heat 382
odour 398
excitement 824, 825
anger 900
in a −
discontented 832
−s of fancy 515
fumid 426
fumigate
vaporize 336
cleanse 652
fumigator 388
fumo, dare pondus − 481
fun 827, 840, 842
make − of 856
funambulist 700
function
algebra 84
office 170
business 625
utility 644
pomp 882
rite 998
duty 926
functionary
director 694
consignee 758
functus officio 756
fund *store* 636
sinking − 802
fundamental
intrinsic 5
base 211
support 215
− bass 413
− note 413
fundamentally 31
funds 800
in − 803
public − 802
funebrial 363

funeral 363
− pace 275
− march 415
funereal
interment 363
dismal 837
fungiform 249
fungology 369
fungosity 250
fungus
projection 250
vegetable 367
fœtor 401
bane 663
funicle 205
funicular 627
funk 860, 862
− hole 530
funnel *opening* 260
conduit 350
air-pipe 351
funnel-shaped 252
funny *odd* 83
boat 273
humorous 842
comic 853
fur *covering* 223
hair 256
warm 384
dirt 653
furacious 791
furbelow 231
furbish
improve 658
prepare 673
adorn 847
furcated 244
furcation 91
furcular 244
furfur 653
furfuraceous 330
Furies *anger* 900
evil-doers 913
demons 980
furious *violent* 173
haste 684
passion 825
anger 900
furiously 31
furl 312
furlong 200
furlough 760
furnace 386
workshop 691
like a − *hot* 382
sighing like −
lament 839
in love 902
furnish
provide 637
prepare 673

give 784
− aid 707
− a handle 617
− its quota 784
furniture 633
− van 272
furor
insanity 503
passion 825
furore
emotion 820, 821
passion 825
desire 865
furrow 259
further
added 37
distant 196
aid 707
go − and fare worse
worse 659
bungle 699
not let it go − 528
furthermore 37
furtive
clandestine 528
stealing 791
furuncle 250
fury *violence* 173
excitation 825
anger 900
demon 980
furze 367
fuscous 433
fuse *join* 43
combine 48
heat 382, 384
torch 388
fuselage 215
fusel oil 356
fusiform 244, 253
fusil 727
fusileer 726
fusillade 361, 716
fusion *union* 48
heat 384
co-operation 709
fuss *agitation* 315
activity 682
haste 684
difficulty 704
excitement 825
ostentation 882
kick up a − 173
make a − about
importance 642
lament 839
disapprove 932
fussy *crotchety* 481
bustling 682
excitable 825

fustian
absurd 497
unmeaning 517
- *style* 577, 579
fustigate 972
fusty 124, 401, 653
futhorc 590
futile 497, 645
future 121
eye to the − 510
− possession 777
− state
destiny 152
heaven 981
futurity 121
fuzzle 959
fuzzy 447

G

gab 284
gift of the − 582
gabardine 225
gabble 517, 583
gabelle 812
gaberlunzie 876
gabion 717
gable *side* 236
− end 67
Gabriel 977
Gaby 501
gad
about 266, 268
gadget 626
gad-so 870
gaff 727
gaffer *old* 130
man 373
clown 876
gag
closure 261
render mute 403, 581
dramatic 599
muzzle 751
imprison 752
gage *measure* 466
security 771
throw down the − 715
gaggle 412
gag-man 844
gaieté de cœur 836
gaiety
[*see* gay] 836
gaillard 844
gain
increase 35
advantage 618
skilful 698

gill 348
gillie 746
gilt 436, 847
 – edged 648
gimbals 312
gimcrack
 weak 160
 brittle 328
 trifling 643
 ornament 847
 ridiculous 853
gimlet 262
gimp
 clean 652
 pretty 845
 decoration 847
gin *trap* 545
 instrument 633
 intoxicating 959
 demon 980
gin mill 189
gin palace 189
gingerbread
 weak 160
 vulgar 851
gingerly 174, 459, 864
gingle 408
gipsy
 wanderer 268
 wag 844
 – lingo 563
giraffe 206
girandole 423
girasol 847
gird *bind* 43
 strengthen 159
 surround 227
 jeer 929
 – up one's loins
 brace 159
 prepare 673
girder 45, 215
girdle *bond* 45
 encircle 227
 circumference 230
 circle 247
 put a – round the
 earth 311
girl 129, 374
girlhood 127
girt 45
girth
 bond 45
 circumference 230
gisarm 727
gist *essence* 5
 meaning 516
 important 642
gît, ci – 363
gittern 417

give *yield* 324
 melt 382
 bestow 784
 discount 813
 – away 782, 784
 in marriage 903
 – back 790
 – birth to 161
 – with both hands 816
 – in charge
 restrain 751
 – chase 622
 – consent 762
 – one credit for 484
 – in custody 751
 – expression to 566
 – forth 531
 – the go by 623
 – a horse his head 748
 – in *submit* 725
 – into *consent* 762
 – light 420
 – the mind to 457
 – notice
 inform 527
 warn 668
 – it one
 censure 932
 punish 972
 – out *emit* 297
 publish 531
 bestow 784
 – over *cease* 142
 relinquish 624
 lose hope 859
 – place to
 substitute 147
 avoid 623
 – play to the im-
 agination 515
 – points to 27
 – quarter 740
 – rise to 153
 – one the slip 671
 – security 771
 – and take
 reciprocate 12
 compensation 30
 interchange 148
 retaliation 718
 compromise 774
 barter 794
 equity 922
 honour 939
 – tongue 531
 – a turn to 140
 – one to under-

 stand 527
 – up
 not understand 519
 unwilling 603
 reject 610
 relinquish 624
 submit 725
 resign 757
 surrender 782
 restore 790
 hopeless 859
 – up the ghost 360
 – way *weak* 160
 brittle 328
 submit 725
 pine 828
 despond 837
 modest 881
given [see give]
 circumstances 8
 supposition 514
 received 785
 – over *dying* 360
 – time 134
 – to 613
giving 784
gizzard 191
 stick in one's – 900
glabrous 225
glacial 383
glaciate 385
glacier 383
glacis 217, 717
glad 827, 829
 give the – eye 441
 would be – of 865
 – tidings 532
gladden 834, 836
glade *hollow* 252
 opening 260
 shade 424
gladiator 726
gladiatorial 361, 713, 720
gladsome 827, 829
Gladstone bag 191
glair 352
glaive 727
glamour 992
glance *look* 441
 sign 550
 see at a – 498
 – at
 take notice of 457
 allude to 527
 censure 932
 – off *deviate* 279
 diverge 291
gland 221

glare *light* 420
 stare 441
 imperfect vision 443
 visible 446
glaring
 [see glare]
 great 31
 colour 428
 visible 446
 manifest 525
glass *vessel* 191
 smooth 255
 brittle 328
 transparent 425
 lens 445
 musical –es 47
 see through a –
 darkly 491
 – of fashion 852
 live in a – house
 brittle 328
 visible 446
 danger 665
 – too much 959
glass-coach 272
glasshouse 191, 371
Glassite 984
glassy [see glass]
 shining 420
 colourless 429
glaucous 435
glave 727
glaver 933
glaze 255
gleam *small* 32
 light 420
glean 609, 775
gleanings 636
glebe *land* 342
 ecclesiastical 995
 church 1000
glee *music* 415
 satisfaction 827
 merriment 836
gleek 929
glen 252
glengarry 225
glib *voluble* 584
 facile 705
glide *lapse* 109
 move 264
 travel 266
 fly 267
 – into
 conversion 144
glider 273
glimmer
 light 420
 dim 422
 visible 446

906
- morrow 292
- name 873
- nature 906
- night 293
- for nothing
  impotence 158
  useless 645
in – odour
  repute 873
  approbation 931
- offices
  mediation 724
  kind 906
- old time 122
- omen 858
- opinion 931
take in – part
  pleased 827
  courteous 894
  kind 906
- pennyworth 815
- at the price 815
to – purpose 731
- repute 873
- sense 498
- society 852
- taste 578, 850
- temper 894
- thing 648
- time *early* 132
  opportune 134
  prosperous 734
- turn
  kindness 906
- understanding
  714
- wife
  woman 374
  spouse 903
- will
  willingness 602
  benevolence 906
- word
  approval 931
  vindication 937
- as one's word
  veracity 543
  observance 772
  probity 939
- works 906
goodie 652, 746
goodly
  great 31
  large 192
  handsome 845
good mixer 892
goodness
  [*see* good] **648**
  virtue 944
  have the –

request 765
- *gracious!* 870
- of heart 906
goods *effects* 270,
  780
  merchandise 798
good taste 868
Goodwin sands 667
goody 374
gooroo 996
goose *hiss* 409
  game of – 840
  giddy as a – 458
  tailor's – 255
  kill the – with
    golden eggs
    699, 818
  a wild – chase 545
gooseberry
  old – 978
  play – 459
  – eyes 411, 443
goosecap 501
goose egg 101
gooseflesh 383
goosequill 590
goose-skin 383
Gordian knot 59,
  704
gore *stab* 260
  blood 361
gorge *ravine* 198
  conduit 350
  fill 641
  satiety 869
  gluttony 957
  raise one's – 900
  – the hook 602
gorge de pigeon 440
gorgeous
  colour 428
  beauty 845
  ornament 847
  ostentation 882
Gorgon 860
gorilla 913
gormandise 298,
  954*a*, 957
gorse 367
gory *red* 434
  murderous 361
  unclean 653
gospel
  certainty 474
  truth 494
  take for – 484
Gospels 985
gossamer
  filament 205
  light 320
  texture 329

gossip *news* 532
  babbler 584
  conversation 588
gossoon 876
Gotama 986
Goth 851, 876
Gotham, wise men
  of – 501
gothic
  amorphous 241
gouache 556
gouge *concave* 252
  perforator 262
goulash 298
gourd 191
gourmand 954*a*,
  957
gourmet 868, 954*a*
gout 378
goût, haut – 392
goutte d'eau, il se
  noyerait dans
  une – 699
govern 693, 737
governess 540
  [*see* govern]
  ruling power 745
  divine – 976
  petticoat – 699
governor
  tutor 540
  director 694
  ruler 745
  keeper 753
gowk 501
gown *dress* 225
  canonicals 999
gownsman 492
grab *take* 789
  miser 819
grabble 379
grace *style* 578
  permission 760
  concession 784
  elegance 845
  polish 850
  title 877
  pity 914
  forgiveness 918
  honour 939
  piety 987
  worship 990
  act of – 784
  God's – 906
  with a bad – 603
  with a good –
    willing 602
    courteous 894
  in one's good –s
    888
  heart of – 861

say – 990
submit with a
  good – 826
- before meat **916**
grâce: coup de –
  914
la – 840
graceless
  inelegant 579
  ugly 846
  vicious 945
  impenitent 951
  irreligious 989
Graces 845
gracile 203
gracious
  willing 602
  courteous 894
  kind 906
  good – 870
grade *degree* 26
  arrange 60
  term 71
  ascent 217
  on the down – **658**
  on the up – 659
gradatim
  gradually 26
  in order 58
  continuous 69
  slow 275
gradation
  degree 26
  order 58
  continuity 69
gradient 217
gradual *degree* 26
  continuous 69
  slow 275
graduate
  adjust 23
  calibrate 26
  arrange 60
  series 69
  measure 466
  scholar 492, 873
graduated scale 466
gradus 86, 562
Græculus esuriens
  886
graft *join* 43
  locate 184
  insert 300
  trees 371
  teach 537
  booty 794
  corruption 940
Grail
  holy – 998
grain *essence* 5
  small 32

land 342
plain 344
evidence 467
teach 537
motive 615
plea 617
above – 359
down to the – 52
dress the – 371
fall to the – 732
get over the – 274
go over the – 302
level with the –
162
maintain one's –
persevere 604a
play– 840
prepare the – 673
stand one's –
defend 717
resist 719
– bait 784
– cut from under
one 732
– floor
chamber 191
low 207
base 211
– on
attribute 155
– plan 554
– of quarrel 713
– sliding from
under one 665
– swell
agitation 315
waves 348
grounded
stranded 732
well– 490
– on _basis_ 211
evidence 467
groundless
unsubstantial 4
illogical 477
erroneous 495
groundling 876
grounds
dregs 653
groundwork
precursor 64
cause 153
basis 211
support 215
preparation 673
group
marshal 60
cluster 72
– captain 745
grouping 60
grouse 852, 901a

grout 45
grove
street 189
glade 252
wood 367
grovel
below 207
move slowly 275
cringe 886
base 940
grow
increase 35
become 144
expand 194
– from
effect 154
– into 144
– less 195
– taller 206
– together 46
– up 194
– upon one 613
grower 164
growl _cry_ 412
complain 839
discourtesy 895
anger 900
threat 909
growler _cab_ 272
discontented 832
sulky 901a
grown up 131
growth [_see_ grow]
development 161
- _in size_ 194
tumour 250
vegetation 367
groyne 706
grub
small animal 193
food 298
– up
eradicate 301
discover 480a
Grub-street writer
593
grudge
unwilling 603
refuse 764
stingy 819
hate 898
anger 900
bear a – 907
owe a – 898
grudging 603
– _praise_ 932
gruel 298
gruesome 846
gruff
harsh sound 410
discourteous 895

grum
harsh sound 410
morose 901a
grumble
cry 411
complain 832,
839
grume 321, 354
grumous 321, 354
grumpy 901a
Grundy, Mrs. 852
grunt 412
complain 839
guano 653
guarantee 768, 771
guard
travelling 268
safety 664
defence 717
soldier 726
sentry 753
advanced – 668
mount –
care 459
safety 664
off one's –
inexpectant 508
throw off one's –
cunning 702
on one's –
careful 459
cautious 864
rear – 668
– against
prepare 673
defence 717
– ship 664, 726
guarda costa 753
guarded
conditions 770
guardian
safety 664
defence 717
keeper 753
– angel
helper 711
benefactor 912
guardless 665
guard-room 752
gubernation 693
gubernatorial 737
gudgeon 547
guerdon 973
guernsey 225
guerre:
nom de – 565
– à outrance &c.
722
guerilla 726
– _warfare_ 720
guess 514

guesswork 514
guest 890
paying – 188
guet:
mot de – 550
–à-pens 545
guffaw 838
guggle
gush 348
bubble 353
resound 408
cry 412
guide
pattern 22
courier 524
teach 537
teacher 540
indicate 550
direct 693
director 694
advise 695
guide-book 527
guided by, be – 82
guideless 665
guide-post 550
guiding star 693
guild 712, 966
guildhall 799
guile
deceit 544, 545
cunning 702
guileless 543, 703
guillotine 972, 975
guilt 947
guiltless 946
guilty:
find – 971
plead – 950
guindé 579
guinea 800
guipure 847
guisard 599
guise
state 7
dress 225
appearance 448
plea 617
mode 627
conduct 692
guiser 599
guitar 417
gulch 198
gules 434
gulf
interval 198
deep 208
lake **343**
gull 545, 547
gullible 486
gullet _throat_ 260
rivulet 348

gully *gorge* 198
  hollow 252
  opening 260
  conduit 350
gulosity 957
gulp *swallow* 296
  take food 298
  – down
  credulity 486
  submit 725
gum *fastening* 45
  fasten 46
  resin 356a
  – elastic 325
  – tree 367
gumbo 298
gummy 352
gumption 498
gun *report* 406
  weapon 727
  great – 626
  blow great –s 349
  sure as a – 474
gunboat 726
gunfire 404
gunman 361
gunner 776
gunnery
  warfare 722
  cannon 727
gunlayer 284
gunpowder
  warfare 722
  ammunition 727
  not invent – 665
  sit on barrel of –
    501
gunroom 193
gun-shot 197
gunwale 232
gurge 312, 348
gurgle
  flow 348
  bubble 353
  faint sound 405
  resonance 408
gurgoyle 350
gush
  flow out 295
  flood 348
  exaggeration 482
  talk 584
gushing
  emotional 821
  impressible 822
gusset 43
gust *wind* 349
  physical taste 390
  passion 825
  moral taste 850
gustation 390

gustful 394
gustless 391
gusto [*see* gust]
  physical pleasure
    377
  emotion 821
gut *destroy* 162
  opening 260
  strait 343
  eviscerate 297
  sack 789
  steal 791
gutling 954a
guts *inside* 221
guttapercha 325
gutter *groove* 259
  conduit 350
  vulgarity 851
guttersnipe 876
guttle 957
guttural
  letter 561
  inarticulate 583
guy
  fastening 45, 752
  fellow 373
  disrespect 929
  grotesque 853
guzzle
  gluttony 957
  drunkenness 959
gybe [*see* jibe]
gymkhana 720, 840
gymnasium 191
  school 542
  arena 728, 840
gymnast 159
gymnastics
  training 537
  exercise 686
  contention 720
  sport 840
gymnosophist
  abstainer 953
  sectarian 984
gynander 83
gynarchy 727
gynecæum 374
gynecology 662
gyniatrics 374
gynics 374
gyp 545, 746
gyre 311
gyrate 312
gyrfalcon 913
gyromancy 511
gyrostat 312
gysart 599
gyve 752

H

habeas corpus 963,
  969
haberdasher 225
habergeon 717
habiliment 225
habilitation 698
habit
  essence 5
  coat 225
  custom 613
  want of – 614
  –s of business 682
  – of mind 820
habitant 188
habitat 189
habitation 189
habit-maker 225
habitual
  unvariable 16
  orderly 58
  ordinary 82
  customary 613
habituate 537, 613
habitude
  state 7
  habit 613
habitué 613
hacienda 189, 780
hack *cut* 44
  shorten 201
  horse 271
  writer 594
  worker 690
  literary – 593
hackle 44
hackney-coach 272
hackneyed
  known 490
  trite 496
  habitual 613
Hades 982
Hadji
  traveller 268
  priest 996
hæ tibi erunt artes
  627
hæret lateri lethalis
  arundo
  displeasure 828
  anger 900
haft 633
hag *age* 128
  ugly 846
  wretch 913
  witch 994
haggard
  insane 503
  tired 688
  wild 824

ugly 846
haggis 298
haggle *cut* 44
  chaffer 794
Hagiographa 985
Hagiolatry 984
Hagiology 983, 985
haguebut 727
ha-ha *trench* 198,
  719
haik 225
hail *welcome* 292
  ice 383
  call 586
  rejoicing 838
  honour to 873
  celebration 883
  courtesy 894
  salute 928
  approve 931
  –fellow well met
  friendship 888
  sociality 892
hailstone 383
hair *small* 32
  filament 205
  roughness 256
  to a – 494
  –'s breadth
  near 197
  narrow 203
  –breadth escape
  danger 665
  escape 671
  –s on the head
  multitude 102
  make one's –
    stand on end
  distressing 830
  fear 860
  wonder 870
hairless 226
hairy *rough* 256
halberd 727
halberdier 726
halcyon *calm* 174
  peace 721
  prosperous 734
  joyful 827, 829
hale 654
half 91
  – the battle
  important 642
  success 731
  – distance 68
  – a dozen *six* 98
  several 102
  see with – an **eye**
  intelligent 498
  intelligible 518
  manifest 525

– a gale 349
– and half
  equal 27
  mixed 41
  incomplete 53
– a hundred 98
– light 422
– measures
  incomplete 53
  vacillating 605
  mid-course 628
– moon 245
– price 815
– rations 640
– scholar 493
– seas over 959
– sight 443
– speed
  moderate 174
  slow 275
– truth 546
half-blind 443
half-blood
  mixture 41
  unconformity 83
  imperfect 651
half-frozen 352
half-hearted
  irresolute 605
  insensible 823
  indifferent 866
half-learned 491
half-melted 352
halfpenny
  trifle 643
half-starved
  insufficient 640
  fasting 956
half-way
  small 32
  middle 68
  between 228
  go – *irresolute* 605
  mid-course 628
  meet –
  willing 602
  compromise 774
half-witted 499, 501
hall *chamber* 189
  receptacle 191
  mart 799
  music – 599
  – of audience 588
  – mark 550
hallelujah 990
halliard 45
halloo *cry* 411
  look here! 457
  call 586
  wonder 870
hallow

celebrate 883
  respect 928
hallowed 976
hallucination
  error 495
  insanity 503
halo *light* 420
  glory 873
Halomancy 511
halser 45
halt *cease* 142
  weak 160
  rest 265
  go slowly 275
  lame 655
  fail 732
  at the – 265
halter *rope* 45
  restraint 752
  punishment 975
  wear a – 874
  with a – round
    one's neck 665
halting
  style 579
  – place 292
halve [*see* half]
halves
  do by –
  neglect 460
  not complete 730
  not do by – 729
  go – 778
ham *house* 189
hamadryad 979
hammam 386, 652
hamlet 189
hammer
  repeat 104
  knock 276
  stammer 583
  under the –
  auction 796
  between the – and
    the anvil 665
  – at *think* 451
  work 686
  – out *form* 240
  prepare 673
  complete 729
hammock 215
hamper *basket* 191
  obstruct 706
hamstring 158, 659
hanaper 802
hand
  measure of
    length 200
  side 236
  transfer 270
  man 372

organ of touch
  379
  indicator 550
  writing 590
  medium 631
  agent 690
  grasp 781
  transfer 783
  at – *future* 121
  destined 152
  near 197
  useful 644
  bad – 590
  bird in – 781
  come to – 292, 785
  fold one's –s 681
  give one's – to
  marry 903
  good –
  writing 590
  skill 698
  proficiency 700
  helping – 707, 711
  hold in – 737
  hold out the – 894
  hold up the –
  vote 609
  in –
  incomplete 53
  business 625
  preparing 673
  not finished 730
  possessed 777
  money 800
  in the –s of
  authority 737
  subjection 749
  lay –s on
  discover 480*a*
  use 677
  take 789
  rite 998
  much on one's –s
    682
  on one's –s
  business 625
  redundant 641
  not finished 730
  for sale 796
  on the other – 468
  no – in 623
  poor – 701
  put into one's –s
    784
  put one's – to 676
  ready to one's –
    673
  shake –s 918
  stretch forth one's
    – 680
  take by the – 707

take in –
  teach 537
  undertake 676
time hanging on
  one's –s
  inaction 681
  leisure 685
  weary 841
try one's – 675
turn one's – 675
turn one's – to 625
under one's
  in writing 590
  promise 768
  compact 769
– back 683
– cart 272
– of death 360
– down
  record 551
  transfer 783
have one's –s full
  682
– gallop 274
– glass 445
– and glove 709,
  888
– in hand
  joined 43
  accompanying 88
  same time 120
  concur 178
  co-operate 709
  party 712
  concord 714
  friend 888
  social 892
– to hand
  touching 199
  transfer 270
  fight 720, 722
– over head
  inattention 458
  neglect 460
  reckless 863
have a – in
  cause 153
  act 680
  co-operate 709
have one's – in
  skill 698
keep one's – in
  613
live from – to
  mouth
  insufficient 640
  unprepared 674
  poor 804
–s off! *avoid* 623
  leave alone 681
  prohibition 761

will of − 601
− forfend! 766
− knows 475, 491
− be praised 838, 916
for −'s sake 765
heaven-born
wise 498
repute 873
virtue 944
heaven-directed 498
heaven-kissing 206
heavenly
celestial 318
rapturous 829
divine 976
of heaven 981
− bodies 318
− host 977
− kingdom 981
heavenly-minded 987
heavens 318
− and earth! 870
Heaviside layer 338
heavisome 843
heavy *great* 31
inert 172
weighty 319
stupid 499
actor 599
sleepy 683
dull 843
brutish 851
− affliction 828
− artillery 726
− cost 814
− dragoon 726
− father 599
− gaited 843
− gun 727
− hand
clumsy 699
severe 739
− on hand 641
− heart *loth* 603
pain 828
dejection 837
− hours 841
− on the mind 837
− news 830
− sea
agitation 515
waves 348
− sleep 683
− type 591
− wet 298
heavy-laden 706, 828

hebdomadal 138
Hebe 845
hebetate 823, 826
hebetude
imbecile 499
insensible 823
inexcitable 826
Hebrew
unintelligible 519
Jew 984
Hecate 994
hecatomb
number 98
sacrifice 991
heckle 830, 900
hectic 382, 821
Hector *brave* 861
rash 863
bully 885, 887
hedge
compensate 30
inclosure 232
− in
circumscribe 229
hinder 706
conditions 770
hedgehog 253
hedonism 377, 827
hedonist 954a
heed *attend* 457
care 459
beware 668
caution 864
heedful 457
heedless
inattentive 458
neglectful 460
oblivious 506
rash 863
heel *support* 215
lean 217
deviate 279
go round 311
iron − 975
lay by the −s 162
turn on one's −
go back 283
go round 311
avoid 623
− of Achilles 665
heel-piece
sequel 65
back 235
repair 660
heel-tap
remainder 40
dress 653
heels *lowness* 207
at the − of
near 197
behind 235

cool one's − 681
follow on the − of 281
laid by the − 751
lay by the − 789
show a light pair of − 623
take to one's − 623
tread on the − of
near 197
follow 281
approach 286
− over head
inverted 218
hasty 684
rash 863
heft *handle* 633
exertion 686
hegemony
influence 175
direction 693
authority 737
heifer 366
heigho! 839
height *degree* 26
altitude 206
summit 210
at its −
great 31
supreme 33
draw oneself up to his full − 307
− finder 206
heighten
increase 35
elevate 307
exaggerate 549
aggravate 835
hegira [*see* hejira]
heinous 945
heir *futurity* 121
posterity 167
inheritor 779
heirloom 780
heirship 777
hejira 293
Helen of Troy 845
heliacal 318
helical 248
Helicon 597
helicon-horn 417
helicopter 273
Heliogabalus 954a
heliograph
signal 550
picture 556
heliography 550
light 420
painting 556
Helios 423

heliotrope 847
heliotype 558
helix 248
hell *abyss* 208
gaming-house 62
gehenna **982**
− upon earth
misfortune 735
pain 828
− broke loose 59
hell-born 945, 978
hellebore 663
hell-hound 913, 949
hellish
malevolent 907
vicious 945
hell 982
helluo librorum 492
helm *handle* 633
sceptre 747
(*authority* 737)
answer the − 743
at the − 693
obey the − 705
take the − 693
helmet 225, 717
helminthology 368
helmsman 269, 694
helot 746
help *benefit* 618
utility 644
remedy 662
aid 707
servant 746
give 784
it can't be −ed
submission 725
never mind 823
content 831
God − you 914
so − me God 535
− oneself to 789
helper 711
helpless 158, 665
helpmate
auxiliary 711
wife 903
helter-skelter 59, 684
helve
throw the − after the hatchet 818
hem *edge* 231
fold 258
indeed! 870
kiss the − of one's garment 886
− in *enclose* 220
restrain 751
hemi- 91
hemisphere 181

hemispheric 250
hemlock 663
hemorrhage 299
hemp 205
hen 366, 374
    female 374
    – with one chicken
      busy 682
henbane 663
hence
    arising from 155
    departure 293
    deduction 476
    – *loathed mel-*
      ancholy 836
henceforth 121
henchman 746
hencoop 370
hendiadis 91
henna 433
henpecked 743, 749
heptagon 244
heptarchy 98
Heraclitus 839
    rideret – 853
herald
    precursor 64
    precession 280
    predict 511
    forerunner 512
    proclaim 531
    messenger 534
heraldry 550
herb 367
herbage 365
herbal 369
herbivorous 298
herborize 369
herculean
    strong 159
    exertion 686
    difficult 704
Herculem, ex pede
    – 550
Hercules 159, 215
    pillars of – 233,
      550
herd 72, 102
herdsman 746
here
    situation 183
    presence 186
    arrival 292
    come –! 286
    – below 318
    – goes 676
    – and there
      dispersed 73
      few 103
      place 182, 183
    – there and

everywhere
diversity 16a
space 180
omnipresence 186
– to-day and gone
  to-morrow 111
hereabouts 183,
  197
hereafter 121, 152
hereby 631
hereditament 780
hereditary
    intrinsic 5
    derivative 154,
      167
heredity 167
herein 221
heresy 495, 984
heretic 984
heretofore 122
hereupon 106
herewith 88, 632
heritage
    futurity 121
    possession 777
    property 780
heritor 779
hermaphrodite 83
  – brig 273
hermeneutics 522
Hermes 534, 582
hermetically 261
hermit 893, 955
hermitage
    house 189
    cell 191
    seclusion 893
hero *brave* 861
    glory 873
    good man 948
    – worship 931, 991
Herod, out-Herod
  – 549
heroic [*see* hero]
    magnanimous
      942
    mock – 853
heroics 884
heroin 663
heroine 861
herpetology 368
Herr 373
herring
    pungent 392
    – pond 341
    draw a – across
      the trail 545
    trail of a red –
      615, 706
herring-gutted 203
hesitate

uncertain 475
sceptical 485
stammer 583
reluctant 603
irresolute 605
fearful 860
Hesperian 236
Hesperides, garden
  of the – 981
Hesperus 423
Hessian boot 225
hest 741
hesterni quirites
  876
heterarchy 737
heteroclite 83
heterodoxy 489,
  984
heterogeneous
    unrelated 10
    different 15
    mixed 41
    multiform 81
    exceptional 83
heterogeneity 15,
  16a
heteromorphism
  16a
hetman 745
hew *cut* 44
    shorten 201
    fashion 240
    – down 308
hewers of wood
    workers 690
    commonalty 876
hexagon 98, 244
hexahedron 244
hexameter 98, 597
hey! 586
heyday
    exultation 838
    festivity 840
    wonder 870
    – of the blood 820
    – of youth 127
hiation 260
hiatus 198
hibernal 383
hibernate 683
Hibernicism 497,
  563
hic:
    – jacet 363
    – labor hoc opus
      704
hick 701, 851, 876
hiccup 349
hid under a bushel
  460

hidalgo 875
hidden 528
  – meaning 526
hide *skin* 223
  conceal 528
  – diminished **head**
    inferior 34
    decrease 36
    humility 879
  – one's face
    modesty 881
  – and seek
    deception 545
    avoid 623
    game 840
hide-bound 751,
  819
hideous 846
hide-out 893
hiding-place
    abode 189
    ambush 530
    refuge 666
hie 264, 274
  – to 266
hiemal 126
hierarch 996
hierarchy 995
hieratic 590
hieroglyphic
    representation
      554
    letter 561
    writing 590
hierographa 985
hieromancy 511
hierophant 996
hieroscopy 511
higgle 794
higgledy piggledy
  59
higgler 797
high *much* 31
    lofty 206
    fetid 401
    treble 410
    foul 653
    noted 873
    proud 878
  from on – 981
  on – 206
  think –ly of 931
  – art 556
  – celebration 998
  – colour
    colour 428
    red 434
    exaggerate 549
  – commissioner
    745
  – days and holi-

days 840
in a – degree 31
– descent 875
– and dry
  stable 150
  safe 664
in – esteem 928
in – feather
  strong 159
  health 654
  cheerful 836
  boasting 884
– glee 836
– hand
  violent 173
  resolved 604
  authority 737
  severe 739
  pride 878
  insolence 885
  lawless 964
– jinks 840
ride the – horse
  878
– hat 225
– life *fashion* 852
  rank 875
– living
  intemperance 954
  gluttony 957
– mass 998
– mightiness 873
– and mighty
  pride 878
  insolence 885
– note 410
– notions 878
– places 210
– pressure
  energy 171
  excitation of
  feeling 824
– price 814
– priest 996
in – quarters 875
– relief 448
– repute 873
–ly respectable
  875
on the – road to
  way 627
  hope 858
on one's – ropes
  excitation 824
  pride 878
  anger 900
– seas 341
in – spirits 836
– tide *wave* 348
  prosperity 734
– time *late* 133

occasion 134
– in tone
  white 430
– treason
  disobedience 742
  dishonour 940
– words
  quarrel 713
  anger 900
high-ball 298
high-born 875
high-brow 492
higher 33
highest 210
highfalutin 884
high-flavoured 392
high-flier
  madman 504
  proud 878
high-flown
  imaginative 515
  style 577
  proud 878
  vain 880
  insolent 885
high-flying
  inattentive 458
  exaggerated 549
  ostentatious 822
highlands 206
high-low 225
high-mettled
  excitable 825
  brave 861
high-minded
  honourable 939
  magnanimous
  942
highness *title* 877
high-pitched 410
high-seasoned 392
high-souled 878
high-sounding
  loud 404
  words 577
  display 882
high-spirited 861,
  939
hight 564
high-toned 852
high-water
  completeness 52
  height 206
  crater 337
– mark
  measure 466
highway 627
–s and byways
  627
– robbery 791
highwayman 792

high-wrought
  good 648
  prepared 673
  excited 824
hike 266
hilarity 836
hill *height* 206
  convexity 250
  ascent 305
  descent 306
  take to the –s 666
  –dwelling 206
hillock 206
hilt 633
hinc illæ lachrymæ
  155
hind *back* 235
  clown 876
  on one's – legs
  elevation 307
  anger 900
– quarters 235
hinder 706
hindermost 67, 235
Hindooism 984
hindrance 706
hinge *fasten* 43
  fastening 45
  cause 153
  depend upon 154
  rotate 312
hinny 271
hint *reminder* 505
  suppose 514
  inform 527
  take a – 498
  – a fault &c. 932
hinterland 235
hip 236
  have on the –
  confute 479
  success 731
  authority 737
  subjection 749
– hip, hurrah! 838
hipped [*see* hypped]
hippocentaur 80
Hippocrates 662
hippocratic 360
hippodrome
  drama 599
  arena 728
  amusement 840
hippogriff 83
Hippolytus 960
hippophagy 298
hippopotamus 192
hirdie-girdie 218
hire
  commission 755
  borrowing 788

  price 812
  reward 973
  on – 763
hireling 746
hirsute 256
hispid 256
hiss *sound* 409
  animal cry 412
  disrespect 929
  contempt 930
  disapprobation
  932
hist! 585, 586
histology 329
historian 553
historic 594
historiette 594
historical:
– painter 559
– painting 556
historiographer 553
historiography 594
history *past* 122
  record 551
  narrative 594
History, Natural –
  357
histrionic 599
hit *chance* 156
  strike 276
  reach 292
  succeed 731
  censure 932
  (*punish* 972)
  good – 626
  make a – 731
– one's fancy 829
– the mark 731
– off 545
– upon
  discover 480*a*
  plan 626
hitch
  fasten 43
  knot 45
  stoppage 142
  hang 214
  jerk 315
  harness 370
  difficulty 704
  hindrance 706
– up 293
hither 278, 292
  come – 286
hitherto 122
hive
  multitude 102
  location 184
  abode 189
  bees 870
  workshop 691

H.M.S. 726
hoar *aged* 128
  white 430
  – frost 383
hoard 636
hoarse
  husky 405
  harsh 410
  voiceless 581
  talk oneself – 584
hoary [*see* hoar]
hoax 545
hob *support* 215
  stove 386
  – and nob
  celebration 883
  courtesy 894
hobble
  limp 275
  awkward 699
  difficulty 704
  fail 732
  shackle 751
  – skirt 225
hobbledehoy 129
hobby
  crotchet 481
  pursuit 622
  desire 865
hobby-horse 272
hobgoblin
  fearful 860
  demon 980
hobo 268
hobnail 876
Hobson's choice
  necessity 601
  no choice 609a
  compulsion 744
hoc genus omne
  876
hock 771
hock shop 787
hockey 840
hockey rink 213
hocus 545
hocus-pocus
  interchange 148
  unmeaning 517
  cheat 545
  conjuration 992
  spell 993
hod
  receptacle 191
  support 215
  vehicle 272
hoddy-doddy 501
hodge-podge 41, 59
hoe 272, 371
hog *animal* 366
  sensualist 954a

glutton 957
(*greedy as a* – 865
  go the whole – 604
hog's back 206
hogmanay 998
hogshead 191
hog-wash 653
hoist 307
  – the black flag
  722
  – a flag 550
  – on one's own
  petard
  retaliation 718
  failure 732
hoity-toity! 815,
  870
hold *cohere* 46
  contain 54
  remain 141
  cease 142
  go on 143
  happen 151
  receptacle 191
  cellar 207
  base 211
  support 215
  halt 265
  believe 484
  be passive 681
  defend 717
  power 737
  restrain 751
  prison 752
  prohibit 761
  possess 777
  retain 781
  enough! 869
  have a firm – 781
  have a – upon 175
  gain a – upon 737
  get – of 789
  quit one's – 782
  take – 175
  – aloof
  stay away 187
  distrust 487
  avoid 623
  – an argument
  476
  – authority 737
  – back *avoid* 623
  store 636
  hinder 706
  restrain 751
  retain 781
  miserly 819
  – one's breath
  wonder 870
  – converse 588
  – a council 695

– fast 751, 781
– forth *teach* 537
  speak 582
– good 478, 494
– one's ground
  141
– in hand 737
– one's hand
  cease 142
  relinquish 624
– hard 265
– up one's head
  861
– a lease 771
– a meeting 72
– off 623
– office 693
– on
  continue 141, 143
  persevere 604a
– out [*see below*]
– one's own
  preserve 670
  defend 717
  resist 719
– oneself in readi-
  ness 673
– in remembrance
  505
– both one's sides
  838
– a situation 625
– in solution 335
– to 602
– together 43, 709
– one's tongue
  403, 585
– up [*see below*]
– oneself up 307
hold out
  endure 106
  affirm 535
  persevere 604a
  resist 719
  offer 763
  brave 861
  – expectation
  predict 511
  promise 768
  – temptation 865
hold up
  continue 143
  support 215
  not rain 340
  aid 707
  rob 791
  display 882
  extol 931
  – one's hand
  sign 550
  threat 609

– to execration
  cures 908
  censure 932
  – the mirror 525
  – to scorn 930
  – to shame 874
  – to view 525
holder 779
holdfast 45
holding
  tenancy 777
  property 780
hole *place* 182
  hovel 189
  receptacle 191
  opening 260
  ambush 530
  – in one's coat 651
  – and corner
  place 182
  peer into – 461
  hiding 528, 530
  – to creep out of
  plea 617
  escape 671
  facility 705
holiday *leisure* 685
  repose 687
  amusement 840
  – task *easy* 705
holiness *God* 976
  piety 987
holloa 411
  – before one is out
  of the wood 884
hollow
  unsubstantial 4
  completely 52
  incomplete 53
  depth 208
  concavity 252
  channel 350
  - sound 408
  specious 477
  false 544
  voiceless 581
  beat – 731
  – truce 723
holm 346
holocaust
  kill 361
  sacrifice 991
  (*destruction* 162)
holograph 590
holster 191
holt 367
holus bolus 684
Holy *of God* 976
  pious 987
  keep – 987
  – breathing 990

home 297
- of cards 160
- of correction
  prison 752
  punishment 975
- of death 363
- of detention 752
- divided against
  itself 713
bring the - about
  one's ears 699
- of Commons
  696, 966
- of God 1000
- of Lords 696,
  875, 966
set one's - in
  order 952
- of peers 696, 875
- of prayer 1000
- built on sand
  160
turn - out of win-
  dow 713
housebreaker 792
housebreaking 791
house-dog 366
household
  inhabitants 188
  abode 189
  - gods 189
  - stuff 635
  - troops 726
  - words
  known 490
  language 560
  plain 576, 849
householder 188
housekeeper 637,
  694
housekeeping 692
houseless 185
housemaid 746
house-organ 531
Houses of Parlia-
  ment 191, 696
house-top 210
proclaim from -
  531
house-room 180
house-warming 892
housewife 682
housewifery 692,
  817
housing
  lodging 189
  covering 223
  horse-cloth 225
hovel 189
hoveller 269
hover *high* 206

rove 266
soar 267
ascend 305
irresolute 605
- about
  move 264
- over
  near 197
how *way* 627
  means 632
- comes it?
  attribution 155
  inquiry 461
- now 870
howbeit 30
however
  degree 26
  notwithstanding
  30
  except 83
howitzer 727
howker 273
howl
  wind 349
  human cry 411
  animal cry 412
  lamentation 839
howler 495
howling wilderness
  169, 893
hoy 273
hoyden *girl* 129
  rude 851
hub 222
hubble-bubble 392
hubbub *stir* 315
  noise 404
  discord 713
huckster 794, 797
huddle
  disorder 59
  derange 61
  collect 72
  hug 197
  - on 225
Hudibrastic 856
- verse 597
hue 428
- and cry *cry* 411
  proclaim 531
  pursuit 622
  alarm 669
  raise a - and cry
  932
hueless 429
huff 885, 900
huffy 901
hug *cohere* 46
  border on 197
  retain 781
  courtesy 894

love 897
endearment 902
- a belief 606
- oneself
  pleasure 827
  content 831
  rejoicing 838
  pride 878
- the shore
  navigation 267
  approach 286
- a sin 945
huge 31, 192
hugger-mugger 528
Huguenot 984
huis clos, à - 528
huissier 965
huke 225
hulk *body* 50
  ship 273
hulks 752
hulky *big* 192
  unwieldy 647
  ugly 846
hull 50
hullabaloo 404, 411
hullo! 292
hum
  faint sound 405
  continued sound
  407
  animal sound 412
  sing 416
  deceive 545, 546
- and haw
  stammer 583
  irresolute 605
busy - of men 682
human 372
- race 372
- sacrifices 991
humane
  benevolent 906
  philanthropic 910
  merciful 914
humanitarian 372,
  910
humanities 560
humanize 894
humano capiti cer-
  vicem jungere
  equinam 24
humation 363
humble *meek* 879
  modest 881
  pious 987
-r classes 876
- oneself
  submit 725
  meek 879
  penitent 950

worship 990
eat - pie 725, 879
your - servant
  dissent 489
  refusal 764
humbug
  falsehood 544
  deception 545
  deceiver 548
  trifle 643
  affectation 855
humdrum 841, 843
humectate 337, 339
humid 339
humiliate 308
humiliation
  adversity 735
  disrepute 874
  sense of shame
  879
  worship 990
self - 950
humility **879**, 987
humming-top 417
hummock 206, 250
humorist **844**
humorous 842
humour *essence* 5
  tendency 176
  liquid 333
  disposition 602
  caprice 608
  aid 707
  indulge 760
  affections 820
  please 829
  wit 842
  flatter 933
  (*fun* 840)
in the - 602
out of - 901*a*
peccant -
  unclean 853
  disease 655
humoursome
  capricious 608
  sulky 901*a*
hump 250
hump-backed 243
humph! 870
Humphrey, dine
  with Duke - 956
Humpty-dumpty
  193
Hun 165, 851, 913
hunch 250, 612
hunch-backed 243
hundred
  number 98
  many 102
  region 181

imaum 745, 996
imbecile 158, 499
imbécile 501
imbecility 499
imbed [*see* embed]
imbedded 229
imbibe 296
  – learning 539
imbrangle 61
imbricated 223
imbroglio
  disorder 59
  difficulty 704
  discord 713
imbrue
  impregnate 300
  moisten 339
  – one's hands in
    blood
    killing 361
    war 722
  – the soul 824
imbue *mix* 41
  impregnate 300
  moisten 339
  tinge 428
  teach 537
imbued
  affections 820
  – with
    belief 484
    habit 613
    feeling 821
imburse 803
imitation
  copying **19**
  copy 21
  representation
    554
immaculate
  perfect 650
  clean 652
  innocent 946
immanent 5, 132
immanity 907
Immanuel 976
immaterial
  unsubstantial 4
immateriality
  spiritual **317**
  trifling 643
immature 123, 674
immeasurable 31,
  105
immediate
  continuous 69
immediately 113,
  132
immedicabile
  vulnus 619
immedicable 859

immelodious 414
immemorial 124
  from time – 122
  ⌐ usage 613
immense *great* 31
  infinite 105
  - *size* 192
immerge⎫
immerse⎭
  introduce 300
  dip 337
immersed in 229
immethodical 59
immigrant
  alien 57
  entering 294
immigration 266,
  294
imminent 152, 286
immiscible 47
immission 296
immitigable
  hopeless 859
  revenge 919
immix 41
immobility 150, 265
immoderately 31
immodest 961
immolation
  killing 361
  giving 784
  sacrifice 991
immoral 923, 945
immortal
  perpetual 112
  glorious 873
  celebrated 883
immotile 265
immovable
  stable 150
  quiescent 265
  obstinate 606
immundicity 653
immunity
  health 656
  freedom 748
  right 924
  exemption 777a,
    927a
immure 751
immutable
  stable 150
  deity 976
imo pectore, ab –
  821
imp 980
impact *contact* 43
  impulse 276
  insertion 300
impair 659
impale *transfix* 260

execute 972
impalpable
  small 193
  powder 330
  intangible 381
impanation 998
impar sibi 608
imparity 28
impart *inform* 527
  give 784
impartial
  judicious 498
  neutral 628
  just 922
  honourable 939
  – opinion 484
impassable
  closed 261
  impossible 471
impasse 706
impassible 823
impassion 824
impassionable 822
impassioned
  - *language* 574
  excited 825
impassive 823
impatient 825
  – of control 742
impawn 771
impeach
  censure 932
  accuse 938
  go to law 969
impeachment,
  soft – 902
impeccability 650,
  946
impecunious 804
impede 706
impediment 706
  – in speech 583
impedimenta 633,
  780
impel *push* 276
  induce 615
impend
  future 121
  imminent 132
  destiny 152
  overhang 206
impenetrable
  closed 261
  solid 321
  unintelligible 519
  latent 526
impenitence 951
imperative
  require 630
  command 737,
    741

severe 739
  duty 926
imperator 745
imperceptible
  small 32
  minute 193
  slow 275
  invisible 447
  latent 526
impercipient 376
imperdible 664
imperfect
  incomplete 53
  failing 651
  vicious 945
imperfection 651
  inferiority 34
  vice 945
imperfectly 32
imperforate 261
imperial
  trunk 191
  beard 256
  authority 737
imperil 665
imperious
  command 737
  proud 878
  arrogant 885
  – necessity 601
imperishable 112
  stable 150
  glorious 873
imperium in
  imperio 737
impermanent 111
impermeable
  closed 261
  dense 321
impersonal
  general 78
  neuter 316
impersonate 19,
  554
impersonator 19
imperspicuity 519
impersuasible 606
impertinent
  irrelevant 10
  insolent 885
imperturbable 823,
  826
impervious
  closed 261
  impossible 471
  insensible 823
  – to light 426
  – to reason 606
impetiginous 653
impetrate 765
impetuous

IN

diffuse 573
– jail 751
– limine 66
– loco 23
– medias res 68
– prison 751
– propriâ personâ 79
– toto 52
– transitu
  transient 111
  transfer 270
– statu pupillari 127
– statu quo 141
– vogue 1
inability 158, 699
inabstinent 954
inaccessible 196, 471
inaccurate 495, 568
inaction 172, **683**
inactivity **683**, 172
inadequate
  powerless 158
  insufficient 640
  useless 645
  imperfect 651
inadmissible
  incongruous 24
  excluded 55
  extraneous 57
  inexpedient 647
inadvertence 458
inadvisable 647
inaffable 895
inalienable
  retention 781
  right 924
inamorata 897
inane *void* 4
  unmeaning 517
  unthinking 452
  insufficient 640
  trivial 643
  useless 645
inanimate 360
– matter 358
inanition 158
inanity [*see* inane]
inappetency 823, 866
inapplicable 10, 24
inapposite 10, 24
inappreciable 33, 193
  unimportant 643
inapprehensible
  stolid 499
  unintelligible 519
inappropriate 24,

INC

647
inapt
  incongruous 24
  impotent 158
  useless 645
  inexpedient 647
  unskilful 699
inarticulate 581, 583
inartificial 703
inartistic 846
inasmuch *whereas* 9
  however 26
  because 476
inattention **458**
inaudible
  silence 403
  faint sound 405
  deaf 419
  voiceless 581
inaugural
  precursor 64
inaugurate
  begin 66
  cause 153
  install 755
  celebrate 883
inauspicious
  untimely 135
  untoward 649
  hopeless 859
inbeing 5
inborn, inbred
  intrinsic 5
  affections 820
– *proclivity* 601
inca 745
incage 751
incalculable 31, 105
incalescence 382
incandescence 382
incandescent 423
incantation
  invocation 765
  sorcery 992
  spell 993
incantatory 992
incapable 158
incapacious 203
incapacitate 158
incapacity
  impotence 158
  ignorance 491
  stupidity 499
incarcerate 751
incarnadine 434
incarnate
  intrinsic 5
  bodily 316
  fleshly 364
  vicious 945

INC

devil –
  bad man 949
  Satan 978
Incarnation 976
incase 223, 229
incautious 863
incendiary
  destroy 162
  burn 384
  influence 615
  malevolent 907
  evil-doer 913
  bad man 949
incense *fuel* 388
  fragrant 400
  hate 898
  anger 900
  flatter 933
  worship 990
  rite 998
incension
  burning 384
incentive 615
inception 66
inceptive 153
inceptor 541
incertitude 475
incessant
  repeated 104
  ceaseless 112
  frequent 136
incest 961
inch *small* 32
  length 200
by –es 275
to an – 494
not yield an – 606
give an – and take an ell 789
– by inch
  by degrees 26
  in parts 51
  slowly 275
not see an – be- yond one's nose 699
inchoation 66, 673
incide 44
incidence 278
incident 151
incidental
  extrinsic 6
  circumstance 8
  irrelative 10
  occurring 151
  casual 156
  liable 177
  chance 621
  trivial 643
– *music* 415
incinerate 384

INC

incipience 66
incircumspect 460
incision 44, 259
incisive *energy* 171
  vigour 574
  feeling 821
incisor 253
incite
  exasperate 173
  urge 615
incivility 895
incivism 911
inclasp 229
inclement
  violent 173
  cold 383
  severe 739
  pitiless 914*a*
inclination
  [*see* incline]
  will 600
  affection 820
  desire 865
  love 897
incline *tendency* 176
  slope 217
  direction 278
  willing 602
  induce 615
– an ear to 457
– the head 308
inclined
  disposed 620
– plane 633
inclose
  surround 227
inclosure 232
include
  composition 54
– *in a class* 76
inclusion 76
inclusive
  additive 37
  component 56
  class 76
incogitancy 452
incognita, terra – 491
incognito 528
incognizable 519
incoherence
  physical **47**
  mental 503
incombustible 385
income *means* 632
  profit 775
  property 780
  wealth 803
  receipt 810
– *tax* 812
incoming

ingress 294
receipt 810
incommensurable 10
– *quantity* 84, 85
incommode 706
hinder 706
incommunicable
unmeaning 517
unintelligible 519
retention 781
incommunicado 528
incommutable 150
incomparable 33
incompassionate 914*a*
incompatible 24
incompatibility 15
incompetence
inability 158
incapacity 499
unskilful 699
dereliction 927
incompleteness 53
non-completion 730
incompliance 764
incomprehensible
infinite 105
unintelligible 519
incomprehension 491
incompressible 321
inconcealable 525
inconceivable
unthinkable 452
impossible 471
improbable 473
incredible 485
unintelligible 519
wonder 870
inconceptible 519
inconcinnity
disagreement 24
ugliness 846
inconclusive 477
inconcoction 674
incondite 851
incongruous
differing 15
disagreeing 24
illogical 477
ungrammatical 568
discordant 713
inconnection 10, 44
inconsequence
irrelation 10
inconsequential 477
inconsiderable 32,

643
inconsiderate
thoughtless 452
inattentive 458
neglectful 460
foolish 699
inconsistent
contrary 14
disagreeing 24
illogical 477
absurd 497
foolish 499
capricious 608
discord 713
inconsolable 837
inconsonant
disagreeing 24
fitful 149
inconspicuous 447
inconstant 149
incontestable 159, 474, 525
incontiguous 196
incontinent 961
incontinently 132
incontrollable 173
incontrovertible 150, 474
inconvenience 647
put to – 706
inconversable 585, 893
inconvertible 143
inconvincible 487
incorporate 48
combine 48
include 76
materialize 316
incorporation 761
incorporeal 317
– *hereditaments* 780
incorrect
illogical 477
erroneous 495
solecism 568
vicious 945
incorrigible
obstinate 606
hopeless 859
vicious 945
impenitent 951
incorruption
probity 939
innocence 946
incrassate
increase 194
density 321
– *fluids* 352
increase
– *in degree* **35**

– *in number* 102
– *in size* 194
incredible
great 31
impossible 471
improbable 473
doubtful 485
wonderful 870
incredulity 487, 989
increment
increase 35
addition 37
adjunct 39
expansion 194
increpation 932
incriminate 938
incrust 223, 224
incubate 370
incubation 673
incubus
hindrance 706
pain 828
demon 980
inculcate 6, 537
inculpable 946
inculpate 938
inculture 674
incumbency
business 625
churchdom 995
incumbent
inhabitant 188
high 206
weight 319
duty 926
clergyman 996
incumber 706
incumbered 806
incunabula 66, 127
incur 177
– *blame* 932
– *danger* 665
– *a debt* 806
– *disgrace* 874
– *a loss* 776
– *the risk* 621
incurable
ingrained 5
disease 655
hopeless 859
incuriam, per – 458, 460
incuriosity 456
incursion 294, 716
incurvation 245
indagation 461
indebted
owing 806
gratitude 916
duty 926
indecent 961

indeciduous 150
indecipherable 519
indecision 475, 605
indecisive 475
indeclinable 150
indecorous
vulgar 851
vicious 945
impure 961
indeed *existing* 1
very 31
assent 488
truly 494
assertion 535
wonder 870
indefatigable
persevering 604*a*
active 682
indefeasible
stable 150, 474
due 924
indefectible 650
indefensible
powerless 158
submission 725
accusable 938
wrong 945
indeficient 650
indefinite
great 31
unspecified 78
infinite 105
misty 447
uncertain 475
inexact 495
vague 519
indeliberate 612
indelible *stable* 150
memory 505
mark 550
feeling 821
indelicate 961
indemnity
compensation 30
restitution 790
forgiveness 918
atonement 952
reward 973
deed of – 771
indenizen 184
indent *scollop* 248
list 86
indentation 252, 257
indenture 769, 771
independence
irrelation 10
freedom 748
wealth 803
Independent 984
indescribable 31,

disorder 59
impossible 471
infallibility 474
assumption of –
885
infamy *shame* 874
dishonour 940
vice 945
infancy 66, 127
infandum renovare
dolorem 505,
833
infant 129
fool 501
– *prodigy* 872
Infanta 745
infanticide 361, 991
infantine 129
foolish 499
infantry 726
infarction 261
infatuation
misjudgment 481
credulity 486
folly 499
insanity 503
obstinacy 606
passion 825
love 897
infeasible 471
infect *mix with* 41
contaminate 659
excite 824
infectâ, re –
shortcoming 304
non-completion
730
failure 732
infection
transference 270
disease 655
infectious 270, 657
infecund 169
infelicity
inexpertness 699
misery 828
infelicitous 24
infer 472
inference 476, 480
by – 467
inferential
demonstrative 478
latent 526
inferiority
in degree **34**
in size 195
imperfection 651
personal – 34
infernal *bad* 649
malevolent 907
wicked 945

satanic 978
– *machine* 727
– *regions* 982
infertility 169
infest 830
infestivity 837, 843
infibulation 43
infidel 487, 989
infidelity
dishonour 940
irreligion 989
infiltrate *mix* 41
intervene 228
interpenetrate 294
moisten 337, 339
teach 537
infiltration
passage 302
Infinite, the – 976
infinite 105
– *goodness* 976
infinitely *great* 31
infinitesimal
small 32
little 193
– *calculus* 85
infinity 105
infirm *weak* 160
disease 655
vicious 945
– of *purpose* 605
infirmary 662
infirmity
[*see* infirm]
infix 537
inflame
render violent 173
burn 384
excite 824
anger 900
inflamed 382
inflammable 384,
388
inflammation
heating 384
disease 655
inflate *increase* 35
expand 194
blow 349
inflated
overestimation
482
style 573, 577
ridiculous 853
vain 880
inflation
[*see* inflate]
rarefaction 322
currency 800
inflect 245
inflexible *hard* 323

resolved 604
obstinate 606
stern 739
inexorable 914*a*
inflexion
change 140
curvature 245
grammar 567
inflict *act upon* 680
severity 739
– *evil* 649
– *pain*
bodily pain 378
mental pain 830
– *punishment* 972
infliction
adversity 735
mental pain 828,
830
punishment 972
influence 153
change 140
physical – **175**
inducement 615
instrumentality
631
authority 737
absence of – **175a**
sphere of – 780
make one's – felt
631
influx 294
infold 232
inform 527
– *against*
accuse 938
go to law 969
informal 83, 964
informality 773
informant 527
information
knowledge 490
communication
527
learning 539
lawsuit 969
pick up – 539
informer 532
informity 241
infra dignitatem
874, 940
infraction
trespass 303
disobedience 742
non-observance
773
exemption 927
– of *usage* &c.
unconformity 83
desuetude 614
infrangible

combined 46
dense 321
infra-red rays 420
infrequency 137
infrigidation 385
infringe
transgress 303
disobey 742
not observe 773
undueness 925
dereliction 927
– a *law* &c. 83
infundibular 252,
269
infuriate
violent 173
excite 824
anger 900
infuscate 431
infuse *mix* 41
insert 300
teach 537
– *courage* 861
– *life into* 824
– *new blood* 658
infusible 321
infusion [*see* infuse]
liquefaction 335
infusoria 193
ingannation 545
ingathering 72
ingemination 90
ingenerate 5
ingenious 515, 698
ingenite 5
ingenium, per-
fervidum – 682
ingénu *artless* 703
ingénue *actress* 599
ingenuity 698
ingenuous 703
ingesta 298
ingestion 296
ingle 388
inglorious 874, 940
ingluvies 191
ingot 800
ingraft *add* 37
join 43
insert 300
teach 537
ingrafted
extrinsic 6
habit 613
ingrain
insinuate 228
colour 428
ingrained
intrinsic 5
combined 48
habit 613

character 820
ingrate 917
ingratiate 897
ingratiating 894
ingratitude 917
ingredient 51, 56
ingress 294
  forcible – 300
ingurgitate 296
ingustible 391
inhabile 699
inhabit 186
inhabitant 188
inhale *receive* 296
  breathe 349
  smell 398
inharmonious
  discord 713
  – colour 428
  – sound 414
inhere 1
inherent 5, 820
inherit 775, 777
inheritance 780
  – of the saints 981
inherited
  intrinsic 5
inheritor 779
inhesion 5
inhibit *hinder* 706
  restrain 751
  prohibit 761
inhospitable 893
inhuman 907
inhume 363
inimaginable
  impossible 471
  improbable 473
  wonderful 870
inimical 708, 889
inimitable
  non-imitation 20
  supreme 33
  very good 648
  perfect 650
iniquity 923, 945
  worker of – 949
inirritability 826
initial 66
  – letter 558
initiate *begin* 66
  admit 296
  teach 537
initiated *skilful* 698
initiative 66
inject 300, 337
injection 662
injudicial 964
injudicious 499, 863
injunction

acquirement 630
advice 695
command 741
prohibition 761
injure *evil* 619
  damage 659
  spite 907
injuria formæ,
  spretæ – 846, 930
injury *evil* 619
  badness 649
  damage 659
injustice 923
ink 431
  pen and – 590
  before the – is dry 132
  – slinging 720
inkle 45
inkling
  knowledge 490
  supposition 514
  information 527
inkstand 590
inland 221
inlay 440, 847
inlet *beginning* 66
  interval 198
  opening 260
  ingress 294
  – *of the sea* 343
inly 221
inmate 188
inmost 221
  to the – core 822
  – soul 820
  – thoughts 451
inn 189
  – s of Court 968
innate 5, 601
innavigable 471
inner 221
  – coating 224
  – man *intellect* 450
  affections 820
innermost recesses 221
innings *land* 342
  acquisition 775
  receipt 810
innkeeper 601
innocence 946
innocent *fool* 501
  good 648
  healthy 656
  artless 703
  guiltless 946
innocuous *good* 648
  healthy 656
  innocent 946

innominate 565
innovation
  variation 20a
  new 123
  change 140
innoxious
  salubrious 656
  innocent 946
innuendo *hint* 527
  censure 932
innumerable 105
innutritious 657
inobservance 773
inoccupation 681
inoculate
  insert 300
  teach 537
  influence 615
inodorous 399
inoffensive 648, 946
inofficious 907
inoperative
  powerless 158
  unproductive 169
  useless 645
inopportune
  untimely 135
  inexpedient 647
inordinate 31, 641
inorganization 358
inornate 849
inosculate *join* 43
  intersect 219
  convoluted 248
inquest 461
inquietude
  changeable 149
  uneasy 828
  discontent 832
  apprehension 860
inquinate 659
inquire 461
  – into 595
inquirer 461
inquiring mind 455
inquiry 461
inquisition
  inquiry 461
  severity 739
  torture 907
  tribunal 966
inquisitive 455
inquisitorial
  prying 455
  inquiry 461
  severe 739
  jurisdiction 965
inroad *ingress* 294
  devastation 659
  invasion 716
inrolment 551

insalubrity 657
insanity 503
insatiable 865
inscribe 590, 873
inscription 551
inscroll 551
inscrutable 519
insculpture 557
insculptured 558
insecable 43, 87
insect *minute* 193
  animal 366
  – cry 412
insecure
  uncertain 475
  danger 665
insensate
  foolish 499
  insane 503
insensibility
  slow 275
  physical **376**
  moral **823**
  – of benefits 917
  – to the past 506
inseparable 43, 46
insert *locate* 184
  interpose 228
  enter 294
  put in 300
  record 551
  – itself 300
insertion 300
  adjunct 39
  ornament 847
inservient 645
inseverable 43, 87
inside 221
  – out 218
  turn – out 529
insidious
  deceitful 545
  cunning 702
  dishonourable 940
insight 465, 490
insignia 550
  – of authority **747**
insignificant
  unmeaning 517
  unimportant 643
insincere 544, 855
insinuate
  intervene 228
  ingress 294
  insert 300
  latency 526
  hint 527
  ingratiate 897
  blame 932
insipid
  style 575

intercept
 hinder 706
 take 789
intercession
 [*see* intercede]
 worship 990
Intercessor 976
interchange 148
 barter 794
 – *visits &c.* 892
interchangeable 12
intercipient 706
interclude 706
intercommunica-
 tion 527
intercommunity
 892
interconnection 9
intercourse
 copulation 43
 friendship 888
 sociality 892
 verbal – 582, 588
intercurrence
 interchange 148
 interjacence 228
 passage 302
interdependence 12
interdict 761
interdictive 55
interdigitate 219,
 228
interest *concern* 9
 influence 175
 curiosity 455
 advantage 618
 importance 642
 property 780
 debt 806
 excite 824
 please 829
 amuse 840
 devoid of – 841
 feel an – in 906
 not know one's
 own – 699
 make – for 707
 place out at –
 lend 787
 economy 817
 take an – in
 curiosity 455
 love 897
 take no – in
 insensibility 823
 indifference 866
 want of – 866
interested
 selfish 943
 – in 457
interesting

lovable 897
interfere *disagree*
 24
 counteract 179
 intervene 228
 activity 682
 thwart 706
 mediate 724
interference
 light 420
interfretted 219
interfusion 41
interim 106, 120
interior 221
 painting 556
interjacence 68,
 228
interject 228, 300
interlace *join* 43
 twine 219
interlacing 41
interlard 41, 228
interleave 228
interline
 interpolate 288
 write 590
interlineation 39
interlink 43, 219
interlocation 228
interlocking direc-
 torate 709
interlocution 588
interlocutor 582
interloper
 extraneous 57
 intervene 228
 obstruct 706
interlude
 time 106
 dramatic 599
intermarriage 903
intermeddle 682,
 706
intermeddling 724
intermediary 534
intermediate
 mean 29
 middle 68
 intervening 228
 ministerial 631
 – *time* 106
intermedium
 mean 29
 link 45
 intervention 228
 instrument 631
interment 363
 insertion 300
intermezzo 415
intermigration 266
interminable

infinite 105
 eternal 112
 long 200
intermingle 41
intermission 106,
 142
intermit
 interrupt 70
 recur 138
 discontinue 142
intermittence
 time 106
intermix 41, 48
intermutation 148
intermural 278
intern 221
internal 5, 221
 – *evidence* 467
international
 reciprocal 12
 sociality 892
 – *law* 963
internecine 361
 – *war* 722
internuncio 534,
 758
interpel 142
interpellation
 inquiry 461
 address 586
 summons 741
 appeal 765
interpenetration
 interjacence 228
 ingress 294
 passage 302
interpolation
 adjunct 39
 analytical 85
 interpose 228
 insertion 300
interpose
 intervene 228
 act 682
 hinder 706
 mediate 724
interposit 799
interplane ary 228
interpretation 522
interpreter 524
interrelation 9, 12
interregnum
 intermission 106
 transient 111
 discontinuance
 142
 interval 198
 laxity 738
interrogate 461
interrupt
 discontinuity 70

cessation 142
 hinder 706
interruption
 derangement 61
 interval 198
intersect 219
interspace 198, 221
intersperse 73, 228
interstellar 228
interstice 198
interstitial 221, 228
intertexture
 intersection 219
 tissue 329
inter-twine, -twist
 unite 43
 cross 219
interval
 – *of time* 106
 – *of space* 198
 – *in music* 413
 at –s
 discontinuously
 70
 at regular –s 138
intervene
 – *in order* 70
 – *in time* 106
 – *in space* 228
 be instrumental
 631
 mediate 724
intervert 140, 279
interview 588, 892
intervolved 43
interweave *join* 43
 cross 219
 interjacence 228
interworking 170
intestate 552
intestine 221
inthral 749, 751
intimacy 9
intimate
 personal 79
 close 197
 inside 221
 tell 527
 friendly 888, 892
intimately
 joined 43
intimidate
 frighten 860
 insolence 885
 threat 909
intitule 564
into: go – 294
 put – 300
 run – 300
intolerable 830
intolerance

prejudice 481
dissent 489
obstinacy 606
impatience 825
insolence 885
malevolence 907
intomb 363
intonation
  sound 402
  musical 313
  voice 580
intone 416, 992
intort 248
intoxicant 663
intoxication
  excitement 824,
  825
  inebriation 959
intra, ab – 221
intractable
  obstinate 606
  difficult 704
  sullen 901a
intramural 221
intransient 110
intransigeance 604
intransitive 110
intransmutable
  110, 150
intrap 545
intraregarding 221
intrench 717
  – *on* 303
intrepid 861
intricate
  confused 59
  convoluted 248
  difficult 704
intrigant
  meddlesome 682
  cunning 702
  libertine 962
intrigue *fascinate*
  615, 897
  plot 626
  activity 682
  cunning 702
  excite 824
  interest 829
  licentiousness 961
intrinsic 5
  – *evidence* 467
  – *habit* 613
  – *truth* 494
intrinsicality 5
introception 296
introduce *lead* 62
  interpose 228
  precede 280
  insert 300
  – *new blood* 140

– *new conditions*
  469
– *to* 888
introduction
  [*see* introduce]
  preface 64
  reception 296
  drama 599
  friendship 888
  courtesy 894
introductory
  precursor 64
  beginning 66
  priority 116
introgression 294
introit 998
intromission 228
intromit
  discontinue 142
  receive 296
introspection 441,
  457
introspective 451
introvert 218
intrude
  interfere 24
  inopportune 135
  intervene 228
  enter 294
  encroach 303
intruder 57
intrusiveness 682
intrust 755, 787
intuition *mind* 450
  unreasoning **477**
  knowledge 490
intumescence 194,
  250
intwine 43, 243
inunction 223
inundate
  effusion 337
  flow 348
  redundance 641
inunderstanding
  452
inurbanity 895
inure 613, 673
inured
  insensible 823
inusitation 614
inutility **645**
invade *ingress* 294
  encroach 303
  attack 716
invalid
  powerless 158
  illogical 477
  diseased 655
  undue 925
invalidate

disable 158
weaken 160
confute 479
invaluable 648
invariable
  intrinsic 5
  uniform 16
  conformable 82
  stable 150
invasion
  ingress 294
  attack 716
invective 932
inveigh 932
inveigle 545, 615
invent
  discover 480a
  imagine 515
  lie 544
  devise 626
invented
  untrue 546
invention 480a
inventive
  skilful 698
inventor 164
inventory 86
inverse 14, 218
inversion
  derangement 61
  change 140
  of position **218**
  contraposition
  237
  reversion 145
  language 577
invertebrate 158
invest
  empower 157
  clothe 225
  besiege 227, 716
  commission 755
  give 784
  lend 787
  expend 809
  – *in locate* 184
  purchase 795
  – *money* 817
  – *with ascribe* 155
investigate 461
investment **225**
  – *trust* 712
  make –s 673
inveterate *old* 124
  established 150
  inborn 820
  – *belief* 484
  – *habit* 613
invidious
  painful 830
  hatred 898

spite 907
envy 921
invigorate
  strengthen 159
invigorating
  healthy 656
invincible 159
inviolable
  secret 528
  right 924
  honour 939
inviolate
  permanent 141
  secret 528
  honourable 939
invious *closed* 261
  pathless 704
invisibility **447**
invisible *small* 193
  not to be seen 447
  concealed 526
  – *ink* 528
  become – 4
invitâ Minervâ 603,
  704
invite *induce* 615
  offer 763
  ask 765
  – *the attention*
  457
inviting
  [*see* invite]
  pleasing 829
invoice 86
invoke *address* 586
  implore 765
  pray 990
  – *curses* 908
  – *saints* 998
involucrum 223
involuntary
  necessary 601
  unwilling 603
  – *servitude* 749
involution [*see*
  involve]
  algebra 85
involve *include* 54
  derange 61
  wrap 225
  evince 467
  mean 516
  latency 526
involved
  disorder 59
  convoluted 248
  obscure style 571
  in debt 806
involvement 704
invulnerable 664
inward *intrinsic* 5

bill 800
fly a – *credit* 805
insolvency 808
– balloon 273, 726
kith 11
kithless 87
kitten *animal* 366
young 129
bring forth 161
playful as a – 836, 840
kleptomania
insanity 502
stealing 791
desire 865
kleptomaniac 504
knack 698
get into the – 613
knacker 361
knag 706
knaggy 901*a*
knap 206
knapsack 191
knave 548, **941**
– of hearts 897
knavery
deception 545
cunning 702
improbity 940
vice 945
knead *mix* 41
mould 240
soften 324
stroke 379
knee *angle* 244
bend the –
stoop 30
submission 725
down on one's –s
humble 879
on one's –s
beg 765
respect 928
atone 952
on the –s of the
gods 121, 152
knee-deep 208, 209
kneel *stoop* 308
submit 725
beg 765
servility 886
courtesy 894
ask mercy 914
respect 928
worship 990
knell 363
strike the death –
361
knickerbockers 225
knicknack 643, 847
knife 253

play a good – and
fork *eat* 298
appetite 865
war to the – 708
knight 875
– errant
madman 504
defender 717
rash 863
philanthropist
910
–'s move 279
– service 777
– of the road 792
– Templar 71
knit 43
well – 159
– the brow
discontent 832
anger 900
disapprobation
932
knitting 847
knob *pendency* 214
ball 249
protuberance 250
knock *blow* 276
sound 406
hard –s 720
– at the door
death 360
request 765
– down
destroy 162
lay flat 213
lower 308
injure 659
dishearten 837
– on the head
kill 361
– one's head
against 699
– off *complete* 729
– out 162
– over 162
– under 725
– up 688
**knock-down argu-
ment** 479
knocked
– to atoms 162
– on the head
failure 732
knocker 936
knock-kneed 243,
244
knoll 206
knot *ligature* 45
entanglement 59
group 72
intersection 219

round 249
dense 321
difficulty 704
hindrance 706
junto 712
ornament 847
marriage 903
true lover's – *love*
897
endearment 902
tie the nuptial –
903
knotted *rough* 256
knout 975
know *believe* 484
knowledge 490
friendly 888
associate 892
I'd have you to –
457, 535
not that one –s
491
– what one is
about 698
– all 474
I – better 536
– no bounds
great 31
infinite 105
redundance 641
– for certain 484
– by heart 505
– one's own mind
604
– one's stuff 465
– one's way about
465
– nothing of 491
– what's what 698
– which is which
465
knowing 702
knowingly 620
knowledge **490**
[*and see* know]
acquire – 539
come to one's –
527
practical – 698
– of the world 698
known:
become – 529
make – *inform* 527
publish 531
well – 490
habitual 613
– as 564
– by 550
knuckle 244
– down 725
knuckle-duster 727

knurl 256
knurr and spell 840
kobold 980
Koh-i-noor 650
kopje 206
Koran 986
kowtow *bow* 308
submission 725
courtesy 894
respect 928
kraal 189, 232
kraken 83
kris 727
Krishna 979
kudos 931
Ku klux klan 712
kursaal 840
kyanize 670
kyles 343

L

laager 717
labarum 550
labefy 659
label 39, 550
labent 306
labial *lip* 231
letter 561
labitur et labetur
112, 143
labor hoc opus, hic
– 704
laboratory 691
laborious
active 682
exertion 686
difficult 704
labour
parturition 161
work 680
exertion 686
hard –
punishment 972
mountain in – 638
– for 620
– of love
willing 602
amusement 840
disinterested 942
– party 712
– under *state* 7
disease 655
difficulty 704
feeling 821
affliction 828
– in vain
fall short 304
useless 645
– in one's voca-

tion 625
- unrest 832
laboured - *style* 579
  prepared 673
  - study 457
labourer 690
labouring
  - man 690
  - oar 686
labyrinth
  disorder 59
  convolution 248
  secret 533
lac *number* 98
  resin 356a
  - of rupees 800
lace *stitch* 43
  netting 219
  ornament 847
  - one's jacket 972
lacerable 328
lacerate 44
  - the heart 830
laches 460, 773
Lachesis 601
lachrymæ, hinc
  illæ - 830
lachrymatory gas
  727
lachrymis, quis
  temperet a - 914
lachrymose 837
lack *require* 630
  insufficient 640
  destitute 804
  desire 865
  - faith 989
  - harmony 708
  - preparation 674
  - wit 501
lackadaisical
  inactive 683
  melancholy 837
  indifferent 866
lackadaisy! 839,
  870
lack-brain 499, 501
lacker [*see* lacquer]
lackey 746
lack-lustre 422, 429
laconic 572
lacquer
  covering 223
  resin 356a
  adorn 847
lacrosse 840
lacteal 352
lacuna 198, 252
lacustrine 343
lad 129
ladder 305, 627

[542]

kick down the -
  604
lade *load* 184
  transfer 185
  contents 190
  dip 270
  - out 297
laden 52
  heavy - 828
  - with 777
ladies' man 897
lading 190, 780
  bill of - *list* 86
ladle *receptacle* 191
  transfer 270
  vehicle 272
lady *woman* 374
  rank 875
  wife 903
  our - 977
  - day 138
  - help 746
  -'s maid 746
lady chapel 1000
ladylike
  womanly 374
  fashionable 852
lady-love 897
lag *linger* 275
  follow 281
  dawdle 683
  - behind 133
laggard 603, 683
lager *beer* 298
lagoon 343
laical 997
laid: - on one's
  back 158
  - by the heels 751
  - low 160
  - up 655
lair 189, 653
laird *master* 745
  proprietor 779
  nobility 875
Lais 962
laisse manger, cela
  se - 394
laisser: - aller,
  - faire
  permanence 141
  neglect 460
  inaction 681
  laxity 738
  freedom 748
  inexcitable 826
laity 997
lake *water* 343
  pink 434
  - of fire and brim-
  stone 982

Lama 745, 996
Lamaism 984
Lamarkism 357
lamb *infant* 129
  animal 366
  gentle 826
  innocent 946
  go out like a - 174
  lion lies down
    with - 721
Lamb of God 976
lambent
  touching 379
  - flame *heat* 382
  light 420
Lambeth 1000
lame *incomplete* 53
  impotent 158
  weak 160
  imperfect 651
  disease 655
  injury 659
  failing 732
  - conclusion
    illogical 477
  failure 732
  help a - dog over
    a stile *aid* 707
  vindicate 937
  - duck 808
  - excuse 617
lamellar 204
lamentable *bad* 649
  painful 830
  sad 837
lamentably *very* 31
lamentation 839
lamia 980, 994
lamina 51, 204
lamination 204
Lammas 998
lamp 423
  rub the - 992
  safety - 666
  smell of the -
    style 577
  prepared 673
lamplighter
  quick 682
lampoon 932, 934
lampooner 936
lanâ caprinâ, de -
  643
lanary 636
lanate 25, 256
lance *pierce* 260
  throw 284
  spear 727
  break a - with
    attack 716
    warfare 722

couch one's - 720
  - corporal 745
lancer 726
  -'s dance 340
lancet 253, 262
lancinate 378, 830
land *arrive* 292
  ground 342
  estate 780
  gone to a better -
    360
  hug the - 286
  make the - 286
  on - 342
  see - 858
  - covered with
    water 343
  - flowing with
    milk and honey
    168
  how the - lies
    circumstances 8
    experiment 463
    foresight 510
  in the - of the
    living 359
landamman 745
landau 272
landed
  - gentry 779
  - estate 780
landgrave 745
landholder 779
landing field 273
landing-place 215,
  292
landlady 779
land-locked 229,
  343
landloper 268
landlord 779
land-lubber 343,
  701
landmark
  limit 233
  indication 550
land-mine 727
landreeve 694
landscape
  prospect 448
  - gardening
    agriculture 71
    beauty 845
  - painting 556
  - painter 559
land-shark 792
land-slip 306
landsman 342
Landsturm 726
land-surveying 466
Landwehr 726

lane 189, 260, 627
langrel 727
lang-syne 122
language 560
  command of – 582
  strong –
    vigour 574
    malediction 908
languid *weak* 160
  inert 172
  slow 275
  - style 575
  inactive 683
  torpid 823
languish
  decrease 36
  ill 655
  inactive 683
  repine 828
  – for 865
languishing
  weak 160
  affected 855
languishment
  lament 839
languor
  [*see* languid]
lank 200
lanky 203, 206
lantern
  window 260
  lamp 423
  magic – 448
  – of Diogenes 461
  – jaws 203
lanterne, à la – 972
lanuginous 256
lanyard 45
Laodicean 822
lap *abode* 189
  support 215
  interior 221
  wrap 225
  encompass 227,
    229
  drink 298
  – of luxury
  pleasure 377
  inactivity 683
  voluptuousness
    954
lap-dog *animal* 366
  servile 886
lapel 39
lapidary 559
lapidate *kill* 361
  attack 716
  punish 972
lapidescence 323
lapis lazuli
  blue 438

jewel 847
lappet 39, 214
lapse *course* 109
  past 122
  conversion 144
  fall 306
  degeneracy 659
  relapse 661
  loss 776
  vice 945
  guilt 947
  – of memory 506
  – of time 109
lapsus calami 495
lapsus linguæ
  mistake 495
  solecism 568
  stammering 583
Laputa, college of –
    538
larboard 239
larceny 791
lard 356
lardaceous 355
larder 636
  contents of the –
    298
lares et penates
  home 189
  idols 991
large
  quantity 31
  size 192
  at – *diffuse* 573
  free 748
  become – 194
  – number 102
  – type 642
large-hearted
  liberal 816
  benevolent 906
  disinterested 942
  larger 194
largest 784
  largest portion 192
larghetto 275, 415
largiloquent 573
largo 275, 415
lariat 45, 247
lark *ascent* 305
  pleasure 827
  spree 840
  with the – 125
larmes:
  fondre en – 839
  – aux yeux 839
larmoyante,
  comédie – 599
larrikin 887, 913
larrup 972
larum 404, 669

larva 129
larynx 351
lascar 269
lasciate ogni spe-
  ranza 859
lascivious 961
lash *tie together* 43
  violence 173
  incite 615
  censure 932
  punish 972
  scourge 975
  under the – *com-*
    pelled 744
  subject 749
  – into fury 909
  – with the tongue
    931
  – the waves 645
lass *girl* 129
lassitude 680, 841
lasso 45, 247
last *model* 22
  - in order 67
  endure 106
  durable 110
  - in time 122
  continue 141
  at – 133
  breathe one's –
    360
  game to the –
    604a
  never hear the –
    of 104
  – but one &c. 67
  die in the – ditch
    604a
  – for ever 112
  at the – extremity
    665
  – finish 729
  – gasp 360
  go to one's – home
    360
  on – legs *weak* 160
  dying 360
  spoiled 659
  adversity 735
  – resort 666
  – rites 998
  – shift 601
  – sleep 360
  – stage 67
  – straw 153
  – stroke 729
  – touch 729
  – word
    affirmation 535
    obstinacy 606
  – year &c. 122

latch 43, 45
latchet 45
latch-key 631
late *past* 122
  new 123
  tardy 133
  dead 360
  too – 135
lately 122, 123
latency 526
lateness 133
latent 172, 526
  – organism 153
later 117
laterality 236
lateritious 434
latest 118
latet anguis in
  herbâ 66
lath 205
  thin as a – 203
lathe
  region 181
  machine 633
lather 332, 353
Latin
  au bout de son –
    704
  perdre son – 704
  thieves' – 563
latitancy 528
latitat 969
latitude *extent* 180
  region 181
  breadth 202
  measurement 466
  freedom 748
  – and longitude
    situation 183
latitudinarian 984,
    989
latration 412
latria 990
latrines 653
latrociny 791
latter *sequent* 63
  past 122
Latter-day Saint
    984
latterly 123
lattice *crossing* 219
  opening 260
laud 931, 990
laudable 944
laudanum 174
laudari a laudato
  viro 931
laudator 935
  – temporis acti
    past 122
    habit 613

discontent 832
detractor 936
laudatory 931
laugh 838
make one – 853
raise a – 840
– at *ridicule* 856
sneer 929
(*undervalue* 483)
– to scorn *defy* 715
despise 930
– in one's sleeve
latent 526
ridicule 856
disrespect 929
contempt 930
– on the wrong
side of one's
mouth
disappointed 509
dejected 837
in disrepute 874
laughable 853
laughing:
no – matter 642
– gas 376
laughing-stock 857
laughter-loving 836
launch *begin* 66
boat 273
propel 284
– forth 676
– into 676
– into eternity
360, 361
– out 573
– out against 716
laundress 652, 746
laundry *room* 191
heat 386
clean 652
– maid 746
– man 652
laureate 875
poet – 597
laurel *trophy* 733
glory 873
decoration 877
repose on one's –s
265
lava *excretion* 299
semiliquid 352
lavatory 652
lave *water* 337
clean 652
lavender *colour* 437
laver la tête 932
lavish *profuse* 641
give 784
squander 818
– of praise 931

law *regularity* 80
statue 697
permission 760
legality 963
court of – 966
give the – 737
go to – 969
Jewish – 985
lay down the –
certainty 474
affirm 535
command 741
learned in the –
968
set the – at
defiance 964
take the – into
one's own
hands 722, 742
– of the Medes
and Persians
80, 148
take the – of 969
law-abiding 743
lawful
permitted 760
due 924
legal 963
lawgiver 694
lawless 59
irregular 83
mutinous 742
non-observant 773
vicious 945
arbitrary 964
lawn *plain* 344
grass 367
agriculture 371
– sleeves 999
– tennis 840
lawsuit 969
lawyer 968
lax *incoherent* 47
soft 324
error 495
- *style* 575
remiss 738
non-observance
773
dishonourable 940
licentious 945
irreligious 989
laxity 738
lay *moderate* 174
place 184
ley 344
music 415
poetry 597
bet 621
secular 997
– about one

active 682
exertion 686
attack 716
contend 720
punish 972
– one's account for
484
– apart
exclude 55
relinquish 782
– aside
neglect 460
reject 610
disuse 678
give up 782
– on the table 133
– the axe at the
root of tree 162
– bare 529
– before 527
– brother 996
– by *store* 636
sickness 655
disuse 678
– to one's charge
938
– claim to 924
– in the dust 162
– eggs 161
– at the door of
155
– down [*see below*]
– at one's feet 763
– figure *nonentity* 4
model 22
representation
554
– one's finger
upon 480a
– the first stone 66
– the flattering
unction to one's
soul 831, 834
– the foundations
153, 673
– ghosts 992
– hands on
use 677
take 789
rite 998
– under hatches
751
– one's head on
the block 942
– heads together
695, 709
– in *eat* 298
store 636
provide 637
– on 972
open *divest* 226

opening 260
show 525
disclose 529
– oneself open to
177
– out
horizontal 213
corpse 363
plan 626
expend 809
– oneself out for
673
– over 133
– reader 996
– under restraint
751
– in ruins 162
– siege to 716
– stress on 642
– to *attribute* 155
rest 265
– it on thick
cover 223
too much 641
flatter 933
– together 43
– train 626
– up *store* 636
sickness 655
disuse 678
– waste 162
lay down *locate* 184
horizontal 213
assert 535
renounce 757
relinquish 782
pay 807
– one's arms
pacification 723
submission 725
– the law
certain 474
assert 535
command 741
insolence 885
– one's life 360
– a plan 626
layer 204
layette 225
layman 699, 997
laystall 653
lazaret 662
lazar-house 662
lazy 683, 927
lazzarone 683
lb. 319
lea *land* 342
plain 344
leach 335
lead *superiority* 33
in order 62

[545]

lee-shore 665, 667
leet, court – 966
lee-wall 666
leeward 236
lee-way *space* 180
 tardy 133
 navigation 267
 deviation 279
 progression 282
 shortcoming 304
left *residuary* 40
 sinistral 239
 over the – 545
 – alone 748
 – in the lurch 732
 – to shift for one-
 self 893
 pay over the –
 shoulder 808
left-handed
 clumsy 699
 – compliment 932
 – marriage 903
leg *support* 215
 walker 266
 thief 792
 best – foremost
 686
 fast as –s will
 carry 274
 have a – to stand
 on 470
 keep on one's –s
 654
 last –s *spoiled* 659
 fatigue 688
 light on one's –s
 734
 make a – 894
 not a – to stand on
 illogical 477
 confuted 479
 failure 732
 off one's –s
 propulsion 284
 on one's –s
 upright 212
 elevation 307
 speaking 582
 in health 654
 active 682
 free 748
 set on one's –s 660
 – bail 623
legacy 270, 780, 784
legal *permitted* 760
 legitimate 924
 relating to law
 963
 – adviser 968
 – estate 780

legality **963**
legate 534
legatee 779, 785
legation 755
legato 415
legend 551, 594
legendary
 imaginary 515
legerdemain 146,
 545
légèreté 605
leggings 225
leghorn hat 225
legible 518
 – hand 590
legion
 multitude 102
 army 726
legionary 726
legislation 693, 963
legislative assem-
 bly 696
legislator 694
legislature 693, 696
legist 968
legitimate *true* 494
 permitted 760
 right 922
 due 924
 legal 963
legume 367
lei 847
leisure **685**
 at one's – *late* 133
leisurely 275
leman 897
lemma 476
lemon *colour* 436
Lemprière 979
lemures 980
lend 787
 – aid 707
 – countenance 707
 – a hand 680
 – oneself to
 assent 488
 co-operate 709
 – on security 789
 – wings to 707
lender *creditor* 805
lending **787**
length **200**
 go all –s
 resolution 604
 activity 682
 exertion 686
 at – *in time* 133
 full – *portrait* 556
 go great –s 549
 – and breadth of
 50

– and breadth of
 the land
 space 180
 publication 531
 – of time 110
lengthen 35, 200
 – out
 diuturnity 110
 late 133
lengthwise 200
lengthy *long* 200
 diffuse 573
lenient
 moderate 174
 mild 740
 compassionate
 914
lenify 174
lenitive
 moderating 174
 remedy 662
 relieving 834
lenity **740**
lens 445
Lent 956, 998
lenten 956
lenticular 245, 250
lentor *slowness* 275
 spissitude 352
 inactivity 683
lentous 352
leonem, ex ungue –
 550
leonine verses 597
leopard
 variegated 440
 –'s spots
 unchanging 150
leprechaune 980
leprosy 655
lerret 273
lèse-majesté 742
less *inferior* 34
 subduction 38
 – than no time
 113
lessee
 possessor 779
 receiver 785
lessen
 – in quantity or
 degree 36
 – in size 195
 – an evil 658
lesson *teaching* 537
 warning 668
 give a – to
 punish 972
 read a – to
 censure 932
 say one's –

memory 505
lessor 805
lest 623
let *hindrance* 706
 permit 760
 lease 771
 lend 787
 sell 796
 apartments to –
 fool 499
 to – 763
 – alone *besides* 37
 permanence 141
 quiescence 265
 avoid 623
 disuse 678
 inaction 681
 not complete 730
 free 748
 – be
 permanence 141
 continuance 143
 inaction 681
 – blood 297
 – 'I dare not' wait
 upon 'I would'
 605
 – down
 depress 308
 humble 879
 – down easily
 forgive 918
 – fall *drop* 308
 inform 527
 speak 582
 – fly *violence* 173
 propel 284
 – fly at 716
 – go *neglect* 460
 liberate 750
 relinquish 782
 restitution 790
 – in *interpose* 228
 admit 296
 trick 545
 – into *inform* 490
 disclose 529
 – one know 527
 – off *violent* 173
 propel 284
 permit 760
 forgive 918
 exempt 927a
 acquit 970
 – out *disperse* 73
 lengthen 200
 eject 297
 disclose 529
 liberate 750
 – out at 716
 – pass 460

in a – with 278
read between the
  –s 522
sounding – 208
straight – 246
troops of the – 726
– of action 692
– of battle 69
– of battle ship
  726
– engraving 558
– of march 278
– of road 627
line**age** *kindred* 11
  series 69
  ancestry 166
  posterity 167
lineament
  outline 230
  feature 240
  appearance 448
  mark 550
linear
  continuity 69
  pedigree 166
  length 200
linen 225
liner 273
lines
  fortification 717
  hard –
    adversity 735
    severity 739
    reins 752
linger *protract* 110
  delay 133
  loiter 275
lingerie 225
lingo 560, 563
lingua franca 563
linguacious 584
lingual 560, 582
linguist 492
linguistics 560
liniment 356, 662
lining 224
link *relation* 9
  connect 43
  connecting - 45
  part 51
  term 71
  crossing 219
  torch 423
  golf –s 840
  missing – 53, 729
linked together
  party 712
linoleum 223
linotype 591
linseed oil 356
linsey-wolsey 41

linstock 388
lint 223
lintel 215
lion
  courage 861
  prodigy 872
  repute 873
  come in like a –
    183
  as dewdrops from
    the –'s mane
    483
  in the –'s den 665
  – lies down with
    the lamb 721
  put one's head in
    the –'s mouth
    665
  – in the path 706
  –'s share *more* 33
  chief part 50
  too much 641
  undue 925
lioness 374
lion-hearted 861
lionize 455, 873
lip *beginning* 66
  edge 231
  side 236
  prominence 250
  between cup and
    – 111
  finger on the –s
    silent 581
    speechless 585
  hang on the –s of
    418
  open one's –s
    speak 582
  seal the –s 585
  smack the –
    taste 390
    savoury 394
  – homage
    flattery 933
  – service
    falsehood 544
    hypocrisy 988
  – wisdom 499
lip salve 847
lipstick 847
lipothymy 688
lippitude 443
liquefaction 335,
  384
liquescence 335
liqueur 298, 396
liquid
  fluid 333
  sound 405
  letter 561

liquidate 807, 812
liquidator 801
liquor *potable* 298
  fluid 333
  in – 959
  – up 959
liquorice 396
liquorish [*see*
  lickerish]
lisp 583
lissom 324
list *catalogue* **86**
  strip 205
  leaning 217
  fringe 231
  hear 418
  record 551
  will 600
  choose 609
  arena 728
  desire 865
  enter the –s
    attack 716
    contend 720
listed 440
listel 847
listen 418
  – in 455
  – to 457
  be –ed to 175
  – to reason 498
listless
  inattentive 458
  inactive 683
  indifferent 866
litany 990, 998
lite, pendente – 969
literæ scriptæ 590
literal
  imitated 19
  exact 494
  manifest 525
  letter 561
  word 562
  orthodox 983a
  – *meaning* 516
  – *translation* 522
literarum
  homo multarum –
    492
  homo trium – 792
literary 560
  – hack 593
  – man 492
  – power 569
literati 492
literatim [*see*
  literal]
literature 490, 560
lithe 324
lithic 323

lithograph 558
lithology 358
lithomancy 511
lithotint 558
litigant
  litigious 713
  combatant 726
  accusation 938
litigation
  quarrel 713
  contention 730
  lawsuit 969
litigious 713
litter *disorder* 59
  derange 61
  multitude 102
  brood 167
  support 215
  vehicle 272
  useless 645
littéraire, la
  morgue – 569
littérateur 492, 593
little
  - *in degree* 32
  - *in size* 193
  darling 897
  mean 940
  cost – 815
  do – 683
  make – of 483
  signify – 643
  think – of 458
  – did one think
    508
  – by little
    degree 26
    slowly 275
  – Mary 191
  – one 129
  to – purpose
    useless 645
    failure 732
littleness 193
littoral 342
liturgy 978
live *exist* 1
  continue 141
  energetic 171
  dwell 186
  life 359
  repute 873
  – apart 905
  – to fight again
    110
  – from hand to
    mouth 674
  – hard 954
  – in hope 858
  – and let live
    inaction 681

– face 832, 837
– for 865
–headed *wise* 498
– life to *glory* 873
  approval 931
–lived 110
– odds *chance* 156
  improbability 473
  difficulty 704
– pending 110
– primer 591
– pull and strong
  pull 285
– range 196
– robe 968
– run *average* 29
  whole 50
  destiny 152
– sea 348
– and the short
  whole 50
  concise 572
–sighted
  dim-sighted 443
  wise 498
  foresight 518
– since 122
– spun 573
– standing
  diuturnal 110
  old 124
–suffering
  lenient 740
  inexcitable 826
  pity 914
– time 110
–winded 573
longanimity
  inexcitable 826
  forgiving 918
longevity 110, 128
longhead 500
longing 865
– lingering look
  behind 833
longinquity 196
longitude
  situation 183
  length 200
  measurement 466
longitudinal 200
longo intervallo
  discontinuity 70
  diuturnity 110
  distance 196
  interval 198
longshore-man
  waterman 269
  plebeian 876
longways 217
loo 840

looby *fool* 501
  bungler 701
  clown 876
look *small degree* 32
  see 441
  appearance 448
  attend to 457
– about 459, 461
– after 459, 693
– ahead 510
– alive 457, 684
– another way 442
– back 122
– beyond 510
– black *or* blue
  feeling 821
  discontent 832
  dejection 837
– down upon 930
– in the face
  sincerity 703
  courage 861
  pride 878
– foolish 874
– for 461, 507
– forwards 121,
  510
– here 457
– into 457, 461
– before one leaps
  864
– like 17, 448
– on 186
– out *view* 448
  attention 457
  care 459
  seek 461
  expect 507
  intention 620
  business 625
  danger 665
  warning 668
  caution 864
– over *examine*
  461
– round *seek* 461
– sharp 682
– to 459, 926
– through 461
– up *prosper* 734
  high price 814
  hope 858
  visit 892
– up to *repute* 873
  respect 928
  approbation 931
– upon as 480, 484
looker-on 444
looking-glass 445
loom *destiny* 152
  dim 422

  dim sight 443
  come in sight 446
  weave 691
– of the land 342
– up 31
loon *fool* 501
  clown 876
  rascal 949
loop 245, 247, 629
– the loop 245
loop-hole
  opening 260
  vista 441
  plea 617
  device 626
  escape 671
  fortification 717
loose *detach* 44
  incoherent 47
  pendent 214
  desultory 279
  illogical 477
  vague 519
– *style* 575
  lax 738
  free 748
  liberate 750
  debauched 961
give a – to
– *imagination* 515
  laxity 738
  permit 760
  indulgence 954
let – 750
on the – 961
screw – 713
– character 961
at a – end 685
– fish 949, 962
– morals 945
– rein 738
– suggestion 514
– thread 495
  leave a - 460
  take up a - 664
loosen 47, 750
loot 791, 793
lop 201
– and top 371
lopped
  incomplete 53
loppet 699
lop-eared 53
lop-sided 28
loquacity **584**
loquendi
  cacoëthes – 584
  jus et norma – 567
  usus – 582
lorcha 273
Lord, lord

  ruler 745
  nobleman 875
  God 976
O – *worship* 990
– Chancellor 967
– of the creation
  372
–'s day 687
–s Justices 966,
  967
the – knows 491
– lieutenant 965
– of Lords 976
– of the manor
  779
– it over 737, 885
–'s prayer 990
–'s supper 998
–'s table 1000
lordling 875
lordly 873, 878
Lord Mayor 745,
  965
–'s show 883
lordship
  authority 737
  property 780
  title 877
  judge 967
lore 490, 539
Lorelei 980
lorette 962
lorgnette 445
lorication
  armour 717
loricated
  clothed 223
lorn 893
lorry 272
lose *forget* 506
  unintelligible 519
  fail 732
  loss 776
no time to – 684
– one's balance
  732
– breath 688
– caste 874, 940
– the clew 475,
  519
– colour 429
– one's cunning
  699
– the day 732
– flesh 195
– ground
  slow 275
  regression 283
  shortcoming 304
– one's head
  bewildered 475

store 636
– rifle 727
Magdalen 950, 962
mage 994
magenta 434
maggot *little* 193
  fancy 515
  caprice 608
  desire 865
maggoty
  capricious 608
  unclean 653
– headed
  silly 499
  excitable 825
Magi *sage* 500
  sect 984
magic 175, 992
– lantern
  instrument 445
  show 448
magician 548, 994
magilp 356*a*
magisterial 878,
  885
magistery 30
magistracy 737, 965
magistrate 745, 967
magistrature 737
magistri, jurare in
  verba – 481
  nullius – 487
magma 41
Magna Charta 769
magna pars fui,
  quorum – 690
magnanimity 942
magnate 875
magnet *attract* 288
  desire 865
magnetism
  power 157
  influence 175
  attraction 288
  motive 615
  animal – 992
magnetize
  influence 175
  motive 615
  conjure 992
magni nominis
  umbra
  wreck 659
  repute 873
  rank 875
magnificent
  large 192
  fine 845
  grand 882
magnifico 875
magnifier 445

magnifique et pas
  cher 815
magnify
  increase 35
  enlarge 194
  over-rate 482
  exaggerate 549
  approve 931
  praise 990
magniloquent 577,
  884
magnitude 25, 31,
  192
magno conatu
  magnas nugas
  638, 643
Magnus Apollo 500
magpie 584
magsman 792
maharajah 745
maharani 745
mah jong 840
mahl-stick [*see*
  maulstick]
mahogany
  colour 433
Mahomet 986
Mahometan 984
maid *girl* 129
  servant 631, 746
  spinster 374, 904
– of all work 690
– of honour 890
maiden *first* 66
  girl 129
  punishment 975
– speech 66
maidenhood 904
maidenly 374
maigre 956
mail *post* 270, 534
  armour 717
– coach 272, 534
– steamer 273
– van 272, 534
maim 158, 659
main *tunnel* 260
  ocean 341
  conduct 350
  principal 642
  coup de – 680
  in the –
  intrinsically 5
  greatly 31
  on the whole 50
  principally 642
  with might and –
  686
  plough the – 267
main-chance 156
  good 618

important 642
profit 775
look to the –
  foresight 510
  skill 698
  economy 817
  caution 864
  selfish 943
main-force
  strength 159
  violence 173
  compulsion 744
mainland 342
main-part 31, 50
mainpernor 771
main-spring 153,
  633
mainstay
  support 215
  refuge 666
  hope 858
maintain
  permanence 141
  continue 143
  sustain 170
  support 215
  assert 535
  preserve 670
– one's course
  persevere 604*a*
– the even tenor of
  one's way 623
– one's ground 717
maintenance
  [*see* maintain]
  assistance 707
  wealth 803
maintien 692
maison de santé
  662
maisonette 189
maître: coup de –
  goodness 648
  skill 698
  l'œil e – 459
majesté, lèse – 742
majestic 873, 882
majesty *king* 745
  rank 873
  deity 976
major *greater* 33
  officer 745
–domo
  director 694
  retainer 746
–general 745
– key 413
– part *great* 31
  all 50
majority
  superiority 33

multitude 102
age 131
join the – 360
majusculæ 561
make
  constitute 54, 56
  render 144
  produce 161
  form 240
  arrive at 292
  complete 729
  compel 744
– acquainted with
  527, 539
– after 622
– its appearance
  446
– away with 162,
  361
– believe 544, 545,
  546
– the best of 725
– bold to differ 489
– a date with 897
– choice of 609
– fast 43
– a fool of 853
– for 278
– one's fortune 734
– fun of 842, 856
– a fuss 642, 682
– good
  compensation 30
  complete 52, 729
  establish 150
  evidence 467
  demonstrate 478
  provide 637
  restore 660
- one's escape 671
- one's word 772
– a go of 731
– haste 684
– hay while the
  sun shines 134
– interest 765
– known 527
– the land 292
– light of 483, 705,
  934
– oneself master
  of 539
– money 775
– a monkey of 853
– much of 549, 642
– no doubt 484
– no secret of 525
– no sign 526, 528
– nothing of
  unintelligible 519
  not wonder 871

[554]

above –ed 104
not worth –ing 643
mentis gratissimus
error 481
mentor *sage* 500
teacher 540
adviser 695
menu 86, 298
Mephistopheles
980
Mephistophelian
945
mephitic 401, 657
mephitis 663
meracious 392
mercantile 794
mercatoria, lex –
963
mercature 794
mercenary
soldier 726
servant 746
price 812
parsimonious 819
selfish 943
mercer 225
merchandise **798**
merchant **797**
merchantman 273
merciful 914
merciless 914*a*
mercurial
changeable 149
mobile 264
quick 274
excitable 825
Mercury 979
traveller 268
quick 274
messenger 534
mercy *lenity* 740
pity 914
at the – of
liable 177
subject 749
cry you – 766
have at one's –
919
have no – 914*a*
– on us! 870
for –'s sake 765
– seat 966
mere *simple* 32
lake 343
trifling 643
– nothing
small 32
trifle 643
buy for a – noth-
ing 815
– pretext 617

– words 477
– wreck 659
merelles 840
meretricious
false 495
vulgar 851
licentious 961
merfolk 980
merge *combine* 48
include 76
insert 300
plunge 337
– in 56
– into *become* 144
merged 228
meridian
region 181
room 125
summit 210
light 420
– of life 131
merit
goodness 648
due 924
virtue 944
make a – of 884
– notice 642
merito, e – 944
meritorious 931
Merlin 994
mermaid 341
monster 83
mythology 979,
980
merman 341
mero motu, ex –
600
merriment
cheerful 836
amusement 840
merry *cheerful* 836
drunk 959
make – *sport* 840
make – with
wit 842
ridicule 856
wish a – Christmas
&c. 896
– and wise 842
merry-andrew 844
merry-go-round
312, 840
merry-making 827,
840, 892
merry-thought 842
mersion 337
meruit ferat, pal-
mam qui – 873
merveille, à – 731
mesa 344
mésalliance 24, 903

meseems 484
mesh 198, 219
meshes *trap* 545
difficulty 704
– of sophistry 477
meshwork 219
mesial
middle 68
mesmerism 992
mesmerist 994
mesne lord 779
mess *mixture* 41
disorder 59
barracks 191
meal 298
difficulty 704
portion 786
make a –
unskilful 699
fail 732
message
intelligence 532
command 741
Messalina 962
messenger 271
envoy **534**
servant 746
– balloon 463
Messiah 976
messianic 976
messmate 890
messuage 189
messy 59
metabolism 140
metacentre 222
metachronism 115
metage 466
metagenesis 140
metagrammatism
561
metal 635
Brittania – 545
metallic *sound* 410
metalepsis 521
metallurgy 358
metamorphosis 140
metaphor
comparison 464
figure **521**
(analogy 17)
metaphrase 522
metaphrast 524
metaphrastic 516
metaphysics 450
metastasis, meta-
thesis
change 140
inversion 218
displacement 270
mete *measure* 466
distribute 786

– out *give* 784
metempsychosis
140
meteor 318, 423
meteoric 173, 420
meteorology 338
meteoromancy 466
meter 466
metheglin 396
methylated spirit
388
methinks 484
method *order* 58
way **627**
want of – 59
methodical 60
Methodist 984
methodist
journalist 988
methodize 60
Methuselah 130
old as – 12
since the days of –
124
meticulous 772
métier 625
métis 83
metonymy 521
metoposcopy
front 234
appearance 44
interpret 522
metre
length 200
poetry 597
metrical
measured 466
verse 597
metrology 466
moderation 174
mid-course 628
metropolis 189
metropolitan
archbishop 996
mettle *spirit* 820
courage 861
man of – 861
on one's –
resolved 604
put on one's –
excite 824
encourage 861
mettlesome
energetic 171
sensitive 822
excitable 825
brave 861
mettre de l'eau
dans son vin 160
meum et tuum 780

disregard distinc-
tion between –
791
mew *moult* 226
 cry 412
 – up 751
mewed up 229
mewl 412
mews 189
mezzanine floor
 191, 599
mezzo rilievo
 convex 250
 sculpture 557
mezzo termine
 middle 68
 mid-course 628
 compromise 774
Mezzofanti 492
mezzosoprano 416
mezzotint 420, 558
miasm 663
mica 425
micacious 204
mi-carême 840
Micawber 460
Michael 977
Michaelmas 998
Micomicon 515
microbe 163, 193
microcosm 193
micrography 193,
 441
micrometer 193
micro-organism
 193
microphone 418
microscope 193, 445
microscopic 32, 193
mid 68
Midas 803
mid-course 628
mid-day 125
midden 653
middle – *in degree*
 29
 – *in order* 68
 – *in space* 222,
 228
 – classes 736
 – constriction 203
 – course 29, 628
 – man *director* 694
 agent 758
 – point 29
 – term 68
 compromise 774
middlemost 222
middling 29, 32, 68,
 651
middy 225, 269

midge 193
midget 193
midland 342
midnight *night* 126
 dark 421
 – oil 539, 689
mid-progress 282
midriff 68, 228
midshipman 269,
 745
midships 68
midst – *in order* 68
 central 222
 interjacent 228
in the – of
 mixed with 41
 doing 680
midsummer **125**
 – day 138
midway 68
midwife
 instrument 631
 remedy 662
 auxiliary 711
midwifery 161, 662
mien 448, 692
miff 900
might *power* 157
 violence 173
 energy 686
mightily 31
mighty *much* 31
 strong 159
 large 192
 haughty 878
migraine 378
migrate 266, 295
mikado 745
milch cow
 productive 168
 animal 366
 store 636
mild *moderate* 174
 warm 382
 insipid 391
 lenient 740
 calm 826
 courteous 894
mildew 653, 663
mildewed
 spoiled 659
mile 200
milestone 550
 whistle jigs to a –
 645
milieu, juste – 174,
 628
militant 722
 church – 983a
military
 warfare 722

soldiers 726
 – authorities 745
 – band 417
 – power 737
 – time 132
 – train 726
militate against 708
militia 726
milk *moderate* 174
 semiliquid 352
 cows &c. 370
 white 430
 mild 740
 – a he-goat into a
 sieve 471
flow with – and
 honey *plenty*
 639
 prosperity 734
 pleasant 829
 – of human kind-
 ness 906
 – the ram 645
 – and water
 weak 160
 insipid 391
 unimportant 643
 imperfect 651
milk-livered 862
milksop
 incapable 158
 fool 501
 coward 862
milky [*see* milk]
 semitransparent
 427
 whiteness 430
 – way 318
mill 330
 notch 257
 machine 633
 workshop 691
 fight 720
 like a horse in a –
 312
millennium
 number 98
 period 108
 futurity 121
 utopia 515
 hope 858
millesimal 99
millet seed 193
milliard 98
milliner 225
 man – 854
millinery *dress* 225
 ornament 847
 display 882
 man – 855
million 98

multitude 102
 people 372
 populace 876
for the –
 intelligible 518
 easy 705
 –s *money* 800
millionaire 803
mill-pond *level* 213
 pond 343
 store 636
mime 19, 599, 844
mimeograph 19
mimeotype 19
mimic 19
mimodrama 599
minacity 909
minaret 206
minatory 668
minauderie 855
mince *cut up* 44
 slow 275
 food 298
 stammer 583
 affected 855
 extenuate 937
 – the matter 868
 not – the matter
 affirm 525
 artless 703
 – the truth 544
mincemeat of
 make – 162
mincing 855
 – steps 275
mind *intellect* 450
 attend to 457
 take care 459
 believe 484
 remember 505
 will 600
 willing 602
 purpose 620
 warning 668
 desire 865
 dislike 867
bear in – 451, 457
bit of one's – 527
food for the – 454
give the – to 457
have a – 602, 865
in the –
 thought 451
 topic 454
 willing 602
make up one's –
 484, 604
never – *neglect* 46)
 unimportant 643
not – 866
out of – 506

set one's – upon
604
speak one's – 582,
703
to one's – *taste* 850
love 897
willing – 602
– one's book 539
– one's business
456, 457
– at ease 827
make one's – easy
826
–'s eye 515
– what one is
about 864
minded 602, 620
mindful 457, 505
mindless
inattentive 458
imbecile 499
forgetful 506
insensible 823
mine
sap 162
hollow 252
open 260
snare 545
store 636
abundance 639
damage 659
attack 716
defence 717
explosive 727
dig a – *plan* 626
prepare 673
spring a –
unexpected 508
attack 716
– of information
700
–layer 726
–sweeper 726
–thrower 727
– of wealth 803
miner 252
sapper and – 726
mineral 358
– oil 356
mineralogy 358
Minerva 979
– invita 603, 709
– press 577, 594
mingle 41
miniature *small* 193
portrait 556
– painter 559
Minié rifle 727
minikin 193
minim *small* 32
music 413

minimize 36, 483,
934
minimum *small* 32
inferior 34
minion 899
type 591
minister *instru-
mentality* 631
remedy 662
director 694
aid 707
deputy 759
give 784
clergy 996
rites 998
– to 746
ministerial
clerical 995
ministering spirit
977
ministration
direction 693
aid 707
rite 998
ministry
direction 693
aid 707
church 995
clergy 996
miniver 223
minnesinger 597
minnow 193
minor *inferior* 34
infant 129
– key 413
Minorites 996
minority *few* 103
youth 127
Minos 694
minotaur 83
minster 1000
minstrel 416, 597
minstrelsy 415
mint *mould* 22
workshop 691
wealth 803
– of money 800
minuend 38
minuet 415, 840
minus *less* 34
subtracted 38
absent 187
deficient 304
loss 776
in debt 806
non-payment 808
minusculæ 561
minute
– *in degree* 32
– *of time* 108
instant 113

– *in size* 193
record 551
compendium 596
to the – 132
– account 594
– attention 457
minuteness
care 459
minutiæ 32, 79, 643
minx 887, 962
mirabile
– dictu &c. 870
mirabilis, annus –
872
miracle 83, 872
– play 599
miraculous 870
mirage 443
mire 653
mirror *imitate* 19
reflector 445
perfection 650
glory 873
hold up the – 525
hold the – up to
nature 554
magic – 443
mirth 836
misacceptation 235
misadventure 735
misadvised 699
misanthropy **911**
misapply
misinterpret 523
misuse 679
mismanage 699
misapprehend 495,
523
misappropriate 679
misarrange 61
misbecome 925
misbegotten 243,
945
misbehave 851, 945
misbehaviour 895,
947
misbelief 485
misbeliever 487,
984
miscalculate
misjudge 481
err 495
disappoint 509
miscall 565
miscarry 732
miscegenation 41
miscellany
mixture 41
collection 72
generality 78
compendium 596

mischance 619, 735
mischief 619
do – 649
make – 649
mischief-maker
913, 941
miscible 41
miscite 544
miscompute 481,
495
misconceive 495,
523
misconduct 699,
947
– oneself 945
misconjecture 481
misconstrue 523
miscorrect 538
miscount 495
miscreance 485
miscreant 949
miscreated 945
misdate 115
misdeed 947
misdemean 945
misdemeanant 949
misdemeanour 947
misdevotion 988
misdirect 538, 699
misdo 945
misdoing 947
misdoubt 485, 523
mise en scène
appearance 448
drama 599
display 882
misemploy 679
miser 819
–'s hoard 800
miserabile dictu 839
miserable *small* 32
contemptible 943
unhappy 828
miserably *very* 31
miserere 215
sing – 950
misericordiam,
argumentum ad
– 914
miseries of human
life 828
miseris succurrere
disco 914
miserly 819
misery 828
put out of one's –
914
misestimate
misjudge 481
misfeasance 699,
947

ugly 846
vulgar 851
ridiculous 853
wonderful 870
mont-de-piété 787
montagne russe
  slope 217
  sport 840
monté *cards* 840
Montgolfier 273
month 108
monthly 138
  magazine 531
  – *nurse* 662
monticle 206
monument *tall* 206
  tomb 363
  record 551
monumentum ære
  perennius 733
moo 412
mood *nature* 5
  state 7
  change 140
  tendency 176
  willingness 602
  temper 820
moods and tenses
  15, 20*a*
moody *furious* 825
  sad 837
  sullen 901*a*
moodish 895, 901
moon *changes* 149
  world 318
  luminary 423
  bay the – 645
  jump over the –
   309
  man in the – 515
  – of green cheese
   credulity 486
moonbeam 420, 422
mooncalf 501
moon-eyed 443
moonshee 493, 540
moonshine
  unsubstantial 4
  dim 422
  absurdity 497
  unmeaning 517
  untrue 546
  excuse 617
moonstone 847
moonstruck 503,
  870
moor *fasten* 43
  open space 180
  locate 184
  highland 206
  plain 344

Moore, Old – 513
moored *firm* 150
mooring mast 184
moorings 45, 184
moorish 345
moorland 180, 206
moot *inquire* 461
  argue 476
  – *point* *topic* 454
  question 461
  discuss 514
mooted 514
mop 243, 652
mope 837
mope-eyed 443
moppet 899
mopsy 962
mopus *dreamer* 515
  drone 683
  money 800
  sad 837
mora nec requies,
  nec – 682
moral *judgment* 480
  maxim 496
  right 922
  duty 926
  virtuous 944
  point a – 537
  – *certainty* 474
  – *courage* 604
  – *education* 537
  – *obligation* 926
  – *support* 707
  – *tuition* 537
  – *turpitude* 940
moral philosophy
  mind 450
  duty 926
morality play 599
moralize 476
morals *duty* 926
  virtue 944
morass 345
moratorium 133
morbid 655
morbific 657
mordacity 907
mordant *keen* 171
  pungent 392
  colour 428
  language 574
more *superior* 33
  added 37
  – than enough 641
  – than flesh and
   blood can bear
   830
  – last words 65
  – or less
   quantity 25

small 32
inexact 495
– than a match
  for 33, 159
– than meets the
  eye 526
– than one 100
more:
  – *majorum* 82
  – solito
   conformable 82
   habitual 613
  – *suo* 613
moreover 37
mores, O – 932
Morgana, Fata –
  423
morganatic mar-
  riage 903
morgue 363
  – *littéraire* 569
mori, memento –
  363
moribund 369, 655
  dying 360
  sick 655
morient 360
morion 717
morisco 840
mormo 860
Mormon 984
Mormonism 903,
  984
morning **125**
  – *coat* 225
  – *dress* 225
  – *noon and night*
   repetition 104
   diuturnal 110
   frequent 136
  – *star* 423, 977
morocco 223
moron 493, 501
moronic 499
morose 895, 901*a*
morosis 503
Morpheus 683
morphew 653
morphia 381, 663
morphology
  form 240
  zoology 368
morra 840
morris
  nine men's – 840
morris-dance 840
morrow 121
morse 45
morsel *small* 32
  portion 51
  food 298

mors aux dents,
  prendre le – 719
mort, guerre à –
  722
mortal
  transient 111
  fatal 361
  man 372
  wearisome 841
  – *antipathy* 867
  – *blow* 619
  – *coil* 362
  – *funk* 860
  – *remains* 362
  – *sin* 947
mortality
  evanescence 111
  death 360
  mankind 372
  bills of – 360
mortar *cement* 45
  pulverizer 330
  cannon 727
mortem, post – 360,
  363
mortgage
  security 771
  lend 787
  sale 796
  credit 805
mortgagee 779, 805
mortgagor 779, 806
mortician 363
mortiferous 361
mortification
  disease 655
  pain 828
  vexation 830
  discontent 832
  humiliation 879
  asceticism 955
mortise *unite* 43
  intersect 219
  interjacence 228
mortmain 748
  in – 781
Morton's fork 475
mortuary 360, 363
mosaic *mixture* 41
  multiform 81
  variegation 440
  painting 556
Moslem 984
mosque 1000
moss *tuft* 256
  marsh 345
  vegetation 367
moss-grown 659
moss-trooper 726,
  792
most 31

at – 32
make the – of
over-estimate 482
exaggerate 549
improve 658
use 677
skill 698
the – 33
– often 136
for the – part 78,
613
make the – of
one's time 682
mot 496
– de l'énigme 522
– du guet 550
– à mot 19
– d'ordre 741
– de passe 550
– pour rire 842
mote *small* 32
light 320
– in the eye
dim-sighted 443
misjudging 481
motet 990
moth *bane* 663
moth-eaten 124,
653, 659
mother *parent* 166
mould 653
– country 189
– of-pearl 440
– superior 996
– tongue 560
– wit 498
motherly *love* 897
kind 906
motif 415, 847
motile 264
motion
change of place
264
topic 454
plan 626
proposal 763
request 765
make a – 763
put in – 284
put oneself in –
680
set in – 677
– downwards 306
– from
recession 287
repulsion 289
– into *ingress* 294
reception 296
– out of 295
– through 302
– towards

approach 286
attraction 288
– upwards 305
motionless 265
motive **615**
absence of – **615a**
– power 264
motivity 264
motley 81, 440
wearer of the – 844
motor 153, 266
vehicle 271, 272
instrument 633
–boat 273
–car &c. 272
–driver 268
–man 694
motorist 268
motory 264
mottled 440
motto *maxim* 496
device 550
phrase 566
motu: ex mero –
737
suo – 600
mouchard 527
mould *condition* 7
matrix 22
convert 144
form 240
structure 329
earth 342
vegetation 367
model 554
carve 557
decay 653
turn to account
677
moulded 820
– on 19
moulder 653, 659
moulding 847
mouldy 653, 659
moulin:
se battre contre
des –s 645
– à paroles 584
moult 226
mound *large* 192
hill 206
defence 717
mount *increase* 35
hill 206
horse 271
ascend 305
raise 307
display 882
– guard *care* 459
safety 664
– up to *money* 800

price 812
mountain *large* 192
hill 206
weight 319
– artillery 726
– in labour
waste 638
make –s of mole-
hills 482
– brought forth
mouse
disappoint 509
mountaineer 268
mountainous 206
mountebank
quack 548
drama 599
buffoon 844
mounted rifles 726
mourn 828, 839
mourner 363
mournful
afflicting 830
sad 837
lamentable 839
mourning *dress* 225
in – *black* 431
lament 839
mouse *little* 193
search 461
mountain brought
forth – 509
not a – stirring
265
mouse-coloured
432
mousehole 260
mouser 366
mousetrap 545
mousseux 353
moustache 256
mouth *entrance* 66
receptacle 191
brink 231
opening 260
eat 298
estuary 343
enunciate 580
drawl 583
deep –ed
resonant 408
bark 412
down in the – 879
make –s 929
open one's – 582
stop one's – 581
word of – 582
– honour
falsehood 544
show 882
flattery 933

pass from – to
mouth 531
– wash 652
– watering 865
mouthful
quantity 25
small 32
food 298
mouthpiece
speaker 524
information 527
speech 582
mouthy *style* 577
moutonné 250
moutons, revenons
à nos – 660
movable 264, 270
movables 780
move *begin* 66
motion 264
propose 514
induce 615
undertake 676
act 680
offer 763
excite 824
get a – on 684
good – 626
on the – 293
– forward 282
– from 287
– in a groove 82
– heaven and
earth 686
– off 293
– on *progress* 282
activity 682
– out of 295
– quickly 274
– slowly 275
– to 894
moveless 265
movement
motion 264
music 415
action 680
activity 682
moved with 821
mover 164
movies 448, 599,
840
movie star 899
moving
keep – 682
self – 266
– pictures 448
mow *shorten* 201
smooth 255
agriculture 371
store 636
– down

destroy 162
moxa 384
M.P. 696
Mr. 373, 877
Mrs. 374
MS. 22, 590
much 31
  make – of
    importance 642
    friends 888
    love 897
    endearment 902
    approval 931
  not say – for 932
  think – of 928, 931
  – ado *exertion* 686
    difficulty 704
  – ado about noth-
    ing
    over-estimate 482
    exaggerate 549
    unimportant 643
    unskilful 699
  – cry and little
    wool 884
  – the same
    identity 13
    similarity 17
    equality 27
  – speaking 584
mucid 352, 653
mucilage 352
muck 653
  run a – *kill* 361
    attack 716
    excitement 825
muckle 31
muckworm 819,
  876
mucor 653
mucosity 352
mucronate 253
muculent 352
mud *marsh* 345
  semiliquid 352
  dirt 653
  clear as – 519
  stick in the – 704
  – guard 666
muddle *disorder* 59
  derange 61
  inattention 458
  absurd 497
  difficulty 704
  failure 732
  – one's brains 475
muddled 959
muddle-headed 499
muddy *moist* 339
  dim 422
  opaque 426

colour 429
  stupid 499
mudlark *dirty* 653
  commonalty 876
muezzin 550, 996
muff *incapable* 158
  dress 225
  bungle 699
  bungler 701
muffettee 225
muffle *wrap* 225
  silent 403
  deaden 408a
  conceal 528
  voiceless 581
  stammer 583
muffled *faint* 405
  latent 526
  – drums
    funeral 363
    non-resonance
    408a
muffler 225, 384
mufti *undress* 225
  judge 967
  priest 996
mug *cup* 191
  face 234, 448
  pottery 384
  dupe 547
mug-house 189
muggy *moist* 339
  dim 422
  opaque 426
mugient 412
mugwump 607
mulatto
  mixture 41
  exception 83
mulct *steal* 791
  fine 974
mule *mongrel* 83
  beast of burden
  271
  obstinate 606
muleteer 694
muliebrity 374
mull
  prominence 250
  sweeten 396
mullah 967, 996
muller 330
mullion 215
mullioned 219
multifarious
  irrelevant 10
  diverse 16a
  multiform 81
  multiferous 102
multifid
  divided 51

multifold 81
multiformity **81**
multigenerous 81
multilateral 236,
  244
multilocular 191
multiloquence 582,
  584
multinomial 102
multiparous 168
multipartite 44
multiple 84, 102
multiplex 81
multiplicand 84
multiplicate 81
multiplication
  increase 35
  arithmetic 85
  multitude 102
  reproduction 163
  productiveness
  168
multiplicator 84
multiplicity 102
multiplier 84
multiply 35
multipotent 157
multisonous 404
multitude 72, **102**
  the – 876
multum in parvo
  596
multure 330
mum 581, 585
  –'s the word 403
mumble *chew* 298
  mutter 583
Mumbo Jumbo
  979, 993
mummer 599
mummery
  absurdity 497
  imposture 545
  masquerade 840
  parade 882
mummify 363
mummy *dry* 340
  corpse 362
  beat to a – 972
mump *mutter* 583
  beg 765
mumper 767, 804
mumpish *sad* 837
mumps 837, 901a
munch 298
Munchausen 549
mundane
  world 318
  selfish 943
  irreligious 989
mundation 652

mundivagant 266
munerary 973
munerate 973
municipal 965
municipality 737
munificent 816
muniment
  evidence 465
  record 551
  defence 717
  security 771
munition
  materials 635
  defence 717
mural 717
murder 361
  – the King's Eng-
  lish
  solecism 568
  stammering 583
  the – is out 529
murderer 361
muricated 253
murky *dark* 421
  opaque 426
  black 431
  gloomy 837
murmur *purl* 348
  sound 405
  voice 580
  complain 839
murmurer 832
murrain 655
Murray *travel* 266
  Lindley – 542
murrey 434
murrion 717
mus, nascitur ridi-
  culus – 509, 643
muscadine 400
muscle 159
muscular 159
muse 451
  [*and see* musing]
Muse *poetry* 597
  historic – 594
  unlettered – 579
musette 417
Muses, the – 416
museum
  collection 72
  store 636
mush 354
mushroom
  new 123
  fungus 367
  upstart 734
  low-born 876
  spring up like –s
  163
  – anchor 666

music **415**
  face the – 861
  set to – 416
  – of the spheres
    order 58
    universe 318
musical **413, 415,**
  416
  – comedy 599
  – ear
    musician 416
    hearing 418
  – instruments **417**
  – note 413
  – voice 580
music-hall 599, 840
musician **416**
musing 451
  – on other things
    458
musk 400
musket 727
  shoulder a – 722
musketeer 726
musketry 727
muslin
  semi-transparent
    427
musnud
  support 215
  council 696
  sceptre 747
muss 59
Mussulman 984
must *necessity* 601
  mucor 653
  compulsion 744
  it – follow 478
  I – say 535
mustachio 256
mustard 392, 393
  after meat – 135
  – gas 663, 727
mustard-seed 193
muster 72, 85
  pass – 639
  not pass – 651
  – courage 861
muster-roll 86
musty 401, 653
mutable 149
mutation 140
mutatis mutandis
  correlation 12
  change 140
  interchange 148
mutato nomine de
  te &c.
  parable 521
  retaliation 718
mute *funeral* 363

silent 403
sordine 405,
  408a, 417
letter 561
speechless 581
taciturn 585
dramatis persona
  599
deaf – 419
render – 581
mutilate
  retrench 38
  deform 241
  injure 659
mutilated 53
mutilation 619
mutineer 742
mutiny 742
mutt 366
mutter
  faint sound 405
  mumble 583
  grumble 839
  threaten 909
mutton-chop
  whiskers 256
mutual 12, 148
mutualize 12
mutual under-
  standing 23
muzzle
  powerless 158
  edge 231
  opening 260
  silence 403
  render speechless
    581
  restrain 751
  gag 752
muzzle-loader 727
muzzy 458
  in liquor 959
my: all – eye 546
  – stars! 870
mycology 369
mynheer 877
myology 329
myomancy 511
myopia 443
myriad 98, 102
myrmidon 726
myrrh 400
myrtle 897
myself *I* 79
  immateriality
    317
mysterious
  invisible 447
  uncertain 475
  obscure 519
  concealed 528

mystery
  [*see* mysterious]
  latency 526
  secret 533
  play 599
  craft 625
  – ship 726
mystic
  uncertain 475
  obscure 519
  latent 526
  concealed 528
  sorcery 992
  puzzle 475
mystify *falsify* 477
  hide 528
  misteach 538
  deceive 545
myth 515, 546
mythology 979, 984

N

nab *deceive* 545
  seize 789
Nabob 745, 803
nacelle 273
nacre 440
nadir 211
nag *horse* 271
  quarrel 713
nager entre deux
  eaux 607
Naiad 341, 979
nail *fasten* 43
  fastening 45
  measure of length
    200
  peg 214
  sharp 253
  hard 323
  retain 781
  on the –
    present 118
    pay 807
  hit the right – on
    the head
    discover 480a
    skill 698
  – polish 847
naïveté 703
naked *denuded* 226
  manifest 525
  simplicity 849
  – eye 441
  – fact 151
  – steel 727
  – sword 727
  – truth 494
namby-pamby 643,

855
name
  indication 550
  appellation 564
  appoint 755
  celebrity 873
  assume a – 565
  call –s
    disrespect 929
    disapprobation
      932
  fair – 873
  good – 873
  in the – of
    aid 707
    authority 737
    due 924
  – to conjure with
    873
nameless 565, 874
namely 79, 522
namesake 564
Nana Sahib 949
Nanny-goat 374
nap *down* 256
  texture 329
  sleep 683
  cards 840
nape *back* 235
napery 652
Napier's bones 85
napkin 652
  buried in a – 460
  lay up in a – 678
napless 226
Napoleon *food* 298
  cards 840
napping
  inattentive 458
  inexpectant 508
  dull 843
nappy *frothy* 353
  tipsy 959
narcissism 897, 943
Narcissus 845
narcosis 376
narcotic 657, 662
nard 356
narration 594
narrow
  contract 195
  thin 203
  intolerant 481
  restrict 761
  – down 42
  – end of the wedge
    66
  – escape 671
  – house 363
  – means 804
  – search 461

narrow-minded
481, 943
narrowness 203
narrows 343
nasal accent 583
nascent 66
nascitur: – ridi-
culus mus 509
– a sociis 82
naso, omnia sus-
pendens – 868
nasty
unsavoury 395
foul 653
offensive 830
cheap and – 815
natâ, pro re – 770
natal *birth* 66
indigenous 188
natation 267
natatorium 652
nathless 30
nation 372
national 188, 372
– guard 726
nationality 372, 910
nations, law of 963
native
inhabitant 188
artless 703
– accent 580
– land 189
– soil 189
– tongue 560
nativity *birth* 66
cast a –
predict 511
sorcery 992
natty 845
natura il fece e po⁚
roppe la stampa
87
naturæ, vis medi-
catrix – 662
natural *intrinsic* 5
musical note 413
true 494
fool 501
– *style* 576, 578
spontaneous 621
not prepared 674
artless 703
simple 849
– course of things
613
– death *death* 360
completion 729
– impulse 601
– meaning 516
– order of things
82

– state 90
– turn 820
Natural – History
357
– Philosophy 316
– Theology 983
naturalist 357
naturalization
conformity 82
conversion 144
location 184
naturalize
habit 613
naturalized
inhabitant 188
naturally 154
nature *essence* 5
rule 80
tendency 176
world 318
reality 494
artlessness 703
affections 820
animated – 357
organized – 357
second – 613
state of –
naked 226
raw 674
in –'s garb 226
naught *nothing* 4
zero 101
bring to – 732
set at –
make light of 483
opposition 708
disobey 742
not observe 773
disrespect 929
contempt 930
naughty 945
naumachia 720
nausea 841, 867
nauseate 395, 830
nauseous
unsavoury 395
unpleasant 830
disgusting 867
nautch dancer 840
nautical 267
naval 267
– authorities 745
– engagement 720
– forces 726
nave *middle* 68
centre 222
church 1000
navel 68, 222
navigation 267
navigator 269
navvy 673, 690

navy 273, 726
– blue 438
nay 536
– rather 14
Nazarene 989
naze 250
N.C.O. 745
ne plus ultra
supreme 33
complete 52
distance 196
summit 210
limit 233
perfection 650
completion 729
neaf 781
neap 195, 207
– tide 36, 340
near *like* 17
- *in space* 197
- *in time* 121
soon 132
impending 152
approach 286
stingy 819
bring – 17
draw – 197
come – 286
– one's end 360
– at hand 132
– the mark 32
– run 32
– side 239
– sight 443
– the truth 480a
– upon 3
sail – the wind
skilful 698
rash 863
nearly 32
nearness 197
neat *simple* 42
order 58
in writing 572,
576, 578
clean 652
spruce 845
–'s foot oil 356
– as a pin 58
neat-handed 698
neatherd 370
neb 250
nebula *stars* 318
mist 353
nebular *dim* 422
nebulous *misty* 353
obscure 519
necessarian 601
necessaries 630
necessarily 154
necessitate 630

necessity *fate* **601**
requirement 630
compulsion 744
indigence 804
make a virtue of
– 698
neck
contraction 195
narrow 203
make love 902
break one's – 360
– and crop
completely 52
turn out - 297
– of land 342
– and neck 27
– or nothing
resolute 604
rash 863
neckcloth 225
necklace 247, 847
necks 980
necrology 360, 594
necromancer 548,
994
necromancy 992
necropsy 363
necroscopic 363
necrosis 49
nectar 394, 396
need *necessity* 601
requirement 637
insufficiency 640
indigence 804
desire 865
friend in – 711
in one's utmost –
735
needful
necessary 601
requisite 630
money 800
do the – *pay* 807
needle *sharp* 253
perforator 262
compass 693
as the – to the
pole
veracity 543
observance 772
honour 939
– in a bottle of
hay 475
needle-gun 727
needle-shaped 253
needless 641
needle-witted 498
needlewoman 690
needlework 847
ne'er-do-well 949
nefarious 945

next
following 63
later 117
future 121
near 197
– friend 759
– of kin 11
– to nothing 32
– world 152
nexus 45
Niagara 348
niais 501
niaiserie 517
nib *cut* 44
end 67
summit 210
point 253
nibble *eat* 298
– at *censure* 932
– at the bait
dupe 547
willing 602
nice
savoury 394
discriminative 465
exact 494
good 648
pleasing 829
fastidious 868
honourable 939
– ear 418
– hand 700
– perception 465
– point 704
nicely
completely 52
Nicene Creed 983*a*
nicety 466
niche *recess* 182
receptacle 191
angle 244
– in the temple of
fame 873
nicher, se – 184
nick *notch* 257
deceive 545
mark 550
– it 731
– of time 124
Nick, Old – 978
nickel
money 800
nicknack 643
nickname 565
nicotine 392, 663
nictitate 443
nidget 862
nidification 189
nidor 398
nidorous 401

nidus 153, 189
niece 11
niggard 819
nigger 431
– in the woodpile 702
niggle *mock* 929
niggling 643
nigh 197
night 421
labour day and – 686
orb of – 318
– and day 136
– school 542
night-cap 225
nightfall 126
nightingale 416
night-gown 225
nightmare
bodily pain 378
dream 515
incubus 706
mental pain 828
alarm 860
nightshade 663
nigrescent 431
nigrification 431
nihil – ad rem 10
– tetigit quod non
ornavit 850
nihilism 989
nihilist 165
nihility 2, 4
nil 2, 4
– admirari
insensible 823
no wonder 871
disapproval 932
– conscire sibi
nullâ pallescere
culpâ 946
– desperandum 858
nill *unwilling* 604
refuse 764
nim 791
nimble 274, 682
nimble-witted 498, 842
nimbus
cloud 353
halo 420
glory 873
nimiety 641
nimis, ne quid – 817
nimium ne crede
colori 485
n'importe 643
Nimrod 361, 622

nincompoop 501
nine 98
tuneful –
music 416
poetry 597
– days' wonder
transient 111
unimportant 643
no wonder 871
– lives 359
– men's morris 840
– points of the
law 777
ninefold 98
ninepins 840
ninety 98
ninny 501
Niobe 839
nip *cut* 44
destroy 162
shorten 201
dram 298
freeze 385
pungent 392
drink 959
– in the bud
check 201
kill 361
hinder 706
– up 789
nipperkin 191
nippers 781
nipple 250
Nirwana 981
nis 980
nisi prius 741, 969
Nisus and Euryalus 890
nisus formativus 161
nitency 420
nitor in adversum 708
nitre 392
nitrous oxide 376
nit-wit 499, 501
niveous *cold* 383
white 430
nixe *demon* 980
nixie *fairy* 979
nizam 745
nizy 501
N or M 78
no *zero* 101
dissent 489
negation 536
refusal 764
unable to say – 605
on – account 761
have – business

there 83
– chicken 128, 131
– choice 601, 609*a*
– conjuror 501, 701
– consequence 643
in – degree 32
at – great distance 197
– doubt 474, 488
have – end 112
– end of *great* 31
multitude 102
length 200
– fear 473
– go 304, 732
at – hand 32
matter of – import 4
with – interval 199
– one knows who 876
– less 639
– longer 122
– love lost be-
tween them 898
– man's land 187, 778
– matter
neglect 460
unimportant 643
and – mistake 474
– more
inexistent 2
past 122
dead 360
– more than 32
have – notion of 489
– object 643
– one 4, 187
– other 13, 87
to – purpose
shortcoming 304
useless 645
failure 732
give – quarter 361
– scholar 493
make – scruple of 602
– great shakes
small 32
trifling 643
imperfect 651
– sooner said than
done 113, 132
– stranger to 490
– such thing
non-existent 2
unsubstantial 4

contrary 14
dissimilar 18
– surrender 606, 717
– thank you 764
at – time 107
– wonder 871
Noah's ark 41, 72
nob 210
nobilitate 873
nobility 875
noble *great* 31
  important 642
  rank 873
  peer 875
  disinterested 942
  virtuous 944
noblesse 875
nobody
  unsubstantial 4
  zero 101
  absence 187
  low-born 876
  – knows
  ignorance 491
  – knows where
  distance 196
  – present 187
  – would think 508
noctambulation 266
noctivagant
  travel 266
  dark 421
noctograph 421
noctuary 421, 551
nocturnal
  night 126
  dark 421
  black 431
nocturne 415
nocuous 649
nod *wag* 314
  assent 488
  signal 550
  sleep 683
  command 741
  bow 894
  – of approbation 931
  – of assent 488
nodding to its fall 162, 306
noddle 210, 450
noddy 501
node 250
nodosity 250, 256
nods and becks and wreathed smiles 894
nodule 250
nodular 256

nodus, dignus vin-dice – 704
Noel 998
noggin 191
noise 402, 404
  – abroad 531
  make a – in the world 873
noiseless 403
noisome
  fetid 401
  bad 649
  unhealthy 657
nolens volens 601
noli me tangere
  defiance 715
  excitable 825
  fastidious 868
nolition 603
nolle prosequi 624
nolumus leges
  Angliæ mutari
  permanence 141
  continuance 143
  preservation 670
nom de: – guerre 565
  – plume 565
nomad 268
nomadic 266
Nomancy 511
nomenclature 564
nominal
  unsubstantial 4
  word 562
  name 564
  – price 815
nomination 564, 755
nominee 758
nominis umbra 4
Nomology 963
non:
  – compos mentis 503
  – constat 477
  – deficit alter 100
  – est in ventus 187
  – hæc in fœdera 536, 610
  – nobis Domine 990
  – obstante 707
  – placet 489
  – possumus
  impossible 471
  obstinate 606
  refusal 764
  – nostrum tantas componere lites 471, 713

lex – scripta 963
  – semper erit æstas 111
  – sequitur 477
  – sum qualis eram 140, 160·
non-addition 38
non-admission 55
nonage 127
nonagenarian 98
non-appearance 447
non-assemblage 73
non-attendance 187
nonce 118
  for the – 118, 134
nonchalance
  neglect 460
  insensibility 823
  indifference 866
non-coincidence 14
non-cohesive 47
non-com. 726
non-commissioned officer 745
non-committal 528, 864
non-completion 730
non-compliance 742, 764
nonconformity
  difference 15
  exception 83
  dissent 489
  sectarianism 984
non-content 489
non-cooperation 489, 927
nondescript 83
none 101
  – else 87
  – to spare 640
  – such
  superior 33
  exceptional 83
  very good 648
  – in the world 4
  – the worse 660
non-endurance 825
nonentity
  inexistence 2
  unsubstantial 4
  unimportant 643
non esse 2
non-essential 6, 643
non-existence 2
non-expectance 508
non-extension 180a
non-fulfilment 730, 732

  – of one's hopes 509
non-imitation 20
non-interference
  inaction 681
  freedom 748
nonius 466
non-juror 489, 984
non-naturals 657
nonny 501
non-observance
  inattention 458
  desuetude 614
  infraction **773**
  dereliction 927
nonpareil 648
  type 591
non-payment 808
non-performance
  non-completion 730
  dereliction 927
non-plus
  uncertain 475
  difficulty 704
  conquer 731
non-preparation 674
non-prevalence 614
non-residence 187
non-resistance 725, 743
non-resonance 408a
nonsense
  absurdity 497
  unmeaning 517
  trash 643
  talk – *folly* 499
non-subsistence 2
non-success 732
nonsuch [*see* none]
nonsuit *defeat* 731
  fail 732
  condemn 971
nonum prematur in annum 133
non-uniformity 16a
noodle 501
nook *place* 182
  receptacle 191
  corner 244
noology 450
noon *mid-day* 125
noon-day *light* 420
  clear as –
  intelligible 518
  manifest 525
nooscopic 450
noose *ligature* 45
  loop 247

snare 545
gallows 975
norma loquendi 567
normal
  intrinsic 5
  mean 29
  regular 82
  perpendicular 212
  – condition
  rule 80
normality 80, 502
Normand, répon-
  dre en – 544
Norns 601
North 278
  – and South 237
Northern 237
  – light 423
  – star
  constant 939
North-west
  passage 311
nose *prominence*
  250
  smell 398
  with one's – in
  the air 878
  lead by the – 615,
  737
  led by the – 749
  not see beyond
  one's –
  misjudge 481
  folly 499
  unskilful 699
  speak through
  the – 583
  thrust one's – in
  interjacence 228
  busy 682
  under one's –
  present 186
  near 197
  manifest 525
  defy 715
  put one's – out of
  joint *defeat* 731
  disrepute 874
  – ring 847
nose-dive 306
nosegay 400, 847
nosey 455
Nosology 655
nostalgia 833
nostril 351
  breath of one's –s
  359
  stink in the –s 401
nostrum 626, 662
not *negation* 536
  what is – 546

what ought – 923
– at all 32
– allowed 964
– amiss 618, 651,
  845
– any 101
– bad 651
– bargain for 508
– a bit 536
– to be borne 830
– a Chinaman's
  chance 471
– come up to 34
– cricket 923
– to be despised
  642
it will – do 923
– of the earth 987
– expect 508
– fail 939
– far from 197
– a few 102
– fit to be seen 846
– following 477
– grant 764
– guilty 946
– to be had 471,
  640
– having 187, 777*a*
– hardened 950
– hear of 764
– included 55
– know what to
  make of 519
– a leg to stand
  on 158
– likely 473
– a little 31
– matter 643
– to mention 37
– mind 823, 930
– often 137
– on your life 489
– one 101
– a particle 4
– particular 831
– pay 808
– a pin to choose
  27
– playing the
  game 923
– within previous
  experience 137
– to be put down
  604
– quite 32
– reach 304
– right 503
– sorry 827
– a soul 101
– on speaking

terms 889
– the thing 925
– to be thought of
  incogitancy 452
  impossible 471
  refusal 764
  hopeless 859
  undue 925
  disapprobation
  932
– trouble oneself
  about 460
– understand 519
– vote 609*a*
– wonder 871
– for the world
  603, 764
– worth
  trifling 643
  useless 645
nota bene 457
notabilia 642
notabilities 875
notable
  manifest 525
  important 642
  active 682
  distinguished 873
notables 875
notably 31
notary 553, 968
notation 85
notch 198, **257**, 550
note *cry* 412
  music 413
  take cognizance
  450
  remark 457
  explanation 522
  sign 550
  record 551
  printing 591
  epistle 592
  minute 596
  money 800
  fame 873
  change one's – 607
  make a – of 551
  of – 873
  take – of 457
  – of admiration
  870
  – of alarm 669
  – of preparation
  673
note-book
  memorandum 505
  record 551
  compendium 569
  writing 590
noted 490, 873

noteworthy
  great 31
  exceptional 83
  important 642
nothing *nihility* 4
  zero 101
  trifle 643
  come to – 304, 732
  do – 681
  for – 815
  go for – 643
  good for – 646
  make – of
  under-estimate
  483
  fail 732
  take – by 732
  think of – 930
  worse than – 808
  – comes amiss 831
  – to do 681
  – to do with 764
  – doing 681
  – to go upon 471
  – in it 4
  – of the kind 18,
  536
  – loth 602
  – on 226
  – more to be said
  478
  – to signify 643
nothingness 2
notice *intellect* 450
  observe 457
  review 480
  information 527
  warning 668
  bring into – 525
  deserve – 642
  give –
  manifest 525
  inform 527
  indicate 550
  short – 111
  take – of 450
  this is to give –
  457
  worthy of – 642
  – is hereby given
  publication 531
  – to quit 782
noticeable 31
notification 527
notion *idea* 453
notional 515
notoriety 531, 873
notorious
  known 490
  public 531
  famous 873

infamous 874
notturno 415
notwithstanding 30
nought
  [see naught]
noun 564
nourish 707
nourishment
  food 298
nous 498
nous avons changé
  tout cela 140
nouveau riche 123,
  734, 876
Nova Zembla 383
novation 609
novel
  dissimilar 18
  new 123
  unknown 491
  tale 594
novelette 594
novelist 594
novice
  ignoramus 493
  learner 541
  bungler 701
  religious 996
novitiate 539, 673
novocaine 376, 381
novus homo 57,
  876
now 118
  – and then 136
  – or never 134
noways 32
nowhere 187
nowise 32, 536
noxious 649, 657
noyade 361, 972
noyerait dans une
  goutte d'eau, il
  se – 699
nozzle
  projection 250
  opening 260
  air-pipe 351
nuance 15, 465
nubibus, in – 2, 515
nubiferous 353, 426
nubile 131, 903
nucleus middle 68
  cause 153
  centre 222
  kernel 642
nuda veritas 494
nude 226, 849
nudge 550
nudity 226
nugacity 499, 645
nugæ canoræ 517,

842
nugas, magno co-
  natu magnas –
  643
nugatory 158
  unimportant 643
nuggar 273
nugget mass 192
  money 800
nuisance 619, 830
null 4
  – and void
  inexistence 2
  powerless 158
  unproductive 169
  illegal 964
  dec'are – and void
  abrogation 756
  non-observance
  773
nulla dies sine
  lineâ 682
nullah 198
nullâ pallescere
  culpâ, nil con-
  scire sibi – 946
nulli secundus 33
nullibiety 187
nullify inexistence 2
  compensate 30
  destroy 162
  abrogate 756
  not observe 773
  not pay 808
nullity 2, 4
nullius jurare in
  verba magistri
  487
numb
  physically insen-
  sible 376, 381
  morally insensible
  823
  –skull 493
number
  part 51
  abstract - 84
  count 85
  plural 100
  - of a magazine
  &c. 593
  – among 76
  take care of – one
  943
  – of times 104
numbered: days –
  kill 361
  necessity 601
  hopeless 859
  – with the dead
  360

numberless 105
numbers many 102
  verse 597
numbness 375, 381
numerable 85
numeral 84, 85
numeration 85
numerator 84
numerical 85
numerose
  many 102
numerous 102
numismatics 800
numps 501
numskull 501
nun 996
nunc dimittis 990
nuncio 534, 758
nuncupation
  naming 564
nuncupatory
  informing 527
nunindation 794
nunnery 1000
nuptials 903
nurse remedy 662
  preserve 670
  help, 707
  servant 746
  custodian 753
  fondle 902
  put to – 537
nurseling 129
nursery infancy 127
  nest 153
  room 191
  garden 371
  school 542
  workshop 691
  – rhymes 597
  – tale 546, 594
nursing home 493
nurture feed 298
  educate 537
  prepare 673
  aid 707
  – a belief 484
  – an idea 451
nut
  – to crack
  fanatic 504
  riddle 533
  difficulty 704
  – oil 365
nut-brown 433
nutmeg 393
nutmeg-grater 330
nuts 618, 829
nutshell small 32
  lie in a – 572
  little 193

compendium 596
nutation 314
nutriment 298
nutrition 707
nutritious food 298
  healthy 656
  remedy 662
nutty 499
nuzzle 902
nyctalopy 443
nymph girl 129
  woman 374
  mythology 979
  sea – 341
nystagmus 443

O

O! wonder 870
  discontent 932
  – for desire 865
oaf fool 501
  bungler 701
  changeling 980
oak strong 159
  heart of –
  hard 323
  brave 861
oakum 205
oar paddle 267
  oarsman 269
  instrument 633
  labouring – 686
  lie upon one's –s
  681
  ply the –
  navigate 267
  exert 686
  pull an – 680
  put in an – 228,
  682
  rest on one's –
  cease 142
  quiescence 265
  repose 687
  stroke – 693
oarsman 269
oasis separate 44
  exceptional 83
  land 342
oast-house 386
oath
  assertion 535
  bad language 908
  on – 543
  rap out –s 885
  upon – 768
oatmeal 298
obbligato 88, 415
obduction 223

– to be met with
136
ogee 847
Ogham 590
ogive 215
ogle *look* 441
  desire 865
  rude 895
  endearment 902
ogpu 696
ogre *bugbear* 860
  evil-doer 913
  demon 980
oil *lubricate* 332
  grease 355, **356**
  pour – on
  relieve 834
– on the troubled
  waters 174, 714
– lamp 423
– stove 386
oiled *drunk* 959
oilcloth 223
oilskin 386
oil-painting 556
oily *smooth* 255
  greasy 355
  servile 886
  courteous 894
  flattery 933
oinomania 959
ointment
  grease 356
  remedy 662
O.K. 58
old 124
  of – 122
– age 128
  die of – age 729
– bachelor 904
– clothes 225
– fashioned 851
– fogey 501, 857
– joke 842
– maid *cards* 840
  spinster 904
– man *veteran* 130
  husband 903
– man of the sea
  706
– Nick 978
– school 124
  obstinate 606
  habit 613
  pay off – scores
  718
– song
  repetition 104
  trifle 643
  cheap 815
– stager

veteran 130
actor 599
proficient 700
– story
  repetition 104
  stale news 532
  love 897
– times 122
  one's – way 613
– woman *fool* 501
  wife 903
Oldbuck 122
olden 124
older 128
oldest inhabitant
  not in memory of
  – 137
old-fashioned 124,
  851
oldness 124
oleagine 356
oleaginous 355
oleomargarine 356
oleum addere
  camino 35, 173
olfactory 398
olid 401
oligarch 745
oligarchy 737
olio 41
olive-branch
  infant 129
  offspring 167
  pacification 723
olive-green 435
olla podrida 41
Olympiad 720
Olympus 981
ombre 840
ombres chinoises
  448
omega *end* 67
omelet 298
omen 512
ominate 511
ominous
  predicting 511
  indicating 550
  danger 665
  hopeless 859
omission
  incomplete 53
  exclusion 55
  neglect 460
  failure 732
  non-observance
  773
  guilt 947
omitted 2, 187
omne tulit
  punctum 731

omnibus 272
omnifarious 81
omnific 168
omniform 81
omnigenous 81
omnipotence 157,
  976
omnipresence 186,
  976
omniscience 490,
  976
omnium gatherum
  mixture 41
  confusion 59
  assemblage 72
omnivorous
  eating 298
  desire 865
  gluttony 957
omphalos 68
on *forwards* 282
– account of 155
– all accounts 52
– that account 155
– approval 463
– an average 29
– the brink of 32
– the cards 152
– foot *duration* 106
  event 151
  doing 170
– the fire 730
– all fours 13, 23
– the other hand
  30
– one's head 218
– the increase 35
– a large scale 31
– these lines 627
– the move 264
– the nail 118
– no account 32
– no occasion 107
– a par 27
– the part of 9
– the point of 111
– the present oc-
  casion 118
– trial 463
– the whole 50
on dit 532, 588
once *past* 119, 122
  seldom 137
  at – 113, 132
– for all *final* 67
  infrequency 137
  tell *one* - 527
  determine - 604
  choose 609
– in a blue moon
  137

– more 90, 104
– over 457
– upon a time
  time 106
  different time 119
  formerly 122
– in a way 137
Ondine 979
one *identical* 13
  whole 50
  unity 87
  somebody 372
  married 903
  all – to 823
  at – with *agree* 23
  concur 178
  concord 714
  make – of 186
  neither – nor the
  other 610
  of – *accord* 488
– and all
  whole 50
  general 78
  unanimous 488
  from – to another
  transfer 783
– thing with
  another 476
– of the best 948
– bone and one
  flesh 903
– consent 178, 488
– of these days 121
– fell swoop 113,
  173
– fine morning 106
– and a half 87
– horse 643
– idea 481
– jump 113
– leg in the grave
  160
  as – man 488, 709
– mind 178, 488
– by one
  separately 44
  respectively 79
  unity 87
  both the – and
  the other 89
  the – or the other
  609
– over the eight
  959
– and the same 13
  on – side 217, 236
– step 840
– in ten thousand
  648, 948
– at a time 87

– or two 100	– out	strings 809	*acting* 170
with – voice 488	*disclosure* 529	– question 461,	*workman* 690
– in a way 83	**opacity 426**	475	operator
– way or another	opal 847	– rupture 713	*surgeon* 662
627	opalescent 427, 440	– sesame 631, 993	*doer* 690
at – with	opaque 426	– the sluices 297	operculated 261
agree 23	open *begin* 66	– space 180	operculum 223
concur 178	*expand* 194	– to suspicion 485	operetta 415
concord 174	*unclose* 260	– to *liable* 177	operose 686, 704
one-eyed 443	*manifest* 525	*facile* 705	ophicleide 417
oneirocritic 524	*reveal* 529	– the trenches 716	ophiology 368
oneiromancy 511	*frank* 543	– up *begin* 66	ophiomancy 511
oneness 13	*artless* 703	*disclose* 529	ophthalmia 443
onerous *bad* 649	break – 173	– to the view 446	ophthalmic 441
difficult 704	lay – 226	– war 722, 889	opiate 174
burdensome 706	lay oneself – to	– warfare 722	opine 484
troublesome 830	177	– the wound 824	opiniative 481
oneself 13	leave the matter –	opening	opiniator 606
have all to – 777	705	*beginning* 66	opinion 484
kill – 361	pry – 173	*opportunity* 134	give an – 480
take merit to –	throw – 296	*space* 180	have too high an –
884	– and above board	*gap* 198	of oneself 880
take upon –	703, 939	*aperture* **260**	popular – 488
will 600	– air 220, 338	open-handed 809,	system of –s 484
undertake 676	– arms *willing* 602	816	wedded to an –
talk to – 589	*friendship* 888	open-hearted	606
true to – 604*a*	*social* 892	*veracious* 543	opinionate 481, 606
be – again 660	*courtesy* 894	*artless* 703	opinionated 474
one-sided	– the ball 62, 66	*liberal* 816	self– 880
misjudging 481	– a case 476	*honourable* 939	opiniâtre 481
wrong 923	– country 344	open-mouthed	opinionist 474, 606
dishonourable 940	in – court 525, 531	*cry* 411	opitulation 707
onion 393	– a discussion 476	*expectation* 507	opium *soothe* 174
onlooker 444	– to discussion 475	*speak* 582	*deaden sense* 376
only *small* 32	– the door to	*loquacious* 584	*bane* 663
simple 42	*cause* 153	*desire* 865	opium-eater 683
single 87	*facilitate* 705	*wonder* 870	oppidan 188
imperfect 651	*permit* 760	opera *music* 415	oppilation 706
if – 865	with – doors 531	*poetry* 597	opponent **710**, 891
– think 870	– enemy 891	*drama* 599	opportune
– yesterday 123	– eyes *see* 441	– glass 445	*well-timed* 134
only-begotten 87	*attention* 457	– hat 225	*expedient* 646
onomancy 511	*discovery* 480*a*	– house 599	opportunism 605,
onomatopœia 560,	*expectation* 507	opéra bouffe 599	646
564	*inform* 527	operculum 261	opportunity 134
onset *beginning* 66	*undeceive* 529	operæ pretium est	lose an – 135
attack 716	*teach* 537	646	oppose *contrary* 14
onslaught 716	*predetermination*	operandi, modus	*counteract* 179
ontology 1	611	627, 692	*evidence* 468
onus *burden* 706	*wonder* 870	operate *cause* 153	*clash* 708
duty 926	– fire 716	*produce* 161	opposite 14
– probandi	– house 892	*act* 170	– scale 30
uncertainty 475	– into	*work* 680	– side 237
doubt 485	*conversion* 144	– upon *motive* 615	opposition
onward 282	*river* 348	operation	[*see* oppose] **708**
onychomancy 511	– the lips 529	[*see* operate]	the – 710
onyx 847	– the lock 480*a*	arithmetical – 85	oppositionist 710
oof 800	– market 799	in – 680	oppress *molest* 649
ooze *emerge* 295	– one's mind 529	put in – 677	*severe* 739
flow 348	– order 194	surgical – 662	*malevolence* 907
semiliquid 352	– one's purse-	**operative**	oppressed with

melancholy 837
oppressive *hot* 382
  painful 830
oppressor 739, 913
opprobrium 874
oppugnation 708, 719
optative 865
optical 441
  – instruments **445**
  – lantern 448
optician 445
optics *light* 420, 445
optics *sight* 441
optimacy 875
optimates 875
optime! 931
optimism 482, 858
optimist 858
  flatterer 935
option 609
optional 600
optometer 443
optometry 445
opulence 803
opuscule 593
or *yellow* 436
  orange 439
  alternative 609
oracle 500, **513**
Oracle, Sir –
  positive 474
  vanity 880
  blusterer 887
oracular
  answering 462
  ambiguous 475
  wise 498
  prediction 511
oral *information* 527
  voice 580
  speech 582
  – communication 588
  – evidence 467
orange *round* 249
  colour **439**
orangery 371
orarium 999
oration 582
  funeral – 363
orator 582
oratoric 415
oratory
  speaking 582
  place of prayer 1000
orb *region* 181
  circle 247
  luminary 423

eye 441
sphere of action 625
– of day *sun* 318
  luminary 423
– of night 318
orbicular 247
orbit *circle* 247
  heavens 318
  path 627
orchard 371
orchestra
  music 415
  musicians 416
  instruments 417
  theatre 599
orchestral 415
orchestrate 60, 413, 416
orchestration 413
orchestrelle 417
ordain
  command 741
  commission 755
  due 924
  legal 963
  God 976
  church 995
ordained *due* 924
  clergy 996
ordeal
  experiment 463
  trouble 828
  sorcery 992
  – of battle 722
order
  regularity **58**
  arrangement 60
  class 75
  record 551
  requisition 630
  direct 693
  command 741
  money 800
  rank 873
  quality 875
  decoration 877
  law 963
  at one's – 743
  call to – 932
  in – 620
  keep in – 693
  money – 800
  out of – 651
  put in – 60
  recur in regular – 138
  set in – 60
  set one's house in – 673
  standing – 613

in working – 673
– of the day
  conformity 82
  events 151
  habit 613
  plan 626
  command 741
  pass to the – of the day 624
orderless 59
orderly
  regular 58, 80
  arrange 60
  conformable 82
  servant 746
  – of succession 63
  – of things 80
orders, holy – 995
  in – 996
ordinal 998
ordinance
  command 741
  law 963
  rite 998
ordinary *usual* 82
  meal 298
  habitual 613
  imperfect 651
  ugly 846
  simple 849
  in – *store* 636
  lie in – 681
  – condition
  rule 80
  – course of things 613
ordinate 466
ordination
  measurement 466
  command 741
  commission 755
  church 995
  rite 998
ordnance 727
ordonnance 963
ordure 653
ore 635
ore rotundo 577
oread 979
orectic 865
organ *music* 417
  voice 580
  instrument 633
  internal –s 221
  – point 413
organic *state* 7
  structural 329
  protoplastic 357
  – change 146
  – chemistry 357
  – remains 357

dead 329
organism 329
organist 416
organization 60
  production 161
  structure 329
  animated nature 357
organize
  arrange 60
  produce 161
  plan 626
organized hypoc-risy 544
organology 329
orgasm 173
orgies 954
oriel *recess* 191
  corner 244
  window 260
  chapel 1000
Orient 236, 420
orifice
  beginning 66
  opening 260
oriflamme 550
Origenism 984
origin 66, 153
  derive its – 154
original
  dissimilar 18
  not imitated 20
  model 22
  initial 66
  individual 79
  exceptional 83
  cause 153
  invented 515
  unaccustomed 614
  laughing-stock 857
  return to – state 660
originality 600
  want of – 843
originate *begin* 66
  cause 153
  invent 515
  – in 154
originator 164
originative 168
Orion's belt 318
orismology 562, 564
orison *request* 765
  worship 990
orlop deck 211
ormoln
  sham 545
  ornament 847
Ormuzd 979
ornament

in writing **577**
adornment **847**
glory 873
excess of – 851
ornamental art 847
  painting 556
ornate
  - writing 577
  ornamental 847
ornavit, nihil tetigit
  quod non – 850
orniscopy 511
ornithology 368
ornithomancy 511
orotundity 577
orphan 893
Orpheus 416
orpiment 436
orrery 318
orthodox
  conformable 82
  - religion 983a
  – *dissenter* 984
orthodoxy 983a
orthoepy 562, 580
orthogonal 212
orthography 561
orthology 494
orthometry 466,
  597
orthopædy 662
orthopraxy 662 ·
orts *remnants* 40
  useless 645
  (*trifles* 643)
oryctology
  minerals 358
  organic remains
  368
oscillation
  change 149
  motion **314**
  centre of – 222
oscitancy
  opening 260
  sleepy 683
osculation
  contact 199
  endearment 902
Osiris 979
Osmanli 984
osmose 302
Ossa on Pelion 72,
  319
osseous 323
ossify 323
ossuary 363
ostensible
  appearance 448
  probable 472
  manifest 525

plea 617
ostentation 882
osteology 329
ostiary
  doorkeeper 263
  mouth 260
  estuary 343
ostler 370, 746
ostracize *exclude* 55
  eject 297
  banish 893
  censure 932
  punish 972
ostrich, stomach of
  an – 957
Othello's occupa-
  tion's gone 757
other 15, 37
  do unto –s as we
  would men
  should do unto
  us 942
  enter into the
  feelings of –s
  906
  every – 138
  put oneself in the
  place of –s 942
  the – day 123
  – extreme 14
  – side of the
  shield 468
  – than 18
  – things to do 683
  – time 119
  just the – way 14
  in – words 522
otherwise 18
otia fecit, Deus
  nobis hæc – 840
otiose 683
otium cum
  dignitate 685
ottar, otto 400
ottoman 215
oubliette
  ambush 530
  prison 752
ough! 874
ought:
  – **to be** 922, 926
ouï-dire 532
oui-ja board 992
ounce *weight* 319
ourselves 372
oust *eject* 297
  dismiss 756
  deprive 789
out *exterior* 220
  in error 495
  come – 446

go – *egress* 295
  cool 385
play – 729
send – 297
time – of joint 735
waters – 337
  – at elbows 874
  – at heels 804
  – of [*see below*]
  – and out 52
  – in one's reckon-
  ing 495
  – upon it
  malediction 908
  censure 932
  – with it
  disclose 529
  obliterate 552
out of *motive* 615
  insufficient 640
get well – 671
  – breath 688
  – cash 804
  – character 24
  – whole cloth 544
  – the common 83
  – conceit with 867
  – countenance
  disrepute 874
  humbled 879
  – danger 664
  – date
  anachronism 115
  old 124
  ill-timed 135
  unfashionable 851
  – one's depth
  deep 208
  shortcoming 340
  difficult 704
  rash 863
  – doors 220, 338
turn – doors 297
  – employ 681
  – favour 867
  – focus 447
  – gear
  disorder 59
  powerless 158
  unprepared 674
  – hand *soon* 132
  completed 729
  – harness 748
  – health 655
  – hearing 196, 419
  – humour
  discontent 832
  anger 900
  – a job 681
  – joint
  disorder 59

impotent 158
evil 619
– luck 735
– one's mind 503
– order·
disorder 59
unconformity 83
imperfect 651
– patience 825
– the perpendi-
  cular 217
– place
disorder 59
unconformable 83
displaced 185
inexpedient 647
– pocket *loss* 776
poverty 804
debt 806
– one's power 471
– print 552
– all proportion 31
– the question
impossible 471
dissent 489
rejection 610
refusal 764
hopeless 859
undue 925
– reach 196, 471
– one's reckoning
uncertain 475
error 495
inexpectation 508
disappointment
  509
– repair 659
– repute 874
– season 135
– shape 243
put – sight
invisible 447
neglect 460
conceal 528
– sorts *disorder* 59
dejection 837
– the sphere of
  196
– spirits 837
– one's teens 131
– time
unmusical 414
imperfect 651
spoiled 659
discord 713
– the way
irrelevant 10
exceptional 83
absent 187
distant 196
ridiculous 853

secluded 893
get – the way 623
go – one's way 629
– one's wits 824
– work 681
– the world
dead 360
secluded 893
outbalance 30, 33
outbid 794
outbrave 885
out-brazen 885
outbreak
beginning 66
violence 173
egress 295
discord 713
attack 716
revolt 742
passion 825
outburst
violence 173
egress 295
revolt 825
outcast
unconformable 83
pariah 876
secluded 893
bad man 949
outcome *effect* 154
egress 295
produce 775
outcry *noise* 411
complaint 839
censure 932
outdo *superior* 33
transcursion 303
activity 682
cunning 702
conquer 731
outdoor 220
outer 220
outermost 220
outface 885
outfit 225, 673
outflank *flank* 236
defeat 731
outgate 295
outgeneral 731
outgo 303
outgoing 295
outgoings 809
outgrow 194
outgrowth 154
out-Herod 33, 174
outhouse 191
outing 266
outjump
transcursion 303
repute 873
outlander 57

outlandish
foreign 10
extraneous 57
irregular 83
barbarous 851
ridiculous 853
outlast 110
outlaw *irregular* 83
secluded 893
reprobate 949
outlawry 964
outlay 809
outleap 303
outlet *opening* 260
egress 295
outline *contour* **230**
form 240
features 448
sketch 554
painting 556
plan 626
outlines
rudiments 66
principles 596
outlive 110, 141
outlook *view* 448
outstare 885
outlying
remaining 40
exterior 220
outmanœuvre
trick 545
defeat 731
outnumber 102
outpost
distant 196
circumjacent 227
front 234
outpouring
egress 295
information 527
abundance 639
output *egress* 295
produce 775
outrage
violence 173
evil 619
badness 649
injury to 659
malevolence 907
disrespect 929
guilt 947
outrageous
excessive 31
violent 173
scandalous 874
outrance: à –
great 31
complete 52
violent 173
guerre – 722

outrank 33, 62
outré
exceptional 83
exaggerate 549
ridiculous 853
outre mer 196
outreach 545
outreckon 482
outride 303
outrider 64
outrigger
support 215
boat 273
outright 52
outrival
superior 33
surpass 303
fame 873
outrun 303
– the constable
debt 806
prodigal 818
outscourings 653
outset 66, 873
outshine 873, 874
outside
extraneous 57
exterior 220
appearance 448
– the gates 893
mere – 544
– car 272
clean the – of the
platter
ostentation 882
outsider 57, 893
outskirts 196, 227
outspan 292
outspeak 582
outspoken *say* 582
artless 703
be – *censure* 932
outspread 202
outstanding
remaining 40
outside 220
– debt 806
– feature 642
outstare 885
outstep 303
outstretched 202
with – arms 894
outstrip 303
outtalk 584
outvie 720, 873
outvote 731
outward 220
– bound 293
outweigh 33, 175
outwit 545, 731
outwork

defence 717
outworn 124
oval 247
ovate 247
ovation 883
oven 386
like an – *hot* 382
over *more* 33
remainder 40
end 67
past 122
high 206
too much 641
all – *completed* 729
all – with
destroyed 162
dead 360
failure 732
adversity 735
danger – 664
get – 660
fight one's battles
– again 594
hand – 783
make – 784
set – 755
turn – 218
– and above
superior 33
added 37
remainder 40
redundance 641
– again 104
– against 237
– the border 196
– head and ears
complete 52
height 206
feeling 821
– the hills and far
away 196
– the mark 33
– one's head 208,
641
– the way 237
overabound 641
overact *bustle* 682
affect 855
overall 225
over-anxiety 865
overarch 223
overawe *sway* 737
intimidate 860
respect 928
overbalance
unequal 28
compensation 30
superior 33
overbear 175
overbearing 885
overboard, throw –

palatial *palace* 189
  ostentatious 882
palatinate 181
palatine 745
Palatine Court 966
palaver
  unmeaning 517
  speech 582
  loquacity 584
  colloquy 588
  council 696
pale *stake* 45
  region 181
  inclosure 232
  limit 233
  dim 422
  colourless 429
  emotion 821
  frightened 860
  turn –
  lose colour 429
  emotion 821
  fear 860
  – of the church
    995
  – its ineffectual
    fire
  dim 422
  out of repute 874
pale-faced 429
paleography
  past 122
  philology 560
paleology *past* 122
  language 160
paleontology 368
paleozoic 124
palestric 686, 720
paletot 225
palette 556
palfrey 271
palimpsest 147, 528
palindrone
  inversion 218
  neology 563
paling 232, 752
palingenesia 163
palingenesis 660
palinode 597
palinody 607
palisade
  wall 212
  defence 717
  prison 752
pall *covering* 223
  mantle 225
  funeral 363
  disgust 395
  insignia 747
  weary 841
  dislike 867

satiety 869
  canonicals 999
palladium
  safety 664
Pallas 979
pall-bearer 363
pallet *support* 215
  painter's - 556
palliament 225
palliate
  moderate 174
  mind 658
  relieve 834
  extenuate 937
palliative 174
  remedy 662
pallid 429
pallium 999
pall-mall 840
pallone 840
pallor 429
palm
  measure of length
    200
  trophy 733
  steal 791
  laurel 877
  bear the – 873
  grease the –
  induce 615
  give 784
  itching – 865
  win the – 731
  – off, – upon 545
  – tree 367
palmated 257
palmer
  traveller 268
  clergy 996
palmist 513
palmistry 511
palmy
  prosperous 734
  pleasant 829
  – days
  prosperous 734
  pleasure 827
palpable
  material 316
  tactile 379
  obvious 446
  manifest 525
  – obscure 421
palpation 379
palpitate
  tremble 315
  colour 440
  emotion 821
  fear 860
palsy
  impotence 158

physical insensi-
  bility 376
  disease 655
  mental insensi-
  bility 823
palter
  falsehood 544
  shift 605
  elude 773
paltry *small* 32
  unimportant 643
  mean 940
paludal 345
pampas 344
pamper 902, 954,
  957
pamphlet 531, 593
pamphleteer 595
Pan 979
pan 191
panacea 662
panache 256, 847
panama *hat* 225
panary 636
pancake 298
pandar [*see* pander]
Pandean pipes 417
pandect
  knowledge 490
  dissertation 595
  compendium 596
  code 963
pandemonium 59,
  404, 982
  inhabitants of –
    978
pandemic 657
pander *pimp* 962
  – to *instrument*
    631
  help 707
  flatter 933
pandiculation
  expansion 194
  opening 260
  sleepy 683
Pandoor 726
Pandora's box 619
  bottom of 858
paned 440
panegyric 931
panegyrize 482
panel *list* 86
  layer 204
  partition 228
  accused 938
  jury 967
  sliding – 545
panelling 847
pang 378, 828
Pangloss 492

panguid 355
panhandle 765, 767,
  876
panic 860
panier 225
Panjandrum 875
pannel 213
pannikin 191
pannier 191
panoply 717, 727
panopticon 752
panorama 448, 556
panoramic 78, 446
  – view 441
pansophy 490
pant *heat* 382
  fatigue 688
  emotion 821
  – for 865
pantaloon
  old man 130
  pantomimist 599
  buffoon 844
pantaloons 225
pantechnicon 272,
  636
pantheism 984
Pantheon 979, 1000
panther 861
pantile 223, 350
pantologist 492, 700
pantology 490
pantomime 550, 599
pantry 191, 636
pants 225
panurgy 698
pap 250, 354
papa *father* 166
Papa *pope* 996
papacy 984, 995
papal 995
paper *cover* 223
  white 430
  writing 590
  book 593
  security 771
  exist only on – 4
  – credit 805
  – money 800
  – pellet 643
  – war 476, 720
Paphian 954, 961
papilla 250
papistry 984
papoose 129
pappous 256
papula 250
papulose 250
papyrus 590
par 27
  above – 648

parse 461, 567
Parsee 984
parsimony **819**
parson 996
parsonage 1000
part *divide* 44
  portion **51**
  diverge 291
  music 413
  book 593
  rôle 599
  function 625
  duty 926
  act a − *action* 680
  take an active −
    682
  bear − in 709
  component − 56
  fractional − 100*a*
  in − *a little* 32
  for my − 79
  on the − of 707
  play a − in 175
  principal − 642
  take the − of 709
  take − with 709
  take a − in 680
  take no − in 623
  − company
    disjunction 44
    avoid 623
    quarrel 713
  − and parcel 56
  − by part 51
  −song 415
  − of speech 567
  − with 782, 784
partake 778
  − of the sacrament
    998
parte, ex − 481
parterre *level* 213
  cultivation 371
Parthis mendacior
  544
parti pris 611
partial *unequal* 28
  incomplete 51
  special 79
  misjudging 481
  unjust 923
  − shadow 422
partiality
  preponderance 33
  desire 865
  friendship 888
  love 897
partially 32, 51
partible 44
particeps criminis
  690, 711

participote 709, 778
  − in *be a doer* 680
participation **778**
participator 690
particle 32, 330
parti-coloured 440
particular *item* 51
  event 151
  attentive 457
  careful 459
  exact 494
  capricious 608
  odd 851
  fastidious **868**
  in − 79
  − account 594
  − estate 780
particularize
  special 79
  describe 594
particularly 31, 33
particulars 79, 594
partie carrée 892
parting 44
partisan
  auxiliary 711
  weapon 727
  friend 890
  sympathizer 914
partisanship
  warped judgment
    481
  co-operation 709
  partiality 923
partition *wall* 228
  allot 786
partlet 366
partly 51
partner
  companion 88
  auxiliary 711
  sharer 778
  friend 890
  spouse 903
  sleeping − 683
partnership
  party 712
join − with 709
parts *intellect* 450
  skill 698
  wisdom 498
parturition 161
parturiunt montes
  482, 509
party *assemblage* 72
  special 79
  person 372
  association **712**
  sociality 892
  − spirit
    warped judgment

  481
  cooperation 709
  wrong 923
  − to *action* 680
  agent 690
  co-operate 709
  − to a suit 969
  − wall 228
parva componere
  magnis 464
parvenu
  new 123
  successful 734
  vulgar 851
  low-born 876
parvitude 193
pas *precedence* 62
  term 71
  precession 280
  rank 873
  − de quatre 840
  − seul 840
pas si bête 498
paschal 998
pasha 875
pashalic 737
pashaw 745
pasigraphie 560
pasigraphy 590
pasquinade 934
pass *conjuncture* 8
  be superior 33
  course 109
  lapse 122
  happen 151
  interval 198
  defile 203
  move 264
  transfer 270
  move through 302
  exceed 303
  vanish 449
  way 627
  difficulty 704
  thrust 716
  passport 760
  gratuity 815
  - as *property* 783,
    784
  barely − 651
  let it − 460
  make a − at 716
  pretty − 704
  − away
    cease to exist 2
    end 67
    transient 111
    past 122
    cease 142
    die 360
  − by *course* 109

  inattention 458
  neglect 460
  disrespectful 929
  − comprehension
    519
  − current 484
  − an examination
    648, 873
  − the eyes over
    457
  − the fingers over
    379
  − into one's hand
    785
  − through one's
    hands 625
  − into 144
  − judgment 480
  − a law 963
  − in the mind 451
  − muster
    conform to 82
    sufficient 639
    good 648
    approbation 931
  barely − muster
    651
  − under the name
    of 564
  − off *be past* 122
    egress 295
  − off for 544
  − on 282
  − an opinion 480
  − to the order of
    the day 624
  − out of 295
  − over
    exclude 55
    cross 302
    give 784
    forgive 918
    exemption 927*a*
  − over to 709
  − and repass 302,
    314
  − in review 457,
    461
  − the Rubicon 609
  − sentence on 971
  − time *exist* 1
    time 106
    do nothing 681
  − one's time in
    625
  − to 144
  − through
    event 151
    motion 302
  − one's word 768
passable *small* 32

firm 604
authoritative 737
rigorous 739
compulsory 744
duty 926
– denial 536
– refusal 764
perennial
continuous 69
diuturnal 110
- *plants* 367
perennius, ære –
873
pererration 266
perfect
great 31
entire 52
excellent 650
complete 729
perfection 650
bring to – 729
perfervidum in-
genium 682
perfidy 874, 940
perflate 349
perforate 260
perforator 262
perforce 601, 744
perform
produce 161
do 170
- *music* 416
action 680
achieve 729
fulfil 772
– a circuit 629
– a duty 926
– the duties of 625
– a function 644
– an obligation
772
– a part 599, 680
– a service 998
performable 470
performance
[*see* perform]
effect 154
performer
musician 416
stage-player 599
agent 690
affectation 855
perfume 400
perfunctory 53, 460
pergola 191
perhaps 470, 514
peri 845, 979
periapt 993
pericranium 450
periculous 665
peridot 847

perihelion 197
peril 665
at your – 909
take heed at
one's – 668
perilepsis 476
perimeter 230
period *end* 67
point 71
- *of time* 106, **108**
recurrence 138
at fixed –s 138
well rounded –s
577, 578
periodical
recurring 138
book 593
periodicity 138
peripatetic 266, 268
periphery 230
periphrase 566, 573
periplus 267
periscope 441, 445
periscopic 446
– *lens* 445
perish
cease to exist 2
be destroyed 162
die 360
decay 659
– with cold 383
– with hunger 956
perishable 111
perissology 573
peristaltic 248
peristyle 189
periwig 225
perjured 940
perjurer 548
perjury 544
perk *dress* 225
– up *elevate* 307
revive 689
perked up
proud 878
perky 880
perlustration 441
permanence
durability 110
unchanging **141**
unchangeable 150
permanent
habitual 613
permeable 260
permeate
insinuate 228
pervade 186
pass through 302
–d with 613
permissible 760
permission 760

permissive 760
permit 760
permitting
weather &c. – 469,
470
permutation
numerical - 84
change 140
interchange 148
pernicious 649
pernicity 274
perorate
diffuse style 573
peroration
sequel 65
end 67
speech 582
perpend *think* 451
perpendicular 212
perpension
attention 457
perpetrate 680
– *a pun &c.* 842
perpetrator 690
perpetua, esto –
928, 931
perpetual 112
frequent 136
– curate 996
– motion 467
perpetuate 112
continue 143
establish 150
perpetuity 69, **112**
perplex *derange* 61
distract 458
uncertainty 475
bother 830
perplexed 59, 248
perplexity
disorder 59
uncertainty 475
unintelligibility
519
difficulty 704
perquisite 775, 973
perquisition 461
perron 627
perscrutation 461
persecute
oppress 649
annoy 830
malevolence 907
perseverance 143,
604a
Persides 215
persiflage 842, 856
persifleur 844
persist *duration* 106
permanence 141
continue 143

persevere 604a
persistence
diuturnity 110
person 3, 372
without distinc-
tion of –s 922
persona grata 890,
899
personable 845
personæ, dramatis
– 599, 690
personage 372
personal
[*see* person]
special 79
subjective 317
– narrative 594
– property 780
– remarks 932
– security 771
personality
[*see* personal]
discourtesy 895
disrespect 929
censure 932
detraction 934
personalty 780
personate 19, 554
personify 521, 554
personnel 56, 590
perspective
view 448
expectation 507
painting 556
aerial – 428
in – 200
perspicacity
sight 441
intelligence 498
fastidiousness 868
perspicuity
intelligibility 518
style **570**
perspiration 295,
299
in a – 382
perstringe 457
persuadable 602
persuade *belief* 484
induce 615
persuasibility
willingness 602
persuasion
class 75
opinion 484
teaching 537
inducement 615
religious – 983
persuasive
reasoning 476
pert

[590]

highway 627
weapon 727
pikeman 726
pikestaff *tall* 206
  plain 525
pilaster
  support 215
  projection 250
  ornament 847
pile *stake* 45
  heap 72
  edifice 161
  post 215
  velvet 256
  money 800
  funeral – 363
  – up 549, 641
pile-driver 276
pilfer *steal* 791
pilferer 792
pilgarlic
  outcast 893
pilgrim 268, 996
pilgrimage 266, 676
pill *sphere* 249
  medicine 662
  bitter – 735
pillage 659, 791
pillager 792
pillar *stable* 150
  lofty 206
  support 215
  monument 551
  tablet 590
  –s of Hercules 550
  – of the state &c.
   873
  from – to post
  transfer 270
  agitation 315
  irresolute 505
  circuit 629
pillion 215
pillory 975
pillow
  support 215
  soft 324
  consult one's –
  temporize 133
  reflect 451
pilot *mariner* 269
  inform 527
  guide 693
  director 694
pilot-balloon 463
pilot-boat 273
pilot-officer 745
pilot-jacket 225
pilous 256
pimp 962
pimple 250, 848

pin *fasten* 43
  fastening 45
  locate 184
  sharp 253
  axis 312
  trifle 643
  might hear a –
   drop 403
  point of a – 193
  not a – to choose
   27, 609a
  – down 744, 751
  – one's faith upon
   484
  – oneself upon
   746, 886
pinafore 225
pince-nez 445
pincers 781
pinch *emergency* 8
  contract 195
  pain 378
  chill 385
  need 630
  difficulty 704
  adversity 735
  grudge 819
  hurt morally 830
  at a – 630, 704
  jack at a – 711
  where the shoe –s
   830
  – of snuff 643
pinchbeck 545, 847
pinched [*see* pinch]
  thin 203
  poor 804
  – with hunger 865
pinching 383, 819
Pindaric 597
ping-pong 840
pine *disease* 655
  dejection 837
  suffer in mind
   828
  – away 837
  – for 865
pinery 371
pinguid 355
pin-hole 260
pinion *fasten* 43
  wing 267
  instrument 633
  restrain 751
  fetter 752
pink *notch* 257
  pierce 260
  thrust 276
  colour 434
  perfection 650
  glory 873

pink of *beauty* 845
  – fashion 852
  – perfection 650
  – politeness 894
pinnace 273
pinnacle 210
pinocle 840
pin-prick 180a
pins *legs* 266
  – and needles
  bodily pain 378
  numb 381
  mental pain 828
pinscher 366
Pinto, Fernam
  Mendez – 548
pioneer
  precursor 64
  leader 234
  teacher 540
  prepare 673
pious 987
  – fraud 546, 988
pip 747
pipe *tube* 260
  conduit 350
  vent 351
  tobacco 392
  sound 410
  cry 411
  music 416, 417
  weep 839
  no – no dance 812
  – one's eye 839
  – of peace 721,
   723
pipeclay *habit* 613
  strictness 739
piper 416
  pay the – 707, 807
piping – hot 382
  – time 721, 734
pipkin 191
piquant
  pungent 392
  - *style* 574
  impressive 821
piquante, sauce –
  393, 829
pique *fly* 267
  excite 824
  pain 830
  hate 898
  anger 900
  – oneself
  pride 878
piqueerer 792
piquet 717, 726
pirate 773, 791, 792
piroque 273
pirouette 218, 312

  turn a – 607
Pisa, tower of – 217
pis-aller 147
piscatorial 366
pisces natare
  docere 538, 641
pisciculture 370
piscina 350, 1000
pish! *absurd* 497
  trifling 643
  excitable 825
  irascible 901
piste 551
Pistol 887
pistol 727
pistol-shot 197
piston 263
pit *deep* 208
  hole 252
  opening 260
  extract 301
  grave 363
  theatre 599
  danger 667
  bottomless – 982
  – of Acheron 982
  – against 708, 713
  – against one
   another 464
pit-a-pat
  agitation 315
  rattle 407
  feeling 821
  excitation 824
pitch *degree* 26
  term 71
  location 184
  height 206
  summit 210
  erect 212
  throw 284
  descent 306
  depression 308
  reel 314
  resin 356a
  musical - 413
  black 431
  absolute – 416
  – of one's breath
   411
  – dark 421
  – into *attack* 716
  contend 720
  punish 972
  – overboard 782
  – one's tent 292
  – and toss 621
  – upon *reach* 292
  discover 480a
  choose 609
  get 775

pitched battle 720
pitcher 191
pitchfork 273, 284
  rain –s 348
pitch-pipe 417
piteous 830
piteously *much* 31
pitfall 545, **667**
pith *gist* 5
  strength 159
  interior 221
  centre 222
  meaning 516
  important part
    642
pithless 158
pithy *meaning* 516
  concise 572
  vigorous 574
pitiable *bad* 649
  painful 830
  contemptible 930
pitied, to be – 828
pitiful
  unimportant 643
  bad 649
  disrepute 874
  pity 914
pitiless **914a**
  revengeful 919
pittance
  quantity 25
  dole 640
  allotment 786
  income 810
pitted 848
pituitous 352
pity **914**
  express – 915
  what a –
    regret 833
    lament 839
  for –'s sake 914
pivot *junction* 43
  cause 153
  support 215
  axis 222, 312
pix *box* 191, 998
  assay 463
pixy 980
pizzicato 415
placable 918
placard 531
placate 723, 918
place
  circumstances 8
  order 58
  arrange 60
  term 71
  situation **182**, 183

locate 184
abode 189
office 625
rank 873
give – to 623
have – 1
in – 183
in – of 147
make a – for 184
out of – 185
take – 151
– to one's credit
  805
– itself 58
– in order 60
– upon record 551
– under
  include 76
placebit, decies re-
  petita – 829
placebo 933
place-hunter 767
placeman 758
placet 488, 741
placid 826
placket 260
plagiarism
  imitation 19
  borrowing 788
  theft 791
plagiarist 792
Plagiary, Sir
  Fretful – 901
plagiedral 217
plague *disease* 655
  pain 828
  worry 830
plague-spot 657
plaguy 704, 830
plaid *shawl* 225
  variegation 440
plaidoyer 476
plain
  horizontal 213
  country **344**
  obvious 446
  meaning 518
  manifest 525
  style 576
  artless 703
  ugly 846
  simple 849
speak –ly 576
tell one –ly 527
– English 576
– dealing 543
– interpretation
  522
– question 461
– sailing 705
– sense 498

– speaking 525,
  703
– terms
  intelligible 518
  interpreted 522
  language 576
– truth 494
– words 703
plainness **576**
plainsong 990
plain-spoken 525,
  703
plaint 411, 839
plaintiff 938
plaintive 839
plaisance
  [*see* pleasance]
plaisanterie 842
plaister 223
plait 219, 258
plan *itinerary* 266
  information 527
  representation
    554
  scheme **626**
  according to – 82
planchette 992
plane *horizontal* 213
  flat 251
  smooth 255
  fly 267
  aeroplane 273
  soar 305
  inclined – 633
planet *world* 318
  luminary 423
  fate 601
planet-struck
  adversity 735
  wonder 870
planimeter 466
planish 255
plank *board* 204
  programme 626
  path 627
  safety 666
plant *place* 184
  insert 300
  vegetable 367
  agriculture 371
  trick 545
  tools 633
  property 780
– a battery 716
– a dagger in the
  breast 830
– oneself 184
– a thorn in the
  side 830
plantation
  location 184

agriculture 371
estate 780
planter 188
planter ses choux,
  aller – 893
plaque 204
plash *lake* 343
  stream 348
  sound 405, 408
plashy 345
plasm 22
plasma 847
plasmic 240
plaster *cement* 45
  covering 223
  remedy 662
– up *repair* 660
plastered 959
plastic *alterable* 149
  form 240
  soft 324
– arts 557
plastron 717
plat *weave* 219
  ground 344
plate *dish* 191
  layer 204
  covering 223
  flat 251
  food 298
  engraving 558
– layer 690
– printing 558,
  591
plateau 213, 344
plated 545
platform
  horizontal 213
  support 215
  stage 542
  scheme 626
  arena 728
– *orator* 582
platinum-blond 430
platitude 517, 843
Platonic
  contemplative 451
  inexcitable 826
  chaste 960
– bodies 244
Platonism 451
platoon 726
– fire 716
platter 191
  layer 204
  flat 251
clean the outside
  of the – 544
plaudit 931
plausible
  probable 472

sophistical 477
false 544
approbation 931
flattery 933
vindication 937
play *operation* 170
influence 175
scope 180
oscillation 314
music 416
drama 599
use 677
action 680
freedom 748
amusement 840
at – 840
bring into – 677
full – 175
full of – 836
in – 842
– along with 709
– one's best card
686, 698
– of colours 440
– at cross pur-
poses 59, 523
– a deep game 702
– the deuce 825
– the devil 907
– one false
disappoint 509
falsehood 544
deception 545
– fast and loose
falsehood 544
irresolute 605
tergiversation 607
caprice 608
– on the feelings
824
– first fiddle 642,
873
– the fool
folly 499
clumsy 699
amusement 840
ridiculous 853
ridicule 856
– for *chance* 621
– a game
pursue 622
conduct 692
pastime 840
– the game 939
– into the hands
of 709
– havoc 659
– hide and seek
528, 623
– a joke 853
give – to the im-

agination 515
– of light 420
– the monkey 499
– off 545
– a part
false 544
drama 599
action 680
– one's part 625,
692
– second fiddle
34, 749
– one a trick 509,
545
– tricks with 699,
702
– truant 623
– upon 545, 856
– with 460
– upon words
misinterpret 523
neology 563
wit 842
play-boy 818
play-day 840
played out
end 67
fatigue 688
completion 729
failure 732
player
musician 416
actor 599
– piano 417
playfellow 890
playful 836
– imagination 515
playground 728,
840
play-house 599
playmate 890
playsome 836
plaything
trifle 643
toy 840
make a – of 749
playwright 599
plea
defence 462
argument 476
excuse **617**
vindication 937
lawsuit 969
plead *argue* 467
plea 617
beg 765
– one's cause 937
– guilty 950
pleader *lawyer* 968
pleading, special –
477

pleadings 969
pleasance 189, 840
pleasant
agreeable 829
amusing 840
witty 842
make things –
deceive 545
induce 615
please 829
flatter 933
pleasantry 840, 842
please 829
as you – 743
do what one –s
748
if you –
obedience 743
consent 762
request 765
– oneself 943
pleasurableness
829
pleasure
physical - **377**
will 600
moral - **827**
dissipation 954
at – 600
at one's – 737
during – 108a
give – 829
man of – 954a
make a toil of –
682
take one's – 840
will and – 600
with –
willingly 602
pleasure-giving 829
pleasure-ground
demesne 189
amusement 840
pleat 258
plebeian 851, 876
plébiscite 480, 609
plectrum 417
plectuntur Achivi
739
pledge *affirmation*
535
promise 768
security 771
borrow 788
drink to 883, 894
hold in – 771
take the – 771, 958
– oneself 768
– one's word 768
pledget 263, 662
Pleiades 72, 318

plenary 31, 52
plenipotent 157
plenipotentiary
consignee 758
deputy 759
plentitude 639
in the – of power
159
plenty
multitude 102
sufficient 639
– to do 682
plenum *substance* 3
matter 316
pleonasm
repetition 104
diffuseness 573
redundance 641
plerophory 484
plethora 64ˉ
plexal 219
plexus 219
pliable 324
pliant *soft* 324
irresolute 605
facile 705
servile 886
plicature 258
pliers 301, 781
plight *state* 7
promise 768
security 771
evil – 735
– one's faith 902
– one's troth 768,
902
plighted love 897,
902
Plimsoll mark 466
plinth 211, 215
plod *journey* 266
slow 275
persevere 604a
work 682
– along 143
plodding 604a, 682
dull 843
plot - *of ground* 181
plain 344
story 594
plan 626
realty 780
the – thickens
assemblage 72
plough *furrow* 259
agriculture 371
– the ground 673
– in 228
– the waves 267
– one's way 266
ploughboy

pointless 843
poise 27, 319, 852
 mental – 498
poison 659, 663
 – gas 722, 727
poisoned 655
 commend the –
  chalice 544
poisonous 657, 665
poke
 pocket 191
 pig in a –
  uncertain 475
  chance 621
  dawdle 683
  rash 863
 – at 276, 716
 – the fire 384
 – fun at 856
 – one's nose in
  682
 – out *project* 250
poker 386
 cards 840
polacca 273
polacre 273
polar 210
 cold 383
 – co-ordinates 466
polarization 420
polariscope 445
polarity
 duality 89
 counteraction 179
 contraposition
  237
pole *measure of*
 length 200
 tall 206
 summit 210
 axis 222
 punt 267
 rotation 312
 greasy – 840
 opposite –s 237
 from – to pole 180
pole-axe 727
polecat 401
pole-star 550, 693
polemic
 discussion 476
 discord 713
 contention 720
 combatant 726
polemoscope 445
police 965
 – court 966
 – magistrate 967
policeman 664, 965
policy 626, 692
polish *smooth* 255

rub 331
furbish 658
beauty 845
ornament 847
taste 850
politeness 894
– off *finish* 729
Polish bank 840
polished
– *language* 578
fashionable 852
polite 894
polisson 949
polite 894
offensive to ears –
 579
– literature 560
– society 852
politic *wise* 498
 cunning 702
 cautious 864
body –
 mankind 372
 government 737
political economy
 692
politician
 director 694
 proficient 700
politics 702
polity *conduct* 692
 authority 737
 duty 926
polka 840
poll 85, 609
 – tax 812
pollard 193, 201
 tree 367
Poll-parrot 584
pollute *soil* 653
 corrupt 659
 disgrace 874
pollution
 disease 655
 vice 945
Pollyanna 858
polo 840
polonaise 840
poltroon 862
polyandry 903
polychord 417
polychromatic 428,
 440
polychrome 440,
 556
polygamy 903
polygastric 191
polyglot 522, 560
polygon
 buildings 189
 figure 244

polygraphy 590
polylogy 573
polymorphic 81
polyphonism 580
polypus 250
polyscope 445
polysyllable 561
polytheism 984
pomade 356
pomatum 356
pommel
 support 215
 round 249
 beat 972
Pomona 369
pomp 882
pom-pom 727
pomposity 882
pompous
 language 577
poncho 225
pond 343, 636
 fish – 370
ponder 451
ponderable 316,
 319
ponderation 319,
 480
ponderous 319
 – *style* 574, 579
 dull 843
pondus fumo, dare
 – 481
poniard 727
pons asinorum 519,
 704
pontifical 995
pontificals 999
pontificate 995
pontiff 996
pontoon
 vehicle 272
 boat 273
 way 627
pony 271
poodle 366
pooh, pooh!
 unimportance 643
 contempt 930
pool *lake* 343
 combination 709
 prize 775
 billiards 840
poop 235
poor *weak* 160
 - *reasoning* 477
 - *style* 575
 insufficient 640
 trifling 643
 indigent 804
 unhappy 828

cut a – figure 874
 – hand 701
 – head 499
 – house 189
 – man 804
 – in spirit 881
 – stick 501
 – thing 914
poorly 160, 655
 – off 804
poor-spirited 862
pop *noise* 406
 unexpected 508
 – at 716
 – in *ingress* 294
 insertion 300
 – off *die* 360
 – a question 461
 – the question
  request 765
 endearment 902
 – upon *arrive* 292
 discover 480a
Pope
 infallibility 474
 priest 996
Popedom 995
Pope Joan 840
Popery 984
pop-gun *trifle* 643
popinjay 854
poplar *tall* 206
poppy *sedative* 174
populace 876
popular
 in demand 865
 celebrated 873
 favourite 897
 approved 931
 – opinion 488
popularis, aura –
 873
popularize
 render intelligible
  518
 facilitate 705
 make pleasant
  829
populate 184
population 188, 372
populi, vox –
 publication 531
 election 609
 authority 737
populous
 crowded 72
 multitude 102
 presence 186
porcelain
 baked 384
 sculpture 557

safety 664
preparation 673
precede
superior 33
- *in order* 62
- *in time* 116
- *in motion* 280
precedence 873
precedent
[see precede]
prototype 22
precursor 64
habit 613
legal decision 969
follow -s 82
precentor 694, 996
precept *adage* 496
maxim **697**
order 641
permit 760
preceptor 540
precession 62, **280**
précieuse ridicule
855
precinct *region* 181
place 182
environs 227
boundary 233
precious *great* 31
excellent 648
valuable 814
beloved 897
- *metals* 800
- *stone* 648, 847
precipice
vertical 212
slope 217
dangerous 667
on the verge of
a - 665
precipitancy 684,
863
precipitate
early 132
sink 308
consolidate 321
refuse 653
haste 684
rash 863
- *oneself* 306
precipitous 217
précis 596
precise *exact* 494
preciosity 578
precisely
literally 19
assent 488
precisianism
affectation 855
heterodoxy 984
over-religious 988

preclude 55, 706
precocious
early 132
immature 674
pert 885
rude 895
precognition
forethought 490
knowledge 510
preconceived idea
481
preconception 481
preconcert 611, 626
preconcertation 673
precursor
- *in order* 62, **64**
- *in time* 116
predict 511
predatory 789, 791
predecessor 64
predeliberation
510, 611
predella 215
predesigned 611
predestination
fate 152
necessity 601
predetermination
611
Deity 976
predetermination
611
predial
land 342
agriculture 371
manorial 780
predicament 8, 75
predicate
affirm 535
preach 998
prediction **511**
predilection
bias 481
affection 820
desire 865
predispose 615, 673
predisposed
willing 602
predisposition 176,
820
predominant 175,
737
predominate 33
pre-eminent 33, 873
pre-emption 795
preen 847
pre-engage 132
pre-engagement
768
pre-establish 626
pre-examine 461

pre-exist 1, 116
preface 62, 64
prefect 745, 759
prefecture 737
prefer *choose* 609
- *a claim* 969
- *a petition* 765
preference 62
preferment
improvement 658
ecclesiastical -
995
prefigure 511
prefix 62, 64
letter 561
pre-glacial 124
pregnable 158
pregnant
producing 161
productive 168
predicting 511
- *style* 572
important 642
- *with meaning*
516
prehensile 789
prehension 789
pre-historic 124
pre-instruct 537
prejudge 481
prejudicate 481
prejudice
misjudge 481
evil 619
detriment 659
prejudicial 481, 649
prelacy 995
prelate 996
prelation 609
prelection 537, 582
prelector 540
preliminaries:
settle - 673
- of peace 723
preliminary 62, 64
prelude 62, 64
beginning 66
music 415
premature 132, 674
premeditate 611,
620
prémices 154
premier 694, 759
- *pas* 66
premiership 693
premise *prefix* 62
precede 116
announce 511
premises
precursor 64
prior 116

ground 182
evidence 467
logic 476
premium
debt 805
receipt 810
reward 783
at a - 814
premonish 668
premonitory 511,
668
Premonstratensian
996
premonstration
appearance 448
prediction 511
manifestation 525
premunire 742, 974
prendre la balle au
bond 134
prenotion
misjudgment 481
foresight 510
prensation 789
prentice 541
prenticeship 539
preoccupancy
possession 777
preoccupation
inattention 458
preoption 609
preordain 152, 601
preparation **673**
music 413
instruction 537
in - 730
in course of - 626
preparatory
preceding 62
prepare the way
facilitate 705
prepared *expectant*
507
ready 698
preparing
destined 152
prepense
spontaneous 600
predetermined
611
intended 620
malice - 907
prepollence 157
πρέπον, τό - 850,
926
preponderance
superiority 33
influence 175
dominance 737
prepossessed
obstinate 606

prepossessing 829
prepossession
  prejudice 481
  possession 777
preposterous
  great 31
  absurd 497
  exaggerated 549
  ridiculous 853
  undue 925
prepotency 157
pre-Raphaelite 122, 124, 556
pre-require 630
pre-resolve 611
prerogative 737, 924
presage 511, 512
presbyopia 443
presbyter 996
Presbyterian 984
presbytery 995, 996, 1000
prescience 510
prescious 511
prescribe *direct* 693
  advice 695
  order 741
  entitle 924
  enjoin 926
prescript 697, 741
prescription
  remedy 662
prescriptive *old* 124
  unchanged 141
  habitual 613
  due 924
presence
  in space **186**
  appearance 448
  breeding 894
  in the – of
  near 197
  real – 998
  saving one's – 928
  – of God 981
  – of mind 826, 864
presence-chamber 191
present
  - *in time* 118
  - *in space* 186
  offer 763
  give 784
  church prefer-ment 995
  at – 118
  these –s 590, 592
  – arms 894, 928
  – a bold front 861

– a front 719
– itself *event* 151
  visible 446
  thought 451
– oneself
  presence 186
  offer 763
  courtesy 894
– to the mind 457, 505
  – *time* **118**
  instant 113
– to the view 448
presentable 852
presentation 883, 894
presentiment
  instinct 477
  prejudgment 481
  foresight 510
presently 132
presentment
  information 527
  law proceeding 969
preservation
  continuance 141
  conservation **670**
  Divine attributes 976
preserve *sweets* 396
preserver 664
preshow 511
preside 693, 737
presidency 737
president 694, 745
press *crowd* 72
  closet 191
  weight 319
  public - 531
  printing 591
  book 593
  move 615
  compel 744
  offer 763
  solicit 765
  go to – 591
  under – of 744
  writer for the – 593
  – of business 682
  – one hard 716
  – in 300
  – on *course* 109
  progression 282
  haste 684
  – into the service 677, 707
  – out 301
press-agent 599
pressed: hard – 704

– for time 684
press-gang 965
pressing *need* 630
  urgent 642
pressure *power* 157
  influence 175
  weight 319
  urgency 642
  exertion 686
  adversity 735
  centre of – 222
  high – 824
  work under – 684
Prester John 515
prestidigitation 545
prestidigitator 548
prestige *bias* 481
  authority 737
  fascination 865
  fame 873
prestigiation 545
prestissimo 415
presto
  instantly 113
  music 415
prestriction 442
presumable 472
presume
  misjudge 481
  believe 484
  suppose 514
  hope 858
  pride 878
presumption
  [see *presume*]
  probability 472
  expectation 507
  rashness 863
  arrogance 885
  unlawfulness 925
presumptive
  probable 472
  supposed 514
  due 924
  heir – 779
  – evidence
  evidence 467
  probability 472
presumptuous 885
presuppose
  misjudge 481
  suppose 514
presurmise 510, 514
pretence
  imitation 19
  falsehood 544
  untruth 546
  excuse 617
  ostentation 882
  boast 884

pretend *assert* 535
  simulate 544, 546
pretended 545
pretender
  deceiver 548
  braggart 884
  unentitled 925
pretending 544
pretension
  ornament 577
  affectation 855
  due 924
pretentious
  affected 855
  vain 880
  ostentatious 882
  boasting 884
  undue 925
preterite 121
preterition **122**
preterlapsed 122
pretermit 460
preternatural 83
preterperfect 122
pretext 546, 617
pretty
  much 31
  imperfectly 651
  beautiful 845
  – fellow 501
  – good 651
  – kettle of fish, pass &c. 59, 704
  – well *much* 31
  little 32
  trifling 643
preux chevalier 939
prevail *exist* 1
  superior 33
  general 78
  influence 175
  habit 613
  succeed 731
  – upon 615
prevailing 78
  – taste 852
prevalence
  [see *prevail*]
prevaricate 544
prévenance 894
prevenient 62, 132
prevention
  prejudice 481
  hindrance 706
  – of waste 817
preventive 55
preventorium 656
previous 116
  move the – question 624
  not within –

nag 271
strike 276
beverage 298
engrave 558
vigour 574
Punch buffoon 844
– and Judy 599,
840
punchbowl
vessel 191
hollow 252
tippling 959
puncheon
vessel 191
perforator 262
punchinello 599
punctated 440
punctilio 852
punctilious
exact 494
observant 772
ostentation 882
scrupulous 939
puncto 882
punctual early 132
periodical 138
exact 494
observance 772
scrupulous 939
punctuation 567
puncture 260
pundit
learned man 492,
500
lawyer 968
pungency 392
physical energy
171
taste 392
pungent taste 392
odour 398
vigour 574
feeling 821
wit 842
Punica fides 940
punishment 972
punition 972
punk 962
punkah 349
punnet 191
punster 844
punt 267, 273
punter 621
puny 193
pup infant 129
give birth 161
dog 366
pupil 541
– of the eye 441
pupilage youth 127
learning 539

pupillari, in statu –
541
puppet little 193
dupe 547
effigy 554
auxiliary 711
tool 746
make a – of 737
be the – of 749
puppet-show 599,
840
puppy dog 366
fop 854
braggart 884
blusterer 887
puppyism 855
pur: – sang 875
Purana 986
purblind 443, 481
purchase
support 215
acquisition 775
buy **795**
purchase-money
147
purchaser 795
purdah 374, 531
pure simple 42
true 494
truthful 543
– style 576, 578
clean 652
artless 703
– taste 850
honourable 939
virtuous 944
innocent 946
chaste 960
devout 987, 990
– accent 580
– colour 428
– and simple 42
purée 298
purely 31, 32
purgation
cleansing 652
atonement 952
purgative 652
purgatory
suffering 828
atonement 952
hell 982
purge cast out 297
clean 652
atone 952
purification 998
purify 652, 658
puris naturalibus,
in – 226
purist style 578
affected 855

Pharisee 988
Puritan 984, 988
puritanical
strict 739
affected 855
ascetic 955
purity 960
[see pure]
purl drink 298
stream 348
faint sound 405
music 416
purlieus 197, 227
purloin 791
purple
violet **437**
insignia 747
– and fine linen
377
purport 516, 600
purpose 620
at cross –s 523
infirm of – 605
to little or no –
645
on – 620
serve a – 644
to some – 731
tenacity of – 604a
purposeless 621
purpure 437
purr 412
purse 800, 802
long – 803
put into one's –
785
– up 195
purse-bearer 801
purse-proud 878
purser 801
purse strings:
draw the – 808
open the – 809
pursuant to 620
pursue continue 143
follow 281
aim 622
– a course 680
– an inquiry 461
– the tenor of
one's way 625,
881
pursuer 622
pursuit 622
pursuivant 534
pursy 194
purulent 653
purvey 637
purview 620
pus 653
Puseyite 984

push exigency 8
impel 276
progress 282
propel 284
essay 675
activity 682
haste 684
come to the – 704
– aside 460, 929
– forward 682, 707
– from 289
– to the last 133
– on haste 684
– out eject 297
pushing 282, 284,
682
pusillanimity 862
puss 366
play – in the
corner 148
pussy-foot 528, 958
pustule 250, 848
put place 184
fool 501
cards 840
clown 876
neatly – 576
– across 484
– about
turn back 283
go round 311
publish 531
– aside
exclude 55
inattention 458
neglect 460
disuse 678
– away
– thought 452
relinquish 782
divorce 905
– back
turn back 283
deteriorate 659
restore 660
– before 527
– by 636
– a case 82, 514
– in commission
755
– a construction
on 522
– on the cuff 806
– down
destroy 162
record 551
conquer 731
compel 744
pay 807
humiliate 874
– an end to

angry 900
censure 932
punish 972
– out *affirm* 535
voice 580
speak 582
– out oaths 885, 908
rapacity
  taking 789
  stealing 791
  avarice 819
  greed 865
rape 791, 961
– oil 356
rapid 274
– slope 217
– strides
  progress 282
  velocity 274
– *succession* 136
rapids 348
rapier 727
rapine 791
rapparee 792
rappel 722
rapping, spirit – 992
rapport 9
rapports, sous tous les – 494
rapprochement 714, 888
rapscallion 949
rapt *attention* 457
  inattention 458
  emotion 821
– in thought 451
raptorial 789, 791
rapture 827, 897
rapturous 827
rara avis
  exceptional 83
  good 648
  famous 873
rare *exceptional* 83
  few 103
  infrequent 137
  light 322
  excellent 648
raree show 448, 840
rarefaction 194, 322
rari nantes 103
rarity **322**
rasa, tabula – 552
rascal 941, 949
rascality 940
rase *obliterate* 552
rash
  skin disease 655
  reckless 863

rasher 204
rashness **863**
rasp 330, 331
rasper *difficult* 704
rasure 552
rat *recant* 607
  smell a –
    discover 480a
    doubt 485
rataplan 407
rat-a-tat 407
ratchet 253
rate *degree* 26
  motion 264
  measure 466
  estimation 480
  price, tax 812
  abuse 932
  at a great – 274
rath *early* 132
  fort 717
rather 32, 643
  have – 609
  – good 651
  have – not 867
ratification
  confirm 467
  affirm 488
  consent 762
  compact 769
ratio *relation* 9
  degree 26
  proportion 84
  apportionment 786
ratiocination 476
ration *quantity* 25
  food 298
  provisions 637
  allotment 786
  short –s 956
rational
  – *quantity* 84
  intellectual 450
  judicious 498
  sane 502
rationale *cause* 153
  attribution 155
  answer 462
  interpretation 322
rationalism 476, 989
rationalization 60
rats in the upper story 503
rattan 975
ratten 158
rattle *noise* 407
  music 417
  prattle 584
  death – 360

  watchman's – 669
– on 584
rattle-snake 913
rattle-traps 780
rattling 836
– pace 274
raucity 405, 410
raucous *hoarse* 581
ravage 162, 659
ravages of time 659
rave *madness* 503
  excitement 824, 825
– against 932
ravel *untwist* 60
  derange 61
  entangle 219
  difficulty 704
ravelin 717
ravelled 59
raven *black* 431
  hoarse 581
  gorge 957
– for 865
ravening 173, 865
ravenous 789, 865
raver 504
ravine *interval* 198
  narrow 203
  dike 259
  channel 350
raving *mad* 503
  feeling 821
  excitement 824, 825
ravish *seize* 789
  please 829
ravished
  pleased 827
ravishment 824
raw *immature* 123
  sensitive 378
  cold 383
  colour 428
  unprepared 674
  unskilled 699
– head and bloody bones 860
– levies 726
– material 635
raw-boned 203
ray 420
– of comfort 831
rayah 745
rayless 421
raze 162
– to the ground 308
razor 253
  cut a whetstone with a – 638

misuse 679
unskilful 699
keen as a – 821
razzia
  destruction 162
  attack 716
  plunder 791
re, in – 9
reabsorb 296
reach *degree* 26
  equal 27
  distance 196
  fetch 270
  arrive at 292
  river 348
  deceive 545
  grasp 737
  take 789
  within – *near* 197
  possible 470
– the ear
  hearing 418
  information 527
– of thought 498
– to *distance* 196
  length 200
reach-me-down 673
reaction
  compensation 30
  reversion 145
  counteraction 179
  recoil 277
  restoration 660
reactionary 145, 607
reactionist 710
read 522, 539
  well – 490
– a lecture 537
readable 578
reader *teacher* 540
  printer 591
  clergyman 996
readership 542
readily 705
reading
  speciality 79
  knowledge 490
  interpretation 522
  learning 539
– glass 445
– in 995
reading-desk 1000
readjust 23, 27
readmit 296
ready
  expecting 507
  willing 602
  useful 644
  prepare 673

assent 488
concord 714
retaliate 718
reciprocity 709
recision 38
recital 415
recitativo 415
recite
  enumerate 85
  speak 582
  narrate 594
reck 459
reckless
  careless 460
  defiant 715
  rash 863
recklessly profuse
  818
reckon *count* 85
  – among 76
  – upon 484, 507
  – with 807
  – without one's
    host
  unskilful 699
  fail 732
  rash 863
reckoning
  numeration 85
  measure 466
  expectation 507
  payment 807
  accounts 811
  reward 973
  day of – 919
  out of one's – 704
reclaim *restore* 660
  command 741
  due 924
  atonement 952
reclaimed
  penitent 950
recline *lie flat* 213
  depress 308
  repose 687
  – on 215
recluse 893
recognition
  [*see* recognize]
  courtesy 894
  thanks 916
  means of – 550
recognizable 446,
  518
  – by 550
recognizance 771
recognize *see* 441
  attention 457
  discover 480a
  assent 488
  know 490

remember 505
understand 518
permit 760
recognized
  influential 175
  customary 613
  – maxim 496
recoil *reaction* 179
  repercussion **277**
  reluctance 603
  shun 623
  from which
    reason –s 471
  – at *hate* 898
  – from *dislike* 867
recollect 505
recommence 66
recommend 695,
  931
  – itself
  approbation 931
recompense 790,
  973
reconcile *agree* 23
  pacify 723
  content 831
  forgive 918
  – oneself to 826
recondite 519, 528
recondition 660,
  790
reconnaissance 441
reconnoitre 441,
  461
reconsideration 451
  on – 658
reconstitute 660
reconstruct 660
reconvert 660
record **551**
  break the – 33
  court of – 966
  gramophone – 551
recorder **553**
  judge 967
recount 594
recoup 30, 790
recourse 677
recovery
  improvement 658
  reinstatement 660
  getting back 775
  restitution 790
  – of strength 689
recreant
  coward 862
  base 940
  knave 941
  vicious 945
  bad man 949
recreation 840

recrement 653
recriminate 932
recrimination 938
recrudescence 661
recruit *strength* 159
  learner 541
  provision 637
  health 654
  repair 658
  reinstate 660
  refresh 689
  aid 707
  auxiliary 711
  soldier 726
  beat up for –s
    673, 707
rectangle 244
rectangular 214,
  244
rectify
  straighten 246
  improve 658
  re-establish 660
rectilinear 346
rectitude 939, 944
rector 694, 996
rectorship 995
rectory 1000
rectus in curiâ 946
reculer pour mieux
  sauter 673, 702
reculons, à – 283
recumbent 213, 217
recuperation 790
recuperative 660
recur
  repeat 104
  frequent 136
  periodic 138
  – to the mind 505
  – to 677
recure 660
recursion 292
recurvity 245
recusant
  dissenting 489
  denying 536
  disobedient 742
  refusing 764
  impenitent 951
  heterodox 984
red 434
  paint the town –
    840
  turn – *feeling* 821
  – book *list* 86
  – coat 726
  – cross 662
  – flag 668
  – hot *great* 31
  violent 173

hot 382
  emotion 821
  excited 824
  – letter 550, 883
  –letter day
  important 642
  rest 687
  amusement 840
  celebration 883
  – light 669
  – rag to a bull 900
  – republican 742
  – tape 613
  – tapist 694
  – and yellow 439
redact 590, 658
redan 717
redargue 479
red cap 271
redden *colour* 434
  humble 879
  angry 900
reddition
  interpretation 522
  restitution 790
redeem
  compensate 30
  substitute 147
  reinstate 660
  deliver 672
  regain 775
  restore 790
  pay 807
  atone 952
  – from oblivion
    505
  – one's pledge
    772, 926
Redeemer 976
redemption
  [*see* redeem]
  liberation 750
  duty 926
  salvation 976
red-handed
  murder 361
  in the act 680
  guilty 947
redict 905
redingote 225
redintegrate 660
redintegratio
  amoris 607
redivivus 660
redness **434**
redolence
  odour 398
  fragrance 400
redouble
  increase 35
  duplication 90

repeat 104
– one's efforts 686
redoubt 717
redoubtable 860
redound to
  conduce 176
  – one's honour
  glory 873
  approbation 931
  honour 939
redress *restore* 660
  remedy 662
  reward 973
red-tape 694, 739
reduce *lessen* 36
  – *in number* 103
  weaken 160
  contract 195
  shorten 201
  lower 308
  subdue 731
  discount 813
  – to ashes 384
  – to demonstra-
    tion 478
  – to a mean 29
  – to order 60
  – to poverty 804
  – to powder 330
  – the speed 275
  – in strength 160
  – to subjection 749
  – to *convert* 144
  – to writing 551
reduced [*see* reduce]
  impoverished 804
  – to the last ex-
    tremity 665
  – to a skeleton 659
  – to straits 704
reductio ad absur-
  dum 476, 479
reduction
  [*see* reduce]
  arithmetical 85
  conversion 144
  at a – 815
  – of temperature
    385
redundance
  diffuseness 573
  too much **641**
redundancy 104
reduplication 19, 90
re-echo *imitate* 19
  repeat 104
  resonance 408
reechy 653
reed *weak* 160
  pan 590
  arrow 727

trust to a broken –
  699
  – *instrument* 417
reef *slacken* 275
  shoal 346
  danger 667
  take in a – 664
  double – topsails
    664
reefer 269
reek *gas* 334
  vaporize 336
  liquid 337
  hot 382
  fester 653
reeking 339, 653
reel *rock* 314
  agitate 315, 851
  dance 840
  – back *yield* 725
re-embody
  junction 43
  combination 48
re-enter 245
re-entrant angle
  244
re-establish 660
re-estate 660
refashion 163
refect
  strengthen 159
refection
  meal 298
  refreshment 689
  (*restoration* 660)
refectory 191
refer to *relate* 9
  include 76
  attribute 155
  cite 467
  allude 521
  take advice 695
referable 9, 155
referee
  judgment 480
  judge 967
reference
  [*see* refer]
referendary 967
referendum 480,
  609
  ad – 461, 605
referrible 9, 155
refine *clean* 652
  – upon 658
refined *colour* 428
  fashionable 852
refinement
  discrimination
    465
  wisdom 498

elegance 578, 845
  improvement 658
  taste 850
  over– 477
refit 660
reflect *imitate* 19
  think 451
  – *dishonour* 874
  – *light* 420
  – upon *censure* 932
reflecting 498
reflection 408, 453
reflector *mirror* 445
reflex *copy* 21
  recoil 277
  regressive 283
reflexion 21, 277
  light 420
refluence *recoil* 277
  regress 283
reflux *decrease* 36
  recoil 277
  regress 283
  current 348
refocillate
  strengthen 159
  refresh 689
reform *convert* 144
  improve 658
reformatory 542,
  752
reformer 658
refound 144
refraction
  deviation 279
  light 420
  fallacy of vision
    443
refractory
  obstinate 606
  difficult 704
  mutinous 742
  ill-tempered 901a
refrain *poetry* 597
  avoid 623
  do nothing 681
  temperate 953
  – from laughter
    837
  – from voting
    609a
refrain 104
refresh
  strengthen 159
  cool 385
  refit 658
  restore 660
  recruit 689
  relieve 834
  – the memory 505

refreshing 377, 829
refreshment
  food 298
  recruiting **689**
  delight 827
refrigeration
  anæsthetic 376
  making cold **385**
refrigerator **387**
reft 44
refuge **666**
refugee 268, 623
refulgence 420
refund 807
refurbish 673
refusal **764**
  pre-emption 795
refuse *remains* 40
  useless 645
  not consent 764
  – *assent* 489
  – to associate with
    893
  – to believe 487
  – to hear 460
refute 479
refuted 495
regain 775
  – breath 689
regal 737
regale *feast* 298
  physical pleasure
    377
  refresh 689
  pleasing 829
  amusement 840
regalia 747
regality 737
regard
  relation 9
  view 441
  attention 457
  judge 480
  credit 873
  love 897
  respect 928
  approbation 931
  have – to 457
  merit – 642
  pay – to
  believe 484
  honour 873
  – as 484
regardful 457, 459
regardless 458, 823
regards 894, 928
regatta 720, 840
regency 755
regenerate
  reproduce 163
  restore 660

– and left 180, 227, 236
– line 246
– man in the right place 23
in one's – mind 498, 502
hit the – nail on the head 480*a*, 698
– owner 779
keep the – path 944
in the – place 646
– thing to do 926
– as a trivet 650
– word in the right place 578
right about: to the – 283
go to the – 311, 607
send to the –
eject 297
reject 610
refuse 764
turn to the – 218, 279
right hand
power 157
dextrality 238
help 711
not let the – know what the left is doing 528
– of friendship 888
righteous 944
the – 987
– overmuch 988
Righteousness:
Lord our – 976
Sun of – 976
rightful 922
– owner 779
rightly served, be – 972
right-minded 939, 944
rights 748
put to – 660
set to – 60
stand on one's – 748
rigid *regular* 82
hard 323
exact 494
severe 739
rigmarole 517, 573
rigor 383
– mortis 360
rigorous *exact* 494

severe 739
revengeful 919
rigour 494, 739
Rigsdag 696
rigueur
de – 744
rile *annoy* 830
hate 898
anger 900
rilievo *convex* 250
sculpture 557
rill 348
rim 231
rime *chink* 198
frost 283
rimer 262
rimple 258
rind 223
ring
fastening 45
pendency 214
circle 247
loud 404
resonance 408
test 463
combination 709
clique 712
arena 728, 840
badge 747
rub the – 992
have the true – 494
– the changes
repeat 104
change 140
changeable 149
– in the ear 408
in a – fence 229, 232
– with the praises of 931
– the tocsin 669
– up 527
ringleader
director 694
mutineer 742
ringlet 247, 256
rink 840
rinse 652
rinsings 653
riot *confusion* 59
derangement 61
violence 173
discord 713
resist 719
mutiny 742
run – *activity* 682
excitement 825
intemperance 954
– in *pleasure* 742
rioter 742

riotous 173
rip 949, 962
– open 260
– up *tear* 44
recall the past 505
excite 824
Rip van Winkle 130
riparian 342
ripe 673
– age *old* 128
ripen *perfect* 650
improve 658
prepare 673
complete 729
– into 144
rippet 713
riposte 462
ripple *ruffle* 256
shake 315
water 348
murmur 405
ripuarian 342
rire, pour – 853
rise *grow* 35
begin 66
slope 217
progress 282
ascend 305
stir 682
revolt 742
– again 660
– in arms 722
– from 154
– to the occasion 612
– in price 814
– up *elevation* 307
– in the world 734
risible 838, 853
rising [*see* rise]
– of the curtain 66, 448
– generation 127, 167
– ground
height 206
slope 217
worship the – sun 886
risk *chance* 621
danger 665
invest 787
at any – 604
risqué 961
rissole 298
risum teneatis amici? 853
rite 963, **998**
funeral – 363
ritornello 64, 104

ritual
ostentation 882
rite 998
ritualism 984
rival
emulate 648
oppose 708
opponent 710
compete 720
combatant 726
outshine 873
rivalry *envy* 921
rive 44
rivel 258
river 348
rivet 43, 45
– the attention 457, 824
– the eyes upon 441
– in the memory 505
– the yoke 739
riveted *firm* 150
rivulet 348
rixation 713
Ro 560
road *street* 189
direction 278
way 627
on the –
transference 270
progression 282
approach 286
on the high – to 278
– to ruin
destruction 162
danger 665
adversity 735
road-book 266
roads *lake* 343
roadstead 154
abode 189
refuge 666
roadster 271
roadway 627
roam 266
roan *horse* 271
colour 433
roar *violence* 173
wind 349
sound 404, 407
bellow 411, 412
laugh 838
weep 839
roaring *great* 31
– trade 731, 734
roast *heat* 384
ridicule 856
rib – 972

roseate *red* 434
　hopeful 858
rose-coloured
　hope 858
Rosetta stone 522
rosette 847
rose-water
　moderation 174
　flattery 933
　not made with –
　704
Rosicrucian
　sect 984
　sorcerer 994
rosin *rub* 331
　resin 356*a*
Rosinante 271
roster 86
rostrum *beak* 234
　pulpit 542
rosy 434
　– *wine* 959
rosy-cheeked 845
rot *decompose* 49
　absurdity 497
　rubbish 517
　putrefy 653
　disease 655
　decay 659
rota 86, 138
Rotarian 892
rotate 138
rotation 312
　periodicity 138
rote, by – 505
　know – 490
　learn – 539
rôti 298
rôtisserie 189
rotogravure 531,
　558
rotten *weak* 160
　bad 649
　foul 653
　decayed 659
　– at the core
　deceptive 545
　diseased 655
　– *borough* 893
rotulorum, custos –
　553
rotund 249
rotunda 189
rotundity 249
roturier 876
roué 949
rouge 434, 847
rouge-et-noir 621
rough *violent* 173
　shapeless 241
　uneven 256

pungent 392
unsavoury 395
sour 397
sound 410
unprepared 674
fighter 726
ugly 846
low fellow 876
bully 887
churlish 895
evil-doer 913
bad man 949
cut up – 900
– copy *writing* 590
unprepared 674
– diamond
uncouth 241
unprepared 674
artless 703
vulgar 851
commonalty 876
good man 948
– draft 626
– guess 514
– it 686
– sea 348
– side of the
　tongue 932
– and tumble 59
– weather 173, 349
rough-cast 256
　covering 223
　shape 240
　scheme 626
　unpolished 674
rough-hew 240, 673
roughly
　nearly 197
rough-neck 876,
　887
roughness 256
rough-rider 268
roughshod over,
　ride – 739
roulade 415
rouleau
　assemblage 72
　cylinder 249
　money 800
roulette 621, 840
round *series* 69
　revolution 138
　- *of a ladder* 215
　curve 245
　circle 247
　rotund 249
　music 415
　fight 720
　all – 227
　bring – 660
　come –

periodic 138
recant 607
persuade 615
dizzy – 312
get – 660
go – 311
go one's –s 266
go the –
　publication 531
make the – of 311
run the – of 682
go the same – 104
turn – *invert* 218
retreat 283
revolve 311
– assertion 535
– a corner 311
– dance 840
– game 840
– hand 590
– like a horse in a
　mill 613
– of the ladder 71
– number 84, 102
in – numbers 29,
　197
– pace 274
– of pleasures
　377, 840
– robin
　information 527
　petition 765
　censure 932
– and round 138,
　312
– sum 800
– terms 566
– trot 274
– up 370
– of visits 892
round about
　circumjacent 227
　deviation 279
　circuit 311
　amusement 840
　– phrases 573
　– way 729
rounded periods
　577, 578
roundelay 597
rounders 840
round-house 752
roundlet 247
round-shouldered
　243
roup 796
rouse 615, 824
　– oneself 682
rousing 171
rout *crowd* 72
　agitation 315

overcome 731
discomfit 732
rabble 876
assembly 892
put to the – 731
– out 652
route 627
en – 270
en – for 282
routine
　uniform 16
　order 58
　rule 80
　periodic 138
　custom 613
　business 625
rove *travel* 266
　deviate 279
rover *traveller* 268
　pirate 792
roving commission
　475
row *disorder* 59
　series 69
　violence 173
　street 189
　navigate 267
　discord 713
　– in the same
　　boat 88
rowdy *vulgar* 851,
　876
　blusterer 887
　bad man 949
rowel 253, 615
rower 269
rowlock 215
royal 737
　– blue 438
　– highness 877
　– road 627, 705
Royal Academician
　559
royalist 737
royaliste que le roi,
　plus 33
royalty 737
Rt. Hon. 877
ruade *impulse* 276
　attack 716
ruat cœlum 908
rub *friction* 331
　touch 379
　difficulty 704
　adversity 735
　painful 830
　– off corners 82
　– down *lessen* 195
　powder 330
　– down with an
　　oaken towel 972

– one's eyes 870
– one's hands 838
– up the memory 505
– off 552
– on *slow* 275
progress 282
inexcitable 826
– out 552
– up 658
– up the wrong way 713
rubadub 407
rubber 325
whist 840
rubber boots 225
rubber hose 975
rubber-stamp 82
rubbish
absurdity 497
unmeaning 517
trifling 643
useless 645
rubble 645
rube 876
rubescence 434
Rubicon *limit* 233
pass the –
begin 66
cross 303
choose 609
rubicund 434
rubify 434
rubigo 653
rubric 550, 697, 998
rubricate
redden 434
ruby *red* 434
gem 648
ornament 847
ruck 29, 258
in the – 235
rucksack 191
ructation 297
rudder 273, 693
rudderless 158
ruddle 434
ruddy *red* 434
beautiful 845
rude *violent* 173
shapeless 241
ignorant 491
inelegant 579
ugly 846
vulgar 851
uncivilized 876
uncivil 895
disrespect 929
– health 654
rudera 645
rudiment 66, 153

rudimental 193, 674
rudimentary 66
rudiments 490, 542
rudis indigestaque moles 59, 241
rue *bitter* 395
regret 833
repent 950
rueful 830, 837
ruff 225
ruffian 876
blusterer 876
maleficent 913
scoundrel 949
ruffianism 851, 907
ruffle *disorder* 59
derange 61
roughen 259
fold 258
feeling 821
excite 824, 825
pain 830
anger 900
rufous 434
rug 215, 223
Rugby
football 840
rugged
shapeless 241
rough 256
difficult 704
ugly 846
churlish 895
rugose 256
ruin *destruction* 162
evil 619
failure 732
adversity 735
poverty 804
ruined
bankrupt 808
hopeless 859
ruinous
painful 830
ruins *remains* 40
rule *mean* 29
regularity **80**
influence 175
length 200
measure 466
decide 480
custom 613
precept 697
government 737
law 963
absence of – 699
as a – 613
by – 82
golden – 697
obey –s 82

– of three 85
– of thumb
experiment 463
unreasoning 477
essay 675
unskilled 699
ruler 745
ruling 697, 969
– passion 606, 820
rum *liquor* 298
queer 853
– running 964
rumba 840
rumble 407
ruminate
chew 298
think 451
rummage 461
rummer 191
rumour 531, 532
rump 235
rumple
disorder 59
derange 61
roughen 256
fold 258
rumpus
confusion 59
violence 173
discord 713
run *generality* 78
repetition 104
continuance 106, 143
course 109
eventuality 151
motion 264
speed 274
sequence 281
liquefy 335
flow 348
habit 613
smuggle 791
contraband 964
have a – 852, 873
have – of 748
near – 197
ordinary – 29
race is – 729
time –s 106
– abreast 27
– after 622, 873
– against 276, 708, 716
– at 716
– away 623
– away with 789, 791
– away with a notion
misjudge 481

credulous 486
– back 283
– a chance
probable 472
chance 621
– counter to 468, 708
– its course
course 109
complete 729
past 122
– into danger 665
– into debt 806
– down
underestimate 483
pursue 622
bad 649
finished 678
attack 716
depreciate 932
detract 934
– dry 638, 640
– the eye over 441, 539
– the fingers over 379
– foul of 276
– the gauntlet 861
– on in a groove 613
– hard *danger* 665
difficult 704
success 731
– in the head 451, 505
– high *great* 31
violent 173
– in *introduce* 228
– into
conversion 144
insert 300
– low 36
– of luck 156, 734
– mad 503, 825
– mad after 865
– like mad 274
– of the mill 29
– amuck
violent 173
kill 361
mad 503
attack 716
– on 143
– out *end* 67
course 109
past 122
antiquated 124
egress 295
prodigal 818
- out on 573
– over *count* 85

saddle 215
  in the – 673
  – on 37, 43
  – on the right
    horse
  discovery 480a
  skill 698
  right 922
  fair 939
  – with *add* 37
  attribute 155
  quarter on 184
  clog 706
  impose a duty
    926
  accuse 938
  – on the wrong
    horse 495, 699
  – up 293
saddle-bags 191
Sadducee 984
sadness, in – 535
safe *cupboard* 191
  hiding place 530
  secure 664
  treasury 802
  cautious 864
  – conduct 631
  – conscience 926,
    946
  – deposit 636
  – keeping 670
  – and sound 654
  on the – side 864
safety 664
  – bicycle 272
  – curtain 599
  – first 665, 864
  – match 388
  – valve 666
saffron *colour* 436
sag 214, 217, 245
saga 594
sagacious 498, 510
sage 498, **500**
  – maxim 496
saggar 386
sagittal 253
sagittary 83
sagum 225
Sahara 169
sahib 373, 745, 875
saick 273
said *preceding* 62
  repeated 104
  prior 116
  it is – 532
  thou hast – 488
  more easily – than
    done 704
sail *navigate* 267

ship 273
set out 293
  easy – 174
  full – 274
  press of – 274
  shorten – 275
  take in – 174
  take the wind out
    of one's –s 706
  too much – 863
  under – 267
  – before the wind
    734
  – near the wind
    698
  – too near the
    wind 863
sailing: plain – 705
  – vessel 273
sailor 269
  fair weather – 701
saint *angel* 977
  revelation 985
  piety 987
  false piety 988
  tutelary – 664
Saint Monday 840
saintly 944, 987
sais quoi, je ne –
  563
sake:
  for the – of 615,
    707
  for goodness – 765
salaam
  bow 308
  submit 725
  courtesy 894
  respect 928
salacity 961
salad 41
  – oil 356
salade 717
salamander 386
salariat 875
salary 973
sale 796
  bill of – 771
  for – *offer* 763
  barter 794
saleable 796
salebrosity 256
salesman 797
salient
  projecting 250
  sharp 253
  manifest 525
  important 642
  – angle 244
  – points 642
saline 392

saliva 299, 332
salivate 297
salle-à-manger 191
sallet 717
sallow
  colourless 429
  yellow 436
sally *issue* 293
  attack 716
  wit 842
sally-port 295, 717
salmagundi 41
salmi 298
salmon-coloured
  434
saloon 189, 191
salt *sailor* 269
  pungent 392
  condiment 393
  importance 642
  preserve 670
  money 800
  wit 842
  below the – 876
  worth one's – 644
  – of the earth
    648, 948
  – water 341
saltation 309
saltatory 315
saltinbanco 548
saltpetre 392, 727
saltum, per – 315
salubrity 656
salutary 656
salutatory 582
salute
  allocution 586
  celebration 883
  courtesy 894
  kiss 902
  respect 928
salutiferous
  [*see* salutary]
salva:
  – res est 664
  – sit reverentia
    928
salvable 946
salvage
  acquisition 775
  tax 812
  discount 813
  reward 973
salvation
  preservation 670
  deliverance 672
  religious 976
  piety 987
  work out one's –
    990

salve *unguent* 356
  remedy 662
  relieve 834
salver 191
salvo *exception* 83
  explosion 406
  qualification 469
  plea 617
  attack 716
  excuse 937
  – of artillery
  celebration 883
Samaritan, good –
  906, 912
same 13
  all the – to 823
  in the – boat 709
  in the – breath
    113, 120
  go over the –
    ground 104
  of the – mind 488
  on the – tack 709
  adds up to the –
    thing 27
  at the – time 30,
    120
sameness 16
samiel 349
samisen 417
Sammael 978
samovar 191
sampan 273
sample 82, 463
Samson 159
sana, mens – 502
  – in corpore sano
    827
sanation 660
sanative 662
sanatorium 662
sanctification 976
sanctify 926, 987
sanctimony 988
sanction
  permission 760
  dueness 924
  approbation 931
sanctitude 987
sanctity 987
sanctuary 666, 1000
sanctum 191
  – sanctorum
  abode 189
  privacy 893
  temple 1000
sand *powder* 330
  –bag 727
  built upon – 665
  –dance 840
  sow the – 645

sandal 225
sand-blind 442
Sandemanian 984
sand-paper 255
sands *danger* 667
 – on the seashore
  multitude 102
sand-storm 330
sandwich-wise 228
sandy *yellow* 436
sane 502
sangar 717
sang-froid
 insensibility 823
 inexcitability 826
 presence of mind
  864
sangrail 998
sanguinary 361
sanguine *red* 434
 hopeful 858
 – expectation 507,
  858
 – imagination 515
sanhedrim 696, 995
sanies 333
sanitaire, cordon –
  670
sanitarian 656
sanitarium 656, 662
sanitary 656
sanity *mental* **502**
 bodily - 654
sans 187
 – cérémonie 888,
  892
 – façon
  simple 849
  modest 881
  social 892
 – pareil 33
 – peur et sans
  reproche
  perfect 650
  heroic 873
  honourable 939
 – souci
  insensible 823
  pleasure 827
  content 831
sans-culotte 742,
  876
Santa Claus 784
santé, maison de –
  662
santon 893, 996
sap *essence* 5
 destroy 162
 excavate 252
 juice 333
 damage 659

attack 716
 – the foundations
  162, 659
sapid 390
sapient 498
sapless 160, 340
sapling 129, 367
saponaceous 355
saporific 390
sapper 252, 726
sappers and miners
 preparers. 673
Sapphic 597
sapphire *blue* 438
 gem 847
sappy
 young 127
 juicy 333
 foolish 499
sarà sarà, che – 601
saraband 840
sarcasm
 disrespect 929
 censure 932
 detraction 934
sarcastic 856, 895
sarcoma 250
sarcophagus 363
sarculation 103
sard 847
Sardanapalus 954a
sardonic 932, 934
 – grin
  laughter 838
  ridicule 856
  discontent 932
sardonyx 847
sark 225
sartorial 225
Sarum, old – 893
sash 247
Satan **978**
satanic
 malevolent 907
 vicious 945
 diabolic 978
satchel 191
sate 869
satellite
 companion 88
 follower 281
 heavenly body 318
 auxiliary 711
 servant 746
satiate 957
satiety
 sufficient 639
 pleasant 829
 cloy **869**
satin 255
satire 521, 856, 932

satirical 546, 932
 detraction 934
satirist 936
satis: jam – 869
 – superque 641
satisfaction
 [*see* satisfy]
 duel 720
 pleasure 827
 atonement 952
 hail with – 931
satisfactorily 618
satisfactory 648
satisfy *answer* 462
 convince 484
 sufficient 639
 consent 762
 observance 772
 pay 807
 gratify 829
 content 831
 satiate 869
 reward 973
 – an obligation
  926
 – oneself 484
satrap 745
saturate *fill* 52
 moisten 339
 satiate 869
Saturn 979
saturnalia
 disorder 59
 games 840
 intemperance 954
Saturnian 829, 946
 – age 734
Saturnia regna 734,
  827
saturnine 837
satyr *ugly* 846
 libertine 962
 demon 980
sauce *adjunct* 39
 mixture 41
 food 298
 condiment 393
 impertinence 885
 abuse 908
 – boat 191
 pay – for all 807
sauce piquante 829
sauce-box 887
saucer 191
 – eyes 441
saucepan 191
saucy 885, 895
saunter 133, 266,
  275
sausage 298
saute aux yeux,

cela – 525
sauvage 893
sauve qui peut
 run away 623
 alarm 669
 haste 684
 cowardice 862
savage *violent* 173
 vulgar 851
 brave 861
 boorish 876
 angry 900
 malevolent 907
 evil-doer 913
savanna 344
savant 490, 492
save *subduct* 38
 exclude 55
 except 83
 store 636
 preserve 670
 deliver 672
 economize 817
 God – 990
 – one's bacon 671
 – and except 83
 – money 817
 – the necessity
  927*a*
 – us 707
save-all 817
saving 817
 – clause 469
 – one's presence
  928
savings 636, 817
saviour 912
Saviour 976
savoir: – faire
  698, 852
 – gré 916
 – vivre *skill* 698
 fashion 852
 sociality 892
savour 390
 – of *resemble* 17
 – of the reality
  780
savouriness **394**
savourless 391
savoury 394
saw *cut* 44
 jagged 257
 maxim 496
 – the air
 gesture 550
sawbuck 800
sawder, soft –
 flattery 933
sawdust 330
sawney 501

sax-horn 417
Saxon
style 576, 578
saxophone 417
say *nearly* 32
assert 535
speak 560, 582
you don't – so 870
go without –ing
525
have one's – 535,
582
that is to – 522
what do you – to
that 870
– by heart 505
– no 489
– nothing 585
– to oneself 589
– one's prayers
990
– what comes up-
permost 612
saying 496, 535
sbirro 965
scabbard 191
throw away the –
resolution 604
war 722
scabby 940
scabrous 256
scaffold
support 215
preparation 673
execution 975
scagliola 545
scalawag 193
scald *burn* 384
poet 597
scale *transcend* 31
portion 51
series 69
term 71
slice 204
skin 223
mount 305
weigh 319
gamut 413
measure 466
hold the –s 480
turn the –
reversion 145
influence 175
counter evidence
468
motive 615
hold the –s even
922
–s of justice 922
– the heights 305
– the walls 716

–s falling from the
eyes 441, 529
scalene 243
scallop 248, 257
scalp 226
scalpel 253
scamble 44
scamp *neglect* 460
shirk 603
rascal 949
scamped *sham* 545
scamper *speed* 274
– *off* 623
scampish 945
scan *see* 441
attend to 457
inquire 461
know 490
prosody 597
scandal *news* 532
obloquy 934
**scandaleuse, chro-
nique** – 934
scandalize 932
scandal-monger
532
scandalous 874, 945
**scandalum magna-
tum**
infamy 874
detraction 934
accusation 938
scandent 305
scansion 597
scant *small* 32
few 103
little 193
narrow 203
insufficient 640
scantling *model* 22
scrap 32
dimensions 192
scanty [*see* scant]
scape 671
scapegoat 147, 952
scapegrace 863, 949
Scapin 548, 941
scapulary 999
scar *shore* 342
record 551
blemish 848
scarab 993
scaramouch 844
scarce
few 103, 137, 640
make oneself –
187, 623
scarcely 32
– any 103
– anything 643
– ever 137

scarcity 103
scare 860
scarecrow 846, 860
scarf 225, 999
scarfskin 223
scarify *notch* 257
torment 830
scarlet 434
– Lady 984
scarp *oblique* 217
defence 717
scathe 649, 659
scatheless 650
scatter *derange* 61
disperse 73
diverge 291
– to the winds
destroy 162
confute 479
scatterbrained 458,
503
scattering 268
scavenger 652
scenario 594, 626
scene
appearance 448
painting 556
drama 599
excitement 825
– of action 728
look behind the
–s 461
scene-painter 559
scene-painting 556
scenery 448, 559
scenic 599, 882
– railway 840
scenography 556
scent *smell* 398
discovery 480a
disbelieve 485
knowledge 490
sign 550
trail 551
get – of 527
put on a new –
279
on the – 622
throw off the –
623
on the right – 462
– from afar 510
scent-bag 400
scent-bottle 400
scented 400
scentless 399
sceptre 747
sway the – 737
schedule 86
schematist 626
scheme *draft* 554

plan 626
schemer 626
scherif 745, 875
scherzo 415
schesis 7
schism *dissent* 489
discord 713
heterodoxy 984
schismless 983a
schistose 204
scholar 492, 541
scholarly 539
scholarship
knowledge 490
learning 539
distinction 873
scholastic
knowledge 490
teaching 537
learning 539
school 542
scholiast 496, 522
scholium 496, 522
school
herd 72
multitude 102
*system of
opinions* 484
knowledge 490
teaching 537
academy **542**
painting 556
go to – 539
send to – 537
schoolboy 129, 541
familiar to every –
490
schooldays 127
schoolfellow 541
schoolgirl 129, 541
schoolman 492, 983
schoolmaster 540
– abroad 490, 537
schoolroom 191
schooner 273
schottische 840
sciatica 378
science 490, 698
scientific *exact* 494
scientist 476, 492
scimitar 727
scintilla *small* 32
spark 420, 423
scintillate 446, 873
scintillation
heat 382
light 420
wit 842
**scintillula forsan,
latet** – 858
sciolism 491

scroll 86, 551
scrub *rub* 331
  bush 367
  clean 652
  dirty person 653
  commonalty 876
scrubby *small* 193
  trifling 643
  stingy 819
  disreputable 874
  vulgar 876
  shabby 940
scruff 235
scruple
  small quantity 32
  weight 319
  doubt 485
  reluctance 603
  probity 939
scrupulous
  careful 459
  incredulous 487
  exact 494
  reluctant 603
  fastidious 868
  punctilious 939
scrutator 461
scrutiny 457, 461
scrutoire 191
scud *sail* 267
  speed 274
  shower 348
  cloud 353
  – *under bare*
    poles 704
scuffle 720
scull *row* 267
  brain 450
scull-cap 225
scullery 191
scullion 746
sculpsit 558
sculptor 559
sculpture 240, **557**
scum *dirt* 653
  – of the earth 949
  – of society 876
scupper 350
scurf 653
scurrilous
  ridicule 856
  malediction 908
  disrespect 929
  detraction 934
scurry 274, 684
scurvy
  insufficient 640
  unimportant 643
  base 940
  wicked 945
scut 235

scutcheon
  standard 550
  honour 877
scutiform 251
scuttle *destroy* 162
  receptacle 191
  speed 274
  – along *haste* 684
Scylla and Charyb-
  dis, between –
  danger 665
  difficulty 704
Scyllam, incidit
  in – 699
scythe *pointed* 244
  sharp 253
'sdeath! *wonder* 870
  anger 900
  disapprobation
    932
se non e vero e ben
  trovato 546
sea *multitude* 102
  ocean 341
  at – 341
  uncertain 475
  erroneous 495
  go to – 293
  on the high –s 41
  heavy – 315
  the seven –s 341
  – of doubt 475
  – of troubles
    difficulty 704
    adversity 735
seaboard 342
seafarer 269
seafaring 267, 273
sea-fight 720
sea-girt 346
sea-going 267, 341
sea-green 435
seal
  matrix 22
  close 261
  evidence 467
  mark 550
  resolve 604
  complete 729
  compact 769
  security 771
  break the – 529
  under – 769
  – the doom of 162
  – one's infamy 940
  – the lips 585
  – of secrecy 528
  – up *restrain* 751
sealed:
  one's fate is – 601
  hermetically – 261

– book
  ignorance 491
  unintelligible 519
  secret 533
sealing-wax 747
seals *insignia* 747
sealskin 223
seam 43
sea-maid 979
sea-man 269
seamanship 692,
  698
sea-mark 550
seamless 50
seamstress 225,
  690
seamy side 651
séance 525, 696
sea-piece 556
seaplane 273, 736
sea-port 666
sear *dry* 340
  burn 384
  deaden 823
  – and yellow leaf
    128, 659
search *inquire* 461
searching
  severe 739
  painful 830
searchless 519
searchlight 423,
  726
seared conscience
  951
searing 830
seascape 556
sea-serpent 83
seaside 342
season *mix* 41
  time 106
  pungent 392
  accustom 613
  preserve 670
  prepare 673
seasonable 23, 134
seasoning 393
seasons 138
seat *place* 183
  locate 184
  abode 189
  support 215
  posterior 235
  parliament 693
  country – 189
  judgment – 966
  – of government
    737
  – of war 728
seated, firmly – 150
seaway 180

seaweed 367
seaworthy 273, 664
sebaceous 355
secant 219
secede *dissent* 489
  relinquish 624
  disobey 742
seceder
  heterodox 984
secern 297
seclusion **893**
second
  duplication 90
  – *of time* 108
  instant 113
  – *in music* 413,
    415
  abet 707
  play or sing a –
    416
  – best 651, 732
  – childhood 128,
    499
  – crop 168, 775
  – edition 104
  play – fiddle
    obey 743
    subject 749
    disrepute 874
  – nature 613
  – to none 33
  one's – self 17
  – rate 659
  – sight
    foresight 510
    sorcery 992
  – thoughts
    sequel 65
    thought 451
    improvement 658
  – youth 660
secondary
  inferior 34
  following 63
  imperfect 651
  deputy 759
  – education 537
  – evidence 467
  – school 542
seconder 711
second-hand
  imitation 19
  old 124
  deteriorated 659
  received 785
secondly 90
second-rate 651
secret *key* 522
  latent 526
  hidden 528
  riddle **533**

sanity 502	semination 673	horse – 498	sept *kin* 11
resolution 604	semi-opaque 427	in no – 565	*class* 75
inexcitability 826	semi-pellucid 427	accept in a par-	*clan* 166
caution 864	semiquaver 413	ticular – 522	Septentrional 237
–praise 880	semitone 413	– of duty 926	septett 415
–preservation 717	semi-transparency	senseless	septic 655, 657
–reliance	**427**	*insensible* 376	septicæmia 655
resolution 604	sempervirent 110	*absurd* 497	septuagenarian 98
hope 858	sempiternal 112	*foolish* 499	Septuagint 985
courage 861	sempstress 225, 690	*unmeaning* 517	septum 228
–reproach 950	senary 98	senses	sepulchral
–respect 878	senate 696	*external* - 375	*interment* 363
–restraint 953	senate-house 966	*intellect* 450	*resonance* 408
–sacrifice 942	senator 695, 696	*sanity* 502	*stridor* 410
–satisfied 880	senatorship 693	sensibility **375, 822**	*hoarse* 581
–seeking 943	senatus consultum	sensible	sepulchre 363
–styled 565	741	*material* 316	whited – 545
–sufficient 880	send 270, 284	*wise* 498	sepulture 363
–taught 490	– adrift 597	sensitive 375, 822	sequacious 63
–tormentor 837	– away	sensorial 821	sequacity *soft* 324
–will 606	*repel* 289	sensorium 450	*tenacity* 327
selfishness **943**	*eject* 297	sensual 377, 954	sequel **65**, 117
self-same 13	*refuse* 764	sensualist 954*a*	sequela 65, 154
sell *convince* 484	– for 741	sensuous	sequence
absurdity 497	– forth 284, 531	*sensibility* 375	- in order **63**
deception 545	– a letter to 592	*pleasure* 377	- in time 117
untruth 546	– off 284	*feeling* 821	*motion* **281**
sale 796	– out *eject* 297	sentence	logical – 476
- for 812	– packing 289	*decision* 480	sequent 63
- one's life dearly	*commission* 755	*maxim* 496	sequester 789, 974
719, 722	– word 527	*affirmation* 535	sequestered 893
- off 796	senescence 128	*phrase* 566	sequestrate
- oneself 940	seneschal	*condemnation* 971	*seize* 789
- out 796	*director* 694	sententious 572,	*condemn* 971
seller 796	*master* 745	574	*confiscate* 974
selon les règles 82	*servant* 746	sentient 375, 821	sequin 847
selvedge 231	seneschalship 737	sentiment 453	serac 383
semaphore 550	senile 128	sentimental	seraglio 961
semblance	senility 158, 659	*sensitive* 822	seraph 948, 977
similarity 17	senior *age* 128	*affected* 855	seraphic
imitation 19	*student* 541	sentinel ⎱ 263	*blissful* 829
copy 21	*master* 745	sentry ⎰	*virtuous* 944
probability 472	seniores priores 62,	*guardian* 664	*pious* 987
wear the – of	380	*watch* 668	seraphina 417
appearance 448	seniority 124, 128	*keeper* 753	seraskier 745
semeiology 522	sennight 108	separate *disjoin* 44	sere and yellow
semeiotics 550	señor 373, 877	*exclude* 55	leaf 128
semester 108	señora 374	*bisect* 91	serein 339, 348
semi- 91	sensation	*diverge* 291	serenade *music* 415
semi-barbarian 913	*physical sensi-*	*divorce* 905	*compliment* 894
semibreve 413	*bility* 375	– the chaff from	*endearment* 902
semicircle 247	*emotion* 821	the wheat	serene
semicircular 245	*wonder* 870	*discriminate* 465	*pellucid* 425
semicolon 142	sensational 574,	*select* 609	*calm* 826
semi-diaphanous	824	– into elements 49	*content* 831
427	sensation drama	– maintenance 905	*imperturbable* 871
semi-fluid 352	599	separation 49	– highness 877
semi-liquidity **352**	sensations of touch	separatist 489, 984	serf *slave* 746
semi-lunar 245	**380**	sepia 433	*clown* 876
seminal 153	sense 498, 516	seposition 44, 55	serfdom 749
seminary 542	deep – 821	sepoy 726	sergeant 745

– of its beams 422, 874
– lamb 828
short
  not long 201
  brittle 328
  concise 572
  uncivil 895
  come – of, fall – of
  inferior 34
  shortcoming 304
  insufficient 640
  in – 572, 596
  – allowance 640
  – answer 895
  – breath 688
  – by 201
  – of cash 804
  – commons
  insufficiency 640
  fasting 956
  – circuit 279, 628
  – cut *straight* 246
  mid-course 628
  – distance 197
  – life and merry 840
  – measure 53
  at – notice 111, 132
  – of *small* 32
  inferior 34
  subtraction 38
  incomplete 53
  shortcoming 304
  insufficient 640
  – sea 348
  make – work of
  destroy 162
  active 682
  haste 684
  complete 729
  conquer 731
  punish 972
shortage 53
shortcoming
  inequality 28
  inferiority 34
  motion short of
  304
  non-completion 730
  deficiency 945
shorten 201
  – sail 275
shorthand 590
short-handed 651
shorthorn 366
short-lived 111
shortly *soon* 132
shortness **201**

for – sake 572
shorts 225
short-sighted
  myopic 443
  misjudging 481
  foolish 499
short-story 594
short-winded 160, 688
short-witted 499
shot *missile* 284
  report 406
  variegated 440
  guess 514
  war material 722, 727
  price 812
  reward 973
  bad – 701
  exchange –s 720
  good – 700
  have a – at 716
  like a – 113
  off like a – 623
  pistol – 406
  random – 463, 621
  round – 727
  – in the locker 632
  not have a – in
  one's locker 804
  – and shell 722
shot-free 815
shot-gun 727
should be:
  no better than
  she – 961
  what – 922
shoulder
  support 215
  projection 250
  shove 276
  broad –ed 159
  cold – 289
  have on one's –s 625
  on the –s of
  high 206
  elevated 307
  instrumentality 631
  shrug the –s
  [*see* shrug]
  rest on the –s of 926
  rub –s with no-
  bility 852
  take upon one's –s 676
  – arms 673
  – a musket 722
  – to shoulder 709,

712
– to the wheel 604, 676
shoulder-knot 847
shoulder-strap 747
shout
  loud 404
  cry 411
  rejoice 838
shove 276
  give a – to
  aid 707
shovel
  receptacle 191
  transfer 270
  vehicle 272
  fire-iron 386
  cleanness 652
  put to bed with
  a – 363
  – away 297
shovel-hat 999
show *visible* 446
  appear 448
  draw attention 457
  evidence 467
  demonstrate 478
  manifest 525
  entertainment 599
  parade 882
  dumb – 550
  make a – 544
  mere – 544
  peep– 840
  – off 525
  – one's cards 529
  – cause 527
  – one's colours, 550
  – one's face
  presence 186
  manifest 525
  disclose 529
  – fight *defy* 715
  attack 716
  defend 717
  brave 861
  – forth 525
  – in front 303
  – one's cards 529
  – one's hand 529
  – a light pair of
  heels 623
  – itself 446
  – of 17, 472
  – off 882, 884
  – one's teeth 715
  – up *visible* 446
  manifest 525
  ridicule 856

  degrade 874
  censure 932
  accuse 938
shower
  assemblage 72
  rain 348
  – bath 386
  – down
  abundance 639
  – down upon 784, 816
showman 524
showy *colour* 428
  beauty 845
  ornament 847
  fashion 852
  vulgar 851
  ostentatious 882
shrapnel 727
shred 32, 205
shredder 260
shrew 901
shrewd
  knowing 490
  wise 498
  cunning 702
shriek 410, 411
shrievalty 965
shrieve 965
shrift
  confession 529
  absolution 952
shriftless 951
shrill 410, 411
shrimp 193
shrine 363, 1000
  receptacle 191
shrink
  decrease 36
  shrivel 195
  go back 283, 287
  unwilling 603
  avoid 623
  sensitive 822
  – from *fear* 860
  dislike 867
  hate 898
shrive 952, 998
shrivel 195
shrivelled *thin* 203
shroud *cover* 225
  funeral 363
  hide 528
  safety 664
  defend 717
  –ed in mystery 519
shrouds 45
Shrove Tuesday 998
shrub *plant* 367

707, 906
- down 174
- over 174
- the ruffled brow
  of care 834
- sailing 705
- water *easy* 705
- the way 705
smooth-bore 727
smoothly, go on -
  prosperous 734
smoothness **255**
smooth-tongued
  544, 933
smother
  repress 174
  kill 361
  stifle sound 581
  restrain 751
smoulder *inert* 172
  burn 382
  latent 526
smous 796, 797
smudge 431, 653,
  848
smug *affected* 855
smuggle
  introduce 228
  steal 791
  illegal 964
smuggler 792
smut
  dirt 653
  impurity 961
smutch 431
snack
  small quantity 32
  food 298
snacks, go - 778
snaffle 752
snag *projection* 250
  sharp 253
  danger 667
  hindrance 706
snail *slow* 275
snake *undulation*
  248
  serpent 366
  hissing 406
  miscreant 913
  scotch the - 640
- in the grass
  hidden 528
  deceiver 548
  bad 649
  source of danger
  667
  evil-doer 913
  knave 941
snake-like
  convoluted 248

snap *break* 44
  eat 298
  brittle 328
  noise **406**
  rude 895
- at *seize* 789
  bite 830
  censure 932
- of the fingers
  trifle 643
- one's fingers at
  defy 715
  insolence 885
  despise 930
- the thread 70
- up *seize* 789
- one up
  censure 932
-shot 554
snap-dragon 840
snappish 901
snare *deception* 545
snarl *growl* 412
  rude 895
  angry 900
  threaten 909
snatch
  small quantity 32
  seize 789
- at *pursue* 622
  seize 789
- a grace beyond
  the reach of art
  845
- from one's grasp
  789
- from the jaws of
  death 662, 672
- from under
  one's nose 702
- a verdict 545,
  702
snatches, by - 70
sneak *hide* 528
  coward 862
  servile 886
  base 940
  knave 941
  bad man 949
- off, - out of 623
sneer *disparage* 929
  contempt 930
  blame 932
sneeze *blow* 349
  snuffle 409
- at *despise* 930
sneezed at, not to
  be - 642
snick 32, 51
snicker 838
sniff *blow* 349

odour 398
  discovery 480a
sniffle 349
snigger *laugh* 838
  ridicule 856
  disrespect 929
sniggle 545
snip
  small quantity 32
  cut 44
  short 201
  tailor 225
sniping 716
snippet 32
snip-snap 713
snip-snap-snorem
  840
snivel *weep* 839
snivelling
  servile 886
snob *vulgar* 851
  plebeian 876
  servile 886
snobbishness
  flattery 933
snood
  headdress 225
  circle 247
snooker 840
Snooks, Mr. - 876
snooze 683
snozzle 250
snore 411, 683
snort 411, 412
snout 250
snow *ship* 273
  ice 383
  white 430
snow-ball 72
snow-blindness 443
snow-drift 72
snow-shoe 272
snow-storm 383
snub *short* 201
  hinder 706
  cast a slur 874
  humiliate 879
  bluster 885
  censure 932
snub-nosed 243
snuff *blow* 349
  pungent 392
  odour 398
up to - 698, 702
go out like the -
  of a candle 360
- out 162, 421
- up 296, 398
snuff-colour 433
snuffing, want -
  pert 885

snuffle *blow* 349
  hiss 409
  stammer 583
  hypocrisy 988
snuffy 653
snug *closed* 261
  comfortable 377
  safe 664
  prepared 673
  content 831
  secluded 893
keep - 528, 893
make all - 673
snuggery 189
snugness 827
so *similar* 17
  very 31
  therefore 476
  method 627
- be it 488, 762
- far so good 618
- let it be 681
- much the better
  831, 838
- much the worse
  832, 835
- to speak 17, 521
soak *immerse* 300
  water 337
  moist 339
  drunkenness 959
- up 340
So-and-so, Mr. -
  neology 563
soap *lubricate* 332
  oil 356
  cleanser 652
soapy *unctuous* 355
  servile 886
  flattery 933
soar *great* 31
  height 206
  fly 267
  rise 305
sob 839
sober *moderate* 174
  wise 498
  sane 502
  style 576
  grave 837
  temperate 953
  abstinent 958
- down 174, 502
  humility 879
in - sadness
  affirmation 535
- senses 502
- truth *fact* 494
sober-minded 502
  calm 826
  humble 879

optical instru-
  ment 445
spectrum
  colour 428
  variegation 440
  optical illusion
   443
speculate
  view 441
  think 451
  suppose 514
  chance 621
  essay 675
  traffic 794
speculation
  experiment 463
  cards 840
speculative 463, 514
speculum 445
  veluti in – 446
sped *completed* 729
speech 582
  figure of – 521
  parts of – 567
speechify 582
speechless 403, 581
speechmaker 582
speed
  velocity 274
  activity 682
  haste 684
  help 707
  succeed 731
  with breathless –
   684
  God – 731, 906
speedily *soon* 132
speedometer 200,
  274, 553
speedway 840
speer 455, 461
spell *period* 106
  influence 175
  read 539
  letter 561
  necessity 601
  motive 615
  exertion 686
  charm **993**
  cast a – 992
  wonder 870
  knurr and – 840
  – for 865
  – out *interpret* 522
spell-bound 601,
  615
spence 636
spencer 225
spend *effuse* 297
  waste 638
  give 784

purchase 795
  expend 809
  – freely 816
  – time 106
  – time in 683
  – one's time in
   625
spender 818
spendthrift 818
spent 160, 688
spermaceti 356
spermatic 168
spermatize 168
spero, dum spiro –
  858
spes sibi quisque
  604
spew 297
sphacelus 655
sphere *rank* 26
  domain 74
  space 180
  region 181
  ball 249
  world 318
  business 625
  – of influence 181,
   780
spheroid 249
spherule 249
sphery 318
sphinx *monster* 83
  oracle 513
  ambiguous 520
  riddle 533
spial 668
spice
  small quantity 32
  mixture 41
  pungent 392
  condiment 393
spiced 390
spicilegium 72, 596
spick and span 123
spiculate 253
spiculum 253
spicy 400, 824
spigot 263
spike *sharp* 253
  pierce 260
  plug 263
  – guns 158, 645
spikebit 262
spikenard 356
spill *filament* 205
  stopper 263
  shed 297
  splash 348
  match 388
  waste 638
  lavish 818

– blood 722
  – and pelt 59
spin *flying* 267
  rotate 312
  pluck 610
  – out *protract* 110
  late 133
  prolong 200
  diffuse style 573
  – the wheel 140
  – a long yarn 549
spindle 312
spindling 203
spindle-shanks 203
spindle-shaped 253
spindrift 353
spine 222, 253
spinel 847
spinet *copse* 367
  harpsichord 417
spinney 367
spinner of yarns
  594
spinosity
  unintelligible 519
  discourtesy 895
  sullenness 901a
spinous *prickly* 253
spinster 374, 904
spiracle 351
spiral 248
spire *height* 206
  convolution 248
  peak 253
  soar 305
spirit *essence* 5
  immateriality 317
  fuel 388
  intellect 450
  meaning 516
  vigorous language
   574
  activity 682
  affections 820
  courage 861
  ghost 980
  bad – 980
  keep one's – up
  hope 858
  with life and – 682
  unclean – 978
  – away 791
  – up 615, 824
Spirit, the Holy –
  976
spirited
  language 574
  active 682
  sensitive 822
  cheerful 836
  brave 861

generous 942
spiritless
  insensible 823
  sad 837
  cowardly 862
spirit-level 213
spiritoso *music* 415
spirit-rapping 992
spirits *drink* 298,
  959
  cheer 836
spirit-stirring 824
spiritual
  immaterial 317
  psychical 450
  heterodoxy 984
  divine 976
  pious 987
  – director 996
  – existence 987
spiritualism
  immateriality 317
  intellect 450
  sorcery 992
spiritualize 317
  reasoning 476
spirituel 842
spirt *eject* 297
  stream 348
  haste 684
  exertion 686
spirtle *disperse* 73
  splash 348
spissitude 321, 352
spit *pointed* 253
  perforate 260
  eject 297
  rotate 312
  rain 348
  – fire *irascible* 901
spite 907
  in – of
  disagreement 24
  notwithstanding
   30
  counteraction 179
  opposition 708
  in – of one's teeth
  unwilling 603
  compulsion 744
spiteful 898, 907
  hating 898
spittle 299
spittoon 191
splanchnology 329
splash *affuse* 337
  stream 348
  spatter 653
  parade 882
  make a –
  fame 873

display 882
–board 666
splay 291
–footed 243
spleen
  melancholy 837
  hatred 898
  anger 900
  sullen 901a
  harbour – 907
spleenless 906
splendour
  bright 420
  beautiful 845
  glorious 873
  display 882
splenetic 837, 901a
splice *join* 43
  cross 219
  interjacent 228
  repair 660
  – the main brace
  tipsy 959
spliced, be –
  marriage 903
splint 215
splinter
  small piece 32
  divide 44
  filament 205
  brittle 328
split *divide* 44
  discontinuity 70
  bisect 91
  brittle 328
  divulge 529
  quarrel 713
  fail 732
  portion 786
  laugh 838
  – the difference
  29, 774
  – the ears } 404
  – the head } 410
  – hairs
  discriminate 465
  sophistry 477
  fastidiousness 868
  – upon a rock 732
  – one's sides 838
splutter *energy* 171
  spit 297
  stammer 583
  haste 684
spoil *vitiate* 659
  hinder 706
  lenity 740
  plunder 791
  booty 793
  deface 846
  satiate 869

– sport 706
– trade 708
spoiled child 869,
  899
– of fortune 734
spoiler 792
spoke *radius* 200
  tooth 253
  obstruct 706
  put a – in one's
  wheel *render*
    powerless 158
  hinder 706
spokesman 524,
  582
spolia opima 793
spoliate 791
spoliative 793
spondee 597
spondulics 800
sponge *moisten* 339
  dry 340
  pulp 354
  clean 652
  despoil 791
  hanger on 886
  drunkard 959
  apply the –
  obliterate 552
  non-payment 808
  – out 552
sponging-house 752
spongy *porous* 252
  soft 324
  marshy 345
sponsion 771
sponsor
  witness 467
  security 771
  be – for
  promise 768
  obligation 926
sponsorship 771
spontaneous
  voluntary 600
  willing 602
  impulsive 612
spontoon 727
spoof 545
spook 980
spool 312
spoon
  receptacle 191
  ladle 272
  bill and coo 902
  born with a silver
  – in one's mouth
  734
Spoonerism 218,
  853
spoonful 25, 32

spoon-like 252
spoon-meat 298
spoony *foolish* 499
  lovesick 902
spoor 551
sporadic 73, 137,
  657
spore 330
sport *killing* 361
  chase 622
  amusement 840
  show off 882
  in – *pastime* 840
  humour 842
  the – of 749
  – of fortune 735
sporting *killing* 361
  contention 720
  amusement 840
  – *dog* 366
sportive 836, 840
sports 686
sportsman 361, 622,
  840
sportulary 784, 785
sportule 784
sporule 330
spot *place* 182
  discover 480a
  mark 550
  dirt 653
  blemish 848
  blot 874
  on the –
  instantly 113
  present time 118
  soon 132
  in one's presence
  186
spotless *perfect* 650
  clean 652
  innocent 946
spot light 423, 599
spots in the sun,
  see – *fastidious*
  868
spotted
  variegated 440
  damaged 659
spousal 903
spouse 88, 903
spouseless 904
spout *egress* 295
  flow out 348
  conduit 350
  speak 582
  act 599
  pawn 771, 787,
  788
sprag 215
sprain 158, 160

sprat to catch a:
  – herring 794
  – whale 699
sprawl *length* 200
  horizontal 213
  descend 306
spray *sprig* 51
  vaporizer 336
  foam 353
spread *enlarge* 35
  disperse 73
  broadcast 78
  expanse 180
  expand 194
  diverge 291
  feast 298
  publish 531
  – abroad 531
  – canvas 267
  – out 194
  – sail 267
  – a shade 421
  – to 196
  – the toils 545
spree 840
spretæ injuria
  formæ *ugly* 846
  disrespect 929
  detraction 934
sprig *branch* 51
  child 129
  shillelagh 727
sprightly 836, 842
spring *early* 125
  source 153
  strength 159
  velocity 274
  recoil 277
  fly 293
  leap 309
  elasticity 325
  rivulet 348
  instrument 633
  store 636
  –s of action 615
  – back 277
  – to one's feet 307
  – from 154
  – a leak 651, 659
  – a mine
  destroy 162
  unexpected 508
  attack 716
  – a project 626
  – up *begin* 66
  event 151
  grow 194
  ascend 305
  visible 446
  hot – 382
  – upon 789

spring balance 319
springe 545
spring-gun 545
spring tide
  greatness 31
  increase 35
  completeness 52
  youth 127
  high 206
  low 207
  wave' 348
  water 337
springy 325
sprinkle *add* 37
  mix 41
  scatter 73
  wet 337
  rain 348
  variegate 440
  baptize 998
sprinkler 348, 385
sprinkling
  small quantity 32
sprint 274
sprit *sprout* 167
  support 215
sprite 979, 980
sprout *grow* 35
  germinate 161
  offspring 167
  expand 194
  – *from result* 154
spruce 652, 845
  – *up* 847
sprue 653
sprung 651, 659
spry 682, 836
spud 272
spume 353
spun out 110, 573
spunk 861
spur
  pointed 250
  sharp 253
  incite 615
  hasten 684
  win –s *succeed* 731
  glory 873
  on the – of the
    moment
  instantly 113
  now 118
  soon 132
  opportune 134
  impulse 612
  – *gearing* 633
  the – *of necessity*
    745
spurious
  erroneous 495
  false 544

deceptive 545
illegitimate 925
spurlos versenkt 2,
  449
spurn *reject* 55
  disdain 930
spurred 253
spurt
  transient 111
  swift 274
  gush 348
  impulse 612
  haste 684
  exertion 686
sputa 299
sputter *emit* 297
  splash 348
  stammer 583
spy *see* 441
  spectator 444
  inquire 461
  informer 527
  emissary 534
  watcher 664
  warning 668
spy-glass 445
squab *large* 192
  short 201
  broad 202
  bench 215
squabble 713
squad 72, 726
squadron 726
  – *leader* 745
squalid 653, 846
squall *violent* 173
  wind 349
  cry 411
  quarrel 713
squalor 653
squamous 204, 223
squander *waste* 638
  misuse 679
  lose 776
  prodigal 818
square
  congruous 23
  compensate 30
  four 95
  limited space 182
  houses 189
  perpendicular 212
  form 244
  sparring 720
  justice 924
  honourable 939
  make all – 660
  on the – 939
  – accounts
  pay 807
  account 811

– dance 840
– deal 922
– the circle 471
– inches 180
– peg into a round
  hole 699
– up 556
– with 23
– yards 180
square-toes 857
squash *destroy* 162
  flatten 251
  blow 276
  soft 324
  marsh 345
  semiliquid 352
  hiss 409
  game 840
squashy 345, 352
squat 308
  locate oneself 184
  little 193
  short 201
  thick 202
  low 207
squatter 188
squaw *woman* 374
  wife 903
squeak }
squeal } 411, 412
squeamish 655
  unwilling 603
  fastidious 868
squeasy 868
squeezable 762
squeeze
  contract 195
  condense 321
  embrace 894
squeeze out 301,
  784
squelch 162
squib *sound* 406
  lampoon 856, 934
squiffy 959
squilgee 652
squint
  peephole 260
  look 441
  defective sight 443
squirarchy 875
squire *aid* 707
  attendant 746
  gentry 875
  – *of Dames* 897
squirm 315
squirrel 274, 682
squirt 297, 348
S.S.C. 968
stab *pierce* 260
  kill 361

pain 378, 649,
  828
injure 659
stabilimeter 150
stabilisator 150
stability 16, **150**
stable *firm* 150
  house 189
  lock the – door
    when the steed
    is stolen
  too late 135
  useless 645
  bungling 699
  – *equilibrium* 150
staccato 415
stack 72, 636
staddle 215
stade 252
stadium 728, 840
stadtholder 745
staff *support* 215
  music 413
  measure 466
  signal 550
  council 696
  party 712
  weapon 727
  chief 745
  retinue 746
  pastoral – 999
  – of life 298
  – of office 747
  – officer 745
stag *deer* 366
  male 373
  defaulter 808
stage *degree* 26
  term 71
  time 106
  position 183
  layer 205
  platform 215
  forum 542
  drama 599
  arena 728
  come upon the –
    446
  on the – 525, 599
  go off the – 293
  revolving – 599
  – business 599
  – coach 272
  – craft 599
  – direction 697
  – effect 882
  – hand 599
  – manager 599
  – name 565
  – play 599
  – player 599

- struck 599
- whisper 580

stager *player* 599
  doer 690
  old – 130

stagger *slow* 275
  totter 314, 821
  agitate 315
  unexpected 508
  dissuade 616
  affect 824
  astonish 870
  – belief *doubt* 485
  – like a drunken
    man 605

staggers 315
stagirite 850
stagnant 265
stagnation 681
stagy 599, 855
staid *wise* 498
  calm 826
  grave 837

stain *paint* 223
  colour 428
  dirt 653
  spoil 659
  blemish 848
  disgrace 874
  – paper *writing*
    590

stained, travel- 266
stainless *clean* 652
  honourable 939
  innocent 946

stair 305, 627
stake *fastening* 45
  wager 621
  danger 665
  security 771
  property 780
  lay down 807
  execution 975
  at – *intended* 620
  in danger 665
  the – *agony* 828
  burn at the – 384

stalactite 224
stalagmite 224
stale *old* 124
  insipid 391
  deteriorated 659
  – flat and unprof-
    itable 645
  – news 532

stale-mate 27, 731
stalk *stem* 153
  support 215
  walk 266
  – abroad
  generality 78

pursue 622
proud 878

stalking-horse
  ambush 530
  plea 617

stall *cease* 142
  abode 189
  receptacle 191
  support 215
  play-house 599
  mart 799
  churchdom 995
  cathedral 1000
  finger– 223

stallion 271, 373
stalwart 159, 192
stamina 159, 604a
stammel 434
stammering 583
stamp
  character 7
  prototype 22
  kind 75
  form 240
  mark 550
  engraving 558
  complete 729
  security 771
  – the foot
  anger 900
  – in the memory
    505
  – out 162, 385

stampede 860
stanch - *a flow* 348
  persevering 604a
  health 654
  reinstate 660

stanchion 215
stanchless 825
stand *exist* 1
  rank 71
  long time 110
  permanent 141
  support 215
  quiescence 265
  difficulty 704
  resistance 719
  brook 821
  patience 826
  brave 861
  at a – 681
  come to a – 704
  make a – 708, 719
  take one's –
  resolve 604
  resist 719
  due 924
  take one's – upon
  reasoning 476
  affirm 535

plea 617
– aghast 870
– aloof 623, 681
– of arms 727
– at attention 507
– the brunt 717
– by *near* 197
  aid 707
  defend 717
– a chance 470,
  472
– committed 754
– at ease 458
– to one's engage-
  ment 772
– fair for 472
– fire 861
– firm 150, 719
– first 66
– for *indicate* 550
  deputy 759
  candidate 763
– forth 446
– one's ground
  preserved 670
  resist 719
– the hazard of
  the die 621
– one in 812
– in need of 630
– no nonsense 604
– off 287, 623
– on 215
– out *project* 250
  visible 446
  obstinate 606
– over 133
– the proof 648
– to reason
  proof 478
  manifest 525
  right 922
– on one's rights
  748
– in the shoes of
  147
– one in good
  stead 644
– still *remain* 141
  stop 265
  difficulty 704
– the test 494, 648
– up [*see below*]
– upon *pride* 878
– upon one's
  rights 924
– in the way of 706
– well in the
  opinion of 931

stand up 212, 307
– against 719

– fight 720
– for 931, 937
– to 459

standard *model* 22
  degree 26
  mean 29
  rule 80
  measure 466
  flag 550
  good 648
  perfect 650
  gold – 800

standard-bearer
  726
standardize 22, 60,
  466
standing *footing* 8
  degree 26
  long time 110
  permanence 141
  situation 183
  note 873
  – army 726
  – dish *rule* 80
  permanent 141
  – jest *wit* 842
  – order 613, 963
  – type 591
  – water 343

stand-pipe 348, 385
stand-point 183,
  441
Stannary Court 966
stanza 597
staple
  fastening 45
  whole 50
  peg 214
  texture 329
  material 635
  trade 794
  mart 799
  – *commodity* 798

star *luminary* 423
  actor 599
  destiny 601
  badge 747
  ornament 847
  glory 873
  noble 875
  decoration 877
  – in the ascendant
  success 731
  prosperity 734
  – of fashion 852
  – it *drama* 599
  fame 873
  display 882
  – shell 423
  – trap 599

starboard 238

starch *stiff* 323
 viscid 352
 affected 855
 proud 878
Star Chamber 966
starched
 ostentatious 882
stare *look* 441
 curiosity 455
 wonder 870
 make one – 870
 – out of counte-
  nance
  humiliate 879
  insolent 885
  discourteous 895
 – one in the face
  destiny 152
  manifest 525
 Death –s one in
  the face 360
stare super anti-
 quas vias
 continue 143
 habit 613
 preservation 670
 inaction 681
star-gazing 318
staring 446
stark *very* 31
 sheer 32
 complete 52
 hard 323
 – blind 442
 – naked 226
stark staring 31
 manifest 525
 – mad 503
starlight 422
starlike
 pointed 253
starry 318
stars [*see* star]
 worlds 318
 bless one's – 916
 – in the firmament
  multitude 102
 – and stripes 550
start *begin* 66
 sudden change
  146
 arise 151
 impulse 276
 move 284
 depart 293
 leap 309
 unexpected 508
 suggest 514
 crack 659
 offer 763
 fear 860

wonder 870
 get the –
  precede 280
  success 731
 give a – to 276
 have the –
  prior 116
  early 132
  get before 280
 – afresh 66
 – a doubt 485
 – game 622
 – off 293
 – a question 461
 – up *project* 250
  arise 305
  appear 446
starting: – hole
 plea 617
 – point
  departure 293
  reasoning 476
 eyes – out of one's
  head 870
startle *doubt* 485
 unexpected 508
 excite 824
 fear 860
 wonder 870
startling 508
startlish 825
starts, by fits and –
 608
starvation 640, 956
starve *cold* 383, 385
 poverty 804
 parsimony 819
 fast 956
starveling *thin* 203
 insufficient 640
 poor 804
state *condition* 7
 speciality 79
 nation 372
 inform 527
 affirm 535
 government 737
 realm 780
 ostentation 882
 robes of – 747
 secretary of – 694
 – of affairs 151
 –'s evidence 529
 – of facts
  description 594
  lawsuit 969
 – paper 551
 – room 191
 – of siege 722
statecraft 693
stated periods, at –

138
stately *grand* 873
 proud 878
 pompous 882
statement 535, 594
statemonger 694
state prison 752
states-general 696
statesman 694
statesmanlike 698
statesmanship 692,
 693
static 404
Statics *strength* 159
 gravity 319
station *degree* 26
 term 71
 place 182
 situation 183
 locate 184
 rank 873
stationary
 permanent 141
 quiescent 265
stationery 590
station-house 752
statist 694
statistics 85, 86
statu:
 in – pupillari 127
 in – quo 141, 660
statuary 557, 559
statue 554
 still as a – 265
stature 206
status *position* 8
 terms 71
 situation 183
 repute 873
status quo
 past 122
 unchanged 145
 restoration 660
 – ante bellum 145
statute 697, 963
staunch *health* 654
 reinstate 660
 honest 939
 – *belief* 484
stave *music* 413,
 415
 contention 720
 – in *concave* 252
 hole 260
 – off 133, 706
stay *remain* 106
 wait 133
 continue 141
 stop 142
 dwell 186
 support 215

not move 265
 prevent 706
 – away 187
 – one's hand
 cease 142
 relinquish 624
 rest 687
 – at home 893
stayed [*see* staid]
stays *corset* 225
stead 644
 in the – of
  substitution 147
  commission 755
  deputy 759
 stand one in
  good – 644
steadfast *stable* 150
 persevering 604a
 – *belief* 484
 – *thought* 457
steady *uniform* 16
 regular 80
 periodic 138
 stable 150
 persevering 604a
 unexcitable 826
 cautious 864
steal 791
 – along 275, 528
 – away 623
 – on the ear 405
 – a march
  prior 116
  early 132
  precede 280
  deceive 545
  active 682
  cunning 702
 – upon one 508
stealing **791**
stealth 528
 do good by – &c.
  881
stealthy 528
 cunning 702
 caution 864
steam *navigate* 267
 gas 334
 vaporize 336
 bubbles 353
 under – 267
 under sail and –
  274
 – car 272
 – up 171
 get the – up 673
steamboat 273
steam-engine to
 crack a nut
 waste 638

long 200
narrow 203
furrow 259
light 420
stripe 440
mark 550
streaked 219, 440
stream *assemble* 72
move 264
– *of fluid* **347**
– *of water* 348
– *of air* 349
– *of light* 420
abundance 639
against the – 708
with the –
conformity 82
progression 282
assent 488
facility 705
concord 714
fashion 852
servility 886
– *of events* 151
– *of time* 109
streamer *flag* 550
streaming 47, 73
streamlet 348
street 189, 627
man in the – 876
streets:
in the open – 525
on the – 961
street-walker 962
strength
quantity 25
degree 26
greatness 31
vigour **159**
energy 171
tenacity 327
animality 364
put all one's –
into 686
lose – 655
tower of – 717
– *of mind* 604
strengthen 35
strengthless 160
strenuous
persevering 604a
active 682
exertion 686
Strephon and Chloe
902
stress *emphasis* 580
requirement 630
importance 642
strain 686
difficulty 704
by – of 601

lay – on 476
– of circumstances
compulsion 744
– of weather 349
stretch *expanse* 180
expand 194
extend 200
exaggerate 549
exertion 686
encroach 925
at a – 69
mind on the – 451
on the – 686
upon the – 457
– away to 196
– forth one's hand
680, 789
– of the imagina-
. tion 515, 549
– the meaning 523
– a point 83, 303
exaggerate 549
severity 739
permit 760
not observe 773
undue 925
exempt 927a
– to *distance* 196
length 200
stretcher 215, 272
strew 73
striæ, striated 259,
440
stricken *pain* 828
terror– 860
be – by 655
– in years 128
strict
in conformity 82
exact 494
severe 739
conscientious 939
orthodox 983a
– inquiry 461
– interpretation
522
– search 461
– settlement 780
strictly speaking
literally 19
exact 494
interpreted 522
stricture
constriction 203
hindrance 706
censure 932
stride *distance* 196
motion 264
walk 266
strident 410
strides: make – 282

rapid – 274
stridor **410**
strife 713, 720
strigil 652
strike *operate* 170
hit 276
resist 719
disobey 742
impress 824
beat 972
– at 716
– a balance
equalize 27
mean 29
pay 807
– a bargain 769,
794
– a blow *act* 680
– dumb *dumb* 581
excitement 824
wonder 870
humble 879
– the eye 457
– the first blow
716
– one's flag 725
– hard 171
– all of a heap
824, 860
– home 171
– in with
imitate 19
assent 488
cooperate 709
– the iron while it
is hot 134
– a light 384, 420
– the lyre 416
– the mind 457
– out something
new 146, 515
– off *exclude* 55
– one 451
– out *exclude* 55
destroy 162
invent 515
obliterate 552
scheme 626
– off the roll 756,
972
– at the root of
162
– root 150
– sail 275
– tents 293
– terror 860
– up 416
– with wonder 870
striker 927
striking 525
– likeness 554

strikingly
greatly 31
string *tie* 43
ligature 45
continuity 69
filament 205
musical note 413
– together 60, 69
stringed instru-
ments 417
stringent
energetic 171
authoritative 737
strict 739
compulsory 744
strings: *music* 417
leading – 541
pull the – 175, 693
two – to one's bow
632
stringy 205, 327
strip *adjunct* 39
narrow 203
filament 205
divest 226
take 780
rob 791
stripe *length* 200
variegation 440
mark 550
badge 747
blow 972
stripling 129
stripped *poor* 804
strive *endeavour*
675
exert 686
contend 720
– against 720
stroke *impulse* 276
touch 379
mark 550
evil 619
expedient 626
disease 655
action 680
success 731
painful 830
at a – 113
good – 626
– of death 360
– of the pen
writing 590
command 741
– of policy 626
– of time 113
– of word 686
– the wrong way
256
stroll 266
strolling player 599

strong *great* 31
  powerful 159
  energetic 171
  tough 327
  taste 390
  pungent 392
  fetid 401
  healthy 654
  feeling 821
  wonderful! 870
  smell − of 398
  − accent 580
  − argument 476
  by a − arm 744
  − box 802
  with a − hand
  resolution 604
  exertion 686
  severity 739
  − language 574
  − pull 686
  − point 476
strong-headed 498
stronghold
  refuge 666
  defence 717
  prison 752
strong-minded 498,
  861
strong-scented 398
strong-willed 604
strop 253
strophe 597
strow 73
struck [*see*
  stricken, strike]
  awe− 860
  − down 732
  − all of a heap
  emotion 821
  wonder 870
  humbled 879
  − with *love* 897
structural *state* 7
structure
  production 161
  form 240
  texture 329
  organization 357
struggle *exert* 686
  difficulty 704
  contend 720
strum 416, 517
strumpet 962
strung
  highly − 825
strut *walk* 266
  pride 878
  parade 882
  boast 884
  − and fret one's

hour upon a
  stage 359, 599
strychnine 663
stub 40, 550
stubbed 201
stubble *remains* 40
  useless 645
stubborn
  strong 159
  hard 323
  obstinate 606
  resistance 719
stubby 201
stucco 45, 223
stuck [*see* stick]
  − fast 150, 704
  be − on 897
stuck-up 878
stud *hanging-peg*
  214
  knob 250
  horses 271
studded *many* 102
  spiked 253
  variegated 440
student 541
stud-farm 370
studied
  predetermined
  611
studio *room* 191
  painting 556
  workshop 691
studious
  thoughtful 451
  docile 539
  intending 620
study *copy* 21
  room 191
  thought 451
  attention 457
  research 461
  learning 539
  painting 556
  intention 620
  retreat 893
  brown − 515
stuff *substance* 3
  contents 190
  expand 194
  line 224
  matter 316
  texture 329
  absurdity 497
  unmeaning 517
  material 635
  trifle 643
  overeat 957
  such − as dreams
  are made of 515
  − gown 968

− in 300
− the memory
  with 505
− and nonsense
  unsubstantial 4
  absurdity 497
  unmeaning 517
− up *close* 261
  hoax 545
stuffed
  redundancy 641
stuffing *contents* 190
  lining 224
  stopper 263
stuffy 321, 382
stultified 732
stultify oneself 699
stultiloquy 497
stumble *fall* 306
  flounder 315
  error 495
  unskilful 699
  failure 732
  − on *chance* 156
  discover 480a
stumbling-block
  difficulty 704
  hindrance 706
stump
  remainder 40
  trunk 51
  walk 266
  drawing 556
  speak 582
  stir your −s
  active 682
  worn to the − 659
  − along *slow* 275
stump orator 582,
  887
stumpy *short* 201
stun *physically*
  insensible 376
  loud 404
  deafen 419
  unexpected 508
  morally insen-
  sible 823
  affect 824
  astonish 870
stung [*see* sting]
  − to the quick 824
stunt *shorten* 201
  performance 680
stunted 193, 195
  insufficient 640
stupe 834
stupefaction 826
stupefy
  - *physically* 376
  - *morally* 823

  astonish 870
stupendous
  great 31
  large 192
  wonderful 870
stupid
  unsubstantial 4
  misjudging 481
  credulous 486
  unintelligent 499
  tiresome 841
  dull 843
stupor
  insensibility 823
  wonder 870
stupration 961
sturdy *strong* 159
  persevering 604a
  − *beggar* 767, 792
stutter 583
sty *house* 189
  enclosure 232
  dirt 653
Stygian *dark* 421
  diabolic 945
  infernal 982
  cross the − ferry
  die 360
  − shore
  death 360
style *state* 7
  time 114
  painting 556
  graver 558
  name 564
  diction **569**
  writing 590
  beauty 845
  fashion 852
stylet
  awl 262
  dagger 727
stylist 578
Stylites, Simon −
  893
stylographic pen
  590
stylography 590
stylus 590
styptic 397
Styx 982
suasible 602
suasion 615
suave mari magno
  664
suaviter in modo
  826, 894
suavity 894
sub 34
  − spe rati 475
subacid 397

suo: – periculo 926
– sibi gladio hunc
jugulo
absurdity 479
retaliation 718
sup *small quantity*
32
feed 298
– full of horrors
828
super *theatrical* 599
superable 470
superabound 641
superadd 37
superannuated 128
superb 845
supercargo 694
supercherie 545
supercilious
proud 878
insolent 885
disrespectful 929
scornful 930
superdreadnought
726
supereminence
648, 873
supererogation 641,
645
superexaltation 873
superexcellence
648
superfetation 37,
168
superficial
shallow 209
outside 220
misjudging 481
ignorant 491
– extent 180
superficies 220
superfine 648
superfluitant 305
superfluity 40, 641
superfluous 645
superhuman 650,
976
superimpose 233
superimposed 206
superincumbent
206, 319
superinduce
change 140
cause 153
produce 161
superintend 693
superintendent 694
superior *greater* 33
– *in size* 194
important 642
good 648

director 694
superiority **33**
superjunction 37
superlative 33
superlatively good
648
superman 33
supernal 206, 210,
981
supernatant 206,
305
supernatural 976,
980
– aid 707
supernumerary
adjunct 39
theatrical 599
reserve 636
redundant 641
superpose 37, 223
supersaturate 641
superscription 550,
590
supersede
substitute 147
disuse 678
relinquish 782
supersensible 317
superstition
credulity 486
error 495
religion 984
superstratum 220
superstructure 729
supertax 812
supertonic 413
supervacaneous
641
supervene
extrinsic 6
be added 37
succeed 117
happen 151
supervise 693
supervisor 694
supination 213
supine
horizontal 213
inverted 218
sluggish 683
mentally torpid
823
suppeditate 637
supper 298
supplant 147
supple *soft* 324
servile 886
supplement
addition 37
adjunct 39
completion 52

publication 531
book 593
suppletory 37
suppliant 765, 767
supplicate *beg* 765
pity 914
worship 990
supplies
materials 635
aid 707
money 800
supply *store* 636
provide 637
give 784
– aid 707
– deficiencies 52
– the place of 147
– and transport
726
support *perform* 170
sustain **215**
evidence 467
preserve 670
aid 707
feel 821
endure 826
vindicate 937
– life 359
supporter 711
–s *heraldic* 550
suppose 514
supposing 469
supposition **514**
supposititious 546
suppress
destroy 162
conceal 528
silent 581
restrain 751
suppression of
truth 544
suppuration 653
suppute 85
supralapsarian 984
supramundane 939
supremacy 33, 737
supreme 33
summit 210
authority 737
in a – degree 31
Supreme Being 976
surbate 659
surbated 688
surcease 142
surcharge 641
– and falsify 811
surcingle 45
surcoat 225
surd *number* 84
deaf 419
silent letter 561

sure *certain* 474
belief 484
safe 664
make – against
673
make – of
inquire 461
take 789
you may be – 535
to be – *assent* 488
on – ground 664
security 771
sure-footed
careful 459
skilful 698
cautious 864
surely 489, 602, 870
sureness 474
surety 474, 664
surf 348, 353
surface *outside* 220
texture 329
below the – 526
lie on the – 518,
525
skim the – 460
Surface, Joseph –
548
surfeit 641, 869
surge *swarm* 72
swell 305
rotation 312
wave 348
surgeon 662
surgery 662
surgit amari
aliquid 651
surly *gruff* 895
sullen 901a
unkind 907
surmise 514
surmount *be*
superior 33
tower 206
transcursion 303
ascent 305
– a difficulty
overcome 731
surmountable 470
surname 564
surpass
be superior 33
grow 194
go beyond 303
outshine 873
surplice 999
surplus 40, 641
surplusage 641
surprint 550
surprise
non-expectation

508
unprepared 674
wonder 870
surprisingly 31
surrebutter &c.
answer 462
pleadings 969
surrender 725, 782
– one's life 360
surreptitious
furtive 528
deceptive 545
untrue 546
surrogate 759
surround 227, 229
surroundings
amidst such and
such – 183
sursum corda 990
surtax 812
surtout *coat* 225
surveillance
care 459
direction 693
under – 938
survene 151
survey 441, 466
surveyor 85, 694
survive *remain* 40
long time 110
permanent 141
susceptibility
power 157
tendency 176
liability 177
sensibility 375
motive 615
impressibility 822
irascibility 901
suscipient 785
suscitate *cause* 153
produce 161
stir up 173
excite 824
suspect *doubt* 485
suppose 514
suspected 938
suspectless 484
suspend *defer* 133
discontinue 142
hang 214
suspended anima-
tion 823
suspender 45, 214
suspense
cessation 142
uncertainty 475
expectation 507
irresolution 605
in – *inert* 172
suspension

cessation 142
hanging 214
music 413
– *of arms* 723
suspicion *doubt* 485
incredulity 487
knowledge 490
supposition 514
fear 860
under – 938
suspiration 839
sustain
continue 143
strength 159
perform 170
support 215
preserve 670
aid 707
endure 821
sustained note 413
sustenance 298
sustentation
[*see* sustain]
food 298
susurration 405
sutler 637, 797
suttee *killing* 361
arson 384
unselfishness 942
idolatry 991
suture 43
suum cuique 780,
922
suzerain 745
suzerainty 737
swab *dry* 340
clean 652
lubber 701
swaddle *clothe* 225
restrain 751
swaddling clothes,
in – *infant* 129
subjection 749
swag *hang* 214
lean 217
curve 245
drop 306
oscillate 314
booty 793
ostentation 887
swag-bellied 194
swage 174
swagger
pride 878
boast 884
bluster 885
swaggerer 887
swain *man* 373
rustic 876
lover 897
swale 659

swallow *gulp* 296
eat 298
believe 484
credulous 486
brook 826
– the bait 547,
602
– *flight* 274
– the leek 607,
725
– *up destroy* 162
store 636
use 677
take 789
– hook, line and
sinker 602
– *whole* 468a, 484
swallow-tail coat
225
swamp *destroy* 162
marsh 345
defeat 731
swamped
failure 732
swampy *moist* 339
swank 845, 882, 884
swan-pan 85
swan-song 360
swap *exchange* 148
blow 276
sward 344
swarm *crowd* 72
multitude 102
climb 305
sufficiency 639
redundance 641
swarthy 431
swash *affuse* 337
spurt 348
swashbuckler 726,
887
swashy 339
swastika 621, 993
swat 276
swath 72
swathe *fasten* 43
clothe 225
restrain 741
sway *power* 157
influence 175
lean 217
oscillate 314
agitation 315
induce 615
authority 737
– to and fro 149
sweal 659
swear *affirm* 535
promise 768
curse 908
just enough to –

by 32
– at 908
– by *believe* 484
– false 544
– a witness 768
sweat *exude* 295
excretion 299
heat 382
exertion 686
fatigue 688
cold – 860
in a – 382
– of one's brow
686
sweater 225
Swedenborgian 984
Swedish dance 840
sweep *space* 180
curve 245
oar 267
rapid 274
bend 279
clean 652
dirty fellow 653
steal 791
make a clean – of
297
– *along* 264
– *away*
destroy 162
eject 297
abrogate 756
relinquish 782
– the chords 416
– off 297
– out 297, 652
– of time 109
sweeper 652
mine– 726
sweeping *whole* 50
complete 52
general 78
– *change* 146
sweepings
useless 645
dirt 653
sweepstakes 775,
810
sweet
saccharine 396
melodious 413
colour 428
clean 652
agreeable 829
lovely 897
look – upon
desire 865
love 897
endearment 902
– smell 400
– tooth 865, 868

on the – 626, 673
turn the –s 218, 468
under the –
  hidden 528
  drunk 959
– of the Lord 1000
– the motion 624
tableau *list* 86
  appearance 448
  painting 556
  theatrical 599
table-cloth 652
table d'hôte 298
table-land 213, 344
tabescent 195
tablet *layer* 204
  flat 251
  record 551
  writing 590
  remedy 662
table-talk 532, 588
tablets of the
  memory 505
table-turning 992
tabloid 531, 662
taboo 762, 992
tabor 417
tabouret 215
tabret 417
tabula rasa
  inexistence 2
  absence 187
  ignorance 491
  obliterated 552
  facility 705
tabulate 60, 69
tabulation 551
tachometer 274
tachygraphy 590
tachy case 191
tacit 526
taciturnity 585
Tacitus
  concise style 572
tack *join* 43
  nails 45
  change course 140
  sharp 253
  direction 278
  turn 279
  food 289
  way 627
  go upon another – 607
  wrong – 732
  – to *add* 37
tackle
  fastening 45
  gear 633
  try 675

undertake 676
manage 693
tacky 352
tact *touch* 379
  discrimination 465
  wisdom 498
  skill 698
  taste 850
  want of – 851
tactful 894
tactician 700
tactics 692, 722
tactless 895
tactile &c. 379
tadpole 129
tædium vitæ 837, 841
tag *small* 32
  addition 37
  adjunct 39
  fastening 45
  sequel 65
  end 67
  point 253
  sheep 366
  – after 281
tagrag and bobtail 876
tail *sequel* 65
  end 67
  pendent 214
  back 235
  aircraft 273
  estate – 780
  turn – 623
  – off *decrease* 36
tail-coat 225
tailor 225, 690
tailoring 225, 882
tail-piece *sequel* 65
  rear 235
  engraving 558
  ornament 847
tail-race 350
taint
  imperfection 651
  dirt 653
  decay 659
  disgrace 874
tainted 401, 655
taintless 652
taj 225
take *eat* 298
  believe 484
  know 490
  understand 518
  succeed 731
  receive 785
  appropriate 789
  captivate 829

give and – 718
– a back 508, 870
– an account of 85
– action 680
– advice 695
– after 17
– aside 586
– away
  annihilate 2
  subtract 38
  remove 185
  seize 789
– back again 790
– a back seat 34
– by [*see below*]
– the cake 33
– care 668, 864
– care of 459, 664
– no care of 460
– off 293
– one's chance 621, 675
– one's choice 609
– things as they come 683, 826
– comfort 831, 834
– the conse-
  quences 154
– coolly 826
– a course 692
– its course 143, 151
– no denial 606, 744
– a disease 655
– down
  swallow 298
  depress 308
  record 551
  write 590
  dismantle 681
  humiliate 874
  censure 932
– easily 826
– effect 151, 170
– an ell 885
– exception 932
– one's fancy 829, 865
– fire 384
– flight 623
– from 38, 789
– for [*see below*]
– the good the gods provide 831
– heart 831, 836
– to heart 828, 832
– heed 864
– a hint 498
– hold of 46, 789

– hold of the mind 484
– ill 832
– in [*see below*]
– an infection 655
– no interest in 823
– into [*see below*]
– it 484, 514
– the lead 62
– a leaf out of an-
  other's book 19
– a lease 788
– leave of 624
– a liberty 748
– away life 361
– a likeness 554
– measures 626
– money 810
– no note of 460
– no note of time 115
– notice 457
– one's oath 535
– off [*see below*]
– oneself off 293
– on [*see below*]
– one with an-
  other 29
– out 301, 552
– over 783
– part with 709
– pattern by 19
– a peep 441
– pen in hand 590
– to pieces 44, 681
– place 151
– the place of 147
– possession of 589
– precedence 33, 62
– its rise 66, 154
– root 150, 184
– the shine out of 33
– ship 267
– steps 673, 680
– stock 85
– time
  duration 106
  late 133
  leisure 685
– time by the
  forelock 132
– to *habit* 613
  pursuit 622
  use 677
  like 827
  desire 865
  love 897
– on trust 484

tape *string* 205
  measure 466
  – machine 553
taper *contract* 195
  narrow 203
  candle 423
  – to a point 253
tapestry 556, 847
tapinois, en – 528
tapis: on the –
  event 151
  topic 454
  intention 620
  plan 626
tap-root 153
taps 550
tapster 746
tar *cover* 223
  sailor 269
  pitch 356a
  – and feather 929,
  972
taradiddle 546
tarantass 272
tarantella 840
tarboosh 225
tardiloquence 583
tardy 133, 275
tare 40a
  – and tret 813
tares 645
targe 717
target 620
  shield 717
tariff 812
tarmac 635
tarn 343
tarnish
  discoloration 429
  soil 653
  deface 848
  disgrace 874
tarpaulin 223
tarry *remain* 110,
  265
  later 133
  continue 141
  – for *expect* 507
tart *pastry* 298, 396
  acid 397
  rude 895
  irascible 901
  harlot 962
tartan 440
tartane 273
Tartar *choleric* 901
  catch a – *dupe* 547
  unskilful 699
  retaliation 718
tartar *dirt* 653
  – emetic 663

Tartarus 982
Tartufe
  hypocrisy 544
  deceiver 548
  impiety 988
task *lesson* 537
  business 625
  put to use 677
  fatigue 688
  command 741
  hard – 704
  set a – 741
  take to – 932
  – the memory 505
taskmaster 694
tass 191
tassel 847
taste *sapidity* **390**
  experience 821
  good taste **850**
  man of – 850
  to one's – *savoury*
  394
  pleasant 829
  love 897
tasteful 850
tasteless *insipid*
  391
tasty 394, 850
tâtonner 463
tatter
  small quantity 32
tatterdemalion 876
Tattersalls 799
tatters *garments*
  225
  tear to – 162
tatting 847
tattle 588
tattler 532, 588
tattoo
  drumming 407
  mottled 440
  summons 741
taught [*see* teach]
  fastened 43
taunt 929, 938
tauromachy 720
taut 43
tautology 104, 573
tavern 189
tawdry 851
tawny 433, 436
tax *inquire* 461
  employ 677
  fatigue 688
  command 741
  compel 744
  request 765
  accounts 811
  impost 812

  discount 813
  accuse 938
  – one's energies
  686
  – the memory 505
taxi 266
taxi-cab 272
taxi-driver 268
taxidermy 368
taxis 60
taxonomy 60
tazza 191
Te Deum 990
te fabula narratur,
  de – *retaliate* 718
  condemn 971
tea 298
teach 537
  – one's grand-
  mother 641, 885
  – one his place 879
teachable 539
teacher **540**, 673
teaching **537**
  false – 538
teacup, storm in a –
  overrate 482, 549
  exaggerate 549
teagown 225
team *assemblage*
  69, 72
teamster 694
tea-party 892
tea-pot 191
tear *separate* 44
  violence 173
  move rapidly 274
  excite 825
  weeping 839
  – away from 789
  – oneself away
  623
  – asunder one's
  bonds 750
  – one's hair 839
  – out 301
  – to pieces
  separate 44
  destroy 162
  – up *destroy* 162
tear-gas 663, 727
tearful 839
tearing passion 839
tears: draw – 830
  shed – 839
  – in one's eyes
  excited 824
  sad 837
tease *annoy* 830
  spite 907
teaser *difficult* 704

teasing 830
teat 250
tea-table talk 588
technic 698
technica, memoria
  – 505
technical
  conformable 82
  workmanlike 698
  – college 542
  – education 537
  – knowledge 698
  – school 542
  – term 564
technicality
  special 79
  cant term 563
  formulary 697
technique 556, 698
technocracy 698
technology 698
techy 901
tedious 841
  while away the –
  hours 681
tedium 841
teem
  produce 161
  productive 168
  abound 639
  – with *multitude*
  102
teemful 168
teeming *crowd* 72
teemless 169
'teens 98
  in one's – 127, 129
teeter 314
teeth 330, 781
  armed to the –
  673, 717, 722
  between the – 405
  cast in one's – 938
  chattering of – 383
  have cut one's eye
  – 698
  in the – of 704, 708
  grind one's – 900
  the run of one's –
  815
  set one's – 604
  show one's – 900
  in spite of one's –
  708, 744
  make one's – chat-
  ter 385, 860
  set the – on edge
  scrape 331
  saw 397
  stridor 410
  pain the feelings

tenter-hook 214
on –s 507
tenth 99
tenths
  tithe 812
tent-pegging 840
tents, O Israel, to
  your – 722
tenue, en grande –
  847, 882
tenuity
  smallness 32
  thinness 203
  rarity 322
tenuous
  shadowy 4
tenure
  possession 777
  property 780
  due 924
tepee 189
tepefaction 384
Tephramancy 511
tepid 382
tepidarium 386
ter quaterque
  beatus 827
teratology
  unconformity 83
  distortion 243
  altiloquence 577
  boasting 884
tercentenary 98,
  138, 883
terceron 41
terebration 260
teres atque rotun-
  dus 249
in seipso – 650
tergiversation 283,
  607
term *end* 67
  place in series **71**
  period of time 106
  limit 233
  word 562
  name 564
  lease 780
termagant 901
terminal 67, 253,
  292
terminate 67, 292
  limit 233
termination 154
termine, mezzo –
  628
terminology 562
terminus *end* 67
  limit 233
  arrival 292
termless 105

terms [*see* term]
  circumstances **8**
  reasoning 476
  pacification 723
  conditions 770
bring to – 723
come to –
  assent 488
  pacify 723
  submit 725
  consent 762
  compact 769
couch in – 566
on friendly – 888
in no measured –
  574
ternary 93
ternion 92
Terpsichore 416,
  840
terra: – cotta
  baked 384
  sculpture 557
– firma
  support 215
  land 342
  safety 664
– incognita 491
terrace *houses* 189
  level 213
terrain 181
terraqueous 318
terre verte 435
terrene 318, 342
terrine 191
terrestrial 318
terrible 860
terribly *greatly* 31
terrier *list* 86
  auger 262
  dog 366
terrific 31, 830, 860
terrify 860
territorial *land* 342
  soldier 726
territory 181, 780
terror 860
  King of –s 360
  reign of – 739, 828
terrorem, in – 860,
  909
terrorism 860
  insolence 885
terrorist
  coward 862
  blusterer 887
  evil-doer 913
terse 572
tertian *periodic* 138
tertiary *three* 92
tertium quid

dissimilar 18
mixture 41
combination 48
unconformable 83
tesselated 440, 847
tesseræ
  mosaic 440
  counters 550
test 463
testa, voce di – 410
testament 771
Testament 985
tester *bedstead* 215
  sixpence 800
testify 467, 550
testimonial 551
testimony 467
testy 901
tetanus 315
tetchy 901
tête: – baissée 863
– exaltée 503
– montée 503, 825
–à-tête *two* 89
  near 197
  confer 588
tether *fasten* 43
  locate 184
  restrain 751
  means of restraint
  752
go beyond the
  length of one's
  – 738
tethered *firm* 150
tetrachord 413
tetractic 95
tetrad 95
tetrahedral 95
tetrahedron 244
tetrarch 745
text *prototype* 22
  topic 454
  meaning 516
  printing 591
–book 542, 596
textile 219, 329
textuary 983*a*, 985
texture *mixture* 41
  roughness 256
  fabric **329**
Thais 962
Thalia 599
Thalmud 985
Thames on fire
  set the – 471
  never set the –
  501, 701
thane *nobility* 875
thank 916
no – you 764

– one's stars 838
– you for nothing
  917
thankful 916
  rest and be – 265,
  831
thankless
  painful 830
  ungrateful 917
thank-offering 916,
  990
thanks to 155
thanksgiving
  gratitude 916
  worship 990
that 79
– is 118
– is to say 79
– being so 8
at – time 119
thatch *roof* 223
thaumatrope 445
thaumaturgist 994
thaumaturgy 992
thaw *melt* 335
  heart 382
  healing 384
  calm the mind 826
  pity 914
Thearchy
  authority 737
  Deity 976
theatre
  spectacle 441
  school 542
  drama 599
  arena 728
  amusement 840
  tribunal 966
théâtre: coup de –
  appearance 448
  prodigy 872
  display 882
jeu de – 448, 872
nom de – 565
theatrical 599
  affected 855
  ostentatious 882
Theban, learned –
  492
theca 223
thé dansant 840
theft 775, 791
theism 984, 987
theistic *of God* 976
theme *topic* 454
  dissertation 595
Themis 922
then *time* 106
  therefore 476
thence

681
under one's –
  authority 737
  subjection 749
  – over 539
  – screw 975
Thumb, Tom – 539
thump
  beat 276
  thud 406
  non-resonance
  408a
  punish 972
thumping *great* 31
  big 192
thunder
  violence 173
  noise 404
  prodigy 872
  threaten 909
look black as –
  832, 900
  – against 908, 932
  – of applause 931
  – forth 531
  – at the top of
  one's voice 411
–s of the Vatican
  908
thunderbolt
  weapon 727
  prodigy 872
thunder-clap 508,
  872
thundering *great* 31
  big 192
thunderstorm 173
thunderstruck 870
thurible 400, 998
thurifer 996
thuriferous 400
thurification
  fragrance 400
  rite 998
thus *circumstance* 8
  therefore 476
  – far *little* 32
  limit 233
thwack 276, 972
thwart
  across 219
  harm 649
  obstruct 706
  oppose 708
  cross 830
thwarted 732
tiara *insignia* 747
  ornament 847
  canonicals 999
Tib's eve 107
tick *graze* 199, 379

  oscillation 314
  sound 407
  mark 550
  credit 805
go on – 806
  – off *record* 551
ticker 553
ticket 86, 550, 609
ticket of leave 760
  – man 754, 949
tickle *touch* 380
  please 829
  amuse 840
  – the fancy 829,
  840
  – the ivories 416
  – the palate 394
  – the palm 784,
  807
ticklish
  uncertain 475
  dangerous 665
  difficult 704
tidal wave 348, 667
tid-bit 648, 829
tide *ocean* 341
  wave 348
  abundance 639
  prosperity 734
against the – 708
drift with the –
  705
go with the – 82
high &c. – 348
stem the – 708
swim with the –
  734
turn of the – 210
  – of events 151
  – over *time* 106
  defer 133
  safe 664
  inaction 681
  succeed 731
  – of time 109
tidings 532
tidy *orderly* 58
  arrange 60
  good 648
  clean 652
  pretty 845
  – up 60
tie *relation* 9
  equality 27
  fasten 43
  fastening 45
  neckcloth 225
  security 771
  obligation 926
  nuptial – 903
  ride and – 266

–s of blood 11
  – down
  hinder 706
  compel 744
  restrain 751
  – the hands 158,
  751
  – oneself 768
  – up *restrain* 751
  condition 770
  entail 771
tie-beam 45
tied up
  busy 135
  in debt 806
tier *continuity* 69
  layer 204
tierce 92
  – and carte 716
tiff 713, 900
tiffin 298
tiger *violent* 173
  servant 746
  courage 861
  savage 907
  evil-doer 913
  bad man 949
tight *fast* 43
  closed 261
  smart 845
  drunk 959
  – grasp 739
  – hand 739
  – rope dancing 698
  keep a – hand on
  751
on one's – ropes
  878
tighten 43, 195
tight-fisted 819
tights 225
tightwad 819
tigress 374
tike 876
tilbury 272
tile *roof* 223
  hat 225
  – loose *insane* 503
till *up to the time*
  106
  coffer 191
  cultivate 371
  treasury 802
  – doomsday 112
  – now 122
  – the soil 673
tiller
  instrument 633
  money-box 802
  – of the soil
  agriculture 371

  clown 876
tilt *slope* 217
  cover 223
  propel 284
  fall 306
  contention 720
full – *direct* 278
  active 682
  haste 684
ride full – at 622,
  716
run a – at 716
  – over 218
  – up 307
  – with 720
tilth 371, 775
tilting at the ring
  840
tilt-yard 728
timber *trees* 367
  materials 635
timbre 413
timbrel 417
time 106
  instant 113
  leisure 685
against – 684
at –s 136
behind the –s 124
course of – 109
doing –
  imprisonment 752
employ one's – in
  625
glass of – 106
in – *course* 109
  early 132
  destiny 152
measure – 114
no – *instantly* 113
  soon 132
no – to lose 630,
  684
no – to spare 684
ravages of – 659
slow – 275
take – *slow* 275
  inaction 681
  inactive 683
true – 113
waste – 683
  – and again 104
  – has been 122
  – being 118
  – to come 121
  – of day 113
  – drawing on 121
  – enough 132
  – gone by 135
  – hanging on one's
  hands

inaction 681
leisure 685
weariness 841
- *immemorial* 122
- of life
  duration 106
  now 118
  age 128
- out of mind 122
- to spare 685
- after time 104
- up 111, 134
- was 122
there being –s
  when 136
timeful 134
time-honoured
  old 124
  repute 873
  respected 928
time-keeper 114
time-recorder 553
timeless 135
timelessness 112
timely 132, 134
timeo Danaos 485,
  864
timeous 134
time-piece 114
time-pleaser 607
timetable 605
times *present* 118
  events 151
  hard – 735
  many – 136
- out of number
  104
time-serving
  tergiversation 607
  cunning 702
  servility 886
  improbity 940
  selfishness 943
time-worn *old* 124
  age 128
  deteriorated 659
timid *fearful* 860
  cowardly 862
  humble 881
timist 607
Timocracy 803
Timon of Athens
  wealth 803
  seclusion 893
  misanthrope 911
timorous [*see* timid]
tin *preserve* 670
  money 800
- hat 717
tinct 428
tinctorial 428

tincture
  small quantity 32
  mixture 41
  colour 428
tinctured
  disposition 820
tinder *fuel* 388
  irascible 901
tine 253
tinge
  small quantity 32
  mix 41
  colour 428
tingent 428
tingle *pain* 378
  touch 380
  emotion 821
  make the ears –
  900
tink 408
tinker
  repair 660
tinkle
  faint sound 405
  resonance 408
tinkling cymbal 517
tinnient 408
tinsel *glitter* 420
  sham 545
  ornament 847
  frippery 851
tinsmith 690
tint 428
tintamarre 404
tintinnabulary 408
tiny 32, 193
- bit 32
tip *end* 67
  summit 210
  cover 223
  give 784
  reward 973
  on –toe *high* 206
  expect 507
- off 527
- the wink 550
tip-cat 840
tippet 214, 225
tipple 298, 959
tippler 959
tipstaff 965
tipsy 959
tip-top 210, 648
tirade 582, 932
tire *dress* 225
  fatigue 688
  worry 830
  weary 841
tiré à quatre épin-
  gles 850
tirer d'affaire 672

se – 731
Tiresias 513
tiresome [*see* tire]
Tisiphone 173, 900
tissue *whole* 50
  assemblage 72
  matted 219
  texture 329
tit *small* 193
  pony 271
tit for tat 718
Titan 159, 980
Titania 979
titanic 192
titbit 291, 394, 829
tithe *tenth* 99
  tax 812
tithing 181
titillate 840, 865
titillation 377, 380
titivate 847
title
  indication 550
  name 564
  printing 590
  right to property
  780
  distinction **877**
  right 924
titled 875
title-deed 771
title-page 66
titter 838
tittle 32
  to a – 494
tittle-tattle 532, 588
titubancy 583
titubate 306, 732
titular 562, 564
tmesis 218
T.N.T. 727
to *direction* 278
  lie – 681
- all intents and
  purposes 27, 52
- a certain degree
  32
- come 121, 152
- the credit of 805
- crown all 33, 642
- do 59
- the end of the
  chapter 52
- the end of time
  112
- and fro 12, 314
- the full 52
- a great extent
  31
- the letter 19
- a man 78

- the point 23
- the purpose 23
- a small extent 32
- some extent 26
- be sure 488
- this day 118
- wit 79
toad 649, 846
- under a harrow
  378
toad-eater 886, 935
toad-eating
  flattery 933
toadstool 367
toady 886
toast *roast* 384
  celebrate 883
tobacco 392
toboggan 272, 840
toby *jug* 191
toccata 415
tocsin 669
tod 319
to-day 118
toddle 266, 275
toddy 298
toe 211
  on the light fan-
  tastic 309, 840
  toes turn up the –
  die 360
toff 854
toffee 396
toga 225, 747
  assume the –
  virilis 131
together 88, 120
  come – 290
  get – 72
  hang – 709
  lay heads – 695
- with 37, 88
toggery 225
toil
  activity 682
  exertion 686
- of a pleasure 682
- s *trap* 545
toilet 225
- water 400
toilette 225
  en grande – 847
toilsome 686, 704
toilworn 688
token 550
  give – 525
- of remembrance
  505
told, do what one
  is – 743
tolderolloll 838

Tories 712
torment
  physical 378
  moral 828, 830
  place of – 982
Tormes, Lazarillo
  de – 941
torn [*see* tear]
  discord 713
tornado 312, 349
torpedo *bane* 663
  sluggish 683
  weapon 727
  evil-doer 913
  – boat 726
  – boat destroyer
   726
  – plane 276
torpid, torpor
  inert 172
  inactive 683
  insensible 823
torque 847
  torrefy 384
torrent
  violence 173
  rapid 274
  flow 348
  rain in –s 348
torrid 382
torsion 248
torso 50
tort 925, 947
tort et à travers, à –
  disagreement 24
  absurdity 497
  resolution 604
tortious 925
tortile 248
tortive 248
tortoise 275
tortoise-shell 440
tortuous
  twisted 248
  dishonourable 940
torture
  physical 378
  moral 828, 830
  cruelty 907
  punishment 972
  – a question 476
torvity 901*a*
toss *derange* 61
  throw 284
  oscillate 314
  agitate 315
  – in a blanket 929
  – the caber 840
  – the head
  pride 878
  insolence 885

contempt 930
– off *drink* 298
– overboard 610
– on one's pillow
  825
– up 156, 621
tosspot 959
tot *child* 129
tot homines, tot
  sententiæ 15
total 50, 84
  sum – 800
  – abstinence 953,
   955
  – eclipse 421
totalisator 621
totality 52
totally 52
totidem verbis 19,
  494
totient 84
toties quoties 136
totis viribus 686
totitive 84
toto: in – 52
  – cœlo 52
totter
  changeable 149
  weak 160
  limp 275
  oscillate 314
  agitate 315
  decay 659
  danger 665
  – to its fall 162
touch *relate to* 9
  small quantity 32
  mixture 41
  contact 199
  sensation **379,
   380**
  music 416
  test 463
  indication 550
  act 680
  receive 785
  excite 824
  pity 914
  – and go
  instant 113
  soon 132
  changeable 149
  easy 705
  – the guitar 416
  – the hat 894
  – the heart 824
  – on 516
  – to the quick 822
  – up 658
  – upon 595
  in – with 9

touched *crazy* 503
  tainted 653
  compassion 914
  – in the wind 655
  – with *feeling* 821
touching 830
touchstone 463
touchwood
  fuel 388
  irascible 901
touchy 901
tough *coherent* 46
  tenacious 327
  difficult 704
toujours perdrix
  repetition 104
  weary 841
  satiety 869
toupee 256
tour 266
tour de force
  skill 698
  stratagem 702
  display 882
touring car 272
tourist 268
tournament 720
tourniquet 263
tournure 230, 448
  belle – 845
tous les rapports,
  sous – 494
tousle 61
tout *solicit* 765
tout: – au contraire
  14
  – court 265
  – ensemble 50
  – le monde 78
touter *agent* 758
  solicitor 767
  eulogist 935
tow 285
  take in – *aid* 707
towage 812
towardly 705
towards 278
  draw – 288
  move – 286
towel *clean* 652
  flog 972
tower
  stability 150
  edifice 161
  abode 189
  height 206
  soar 305
  defence 717
  – of strength
  strong 159
  influential 175

  safety 664
towering *great* 31
  furious 173
  large 192
  high 206
  – passion 900
  – rage 900
town *city* 189
  fashion 852
  man about – 854
  on the – 961
  all over the – 532
  talk of the – 873
  – council 696
town-hall 189, 966
township 181
townsman 188
  fellow – 892
town-talk 532, 588
toxic 657
toxicology 663
toxophilite 284
toy *trifle* 643
  amusement 840
  fondle 902
toy-dog 366
toy-shop 840
trabant 717
tracasserie 713
trace *inquire* 461
  discover 480*a*
  mark 550
  record 551
  delineate 554
  – back 122
  – out 480*a*
  – to 155
  – up 461
tracery
  lattice 219
  curve 245
  ornament 847
traces *harness* 45
trachea 351
tracing 21
track *trace* 461
  record 551
  way 627
  cover up one's –s
   528
  in one's –s 113
  racing – 840
  – meet 840
  – racing 728
trackless
  space 180
  difficult 704
  – trolley 272
tract *region* 181
  book 593
  dissertation 595

- of time 109
tractable
 malleable 324
 willing 602
 easy 705
tractarian 984
tractile
 traction **285**
 soft 324
traction 285
tractor 271
trade *exchange* 148
 business 625
 traffic 794
 drive a – 625
 learn one's – 539
 tricks of the – 702
 two of a – 708
 – with 794
trader 797
trade-mark 550
tradesman 797
trade-publication 531
trade-union 712
trade-wind 349
tradition *old* 124
 description 594
 custom 613
traduce 934
traducer 936
traffic 794
tragedian 599
tragedy
 drama 599
 evil 619
tragic *drama* 599
tragical 830
tragi-comedy 599
tragi-comic 853
trail *sequel* 65
 pendent 214
 slow 275
 follow 281
 traction 285
 odour 398
 inquiry 461
 record 551
 highway 627
 follow in the – of 281
 – of a red herring 615, 706
train *sequel* 65
 series 69
 pendent 214
 vehicle 272
 sequence 281
 traction 285
 - *animals* 370
 teach 537

accustom 613
 prepare 673
 bring in its – 615
 in – 673
 in the – of 281, 746
 lay a – 626, 673
 put in – 673
 siege – 727
 – de luxe 272
 – of reasoning 476
 – of thought 451
train-band 726
train-bearer 746
train-ferry 272
trained 698
trainer
 - *of horses* 268
 - *of animals* 370
 teacher 540
training
 education 537
 – college 542
train-oil 356
traipse 275
trait *speciality* 79
 appearance 448
 mark 550
 description 594
traitor
 disobedient 742
 knave 941
 enemy 891
trajection 297
trajectory 627
tra-la-la 838
tralatitious 521
tralineate 279
tralucent 425
tram 272
trammel *hinder* 706
 restrain 751
 fetter 752
 cast –s off 750
tramontane
 foreign 57
 distant 196
 wind 349
 outlandish 851
tramp *stroll* 266
 stroller 268
 idler 683
 vagabond 867
 on the – 264
trample
 – in the dust
 destroy 162
 prostrate 308
 – out 162
 – under foot
 vanquish 731

not observe 773
 disrepute 874
 insolence 885
 dereliction 927
 contempt 930
 – upon 649, 739
tramway 627
trance *insensibility* 376
 dream 515
 sleep 683
 lethargy 823
tranquil *calm* 174
 quiet 265
 peaceful 721
 calmness 871
 – *mind* 826
tranquillize
 moderate 174
 pacify 723
 soothe 826
transact *act* 680
 conduct 692
 – *business* 625
 – business with 794
transaction 151, 625, 680, 769
transactions 551
transalpine 196
transanimation 140
transatlantic 196
transcalency 384
transcend *great* 31
 superior 33
 go beyond 303
transcendency 641
transcendent 33, 873
transcendental 78, 519
transcendentalism 450
transcolate 295
transcribe 19, 590
transcript 21, 590
transcursion **303**
transept 1000
transfer
 copy 21
 displace 185
 - *of things* 270
 - *of property* **783**
 transference **270**
transfiguration
 change 140
 divine - 998
transfix 260
transfixed *firm* 150
transform 140
transformation

scene 599
transfuse 41, 270
 – the sense of 522
transgress
 go beyond 303
 infringe 773
 violate 927
 sin 945
transgression 947
transi de froid 383
transient 111, 149
transientness 111
transilience 146, 303
transit
 conversion 144
 motion 264
 transference 270
 - *circle* 244
transit gloria mundi, sic – 735, 874
transition 144, 270
transitional 140
transitory 111
transitu, in –
 transient 111
 journey 266
 transference 270
translate
 interpret 522
 promote 955
translator 524
translation
 transference 270
 resurrection 981
translocation 270
translucence 425
transmarine 196
transmigration 140, 144
transmission
 moving 270
 passage 302
 - *of property* 783
transmit light 425
transmogrify 140
transmutation 140, 144
transom 215
transparency 425
transparent
 transmitting light 425
 obvious 518
transpicuous
 transmitting light 425
 obvious 518
transpierce 260
transpire

evaporate 336
appear 525
be disclosed 529
transplace 270
transplant 270
transplendent 420
transpontine 196
transport
transfer 270
ship 273
war vessel 726
excitement 825
delight 827
please 829
punish 972
– of love 897
– plane 273
transpose
exchange 148
displace 185
invert 218
transfer 270
- *music* 413
transubstantiation
change 140
sacrament 998
transude 295, 302
transume 140
transumption 270
transverse 217, 219
tranter 271
trap *closure* 261
gig 272
snare 545
stage – 599
pitfall 667
fall into a – 547, 699
lay a – for 545
trap bat and ball 840
trap-door
opening 260
snare 545
pitfall 667
trapan 545
trapes 701
trappings
adjunct 39
clothes 225
equipment 633
ornament 847
Trappist 996
traps
clothes 225
baggage 780
trash
unmeaning 517
trifling 643
useless 645
trashy – style 575

traulism 583
traumatic 662
travail 161, 686
trave 215
travel 266
– out of the record 477
traveller 268
bagman 758
tricks upon –s 545, 702
–'s tale 546, 549
travelling bag 191
traverse *move* 266
pass 302
negative 536
obstruct 706
travesty
imitate 19, 21
misinterpret 523
misrepresent 555
ridicule 856
travis 215
trawl 285, 463
trawler 273
tray 191
treacherous 907, 940
– memory 506
treachery 545, 940
treacle 352, 396
tread 264, 266
– the beaten track 82, 613
– the boards 599
– down 739, 879
– on the heels of 281
– a path 266, 622
– the stage 599
– in the steps of 19
– under foot
destroy 162
subjection 749
disrepute 874
insolence 885
contempt 930
– upon 649
treadle 633
treadmill 975
treason 742, 940
treasure *cherish* 897
store 636
goodness 648
money 800
– trove 618
– up in the memory 505
treasurer **801**
treasury **802**
– note 800

treat *physical pleasure* 377
manage 692
bargain 769
delight 827, 829
amusement 840
– of 595
– oneself to 827
– well 906
treatise 593, 595
treatment
painting 556
conduct 692
ill – 649
medical – 662
treaty 769
treble
three 93
shrill 410
childish – 581
tree *pedigree* 166
plant 367
gallows 975
top of the – 210
up a – 704
as the – falls 151
– of knowledge 493
treenail 45
trefoil 92
trek 266
trellis 219
tremble
fluctuate 149
weakness 160
shake 315
cold 383
emotion 821
fear 860
make one – 860
trembling:
– in the balance 475, 665
– to its fall 160
tremblingly alive 822
tremendous 830, 860
tremendously 31
tremolo 415
tremor
agitation 315
emotion 821
fearful 860
tremulous
agitated 315
- *voice* 583
irresolute 605
fear 860
trench *moat* 232
furrow 259

concavity 252
defence 717
– *mortar* 727
– on *near* 197
trespass 303
moral trespass 925
trenchant
energetic 171
assertive 535
concise style 572
vigorous language 574
important 642
emotion 821
discourteous 895
censure 932
trench-coat 225
trencher *plate* 191
layer 204
trenches, open the – 716
trend *tendency* 176
bend 278
deviate 279
trennel 45
trepan 260
snare 545
borer 262
trephine 260, 267
trepidation
agitation 315
emotion 821
excitement 825
fear 860
tres juncta in uno 92
trespass
go beyond 303
vice 945
guilt 947
tress 256
trestle 215
trevet 215
[*and see* trivet]
trews 225
trey 92
triad 92
triagonal 244
trial *inquiry* 461
experiment 463
essay 675
difficulty 704
adversity 735
suffering 828, 830
lawsuit 969
punishment 972
– of temper 824
triality **92**
trialogue 588
triangle 92, 244

music 417
punishment 975
triangular duel 720
triarchy 737
tribe *race* 11
  assemblage 72
  class 75
  clan 166
tribulation 828
tribunal **966**
tribune
  rostrum 542
  judge 967
tributary *river* 348
  giving 784
tribute
  compensation 30
  donation 784
  money paid 809
  reward 973
  pay – *to* 928, 931
trice 113, 633
 – up 43
 in a – 113
trichotomy 94
trichroism 440
trick *deception* 545
  trait 550
  habit 613
  contrivance 626
  skill 698
  artifice 702
 – *at cards* 775
 play –s
  bungle 699
  cunning 702
  amusement 840
  ridicule 856
 – of fortune 509
 – out 847, 851
 –s of the trade 702
trickery *deceit* 545
  finery 851
trickle 295, 348
trickster
  deceiver 548
  cunning 702
  rogue 792
tricksy *cheery* 836
  pretty 845
  ornamented 847
tricolour
  variegated 440
  flag 550
tricycle 272
trident 92, 341
triennial
  periodical 138
  plant 367
triennium 92
trifid 94

trifle *small* 32
  neglect 460
  folly 499
  unimportant 643
 not to be –d with
  744
 not stick at –s 604
 – time away 683
 – with *neglect* 460
  deceive 545
  disrespect 929
trifler 460, 501
trifling 499, 643
  wit 842
triforium 1000
triform 92
trifurcate 94
trigamy 903
trigger 633
 draw the – 722
Trigger, Sir Lucius
  O' – 887
trigon 244
trigonometry 244
trihedral 93
trilateral 236, 244
trilogistic 93
trilogy 93
  drama 599
trill *stream* 348
  sound 407
  music 416
trillion 98
trim *state* 7
  adjust 27
  dress 225
  form 240
  lie 544
  waver 605
  change sides 607
  clean 652
  beautify 845
  adorn 847
  scold 932
  flog 972
 in – order 58
trimmer *fickle* 607
  apostate 941
  selfish 943
trimming
  border 231
  ornament 847
  dishonesty 940
trinal 92
trine 93
trinitrotoluene 727
trinity 92
 – Sunday 998
Trinity, Holy – 976
trinket 643, 847

trinkgeld 784
trinal 93
trinomial 92
trio *three* 92
  music 415
triolet 597
trip *jaunt* 266
  run 274
  fall 306
  leap 509
  mistake 495
  bungle 699
  fail 732
  vice 945
  guilt 947
 – up *deceive* 545
  overthrow 731
tripartition 94
triplane 273
triple 93
 – crown 747, 999
triplet *three* 92
  verse 597
triplex 93
triplication **93**
triplicity 93
tripod 215
tripos 461
tripotage 588
tripping [*see* trip]
  style 578
  nimble 682
 caught – 491
trippingly on the
  tongue 584
Triptolemus 371
trireme 273
trisection **94**
triste 837
tristful 837
trisulcate
  trisected 94
  furrow 259
trite
  known 490
  conventional 613
 – saying 496
tritheism 984
Triton *sea* 341
 – among the
  minnows
  superior 33
  huge 192
  important 642
trituration 330
trium literarum,
  homo – 792
triumph
  success 731
  trophy 733
  exult 838

celebrate 883
  boast 884
triumvirate 92, 737
triune 93
Triune God 976
trivet 215, 386
 right as a – 650,
  924
trivia 643
trivial
  unmeaning 517
  trifling 643
  useless 645
troat 412
trocar 262
trochaic 597
trochee 597
trochilic 312
trodden: down–
  749
 well – 613, 677
Troglodyte 893
troika 92
troll
  roll 312
  fairy 980
trollop 962
trolley 272
 – omnibus 272
trombone 417
tronk 752
troop 72, 726
 raise –s 722
 – carrier
  aeroplane 726
trooper 726
 lie like a – 544
 swear like a – 908
troop-ship 726
trop, de – 641
trope 521
Trophonius, cave
  of – 837
trophy 551, **733**
tropical 382
troposphere 338
trot 266, 274
 – out 525, 882
troth *belief* 484
  veracity 543
  promise 768
 by my – 535
 plight one's – 902
trothless 544, 940
trotters 266
trottoir 627
troubadour 597
trouble *disorder* 59
  derange 61
  exertion 686
  difficulty 704

adversity 735
pain 828
painful 830
bring into – 649
get into – 649, 732
in – 619, 735
take – 686
– one's head
about 682
– one for 765
– oneself 686
troubled waters,
fish in – 704
troublesome 686,
704, 830
troublous 59, 173
– times 713
trough *hollow* 252
trench 259
conduit 350
trounce 932, 972
troupe 72
trousers 225
trousseau 225
trouvaille 775
trouvère 597
trover 775, 964
trow *think* 451
believe 484
know 490
trowel 191
troy-weight 319
truant *absent* 187
runaway 623
idle 682
apostate 941
truce *cessation* 142
deliverance 672
peace 721
pacification 723
flag of – 724
trucidation 361
truck *summit* 210
vehicle 272
barter 794
truck driver 268
truck farm 371
truckle to
submit 725
servile 886
flatter 933
truckle-bed 215
truck-load 31
truckman 268
truculent 907
trudge 266, 275
truditur dies die
109
true *real* 1
straight 246
assent 488

accurate 494
veracious 543
faithful 772
honourable 939
orthodox 983a
– bill
vindicate 937
accuse 938
lawsuit 969
see in its –
colours 480a
– meaning 516
– to nature 17
– to oneself 604a
– saying 496
– to scale 494
true-hearted 543,
939
true-love 897
true-lover's knot
897, 902
true-penny 939
truism *axiom* 496
unmeaning 517
trull 962
truly *very* 31
assent 488
really 494
indeed 535
trump *perfect* 650
honourable 939
good man 948
turn up –s 731
– card *device* 626
success 731
– up *falsehood* 544
accuse 938
trumped up 468,
545, 546
trumpery 517, 643
trumpet *music* 417
war cry 722
boast 884
flourish of –s
ostentation 882
celebration 883
boasting 884
ear– 418
penny –
skill 410
sound of –
alarm 669
speaking – 418
– blast 404
– call 550, 741
– forth 531
trumpeter
musician 416
messenger 534
boaster 884
trumpet-toned 410

trumpet-tongued
404, 531
truncate 201, 241
truncated 53
truncheon
weapon 727
staff of office 747
instrument of
punishment 975
trundle 284, 312
trunk *whole* 50
origin 153
paternity 166
box 191
trunk-hose 225
trunnion
support 215
projection 250
truss *tie* 43
pack, packet 72
support 215
trust
belief 484
combination 709
property 780
credit 805
hope 858
– to a broken reed
699
– to the chapter of
accidents 621
trustee
consignee 758
possessor 779
treasurer 801
trustful 484
trustless 940
trustworthy
certain 474
belief 484
- *memory* 505
veracious 543
honourable 939
truth
exactness **494**
veracity 543
probity 939
arrive at the –
480a
in – *certainly* 474
love of – 543
of a – 535, 543
prove the – of 937
religious – 983a
speak the – 529,
543
in very – 543
Truth, Spirit of –
976
truthless 544
trutination 319

try *experiment* 463
adjudge 480
endeavour 675
use 677
lawsuit 969
– a case 967
– a cause 480
– conclusions
discuss 476
quarrel 713
contend 720
– one's hand 675
– one's luck 621
– one 704
– out 463
– the patience 830
– a prisoner 967
– one's temper 824
– one's utmost 686
trying 688, 704
tryst 892
trysting-place 74
tsar [*see* czar]
tu quoque 718
– argument
counter-evidence
468
confutation 479
accuse 938
tub 191
– thumper 582
– to a whale 545,
617
tuba 417
tubam trepidat,
ante – 860, 862
tubby 202
tube 260
test – 144
tubercle 250
tuberculous 655
tuberosity 250
tubman 968
tubular 260
tubulated 260
tubule 260
tuck *fold* 258
dagger 727
– in *locate* 184
eat 298
insert 300
tucker 225
tuft *collection* 72
rough 256
tufted 256
tuft-hunter 836,
943
tuft-hunting 886,
933
tug *ship* 273
pull 285

unbesought 766
unbetrayed 939
unbewailed 932
unbiassed 498, 748
unbidden 600, 742
unbigoted 498
unbind 44, 750
unblamable 946
unblamed 946
unblemished 650,
 946
unblenching 861
unblended 42
unblest 735, 932
 – with 777a
unblown 674
uncommenced 67
unblushing
 proud 878
 vain 880
 imprudent 885
unboastful 881
unbodied 317
unboiled 674
unbolt 750
unbookish 491
unborn 2, 152
unborrowed 787,
 788
unbosom oneself
 529
unbought
 not bought 796
 honorary 815
 honourable 939
 unselfish 942
unbound 748, 927a
unbounded 105
unbrace 160, 655
unbreathed 526
unbred 895
unbribed 939, 942
unbridled
 violent 173
 lax 738
 free 748
unbroken
 entire 50
 continuous 69
 preserved 670
 unviolated 939
unbruised 50
unbuckle 44
unburden
 – one's mind 529
unburdened 705
unburied 362
unbusinesslike 699
unbuttoned 748
uncalculating 863
uncalled for

redundant 641
useless 645
not used 678
uncandid 544, 907
uncanny 846, 980
uncanonical 984
uncared for
 neglected 460
 indifference 866
 disliked 867
 hated 898
uncase 226
uncaught 748
uncaused 156
unceasing 112
uncensured 931
unceremonious
 880, 895
uncertain
 irregular 139
 not certain 475
 doubtful 485
in an – degree 32
uncertainty 475
unchain 44, 750
unchained 748
unchallenged 488,
 924
unchangeable 150,
 604a
unchanged 16, 141
unchanging 5
uncharitable 907
unchartered 925,
 964
unchaste 961
unchastised 970
unchecked 748
uncheckered 141
uncheerful 837
unchivalric 940
unchristian 984,
 989
uncial 590
uncinated 244
uncircumscribed
 180
uncircumspect 460
uncivil 851, 895
uncivilized 876, 895
unclaimed 748
unclassical 851
uncle kin 11
 my –'s
 pawnshop 787
unclean 653
 – spirit 978, 980
uncleanness 653
unclipped 50
unclog 705, 750
unclose 260, 750

unclothe 226
unclouded 420, 446
unclubbable 893
unclutch 790
uncoif 226
uncoil 313
uncoloured
 achromatic 429
 true 494
uncombed 653, 851
uncombined
 simple 42
 incoherent 47
uncomeatable 471
uncomely 846
uncomfortable 828,
 830
uncommenced 67
uncommendable
 blamable 932
 bad 945
 guilt 947
uncommensurable
 24
uncommon 31, 83,
 137
uncommonly 31
uncommunicated
 781
uncommunicative
 528
uncompact 322
uncompassionate
 914a
uncompelled 748
uncomplaisant 764
uncompleted
 incomplete 53
 unfinished 730
 failure 732
uncomplying 742,
 764
uncompounded 42
uncompressed 320,
 322
uncompromising
 conformable 82
 severe 739
unconcealable 525
unconceived
 uncreated 12
 unintelligible 519
unconcern 823, 866
unconcocted 674
uncondemned 970
unconditional
 complete 52
 free 748
 permission 760
 consent 762
 release 768a

unconducive 175a
unconfined 748
unconfirmed 475
unconformity
 disagreement 24
 irregularity 83
unconfused
 methodical 58
 clear 518
unconfuted 478,
 494
uncongealed 333
uncongenial 24, 657
unconnected
 irrelative 10
 disjointed 44
 discontinuous 70
 illogical 477
unconquerable
 strong 159
 persevering 604a
 – will 604
unconquered 719
unconscientious
 940
unconscionable
 excessive 31
 unprincipled 945
unconscious
 ignorant 491
 insensible 823
unconsenting 603,
 764
unconsidered 452
unconsolable 837
unconsolidated 47
unconsonant 24
unconspicuous 447
unconstitutional
 925, 964
unconstrained 748,
 880
unconsumed 40
uncontested 474
uncontradicted 488
uncontrite 951
uncontrollable
 violent 173
 necessity 601
 emotion 825
uncontrolled
 free 748
 excitability 825
uncontroverted 488
unconventional 83,
 614
unconversant 491,
 699
unconverted
 dissenting 489
 irreligious 989

unconvinced 489
uncooked 674
uncopied 20
uncork 750
uncorrupted 939
uncounted 475
uncouple 44
uncourteous 895
uncourtly 851, 895
uncouth
  - style 579
  ugly 846
  vulgar 851
uncover
  denude 226
  open 260
  disclose 529
  bow 894
uncreated 2
uncritical 931
uncropped 50
uncrown 756
unction
  emotion 821, 824
  divine functions
  976
  piety 987
  extreme – 998
  lay the flattering
  – to one's soul
  834, 858
unctuous *oily* 355,
  894
  flattering 933
  hypocritical 988
unctuousness **355**
unculled
  unused 678
  relinquished 782
unculpable 946
uncultivated
  vulgar 85
  ignorant 491
  unprepared 674
uncurbed 748
uncurl 246
uncustomary 83
uncut 50
undamaged (648)
undamped 340
undated
  without date 115
  waving 248
undaunted 861
undazzled 498
undebauched 939
undeceive 527, 529
undeceived 490
undecided
  inquiring 461
  uncertain 475

irresolute 605
leave – 609*a*
undecipherable 519
undecked 849
undecomposed 42
undefaced 845
undefended 725
undefiled
  honest 939
  innocent 946
  chaste 960
undefinable
  uncertain 475
  unmeaning 517
  unintelligible 519
undefined
  invisible 447
  uncertain 475
undeformed 845
undemolished 50
undemonstrable
  485
undemonstrated
  475
undemonstrative
  826
undeniable 474, 478
undeplored 898
undepraved 939
undeprived 781
under *less* 34
  below 207
  subject to 749
  range – 76
  – advisement 454
  – age 127
  – agent 758
  – arrest 751
  – breath 405
  – the conditions 8
  – one's control 743
  – cover
  covered 223
  hidden 528
  safe 664
  – the domination
  of 737
  – one's eyes 446
  – foot [*see below*]
  – full strength 651
  – the head of 9
  – lock and key 664
  – the mark 34
  – press of 744
  – protest 489, 744
  – restraint 751
  – the rule of 737
  – seal 467
  – subjection 749
  – the sun 1
  – way 282

underbid 794
underbreath 405
underbred 851
underclothing 225
undercurrent
  cause 153
  stream 348, 349
  latent 526
  opposing 708
underestimation
  483
underfed 640
underfoot 207
  tread – 739
undergo 151
  – a change 144
  – pain 828
undergraduate 541
underground
  low 207
  deep 208
  latent 526
  hidden 528
underhand 526, 528
  – dealing 528
underhung 250
underived 20
underlessee 779
underlet 787
underlie 207, 526
underline
  mark 550
  emphatic 642
underling
  servant 746
  clown 876
undermine
  weaken 158
  burrow 252
  damage 659
  stratagem 702
  hinder 706
undermost 211
underneath 207
undernourished
  640
underpaid 817
underpin 215
underplot 626
underprop 215
underrate 483
underreckon 483
undersell 796
underset 215
undershot 250
undersign 467
undersized 193
understand
  know 490
  intelligible 518
  latent 526

be informed 527
give one to – 572
  – by 516, 522
  – one another
  709, 714
understanding
  agreement 23
  intellect 450
  intelligence 498
  come to an – 488
  intelligible 518
  agree 714
  pacification 723
  compact 769
  good – 714, 888
  by a mutual – 526
  with the – 469
understate 489
understood
  meaning 516
  implied 526
  customary 613
understrapper 746
understudy 134
undertake
  endeavour 676
  promise 768
undertaker 363
undertaking 625,
  676
undertone 405
undertow 348
undervalue 483
underwood 367
underwrite
  promise 768
  compact 769
  insurance 771
underwriter 758
undescribed 83
undeserved 925
undeserving of be-
  lief 485
undesigned 621
undesigning 703
undesirable 647,
  830
undesired 830, 866
undesirous 866
undespairing 858
undestroyed
  existing 1
  whole 50
  persisting 141
undetermined
  chance 156
  inquiry 461
  uncertain 475
  unintelligible 519
  irresolute 605
undeveloped 526

unforfeited 781
unforgettable 505
unforgiving 919
unforgotten 505
unformed 241, 674
unfortified
  pure 42
  powerless 158
unfortunate
  ill-timed 135
  failure 732
  adversity 735
  unhappy 828
  – woman 962
unfounded 546
unfrequent 137
unfrequented 893
unfriended
  powerless 158
  secluded 893
unfriendly
  opposed 708
  hostile 889
  malevolent 907
unfrock 756, 972
unfrozen 382
unfruitful 169
unfulfilled 713, 925
unfurl
  unfold 313
  – a flag 525, 550
unfurnished 640,
  674
ungainly 846, 895
ungallant 895
ungarnished 849
ungathered 678
ungenerous 819,
  943
ungenial 657
ungenteel 851, 895
ungentle 173, 895
ungentlemanly
  vulgar 851
  rude 895
  dishonourable 940
ungifted 499
unglorified 874
unglue 47
ungodly 989
ungovernable
  violent 173
  disobedient 742
  passionate 825
ungoverned 748
ungraceful
  - language 579
  ugly 846
  vulgar 851
ungracious 895, 907
ungrammatical 568

ungranted 764
ungrateful 917
ungratified 832
ungrounded
  unsubstantial 4
  erroneous 495
ungrudging 816
unguarded
  neglected 460
  spontaneous 612
  unprepared 674
  in an – moment
  unexpectedly 508
unguem, ad – 494,
  650
unguent 356
unguibus et rostro
  686
unguided
  ignorant 491
  impulsive 612
  unskilled 699
unguilty 946
unhabitable 187
unhabituated 614
unhackneyed 614
unhallowed 988,
  989
unhand 750
unhandseled 123
unhandsome 940
unhandy 699
unhappy
  adversity 735
  pain 828
  dejected 837
  make – 830
unharbored 185
unhardened
  tender 914
  innocent 946
  penitent 950
unharmonious 24,
  414
unharness 750
unhatched 674
unhazarded 664
unhealthy 655, 657
unheard of
  exceptional 83
  improbable 473
  ignorant 491
  wonderful 870
unheated 383
unheed, -ed 460
unheeding 458
unhesitating
  belief 484
  resolved 604
unhewn 241, 674
unhindered 748

unhinge 61, 158
unhinged
  impotent 158
  insane 503
  failure 732
unhitch 44
unholy 989
unhonoured 874
unhook (44)
unhoped 508
unhorsed 732
unhostile 888
unhouse 297
unhoused 185
unhurt 670
unicorn
  monster 83
  carriage 272
unideal *existing* 1
  no thought 452
  true 494
unification 48, 87
uniform
  homogeneous 16
  simple 42
  orderly 58
  regular 80
  dress 225
  symmetry 242
  livery 550
uniformity **16**
unilluminated 421
unimaginable 471,
  473
  wonderful 870
unimaginative 576,
  843, 868
unimagined 1, 494
unimitated 20
unimpaired 670
unimpassioned 826
unimpeachable
  certain 474
  true 494
  due 924
  approved 931
  innocent 946
unimpeached 931,
  946
unimpeded 705, 748
unimportance **643**
unimpressed 838
unimpressible 823
unimproved 659
unincreased 36
unincumbered
  easy 705
  exempt 927a
uninduced 616
uninfected 652
uninfectious 656

uninflammable 385
uninfluenced
  obstinate 606
  unactuated 616
  free 768
uninfluential 172,
  175a
uninformed 491
uningenuous 544
uninhabit, -able,
  -ed 187, 893
uninitiated 491, 699
uninjured
  perfect 650
  healthy 654
  preserved 670
uninjurious 656
uninquisitive 456
uninspired 823
uninstructed 491
unintellectual 452,
  499
unintelligent 499
unintelligibility **519**
unintelligible 519
  - style 571
  render – 538
unintentional
  necessary 601
  undesigned 621
uninterested 456,
  841, 843
unintermitting
  unbroken 69
  durable 110
  continuing 143
  persevering 604a
uninterrupted
  continuous 69
  perpetual 112
  unremitting 893
unintroduced 893
uninured 614
uninvented 526
uninvestigated 491
uninvited 893
uninviting 830
union
  agreement 23
  junction 43
  combination 48
  concurrence 178
  workhouse 189
  party 712
  concord 714
  marriage 903
unionist 712
union-jack 550
union-pipes 417
unique
  dissimilar 18

unforfeited 781	ungranted 764	unhinge 61, 158	uninflammable 385
unforgettable 505	ungrateful 917	unhinged	uninfluenced
unforgiving 919	ungratified 832	*impotent* 158	*obstinate* 606
unforgotten 505	ungrounded	*insane* 503	*unactuated* 616
unformed 241, 674	*unsubstantial* 4	*failure* 732	*free* 768
unfortified	*erroneous* 495	unhitch 44	uninfluential 172,
pure 42	ungrudging 816	unholy 989	175a
powerless 158	unguarded	unhonoured 874	uninformed 491
unfortunate	*neglected* 460	unhook (44)	uningenuous 544
ill-timed 135	*spontaneous* 612	unhoped 508	uninhabit, -able,
failure 732	*unprepared* 674	unhorsed 732	-ed 187, 893
adversity 735	in an – moment	unhostile 888	uninitiated 491, 699
unhappy 828	*unexpectedly* 508	unhouse 297	uninjured
– *woman* 962	unguem, ad – 494,	unhoused 185	*perfect* 650
unfounded 546	650	unhurt 670	*healthy* 654
unfrequent 137	unguent 356	unicorn	*preserved* 670
unfrequented 893	unguibus et rostro	*monster* 83	uninjurious 656
unfriended	686	*carriage* 272	uninquisitive 456
powerless 158	unguided	unideal *existing* 1	uninspired 823
secluded 893	*ignorant* 491	*no thought* 452	uninstructed 491
unfriendly	*impulsive* 612	*true* 494	unintellectual 452,
opposed 708	*unskilled* 699	unification 48, 87	499
hostile 889	unguilty 946	uniform	unintelligent 499
malevolent 907	unhabitable 187	*homogeneous* 16	unintelligibility **519**
unfrock 756, 972	unhabituated 614	*simple* 42	unintelligible 519
unfrozen 382	unhackneyed 614	*orderly* 58	- *style* 571
unfruitful 169	unhallowed 988,	*regular* 80	render – 538
unfulfilled 713, 925	989	*dress* 225	unintentional
unfurl	unhand 750	*symmetry* 242	*necessary* 601
unfold 313	unhandseled 123	*livery* 550	*undesigned* 621
– *a flag* 525, 550	unhandsome 940	uniformity **16**	uninterested 456,
unfurnished 640,	unhandy 699	unilluminated 421	841, 843
674	unhappy	unimaginable 471,	unintermitting
ungainly 846, 895	*adversity* 735	473	*unbroken* 69
ungallant 895	*pain* 828	*wonderful* 870	*durable* 110
ungarnished 849	*dejected* 837	unimaginative 576,	*continuing* 143
ungathered 678	make – 830	843, 868	*persevering* 604a
ungenerous 819,	unharbored 185	unimagined 1, 494	uninterrupted
943	unhardened	unimitated 20	*continuous* 69
ungenial 657	*tender* 914	unimpaired 670	*perpetual* 112
ungenteel 851, 895	*innocent* 946	unimpassioned 826	*unremitting* 893
ungentle 173, 895	*penitent* 950	unimpeachable	unintroduced 893
ungentlemanly	unharmonious 24,	*certain* 474	uninured 614
vulgar 851	414	*true* 494	uninvented 526
rude 895	unharness 750	*due* 924	uninvestigated 491
dishonourable 940	unhatched 674	*approved* 931	uninvited 893
ungifted 499	unhazarded 664	*innocent* 946	uninviting 830
unglorified 874	unhealthy 655, 657	unimpeached 931,	union
unglue 47	unheard of	946	*agreement* 23
ungodly 989	*exceptional* 83	unimpeded 705, 748	*junction* 43
ungovernable	*improbable* 473	unimportance **643**	*combination* 48
violent 173	*ignorant* 491	unimpressed 838	*concurrence* 178
disobedient 742	*wonderful* 870	unimpressible 823	*workhouse* 189
passionate 825	unheated 383	unimproved 659	*party* 712
ungoverned 748	unheed, -ed 460	unincreased 36	*concord* 714
ungraceful	unheeding 458	unincumbered	*marriage* 903
- *language* 579	unhesitating	*easy* 705	unionist 712
ugly 846	*belief* 484	*exempt* 927a	union-jack 550
vulgar 851	*resolved* 604	uninduced 616	union-pipes 417
ungracious 895, 907	unhewn 241, 674	uninfected 652	unique
ungrammatical 568	unhindered 748	uninfectious 656	*dissimilar* 18

original 20
exceptional 83
alone 87
unirritating 174
unison
  agreement 23
  melody 413
  concord 714
unit 51, 87
Unitarian 984
unite *join* 43
  combine 48
  assemble 72
  concur 178
  converge 290
  party 712
  – one's efforts 709
  – in pairs 89
  – with 709
united 46, 714
unity *identity* 14
  uniformity 16
  whole 50
  complete 52
  single 87
  concord 714
  – of time 120
Unity, Trinity in –
  976
universal 78
  – Church 983*a*
  – favourite 899
universality 52
universe 318
university 542
  – education 537
  – extension 537
  go to the – 539
unjust *wrong* 923
  impious 988
unjustifiable
  wrong 923
  inexcusable 938
  wicked 945
unjustified 923
  undue 925
unkempt
  unclean 753
  vulgar 851
unkennel *eject* 297
  disclose 529
unkind 907
  –est cut of all 828
unknightly 940
unknit (44)
unknowable 519
unknowing 491
unknown
  ignorant 491
  latent 526
  – to fame

inglorious 874
low-born 876
– quantities 491
unlaboured
  - *style* 578
  unprepared 674
unlace (44)
unlade 297
unladylike
  vulgar 851
  rude 895
unlamented
  hated 898
  disapproved 932
unlatch 44, 750
unlawful
  undue 925
  illegal 964
unlearn 506
unlearned 491
unleavened 674
unless
  circumstances 8
  except 83
  qualification 469
unlettered 491
  – Muse 579
unlicensed 761
unlicked
  unprepared 674
  vulgar 851
  clownish 876
  – cub
  youngster 129
  shapeless 241
  unmannerly 895
unlike 18
unlikely 473
unlikeness 15
unlimber 323
unlimited
  great 31
  infinite 105
  free 748
  – space 180
unliquefied 321
unlively 837, 843
unload
  displaced 185
  eject 297
  disencumber 705
unlock *unfasten* 44
  discover 480*a*
unlooked for 508
unloose
  unfasten 44
  liberate 750
unloved 898
unlovely 846
unlucky
  inopportune 135

bad 649
unfortunate 735
in pain 830
unmade 2
unmaimed 654
unmake 145
unman
  mutilate 38
  render powerless
  158
  madden 837
  frighten 860
unmanly
  effeminate 374
  dishonourable 940
unmanageable
  unwieldy 647
  perverse 704
unmanned
  dejected 837
  cowardly 862
unmannered 895
unmannerly 895
unmarked 460
unmarred 654, 670
unmarried 904
unmask 529
unmatched
  different 15
  dissimilar 18
  unparalleled 20
unmeaningness 517
unmeant 517
unmeasured
  infinite 105
  undistinguished
  465*a*
  abundant 639
unmeditated 612
unmeet 925
unmellowed 674
unmelodious 414
unmelted 321
unmentionable 874
  –s 225
unmentioned 526
unmerciful 914*a*
unmerited 925
unmethodical 59
unmindful
  inattentive 458
  neglectful 460
  ungrateful 917
unmingled 42
unmissed 460
unmistakable
  certain 474
  intelligible 518
  manifest 525
unmitigable 173
unmitigated

great 31
complete 52
violent 173
unmixed 42
unmolested 664,
  831
unmoneyed 804
unmoral 823
unmourned 898
unmoved
  quiescent 265
  obstinate 606
  insensible 823
unmusical 424
  – voice 581
unmuzzled 748
unnamed 565
unnatural
  exceptional 83
  affected 855
  spiteful 907
unnecessary
  redundant 641
  useless 645
  inexpedient 647
unneeded 645
unneighbourly 895
unnerved
  powerless 158
  weak 160
  dejected 837
unnoted } 460
unnoticed } 874
unnumbered 105
unnurtured 674
uno saltu 113
unobeyed 742
unobjectionable
  good 648
  pretty good 651
  innocent 946
unobnoxious 648
unobscured 420
unobservant 458
unobserved 460
unobstructed 705,
  749
unobtainable 471
unobtained 777*a*
unobtrusive 881
unoccupied
  vacant 187
  unthinking 452
  doing nothing 681
  inactive 683
  untenanted 893
unoffended
  enduring 826
  humble 879
unofficial 964
unoften 137

unopened 261
unopposed 709
unorganized 674
– matter 358
unornamental 846
unornamented
- *style* 576
simple 849
unorthodox 984
unostentatious 881
unowed 807
unowned 782
unpacific 713, 722
unpacified 713
unpack
unfasten 44
take out 297
unpaid *debt* 806
honorary 815
the great –
magistracy 967
– worker 602
unpalatable 395,
830
unparagoned
supreme 33
best 648
perfect 650
unparalleled
unimitated 20
supreme 33
exceptional 83
unpardonable 938,
945
unparliamentary
language 895,
908
unpassable 261
unpassionate 826
unpatriotic 911
unpeaceful 720, 722
unpeople
emigration 297
banishment 893
unperceived
neglected 460
unknown 491
unperformed 730
unperjured 543,
939
unperplexed 498
unpersuadable 606
unpersuaded 616
unperturbed 826
unphilosophical 499
unpierced 261
unpin (44)
unpitied 932
unpitying 914*a*
unplaced 185
unplagued 831

unpleasant 830
unpleasing 830
unpoetical 598, 703
unpolished
rough 256
inelegant 579
unprepared 674
vulgar 851, 876
rude 895
unpolite 895
unpolluted
good 648
perfect 650
unpopular 830, 867
unpopularity 898
unportioned 804
unpossessed 777*a*
unpractical 699
unprecedented 83,
137
unprejudiced 498,
748
unpremeditated
impulsive 612
undesigned 621
unprepared 674
unprepared 508,
674
unprepossessed 498
unprepossessing
846
unpresentable 851
unpretending 881
unprevented 748
unprincipled 945
unprivileged 925
unprized 483
unproclaimed 526
unproduced 2
unproductive 645
unproductiveness
169
unproficiency 699
unprofitable
unproductive 169
useless 645
inexpedient 647
bad 649
unprolific 169
unpromising 859
unprompted 612
unpronounceable
519
unpronounced 526
unpropitious
ill-timed 135
opposed 708
hopeless 859
unproportioned 24
unprosperous 735
unprotected 665

unproved 477
unprovided
scanty 640
unprepared 674
unprovoked (616)
unpublished 526
unpunctual
tardy 133
untimely 135
irregular 139
unpunished 970
unpurchased 796
unpurified 653
unpurposed 621
unpursued 624
unqualified
incomplete 52
impotent 158
certain 474
unprepared 674
inexpert 699
unentitled 925
– truth 494
unquelled 173
unquenchable
strong 159
desire 865
unquenched
violence 173
heat 382
unquestionable 474
unquestionably 488
unquestioned 474,
488
unquiet
motion 264
agitation 315
excitable 825
unravel *untie* 44
arrange 60
straighten 246
evolve 313
discover 480*a*
interpret 522
disembarrass 705
unreached 304
unread 491
unready 674
unreal
not existing 2
erroneous 495
imaginary 515
unreasonable
impossible 471
illogical 477
misjudging 481
foolish 499
exorbitant 814
unjust 923
unreclaimed 951
unrecognizable 146

unreconciled 713
unrecorded 552
unrecounted 55
unreduced 31
unrefined 851
unreflecting 458
unreformed 951
unrefreshed 688
unrefuted 478, 494
unregarded
neglected 460
unrespected 929
unregenerate 988
unregistered 552
unreined 748
unrelated 10
unrelenting 914*a*,
919
unreliable
uncertain 475
irresolute 605
dangerous 665
unrelieved 835
unremarked 460
unremembered 506
unremitting
continuous 69
continuing 110
unvarying 143
persevering 604*a*
unremoved 184
unremunerated 808
unrenewed 141
unrepealed 141
unrepeated 87, 103
unrepentant 951
unrepining 831
unreplenished 640
unrepressed 173
unreproached 946
unrequited 806, 917
unresented 918
unresenting 826
unreserved
manifest 525
veracious 543
artless 703
unresisted 743
unresisting 725
unresolved 605
unrespected 929
unrest 149, 264
unrestored 688
unrestrained
capricious 608
unencumbered
705
free 748
unrestricted
undiminished 31

free 748
unretracted 535
unrevenged 918
unreversed 143
unrevoked 143
unrewarded 806,
  917
unrhymed 598
unriddle 480a, 529
unrig 645
unrighteous 945
unrip 260
unripe
  young 127
  sour 397
  immature 674
unrivalled 33
unroll *evolve* 313
  display 525
unromantic 494
unroot 301
unruffled
  calm 174
  quiet 265
  unaffected 823
  placid 826
unruly *violent* 173
  obstinate 606
  disobedient 742
unsaddle 756
unsafe 665
unsaid 526
unsaleable
  useless 645
  selling 796
  cheap 815
unsaluted 929
unsanctified 988,
  989
unsanctioned 925
unsated 865
unsatisfactory
  inexpedient 647
  bad 649
  displeasing 830
  discontent 832
unsatisfied 832, 865
unsavouriness **395**
unsay *recant* 607
unscanned 460
unscathed 654
unschooled 491
unscientific 477
unscoured 653
unscriptural 984
unscrupulous 940
unseal 529
unsearched 460
unseasonable 24,
  135
unseasoned 614,

674
unseat 756
unseemly
  inexpedient 647
  ugly 846
  vulgar 851
  undue 925
  vicious 945
unseen
  invisible 447
  neglected 460
  latent 526
unseldom 136
unselfish 942
unseparated 46
unserviceable 645
unsettle *derange* 61
unsettled
  mutable 149
  displaced 185
  uncertain 475
  – in one's mind
   503
unsevered 50
unsex 146
unshaded 525
unshaken 159
  – belief 484
unshapely 846
unshapen 241
unshared 777
unsheathe
  – the sword 722
unsheltered 665
unshielded 665
unshifting 143
unship 185, 297
unshocked 823
unshorn 50
unshortened 200
unshrinking 604,
  861
unsifted 460
unsightly 846
unsinged 670
unskilfulness **699**
unslaked 865
unsleeping 604a,
  682
unsmooth 256
unsociable 893
unsocial 893
unsoiled 652
unsold 777
unsoldierlike 862
unsolicitous 866
unsolved 526
unsophisticated
  simple 42
  genuine 494
  artless 703

unsorted 59
unsought
  avoided 623
  unrequested 766
unsound
  illogical 477
  erroneous 495
  deceptive 545
  imperfect 651
  – mind 503
unsown 674
unsparing
  abundant 639
  severe 739
  liberal 816
  with an – hand
   818
unspeakable 31,
  870
unspecified 78
unspent 678
unspied 526
unspiritual 316, 989
unspoiled 648
unspotted
  clean 652
  beautiful 845
  innocent 946
unstable 218
  changeable 149
  uncertain 475
  irresolute 605
  precarious 665
  – equilibrium 149
unstaid 149
unstained
  clean 652
  honourable 939
unstatesmanlike
  699
unsteadfast 605
unsteady
  mutable 149
  irresolute 605
  in danger 665
unstinted 639
unstinting 816
unstirred 823, 826
unstopped
  continuing 143
  open 260
unstored 640
unstrained
  turbid 653
  relaxed 687
  – meaning 516
unstrengthened 160
unstruck 823
unstrung 160
unstudied 460
unsubject 748

unsubmissive 742
unsubservient
  useless 645
  inexpedient 647
unsubstantial 4
  weak 160
  rare 322
  erroneous 495
  imaginary 515
unsubstantiality **4**
unsuccessful 732
unsuccessive 70
unsuitable
  incongruous 24
  (*inexpedient* **647**)
  – time 135
unsullied *clean* 652
  honourable 939
  (*guiltless* 946)
unsung 526
unsupplied 640
unsupported
  weak 160
  (*unassisted* 706)
  – by evidence **468**
unsuppressed 141
unsurmountable
  471
unsurpassed 33
unsusceptible 823
unsuspected
  belief 484
  latent 526
unsuspecting
  hopeful 858
unsuspicious
  belief 484
  artless 703
  hope 858
unsustainable 495
unsweet 395
unswept 653
unswerving
  straight 246
  direct 278
  persevering 604a
unsymmetric 83
unsymmetrical 59,
  243
unsystematic 59
untainted *pure* 652
  healthy 654
  honourable 939
untalked of 526
untamed 851, 907
untarnished 939
untasted 391
untaught 491, 674
untaxed 815
unteach 538
unteachable 499,

699
untenable
  powerless 158
  illogical 477
  undefended 725
untenanted 187,
  893
unthanked 917
unthankful 917
unthawed 321, 383
unthinkable 471
unthinking
  unconsidered 452
  involuntary 601
unthought of 452,
  460
unthreatened 664
unthrifty
  unprepared 674
  prodigal 818
unthrone 756
untidy 59, 653
untie 44, 750
  – the knot 705
until 106
  – now 118
untilled 674
untimely 135
  – end 360
untinged 42
untired 689
untiring 604a
untitled 876
untold
  countless 105
  uncertain 475
  latent 526
  secret 528
untouched
  disused 678
  insensible 823
untoward
  ill-timed 135
  bad 649
  unprosperous 735
  unpleasant 830
untraced 526
untracked 526
untractable 606,
  699
untrained
  unaccustomed 614
  unprepared 674
  unskilled 699
untrammelled 705,
  748
untranslatable 523
untranslated 523
untravelled 265
untreasured 640
untried *new* 123

not decided 461
untrimmed 674,
  849
untrodden *new* 123
  impervious 261
  not used 678
untroubled 174, 721
untrue 495, 546
untrustworthy
  uncertain 475
  erroneous 495
  danger 665
  dishonourable 940
untruth 544, **546**
untunable 414
unturned 246
untutored
  ignorant 491
  unprepared 674
  artless 703
untwine 313
untwist 313
unused
  new 123
  unaccustomed 614
  unskilful 699
unusual 83
unusually *very* 31
unutterable 31,
  519, 870
unvalued
  underrated 483
  undesired 866
  disliked 898
unvanquished 748
unvaried
  continuing 143
  - *style* 575, 576
unvarnished
  true 494
  - *style* 576
  unreserved 703
  simple 849
  – *tale* 494, 543
unvarying 16, 143
unveil 525, 529
unventilated 261
unveracious 544
unversed 491
unvexed 831
unviolated 939
unvisited 893
unwakened 683
unwarlike 862
unwarmed 383
unwarned 508, 665
unwarped judg-
  ment 498
unwarrantable 923
unwarranted
  illogical 477

undue 925
  illegal 964
unwary 460
unwashed 653
  great – 876
unwatchful 460
unwavering 604a
unweakened 159
unwearied
  persevering 604a
  indefatigable 682
  refreshed 689
unwedded 904
unweeded garden
  674
unweeting 491
unweighed 460
unwelcome 830,
  893
unwell 655
unwept 831
unwholesome 657
unwieldy
  large 192
  heavy 319
  cumbersome 647
  difficult 704
  ugly 846
unwilling 489
unwillingness **603**
unwind *evolve* 313
unwiped 653
unwise 499
unwished 866
unwithered 159
unwitting
  ignorant 491
  involuntary 601
unwittingly 621
unwomanly 373
unwonted 83, 614
unworldly 939
unworn 159
unworshipped 929
unworthy
  shameful 874
  vicious 945
  – of belief 485
  – of notice 643
unwrap 246
unwrinkled 255
unwritten
  latent 526
  obliterated 552
  spoken 582
  – law 697, 963
unwrought 674
unyielding
  tough 323
  resolute 604
  obstinate 606

resisting 719
up
  aloft 206
  vertical 212
  effervescing 353
  excited 824
  the game is – 735
  prices looking –
    814
  time – 111
  – in arms
    prepared 673
    active 682
    opposition 708
    attack 716
    resistance 719
    warfare 722
  – and at them 716
  – and doing 682
  – and down 314
  – on end 212
  – in 698
  – to [*see below*]
  all – with
    destruction 162
    failure 732
    adversity 735
up to
  time 106
  power 157
  knowing 490
  skilful 698
  brave 861
  – the brim 52
  – date 123
  – one's ears 641
  – one's eyes 641
  – the mark
    equal 27
    sufficient 639
    good 648
    due 924
  – snuff 702
  – this time
    time 106
    past 122
Upas tree 663
upbear 215, 307
upbraid 932
upcast 307
upgrow 206
upgrowth 194, 305
upheaval 146
upheave 307
uphill
  acclivity 217
  ascent 305
  laborious 686
  difficult 704
uphoist 307
uphold

deviating 279
vague
　unsubstantial 4
　uncertain 475
　unreasoning 477
　unmeaning 517
　obscure 519
　- *language* 571
　- *suggestion* 514
vail *panel* 228
　donation 784
　reward 973
vain *unreal* 2
　unprofitable 645
　unvalued 866
　conceited 880
　in - *failure* 732
　labour in -
　come *short* 304
　useless 645
　fail 732
　take a name in -
　895
　- attempt 732
　use - efforts 645
　- expectation 509
vainglorious
　haughty 878
　vain 880
　boasting 884
vaivode 745
valance 231
vale 252
　- of years 128
valeat quantum 467
valediction 293, 894
valedictory 293
valentine 902
valet 631, 746
valet
　- de chambre 746
　- de place 524, 527
valetudinarian 655,
　656
Valhalla 981
valiant 861
valid *confirmed* 150
　powerful 157
　strong 159
　true 494
　sufficient 639
　- *reasoning* 476
valise 191
valley 252
　- of the shadow of
　death 360
vallum 717
valoir, se faire -
　884
valorem, ad - 812
valour 861

valuable 644, 648
value *colour* 423
　measure 466
　estimate 480
　importance 642
　utility 644
　goodness 648
　price 812
　approbation 931
　of priceless - 814
　set a - upon 482
　- received 810
　-s *painting* 556
valueless 645
valve *stop* 263
　conduit 350
　safety - *safety* 664
　refuge 666
　escape 671
vamp *change* 140
　music 463
　- up *improve* 658
　restore 660
　prepare 673
vampire 913, 980
vampirism 789, 992
van *beginning* 66
　front 234
　wagon 272
　in the - 234
　precession 280
van-courier 64
Vandal
　destroyer 165
　vulgar 851
　commonalty 876
　evil-doer 913
vandalism 851
vandyke 257
Vandyke brown 433
vane *wind* 349
　indication 550
vanguard 234
vanish
　unsubstantial 4
　transient 111
　disappear 449
vanishing 32, 193
vanity *useless* 645
　conceit **880**
　- *bag* 191
Vanity Fair 852
vanquish 731
vantage ground
　superiority 33
　power 157
　influence 175
　height 206
vapid *insipid* 391
　- *style* 575
vaporization **336**

vaporous
　imaginary 515
　opaque 426
vapour *gas* 334
　bubbles 353
　fancy 515
　boast 884
　insolence 885
　- *bath* 386, 652
vapourer 887
vapours
　dejection 837
variable 149, 605
variance
　difference 15
　disagreement 24
　discord 713
　at - *enmity* 889
　at - with 489
variant 15
variation
　difference 15
　diverseness **20a**
　number 84
　chance 140
　music 415
varied 15
variegated 16a, 440
variegation **440**
variety
　difference 15
　class 75
　multiformity 81
　exception 83
　entertainment 599
variform 81
various 15, 102
　- *places* 182
　- *times* 119
varlet 949
varnish
　overlay 223
　resin 356a
　sophistry 477
　falsehood 544
　painting 556
　decorate 847
　excuse 937
vary *differ* 15
　dissimilar 18
　variation 20a
　change 140
　fluctuate 149
vascular *cells* 191
　holes 260
　pipes 350
vase 191
vassal 746
vassalage 749
vast *great* 31
　spacious 180

　large 192
　- *learning* 490
vasty deep 341
vat 191
Vatican 995, 1000
　thunders of the -
　908
vaticination 511
vatum, genus irri-
　tabile - 597
vaudeville 599, 840
vault
　cellar 191
　curve 245
　leap 309
　tomb 363
　store 636
　- of heaven 318
vaulted 245, 252
vaulting 33, 865
vaunt 884
vaurien 949
vavasour
　possessor 779
　nobleman 875
V.C. 733
vection 270
Vedas 986
vedette 668
Vedidad 986
veer
　change 140
　deviate 279
　go back 283
　change intention
　607
vegetability **365**
vegetable **367**
　- *kingdom* 367
　- *life* 386
　- *oil* 356
　- *physiology* 369
vegetarian 298, 953
vegetate 365
　exist 1
　grow 194
　stagnate 265
　inactive 681, 683
　insensible 823
vegetation 365
vehemence
　violence 173
　feeling 821
　emotion 825
vehement
　- *language* 574
vehicle
　carriage **272**
　instrument 631
veil *covering* 225
　shade 424

vindicator 919
vindictive 901, 919
vine 367
– grower 371
vinegar 397
– aspect 846
vinery 191
vineyard 371, 691
vingt et un 840
vintage 371, 636
vintner 637
viol 417
violate
 disobey 742
 non-observance
  773
 undue 925
 dereliction 927
 ravish 961
 – a law 83
 – the law 964
 – a usage 614
violence **173**
 arbitrary 964
 do – to *bad* 649
 non-observance
  773
 undue 925
violent 173
 excitable 825
 – death 360, 361
 in a – degree 31
 lay – hands on 789
violet 437
violin 417
violinist 416
violoncello 417
viper *snake* 366
 bane 663
 evil-doer 913
 bad man 949
 – in one's bosom
  667
virago 901
virent 435
vires acquirit
 eundo
 increase 35
 energy 171
 velocity 274
virescence 435
Virgilianæ, sortes –
 621
virgin *new* 123
 girl 129
 woman 374
 spinster 904
 good 948
 pure 960
 – forest 367
 – soil

ignorance 491
untilled 674
the – Mary 976
virginals 417
virginibus
 puerisque 960
viribus, totis – 686
viridity 435
virile
 adolescent 131
 strong 159
 manly 373
virtu 850
 article of – 847
virtual 2, 5
 – image 443
virtue *power* 157
 courage 861
 goodness **944**
 purity 960
 by – of 157, 631
 in – of 737
 make a – of neces-
  sity *no choice*
  609a
 skill 698
 submit 725
 compromise 774
 bear 826
virtueless 945
virtuoso 416, 850
virtuous 944, 960
virulence
 energy 171
 noxiousness 649
 insalubrity 657
 discourtesy 895
 anger 900
 malevolence 907
virulent 932
virum volitare per
 ora 531
virus 655, 663
vis:
 – comica 842
 – conservatrix 670
 – inertiæ
 power 157
 inertness 172
 insensibility 823
 – medicatrix 660,
  662
 – mortua 157
 – a tergo 284
 – viva 157
visa 488
visage 234, 448
vis-à-vis *front* 234
 opposite 237
 carriage 272
viscera 221

viscid 352
viscount 875
viscous 352
vise 781
Vishnu 979
visibility **446**
visible 446
 be – 448
 become – 448
 darkness – 421
 – radiation 420
vision *sight* **441**
 phantasm 443
 dream 515
 spectre 980
 organ of – 441
visionary
 inexistence 2
 unsubstantial 4
 impossible 471
 imaginary 515
 heterodox 984
visionless 442
visit *arrival* 292
 social 892
 courtesy 894
 – upon 972
 pay a surprise –
  647
visitation
 disease 655
 adversity 735
 suffering 828
 –s of Providence
  976
 – of the sick 998
visiting:
 – card 550
 on – terms 888,
  892
visitor *incomer* 294
 director 694
 friend 890
visor 530
vista
 convergence 260
 sight 441
 appearance 448
 expectation 507
visual 441
 – organ 441
vitability 359
vitæ, elixir – 662
vital *life* 359
 important 642
vitality
 stability 150
 strength 159
 life 359
vitalize 359
vitals 221

vitamin impendere
 vero 535, 939
vitamines 298
vitiate 659
vitiated 655
viticulture 371
vitreous 323, 425
vitrify 323
vituperate 908, 932
vituperator 936
viva! 873, 931
vivace *music* 415
vivacious
 active 682
 sensitive 822
 cheerful 836
vivamus, dum
 vivimus – 840
vivandière 797
vivarium 370
vivâ voce 582
vive *glory be to* 873
 on the qui – 824
vivendi
 modus – 723
 – causa 359
vivid *energetic* 171
 sensibility 375
 light 420
 colour 428
 distinct 518
 – memory 505
vivify 159, 359
vivisection 378
vixen *fox* 366
 female 374
 shrew 901
viz. [see videlicet]
vizier *director* 694
 mask 530
 shield 717
 deputy 759
vizor 530
vobis, sic vos non –
 791
vocable 562
vocabulary 562
vocal 415, 580
 – training 537
vocalist 416
vocalize 580
vocation 625
voce, sotto – 581
vociferation
 loud 404
 cry 411
 voice 580
vogue *custom* 613
 fashion 852
 fame 873
vogue la galère

[693]

inquiry 461
reasoning 476
where 186, 461
– am I? 870
whereabouts 183, 197
whereas 9, 476
whereby 631
wherefore
  attribution 155
  inquiry 461
  reasoning 476
  motive 615
wherein 221
whereness 186
whereupon 106, 121
wherever 180, 182
wherewith 632, 800
wherret 830
wherry 273
whet *sharpen* 253
  meal 298
  incite 615
  excite 824
  take a –
  tipple 959
  – the appetite 865
  – the knife 673
whether or not 609
whetstone, cut a –
  with a razor 638
which:
  at – time 119
  know – is which 465
whiff 349, 825
whiffle 349
Whig 712
while *time* 106
  in a – 132
  worth – 646
  – away time
  inaction 681
  pastime 840
  – speaking of 9, 134
whilom 122
whilst 106
whim *fad* 481
  fancy 515
  caprice 608
  wit 842
  desire 865
whimper 839
whimsey 515, 865
whimsical [*see* whim] 853
whimwam 608, 643
whin 367
whine 411, 839
whinyard 727

whip *collect* 72
  coachman 268
  strike 276
  stir up 315
  urge 615
  hasten 684
  director 694
  flog 972
  scourge 975
  – and spur 274
  – away 293
  – hand 731, 737
  – in 300
  – on 684
  – off 293
  – up 789
whipcord 205
whipper-in 694
whippersnapper 129
whipping-post 975
whipster 129
whir *rotate* 312
  sound 407
whirl *rotate* 312
  flurry 825
whirligig 312
whirlpool *rotate* 312
  agitation 315
  water 348
  danger 667
whirlwind
  disorder 59
  agitation 315
  wind 349
  reap the –
  product 154
  fail 732
  ride the –
  resolution 604
  authority 737
whisk *rapid* 274
  circuition 311
  agitation 315
  – off 297
whisker 256
whisket 191
whisky
  vehicle 272
  drink 298
whisper
  faint sound 405
  tell 527
  conceal 528
  stammer 583
  stage – 580
  – about
  disclose 529
  publish 531
  – in the ear
  voice 580
whist *hush* 403

  cards 840
whistle *wind* 349
  hiss 409
  play music 416
  musical instru-ment 417
  clean as a –
  thorough 52
  perfect 650
  neatly 652
  pay too dear for one's –
  inexpedient 647
  unskilful 699
  dear 814
  police – 669
  wet one's –
  drink 298
  tipple 959
  – at 930
  – for *request* 765
  desire 865
  – jigs to a mile-stone 645
  – for want of thought
  inaction 681
whit *small* 32
whit-leather 327
Whit-Monday 840
white 430
  – of the eye 41
  – feather 862
  – flag 723
  – frost 383
  – heat 382
  – horses 348
  – lie *equivocal* 520
  concealment 528
  untruth 546
  plea 617
  – liver 862
  – as a sheet 860
  – slave 962
  stand in a – sheet 952
  mark with a – stone 642, 931
whitechapel
  vehicle 272
Whitefriars 996
whiteness **430**
whitewash
  cover 223
  whiten 430
  cleanse 652
  ornament 847
  justify 937
  acquit 970
whitewashed
  get – 808

whitewasher 935
white wings 652
whitey-brown 433
whither
  tendency 176
  direction 278
  inquiry 461
whitlow 655
whittle 44, 253
whittled
  drunk 959
Whitsuntide 998
whiz 409
who 461
  – goes there? 669
  – would have thought? 508, 870
whoa! 265
whole *entire* **50**
  healthy 654
  make – 660
  as a – 50
  on the – 476, 480
  go the – hog 729
  the – time 106
  – truth
  truth 494
  disclosure 529
  veracity 543
wholesale
  large scale 31
  whole 50
  abundant 639
  trade 794
wholesome 656
wholly 50, 52
whoop 411
  war – 715, 722
whop *flog* 972
whoopee 840
whopper *lie* 546
whopping *huge* 192
whore 962
whoredom 961
whoremonger 962
whorl 248
why *cause* 153
  attribution 155
  inquiry 461
  indeed 535
  motive 615
  – not 868
wibble-wabble 314
wick 388, 423
wicked 945
  the – *bad men* 949
  impious 988
  the – one 978
wicker 219
wicket 66, 260

wide 202
– apart 15
–awake *hat* 225
intelligent 498
– away 196
– berth 748
– of the mark
distance 196
deviation 279
error 495
– of *distant* 196
– open 194, 260
– of the truth 495
– world 180, 318
in the – world 180
widen 194
– the breach 713,
900
wide-spread
great 31
dispersed 73
space 180
expanded 194
widow 905
widowhood 905
width 202
wield
brandish 315
handle 379
use 677
– authority 737
– the sword 722
wieldy 705
wife 903
wig 225
wigging 932
wiggle 315
wight 373
wigwam 189
wild 851
unproductive 169
violent 173
plain 344
inattentive 458
mad 503
shy 623
unskilled 699
excited 824, 825
untamed 851
rash 863
angry 900
licentious 954
run – 825
– animals 366
– beast *fierce* 173
evil-doer 913
– goose chase
caprice 608
useless 645
unskilful 699
– imagination 515

sow one's – oats
grow up 131
improve 658
amusement 840
vice 945
intemperance 954
Wild, Jonathan –
thief 792
bad man 949
wilderness
disorder 59
unproductive 169
space 180
solitude 893
wild-fire 382
spread like –
violence 173
influence 175
expand 194
publication 531
wile 545, 702
wilful
voluntary 600
obstinate 606
will
volition **600**
resolution 604
testament 771
gift 784
at – 600
at one's own
sweet – 608
have one's own –
600, 748
make one's – 360
tenant at – 779
– be 152
– for the deed
774, 937
– of Heaven 601
– he nil he 601
– power 600
– and will not 605
– you 765
Will o' the wisp
luminary 423
imp 980
willing or unwilling
601
willingness **602**
willow 839
willy-nilly 601, 744
wilted 659
wily 702
wimble 262
wimple 225
win 731, 775
– the affections
897
– golden opinions
931

– the heart 829
– laurels 873
– out 33
– over *belief* 484
induce 615
content 831
wince
bodily pain 378
emotion 821
excitement 825
mental pain 828
flinch 860
winch 307, 633
wind *convolution*
[*see below*]
velocity 274
blast **349**
life 359
against the – 278,
708
before the – 278,
734
cast to the –s
repudiate 610
disuse 678
not observe 773
relinquish 782
close to the – 278
fair – 705
to the four –s 180
get – 531
get the – up 860
see how the –
blows
direction 278
experiment 463
foresight 510
fickle 607
in the – 151, 152
lose – 688
sail near the –
direction 278
skill 698
sharp practice 940
outstrip the – 274
preach to the –s
645
raise the – 775
scatter to the –s
756
see where the –
lies 698
short –ed 688
sport of –s and
waves 315
sound of – and
limb 654
take the – out of
one's sails
render powerless
158

hinder 706
defeat 731
touched in the –
655
what's in the – ?
461
– ahead 708
– bag 584
in the –'s eye 278
– the horn 416
hit between – and
water 659
– and weather
permitting
qualification 469
possibility 470
wind *blast* [*see
above*]
convolution 248
deviate 279
circuition 311
– round the heart
897
– up *strengthen* 159
prepare 673
complete 729
- *accounts* 811
windbag 884
wind instruments
417
wind-bound 706
windfall 618
wind-gauge 349
wind-gun 727
winding 248, 311
winding-sheet 363
**windings and turn-
ings** 248
wind-jammer 273
windlass 307, 633
windless 688
windmill 312
tilt at –s 638
window 260
make the –s shake
loud noise 404
– dressing 544
wind-pipe 351
wind-up 67
windward, to – 236,
278
windy 349
wine 298, 959
put new – into old
bottles 699
look upon the –
when it is red
953
wine-bibbing 959
wine-cooler 387
wineglass 191